THE

MARCUS GARVEY

AND

UNIVERSAL NEGRO
IMPROVEMENT ASSOCIATION

PAPERS

SUPPORTED BY
The National Endowment for the Humanities
The National Historical Publications and Records Commission
The Ford Foundation
The Rockefeller Foundation

SPONSORED BY
The University of California, Los Angeles

Marcus Garvey presiding at 1922 convention, Liberty Hall

THE
MARCUS GARVEY
AND
UNIVERSAL NEGRO
IMPROVEMENT ASSOCIATION
PAPERS

Volume V
September 1922–August 1924

Robert A. Hill, *Editor*

Deborah Forczek, *Senior Editor*
Devra Weber, *Assistant Editor*
Michael Furmanovsky, *Editorial Assistant*
Robin Dorman, *Publications Assistant*
Diane L. Hill, *Administrative/Production Assistant*

University of California Press
Berkeley   Los Angeles   London

University of California Press
Berkeley and Los Angeles, California

University of California Press, Ltd.
London, England

This volume has been funded in part by the National Endowment
for the Humanities, an independent federal agency. The volume has
also been supported by the National Historical Publications and
Records Commission, the Ford Foundation, the Rockefeller Foundation, and the University of California, Los Angeles.

Documents in this volume from the Public Record Office are
©British Crown copyright 1986 and are published by permission
of the Controller of Her Britannic Majesty's Stationery Office.

Designed by Linda M. Robertson and set in Galliard type.
This volume has been typeset by the Garvey Papers Project using the
TYXSET software system supplied by TYX Corp., Reston, Virginia.

Library of Congress Cataloging in Publication Data

Main entry under title:

The Marcus Garvey and Universal Negro Improvement Association
    papers.

    1. Garvey, Marcus, 1887–1940. 2. Universal Negro Improvement
    Association—History—Sources. 3. Black power—
    United States— History—Sources. 4. Afro-Americans—Race
    identity—History— Sources. 5. Afro-Americans—Civil rights—
    History—Sources. 6. Afro-Americans—Correspondence.
    I. Hill, Robert A., 1943–   . II. Garvey, Marcus, 1887–1940.
    III. Universal Negro Improvement Association

E185-97.G3M36   1986   305.8'96073   82-13379
ISBN 0–520–05817–8

Printed in the United States of America

1 2 3 4 5 6 7 8 9

To
Winston Rodney–Burning Spear
Garvey Disciple

CONTENTS

ILLUSTRATIONS   xxvii

ACKNOWLEDGMENTS   xxix

INTRODUCTION   xxxiii

EDITORIAL PRINCIPLES AND PRACTICES   xxxix

TEXTUAL DEVICES   xlv

SYMBOLS AND ABBREVIATIONS   xlvii
 Repository Symbols xlvii
 Manuscript Collection Symbols xlviii
 Descriptive Symbols xlix
 Published Works Cited xlix
 Other Symbols and Abbreviations l

CHRONOLOGY   li

DOCUMENTS

1922

1 September Maurice Peterson, British Embassy, to William L.
Hurley, Department of State 3

2 September Article by Hodge Kirnon 3

6 September Report by Special Agent James E. Amos 6

7 September Charles L.C.M.P. Barret, French Consul
General, New York, to M. La Rocca, French
Ministry of Foreign Affairs 7

8 September	Report by Special Employee Andrew M. Battle	7
ca. 8 September	L. A. Johnson to the Editor, *New York Age*	8
11 September	Article in the *New York Times*	9
12 September	G. O. Marke, Chairman of UNIA Delegation, to Sir Eric Drummond, Secretary General, League of Nations	11
12 September	Emmett J. Scott to W. E. Mollison	12
13 September	Report by Special Employee Andrew M. Battle	13
15 September	Memorandum to the United States Shipping Board	15
15 September	G. O. Marke to William Rappard, Director, Mandates Section, League of Nations	16
15 September	Sir Eric Drummond to G. O. Marke	17
16 September	William Rappard to G. O. Marke	17
17 September	Speech by Marcus Garvey	19
18 September	Lewis W. Haskell, American Consul, Geneva, to Joseph C. Grew, American Minister, Berne	27
19–20 September	Report by Special Employee Andrew M. Battle	27
21 September	G. O. Marke to Sir Eric Drummond	28
21–24 September	Report by Special Employee Andrew M. Battle	29
23 September	Report by Special Agent Joseph G. Tucker	31
post-26 September	Henri Jaspar, Belgian Minister of Foreign Affairs, to Mr. Le Tellier, Belgian Chargé d'Affaires, London	32

CONTENTS

28 September	G.O. Marke to Prince Mirza Riza Khan Arfa-ed-Dowleh of Persia	32
September	Article by W.E.B. Du Bois	33
5 October	Report by Bureau Agent H.L. Morgan	41
7 October	Report by Special Agent Joseph G. Tucker	43
ca. 7 October	Circular by Chandler Owen	44
10 October	Thomas W. Anderson, UNIA Second Assistant Secretary General, to William Phillips, Executive Secretary, New Orleans Division, UNIA	45
14 October	Report by Special Agent Joseph G. Tucker	46
ca. 14 October	Article in the *New York Age*	48
17 October	Editorial Letter by Marcus Garvey	51
19 October	Report by Special Agent James E. Amos	54
21 October	Article in the *Chicago Whip*	55
27 October	Florent de Sélys-Fanson, Chargé d'Affaires, Belgian Embassy, Washington, D.C., to Henri Jaspar	56
27 October	Summary Report of the Books and Records of the Black Star Line and UNIA by Thomas P. Merrilees, Expert Bank Accountant	58
30 October	Articles in the *Savannah Tribune*	115
31 October	Anonymous Letter to James Weldon Johnson	116
	25 October Clipping from an Unidentified Raleigh, North Carolina, Newspaper 117	
	Editorial Cartoon in the *Messenger*	121
31 October	Thomas P. Merrilees to William Hayward, United States Attorney, New York	122
5 November	Speech by Marcus Garvey	127

9 November   Marcus Garvey to William Phillips   133

11 November   Baron Emile de Cartier de Marchienne, Belgian Ambassador, Washington, D.C., to Henri Jaspar   134

12 November   Speech by Marcus Garvey   135

19 November   William Phillips to Marcus Garvey   141

21 November   William Phillips to Enid H. Lamos, Secretary to Marcus Garvey   142

25 November   Speech by Marcus Garvey   143

25 November   Article by Marcus Garvey   149

November   Article in the *Crisis*   150

ca. November   Luc Dorsinville to the Editor, *Crisis*   153

2 December   Enid H. Lamos to William Phillips   153

2 December   Article in the *Omaha New Era*   154

11 December   Speech by Marcus Garvey   155

12 December   Report by Special Agent Mortimer J. Davis   160

12 December   William Phillips to Joseph Martin, President, UNIA New Orleans Chapter   161

1923

2 January   Article in the *New Orleans Times-Picayune*   161

3 January   UNIA Press Release   162

4 January   Marcus Garvey to William Phillips   163

4 January   Report by Special Agent Mortimer J. Davis   164

4 January   Bureau of Investigation Report   164

6 January   Report by Special Agent James E. Amos   165

6 January   Report by Special Agent Mortimer J. Davis   166

9 January   Editorial Letter by Marcus Garvey   169

10 January   Editorial in the *New York Amsterdam News*   170

10 January   Editorial in the *New York News*   170

12 January   Thomas W. Anderson to William Phillips   172

13 January   Article in the *Negro World*   172

13 January   Report by Bureau Agent William E. Dunn, Jr.   173

13 January   Dr. Joseph D. Gibson to Albert D. Lasker, Chairman, United States Shipping Board   173

13 January   Report by Special Employee Andrew M. Battle   174

16 January   Report by Bureau Agent Harry D. Gulley   174

16 January   Report by Special Employee Andrew M. Battle   181

17 January   Report by Special Agent James E. Amos   182
15 January   Circular Letter to Harry M. Daugherty, Attorney General   182

17 January   Albert D. Lasker to Dr. Joseph D. Gibson   189

17–18 January   Report by Special Employee Andrew M. Battle   189

19 January   W. W. Grimes to J. Edgar Hoover   190

20 January   Bureau Agent George R. Shanton, Chief, Department of Justice, New Orleans, to William J. Burns, Director, Bureau of Investigation   191

20 January   Marcus Garvey and Robert L. Poston to Harry M. Daugherty   192

23 January   Editorial Letter by Marcus Garvey   193

23 January   William J. Burns to Bureau Agent George R. Shanton   195

23 January   Report by Special Agents Mortimer J. Davis James E. Amos   196

26 January   Report by Special Employee Andrew M. Battle   197

27–29 January   Reports by Confidential Informant Capt. J. W. Jones to William J. Burns   197

31 January   Thomas W. Anderson to Robert L. Poston   201

January   Marcus Garvey to the White Press of the World   202

January   Article by W. E. B. Du Bois   208

3 February   Perry W. Howard to William J. Burns   212

4 February   Confidential Informant Capt. J. W. Jones to William J. Burns   213

4 February   Speech by Marcus Garvey   214

4 February   Marcus Garvey to Harry M. Daugherty   217

5 February   C. B. Smith, Chief, Office of Extension Work, States Relations Service, Department of Agriculture, to Luther N. Duncan, Director of Extension Service, Alabama Polytechnic Institute   219

6 February   Editorial Letter by Marcus Garvey   220

11 February   Report by Special Employee Andrew M. Battle   229

13 February   Report by Special Agents James E. Amos and Mortimer J. Davis   230

13 February   J. Edgar Hoover to William J. Burns   232

13 February   Editorial Letter by Marcus Garvey   232

14 February   Confidential Informant Capt. J. W. Jones to William J. Burns   242

14 February	Report by Special Agent Mortimer J. Davis	243
16 February	Carl Murphy, Editor, *Baltimore Afro-American*, to Harry M. Daugherty	245
18 February	Confidential Informant Capt. J. W. Jones to William J. Burns	246
23 February	Speech by Marcus Garvey	247
24 February	Article in the *Norfolk Journal and Guide*	254
24 February	William J. Burns to Carl Murphy	256
24 February	*Negro World* Advertisement	257
25 February	Speech by Marcus Garvey	258
26 February	Chandler Owen to John W. H. Crim, Assistant Attorney General	263
28 February– 1 March	Reports by Special Employee Andrew M. Battle	263
4 March	Speech by Marcus Garvey	266
15 March	Report by Special Employee Andrew M. Battle	273
15 March	Report by Special Agent James E. Amos	275
16 March	William J. Burns to Edward J. Brennan, Special Agent in Charge, New York Office, Bureau of Investigation	276
18 March	Speech by Marcus Garvey	277
24 March	Article in the *Negro World*	283
27 March– 5 April	Reports by Special Agent Mortimer J. Davis	285
9 April	Report by Bureau Agent Rocco C. Novario	288
13 April	Speech by Marcus Garvey	289

27 April	Report by Special Employee Andrew M. Battle	293
30 April	Report by Bureau Agent W. L. Buchanan	294
5 May	Agreement Between the UNIA, Marcus Garvey, and Amy Jacques Garvey	295
10 May	Report by Special Agent Mortimer J. Davis	298
12 May	Report by Special Agent Joseph G. Tucker	301
14 May	Petition of Marcus Garvey	301
17 May	James Weldon Johnson to Judge Julian W. Mack	305
18 May	Report of the Opening Address of Assistant U.S. Attorney Maxwell S. Mattuck	306
20 May	Speech by Marcus Garvey	308
22 May	Editorial Letter by Marcus Garvey	312
25 May	Report by Special Agent Mortimer J. Davis	316
	Government Exhibit from Garvey's Trial	318
1 June	Anonymous Letter to William J. Burns	319
11 June	Editorial Letter by Marcus Garvey	320
12 June	Report of Angus Fletcher, British Library of Information, on His American Tour	321
ca. 14 June	Report of Closing Address to the Jury by Henry Lincoln Johnson	323
15 June	Closing Address to the Jury by Marcus Garvey	330
17 June	Speech by Marcus Garvey	359
ca. 18 June	Composite of Headlines from the *Negro Times* and the *Negro World*	363
19 June	Article in the *New York Evening Post*	364

19 June	Message from Marcus Garvey	365
20 June	Rev. E. Ethelred Brown to the *New York World*	367
20 June	Marcus Garvey to the Members and Friends of the UNIA	368
20 June	Last Will and Testament of Marcus Garvey	369
21 June	Salary Accounts of Marcus Garvey	370
21 June	*Negro World* Notice	373
21 June	Article in the *Kansas City Call*	373
23 June	Article in the *Pittsburgh Courier*	376
23 June	Editorial by George W. Harris	377
24 June	Jean-Jules Jusserand, French Ambassador, to the President of the Council, French Ministry of Foreign Affairs	378
24–26 June	Report by Special Employee Andrew M. Battle	379
25 June	Report by Bureau Agent Harry D. Gulley	380
25–27 June	Report by Special Agent Mortimer J. Davis	381
27–28 June	Report by Special Employee Andrew M. Battle	383
28 June	William J. Burns to W. W. Husband, Commissioner General of Immigration	384
28 June	Article in the *Kansas City Call*	385
30 June	Article in the *Financial World*	386
30 June	*Negro World* Notice	387
1 July	Message from Marcus Garvey	388
3 July	Editorial Letter by Marcus Garvey	389

5 July   The Marcus Garvey Committee on Justice to
          Henry C. Wallace, Secretary of Agriculture   390
          ca. 5 July   Petition to the President of the
          United States of America for Justice   390

7 July   Aaron P. Prioleau, UNIA National Political
          Director General, to Harry M. Daugherty   394

8 July   Meeting Announcement   395

10 July   W.E.B. Du Bois to Ida May Reynolds   396

10 July   John E. Bruce to George B. Christian, Jr.,
          Secretary to President Warren G. Harding   396

10–16 July   Report by Bureau Agent Adrian L. Potter   397

15 July   Vernal J. Williams to the UNIA Executive
          Council   397

16 July   Robert L. Poston to Vernal J. Williams   398

16 July   Amy Jacques Garvey to the *Negro World*   398

ca. 17 July   William Hayward to Judge Martin Manton   400
          17 July   Affidavit of Maxwell S. Mattuck   401
          17 July   Affidavit of James E. Amos   402

17–23 July   Report by Bureau Agent Adrian L. Potter   404

19 July   Affidavit of Marcus Garvey   404

ca. 19 July   Marcus Garvey to Vernal J. Williams   411

1 August Editorial Letter by Marcus Garvey   413

2 August Marcus Garvey to Mrs. Warren G. Harding   416

4 August Editorial Letter by Marcus Garvey   417

6 August President Calvin Coolidge to Rudolph E.B.
          Smith, Third Assistant President General, UNIA   418

6 August Marcus Garvey to Vernal J. Williams   419

6 August	Vernal J. Williams to the UNIA Committee of Management	421
9 August	Vernal J. Williams to Marcus Garvey	421
12 August	Sermon by Rev. E. Ethelred Brown	423
14 August	Marcus Garvey to Sir Eric Drummond	432
ca. 17 August	Marcus Garvey to Henry E. Manghum, Commerce Counsel, United States Shipping Board	432
18 August	Marcus Garvey to President Calvin Coolidge	433
21 August	G. Emonei Carter, First Vice President, New York Division, UNIA, to President Calvin Coolidge	434
25 August	Article in the *Dawn of Tomorrow*	435
29 August	Robert L. Poston to the *Negro World*	436
31 August	Editorial Letter by Marcus Garvey	437
6 September	Marcus Garvey to Emperor Yoshihito of Japan	442
8 September	Report by Special Agent Joseph G. Tucker	443
8 September	*Negro World* Notice	445
10 September	Statement by Marcus Garvey	446
13 September	Speech by Marcus Garvey	448
16 September	Speech by Marcus Garvey	456
29 September	Report by Special Agent Mortimer J. Davis	463
September	Article by Rev. George Alexander McGuire	463
2 October	Speech by Marcus Garvey	464
3 October	Marcus Garvey to Harry M. Daugherty	468

6 October   *Negro World* Front Page   471

6–27 October   Account of the Black Star Line by Capt. Hugh
             Mulzac in the *Cleveland Gazette*   472

8 October   Godfrey E. P. Hertslet, British Consul, St. Louis,
             to Sir Henry Getty Chilton, British Embassy   479
             6 October   Article in the St. Louis Star   *480*

19 October   Report by Special Agent James E. Amos   482

19 October   Sen. William E. Borah to Marcus Garvey   482

20 October   Henry C. Wallace to Marcus Garvey   483

23 October   John W. H. Crim to Marcus Garvey   483

23 October   Marcus Garvey to R. R. Moton   484

23 October   Editorial Letter by Marcus Garvey   484

27 October   Robert L. Vann to James Weldon Johnson   488

30 October   James Weldon Johnson to Robert L. Vann   489

31 October   Robert L. Vann to James Weldon Johnson   489

1 November   Address by Marcus Garvey   490

2 November   Marcus Garvey to R. R. Moton   496

5 November   Sen. Frank B. Willis to Marcus Garvey   496

6 November   R. R. Moton to Marcus Garvey   497

9 November   James Weldon Johnson to Robert L. Vann   497

10 November   Editorial by Robert L. Vann   498

11 November   Speech by Marcus Garvey   498

15 November   Marcus Garvey to Sen. Frank B. Willis   506

CONTENTS

5 December	Marcus Garvey to President C.D.B. King of Liberia	507
7 December	Dr. Theodore M. Kakaza to Rep. Clarence MacGregor	510
18 December	Marcus Garvey to Nicholas Murray Butler	511

1924

1 January	Editorial Letter by Marcus Garvey	512
1 January	*Negro World* Notice	512
2 January	John E. Bruce to Florence Bruce	513
	2 January John E. Bruce to Marcus Garvey 513	
6 January	Speech by Marcus Garvey	513
15 January	Speech by Marcus Garvey	520
16 January	Editorial Letter by Marcus Garvey	534
20 January	Speech by Marcus Garvey	536
22 January	Report by Bureau Agent H.J. Lenon	548
25 January	Marcus Garvey to J.H. Thomas, British Colonial Secretary	548
27 January	Speech by Marcus Garvey	549
2 February	Report by Special Agent Joseph G. Tucker	556
ca. 12 February	Workers Party Resolutions for the Negro Sanhedrin	557
28 February	A.L. Woodley, Marcus Garvey Release Committee, to J.R. Ralph Casimir	559
February	British Colonial Office Report on the UNIA	560

1 March Report by Special Agent Joseph G. Tucker 562

16 March Speech by Marcus Garvey 563

18 March Special Agent Frank C. Higgins to Robert S.
Sharp 568
17 March Article in the New York World *572*

20 March Black Cross Navigation and Trading Company
Certificate 574

22 March *Negro World* Announcement 575

ca. March Application for Transportation to Liberia 576

ca. March UNIA Registration Card 577

3 April James Weldon Johnson to John Mitchell, Jr.,
Editor, *Richmond Planet* 578

ca. 19 April Eunice Lewis to Amy Jacques Garvey, Associate
Editor, *Negro World* 579

May *Negro World* Advertisements 581

May Article by W.E.B. Du Bois 583

3 June Marcus Garvey to Thomas V. O'Connor,
Chairman, United States Shipping Board 586

4 June Speech by Marcus Garvey 586

6 June Esme Howard, British Embassy, Washington,
D.C., to Ramsay MacDonald, Prime Minister
of Great Britain 591

7 June Report by Special Agent Joseph G. Tucker 592

7 June Articles in the *Negro World* 595

11 June J. Harry Philbin, Manager, Ship Sales Division,
United States Shipping Board, to General
Counsel 600

15 June	Speech by Marcus Garvey	601
16 June	Memorandum by J. Harry Philbin	606
23 June	Letter of Introduction for James O'Meally	608
23 June	Livingston, Paperne and Wachtell, Accountants and Industrial Engineers, to Marcus Garvey	609
25 June	*New York World* Advertisement	610
10 July	Press Release by Ernest Lyon	611
12 July	*Negro World* Announcement	612
20 July	Otey J. Porter, M.D., to Robert Watson Winston	613
31 July	UNIA Membership Loan Booklet	614
1 August	Report on the UNIA Convention Opening	616
1 August	Speech by Marcus Garvey	631
2 August	Editorial in the *New York Evening Bulletin*	639
3 August	Marcus Garvey to President Calvin Coolidge	640
3 August	Marcus Garvey to Ramsay MacDonald	641
3 August	Marcus Garvey to Sir Eric Drummond	641
3 August	Marcus Garvey to Premier Édouard Herriot of France	641
3 August	Marcus Garvey to Premier Zaghlul Pasha of Egypt	642
3 August	Marcus Garvey to President Louis Borno of Haiti	642
3 August	Marcus Garvey to Premier Benito Mussolini of Italy	643

3 August	Marcus Garvey to Empress Zauditu of Ethiopia	644
3 August	Marcus Garvey to Pope Pius XI	645
3 August	Marcus Garvey to Mahatma Gandhi	645
3 August	UNIA to President C. D. B. King	646
3 August	Convention Addresses by Marcus Garvey, J. J. Peters, and Bishop George A. McGuire	646
4 August	Convention Report	650
5 August	Convention Report	661
6 August	Convention Report	669
7 August	Convention Report	677
7 August	Report by Special Agent James E. Amos	682
8 August	Convention Report	684
9 August	Report by Special Agent James E. Amos	688
9 August	Report by Special Agent Joseph G. Tucker	689
11 August	Address by Marcus Garvey	690
11 August	Convention Report	713
12 August	Convention Report	717
12 August	Enid Lamos to President Calvin Coolidge	723
12 August	Resolution of Confidence Presented to Marcus Garvey	723
13 August	Editorial Letter by Marcus Garvey	724
13 August	Convention Report	729
14 August	Convention Report	733

CONTENTS

14 August   Article by Robert Minor   738

15 August   Convention Report   742

18 August   Convention Report   747

18 August   Article by Robert Minor   753

19 August   Editorial Letter by Marcus Garvey   756

19 August   Convention Report   760

20 August   Convention Report   762

21 August   Convention Report   763

22 August   Convention Report   766

22 August   Article by Robert Minor   768

25 August   William R. Castle, Jr., Chief, Division of Western European Affairs, Department of State, to Charles Evans Hughes   773
25 August   Statement for the Press by Edwin Barclay   774

25 August   Convention Report   775

26 August   Convention Report   778

27 August   Convention Report   784

27 August   Report of the UNIA Delegation to Liberia   786

ca. 27 August   "West Indies Blues"   803

28 August   Convention Report   805

28 August   Speech by Marcus Garvey   810

29 August   Convention Report   813

30 August   Convention Announcement   821

31 August   Convention Reports   822

APPENDIXES

APPENDIX I   Delegates to the 1924 UNIA
                  Convention   833

APPENDIX II   Delegates to the 1924 UNIA
                  Convention Listed by Division   835

APPENDIX III   The Comintern and American
                  Blacks, 1919–1943   841

INDEX   855

ILLUSTRATIONS

Marcus Garvey presiding at the 1922 convention,
Liberty Hall
Culver Pictures, Inc.

UNIA delegation to the League of Nations
NW, 9 December 1922

Joel A. Rogers
WWCA

S. V. Robertson
Courtesy of Joyce Jones

Esau Ramus
Courtesy of the Department of Justice

James A. Amos
Courtesy of the Department of Justice

Julian W. Mack
The Maccabean, August 1918

Garveyites, New York, 1924
Collection of James Van Der Zee

J.J. Dossen
Momalou Massaqoi, The Republic of Liberia (Hamburg, 1926)

UNIA delegation to Liberia in Lisbon
NW, 21 June 1924

UNIA delegation to Liberia, 1924
P&O

Rupert Christian, Reginald Hurley, James Nichols,
James C. Roberts, William W. Strange, and James N. Walcott
NW, 14 June 1924

Marcus Garvey and Amy Jacques Garvey
Ebony, June 1971

Marcus Garvey in Universal African Legion uniform
Courtesy of Tuskegee Institute Archives

George O. Marke, Kojo Tovalou-Houénou, and Marcus Garvey
Collection of James Van Der Zee

Marcus Garvey in academic robes
Courtesy of the West India Reference Library

Marcus Garvey and UNIA officials on viewing stand,
convention parade, 1924
Collection of James Van Der Zee

UNIA marching band, 1924
Collection of James Van Der Zee

Marchers in UNIA convention parade, 1924
Collection of James Van Der Zee

UNIA juvenile division
P&O

Marcus Garvey in regalia, 1924
Collection of James Van Der Zee

Booker T. Washington University, 1924
Collection of James Van Der Zee

Funeral of John E. Bruce, 1924
The Schomburg Center for Research in Black Culture

Crowd at the 1924 UNIA convention
Collection of James Van Der Zee

Marcus Garvey at Liberty Hall, 1924
Collection of James Van Der Zee

Marcus Garvey and UNIA officers reviewing the convention parade
Brown Brothers

ACKNOWLEDGMENTS

The editors wish to thank the many institutions and individuals whose generous assistance contributed to the historical research and editorial preparation of the present volume. Important documents were provided by the Archives of the Belgian Ministry of Foreign Affairs, Brussels; Archives of the French Ministry of Foreign Affairs, Paris; Federal Bureau of Investigation, Washington, D.C.; League of Nations Archives, Geneva; Library of Congress; Hall of Records of the New York Supreme Court, New York; and the Public Record Office, Kew, England. The archivists and their staffs at these institutions have been most responsive to our many requests, and we are grateful for their continued interest in our work.

The following institutions or individuals have graciously granted the project permission to reprint their documents: Columbia University; David Graham Du Bois, Cairo, Egypt; Fisk University, Nashville; Her Majesty's Stationery Office, Norwich, England; Morgan State University, Baltimore; Ohio Historical Society, Columbus; Universal Negro Improvement Association Collection of the Schomburg Center for Research in Black Culture, the New York Public Library, Astor, Lenox, and Tilden Foundations, New York; and Tuskegee Institute, Alabama.

The process of annotating the many people, places, and historical events that appear in the documents is an arduous one. Our burden has been eased by the helpful information provided by many different institutions. We would like to thank the staffs of the following libraries for their assistance: Armstrong Library, Natchez, Mississippi; City of Chicago Library; City of New Orleans Public Library; Cleveland Public Library; Indianapolis–Marion County Library, Indianapolis; Kansas City Public Library, Kansas City, Kansas; Library of Congress; Maury County Public Library, Columbia, Tennessee; Newark Public Library, Newark, New Jersey; Norfolk Public Library, Norfolk, Virginia; Prichard Public Library, Prichard, Alabama; St. Louis Public Library; Springfield City Library, Springfield, Massachusetts; and the Tokyo Metropolitan Central Library.

The following historical societies and museums have provided us with helpful information: American Baptist Historical Society, Rochester, New York; Amistad Research Center, New Orleans; Chicago Historical Society; Cincinnati Historical Society; Florida Historical Society, Tampa; Illinois State

Historical Library, Springfield; Los Angeles Archives; Mariners' Museum, Newport News, Virginia; Missouri Historical Society, St. Louis; Museum and Library of Maryland History, Baltimore; Mystic Seaport Museum, Mystic, Connecticut; Newark Museum, Newark, New Jersey; Ohio Historical Society, Columbus; Pasadena Historical Society, Pasadena, California; Pemiscot County Historical Society, Caruthersville, Missouri; St. Augustine Historical Society; Schenectady County Historical Society, Schenectady, New York; Virginia Historical Society, Richmond; and the Western Reserve Historical Society, Cleveland.

We also thank the following educational institutions for their assistance: Columbia University; Hampton Institute, Hampton, Virginia; Mississippi State University; Occidental College, Los Angeles; Temple University, Philadelphia; Tulane University, New Orleans; Tuskegee Institute, Tuskegee Institute, Alabama; University of North Carolina, Chapel Hill; and Wake Forest University, Winston-Salem, North Carolina.

The following institutions deserve the project's thanks as well: American Jewish Archives, Cincinnati; Archives of the Episcopal Church, Austin, Texas; Catholic Church Extension Society, Chicago; City of New York Municipal Archives; Federal Archives and Records Center, Bayonne, New Jersey; Interdenominational Theological Center, Atlanta; Italian Ministry of Foreign Affairs, Rome; Labour Party, London; National Diet Library, Tokyo, Japan; New York Supreme Court Appellate Division, New York; North Carolina State Archives, Raleigh; Office of the Clerk of Court, New Orleans; Southern Tenant Farmers Union, Montgomery, Alabama; State of Mississippi Department of Archives and History, Jackson; State of New York Court of Appeals, Albany; and the United States Coast Guard.

We should also like to thank the staff of the University Research Library at the University of California, Los Angeles, for their assistance. The archival staff of the National Historical Publications and Records Commission, Washington, D.C. has given indispensable sustenance to the project, and we gratefully acknowledge their help.

The following individuals have assisted the project with their research knowledge: Helga Rogers Andrews, St. Petersburg, Florida; R.L. Beall, Greensboro, North Carolina; Prof. Randall K. Burkett, College of the Holy Cross, Worcester, Massachusetts; Judith Conlin, St. Augustine; W.F. Elkins, London; Prof. Lorenzo J. Greene, Lincoln University, Jefferson City, Missouri; Prof. Harvey Klehr, Emory University, Atlanta; Steve Lavere, Rare Records, Glendale, Calif.; Prof. Alexander Muller, California State University, Northridge; Prof. Mark Naison, Fordham University, Bronx, New York; Prof. Fred Notehelfer, University of California, Los Angeles; Peter S. Ridley, Washington, D.C.; Prof. Mark Solomon, Simmons College, Boston; and Patrick Stanton, Deputy Auditor General, Smithsonian Institution, Washington, D.C. For assistance with translation of French documents, thanks are due to Josephine Wilson, Staines, Middlesex, England. John P. Kaminski, Editor of the Documentary History of the Ratification of the Constitution Project, University of Wisconsin, Madison, has kindly advised us on a particular editorial problem of this volume.

For photographs used in this volume, the project acknowledges Brown Brothers of Sterling, Pennsylvania, Culver Pictures, Inc., New York, Joyce Jones, Donna Mussenden Van Der Zee, and the West India Reference Library.

This volume has been computer typeset by the project using the TYXSET system. The editors wish to thank the staff at the TYX Corporation, Reston, Virginia, for all their assistance, especially James Gauthier, Benell Trahan, and Mark Hoffman.

It has been a pleasure as always to work with the editors at the Los Angeles office of the University of California Press. The project thanks James Kubeck and Shirley Warren for their patience and support. We extend thanks to Sylvia Tidwell, who copyedited the manuscript, Robin Haller, who prepared the index, and Linda Robertson, the designer of the Garvey Papers volumes.

The editors wish to thank the Garvey Papers' exemplary staff; without their critical support we could not imagine carrying out our tasks as editors. Our special gratitude is due to Diane Lisa Hill, Administrative/Production Assistant who managed the complex computer typesetting of this volume with great skill and diligence, and has been an integral and sustaining force throughout the editorial and production phases of the project. Robin Dorman, Publications Assistant, conducted much of the research for the annotations, following many an obscure path to uncover material on previously little-known individuals and events. Teresa Meade, Research Assistant, also contributed to the research phase of the volume, and Tracy Chriss, Senior Typist Clerk, was responsible for the computer-coding of the documents in their conversion to the TYXSET process. Gregory A. Pirio, former Senior Editor of the African Series, assisted with the annotations of African subjects. Michael W. Fitzgerald, Research Assistant, contributed annotations dealing with a variety of black communities involved in the larger Garvey phenomenon. The process of revision in the draft manuscript was aided by Charles F. Bahmueller, who joined the project in August 1984 as Associate Editor. The critical eye of R. Kent Rasmussen, Senior Publications Coordinator since February 1986, has improved the quality of the final work in all its aspects. Barbara Bair, the project's NHPRC-Mellon Fellow in Historical Editing for 1984–1985, and Senior Editor since January 1986, has also contributed substantially to the editing and production of this volume.

The National Endowment for the Humanities, the National Historical Publications and Records Commission, and the University of California, Los Angeles, have sustained the project with their support, and we are deeply grateful for their continuing commitment. In addition, we would like to acknowledge Sheila Biddle of the Ford Foundation, Lynn Szwaja and Alberta Arthurs of the Rockefeller Foundation, and Dr. Cuthbert Pyne, Los Angeles, who have greatly assisted the project with their support.

INTRODUCTION

The fifth volume of *The Marcus Garvey and Universal Negro Improvement Association Papers* opens in the aftermath of the tumultuous 1922 convention, a convention replete with internal strife, impeachment trials, and a protest by the women delegates regarding their role in the organization. Outside the ranks of the UNIA, a growing list of opponents, including A. Philip Randolph and Chandler Owen, editors of the *Messenger*, and Robert Bagnall and William Pickens of the NAACP, launched renewed criticism of Garvey under the slogan "Garvey Must Go." Meanwhile, the United States government continued to press its mail fraud case against Garvey.

This was a period of heightened crisis for the UNIA, the most difficult the movement had ever faced. Nonetheless, the UNIA's delegation to the League of Nations, mandated by the 1922 convention, scored something of a propaganda coup during its three-month stay in Geneva, as a visible sign of the UNIA's self-proclaimed status as a sort of African government in exile. Although the delegation achieved no tangible results, its members were welcomed home at a triumphant Liberty Hall meeting on 30 November 1922. Other officials were similarly dispatched to European capitals, and Garvey himself proposed to making a worldwide speaking tour in 1923.

During the 1922 convention, Garvey gained virtually complete control of the UNIA by silencing his opposition, but he gained this control at the cost of increasing disaffection inside, and dissent outside, the movement. By 1924, of the officers elected at the original 1920 convention, only two—Garvey and Henrietta Vinton Davis—remained. Rev. J.W.H. Eason, impeached during the 1922 convention, emerged as an open rival, and, with J. Austin Norris, another former UNIA stalwart, he attempted to constitute a competing UNIA under the name of the Universal Negro Alliance.

Eason, by then a potential prosecution witness in Garvey's mail fraud trial, was assassinated in New Orleans in January 1923, and two UNIA adherents, William Shakespeare and Constantine F. Dyer, were charged with the crime. Although initially convicted of manslaughter, they were acquitted in August of the following year. The Bureau of Investigation's agents believed that Esau Ramus, a minor UNIA official who had recently been sent by Garvey to the New Orleans division, was the real assassin. While it is impossible to determine Garvey's role in the killing (he denounced it, and attributed the murder to Eason's "woman affair") (*NW*, 13 January 1923), the publicity surrounding the assassination of Eason cast a pall over the movement and did Garvey no small damage.

Garvey's relations with colleagues such as William H. Ferris were never the same after the Eason incident. Many in the UNIA leadership opted to give confidential statements to the government. For some of Garvey's internal critics, Eason's murder was implicitly the culmination of the ever-widening split between the West Indian and Afro-American factions. Meanwhile, the delays in Garvey's mail fraud trial (caused by both prosecution and defense) became a new focal point for his critics outside the movement. Eight prominent Afro-Americans, among them William Pickens, Chandler Owen, Robert Bagnall, and Robert Abbott, petitioned the attorney general demanding the deportation of the black leader. Garvey responded quickly to the "Garvey Must Go" campaign with a flurry of press releases, articles in the UNIA's *Negro World*, and public speeches, attacking his black opponents and questioning both their political motivation and their racial character.

As Garvey awaited bail in Manhattan's Tombs Prison following his conviction, a series of internecine feuds, fueled in part by his own actions, erupted within the UNIA. His frequent absences from the UNIA's New York headquarters in order to raise funds for his defense had already opened the way for dissent among subordinates. In an attempt to quell such internal dissension, in June 1923 Garvey unseated four UNIA officials—E.L. Gaines (international organizer), Rudolph Smith (third vice-president), G.O. Marke (supreme deputy), and Henrietta Vinton Davis (fourth vice-president). The following month Vernal Williams departed as attorney for the UNIA, leaving behind a variety of legal entanglements, and in September William H. Ferris resigned as literary editor of the *Negro World*. While Davis and Smith remained loyal to Garvey (and were reelected by the 1924 convention), the other departing officers successfully sued the UNIA for back salaries. Garvey canceled the 1923 conclave, most likely because he was fearful of losing control of a convention that, because of his incarceration, he was unable to attend. Instead, he instructed local UNIA divisions to meet regionally. The cancellation of the by-then-traditional August convention contributed both symbolically and structurally to the movement's deepening demoralization.

Released on bail in September 1923 pending his appeal against conviction, Garvey moved quickly to consolidate his hold over the movement, while simultaneously developing a new political strategy. This new strategy involved, first, a repackaging of his old message, the need for ships. The defunct Black Star Line became officially reconstituted in March 1924 as the Black Cross Navigation and Trading Company, which finally succeeded in acquiring the S.S. *General Goethals* from the United States Shipping Board. The acquisition came just in time for UNIA convention delegates to tour the ship in August 1924, although it was not officially launched until mid-January of the following year.

The second part of Garvey's new strategy took the form of his attempting to reduce white antagonism against him. His speech "An Appeal to the Soul of White America" was later reprinted as a pamphlet. As a means of furthering his legal appeal, Garvey also mounted an extensive letter-writing campaign to U.S. government officials, enclosing copies of his latest book, *Philosophy and Opinions of Marcus Garvey*, the first volume of which appeared in December 1923. Consisting largely of epigrams and speeches by Garvey that had been published in the *Negro World*, the volume was subtly edited to enhance his image among the white public. It was at this time that Garvey also announced his intention of entering the political arena. By marshaling black voters, Garvey hoped to offset the perceived influence of his black opponents.

Although this period saw Garvey making his most explicit antisocialist denunciations—indeed, Garvey's speeches after 1922, immediately following Benito Mussolini's accession to power in Italy, resonated with rhetoric characteristic of the Italian Fascist movement—he nonetheless greeted with optimism the formation, in January 1924, of Britain's short-lived first Labour government, under Prime Minister Ramsay MacDonald. "I knew that as soon as I was able to get out of this country, and approach the British Government, especially the present Labour Government," Garvey told the convention in August of that year (referring to his earlier announcement that he intended to undertake a worldwide speaking tour, which was never to materialize), "I felt sure that we would have had Southern Nigeria or somewhere else, and we would have had more land than we want[,] to carry out the program of the UNIA." Garvey now seemed to change his tack from its rightward course and welcomed the momentary British turn to the left.

Not all of Garvey's efforts met with failure, and many reforms proposed at the 1922 convention were instituted. The publication of special Spanish and French *Negro World* sections attested to the growing Garveyite movement in non-English-speaking areas abroad. Likewise, the establishment of the *Negro World*'s women's page, edited by Amy Jacques Garvey, helped meet the needs of women members. Entitled "Our Women and What They Think," the special page presented a broad overview of women's issues, featuring articles on the achievements of women college graduates, a woman who retained her name after marriage, and the role of women in the Philippines. These items all shared the limelight with recipes, cosmetics advertisements, and advice on such questions as the proper age for matrimony. More important, this official recognition of Amy Jacques Garvey on the *Negro World*'s editorial masthead signified her own increased position within the movement. As her husband's personal emissary, she wielded influence as well as direct power.

The *Negro World* during this period was not immune to the tensions faced by the UNIA. Compared to other black newspapers of the time—papers such as the *Chicago Defender* and the *New York Age*—early issues of the *Negro World* had been noteworthy for their lack of advertisements for skin-lightening and hair-straightening products. It would seem that financial problems, exacerbated by Garvey's legal costs, forced a change in policy; by November 1923 the *Chicago Whip* noted that Garvey "has been quite successful in cluttering up his paper, the *Negro World*, with hair straightening advertisements and face bleaches."

Although Garvey had announced at the outset of 1923 that "the Executive Council of the Association and myself personally are contemplating holding the next convention in Liberia," the August 1924 convention took place as was customary, in the UNIA's Liberty Hall in Harlem. Liberia did, however, prove to be the convention's most pressing problem. In December 1923 the UNIA sent Robert Lincoln Poston, Henrietta Vinton Davis, and J. Milton Van Lowe to attempt to negotiate its second colonization plan with Liberian officials. The UNIA delegates believed that its meetings with the Liberians boded well, so much so that Poston cabled Garvey his news in a single word—"success." However, by the following July the UNIA's hopes for a base in Liberia lay in ruins. Only a few weeks before the convention opened, the Liberian consul general in the United States, Ernest Lyon, issued a press release announcing his government's refusal to grant visas for colonization purposes to UNIA members.

Some comparisons between the 1924 convention and the previous meeting in 1922 reveal the political tensions and demographic shifts within the movement at this juncture. Although the size of the New York local's delegation, the largest at both conventions, remained virtually the same—with thirty members in 1924, as opposed to thirty-one two years earlier—the local itself had become so merged with the UNIA parent body that its growing lack of a separate identity was proving to be problematic. According to Bureau of Investigation reports, members of the New York local resented the parent body's reliance on their contributions; they likewise objected to their division's president blending local and parent-body concerns to such an extent that "it is practically impossible for the local to function independently" (special report, 12 April 1923, DJ-FBI). Even the Garvey Defense Fund reflected the shift in UNIA membership, as contributors were more likely to be coal miners from western Pennsylvania or West Indian migrant workers in Central America than the old reliable crowd from New York and the eastern seaboard of the United States (special report, 30 December 1922, DJ-FBI). Another indication of change was the reduction of the California and Pennsylvania delegations from their 1922 levels, because of disputes within their two principal divisions. Conversely, a number of the black belt southern states (Arkansas, Georgia, and Mississippi), as well as coal-mining West Virginia, markedly increased the size of their convention delegations.

In all, nearly a hundred new charters were issued in 1924; together with the 105 charters that were then also pending, the movement now encompassed some fourteen hundred separate branches, more than half of which were located in the United States and Canada, with the remainder spread throughout the Caribbean, Central and South America, and Africa.

In general the 1924 convention was peacefully conducted; it was also the largest and the best-documented of Garvey's meetings, to which James Van Der Zee's famous photographs give eloquent visual testimony. Some of the movement's elder statesmen, however, were absent: Gabriel M. Johnson, the former potentate, had by now broken with Garvey and held a lucrative post in the Liberian government as its consul to Fernando Po; and death had claimed the venerable black journalist John E. Bruce at the age of sixty-eight. More significant was the premature passing of Robert Lincoln Poston, who died at the age of thirty-three aboard ship, as he returned from Liberia with the UNIA delegation in March 1924.

Nevertheless there was a noteworthy addition to the convention in the person of a distinguished African guest, Prince Kojo Tovalou-Houénou of Dahomey, editor of the Paris-based black nationalist newspaper *Les Continents*, who addressed the convention and attended the UNIA's court reception. Called "the Garvey of Africa," he was a living symbol of the interest that the UNIA had generated in francophone Africa. Moreover, former members who had long been absent from the UNIA, notably Fred A. Toote of Philadelphia and Rev. George Alexander McGuire, founder of the African Orthodox Church, returned to the fold. McGuire, indeed, led the convention to take one of its most controversial stands, in the form of "the canonization of the Lord Jesus Christ as the Black Man of Sorrows" ("seeing Him through the eyes of blackness") and "the canonization of the Blessed Virgin Mary as a black woman" (report of Special Agent Joseph G. Tucker, 7 June 1924, DJ-FBI). The convention also formulated plans for organizing the Universal Negro Political Union, a step ironically out of keeping with Garvey's previous policies, since he had urged his followers to eschew politics.

Despite the UNIA's despair over the failure of its Liberian plan, the convention ended with membership of the movement diminished but intact, and with internal dissent quelled, at least temporarily. Garvey's Afro-American critics, pleased at his federal conviction, now entered a period of quiescence. And although Garvey's energies would have to continue to be employed in fighting his appeal, the movement's ideas still continued to spread, taking root in new places and informing new struggles.

EDITORIAL PRINCIPLES AND PRACTICES

I. Arrangement of Documents

Documents are presented in chronological order according to the dates of authorship of the original text. Enclosures and attachments to documents, however, do not appear in strict chronological sequence, but are printed with their original covering documents. Enclosures have been set in italic type in the table of contents for identification.

The publication date of news reports, speeches, and periodical articles is given on the place and date line within square brackets. In the case of news reports, speeches, and periodical articles containing the date of original composition, that date chronologically supersedes the date of eventual publication and is printed within double square brackets on the place and date line of the document.

Bureau of Investigation reports that give both the date of compostion and the period covered by the report are arranged according to the date of composition.

Documents that lack dates and thus require editorial assignment of dates are placed in normal chronological sequence. When no day within a month appears on a document, it is placed after the documents specifically dated on the lates date within that month. Documents that carry only the date of a year are placed according to the same principle. Documents that cover substantial periods, such as diaries, journals, and accounts, appear according to the dates of their earliest entries.

When two or more documents possess the same date, they are arranged with regard to affinity to the subject of the document that immediately precedes them or that which immediately follows them.

II. Form of Presentation

Each document is presented in the following manner:

A. A caption introduces the document and is printed in a type size larger than the text. Letters between individuals are captioned with the names of the individuals and their titles; captions, however, include a person's office only upon that person's first appearance. The original titles of published materials are retained with the documents; however, the headlines of some news reports are abbreviated or omitted, in which case this is indicated in the descriptive source note to the document.

B. The text of a document follows the caption. The copy text of letters or reports is taken from recipients' copies whenever possible, but in the absence of a recipient's copy, a file copy of the letter or report is used. If the file copy is not available, however, and a retained draft copy of the letter is found, the retained draft copy is used as the basic text.

C. Following the body of the text, an unnumbered descriptive source note describes editorially the physical character of the document by means of appropriate abbreviations. Moreover, a repository symbol gives the provenance of the original manuscript or, if it is rare, printed work. Printed sources are identified in the following manner:

1. A contemporary pamphlet is identified by its full title, place and date of publication, and the location of the copy used.

2. A contemporary essay, letter, or other kind of statement that appeared originally in a contemporary publication is preceded by the words "Printed in . . . ," followed by the title, date, and, in the case of essays, inclusive page numbers of the source of publication.

3. A contemporary printed source reprinted at a later date, the original publication of which has not been found, is identified with the words "Reprinted from . . . ," followed by the identification of the work from which the text has been reproduced. The same applies to any originally unpublished manuscript printed at a later date.

D. Numbered textual annotations that explicate the document follow the descriptive source note. The following principles of textual annotation have been applied:

1. Individuals are identified upon their first appearance, with additional information about them sometimes furnished upon their later appearance in a document where such data provide maximum clarification. Pseudonyms are identified, wherever possible, by textual annotations.

2. Reasons for the assignment of dates to documents or the correction of dates of doucments are explained in those instances where important historical information is involved.

3. Obscure allusions in the text are annotated whenever such references can be clarified.

4. Printed works and manuscript materials consulted during the preparation of textual annotations appear in parentheses at the end of each

annotation. Frequently used reference works are cited in an abbreviated form, and the complete table may be found in the list of abbreviations of Published Works Cited on p. xlix.

5. Garvey's appeal case (*Marcus Garvey* v. *United States of America*, no. 8317, Ct. App., 2d Cir., 2 February 1925) contains the complete transcript of his original mail fraud trial (*United States of America* v. *Marcus Garvey et al.*, C31-37 and C33-688, U.S. District Court, Southern District of New York, May 1923). Trial documents reprinted in the volume and references to the trial in annotations are taken from the transcript used in the appeal case. A microform copy of this trial transcript will be available with the next volume of the *Garvey Papers*.

III. Transcription of Text

Manuscripts and printed material have been transcribed from the original text and printed as documents according to the following principles and procedures:

A. Manuscript Material

1. The place and date of composition are placed at the head of the document, regardless of their location in the original, but exceptions are made in the cases of certificates of vital registration and documents in which original letterhead stationery is reproduced. If the place or date of a letter (or both) does not appear in the original text, the information is supplied and printed in italics at the head within square brackets. Likewise, if either the place or date is incomplete, the necessary additional information is supplied in italics within square brackets. Superscript letters are brought down to the line of type, and terminal punctuation is deleted.

2. In the case of Bureau of Investigation reports that were submitted on printed forms, the place and date are abstracted and placed at the head of each document, while the name of the reporting agent is placed at the end of the document on the signature line.

3. The formal salutation of letters is placed on the line below the place and date line, with the body of the text following the salutation.

4. The complimentary close of letters is set continuously with the text in run-in style, regardless of how it was written in the original.

5. The signature, which is set in capitals and small capitals, is placed at the right-hand margin on the line beneath the text or complimentary close, with titles, where they appear, set in uppercase and lowercase. Terminal punctuation is deleted.

6. When a file copy of a document bearing no signature is used to establish

the text but the signatory is known, the signature is printed in roman type within square brackets.

7. The inside address, if significant and not repetitive, is printed immediately below the text.

8. Endorsements, docketings, and other markings appearing on official correspondence, when intelligible, are reproduced in small type following the address, with appropriate identification. In the case of other types of documents, such as private correspondence, endorsements and dockets are printed only when they are significant.

9. Minutes, enclosures, and attachments are printed in roman type following their covering documents and placed after the annotation material of their covering documents. Whenever minutes, enclosures, or attachments are not printed, this fact is always recorded and explained. Whenever a transmission letter originally accompanying an enclosure or attachment is not printed, the omission is noted and the transmission document identified and recorded in the descriptive source note.

10. Printed letterheads and other official stationery are not reproduced, unless they contain significant information, in which case they are reprinted above the date line. In cases where they are not reprinted, they are sometimes abstracted, and the information is placed in the descriptive source note. Printed addresses are reproduced only upon the first appearance.

11. In general, the spelling of all words, including proper names, is preserved as written in the manuscript and printed sources. Thus, personal and place names that are spelled erratically in the original texts are regularized or corrected only in the index. However, serious distortion in the spelling of a word, to such an extent as to obscure its true meaning, is repaired by printing the correct word in square brackets after the incorrect spelling. Mere "slips of the pen" or typographical errors are corrected within the word and printed within square brackets; however, some typographical errors that contribute to the overall character of documents are retained.

12. Capitalization is retained as in the original. Words underlined once in a manuscript are printed in italics. Words that are underlined twice or spelled out in large letters or full capitals are printed in small capitals.

13. Punctuation, grammar, and syntax are retained as found in the original texts. In the case of punctuation, corrections that are essential to the accurate reading of the text are provided within square brackets. If, however, a punctuation mark appears in a document as a result of typographical error, it is corrected in square brackets, or in some instances, silently deleted.

14. All contractions and abbreviations in the text are retained. Abbreviations of titles or organizations are identified in a list of abbreviations

that appears at the front of the volume. Persons represented by initials only will have their full names spelled out in square brackets after each initial on their first appearance.

15. Superscript letters in the text are lowered and aligned on the line of print.

16. Omissions, mutilations, and illegible words or letters have been rendered through the use of the following textual devices:

   a) Blank spaces in a manuscript are shown as [   ]. If the blank space is of significance or of substantial length, this fact is elaborated upon in a textual annotation.

   b) When a word or words in the original text must be omitted from the printed document because of mutilation, illegibility, or omission, the omission is shown by the use of ellipses followed by a word or phrase placed in square brackets in italics, such as: . . . [*torn*], . . . [*illegible*], . . . [*remainder missing*].

   c) Missing or illegible letters of words are represented by suspension points within square brackets, the number of points corresponding to the estimated number of letters omitted. The same holds true for missing or illegible digits of numbers.

   d) All attempts have been made conjecturally to supply missing items in the printed document, according to the following rules:

      (1) If there is no question as to the word, the missing letter is supplied silently.

      (2) If the missing letter(s) can only be conjectured, the omission is supplied within square brackets and printed in roman type. Uncertainty of the conjecture, however, is indicated by a question mark within square brackets in the document.

      (3) If the conjectured word(s) is highly uncertain, it is rendered in italics within the square brackets.

17. Additions and corrections made by the author in the original text have been rendered as follows:

   a) Additions between the lines are brought onto the line of type and incorporated into the body of the text within diagonal lines / /.

   b) Marginal additions or corrections by the author are also incorporated into the printed document and identified by the words [*in the margin*] italicized in square brackets. Marginal notes made by someone other than the author are treated as endorsements and are printed following the text of the document.

   c) Words or groups of words deleted in the original, as in a draft, are restored in the printed document. The canceled word or phrase is indicated by canceled type at the place where the deletion occurs in the original text. If a lengthy deletion is illegible, this in indicated by the words [*deletion illegible*].

B. Printed Material

Contemporary printed material is treated in the same manner as are original texts and is transcribed according to the same editorial principles as manuscript material.

1. In the case of originally published letters, the place and date of composition are uniformly printed on the place and date line of the document, regardless of where they appear in the original, and placed within double square brackets. Those elements that have been editorially supplied are italicized.

2. Newspaper headlines and subheads are printed in small capitals. Headlines are punctuated as they are in the original; however, they are reproduced in the printed document in as few lines as possible.

3. Words originally printed in small capitals for emphasis or for other reasons are usually printed in small capitals. Boldfaced type that appears within the text is retained.

4. The signature accompanying a published letter is printed in capitals and small capitals.

5. Obvious typographical errors and errors of punctuation, such as the omission of a single parenthesis or quotation mark, are corrected and printed within square brackets in roman type.

6. In the case of a printed form with spaces to be filled in, the printed words are designated in small capitals, while the handwritten or typewritten insertions are designated in italics with spaces left before and after the small capitals to suggest the blank spaces in the original form.

TEXTUAL DEVICES

[   ]   Blank spaces in the text.

[[   ]]   Double square brackets are used to give the composition date of a published letter or news report if the publication date differs.

/   /   Incorporation into the text of an addition or correction made above or below the line by author.

[roman]   Conjectural reading for missing, mutilated, or illegible matter, with a question mark inside the square bracket when the conjectural reading is doubtful. Also used in editorial correction of typographical errors in original manuscript or printed document. Also used to indicate the publication date of a news report or periodical article.

[*italic*]   Assigned date of any undated document; editorial comment inserted in the text, such as [*endorsement*], [*illegible*], [*remainder missing*], [*sentence unfinished*], [*torn*], [*enclosure*], [*attachment*], [*in the margin*]. Also used for a conjectural reading that is highly uncertain.

~~canceled~~   Textual matter deleted in the original but restored in the text.

SYMBOLS AND ABBREVIATIONS

Repository Symbols

The original locations of documents that appear in the text are described by symbols. The guide used for American repositories has been *Symbols of American Libraries*, eleventh edition (Washington, D.C.: Library of Congress, 1976). Foreign repositories and collections have been assigned symbols that conform to the institutions' own usage. In some cases, however, it has been necessary to formulate acronyms. Acronyms have been created for private manuscript collections as well.

Repositories

ANSOM	Archives Nationales, Section d'Outre-Mer, Paris
AMAE	Archives du Ministère des Affaires Étrangères, Paris
ADSL	Archives of the Department of State, Ministry of Foreign Affairs, Monrovia, Liberia
ATT	Hollis Burke Frissell Library, Tuskegee Institute, Tuskegee Institute, Alabama
DJ-FBI	Federal Bureau of Investigation, United States Department of Justice, Washington, D.C.
DLC	Library of Congress, Washington, D.C.
DNA	National Archives, Washington, D.C.

RG 16	Records of the Office of the Secretary of Agriculture
RG 32	Records of the United States Shipping Board
RG 38	Records of the Office of the Chief of Naval Operations
RG 59	General Records of the Department of State
RG 60	General Records of the Department of Justice
RG 65	Records of the Federal Bureau of Investigation

	RG 165	Records of the War Department, General and Special Staffs; Records of the Office of the Chief of Staff
	RG 233	Records of the United States House of Representatives
JA	Jamaica Archives, Spanish Town, Jamaica	
LNA	League of Nations Archives, Geneva	
MdBMC	Morgan State University Library, Baltimore	
MU	University of Massachusetts Library, Amherst	
NCU	University of North Carolina, Chapel Hill	
NN-Sc	The Schomburg Center for Research in Black Culture, New York Public Library, New York	
NNC	Butler Library, Columbia University	
NNHR	New York Supreme Court, Hall of Records, New York	
OC-HS	Ohio Historical Society, Columbus	
PRO	Public Record Official Office	
	CO	Colonial Office
	FO	Foreign Office
SAMAE	Service des Archives du Ministère des Affaires Étrangères, Brussels	
TNF	Fisk University, Nashville	
WNRC	Washington National Records Center, Suitland, Maryland	
	RG 204	Records of the Pardon Attorney

Manuscript Collection Symbols

CC	Calvin Coolidge Papers, *DLC*
JRRC	J. R. Ralph Casimir, Roseau, Dominica
MGMC	Marcus Garvey Memorial Collection, *TNF*
NAACP	National Association for the Advancement of Colored People Papers, *DLC*
NMB	Nicholas Murray Butler Papers, *NNC*
RRM	Robert R. Moton Papers, *ATT*
WEBDB	W. E. B. Du Bois Papers, *MU*
WP	William Pickens Papers, *NN-Sc*

Descriptive Symbols

The following symbols are used to describe the character of the original documents:

ALS	Autograph letter signed
AMS	Autograph manuscript
PD	Printed document
TD	Typed document
TDS	Typed document signed
TG	Telegram
TL	Typed letter
TLI	Typed letter initialed
TLS	Typed letter signed
TMS	Typed manuscript
TN	Typed note
TNI	Typed note initialed

Published Works Cited

BFQ	*Bartlett's Familiar Quotations,* fifteenth edition
BM	*Black Man*
CD	*Chicago Defender*
DAB	*Dictionary of American Biography*
DANB	*Dictionary of American Negro Biography*
DG	*Daily Gleaner*
DNB	*Dictionary of National Biography*
EA	*Encyclopedia Americana*
EB	*Encyclopaedia Britannica*
EWH	*Encyclopedia of World History*
HJ	*Handbook of Jamaica*
JNH	*Journal of Negro History*
NCAB	*National Cyclopedia of American Biography*
NW	*Negro World*
NYB	*Negro Year Book*
NYT	*New York Times*

P&O	*Philosophy and Opinions of Marcus Garvey*
WBD	*Webster's New Biographical Dictionary*
WWCA	*Who's Who of Colored America*
WWCR	*Who's Who of the Colored Race*
WWJ	*Who's Who in Jamaica*
WWW	*Who Was Who*
WWWA	*Who Was Who in America*

Other Symbols and Abbreviations

Included are abbreviations that are used generally throughout annotations of the text. Standard abbreviations, such as those for titles and scholastic degrees, are omitted. Abbreviations that are specific to a single annotation appear in parentheses after the initial citation and are used thereafter in the rest of the annotation.

ABB	African Blood Brotherhood
ACL	African Communities League
AFL	American Federation of Labor
AME	African Methodist Episcopal Church
AMEZ	African Methodist Episcopal Zion Church
BSL	Black Star Line, Incorporated
BWI	British West Indies
GPO	Government Printing Office
MID	Military Intelligence Division
NAACP	National Association for the Advancement of Colored People
NFC	Negro Factories Corporation
RG	Record Group
UNIA	Universal Negro Improvement Association
USSB	United States Shipping Board

CHRONOLOGY

September 1922–August 1924

1922

11 September	UNIA League of Nations delegates arrive in Geneva.
ca. 11 September	J.W.H. Eason forms rival organization, Universal Negro Alliance.
25 September	First issue of *Daily Negro Times* is published.
1 October	Garvey speaks in Pittsburgh.
19 October	Garvey is rumored to own a house in Larchmont, N.Y.
ca. 26 October	UNIA announces suspension of *Daily Negro Times*.
1–5 November	UNIA announces opening of its first educational and commercial exposition and fair.
9 November	Garvey sends Esau Ramus, formerly third vice-president of Philadelphia UNIA, to New Orleans division.
27 November	Marcus Garvey's mail fraud trial, scheduled to be heard in the United States District Court for the Southern District of New York, is postponed.
30 November	UNIA League of Nations delegates return to New York.
2 December	Reported closing of UNIA's restaurant.
26 December	Garvey's case is postponed again.

1923

1 January	Eason is shot in New Orleans.
4 January	Eason dies of gunshot wounds.
5 January	William Shakespeare and Fred Dyer are arrested for Eason's murder.
12 January	Garvey has Elie Garcia arrested for petty larceny.
15 January	Chandler Owen and others send letter of complaint against Garvey to Attorney General Harry M. Daugherty.
20 January	UNIA announces formation of Dyer and Shakespeare Defense Fund.
23 January	J. W. Jones (Confidential Informant 800) is assigned by Bureau of Investigation to investigate Eason's murder.
31 January	Because of failure to pay rent, UNIA's laundry enterprise is evicted and ceases operation.
January	Garvey publishes an answer to his critics.
1 February	Garvey contemplates taking world tour.
5 February	Garvey requests postponement of his case from 2 January until 5 February.
21 February	Esau Ramus is arrested in Detroit in connection with Eason's murder.
23 February	Garvey holds meeting at Carnegie Hall and invites three hundred prominent white citizens.
25 February	Garvey speaks in Chicago.
4 March	Elie Garcia is convicted of larceny.
22 March	Shakespeare and Dyer are found guilty of manslaughter in Eason's killing.
27 March–2 April	Bureau of Investigation reports that the Pittsfield, Massachusetts, UNIA has disbanded and affiliated with the Workers Party of America.

2 April	Shakespeare and Dyer are each sentenced to eighteen-to-twenty-year prison terms for Eason's death.
11–30 April	New York UNIA division sponsors series of educational meetings at Liberty Hall.
29 April	Garvey speaks in Buffalo.
3 May	Garvey speaks in Pittsburgh.
14 May	Garvey files writ to have Judge Julian Mack dismissed from his case because of Mack's affiliation with the NAACP.
18 May	Government's case consolidates both indictments; Garvey's trial for mail fraud begins.
15 June	Garvey makes final address at his trial.
16 June	Shakespeare and Dyer lose the appeal of their case.
21 June	Garvey is sentenced to five years in jail for mail fraud.
25 June	Garvey's appeal for bail is rejected by Judge Henry Wade Rogers.
27 June	Garvey discharges UNIA officers E.L. Gaines, Rudolph Smith, G.O. Marke, and Henrietta V. Davis; William Ferris resigns from *Negro World*, but is listed on masthead until September.
ca. 5 July	Formation of Marcus Garvey Committee on Justice, beginning of petition drive to free Garvey.
6 July	Pro-Garvey petition is delivered to attorney general in Washington, D.C.
15 July	Vernal J. Williams resigns as UNIA's attorney.
17 July	United States government opposes Garvey's bail request.
2 August	President Warren G. Harding dies in San Francisco; Garvey sends condolences to Mrs. Harding.
5 August	*New York World* publishes Garvey's autobiographical article; it later appears in the September issue of *Current History*.

7 August	Garvey appoints Maurice Nagler to take over as UNIA's attorney.
12 August	Rev. E. Ethelred Brown writes anti-Garvey sermon.
14 August	J. J. Adam is reelected as UNIA's delegate to League of Nations and is named by Garvey as first provisional ambassador of the Negro peoples of the world to France.
19–26 August	Montreal UNIA division holds its convention meetings.
27–29 August	Washington, D.C., UNIA division holds its convention meeting.
29–31 August	New York local UNIA division holds three-day convention.
10 September	Garvey is released on bail after three-month imprisonment in Tombs Prison.
13 September	New York local welcomes Garvey to Liberty Hall with mass meeting.
25 September	Immigration Department begins preparing deportation case against Garvey.
September	*Current History* magazine publishes Garvey's essay "The Negro's Greatest Enemy."
2 October	Garvey delivers speech, "An Appeal to the Soul of White America," in Youngstown, Ohio.
3 October	Garvey begins letterwriting campaign to senators and other United States government officials on the "Negro problem."
5 October	Garvey speaks in St. Louis.
6–27 October	Capt. Hugh Mulzac begins publishing his exposé of BSL in *Cleveland Gazette*.
23 October	Garvey is in Oakland, California, on a speaking tour.
31 Oct–2 Nov	Garvey and Amy Jacques Garvey visit Tuskegee Institute.
1 November	Garvey addresses students and faculty at Tuskegee Institute.

6 November	Garvey to speak in Washington, D.C.
6 November	Garvey contributes $50 to Tuskegee Institute.
26 November	Garvey speaks in Philadelphia's Salem Baptist Church.
5 December	Garvey writes a letter of introduction to President C.D.B. King of Liberia for UNIA delegation of Robert L. Poston, Henrietta V. Davis, and Milton Van Lowe.
11 December	UNIA delegation (Davis, Poston, Van Lowe) leaves for Liberia.

1924

17 January	Garvey addresses students and faculty at Howard University.
2 February	*Negro World* adds two sections, one in French, the other, edited by Amy Jacques Garvey, devoted to interests of women; Amy Jacques Garvey becomes assistant editor of *Negro World*.
ca. 2 February	Garvey congratulates Ramsay Macdonald on his election as prime minister of Great Britain.
16 March	UNIA mass meeting held at Madison Square Garden.
22 March	Announcement is made that Black Cross Navigation and Trading Company is to replace BSL.
31 March	Garvey writes to President C.D.B. King.
10 April	Garvey to speak at Carnegie Hall.
May	Du Bois writes editorial calling Garvey "lunatic or traitor."
3 June	Garvey seeks appointment with United States Shipping Board to purchase new ships.
7 June	Garvey announces program for August 1924 convention.
25 June	Garvey wants first ship of Black Cross Navigation and Trading Company to sail in September.
3–4 July	Garvey to speak in Newark, New Jersey.

10 July	Ernest Lyons, Liberian consul general to United States, announces that Liberia refuses to grant visas to UNIA members.
1 August	Fourth International Convention of the Negro Peoples of the World is opened.
3 August	Garvey cables messages to various world leaders, including MacDonald, Gandhi, Mussolini, and Pope Pius XI.
7 August	John E. Bruce dies.
8 August	Dyer and Shakespeare are finally acquitted of Eason's murder, after a year and a half of court battles.
13 August	Garvey claims to have acquired S. S. *General Goethals* for Black Cross Navigation and Trading Company.
17 August	Garvey announces that inspection of S. S. *General Goethals* by UNIA members will occur.
18 August	Prince Kojo Tovalou-Houénou addresses UNIA convention.
23 August	Garvey makes annual report to convention.

THE PAPERS

VOLUME V
September 1922–August 1924

Maurice Peterson, British Embassy, to William L. Hurley, Department of State

[*Washington, D.C.*] September 1, 1922

My dear Hurley,

I think it was with you that we had some time ago some conversations and correspondence with regard to the negro movement in this country headed by Marcus Garvey. In this connection I think it well to call your attention to an article in the "New York World" of August 29th[1] which reports that a message from the King and Queen of Abyssinia was conveyed to the meeting under Garvey's auspices by the Persian Consul General in New York, H.H. Topakyan, who apparently claimed to represent Abyssinia in this country.[2]

I should be very grateful if you would let me know whether this claim is justified or, if not, what power, if any, does represent Abyssinian interests in the United States. Yours sincerely,

MAURICE PETERSON

PRO, FO 115/2766. TL, carbon copy.

1. The message was printed in *The Marcus Garvey and Universal Negro Improvement Association Papers* 4 (Berkeley and Los Angeles: University of California Press, 1985), pp. 1,005–1,007; hereafter cited as *Garvey Papers*. The *New York World* article of 29 August 1922 was entitled "Abyssinia's King Elates Negroes by His Invitation"; it implied that Topakyan delivered the message in person; according to *Negro World* accounts of the speech, however, Topakyan was in Washington, D.C., and sent his message, which Garvey read to the convention (*NW*, 9 September 1922).

2. No records have been found that indicate an official relation between H.H. Topakyan and the Abyssinian (Ethiopian) government. In response to a letter Topakyan wrote to President Warren G. Harding asking that an American consulate general be established in Addis Ababa, an interoffice memo of the State Department said simply, "Who is Mr. Topakyan . . . ?" While the Department of State replied to Topakyan that they would consider the matter, an embassy was not opened in Addis Ababa until 1 March 1928 (DNA, RG 59, file 125.121/3, H.H. Topakyan to Warren G. Harding, 4 October 1922; unsigned letter from Department of State to H.H. Topakyan, 19 October 1922; unsigned memo, 21 October 1922).

Article by Hodge Kirnon

[*Negro World*, 2 September 1922]

HODGE KIRNON[1] ANALYZES RESULTS OF ANTI-GARVEY CAMPAIGN

The campaign against Garveyism waged by Randolph, Owen and Pickens ought to be productive of beneficial results. I enumerate the following as characteristic ones:

1. It should provoke discussion as to whether Pickens' platform buffoon oratory was taken seriously as against Garveyism.

2. It should tend to modify the exuberance of optimism and idealism of the Garveyites, thus rationalizing Garveyism to some degree.

3. It should tend to prove a corrective against injudicious and thoughtless election and appointment of officers and leaders of the Garvey movement.

4. It should awaken and stimulate a keener interest in questions affecting the Negro.

5. It should tend to stimulate more interest in the Garvey movement.

6. It should tend to emphasize the fact that while the Garvey movement received its impetus from economic considerations, a spiritual and racial idealism has been evolved which transcends economic interests, and which is fast getting beyond the assaults of logic.

7. It should tend to force Randolph and Owen to eventually recognize Garvey as a potent factor in the life of the Negro, just as they have at this very late date begun to recognize J.A. Rogers[2] and Wm. H. Ferris.

8. It should teach Randolph and Owen that Garveyism is a spiritual power which has enveloped and stimulated the racial soul of the Negro, and therefore cannot be thrown, bag and baggage, out of America.

9. It should teach Randolph and Owen that class consciousness could and should be developed alongside race consciousness.

10. It should teach Randolph and Owen to ponder seriously over the following words of Dr. Henry Maudsley,[3] the great English scientist and author, before sweeping Garvey too abruptly aside with an air of finality: "What right have we to believe Nature under any obligation to do her work by means of complete minds only? She may find an incomplete mind a more suitable instrument for a particular purpose. It is the work that is done, and the quality in the worker by which it is done, that is alone of moment; and it may be no great matter from a cosmical standpoint, if in other qualities of character he was singularly defective—if, indeed, he were hypocrite, adulterer, eccentric or lunatic."

11. It should teach Randolph and Owen that they do not know it all.

Printed in *NW*, 2 September 1922.

1. Hodge Kirnon was born in Montserrat, West Indies, in 1891; he immigrated to the United States in 1908, and was an early follower of Hubert H. Harrison. Kirnon drifted into the Garvey movement in 1920, at the same time that he began to edit a journal entitled the *Promoter*, which the *Negro World* praised as being both "radical and racial" (*NW*, 21 August 1920). Despite leveling periodic criticism at the Garvey movement, Kirnon contributed articles to the *Negro World*, spoke at occasional UNIA meetings, and supported Garvey in the early days of his trial. Kirnon felt that the "racial radicalism" of the Garvey movement was part of an "evolutionary process in the life of the Negro" and recognized that this "racial patriotism" held a spiritual power that had a profound appeal among blacks in the United States as well as having the potential to unite blacks around the world (*NW*, 17 June 1922). He felt, however, that the struggle of American blacks was in the United States, not abroad, and called it "downright ignorance and unspeakable folly" not to work with progressive whites in the fight to improve conditions for all American workers, both white and black. Racial consciousness should, he believed, be developed alongside of class consciousness (Hodge Kirnon, "Racialism and Radicalism," *Promoter* 1, no.3 [July 1920]). Kirnon wrote a book on his homeland in 1925 entitled *Montserrat and the Montserratians* and by 1928 was chairman

of the publicity committee for the Montserrat Progressive Society. Kirnon became a naturalized U. S. citizen in 1928. Still interested in the West Indies, Kirnon became an active member of the American-West Indian Association on Caribbean Affairs in 1942 (Hodge Kirnon, *Montserrat and the Montserratians* [New York: n.p., 1925]; Ben Waknin, "Garvey Among the Intellectuals" [unpublished manuscript]; *NW*, 20 August 1920, 16 July and 30 July 1921, 14 January, 28 January, 3 June, 17 June and 2 September 1922, 5 September 1925, 6 October 1928, 16 August 1929; *NYT*, 8 October 1922; U. S. Department of Labor, declaration of intention no. 154866, May 1928; NN-Sc, UNIA Records, box 11, e.18).

2. Joel Augustus Rogers (1880–1966), a self-educated journalist and historian, helped pioneer the study of black history in the early twentieth century. Born in Negril, Jamaica, Rogers migrated to the United States, where in 1911 he began his lifelong research in black history. In 1917 Rogers published *From "Superman" to Man*, which attacked racist assumptions of black inferiority. This was followed in 1919 by the publication of *As Nature Leads*. These self-published books brought Rogers to the attention of the black press and helped launch his career in journalism. He began writing a weekly column for the *Pittsburgh Courier* and became a contributing editor to the *Chicago Enterprise*. He served as subeditor of Garvey's short-lived *Daily Negro Times* in 1922 and wrote occasionally for the *Negro World*. In 1926, writing for the *New York Amsterdam News*, Rogers interviewed Garvey in prison (*New York Amsterdam News*, 17 November 1926).

In 1925 Rogers went to Europe as a correspondent. He sent back articles on life in Europe and the rise of fascism that were published in black American newspapers. He was the only war correspondent for a black weekly to cover the Italian invasion of Ethiopia in 1935–1936; Rogers's detailed accounts of Ethiopian bravery and his interview with Emperor Haile Selassie, by then the beleaguered symbol of resistance to the onslaught of Italian fascism, made him a celebrity.

In spite of his support of Garvey's efforts to build black racial pride and the UNIA's appeal to black workers, Rogers was critical of Garvey's leadership, and in 1922 he attended at least one meeting of the anti-Garvey group, the Friends of Negro Freedom. In 1947 he chose to label the Garvey movement "racial fascism," comparing Garvey with Mussolini and Hitler. Whatever his political differences, however, Rogers was to remain in contact with Garvey until Garvey's death in London in 1940.

The culmination of Rogers's historical research found expression in 1947, when he published *World's Great Men of Color*, a two-volume series of biographical essays on black historical figures which he had begun publishing in black newspapers in 1924. Although Rogers wrote the essays as inspirational success stories aimed at black youth, the volumes found a much broader audience, bringing to light neglected areas of the past and laying the basis for a later resurgence of interest in black history. Rogers continued to write books and articles on various aspects of black history until his death in 1966 (*WWCA*; Augustus Low and Virgil Clift, *Encyclopedia of Black America* [New York: McGraw-Hill, 1981], p.735; Earl E. Thorpe, *Black Historians: A Critique* [New York: William Morrow, 1971], p. 153; Robert L. Southgate, *Black Plots and Black Characters* [Syracuse, N.Y.: Gaylord Professional Publications, 1979], p. 288; *NW*, 7 May 1921, 7 January and 17 June 1922, 22 August and 12 December 1925, 3 November 1928, 16 June 1932; *Pittsburgh Courier*, 9 April 1966; *New York Amsterdam News*, 2 April 1966; *NYT*, 27 April 1966; *JNH* 51, no. 3 [July 1966]: 236; Valerie Sandoval, "The Bran of History: An Historiographic Account of the World of J. A. Rogers," *Schomburg Center Journal* 1, no.4 [spring 1978]: 5–7, 16–19; W. Burghart Turner, "Joel Augustus Rogers: An Afro-American Historian," *Negro History Bulletin* 25, no. 2 [February 1972]: 35–38; Ralph L. Crowder, "Street Scholars: Self-Trained Black Historians," *Black Collegian* [January/February 1979]: 8–23; Jervis Anderson, *A. Philip Randolph: A Biographical Portrait* [New York: Harcourt, Brace, Jovanovich, 1972], p. 140; Andrew Buni, *Robert L. Vann of the "Pittsburgh Courier": Politics and Black Journalism* [Pittsburgh: University of Pittsburgh Press, 1974], pp. 141, 246–249; William R. Scott, "A Study of Afro-American and Ethiopian Relations, 1896–1941," [Ph.D. diss., Princeton University, 1971], pp. 294–300; John Henrik Clarke, Introduction to *World's Great Men of Color* [New York: Macmillan, 1972], 1: ix–xv, 2: xi–xxiv). For Joel A. Rogers's own works, see *From "Superman" to Man* (published by the author, 1917); *As Nature Leads* (published by the author, 1919); *History of the Maroons of the West Indies* (published by the author, 1921); *World's Great Men of African Descent* (published by the author, 1930); *Real Facts About Ethiopia* (published by the author, 1935); *One Hundred Amazing Facts about the Negro* (published by the author, 1940); *Your History from the Beginning of Time to the Present* (Pittsburgh: Pittsburgh Courier Co., 1940); *Sex and Race*, 3 vols. (published by the author, 1944); *World's Great Men of Color* (published by the author, 1947; reprint, New York: Macmillan, 1972); *Nature Knows No Color Line* (published by the author, 1952); *Africa's Gift to America* (published by the author, 1961); *She Walks in Beauty* (Los Angeles: Western Publishers, 1963); *Facts about the Negro* (Pittsburgh:

Lincoln Park Studios, 1964); *Five Negro Presidents* (published by the author, 1965).

3. Dr. Henry Maudsley (1835–1918), English physician, academic, and author, was a pioneer of research into mental illness and psychiatry (*Allibone's Dictionary of English Literature and British and American Authors*, supp., vol. 2 [Philadelphia: J. B. Lippincott Co., 1897], p. 1,092).

Report by Special Agent James E. Amos

New York, N.Y. Sept. 6, 1922

U.S. vs. Marcus Garvey et al.

Continuing on the above entitled matter, Agent interviewed the REV. [J.D.] GORDON, 385 Herkimer Street, Brooklyn, N.Y. GORDON has given to Agent all papers he had in connection with this matter, but did not want to appear on the stand as he is a minister, but after talking to Agent, he promised to testify at any time the Government wanted him to, as he now feels that GARVEY is a menace to the negro race.

Agent interviewed DR. J.D. GIBSON, 140 West 128th Street, N.Y. City, former Surgeon General of the U.N.I.A., and he has promised to come to the Bureau office with letters, papers and anything he has that he thinks will be of service to the Government when GARVEY is tried, and is also willing to go on the stand at any time.

Agent also interviewed J.D. BROOKS, 72 Wickliffe Avenue, Newark, N.J., whom GARVEY had arrested for stealing $400.00. BROOKS was tried in Part 4, General Sessions, before Judge [N]ott,[1] but was found not guilty. BROOKS told Agent he intended to sue GARVEY for $100,000 for false arrest and defamation of character. BROOKS was general secretary of the U.N.I.A., and went through the count[r]y selling stock for the myth ship "PHILIS WHEATLY." He testified on the stand before Judge Knott that he sold $2,000 worth of stock certificates for the "PHILS WHEATLY." BROOKS is ready and willing to testify at any time for the Government.

Agent interviewed J.W. [H]. EASON, who was leader of American negroes in the U.N.I.A. He has promised to come to this office and give a statement concerning the U.N.I.A., also of moneys he sent by mail to GARVEY for his fraudulent stock sales. All of these men and hundreds of others are willing to testify for the Government any time they are called.

Agent will forward statements of these men as soon as same are obtained.

JAMES E. AMOS

DJ-FBI, file 61. TD.

1. Charles C. Nott, Jr. (1869–1957), Massachusetts-born judge, graduated from Harvard Law School in 1894. In 1903, following several years of practice in New York, he was appointed assistant district attorney, a position he held until his election in 1913 to the general sessions bench. He served twenty-five years on the bench and presided over the trial and eventual acquittal of George A. McManus, accused of murdering the gambler Arnold Rothstein, and of James H. Hines, Tammany Hall leader charged with protecting the racketeer Arthur "Dutch Schultz" Flegenheimer (*NYT*, 11 May 1957).

Charles L.C.M.P. Barret, French Consul General, New York, to M. La Rocca,[1] French Ministry of Foreign Affairs

New York, 7 September 1922

RE CERTAIN ATTACKS AGAINST
THE U.N.I.A.

The Pan-African Movement organized by the U.N.I.A. has not been without strong opposition from black Americans, as I have already informed Your Excellency.

The society, "The Friends of Negro Freedom," held last Sunday an important meeting at which A. Philip Randolph, Secretary General of the organization and editor of "The Messenger" (a Negro newspaper published in New York), violently attacked Marcus Garvey who, he said, had assembled at this recent convention far less delegates than he had boasted of and that these delegates "did not represent the leading black organizations and the Negro churches of the country."

He concluded with the prediction that a day would come "when all men will fight for the good of humanity, without taking differences of race and color into consideration."

[CHARLES L.C.M.P. BARRET]
[French Consul General, New York]

ANSOM, Service de Liaison avec les Originaires des Territoires de la France d'Outre-Mer, [88] series III, carton 84(2). TL, carbon copy (translated from the French).

1. M. La Rocca served as the director of Political and Commercial Affairs, a subdivision of the French Foreign Ministry, from 1920 to 1925 (Paul Gordon Lauren, *Diplomats and Bureaucrats* [Stanford, Calif.: Hoover Institution Press, 1976], p. 239).

Report by Special Employee Andrew M. Battle

New York, N.Y. 9/8/22

. . . In the evening [6 *September*] [Rev. G.E. Stewart,] former High Chancellor of the U.N.I.A.[,] called on me and informed me that he had been to the office of the Department of Justice during the day and had talked with Agent [Amos], but had not told him the truth. He also said that he had omitted to tell [Amos] anything about the letters which he had written to Marcus Garvey in April regarding the reckless manner in which Garvey was spending the organization's money. He informed me that in his opinion Garvey was mixed up in the matter of the human hand being sent to Philip Randolph through the mail.[1] He said that Garvey had been very foolish when he committed himself in a speech made at the convention on the 6th of August when he advised Owen and others who disagreed with him to "get themselves another job," as he, Garvey, "could not be responsible for anything that might happen to them because they might come up with a hand off or a leg off or a broken head."

ANDREW M. BATTLE

DJ-FBI, file 61-746-11. TD.

1. On 5 September 1922, A. Philip Randolph received a package containing a human hand that had been cut off below the wrist. The *New York Times* reported that it was the hand of a white man, the *New York World* that it was the hand of a black. The package was marked "From a Friend, New Orleans" and contained a letter, signed allegedly by the Ku Klux Klan, ordering Randolph to join the UNIA. The letter read in part: "We have sent you a sample of our good work, so watch your step or else you. . . . Now let me see your name in your nigger improvement association as a member, paid up too, in about one week from now . . . if you can't unite with your own race we will find out what's the matter with you all. Don't be selfish . . ." (*New York World*, 6 September 1922). Marcus Garvey called the incident a "publicity stunt" by black socialists, saying, "They have been trying to steal some of my own publicity for a long time" (*New York Age*, 9 September 1922). In a *Messenger* column, Randolph said the Klan had sent the letter to "come to the rescue of its Negro leader, Marcus Garvey, as is indicated in the letter of warning." Randolph was quoted by the *New York World* as saying, "I am inclined to believe that the package was sent by a white man or men and by someone really connected with the Ku Klux Klan. A Negro would hardly be so calculating in a thing of this kind, and a Negro wouldn't be likely to get hold of the hand." Police at the 139th Street station, however, suspected the package might have been sent by a black supporter of Garvey (*New York World*, 6 September 1922; *NYT*, 6 September 1922; *New York Age*, 9 September 1922; *NW*, 23 September 1922; *Messenger* 4, no. 10 [October 1922]: 499).

L.A. Johnson to the Editor, *New York Age*

[[2[5]5 1-2 W. 114th St. New York City,
ca. 8 September 1922]]

Editor of THE NEW YORK AGE:

In your editorial of the Age under date of September 8, under caption, "Unearned Salaries,"[1] you underestimate the salary budget of the Hon. Mr. Garvey. Being a former member of the U.N.I.A., I'm in position to speak with certainty as to these wasteful policies.

The salary list of high executives should really stand as follows:

The Potentate, $12,000; President General, $10,000; Supreme Deputy, $6,000; First Assistant President General, $7,500; 2nd Assistant President General, $4,000; 3rd Assistant President General, $4,000; 4th Assistant General, $4,000; Coun[se]l General (to be supplied) $6,000; Assistant Coun[se]l General[,] $3,500; 1st Delegate to League, $12,500; 2nd Delegate to League[,] $12,500; Secretary General[,] $3,600; 1st Assistant Secretary General, $3,250; 2nd Assistant Secretary General, $2,500; High Chancellor, $4,000; Auditor General[,] $4,000; International Organizer, $4,000; Minister of U[*niversal*] A[*frican*] Leg[*ion*,] $3,500; Minister of Industry, $3,000; High Commissioner General, $6,000; total $110,250.

Many of these high executives have private secretaries paid by the people.

The Hon. Mr. Garvey is not by any means equal to the task he assumes. He has no knowledge of the economic fitness of things; over estimates the value of propaganda; tries to fool the public concerning the numerical strength of his organization by claiming 5,000,000 members when their books at headquarters show an awful shrinkage to less than 100,000 paid up, and they are quitting every day—(not in New York but out in the country).

Hon[.] Mr. Garvey is a great organizer and if the race was allowed to run it, it could be made a great organization. But with the nonsensical dreams of this wild man, who will do anything for notoriety from wasting $12,500 each on a group of delegates to carry a petition to the League of Nations (which of course will be thrown in the trash basket before they get out of the door) to $10,000 on a press for [a] daily paper which will be an impossibility, because the same thing that is gradually killing "The Negro World" will kill Mr. Garvey's daily paper. That is, there will be nothing in it but Garvey, Garvey, Garvey. The world wants news and there'll be no news in it, it will begin with Garvey and end with Garvey.

It wil[l] simply be a few more wasted thousands of the people's money. But why should he worry? Barnum assures him that one is born every minute.[2]

The movement is rapidly caving [in] on the inside and hence unless a few able men with common sense set up a similar movement the final crash is just over the hill.

This time last year, I was a most enthusiastic member and I still believe that a powerful Negro state somewhere in the World will be the final and ultimate so[l]ution of our problems. But as I see it, [it is] Garvey's own affair from bottom to top and the race is not allowed to exercise its will in any important way or at any time. I quit and hundreds of my friends quit and hundreds more are quitting every day. Yours,

L. A. JOHNSON
A lover of the race

Printed in the *New York Age*, 23 September 1922. Original headlines omitted.

1. The editorial, which appeared on 9 September 1922, had placed Garvey's salary at $10,000 and stated that the salaries of all other officials had been cut by about 30 percent (*New York Age*, 9 September 1922).

2. A reference to a saying attributed to P. T. Barnum (1810–1891), "There's a sucker born every minute" (*BFQ*).

Article in the *New York Times*

[11 September 1922]

"GARVEY MUST GO," NEGROES DECLARE

"Marcus Garvey Must Go" was the slogan of three meetings of negroes held in Harlem yesterday [*10 September*] by men and women who expressed dissatisfaction with Garvey's handling of the affairs of the Universal Negro

Improvement Association.

A. Philip Randolph, an editor of The Messenger, speaking under the auspices of the Friends of Negro Freedom at New Douglass Hall, Lenox Avenue and 142d Street, discussed Garvey's reported visit to the headquarters of the Ku Klux Klan in Atlanta.

Randolph, answering the implied threat of those who sent him a human hand through the mails, declared that the incident would not cause him to stop his agitation against Garvey and the Ku Klux Klan. He discussed the affairs of the Black Star Line and other ventures headed by Garvey, and announced that meetings under the auspices of his organization would be held in all parts of the United States.

J.W.H. Eason, at the National Baptist Church, 125th Street and Fifth Avenue, told why he severed his connection with Garvey's organization and formed the Universal Negro Alliance. He opposed Garvey's action in sending a delegation of negroes to the League of Nations Assembly in Geneva to ask for a mandate over parts of Africa. Mr. Eason said that the negroes of the United States had plenty of problems of their own and his organization aimed to stimulate negroes to face their immediate pressing problems and not to go to other countries to take up problems there.

J. Austin Norris of Philadelphia asserted that Garvey's assertion that his organization contained 4,000,000 members caused the British Government to refuse passports to African students intent on coming to this country[1] and working their way through college.

Another meeting where Garvey's methods were criticised was held at Lafayette Hall, Seventh Avenue and 131st Street.

Garvey himself held a mass meeting at Liberty Hall, 120 West 138th Street. He announced the issue of the first number of The Daily Negro Times[2] and reported in behalf of the delegation of his association to the League of Nations Assembly.

"The delegation reports that it is making splendid headway and has met with great success through the reception accorded its members by the various national groups that form the League," he declared in a statement. "The delegation was successful in drawing the attention of the League Assembly to the atrocities perpetrated upon the natives of the late German Southwest African colonies, now under British mandate.[3] The matter was brought before the League by Delegate [*Louis Dantès*] Bellegarde. The delegation now at Geneva is asking to have the late German colonies in Africa turned over to the negro peoples of the world under the auspices of the Universal Negro Improvement Association."

Printed in the *New York Times*, 11 September 1922. Original headlines abbreviated.

1. A policy concerning higher education established by the British colonial authorities for the protectorate of Uganda confirmed Norris's assertion regarding the British government's refusal to issue passports to African students. In the early 1920s a debate on higher education began as Baganda, Basoga, and Batoro chiefs petitioned the colonial government about providing advanced education opportunities for their young men. British colonial authorities questioned where these

students might be educated with a minimum of political risk. Out of a concern for the UNIA's influence among the black American community, on 30 May 1922 the governor of Uganda, R.T. Coryndon, requested authority to refuse passports to those wishing to study in the United States. The colonial secretary, Winston Churchill, consented to this ban, which lasted for a number of years (PRO, CO 536/119/02501; Kenneth James King, *Pan-Africanism and Education: A Study of Race Philanthropy and Education in the Southern States of America and East Africa* [Oxford: Clarendon Press, 1971], pp. 69–73).

2. The staff of the *Daily Negro Times* included Garvey, executive editor; T. Thomas Fortune, editor; Ulysses S. Poston, managing editor; W.A. Stephenson, news editor; Joel A. Rogers, sub-news editor; John E. Bruce, H.G. Mugdal, and Robert L. Poston, editorial writers; Romeo L. Daugherty, sports editor; and Robert Cross and Arnold de Petrie, reporters (*New York Age*, 21 October 1922). The *Daily Negro Times* failed after twenty-six issues; after its demise, Fortune and Stephenson joined the staff of the *Negro World* (*NW*, 6 October 1923). Mugdal later served as the *Negro World*'s acting managing editor from May 1930 until June 1932 (*NW*, 31 May 1930, 11 June 1932). Joel A. Rogers reported that Garvey had bought a second-hand newspaper press to produce the *Daily Negro Times*. Garvey also acquired a regular United Press ticker, making the *Daily Negro Times* "probably the first Negro newspaper in America with a ticker that gave the news of the world" (J.A. Rogers, "Additional Facts on Marcus Garvey and His Trial for Using the Mails to Defraud," Negroes of New York Writers Program, New York, 1939, NN-Sc).

3. Actually under South African mandate.

G.O. Marke, Chairman of UNIA Delegation, to Sir Eric Drummond, Secretary General, League of Nations

Hotel Suisse, Place Cornavin Geneva, Switzerland,
September 12, 1922

DELEGATION OF NEGRO PEOPLES OF THE WORLD TO THE LEAGUE OF NATIONS

Sir,

With reference to previous communications that have passed between you and the honourable Marcus Garvey,[1] President-General of the Universal Negro Improvement Association, I have the honour to inform you that the Delegation of gentlemen elected by the third International Convention of the Negro Peoples of the World to attend the September sitting of the Assembly of the League of Nations for the purpose of representing the interests of the Negro Peoples of the world, arrived in this city on the 11th instant and are, at present, staying at the Hotel Suisse.

2. As Chairman of the Delegation, I am, conform[ing] with the instructions of the Administrator of my association, respectfully requesting you kindly to reserve four seats for the Delegation at the forthcoming meeting of the League.

3. I am furthermore respectfully requesting you to be good enough to grant us an interview at your earliest convenience to enable us, without any undue encroachment on your invaluable time[,] to discuss the object of our mission.

4. To expedite matters I herewith enclose my letter of introduction from the President-General of my Association to yourself together with my card, the letters of introduction of the other members of the Delegation to be handed in at the prospective interview.

5. I may add for your information that the number of Delegates has, through unavoidable circumstances, been reduced from five to four, Mr. [*Henry*] Hodge being the absentee Delegate. I have the honor to be, Sir, Your obedient Servant,

G.O. MARKE
Chairman of the Delegation

LNA, file 1/21159/21159. TLS on UNIA letterhead, recipient's copy.

1. Printed in *Garvey Papers* 4: 950–951.

Emmett J. Scott to W.E. Mollison

[*Washington, D.C.*] Sept 12, 1922

Dear Mr. Mollison:

I thank you for your kind letter of August 31st which is called to my attention upon my return. I am enclosing a newspaper containing a report of my telegram to Fred Moore disclaiming my acceptance of Garvey's foolish decoration.[1]

I am pleased to learn that you gave me credit for having sense enough not to fall in with Garvey's foolish schemes. When I see you I can tell you of the many efforts that were made to inveigle me into an association with this organization. . . . Very truly yours,

[EMMETT J. SCOTT][2]

[*Address*] Mr. W.E. Mollison,
603 Firmenich Bldg., 184 W. Washington St.,
Chicago, Ill.

MdBMC, Emmett J. Scott Papers. TL, carbon copy.

1. The *New York Age* of 26 August 1922 quoted a telegram from Scott that called upon the editor to "deny, repudiate and contradict . . . the wholly false, misleading, and derisive article [of 19 August 1922]. . . . I was not present at any meeting held by Mr. Garvey. I did not kneel. I received no decoration. . . . What the motive of this misrepresentation is, I do not at this moment undertake to characterize. I only know that a false and misleading story has been chronicled so far as I am personally concerned. Mr. Garvey was informed by me in response to his letter that I would not be present at his exercises to receive one of his titles or decorations, and I was not present as I advised him I would not be."

2. Scott was serving as secretary-treasurer of Howard University at the time he wrote this letter (*WWCA*).

Report by Special Employee Andrew M. Battle

New York City 9/13/22

In Re: General Negro Activities

Sept. 8th:

This morning I called on Arnold J. Ford, Musical Director of the U.N.I.A., and had a talk with him. He said that he and his friends were going to start another organization¹ and take up the first program which had been proposed at the formation of the U.N.I.A. four years ago. He said that the new organization would gather all the negroes together and make them understand themselves and then, having formed a strong union, would rise up and demand that this government change its policy toward the negro, stop lynching and give the negro a better deal all around.

J.W.H. Eason, former leader of American negroes with the U.N.I.A., and J. Austin Norris of Philadelphia, are starting a movement which will be called the United [*Universal*] Negro Alliance and will speak on Sunday at the New York Baptist Church at 3:30 P.M. and 10:00 P.M.

There seems to be an impression amongst the West Indians that Anderson of New Orleans, the newly elected Secretary of the U.N.I.A., had something to do with the sending of the human hand to A. Philip Randolph some time ago as he was one of the first men to say that something should be done to those persons who were going around the country speaking against Garvey and the U.N.I.A.

Sept. 9th:

Today I had talks at different times with Rev. William Moses, R.R. Wilson, M.L. Campbell, Clarence Carpenter, Cyril Briggs, Rev. G.W. Stewart and others, but learned nothing of value. The first mentioned persons seemed to be much in favor of the proposed new organization of negroes which will be founded by J.W.H. Eason, former leader of American negroes with the U.N.I.A.

Sept. 10th:

Today I talked with several negroes regarding the Garvey movement and the consensus of opinion seems to be that Garvey is doing a great deal more harm to the negro race than good. Amongst those I interviewed were Franklin C. Carr, R.R. Wilson, Thomas [*Theo?*] Burrell and Domengo H. Wizzard.

This afternoon I attended a meeting held at 125th St. and 5th Avenue by J.W.H. Eason, former Leader of American Negroes. J. Austin Norris of Philadelphia was also a speaker at this meeting. Norris, in his speech[,] sharply criticised Garvey and his organization and stated that he had tricked negroes out of more than half a million dollars in the last year and that he had collected over two hundred thousand dollars of that money for a sawmill. He stated that

Garvey had hurt the colored race as no other man had in the last twelve years and had been responsible for creating strife between the white and colored races.

J. W. H. Eason also spoke and stated that the American negroes, members of the Uni[v]ersal Negro Improvement Association, would, in a large part, be taken over eventually by the new organization of which he is the head, the United [*Universal*] Negro Alliance. He stated that he had just received a telegram from the National Baptist Publication Society of America[2] which stated that every Baptist preacher would help the organization to carry out its program. He stated that, unlike the Garvey Association[,] the new one would transact some of its business behind closed doors and told his hearers that when they were properly organized they could demand a place in Congress and in the commercial world.

At the evening meeting, which opened at eight o'clock, Rev. William H. Moses addressed the audience and told the audience that they were making a big mistake by keeping nagging at Marcus Garvey as he had done more to show the world that the negro could get together than any man since the coming of Christ and that until they got some ships and got into the commercial world they would never amount to anything. Norris later said, in the course of remarks, that he too had felt toward Garvey as the Rev. Mr. Moses until he had found Garvey out. He also said he would have a private talk with Rev. Moses after which he thought the Rev. Moses would think as he, Norris, did.

ANDREW M. BATTLE

DJ-FBI, file 61-746-13. TD.

1. Ford appears to have remained as UNIA musical director of Liberty Hall until 1926. When factional disputes threatened to split the organization in 1925, he attempted to mediate. When these attempts failed, he left Liberty Hall to devote full attention to his Harlem congregation, Temple Beth B'nai Abraham (William R. Scott, "Rabbi Arnold Ford's Back-to-Ethiopia Movement: A Study of Black Emigration, 1930–1935," *Pan African Journal* 7, no. 2 [summer 1975]: 194).

2. No telegram has been located to this effect. This is probably a reference to the National Baptist Publishing Board of the National Baptist Convention (unincorporated). The original National Baptist Publishing Board was created in 1893 in response to the refusal of the American Baptist Publication Society, a white organization, to publish the works of black authors. The publishing board became the arm of the black organization of Baptists, the National Baptist Convention, formed in 1895. When in 1915 the National Baptist Convention split, the publishing board became part of the unincorporated branch (John P. Davis, *The American Negro Reference Book* [Englewood Cliffs, N.J.: Prentice Hall, 1969], pp. 402–403; Lewis G. Jordan, *Negro Baptist History, USA* [Nashville: Sunday School Publishing Board, 1930], pp. 242–255; J. H. Jackson, *A Story of Christian Activism: A History of the National Baptist Convention, USA, Inc.* [Nashville: Townsend Press, 1980], pp. 90–118; James M. Washington, "The Origins and Emergence of Black Baptist Separatism, 1863–1897" [Ph.D. diss., Yale University, 1979]; Susan M. Eltscher, American Baptist Historical Society, Rochester, N. Y., to Robert A. Hill, 13 January and 28 August 1984).

Memorandum to the United States Shipping Board

[*Washington, D.C.*] 9/15/22

[Re:] Black Star Line, Inc.—
SS ORION

The following memorandum from General Counsel Freund, Emergency Fleet Corporation, dated September 14, 1922, is placed before the Board for such action as it may deem proper:

"On July 8th, 1921, the New York Ship Exchange acting for the Black Star Line, Incorporated, submitted a written offer to purchase the SS. ORION, ex. PRINZ OSKAR 'as is where is' for the sum of $225,000 on terms of ten percent (10%) cash on delivery and ten percent (10%) each month thereafter until the entire purchase price was paid, together with interest on deferred payments at five percent (5%) per annum and further offering to furnish a performance bond satisfactory to the Shipping Board guaranteeing the fulfillment of the contract. The Shipping Board on August 2nd, 1921 passed a resolution authorizing the acceptance of the above offer and on the following day the New York Ship Exchange was advised by telegram of the acceptance of the offer. On August 3rd, there was deposited with the Treasurer a check in the sum of $12,500 on account of the purchase price. Apparently, the purchaser experienced considerable difficulty in attempting to secure the performance bond. On December 22nd, 1921, there was forwarded to the Board by the purchaser an additional check in the sum of $10,000 on account of the purchase price. In the meantime, the Board incurred an expense of $875.34 for shifting stores, officers and personnel from the SS. ORION to the SS. WOMACHICHI by reason of the contemplated sale. The Black Star Line, Incorporated, is a corporation whose stockholders are entirely negroes and there has been dissension in the organization. The attorney for the Black Star Line, req[u]ested the Shipping Board to send the SS. ORION to New York City in order that the stockholders of this corporation might see the vessel but this request was refused. The Black Star Line, Incorporated, did not execute the contract of sale as submitted to it by the Shipping Board. Thereafter, the Black Star Line, Incorporated, requested that the Board release it from its obligations under the contract to purchase and return to it the sum of $22,500 paid on account, it agreeing to execute any and all instruments required by the Shipping Board. While there was quite a delay in the submission of papers to the purchaser, this was occasioned by the fact that the forms to be used were being revised by the Legal Department in accordance with the policy laid down by the General Counsel. When the final papers were submitted to the purchaser, they refused to execute the same and the parties could not agree on the final terms for the consummation of the sale.

"I attach herewith a form of resolution, should it be the desire of the Board to cancel the sale and return the deposit less expenses to the Black Star Line, Incorporated."[1]

Should the Board approve of the recommendations of General Counsel Fr[e]und, there is attached a copy of proposed resolution submitted with the above memorandum.

DNA, RG 32, file 605-1-653. TN, carbon copy.

1. By 30 October 1922, Commissioner Frederick I. Thompson wrote to Clifford Smith, secretary of the U.S. Shipping Board, that "If this money is rebated, it should be rebated to those who actually subscribed to it" rather than to the Black Star Line, Inc. The U.S. Shipping Board had tried without success, however, to obtain a list of the subscribers from the lawyers in the case (DNA, RG 32, file 605-1-653).

G.O. Marke to William Rappard, Director, Mandates Section, League of Nations

Hotel Suisse, Place Corn[a]v[i]n
Genève, Switzerland, September 15 1922

Your Excellency,

I am indebted to the courtesy and kindness of his Excellency the Hon. Louis Dantès Bellegard[e], Haitian Envoy Extraordinary and Minister Plenipotentiary at Paris for the liberty that I, an utter stranger, am now taking in thus trespassing on your Excellency's invaluable time.

I am the Chairman (President) of a Delegation of Negroes elected, at the Third International Convention of the Negro peoples of the World, to represent the interests of those peoples at this year's Assembly of the League of Nations (La Société des Nations).

A few days ago our Delegation enjoyed the privilege of interviewing the Hon. M. Bellegard[e] when I was enabled to explain to him the object of our mission to Genève.[1]

Monsieur Bellegarde[,] who spoke to us in high terms of your Excellency's goodness of heart and genuine benevolence towards our race and its aspirations, fortified the belief in me that in you we should find a sympathetic friend and a wise counsellor. Thus encouraged, I venture to approach your Excellency with the hope that you may grant us an interview at a time and place convenient to yourself in order that we may explain the object of our mission and profit by your wisdom.

With every assurance of the profound regard of our Delegation, I have the honour to be, Your Excellency's Obedient Servant,

G.O. MARKE
Chairman of Delegation

LNA, file 1/21159/21159. TLS on UNIA letterhead, recipient's copy.

1. A note in the *Negro World* of 9 December 1922 inaccurately attributed Bellegarde's speech to the League of Nations to the efforts of the UNIA delegation. Bellegarde, in a letter printed in the *Crisis* in February 1923, denied there was any connection, noting that he had addressed the League on 9 September 1922, several days before meeting with the UNIA delegation. In a

subsequent meeting, he added, the UNIA representatives "frankly admitted there must have been a misunderstanding, since I had already made my speech before the president of the delegation, Mr. Marke, called at my hotel in Geneva" (*Crisis* 25, no. 4 [February 1923]: 152–153; *NW*, 9 December 1922).

Sir Eric Drummond to G.O. Marke

GENEVA September 15th, 1922

Sir:—

I have the honour to acknowledge the receipt of your letter of September 12th, together with the enclosures thereto.

I have given the necessary instructions for seats in the Assembly Hall to be placed at the disposition of your Delegation.

I should have been very glad to have taken the opportunity of receiving you and hearing the object of your mission to Geneva, but the calls made upon my time by the simultaneous meetings of the Council and of the Assembly, together with the work necessary for the preparation of those meetings and the execution of the decisions taken, make it unfortunately impossible for me to foresee any moment in the near future when I shall have the necessary time at my disposal.

I have, therefore, requested Monsieur Rappard, Director of the Mandates Section, and Mr. Colban,[1] Director of the Administrative Commissions and Minorities Section, of the Secretariat, to represent me for this purpose, and I am requesting these gentlemen to get into touch with you in order that the necessary arrangements may be made without delay. I have the honour to be, Sir, Your obedient Servant,

[ERIC DRUMMOND]
Secretary-General

LNA, file 1/21159/21159. TL, carbon copy.

1. Erik Colban (1876–1956), a Norwegian lawyer, served in a variety of diplomatic posts before being appointed to the League of Nations; from 1919 to 1927 he served as director of the administrative and minorities section under Sir Eric Drummond, and from 1927 to 1930 he served as director of disarmament. He retired from the league in 1930, and in 1942 became ambassador to Great Britain (*Times* [London], 29 March 1956; *WWW*; *League of Nations Official Journal*, September 1922, p. 1,067).

William Rappard to G.O. Marke

Geneva, September 16th, 1922

Sir,

I have the honour to acknowledge the receipt of your letter of September 15TH and of the accompanying petition of the Universal Negro Improvement Association and African Communities['] League to the League of Nations.

When your delegation approached the Secretary-General of the League of Nations with the request that it might be given an opportunity of placing its views before the League of Nations, he informed you that, on account of the pressure of urgent work entailed by the meetings of the Council and the Assembly of the League, he was, to his regret, unable to receive you. He added that my colleague, Mr. Colban, and I would be at your disposal for an interview. Accordingly, we had the pleasure of meeting today two delegates, Mr. William Le Van Sher[r]ill, and Mr. Jean Joseph Adam. These gentlemen, on behalf of your organization expressed two requests: first, that the League of Nations might entrust the Universal Negro Improvement Association and African Communities['] League with a mandate over one or more of the former German colonies, and, second, that a negro might be appointed to the Permanent Mandates Commission of the League of Nations.[1]

I have the honour hereby briefly to confirm the declarations which I made to your delegates on these two points. It was pointed out, in the first place, that as Germany had, by the Treaty of Versailles, ceded her rights to her overseas possessions to the Principal Allied and Associated Powers, the League of Nations could not consider any requests concerning the disposal of these territories. As a matter of fact, the administration of all the f[or]mer German colonies had been entrusted by the Representatives of the Principal Allied and Associated Powers to certain States which are administering them as Mandatories on behalf of the League of Nations in accordance with the principles laid down in Article 22 of the Covenant of the League.

[The Permanent Mandates] Commission consists of nine members[2] who have been chosen by the Council of the League of Nations for an indefinite period and should a candidate of the negro race possessing the necessary qualifications be presented and authoritatively recommended, I am sure the Council of the League of Nations would not fail to consider the application made on his behalf with the same spirit of impartiality which they would bring to the consideration of all concurrent proposals.

I must add that I have written you so fully on these two points because your two delegates expressly requested me to make the situation quite clear to you. I have the honour to be, Sir, Your obedient Servant,

[WILLIAM RAPPARD]
Director of the Mandates Section

LNA, file 1/21159/21159. TL, carbon copy.

1. On 16 September 1921, W.E.B. Du Bois, on behalf of the Second Pan-African Congress, asked the league to appoint a black to the Permanent Mandates Commission (PRO, FO 371/7065, W10614/19614/98; W.E.B. Du Bois to Sir Eric Drummond, 16 September 1921, LNA, 1/15865/13940; report of 26 September 1921, LNA, file A 148.1921).

2. The original members were Alberto Theodoli, chairman, Italy; D.F.W. van Rees, vice-chairman, Netherlands; Ramon Pina, Spain; Freire d'Andrade, Portugal; Anna Bugge-Wicksell, Sweden; W.G. Ormsby-Gore, Great Britain; J.B.P. Beau, France; Kunio Yanaghita, Japan; and Pierre Orts, Belgium. Rappard became a tenth member when he retired as mandates section director in 1925 (Quincy Wright, *Mandates Under the League of Nations* [Chicago: University of Chicago Press, 1930], pp. 137–155, 626–627; Elizabeth van Maanen-Helmer, *The Mandates System in Relation to Africa and the Pacific Islands* [London: P.S. King, 1929], pp. 79–85).

Speech by Marcus Garvey

[[LIBERTY HALL, New York, September 17, 1922]]

. . . We have a report coming from Geneva as published in the "Tribune" of New York.[1] We have our own private communications, but colored people do not believe anything that comes from themselves. They are always disposed to doubt the veracity of anything that emanates or comes from themselves. But in this instance I am going to read to you not what comes from us but what comes through other channels and channels not very friendly towards us, and channels not very desirous of presenting us to the world in the proper light. You will therefore give them credit for publishing that part of the truth that they have finished tarnishing to satisfy their own desires as working in opposition to the organization. Every bit of news and facts relating to us is cut down and dressed up and tarnished before it goes to the public, because the opposition forces desire to place the Universal Negro Improvement Association in an unfavorable light. The article which I will read to you is a special article to "The Tribune," which they have copyrighted:

> Geneva, Switzerland, Sept. 13.—A contingent of Negroes representing Marcus Garvey, Provisional President of Africa, appeared before the League of Nations today and demanded that it grant to the Negroes of the world a mandate for South Africa. The spokesmen of the party were Jean Joseph Adam, a Haitian Negro, and Lee Van Sherrill, of New York. They declared that the Negroes would demonstrate their ability to run a government if the league granted them authority to do so. The New York spokesman said that the delegation was acting under the authority of the United Negro Congress, recently held in that city. The League Secretariat acknowledged the receipt of the petition.

Now that proves that our delegates are not gone to California or to New Orleans or to Haiti, but in truth they are gone where we sent them. We sent them to the assembly of the League of Nations at Geneva, Switzerland, and you will see that they are very much there; insomuch so that the league gave them a hearing through Prof. Adam and the Hon. William Sherrill, whom you all saw during the convention. Mr. Sherrill is the gentleman that we elected here as Second Assistant President-General and titular leader of American Negroes, and Prof. Adam is the gentleman who came to us from San Francisco as the president of the San Francisco Division of the Universal Negro Improvement Association. They were the spokesmen before the league on the 12th of this month in behalf of the association in our demand for the turning over to us of the mandates affecting German Southwest Africa, German East Africa, and Togoland. The whole delegation is there, but these gentlemen spoke before the league. They are in Europe at the right time—the psychological moment— and it is most likely we have to keep them there longer than we anticipated.

19

THE NEGRO'S ATTITUDE IN THE NEXT WAR

My subject for tonight is "The Negro's Attitude in the Next War." I feel sure that each and every one within the reach of my voice tonight realizes the seriousness of the hour. For four and a half years we have been preaching preparedness and organization among the Negro peoples of the world. We did not prophesy; we simply told them that the greatest of wars was yet to come, and that there would be many more wars other than the great world war of 1914–18. We preached it from the hilltops; we proclaimed it throughout the land. When Wilson of America, Lloyd George of England, Clemenceau of France, Orlando of Italy and others met at the Versailles conference and other places in Europe and declared to the world that the 1914 holocaust was the last of wars and that we were to have a reign of peace they knew well that they were camouflaging the people of the world. They knew well that they were saying what they did not believe. They knew well, if they had the vision of statesmen, that Europe was then in a worse political condition than she ever was in, and that at that time there were more grounds and reasons for war than prior to 1914. All sensible men, all students of political science knew then that Europe was but setting the stage for the greatest war of humanity—the greatest war of the ages. I am not saying that the war clouds of today will usher in the greatest war of the ages. I do not believe it; behind what is happening now will come that great conflict—that bloody war. And it was with the realization of that truth why we of the Universal Negro Improvement Association started a world-wide universal propaganda to draw together into one mighty whole— into one great bond—the 400,000,000 Negroes of the World in readiness.

PREPARING TO STAND TOGETHER

Not longer than a couple of weeks ago I told you that the news of war was in the wind—coming, coming, coming, and will soon be here. I told you that coming may mean a day or a week or a year or five years, but it is coming as sure as you live, as sure as there is a God that day is coming; and the Universal Negro Improvement Association is preparing the minds of 400,000,000 Negroes to stand together, die together if we must die, but before that death there shall be an emancipated race, a redeemed Africa.

SOME REFLECTIONS ON THE EASTERN SITUATION

Mustapha Kemal[2] has become the man of the hour, even as the Kaiser was in 1914. Around Kemal and his army the world revolves at this hour. The Kaiser laid the foundation for a changed Europe; Kemal is going to lay the foundation for a changed world, and the whole world is crazy if they think they are going to use Negroes now as they used them in the past. (Great applause.) England before the real sound of battle has started to cry out for help from her dominions.[3] The help shall include everybody else except the new Negro. (Applause.)

COUNTING WITHOUT THEIR HOSTS

And not only England, but all the powers of the world will be counting without their hosts this time if they think they are going to use Negroes in 1922 and 1925 or 1930, as they used them between 1914 and 1918. Now some of us are ready and willing to go to jail this time. (Cries of Yes! Yes!)

NEGROES ARE ON STRIKE

We have nothing to hide. We are on strike, that is all, all over the world. (Loud and prolonged applause.) They may start their fight over there, but let me tell them to count on everybody else except the Negro, except you are going to come across and deliver the goods before the Negro moves. We do not object to fighting, because we are not cowards; the world knows that; but, brother we are going to fight for something, and you will have, because of the distrust that you have caused through your own acts in the past, you will have to deliver the goods first. Sometimes in dealing with a man he credits you and trusts you upon your honesty and you dodge him and you make believe you do not remember him, and after he collects that first debt and you go back and want some more credit you have to pay in advance. Somebody will have to pay in advance this time, if you are expecting Negroes' help in any war between now and eternity. (Applause.)

They have touched a hornets' nest. They have aroused the religious patriotism of 250,000,000 Mohammedans.[4] We do not say a holy war; we said a race war, but a holy war may be the sign by which we shall see liberty through the race war that will follow.

WHERE THE NEGRO STANDS

Now, we are Christians, and I suppose later on they are going to tell us that Christianity is attacked; that it is a fight between the Cross and the Crescent. They told us all the time that Jesus Christ was a white man; now everybody knows that Mohammed was a Negro, and if we are not going to take sides because of religion I am sure we are going to take sides because of race; that is all. (Applause.) We are not in a holy war; therefore we will not go out either as Christians or as Mohammedans, because as Christians we love our faith and by the sign of the cross we hope to see salvation. No one shall engage us, though, because of our religion, to fight a holy war. We are not interested in the holy war, we are not interested by which means a man gets into heaven so long as he gets there; so nobody is going to interest us to kill anybody because he does not believe in his way of getting to heaven. Let me get to heaven in the best way I can. So I want you always to have that before your mind. Jesus Christ was not a white man; we know that well. Jesus Christ was the embodiment of all humanity, but for nearly 2,000 years they have been trying to make him white; now if he was white, then I suppose for them he is still white now. We believe in Christianity for the purity of Christianity, for the good of Christianity, but, knowing the history of the whole human race, we all know that Mohammed was of our blood; therefore if we cannot do any good we are not going to do any bad to the faith he founded.

Two hundred and fifty million Mohammedans! And Kemal has called upon them to stand in defense of Turkey and of Constantinople, and England tells us that we in the dominions must go and fight for the Cross. Since when did they remember the Cross? We know the Cross of Calvary; we have been bearing that burden and we know it more than the Anglo-Saxon, because when his own race despised the Cross and the Man on the Cross, it was the man of Mohammed's people and of our blood who took up the Cross and bore it up the heights to Calvary.[5] Therefore we know more about the Cross than they do, and we know when it is necessary to go to war for the Cross. So they are not going to camouflage us now and tell us about the Cross as against the Crescent, because after we will have done our duty they won't remember the Cross any more until somebody starts something again.

THE PROPAGANDA AGAINST THE TURKS

Now they tell us—the vile and wicked propaganda—that Kemal and the Turks are barbarians, as they told us that the Kaiser was a barbarian. They tell us that Kemal is a barbarian and the Turks are barbarians and cannot be allowed even to live in Europe because they burned Smyrna and killed so many people in Smyrna.[6] Were not they barbarians when they bombed the natives of East Africa and South Africa?[7] If it was a barbarous act for Kemal and his army to overrun S[my]rna then it was also a barbarous act for the British men to have gone in the air in airplanes and bombed the natives of Southwest Africa when they had nothing else than sticks and stones to fight with.

A NEW RACE TO DEAL WITH

Let them realize that they have a new race to deal with and not a race of fools. They are counting without their hosts. England has bluffed her way through the world for hundreds of years. You cannot bluff your way any longer, and I pray that the better judgment of America, the better sense of America, will keep out of this new war. I trust that the united opinion of America will be made so manifest that no one will take us into war again, because somebody is doomed for a new war; somebody is going to be burned this time if a real war starts, and England is not going to start anything, believe me; she has better sense. She was along with Greece—behind Greece and was willing to stand along with and behind Greece to fight the Turk until Kemal's army whipped Greece into submission, and then, when she found out that Greece was licked, she was independent no more. You know she was independent when Greece stood alone and France stood behind Turkey, and she was even willing to break off her friendly relationship with France,[8] believing that Greece would have licked Turkey; but when Turkey licked Greece she changed her mind and raised a howl of the cross! the cross! the cross! It is the cross against the crescent. Can you allow Turkey to overrun Southwestern Europe? That is her cry. And now she has appealed to the religious sentiment of Europe,[9] with the hope of lining up Italy and France along with her to defeat the Turks.[10] But Trotsky has something to say. (Applause.) Trotsky makes the whole world understand today that he has 1,300,000 well-prepared soldiers that Kemal can use if he wants.[11] Balfour says it is a bluff. He knows better than anybody else in Europe the result of that bluff if he allows that bluff to stick. Therefore we read between the lines where England is endeavoring to satisfy the Turk, and if they can come to some agreement there will be no war,[12] because she knows that if she goes to war against the Crescent she is licked. She will be licked in India; she will be licked in Egypt; she will be licked throughout Africa, because 75 per cent. of the Africans are Mohammedans,[13] and there will be no more of British dominions after thirty days. England knows that and the whole world knows that, too. So we would not be surprised that tomorrow morning we pick up the papers and read that the misunderstanding has been settled. So do not be too sure that this is the real war. It may be an entering wedge to that bigger war and the real war that is bound to come.

GERMANY COMING BACK

Did I not tell you that Germany would come back and that Germany would not come back through Germany. The crazy idea that they could defeat a race like Germany, levy an indemnity and reduce Germany to impotence! They are crazy if they think so. The greatest mind of the twentieth century, the greatest genius of the twentieth century, the greatest scientist of the twentieth century are the Germans, and they are crazy enough to believe that they can put down Germany and keep Germany down for ever. I told you that Germany will come back; if not through Germany, through somewhere else; a thousand miles, five thousand miles or ten thousand miles from Germany, but Germany will come back, and not only Germany, but wheresoever injustice is done to humanity, humanity will come back because it is of the human nature to revenge. If you put me down today I am going to prepare to put you down tomorrow. Why Kemal's teacher was one of the men who fought in the German war as a German general[14] and he taught Kemal the perfection of war so that Germany could come back through Turkey, through Asia Minor or somewhere else, but Germany will be coming back anyhow. I will not be surprised if Germany comes back through Brazil. All that is in the game of diplomacy; all that is in the game of statesmanship, and, Negroes, all that you have to do is to interfere with nobody's business, but mind your own business. If Germany comes back through Turkey or Brazil or Mexico it is their business; all that you want is UNIVERSAL EMANCIPATION AND AFRICAN FREEDOM[.] And we do not care whether we get it through the Crescent or through the Cross, because to the Mohammed[an,] Allah is God, to us God is God; the same God, and He is the same God who is saying, "Princes shall come out of Egypt, and Ethiopia shall stretch out her hand"; and methinks at this hour Ethiopia is in a splendid way of stretching forth her hands unto God.

WE ARE OUR OWN ENEMIES

I am only sorry that we become our own enemies. The very thing that we have been preaching—unity in organization, steadfastness in opinion—is the same thing that our own race is endeavoring to defeat by this division. But thank God there are more of us organized now than in 1914. In 1914 all of us were divided; today we have millions of members who profess the faith of the Universal Negro Improvement Association, and after all sometimes it is not very good to prepare the soldier in advance; prepare the generals and they will mobilize the soldiers when the crisis comes, and anywhere you go, from the Western World to the Eastern World, you have a general of the Universal Negro Improvement Association who is ready to marshall the soldiers when the bugle sounds. So, after all, if we have 200 generals organized in Africa, we have and know we have an army of 280,000,000 men in Africa anyhow, because 280,000,000 cannot lead themselves, but the 200 generals will lead the army of 280,000,000 men.

THE HOUR FAST APPROACHING

So men, you realize the hour is fast approaching; the war clouds are gathering; the news of battle is coming; I repeat, it is in the wind. It may be here in an hour, a day, a week, a month, a year, or five or ten years, but it is coming, and one day it will come with the speed of a hurricane; it will travel with the speed of a great storm, and will reach its destination over night. Prepare yourselves and realize that your worst enemy at this time is the Negro who will try to divide you; because to divide you are bound to fall; united you are bound to stand. The Negro who tries to preach disunity at this time in this race, when the war clouds are gathering, is a worse enemy than any you have ever had, because this is the hour when all Negroes must stand together. Our great leader of the past—Booker Washington—made the mistake of his life. Our great leader of the past, Frederick Douglass, made the mistake of his life; Sir Conrad Reeves, of Barbados, made a mistake; Sir Samuel Lewis, of Africa, made the mistake when fifty years ago, forty years ago, thirty years ago, twenty years ago they did not organize the Negroes of the world to stand together for a crisis as that came in 1914. Surely we shall not make the mistake now when another war becomes imminent. If it comes tomorrow let the 400,000,000 Negroes of the world stand together as one man. Freedom or death shall be the slogan of the Negro in the next world war.

We shall not forsake the ship at the hour of peril and of danger. Others will desert us when the hour comes when we must take a stand, but if war comes tomorrow and the question is asked the Negro, "Where art thou?" the answer of the Universal Negro Improvement Association shall be, "We are here; we refuse to march until Africa has been properly arranged for; until all the ills the Negro has suffered from have been properly corrected; until then you appeal to a deaf man who cannot hear you at all." (Applause.)

Now, whether you are a government or whether you are a race, if you intend to approach the Negro in the next world war you will better come clean, come with the intention of delivering the goods, and if you want us to fight we shall know first of all what we fight for before one drop of Negro blood is shed. In the past they told us to go to war and we will arrange the settlement; but today you will have to sign the papers first, otherwise 400,000,000 are going to jail (applause) when the time comes for upholding the principles of the Universal Negro Improvement Association we have preached for the last four years.

I thank you for your patience you have exhibited in hearing me through tonight as Europe's battle clouds gather. Go away and send the news to your friends throughout the length and breadth of the world to stand fast under the colors of the Red, the Black and the Green, and not to yield one inch until Africa is redeemed. (Applause.)

Printed in *NW*, 23 September 1922. Original headlines omitted.

1. The article appeared on the front page of the *New York Tribune*, 14 September 1922. A similar article also appeared in the *New York Times* on the same day.

2. Mustapha Pasha Kemal (1881–1938), nationalist leader and war hero of Turkey, led his country's resistance to the Allied plans of dismemberment directed against Turkey after World War I. Kemal also played a major role in the nationalist war against Greece to regain Asia Minor, the broad peninsula that comprises most of modern Turkey. He was also a central figure in the movement to abolish the Turkish sultanate. On 29 October 1923, he became the first president of the new Turkish republic and adopted the name Kemal Ataturk (Geoffrey Lewis, *Modern Turkey* [New York: Praeger, 1974], pp. 66–127).

3. The British government took an aggressive stand in defense of the neutral zone established in the Dardanelles and Bosporus straits. When the Turks threatened to invade the area they claimed as part of Turkey, Lloyd George declared that freedom of the straits was essential to British interests and appealed not only to European allies but to the British dominions for support in the event of an open conflict. Only New Zealand, however, promised to send troops in the event of military action against the Turkish Nationalist army (*NYT*, 20 September 1922; "The New Turkish Crisis," *Current History* 17, no. 2 [November 1922]: 185; Donald McCormick, *The Mask of Merlin: A Critical Study of David Lloyd George* [London: McDonald Press, 1963], pp. 227–230; John Campbell, *Lloyd George* [London: Jonathan Cape, 1977], pp. 66, 94).

4. The Greco-Turkish War was waged in part as a religious conflict. Lloyd George had initially fabricated a report that a Turkish guerrilla uprising around Smyrna was endangering the lives of Greek and other Christian minorities. The report, aimed at engendering European and United States sympathy, helped rally President Woodrow Wilson and Clemenceau of France to support the Greek occupation of Smyrna. The original Greek invasion of the area exacerbated religious strife: fezzes were pulled from the heads of Turkish men and trampled underfoot, veils were torn from the faces of Muslim women, and Christian mobs plundered the homes of Muslims. The Turks responded in kind, declaring the conflict a war to regain Muslim land taken by Christian armies. The Turkish army, initially heavily outnumbered and disorganized, reorganized into a strong fighting force and regained the territory taken by Greece. Because the war had been fought largely to regain Muslim lands taken by Christian forces, the Turkish victory increased Pan-Islamic feeling in many Muslim countries. In India, Islamic members of the council of state and legislative assemblies sent a message to Lloyd George, declaring it a political necessity that Great Britain maintain strict neutrality in the conflict between the Greeks and the Turks, and urging him to use the opportunity to restore Anglo-Turkish friendship. In Cairo, mosques were illuminated in celebration, Islamic flags were displayed, and Muslim papers rejoiced in the victory (*NYT*, 13 and 14 September 1922; Roger Kincaid Jensen, "The Greco-Turkish War, 1920–1922," *International Journal of Middle East Studies* 10 [1979]: 553–565; Dagobert Von Mikusch, *Mustafa Kemal*, trans. J.

Linton [Garden City, N.Y.: Doubleday, Doran, and Co., 1931], pp. 192–193, 210–215).

5. A reference to Simon of Cyrene.

6. The Greek army captured the city of Smyrna (Izmir) in November 1919. On 9 September 1922 it was retaken by the Turkish army, led by Kemal. Three days later, an incendiary fire that began in the Greek and Armenian quarters swept the city, reducing much of Smyrna to ruins. By 14 September an estimated 1,000 had lost their lives and 300,000 were homeless ("The New Turkish Crisis," *Current History* 17, no. 2 [November 1922]: 181–184).

7. A reference to a shooting attack against Africans in Nairobi, Kenya, and to the bombing of the Bondelswarts people in South-West Africa (See *Garvey Papers* 4: 676–677).

8. On 9 March 1921 the French government reversed its earlier policy on the Greco-Turkish conflict and concluded a military and political alliance with Kemal and the nationalists. The French decision was followed by a similar agreement between Kemal and the Italians, in which the Italians agreed to evacuate the province of Anatolia. These agreements left Britain as the sole ally of Greece in the conflict, although all the Allied powers continued to oppose the threatened Turkish occupation of Constantinople, then under joint Allied supervision (*EWH*).

9. The religious dimension of the Greco-Turkish conflict emerged after the occupation of Smyrna and the alleged massacres of the city's Christian minorities by Turkish soldiers. Greek appeals for the "intervention of the fleets of the Christian States" stressed the threat to the "civilized world" posed by "Moslem fanaticism" and "non-progressive, retrograde races, whose whole doctrine is founded on domination" (*NYT*, 24 September and 25 September 1922; *EWH*; Geoffrey Lewis, *Modern Turkey*, pp. 75–84).

10. On 12 September, after several British appeals to France to restrain her Turkish allies, the French government notified the British that it was in full accord with them concerning the freedom of the Dardanelles and Bosporus straits. The French government also stated its willingness to participate in negotiations to settle the Greco-Turkish conflict, provided that the legitimate aspirations of the Turks were safeguarded (*NYT*, 13 September 1922).

11. On 16 September 1922 the front page of the *New York Times* announced that "the Russian Revolutionary Military Council, presided over by Leon Trotsky, is reported to have decided to prepare immediately for action all the forces in the Caucasian republics and Moscow Government forces stationed in other parts of the Caucasus and the Soviet Black Sea Fleet . . . ready to march to the assistance of Mustapha Kemal in case the Turkish Nationalist leader advances on Constantinople." The Soviet Union and Turkey had signed a treaty on 16 March 1922, and the Soviet Union was generally acknowledged as a major arms supplier to the Turkish nationalists during the war with Greece. The Red Army was estimated at "about 1,000,000 effective fighters" by British and American experts in 1922 (*NYT*, 2 April, 10 April, and 12 December 1922).

12. Tentative discussions between Britain and France on a compromise agreement with the Turks to revise the unratified Treaty of Sèvres began in mid-September 1922. While both sides agreed on the necessity of maintaining the neutrality of the straits, the British government insisted upon a cessation of Turkish threats to the neutral zones under which Constantinople, the Bosporus, and the Dardanelles were protected, before any general conference to restore Turkish claims could be held. On 11 October an armistice was signed under which Constantinople and Eastern Thrace were handed to the Nationalists, while the Nationalists accepted the neutralization of the straits under international accord. Further negotiations between the Allies and Turkey culminated with the Treaty of Lausanne on 24 July 1923, and three months later the Nationalists formally proclaimed Turkey a republic (*EWH*, pp.1,086–1,087; Geoffrey Lewis, *Modern Turkey*, pp. 84–88).

13. The population of North Africa has long been nearly 100 percent Muslim. Islam historically expanded from the north, having its greatest impact in West Africa. Demographic estimates made in French West Africa in the late 1920s give a figure of about 38 percent Muslim for that region (Raymond Leslie Buell, *The Native Problem in Africa* [New York: Macmillan Co., 1928], 2: 65). Even though Islamic expansion accelerated during the colonial period, few black African countries today have Muslim populations approaching 50 percent, and most of those south of the equator have only tiny Muslim minorities (J. S. Trimingham, *The Influence of Islam upon Africa*, 2d ed. [London: Longman, 1980], pp. 103ff.; Guy Nicolas, *Dynamique de L'Islam au Sud du Sahara* [Paris: Publications Orientalistes de France, 1981], p. 267).

14. A possible reference to Marshal Colmar von der Goltz, head of the German military mission in Turkey (Lord Kinross, *Ataturk* [New York: William Morrow and Co., 1965], p. 34).

Lewis W. Haskell, American Consul, Geneva, to Joseph C. Grew,[1] American Minister, Berne

AMERICAN CONSULAR SERVICE, Geneva, Switzerland
September 18, 1922

Sir:

I have the honor to report that I have just had a short visit from Mr. Wm. Le Van Sher[r]ill, Lecturer, Delegate from the Congress of the Negro Peoples of the World to the Assembly of the League of Nations at Geneva, of New York City. He has a petition which he is presenting to the League of Nations, and while I received him politely and courteously, I immediately let it be known that I could in no wise, directly or indirectly, concern myself with this petition.

I added that if, as an American citizen, he desired to see any government official in Switzerland, that I thought you, as the American Minister, would be the proper official to see. I further added that I did not in any measure attempt to advise him to go to Berne as I would not, in any sense, attempt to say that you could or would concern yourself in the matter of his petition.[2]

I am sending this letter to you in order that you may understand that I have done nothing whatsoever in the matter. I thought too, that as the American diplomatic representative, you would like to know of this agitation on the part of what seems quite a large number of American negro[e]s. I have the honor to be, Sir, Your obedient servant,

LEWIS W. HASKELL
American Cons[u]l

DNA, RG 59, file 800.4016/19. TL, carbon copy.

1. Joseph Clark Grew (1880–1965) had been a secretary at the Paris Peace Conference and a minister in Brussels before taking his position at Berne (*NYT*, 27 May 1965).
2. On 25 September 1922 Grew informed Charles Evans Hughes, the U.S. secretary of state, about the matter of the UNIA's petition. Grew told Hughes that he concurred with Lewis W. Haskell's actions not to become involved, directly or indirectly, with the petition (Joseph C. Grew to Charles Evans Hughes, 25 September 1922, DNA, RG 59, file 800.4016/20).

Report by Special Employee Andrew M. Battle

New York City [19–20 September 1922]

Sept. 19th:

. . . I also talked with William Ferris, editor of the "Negro World," who informed me that he had advised Marcus Garvey to be very careful in his dealings with the Ku Klux Klan, as the American negro was strongly against it.

During the course of the day I also spoke with Arnold J. Ford of 38 West 131st St.[,] who, in the course of conversation I had with him, said that Garvey had stolen all the money of the Universal Negro Improvement Association and that as a result of these thefts he would probably be a rich man.

Sept. 20th:

Today I called at the office of the "Negro World" and made inquiries regarding the forthcoming issue of "The Negro Daily Times." William Ferris, editor of the "Negro World" showed me through the offices and I gathered the impression that the daily paper will not be published for some time to come.

I also had a talk with Captain Gaines of the U.N.I.A. who informed me that in his opinion Marcus Garvey would not remain head of the organization for any length of time as he was considered unfit to manage the business of the U.N.I.A. . . .

ANDREW M. BATTLE

DJ-FBI, file 61-746-16. TD.

G.O. Marke to Sir Eric Drummond

Hotel Suisse, Place Corn[a]v[i]n,
Genève September 21, 1922

Sir,

I have the honour to acknowledge with thanks the receipt of your letter No. L/21159/21159 of the 15th inst., in which you expressed regret at your inability, through pressure of work, personally to receive our Delegation, but informed us that you had, for this purpose, requested Monsieur Rappard, Director of the Mandates Section, and Mr. Colban, Director of the Administrative Commissions and Minorities Section, of the Secretariat to represent you.

2. In reply, I beg leave to inform you that I received a letter, dated September 16, from Monsieur Rappard informing me that he had that day met two of our Delegates to wit, Mr. William Le Van Sherrill and Monsieur Jean Joseph Adam and that these gentlemen made certain requests which he pointed out to them could not be considered by the League of Nations.

3. I may remark for your information that my letter to which Monsieur Rappard's is a reply was a purely private and informal communication written to him on the advice of a friend and dispatched before your letter of the 15th inst[.] came to hand.

4. Our secretary, Monsieur Adam[,] was directed by me to see to it that the letter reached Monsieur Rappard's hand safely. Accompanied by Mr[.] Sherrill he called at your Secretariat to deliver the letter when Monsieur

Rappard invited them in and engaged them in conversation. During their absence your letter above alluded to came to hand.

5. Had I received your letter earlier, I would undoubtedly have awaited Monsieur Rappard's Official communication, conveying your request to him and Mr. Colban in respect of the proposed interview.

6. It thus happened that, through this unfortunate contretemps, Monsieur Rappard deemed his colloquy with Monsieur Adam and Mr. Sherrill as official conversation conducted on your behalf while the latter gentlemen, who were blissfully innocent of the contents of your letter regarded the conversation as /of a/ purely informal and private character.

[7]. You will hence note that the interview sought by me, for which you kindly made arrangements through proxies, has never taken place.

[8]. I am therefore respectfully requesting you, kindly to exercise your good offices in respect of the Petition of the Negro Peoples of the World /so/ that it may, without /further/ delay, be submitted to the Assembly of the League of Nations.

[9]. Should you require them, I would gladly furnish you with as many copies of the Petition as you may deem necessary. I have the honour to be, Sir, Your obedient Servant

G. O. MARKE
Chairman of Delegation

LNA, file 1/21159/21159. TLS on UNIA letterhead, recipient's copy.

Report by Special Employee Andrew M. Battle

New York City [*21–24 September 1922*]

IN RE: U.S. VS. MARCUS GARVEY ET AL.
NEGRO RADICAL ACTIVITIES

September 21st, 1922

This morning I interviewed CAPTAIN GAINES of the UNITED [*Universal*] NEGRO IMPROVEMENT ASSOCIATION and among other things he stated that he had had a personal talk with J. W. H. EASON, former American Leader of the U.N.I.A. and that EASON had informed him that he was going to "wrench" the U.N.I.A. out of GARVEY's hands and see that the organization carried out the aims and objects for which it was first formed. He added that as soon as he could get GARVEY out of the way he would rejoin the U.N.I.A. and bring with him the UNITED [*Universal*] NEGRO ALLIANCE, the recently formed organization of which he is at present the head. GAINES further informed me that he and WILLIAM FERRIS of the "Negro World" were also siding with EASON.

FRED A. TOOT[E,] the Asst. Secretary General and now Field Organizer of the U.N.I.A.[,] stated that as soon as the members could get GARVEY out of the way they hoped to elect G. E. STEWART as President General.

SYDNEY DE BOURG, a West Indian, in the course of a conversation I had with him informed me that he had had a talk with MRS. H[ENRIETTA] VINTON DAVIS, the Third Asst. V.P. of the U.N.I.A.[,] and that she had said that she and R[U]DOLPH SMITH, the Second Asst. V.P. of the U.N.I.A. were going to do all they could to displace GARVEY and in his stead elect LEROY BUNDY.

September 22nd, 1922

This morning I had an interview with ULYSSES S. POSTON, the Minister of Labor and Industries of the U.N.I.A. In the course of the conversation he informed me that the reason DUSE MOHAMED ALI left the Negro World was because GARVEY had asked ALI to let him see all of the matter that was to be printed in the NEGRO TIMES, the new daily paper which is soon to be printed. This ALI refused to do and he told GARVEY that before he would do so he would quit the job, which he did. It seems that GARVEY had been informed that ALI intended to use the columns of the Daily Times for the purpose of spreading Egyptian propaganda[1] and this GARVEY objected to. POSTON stated that ALI went immediately to the office of the persons who are spreading the Egyptian propaganda and is now employed there. . . .

September 24th, 1922

This morning I interviewed J. W. H. EASON, Former American Leader of the U.N.I.A. EASON informed me that he had started a new organization which is called the UNIVERSAL NEGRO ALLIANCE, with office[s] at no. 2294 Seventh Avenue. He said the initiation fee is $1.00 with monthly dues of 40 cents. He stated that they would have branches in every county and offices in every State and later would have County and State meetings and eventually an International meeting once every two years. He added that they would have what he called a "Secret Department" the members of which would only be admitted after having taken a certain oath. EASON informed me that he would like to have me the head of the Commerce Department. I told him that I would think the matter over and let him know later. EASON said that J. AUSTIN NORRIS would be here later in the day and would bring with him a copy of the by-laws which he (Eason) would give me later. NORRIS, Eason said, is a Philadelphian and will handle the affairs of the organization in that City.

I later met WILLIAM FERRIS, Editor of the "Negro World[,]" who informed me that he had known for some time that DUSE MOHAMED ALI had been connecting the Egyptians in Wall Street whose propaganda he was being paid to spread. FERRIS also said that he would make an engagement with me to meet GARVEY as he thought I could advise him along many lines. He also informed me that the "Daily Times" would come out on Monday next.[2]

ANDREW M. BATTLE

DJ-FBI, file 61. TD.

1. In his column, "Foreign Affairs," which appeared in the *Negro World* in 1922, Dusé Mohamed Ali wrote primarily on issues pertaining to Turkey, Egypt, and Islam (*NW*, 25 March, 1–29 April, 20 May, 27 May, 10–24 June, 1–29 July, 5 August, 12 August, and 26 August 1922).

2. According to Special Agent Joseph G. Tucker, "Volume one, number one, of 'The Negro Times,' the new daily which Garvey has launched, appeared on Monday, September 25th. It is published by the Negro Times Publishing Co." (report by Special Agent Joseph G. Tucker, 30 September 1922, DJ-FBI, file 61-189). To date, no issues of the *Daily Negro Times* have been found.

Report by Special Agent Joseph G. Tucker

[*New York*] Sept. 23, 1922

FRIENDS OF NEGRO FREEDOM

William Pickens addressed an audience at Douglass Hall, Lenox Avenue and 143rd St.[,] on the 17th inst. under the auspices of the above organization and sharply criticised Marcus Garvey and his activities. He stated that he had just returned from a tour which included the cities of Detroit, Toledo, Rochester and Toronto, and that while in the latter city where he was scheduled to address a meeting under the auspices of the African Methodist Episcopal Conference, he was accosted by a number of negroes as he was about to enter the Church and was warned to be careful of what he might say about Garvey if he wanted to avoid getting hurt. He made the further statement that in other cities he had been heckled and interrupted. He branded as a "barrage of lies" the charges that Garvey has been making that he appealed to him, Garvey, for a position with the Universal Negro Improvement Association and in proof of his contention read a letter dated in May last addressed to him from Garvey in which the latter invited him to become a member of his "cabinet."

Pickens ridiculed the "Back to Africa" movement and said that there were enough negroes there already and the mere presence of any more from the United States would not ameliorate conditions in the dark continent. He added that, "Garvey and his followers have more privileges in New York and South Carolina than they will ever have in Africa." . . .

JOSEPH G. TUCKER

DJ-FBI, file 61-187. TD.

Henri Jaspar,[1] Belgian Minister of Foreign Affairs, to Mr. Le Tellier, Belgian Chargé d'Affaires, London

Brussels [*n.d.; post-26 September 1922*]

Black agitator, Marcus Garvey, leader of the Pan-Negro Movement in the United States, has addressed a request to His Majesty's government for support of his petition before the League of Nations.[2] This is the petition that the Executive Council of the U.N.I.A. addressed to the League of Nations from which it was hoped to obtain the mandate for the former German Colonies in the East and West.

I do not need to state that there is no question of His Majesty's government favoring such an initiative. But it is a question of finding out what attitude would be suitable to adopt vis à vis Marcus Garvey as a result of his letter to the government. Must receipt of it be acknowledged?

I opt for a negative reply—but I would like to know what the British and French governments have done under the circumstances, as they will have received similar letters.

In these matters it is useful for me to be seen to adopt a course in keeping with the different governments concerned.

Please try to obtain the desired information.

Enclosed is a copy of a letter sent by me to Mr. Hymans to refute Garvey's statement.

[HENRI JASPAR]

SAMAE, no. 617. TN, recipient's copy (translated from French).

1. Henri Jaspar (d. 1939), Belgian statesman and leader of the Catholic party, became foreign minister in November 1920; he played a major role in the Allied negotiations over German reparations at the conference held in London in 1921. Jaspar became prime minister of Belgium in 1926, but held the office for only a short while. He later became minister for the colonies and, in 1932, minister of finance (Jane K. Miller, *Belgian Foreign Policy Between Two Wars, 1919–1940* [New York: Bookman Associates, 1951]; *Biographie Nationale* [Brussels: L'Academie royale des sciences, des lettres, et des beaux-arts de Belgique, n.d.], 31: 480–491).

2. This letter has not been found.

G.O. Marke to Prince Mirza Riza Khan Arfa-ed-Dowleh of Persia[1]

Hotel Suisse, Genève, Switzerland
September 28, 1922

Your Highness,

With reference to my previous communication to you on the subject of the Petition of the Universal Negro Improvement Association to the League of Nations, I beg leave, on behalf of the Delegation of the said organization, sent to Genève for the purpose of presenting that Petition, respectfully to request

Your Highness as head of the Persian Delegation, kindly to submit our Petition to the Assembly of the League of Nations during its present session in Genève, conformably with its rules of procedure.[2]

Our Delegation, assured of your well known sympathy with the aspirations of the less favoured races of the world and of your devoted interest in the cause of peace and goodwill among men, feel more than confident that in submitting this Petition to the Assembly of the League of Nations, Your Highness will contribute in a large measure to the acceleration of that modern tendency to solidarity of interest among the different races of Mankind, of which the League of Nations is a monumental outcome.

For this purpose I submit herewith seventy copies of the said Petition. I have the honour to be, Your Obedient Servant,

G. O. MARKE
Chairman of Delegation

LNA, file 1/21159/21159. TLS on UNIA letterhead, recipient's copy.

1. Prince Mirza Riza Khan Arfa-ed-Dowleh was the representative of Persia to the League of Nations, Persia being the only Islamic country represented at the league. In September 1922 Arfa-ed-Dowleh made national headlines when Lord Balfour interrupted the proceedings to raise the issue of 200,000 destitute Greek and Armenian refugees left in Smyrna in the wake of the Turkish invasion. Offering British and European relief, Balfour appealed to Arfa-ed-Dowleh to communicate with Persia and urge his government to intercede with its Turkish allies to facilitate relief. In response, Arfa-ed-Dowleh cabled, urging Persia to intercede with the Turks and act as the link between Turkey and the league to take charge of the refugees (*NYT*, 26 September 1922; *Current History* 17, no. 1 [October 1922]: 161).

2. On 30 September 1922 William Rappard officially requested that the UNIA petition be distributed and its title mentioned in the *League of Nations Official Journal* (William Rappard to registry of delegates, 30 September 1922, LNA, file 1/21159/21159).

Article by W. E. B. Du Bois

[*Crisis*, September 1922]

THE BLACK STAR LINE

The main economic venture of Marcus Garvey was the Black Star Line.

This steamship venture was the foundation stone of Garvey's rise to popularity among Negroes. African migration is a century old and a pretty thoroughly discredited dream. Autonomous African Negro States have been forecast by scores of Negro leaders and writers. But a definite plan to unite Negrodom by a line of steamships was a brilliant suggestion and Garvey's only original contribution to the race problem. But, asked the critic, can it be done? Has Garvey the business sense, can he raise the capital, can he gather the men?

The answer lies in the history of the Black Star fleet. The *Yarmouth* was a steamer of 1,452 gross tons, built in 1887. The Black Star Line bought this boat in 1919 and in its report for the year 1920, it was put down as worth $178,156.36. At the Orr trial, Garvey swore under oath that he paid $140,000 cash for it. We will tell the rest of this story in Garvey's own words [*Footnote in article*:

"Orr, a stockholder, sued Garvey. The following extracts are from a certified copy of the sworn testimony at this trial.]¹:

> We contracted to bring a carload of whiskey valued at five million dollars and the ship, in sailing out between here and Sandy Hook, was caught in a gale and was damaged badly and put back into port, and there were several raids on the whiskey; when it came back, Prohibition was in effect; the ship was raided several times, whiskey was stolen; we had a great deal of trouble with the Federal Government, costing us thousands of dollars; ultimately the ship was repaired in Cuba; we experienced a tie-up of two months with this cargo of whiskey with a crew of over fifty men and we experienced some trouble in Cuba in handling the whiskey; when she did clear from Cuba, she went to the West Indies and also had an accident there and returned, and we lost on that trip from 250 to 300 thousand dollars, and on another trip we lost about 75 thousand dollars; there were extensive repairs done on the boat, and even against our instructions because the captain of the boat did things on his own account, and we were held liable for it.

> Q. What did you mean by testifying you lost about a quarter of a million dollars on that cargo? A. Because we had to pay the cost of the undelivered cargo; we had to pay the cost of the repairs of the boat.

> THE COURT: You had to pay for what disappeared?

> A. Yes.

> Q. Did all of that cargo disappear, or a few cases?

> A. Part of the cargo.

> Q. Do you mean for the Court to understand that you, at the head of a corporation that had a load of whiskey on their boat, that because it was destroyed or confiscated, you had to pay for it, is that what you want the Court to believe? A. We had to pay for the cargo that was not delivered for which we contracted to deliver.

> Q. Did you insure the cargo? A. No, I did not.

> Q. You mean for the Court to believe you had to pay for the cargo of whiskey?

> THE COURT: That is what he said.

On another voyage, Luc Dorsinville, who claimed to have been Haitian agent of the line, stated that it took the *Yarmouth* three months to make a single voyage between New York, Cuba, Haiti and Jamaica; that the voyage cost between fifteen and twenty thousand dollars and that at the end of the three months the cargo did not pay half the cost. This agent claims that he had 77 passengers booked for passage and a cargo of freight, but the boat was so dirty that most of the people would not take passage. He said that he sold 27 passages beside paying many bills for the ship. Nevertheless, the ship went to Jamaica instead of New York and left the agent to settle the claims for passage money paid and other matters. There was a good deal of controversy as to just who was to blame for all this and why the *Yarmouth* did not return to ship the cargo worth over $30,000 which the agent claims was waiting for her.

Of the staggering losses on the *Yarmouth* no hint appears in Mr. Garvey's glowing speeches concerning the Black Star Line, or in the advertisements in the *Negro World*, or even in the first annual financial report issued in 1920— July 26. No losses whatsoever are recorded there. The *Yarmouth* is entered at full value and an organization expense of $289,066.27 is put down as an asset because it is an "organization expense." It was also recorded: "We have much to be thankful for in that no unfortunate accident has befallen us"!

The *Yarmouth* made three trips to the West Indies in three years. It was then docked for repairs. This bill was apparently not paid, for the *Nauticus*[2] announced, October 15, 1921, an attachment against the Black Star Line for $20,285.57 by the National Dry Dock and Repair Company [*Footnote*: A judgment of $526.70 was also obtained by the Garcia Sugar Corporation.]. This was presumably for unpaid repairs on the *Yarmouth*, although it may have applied to other boats also. At any rate, in the *Nauticus* of December 10, 1921, appears this obituary of the first boat of the Black Star Line:

> *Yarmouth* (S.S.) 1452 tons gross[,] 725 net, built at Dumbarton 1887 and owned by the B.S.L., N.Y., was sold by U.S. Marshall as she lay at the National Dry Dock, N.Y., December 2 (1921), to Frederic Townsend, c/o Walter Welsh, 32 Broadway, for $1,625 [*Footnote*: In addition to this sum the buyer probably had to pay the attachment noted above, making the total selling price of the ship at auction $21,910.57.].

The *Kanawha* or *Antonio Maceo* was listed in the Black Star report as worth $75,359.01. Garvey swore that he paid $60,000 for it. It was apparently bought to do a small carrying trade between the West Indian Islands. The *Kanawha* left New York about Easter time 1921 and sailed for Cuba and the West Indies. Garvey testified that she with another ship "was repaired in dry dock and sailed from here; she broke down between Cuba and the Virginia Coast and we had to tow her back to New York. We had to spend seventy or eighty thousand dollars on that boat." The *Negro World* announced that this boat "arrived in Cuba in a blaze of glory, April 16."

According to the New York *Evening World*, the boat was held up in Cuba because of boiler troubles, although several thousand dollars had been recently spent on new boilers. Finally she was tied up in Santiago de Cuba and the United States Government brought the crew back. The boat itself has never reappeared.

The *Shadyside* was listed by the Black Star Line as worth $35,000. It did a small excursion business up the Hudson during one summer.

In March, 1921, the *Shadyside* lay on the beach beside North River at the foot of 157th Street and was in a hopeless condition, quite beyond repair.

Thus the three first boats of the Garvey fleet disappeared and if the Black Star's own figures and Mr. Garvey's statements of losses are true, this involves a total disappearance of at least $630,000 of the hard-earned savings of colored folk.

But this is not all.

On Sunday night, April 10, according to the *Negro World* of April 16, 1921:

> Unexpectedly, like a bolt of lightning, came the announcement at Liberty Hall tonight that the Black Star Line Steamship Corporation expected by May 1, next, to float the *Phyllis Wheatley*, its latest addition to the corporation's line of steamships to engage in transportation between this country and Africa. The news was hailed with wild expressions of joy and delight by the immense audience that filled the great hall.

The ship was said to carry 4,500 tons of cargo and 2,000 passengers, was equipped with electric lights, fans, music and smoking rooms and refrigerating machinery [*Footnote*: In the Orr trial.].

Already, as early as January, 1921, Black Star Line sailings for Liberia, West Africa, had been given display advertising in the *Negro World*. They were announced for "on or about the 27th of March, 1921, at 3 P.M." Beginning in April and continuing for seven or more months, there appeared advertisements announcing "passengers and freight" for the West Indies and West Africa by the S.S. *Phyllis Wheatley*, "sailing on or about April 25" or without definite date.

When the delegates came to the convention August 1, they naturally asked to see the *Phyllis Wheatley*, but a delegate, Noah Thompson, says in the California *New Age* of September 23, 1921:

> None of the boasted ships were shown the delegates, who were daily promised that on "tomorrow" the ships would be shown. Mr. Thompson said that he was in New York thirty-five days, and with others persisted in demanding to be shown the ships, but was told daily that they could see the ships "tomorrow," and "later," but "tomorrow" never came.

September 30, 1921, Mr. Garvey defended himself, declaring:

> It was announced before the convention adjourned, that the United States Shipping Board had awarded the S.S. *Orion* to the Black Star Line, Inc., the ship for which we are to pay $250,000 and on which we have a deposit of $25,000.

Finally the truth came out. In an editorial in the *Negro World*, February 18, 1922, Mr. Garvey alleges:

A "group" ha[s] robbed the Black Star Line and desires to cover up their robbery, in that within recent months a thorough investigation has been started to find out what has been done in the matter of over $25,000 which is said to be deposited with the United States Shipping Board for the purchase of a ship, and the continuous deception of the said parties in promising the president of the Black Star Line, the Board of Directors and stockholders, that a ship by the name of the S.S. *Orion*, which should have been named the S.S. *Phyllis Wheatley*, should have been delivered since April of 1921 and is not yet delivered up to the time of writing, and for which over a thousand and one excuses have been given.

Moreover, Mr. Garvey virtually acknowledged that the Black Star Line after collecting nearly three-quarters of a million dollars did not have in 1921 enough money to deposit $25,000 on the new ship, but said that part of the purchase money of the ship was to be raised in America and that he went to the West Indies to raise the balance. No sooner had Mr. Garvey left, however, than, as he alleges:

Certain parties who assumed the active management of affairs of the Black Star Line in the United States planned, in conjunction with others, that I should never return to America, and that during my absence from the country, plunderings of all kinds would have been indulged in. . . .

Changes were made in the plans that were laid out for the acquirements of the African boat; new arrangements were made, contracts were signed and for four months, whilst all these changes had been going on, not even a word of information was sent to me to acquaint me of what was being done.

The S.S. *Phyllis Wheatley* that should have been secured since April, and which I had every reason to believe was either at anchor in New York, or had sailed for Africa, was nowhere to be found!

Finally Mr. Garvey concludes:

Patience dragged on and on, until I took definite steps to locate either the money or the ship, and then to my surprise where $25,000 should have been only $12,500 was credited.

In other words, Mr. Garvey says that officials of the Black Star Line, whom he is careful not to name, stole so much of the deposit money that the *Phyllis Wheatley* could not be secured for the line!

Just when Mr. Garvey made this astonishing discovery, we are not informed; but after he returned to America in July, the sailing of the *Phyllis Wheatley* continued to be advertised until October and tickets offered for sale. As a result, Mr. Garvey and three of his chief officials were indicted by the Grand Jury of the District Court of the United States for the Southern District of New York, for "using the mails in furtherance of a scheme to defraud and conspiring so to do."

Several states questioned the honesty of the corporation and refused to let Mr. Garvey sell stock. In the city of Chicago, he was convicted of violating the Illinois Stock Law and fined one hundred dollars. In Virginia, John A. George was sent to jail for selling stock after the Corporation Commission had investigated the scheme through Pinkerton detectives. This was in February, 1921.

What excuses does Mr. Garvey offer for his failure? His excuses are various and extraordinary. *First* and perhaps the most astonishing is the following statement in the *Negro World* of January 21, 1922:

> All the troubles we have had on our ships have been caused because men were paid to make this trouble by certain organizations calling themselves Negro Advancement Associations. They paid men to dismantle our machinery and otherwise damage it so as to bring about the downfall of the movement.

Secondly, Mr. Garvey alleges gigantic "conspiracies." He said, as reported in the *Negro World*, May 13, 1922, at Liberty Hall:

> Millions of dollars were expended in the shipping industries to boycott and put out of existence the Black Star Line.

In the *Negro World* of January 28, 1922, he adds:

> The matter of my arrest last week for the alleged fraudulent use of the mails is but a concoction decided upon by the unseen forces operating against us to find some criminal excuse by which the promot[e]r of the greatest movement among Negroes could be held up to world scorn and ridicule, thereby exposing the movement to contempt. It is a mean, low-down, contemptible method of embarrassing any movement for human uplift.

He also says that "Bolshevists" are paying for attacks on the line. (*Negro World*, December 14 [24?], 1921.)[3]

Thirdly and chiefly, Mr. Garvey accuses his associates and employees of dishonesty. In the *Negro World* of February 18, 1922, Mr. Garvey writes of a "treacherous plot" against him and a "great state of demoralization" in the Black Star Line during his absence, and of "the tricks and dishonesty of a few employees of the Black Star Line."

In the *Negro World* of December 24, 1921, he says:

Through the dishonesty of some of the "so-called educated," Garvey has had to suffer many reverses. Business transactions and financial arrangements which Garvey was too busy to attend to himself and left to others opened the door for several of these "so-called educated" (whom he trusted to represent him) to rob and cheat the organization, and thus make it harder for Garvey to protect and represent the interests of the people.

As often as found out the "so-called educated" tramps and villains have been kicked out of the organization. Several of them have formed new organizations, started newspapers and journals. And some of the organizations, newspapers and journals, after collecting a few thousand dollars from the poor, innocent people, have gone out of existence; but the villains still hover around, connecting themselves with other papers and organizations that keep up a fight against the Universal Negro Improvement Association and Garvey.

Observe carefully the composition of any anti-Garvey organization or paper and you will find there a congregation of dismissed, disgraced and so-called resigned employees of either the Universal Negro Improvement Association, the *Negro World* or the Black Star Line Corporation. All birds of a feather flock together. All villains keep together.

In the *Negro World* of July 8, 1922, he writes:

No head of any steamship company can guarantee what will be the action of the captain of one of his ships when he clears port. If a captain wants to sell or confiscate your goods; if a captain wants to pile up debts on a steamship company for his own selfish profit, what can the president of that corporation do, especially when the individual may be in league with some powers that be, and especially the only powers that could punish him if he creates a criminal offense against the corporation? . . .

What can Marcus Garvey do if men are employed to do their work and they prove to be dishonest and dishonorable in the performance of that work? What could Jesus do dealing with a dishonest man but to wait and punish him at His judgment? And judgment is not just now. What will happen in the meanwhile—Jesus would be robbed.

Finally, Mr. Garvey alleges his own lack of experience in the shipping business:

Marcus Garvey is not a navigator; he is not a marine engineer;

he is not even a good sailor; therefore the individual who would criticize Marcus Garvey for a ship of the Black Star Line not making a success at sea is a fool.—(*Negro World*, July 8, 1922.)

Mr. Garvey consequently writes in the *Negro World* of April 1, 1922, "We have suspended the activities of the Black Star Line."

Here then is the collapse of the only thing in the Garvey movement which was original or promising. Of course, Mr. Garvey promises repayment, reorganization and a "new" Black Star Line.

What are his statements and promises worth? Knowing, as he did, that he had lost $250,000 on a single voyage and $75,000 on another and that his capital had practically disappeared, he declared according to a report in the *Negro World*, March 5, 1921:

> Nothing engineered by Negroes within the last 500 years has been as big or as stupendous as the Black Star Line. . . .
>
> Today we control three-quarters of a million dollars (applause); not three-quarters of a million on mere paper, but in property value—money that can be realized in twenty-four hours if the stockholders desire that their money be refunded to them. By a majority vote at any meeting we can sell out the property of the Black Star Line and realize every nickel we have placed in it.

In spite of this, Mr. Garvey made the following statements under oath in the Orr trial:

> THE COURT: The people in your community have a great deal of faith in you?
>
> A. Yes, they have.
>
> THE COURT: Any statements you made in 1919 were relied on by the members of your community?
>
> A. Yes. THE COURT: *You did not paint the possibilities of the Black Star Line in hues of rose color, did you?*
>
> A. *No, I did not; it was still a business proposition like any other business proposition.*—(*Italics ours.*)

Small wonder that at the end of this trial Judge Panken said:

> It seems to me that you have been pr[e]ying upon the gullibility of your own people, having kept no proper accounts of the money received for investment, being an organization of high finance in which the officers received outrageously high salaries and were permitted to have exorbitant expense accounts for pleasure jaunts throughout the country. I advise these "dupes" who have

contributed to these organizations to go into court and ask for the appointment of a receiver. You should have taken this $600,000 and built a hospital for colored people in this city instead of purchasing a few old boats. There is a form of paranoia which manifests itself in believing oneself to be a great man.

To this let us add this pitiful document from San Diego, Cal., to Noah Thompson:

> I am forced to write you, asking if it is wise for a widow-woman who makes her living by working in service and doing day's work, to continue to make the sacrifice by sending $5.00 per month on payment of shares in the Black Star Line.
>
> After reading that part of your report, stating that you and many other delegates were unable to see the ships supposed to be owned by said company, I began to think, maybe I had better keep my hard earnings at home, for I have an aged mother to support and I haven't one penny to throw away. So I am writing you for facts in regard to what I have asked you.
>
> ELLA ROSS HUTSON

Printed in the *Crisis* 24, no. 5 (September 1922): 210–214.

1. This footnote appears in the original document. Subsequent footnotes from the original appear here in square brackets.
2. *Nauticus*, a journal of shipping, insurance, investments, and engineering, began publication in New York in 1918.
3. In a front-page editorial letter, Garvey declared, "Some of these cheap good-for-nothing Negroes are now trying to turn our race into Bolsheviks, through money they receive from anarchistic quarters" (*NW*, 24 December 1921).

Report by Bureau Agent H.L. Morgan

Pittsburgh, Pa. Oct. 5, 1922

MARCUS GARVEY, PRESIDENT GENERAL OF UNIVERSAL NEGRO IMPROVEMENT ASSOCIATION

This office was advised by CAPTAIN MAUK, of the Jones & Laughlin Steel Company Police Force, Woodlawn, Pa., that a meeting was to be held by the UNIVERSAL NEGRO IMPROVEMENT ASSOCIATION, on Sunday, October 1st, 1922, and that it had been advertised that subject would speak.

Agent proceeded to Woodlawn, Pa., accompanied by CAPTAIN MAUK and Chief of Police Kane, at Woodlawn, Pa., and went to the meeting which was held in the Polish Hall at 120 Third Avenue, Woodlawn, Pa.

Agent secured one of the leaflets put out by the Committee advertising the meeting, which reads as follows:—

LECTURE

BY

RIGHT HONORABLE MARCUS GARVEY

PRESIDENT GENERAL OF UNIVERSAL NEGRO IMPROVEMENT
ASSOCIATION AND

PROVISIONAL PRESIDENT OF AFRICA

SUNDAY, OCT. 1 AT 3 O'CLOCK P.M.

THE PUBLIC IS CORDIALLY INVITED TO HEAR THIS LECTURE

The meeting was opened by WALTER GREAVES, President of the Woodlawn Branch of the UNIVERSAL NEGRO IMPROVEMENT ASSOCIATION. MR. GREAVES introduced MERWIN OWENS, Secretary of the Woodlawn Branch, UNIVERSAL NEGRO IMPROVEMENT ASSOCIATION.

MR. OWENS made a short address; about the only thing he said was in criticism of the colored people of Woodlawn who did not belong to the UNIVERSAL NEGRO IMPROVEMENT ASSOCIATION.

MR. GREAVES then introduced GEORGE WESTON, stating that he was the Chief Arbitrator of the UNIVERSAL NEGRO IMPROVEMENT ASSOCIATION of Western Pennsylvania and that MR. WESTON had been sent as a substitute for MARCUS GARVEY.

MR. WESTON stated that he was very sorry to have to disappoint the crowd, but that MR. GARVEY was a very busy man, in fact, the most busy person in all the world; that he was even more busy than Lloyd George, the Welsh wizard and chief tyrant of the negro race.

WESTON stated that GARVEY fully intended to address the meeting at Woodlawn, but that he had been unexpectedly called to New York City, where it was necessary for him to make an address that night.

WESTON explained the object of the UNIVERSAL NEGRO IMPROVEMENT ASSOCIATION, criticized the colored preachers and other colored people who were opposed to this organization, and impressed this Agent as being a very intelligent colored man.

There was nothing in MR. WESTON'S address which was in any way offensive, as he lauded the United States and stated that the hopes of the UNIVERSAL NEGRO IMPROVEMENT ASSOCIATION were centered in the American flag.

MR. GREAVES then closed the meeting, after asking for a collection which was to be used in defense of GARVEY, who, GREAVES stated, through prejudice had to stand trial the coming week. Most all those present contributed to the collection, how generously could not be ascertained.

The meeting was attended by 56 women and 36 men.

It was the general impression of the people of Woodlawn that there was no intention of ever having GARVEY come there and that advertising him to be there was just done by the Committee in order to assure a crowd for GEORGE WESTON.

H. L. MORGAN

DJ-FBI, file 61. TD.

Report by Special Agent Joseph G. Tucker

[New York] OCT. 7, 1922

. . . U.N.I.A.

Marcus Garvey, through the above organization, is claiming that the enemies of the organization have organized throughout the country to spread propaganda against him in his forthcoming trial in New York and thus endeavor to disorganize the U.N.I.A.

The organization held its usual meeting on the 1st inst. at which William H. Ferris, R.L. Poston, F.A. Toot[e], Henrietta Vinton Davis and Marcus Garvey were the speakers. Garvey, as usual, was the principal speaker. His subject was "The Coming Conflict." He discussed the possibility of war between England and Turkey. In the course of his later remarks he said: "Every white man is welcome to put me in jail if it is done in the cause of African freedom. I do not know whether they understand it or not, that if Marcus Garvey dies, Marcus Garvey's son shall revenge every drop of blood and every ounce of flesh and the family record of Garvey shall go on until eternity.

"I feel sure we are well prepared for the work that is ahead of us. We will face the future as never before. We will watch developments in Europe as never before. I do hope for war; I am not such a Christian as not to desire war at this time. I am that Christian that believes that [*except*] for the shedding of blood there will be no remission of sins, and I believe that the unspeakable Turk is going to be the agent through whom four hundred million negroes will see salvation, and if it comes to-morrow, or the next day or a month from now, I am praying that it will come because only through the coming of another great war in Europe will we get the opportunity to strike the blow for our freedom."

In his early remarks, touching upon the probability of England warring with Turkey, he said the answer to England's plea for colonial help this time will be far different from that which was given during the world war and that after the coming war there will be no more British Empire. He also added:

"They are calling upon colored folks to help them, too. I suppose, since my naturalization papers are not yet complete, I am still a British subject and therefore, when David Lloyd George calls, he includes me." . . .

JOSEPH G. TUCKER

DJ-FBI, file 61-190. TD.

Circular by Chandler Owen

[*New York, ca. 7 October 1922*]

DO YOU WANT GARVEY CONVICTED?
MARCUS GARVEY IS OUT OF JAIL ON BOND

In a short while he will be placed on trial for defrauding through the United States mails. (*He did this by selling passage on a ship he never owned.*)

The Government is traditionally slow. Marcus would probably not be brought into court for a year or more were it not for the strong public sentiment created against him by the meetings of the Friends of Negro Freedom, with the hearty co-operation of the combined Negro press.

Now that you have succeeded in getting Garvey into Court, do you want him to get off lightly, or do you want him to get both fine and imprisonment?

We want him stuck for all he's worth. Now that we have him going, we want to finish the job right.

Nothing could impress the Court and Jurors more than a long petition praying that this trickster be put out of the way for good.

Practically all the New York Judges are Irish or Jewish. The Ku Klux Klan fights them. Garvey supports the Klan. Therefore he fights the Irish and Jewish people. They know this. They will be glad to help you put Garvey out of the way if you let them know you want it done. Will you sign a petition saying you want it done? Sunday will be your opportunity.

The meeting, as usual, will be held at NEW DOUGLAS[S] HALL, 142nd STREET and LENOX AVENUE, 3 o'clock sharp.

SUNDAY, OCTOBER 8th, 1922. CHANDLER OWEN, Co-Editor of the Messenger, will discuss "A NEW APPROACH TO THE SOLUTION OF THE NEGRO PROBLEM" in conjunction with which he will show the necessity for getting rid of the menace of MARCUS GARVEY and why he should be convicted.

Mr. J.B. Brown, brilliant Negro baritone, will sing. Robert W. Bagnall will preside.

READ THE MESSENGER

[CHANDLER OWEN]

NNHR, *Marcus Garvey* v. *Chandler Owen*, no. 37747-22, 22 November 1922.

Thomas W. Anderson, UNIA Second Assistant Secretary General, to William Phillips, Executive Secretary, New Orleans Division, UNIA

New York City, Oct. 10, 1922

My dear Mr. Phillips:

You state that notice has been served on your divi[sion] that "Mr. Garvey is sending another West Indian [N]egro to live on the people" of New Orleans. Let us say here we do not know how you could have received such a report, because such a thing is not in the mind of the Executive Council or the President General. If another man is sent to the New Orleans division he will not be a West Indian. But we do not have in mind sending anyone there just now. But even if we were to send a West Indian Negro there[,] now what is there against a West Indian Negro[?] A West Indian Negro is just as good as a black person of America. This is the thing that our divisions must be gotten out of, making distinction between the various groups of black people when we are all classed by the world, and even high Heaven as Negroes. We do not wish to hear any such thing again from the New Orleans Division.

THOS. W. ANDERSON
2nd Asst. Secretary General

[*Address*] Mr. William Phillips,
2068 Jackson Ave., New Orleans, La.

DJ-FBI, file 61-50-195. TL, transcript.

New York City, Oct. 10, 1922

My dear Mr. Phillips:

By instructions of the President General I am writing you. We are informed here that you are giving undue attention to Mr. J.W. Eason, whom you know to be an enemy of the President General's which means he is an enemy to the Organization.

The President General does not feel a bit pleased over this incident and he is not inclined to overlook it, but we have asked him to be patient until the facts are before us.

We are informed that dissatisfaction is creeping into the division because of your association with Mr. Eason. It is reported here that he was seen in the office with you and we are wondering how this happened. Of course we know that you could not keep him out of the office if he chose to walk in, but you could refuse to have conference with him. You could further have asked him to leave the office because of known conditions. It appears that he remained with you some time.

Further information has reached the President General that you were very active with him while in New York, and that you had certain ambitions, which you hoped to realize but because of actions taken in Mr. Eason's case your ambitions were blasted. Now you know the President General has a peculiar way of receiving information, and at this time the Parent Body is not in attitude to tolerate the slightest suspicion of disloyalty on the part of its representatives.

We are informed that the Vice-President of your division is not executing the work of the division as he should. They claim that your influence can be seen in the Actg. President's actions. Now you will please send to this office a complete statement of conditions as affect[s] yourself in this case.

We are reminded that your division is behind in its reports to the Parent Body. We are informed that the members are very doubtful whether the intention to buy property is honest or not. It is your business to see that members do not become dissatisfied with the work and that the division progresses properly. The slightest act of disloyalty will not be tolerated on the part of any representative of this Organization.

The President General has planned to take care of this matter but he has deferred it for the time being, pending your report in this matter and evidence of the progress of the New Orleans Division in form of proper financial reports and otherwise.

Now if Mr. Eason is still in your community, as a representative of this Organization you know what attitude you should assume, and this is expected of you. We are, with very best wishes, Fraternally yours,

Universal Negro Improvement [As]sociatio[n]
THOS. W. ANDERSON
2nd Assistant Secretary General

DJ-FBI, file 61-50-195. TL, transcript.

Report by Special Agent Joseph G. Tucker

[*New York*] OCTOBER 14, 1922

NEGRO ACTIVITIES

. . . From a confidential source it is reported that Marcus Garvey recently sent to Lincoln Johnson, who is a Republican State Committeeman, at present located in Washington, a check for a thousand dollars which money is to be used by Johnson in endeavoring to extricate Garvey from his present difficulties with the Government.

The same source is also responsible for the statement that one Belgrade, who was former Chief Bodyguard for Garvey and head of his so-called "Secret Service," left Garvey's employ about two weeks ago, after a disagreement with him. Belgrade is said to have made the statement that he knows a great deal about Garvey's financial condition and that the latter draws his salary weekly and is placing it where he will be able to get his hands on it in the event of needing it in a hurry. Efforts are being made to obtain information additional to the foregoing with regard to this matter.

Through the Negro World, Marcus Garvey is raising a fund for the defense, which is known as "The Marcus Garvey Defense Fund." Up to date the fund amounts to over $500.00.

Universal Negro Improvement Association

The usual Sunday night meeting of the above organization was held at Liberty Hall on the 8th instant and as usual, MARCUS GARVEY was the principal speaker, his subject being "The Consciousness of an Ideal." In opening his address, Garvey warned his enemies, whom he enumerated as BAGNELL, WILLIAM PICKENS, PHILIP RANDOLPH and CHANDLER OWEN, to be careful of what they said about him or his organization. In the course of his remarks he said in part:

"I have come to ask you to follow me in the things physical for the emancipation of the 400,000,000. Therefore, in the fight for this [e]mancipation, no one will expect us to read the Sunday School chapter in going forward, but we may read the chapter of something else much more in keeping with the physical side of man's emancipation, and those who place themselves in the way of the Universal Negro Improvement Association, let me tell you this—That you are attempting to place yourself in the physical on-rush of a mighty race that seeks its liberty, not so much by spiritual force as by physical force."

THOMAS W. ANDERSON, Second Assistant Secretary-General, another speaker said in the course of his remarks:

"The Black man has endured hardships long enough. All we have had is hardships. We are tired of hardships now; we are tired of eating the hog[']s head. Now we are going to eat further down. And it is for you to say how far off that is. If the Negroes of this World will unite tonight, tomorrow we can march on singing the song of victory. . . . We are not opposed to fighting, but we are opposed to fighting for other men and getting nothing for it. . . . You [were] asked to go and fight the Germans who had done you no wrong. You were told to give the Germans hell, while they were giving you hell over here, and while you were giving the Germans hell, they were giving your mothers, sisters and sons hell in Mississippi, Georgia, Alabama, and then the Negro asked which was better, to make the World safe for democracy, or to make his home safe for his wife and children. That is what he asked then and what he is asking now."

UNIVERSAL NEGRO ALLIANCE

J. W. H. EASON, Founder and President of the above organization, which is opposed to the Universal Negro Improvement Association, is at present on a tour of the Middle West, where he has been endeavoring to organize branches of the Alliance.

JOSEPH G. TUCKER

DJ-FBI, file 61-50-191. TD.

Article in the *New York Age*

[[New Orleans, *ca. 14 October 1922*]]

DR. EASON, FORMER GARVEYITE, MAKES EXPOSURES OF UNIA

"I could today be still in the Garvey group of the Universal Negro Improvement Association, Factories Corporation, and other concerns, if I would only keep my mouth shut, not come out publicly and call upon Mr. Garvey, as I have done, as I intend to continue to do, to tell the truth to the members of the association as to what has become of the nearly a million dollars collected from the members, with absolutely nothing to show for it on hand," was the opening crack of the thundering things that the Rev. J. W. H. Eason, who last year came to New Orleans and put the Garvey movement in good shape in this city, said in Longshoremen's Hall, Jackson avenue and Franklin street, on Monday night to about one hundred representative citizens gathered there to hear the Eason side of the reason why he was expelled for ninety-nine years and one day from the Garvey movement during Garvey's August convention in New York.

Another of Mr. Eason's strong and ripping cracks which brought long and loud applause was when he said:

I am an American citizen, with rights and privileges in the part of the country where I live equal before the law to those of every other American citizen there, and it has never occurred to me in all my life that any man has the right to deny me the exercise of those sacred rights and privileges; so when Garvey seemed to require of me as a fair price for my remaining in his good graces that I should never question him about the use he was making of the money I put in the association, of the money I raised from others and put into his hands for buying and paying for ships to carry on trade and commerce between this and other countries, in keeping with the program which he had shown me, while time was passing and our money going, too, as in a hole, I told Garvey in as forceful language as I could utter, that I would never surrender my manhood, my sacred rights and privileges to question him on such vital matters for the biggest office that he had in the U.N.I.A. to give me.

Mr. Eason said that when he found on close investigation that nearly a million dollars of members['] money appeared to have been foolishly spent, wantonly squandered or made away with, and that there was absolutely nothing to show in ships or anything else for the money that was all gone, there was nothing he could think of to do but to question Garvey about the missing money, because Garvey received all the money and permitted none of it to get out without knowing what it was going for, who it was going to and when it was going. Eason said that there was no one else for him to question about it, and of course he questioned Garvey as the one responsible for it.

Mr. Eason said that this made him a bad man, and [a] dangerous man in the opinion of Mr. Garvey,—a man that Garvey had to get rid of in the U.N.I.A., and Garvey's convention, at the dictation and order of Garvey, expelled him for ninety-nine years and one day.

"One thing," said Mr. Eason, "that Garvey and his convention in expelling me did not do was to give me back the five thousand dollars which I loaned the movement through the solicitation of Garvey in order to help Garvey get it on its feet. I hold duly signed notes, notes signed by Garvey as president and by his secretary of the U.N.I.A., for this money and I mean to get back my money."

Mr. Eason said he went to see Garvey after the convention in his office and demanded a return of his money and that Garvey told him, he said, that they could not pay him because they had no money in the treasury to pay him with.

Mr. Eason seemed inclined to believe that there was very little money in the U.N.I.A. treasury because the treasurer's report read at the recent convention showed a balance on hand of a little over $700, and because he himself had figures to show that the U.N.I.A. and allied concerns were in debt for over $285,718 today, with absolutely nothing in the way of unencumbered property of any kind to set up against the debt.

Charges that a plantation in the West Indies, costing $25,000 had been bought by Garvey, and $4,000 or $5,000 had been invested in some concern in Liberia or other part of Africa by Garvey, and the U.N.I.A. and allied concerns are in debt over $285,700, were made by the speaker. Mr. Eason said Garvey vaunts himself as the only man in the U.N.I.A. who has sense enough to manage a big affair like the U.N.I.A. and its allied concerns properly, and yet Eason says, nearly a million dollars of the members' money can neither be found in the banks in the shape of ships, realty or other assets of the U.N.I.A. And Eason asks where is this money if it has not been foolishly squandered, recklessly spent or dishonestly made away with?

"No doubt," Eason said, "Garvey spent much of this money advertising Garvey."

During the convention, Mr. Eason alleged, one day Garvey paid out in a check to a representative of a big New York daily paper $250 to announce in its colum[n]s that the "Hon Marcus Garvey, the greatest Negro orator [that] the Negro race ever produced will speak" on a certain occasion, naming the occasion.

That was money, Eason said, that was foolishly spent out of the funds of the U.N.I.A. But he added, there is no doubt that this $250 which Garvey wast[e]fully threw away that day was only a small fraction of the members' money that Garvey has used to advertise the "Hon. Marcus Garvey" and Marcus Garvey alone, at the expense of members who are too craven to question Garvey's right to do so.

Mr. Eason said that the report of the general treasurer of the U.N.I.A., read to the convention in August was, by a motion made and adopted, to be printed and a copy of it placed in the hands of every member of the convention, but that Garvey knew when the motion was entertained that no printed copy of this report was ever to get into the hands of any member and none ever did. This report showed a balance of a little over $700 on hand of an aggregate amount collected for the year of over $187,000, he said. Mr. Eason said that although Garvey did not want any one to have a copy of this report, he (Eason) managed to get one just the same and that he obtained it from one of Garvey's confidential and trusted employees for ten dollars. Mr. Eason read essential parts of the report from what he declares was a true copy of the original and what he read bore out what he had said of the condition of the U.N.I.A. and allied concerns as to funds.

Mr. Eason is in New Orleans organizing the Negro Improvement Alliance under charter granted by the State of Louisiana. Every State is [t]o have a chartered organization of its own and the state organizations are to form a national organization like the national convention like the great political parties of this country.

Mr. Eason said that Garvey's claims that there were four million Negroes in the U.N.I.A. was not borne out by the true membership roll which shows only about fifty thousand members.

Printed in the *New York Age*, 14 October 1922.

Editorial Letter by Marcus Garvey

[[New York, October 17, 1922]]

Moton And His Mission To Europe

FELLOW MEN OF THE NEGRO RACE, GREETING:

Our friend, Dr. Robert R. Moton, Principal of Tuskegee Institute, has been called by the white race to speak in Edinburgh and Glasgow, Scotland, and in parts of England.[1] He is supposed to tell the people he will address of Africa's needs. This in itself seems harmless, on the surface, but we are not disposed to take this call of Mr. Moton to speak in Europe at this time at its face value. This is really the time when we must be saved from our friends. As we see it, the case is as follows:

At The Bottom Of It

The white nations interested in the exploitation of Africa have suddenly discovered that there is a universal agitation for the redemption of Africa by the black peoples of the world and that the Africans themselves at home are taking an active part in fostering this agitation. Their brothers in America, the West Indies, South and Central America, Asia, and Europe are giving them a strong helping hand. Millions of Negroes in the western world are now working toward the end of African redemption. Not very long ago the Universal Negro Improvement Association sent to the League of Nations at Geneva, Switzerland, a delegation of representative Negro men to lay before that august body the claims of the entire race for the freedom of Africa. Great publicity has been given to the matter in Europe, to the extent of stirring up sentiment among the Europeans, at least the working classes. To offset this forward movement of the Negro peoples of the world, the white capitalists, working through their various Christian Missionary Societies, have decided to give a new aspect to the African question. They desire to convince the world that Africa does not need an independence all her own, but that Africa's development should be dependent upon the good Christian graces of the white Missionary Societies, supported by the good white Christian philanthropists. They calculate that if they can get the world to see Africa's future from this viewpoint, there would be very little likelihood of the masses of white people sympathizing with this new claim advanced by the Universal Negro Improvement Association for Africa's redemption. Now, what is behind all this? The answer is, it is simply that the white capitalists of Wall Street, the bank district of London, and the financial centers of France and Italy are determined to strengthen their grip upon Africa's throat, and throttle her until every ounce of gold, silver, copper, coal, iron, oil, and all minerals are squeezed out of her through the sweat and blood of the African natives themselves. To successfully do this, the Africans at home and the Africans abroad must be convinced that it is a right thing for them to welcome the foreign Christian

Missionary agencies from Europe, and the protecting influence of the great European Governments.

BLOOD MONEY

Now that the Negro has started to think for himself, the white Christian leaders and philanthropists realize that it will be very hard for them to convince us to accept their "friendly (?) protection." Hence they feel that the best that can be done would be to get a representative Negro to say for them what they would very much like to have said. Our friend Dr. Moton is the fittest man for such a job, because he and his institution, as well as the Hampton Institute (which, by the way, sent Major Allen Washington[2] to accompany Dr. Moton), are the two Negro institutions that have received millions of dollars from white philanthropists to teach Negroes in the way they should go.

When our late lamented friend, Dr. Washington, and our friend Dr. Moton received their millions of dollars from white philanthropists, in America, they little calculated that they were receiving but the blood money for which their race must be sold. No white man gives away money in the thousands without a purpose behind it. The purpose behind all the philanthropy among Negro schools and institutions is that these institutions would give Negroes the kind of education that would alienate them from all those things that tend to make them a united, strong and independent race. Tuskegee was never encouraged to teach the liberated slaves even of to-day their relationship with Africa; neither did Hampton teach this. If these two institutions had taught the thousands of black students who passed through them their racial and national kinship to Africa, to-day Africa would not be so parceled out among the alien races and nation[s] of Europe. But Africa would have been a vast native commonwealth, controlled and governed by Africans themselves.

A $5,000 CHECK—WHAT IT MEANS!

The lessons of racial and national love for Africa that should have been imparted to the thousands of liberated slaves would have inspired them to return to their Motherland, to help in her development. White philanthropists saw to it that no such thing was taught neither the liberated slaves of America, nor those of the West Indies, but that they subsidized these Negro institutions for the purpose of inspiring our race to love everybody and everything except ourselves and our country, during which time they redoubled every effort to grab every inch of African territory, until to-day Africa, north, south, east and west, and central, is all the property of the white man, which he intends to exploit for the enrichment of himself and his race.

When Julius Rosenwald[3] gives his check for $5,000 and Carnegie for $10,000, it all means that you, the black man, and your country, must repay it one hundred fold, because later on I intend to invest so much in African rubber, diamonds, copper, iron, gold, or coal, and so as to be able to secure my investment and make the profit that I hope to gain, either myself personally or my posterity, I will call upon the leaders of your race, whom I have subsidized through their institutions, to tell you just what I want done. You will naturally believe your own. Hence we find Dr. Moton going to Scotland and England to tell the world of Africa's needs, under the direction of the white philanthropists and Christian Missionaries.

WHAT IS GOING TO HAPPEN

I hardly believe that Dr. Moton is conscious of what he is about to do, because he looks upon it as a great honor bestowed upon the Negro race for a black man to be called to speak before a white missionary society in Edinburgh, and a Christian Endeavor convention in Glasgow. That is all he sees of it, but the white man has a deeper meaning than that. Those of us on this side of the Atlantic will expect to read in the New York World, the New York Times, and other white daily papers, the advice of our good friend Dr. Moton, as released by the Associated Press from Edinburgh, Glasgow and London. These American papers that are but carriers of the capitalist program will tell us how great a leader Dr. Moton is, how sane and sober his advice to the colored people, and that the colored people should follow him in the direction given. The unthinking colored press will take it up, and convey it to the home of every colored man in the United States of America and elsewhere, and thus the white capitalist propaganda will be put over, to the detriment of the race, without our knowledge of it.

Fortunately, the Universal Negro Improvement Association is here to expose these little tricks that have been practised to the detriment of Africa. We hope that no member of our race will pay any attention to what Dr. Moton says in the matter of Africa's needs, because it is strange that he had nothing to say about Africa until he was called by these white missionaries and philanthropists to speak.

Africa needs very little of the advice that the so-called Christian nations are giving to her at the present time. They have had hundreds of years for Christianizing Africa, and all that they have done during that time was to rob, ravish and exploit her. We will no longer trust ourselves to their advice.

Let every member of the Universal Negro Improvement Association cling firmer to the program we have initiated—that of an emancipated Negro race, and a free and redeemed Africa. Support this with your moral, physical and financial strength, and if all of us will loyally obey the dictates of this great world movement, there is absolutely no reason why we shall not, in a short while, defeat the enemies at their game. Send in whatever financial support you can to the Parent Body, Universal Negro Improvement Association, 56 West 135th Street, New York City, N.Y., and help us put over the program. With very best wishes, I have the honor to be Your obedient servant,

MARCUS GARVEY
President-General
Universal Negro Improvement Association

Printed in *NW*, 21 October 1922. Original headlines abbreviated.

1. Moton's visit was sponsored by the Glasgow-based Scottish Churches Missionary Congress. Moton opened the Congress on 17 October with a lecture on "Africa in Transformation" and later spoke before the African Races Association of Glasgow (*Baltimore Afro-American*, 20 October 1922; *New York Age*, 23 September 1922). In his speech at Liberty Hall, Garvey claimed that the Congress was using Moton as a vehicle to convince "the Africans at home and the Africans abroad . . . that it is a right thing for them to welcome the foreign Christian missionary agencies from Europe, and the protecting influences of the great European governments" (*New York Age*, 28 October 1922).

2. Maj. Allen W. Washington (1870–1930), an administrator for forty-five years at the Hampton Institute, was born and reared in Zanoni, a town in Gloucester County, Virginia. In 1885 he matriculated at Hampton, where he studied harness making and worked at the institute's sawmill. In his first year he met and roomed with fellow student Robert Moton, with whom he developed a lifelong friendship. He graduated from Hampton in 1891 and upon graduation was made associate commandant of Hampton under Maj. Robert Moton. When Moton left Hampton to join Tuskegee, Washington replaced Moton as major at Hampton. In 1913, along with Moton, he helped to found the Negro Organization Society, a self-help organization for blacks in Virginia. He served as the organization's treasurer and then as its president and was a frequent participant at meetings of the National Negro Business League (*Southern Workman* 46, no. 7 [July 1917]: 402–404; ibid., 51, no. 11 [November 1922]: 532–533; ibid., 55, no. 1 [January 1926]: 12–13; ibid., 55, no. 12 [December 1926]: 533–534; ibid., 59, no. 11 [November 1930]: 482–483, 492–494).

3. Julius Rosenwald (1862–1932), Chicago merchant and philanthropist, got his start in the wholesale clothing business in 1885. By 1895 he was vice-president and treasurer of Sears Roebuck and Co.; he served as president from 1910 to 1925 and as chairman of the board from 1925 until his death. A religious Jew but never a Zionist, Rosenwald contributed millions to philanthropy. The Julius Rosenwald Fund, created in 1917, totaled over $30,000,000, and he gave liberally to Jewish and civic organizations. His contributions to blacks were considered "the outstanding feature of his philanthropy." He contributed over $3 million toward the cost of building twenty-five YMCAs and three YWCAs for blacks in various cities, and gave over $3.5 million toward the building of black public schools in the south (*DAB*; *NYT*, 7 January 1932).

Report by Special Agent James E. Amos

New York, N.Y. Oct. 19, 1922

Agent interviewed LOUIS LA MOTHE, 221 West 141st Street, who informed Agent that GARVEY expected to go to jail, but that he was preparing a home for himself when he got out; that he was building a house somewhere near Larchmont, N.Y., which was to cost $45,000. Agent will investigate this matter.

Agent also went to the 7th District Court, where ADRIAN JOHNSON of 438 St. Nicholas Avenue had a suit against Garvey for $300.00, in part 3 before JUDGE WM. YOUNG. GARVEY testified that the U.N.I.A. had a membership of 4,000,000 negroes. The jury was out fifteen minutes and brought in judgment for JOHNSON of $300.00 and interest.

Agent received from a confidential source, information to the effect that GARVEY has offered to pay stockholders of the BLACK STAR LINE with the funds of the U.N.I.A., and for all stockholders to turn over their shares to him. Of course, the U.N.I.A. has only about $3,000. to their credit, so Agent is of the opinion that this is a scheme to get the stock from the people.

Agent also interviewed WALTER WHITE, Ass[istan]t Sec[retar]y of the NATIONAL ASSN. FOR THE ADVANCEMENT OF COLORED PEOPLE, and he thinks that GARVEY has and is doing more to hurt the negro than anyone has ever done, also if GARVEY doesn't go to jail it will be the worst calamity the negroes have ever experienced.

JAMES E. AMOS

DJ-FBI, file 61-50. TD.

Article in the *Chicago Whip*

[[Cincinnati, Ohio, Oct. 21, 1922]]

In deciding the cases following a riot at the Sterling Hotel, Sixth and Mound streets, several nights ago, Judge William D. Alexander,¹ in Police Court yesterday [*20 October*] said that he favored the advancement of the Negro race, but that as long as Negroes cannot get together and talk things over in a sensible way such advancement will be impossible.

William Ware, of 927 Barr street, president of the Cincinnati Division of the Universal Negro Improvement Association, was found guilty of assault and battery upon Samuel Saxon, lecturer of New York. Ware was fined $50 and costs, and Judge Alexander said he was convinced it was Ware's fault that the riot was started.

Willie Davis, of 409 Carlisle avenue, charged with disorderly conduct, was found guilty and fined $10 and costs, while Clarence Turner, of 1029 Foraker avenue, was found guilty of the same offense and fined $25 and costs. Archie Simmons, of 917 Barr street, Loui[s] Hancock of 550 West Sixth street, George Miller of Carlisle avenue and Samuel Saxon of the Sterling Hotel were dismissed.

Samuel Saxon, lecturer, his head [w]rapped with bandages, took the witness stand and said that he had planned the meeting at the Sterling Hotel for the exposure of Marcus Garvey, as Saxon said, "the self-styled President of Africa." He said that he opened the meeting and read from a newspaper a threat by Marcus Garvey against any who would oppose the Garvey movement. When Saxon said that, a riot suddenly started in the meeting place. He told of William Ware having struck at him with a knife.

At this time there were "boos" and jeers from the audience. Judge Alexander rapped for order and had the police eject all from the courtroom. Saxon told a story of fighting his way out of the auditorium while men struck at him with chair legs and their fists.

Numerous witnesses told their versions of the riot and the case was continued until the afternoon session of court. When court convened at 2 o'clock in the afternoon, Judge Alexander warned all spectators that the slightest comment from any person in the audience would mean ejection from the courtroom.

After all arguments had been submitted and Judge Alexander was about to rule in the case, he said: "The colored folks have been too much worked up about a matter which could be argued out without any cutting or head busting. I don't know what the Garvey movement is, but I do know that any movement that can not stand criticism can not stand. There is no doubt in my mind but that Ware is responsible for this riot. There has [been] testimony about a wrong impression given out by a newspaper article, but this newspaper on the next day printed a correct statement of the facts and that is all that can be asked. This corrected statement was printed before the meeting took place. The Negroes cannot expect to progress unless they can argue out matters as men."

Printed in the *Chicago Whip*, 21 October 1922. Original headlines omitted.

1. William D. Alexander (1871–1954), an Ohio-born judge, graduated from the University of Cincinnati Law School in 1900. A lifelong Republican, he was elected to the Ohio legislature in 1911; he became a municipal court judge in 1918, a position he held until his death (*Cincinnati Enquirer*, 27 May 1954).

Florent de Sélys-Fanson,[1] Chargé d'Affaires, Belgian Embassy, Washington, D.C., to Henri Jaspar

Belgian Embassy, Washington 27 Oct. 1922

Following on from my letter dated 16th Oct. No. 1530/621 enclosed please find:

1) The only issues of "Daily Negro Times" that our Consul-General in New York was able to get are dated 12th & 19th October. You will observe that very little information on the Negro question is included, although on the first page beside the title there is "Daily Voice of the Negro." It is a genuine newspaper, and contrary to its colleague, the "Negro World," it is not solely concerned with spreading propaganda in favor of Marcus Garvey;

2) Extract of New York newspaper "The Sun," of 26 October,[2] announcing that the publication of the "Negro Times" has been suspended after the 26th issue. This is due to an increase in publication costs which have surpassed the daily returns;

3) A copy of "Negro World" of 21st October in which it is announced that Dr. Robert Moton, Principal of Tuskegee Institute, has been invited by the English to give lectures in Edinburgh, Glasgow[,] etc. He will speak of "The Needs of the African Negro" and it is likely that His Majesty's Ambassador in London will eventually inform you about the activities of this lecturer.

Mr. Garvey sees Dr. Moton's mission as a plot of the enemies of the U.N.I.A. He recalls that this association [*UNIA*] has sent delegates to the

Geneva Conference (League of Nations) to demand a part of the former German colonies. Also, these delegates are to make a propaganda tour of Germany, France, and England to spread propaganda in favor of the U.N.I.A.; the last Negro convention had voted funds to cover the cost of this mission.[3]

Dr. Moton's ideas on the Negro question are not the same as those of Garvey's, who wishes Negro emancipation with the exclusion of white participation, while Dr. Moton thinks that it is impossible for Negroes to make progress in civilization without white help. Garvey thinks that Dr. Moton will speak in favor of whites. He finds it strange that the English would appeal for Dr. Moton's intervention at the time when the U.N.I.A.'s delegates are traveling in Europe.

In short, Marcus Garvey, in his speech delivered in Liberty Hall on 15th October, did not openly accuse Dr. Moton but suspects him of betraying the Negro cause and of playing into the hands of the English and other powers who have mandates in Africa. The "Tuskegee Institute," he says, receives subsidies from whites. It is likely that Dr. Moton will not speak against those who support his Institute, and Garvey concludes "a Negro Institute that has been started on white people's philanthropy must naturally be willing to be used by that same class of people to put over the program they have for ruling the world and the entire human race."

I received your dispatch "Direction P.B. (Congo) no. order 574," dated 10th of this month[,] with copy of the letter sent to the Belgian delegate at the League of Nations re Garvey's statement. I would like to know what the League of Nations has decided to do about the appeal from the black agitator. . . .

FLORENT DE SÉLYS-FANSON

SAMAE, no. 1638/654. TLS, recipient's copy (translated from French).

1. The baron Florent de Sélys-Fanson (1884–1941), doctor of law, began his diplomatic career in 1909 as an attaché. He served as secretary to the legation in London, St. Petersburg (now Leningrad), and Bucharest before being assigned as adviser to the delegation in Washington, D.C., in 1921, where he served until 1923. From 1923 to 1940 Sélys-Fanson served in Ottawa and the Soviet Union; he left in the wake of World War II and fled to Stockholm, where he died the following year (G. De Klerck, director general, Ministry of Foreign Affairs, Brussels, to Robert A. Hill, 28 March 1983).

2. On 26 October 1922 an article appeared in the *New York Sun* stating that "Publication of Marcus Garvey's daily newspaper, *The Negro Times*, has been definitely suspended, according to an announcement made by the Universal Negro Improvement Association at 56 West 135th St. Only twenty-six issues of the paper were published, and the cost is said to have greatly exceeded the daily receipts" (*New York Sun*, 26 October 1922).

3. According to the Office of Political Affairs of the French Ministry of Colonies, the UNIA delegates (Sherrill, Marke, O'Meally, and Adam) stayed in Geneva "to attend the meetings of the International Labor Conference," which was held in November under the auspices of the League of Nations International Labor Organization. On 3 November the UNIA delegation left Geneva for Paris (memorandum to the Office of Political Affairs, French Ministry of Colonies, 13 November 1922, AMAE, file S.C.R. 2/11).

Summary Report of the Books and Records of the Black Star Line and UNIA by Thomas P. Merrilees, Expert Bank Accountant

New York City, N.Y. October 27th, 1922

BLACK STAR LINE, INC.

Organization:

The "BLACK STAR LINE, INC." was incorporated under the laws of the State of Delaware on June 27, 1919, with an authorized capital of $500,000.

Shares   100,000.

Par Value $5.

The amount of capital declared to commence business $1,000.[,] the subscribers being:

Marcus Garvey	40 shares
Edgar M. Grey	40 shares
Richard E. Warner	40 shares
George Tobias	40 shares
Janie Jenkins	40 shares

Transfer of Subscription:

At a meeting of the Board of Directors held June 27, 1919, the Secretary presented transfer of subscription by the above named subscribers to Universal Negro Improvement Association, Inc., for the total of 200 shares.

Control of Corporation:

At a meeting of the Board of Directors held September 11, 1919, it was stated by the President (MARCUS GARVEY) that it was the intention to have the BLACK STAR LINE controlled by the U.N.I.A., but having had no money the public had to be appealed to. He proposed to enlarge the directorate of the BLACK STAR LINE so as to have the Association protected by not allowing persons who were not members to be on the directorate to control the stock.

Increase of Capital Stock:

The increase of the capital stock and capitalization of the corporation from $500,000. to $10,000.000. was first raised at a meeting of the Board of Directors held November 14, 1919.

On December 22, 1919, the first stockholders['] meeting was held and the President (Marcus Garvey) reported purpose of meeting as being to increase capital from $500,000. to $10,000,000. and that according to the by-laws there should be an annual (stockholders[']) meeting, but finding it necessary and in the interest of the corporation he took the opportunity by the authority vested in him to call the meeting[,] and as it was only by a majority vote that such action could be authorized, it was left with the stockholders assembled after considering the proposition to deal with same according to their conviction which will be manifested by the votes. A motion to increase capital stock from $500,000. to $10,000,000. was unanimously carried, the shares to be sold at $5. each par.

Control of Corporation:

At the first annual meeting of stockholders held July 26, 1920, the President, (MARCUS GARVEY) stated we are here principally as members of the U.N.I.A. who incorporated the BLACK STAR LINE to achieve the objects it set itself out to do. We entered as a people of but little experience. The policy of the U.N.I.A. is to control this corporation to help the Parent Body in achieving its objects.

Directors:

At the first meeting of the incorporators on June 27, 1919, the following directors were elected: Marcus Garvey, Edgar M. Grey, Richard E. Warner, George Tobias, Jeremiah Certain, Henrietta Vinton Davis, Janie Jenkins.

Officers:

At the first Directors['] meeting, held June 27, 1919, the following officers were elected:

President—Marcus Garvey, First Vice President—Jeremiah Certain, Second Vice President—Henrietta Vinton Davis, Treasurer— George Tobias, Secretary—Richard E. Warner, Assistant Secretary—Edgar M. Grey, Assistant Treasurer—Janie Jenkins.

Changes in Directors and Officers, 1919–1920:

On August 2, 1919, Richard E. Warner and Edgar M. Grey expelled as Directors and Officers.

Fred Powell and Edward Smith-Green elected Directors.

Edward Smith-Green elected Secretary.

Fred Powell elected Assistant Secretary.

On August 8, 1919, Fred D. Powell elected Assistant Treasurer in place of Miss Jenkins.

On September 20, 1919, four directors were added: Miss Ashwood, Cyril Henry, J.G. Bayne, D.D. Shirley; and Fred D. Powell resigned as Assistant Treasurer[;] Cyril Henry elected as Assistant Treasurer.

On February 14, 1920, Fred D. Powell, Assistant Secretary, resigned.

June 3, 1920, J.G. Bayne (Director) protested his dismissal as unfair.

Directors: Second election:

At the first annual meeting of stockholders, July 27, 1920, the following Directors were elected:

Miss Henrietta Vinton Davis, Miss J[a]nie Jenkins, George Tobias, C. Henry, Professor Ferris, Fred Toote, Elie Garcia, J. Certain, C. Benj. Curley.

By acclamation the name of MARCUS GARVEY was added to the list.

Wilford H. Smith and William Matthews are listed as among the Directors present at a meeting of the Board of Directors on May 28, 1921, but there is no record of their election or appointment until October 26, 1921. Again Wilford H. Smith and J.D. Gordon are listed as among the Directors present at a meeting of the Board of Directors on July 2, 1921, and again there is no record of the election or appointment of Smith until October 26, 1921, and in the case of Gordon, ever.

Officers: Second election:
At a meeting of Directors held on August 7, 1920, the following officers were elected:

> President—Marcus Garvey, First Vice President—O.M. Thompson, Second Vice President—Henrietta Vinton Davis, Treasurer—George Tobias, Secretary—C.B. Curley, Assistant Treasurer—C. Henry, Assistant Secretary—Elie Garcia.

Changes in Directors and Officers—1920–1921:
On October 11, 1920, C. Benj. Curley, Secretary, having resigned, Elie Garcia, Assistant Secretary, was appointed Acting Secretary.

Second annual meeting of stockholders:
Held July 26, 1921, and adjourned to October 26, 1921, apparently without action in regard to Board of Directors.

Directors: Third election:
At an adjourned meeting of stockholders held October 26, 1921, the following Directors were elected:

> Marcus Garvey, O.M. Thompson, Elie Garcia, George Tobias, Henrietta Vinton Davis, Wilford H. Smith, William C. Matthews, William H. Ferris, Fred A. Toote, J[a]nie Jenkins.

Officers:
The minute book does not record any election of officers at or about this date (October 26, 1921).

Stock selling plans (from Minute Book):
It has already been shown that MARCUS GARVEY and the other 4 incorporators assigned their subscription of 40 shares each—200 in all—to the Universal Negro Improvement Association on June 27, 1919, the date of incorporation. This stock never was issued or paid for, notwithstanding it was

the declared capital with which they were to commence business.

At a second meeting of the Board of Directors held June 27, 1919, the President (MARCUS GARVEY) stated it was his intention to visit the State of Virginia and that during his stay there stocks should be sold starting on Sunday, June 29th, and further that stocks should be sold at the Palace Casino in New York at the same time. Edgar M. Grey (Director and Assistant Secretary) was empowered to do so.

At a meeting of the Board of Directors August 1, 1919, the President (MARCUS GARVEY) stated the time was at hand for a proper organized campaign for the selling of the stock of the corporation.

At a meeting of the Board of Directors August 8, 1919, it was resolved that a Rally be given by the BLACK STAR LINE for the swelling of its funds by the sales of stock.

At a meeting of the Board of Directors August 26, 1919, the results of the campaign waged during the past week for the BLACK STAR LINE, INC., were discussed. The Treasurer could not furnish a financial statement as all the applications for stock at Carnegie Hall had not been posted.

At a meeting of the Board of Directors August 30, 1919, it was resolved that meetings be held for the sale of BLACK STAR LINE stock, as follows:

Olympia Theatre, Philadelphia, Sunday afternoon, August 31st, Peoples Church, Philadelphia, Monday evening, Sept. 1st, Faneuil Hall, Boston, Thursday evening, Sept. 4th.

It was also resolved that the President (MARCUS GARVEY) secure Madison Square Garden, New York City, for a meeting in the interest of the BLACK STAR LINE.

At a meeting of the Board of Directors September 11, 1919, Captain Cockburn reported on his negotiations relative to the purchase of the s.s. "YARMOUTH" and advised the Board to negotiate a charter for the ship on Saturday morning, September 13, at which time it is intended to make the first payment of $16,500. The cost of the charter will be about $2,000. per month and he explained even if the Corporation did not make money on her charter the p[sych]ological effect on the people would be so great that the chartering of the ship alone [would] boost the sales of stocks whereby the finances of the corporation would be augmented.

At a meeting of the Board of Directors September 19, 1919, the President (MARCUS GARVEY) reported that Mr. Lemam, counsellor-at-law, gave the opinion that the article in the Chicago Defender, postdated Saturday, 20th inst., was libellous, that it was apparently intended to influence the public mind against the purchase of the shares of the BLACK STAR LINE SHIPPING CORPORATION. He advised a suit for damages of $20,000. It was approved that Mr. Lemam proceed with the action which was sworn to by the Secretary.

At a meeting of the Board of Directors, September 20, 1919, the contemplated trip of some of the Directors and Officers to the West in the interest of the U.N.I.A. and the BLACK STAR LINE was approved. The cities to be *touched* are Philadelphia, Chicago and Pittsburgh.

At a meeting of the Board of Directors, October 13, 1919, the President (MARCUS GARVEY) made report of his trip to the West and informed the Directors of his financial success in Philadelphia in the interest of the BLACK STAR LINE. But on account of the propaganda waged by the Chicago Defender in Chicago he was not as successful there. Before leaving New York the attorney for the corporation advised him that it was not necessary to obtain a license to do business in Chicago but after his arrival there he was arrested for violation of the "Blue Sky Law" which prevented him from doing business without the permission of the authorities; through this the financial [*aspect?*] of the trip was damaged.

The President (MARCUS GARVEY) again explained that the Chicago Defender made a publication which counsel deemed libellous and was intended to work harm against the interests of the BLACK STAR LINE. A suit for damages, $300,000.[,] was brought against the Defender in Chicago. Action approved.

Application made through Mr. Lemam, counsel, for license in Maryland, Illinois and West Virginia to enable him (President) to do business in interest of BLACK STAR LINE, approved.

At a special meeting of the Board of Directors, November 20, 1919, Henrietta Vinton Davis and Cyril Henry were appointed agents of the BLACK STAR LINE, INC., in the Republic of Panama, Canal Zone, to sell the shares of stock and issue certificates of stock for shares so sold.

At a meeting of the Board of Directors November 21, 1919, the President (MARCUS GARVEY) reported that Miss Davis, 2nd Vice President, and Cyril Henry, Assistant Treasurer, were being sent to the West Indies, Central and South America.

At a special stockholders['] meeting, December 22, 1919, capital stock authorized increased from $500,000. to $10,000,000.

At a meeting of the Board of Directors January 30, 1920, President (MARCUS GARVEY) authorized to appoint Agents and lawyers in the Republic of Panama and the Canal Zone to act for and on behalf of the corporation and that the authority given Henrietta Vinton Davis [and] Cyril Henry remains unrevoked.

At a meeting of the Board of Directors February 14, 1920, the sending of Secretary E.D. Smith-Green to Havana, Cuba and Jamaica, B.W.I., to represent interest of corporation approved.

At a meeting of the Board of Directors March 22, 1920, the President (MARCUS GARVEY) stated he had received report from Mr. Smith-Green that he had done business to the extent of $6,000.; that he had remitted $3,000. to New York having in hand $2,000. which he had received when going to Cuba and $3,000. balance out of the $6,000. Owing to the strike in Cristobal he (GARVEY) had instructed Capt. Cockburn to coal the ship (S.S. "YARMOUTH") in Havana and had cabled Smith-Green $3,000.

The President (MARCUS GARVEY) suggested that the S.S. Yarmouth should go to Philadelphia, Baltimore and Boston on her return so as to boom the stocks of the corporation. Carried.

At a meeting of the Board of Directors May 17, 1920, the President (MARCUS GARVEY) stated that the Secretary (Smith-Green) had been sent to Cuba in February mainly to see to the unloading of the whisky cargo of the S.S. Yarmouth, that he had returned in April and that according to the Auditor, Mr. Thompson, the account presented by Mr. Smith-Green showed a shortage. The Secretary (Smith-Green) in reply stated he was ready to make all explanations and had placed himself at the disposal of the accountant but that ever since his return from Cuba he was taken around the country touring with the President in the interests of the Corporation and has been given little or no chance to prepare his report. The President charged that large expenditures were shown without adequate vouchers and special mention was made of 40 shares of stock being issued without the corresponding amount being produced. Mr. Smith-Green pointed out in the special instance of the stock sale that it was owing to lack of proper recording in the home office (in that instance and others not brought to notice of Directors) as he had accepted receipts or other evidence of parties having paid up their subscriptions on shares and issued certificates to cover, consequently no amount would be presented for such stock. Due note of such transaction was made and could be shown.

At a meeting of the Board of Directors June 3, 1920, the President (MARCUS GARVEY) remarked that complaints had come from everywhere of reckless waste. In consequence support had fallen off considerably and he attributed it to the reckless handling of the ship (S.S. Yarmouth) by Capt. Cockburn. As a result he thought it best to remove Capt. Cockburn, which he had done by making a deal with him to remain ashore for a few months and help in another strenuous campaign.

At a meeting of the Board of Directors July 22, 1920, the President (MARCUS GARVEY) said that owing to the fact that we have never received any report from Mr. Wilson (Agent, Kingston, Jamaica) relative to the sales of stock and other business of the line we were not able to say just where we stood. We did not know whether the Kingston agency owed us money or we them. Further that Mr. Smith-Green was sent to adjust the accounts of the Kingston Agency[,] which was not done. However, with the coming of Mr. Evans the account will be gone into by the accountant and proper adjustments made.

At the first annual meeting of stockholders July 26, 1920, the President (MARCUS GARVEY), alluding to subscriptions to the BLACK STAR LINE[,] said that $500,000. as subscribed is but a drop in the bucket. But because we desire to show to the world that we can achieve, we are satisfied to purchase small boats so as to show that we can run them, etc. etc.

At a meeting of the Board of Directors October 20, 1920, the President (MARCUS GARVEY) informed the Board of the conduct of H.R. Watkis, salesman for the BLACK STAR LINE[,] who in his report of receipts and disbursements had submitted an item of $300. as "Paid to Court." The President denied knowledge of any case that required payment of such an amount or that he had authorized it. Mr. Watkis stated that he was arrested in Youngstown, Ohio, on suspicion together with Dr. J. D. Brooks and on the following morning paid $300. to two men and were released. Ordered that Watkis give a note for $300. to be paid in instalments of $5. a week.

At a meeting of the Board of Directors May 28, 1921, Mr. Garcia (Secretary) requested the Board to outline the statement to be made to the public; since the various announcements made (of the sailing of the S.S. Phyllis Wheatley) were not going to be kept. Mr. Garcia also stated that owing to the conditions created by the delay in having the boat and the failure of the company to produce said boat on the various dates given to the public, the returns from the field were decreasing rapidly with but very little hope of improvement unless a sound and reasonable explanation was given.

Matthews, Toote and Garcia appointed a committee to prepare such statement, Smith and Thompson added and to consult with Mr. Nolan about the whole matter.

. . . [*Words mutilated*] the whole matter to Mr. Nolan and pointed out that owing to the fact that the N.Y. Shipping Exchange had defaulted their contract the company was considering to call off the negotiations for the purchase of the S.S. Phyllis Wheatley and withdraw its deposit in escrow. Mr. Nolan advised the company not to do so, etc.

Mr. O. M. Thompson informed the Board that a communication had reached him the night before from the N.Y. Shipping Exchange through Mr. Silverston that the papers were signed in Washington and the vessel secured. He made known that since the contract with the N.Y. Shipping Exchange calls for delivery in New York[,] all expenses in connection with bringing the ship to New York were to be met by the N.Y. Shipping Exchange but that to help our propaganda he had obtained the authorization to place on the ship our own crew.

After weighing carefully the prospects of financial results in Philadelphia, the Board decided that the S.S. Phyllis Wheatley stop at Philadelphia, also that the boat stop at Norfolk half a day. Committees appointed to stage meetings at both places and take care of campaign to be waged in connection with the visit of the boat:

For Norfolk—Mr. Toote and Dr. Gordon
Philadelphia—Dr. Eason, Captn. Gaines and Mr. Garcia.

Mr. Thompson suggested and the Board approved that invitations be sent to a number of prominent men of the Race to a luncheon on the S.S. Phyllis Wheatley on July 4th pointing out that the high standard of the ship cannot fail to impress their minds to our benefit and therefore secure their future financial and moral support. Committee on invitations—Mr. Smith, Mat[t]hews, Dr. Ellegor and Thompson.

Understanding that the S.S. "Phyllis Wheatley" would reach New York about June 26th, it was decided that a campaign be launched in New York from June 26 to July 4th. During this period effort to be made for the sales of stock and the sale of 30,000 tickets of admission on the ship at the cost of one dollar, Campaign committee—Dr. Stewart, Mr. Yearwood, Dr. Brooks, Mr. Walters, Mr. H.V. Plummer, Dr. Ellegor, Mr. Tobias, Miss Jenkins and Mr. Garcia.

At the regular stockholders meeting held July 26, 1921, the President (MARCUS GARVEY) gave stockholders a lengthy report of his trip to the West Indies and Central America for the purpose of developing new business and bringing new investment and related some of his unfortunate experience on board the S.S. "Kanawha" due to the incompetency and disloyalty of the crew.

Stock Sales:

In the Daily Reports of Receipts and Disbursements made by the Treasurer to the President's office the receipts from the sale of stock were shown under the heads of:

Office
[*Liberty*] Hall
Mail

and in case of Special Drives or from Special Agents under those heads.

It seems to have been the custom to outfit their Agents on trips with stock certificate books all signed up and ready to be filled out and notwithstanding protest on the part of Secretary Curley at a meeting of the Board of Directors on August 28, 1920, the Board authorized the practice continued. This prevailed until February 28, 1922, when it is known Secretary Garcia ordered the sale of stock stopped.

Although subpoenaed on January 12, stock certificate books had to be called in from Agents on the road and the last of them were not received until March 10th. Even now there are still 41 missing, as follows:

LIST OF STOCK CERTIFICATE BOOKS MISSING.
SERIAL NUMBER.

1 to 50	40501 to 40600
5122 to 5150	40701 to 40800
10201 to 10300	40801 to 40900
10301 to 10400	41101 to 41200
10401 to 10500	41401 to 41500
15301 to 15400	41701 to 41800
23001 to 23119	41801 to 41900
23501 to 23600	42501 to 42600
25474 to 25500	42601 to 42700
28901 to 29999	43001 to 43100

29701 to 29800	43101 to 43200
30701 to 30800	43201 to 43300
31501 to 31600	43501 to 43600
34601 to 34700	43601 to 43700
37201 to 37300	43801 to 43900
37401 to 37500	44001 to 44100
38001 to 38100	44101 to 44200
39401 to 39500	44201 to 44300
39601 to 39700	44401 to 44500
39701 to 39800	44501 to 44600
39901 to 40000	44701 to 44800
	40201 to 40300

In addition there are numerous certificates in lots of two to five missing from the books and stubs received.

Below is a summary of shares issued, cancelled, transferred and outstanding by months from July, 1919, to February, 1922, inclusive, compiled from the stock certificate stubs received under subpoena, but no estimate even can be made of the number issued through the 41 missing books.

Black Star Line, Inc.
Monthly Summary of Shares of Stock
Issued, Cancelled, Transferred and Outstanding.

1919	Shares Issued	Shares Cancelled	Shares Transferred	Shares Outstanding
July	587	4		583
August	1,401	60		1,341
September	5,530	147		5,383
October	11,182	172		11,010
November	8,090	77		8,013
December	10,352	121		10,231
	37,142	581		36,561
1920				
January	9,694	150	36	9,508
February	8,192	127	115	7,950
March	10,494	55	254	10,185
April	8,357	18	36	8,303
May	6,856	135	82	6,639
June	5,146	58	6	5,082
	85,881	1,124	529	84,228
July	5,690	41	46	5,603
August	4,714	35	14	4,665
September	5,233	44	25	5,146
October	4,303	86	37	4,180
November	2,615	34	16	2,565
December	2,971	13		2,958
	111,407	1,377	667	109,363
1921				
January	3,526	107	18	3,401
February	4,369	52	51	4,266
March	5,087	42	13	5,032
April	5,188	65	9	5,114
May	2,560	7	2	2,551
June	2,830	16	1	2,813
	134,967	1,666	761	132,540

1921	Shares Issued	Shares Cancelled	Shares Transferred	Shares Outstanding
July	15,389	13	5	15,371
August	1,074	11	1	1,062
September	1,046	10	2	1,034
October	1,146	7		1,139
November	645	1		644
December	670			670
	154,937	1,708	769	152,460
1922				
January	323		323	
February	250	7		243
	155,510	1,715	769	153,026

Herewith is a comparative statement of the amount of stock issued, in dollars, as shown by preceding statement, by Capital Stock issued and outstanding account ledger page 220 and in balance sheets prepared by Accountants Simonoff, Peyser and Citrin for the BLACK STAR LINE, Inc., at different stated periods.

VALUE OF CAPITAL STOCK

	Our Analysis	Ledger A/C.	Simonoff, Peyser & Citrin.
December 1919	$182.805		
June 1920	421,140	442,625	442,625
December	546,815	536,081	
June 1921	662,700	622,235	622,255
December	762,300		
February 1922	765,130		

For a possible partial explanation of the differences in above see page 21 of this report.[1]

Partial Payments:

On June 30, 1921, $35,115.61 of partial payments on stock was credited to Profit and Loss account, ledger p. 395 and J[ournal] p. 40, under the title of "Premiums on Stock forfeited."

In no sense were the amounts premiums, they were partial payments.

At a meeting of the Executive Council of the U.N.I.A. and A.C.L.,

July 20, 1921, it was unanimously carried that all loans to the BLACK STAR LINE, INC., by the Parent Body be invested in B.S.L. stock held by the Parent Body, but there is no mention of this proposed transaction in the Minute Book of the Black Star Line, Inc.

As a result two checks were drawn by the BLACK STAR LINE, INC.:

no. 4227 dated July 27, 1921, to Universal Negro Improvement Association for $32,820. and
no. 4233 dated July 29, 1921 to Parent Body U.N.I.A. for $34,780.

which amounts represented practically the sums borrowed at different times from the concerns named. In turn these concerns issued their checks (missing) for like amounts which were deposited to the credit of the BLACK STAR LINE, INC. the first for 6554 shares of their Capital Stock certificate No. 36425, and the second for 6956 shares, certificate No. 36438.

At this time the BLACK STAR LINE, INC., was hopelessly bankrupt and everyone connected with it knew it.

Books of Account:

At the first meeting of the Board of Directors June 27, 1919, the Secretary was authorized and directed to procure the proper corporate books.

At a meeting of the Board of Directors August 8, 1919, the President (MARCUS GARVEY) was authorized to engage a Certified Public Accountant to start a proper set of books for the BLACK STAR LINE, and to purchase all the necessary material for the clerical work in the office of the Corporation.

During the first year, July, 1919 to June, 1920 inclusive, a Cash Received and Disbursed Book was kept in a crude and haphazard manner and with no ledger being kept during this period[,] no accounts were set up in detail. It does appear that the accounting firm of Simonoff, Peyser and Citrin (1 Madison Avenue) were called in early in 1920, probably in March, and one of their employees, H.S. Chirlian, spent some time at the office of the BLACK STAR LINE in an endeavor to install a proper method of bookkeeping and keeping of records, but in this he was not successful. Mr. Chirlian, however, did set up a Balance Sheet as of June 30, 1920, (Journal p. 26 and page 20 of this report)[2] and opened a ledger as of July 1, 1920, the accounts in which are written up for the next fiscal year (to June 30, 1921) but on which no postings have been made after September 30, 1921.

Financial reports to Stockholders:

FIRST:

The President (MARCUS GARVEY) had called (?) special meeting of stockholders on December 22, 1919, for the purpose of increasing the capital stock from $500,000. to $10,000,000., and at this meeting the Treasurer (George Tobias) was called upon for the financial report of the corporation and submitted the following which appears in the Minute Book:

Black Star Line, Inc.
Financial Report,
June, 1919 to December 20, 1919.

Debit:

By Cash Sales of Stock—28,860 shares	$144,300.00
Deposit on Stock 47,586 shares	46,222.64
Freight on Yarmouth to Cuba	5,700.00
Passenger Tickets	570.00
Sundry receipts	125.00
	196,917.64
To approximate Revenues (N[*ot*] O[*therwise*] S[*pecified*])	10,000.00
	$206,917.64

Credit:

Working Capital	$20,606.20	
Rent & Sundry Liabilities	4,040.00	
Legal Expenses	1,963.50	
Real Estate Holdings	6,725.55	
Purchase & Repairs of S.S. Yarmouth	132,734.28	
Sundries supplied to ship	50,010.97	181,079.44 (A)
To balance on hand		$27,838.20 (B)

Note: (A) This total, $181,079.44 should read $216,079.44, or $35,000. more.
Note: (B) This total, $27,838.40[,] if total debit and credit figures are correct, should read only $25,838.20, but if $35,000. referred to in note (A) be granted[,] then there would be an excess of disbursements over receipts of $9,161.80.

Your accountant, with the aid of Accountant Mendenhall, analyzed the Cash Books of the BLACK STAR LINE, INC. from June, 1919, to and including January, 1922, and from that analysis built up monthly statements of Income and Expenses as well as assets and liabilities and as of December 20, 1919, this analysis shows as follows:

STATEMENT OF INCOME AND EXPENSES.
JUNE, 1919, TO DECEMBER 20, 1919.

Income:

Freight S.S. Yarmouth		$5,705.26
Passenger S.S. Yarmouth		628.00
		$6,333.26

Expense:
Stock Selling Expense.

Rent	$5,407.25	
Music	1,824.73	
Travelling	4,757.12	
Com. & Salaries	918.18	
Stamp Tax	306.00	
Advertising	8,595.90	
Miscellaneous	150.00	
	21,959.18	

Office Expense.

Rent	475.00	
Salaries	7,339.52	
Books, stationery, printing & postage	4,304.93	
Light & Heat	64.12	
Telephone & Telegraph	563.63	
Legal	2,136.50	
Interest & Discount	17.95	
General	4,179.69	
	19,081.34	

Operating Expense.

S.S. Yarmouth	30,589.42	$71,629.94
Deficit		$65,296.68

STATEMENT OF ASSETS AND LIABILITIES
DECEMBER 20, 1919

Assets:

S.S. Yarmouth	$108,201.95
Furniture & Fixtures	1,093.73
Real Estate	2,500.00
Motor Truck	1,262.81
Cash	8,213.04
Loans Receivable	1,902.64
	$123,174.19

Liabilities:

Capital Stock (fully paid) and part payments thereon	$188,470.87
Less deficit	65,296.68
Net Stock worth	$123,174.19

A comparison of the two will show that the statement submitted to the stockholders was false in many important particulars, chief among them being

Purchase & repairs of S.S. Yarmouth	$132,734.28
Sundries supplied to ship	50,010.09
Balance on hand	27,838.20

It is not believed that this false statement ever was published in the Negro World or sent through the mails to stockholders for the purpose of procuring new subscriptions.

Treasurer's Reports:

At a meeting of the Board of Directors February 14, 1920, the Treasurer's Financial Statement was read and accepted. The minute book does not reflect this statement.

At a meeting of the Board of Directors March 22, 1920, the Treasurer (George Tobias) said he would have financial statement ready for next meeting and that the Corporation was in a healthy financial state.

It was about this time that Mr. Chirlian[,] of the accounting firm of Simonoff, Peyser and Citrin, was called in, it is believed through the efforts of O.M. Thompson, who was acting as a sort of an accountant at this time and who, on August 7, 1920, was elected first vice president, to install, it is said by Mr. Chirl[ia]n, proper methods of bookkeeping.

At a meeting of the Board of Directors April 6, 1920, the Treasurer (George Tobias) read the financial report, but the minute book does not reflect it.

At a meeting of the Board of Directors June 3, 1920, the President (MARCUS GARVEY) reminded the Board that the financial year ended this month and as that entailed a stockholders['] meeting, it was necessary for the corporation to be very active in getting a balance. The President suggested that the Treasurer furnish a complete statement of the finances of the corporation at the next meeting.

Stockholders Meeting July 26, 1920:

Mr. Chirlian and O.M. Thompson together endeavored to build up a balance sheet as of June 30, 1920, for submission to stockholders at their first annual meeting held on July 26, 1920, when the President (MARCUS GARVEY) called upon the accountant (O.M. Thompson) to read the balance sheet, which was done. At this meeting it was decided to publish the report in the Negro World in which publication it appeared in the issue of Saturday, August 14, 1920.

Following appears the balance sheet in question compared with one set up in the Journal by Mr. Chirlian and also with one set up by your accountants from analysis of Cash Books, etc.

At this meeting the President (MARCUS GARVEY) among other things stated: "Because of our determination, we have been able to bring it to this point as solvent and as intact as any corporation can be."

Comparative Statement of three Balance Sheets of the Black Star Line, Inc. June 30, 1920

	Balance Sheet June 30, 1920, as set up in MINUTE BOOK and published in NEGRO WORLD	Balance Sheet June [30], 1920, as set up in JOURNAL, page 26 by MR. CHIRLIAN.	Balance sheet June 30, 1920, as set up by Your Accountants from Analysis of CASH BOOKS, etc.
Assets			
Invested Assets			
Real Estate 54-56 W. 135 St. Schedule II	26,000.00	27,823.10	26,665.00
Delivery Equipment Sch. III	4,620.27	4,620.27	
Furniture & Fixtures	8,354.74	8,354.74	4,681.44
(A) S.S. Yarmouth Sch. IV	178,156.36	200,000.00	189,361.65
" Kanaw[ha] "	75,359.01	77,053.57	66,761.47
" Shadyside "	35,000.00	35,000.00	35,000.00
Total Invested Assets	328,190.38		
(A) (Should be $700. more)			
Deferred Charges			
Prepaid insurance on steamships, property, etc.	5,729.00		
Due from Subscribers to Capital Stock	118,153.28	118,153.28	118,153.28
Current Assets			
Cash in Bank	1,933.48	1,933.48	2,025.23
Deposit (security)	5,500.00	5,500.00	
Loans Receivable (Schedule L)	14,551.73	14,551.73	13,742.44
Organization expense	21,985.21		
Deficit on operations		65,334.05	
Loss on operations			102,890.07
Organization & promotion	289,066.27	104,799.92	
Office & Stock selling expense			131,905.84
	763,124.14	663,124.14	342,677.39

Liabilities

Capital

Capital Stock issued	442,625.00	442,625.00		406,310.50
Subscriptions to Capital stock	168,235.00	168,235.00		32,585.98
Total Capital	610,860.00			438,896.48
			Deficit	234,795.91
Mortgages payable (Schedule VI)	21,500.00	21,500.00	Stock Worth	204,100.57
("itemized")	21,500.00			21,500.00

Current and other Liabilities

Accounts payable (Schedule V)	12,148.02	12,148.02	
Accrued salaries & wages	1,539.30	1,539.30	
Notes Payable, Schedule VII	117,076.82	117,076.82	117,076.82
Total Current & other Liabilities	130,764.14	663,124.14	342,677.39
	763,124.14		

(1) Under "Liabilities" they show

Capital Stock issued		$442,625.00
Subscriptions to		
Capital Stock	$168,235.00	
Less due from		
Subscribers	118,153.28	50,081.72
Total capital & subscriptions paid		$492,606.72
while we show		
Capital stock issued		406,310.50
Subscriptions to Capital		
stock (paid)		32,585.98
		$438,896.48
Difference		$53,710.24

Their figures in the case of Capital Stock issued[,] Mr. Chirlian states[,] were arrived at by the office force of the BLACK STAR LINE taking the stock certificate books and ascertaining the number of shares issued and multiplying that figure by 5, giving the amount in dollars and at the same time compiling the same information from the stock ledgers. Mr. Chirlian told me that because of many of the stock certificate books being out in the hands of Agents on the road, there was a large difference between the two sets of figures and to be on the safe side he took the largest. Our analysis of the stock certificate books (6 missing) showing shares issued to June 30, 1920, prepared by accountant Jamison[,] shows 84,228 shares, equal in amount to $421,140.00.

Our figures, however, are based on what actually appears in the Cash Book and Mr. Chirlian in explanation of the difference advances the theory that it is probably due to the method of Agents reporting stock sales and improper bookkeeping by the office force of the BLACK STAR LINE, INC. in not showing under Cash Received the full amount of the stock sales and contra under Cash Disbursed, Agents' salary and commission, but instead posting only under Cash Received the net amount received from Agent. This theory is supported in a report by the Accountants dated October 4, 1920, in which they state: "V. We again call to your attention the fact that stock sales by Agents, salesmen, etc., are not being treated in accordance with our recommendation."

I hardly think we would be justified in charging wilful misrepresentation in this particular instance, although it does show utter incompetence.

(2) Under head of "Current Assets" they show

Deposit Security $5,500.00

This item had actually been merged into the General Cash on June 18, 1920 (See Cash Receipts page 69) and had been taken into account in arriving at their "Cash in Bank, $1933.48," in which it was included.

Again I do not believe this misrepresentation was wilful.

(3) But in trying to balance the "Assets" with the "Liabilities" they show on Assets side:

Organization Expense $289,066.27

and this Garvey, Tobias and Thompson knew to be false and a wilful misrepresentation. Garcia was elected a Director immediately following the reading of the report by Thompson and a resolution by the stockholders to have it published, so he seemingly escapes participation in it.

The item really represents their Deficit for the year, but according to our analysis of Cash Books this amounted to $234,795.91 and is made up of

Operating Loss $102,890.07

Stock selling & office expense 131,905.84

as appears by the following:

STATEMENT OF INCOME AND EXPENSE
FISCAL YEAR ENDING JUNE 30, 1920.

Income.		*Total.*
Freight S.S. Yarmouth	$32,201.66	
Passenger S.S. Yarmouth	12,578.05	
Passenger S.S. Shadyside	2,882.63	
Passenger S.S. Kanawha	98.25	
Miscellaneous	7,024.32	
		$54,784.91
Expense:		
Rent, halls, etc.	6,437.47	
Music	10,518.20	
Travelling	10,649.26	
Com. & Salaries	2,397.45	
Stamps, revenue	505.00	
Advertising	23,369.63	
Miscellaneous	16,724.13	
Stock selling expense total	70,601.14	

Rent (office)	550.00
Salaries	34,783.61
Books, stationery, postage, printing	9,283.54
Light & Heat	355.96
Telephone & Telegraph	1,119.76
Legal & Prof.	8,539.56
Interest & Discount	288.17
Real Estate Expense	3,764.71
General	9,643.71
Office expense total	68,329.02
S.S. Yarmouth	138,469.55
S.S. Kanawha	4,060.83
S.S. Shadyside	8,120.28
Operating expense total	150,650.66
	289,580.82
Deficit for Year	$234,795.91

Organization expense, usually made up of incorporation fee, legal expenses in connection with the formation of the corporation, and the numerous other expenses incident to putting the corporation into operation and on a revenue producing basis is generally recognized as a legitimate Deferred Charge until such time as it can be charged off from Revenue, although some authorities maintain it should be charged off at once or divided over two years at most.

In this case, however, the corporation had purchased a boat in September, and was in receipt of income therefrom in November, so that at the utmost the maximum expense therefore properly chargeable to Account of Organization Expense would be that incurred to and including November, viz.:

Stock selling expense	$18,288.11
Office expense	14,358.52
Total	$32,646.63

Financial distress:

The following instances tend to prove the knowledge of the Directors as to the financial distress of the corporation prior to the publication of the balance sheet.

At a meeting of the Board of Directors June 3, 1920, "the President (MARCUS GARVEY) suggested that the Treasurer (GEORGE TOBIAS) furnish a complete statement of the finance of the corporation at the next meeting

(Stockholders, July 26th). At this juncture he spoke with seriousness of the present situation which was saved by our not relaxing. Had we not been vigilant the BLACK STAR LINE would have collapsed."

At the same meeting: "Mr. Shirley was for bringing Capt. Cockburn to terms, but others present were against antagonizing Capt. Cockburn as they claimed he would be in a position to cause much harm and embarrassment in consequence of their present delicate situation.["]

Later, at the same meeting, he said:

> * * * was annoyed in that Mr. Bayne allowed the employees to contract debts without his (Mr. Garvey's) sanction. Said he—we have been embarrassed many times. He further said that at the present time many ugly rumors were going about, such as graft upon contracts, etc., and considering the seriousness of our present financial situation he had given word to contract no debt without his supervision.

while the following instance makes clear their knowledge that the Operating loss for the year had been included purposely in Organization Expense.

In Journal, page 34, under date of November 30, 1920, appears in the handwriting of Mr. Chirlian:

Ships['] Fixtures and Supplies	253	$63,000.	
to Organization Expense	106		$63,000.

> To adjust Promotion and Organization Exp. account balance as at June 30, 1920, due to the impossibility of making a correct analysis of income and expenses, because of the urgent need of the balance sheet at the time, a statement of Assets and Liabilities was drawn up as of June 30, 1920.
>
> The amount by which the Liabilities and Capital exceeded the Assets was called Organization Expense, which included the Operating Deficit for the fiscal year ended June 30, 1920.[3] Later it was discovered that large expenditures for ships['] supplies had not been taken into consideration on the published balance sheet as of June 30, 1920. Such items as beds and bedding, chairs, tables, kitchen equipment, hardware, tools, railings, rope and sundry other supplies were not included among the assets on the above balance sheet. This entry is made to set up on the books the estimated cost of the above mentioned fixtures and supplies for all ships and to reduce the excess of Liabilities and Cap. over Assets on June 30, 1920.
>
> (Signed) Authorized by O.M. Thompson
> V. Prest & Manager.

Incidentally this transfer of $63,000. to ships['] Fixtures and Supplies for the year ended June 30, 1920, is beyond all reason. Their figures in the published statement under Invested Assets are:

S.S. Yarmouth	$178,156.36—while our analysis shows	$189,361.65
S.S. Kanawah	75,359.01—while our analysis shows	66,761.47
S.S. Shadyside	35,000.00—while our analysis shows	35,000.00
	$288,515.37		$291,123.12

a difference of only $2,607.75 to be so transferred.

Furthermore as of June 30, 1920, they set up in the journal and opened ledger accounts with the following set of figures:

S.S. Yarmouth	$200,000.00
S.S. Kanawah	77,053.57
S.S. Shadyside	35,000.00
Total	$312,053.57

an additional overcharge of $20,930.45.

Subsequent to the first annual meeting of stockholders on July 26, 1920, the following instances of financial distress are evidenced by the Minute Book:

At a special meeting of the Board of Directors August 28, 1920, the President (MARCUS GARVEY) laid before the Board the financial distress of the corporation due to previous bad management and to adverse activity of Capt. Cockburn, a former master. Present claims or libels against the ship (S.S. Yarmouth) amount to about $60,000.

At this meeting it was carried that active operation of the Yarmouth and Shadyside be discontinued until further instructions of the Board except that the Shadyside be used on or about Labor Day in the discretion of the President and the Vice President.

The S.S. Yarmouth had ceased to earn after September 1, 1920, the S.S. Shadyside after September 13, 1920 and the S.S. Kanawha apparently some time in March, 1921.

At a meeting of the Board of Directors July 16, 1921, it was resolved to accept the offer of the U.N.I.A. to purchase the office furniture and paraphernalia for $3500. in Cash as the company is pressed by numerous creditors for payments of claims which it is unable to pay on account of lack of funds. Contrast this with what took place at a meeting of the Board of Directors the next day, July 17, 1921, at which it was stated that funds were needed to purchase a steamer for the African trade and the U.N.I.A. has offered to lend $10,000. if loan is secured by a mortgage on the properties of the company at 56 W. 135th to run for one year at 6%. This was carried and officers instructed and empowered to sign all proper instruments.

At a meeting of the Board of Directors October 11, 1921, O.M. Thompson, Vice President, stated he had been unable to get a surety (on a performance bond to guarantee that the Shipping Board would receive the $10,000. monthly payments for the purchase price of the S.S. "Orion") because of the financial condition of the company and because of the inability of the company as operators.

At a meeting of the Board of Directors October 31, 1921, it is recorded that the corporation was being pressed by claims from numerous creditors threatening suits and attachments. That the corporation was without means to pay said claims or any part thereof without selling such of its personal property and effects not previously disposed of and the African Communities['] League has offered to purchase the Auto Truck for $3,000. cash.

Stockholders meeting July 26, 1921:

A letter from Elie Garcia, Secretary[,] and George Tobias, Treasurer, was read by the President (MARCUS GARVEY):

Hon. Marcus Garvey, President, B.S.L., New York City
Honorable Sir:

Owing to the numerous transactions pending for settlement, it is almost impossible for me to furnish you with a balance sheet which will reflect the true conditions of the company, therefore I am asking that you use your influence to bring about an adjournment of the stockholders['] meeting. Respectfully yours,

ELIE GARCIA
Secretary

Same letter signed by Tobias, Treasurer.

with the result that the meeting was adjourned until October 26, 1921.

This representation was utterly false, as a ledger started June 30, 1920, had been written up to and including June 30, 1921, further there is in our possession a full report of all operations for the year by Simonoff, Peyser & Citrin, accountants, including statement of Income, Profit and Loss, as well as a Balance Sheet supported by various schedules together with an unsigned letter dated July 26, 1921, with comment on various accounts and the audit addressed to the BLACK STAR LINE, INC., Attention—Mr. Marcus Garvey, President General—stating that they had audited the books for the year ended June 30, 1921, and submitted report therewith.

Following appears the statements referred to compared with one set up by your accountants from their analysis of Cash book, etc.

BLACK STAR LINE, INC.
STATEMENT OF INCOME, PROFIT AND LOSS
FOR [JUNE] 30TH, 1921.[4]
AS SET UP BY ACCOUNTANTS
SIMONOFF, PEYSER & CITRIN.

Income

Freight S.S. Yarmouth	8,087.35	
Freight S.S. Kanawah	133.08	8,220.43
Passengers Transportation		
Passengers S.S. Yarmouth	3,521.39	
Passengers Kanawah	958.05	
Passengers Shadyside	3,312.17	7,791.61
Gross Income, Operations		16,012.04
Deduct Steamship Operation Expenses		
Schedule I		110,885.80
Net loss on Steamship Operations		94,873.76

Expenses

General & Administrative Expense		
Schedule 2.	39,623.77	
Maintenance of Real Estate		
Schedule 3.	2,882.48	
Officers Salaries, Schedule 4.	7,555.97	
Capital Stock Tax	232.19	50,294.41
Add. Profit & Loss charges		11,931.36
		157,099.53

Deduct:

Premiums Stock Forfeitures	35,115.61	
Misc. Income		
Gate Receipts	6,779.43	41,895.04
		115,204.49

As Set up by your Accountants
from Analysis of Cash Books, etc.

Assets:

S. S. Yarmouth	189,842.90
S. S. Kanawha	75,339.45
S. S. Shadyside	35,000.00
Real Estate	26,665.00
Furniture & Fixtures	6,120.23
Motor Truck	4,440.16
Cash	1,550.31
S. S. Phyllis Wheatley	25,000.00
Building Fund Notes	1,378.57
Loans Receivable	14,814.99

Liabilities

Capital Stock Issued		584,812.70
Capital Stock payments		14,611.15
Capital Stock Agents returns		38,782.43
		638,206.28

Less Deficit

1919–1920	234,795.91	
1920–1921	209,456.34	444,252.25
		193,954.03

Mortgages Payable	19,400.00
Loans Payable	84,078.11
Accounts Payable	4,500.00
Notes Payable	70,930.22
Unearned Passage Liberia	7,289.25

Purchase and Operation of Ships:

Purchase S. S. "Yarmouth"

At a meeting of the Board of Directors August 26, 1919, the President (MARCUS GARVEY) stated that in consultation with Capt. Cockburn, Commander elect of the BLACK STAR LINE, the latter informed him of a shipping firm in Philadelphia which had two ships, one steel and one wooden, for sale.

This firm had submitted tenders and asked $30,000. for the wooden ship. The Captain had suggested that this be negotiated for provided the directorate assented. It was resolved that Capt. Cockburn be authorized to approach the said Shipping Company to negotiate the purchase of the wooden ship and if necessary to close the deal provided the seaworthiness of said ship be guaranteed by expert investigators.

At a meeting of the Board of Directors August 27, 1919, the President (MARCUS GARVEY) stated that he was informed by Capt. Cockburn the wooden ship at Philadelphia was not suitable and the Captain did not advise the purchase, it not being seaworthy. The Captain was then called upon for his advice and he stated the firm of Johnsons, Shipbrokers, w[as] approached by him and they had given him the plans of a ship of 1,000 tons cargo capacity and accommodations for 125 passengers were in process or proposed by this firm. The cost of the vessel, or the sum asked, was $85,000. as she now is, or when converted so as to have passenger accommodations, $55,000. more, or a total of $140,000.

The Directors then by motion authorized Capt. Cockburn to interview the firm of Johnsons and after necessary examination of the vessel had been completed, to make an offer of $5,000. down and sign the contract to pay down another $20,000. in 30 days and $60,000. on the 20th of October and that the balance of $55,000. be paid 90 days after the ship had been delivered. The Captain to make his report Friday evening.

At a meeting of the Board of Directors September 11, 1919, Capt. Cockburn reported the S.S. Yarmouth when examined by himself and the engineer was in seaworthy condition and advised the Board to negotiate a charter for the ship on Saturday morning, September 13th, at which time it is intended to make the first payment of $16,500. The cost of the charter will be about $2,000. per month. It was resolved that the Charter be negotiated on Saturday morning at 10:30 and for one month besides making the first payment of the ship.

At a meeting of the Board of Directors September 12, 1919, it was decided that the deal to purchase the S.S. Yarmouth be put through and contract signed and that the President, the Secretary and the Treasurer be the representatives of the Corporation to negotiate the terms of purchase, also that expert advisors be obtained to assist in the negotiation.

At a meeting of the Board of Directors September 15, 1919, the Corporation was authorized to contract with Harris[s], Magill & Co. for the purchase of the S.S. Yarmouth on the following terms and conditions:

$16,500. on signing of contract.
83,500. on date of delivery of ship between October 31, 1919, and November 10, 1919 and the execution of a chattel mortgage for 65,000. to be paid on equal monthly instalments of $6,500. until the purchase price of $165,000. is fully paid.

Board of Directors through the duly authorized officers of the Corporation authorized and empowered to sign a contract of purchase with the North American Steamship Co. (represented in New York by Harriss, Magill & Co.) a Canadian corporation.

At a meeting of the Board of Directors September 20, 1919, the Secretary read the contract in re Harriss, Magill & Co., Inc., and the Black Star Line, Inc. Approved by Directors.

At a meeting of the Board of Directors, October 20, 1919, it was resolved as certain circumstances had arisen which might delay the payment of the purchase price of the S.S. Yarmouth and negotiations have been had with the owners for a modification of the agreement for its purchase made on September 17, 1919, and the owners have agreed to modify the said agreement provided the additional sum of $3,500. be paid, that the officers of the Corporation be and are authorized to enter into a new agreement with the North American Steamship Corporation, Ltd., modifying the agreement of September 17, 1919, by making the purchase price $168,500. instead of $165,000. and extending the time of payment of the sum of $98,500. in monthly payments of $9,850., the balance of the purchase price to be paid after the delivery of the steamship.

The following payments had so far been made:

$16,500. on September 19, 1919, by certified check no. 127, dated September 15, 1919, to Harriss, Magill & Co., Inc.

3,500. on October 23, 1919, by certified check no. 287, dated October 20, 1919, to Harriss, Magill & Co., Inc.

At a meeting of the Board of Directors October 31, 1919, it was resolved, as the S.S. Yarmouth had arrived at New York and the time to complete its purchase has arrived, but it will take about one month to change the registry to United States Registration and the Company (corporation) desires to operate the steamer, that the President be and is authorized to pay to the North American Steamship Corporation the sum of $50,000. on account of the purchase price and to enter into an agreement chartering the vessel for a round trip from New York to West Indies and Central America and return to a monthly hiring of $700. and to adjourn a final closing of the purchase of said steamship to a time 15 days after the return of the steamer to New York.

$50,000. paid by certified check no. 344 dated October 31, 1919, to Harriss, Magill & Co., Inc.

At a meeting of the Board of Directors November 14, 1919, the President (MARCUS GARVEY) stated that the S.S. Yarmouth was taken over [from] the North American Steamship Corporation and that the route mapped out for her was Cuba, Jamaica and Colón. Arrangements were being made to renovate the boat after which time she would be ready to take passengers and cargo to above places.

$20,000. paid by certified check no. 585 dated November 24, 1919, to Harris[s], Magill & Co., Inc.

3,000. paid by certified check no. 586 dated November 24, 1919, to
Harris[s], Magill & Co., Inc.

At a meeting of the Board of Directors February 14, 1920, the transactions
carried out by the President (MARCUS GARVEY) relative to new contracts
entered into on January 10th, 1920, between the North American Steamship
Corporation and the Black Star Line were unanimously approved.

$20,000. paid by certified check no. 980 dated January 10, 1920, to
Harris[s], Magill & Co., Inc.
9,000. paid by check no. 1854 dated May 17, 1920, to the North
American Steamship Co., endorsed to Harris[s], Magill & Co. Inc.

At a meeting of the Board of Directors June 3, 1920, it is noted that there
are payments to be made on the S.S. Yarmouth of $4,500. per month for 10
months while ledger P. 164 indicated 10 notes of $4,950.

On the first voyage the S.S. Yarmouth cleared from New York on
November 20, 1919, and on the second (the whisky cargo trip) on January
17, 1920. The receipts from freight indicate a third trip.

The operation of this vessel was discontinued by the Board of Directors
August 28, 1920, the vessel having been in use less than one year.

The amounts invested are as follows:-

Purchase price	$171,500.00
Fixtures	10,296.16
Repairs (first)	8,046.74
Total Investment	$189,842.90

On the purchase price the following payments were made:

January 10, 1920	20,000.00
September 18, 1919	16,500.00
October 18	3,500.00
October 31	50,000.00
November 24	23,000.00
May 17, 1920	9,000.00
By Cash	$122,000.00
By Notes	49,500.00
	$171,500.00

On the notes the following payments have been made:

July 17, 1920	$4,950.
July 26	4,950.
November 3	2,000.
November 9	950.
December 3	1,000.
December 11	1,000.
December 21	500.
January 15, 1921	1,000.
January 24	500.
January 31	500.
February 8	500.
February 18	500.
March 3	1,000.
March 10	500.
March 18	500.
March 25	500.
	$20,850.

leaving $28,650. still unpaid and owing on purchase price.

Note that the first indicated price was $140,000; the second $165,000. and the third $168,500., while the actual payment cash and notes reaches the sum of $171,500.

In addition, Check No. 2844, certified and dated November 24, 1919, (but not entered in Cash Book) to order of Harris[s], Magill & Co., purpose unknown, check stub no. 1325, February 6, 1920, to Harriss Magill & Co., for $1,000., reads "Hireage charter of Yarmouth" and check stub no. 1766 A, March 16, 1920, to same for $765.91 reads "Balance due on charter hire of Yarmouth per contract" all of which checks were paid.

OPERATION S.S. YARMOUTH.
STATEMENT OF INCOME AND EXPENSE OF S.S. YARMOUTH.

Expense.	Year ending June 30, 1920	Year ending June 30,1921	Period ending Jan. 5, 1922	Total entire Period
Repairs(A)	$18,276.86	2,161.30	—	$20,438.16
Wages	35,755.45	15,944.09	743.41	52,442.95
Fuel	28,493.41	6,026.41	—	34,519.82
Supplies & Provisions	16,118.21	4,697.79	—	20,816.00
Port, Pilot, Towing, Wharf	7,799.47	998.39	—	8,797.66
Insurance	7,741.66	4,042.50	—	11,784.16
Claims, Libels, etc.	6,613.82	11,945.77	275.00	18,834.59
Miscellaneous	17,670.67	8,827.87	—	26,498.54
(B)	138,469.55	54,644.12	1,018.41	194,132.08

Income.				
Freight	32,201.66	8,644.11	—	40,845.77
Passenger	12,578.05	4,696.64	—	17,274.69
	44,779.71	13,340.75	—	58,120.46
Operating Loss.	93,689.84	41,303.37	1,018.41	136,011.62

Notes:
(A) Repairs to January 1920 charged to Investment account.
(B) No office expense, overhead or depreciation charged.

Office Expense.	$68,329.02	55,865.89	15,553.70	139,748.61

PURCHASE S.S. SHADYSIDE.

At a meeting of the Board of Directors March 22, 1920, the President (MARCUS GARVEY) stated he was interested in a Pleasure Excursion boat, to accommodate 500 passengers and 400 tons of cargo, for $35,000., and could purchase same by paying $10,000. cash and the balance in notes.

Mr. Johnson and himself had inspected the same. The boat in their opinion would be a wonderful asset as it could be used here in summer and taken to the West Indies in winter.

$2,000. paid by check no. 1829 A dated March 24, 1920, to Leon R. Swift.

8,000. paid by certified check no. 1556, dated April 10, 1920, to Leon Swift.

2,000. paid by check no. 1749 dated May 4, 1920, to Leon R. Swift.

At a meeting of the Board of Directors June 3, 1920, it is noted that there are payments to be made on the S.S. Shadyside of $2,000. per month for 10 months.

$2,000. paid by check no. 1978 dated June 7, 1920, to Leon R. Swift.

Ledger account, page 166, July 1, 1920, shows 9 notes of $2,000.– the first due July 1st and one on the first of each month thereafter until April 1st, 1921, when a tenth note of $3,000. is due.

Payments on these notes had been made, as follows:

July 14, 1920	$2,000.	(Check missing C.B. 32)
Aug. 25	2,000.	(Check missing C.B. 44)
Nov. 17	1,000.	(Check missing C.B. 66)
Nov. 30	1,000.	(Check missing C.B. 66)

leaving $15,000. unpaid.

At a meeting of the Board of Directors August 28, 1920, the operation of the Shadyside was discontinued except for use on or about Labor Day. The Cash Book shows she ceased to earn after September 13, 1920.

During the winter of 1920–1921, it is reported the Shadyside was badly damaged by ice and is said to be fully insured for $35,000. It is also said the policy has been assigned to Leon R. Swift, but no mention of any of these facts is to be found in the records.

OPERATION S.S. SHADYSIDE.
STATEMENT OF INCOME AND EXPENSE S.S. SHADYSIDE.

	Period ending June 30, 1920	Year ending June 30, 1921	Period ending Jan. 5, 1922	Total entire Period
Expense	$8,120.28	$8,946.45	$75.00	$17,141.73
Income	2,882.63	3,306.67	—	6,189.30
Operating Loss	5,237.65	5,639.78	75.00	10,952.43

PURCHASE S.S. KANAWHA.

At a meeting of the Board of Directors April 6, 1920, the President (MARCUS GARVEY) said he had called the meeting for the purpose of discussing whether or not they should purchase a ship of 4050 tons. After going over the specifications it was decided that having regard to the fact they would have to pay a large amount of money on the Yarmouth, also the Shadyside, it would not be wise to purchase, it being a Government ship and the terms very stringent.

At a meeting of the Board of Directors April 23, 1920, the matter of the purchase of a third ship was then brought up by the President (MARCUS GARVEY) who said there was a great demand for a ship of small tonnage for the Inter-Colonial Trade and as the Yarmouth was not fitted for long voyages, it would be, in his estimation, advisable that such a ship be acquired to take passengers and collect freight between the islands, so that the Yarmouth would be able to make short and payable trips to Jamaica via Cuba and back to New York. He then said that there was a steam yacht, the Kanawha, now for sale, that it had already been inspected and found to be seaworthy and that he would advise its purchase. Unanimously carried that negotiations be entered into for the purchase of said ship.

> $5,000. paid by check no. 1660, dated April 24, 1920, to James M. Briggs.
> 10,000. paid by certified check no. 1899, dated May 25, 1920, to James M. Briggs.

At a meeting of the Board of Directors June 3, 1920, it is noted that there are payments to be made on the S.S. Kanawha of $7500. per month for 6 months.

> Left New York in August, 1920, for Norfolk.
> Left New York March 25, 1921, for Cuba.

In August, 1921, this vessel put into the port of Antilla, Cuba, in bad condition and at latest reports was still there.

The amounts invested are as follows:

Purchase price	$61,000.00
Fixtures	5,890.39
Repairs (first)	9,649.06
	$76,539.45

On the purchase price the following payments were made:

April 24, 1920	5,000.00
May 25	10,000.00
By Cash	15,000.00
By Notes	45,000.00
	$60,000.00

On the notes the following payments have been made:

June 29, 1920	$1000.
July 10, 1920	7500.
Aug. 6	5000.
Aug. 12	2500.
Dec. 3	1500.
Dec. 28	7500.

Jan. 20, 1921	5000.
Jan. 31	2500.
Feb. 21	4000.
April 26	2000.
May 2	2000.
May 17	1000.
May 21	1000.
May 25	1000.
May 28	1000.
June 18	1000.
July 9	1000.

$46,500.

Of this, $500. was reversed by Journal entry June 30, 1921, page 39, and charged as a payment to the Massachusetts Bonding Co., on a $5,000. libel against the Kanawha. The remaining $1,000. seems to be an overpayment on the purchase price of the Kanawha.

Operation of Ships:

S.S. KANAWHA

Expense.	Period Ending June 30, 1920	Period Ending Sept. 8, 1920	Period Ending June 30, 1921	Period Ending Dec. 31, 1921	Total Entire Period
Repairs (A)	—	—	$57,790.08	$ 200.00	$57,990.08
Wages	$1,883.37	$3,531.74	19,049.87	6,188.81	30,653.79
Fuel	63.50	—	7,944.15	—	8,007.65
Supplies & Provisions	808.93	4,088.77	13,119.31	1,555.22	19,752.23
Port & Towing	515.00	—	2,921.25	—	3,436.25
Pilot & Wharfage	282.35	107.89	194.42	—	584.66
Insurance	—	622.50	—	—	622.50
Claims, Libels	343.25	—	6,480.00	3,000.00	9,823.25
Miscellaneous	164.43	222.00	1,606.38	1,257.89	3,250.70
(B)	4,060.83	8,572.90	109,105.46	12,201.92	133,941.11

Income.

Freight	—	133.08	—	—	133.08
Passenger	98.25	210.05	766.25	—	1,207.63
	98.25	343.13	766.25	—	1,207.63

Operating Loss.	$3,962.58	8,229.77	108,339.21	12,201.92	132,733.48

Notes:
(A) Repairs to September 8, 1920, charged to Investment Account.
(B) No office expense, overhead or depreciation charged.

Office Expense.	68,329.02	—	55,865.89	15,553.70	139,748.61

Fourth Ship—S.S. "Phillis Wheatley."

See first paragraph S.S. Kanawha.

At a meeting of the Board of Directors June 3, 1920, the question of chartering a ship was discussed. The President (MARCUS GARVEY) said that so far, he had found that chartering ships usually cost[s] more than buying them outright and the matter of chartering was dropped.

The Minute Book shows MARCUS GARVEY to have been present at a Special Meeting of the Board of Directors held on October 20, 1920, and meetings were subsequently held, at which he does not appear to have been present as follows:

April 19, 1921 (Next of record.)
May 28
June 9
July 2
July 16

but on that of July 20, it is indicated he was present.

In the books and records of the Black Star Line, Inc., the *first* indication of the proposed purchase of this vessel appears in check stub book of checks drawn on the Chelsea Exchange Bank, on check stub no. 4029-A, dated March 11, 1921, to New York (Ship) Exchange for $500. "in part payment on the Phyllis Wheatley"; *the second*, on check stub no. 4090-A dated March 21, 1921, to New York Ship Exchange for $1200. in "payment on new ship Hong Keng"; *the third*, on check stub no. 4146-A dated April 8, 1921, to New York Ship Exchange for $2,000. for "on purchase price S.S. Phyllis Wheatley"[.]

None of the checks pertaining to this transaction were produced on service of subpoena, but it would appear from the minutes of a Special Meeting held April 19, 1921, that the President (MARCUS GARVEY) had signed the above three checks and others before he left for the West Indies, as the Treasurer (George Tobias) explained that the number of checks signed by the President before leaving the country were exhausted and that no funds could be drawn unless the Vice President was authorized to sign checks, which he was thereupon authorized to do; *the fourth*, on check stub no. 4170-A dated April 19, 1921, to New York Ship Exchange for $15,000.— "in part payment S.S. Phyllis Wheatley, certified"; *the fifth*, on check stub no. 4171-A dated April 19, 1921, to New York Ship Exchange for $1300. "in part payment on S.S. Phyllis Wheatley."

At a meeting of the Board of Directors May 28, 1921, O.M. Thompson (Vice President and General Manager) in charge of the negotiations for the purchase of the S.S. Phyllis Wheatley[,] reported he had just returned from Norfolk where he had visited the S.S. "Phyllis Wheatley," which was satisfactory and whose acquisition would bring much credit to the Company, that owing to circumstances beyond his control the Bill of Sale for the ship was delayed in Washington but that the buyers (New York Ship Exchange) were not sparing any effort to rush the closing of the deal and while he was expecting the papers to be signed any minute, it was not possible to name any day or date.

Carried unanimously that because of the fact that the New York Ship Exchange had twice forfeited their contract[,] the negotiations with them be called off, and the amount in escrow with the Farmers Loan & Trust Co. withdrawn.

Mr. Garcia (Secretary) requested the Board to outline the statement to be made to the Public since the various announcements made were not going to be kept. A Committee to prepare such a statement was appointed, as follows: Mr. Mat[t]hews, Mr. Toote and Mr. Garcia. It was also unanimously carried that before execution of this motion a Committee, consisting of Messrs. Smith, Mat[t]hews, Toote, Thompson and Garcia, consult Mr. Nolan about the whole matter.

At a meeting of the Board of Directors June 9, 1921, Mr. Wilford Smith speaking, the Committee reported that Mr. Nolan emphatically advised against calling off negotiations for purchase of S.S. Phyllis Wheatley and withdrawing its deposit in escrow and promised to see Mr. Barnett next day to hasten the transaction and secure a pledge of consideration should the company be unable to meet the full payment of $20,000. as stated in the contract.

Mr. Thompson stated that the New York Ship Exchange had communicated with him the night before through Mr. Silverston that the papers were signed in Washington and the vessel secured. That it would take two days to unload the vessel and as soon as that was done he would take the Captain and Chief Engineer to Norfolk and have them make the trip from Norfolk to New York on the boat.

At this point it may be stated that from June 1 to 17, 1921, the largest balance of cash available was $826.51 on June 13th, and at the meeting of the Board of Directors on June 9th it was carried that as the Phyllis Wheatley would reach New York about June 26, a campaign be launched in New York June 26 to July 4, for the sale of stock and the sale of 30,000 tickets of admission on the ship at $1. each, the dates for public inspection to be July 3rd and 4th. As a result of this dollar drive the Parent Body of the U.N.I.A. collected, as follows:

June, 1921	$5,959.18
July	62.00
August	102.50

of which, on June 18th, they turned over to the Black Star Line, Inc., $5,000., which amount was immediately applied as follows:

Fifth: on check stub no. 4141 dated June 18, 1921, to order United States Shipping Board for $5,000. "by order of New York Ship Exchange a/c purchase price S.S. Phyllis Wheatley, check certified."

At a meeting of the Board of Directors July 2, 1921, it is stated that owing to the indefinite postponement of the closing of the purchase of the "Phyllis Wheatley" Mr. Garcia (Secretary) after consulting with [M]r. Wilford Smith, decided to write to the U.S. Shipping Board concerning the nature of Mr. Silverston's transactions with them and what result was to be expected, the letter written being as follows:

Mr. Philb[in],
Manager, Ship Sales Department,
United States Shipping Board,
Washington, D.C.

Dear Sir:

In the course of our investigation at the United States Shipping Board office, of 45 Broadway, New York City, Mr. Foster, head of the Contract Department has referred us to you for information in the following matter.

About two months ago, the above named company entered into a contract with Mr. Rudolph Silverston, doing business under the name of the New York Ship Exchange, to purchase for it a ship from the said Exchange. After some negotiations with Mr. Silverston, he stated to us that he could purchase for us from the United States Government the steamship Porto Rica, then in Dry Dock at Brooklyn and after several trips to Washington he came back and stated that the said steamship Porto Rica had been awarded to the Black Star Line, Inc., through his efforts. He further stated that he had deposited with the United States Shipping Board $5,625. on an option, which was 2% on the sum of $225,000., the purchase price of said ship. He stated that the United States Shipping Board required a cash payment of $25,000., which amount was turned over to him to secure title to said steamer and a certified check of $5,000. of said amount was made payable to the order of the said United States Shipping Board.

After receiving the said $25,000. the said Silverston reported that the papers for the full transfer of said steamship would be signed and approved within ten days and on June 17, 1921, the said Silverston signed a contract that the full transfer and delivery of said ship would be made not later than June 23, 1921. On June 23, when questioned about the progress of the negotiations for said ship, Mr. Silverston stated that as the new Heads of the Shipping Board were in New York, the papers could not be approved before Monday, June 27th, when they would return to Washington. On June 27, the Black Star Line was informed by him that owing to developments we would have to continue to wait longer, before the ship could be transferred and from time to time we have been put off.

In view of the fact that the acquisition of this ship is urgent and that more than five weeks have elapsed since we began negotiations for the purchase of the same, we would be very grateful to your Department if you would furnish us with information concerning the nature of Mr. Silverston's transactions with the Shipping Board and what results we may expect from the same.

We would like further to know if the said steamship Porto Rica is still for sale, and if there is any possibility of the same being purchased by the Black Star Line if it should turn out that the negotiations claimed by Mr. Silverston did not take place. Hoping that you will oblige us with a prompt reply, we beg to remain, Yours respectfully,

Black Star Line, Inc.
ELIE GARCIA
Secretary

EG.BB.

Mr. Garcia left for Washington and next day met Mr. J.H. Philb[in], Manager of Sales Division of Shipping Board, who after having read the letter stated that after negotiating with Mr. Silverston for a few days in the matter of the Porto Rica, the latter was informed by official letter signed by the Chairman of the Shipping Board that the S.S. Porto Rica was chartered by the Board to the Porto Rica Line, Inc., and therefore his offer in behalf of the Black Star Line was rejected. He also stated that after being so informed[,] Mr. Silverston, however, refused to take back the sum of $12,500. placed by him as an option on the S.S. Porto Rica, but manifested some interest in the S.S. Freedom and authorization was given him to inspect said boat with a view of later on making an offer for same.

Mr. Philb[in] confirmed this in writing and the letter was read to the Directors. (Letter not in Minute Book.)

Carried that Mr. Thompson (Vice President) at once cease all negotiations with the New York Ship Exchange represented by Mr. Silverston and revoke the credential given him as our Agent and demand the immediate refund of $25,000. advanced for the purchase of a steamship. In case it is not forthcoming the matter to be placed in the hands of Mr. Nolan, our attorney, for collection and if necessary referred to the District Attorney.

Mr. Garcia (Secretary) stated that his conversation with the Shipping Board led him to believe it was possible and even more desirable for the Company in the future to deal directly with the Shipping Board and recommended that the matter of purchasing a steamer be not dropped. A committee was formed to investigate about ships on sale to consist of Mr. Garcia, Dr. Stewart and Mr. Matthews.

Mr. Garcia was requested by the Board to draw a statement for the public to make clear their situation.

At a second meeting of the Board of Directors July 2, 1921, Mr.

Thompson (Vice President and General Manager) was informed of the proceedings at the morning session and called upon to state his views. He stated that after taking a copy of the letter from the Shipping Board he saw and spoke with Mr. Silverston and was positively convinced by the latter that the letter written by the Shipping Board to the Black Star Line was without foundation and that the one written to Mr. Silverston by the same Board and signed by Mr. Lasker, was a material impossibility, since on the date stated in the letter, Mr. Lasker, Chairman of the Board, was in Chicago. That it still was his belief that the New York Ship Exchange is able to secure the Porto Rica and requested the Board to postpone withdrawal action and statement to the public until July 7th.

Mr. Smith requested Mr. Thompson to make such statement in writing, which he did, as follows:

> I honestly believe through my constant contact with the New York Ship Exchange et al[.], that they have as much opportunity to secure either the Prinz Joachim or the Prinz Oskar for the Black Star Line as ever. I have seen the correspondence between Hwibburt representing the Baltimore Transatlantic Co. and the New York Ship Exchange and know something of the influence of Mr. Duff, Mr. Barnett and Mr. Nottingham have with the Board to represent the justice of the case in behalf of the Black Star Line. I respectfully ask to [counsel] while presenting the case to our lawyer to withhold withdrawal action and statement to the public.
>
> O. M. THOMPSON

Request not granted.

Mr. Garcia made the following statement which he was instructed to prepare for the public.[5] (Note—statement does not appear in Minute Book.)

At a meeting of the Board of Directors July 17, 1921, it is stated that funds are needed by the company to finance the purchase of a steamer for the African trade and that the U. N. I. A. has offered to lend $10,000.—provided loan is secured by a mortgage on the properties of the company at 56 West 135th Street for a period of one year.

At a meeting of the Board of Directors July 20, 1921 (MARCUS GARVEY present for the first time since October 20, 1920) the minutes of June 9, 1921, were corrected by the addition of "the amount of $16,300. lodged in trust with the Farmers Loan & Trust Co. and paid to the New York Ship Exchange by the Vice President, Mr. Thompson, without the knowledge and approval of the Board" which had been omitted.

Marcus Garvey pointed out that since his return[6] he had not as yet interfered with the work of any of the departments of the Black Star Line and that it was unfair for anyone to spread a rumor that he as President, as well as other officers of the Company, have interfered with the long delayed transactions for the purchase of the Phyllis Wheatley in a way to prevent or cause further delay. Mr. Thompson, Vice President and Traffic Manager, denied that his department had been interfered with by the President, but the trips of the Secretary to Washington on June 22 and 30 had done so unintentionally or not *by disclosing the name of the buyer.*

Mr. Garcia (Secretary) took exception and certified that on his first trip to Washington on June 22, he did not approach the Shipping Board, even had he done so he would not have been the first one to disclose the name of the buyer since the records of the Shipping Board can prove that a day prior to his going to Washington a bid in the name of the Black Star Line and 4,000,000 black citizens of America was filed with the Shipping Board. As to the effect of his last trip June 30 on refusal of Board to award S.S. Porto Rico to the Black Star Line, the records of the Shipping Board show that such decision was rendered on June 29th.

At a meeting of the Board of Directors October 11, 1921, the President (MARCUS GARVEY) stated that the meeting was called to decide action to be taken in the matter of a boat we were supposed to have had—S.S. Phyllis Wheatley—negotiations for which have been going on for over 6 months and not yet consummated. Mr. O.M. Thompson (Vice President) asked to state present position: said the Shipping Board on August 2 recorded the sale of the S.S. Orion to the Black Star Line, Inc. and sent a form asking for the balance of 10%—$10,000.—and a performance bond to complete the sale, then we would get title to the ship. He had paid the $10,000., but had failed to get the performance bond, i.e., a surety from someone capable of backing such an amount to guarantee that the Shipping Board would receive the monthly payments of 10% of the purchase price of the ship. *He had been unable to get such surety because of the financial condition of the Black Star Line and because of the inability of the Company as operators.*

Note: There follow about eight pages of recriminations with Marcus Garvey making it appear that the early negotiations for the S.S. Phyllis Wheatley were outside of his knowledge.

At a meeting of the Board of Directors October 16, 1921, a proposition made by the *Black Star Line Steamship Co. (N.J.)* to sell 45,000 shares of their common stock for $200,000.—[i]n cash, was accepted on terms set forth in writing dated October 5th. and President and Treasurer were empowered and instructed to execute all proper instruments to carry this into effect and to immediately transfer to Black Star Steamship Co. the $22,500. on deposit with the United States Shipping Board as first payment on said purchase of stock and thereafter pay each month the sum stipulated, ($10,000).

At a meeting of the Board of Directors October 17, 1921, *the Black Star Steamship Company (New Jersey)* having proposed to assume and carry out all obligations of the Black Star Line, Inc. to the U.S. Shipping Board for the purchase of the S.S. Orion which has been awarded to the Black Star Line, Inc., and in consideration of the assignment by the Black Star Line, Inc., of such award and the assignment of the deposit by the Black Star Line, Inc. to the United States Shipping Board at the time of the award and to secure the same and the Black Star Line, Inc., finding itself unable to comply with the requirements of the Shipping Board and to carry out its contract and obligations to said Shipping Board.

Carried, that the Black Star Line, Inc. accept the proposition of the Black Star Steamship Co. and assign to it all right[s], title and interest in and to the award of the S.S. Orion made to it by the United States Shipping Board and that the Black Star Line, Inc., also assign to the Black Star Steamship Co. all monies in the hands of the United States Shipping Board deposited to secure the S.S. Orion in consideration of the Black Star Steamship Co. assuming the debts and obligations of the Black Star Line, Inc. to the United States Shipping Board.

At a meeting of the Board of Directors January 3, 1922, the purchase of the S.S. Orion from the U.S. Shipping Board was discussed[,] also terms of contract and proposed bond and mortgage. The President (MARCUS GARVEY) stated that officers of the company, acting under his instructions, had been negotiating with individuals to advance sufficient money to complete the purchase of the S.S. Orion by cash payments to the U.S. Shipping Board, that to do so it was necessary to assure the lenders of a profit but that the cost price of the ship delivered to the company at New York, fully repaired, was not to exceed the original proposed cost price of $350,000.

Carried: That O.M. Thompson, Vice President[,] and Joseph P. Nolan, Admiralty Counsel, be authorized to continue negotiations with J. Wolff and others for a loan sufficient to enable the Black Star Line, Inc. to complete purchase of S.S. Orion and that Thompson and Nolan be authorized to negotiate further with U.S. Shipping Board for reducing the net price charged and that Thompson and Nolan be authorized to agree to pay such sum of money for services, or bonus, to proposed lenders and to Wolff and associates as brokers, as may be necessary to pay to complete the transaction provided that the cost price of the S.S. Orion fully repaired and delivered to the Black Star Line, Inc. at New York shall not exceed the original price fixed for the S.S. Orion in a certain contract with one Rudolph Silverston. Officers authorized and directed to execute necessary contracts, mortgage and place a bond issue[,] if necessary against mortgage.

Officers' Salaries:

MARCUS GARVEY, PRESIDENT.

The first payment to Marcus Garvey, as President of the Black Star Line, Inc., was $25. on August 12, 1919, thereafter $50. a week for the fifteen weeks to and including November 24, 1919, thereafter $100. a week from December 1, 1919 to and including December 31, 1920, after which no payments appear to have been made. In total for the periods mentioned

August 12 to December 22, 1919	$1175.00
January 10 to December 31, 1920	5168.84

At a meeting of the Board of Directors August 8, 1919, it was resolved that the President be allowed a salary of $50. a week, a raise in three months and travelling expenses.

In addition the Parent Body of U.N.I.A. and A.C.L. paid Marcus Garvey as salary (See Minute Book November 3, 1920) as follows:

November–December, 1920	$1016.68
January–December, 1921	7950.14

O.M. THOMPSON (LATER VICE PRESIDENT AND GENERAL MANAGER).

First appears on payroll	April 9, 1920 at $25. per week
	May 21, 1920 at 30. per week
	Oct. 22, 1920 at 40. per week
	Oct. 29, 1920 at 50. per week
and thereafter.	

GEORGE TOBIAS, TREASURER.

First appears on payroll	August 26, 1919 at $30. per week
	November 29, 1920 $50. per week
and thereafter until January 13, 1922.	

ELIE GARCIA, SECRETARY.

No record of any salary being paid to him by the Black Star Line, Inc.

Unearned passage money S.S. "Phyllis Wheatley":
On their ledger to June 30, 1921, this is carried under the head of "Sale of Passenger tickets S.S. Kanawah," page 368, with a credit balance (or liability) of $7582.50, and on September 30, of $7280.25.

Below are the actual receipts, refunds and net amounts that should appear in this account:

	Received.	*Refunded.*	*Balance.*
February, 1921	$169.25		$169.25
March	460.00		629.25
April	4,335.00	$230.00	4,734.25
May	2,275.00	180.00	6,829.25
June	460.00		7,289.25
July	230.00	75.00	7,444.25
August	672.50	20.00	8,096.75
September		240.00	7,856.75
October		254.00	7,602.75
November		650.00	6,952.75
December	330.00	1,120.00	6,162.75
January, 1922		20.00	6,142.75

As this boat was advertised to sail for West Africa on a given date in April, 1921, the collection of these moneys was a palpable fraud.

UNIVERSAL NEGRO IMPROVEMENT ASSOCIATION.

Its objects and aims as outlined in Article 1, Sect. 3 of its Constitution and Book of Laws, New York, July, 1918 are as follows:

"OBJECTS AND AIMS"

Sec. 3. The objects of the Universal Negro Improvement Association and African Communities' League shall be: to establish a Universal Confraternity among the race; to promote the spirit of pride and love; to reclaim the fallen; to administer to and assist the needy; to assist in civilizing the backward tribes of Africa; to assist in the development of Independent Negro Nations and Communities; to establish Commissionaries or Agencies in the principal countries and cities of the world for the representation and protection of all Negroes, irrespective of nationality; to promote a conscientious Spiritual worship among the native tribes of Africa; to establish Universities, Colleges, Academies and Schools for the racial education and culture of the people; to conduct a world-wide Commercial and Industrial Intercourse for the good of the people; to work for better conditions in all Negro communities.

OFFICIALS

Leaders and High Officials were elected as follows:

EXECUTIVE COUNCIL
AUGUST 19, 1920.

His Excellency, the American Leader	J.W.H. Eason
His Excellency, the West Indian Leader	R.H. Tobitt
His Excellency, the West Indian Leader	J.S. De [B]ourg
His Excellency, the Provisional President of Africa	Marcus Garvey

AUGUST 26TH & 27TH.

His Highness, the Potentate	Gabriel Johnson
His Highness, the Supreme Deputy	G.O. Marke
His Excellency, the President-General	Marcus Garvey
Rt. Hon. Assistant President-General	J.D. Gordon
Rt. Hon. Secretary-General	J.D. Brooks
His Hon. Asst. Secretary-General	J.B. Yearwood
Rt. Hon. Chancellor	Gabriel Stewart

Rt. Hon. Counsellor-General	Wilford H. Smith
His Hon. Asst. Counsellor-General	Wm. C. Matthews
Rt. Hon. Auditor-General	Eli[e] Garcia
Rt. Hon. Commissioner-General	F.W. Ellegor
His Grace, the Chaplain-General	Geo. A. McGuire
Rt. Hon. International Organizer	Miss H.V. Davis
Rt. Hon. Surgeon-General	D.D. Lewis
Rt. Hon. Speaker in Convention	F.A. Toote
Rt. Hon. Minister of Legions	[E.] L. Gaines

Article VII of Constitution and Book of Laws, New York, July 1918, reads:

> Sec. 1. The salary of the Potentate and Supreme Commissioner shall be in keeping with his high office and responsibilities, which salary shall be granted by the convention. The Potentate shall labor for the good and welfare of the organization, irrespective of salary or other consideration.

> Sec. 2. The Supreme Deputy shall be subjected to the same conditions on matter of salary as the Potentate.

HIGH OFFICERS.

> Sec. 3. All officials and high officers of the Universal Negro Improvement Association and African Communities' League other than the Potentate and Supreme Commissioner and Supreme Deputy shall be granted salaries commensurate with the work they perform, which shall be voted by the convention.

The books of account of this Association are not in any better shape than those of the BLACK STAR LINE, INC. The Cash Books start with February 17, 1920, and continue to January, 1922, at which time they were obtained under subpoena.

Their bank balances July to November, 1920, were, as follows:

July 31, 1920	$4,030.23
Aug. 31	3,256.27
Sept. 30	2,669.03
October 31	1,675.53

At a meeting of the Executive Council November 3, 1920, it was stated, referring to salaries, "we have sufficient assets to make a start, but that this be successfully continued, each member would have to work conscientiously thus measuring up to his salary."

At this time, however, they had pledges up to date for the purchase of $15,699. bonds to be issued: "for use in the furtherance of the Industrial, Commerical and Agricultural purposes of the Association in its Construction plans in Africa."

Their total receipts for November, 1920, were $14,883.70 of which $11,103.55 was from the sale of the above bonds[:]

Pages 35–37 of Cash Book for November show the following payments for salaries to officers[:]

SALARY 1–15TH INST. (NOV.)

Marcus Garvey	$229.17
G.A. McGuire, Chaplain	104.16
J.D. Brooks, Secretary	125.00
Jas. W.H. Eason, Am. Leader	208.32
G.E. Stewart, High Chancellor	125.00
J.B. Yearwood, Asst. Sec.	83.33
Wilford H. Smith, Counsel Gen.	145.88
J.D. Gordon, Asst. Pres. Gen.	125.00
[F.] Willcom Ellegor, Comm. Gen.	83.33
J[ohn] Sydney De [B]ourg, W.I. Leader	125.00
[E.] L. Gaines, Min. of Legions	62.50
Fred A. Toote, Speaker in Con.	62.50
Wm. C. Matthews, Asst.Co[u]ns[e]l Gen.	125.00
Elie Garcia, Auditor Gen.	104.16
Total	1,708.35

The balance on hand November 30th was $6,760.41, but out of this, under date of December 1 (Cash Book, p. 38) all of the salaries enumerated above are doubled and read for "Salary to November 30th," indicating overpayment of 1/2 of a month's salary in each instance and in addition, the following

Miss H.V. Davis—salary to Nov. 30th	$250.00
G.O. Marke—salary to Nov. 30th	125.00
Total	$3,791.70

showing that $5500. had been paid out of the receipts of the sales of bonds for officers['] salaries, for the month of November alone.

That this practice continued will be shown in the analysis of the published reports following.

BALANCE SHEET OF THE UNIVERSAL NEGRO IMPROVEMENT ASSOCIATION, AS PUBLISHED

Assets.

Balance in Bank July 30 [*1921*]	10,913.67	
Furniture & Fixtures	2,154.00	
Uncollected checks	3,494.30	16,561.97

Machineries.

Saw Mill Equipment	4,463.42
Invested in building material, Liberia	4,000.00

Inventory.

Supplies on hand	4,500.00

Stocks.

6888 shares common stock		
B.S.L.	34,440.00	
604 shares common stock		
N.F.C.	3,020.00	37,460.00

Good Will.

Negro World, estimated worth	60,000.00
Negro World Purchase price	

Accounts Receivable.

Arrears from branches on dues	37,690.52
Death Tax unpaid by branches	68,664.80

Loans Receivable.

B.S. Line
A.C.L.
N.F.C.
U.N.I.A. Local
Personal

Total	233,340.71

Liabilities.

Notes Payable	144,450.58	
Computed interest	6,500.00	150,950.58
Death Tax		
Loan U.N.I.A. special		
Dollar Drive		
[Total]		150,950.58
[Ne[t] Worth]		[82,390.13]

BALANCE SHEET OF THE
UNIVERSAL NEGRO IMPROVEMENT ASSOCIATION,
OUR ANALYSIS SHOWS:

Receipts.	*Disbursements.*	
3,250.65		
3,545.52		
8,502.88		
16,523.62		
7,460.23		
2,848.61		
1,778.48		
6,844.73		
13,080.42		From Secretary General
31,785.89		General
6,021.18		
35,536.00		Loans, etc. refunded
500.00		Loans, U.N.I.A. special
1,500.53		Bank collections and general equipment
	7,723.42	
	209.00	
	4,653.59	
	75,789.11	Salaries (all)
	12,403.53	
	9,029.37	
	5,356.45	Buttons, Banners, Badges, Gowns, Uniforms, Crosses & Decorations.
	793.89	Other loans
	3,194.71	Loans Negro F[*actories Corp.*]
	318.61	Loans Personal
	1,350.00	
	1,313.16	

105

Receipts.	*Disbursements.*	
	40,440.00	Loans Black Star Line
	2,178.90	Rec[e]ption, Parade, Convention
	439.91	Com. Legal & Prof.
	2,954.01	Refunds
3,250.87		
	4,000.00	Real Estate
	4,463.42	
	4,950.00	
	34,780.00	
	46,555.20	

PARENT BODY UNIVERSAL NEGRO IMPROVEMENT ASSOCIATION
CHANCELLOR'S REPORT—
SEPTEMBER 1, 1920 TO JULY 30, 1921.

General Funds.

Balance in Bank, Sept. 1, 1920	3,324.31	
Membership fees	3,891.84	
Sales Supplies to Branches	9,043.49	
Death Tax	19,562.80	
Twenty percent due from branches	7,471.26	
Convention Funds	3,993.37	
Sales of almanacs & pictures	2,102.10	
Dollar Assessment Tax	8,996.66	
Fees of charters	5,901.40	
Contributions (Voluntary)	19,802.56	
Dollar Drive for Black Star Line	5,959.11	90,048.90

Expenditures.

Petty Cash expenses for coal, gas, telephone bills, light, postage, expressage, etc. (223.40)	5,735.67
Furniture & fixtures	1,154.00
Returned checks	3,494.30
Salaries of officers (17,206.42)	35,519.74
Salaries of employees (9,740.61)	10,105.00
Travelling expenses (10,872.19)	5,346.39
Printing, stationery and adv.	9,930.56
Cost of Supplies	4,956.37
Loans to N.Y. Local	643.89
Purchase of Stock of Negro F[*actories Corp.*]	3,019.71

Loans, Sundries	227.00	
Death Benefits paid	1,275.00	
Telegrams & cables	1,258.00	
Refund Black Star Acct.		
Dollar Drive	5,000.00	87,665.57(A)
Balance in Bank July 30th.		2,383.33

Construction Loan.

Notes sold	137,458.22	
	6,992.36	144,450.58

Expenses.

Building Liberia	4,000.00	
Sawmill Equipment	4,463.42	
General Expenses	2,238.40	

Cost of various Sales campaigns.

Salaried officers	17,206.42	
Salaried employees	9,740.61	
Travelling expenses	10,872.19	
Advertising	6,400.00	
Invested in B.S.L. stock	34,440.00	
Purchase Acct. Negro World good will	46,555.20	135,920.24(B)
Balance in Bank		8,530.34

Condensed Statement of Receipts and Expenses.

General Receipts	90,048.90	
Sales of Bonds	144,450.58	234,499.48

Disbursements.

General Expenses	87,665.57	
Construction Funds	139,920.24	223,585.81
Balance in Bank		10,913.67
Balance Parent Body	2,383.33	
Balance Acct. Loans	8,530.34	10,913.67

(A) Should be .o6 more
(B) Should be 4.oo less

The following appeared in "The Negro World" under date of August 13, 1921:

UNIVERSAL NEGRO IMP. ASSOCIATION
AUDITOR-GENERAL'S REPORT

To the Honorable Delegates and Deputies to This Convention
Honorable Gentlemen:

It is not customary for the auditor of a company or an organization to submit any detailed report of his own, when statements and balance sheet submitted by the treasurer of said concern, are satisfactory to those who represent the financial interest of the business.

However, I may say that I have audited the reports as read by the High Chancellor, and that I have found all the items mentioned in the statement of receipts and disbursements to be true and correct and supported by proper vouchers and that all payments were made by the order of the President-General of the Association according to our constitution.

Nevertheless, it is always the duty of the auditor when such statement and reports have passed through his hands, to convey to the interested parties the impression that said report and balance sheet has made upon him, and also the true significance of the figures as lined up in the reports. It is also his duty to reveal to those in authority the various reasons why the report is good or bad, also the causes of loss of profit as found out by him, throughout his investigation and auditing of the transactions of the concern.

For the benefit of those who may not have fully understood the true significances of the report read by the chancellor, I will make the following comments:—

REPORT OF PARENT BODY.

You have noticed that two separate and distinct reports have been made for the funds received by the parent body, the general funds, and the construction funds. The general funds include the natural resources of the parent body coming from the branches, such as membership fees, dues, assessment tax, and so forth, while the construction funds represent only the amount of monies received through sales of bonds for construction in Liberia.

The disbursements made from the funds of the parent body need no comment, as they are entirely in keeping with the maintenance and operation of the association.

In the expense made out of the construction funds, the items of $4,000 represent the amount invested in materials for the building of our headquarters in Liberia.

The item of $4,463.42 represents the cost of sawmill equipment, which was purchased by the Executive Council on the request of his Highness, the Potentate, and which is at the present time in Hoboken, N.J., ready to be shipped to Monrovia, Liberia, at the first opportunity.

The items of $17,206.42, as also the one of $9,740.61[,] represent the salaries of the staff, both members of the Council and ordinary employees, who have labored for the sales of the bonds.

The items of $10,872.19 is the cost of railway tickets, car fares, and other conveyances of the staff throughout this country, and abroad, also for the disposition of the bonds.

The item of $6,400.00 for advertising is self explanatory.

The item of $34,440.00 represents the investment of the parent body in the Black Star Line, Inc.

The item of $46,555.20 represents the cost of purchase of the good will of the Negro World, the official organ of the Universal Negro Improvement Association, from the New York Local for $60,000.00.

BALANCE SHEET—ASSETS.

The general funds of the parent body and the construction funds amounts to $10,913.67, which was the bank balance as per July 31st.

There is also a bank balance of $1,436.00 to the credit of the Negro World which is also to be credited to the parent body by virtue of the purchase of the good will of said Negro World.

The item of $2,154.00 for furniture and fixtures, represents the value of the furnitures of the various offices of the parent body, less a reasonable amount for depreciation.

The item of $3,494.30 mentioned as uncollected checks represent the aggregate amount of numerous checks returned by the bank and not yet collected from the makers.

The item of $4,463.42 is, as stated, the value of the sawmill equipment, which, being new, has no depreciation.

The item of $4,500 mentioned as inventory represents the cost value of the supplies on hand in the Chaplain General's office, the Commissioner General's office and the Secretary General's office, to be sold to the various branches of the U.N.I.A.

The item of $37,690.52 represents the balance due by the

various branches of the U.N.I.A. to the parent body on the 20 per cent dues.

The item of $68,664.80 represents the correct amount of death tax due by the various branches to the parent body. The amount which should have been received from death tax is $88,227.00, and only $19,562.80 ha[s] been received, which gives the uncollected balance of $68,664.80 above stated. Therefore the total assets of the parent body as per balance sheet is $233,340.71.

LIABILITIES.

The parent body has no other liabilities except the amount of $144,450.58, which is the amount of bonds sold during the year. This liability is extended over a period of ten years and the books show that there will be no more than $20,000. to be paid out in one year. The computed interest on said notes is $6,500. The total liabilities being, therefore[,] $150,950.58, showing a net worth of $82,390.13, on July 31, 1921.

Before closing my comments I should like to say that the net worth of $82,390.13 is only the net worth of the central office of the association, but is not the net worth of the Universal Negro Improvement Association, which is to include the net worth of all the branches of the Universal Negro Improvement Association throughout the world.

I want also to call the attention of the honorable delegates to the important fact that the parent body has no other income but what is paid by the branches to its treasurer, and when the branches fail to maintain their obligations or fail to keep up their payments the parent body receives nothing.

I want also to bring to the attention of the honorable delegates that it is important for the presidents of the various branches to devise means and ways by which they can collect dues and death tax from the largest number of members in their branches.

The Secretary General's report shows a large membership throughout the world, but I have found that only a portion of the membership is financially connected with the parent body.

In conclusion I want to state that owing to the economic condition of the world at this time, and especially of our people, it is my opinion that the year just ended has been a successful one and that the operations carried out as well as the investments made are all going to bring great profit in the future. It must be understood that to maintain an organization as broad in its scope as the Universal Negro Improvement Association, large sums of money are required to meet the expenses.

If I should base my estimation on the experiences of the previous year I would say that a budget of no less than $300,000 a year is to be met by the Universal Negro Improvement Association if our construction work in Liberia is to go on and if we are to have a large enough staff to attend to the work and if we are to maintain the propaganda that we have launched throughout the world.

I therefore recommend to the honorable delegates that before the rising of this convention you take into consideration the discussion of the budget for the following year, so that each branch or each district of the country where the Universal Negro Improvement Association is represented can be allotted a certain portion of the total amount, and that on your return to your respective homes you may see to it that they carry their part as decided by you at this convention. Respectfully yours,

ELIE GARCIA
Auditor General

Exceptions:
The receipts of the General Funds and from the Sale of Bonds are, of course, shown under their respective heads separately but in the case of Disbursements there is nothing in the Cash Book indicating whether on account of the Parent Body or on account of the Construction Loan. Your accountant is unable to determine by what process the division was arrived at. This has particular reference to the division of Salaries, and Travelling Expenses, summarized as follows:

	They Show:	We Show:
Officers' salaries (gen. funds)	$35,519.74	
Officers' salaries (bonds)	17,206.42	
Employees['] salaries (gen. funds)	10,105.00	
Employees['] salaries (bonds)	9,740.61	
All salaries	$72,571.77	$75,789.11
Travelling Expenses	5,346.39	
Travelling Expenses (bonds)	10,872.19	
All Travelling Expenses	16,218.58	12,403.53
Total.	$88,790.35	$88,192.64

The amount received from the Sale of Bonds according to their Cash Book to July 30, 1921, was $133,250.87 (while they show $144,450.58) but from this should be deducted the $46,555.20 used for the purchase of the Negro

World, the $4,000. for Real Estate and $4,463.42 for Sawmill, a total of $55,018.62, leaving $78,232.25 of bond receipts to be accounted for, while their actual cash balance on July 31 was but $8,286.41 (not $10,913.67 as stated). It at once becomes evident that all of the salaries paid to the officers from November, 1920 ($52,726.16)[,] as well as about $17,000. of the loans made to the Black Star Line came from the proceeds of the Sale of the bonds. Incidentally their division of employees salaries and travelling expenses has yet to be taken care of and this completely wipes out the Death Tax Fund, a fund which should have been held separate and intact.

It may be noted here that it is claimed it cost $44,219.22 to dispose of $86,695.67 worth of bonds, the $46,555.20 sold by the New York Local being left out of the computation.

$34,440. invested in Black Star Line stock:

This actually represents loans made at various times from July, 1920, to July, 1921, to the Black Star Line. Inc., without security and on July 20, 1921, at a meeting of the Executive Council, it was carried "that all loans to the Black Star Line by the Parent Body be invested in B.S.L. stock held by the Parent Body."

On July 29, 1921, this was consummated by the Black Star Line, Inc.[,] giving its check no. 4233 of that date to order of Parent Body U.N.I.A. for $34,780. and receiving the same check, endorsed, in return for the issue of 6956 shares of its capital stock, at the time worthless and which fact was known to everyone concerned with the transaction.

$46,555.20 Purchase account Negro World good will

At a meeting of the Executive Council July 20, 1921, it was decided that the New York Local turn over to the Parent Body all monies due her for Construction Loan, that the Parent Body in turn buy out the interest in the "Negro World" held by the New York Local.

This transaction appears to have been consummated by the making of offsetting entries in Cash Received and Disbursed books under date of July 27, 1921, although it may be that the New York Local gave their check and the Parent Body may have used the same check in payment of the purchase price. At any rate the Parent Body did not deposit the check to their credit or issue another of like amount.

It will be observed that in their statement of Assets they estimated the worth of the good will of the Negro [W]orld at $60,000. in arriving at their Net Worth of $82,390.13—an appreciation of $13,444.80 in four days['] ownership.

Balance Sheet Assets:

It is stated that the General funds of the Parent Body and the Construction [*Loan*] funds amounts to $10,913.67 which was the bank balance as of July 31st. Both statements are false. The book balance (Cash Book p. 17) shows $8,286.41 and adding the amount of checks not yet paid by bank on July 31st of $1,249.84, the true bank balance of $9,536.25 is arrived at.

It is stated that there is also a bank balance of $1436. to the credit of the Negro World which is also to be credited to the parent body by virtue of the purchase of the good will of said Negro World. If a corporation, this cannot be[;] if privately owned, as appears to be the case, there are also the liabilities, if any, to be considered.

Accounts Receivable:

It is stated that the item of $37,690.52 represents the balance due by the various branches of the U.N.I.A. to the Parent Body on the 20 percent dues, but the fact that they are [in] arrears militates against considering the item a live asset.

It is stated that the item of $68,664.80 represents the correct amount of the Death Tax due by the various branches to the Parent Body. The amount which should have been received from Death Tax is $88,227.60 and only $19,562.80 ha[s] been received, which gives the uncollected balance of $68,664.80 above stated. If this is to be considered an asset and the fact that the arrears are so large in proportion to the amount paid in indicates its worthless character when the

arrears	$68,664.80
and the amount claimed to have been paid in	19,562.80
	88,227.60
less Death Grants paid	1,275.00
	$86,952.60

[s]hould be charged as a liability in view of General Law, Article 1, [Sec]t. 28, reading as follows:

> Sect. 28. A death tax of 10 cents per month shall be levied on each member, which shall be separate and distinct from the regular monthly dues, and the death tax so levied by each local Division or society shall be forwarded to the Secretary General of the Universal Negro Improvement Association and African Communities' League to be lodged to the credit of the Association's death fund; and on the death of a member who has paid up his or her last month's complete dues a sum of seventy-five dollars shall be granted from the death fund for his or her burial.

According to our analysis of Cash Books only $16,523.62 was paid in to July 31 and $1500. paid out.

It is stated "therefore the total assets of the Parent Body as per balance sheet is $233,340.71" but it would [be] much nearer the truth to say they were only $90,000, as shown by our comparative analysis['] which against the Net Worth as shown in published statement of $82,390.16, shows a deficit of $67,082.43 represented chiefly by the official salaries and loans to the bankrupt Black Star Line, Inc.

Books and Witnesses:

Practically all the books needed are in possession of the writer, being obtained under subpoena duces tecum on January 12th.

The witnesses necessary will have to be decided upon in conference with the United States Attorney. Respectfully submitted,

THOMAS P. MERRILEES
Expert Bank Accountant

DJ-FBI, file 61-157. TDS, recipient's copy.

1. See p. 76 in the present volume.
2. See pp. 74–75 in the present volume.
3. This is a key point, which Merrilees includes but does not emphasize in his report. The net result of this method of formulating the organization expense was concealment of the corporation's deficits. In taking this approach, BSL accountants were burying the fact that the capital the company possessed at the beginning of the year had been substantially diminished, thus leading to a false depiction of the total capitalization. The accounting procedure "did two things—it covered up the deficit, and it also presented a corporation that looked much healthier than in fact they were. . . . It looks very much like woeful misrepresentation, which is another way of saying fraud." Both the BSL officials who prepared the financial statement and Mr. Chirlian, the accountant who reviewed it, could be said to "be guilty of gross negligence" in their preparation of the report (Patrick Stanton, Deputy Auditor General, the Smithsonian Institution, interview with Robert A. Hill, Washington, D.C., 16 November 1984).
4. A statement of income or profit and loss differs from a balance sheet in that it reports the financial dealings of a company over a period of time, in this case the fiscal year 30 June 1920–30 June 1921. The balance sheets cited elsewhere in Merrilees' report were designed to show the financial status of a company on a given day. Short-term fluctuations in the standing of a corporation are not reflected in either type of financial statement, and are best determined by a comparison of a series of balance sheets over a period of time (Patrick Stanton, interview with Robert A. Hill, Washington, D.C., 16 November 1984; see also H. A. Finney, *Introduction to Principles of Accounting* [New York: Prentice-Hall, 1932], and George E. Bennett, *Accounting Principles and Practice* [New York: Biddle Business Publications, 1920]).
5. Garcia's "statement to the public" appeared in the *Negro World* of 9 July 1921. In it, he declared:

> Notice is hereby given that the annual meeting of the stockholders of the Black Star Line, Inc., will be held at 120 West 138th street, New York city, State of New York, Tuesday, July 26th, 1921, at 8 p.m., for the election of eleven directors and for the transaction of such other business as may be brought before said meeting.
>
> The stock transfer books of the company will be closed at 8 o'clock p.m., July 21, 1921, and remain closed until 10 a.m., July 27, 1921.

6. Garvey returned from the Caribbean on 13 July 1921.

Articles in the *Savannah Tribune*

[[New York, Oct. 30, 1922]]

Garvey's Daily Has Brief Life

The "Negro Daily Times," with which Marcus Garvey had hoped to combat the rising tide of public resentment against him for his alleged deal with the Ku Klux Klan, and which was launched with a flourish of trumpets and a hot-air blast against his "enemies," has failed to make its appearance for the past week. Announcement was made at the offices of the Universal [*Negro*] Improvement Association, 56 West 135th Street, that publication had been indefinitely suspended.

Garvey's daily had a brief and stormy career, twenty-six issues having been published. Publication of the first issue took Garvey and his staff something like three weeks, even after the plant had been installed. What Garvey will do with the plant, which is a white elephant on his hand, is problematical. Should he decide to dispose of it, he would be unable to raise one-fourth of the price paid for it. A peculiar feature of the business management of this plant is that the "Negro World," Garvey's weekly propaganda organ, is still being printed downtown, in spite of the fact that Garvey's plant undoubtedly has facilities for its printing, and could have saved money and supplied work for the force in his plant by having it printed at his own plant. This would be a shocking piece of mismanagement on the part of anybody but Marcus Garvey. From Marcus Garvey the public has learned to expect anything in the line of blunders and mismanagement.

Printed in the *Savannah Tribune*, 2 November 1922; from the Crusader News Service, 30 October 1922.

[[New York, Oct. 30, 1922]]

Black Star Line Has No Ships

Quite a furore has been created in this city by the publication of the records of a supplementary examination of Marcus Garvey, president of the "Black Star Line," held in the Supreme Court of the Bronx, August 19, when Mr. Garvey, under oath, was forced to admit that the "Black Star Line" was a line without ships and that it at present possessed only an interest in two boats one of which, the "Kanawha," is abandoned in the port of Antilla, Cuba, as a wreck; and the other, the "Shadyside," also a wreck "somewhere in New York Harbor." In both these vessels, the Garvey concern has only an interest and in both cases that interest is mortgaged. Both vessels are useless wrecks, according to Garvey's own admission.

Asked "should this matter be settled how much money would the Black Star Line receive individually," Garvey replied "the Black Star Line would not receive anything, because its interest is mortgaged to others to cover liabilities."

Questioned as to whether the Black Star Line had any accounts outstanding, Garvey replied, "No, it has no outstanding accounts." Garvey was then asked if anybody owed money to the Black Star Line and replied in the negative. He also replied in the negative to the question whether the Black Star Line was doing any business at the present time.

Garvey told the court that "about $900,000" had been collected on sale of stock and that the Black Star Line has never paid any dividends, and that what property it has in its name is all mortgaged, said property being that at 56 West 135th Street. The present indebtedness of the line was "approximately $200,000," he said, and there were no assets. Questioned as to whether there were any other judgments outstanding against the Black Star Line, and to name them, Garvey answered that "there are so many I cannot name them. There are judgments from the crew, aggregating about $40,000. That is, I am giving you what I can remember. We have several wage cases aggregating about $20,000. Also the Green River Distilling Company libel for $52,000." He told the court that the line had about $500 in the bank, but that this had been attached by one of his creditors.

Thus endeth the bubble of the "Black Star Line," and the marvellous things that Marcus Garvey, self-appointed Negro Moses, was going to do for the race if only they would "buy shares in the Black Star Line and support the Universal Negro Improvement Association."

In the meantime, the Federal case against Garvey, growing out of the exposure by the "Crusader Magazine" that his company had been advertising and selling passage on a "ghost steam ship," the "Phyl[l]is Wheatley," and the subsequent charges by Federal agents that he used the mails to misrepresent and defraud, is scheduled to come to trial November 6, 1922.

Printed in the *Savannah Tribune*, 2 November 1922; from the Crusader News Service, 30 October 1922.

Anonymous Letter to James Weldon Johnson

New York City 10/31/22

Mr. J. Weldon Johnson,

The Negro race is much beholden to you for the keen interest that you take in everything pertaining to its welfare and happiness, and for which I am profoundly grateful.

I am enclosing a report of a speech made by Marcus Garvey in Raleigh, N.C. which shows the kind of belly-crawling chameleon that he is.

Are these southern whites of such memories as to forget that only two years ago a speech was made in Liberty Hall in which this same Garvey or one of those then associated with him declared in substance that they (the Garvey organization) would democratize this country if it had to kill every white man in it? I think that Rev. E. V. Daniels, then a curate in St. Philip's Church, condemned the utterance in the New York Globe.[1] It is time that this blatant demagogue and traducer of men much better than himself should be shown in all his h[i]deousness, that decent self respecting men will know and despise him.

DLC, NAACP. TL, recipient's copy.

1. Rev. Everard W. Daniel of St. Philip's Protestant Church, 134th Street and Seventh Avenue, made a speech on 22 August 1920 denouncing "the plans of Garvey and his followers for the redemption of Africa" that were put forward during the UNIA's August 1920 convention. In his speech, Daniel, an assistant to the rector of the church (many of whose members were Garveyites), stated that he had heard one speaker at Liberty Hall say, "We are going to have democracy in this country if we have to kill every white man in it." Daniel's speech took place on the same day as a "near riot" occurred outside the outdoor meeting tent of Rev. Adam Clayton Powell, Sr., adjacent to Liberty Hall, following an anti-Garvey speech by the Rev. Charles S. Morris of Norfolk, Va. (*New York Age*, 28 August 1920).

Enclosure

[[Raleigh, Oct. 25, 1922]]

WEIGHED IN BALANCE NEGRO FOUND WANTING SAYS MARCUS GARVEY

PROVISIONAL PRESIDENT OF AFRICA MAKES STIRRING ADDRESS AT NEGRO FAIR[1]

BLAMES THE RACE FOR ITS PRESENT PLIGHT

THE NEGRO LEADER LITERALLY TAKES THE HIDE OFF A CHEERING MASS OF BLACKS

BY BROCK BARKLEY

Weighing his race in the balance and finding it wanting, Marcus Garvey, "provisional president of Africa[,]" treated five hundred negroes attending their state fair here today to a full relation of his ideas and ideals for founding a nation where they might be truly free men, mingle with one another on an equal plan[e], practice self reliance and become [as] unified as "the great white man" or the "great yellow man."

Introduced as "his excellency, the provisional president of Africa" this negro Moses literally, "took the hide" off his hearers as they cheered almost his every word. Men shouted and some even gave vent to an emotional "amen."

Garvey thought it was time the negro was up and doing. He had done nothing for himself. He had taken the customs of his former slave master, and if he should be forced to depend on his own creations the very clothes upon his back would be lost to him. He gave America as the great example in support of his African colonization scheme. In two hundred years this country has been built up from a band of pilgrims to a nation of 105,000,000 people. Why could not the same be done in Africa, he wanted to know.

With "his excellency" was "Sir" Robert Po[s]t[o]n, of Cleveland, Ohio, evidently a member of the African provisional aristocracy. "Sir Robert" was the very picture of dignity with a swallow tail coat and a chivalrous grace in his bow to the audience [and] made a five minute speech, preceding his chieftain and while Garvey spoke "Sir Robert" lent enthusiasm to the crowd by constantly chiming a string of approving "all right's."

As for his "excellency," he was dressed in [his?] citizenship clothes, and his . . . [*several lines mutilated*].

He pronounced such words as "master" with the use of a long "R" but ordinarily his flow of language was that of the educated southern negro. He spoke very rapidly and used as many gestures as Billy Sunday.[2]

Leaning far over the banisters on the floral hall balcony, from which he spoke, he pounded his fists vig[or]ously against the railing as a pair of extraordinarily thick lips parted to let pour f[ro]m an over sized mouth words of condemnation for his race.

He damned the negro's indolence, his dependence and his failure to do anything whatsoever for himself. It has been depending too much on the Lord, Garvey said, whereas the Lord quit after he had made the white man, the yellow man and the black man equal and started them all on the same road and from the same starting tape.

He chose as his subject, "Race Uplift," and inaugurated his address with the explanation that he represented an organization known as the [U]niversal [N]egro [I]mprovement [A]ssociation, bent upon "uniting in one great home the four hundred million negroes of the world." Two hundred and eighty million of them are already in Africa, and he proposes taking the remaining 120,000,000 over.

Nobody wants the negro, Garvey cried. Austria doesn't want him; Europe doesn't want him; Canada doesn't want him and even his home of fifteen million negroes doesn't want him.

"I am building a civilization of my own; I am building a civilization to hand down to the posterity of my own race," Garvey declared these countries would say.

And the negro cannot build up on the civilization of another race. "When you build on the civilization of another race you are building on sandy ground," he told them.

"The white man hates you not because of your color but because you will not do anything for yourself. It is not a matter of color but of condition. The [U]niversal [N]egro [I]mprovement [A]ssociation preaches the doctrine of race equality. I do not mean social equality; I do not give a rap about that if a man doesn't want to associate with me, I don't want to associate with him.

"Man is the Lord, master and architect of his own destiny. God never placed a superior man on earth. God gave him the right to do whatsoever he wanted to do. God is not responsible for your economic or political condition. God is not a politician. He is your spiritual overlord. You create your own destiny. The white man had no better chance than you have. If the white man gathers up the world and puts you in slavery don't blame him. Blame yourself and your own laziness.

"Don't wait for the Lord to do anything for you, you must do it yourself. An angel didn't bring me here. Jesus didn't send down a machine to carry me. A train of the white man brought me here by laying the rails from New York to Raleigh and building the engine that pulled the cars. If I waited for negroes to convey me from New York to Raleigh I would be walking for six month[s].

"The white man's superiority to us is not physical but material." Here, Sir Robert broke in with a chorus of "all right's" and the audience joined him with shouts.

"You will never get up the ladder until you get to and build a civilization that can compare with the white man's," Garvey went on. ["]Till you do that you may talk equality until doomsday and you'll still be at the bottom of the ladder. You must do it yourself. Jesus did all he could for you when he created you. It's up t[o] you to better your own conditio[n.] 'What do we want?' All we want [is a] government of our own. Why, because both races cannot live togethe[r] in peace and seek the same thing[.] The weaker race must die or give awa[y.] Nothing happens now but what of th[e] next two hundred years."

Here Garvey told of the arrival o[f] the band of pilgrims and of the growt[h] of the white man's country from tha[t] day. Now the white man owns th[is] country and he is not going to give [it] away. Consequently, Garvey declare[d] the negro must establish a country of his own. He failed to state ho[w] he proposed getting Africa away fro[m] the white man of the European nations.

"Physically I may be the equal [of] the white man, but materially I woul[d] find myself naked. If the white ma[n] said to me: Well, Garvey, if you wan[t] to really be my equal give me m[y] clothes there and my shoes, and the[n] Marcus Garvey would be as naked a[s] when he came into the world."

Berry O'Kelly[3] presided over the meeting and Rev. Lee Walker, pasto[r] of one of the negro churches here, introduced Garvey as [on]e of two me[n] in the world most [oppre?]ssed and misunderstood. "Gandh[i of] India and Garvey of America."

DLC, NAACP. Unidentified newspaper clipping.[4]

1. Garvey's speech at the Negro State Fair in Raleigh, N. C., was described by the white *Greensboro Daily News* as "quite the cleverest speech ever heard" at the annual event (*New York Age*, 11 November 1922). The address came under attack, however, from the *Baltimore Afro-American*, which headlined its report, "Marcus Garvey Thanks White Southerners for Lynching Negroes" (*Baltimore Afro-American*, 3 November 1922), and in January 1923 the *Messenger* condemned Garvey's use of the word *nigger* in a scathing editorial entitled "A Supreme Negro Jamaican Jackass" (*Messenger* 5, no. 1 [January 1923]: 561).

2. Billy Sunday (1862–1935) was an American preacher and revivalist renowned for his rousing pulpit style. After an early career as a baseball player in Chicago, Sunday became one of the nation's

most prominent Protestant evangelists. As a reporter observed of one sermon, "He raced up and down the green-carpeted platform . . . waving his hands, kicking up one knee now and again . . . brandishing a chair, standing with one foot on the chair and another on the pulpit . . . bobbing back and forth and waving a handkerchief between his legs." Another newspaper account pointed out that Sunday was "not afraid to wave his hands and shout" (cited in William G. McLoughlin, Jr., *Billy Sunday Was His Real Name* [Chicago: University of Chicago Press, 1955], pp. xx, 26).

3. Berry O'Kelly (1861–1931), businessman and educator, was educated in Chapel Hill, N.C. Founder of the Berry O'Kelly Training School for Negroes and president of the Acme Realty Co. of Raleigh, N.C., he also served as president of the North Carolina Negro State Fair. O'Kelly and Booker T. Washington together founded the National Negro Business League. Known as a race leader, O'Kelly was associated with the philanthropist Julius Rosenwald and the black educator Robert R. Moton; he also served on the executive committee of the North Carolina State Interracial Commission (*Raleigh News and Observer*, 15 March 1931; Louis R. Harlan, *Booker T. Washington: The Making of a Black Leader, 1856–1901* [New York: Oxford University Press, 1972], pp. 266–271).

4. Above the author's byline a subhead reads, "Star's News Bureau[,] 312 Tucker Building." It has proven impossible, however, to confirm the identity of the newspaper in which this article actually appeared. Other North Carolina newspapers also carried accounts of Garvey's visit. The *Greensboro Daily News*, for example, in a pro-segregationist article, headlined Garvey's visit as "Garvey Thanks White People for Lynching Black Pride into the Black." The article said that Garvey's speech thanked "the southern white man for having lynched the black man into a race consciousness which a mendacious northerner never could have given him by flattery or dissembled love." The black crowd at the meeting was divided in their response to Garvey's talk. While some "cheered every sentence," others in the audience "talked down Garvey" (*Greensboro Daily News*, 26 October 1922; R. L. Beall, *Greensboro Daily News*, to Robert A. Hill, 24 January 1984; *Raleigh News and Observer*, 26 October 1922).

Editorial Cartoon in the *Messenger*

Thomas P. Merrilees to William Hayward, United States Attorney, New York

New York City, N.Y., October 31, 1922

Sir:

In the case of U.S. vs MARCUS GARVEY, et al., and further to summary report of October 26th thereon, the following may prove of interest:

POINT ONE

In a supplementary proceedings examination of Marcus Garvey held in the Supreme Court of Bronx County, New York City, August 19, 1922, Mr. Garvey made the following statements under oath (THE CRISIS Vol. 25 No. 1 November, 1922 Whole No. 145.)

Q. Has the Black Star Line any property whatsoever at the present time?

A. It has property in its name, but it is all mortgaged.

Q. What property is that?

A. At 56 West 135th Street.

Q. What do you mean by the property being all mortgaged?

A. Well, there are three mortgages on it, first, second, and third.

Q. Who holds the first mortgage?

A. Some outside corporation. The secretary can give you the name of that corporation.

Q. Who owns the second mortgage?

A. The second mortgage is owned by the person we bought the property from.

Q. And who owns the thir[d mortgage?]

A. The Universal Negro Improvement Association.

Q. [*line mutilated*]

A. [*several lines mutilated*]

[Q.] [H]ow long ago was this money borrowed?

[A.] Wit[hin] two ye[ar]s.

[Q.] Has the Universal Negro Improvement Association received any of its money in return?

A. No, it has not.

Q. Has the Black Star Line paid any interest on that loan?

A. No.

Q. What is the present indebtedness of the Black Star Line?

A. Approximately [$]200,000.

Q. And what are the assets of the Black Star Line?

A. There are no assets.

Q. What is the equity in this building at 56 West 135th Street?

A. Well, we have no equity, because it is all mortgaged. Even if the building were to be sold we would not get anything because the mortgage is out of our control.

In making the statement that the consideration for the $10,000.00 third mortgage was received in cash and that it actually went into the Treasury of the Black Star Line, he testified falsely, as will be subsequently shown.

Furthermore, it is apparent from all the surrounding circumstances that his real object in going through the motions he did was to put the equity of the Black Star Line, Inc., in the property at 56 West 135th Street beyond the reach of its creditors as will also be subsequently shown.

The first indication of this transaction appears in the Minute Book under date of July 17, 1921, (it is not indicated whether Garvey was present at this meeting, which was about the time he returned from the West Indies, but he is shown to be present at the next meeting on July 20, 1921,) where it is stated that funds are needed by the company to finance the purchase of a steamer for the African trade and the U.N.I.A. offered to lend the sum of ten thousand dollars to the Company provided said loan is secured by a mortgage on the property of the company located at 56 West 135th Street, Borough of Manhattan, County of New York, which mortgage shall be for a period of one year with interest at 6%. It was resolved and adopted that the offer be accepted and that the officers of the company be fully authorized, instructed and empowered to execute all proper instruments to carry such acceptance into effect on behalf of the company, to receive said $10,000. in cash and to do all other things in connection with such mortgage as may be found necessary for its proper consummation.

This minute was read at the meeting on July 20, 1921 (Garvey present) and accepted without correction.

On the same day, July 20, 1921, at a meeting of the Executive Council of the U.N.I.A. and A.C.L. (Garvey . . . [*several words mutilated*] it was unanimously carried that all loans to the Blac[k] [Star Line by] the Parent Body be inv[es]ted in BSL stock. [*Two lines mutilated*].

At this time, July 20, 1921, the ledger of the Black Star Line, Inc., page 457, shows a balance due in account "Loans payable U.N.I.A. Parent Body" of $34,780. and on July 20, 1921, the Black Star Line, Inc., issued their check no. 4233, to the U.N.I.A. Parent Body for [$]34,780. in payment.

The books of the U.N.I.A. Parent Body show loans made to July 20, 1921, to the Black Star Line, Inc., in the total of $38,440 but as a matter of fact, neither are correct, the actual amount loaned to this time being [$]39,290.

Thus a balance of $4510.was still owing by the Black Star Line, Inc., although there is every indication they all believed they had cleared all indebtedness. In addition to which the following loans were subsequently received by the Black Star Line:

July 21, 1921	$1000.00
Aug. 5, 1921	1000.00
[Aug.] 13, 1921	1000.00
[Aug.] 31, 1921	1000.00
Sept. 8, 1921	130.00
Oct. 15, 1921	50.00
Dec. 13, 1921	200.00
Jan. 6, 1922	200.00

a total of $4580.00, which added to the previous balance of $4510.00 leaves $9,090.00 due by the Black Star Line, Inc., to the U.N.I.A. Parent Body as of January 6, 1922, but again from this should be deducted the following loans made to the U.N.I.A. Parent Body by the Black Star Line, Inc., and never repaid:

July 14, 1919	$266.44
[July] 17, 1919	85.00
[July] 18, 1919	262.00
Aug. 16, 1919	135.00
Dec. 3, 1919	150.00
May 13, 1920	50.00
June 24, 1920	50.00
[June] 24, 1920	10.00
Oct. 7, 1920	18.56
June 30, [1921]	48.00
Nov. 7, 1921	400.00
	$1475.00

and in addition a balance of $250.50 in loans made to and by the U.N.I.A. Special, leaving in the final accounting a balance of $7364.50 due by the Black Star Line, Inc. to the U.N.I.A. Parent Body from which, however, $3500 should be deducted for the purchase price of office furniture, leaving a net of $3,864.50 still due.

But all this is beside the mark and is only given so that a true picture of all the conditions will be shown.

On July 16, 1921, their office furniture, etc., was ordered sold to the

U.N.I.A. for $[3]500. cash, which payment was never directly made.

[A]l[so] [o]n July [17?] 1921, t[he] property at 56 West 135th Street was authorized to be mort[gag]ed for $10,000. cash.

[*Several words mutilated*] balance in the Chelsea Exchange Bank was attached.

At a meeting of the Board of Directors on October 31, 1921, it was resolved that as the corporation was being pressed by claims from numerous creditors threatening suits and attachments and that as the corporation was without means to pay said claims, or any part thereof, without selling such of its personal property and effects as it had not previously disposed of and the African Communities League, a domestic corporation, has offered to purchase the automobile truck owned by this Company and to pay therefor the sum of $3000. cash, which offer is fair and reasonable, that this company accept the offer of said African Communities League to purchase said auto truck and that the President of this corporation be and he is hereby authorized and decided to make proper transfer and sale of said auto truck to said African Communities League upon receipt of amount offered.

Except a loan of $200. from the African Communities League on December 15, 1921, and $100. of this was repaid December 30, their Cash Book to January 6, 1922, does not indicate the payment of any part of this $3,000. It is true that in April, May and June 1921, they had borrowed $1700. from the A.C.L. which was never repaid.

It has been stated to the writer by Elie Garcia, Secretary of the Black Star Line, that after the bank balance was attached in October, 1921, all moneys received were turned over to the Black Star Steamship Co. of New Jersey and checks would be taken from the latter as needed.

On November 16, 1921, at which time the balance in the Chelsea Exchange Bank was only $592.05, check no. 1566 of the Parent Body of the U.N.I.A., bearing date of November 16, 1921, to order of the Black Star Line, bearing the words: "Balance mortgage 54–56 West 135th Street and purchase price of office furniture" in the amount of $9340, signed by Marcus Garvey, President General and G.E. Stewart, High Chancellor, was issued. This check bears the endorsement, in blank, "Black Star Line, Inc., George Tobias, Treasurer" and is followed by the endorsement of the Parent Body, also in blank, "Parent Body, U.N.I.A. & A.C.L., 54–56 West 135th Street, New York City, N.Y., U.S.A. G.E. Stewart, High Chancellor, U.N.I.A. & A.C.L."

It is true this check appears in the Cash Book (Receipts) . . . [*word mutilated*] but it was not deposited to the credit of the Black Star [Line] [account?] for the very good reason that there were not sufficient [funds to cover?] it, instead, Tobias, the Treasurer, as has been shown, [endorsed it in?] blank and turned it back to the Parent Body of the [U.N.I.A.] so the Cash Book (Disbursements) page 120, under date of [November 16?] 1921, shows for the "Purchase of U.N.I.A. Const. Bonds, $9340.00." [The Cash] Book of the Parent Body of the U.N.I.A., under date of November 16, 1921, page 24, records the sale of $9340 in Bonds to the Black Star Line and the receipt of their check on November 19, 1921, for $9340.00—(It being their own check) and which check was deposited by the Parent Body of the U.N.I.A. to their credit in the Chelsea Exchange Bank on November [21,?] 1921. Of course it being their own check the bank also charged their own account at once.

Thus neither the U.N.I.A. Parent Body or the Black Star Line, Inc., having $9340. in cash, the true status of the transaction is merely that of book [entries] and as disclosed by the minutes of the Black Star Line, Inc., was merely for the purpose of putting their equity in the property at 54–56 West 135th Street beyond reach of the creditors, as the concern was bankrupt and had always been so. Further, the so-called bonds were not bonds at all, but merely promises to pay, without security, and their purchase was not authorized at any meeting of the directors of the Black Star Line, Inc. On the contrary, the $10,000. was to be used in the purchase of a steamer for the African trade.

POINT TWO

The Cash Book of the Parent Body of the U.N.I.A., page 36, under date of November 19, 1920, indicates a loan of $2050. in cash to the Black Star Line, Inc., but no record is to be found anywhere in the records of the Black Star Line, Inc., of its receipt.

This amount was part of check no. 534 dated November 19, 1920, of the Parent Body of the U.N.I.A., on the Chelsea Exchange Bank to order of Cash in the amount of $[2]534.00, signed by Marcus Garvey, President General and G.E. Stewart, Chancellor, without endorsement and was paid by the Bank, November 20, 1920.

As to what became of it?

POINT THREE

As to what became of the $[3],000.00 cash for sale of truck mentioned on page 4, which Garvey alone was authorized to negotiate. Respectfully,

THOMAS P. MERRILEES
Expert Bank Accountant

DJ-FBI, file 61. TLS, recipient's copy.

Speech by Marcus Garvey

[[LIBERTY HALL, New York, November 5, 1922]]

My subject for tonight is: "A People Who Are Enemies to Themselves." For near on five years a new doctrine was given to the world—one that sought to liberate the souls and minds of black men the world over. We sponsored the doctrine under the organized movement known as the Universal Negro Improvement Association. The placing of this doctrine among men called for the same amount of effort, the same amount of sacrifice, the same amount of misunderstanding, the same amount of persecution as all other doctrines have called for in their growth in the minds and hearts and souls of the people.

Tracing the human race back for centuries and the movements that they have helped to formulate for the good of society that holds the entire family together, you will find hundreds and thousands of other movements similiar to the movement of the Universal *Negro* Improvement Association. Each and every one has had a history; as for instance: the doctrine of the movement of Mohammed has its history, the doctrine of the movement of the Man of Galilee has its history, the movement of the reformers has its history. Those were social and religious movements. Then we had the great political movements—the movement of the people of Israel that sought to liberate them from Egyptian bondage. Coming down, we have had many kinds of liberation movements seeking to free the physical body, the spiritual soul, the mental mind of man. We have been as much enslaved mentally, spiritually and physically as any other race and a fair comparison is the race that Moses led out of Egyptian bondage. You are as well acquainted with the history of each and every one of these movements as I am. You know as well as I do that if your movement is to merit the success that you desire—if your movement is to hold the place that you have planned for it—you must expect to pass under the same shadows, pass under the same misunderstanding, pass under the same persecutions, pass under the same hardships. The man or the woman who enters the fold of the Universal Negro Improvement Association without taking to himself or herself the thought of the cost has really been misplaced in a great gigantic crusade for the liberation of humanity.

I was fully cognizant and fully aware of all the cost before I entered into service for the Universal Negro Improvement Association. The cost is ingratitude; the cost is persecution; the cost is death and those who have led great movements counted the cost and were prepared for the extreme of it. Those of us who led the Universal Negro Improvement Association must have counted the cost and must have prepared ourselves for the extreme penalty. But even though leaders of great reform movements prepared themselves for all that came their way they have always expressed surprise and dissatisfaction over the attitude of the people whom they make an effort to lead. That same surprising attitude now takes hold of me even though I counted the cost; even though I knew beforehand the attitude of the people, the attitude of the great mob, generally that of ingratitude; yet it is surprising that the people whom you want to lead, the people whom you want to serve are the ones most active in doing everything to inflict injury and pain on those who lead them.

We Are Our Greatest Enemies

Characteristically it has been said of us that we are our greatest enemies, and, indeed, it is true. The struggle of the Universal Negro Improvement Association to hold a place among men—the struggle to place the race on a pinnacle of exaltation and eminence is a struggle made most difficult, most hard and tiresome by the people within the very race that desires to be elevated. We ourselves contribute most toward our own difficulties, to our own condition because of lack of patience with ourselves; because of lack of understanding among ourselves. As I said before, you are not singular; the people of Israel exhibited the same amount of disgust and dissatisfaction and impatience as this race of ours exhibits now in the desire to reach the new Promised Land. When Moses started out with the people, pointing them in the direction of the Promised Land, the millions of them started with buoyant hopes, but when they had gone not even half of the journey some of them started propaganda against Moses. They started to question his authority; they started to doubt his ability to lead them to the Promised Land. You know what happened to them because of the wicked agitation that they carried on among themselves. Even the Spiritual Director of the movement, who was to lead them into liberty and freedom out of capitivity, became disgusted with them.

Are we not pursuing the same course? Are we not every day duplicating just that which happened centuries before and probably will happen centuries again to come? A people cannot successfully carry themselves except they first understand themselves.

Environment the Cause

It is the belief of the Universal Negro Improvement Association—I am not going to blame you for this—that no people can well understand themselves surrounded by an environment not created by themselves in an alien land. That takes me back to what I said last Sunday night—that so long as the Negro forms a part of another man's civilization he shall ever be a slave, mentally, physically and spiritually. It was the environment of Egypt that caused the Israelites to doubt the leadership and possibilities of Moses. They were unable to get away from the old environment and influence of Egypt even though they had left the old land and were following in another direction.

It is not a prophecy; it is but a conclusion reached from close study and observation of conditions as they are and as they affect this race of ours. I repeat and say that so long as the Negro forms a part of the white man's civilization; so long as the Negro forms a part of alien environment, alien culture, so long shall he remain a mental, spiritual and physical slave. In slavery we shall remain until that day of Ethiopia's stretching forth her hands unto God arrives, until that day of princes coming out of Egypt is ushered in.

NOVEMBER 1922

THE PROGRESS OF RACES

The true progress of a race depends upon its own energy, its own effort, its own initiative. The race that has no initiative has absolutely no future. Look at things as they are. In this Western world we find the race without any initiative; we find the race without a vision but that supplied by the Universal Negro Improvement Association. In trying to place this initiative, in trying to place this vision, what do we come in contact with? Because of the lack of understanding among the races we come in direct contact with the enemies who seek to destroy our vision and to deprive us of this outlook. The Universal Negro Improvement Association finds itself in this position at this time: In nearly every section of this Western world, and for that matter in every popular section of the world where Negroes live, there springs up a voluntary opposition to our program, not so much from among others, because, as I have said before, we know our enemies among the people that we have to fight in the great conflict to reach destiny. But what I am speaking of is this opposition that springs from within, wherein this community as well as in this country and all over the world we have men of our race who have made it their duty to place as many barriers as possible in the way of the Universal Negro Improvement Association to prevent this vision taking hold of all the people and directing the people in one direction.

Who would believe it that in this community—because we are so near home we will speak of this community, and what is true of this is true of all—that men take special pains in misrepresenting the aims and objects of this Association to the powers that be; to the forces that control, because of their selfishness in believing that through a movement so gigantic, so attractive to which millions of people rush, will come a recognition that probably would be justly merited that would not be attracted their way. And because that recognition goes not their way, in spite of the things that can be achieved, they seek to destroy the vision and the purpose in view. Here we have little groups of men, and we have had them for a long time, who have tried to lead the people. They have probably failed in getting that understanding among the people as to have them directed in one channel. Because of their failure some one else comes on the scene and places before the people an ideal, attracts the multitude and in the attracting of the multitude[,] in the placing of the ideal[,] there is created a malice, an envy, that gives expression in a way as not only to injure the person who gives the ideal, but to injure the entire race that sees in that ideal the hope of a new life. That is the situation as it is today. That is where the Universal Negro Improvement Association has found itself because of the desire to spite one individual who probably by some chance has been able to arouse the attention of the multitude. The men who should be most on the alert to lift as we go have placed obstructions in the way, hoping that by those obstructions they will be able to defeat the one who has in some way or other incurred their displeasure.

You will better understand me when I say this: that probably through me the great ideal of the Universal Negro Improvement Association is being fought; through me the great vision of millions of people for a new day and for a new life is to be obstructed. That fight that has centered around me is the fight that will be centered around any other leader, any other idealist who sets out to lead the people into a new vision, into a new light. It was the same kind of fight that was centered around Mohammed when he enuciated his doctrine; it was the same kind of fight that was centered around Martin Luther when he declared for the reformation; it was the same kind of fight that was centered around the great political leaders of Ireland who sought to arouse the people for Irish freedom; it was the same kind of fight that was centered around the Man of Nazareth who attempted to assemble the multitude and teach them the new doctrine of salvation; it is the same kind of fight that will be centered around any man or any woman who seeks to place an ideal among the people. The fight is one that will go on probably forever, but those who have got the vision, those who have got the ideal, are the ones to give consolation and hope to the one who leads, who becomes the target of abuse and persecution. It was through the sympathy of the lowly people that the Nazarene became inspired to perform the best part of His work. It was through the loyalty of the people who followed Mohammed that he placed himself on the altar of sacrifice to carry on the doctrine that he taught. It was through the faithful who held up the hand of Moses as others pressed around him that inspired him to march on and on with the hope of seeing the Promised Land. It is on the hope of the multitude that causes me to fight on and fight on for the achievement of the ideals of the Universal Negro Improvement Association. Human as I am, human as all the reformers probably have been with the exception of the Nazarene, who would not become tired, who would not become disgusted leading a people who have no gratitude, but whenever the reformers would give up, that silent multitude who suffers, who cries, who always felt willing to encourage and to help, appeals, and because of that appeal a new life comes to the leader, a new vision takes hold of him and he seems to forget the trials and tribulations; he seems to forget the ingratitude of the many as they spring up day after day and time after time.

And as I am about to close let me say this: that but for the suffering of the silent multitude, the suffering that I see in every community that I visit, but for the great pain and anguish of heart in the millions that I know, I too could have been on strike, I too could have given up, but for a moment the thought comes to me—why exhaust your energy, why dissipate your life, why give up [al]l your precious time, to a people who have no thanks? And I see the old suffering mother in the corner; I see the unprotected child growing up without hope; I see the suffering of the untold multitude, and then another vision comes to me and it says, "You must go on; you must go on because it is your duty." But understand, men and women, that it is not more the duty of one than it is the duty of all. Moses could have remained in Egypt and have become the elect of the Pharaohs; Martin Luther could have remained in the monastery and become one of the Popes; Robert Emmet could have remained in the society of Irish aristocracy and become one of the elect of the land. I also could remain in my own literary circle and become one of the privileged few. But Moses decided for the people; Martin Luther decided for the people; Robert Emmet decided for the people; I also have decided for the people. (Applause.) So long as the people live I will find cause to perform my duty. (Applause.) So long as the people suffer I will find cause to wage a relentless warfare for their emancipation. So long as Africa is held in bondage by an alien race I will find cause to strike the blow for her freedom. Therefore, painful though it may be to see those who should be nearest the firing line doing things and saying things to make you feel disgusted and dissatisfied, yet we cannot give up.

And just a word about those who seek to ruin the Universal Negro Improvement Association by propaganda even as they [s]ought to ruin the cause of Moses through propaganda. They said many things against Moses when he made his effort, but they did not say that Moses was building a house in Larchmont, N.Y., costing $45,000; but they say that Marcus Garvey is building a palace in Larchmont, N.Y., costing $45,000. Why do they say these things? They say these things to dishearten the people and disturb the minds of the people. I have been in New York about five years, and if a man gave me ten million dollars to go to Larchmont myself I would not be able to find the place because I do not know where it is; but they have me there as building a house costing $45,000. Why did they publish that in the Chicago Defender and in the Amsterdam News and in the Negro publications all over the country, and made big headlines of it?[1] Because by that very propaganda they caused the temporary setback and failure of the Black Star Line; because they were able through their ingenuity and machinations to deceive the people and cause the government to arrest Marcus Garvey for the Black Star Line and its activities, and because they knew just at this time the case of the Black Star Line will be called and because they knew that the people are contributing to the defense of Marcus Garvey, they desire to show that Marcus Garvey has so much money that he can build a mansion in Larchmont and therefore he must be guilty of something. That is the propaganda of the enemy and that does not come from the white man; it comes from those so-called educated Negroes that we have been talking of last Sunday night[2] and who are the avowed enemies of their own race—the Negro who has an education that fits him to be nothing else but a member of the white man's civilization. Education without preparation is a dangerous thing, and it is the duty of the Universal Negro Improvement Association to safeguard the race against that danger. We desire the higher education, the education that will teach the Negro to be loyal and true to himself.

It is immaterial what happens to Marcus Garvey; it was immaterial what happened to Robert Emmet; it was immaterial what happened to Martin Luther; it was immaterial what happened to Moses; it was immaterial what happened to the lowly Nazarene, Jesus the Christ. The thing that counted was the salvation of the people; the righteousness of the cause. Marcus Garvey calculated for all those things. I knew all those things would be said; I knew all those lies would be told, but because of that I am not disturbed. Let me tell you, you cannot go further than the confidence you have in yourself and the confidence you have in those who lead you. If you believe that I am capable at this time of building a mansion in Larchmont, N.Y., for $45,000 at the time that the Universal Negro Improvement Association needs money to put over its program, then you will be big fools to follow Marcus Garvey in the Universal Negro Improvement Association. When I am going to build a mansion I am going to build it on the banks of the Nile. (Applause and laughter.) The day may come, and it may never come; but I would do no more probably or do no less than human beings situated in my place would do. M[o]h[a]mmed did not build a mansion; Moses did not build a mansion while the people were passing in the wilderness, and I hardly would build a mansion around here. Suffice it to say that the kind of propaganda that you have heard and read of is the method by which you are to lose sight of that vision which will lead us into salvation. If you lose the vision it will not be my fault. I have done everything to keep you seeing always the vision, and I trust you will keep close to that vision whether Marcus Garvey goes up or down. Let the vision always be that which we have followed for the last five years.

They say my case comes up tomorrow, and believe me when I say that I have never even had time to consult a lawyer. I have been kept so busy attending to the affairs of the Universal Negro Improvement Association that I have never had time even to think of my own personal safety or protection. But the greatest protection a man can have anywhere is his conscience, a clean soul with man and with his God. A man stands convicted on his own conscience. If his soul is guilty even though he may be set free through the assistance of a hundred lawyers he is still convicted; but when a man's conscience is clear no conviction can make him a criminal; and I want to say that Marcus Garvey has never robbed a man in all his life; he believes too much in his own strength[,] is too much conceited about his own ability to find a place in the world to rob the other fellow. I promise you this, that when the case of Marcus Garvey comes to trial the whole world will read of the truth and the sacrifice and the persecution of the Universal Negro Improvement Association. I have nothing to hide and am willing to face the world and let the world tell me what they know about me. We shall fight on as never before, and if any one thinks that anything in the world can intimidate and curb the spirit that leads the Universal Negro Improvement Association they make a tremendous mistake. No crosses, no shadows of the gallows, no persecution can intimidate and curb the spirit that leads the movement that seeks to liberate suffering humanity. Others have suffered in the past, and I know that I can do no less than pay the supreme sacrifice for the cause that is dearest to my heart and to 400,000,000 Negroes throughout the world. (Applause.)

Printed in *NW*, 11 November 1922. Original headlines omitted.

1. The *Chicago Defender* reported on 28 October 1922 that "Garvey is building a palatial mansion to cost $45,000 in Larchmont, N.Y., one of the most exclusive and fashionable colonies in the country."

2. On 29 October 1922 Garvey spoke on "The Negro—His Greatest Enemy, His Environment, His Rise to Power." In the speech he said, "Do you know that the educated Negro today unconsciously is the greatest danger to this race of ours? Why? Because he has imbibed the education of the other fellow without first preparing himself for leadership. He has prepared himself with an education, an environment that was not his, and he has failed to grasp the vision of his race. He has failed to fit himself with that vision that will lead his people in the right way" (*NW*, 4 November 1922).

Marcus Garvey to William Phillips

New York City, Nov. 9, 1922

Dear Mr. Phillips:

This letter introduces to you Mr. Esau Ramus,[1] up to recently, 3rd Vice President of the Philadelphia Division.

Mr. Ramus is going to live in New Orleans and desires to work in the interest of the Association. I ask that you be good enough to help him in whatsoever way you can to serve the Association. I will appreciate it very much if you can find some organizing work for him to do for the Division in going around enlisting new members and helping generally. I have the honor to be, Your obedient servant,

MARCUS GARVEY
President General
Universal Negro Improvement Association

DJ-FBI, file 61-50-195. TL, transcript.

1. When questioned by Bureau of Investigation agents in New York on 23 February 1923, Ramus, who also used the names John Jefferies, Jeffries, and Prince, said that he was born in St. Kitts, BWI, and came to the United States in 1910. He first arrived in Boston, but then went to New York, where he joined the UNIA after hearing Garvey speak on a street corner. He eventually moved to Philadelphia, where he joined the UNIA and was employed at the local Liberty Hall as a janitor. Using the name Jefferies, Ramus attended the 1922 UNIA convention as a delegate; later in the year he went to New Orleans allegedly in order to organize a police department for the local UNIA division. He testified that there were between thirty and thirty-five men on the force and that their purpose was to keep order at local UNIA meetings. Shortly after this, Rev. J.W.H. Eason was assassinated, and Ramus was arrested in Detroit. When New Orleans officials refused to request his extradition, New York police enforced an outstanding warrant for his arrest on charges of felonious assault and robbery. He was convicted and served his sentence at Clinton Prison in Dannemora, N.Y., from which he was released on parole on 16 June 1926. In 1942 Ramus wrote to the bureau claiming to have invented a method of preventing torpedoes from hitting American ships (DJ-FBI, file 61-54-175).

Baron Emile de Cartier de Marchienne,
Belgian Ambassador, Washington, D.C.,
to Henri Jaspar

Belgian Embassy, Washington, D.C.
11 November 1922

RE: "NEGRO WORLD," ETC.

Following on from our report No. 1638/654, 27 October, enclosed please find:

1. Extract from the "New York Age," of 21 October 1922, containing interesting information on the U.N.I.A.;[1] the author of the article lets us know who is on the "Literary Staff" of the "Negro World" and the "Daily Negro Times." The "New York Age" announced in a previous issue that Marcus Garvey spent $10,000 to purchase a new press needed for the publication of the "Daily Negro Times." The author also gives information on the financial situation of the U.N.I.A. He adds that information was provided *by the treasurer* of this association: the U.N.I.A.'s bank balance on the 31st July 1922 was $20,888.24, of which $19,667.05 belonged to reserve funds.

2. Copy of the "Negro World" of 4 November. In previous speeches Marcus Garvey always puts Negroes on guard against whites, who, he says, will always be enemies of the Negro race. In his speech on 29 October at Liberty Hall, he states that the greatest enemy of the Negro is not the white but the Negro himself.

There is a lot of truth in these words. The well educated Negro hardly enjoys the company of his Harlem brothers who do not have the same standard of education. He seeks the company of whites, to improve himself from contact with them, be it to take place in their industry or their commerce.

Moreover, the Negro commercial and industrial enterprises are of so little importance that they do not offer him the opportunity of realizing his ambitions. And so Marcus Garvey would like all Negroes, who have had the opportunity of education, to devote themselves to the cause of their race, but to beware of contact with the white race.

Despite repeated efforts to find the "Negro World" on different newsstands in the Negro quarter, our Consulate General in New York has been unable to obtain a copy of the 28 October issue of the "Negro World."

[BARON DE CARTIER DE MARCHIENNE][2]

SAMAE, file no. 843/1710/687. TLS, recipient's copy (translated from French).

1. The article was entitled "Marcus Garvey the Man: An Intimate Study of a Leader's Personality" (*New York Age*, 21 October 1922).

2. Baron Emile de Cartier de Marchienne (1871–1946) was named ambassador to the United States in 1919, serving in this post until 1923. De Cartier was the Belgian delegate to the Washington

Conference of 1921–1922 and a member of the Belgian delegation at the 1925 conference for the regulation of Belgian war debts. In 1927 he was appointed ambassador to London, where he served until his death in 1946.

The Belgian government, concerned about the impact of the UNIA on its African colonies, followed Garvey's activities closely. De Cartier received regular reports of UNIA activity, and in 1921 he attempted to take out a subscription to the *Negro World*. In 1921 the Ministry of Colonies requested that de Cartier not sign any passports for blacks without first consulting the minister of foreign affairs in Brussels (G. De Klerck, director general, Belgian Ministry of Foreign Affairs, to Robert A. Hill, 28 October 1983; SAMAE, file 10183, memorandum to de Cartier, 20 April 1921; SAMAE, file 10185, de Cartier to Henri Jaspar, 18 May 1921; Jane K. Miller, *Belgian Foreign Policy Between Two Wars, 1919–1940* [New York: Bookman Associates, 1951]).

Speech by Marcus Garvey

[[LIBERTY HALL, New York, Nov. 12, 1922]]

My subject for tonight is "The International Attitude Toward the Negro." Prof. Ferris touched on a very significant and important matter which I spoke on myself this afternoon—about the banning of Siki not only in France but in England.[1] I am myself not interested in prize-fighting and probably if it were for me there would be very little collecting at the ring or at the door where the fight is on; so I am not interested in Siki from the pugilistic viewpoint, but I am interested in him from the racial viewpoint. Things that confirm the policy of the Universal Negro Improvement Association are things that we should draw your attention to as they do occur.

THE ATTITUDE OF OTHER PEOPLE
TOWARDS THE NEGRO

We have been preaching through our entire existence the attitude of the other people towards us and stating that attitude was not only domestic, but that attitude was international, and those who believed in our viewpoint joined the Universal Negro Improvement Association. Those who do not believe in our viewpoint keep out of the association and indulge in severe criticism of the movement. We have often heard even among ourselves that the English are more kindly disposed toward the Negro than the Americans and that the French are more liberal to the Negro than the English. We have heard that all over the world that the English people are better in dealing with the Negro than the American people, but we have always held to the opinion that there was absolutely no difference between the Englishman and the Frenchman and the American when it comes to the race. That has been always our attitude and those of you who have followed me in my speeches long enough and have taken note of all that I have said will recall years ago when I said that the attitude of France toward the Negro as against the American is simply because the French do not come in direct contact with the situation as the American does and also the English do not come in contact with the situation as the

American does, and that only accounts for the difference as against the attitude of the American. If you would transport 12,000,000 Negroes from America to England you would have the same lynching and burning in places like London and Manchester as we have in Texas and Georgia and Mississippi and Alabama, and if we would transport them to France we would have lynching and burning in places like Paris and Bordeaux as we have in the States of the United States of America I have mentioned, and more and more as the Negro comes in direct contact with European civilization we are getting to realize the truth of that statement made by us years ago. The truth of that belief has driven us into close association and kinship in the Universal Negro Improvement Association.

As to Siki

Now what of the matter of Siki? It happened that a few weeks ago a black man from Senegal was brought in a pugilistic combat with a white man from France by the name of Carpentier. Carpentier was then regarded as the light-heavyweight champion of Europe, and there was very little belief that Carpentier would have lost out to this black man from Senegal, because he was not properly trained, and they did not believe he could whip this white man. They thought this white man would have had an easy time, and for the sake of making money some of the promoters of the ring got this black Senegalese to sign up with Carpentier, believing that Carpentier would have an easy walkover.[2] It happened to the contrary. This black man knocked out Carpentier and knocked him out hopelessly (applause), and then after the knocking out was done France found out her mistake. They promoted the game for what was in the game, and everybody because of the reputation of Carpentier thought that Carpentier would have come out the victor. But the thing turned the other way, and then France suddenly saw her mistake—that a black man was allowed to knock out a white man in Europe and in a country that held millions of black men as slaves and as serfs. The psychology of the thing was that France allowed a black man from Africa—a man who was not regarded as a full man—a man who was not regarded as being entitled to any consideration at all, a man whom they said was just next door to the ape or the monkey—they allowed that man to go to Europe and knock down a white man and keep him down, looking over him. (Applause.)

The Psychology of the Affair

It was not as much the fight between the two men, but it was the psychology of having a white man down and a black man up looking in his face after knocking him down. Then all of a sudden Europe went in an uproar. England was very mad; Italy was mad. The whole continent immediately took fire. America was mad, because from the time of Jack Johnson America had made up her mind that she never would allow a black man to knock out a white man for the championship of anything, and that is why in America we had such a hard time in getting a match between Wills and Dempsey.[3] In America that is why we had the hounding of Jack Johnson, not that Johnson had committed a crime worse than any other man, because men in higher positions than Jack Johnson committed greater crimes than he had committed. Some of the very men who convicted Jack Johnson might have committed worse crimes against society. It was not that Johnson had so much outraged society, because he had not outraged society more than Rev. Hall (applause), but Jack Johnson had committed a crime of knocking out a white man and winning the heavyweight championship of the world. They had to find some excuse to get rid of Johnson to restore the championship to the white man, because they could not allow a Negro to hold such an honor, as it would make the Negro realize that he is really a man. You know no monkey can knock down a man. (Laughter.) It takes a man to knock down a man, and it does not only take a man but it takes a superior man to knock down a man. (Applause.) So when Johnson knocked them out he had declared for the superiority physically of the Negro race. They could not afford that; they could not allow that.

Well, America had her lesson, and she decided that it would not happen again, and she made all kinds of laws within the ring to regulate it so that even the government should have a say in who should fight,[4] so that no adventurer could come along and match any Negro against any white man with the chance of the black man whipping the white man. America said that she would not allow a black man another chance to knock out a white man; but France had not the lesson, so some adventurer—just as some adventurer organized the Johnson bout which caused him to become the heavyweight champion of the world—organized this light-heavyweight bout between Siki and Carpentier, and France did not concern herself about it because she had not the experience of America. But the same thing happened in France as happened in America— the black man by his physical prowess and superiority knocked out the white man, and then France found out the same mistake that America did.

Then France sought ways and means of getting rid of Siki. I knew it would come. When I heard of Siki's victory and how he was visiting the cabarets in France, I knew his doom was at hand. That is the white man's way of getting rid of the Negro. They dissipated Siki; they got him drunk and they created an environment by which they could trap him and he fell into it, and the championship that he won and should have maintained, by the plot that they laid for him, they have taken away, just as they have taken it away from Jack Johnson, so that he will never have the chance of fighting anybody as the light-heavyweight champion of Europe; so that the championship will go back to white men, just as the heavyweight championship of the world has gone back to white men.[5]

FRANCE'S ATTITUDE TOWARD THE NEGRO

And that is France's attitude—France that loves the Negro so. When France found out her mistake, she played the dirty game of tricking Siki. I do not doubt that Siki was drunk when he knocked that manager down, and they tricked him so as to get him to do the thing he did so as to get the opportunity of taking away from him the laurels he had won for his race.

NO PERSONAL REGARD FOR SIKI

Personally I do not give a snap of my fingers for Siki, because to me Siki has lost his pride of race. Any black man who will go out of his way to marry a white woman is a Negro I do not want to see at all.[6] (Applause.) I am interested in Siki not because of Siki himself, but because of the race of which he is a member and could not get away from even though he has offered $50,000 if he could change his color.[7]

However, France's treatment of Siki reveals that the racial attitude of France is no different from the racial attitude of America so far as the black man is concerned. The black race must be kept down in an inferior position. We all knew that it was the attitude of America, but some of us did not believe it was the attitude of France. Now you have it open before you. It is as much the attitude of France as it is of America and as it is of England. Before they took away the championship from Siki, his manager, so as to make more money, arranged a bout with Beckett, an Englishman, for the maintenance of the championship that he had won. The bout was arranged, and let me say that up to that time there was no government regulation in England to prevent black men from fighting white men, but when the English government saw that the same thing would repeat itself in England, they immediately called a conference among themselves and the Secretary for Foreign Affairs (I think) stepped right in and interfered with the arrangements and they made a law that the fight could not come off, and the reason was because they had black subjects in their colonies, and if Siki should lick Beckett they would stick out their chests and it would impair the reputation of England and Englishmen in the colonies.[8]

A SET POSITION FOR THE NEGRO

It means this: That there is a set position for the Negro not only in America, but all over the white world, and any man who flatters himself to believe that his position is one of equality depending upon conditions as they are has a false opinion and a false idea of life. The only position you can keep on equality is that position that you create for yourself, and that brings me back to what I said this afternoon as to how misguided some of our leaders are, believing in the professed friendship of the white man.

A MISINTERPRETATION

Now when I talk about the white man some people misinterpret me and try to make capital out of it to create prejudice against me on the part of the white man. They say I hate the white man. I do not hate the white man, but I do not love anybody better than I love myself. I have to speak of the white man because he is the fellow that this race has to knock up against for its future or present condition. And when I speak of the white man I speak of him in respect because I respect him, because if I were white I would do just what he has done. If I were white, I would do just what he is doing—keep Negroes down; keep everybody down. So I am not blaming him for doing it. I blame the fool who will allow himself to be kept down, and since I am not one of those being kept down the fellow who is keeping me down must be eternally vigilant—he must be always watching because as soon as he turns his back I am going to knock him down. So that when I talk of the white man I do not talk in the spirit of hate. I do not want to encourage the spirit of hate. I love the white man just as much as he loves me. I respect him for his power because power is strength and strength is power. You cannot separate them. The fellow who is strong can maintain his equilibrium and maintain his stand anywhere, but the fellow who is weak is at the mercy of everybody who passes by. So that if this white man is strong and we know it we have to respect him for it, and we are crazy if we think he is going to share that power with us. If you have some secret by which you can enjoy happiness, the moment you impart that secret to somebody else you will be sharing your happiness. So that any man who expects that the white man is going to admit him into his sanctum of happiness and satisfaction makes a big mistake. There is no white man in the world, whether he be the Pope of Rome or the Archbishop of Canterbury, who loves anybody else better than he loves himself or his race, and when it comes down to a question of who shall enjoy or who shall benefit, surely he is going to decide on his own kind. So when we flatter ourselves in America—a large number of us do so as leaders—that the white man is going to be kind to us and help us to become a better people and more prosperous, we are making a tremendous mistake. If we have thought that this man is going to be more considerate of our interests we are making a tremendous mistake because here we have his attitude—an attitude that he must maintain a position of supremacy and dominance—and so long as you assist him in that position he is your friend. When you attempt to draw the line in your own interest you are an enemy to society.

Now, who are the worst Negroes in America? The worst Negroes in America are those who believe that the Negro should fight for himself and do for himself and be independent of the white man. Why? Because such a Negro threatens the supremacy of the white man. But he is the best Negro in America or anywhere else who is willing always to take off his hat and bow before Massa George. That is why Garvey is a bad man and shall be a bad man always, because he is not going to take off his hat and bow and scrape before anybody. I prefer to die than to apologize or compromise for anything where my race is concerned. That is my attitude, and the world knows it. I refuse to bow to any one else but the Christ. I refuse to bow to any other power in the world but the Almighty Architect, the Creator of Mankind. When it comes to man, you could be as white as snow or as black as night, if you expect me to go on the knee you are wrong in your judgment, because I am not going to do it, and the Negro who takes such a stand is a dangerous character and a dangerous member of society. But that is the only thing that will lift a people out of the condition of serfdom and peonage to a position of liberty, freedom and the enjoyment of human rights. If we must go the way, we must go it as men. If we must continue the course of freedom and liberty we must make up our minds as the martyrs and heroes of old who have led the people on to the brighter day of freedom and liberty. Marcus Garvey has no apology to make to man on earth, I do not care where he comes from, let him be British, French, American, because Marcus Garvey is very much grieved at the condition of this race of mine, and the only regret that Marcus Garvey has now [is] that he was not born in the days of slavery, when he would have taken up the sword like Toussaint l'Ouverture to free myself out of a slavery that I did not bring upon myself. Since I was not born in that age, and born in another age, I am going to give some kind of trouble to those who brought me away from my country against my will; and the best thing they can do is to make arrangements to take me back from whence they brought me. (Applause.)

We have now the attitude of England; we have the attitude of France; we have now the attitude of America. Now it is an open book, and it is for you to decide what your attitude shall be. (Applause.)

Printed in *NW*, 18 November 1922. Original headlines omitted.

1. "Battling" Siki, a black Senegalese light-heavyweight boxer, unexpectedly knocked out the French champion, Georges Carpentier, in Paris on 24 September 1922. On 9 November the French Boxing Federation stripped Siki of his title and suspended him for nine months for assaulting Fernand Ouny, a well-known boxing manager. On the same day the British Home Office canceled a projected fight between Siki and the British boxer Joe Beckett, stating that "all sorts of passions are aroused" as a result of "the introduction of the color question" (*New York Age*, 20 September and 19 November 1922; *Times* [London], 17 October and 10 November 1922; *NW*, 30 September, 28 October and 18 November 1922).

2. Although Siki had originally made a prefight agreement to lose the match, during the course of the fight he decided to "go in and win" because he "could not lie down before 50,000 acclaiming me." When the French Boxing Federation suspended Siki and attempted to sue him, the French Senegalese deputy, Blaise Diagne, took the case to the Chamber of Deputies in an attempt to have the funds of the French Boxing Federation suspended. Diagne remarked that "the white man refuses to be reconciled to the idea that the black man may be his equal, either physically or mentally." Diagne's proposal was defeated by a wide margin (*New York Age*, 9 December 1922; *Messenger* 5, no. 1 [January 1923]: 563; *Times* [London], 11 November 1922; *Echo de Paris*, 1 December 1922).

3. Arthur John [*John Arthur*?] "Jack" Johnson (1878–1946) was the world heavyweight boxing champion from 1908 to 1915. Johnson was the first black pugilist to attract widespread publicity, especially after his victory over James J. Jeffries, the "Great White Hope," in 1910. Johnson married a white woman, prompting widespread calls for further legislation banning interracial marriage. In 1913, the fighter was indicted under the federal Mann Act for having transported a woman across state lines for immoral purposes, despite the fact that the law was not in effect when the incident took place (Randy Roberts, *Papa Jack: Jack Johnson and the Era of White Hopes* [New York: Free Press, 1983]). Harry Wills (1889–1958) was the leading black American heavyweight, known as the "Brown Panther." Jack Dempsey (1895–1983), the white heavyweight champion, wanted to fight Wills, but Dempsey's promoter and manager, Ted Rickard, blocked the match. Since Rickard had been accused of "humiliating the white race" by promoting the Johnson-Jeffries fight, he was reluctant to sponsor another interracial bout. He was not alone, however, in opposing the match. William Muldoon of the New York State Athletic Commission opposed the fight on the grounds that it might precipitate a riot. Those with financial interests in the sport claimed that their business would plummet if Dempsey lost, while white New York politicians feared losing black votes if Dempsey won (*NYT*, 22 December 1958; Bob Considine and Bill Slocum, *Dempsey: By the Man Himself* [New York: Simon and Schuster, 1960], pp. 179–184).

4. No laws at the time specifically prohibited boxing matches between white and black fighters.

The 1910 Johnson-Jeffries fight, however, occurred in the midst of a reform movement to ban boxing, and Jeffries' defeat contributed to the efforts to ban the sport. (To the reformers, boxing epitomized a social threat to the established order: it attracted immigrants and blacks, and it was closely linked with Democratic ward politics. Johnson, a black man who openly challenged the racial order of the United States, epitomized both the moral and the social threats that boxing posed.) Prior to the Johnson-Jeffries fight, laws had been passed that banned boxing, but they were often circumvented in practice. Johnson's victory, however, increased support for legislation to ban boxing, which became used as a de facto tool to stop interracial fights.

Following the fight, former president Theodore Roosevelt predicted that with the interracial bout "public sentiment will be so aroused . . . as to guarantee that this is the last prize fight to take place in the United States" (Al-Tony Gilmore, *Bad Nigger!* [London: Kennikat Press, 1975], p. 71). The *Dallas News* recommended that even if boxing itself were not outlawed, interracial bouts be forbidden, because they incited race riots. Moreover, films of the Johnson-Jeffries fight were banned in the United States and abroad. In the ensuing months local ordinances were passed to ban boxing, and although the sport continued illegally, matches between black and white fighters were prevented through selective use of the laws and tacit agreement among the major boxing promoters (Randy Roberts, *Papa Jack: Jack Johnson and the Era of White Hopes*; Bert Sugar, *One Hundred Years of Boxing* [New York: Rutledge Press, 1982], pp. 70–74; John Lardner, *White Hopes and Other Tigers* [Philadelphia: J. B. Lippincott, 1951]; Thomas Elton Foreman, *Discrimination Against the Negro in American Athletics* [San Francisco: R and E Research Associates, 1975]; Jack Johnson, *Jack Johnson: In the Ring and Out* [London: Proteus, 1977]; *NYT*, 29 June, 6 July, 8 July, 13 July and 21 July 1910, 8 July, 9 July and 19 September 1911, 17 January and 9 February 1912; *San Francisco Chronicle*, 19 July 1910).

5. The American press, particularly the *New York Age*, published accounts of Siki's alleged drunkenness while patronizing an American café in Paris. The Americans in the bar apparently objected to Siki being served and later gave Carpentier a warm welcome (*New York Age*, 4 November 1922).

6. The *New York World* made much of Siki's white wife, printing a photograph of the couple with the headline "Siki Victory Forces French Army into Turmoil over Color Line" (*New York Age*, 4 November 1922).

7. The *World* reported that Siki said, "I would give 50,000 francs to be changed into a white man." The *New York Times* and the *Messenger* also printed the story (*World*, 27 September 1922; *NYT*, 27 September 1922; *Messenger*, October 1922, p. 499).

8. Although the British Home Office stopped the 1911 match between Jack Johnson and "Bombadier" Wells, subsequent fights between white and black fighters had been permitted. However, the Home Office forbade the Siki-Beckett fight on the basis that "all sorts of passions" would be aroused "which it is not advisable to excite" among the "large number of men of color within the British Empire" (*NYT*, 14 September 1911, 10 November 1922; Randy Roberts, *Papa Jack*, pp. 126–127).

William Phillips to Marcus Garvey

[*New Orleans*] Nov. 19, 1922

May it please His Excellency. Sir:

I am glad to inform you of the safe arrival of Mr. Esau Ramus.

I wish to assure you that everything possible will be done for him as mentioned in his letter of introduction.

Miss Mary Prince will call at the office for mail for Mr. Ramus, which will be sent in an envelope addressed to you. I remain your humble servant,

WILLIAM PHILLIPS
Exect. Sec'y

DJ-FBI, file 61-50-195. TL, transcript.

[*New Orleans*] Nov. 19, 1922

My Dear Sir:

I am asking that you allow Mr. Ramus to handle as many of the items of the repository as possible[,] along with new constitution, buttons, anthems, etc. on his personal account so as to assist him.

If this suggestion meets with your approval, I suggest that a supply of same be sent him as soon as possible.

I am arranging for him to get in contact with the members by visiting their homes and I think he can do well selling such articles as he can get from the Parent Body. I remain Your Humble Servant,

WILLIAM PHILLIPS
Exect. Sec'y

P.S. Is it possible to give Mr. Ramus a special rate on supplies?

DJ-FBI, file 61-50-195. TL, transcript.

William Phillips to Enid H. Lamos, Secretary to Marcus Garvey

[*New Orleans*] Nov. 21, 1922

My Dear Miss Lamos:

I am writing you in behalf of Mr. Esau Ramus who recently came to New Orleans with letters of recommendation from the President General.

Mr. Ramus is endeavoring to organize a police and secret service unit here but it has not met the approval of the majority of the officers. We need all the units Mr. Ramus has spoken of but we must have an order from the President General in order to minimize the obstacles which usually confront a stranger to this people.

Mr. Garvey has asked that we do everything possible to enable Mr. Ramus to be well taken care of and as it has always been my rule, I am doing so, but I cannot do it well in opposition to the other officers.

I have gone through every obstacle I met here and I am sure I can assist Mr. Ramus in doing the same and eventually succeed, but his position, being different from mine, it is advisable in my opinion to secure an order or a specific request from Mr. Garvey.

I am therefore asking that you take up this matter with the President General and let us hear from you on this matter by return mail. I remain yours fraternally,

WILLIAM PHILLIPS
Exect. Sec'y. New Orleans Div. 149

DJ-FBI, file 61-50-195. TL, transcript.

Speech by Marcus Garvey

[[New York City, U.S.A., November 25, 1922]]

THE PRINCIPLES OF THE
UNIVERSAL NEGRO IMPROVEMENT ASSOCIATION

Over five years ago the Universal Negro Improvement Association placed itself before the world as the movement through which the new and rising Negro would give expression of his feelings. This Association adopts an attitude not of hostility to other races and peoples of the world, but an attitude of self-respect, of manhood rights on behalf of 400,000,000 Negroes of the world.

We represent peace, harmony, love, human sympathy, human rights and human justice, and that is why we fight so much. Wheresoever human rights are denied to any group, wheresoever justice is denied to any group, there the U.N.I.A. finds a cause. And at this time among all the peoples of the world, the group that suffers most from injustice, the group that is denied most of those rights that belong to all humanity, is the black group of 400,000,000. Because of that injustice, because of that denial of our rights, we go forth under the leadership of the One who is always on the side of right to fight the common cause of humanity; to fight as we fought in the Revolutionary War, as we fought in the Civil War, as we fought in the Spanish-American War, and as we fought in the war between 1914–18 on the battle plains of France and Flanders. As we fought up the heights of Mesopotamia; even so under the leadership of the U.N.I.A., we are marshaling the 400,000,000 Negroes of the world to fight for the emancipation of the race and of the redemption of the country of our fathers.

We represent a new line of thought among Negroes. Whether you call it advanced thought or reactionary thought, I do not care. If it is reactionary for people to seek independence in government, then we are reactionary. If it is advanced thought for people to seek liberty and freedom, then we represent the advanced school of thought among the Negroes of this country. We of the U.N.I.A. believe that what is good for the other fellow is good for us. If government is something that is worth while; if government is something that is appreciable and helpful and protective to others, then we also want to experiment in government. We do not mean a government that will make us citizens without rights or subjects without consideration. We mean the kind of government that will place our race in control, even as other races are in control of their own governments.

That does not suggest anything that is unreasonable. It was not unreasonable for George Washington, the great hero and father of the country, to have fought for the freedom of America giving to us this great republic and this great democracy; it was not unreasonable for the Liberals of France to have fought against the Monarchy to give to the world French Democracy and French Republicanism; it was no unrighteous cause that led Tolstoi to sound the call of liberty in Russia, which has ended in giving to the world the social democracy of Russia, an experiment that will probably prove to be a boon and a blessing to mankind. If it was not an unrighteous cause that led Washington to fight for the independence of this country, and led the Liberals of France to establish the Republic, it is therefore not an unrighteous cause for the U.N.I.A. to lead 400,000,000 Negroes all over the world to fight for the liberation of our country.

Therefore the U.N.I.A. is not advocating the cause of church building, because we have a sufficiently large number of churches among us to minister to the spiritual needs of the people, and we are not going to compete with those who are engaged in so splendid a work; we are not engaged in building any new social institutions, and Y.M.C.A.'s or Y.W.C.A.'s[,] because there are enough social workers engaged in those praise-worthy efforts. We are not engaged in politics because we have enough local politicians, Democrats, Socialists, Soviets, etc., and the political situation is well taken care of. We are not engaged in domestic politics, in church building or in social uplift work, but we are engaged in nation building.

MISREPRESENTATIONS

In advocating the principles of this Association we find we have been very much misunderstood and very much misrepresented by men from within our own race, as well as others from without. Any reform movement that seeks to bring about changes for the benefit of humanity is bound to be misrepresented by those who have always taken it upon themselves to administer to, and lead the unfortunate, and to direct those who may be placed under temporary disadvantages. It has been so in all other movements whether social or political; hence those of us in the Universal Negro Improvement Association who lead, do not feel in any way embarrassed about this misrepresentation, about this misunderstanding as far as the Aims and Objects of the Universal Negro Improvement Association go. But those who probably would have taken kindly notice of this great movement, have been led to believe that this movement seeks, not to develop the good within the race, but to give expression to that which is most destructive and most harmful to society and to government.

I desire to remove the misunderstanding that has been created in the minds of millions of peoples throughout the world in their relationship to the organization. The Universal Negro Improvement Association stands for the Bigger Brotherhood; the Universal Negro Improvement Association stands for human rights, not only for Negroes, but for all races. The Universal Negro Improvement Association believes in the rights of not only the black race, but the white race, the yellow race and the brown race. The Universal Negro Improvement Association believes that the white man has as much right to be considered, the yellow man has as much right to be considered, the brown man has as much right to be considered as well as the black man of Africa. In view of the fact that the black man of Africa has contributed as much to the world as the white man of Europe, and the brown man and yellow man of Asia, we of the Universal Negro Improvement Association demand that the white, yellow and brown races give to the black man his place in the civilization of the world. We ask for nothing more than the rights of 400,000,000 Negroes. We are not seeking, as I said before, to destroy or disrupt the society or the government of other races, but we are determined that 400,000,000 of us shall unite ourselves to free our motherland from the grasp of the invader. We of the Universal Negro Improvement Association are determined to unite 400,000,000 Negroes for their own industrial, political, social and religious emancipation.

We of the Universal Negro Improvement Association are determined to unite the 400,000,000 Negroes of the world to give expression to their own feeling; we are determined to unite the 400,000,000 Negroes of the world for the purpose of building a civilization of their own. And in that effort we desire to bring together the 15,000,000 of the United States, the 180,000,000 in Asia, the West Indies and Central and South America, and the 200,000,000 in Africa. We are looking toward political freedom on the continent of Africa, the land of our fathers.

Not Seeking a Government Within a Government

The Universal Negro Improvement Association is not seeking to build up another government within the bounds or borders of the United States of America. The Universal Negro Improvement Association is not seeking to disrupt any organized system of government, but the Association is determined to bring Negroes together for the building up of a nation of their own. And why? Because we have been forced to it. We have been forced to it throughout the world; not only in America, not only in Europe, not only in the British Empire, but wheresoever the black man happens to find himself, he has been forced to do for himself.

To talk about Government is a little more than some of our people can appreciate just at this time. The average man does not think that way, just because he finds himself a citizen or a subject of some country. He seems to say, "Why should there be need for any other government?" We are French, English or American. But we of the U.N.I.A. have studied seriously this question of nationality among Negroes—this American nationality, this British nationality, this French, Italian, or Spanish nationality, and have discovered that it counts for nought when that nationality comes in conflict with the racial idealism of the group that rules. When our interests clash with those of the ruling faction, then we find that we have absolutely no rights. In times of peace, when everything is all right, Negroes have a hard time, wherever we go, wheresoever we find ourselves, getting those rights that belong to us, in common with others whom we claim as fellow citizens; getting that consideration that should be ours by right of the constitution, by right of the law; but in the time of trouble they make us all partners in the cause, as happened in the last war, when we were partners, whether British, French or

American Negroes. And we were told that we must forget everything in an effort to save the nation.

We have saved many nations in this manner, and we have lost our lives doing that before. Hundreds of thousands—nay, millions of black men, lie buried under the ground due to that old-time camouflage of saving the nation. We saved the British empire; we saved the French empire; we saved this glorious country more than once; and all that we have received for our sacrifices, all that we have received for what we have done, even in giving up our lives, is just what you are receiving now, just what I am receiving now.

You and I fare no better in America, in the British empire, or in any other part of the white world; we fare no better than any black man wheresoever he shows his head. And why? Because we have been satisfied to allow ourselves to be led, educated, to be directed by the other fellow, who has always sought to lead in the world in that direction that would satisfy him and strengthen his position. We have allowed ourselves for the last 500 years to be a race of followers, following every race that has led, in the direction that would make them more secure.

The U.N.I.A. is reversing the old-time order of things. We refuse to be followers any more. We are leading ourselves. That means, if any saving is to be done, later on, whether it is saving this one nation or that one government, we are going to seek a method of saving Africa first. Why? And why Africa? Because Africa has become the grand prize of the nations. Africa has become the big game of the nation hunters. To-day Africa looms as the greatest commercial, industrial and political prize in the world.

THE DIFFERENCE BETWEEN THE U.N.I.A. AND OTHER ORGANIZATIONS

The difference between the Universal Negro Improvement Association and the other movements of this country, and probably the world, is that the Universal Negro Improvement Association seeks independence of government, while the other organizations seek to make the Negro a secondary part of existing governments. We differ from the organizations in America because they seek to subordinate the Negro as a secondary consideration in a great civilization, knowing that in America the Negro will never reach his highest ambition, knowing that the Negro in America will never get his constitutional rights. All those organizations which are fostering the improvement of Negroes in the British Empire know that the Negro in the British Empire will never reach the height of his constitutional rights. What do I mean by constitutional rights in America? If the black man is to reach the height of his ambition in this country—if the black man is to get all of his constitutional rights in America—then the black man should have the same chance in the nation as any other man to become president of the nation, or a street cleaner in New York. If the black man in the British Empire is to have all his constitutional rights it means that the Negro in the British Empire should have at least the same right to become premier of Great Britain as he has to become street cleaner in the city of London. Are they prepared to give us such political equality? You and I can live in the United States of America for 100 more years, and our generations may live for 200 years or for 5000 more years, and so long as there is a black and white population, when the majority is on the side of the white race, you and I will never get political justice or get political equality in this country. Then why should a black man with rising ambition, after preparing himself in every possible way to give expression to that highest ambition, allow himself to be kept down by racial prejudice within a country? If I am as educated as the next man; if I am as prepared as the next man, if I have passed through the best schools and colleges and universities as the other fellow, why should I not have a fair chance to compete with the other fellow for the biggest position in the nation? I have feelings, I have blood, I have senses like the other fellow; I have ambition, I have hope. Why should he, because of some racial prejudice, keep me down and why should I concede to him the right to rise above me, and to establish himself as my permanent master? That is where the U.N.I.A. differs from other organizations. I refuse to stultify my ambition, and every true Negro refuses to stultify his ambition to suit any one, and therefore the U.N.I.A. decides if America is not big enough for two presidents, if England is not big enough for two kings, then we are not going to quarrel over the matter; we will leave one president in America, we will leave one king in England, we will leave one president in France and we will have one president in Africa. Hence, the Universal Negro Improvement Association does not seek to interfere with the social and political systems of France, but by the arrangement of things to-day the U.N.I.A. refuses to recognize any political or social system in Africa except that which we are about to establish for ourselves.

NOT PREACHING HATE

We are not preaching a propaganda of hate against anybody. We love the white man; we love all humanity, because we feel that we cannot live without the other. The white man is as necessary to the existence of the Negro as the Negro is necessary to his existence. There is a common relationship that we cannot escape. Africa has certain things that Europe wants, and Europe has certain things that Africa wants, and if a fair and square deal must bring white and black with each other, it is impossible for us to escape it. Africa has oil, diamonds, copper, gold and rubber and all the minerals that Europe wants, and there must be some kind of relationship between Africa and Europe for a fair exchange, so we cannot afford to hate anybody.

NEGROES EVER READY TO ASSIST HUMANITY'S CAUSE

The question often asked is what does it require to redeem a race and free a country? If it takes man power, if it takes scientific intelligence, if it takes education of any kind, or if it takes blood, then the 400,000,000 Negroes of the world have it.

It took the combined manpower of the Allies to put down the mad determination of the Kaiser to impose German will upon the world and upon humanity. Among those who suppressed his mad ambition were two million Negroes who have not yet forgotten how to drive men across the firing line. Surely those of us who faced German shot and shell at the Marne, at Verdun, have not forgotten the order of our Commander-in-Chief. The cry that caused us to leave America in such mad haste, when white fellow citizens of America refused to fight and said, "We do not believe in war and therefore, even though we are American citizens, and even though the nation is in danger, we will not go to war." When many of them cried out and said, "We are German-Americans and we cannot fight," when so many white men refused to answer to the call and dodged behind all kinds of excuses, 400,000 black men were ready without a question. It was because we were told it was a war of democracy; it was a war for the liberation of the weaker peoples of the world. We heard the cry of Woodrow Wilson, not because we liked him so, but because the things he said were of such a nature that they appealed to us as men. Wheresoever the cause of humanity stands in need of assistance, there you will find the Negro ever ready to serve.

He has done it from the time of Christ up to now. When the whole world turned its back upon the Christ, the man who was said to be the Son of God; when the world cried out "Crucify Him," when the world spurned Him and spat upon Him, it was a black man, Simon, the Cyrenian, who took up the cross. Why? Because the cause of humanity appealed to him. When the black man saw the suffering Jew, struggling under the heavy cross, he was willing to go to His assistance, and he bore that cross up to the heights of Calvary. In the spirit of Simon, the Cyrenian, 1900 years ago, we answered the call of Woodrow Wilson, the call of a larger humanity, and it was for that that we willingly rushed into the war from America, from the West Indies, over 100,000; it was for that that we rushed into the war from Africa, 2,000,000 of us. We met in France, Flanders and in Mesopotamia. We fought unfalteringly. When the white men faltered and fell back on their battle lines, at the Marne and at Verdun, when they ran away from the charge of the German hordes, the black hell fighters stood before the cannonade, stood before the charge, and again they shouted, "There will be a hot time in the old town to-night."

We made it so hot a few months after our appearance in France and on the various battle fronts, we succeeded in driving the German hordes across the Rhine, and driving the Kaiser out of Germany, and out of Potsdam into Holland. We have not forgotten the prowess of war. If we have been liberal minded enough to give our life's blood in France, in Mesopotamia and elsewhere, fighting for the white man, whom we have always assisted, surely we have not forgotten to fight for ourselves, and when the time comes that the world will again give Africa an opportunity for freedom, surely 400,000,000 black men will march out on the battle plains of Africa, under the colors of the red, the black and the green.

We shall march out, yes, as black American citizens, as black British subjects, as black French citizens, as black Italians or as black Spaniards, but we shall march out with a greater loyalty, the loyalty of race. We shall march out in answer to the cry of our fathers, who cry out to us for the redemption of our own country, our motherland, Africa.

We shall march out, not forgetting the blessings of America. We shall march out, not forgetting the blessings of civilization. We shall march out with a history of peace before and behind us, and surely that history shall be our breastplate, for how can man fight better than knowing that the cause for which he fights is righteous? How can man fight more gloriously than by knowing that behind him is a history of slavery, a history of bloody carnage and massacre inflicted upon a race because of its inability to protect itself and fight? Shall we not fight for the glorious opportunity of protecting and forever more establishing ourselves as a mighty race and nation, never more to be disrespected by men[?] Glorious shall be the battle when the time comes to fight for our people and our race.

We should say to the millions who are in Africa to hold the fort, for we are coming 400,000,000 strong.

Printed in *P&O*, 2: 93–100.

Article by Marcus Garvey

[*Negro World*, 25 November 1922]

THE WORLD AS IT IS
"NEGRO TIMES" TO "HEW TO THE LINE"

The publication of The Daily Negro Times was suspended for three weeks for the purpose of installing new machinery to accommodate its continuous output. During the time of readjustment the malicious and wicked weeklies that have been fighting the Universal Negro Improvement Association for the last two years seized the opportunity of publishing broadcast the falsehood that the paper was permanently suspended, which report has caused a great deal of annoyance through the many inquiries that have been made as to its truthfulness.

The Daily Negro Times is to fill a great gap in Negro journalism. Unfortunately, we cannot recommend the colored press for its honesty and truthfulness in racial and public matters. The average colored newspaperman will sell his best friend in exchange for the dollar. He has absolutely no principle nor policy, and that accounts for the many vicious attacks that have been made upon the Universal Negro Improvement Association and its allied interests. Ninety per cent. of the colored newspapers have been subsidized to keep up the malicious and wicked propaganda against the most progressive Negro movement of the 20th century. The Daily Negro Times will be used for the purpose of honestly defending the rights of the race, as well as of educating our people to the higher standards of our civilization.

Unfortunately the Negro journalist stepped into the most important profession in the moulding of public sentiment, and in the educating of the human race, like the ante-bellum Negro preacher who started to save souls and preach religion without being able to conjugate a verb, or to read intelligently a passage of the Holy Scriptures; hence, they have absolutely no regard for the ethics of the profession. They care nothing about principles or policies, and that is why the opinion of the average Negro newspaper can be bought at any price, from 50 cents up.

The Daily Negro Times will always maintain the policy as enunciated in our first issue, and now that we again make our appearance our friends and well-wishers[,] as well as the public at large, will expect us to "hew to the line."

MARCUS GARVEY

Printed in *NW*, 25 November 1922.

Article in the *Crisis*

[November 1922]

"SEE WHAT GARVEY HAS DONE"

In a circular recently thrown about Harlem, Messrs. Pickens, Bagnall and Owen and others were severely criticized for attacking a great man and after asserting that none of these men had done anything, the circular ended with "See What Garvey Has Done!"

Well, let us see.

In a supplementary proceedings examination of Marcus Garvey held in the Supreme Court of Bronx County, New York City, August 19, Mr. Garvey made the following statements under oath:

(Italics are ours.)

Q. Can you tell me at this time whether or not the Black Star Line owns and operates any boats? A. It has interest in *one boat that is floundered at Antilla, Cuba*.

Q. By floundered, do you mean it is wrecked? A. Yes, *it is no use*. It cannot be reached from where it is.[1]

Q. Who controls that boat? A. The Black Star Line, but other people have interest in it. *Our interest is mortgaged*. The National Drydock has interest in the boat and the Massachusetts Bonding Company.

Q. What is the extent of the interest of the National Drydock Company? A. I believe $4,000 or $5,000.

Q. And the extent of the Massachusetts Bonding Company? A. I believe it is $15,000 or $20,000, I am not sure.

Q. What is the value of the boat? A. Well, the appraised value on the last statement given to me was $5,000.

Q. What is the name of this boat? A. *S.S. Kanawha. . . .*[2]

Q. *Does the Company own any other boats at the present time? A. No.*

Q. Did you own the *S.S. Yarmouth?* A. Yes.

Q. What happened to it? A. It was libeled by the National Drydock Company and held by the United States Marshall for about $1,800.

Q. And do you own and operate any other boat at the present time? A. No. We have interest in a boat called the *Shady Side, which is a wreck.*

Q. Where is this wreck? A. It is somewhere in New York Harbor; I do not know the exact location now. . . . You see, *we purchased [the] boat off Leon Swift for $35,000, on which we paid, I believe, $16,000. Our interest in it has been mortgaged* to a bonding company and individuals.[3]

Q. What is the extent of the mortgage, Mr. Garvey? A. The extent of the mortgage is $16,000. . . .

Q. Should this matter be settled, how much money would the Black Star Line receive individually? A. The Black Star Line would not receive anything, because its interest is mortgaged to others to cover liabilities. . . .

Q. Has the Black Star Line any accounts outstanding? A. *No, it has no outstanding accounts.*

Q. *Does anybody owe any money to the Black Star Line? A. No. . . .*

Q. What was the capital stock of the Black Star Line? A. $10,000,000.

Q. Any paid-up stock? A. About $900,000. . . .

Q. *Is the Black Star Line doing any business at the present time? A. No, no business. . . .*

Q. Has the Black Star Line any bank account? A. Yes, it has; but it is attached.

Q. Who attached your bank account? A. The National Drydock Company.

Q. Did you owe them any money? A. Yes, it is alleged that we owe them $45,000.

Q. How much did they attach? A. *We only had $500 in the bank.* . . .

Q. The Black Star Line has no funds at that bank at the present time? A. *No, they haven't.*

Q. No other money whatsoever? A. No.

Q. Has the Black Star Line any money in any other bank? A. No other money in any other bank. . . .

Q. Do you know where the books of the corporation are at the present time? A. *They are at the Department of Justice.* . . .

Q. Has anybody any access to these books? A. I do not know. The Department of Justice controls them.

Q. *Has the Black Star Line at any time paid any dividends? A. No, never.*

Q. *Do you know when the Insurance Company money had been assigned to the various creditors?* A. No, I do not.

Q. How long ago had it been assigned? A. *Almost two years.* . . .

Q. Has the Black Star Line any property whatsoever at the present time?
A. It has property in its name, but it is all mortgaged.

Q. What property is that? A. At 56 West 135th Street. . . .

Q. What do you mean by the property being all mortgaged? A. Well, there are three mortgages on it, first, second and third.

Q. Who holds the first mortgage? A. Some outside corporation. The secretary can give you the name of that corporation.

Q. And who owns the second mortgage? A. The second mortgage is owned by the person we bought the property from.

Q. And who owns the third? A. The Universal Negro Improvement Association. . . .

Q. For what consideration was this third mortgage given? A. The Universal Negro Improvement Association loaned the Black Star Line money.

Q. How much money did they loan? A. $10,000.

Q. Was that in cash or in the form of services? A. Cash.

Q. Did that money actually go into the treasury of the Black Star Line?
A. Yes.

Q. *How long ago was this money borrowed? A. Within two years.*

Q. Has the Universal Negro Improvement Association received any of its money in return? A. No, it has not.

Q. Has the Black Star Line paid any interest on that loan?
A. No. . . .

Q. What is the present indebtedness of the Black Star Line?
A. Approximately $200,000.

Q. What are the assets of the Black Star Line? A. There are no assets.

Q. What is the equity in this building at 56 West 135th Street? A. Well, we have no equity, because it is all mortgaged. *Even if the building were to be sold we would not get anything because the mortgage is out of our control.* . . .

Q. Are there any other judgments outstanding against the Black Star Line? A. Yes.

Q. Name them. A. *There are so many I cannot name them. There are judgments from the crew, aggregating about $40,000.* That is, I am giving you what I can remember. *We have several wage cases aggregating about $20,000. Also the Green River Distilling Company libel for $52,000.*

Printed in the *Crisis* 25, no. 1 (November 1922): 34–36.

1. A reference to the *Kanawha*. See Henry C. Von Struve, U. S. consul, Antilla, Cuba, to Black Star Line, New York, 1 September 1921, *Garvey Papers* 4: 5–7.

2. Ellipses throughout are in the original document.

3. Leon Swift held a mortgage for $25,000. The names of other mortgagees have not been uncovered (*BSL and Leon Swift* v. *Baltica Insurance Co. et al.*, N.Y. Supreme Court, 27 August 1926, plaintiff exhibit no. 3, p. 765).

Luc Dorsinville to the Editor, *Crisis*

[[Port-au-Prince, Haiti, ca. November 1922]]

In your article appearing in the September, 1922, issue of THE CRISIS you say that there has been a great deal of discussion as to who was responsible for the loss of the freight which I had prepared for the S.S. Yarmouth of the Black Star Line; freight whose value mounted up to around $30,000.

I am in a position to assure you that all the blame in this affair falls upon the management of the Black Star Line, which was very bad, and upon the ship's crew, which was the most undisciplined that I have ever seen in my life.

The *Tribunal de Paix* (law court) in the northern section of Port-au-Prince condemned last year the Black Star Line in an action which a passenger, Malval, had brought against the Line; the judge in Chambers of the Lower Court of Port-au-Prince rendered judgment against the Black Star Line; the Lower Court itself of Port-au-Prince likewise condemned the management of the Black Star Line and all three judgments particularly pointed out that I personally was absolved from any fault.

LUC DORSINVILLE

Printed in the *Crisis* 25, no. 1 (November 1922): 36.

Enid H. Lamos to William Phillips

New York City Dec. 2, 1922

My dear Mr. Phillips:

Your several letters regarding Mr. Ramus have been receive[d] and I have to thank you for same.

We are glad to know that he arrived safely in New Orleans, and that you will do all in your power to help him.

Regarding the police and secret service units that Mr. Ramus is endeavoring to organize in your division I have to advise that he was very successful in Philadelphia when he organized these units. I have no doubt if he was permitted to do the same thing in New Orleans that he would be very successful, still I have no authority to authorize the organization of such units, and inasmuch as Mr. Garvey is away from the city I would have to wait until his return so that he could send you the authority for doing so.

Regarding the matter of supplies I have taken that up with the Secretary-General's Department, they have promised to give me an answer today. We hope you will continue doing all you can to assist Mr. Ramus as it is our desire that he continue work in the cause of the Association as he has always done.

With very best wishes for the continued success of your division, we remain Yours fraternally,

Universal Negro Improvement Association
E. H. LAMOS
Secretary to President-General

DJ-FBI, file 61-50-195. TL, transcript.

Article in the *Omaha New Era*

[[New York City, Dec. 2, 1922]]

SHERIFF THROWS GARVEY'S STUFF
INTO STREETS

The branch office of the U.N.I.A., the defunct "Daily Negro Times" and the monthly "Blackman,"[1] which has not appeared as yet although Garvey announced it for publication in September, located at 504 Lenox Avenue[,] was closed by the sheriff last week and the office furniture placed on the sidewalk.

During the convention last August, Mr. Garvey rented the store which is less than a block from his main office and placed flaming red-lettered signs in the window announcing that a new enterprise would be located there. Less than two months after actually occupying the "branch office" he and his office were incontinently thrown out for inability to pay the $250.00 monthly rent due the white landlord.

CLOSE RESTAURANT TOO

The restaurant at 73 West 135th Street has also been forced to close its doors. No reason has as yet been given by Mr. Garvey, and probably none will be forthcoming. The apparent fact is that ever since Garvey's flirtation with the Ku Klux Klan and his advocacy of its plan for a white man's country in the United States, the few thousands of members who had weathered the failure of the Black Star Line and the many evidences of bad business management have been steadily dropping away.

With the closing of three of his "businesses" in Harlem in less than a week many of his followers are losing faith in the "Negro Moses" whom they were forme[r]ly wont to describe as "a man sent by God to redeem the race."

Printed in the *Omaha New Era*, 8 December 1922.

1. Two later publications edited by Garvey eventually bore this title. The *Blackman*, a daily newspaper, was published in Jamaica from 30 March 1929 until 14 February 1931. Garvey's last publication, *The Black Man*, a monthly magazine, first appeared in December 1933 in Jamaica. He moved the magazine with him to London in 1935 and edited its last issue in the summer of 1939 (*The Black Man: A Monthly Magazine of Negro Thought and Opinion*, ed. and comp. Robert A. Hill [Millwood, N.Y.: Kraus-Thomson Organization, 1975], pp. 5–6).

Speech by Marcus Garvey

[[New York, December 11, 1922]]

THE PRESENT POSITION OF THE NEGRO

. . . What is the present position of the Negro in the world? In his relationship to other races and nations he is still discounted and discarded. Wheresoever we turn, whether to America or to France or England, or any of the controlling nations, we find the same attitude when it comes to a question of our rights. But recently we had a fair example in the Senate of the United States when an association known as the National Association for the Advancement of Colored People made an effort for getting the highest legislative body in the nation to pass a law making lynching of human beings a crime against the nation, a crime against humanity. When the bill was brought up before the supreme body of the nation, what did they do? They blockaded the bill and destroyed all hope of its passage, proving to us just what we of the Universal Negro Improvement Association knew all along, that it is a lost hope to have faith and confidence in the white man's government; proving that it is a mistake for any race to place their hope in an alien race for the adjustment of the wrongs that affect the race. We of the Universal Negro Improvement Association advise that no such confidence be placed in any other race but ourselves. We knew all along that when it came to the supreme test that neither the American Government, [n]or the French Government, [n]or the English Government would do anything against themselves or against their people for the interest of Negroes or for the interest of any race that seeks freedom or liberty at the hands of the people that oppress them. We therefore say that the only hope of the Negro is that of creating a government of his own. The question nationally as it affects us here in America is a very serious one. It has become more serious from the failure of the Dyer Anti-Lynching bill. It places us in a very unfavorable position, in that those of you who have been following the history of the Dyer Anti-Lynching bill will recollect that the National Association for the Advancement of Colored People conducted certain propaganda in their effort to pass the bill and adopted methods that were calculated to offend the present government or the people who constitute the government.

You remember that during the last election they issued a threat not only to the President of the United States, but to the Senators and Congressmen who were seeking election, that if they did not vote for the Dyer Anti-Lynching bill that the National Association for the Advancement of Colored People would see to it that they were not returned to the Senate or to Congress,[1] making the issue one of either supporting the Dyer Anti-Lynching bill or making up their minds to go down to defeat before the electors. That was the threat held out by the men who represented the National Association for the

Advancement of Colored People. The association thus brought out that the Negro constituted a balance of power politically. At no time in the history of America was the white man willing to admit the Negro as a political entity, as a political power, as a political factor to be reckoned with. During the time of the emancipation or immediately after, when the Negro was given the vote in the South,[2] it was done without previous calculation as to how it would effect the white man in his relations with the black man. The question of emancipation was an accident and a matter of the moment, and Abraham Lincoln, in signing the Emancipation Proclamation, laid the foundation for admitting 4,000,000 black men to full citizenship in the country. The majority of these black men were to be found in the slave States. Lincoln did not calculate on the political consequences which would result from giving the Negro political rights co-equal with the white man. The Negro was called upon by his compatriots and by the political exploiters of the other race to use his ballot not only to his own advantage but to the disadvantage of those who liberated him because of the capital that could be made out of it. The result was that hundreds of Negroes were elected to the State Legislatures and Assemblies as well as to the National Legislature of the country. Owing to the Negroes having elected their representatives to the different legislative assemblies of the States and of the nation, the eyes of the white people were opened up to the great menace. The result was that in the period of a couple of years the white people of the South were able to devise ways and means by which they could pass laws depriving the Negro of his political power, and the vote was taken away from him and has not been restored.[3] The North was not interested because at that time the North had no similiar problem. The majority of our people were in the South, hence the North had no need to resort to such measures in depriving the Negro of his vote. What has happened? The Negro has transferred his residence from the South to the North, and in the big Northern and Western industrial communities we find large bodies of Negroes established. In New York, where ten or twenty years ago we had 10,000 Negroes, today we have 150,000; in Chicago, where we had about 50,000, we have 125,000 Negroes; in Philadelphia, where we had a few Negroes, we have nearly 100,000, and in many of the big cities of the North and Northwest, where we had no Negro population, we now have a Negro population ranging from 50,000 to 150,000. In these respective centers we started just a few years ago to seek representation in the Legislatures, and in New York and Chicago we were able to elect Negroes to the city councils and State Legislatures.[4]

The question was local and the problem of the Negro and his voting power was only local. But what has happened? For the purpose of getting the Dyer Anti-Lynching bill passed—whether the National Association for the Advancement of Colored People was in earnest or not—I believe they were not in earnest as I will explain later on. They raised a great national howl, and made every Congressman and every Senator throughout the nation to understand that the Negro in the North had constituted himself a political power, a political factor, and that no Senator or no Congressman could continue his career except with the good will of the Negro. No white man is going to stand for that. What has happened, therefore? The turning down of the Dyer Anti-Lynching bill in the Senate was but an act of resentment on the part of the Legislators of this country to prove to the Negro that they were not going to pass anything on the threat of our race.

The Negro Problem a National Issue

What is going to happen? Where the problem of the Negro politically was a local issue they have made it a national issue, and Marcus Garvey prophesies that unless we take steps to change things, that in the next few years the Negro in the North will be in the same condition as the Negro in the South in respect to his vote, for the simple reason that the National Association for the Advancement of Colored People has opened up the eyes of the big politicians of the nation to the danger of having the Negro the balance of power in politics.

Is the N.A.A.C.P. an Honest Organization?

Now the question comes whether the National Association of the Advancement of Colored People is an honest organization towards Negroes or not? And Marcus Garvey maintains the opinion that it is not honest in its intention. I believe that the National Association for the Advancement of Colored People staged the act of this Dyer Anti-Lynching bill for the results they were going to have. You will say, how is that and they are an organization organized for the advancement of Negroes? The motive of this organization as I can see is this: As you all know the National Association for the Advancement of Colored People is an organization that is controlled by white executives. The president is a white man, the treasurer is a white man, the chairman of the Board of Directors is a white man, many of the vice-presidents are white men; until recently the secretary was a white man. It was not until the Universal Negro Improvement Association started to criticize them, and when their white secretary was assaulted down in Texas that they changed the secretary from a white man to a colored man and the only executive officer who is a colored man is the secretary.[5] All the executive officers are white men and white women.

The N.A.A.C.P. a Subterfuge

Now what is the object of it? The object of it is this: that this National Association for the Advancement of Colored People is not a Southern institution; it was of Northern origin, but when the South found out its mistake—the mistake of Lincoln in emancipating four million Negroes to full citizenship with the power of the ballot and then the North saw what had happened in the South in depriving the Negro of the use of the ballot, the North regretted its act of fighting for the freedom of the Negro, but it was too late. The North therefore sought to devise some ways and means of circumventing the Negro, and the way they decided to do it was by the formation of an organization to which Negroes would look as the only rock of hope and that these white people would get control of such an organization under the disguise of philanthropy. They would get hold of that organization and make Negroes believe that it was only through this organization that they could enjoy all the rights which they want. And they so arranged it that they were able to get the influence desired.

More Lynchings Have Occurred

That association has been fighting lynching for thirteen years, and every year more people have been lynched.[6] They have been talking about social equality, and they have drawn the line of prejudice more and more every year. That organization has been talking about political rights, and we find out now that year after year they are redistricting those districts where Negroes have the balance of power in politics.[7] That is what we have got through the advocacy of the National Association for the Advancement of Colored People. It is nothing else but the trick of the white man to control the rising ambition of the Negro.

If the National Association were in earnest about the Dyer Anti-Lynching bill they never would have gone about it in the way they went, but they went about it that way because they knew they would arouse the suspicion of the great politicians who are directing the destinies of the country, and at this time I know that such politicians are devising ways and means by which in another few years every Negro will be deprived of his ballot in the North even as the Southern Negro has been deprived of his ballot. . . .

Printed in *NW*, 23 December 1922. Original headlines omitted.

1. By 1921 the NAACP had dropped legal and ethical arguments in its campaign to obtain congressional support for the Dyer antilynching bill. In November NAACP secretary James Weldon Johnson sent letters to congressmen with a thinly veiled warning that opposition to the bill would cost them black votes in the upcoming elections. At its 1922 annual conference, the NAACP publicly pledged it would "punish" those who opposed the bill, and advertisements were taken out in major newspapers to this effect. As the final vote on the bill approached, Johnson flooded first the House and then the Senate with telegrams emphasizing that black voters "could not be expected to overlook or excuse" any who voted against the bill (*Crisis* 25, no. 3 [January 1923]: 119). In Delaware, New Jersey, Wisconsin, and Michigan the NAACP actively campaigned against local congressmen who voted against the bill. The *Crisis* claimed that black voters were responsible for the defeat of five anti-Dyer congressmen (*NYT*, 2 March and 24 June 1922; *Crisis* 25, no. 3 [January 1923]: 117–119; Ira Katznelson, *Black Men, White Cities* [London: Oxford University Press, 1973], pp. 56–61; Bernard Ersenberg, "James Weldon Johnson and the National Association for the Advancement of Colored People, 1916–1934" [Ph.D. diss., Columbia University, 1968]; Robert L. Zangrando, *The NAACP Crusade Against Lynching, 1909–1950* [Philadelphia: Temple University Press, 1980], pp. 51–72).

2. The Fifteenth Amendment, ratified in 1870, banned denial of suffrage on the basis of race (Kenneth M. Stampp, *The Era of Reconstruction: 1865–1877* [New York: Alfred A. Knopf, 1978], p. 142).

3. After Radical Reconstruction in the South came to an end in 1877, white Democrats devised ways of limiting black political participation. These techniques included intimidation, gerrymandering, and outright fraud. Though the number of black voters dwindled, they played a significant role in southern politics for some years. From 1870 to 1901 the South elected 22

black representatives to Congress; a full 15 percent of southern public officials were black (Arthur Link et al., *The American People: A History* [Arlington Heights, Ill.: AHM Publishing Co., 1981], p. 495). The continuing importance of the black vote stemmed in large part from social divisions among southern whites. Agricultural depression in the 1870s, and again in the 1890s, fueled a class-based movement against conservative "Bourbon" rule. The unrest among poor white farmers, culminating in the Populist revolt of the 1890s, led to efforts by both the Populists and their conservative opponents to gain control of the black vote; after the Democrats turned back the Populist challenge, however, they moved to eliminate the potential threat of black suffrage. Beginning in 1890 in Mississippi, and spreading to most of the other southern states over the next few decades, conservative Democrats deprived blacks of effective suffrage through a variety of legislative enactments; the most important among these were poll taxes, literacy requirements, the "White Primary," and a variety of similar measures. By these means a large number of poor whites were effectively disfranchised as well (John Hope Franklin, *From Slavery to Freedom: A History of Negro Americans*, 5th ed. [New York: Alfred A. Knopf, 1980], pp. 251–267; C. Vann Woodward, *The Strange Career of Jim Crow*, 3rd rev. ed. [New York: Oxford University Press, 1974], pp. 35–101; J. Morgan Kousser, *The Shaping of Southern Politics: Suffrage Restriction and the Establishment of the One Party South, 1880–1910* [New Haven: Yale University Press, 1974]).

4. As blacks migrated to cities during and following World War I, they played an increasingly important role in municipal and state politics. By the late teens, a small number of blacks began to be elected to offices in the state assemblies and local city councils in New York and Chicago. In New York the first black official was elected in 1918. By the 1920s blacks were nearly a majority of the population in Harlem's two central assembly districts. By 1921 New York's Democratic and Republican parties began to run black candidates. The number of black representatives increased to two assemblymen and two aldermen, but from the 1921 reapportionment until 1929, the number of elected black officials remained the same. Chicago held out more promise for the possibilities of black political representation, because of the ethnic heterogeneity of the city, which served as a basis for ethnic coalitions, and because of the size of electoral areas that contained discrete ethnic communities; as a result, each ethnic group functioned as a pressure group, and blacks were able to develop a separate power base. Between 1906 and 1915 black politicians, such as Edward Wright and Oscar De Priest, had laid the basis for black political organizations. In 1912 and 1914 the first two black state senators were elected, and by 1915 the black political coalition had amassed enough power to elect Oscar De Priest as the first black alderman in Chicago. From 1918 to 1924 four blacks served in the Illinois General Assembly. By 1922 three black aldermen (Oscar De Priest, Louis Anderson, and Robert R. Jackson) were elected to the city council from the second ward of the South Side black belt (Edwin R. Lewinson, *Black Politics in New York City* [New York: Twayne Publishers, 1974], pp. 58–80; Ira Katznelson, *Black Men, White Cities*, pp. 62–104; Allan H. Spear, *Black Chicago: The Making of a Negro Ghetto* [Chicago: University of Chicago Press, 1967], pp. 111–126, 181–200; Ernest R. Rather, *Chicago Negro Almanac and Reference Book* [Chicago: Chicago Negro Almanac Publishing Co., 1972], pp. 5, 113, 140; Harold S. Gosnell, *Negro Politicians: The Rise of Negro Politics in Chicago* [Chicago: University of Chicago Press, 1935], pp. 375–376; James R. Barrett, "Unity and Fragmentation: Class, Race, and Ethnicity on Chicago's South Side, 1900–1922," *Journal of Social History* 18 [fall 1984]: 37–56).

5. Garvey is referring to James Weldon Johnson, secretary of the NAACP, who succeeded John R. Shillady in 1920. The previous year Shillady, in Texas in an unsuccessful attempt to meet with the governor and attorney general, was beaten unconscious by a group of men. He never fully recovered from the attack and resigned from the NAACP in 1920. Contrary to Garvey's assertion, however, Johnson was not the only black executive in the NAACP; others included Assistant Secretary Walter White and executive officers W. E. B. Du Bois, Robert Bagnall, William Pickens, and Addie W. Hunton (Charles Flint Kellogg, *The NAACP*, pp. 234–241, 291–292; Elliott Rudwick and August Meier, "The Rise of the Black Secretariat in the NAACP, 1909–1935," in Meier and Rudwick, eds., *Along the Color Line: Explorations of the Black Experience* [Urbana: University of Illinois Press, 1976], pp. 94–127; Robert L. Zangrando, *The NAACP Crusade Against Lynching, 1909–1950*, pp. 51–53).

6. In 1909 the NAACP launched a vigorous campaign against lynching. But although lynchings continued, their numbers actually decreased slightly from 1909 to 1920, and they declined steadily after 1921. The lessening was in part due to the organized pressure the NAACP brought to bear through exposés, investigations, and campaigns for federal antilynching laws. Other factors were important as well: economic changes in the South, the diminishing of southern isolation, and the migration of blacks to northern areas during and after World War I. While violence against blacks continued, it began to take different forms in the South as well as the North (NAACP,

Thirty Years of Lynching in the United States: 1889–1918 [New York: NAACP, 1919], p. 8; Arthur F. Raper, *The Tragedy of Lynching* [Chapel Hill: University of North Carolina Press, 1933]; Robert L. Zangrando, *The NAACP Crusade Against Lynching, 1909–1950*, pp. 51–71).

7. No evidence has been found that redistricting to reduce black political strength occurred in areas where blacks held a balance of power. In fact, in the two major centers of black political strength, New York and Chicago, the basis for black political power increased during this period. The degree to which the black political base was effective in benefiting the population as a whole economically or politically stemmed from machine party politics and the patronage system. In New York, for example, the influx of blacks to Harlem created two assembly districts that by 1920 were dominated by blacks. At the same time, however, blacks began to vote Democratic, and the growing political base became dominated by the Tammany Democratic machine, controlled by whites. Direct political benefits accrued to a handful of middle-class blacks through party patronage. In Chicago, where ethnic blocs were the basis for politics, the black political power base was even stronger. By 1920 blacks had built a powerful black political machine on the South Side of the city, which was controlled by blacks who managed to capture major ward patronage positions (Ira Katznelson, *Black Men, White Cities*, pp. 62–104; Edwin R. Lewinson, *Black Politics in New York City*, pp. 58–80; Richard B. Sherman, *The Republican Party and Black America* [Charlottesville: University Press of Virginia, 1973], pp. 145–173, 200–223).

Report by Special Agent Mortimer J. Davis

New York City 12/12/22

IN RE: U.S. VS. MARCUS GARVEY, ET AL.
VIO. SEC. 215 U.S.C.C.

On the 4th inst., in company with Bank Accountant Merril[e]es, Post Office Inspector Shea and Agent Amos, the writer started examining prospective witnesses in this case in the office of Asst. U.S. Attorney Mattuck and was so engaged during the entire week.[1]

It is probable that the case will go to trial shortly after January 1st, by which time it is expected that all details in the way of evidence and witnesses will have been concluded. The witnesses are being examined and selected by Mr. Mattuck personally, and the writer, in addition to assisting in the questioning of same, has been requested by Mr. Mattuck to make such investigations based on their testimony, as appear necessary.

MORTIMER J. DAVIS

DJ-FBI, file 61. TD.

1. Agents Mortimer Davis and James E. Amos began their preparation for the case in late November, the trial date being initially set for 15 December 1922. Inquiring about the subsequent delay in bringing the case to trial, Amos was informed by the U.S. attorney's office that the calendar of the federal courts of the Southern District of New York was crowded, but every effort was being made to bring the case to an early trial (27 November 1922 and 10 January 1923, DJ-FBI, file 61).

William Phillips to Joseph Martin, President, UNIA New Orleans Chapter

[*New Orleans*] DEC. 12, 1922

Dear Sir:—

Mr. Smyer has requested Deputy Esau Ramus to visit your chapter Friday night to assist in whatever way possible in arousing more interest in your chapter. You are therefore asked to do all you can to get a big crowd out to your meeting this week. I am yours truly,

WILLIAM PHILLIPS
Exect. Sec'y. N.O. Division 149

DJ-FBI, file 61. TL, transcript.

Article in the *New Orleans Times-Picayune*

[2 January 1923]

NEGRO PREACHER IS SHOT IN BACK

EASON TELLS POLICE HE'S A WITNESS AGAINST MARCUS GARVEY

J.W.H. Eason, negro preacher who was to have left for New York this morning to testify in the trial of Marcus Garvey, negro, self-styled, president of the negro republic, was shot twice from behind by unidentified assailants as he was leaving church last night.[1] His condition was reported serious at Charity Hospital.

Although one of the bullets struck him in the head above the right eye and the other entered his back, Eason was able to tell the police of the attack upon him. He attended services at the negro church at First and Freret streets,[2] he said, and was walking home along First street when two negroes stepped out of an alley after he passed. He heard the men and turned as one of them opened fire with a revolver.

Eason arrived in New Orleans Sunday night and was staying at 2804 Phillip street. He told the police that he intended leaving for New York this morning to give evidence against Garvey, who he said is to be tried there on charges relating to the funds of the Black Star Steamship Company, a firm Garvey promoted for the purpose of transporting negroes to Liberia.

Garvey was in New Orleans several months ago and spoke before a large gathering of negroes.[3]

In describing the attack last night, Eason said he had no doubt as to the motive of the shooting.

"I am positive," he asserted, "that my assailants were acting on instructions to put me out of the way and prevent my appearing as a witness against Garvey at the trial. I have already been threatened several times."

Eason, who is pastor of the Zion African Methodist Episcopal Church in New York, said that he was formerly associated with the Negro Improvement society, in which organization the plans for the formation of the Black Star Line originated. He declared that he and several others in the organization became dissatisfied with the way in which Garvey handled the funds and dropped out some time ago.

Garvey's trial is scheduled for the latter part of the week in the United States court at New York. According to Eason there are federal charges against Garvey for using the mails to defraud, in connection with obtaining money for the Black Star Line.

Printed in the *New Orleans Times-Picayune*, 2 January 1923.

1. Eason, who had just finished delivering an address as part of the emancipation anniversary celebration, was apparently returning home to change his clothes before returning to speak again (telephone report by Horten to NAACP, DLC, NAACP Papers).
2. A reference to St. John's Baptist Church.
3. Garvey spoke in New Orleans on 23 June 1922; he was enabled to speak after a court order was issued prohibiting the police from interfering with his meeting (*Garvey Papers* 4: lv).

UNIA Press Release

[[*New York, 3 January 1923*]]

HON. MARCUS GARVEY, PRESIDENT-GENERAL OF THE U.N.I.A. AND PROVISIONAL PRESIDENT OF AFRICA, AND PARTY TO MAKE TRIP AROUND THE WORLD IN INTEREST OF THE ORGANIZATION

Owing to the continuous general misrepresentations made of the aims and objects of the Universal Negro Improvement Association by the enemies of the movement and by the false opinion that certain Negro organizations, so-called leaders and exploiters have created in the minds of a large number of the white people of America for the purpose of such organizations and individuals fleecing from the white race through patronage and charity contributions and support for their own movements and themselves, the Honorable Marcus Garvey, President-General of the Universal Negro Improvement Association, has decided for the purpose of presenting the association before the world in a proper light, to make a speaking tour of the world, starting from February next and continuing for several months. He will speak for five months in all the principal cities of the United States, to white and colored audiences, one month in the Dominion of Canada, two months in South and Central America, one month in the West Indies, two months in England, Scotland, Wales, Ireland, France, Italy, Switzerland, Spain and Germany, one month in Africa, one month in Australia and one month in Japan.[1]

In America Mr. Garvey will speak to the majority of white people for the purpose of honestly informing them of the real program of the Universal Negro Improvement Association. In Europe he will lay before the working classes the need for co-operation among them to make Africa the land of the blacks. Mr. Garvey shall also, while in Europe, continue the work of the delegation from the association recently returned from the League of Nations. It is rumored that among those to accompany Mr. Garvey on the trip around the world in the interest of the association will be Sir William Ferris, editor of the Negro World; Lady Henrietta Vinton Davis, Fourth Assistant President-General, and several secretaries and reporters.

Already arrangements are on the way for Mr. Garvey to speak in some of the largest halls in Europe, and arrangements will be made for him to speak in the Royal Albert Hall in London, England.

All branches of the Universal Negro Improvement Association in America and the West Indies desiring Mr. Garvey to visit their cities or towns are requested to communicate immediately with Miss Enid Lamos, secretary to the President-General, 56 West 135th street, New York city.

Printed in *NW*, 20 January 1923.

1. Garvey never made this proposed trip; however, he made a speaking tour of Europe in 1928.

Marcus Garvey to William Phillips

New York. Jan. 4. [*1923*]

Arrange immediately for big meeting at church or hall in New Orleans for Friday night January nineteenth for return delegates from League of Nations to speak Honorable G.O. Mark[e] and Honorable William Sherrill admission fifty cents advertise immediately inform President.

GARVEY

DJ-FBI, file 61-50-195. TG, transcript.

Report by Special Agent Mortimer J. Davis

New York City 1/4/23

IN RE: U.S. VS. MARCUS GARVEY ET AL.,
VIOLATION SEC. 215, U.S.C.C. USING THE MAILS TO DEFRAUD

As advised in a previous report, Expert Bank Accountant Mer[r]ilees and the writer have been in constant conference with Asst. U. S. Attorney Mattuck in the preparation for trial of this case.[1]

The case was on the court calendar for December 26th, but due to various circumstances, particularly the fact that Judge Knox would not sit long enough in this district to hear the case, and the further fact that O. M. Thompson, one of the defendants, was without counsel, it was postponed until January 2nd, although Mr. Mattuck at the time advised me it would probably be again postponed by him until January 8th.

On January 2nd the case again came up and has been indefinitely postponed, Mr. Mattuck explaining that Judge Learned Hand,[2] who is now sitting, will not be in this district long enough to hear the case. However, several new judges will probably be appointed in February and it will not be until that time, therefore, that a judge who will sit a sufficiently long time to hear this matter will be available.

MORTIMER J. DAVIS

DJ-FBI, file 61. TD.

1. During this time, the Bureau of Investigation also monitored Garvey's official defense fund. A bureau agent noted: "Garvey's Defense Fund has now reached the sum of $6,619.39 and it is particularly noticeable that practically no part of recent contributions to the fund have come from New York. The last list of contributions shows that they have come largely from coal mining districts of Western Pennsylvania and also from Central America and the West Indies" (DJ-FBI, special report, 30 December 1922).

2. Billings Learned Hand (1872–1961) was born in Albany, N. Y., and educated at Harvard Law School. He was appointed to the federal bench in New York in 1909. He served for fifteen years as a federal district judge before President Calvin Coolidge nominated him as a judge on the U. S. Circuit Court of Appeals in 1924. At the end of his career Hand was considered among the great jurists of his time (*NYT*, 19 August 1961).

Bureau of Investigation Report

Los Angeles, Cal. 1/4/23

UNIVERSAL NEGRO IMPROVEMENT ASSOCIATION

On [J]une 4th 1922 the paid up membership of the Los Angeles Branch of the U.N.I.A. was 390 members. [*The confidential informant?*] in contact with the Los Angeles Branch of the U.N.I.A. reports that the paid up membership of the local branch as of January 1st 1923 is approximately 80 members, of whom about 50 are men and 30 women. [T]he [*confidential informant?*] states that the local U.N.I.A. is virtually on the rocks, that there has been considerable internal dissen[t]ion in the organization lately resulting in the resignation of . . . [*two lines deleted*] of the Los Angeles Branch. In an effort to revive interest and enthusi[as]m in the organization meetings were arranged at the U.N.I.A. Hall[,] 1824 Central Ave[.], Los Angeles[,] on the nights of Dec[.] 26–27th 1922, at which meetings a welcome was given to and speeches made by the "Negro Delegates to the League of Nations at Geneva[,] Switzerland[.]" Informant covered these meetings and states that by actual count there were 67 persons present at the first meeting and 45 at the second meeting[;] he states that there was nothing said in these speeches that might be considered as "Radical" and that it was principally the old U.N.I.A. "bunk."

The following is quoted from an article by [*name deleted*] of the "Negro Messenger"[;][1] the article is entitled "The New Year".

> Probably the most hopeful phase of the year just passed has been the tendency of leaders of different political religious and social faiths, to get together; we refer of course to the honest men. Honest and clean men of all faiths have therefore joined hands against the blackest (inside) of all negro race traitors in history, the conscienceless renegade, the unspeakable negro vill[ai]n, that indescribable clown, that monumental mountebank, that libidinous liar, that lusty lunged leech, that—as Cicero would say: Oh what shall I call him?—infamous MARCUS GARVEY. This Negro[']s influence has been killed, his schemes have fallen through, the fanaticism of his followers has now changed to wrath against him. Ere you have read this gentle reader, MARCUS GARVEY will be on trial, and the New Year will be happier when justice is meted out to him. In this New Year may the old demagogic devil be driven out of the life of the Negro and held in such check that he can sin no more.

CONTINUED.

DJ-FBI, file 61. TD.

1. This journal has not been found; it should not be confused with the *Messenger*, edited and published by A. Philip Randolph and Chandler Owen.

Report by Special Agent James E. Amos

New York, N.Y. Jan. 6, 1923

RE: U.S. VS. MARCUS GARVEY, ET AL.: VIOLATION SECTION
215 U.S.C.C. (USING THE MAILS TO DEFRAUD)

Continuing the writer's previous reports on this matter, Agent wishes to state that when this case was called for trial in the Federal Court, Southern

District of New York, on January 5th, 1923, it was again postponed to January 8th. Commencing with the adjournment taken on December 26th, 1922, this is the third postponement of the trial of this case within two weeks. Previous records will point out that the case shows a long series of adjournments ever since it was first moved for trial. Agents are having great difficulty in holding the witnesses for the Government and one of our principal witnesses has been shot by, we think, some of GARVEY's fanatics, and if this case drags along much longer, we will have no witnesses left for the Government. (REV. J.W.H. EASON, shot at New Orleans, La., died Jan. 4, 1923.)

This report is submitted at the especial request of Mr. J.B. Cunningham, Asst. Director, with whom Agent conferred at this office today.

JAMES E. AMOS

DJ-FBI, file 61. TD.

Report by Special Agent Mortimer J. Davis

New York City 1/6/23

IN RE: U.S. VS. MARCUS GARVEY, ET AL.,
VIOLATION SEC. 215, U.S.C.C.
(USING MAILS TO DEFRAUD)

The writer's attention has been called to the following news account, received from Agent J.E. Amos, which was clipped from a Washington, D.C. newspaper:

SLAIN TO SEAL LIPS
PASTOR SAYS HE WAS SHOT TO PREVENT
TESTIFYING IN FRAUD TRIAL

NEW ORLEANS, La. January 5—Rev. J.W.H. Eason, negro, who was shot and wounded as he was leaving his church Monday night, died in a hospital yesterday. In a statement after the shooting Eason told the police he was convinced that his assailants were sent to kill him to prevent his testifying at the trial in federal court in New York of Marcus Garvey, negro promoter, on a charge of using the mails to defraud in connection with the promotion of the Black Star Line. Eason was to have left for New York last Tuesday.

WILLIAM SHAKESPEARE, negro "chief of police" of the United Negro Improvement Association, a Garvey project, and FRED DYER, negro member of the "force[,]" were arrested and charged by the police with the killing of Eason.

Eason, it was said, dropped out of the Garvey projects when he became dissatisfied with the promoter's methods.

The New Orleans office is undoubtedly aware of the fact that Marcus Garvey and three other officers of the Black Star Line, Inc., which is an adjunct of the U.N.I.A., have been under indictment in this district for some time, charged with using the mails in a scheme to defraud. Several weeks ago I requested Dr. Eason to come to the U.S. Attorney's office, which he did, and at which time he gave us a statement of his connection with the various Garvey projects. His remarks were of importance and interest, and he was looked upon as one of the Government's leading witnesses in the case. Shortly before Christmas Dr. Eason, on the telephone, informed me that he was going to New Orleans but would return to New York on January 2nd, and I heard no more from him.

Yesterday, while in the U.S. Attorney's office here, I was informed by [*name deleted*], who had been summoned as a witness in this case, that Dr. Eason had been shot in New Orleans. [*Name deleted*] stated that at about 10.30 P.M. on the night of January 2nd, he accidently met [*name deleted*] on the street, and they informed him they had just come from Liberty Hall (the U.N.I.A. headquarters in this city), where the shooting of Dr. Eason had been announced. Thus, it will be noticed, Garvey must have had the news of the affair within an hour after its occurrence.[1] It is also alleged that Garvey, upon hearing of it, stated "that's the way they treat them in the West!"

Agent Amos and the writer will, on Monday, endeavor to locate [*name deleted*] and obtain from him a correct statement of the facts with a view to determining whether or not the shooting and death of Dr. Eason were inspired at New York and whether it was the result of his willingness to testify for the Government against Garvey.

Today, Agent Amos and the writer interviewed John J. Fitz[si]mmons, Deputy U.S. Marshal at New York, who handed to agents a letter and attached statement, quoted below. These papers were turned over to him by Mr. Fred Moore, Editor of the New York "Age[,]" a colored newspaper here, with the request that they be copied and returned as they will be published in the paper on Monday. The papers read:

New Orleans, La.
Jan. 2, 1923

Editor, New York Age
New York, N.Y.

Dear Sir:—

Inclosed herewith you will please find an accurate account of the attempt on the life of the Hon. Dr. Eason of your city. The writer is [*editor?*] of the Negro Advocate[2] and at the time of this letter learned that one of the assailants' bullets entered the Doctor[']s head just above the left eye and one entered the back. Exray pictures will be taken today in order to determine the location of the bullets.

Trusting same will prove of use to you and while wishing you a Happy New Year, I am Yours very truly

[*signature deleted*]

New Orleans, La.
Jany. 2, 1923

NOTED COLORED PREACHER SHOT

Dr. J.W.H. Eason, Pastor of the A.M.E. Zion Church in New York was shot last night as he left the Church at Freret and First Sts.

It is believed by those who witnessed the shooting that it was purely an attack on the Pastor's life. The writer rushed to the scene of the affair which happened about 9.45 P.M., and at 8.45 A.M. the next morning succeeded in having an interview with the wounded man in the Charity Hospital. Dr. Eason's statements to the reporter are as follows:

["]I arrived in New Orleans from New York where several friends and myself were to arrange a series of meetings in the interest of colored people. These meetings were to be held purely for American Negroes. I, at the request of these friends, went to the Church of Rev. [*Frederick H.*] Collins to have a short talk with the people. This being accomplished the meeting came to a close. As I was leaving the Church being greeted by my many friends, my assailants fired point blank into the crowd. I fell. Some of my friends, as far as I can remember[,] made an attempt to catch the assailants but they fired back at their pursuers as they made their escape. I was then rushed to the Hospital where I became unconscious until just a while ago. That is all I can remember about the affair now.["]

After quite a bit of efforts upon the part of the reporter it developed that Dr. Eason was to have returned to New York and to have been a Government witness in the case of Marcus Garvey, the self st[y]led President of Africa, versus the U.S. Government. The writer also learned that while Dr. Eason was a prominent figure in the case, he was in possession of some valuable information concerning his Excellency's fraudulent use of the mail and for these reasons, the assailants acted on instructions received from the Garvey camp. Garvey's trial is scheduled for the latter part of the week in the U.S. Court in New York where several federal charges are pending. Dr. Eason's condition according to physicians is serious. But at the time do[es] not appear dangerous.

Since this case has been in progress there have been several reports of threats and intimidation of Government witnesses, but this, of course, is the most disastrous incident recorded and the Asst. U.S. Attorney at New York has requested that all facts be obtained, particularly any statements which the arrested men ma[y] make as to their connection with any of the Garvey organizations, and such information which may tend to indicate that they committed the act under orders from New York, as is alleged.

MORTIMER J. DAVIS

DJ-FBI, file 61-50-176. TD.

1. According to Special Agent James Amos, Garvey learned of the Eason assassination within "a few minutes after the shooting took place" by means of "a telegram . . . sent to Mrs. Garvey, stating that the work had been done" (report by Special Agent James Amos, 13 January 1923, DJ-FBI, file 61). Eason died of his wounds on 4 January 1923.

2. The *Negro Advocate*, edited by Milton S. Hampton, was published briefly in New Orleans in 1922 and 1923 (Colin B. Hamer, Jr., City of New Orleans Public Library, to Robert A. Hill, 5 August 1983).

Editorial Letter by Marcus Garvey

[[NEW YORK, January 9, 1923]]

FELLOW MEN OF THE NEGRO RACE, Greeting:

The war clouds of Europe are once more gathering, and it is most likely that at any time a Continental conflict will break out and force through the militaristic tendencies and designs of France,[1] which will ultimately engulf the world in another holocaust.

It is for such a time that the four hundred million Negroes of the world are preparing themselves, when the opportunity will be presented to strike the blow in Africa for our liberation. It is hoped that Negroes everywhere will prepare themselves for the time when they will be called upon to stand together as one mighty whole to blast a way toward those changes that are desired by us universally. Critics have speculated as touching the program of the Universal Negro Improvement Association, claiming how impossible it will be for us to accomplish the things that we have set out to do, but all reasonable minds can see and readily admit that the changes that will bring about better conditions among Negroes will not so much be instigated through war by the Negro himself as by the very people who have robbed, exploited and killed us for hundreds of years. The great Colonial governments of Europe will of themselves strike the blow by which the four hundred million Negroes of the world will be made free, and France is just lining up for such a contingency. Whether France is gone mad or not, we are not inclined to say, but we feel sure that she is going to continue to provoke Europe until they bring down the pillars of the temple upon themselves. . . .

MARCUS GARVEY
President-General
Universal Negro Improvement Association

Printed in *NW*, 13 January 1923. Original headlines omitted.

1. A reference to the increasingly bellicose French threats to invade the coal-rich Ruhr area of Germany in order to extract reparation payments after World War I. While France had threatened to take over the area, not until 1922 did the French government, under the nationalist leadership of Prime Minister Raymond Poincaré, begin serious discussion of military occupation. By December of that year the French press began to clamor for payment of German war debts. On 11 January 1923, two days after Garvey's speech, French and Belgian troops occupied the Ruhr. The Germans responded with massive strikes and refused to cooperate with the occupying forces. The German government's financial support of the strikers, combined with the loss of income from Ruhr coal, helped undermine the German economy. This humiliation to German national pride has been viewed as a significant contribution to the growth of German fascism (Ellis Barker, "The Franco-German Feud," *Current History* 17, no. 3 [December 1922]: 445–451; Walter A. McDougall, *France's Rhineland Diplomacy* [Princeton, N.J.: Princeton University Press, 1978]; A.J. Ryder, *Twentieth-Century Germany: From Bismarck to Brandt* [New York: Columbia University Press, 1973], pp. 223–231).

Editorial in the *New York Amsterdam News*

[10 January 1923]

DEATH BLOW TO U.N.I.A.

We are not willing to go so far as to say that Marcus Garvey was implicated directly or indirectly in the cowardly assassination of J.W.H. Eason, former leader of American Negroes in the Universal Negro Improvement Association of which Garvey is President.

We will not go so far as to say that such an extreme measure would be approved by officers of his Association.

We do say, however, and most emphatically, that the murder of Mr. Eason will not do the U.N.I.A. any good, even if he was one of the outstanding opponents of Garvey and his enterprises. Such methods have never been known to do any good.

The men who actually shot Mr. Eason may have thought they were doing the U.N.I.A. a service, but they are mistaken. What they actually did was to give it its first serious blow—a blow from which it will never, never recover.

Printed in the *New York Amsterdam News*, 10 January 1923.

Editorial in the *New York News*

[*New York, N.Y., 10 January 1923*]

THE MURDER OF DR. EASON

There are many circumstances connected with the cold-blooded murder of Dr. J.W.H. Eason which demand the attention of the authorities. That he was to have been the star witness against Marcus Garvey in the trial on the calendar for last Monday is not the least of these. That he was killed, as it is alleged, by two policemen of the Garvey association whom Dr. Eason in his antemortem statement named as his assassins is another of the suspicious circumstances. That this was a second time, as he alleged in that statement, that he had been so attacked since his severance of relations with the Garvey association adds to the chain of circumstantial evidence. That this was only one of a series of many offenses alleged to have been committed by the adherents of the Universal Negro Improvement Association makes the chain apparently complete in the case that argued against the culpability of the radical racial propagandist. For these reasons the colored citizens of this country demand that the killing of Dr. Eason be probed to the bottom. The murder of a Federal witness in the face of an impending trial by the adherents of the accused brings the assassination properly within the purview of the Federal government. It is now time to call a halt to this program, which has resulted in such widespread dissension and discord within the race. There is no place in this country for any policy which justifies the commission of crime for the accomplishment of any end. The U.N.I.A. Constitution forbids membership in that organization to any person who has committed a crime except that crime was committed in behalf of that organization.[1] The colored people of this country regret and lament the untimely death of the brilliant Eason. It was, however, the logical conclusion of the program and policy of the organization which he so long and willfully supported. Those who play with fire cannot complain when they are burned. There is no excuse by justification for any man of color, native born or foreign born, professional or layman, to further support the U.N.I.A. if these things are proven, to which all of these damaging testimonies so conclusively point.

There can be no question in the minds of any fair-minded citizens as to the value of this organization if these things are true. These things being true, it must be routed out of the life of the people of this community and this country. It is more dangerous to the people of color than the Ku Klux Klan. We have long withheld our condemnation of the U.N.I.A., but forbearance at this time is no virtue. We ask the Government to probe the dastardly murder of Dr. Eason and to prosecute the conspirators, whoever they may be, to the full extent of the law.

Printed in the *New York News*, 10 January 1923, found in DJ-FBI, file 61. TD.

1. The original UNIA *Constitution and Book of Laws* of 1918 read: "No one shall be received by the Potentate and his Consort who has been convicted of crime or felony, or whose morality is not up to the standard of social ethics" (art. 5, sect. 3). In August 1920 it was amended to read ". . . except such crime or felony was committed in the interests of the UNIA" (*Garvey Papers* 1: 260, 2: 678). Although the constitution specified that officers "shall be free from criminal conviction," it did not apply this restriction to members. Ordinary members were defined as "all persons of Negro blood and African descent," and active members as "those who pay the monthly dues" (*Garvey Papers* 1: 264, 266).

Thomas W. Anderson to William Phillips

New York City January 12 [*1923*]

By order of the President General you are instructed to retain Woodville [&] Woodville on behalf of Dyer et al[.] Keep up morale and urge big meetings you will receive further instructions later.

THOMAS W. ANDERSON
Asst. Sec[']y General

DJ-FBI, file 61-50-195. TG, transcript.

Article in the *Negro World*

[13 January 1923]

EASON, AT ONE TIME CONNECTED WITH THE U.N.I.A., SHOT AND KILLED IN NEW ORLEANS

J.W.H. Eason, one time connected with the Universal Negro Improvement Association, who was dismissed from the organization at the last convention in August, 1922, for plotting and consorting with enemies, and for conduct unbecoming a gentleman, was shot and killed in New Orleans last week.

From information gathered, the man was killed over an alleged woman affair. It is alleged that he got mixed up in the domestic affairs of the usual crowd of women whom he frequented, and chiefly on which conduct he was disgraced and dismissed from the Universal Negro Improvement Association for ninety-nine years.

The usual enemy crowd of the association is endeavoring to fasten his death upon the organization, and the unfortunate man himself, true to his character, lied up to the time of his death in endeavoring to make out that he was killed by someone associated with the Universal Negro Improvement Association. He, more than anyone else, knew that the association does not indulge in lawlessness and murder, but Eason's own conscience no doubt led him to fear the association after he took, like all other executive officers, a solemn oath to be a true and faithful servant of his race and the organization.

All those who knew the man intimately are not surprised at the news, but cannot but pity him for his sad end.

Men who claim to be race leaders ought at least to so live as to make their lives an example to others.

The Negro World extends its sympathy to those bereaved.

Printed in *NW*, 13 January 1923. Original headlines abbreviated.

Report by Bureau Agent William E. Dunn, Jr.

[*New York*] JAN. 13, 1923

. . . On the 12th instant Elie Garcia, Auditor-General of the above organization and Secretary of the Black Star Steamship Line, was arrested charged with petty larceny by Marcus Garvey.[1] He was held for trial under $500.00 bail in the West Side Court.

According to Garvey, Garcia substituted an alleged bogus check for $40.00 in cash at the Association's office. Garvey also intimated that alleged irregularities in the handling of $1,500,000 worth of securities entrusted to Garcia will also figure in the trial.

Garcia is a co-defendant with Garvey, Tobias and Thompson in the case of U.S. vs. Marcus Garvey et al. and this is the second defendant with whom Garvey has had differences, Thompson having had a lawyer appointed by the Court to defend him.

The Marcus Garvey Defense Fund has now reached the total of Six thousand seven hundred forty-six dollars and seventy cents.[2]

WILLIAM E. DUNN, JR.[3]

DJ-FBI, file 61-206. TD.

1. Garvey charged Garcia with two counts of larceny. Garcia was found innocent of charges of stealing $175.00, but the court declared him guilty of stealing $47.00 from UNIA accounts by replacing the funds with a forged check. The New York Court of Special Sessions found Garcia guilty on 14 March 1923 (DJ-FBI, report of Special Agent Joseph G. Tucker, 15 March 1923).
2. Six weeks earlier, the bureau reported that the African Redemption Fund had reached $20,476.25; the Convention Fund, $10,874.85 (DJ-FBI, file 61-206, 2 December 1922).
3. William Edwin Dunn, Jr. was engaged in the New York office of the Bureau of Investigation as a stenographer from July 1919 until May 1920, when he was appointed a special agent. He resigned from the bureau in October 1925 (U.S. Department of Justice, personnel files).

Dr. Joseph D. Gibson to Albert D. Lasker, Chairman, United States Shipping Board

P.O. Box Logan W. Va., January 13, 1923

Dear Sir

I beg to inform you that word has just reached me that the U.S.A. Ship[p]ing Board now holds [$]25,000 for the Black Star line, said money was paid as part payment on the SS Orion. I am informed that the shipping board will return that money to the owners of said money. If that is true I may beg that I loaned the Black star line people [$]500.00 towards the buying of said ship, which has not yet be[en] given back to me. I have got the promis[s]ory note. Will you kindly advise me on this matter. Thanking you in advance I am respectfully yours

J[OSEPH] D[.] GIBSON

DNA, RG 32, file 605-1-653. ALS on letterhead.

Report by Special Employee Andrew M. Battle

New York, N.Y. [*13 January 1923*]

Continuing the above matter, Agent, in order to ascertain whether or not MARCUS GARVEY, President of the U.N.I.A. and Black Star Line, had been detained at home by sickness for the last three days, talked to MR. R.L. POST[ON], one of the editors, who said that GARVEY hadn't been in his office for the last three days because he was dodging his creditors. However, POST[ON] said he was going after GARVEY on Monday (January 15th), and further said that if GARVEY didn't "come across to him" he would serve him with a summons. POST[ON] also said it was too bad that GARVEY had EASON killed and also that if he finds that GARVEY ever threatens him, he will take his gun, go to his (GARVEY'S) office and get him first.

In talking to D. T. TOBIAS, once manager of the Forum, 131st Street & 7th Avenue, he said it was too bad about GARVEY having EASON "knocked off," but that GARVEY can't stand up under the charges against him. MR. TOBIAS also said that GARVEY was very foolish to make the remarks he did, on or about August 1[3?]th, which were to the effect that GARVEY would not be responsible for anyone who started out against the U.N.I.A., if they should lose an eye, an arm, a leg, or head. GARVEY further said, "when they get in the crowd you can't tell who will get you, for the U.N.I.A. are all over the world and they know you." Continued.

ANDREW M. BATTLE

DJ-FBI, file 61. TD.

Report by Bureau Agent Harry D. Gulley

New Orleans, La. 1/16/23

U.S. VS. MARCUS GARVEY ET AL. (NEGRO RADICALS):
USING MAILS TO DEFRAUD
PROBABLE CONSPIRACY TO KILL GOVT. WITNESS

Attention Mr. Hoover—
Reference is made to report of Agent Mortimer J. Davis, New York City, dated January 6, 1923.

Interviewed CAPTAIN GEORGE REED, 12th Precinct Police Station, who stated that on the night of January 1st, in company with Corporal Alix Scherer, at 10:50 P.M., he received a telephone message that J.W.H. EASON, Field Editor of the Negro Advocate, Pastor A.M.E. ZION CHURCH of New York City, and also Organizer of the Universal Negro Alliance, had been shot at the corner of 1st and S. Robertson Sts.; that investigation showed that REV. J[A]S.W.H. EASON had left St. John[']s Baptist Church no. 4, located on 1st and F[re]ret Sts., in company with Frederick H. Collins, 2610 Velmont Place, W.A. Thomas, 2230 Jackson Avenue, and Henry Scott, 2909 2nd Street, and upon reaching the corner of 1st and S. Robertson St., he was shot from behind. EASON made a statement to CAPTAIN REED that he did not know who shot him, but suspected members of the Universal Negro Improvement Association of which MARCUS GARVEY is president. He also told Captain Reed that he was opposed to the GARVEY FACTION, and was a witness against GARVEY, who was charged in New York City with "USING THE MAILS TO DEFRAUD," and was subpoenaed to be in New York on Wednesday or Thursday of that week to testify against GARVEY. After the shot, two unknown negroes ran up S. Robertson Street, jumped the fence at Magnolia, but search for these men proved fruitless. EASON died in the Charity Hospital on January 4th.

Later, WILLIAM SHAKESPEARE (Col.) laborer, age 39, residing at 1532 Iberville Street, and CONSTANTINE F. DYER,[1] age 39, resident at 1538 Iberville Street, were identified by witnesses, and charged with "MURDER."

From the person of CONSTANTINE F. DYER were taken the following evidence:—

1 Badge with the following inscription:
"JUSTICE–U.N.I.A. POLICE 47."
On this badge is the figure of an eagle and two policemen, and in the center is a tri-color button red, black and green.
1 Membership card—JUSTICE COUNCIL,
G.E.K.K.H.
JUR. S.C. of L.A.
A.A.S.R.F.M.
Name of Knight FRED C. DYER,
No.—Page—Year 1922. No.—Page—Year—
January February March—25¢
Sec. P. Domínguez, Act.
April May June—25¢
Sec. O. Colon
July, August, September—25¢
Sec. Geo. Beyer, Act.
October, November, December
Sec.

Also several samples of police badges which were obtained from the George S. Gethen Company, 1616 Arch St., (City Unknown) from whom it is possible that the above badge was obtained.

Also a newspaper clipping showing photograph of negro delegates attending assembly of the League of Nations, to urge that a former Germany colony in Africa be set aside for the founding of a new native African Republic, probably taken from the "Chicago Defender."[2]

Also memorandum of the following address:

W. T. Domingue, 3017 Perdido St.

DYER was identified as the negro who actually shot EASON. The following are witnesses:—

John Riley,	2223 3rd St.
W. A. Thomas,	2230 Jackson St.
Benjamin Dujas,	2909 2nd St.
Henry Scott,	2808 Philip St.
Minnie Reason,	906 7th St.
Alice A. Williams,	1305 S. Robertson St.

Statements were obtained by CAPTAIN REED from the REV. J. W. H. EASON as follows:—

My name is James W. H. Eason (C[*olored,*]) age 36 years, residing at 2808 Philip St. I form[e]rly resided at 245 West 136 Street New York[.] I am a Preacher and preached in the Second Baptist Church on First near Freret Streets relative to being shot on First near S. Robertson Sts. upper side about 10:50 P.M. Monday January 1st, 1923 by some unknown party.

I was invited by a committee of members of the Universal Negro Alliance to preach to the congregation of the Second Baptist Church which is on First St. near Freret St. of which Rev. A. Hubs is the regular preacher of this chur[c]h. The following invited him down from New York to preach in the, church: James Crawford (C)[,] 2062 Jackson Ave.[,] Mrs. Mamie Reason (C)[,] 900 Seventh St., Rev. Burrel[l], Rev. Collins, and Rev. A. Hubs[,] all colored and residents of New Orleans. After the services about 10.35 P.M. Monday January 1st, 1923 while walking out First St. Upper Side with Rev. Collins[,] when a shot struck the pavement I turned around to see where the shooting was coming from. I was shot in the back first and turning around I was struck in the forehead and knocked me down. I then asked Dr. Collins to ring up for the Ambulance as I knew I was shot. 3 men followed me and one man did the shooting. I could identify the man that shot me. [[Attended Sunday night in Dr. Hubs Church and Monday night I.]] That is all I know until I woke up in the Hospital this morning.

J.W.H. EASON
2808 Philip St. form[e]rly resided
at 245 West 136 St., New York City

This statement was taken in the presence of Patrolman Leonard Salath.

HENRY LEDIG, SUPY. CLERK

Also statement of SYLVE[S]T ROBERTSON[3]:—

My name is Sylvest Robertson (C)[;] my age is 40 years. I reside at 2222 Philip St. My occupation is porter employed in the Carondelet St. My wife and I are the Organizers of the Universal Negro Imp. Association.

On Monday January 1st, 1923 I went to the St. John's Baptis[t] Church on First St. bet. Howard & Freret Sts., about 9:30 P.M., to hear Rev. Joseph [*James*] W.H. Eason lecture, and remained until after the lecture was over about 10:45 P.M. During the lecture I seen Constantine F. Dyer setting in the church. It is the first time I have seen him in the church. I left the church in company with Rev. H. Fisher, going towards the river, on my way home I did not hear any shots fired or see any one running. I was informed Tuesday morning January 2nd, 1923 at the building where I work by one of the porters named Emile.

SYLVEST ROBERTSON,
2222 Philip St.

This statement taken in the presence of George Reed, Captain Commanding 12th Precinct.

HENRY LEDIG, SUPY. CLERK

CAPTAIN REED also stated that he had received the following letter by mail:—

Jan. 5, 1923

I will inform you that A.N. Webley 1420 Iberville St., his one of them that shot the preacher he is one of the member of Garvey and it was puting up a long time to kill him, so you see I am going to get all of them an repot them. Aubley [*Webley?*] say if he did have one more shot he would shot you when you made the rest of those to men he said it at the club the same man should die long time be fo now.

I AM FRANCIS.

He stated that he had made investigation, but was unable to learn the name of the writer. He had located the negro mentioned therein, but pending further developments had not questioned him.

REV. NOEL OLIVER (Col), who lives at 2222 South Rampart Street, stated that he was Pastor of the A.M.E. CHURCH, and had joined the UNIVERSAL NEGRO IMPROVEMENT ASSOCIATION and AFRICAN COMMUNIT[IES' LEAGUE] located at New Orleans in May 1921, and that he was elected CHAPLAIN; that SYLVEST ROBERTSON and wife were organizers of the local order, and that a "HIGH COMMISSIONER" of the local order by the name of GIBSON was in charge of this District out of the New York office; that he resigned Sept. 1921 because of the radical addresses or lectures in which they tried to incite ignorant negroes, and he believed that in the event that some step is not taken to curb the activities of this league, that it will eventually lead to numerous riots between the whites and blacks. He stated also that each of the officers of this organization would publicly as well as at private meetings proclaim that any one opposing MARCUS GARVEY, Provincial [*Provisional*] President, had to be put out of the way, that he deduced that that meant that they would be killed in the event that they would in any way oppose GARVEY. He stated that another "HIGH COMMISSIONER" by the name of ANDERSON came down from New York later, and had charge of this district; that at that time there were probably 3000 members in the league in New Orleans, and that he would estimate that the present membership was about 2000; that they did at that time and now hold meetings at the Negro Longshoremen's Hall in New Orleans; that another subdivision of the League is at Algiers, but he did not know the meeting place; that a negro by the name of PHIL[L]IPS is now the Acting Secretary and leader in this district, and was sent to New Orleans from New York on August, 1922; that he is of the opinion that SYLVEST ROBERTSON above referred to is acting as confidential informant for MARCUS GARVEY, and if any conspiracy existed between the New York organization and the New Orleans organization for the purpose of putting out of the way EASON, ROBERTSON and another negro by the name of FRANK JOHNSON, who operates a shoe shop across the street from the negro Y.M.C.A., probably are "in on it"; that ALLEN THOMAS, who lives at First Street between Dryades and Rampart, is supposed to be at the head of the "UNIFORM RANK," a military organization for the League. He did not know DYER or SHAKESPEARE, nor does he know the present officers except as stated above.

W. A. THOMAS (COL.)[,] 2230 Jackson Ave., stated that he joined the U.N.I.A. July 1921, and resigned in October 1922; that his reason for sending in his resignation was because of the inciting lectures of blacks against the whites; that WILLIAM PHIL[L]IP[S], who resides at 2068 Jackson Avenue, is now "HIGH COMMISSIONER" in charge of the local district. The president of the local order, whose name he does not know, is in the hospital. Among other radical remarks that have been made by the lecturers in mass meetings and at the business meetings, which are held every Thursday night, was "THE WHITE MEN ARE MASTERS AND NOT FRIENDS OF THE NEGRO, YOU ARE NOT

AMERICAN CITIZENS but are CITIZ[EN]S OF AFRICA. THE AMERICAN FLAG IS NOT OUR FLAG, AWAY WITH [THE] AMERICAN FLAG." He stated that the "HIGH COMMISSIONER in charge of this district had on numerous occasions stated that any man who was against MARCUS GARVEY and his teachings is not worthy of living and must go; that a man by the name of THOMAS is now CAPTAIN of the Legions, being a Division Head, and lives somewhere on General Taylor Street, exact address unknown.

He stated that he first met DR. EASON in October, 1922 on his first visit to New Orleans; that EASON was formerly connected with MARCUS GARVEY, but had organized a new fraternity known as the "UNIVERSAL NEGRO ALLIANCE["]; that EASON made several addresses in the different negro churches, and on each occasion five or six GARVEYITES, mostly JAMAICAN NEGROES, would follow him; that DYER, who shot EASON on the night of January 1st, was among these, and he lectured here for fifteen days, and that this was a common occurrence noticed by all; that on one occasion a GARVEYITE interrupted and threatened him while on the platform, but was put out of the church. He stated that on the night EASON was killed, that he saw about six of these GARVEYITES together at the church where EASON had lectured, and among them were DYER and SHAKESPEARE; that he also saw S.E. ROBERTSON above referred to, among this group of men; that THOMAS, who is the Division head of the Legion, was also there; that EASON came out of the church with him, and at the time he was shot was probably forty or fifty feet in front; that he recognized DYER as the negro who had shot EASON, DYER being with SHAKESPEARE, and both of them hurried away after the shot was fired; that both of these negroes rushed by him in an effort to get close to EASON after they had come out of the church and that he could positively identify the two as being the murderers of EASON.

REV. A. HUBS (Col.)[,] 2217 Willow Street, stated that he was pastor of the 2nd Baptist Melpomene Church; that the day after EASON was shot, he went to the hospital to see him, and had a long talk with him; that EASON stated he believed that GARVEY had planned his murder because he was the star witness in the case of the UNITED STATES VS. GARVEY, who was to come to trial on Thursday following in New York City, and that he intended to leave New Orleans Tuesday in order to be in New York City on that date; that EASON requested him to telegraph his (EASON's) brother who lives in ELIZABETH, N.J. he did not recall his name, to come to New Orleans at once, as he desired to tell him something about GARVEY; that he sent the telegram to EASON's brother, who came to New Orleans, but did not get here until after his death; that he was of the opinion that there was a collusion between GARVEY and his (Garvey's) followers in this city who murdered DR. EASON; that he had heard it rumored among the different negroes that GARVEY sent a telegram to PHIL[L]IPS the day preceding the murder, but this was only a rumor and thinks it unfounded; that he recognized several of GARVEY's followers on the night of the murder in the church where EASON had lectured; that he recognized these same men who had formerly attended the various other churches in the city where EASON had lectured when he was here on a former visit; that at his church, while EASON was lecturing sometime in October and November[,] several of the GARVEYITES went to attack him at that time, but were prevented from doing so. He did not know the names of these men, but knew their faces. He stated that the JAMAICAN NEGROES were hard to handle, and that most of the resident negroes were deserting the GARVEY Organization. CONTINUED.

HARRY D. GULLEY[4]

DJ-FBI, file 61-50-187. TD.

1. Little information is available on either William Shakespeare or Constantine Dyer, other than that Dyer, forty-two, was a longshoreman, and Shakespeare, twenty-eight, was a house painter and that both were Jamaicans; they were neighbors and were known to have been Garvey supporters. According to the *Chicago Defender*, Dyer was regarded as the "grand chief of police" for the Garveyites. Although Dyer was indicted and convicted of Eason's murder, the Louisiana Supreme Court remanded the case for retrial. At the second trial, both men were acquitted. While the *Negro World* acclaimed the reversal, the *Chicago Defender* called the acquittal "the most flagrant case of miscarried justice in the history of the local bar" (*Chicago Defender*, 16 August 1924; *NW*, 9 August 1924; *New York Amsterdam News*, 10 January 1923).

2. No such article is to be found in the *Chicago Defender*. The article was probably a clipping from the 9 December 1922 edition of the *Negro World*, which featured a photograph of the four UNIA delegates at the League of Nations in Geneva. The accompanying article reported the UNIA welcoming reception held at Liberty Hall for the returning delegates; it also reported that the British government had just issued executive orders abolishing slavery in former German East Africa which, it was claimed, was "due to the delegation's splendid representations before the League" (*NW*, 9 December 1922).

3. Sylvester R. Robertson (1881–1931) a native of New Orleans, was one of eight children in a family reportedly partly Dutch; at an early age, Robertson changed his original family name from Dewey to that of the grandmother who raised him. He began his career as a bank porter, working his way up to becoming a mail clerk, and over time he picked up a smattering of bookkeeping. After joining Garvey, he traveled extensively for the UNIA; eventually he settled in Cleveland where he was employed as president of the local UNIA division. It is believed that at one point he spent several months in Nigeria and Liberia. He was twice married: his first wife, Eleanora Martines, who worked as a domestic in New Orleans, was the mother of James Dewey Robertson, the couple's only child (reputation has it that the young Robertson was frequently mistaken for white; after studying music at Tuskegee Institute in Alabama, and while working in the stockyards in Chicago, he formed a jazz band under the name "Specks" Robertson.) A second wife, Aladia Robertson, generally known as "Miss Spanish," was from Panama. Robertson died in Cleveland at the age of forty-nine and was buried in New Orleans (Annie Joe Robertson [daughter-in-law] and Mrs. Joyce Jones [granddaughter], interview with Robert A. Hill, 16 August 1985, Los Angeles; Division of Vital Statistics, Ohio Department of Health, death certificate of Sylvester Robertson, Cleveland, Ohio, 21 March 1931).

4. Harry DeWitt Gulley, a lawyer by training, was a local officer for the Bureau of Investigation in Meridian, Miss., from 1913 until December 1919. In January 1920 he was appointed special agent in charge of the New Orleans office, where he served until July 1924. Gulley returned to the bureau for another tour of duty, from April 1926 until January 1927 (U.S. Department of Justice, personnel files).

Report by Special Employee Andrew M. Battle

New York, N.Y. [*16 January 1923*]

Continuing in this matter, in an interview with S[Y]DNEY DE BOURG, of 104 West 138th Street, one of the West Indian leaders of the U.N.I.A., the writer was informed that GARVEY sent ANDERSON (one of the secretaries) to New Orleans, just a few days before EASON was shot, and that ANDERSON remained in New Orleans until after EASON was killed; then ANDERSON returned to GARVEY'S office.

On arriving at GARVEY'S office, ANDERSON was asked if he killed EASON. ANDERSON said, "No, but he got what was coming to him," also that there had been a big uproar in [the] office of the U.N.I.A. ever since EASON's death.

Agent was again talking to DE BOURG near 138th Street & Lenox Avenue, and DE BOURG stated that in a conference he had with MR. R.L. POST[ON], at 264 West 135th Street, POST[ON] stated that his brother [*Ulysses S. Poston*], who is now working with the U.N.I.A., was going to resign for the following reasons: That up at Liberty Hall the other night, GARVEY bragged about the death of EASON and then took up money to defend the men who did the killing and he said it was true that ANDERSON did go to New Orleans a few days before the shooting of EASON and had remained in New Orleans until EASON was shot and then returned to the New York office of the U.N.I.A.

POST[ON] further stated that immediately after the shooting a telegram had been sent direct to GARVEY, notifying him of same, and made this remark, "You see, MR. BATTLE, ANDERSON went down a few days before EASON went to New Orleans and made the necessary arrangements for the killing, and then returned and ANDERSON had some bitter words with EASON last year."

In talking to W.H. FERRIS, Editor of the "[*Negro*] World," of the U.N.I.A., FERRIS said that one of the reasons that GARVEY had it in for EASON was that EASON blocked GARVEY in New Orleans by going down there last year and telling the police force that GARVEY, on his return to New York in 1922, bragged of the way he had bluffed the entire police force there and had managed to give lectures against their orders, and that when GARVEY went down the second time he received a "warm" reception from the police.

FERRIS further stated that it looked very bad for ANDERSON from the remarks that he made when he came back to New York and that it looked bad also for GARVEY, as GARVEY had taken up $200. through contributions and had stated it was to defend those men who had been arrested in New Orleans and that GARVEY is asking practically every member of the U.N.I.A. through the "Negro World" to help to defend those men by sending money to the U.N.I.A. office.[1] Continued.

ANDREW M. BATTLE

DJ-FBI, file 61. TD.

1. On 20 January the *Negro World* launched a defense fund for the two defendants, urging all members and divisions to send in contributions. The campaign evidently had an early start. In a

report of 17 January, Special Agent Amos reported that "Garvey has collected a fund of $250 for the defense of Frederick Dyer and William Shakespeare" (*NW*, 20 January 1923; report by Special Agent James Amos, 17 January 1923, DJ-FBI, file 61).

Report by Special Agent James E. Amos

New York, N.Y. Jan. 17, 1923

RE: U.S. VS. MARCUS GARVEY, ET AL.

In connection with the above entitled matter, Agent received a telephone call on January 15th, 1923, from CHANDLER OWEN, Editor of the "MESSENGER" Negro Magazine, requesting that Agent call on him as he had some information in regard to a letter or communication which he was going to send to the Attorney General, and also to the press of the country, concerning MARCUS GARVEY.[1]

Agent proceeded to the office of the "MESSENGER," 2305–7th Avenue, New York City[,] and there received a copy of the letter referred to above, copy of which is attached hereto, and which is self-explanatory. This document is to be signed by CHANDLER OWEN, PHILIP RANDOLPH, Asst. Editor of the "MESSENGER"[,] and WILLIAM PICKENS, Asst. Editor of the "MESSENGER" and Field Secretary of the NATIONAL ASSOCIATION FOR THE ADVANCEMENT OF COLORED PEOPLE. Continued.

JAMES E. AMOS

DJ-FBI, file 61. TD.

1. Along with this letter to Attorney General Daugherty, Owen sent a note, "Please do not give this letter to the press as copies have been sent over the country for a definite date (Feb. 1) for release" (Chandler Owen to Harry M. Daugherty, 26 January 1923, DNA, RG 60, file 198940-283).

Enclosure

2305 Seventh Avenue New York City
Jan. 15, 1923

As the chief law enforcement officer of the Nation, we wish to call your attention to a heretofore unconsidered menace to harmonious race relationships. There are in our midst certain Negro criminals and potential murderers, both foreign and American born, who are actuated by intense hatred against the white race. These undesirables continually proclaim that all white people are enemies to the Negro. They have become so fanatical that they have threatened and attempted the death of their opponents, actually assassinating in one instance.

The movement known as the Universal Negro Improvement Association has done much to stimulate the violent temper of this dangerous element. Its president and moving spirit is one Marcus Garvey, [[a negro from Jamaica,

British West Indies, not a citizen of the United States and]] an unscrupulous demagogue who has ceaselessly and assiduously sought to spread among Negroes distrust and hatred of all white people.

The official organ of the U.N.I.A., "The Negro World," of which Marcus Garvey is Managing Editor, sedulously and continually seeks to [[undermine the loyalty of all Negroes to this country]] arouse [[antipathy towards whites]] ill-feeling between the races. Evidence has also been presented of an apparent alliance of Garvey with the Ku Klux Klan.

An erroneous conception held by many is that Negroes try to cloak and hide their criminals. The truth is that [[decent]] the great majority of Negroes are bitterly opposed to all criminals and especially to those of their own race, because they know that such criminals will cause increased discrimination against themselves.

The U.N.I.A. is composed chiefly of the most primitive and ignorant element of West Indian and American Negroes. The so-called respectable element of the movement are largely ministers without churches, physicians without patients, lawyers without clients and publishers without readers, who are usually in search of "easy money." In short, this organization is composed in the main of Negro sharks and ignorant Negro fanatics.

This organization and its [[leader Marcus Garvey]] fundamental laws encourage violence. In its constitution there is an article prohibiting office holding by a convicted criminal, EXCEPT SUCH CRIME IS COMMITTED IN THE INTEREST OF THE U.N.I.A. Marcus Garvey is intolerant of free speech when it is exercised in criticism of him and his movement, his followers seeking to prevent such by threats and violence. Striking proof of the truth of this assertion is found in the following cases:[1]

In 1920 Garvey's supporters rushed into a tent where a religious meeting was being conducted by Rev. A. Clayton Powell in New York City and sought to do bodily violence to Dr. Chas. S. Morris,[2] the speaker of the evening—who[m] they had heard was to make an address against Garveyism—and were prevented only by the action of the police. Shortly afterwards members of the Baltimore branch of the U.N.I.A. attempted bodily injury to W. Ashbie Hawkins,[3] one of the most distinguished colored attorneys in America, when he criticised Garvey in a speech. During the same period an Anti-Garvey meeting held by Cyril Briggs, then editor of a monthly magazine, The Crusader,—in Rush Memorial church, New York City, on a Sunday evening—was broken up by Garveyites turning out the lights.[4]

Several weeks ago the Garvey division in Philadelphia caused such a disturbance in the Salem Baptist church where Attorney J. Austin Norris, a graduate of Yale University, and the Rev. J.W.H. Eason, were speaking against Garvey that the police disbanded the meeting to prevent a riot and bloodshed.[5] Reports state the street in front of the church was blocked by Garveyites who insulted and knocked down pedestrians who were on their way to the meeting.

In Los Angeles, Cal., Mr. Noah D. Thompson, a distinguished colored citizen of that city, employed in the editorial department of the Los Angeles Daily "Express," reporting adversely on the Garvey movement as a result of his visit to the annual convention, was attacked by members of Garvey's Los Angeles division, who, it is alleged, had been incited to violence by Garvey himself, and only through the help of a large number of police officers was Thompson saved from bodily harm.[6]

A few months ago when some persons in the Cleveland, Ohio, division of the U.N.I.A. asked Dr. LeRoy Bundy, Garvey's chief assistant, for an accounting of funds, a veritable riot took place, led, according to the Pittsburg[h] "American," by Bundy himself.[7]

In Pittsburg[h], Pa., on October 23d, last, after seeking to disturb a meeting conducted by Chandler Owen, Editor of The Messenger Magazine, Garveyites who had lurked around the corner in a body, rushed on the street car after the meeting, seeking to assault him, but were prevented by the interruption of the police.

When William Pickens, who had cooperated in the exposé of the Garvey frauds, was to deliver an address in Toronto, Canada, Garveyites met him on the steps of the church with hands threateningly on their hip-pockets, trying to intimidate him, lest he should further expose that movement.[8]

In Chicago, after seeking to break up an Anti-Garvey meeting, a Garvey supporter shot a policeman[9] who sought to prevent him from attacking the speaker as he left the building.

In New York last August during a series of meetings conducted by the Friends of Negro Freedom to expose Garvey's schemes and methods, the speakers were threatened with death. Scores of Garveyites came into the meetings with the avowed intention of breaking them up. This they were prevented from doing by the stern determination on the part of the leaders, the activities of the New York police and the great mass of West Indians and Americans who clearly showed that they would not permit any cowardly ruffians to break up their meetings.

In fact, Marcus Garvey has created an organization which [[is fundamentally and wilfully criminal.]] in its fundamental law condones and invites to crime[.] This is evidenced by Section 3 of Article 5, of the Constitution of the U.N.I.A., under the caption, "Court Reception At Home." It reads, "No one shall be received by the Potentate and his Consort who has been convicted of felony, EXCEPT SUCH CRIME OR FELONY WAS COMMITTED IN THE INTEREST OF THE UNIVERSAL NEGRO IMPROVEMENT ASSOCIATION AND THE AFRICAN COMMUNITIES LEAGUE."[10]

Further proof of this is found in the public utterances of William Sherrill, one of the chief officials in the organization and Garvey's envoy to the League of Nations Assembly at Geneva. Speaking at the Goldfield Theatre in Baltimore, Md. on August 18, 1922, he is quoted as saying: "BLACK FOLK AS WELL AS WHITE WHO TAMPER WITH THE U.N.I.A. ARE GOING TO DIE."[11]

What appears to be an attempt to carry out this threat is seen in the assault and slashing with a razor of one S.T. Saxon, by Garveyites, in Cincinnati,

Ohio, when he spoke against the movement there last October.[12]

On January 1, this year, just after having made an address [[~~scoring Garvey~~]] in New Orleans, the Rev. J. W. H. Eason, former "American Leader" of the Garvey movement, who had fallen out with Garvey and was to be the chief witness against him in the Federal Government's case, was waylaid and assassinated, it is reported in the press, by the Garveyites. Rev. Eason identified two of the men as Frederick Dyer, 42, a longshoreman, and William Shakespeare, 28, a painter. Both of them are [[~~said to be~~]] prominent members of the U.N.I.A. in New Orleans [[~~and are immigrants from Jamaica, B.W.I.~~]], one wearing a badge as chief of police and the other as chief of the fire department of the "African Republic." Dr. Eason's dying words, identifying the men whom he knew from long acquaintance in the movement, were:

"I had been speaking at Bethany and was on my way home when three men rushed out at me from an alley. I saw their faces and (pointing at Dyer and Shakespeare) I am positive that these two men here are two of the three."

The vicious inclination of these [[~~alleged~~]] Garvey members is seen in their comments in an interview:

(The N. Y. Amsterdam News reports:) "Both Dyer and Shakespeare have denied the attack, but declared they were glad of it as they said Eason richly deserved what he got. 'Eason,' said one of them, 'was a sorehead. The Association made him what he was. When he was expelled because of misconduct he went up and down the country preaching against Marcus Garvey who is doing great good for our race. Someone who evidently thought it was time to stop his lies took a crack at him. I don't blame the one that did it. Eason richly deserved what he got.'"

Eason says he knew the men who shot him were directed to do so. Insomuch, however, as the assassination of Mr. Eason removes a federal witness, we suggest that the Federal Government probe into the facts and ascertain whether Eason was assassinated as the result of an interstate conspiracy emanating from New York. It is significant that the U.N.I.A. has advertised in its organ, "The Negro World," the raising of a defense fund for those indicted for the murder, seemingly in accordance with its constitution.

Not only has this movement created friction between Negroes and whites, but it has also increased the hostility between American and West Indian Negroes [[~~due to the fact that Marcus Garvey, their leader, is a West Indian~~]].

Further, Garvey has built up an organization which has victimized hordes of ignorant and unsuspecting Negroes, the nature of which is clearly stated by Judge Jacob Panken of the New York Municipal Court, before whom Garvey's civil suit for fraud was tried. Judge Panken said: "It seems to me that you have been preying upon the gullibility of your own people, having kept no proper accounts of the money received for investments, being an organization of high finance in which the officers received outrageously high salaries and were permitted to have exorbitant expense accounts for pleasure jaunts throughout the country. I advise those 'dupes' who have contributed to these organizations to go into court and ask for the appointment of a receiver."

For the above reasons we advocate that the Attorney General use his full influence [[to]] completely to disband and extirpate this vicious movement, and that he vigorously and speedily push the Government's case against Marcus Garvey for using the mails to defraud. [[when convicted we urge that he be severely punished.]] This [[must]] should be done in the interest of justice; even as a matter of practical expediency.

The Government should note that the Garvey followers are for the most part voteless—being either largely unnaturalized or refraining from voting because Garvey teaches that they are citizens of an African Republic. He has greatly exaggerated the actual membership of his organization, which is conservatively estimated to be much less than 20,000 in all countries, including the United States and Africa, the West Indies, Central and South America. (The analysis of Garvey's membership has been made by W. A. Domingo, a highly intelligent West Indian from Jamaica, Garvey's home, in "The Crusader" magazine, New York City;[13] also by Dr. W. E. B. Du Bois, a well known social statistician, in "The Century Magazine," February, 1923, New York City.)[14] On the other hand, hosts of citizen voters, native born and naturalized, both white and colored, earnestly desire the vigorous prosecution of this case.

Again, the notorious Ku Klux Klan, an organization of white racial and religious bigots, has aroused much adverse sentiment,—many people demanding its dissolution, as the Reconstruction Klan was dissolved.[15] The Garvey organization, known as the U.N.I.A., is just as objectionable and even more dangerous, inasmuch as it [[deals with an even lower level]] naturally attracts an even lower type of cranks, crooks and racial bigots among whom suggestibility to violent crime is much greater.

Moreover, since in its basic law—the very Constitution of the U.N.I.A.—the organization condones and encourages crime, its future meetings should be carefully watched by officers of the law and infractions promptly and severely punished.

We desire the Department of Justice to understand that those who draft this document, as well as the tens of thousands who will endorse it in all parts of the country, are by no means impressed by the widely circulated reports which allege certain colored politicians have been trying to use their influence to get the indictments against Garvey quashed. The signers of this appeal represent no particular political, religious or nationalistic faction. They have no personal ends or partisan interests to serve. Nor are they moved by any personal bias against Marcus Garvey. They sound this tocsin only because they foresee the gathering storm of race prejudice and sense the imminent menace of this insidious movement which, cancer-like, is gnawing at the very vitals of peace and safety–of civic harmony and inter-racial concord.

The signers of this letter are:
HARRY H. PACE,[16] 2289 Seventh Avenue, New York City
ROBERT S. ABBOTT, 3435 Indiana Avenue, Chicago, Ill.
JOHN E. NAIL,[17] 145 West 135th Street, New York City
DR. JULIA P. COLEMAN,[18] 118 West 130th Street, New York City

WILLIAM PICKENS, 70 Fifth Avenue, New York City
CHANDLER OWEN, 2305 Seventh Avenue, New York City
ROBERT W. BAGNALL, 70 Fifth Avenue, New York City
GEORGE W. HARRIS, 135 West 135th Street, New York City

Harry H. Pace is President of the Pace Phonograph Corporation.

Robert S. Abbott is Editor and Publisher of the "Chicago Defender."

John E. Nail is President of Nail & Parker, Inc., Real Estate.

Julia P. Coleman is President of the Hair-Vim Chemical Co., Inc.

William Pickens is Field Secretary of the National Association for the Advancement of Colored People.

Chandler Owen is co-Editor of "The Messenger" and co-Executive Secretary of the Friends of Negro Freedom.

Robert W. Bagnall is Director of Branches of the National Association for the Advancement of Colored People.

George W. Harris is a member of the Board of Aldermen of New York City and Editor of the "New York News."

> Address reply to Chandler Owen, Secretary of Committee, 2305 Seventh Avenue, New York City.

DNA, RG 60, file 198940-282. TLS, recipient's copy. Also found in DLC, NAACP. The author(s) of this letter edited it significantly. The final version served as the copy text, and the deleted material has been reinstated and printed in cancelled type in brackets.

1. For a more detailed description of the events alleged see "Garveyism and Anarchism," *Messenger* 4, no. 10 (October 1922): 500–501.

2. Morris was the pastor of the Abyssinian Baptist Church when it moved from Waverly Place to 40th Street. Evangelistic tent meetings were held in the summers of 1920 and 1921 on the Harlem property, where the new church building was erected in 1922–1923 (A. Clayton Powell, Sr., *Against The Tide: An Autobiography* [New York: Richard R. Smith, 1938], pp. 160–161).

3. William Ashbie Hawkins (1862–1941) was born in Lynchburg, Va. He briefly attended the University of Maryland Law School; in 1890 he was one of two black students forced to leave in the face of an antiblack petition signed by most of the school's white students. He subsequently attended Howard University Law School, graduating in 1892. Hawkins became a newspaper editor while studying law, publishing the *Cambridge Advance* in 1887 and becoming editor of the *Baltimore Spokesman* from 1893 to 1895; he was editor of the *Baltimore Lancet* from 1902 to 1905. He later became the senior member of the Baltimore law firm Hawkins and Mechen. In 1920 Hawkins ran as an independent candidate for the U.S. Senate (*NYT*, 15 September 1890; *Baltimore News-Post*, 7 April 1941).

4. See *Garvey Papers* 4: 299–300.

5. A possible reference to a meeting of the Universal Negro Alliance, the organization formed in September 1922 by former Philadelphians Eason and Norris to combat Garvey (ibid., p. 501).

6. The deep division among Los Angeles Garveyites after Thompson's report led to bitter feelings between the faction that supported Thompson and the group that chose to remain loyal to the parent body of the UNIA. Garvey reportedly sent telegrams to Los Angeles UNIA members urging them to support him and to oppose Noah Thompson. The Thompson faction passed a series of resolutions against Garvey and the parent body, but none of them mentioned violence or threats of violence (Emory J. Tolbert, *The UNIA and Black Los Angeles* [Los Angeles: Center for Afro-American Studies, University of California, Los Angeles, 1980], pp. 65 ff.).

7. On his return to Cleveland from the 1922 UNIA convention, Bundy found a "For Rent" sign on the local Liberty Hall. A UNIA committee subsequently charged that bills for expenses of the building had been left unpaid for six months, while excessive convention expenses had been incurred by Bundy; on 16 September 1922 a fight broke out, which resulted in the hospitalization of two men (*Baltimore Afro-American*, 22 September 1922).

8. While attending a conference of the AME church convention in Toronto, Garveyites apparently met Pickens at the church entrance and "fingering their hip-pockets" warned him not to "do any knocking." According to the *Baltimore Afro-American*, Pickens then lectured them for several minutes, stating that he would not "be frightened for the millionth part of a second by any lily-livered, cocoanut busting monkey chasers, even in Canada." After the confrontation Pickens delivered his speech before the AME conference, in which he claimed that while he had not intended to mention Garveyism, he felt it necessary to "pay his respects" to the "bunch of cowards" he had encountered at the door. Pickens was apparently cheered by most of the audience following his speech (*Baltimore Afro-American*, 29 September 1922).

9. Charles Springfield of Chicago was given a one-year sentence for the attempted shooting. The anti-Garvey meeting, which was held on 28 September 1922, was addressed by Rev. J. W. H. Eason (*New York Age*, 27 January 1923).

10. Art. 5, sect. 3, of the UNIA Constitution and Book of Laws.

11. It has not been possible to verify this statement. Chandler Owen, in an article entitled "Should Marcus Garvey Be Deported?" claimed that the *Baltimore Afro-American* of 18 August 1922 reported Sherrill as saying, "Black folks as well as white who tamper with the Universal Negro Improvement Association are going to die" (*Messenger* 4, no. 9 [September 1922]: 480). Searches of the *Baltimore Afro-American* for this period, however, do not reveal any account of such a speech by Sherrill. In fact, Sherrill was a delegate to the UNIA's August 1922 convention in New York, and he addressed the 18 August 1922 session (*NW*, 26 August 1922).

12. For an account of this incident, see the *Chicago Whip*, 21 October 1922.

13. Domingo's article was entitled "Figures Never Lie, But Liars Do Figure." Basing his estimate on the fact that $19,562.80 in death taxes were paid in ten months, he judged from the UNIA chancellor's report that there were fewer than twenty thousand members. Domingo's article went on to condemn the handling of the "convention funds" and the Liberian Construction Loan, claiming that less than 3 percent of the funds collected for the Liberian Construction Loan were actually used for the stated purpose (*Crusader* 5, no. 2 [October 1921]: 13–14).

14. In the *Century* article, which was entitled "Back to Africa," Du Bois estimated the UNIA membership at eighty thousand (*Century*, 105 [February 1923]: 539–548.

15. This is a reference to federal attempts to suppress the Klan in the 1870s. In 1869 the Klan formally dissolved itself, but organized violence against blacks continued in the South. In response, Congress passed three federal acts in 1870 and 1871 to protect black voters and suppress the Klan. A congressional investigation was launched into Klan activities, and federal troops were sent to the South. Hundreds of Klan members were arrested, tried, and imprisoned, and by 1872 the Klan had virtually disappeared. By 1875 the federal government was no longer willing to enforce the acts and withdrew its troops. Organized violence against blacks continued, despite the dissolution of the Klan (Kenneth M. Stampp, *The Era of Reconstruction: 1865–1877*, pp. 199–201; John Hope Franklin, *Reconstruction after the Civil War* [Chicago: University of Chicago Press, 1961], pp. 153–177; David M. Chalmers, *Hooded Americanism: The History of the Ku Klux Klan* [New York: Franklin Watts, 1981], pp. 8–21).

16. Harry Herbert Pace (b. 1884) was born in Covington, Ga., and educated at Atlanta University. Pace served as managing editor for W. E. B. Du Bois's first newspaper, the *Moon*, published in Memphis from 1905 to 1906. He served as professor of Latin and Greek at Lincoln Institute in Jefferson City, Mo., in 1906–1908, leaving to establish the Standard Life Insurance Co. of Atlanta. In 1920 he joined the famous blues composer W. C. Handy to form the Pace and Handy Music Co. of Memphis. Afterward he became an influential community organizer in Memphis and organized the Colored Citizens Association of Memphis. In 1925 Pace moved to Newark, N. J., where he founded the Northeastern Life Insurance Co., serving as its first president (*WWCR*; *WWCA*).

17. John E. Nail (1883–1947), brother of Grace E. Nail, who married James Weldon Johnson, was a prominent Harlem real estate investor who hoped to develop a Harlem dominated by middle-class black homeowners. Along with Henry Parker, Nail began the real estate firm of Nail and Parker in 1907. As blacks migrated into the city during World War I, the company acquired property and was central to many of the largest real estate transactions in the rapidly growing community. James Weldon Johnson and other prominent blacks invested in the company to support black entrepreneurship and the building of homes for blacks. By 1925, Nail managed fifty apartment complexes, and the company boasted an income of $1 million. And as Harlem's leading realtor, Nail was also one of the most influential realtors in New York. He was the first black to serve on the Real Estate Board of New York; he was the only black on the Housing Committee of New York and he also served on the board of the Uptown Chamber of Commerce.

Influenced by his brother-in-law, Nail was active in civil rights causes, serving as national treasurer for the NAACP, a member of the board of directors, and the first lifetime member of the organization. With the onslaught of the Depression, however, Harlem real estate business began to decline, and in 1933 the company went bankrupt and was dissolved. Nail opened a new firm, and although he continued his attempts to revitalize a now-deteriorating Harlem with New Deal funding, the plans never materialized (*WWCA*; *DANB*; *NYT*, 5 January 1926, 6 March 1947; David Levering Lewis, *When Harlem Was in Vogue* [New York: Alfred A. Knopf, 1981], pp. 44, 146, 174, 241; Charles Flint Kellogg, *The NAACP*, p. 226; Langston Hughes, *Fight for Freedom: The Story of the NAACP* [New York: W. W. Norton, 1962], pp. 132–133; Maceo C. Dailey, "Booker T. Washington and the Afro-American Realty Company," *The Review of Black Political Economy* 8, no. 2 [winter 1978]: 184–201).

18. Julia P. H. Coleman was a pharmacist who was born in North Carolina. She received her degree in pharmacology at Howard University in 1897 and later worked as president and manager of the Hair-Vim Chemical Co., a Washington, D.C., concern specializing in hair preparations for blacks (*WWCR*).

Alfred D. Lasker to Dr. Joseph D. Gibson

[*Washington, D.C.*] January 17, 1923

My dear Sir:

Replying to your letter of January 13th, addressed to the Chairman of the United States Shipping Board, the Board has not determined that the original payment on the ss "ORION" was to be returned, but it is the opinion of the Committee to whom the matter was referred for consideration that if this payment should be returned, it should be rebated to those who originally subscribed their money.[1] Very sincerely yours,

[ALBERT D. LASKER]
Commissioner

DNA, RG 32, file 605-1-653. TL, carbon copy.

1. This rebate policy of returning the money to the subscribers of the *Orion* was first reiterated by Commissioner Frederick I. Thompson on 30 October 1922 (Frederick I. Thompson to Clifford Smith, 30 October 1922, DNA, RG 32, file 605-1-653).

Report by Special Employee Andrew M. Battle

New York, N.Y. [*17–18 January 1923*]

Continuing the above matter, Agent was called upon by WM. FERRIS, Editor of the "Negro World" and during the conversation WM. FERRIS stated that THOMAS ANDERSON, Asst. Secretary General of the U.N.I.A. whose home is in New Orleans, but who has a room at the "Phyllis Wheatley" Hotel, 3–5 West 136th Street, New York City, was once a preacher in Detroit, Mich.,[1] and that ANDERSON went to New Orleans last fall to conduct two meetings for the U.N.I.A., and that the first night the meeting was conducted with the help of R. L. POST[ON], but that on the second night DR. EASON had the meeting blocked by the police force and that ANDERSON had become very angry and when EASON returned to New York and went to the U.N.I.A. office for a conference with GARVEY, EASON told GARVEY that he had fixed it so that GARVEY would not be able to do any more business in New Orleans. GARVEY told EASON that he heard that he (EASON) came near getting a beating for the trouble he had taken to block the meeting at New Orleans.

FERRIS further stated that the reason things looked so black for GARVEY was because of the fact that when S[Y]DNEY DE BOURG was arrested in Panama² last year for holding a meeting in behalf of the U.N.I.A., GARVEY made no effort to get DE BOURG out of jail and when ABRAHAM [*Adrian*] JOHNSON was stranded down south last fall, GARVEY gave him no help, and then FERRIS asked this question: "Why do you suppose GARVEY should take so much interest in those men that killed EASON, even to the extent of taking up money to be used for their defense?" "Those two men who killed EASON are from Jamaica, W.I., and another thing that is going to harm GARVEY—the Government will surely get the telegram that was sent to GARVEY notifying him that EASON had been killed.³ The telegram, as you know, will do much to show whether GARVEY had anything to do with the killing or not."

The writer also had a conference with DE BOURG of 104 W. 138th Street, N.Y. City and DE BOURG stated that [*J.B.*] YEARWOOD was the one who told of GARVEY getting the telegram at his (GARVEY'S) house regarding the shooting of EASON, as soon as it was done.

In talking with F. A. TOOTE, the Field Organizer of the U.N.I.A.[,] he said that it was a dead give-away for GARVEY to start a fund to defend the men who shot EASON; that it was also very foolish for ANDERSON to come to the New York Office and say he didn't kill EASON but that EASON got what was coming to him, and that GARVEY would have some time explaining the telegram that he received from New Orleans as soon as the trick was pulled.

The above remarks of TOOTE were made to Agent, A.M. Battle, on January 18th at about 3:00 P.M. Continued.

ANDREW M. BATTLE

DJ-FBI, file 61. TD.

1. Anderson was ordained a Baptist minister in Detroit in 1918 (*NW*, 29 December 1923).
2. De Bourg was actually arrested in San Pedro de Macoris, Dominican Republic, on 16 February 1922, for conducting a UNIA meeting (DNA, RG 38, file 1400-60-35).
3. This telegram was never produced; it still has not been found.

W.W. Grimes to J. Edgar Hoover

Washington, D.C. January 19, 1923

MEMORANDUM FOR MR. HOOVER

On the 16th you sent me a report from Agent Davis in the New York office indicating that MARCUS GARVEY contemplated making a world tour about the first of February. His case is fixed for hearing on February 5th. Mr. Davis suggested, and you and Mr. [*John B.*] Cunningham both relayed the desire, that arrangements be made with the State Department to block any request for passport. Marcus Garvey is an alien and would not apply for a passport to the American State Department. There is no action that we could take to keep him from leaving the country, other than to have his bond raised, which seems to be a very sensible thing to do, as the report that he is to leave the country emanates as a press notice from his own office. He is now out on $2500 only. His bond should be promptly increased to $10[,]000, which he could not raise, and he would be put in the place where he should have been long ago. Should he be able to raise the bond he probably would skip and he should be kept under strict surveillance as it is only a short time now.

[W. W. GRIMES]

DJ-FBI, file 61. TN, recipient's copy.

Bureau Agent George R. Shanton, Chief, Department of Justice, New Orleans, to William J. Burns, Director, Bureau of Investigation

New Orleans, La., January 20, 1923

Re Marcus Garvey et al. have secured valuable information which will probably connect subject with police or Secret Service Agency attached Garvey Organisms headed by Esau Ramus formerly third Vice President of a Philadelphia Division Universal Negro Improvement Association deliberately planned death of Eason January first through raid conducted by police department documentary evidence secured showing Garvey sent Ramus to New Orleans stop Similar Secret Service organization at Philadelphia stop Ramus left city immediately after murder of [E]ason stop Above information wired New York and Philadelphia offices.

[GEORGE] SHANTON[1]

DJ-FBI, file 61. TG.

1. Colonel George R. Shanton (1868–1930) was commissioner of police in the Panama Canal Zone in 1904, joining the Department of Justice in 1922 after a distinguished military career. He was sent to Louisiana in 1923 to investigate the Ku Klux Klan and charges of debt peonage among sharecroppers (*NYT*, 25 September 1930).

Marcus Garvey and Robert L. Poston to Harry M. Daugherty

56 West 135th, New York City, January 20, 1923

On behalf of two and a half million loyal citizens[,] members of the [U]niversal Negro Improvement Association who have at all times proved their loyalty to the government of the United States[,] and on behalf of four hundred million Negroes throughout the World who look to the United States of America for justice[,] we protest against the scandalous and unfair attitude adopted toward the Universal Negro Improvement Association[,] a legal organization in the United States of America[,] in the raiding of the meeting place and the arrest of its members of the New Orleans division number one hundred and forty nine by officers of your department[1] who are being instigated to act against the Universal Negro Improvement Association by rival negro organizations[,] namely the National Association for the Advancement of Colored People[,] a group of socialists[; F]riends of [N]egro [F]reedom[,] a red socialist organization[;] and the African Blood Brotherhood[,] representatives of the [B]olshevists of Russia[. T]he Universal Negro Improvement Association is neither [S]ocialist[,] Bolshevist or Anarchist as your representatives are endeavoring to make out.[2] We have absolutely no connection with any disloyal movement and in our records of five years there can be found absolutely no trace of disloyalty to the United States of America in any of our utterances or communications[. W]e believe it unfair that a Department of the government should be used by rival organizations for the purpose of injuring those whom they desire to embarrass[. Y]ours truly,

MARCUS GARVEY, PRESIDENT GENERAL
Universal Negro Improvement Association
ROBERT L. POSTON, SECRETARY GENERAL

DNA, RG 60, file 198940-281. TG.

1. In a raid of the UNIA meeting held at the longshoremen's hall, police seized UNIA literature, including letters, New Orleans division papers, and documents pertaining to the Dyer and Shakespeare defense fund. Ike Whittmore, acting president of the UNIA division; Lawrence J. Davis, treasurer; Thomas Anderson, assistant secretary-general from the New York office (recently sent by Garvey to New Orleans); William Phillips, executive secretary; Rev. James Hill; John Carey, Jr., chairman of the board of trustees; Henry Lee, trustee; Thomas Franklin; James Hamilton; and Tiezekiah Griffith were arrested in the raid (*NYT*, 20 January 1923; *New Orleans Times-Picayune*, 20 January, 21 January, and 12 February 1923).

2. On 21 January 1923 Garvey was quoted in the *New York Times*:

There is absolutely no truth in the statement of the New Orleans police that they have seized anarchistic literature at a meeting of the Universal Negro Improvement Association. The association has no such literature, neither does it preach hatred for any one.

We have absolutely no connection with the murder of J.W.H. Eason, and the statement that Eason was a star witness against me is without foundation, for there was nothing the man could have said that would injure me. I have paid but little attention to the charge of using the mails to defraud, in that I know the whole affair to be a "frame-up" among jealous negroes who have been trying for some time to embarrass me. There is no more loyal American organization than the Universal Negro Improvement Association. (*NYT*, 21 January 1923)

Editorial Letter by Marcus Garvey

[[NEW YORK, January 23, 1923]]

FELLOW MEN OF THE NEGRO RACE, Greeting: . . .

THE ENEMIES OF THE U.N.I.A.

These Negroes who have been unable to do any harm to the Universal Negro Improvement Association because of its potency, and because of the impotence of Negroes to harm each other, have sought the majesty of the United States Government to get the Federal authorities to do what they of themselves could not do. But there may be a sad disappointment in store for somebody. The Jews were disappointed, because after the crucifixion of Jesus the doctrine He taught took a greater turn and scattered itself around the world, and today man in every clime professes His faith. I wonder if these Negroes realize that they are but laying the foundation for a greater Universal Negro Improvement Association when they attempt by their wicked propaganda and tactics to hold up the only movement through which the race will see salvation. We are not disturbed, we are only amused at the action of these traitors of the race. They have written all kinds of letters, they have made all kinds of misrepresentations to the white press and to the Government authorities, but it generally turns out that the fellow who digs the pit for the other falls into it himself. What these Negroes hope to achieve by so designedly and wickedly misrepresenting a Negro movement that is seeking the interest of the four hundred million Negroes of the world it is impossible to imagine. If it were possible for them to do harm to the Universal Negro Improvement Association what would be the result but that in time harm would be done to themselves by the very agency that they are using now to defeat this great organization. If you show a thief how to break into your neighbor's house it is only a question of time when he will break into yours. So that we are giving these fellows all the rope they want; one of these days they will hang themselves.

THE U.N.I.A. NOT ANARCHISTIC

It is strange, however, to see that the officials of the Government could be so carried away with mis-information as to allege that the Universal Negro Improvement Association is anarchistic and desires to overthrow the government. Why, the very people who gave them the information are the ones who are anarchists and who are no doubt plotting to overthrow the Government. If they want anarchistic literature they will not look for it in the meeting places or offices of the Universal Negro Improvement Association, but if they will investigate a little more they will find that their informants, who are agents of the Bolshevists, are the ones who have all the anarchistic literature in their possession, in that they openly receive money from Moscow and consort with the Soviet Government for the destruction of all other governments. The Universal Negro Improvement Association is not Socialist, Bolshevist nor anarchistic. We have absolutely no connection with any other organization but ourselves—we are pro-Negro. We believe that to be Socialists, Soviets, or what not, would be like being anything else among other people, and we are tired of following; we lead ourselves. The only connection we have is that which will make us a free and independent race of people on the continent of Africa. We have not to go to Russia for that; we have not to join the Socialist party for that. We can work for that ourselves.

No one need fear that the Universal Negro Improvement Association would waste its time joining any radical group of white men in any way for the overthrow of any government. No one could claim ever giving the Universal Negro Improvement Association one penny for spreading propaganda. Everything that we have done came through our own dimes and dollars, so that we have absolutely no obligation to anyone to make us anything else than what we are.

THE CRITICS OF THE U.N.I.A.

The Negroes who lead the anti-Universal Negro Improvement Association movements are of the type who have never been any use to the race, and will never be any, in that they fear the success of any real Negro movement which would detract from them the notoriety that they desire, which they generally use for the purpose of exploiting the ignorant of the race by presenting themselves as great leaders. The people are, however, gradually being awakened, and one of these fine mornings it would not be surprising if these so-called leaders find themselves deserted and despised by those whom they have deceived for so long.

Since these enemy organizations are determined to fight the Universal Negro Improvement Association by foul and unfair means, we promise them that we shall spare some time to present our case to the world as it should be and make it much harder for them to collect from the philanthropic whites whom they have tried to exploit for the last fourteen years. We shall let some of these men find useful occupations after we are through with them and not continue to live upon the charity of the sympathetic white people who have fed them under the belief of helping the race. Each of these leaders has his own pet group of white patrons to collect from, and that is why they viciously attack the Universal Negro Improvement Association, in that they realize that their occupations are going, and it is not so easy to collect now as before the organization came upon the scene, in that the white race is getting to understand that all Negroes are not beggars and that the representations that have been made to them before are false and inaccurate; hence, the tightening up upon these fellows who have had an easy time in collecting for philanthropic and uplift movements among Negroes.

THE NEED OF UNITY

Let all members of the Universal Negro Improvement Association unite the more throughout America and the world for the carrying through of the principles of this great organization. Now is the time for every loyal member to stand firm to the colors. The organization must be protected, and now is the time to do it. All divisions and members are requested to make an effort to pay their $1.00 assessment tax for this month of January, so as to enable the Parent Body to meet its annual budget. It is understood that no member will be regarded as financial except that $1.00 tax is paid. Pay this tax to your local immediately. With very best wishes for your success, I have the honor to be Your obedient servant,

MARCUS GARVEY
President-General
Universal Negro Improvement Association

Printed in *NW*, 27 January 1923. Original headlines omitted.

William J. Burns to Bureau Agent George R. Shanton

[*Washington, D.C.*] January 23, 1923

Dear Sir:

Special Agent J.W. Jones[1] is leaving Washington at once on a special assignment at New Orleans in connection with the murder of J.W.H. Eason, a material witness in the case of United States v. Marcus Garvey. Agent Jones will work undercover and submit his reports directly to the Bureau. He will report to you promptly upon arrival for the benefit of any information already procured by you on the case and it is probable that at various times he will need assistance or advice, which of course you will give. Should he desire to communicate with the Washington office by telegraph, he would be accorded that privilege and it may be necessary for you to keep in touch with the Philadelphia and New York offices for assistance in running out leads. Very truly yours,

W[ILLIAM]. J. B[URNS]
Director

DJ-FBI, file 61-50-192. TLI, carbon copy.

1. J.W. Jones was Confidential Informant 800.

Report by Special Agents Mortimer J. Davis and James E. Amos

New York, N.Y. Jan. 23, 1923

. . . The death of DR. EASON is but the culmination of many threats which have been made against Government witnesses in this case. Allied with DR. EASON was a woman by the name of MRS. DOROTHY LAWSON, of 2092 Madison Avenue, New York City, who is at the present time under subpoena in this case. Some time ago MRS. LAWSON and her husband were met on the street by a colored man, who, after drawing a revolver, threatened both MR. and MRS. LAWSON with death if they did not cease their attacks on GARVEY. This man was later identified and arrested and during the trial it was learned that he was a member of GARVEY's so-called "secret service." He is now serving a term in State's prison.

MRS. LAWSON, within the last few days has complained to Agent Amos that she is again being molested, the particular instance in question having occurred on Saturday last (January 20th) when two unknown men accosted her on the street.[1] Today Agents interviewed MRS. LAWSON, but outside of stating that she had seen one of these men previously around Liberty Hall, GARVEY's headquarters, she could furnish no further identification. Agents instructed MRS. LAWSON to walk through the section where GARVEYITES are strong, at which time we followed her, but she was not molested, neither could she locate either of the men alleged to have interfered with her.

Agents also interviewed CAPT. JOSHUA COCKBURN, who is also a Government witness. He advises us that new threats have been made against him. CAPT. COCKBURN has been previously threatened. The threats against him have also come from an unknown source.

Agents have instructed these witnesses to endeavor to obtain the names of persons threatening them or some identification through which they can be picked up. We have instructions from Asst. U.S. Attorney Mattuck to call to his immediate attention any attempts to interfere with the witnesses in this case. . . .

MORTIMER J. DAVIS
JAMES E. AMOS

DJ-FBI, file 61. TD.

1. Special Agent Amos reported on 22 January 1923:

> Mrs. [Dorothy] Lawson, a government witness in the Garvey case . . . claimed that two men whom she stated belong to the Garvey organization, had been following her and when she recognized them she immediately went up to a traffic policeman at the corner of 135th Street and Lenox Avenue and called his attention to this fact and the traffic officer told her to point them out and he would arrest them. The two parties in question, on seeing her talking to the traffic policeman, ran down the steps of the subway where it was impossible to follow and apprehend. (DJ-FBI, file 61)

Report by Special Employee Andrew M. Battle

New York City [*26 January 1923*]

Continuing on the above matter, the writer, in an interview with J.B. YEARWOOD, 620 Lenox Avenue, New York City, ascertained that YEARWOOD actually saw the letter given to RAMUS by GARVEY when RAMUS was sent to New Orleans and YEARWOOD also stated that it was absolutely true that RAMUS was the third party in the killing of DR. EASON, and in reply to whether a telegram had actually come to GARVEY after the shooting of DR. EASON and if GARVEY had put on the books of the U.N.I.A. $60. and classified it as bond money, YEARWOOD replied, "Yes."

The writer then advised YEARWOOD that it would be to his advantage to be absolutely open and above board in telling all he knew if called on to verify the conversations and facts stated by YEARWOOD to Agent. YEARWOOD replied that if he was called on he would give to the best of his recollection all the facts as known by him and further stated that he had opposed GARVEY in many ways and that GARVEY had no liking for him, and if it had been left to GARVEY he (YEARWOOD) would not be there today talking with the writer. He also said, "And I very much fear from the way GARVEY has managed things, that there is a possibility of all of us being arrested and I am very sorry that I ever took the job at the last convention and GARVEY is not fit to be at the head of the U.N.I.A." Yearwood then showed the writer four Liberian Loan Bonds of $2,000. each and a note in African Communities League of $500. . . .

In a conversation had with S[Y]DNEY DE BOURG, 104 West 138th Street, DE BOURG informed the writer that the telegram sent by RAMUS from New Orleans after the killing of DR. EASON was sent to A.M. CARTER, residing at 56 West 136th Street, New York City, and that YEARWOOD had destroyed the letters coming from the manager of the New Orleans Division in reply to the letter sent by GARVEY relative to giving RAMUS work.

ANDREW M. BATTLE

DJ-FBI, file 61. TD.

Reports by Confidential Informant Capt. J.W. Jones to William J. Burns

123 No. Roman St. New Orleans, La.
Jan, 27, 1923

Sir:

After a conference with agent Harry Gulley, I proceeded to investigate the case assigned to me undercover. I have interviewed S.V. Robinson and his wife[,] who at one time were the organizers for the Universal Negro Improvement Association in this state and are, at the present, active members of the organization in this City. I know Robinson and his wife as they came to the New York headquarters several times while I was working there. Both Robinson and his wife were very free in talking to me as they know me only as a loyal member of the organization. Robinson says that the police have the right men but he believes these men were the tools of Esau Ramus. Esau Ramus was the agent sent down here by Garvey, from Philadelphia.[1] The police have in their hands a letter address[ed] to the president of the organization in this city signed by Garvey, telling the president that Ramus will reside in New Orleans in the future and to give him any work that he could find for him to do, not saying that Ramus was to establish a police force. After Ramus was here for a few weeks the president of the organization here wrote to New York to find out just what Ramus was to do here, as the members did not approve of this police force that Ramus was trying to organize. This letter was answered by Garvey's secretary saying that Garvey was out of town, but, that Ramus had organized a police force in Philadelphia and no doubt that Mr. Garvey would approve of his organizing a police force here. This appears to be all the communication that took place between Garvey's office and this city in regards to Ramus. All of these communications are in the hands of the local office of this department. The contents of these communications were confirmed to me in my interview with Robinson. During my interview I tried to learn from Robinson the whereabouts of Ramus. Robinson says that Ramus has left the city and is likely in Philadelphia, or New York, but did not know his address. Since the two men that are arrested for the murder of Eason are local men and the fact that these people here bel[ie]ve them to have been the tools of Ramus, and the arrest of Ramus will help to clear these local members, if they knew the whereabouts of Ramus they would turn him up.

After my interview with Robinson I interviewed Willia[m] Phillips secretary to the local division. Phillips who was a secretary to the Boston division at one time, is also known to me personally. Phillips talked to me very freely and deplores the murder of Eason as Eason was a personal friend of his. He says that before the arrest of these two men he received a threat[en]ing letter because he had made a statement that if he knew who the men were that had killed Eason he would turn them over to the police. Phillips seems to be very much disgusted with the organization and says as soon as this trial is over he is going to leave here. Phillips says that he thinks that Ramus has left the country for some part of the West Indies.

After going over the evidence in this case with agent Gulley, agent in charge of this office sent a telegram to New York and Philadelphia to apprehend if possible Esau Ramus. Pictures of Ramus were sent along with reports to these offices. I am enclosing picture of Ramus with this report. I believe Ramus can give the necessary evidence in this case to secure an indictment against certain parties as an "a[cc]essory before the fact." I will continue my investigation and attend all meetings of the association while here as I have been invited to attend by both Phillips and Robinson. Respectfully,

J. W. JONES

DJ-FBI, file 61. TLS, recipient's copy.

1. A memorandum written for the director of the Bureau of Investigation by J. Edgar Hoover, who was then assistant director, stated: "The head of Garvey's organization in Philadelphia, one Ramus, made a mysterious trip to New Orleans; and shortly after Eason left the building, he was murdered by three Garvey men, two of whom he identified before he died. Ramus got away, but the others are now held" (DJ-FBI, file 61, 27 January 1923).

123 Roman St., c/o Turner,
New Orleans, La., Jan. 29, 1923

Sir:

In continuance of my investigation undercover, I again interviewed S. V. Robinson[,] 2222 Phillips St.[,] in hopes that I would learn the whereabouts of Esau Ramus, and any other information concer[n]ing this case. I attended the meeting at 2029 Jackson Ave. and freely mingled with members of the organization in hopes of picking up some lead in this case. The members freely talked of the murder of Eason and they all seem to think that a good deed had been done. In discussing the case with Robinson, who seems to be possessed of more facts than anyone else, he said that Ramus lived at Dyer's (one of the men arrested for this crime) house, and that Dyer, after not receiving much encouragement at the meeting in organizing this police force of his, took the matter up with a few members, at his, Dyer's[,] house. He says that he doesn't believe that Ramus made known to these men what his real mission here was. Said that Ramus was a good talker and that he used these men as tools. These men are denying their guilt as they think they will get more support if they do so. Then, Mrs. Dyer is saying that Ramus came to her house after Eason had been killed and said, that he, Ramus, "had killed the S—— B—."[1] It is very doubtful if Ramus made use of any such expression but Mrs. Dyer is using this to help clear her husband. Robinson is of the opinion that if Ramus is arrested Dyer and Shakespe[a]re will be released. I have encouraged this idea as I think it will help to locate Ramus.

At the meeting last night they took up a collection for a defense fund and collected $115.00 (one hundred and fifteen dollars[)]. They have collected and had pledged a total of $915.00 (nine hundred and fifteen dollars) for a defense fund from this division, and Garvey is collecting a sim[i]lar fund from all divisions.

Robinson told me last night that the last time that Garvey was down here they expected to have some trouble with the police, but they were prepared for the police as they had about twenty men across the street from the hall at which Garvey was speaking, with plenty arms, and ammunition, and if the police had attempted to arrest Garvey that night the streets would have been run[n]ing with blood. I have no doubt of the truthfulness of this statement, that is[,] about being prepared, and I am sure it would have been the starting of one of the country's wors[t] riots.

At the present I am trying in some way to be arrested so that I can be put in the cells with Dyer and Shakespe[a]re. Agent Gulley and myself will likely have to arrange another raid and let me be caught in the raid, otherwise I am afraid they would not talk to me even if I was put in the cell.[2]

I am very careful not to uncover myself as it would kill what chances I may have in the future with this and other organizations of a sim[i]lar kind.

A telegram was received from New York today telling this office to send warrant up there for Ramus' arrest. Agent Gulley went over to court this afternoon to arrange about this warrant.

I would add that every effort be used to locate Ramus. He is well known to both the Philadelphia and the New York divisions of this organization. Agent Gulley is checking this afternoon on all steamship lines to see if he has left the country from this port. If he is in New York, Harold Saltus, who is the head of Garvey's police force in that city, will be in touch with Ramus. Saltus is the advertising manager for the Negro World, Garvey's paper. He is the most likely man for Ramus to get in touch with, and then I know that Garvey will trust Saltus a little more than anyone that is working for him.

Will continue this investigation and attend another meeting of the organization on Thursday night. Respectfully,

J. W. JONES

DJ-FBI, file 61. TLS, recipient's copy.

1. Agent Harry D. Gulley later reported on a conversation with E. Strain, who stated that "she was present at the home of Cornelius Dyer on January 3rd, 1923 when Esau Ramus entered the rooming house . . . and in her presence stated that he had killed Eason." Ramus then "left hurriedly and had not been seen nor heard of since" (report of Special Agent Harry D. Gulley, 8 February 1923, DJ-FBI, file 61).

2. Another raid occurred on 11 February, when twenty police armed with tear gas guns raided a UNIA meeting of five hundred men and women held at the longshoremen's hall. Police arrested Thomas Anderson and others who were on the podium—Mrs. Anderson, William Phillips, Henry Lee, Lawrence Davis, Rev. James Hill, Effie Hathaway, and Florence Watterhouse. They were charged with inciting a riot and unlawful assembly. Police seized papers showing the UNIA was raising defense funds for Dyer and Shakespeare, and Anderson was reported to have shown the police, as he was being led from the hall, a letter signed by the Ku Klux Klan warning him to stop putting "dangerous ideas into the heads of ignorant negroes." There is no evidence that Jones was arrested in the raid.

Five days after the raid a group of UNIA women, two of whom had been arrested in the raids, launched a formal protest with the mayor. Contesting the charge that they were "dangerous characters," the women based their protest on the grounds that they were property owners, taxpayers, and good citizens. They called the UNIA "our church, our clubhouse, our theatre, our fraternal order and our school" and invited the mayor to the next meeting to assure UNIA members that New Orleans "is a city of fair play, even for the most humble and ignorant law-abiding citizens as well as law-abiding black strangers." When those arrested were brought to trial, they were found innocent of all charges (*NYT*, 20 January 1923; *New Orleans Times-Picayune*, 20 January, 21 January and 12 February 1923; *NW*, 10 March, 24 March and 14 April 1923).

Thomas W. Anderson to Robert L. Poston

2059 Jackson Ave., New Orleans, La.,
January 31, 1923

My Dear Mr. Poston:—

I am informed that early in the month of December, Mr. Wm. Phillips, Executive Secretary of Division no. 149, placed into the hands of the Commissioner, Mr. Smyer, a money order for twenty-six dollars and seventy-five cents ($26.75) with a request that this be sent to the Parent Body as price of charter and membership fee for the Gentilly Chapter, New Orleans, La.

This application has been ignored by the Commissioner for some time and it was only after a third urgent demand by this Chapter that Mr. Phillips accepted the money, secured the money order and placed it in the Commissioner's hands, who promised to have charter here within two weeks. To date, we are informed that nothing has been heard as to this matter from any source, Mr. Smyer nor the Parent Body.

Mr. Smyer keeps himself away from this part of the state, letters do not reach him and we are asking you, if such an order has been sent in by him and also as regards [one] hundred and twenty dollars given him to be sent to the parent body, by this Division. Several Divisions report that they have turned money over to him for the Parent Body. Tell us if this man has sent any money in at all to the Parent Body.

Dyer and Shakespear[e] were indicted yesterday for Murder.[1] Federal authorities are making frantic efforts to involve the organization. My case, I believe, is being held up pending the outcome of this effort. It is a futile effort for our hands are clean as well as our conscience.

That man, stout bright fellow, formerly connected with the Negro World, is here and is making himself active, we are informed, as regards this Eason matter.[2] We are convinced that he is in Federal employ.

The morale of this Division is 100%, sorry we can't say same of some of the officers. The membership has pledged nearly a thousand dollars for defense of this case of the officers and myself. A thousand dollars is the attorney's fee. As to the Dyer matter the defense fund now being subscribed on the President General's appeal will have to be used for Dyer and Shakespear[e]. I believe that four hundred dollars all told, will be sufficient, which will be used to refund to the source now supplying funds. We are doing our best here and will call upon the Parent Body only in cases of actual necessity[,] but when we do it should not be necessary for us to make a second appeal. Please impress this upon the President General. I wrote him last night, myself.

The long-promised funds are a long time reaching us. It appears that it is hard for the Parent Body to realize the necessity of immediate action. For God's sake let us get down to business. Anything else isn't worth a tinker's d———.

Our members jammed the court last Tuesday when we thought the preliminary hearing of the men was to be had. They did themselves fine. It is an inspiration to be among these people yet I will be happy when I can say, Good-bye, to this part of the field. Not that I am afraid but I know that I am needed in the office.

Ask the President General to prepare copies of articles of incorporation and other necessities for we must register in this state. I want to take care of that before I leave here. It is a feather in these people's cap that they purchased property, they desire to build[,] which will mean more to them and the organization than I can now tell you. After registering here they can build. It is unwise to do so before then. Urge this upon the Chief, I asked him in my letter not to lay this aside and forget it as he usually does. Also return that bill of sale, sent up by the Division. The other changes referred to by myself must be suspended protem. We are all working together in interest of the organization.

Send me some letterheads by the way, P.D.Q. Madame sends her regards. Well[,] boy, I am the first of the great host to go behind the bar, I'll tell you how it feels when I see you, but we are anything but down-hearted. The local department of justice said that Garvey and Anderson were the two most dangerous men in the organization. I have gained seven pounds since he made that statement. Awaiting your reply, I am Sincerely yours,

THOS W. ANDERSON

DJ-FBI, file 61. TL, transcript.

1. Shakespeare and Dyer were indicted in New Orleans on 30 January 1923. The *New York Times* reported that on his arrest Shakespeare was wearing "ponderous gold epaulets, a grotesque uniform and much silk braid, his official regalia as Police Chief . . . in Marcus Garvey's proposed Black Republic" (*NYT*, 31 January 1923).
2. A reference to Confidential Informant Capt. J.W. Jones.

Marcus Garvey to the White Press of the World

[*New York*] January 1923

PRESS RELEASE

News for Publication:
You may use this bit of news to your advantage

IMMEDIATE RELEASE

The Following Letter is Released At The American Headquarters of the Universal Negro Improvement Association, 52–54–56 West 135th Street, New York City[,] To The White Press Of The World by MARCUS GARVEY As An Explanation Of The Aims And Objects Of The Universal Negro Improvement Association of which he is President-General.

AN ANSWER TO HIS MANY CRITICS.

THE EDITOR

Sir:

You have, for quite some time, been publishing news, letters and other articles in your paper purporting to be information about the activities of the Universal Negro Improvement Association, the "Back to Africa Movement," so named by critics, the Black Star Line Steamship Corporation and myself, but you have never been fair enough to give to the public and your readers the other side of the story of the picture painted by you.

It has been my policy not to pay any attention to prejudiced and unfair criticism, in that I always believed that truth of any kind cannot be permanently crushed; but whilst I personally still feel this way, a large number of my friends and well wishers have for more than a thousand times endeavored to have me place the Association I represent in a proper light before the public so that the general misrepresentations of the Movement can be clarified, I still would not have yielded but for the increasing demands made upon me by those whose interest I serve, and because this misrepresentation has been conveyed to a large number of your readers who seem to regard me as some "hideous" person who hates all white people.

I am not blaming you for the stand you have taken against me and against the Movement I represent because I know that you have arrived at your conclusions through the misrepresentations made to you directly or indirectly by my enemies within my own Race who, being jealous of my success in assembling together more members of my Race throughout this Country and the world than any other person has done, have been and are endeavoring to so misrepresent me as to cause an opposition sentiment to develop that would eventually handicap and thwart the objects of the Organization I am leading.

The real function of the Press is public service without prejudice or partiality; to convey the truth as it is seen and understood without favoritism or bias.

You have already by your many reports published one side of my activities; I feel that you will be honest enough to now publish at least a part of the other side.

First of all, let me say that all that ha[s] been published about the Universal Negro Improvement Association and about me, tending to show that there is any hatred of other peoples, any scheme for personal gain, any desire to stir up Race antagonism, and that my Organization tends to promote Race friction, are all false.

The following Preamble to the Constitution of the Universal Negro Improvement Association speaks for itself:

> The Universal Negro Improvement Association and African Communities' League is a social, friendly, humanitarian, charitable, educational, institutional, constructive and expansive society, and is founded by persons desiring to the utmost to work for the general

uplift of the Negro peoples of the world, and the members pledge themselves to do all in their power to conserve the rights of their noble Race and to respect the rights of all mankind, believing always in the brotherhood of man and the Fatherhood of God. The motto of the Organization is: "One God! One Aim! One Destiny!["] Therefore, Let justice be done to all mankind, realizing that if the strong oppresses the weak, confusion and discontent will ever mark the path of man, but with love, faith and charity towards all, the reign of peace and plenty will be heralded into the world and the generations of man shall be called blessed.

Surely you will not find hate or anything unworthy in the above declaration.

The oft repeated statement that the Movement is sponsored and supported by the ignorant and gullible is so frivolous as to need no comment. Our Movement reflects the highest intelligence of the Race and as proof of this, we have challenged and still challenge anyone within the Race to debate our differences. No one has been manly enough out of the critics to accept the challenge.

Among our bitterest critics and opponents are W.E.B. Du Bois, James Weldon Johnson and their National Association for the Advancement of Colored People, yet, these persons have not the manhood to match the intelligence of their Association with that of the Universal Negro Improvement Association by accepting the challenge.

Our Organization stands for the highest in Racial ideals, yielding to all Races the right to ascend to the loftiest peak of human progress and demanding for ourselves a similar privilege.

Starting our Organization in New York four and one half (4 1/2) years ago with Thirteen (13) members, we have now grown into an approximate membership of five million (5,000,000) people scattered all over the World, but principally to be found in the United States of America, Canada, South and Central America, the West Indies and Africa. It is because of the rapid growth and success of this Organization that other Negroes have sought to defeat me by hostile propaganda in their own newspapers and with the misrepresentations they supply to the White Press from time to time against which I am now complaining.

Every effort among Negroes has been made and exhausted by my enemies to defeat me and yet they have failed, hence they resort to the Government and the White Press for the accomplishment of this purpose. To repeat, it is not because I fear defeat or the sting of unfriendly or unfair criticism that I write to you because I owe my success in organization to no one. Neither the Press nor my enemies made me, so neither can they break me. No influence, caring not how great, can defeat a righteous cause so I am not personally disturbed, but I would like the public to be correctly informed about the Movement I represent for the good of the members and those interested.

The Negro problem in America and elsewhere must be solved. We cannot do this by postponing the issue or by sidetracking it. We might as well face it now.

Some Negroes, such as the faction of the mulatto W.E.B. Du Bois, believe that the problem will be solved by assimilation and miscegenation; at least they believe that the black Race will become, through social contact and intercourse, so mixed up with the white Race as to produce a new type, probably like Du Bois himself, which will in time be the real American. It is for such a contingency that he and his associates are consciously or unconsciously working.

We of the Universal Negro Improvement Association believe in a pure black Race, just as how all self-respecting whites believe in a pure white Race as far as that can be.

We are conscious of the fact that slavery brought upon us the curse of many colors within our Race, but that is no reason why we of ourselves should perpetuate the evil, hence, instead of encouraging a wholesale bastardy in the Race, we feel that we should now set out to create a Race type and standard of our own which could not, in the future, be stigmatized by bastardy but could be recognized and respected as the true Race type anteceding even our own time.

We believe that the Negro has at least, a social[,] cultural and political destiny of his own and any attempt to make a white man of him is bound to fail in the end. In like manner, we believe that you cannot successfully make a Negro out of a white man in that he too has at least a social, cultural and political destiny of his own. Therefore, the fullest opportunity should be given to both Races to develop independently a civilization of their own, meaning not to infer thereby that either Race should not, in a limited degree, become a part of the civilization of each without losing their respective Racial, cultural, social and political identities.

If this can be done, then we feel that the Negro too should have a Government of his own and not remain in the Countries of whites to aspire for and to positions that he will never get under the rule of the majority group upon his merely asking for or demanding such positions by an accidental Constitutional right.

If the Negro is to have a Government of his own of any importance, then there can be no better place than Africa, the land to which centuries ago he was born a Native. Admitting that this is right, is the reason why the Universal Negro Improvement Association[,] of which I am President-General, raises the cry of: "Africa For the Africans at Home and Abroad." I see [*that this*] will be the only solution of the Negro problem not only in America but all over the world.

We have been brutally criticized for advancing this programme as a solution of the Race problem. Some critics have been honest enough to give their reason for attacking us, others have done so, as I have already stated, through jealousy and prejudice.

Within the Negro Race, if I must repeat, there is as much prejudice, and

I believe probably more, than is exercised against us by other Races. Some mulattos and other types within the Race do not want to be classified with Negroes and hate to be identified with anything African in color or in spirit except for immediate personal benefit. Such persons are mainly responsible for the general opposition to the African programme in that they claim that they are not to be personally benefited; that they have "not lost anything in Africa." The[y] believe that being the offsprings of black and white in America, they constitute the only true America.

How far the two Races will travel together socially, industrially and politically in America before a serious civil clash ensues is the speculation of all earnest thoughtful people. It is because I personally want to prevent such a clash that I am advocating the cause of the Universal Negro Improvement Association.

My interest in the Negro peoples of America and of the world is purely Racial, because I feel proud of my Race; I have the highest regard for the Motherhood of the Race and I see absolutely no reason why all Negroes should not be as proud of themselves as other Races are.

Now let us look at the Race problem reasonably.

We are educating the Negro, the slave of the last century. He is so advanced educationally that he claims scholastic recognition everywhere. Place him in any school, college or university and he comes out with honors. In Science, Music, Art and Literature, he is holding a place of equality with other Races everywhere. His ability fits him no longer for the farm, cotton field, or plantation as a Race. He seeks broader opportunities in every field. He is a Citizen. He pays Taxes. He observes the Law. He supports the Government. He applies for and seeks the position that attracts him.

"Why shouldn't I be President?" he asks himself. "I have the education and the ability."

"Why shouldn't I be a member of the Cabinet, a Post-Master General, Attorney-General, Secretary of War or Secretary of State?["]

"Why shouldn't I be Governor of the State, Mayor of the City, a Judge of the Supreme Court, Police Commissioner o[r] President of the Board of Aldermen?["]

"Why shouldn't I be Chief in Gimbel Brothers,[1] Macy's[2] or Wanamaker's?"[3]

"Why shouldn't I be a Conductor on the Railroad, or the Pullman Car or Tramp Car service?"

"Why shouldn't I be employed in all useful and productive industries of the Nation?"

All these are positions and jobs sought by the majority group of whites in America and elsewhere. As the Negro becomes more insistent on these demands for Constitutional rights and privileges and threatens the more to compete with the white man for the job that the latter seeks and believes worthwhile having, then the inevitable conflict will come, and the group that is not strong enough to hold its own will go down, irrespective of the law and of the Government because the law and the Government are but executive expressions of the sober will of the people, but when the people, through prejudice or any mass opinion, become dissatisfied, the law and the Government are no longer able to control them in their action.

In this respect, I would refer you to the industrial riots of East St. Louis and Chicago;[4] the political riot of Washington[5] and the commercial riot of Tulsa, Oklahoma.[6] The things that the white majority want in their own Countries they will not yield to the Negro or to ANY OTHER RACE and that is natural.

The only sensible thing for the Negro to do, therefore, is to "BUILD" for himself. This can be done without friction or animosity between the Races and that is why the Universal Negro Improvement Association believes in the building up of Africa for the Negro Race.

Those Negroes who are too lazy to work and lay the foundation for such a Government are among those who criticize us.

Pilgrim Fathers we had in America before we enjoyed the delights of New York, Chicago or Boston. Pilgrim Fathers we must have if Africa is to rise from her slumber and darkness.

We of the Universal Negro Improvement Association are satisfied to be called ignorant and gullible in working toward this end.

The Black Star Line's failure has been made much of by the Press and our critics. In another letter, I will explain to the public, through you, the cause of the failure of this Corporation.[7] Yours truly,

MARCUS GARVEY
President General
Universal Negro Improvement Association

PRO, FO 371/8513. TDS. MU, WEBDB, 1923 general file. The copy of the statement sent to Du Bois in February bears the handwritten endorsement "This is it." The document's letterhead contains the following:

Universal Negro Improvement Ass'n
Cable Address: "Unimpro"; American Headquarters: 56 West 135th Street, New York City; Telephone Harlem 2877
African Headquarters: Monrovia, Liberia, West Africa
West Indian Headquarters: Kingston, Jamaica
Central American Headquarters: Panama City, Panama
South American Headquarters: Demerara, British Guiana
International Officers
His Supreme Highness Gabriel Johnson, Potentate;
Hon. Marcus Garvey D.S.O.E., President-General;
Sir Leroy Bundy, D.D.S. D.S.O.E., Asst. President General;
Sir Robt. L. Poston, K.C.O.N., Secretary-General;
Sir Clifford Bourne, D.S.O.E., High Chancellor.

1. The Gimbel brothers, Jacob (1850–1922), Charles (1861–1932), Ellis (1865-1950), and Bernard (1885–1966), were merchants who established department stores in Philadelphia, New York, and several other cities (*WBD*).

2. Rowland H. Macy (1822–1877) opened the original Macy's department store in New York in 1857 (*NYT*, 31 March 1877).

3. John Wanamaker (1838–1922) started his men's clothing business in 1861 in Philadelphia and opened a large department store in New York in 1896. He was succeeded in 1922 by his son, Lewis Rodman Wanamaker (*WBD*).

4. An explosion of racial tensions between white ethnic European workers and black migrants from the South triggered both the East St. Louis and Chicago race riots. These tensions were largely a product of intense competition for jobs in local industry as well as for housing, which involved conflict over residential boundaries (Elliott Rudwick, *Race Riot at East St. Louis, July 2, 1917* [Carbondale: Southern Illinois University Press, 1964], chap. 1; Arthur I. Waskow, *From Race Riot to Sit-in, 1919 and the 1960's* [Gloucester, Mass.: Peter Smith, 1975], pp. 39–41).

5. The underlying causes of the Washington riot have been attributed to "the accession of the southern-oriented Wilson administration," the rapid influx of southern whites into the city, and their resentment at the entrance of blacks into higher-paying jobs during wartime (Arthur I. Waskow, *From Race Riot to Sit-in*, pp. 21–22).

6. During the 1921 Tulsa riot, white mobs burned the city's black business and residential districts to the ground (Scott Ellsworth, *Death in a Promised Land: The Tulsa Race Riot of 1921* [Baton Rouge: Louisiana State University Press, 1982], pp. 45–70).

7. This second letter does not appear to have been sent.

Article by W.E.B. Du Bois

[*Crisis*, January 1923]

THE U.N.I.A.

What are the facts concerning the membership and finances of the Universal Negro Improvement Association under the leadership of Marcus Garvey?

We do not know and we have asked in vain for information, stating[,] as we still insist, that a public organization claiming to represent the Negro race, collecting monies not only from its own membership but broadcast, owes a regular and specific accounting to the public.

We must therefore depend: 1st, on the published report of 1921 and its analysis made first by W. A. Domingo[1] in the *Crusader* and afterwards corrected in minor details in our own office. 2nd, on the suppressed report of 1922, ordered printed by the Congress but not yet issued. This report we now print for the first time.

Mr. Garvey's claims of membership for the U.N.I.A. have been untrue and even fantastic. In the CRISIS articles of December, 1920, and January, 1921, we were unable to say how widespread the Garvey movement was, but, believing then part of its published assertions, assumed that it had less than 300,000 paid-up members. Since that, Mr. Garvey has reiterated his statements as to the large membership of his association. At Port Antonio, Jamaica, April 4th, 1921, he claimed "an active membership of four million scattered the world over." In a letter in the Kingston, Jamaica, *Daily Gleaner*, March 26th, 1921, he wrote: "There are two million members of the Universal Negro Improvement Association in the United States." The only chance for checking these statements up until now, has been furnished by the reports of officials at his second annual conference. [J.] B. Yearwood, the Assistant Secretary General, says there were, August 1st, 1921, 418 chartered Divisions and in addition to these there were 422 not yet chartered; but he made no statement as to the number of members.

W. A. Domingo in the *Crusader* of October, 1921, called attention to the report of the Chancellor and auditor. According to this report, which covers the period from September 1st, 1920, to July 30, 1921, the sum of $19,562.80 was paid in as "death tax." Mr. Domingo says that this death tax is a tax of ten cents per month per member remitted by the branches to the parent body. As the report covers eleven months, this shows a paid-up membership of 17,784 persons.

Another method of estimating the membership is from the dues received from the branches. These dues, according to a statement from Mr. Garvey, are thirty-five cents a month, or four dollars and twenty cents a year. Four-fifths of the dues remain with the branches and one-fifth is remitted to the parent body. This one-fifth for the eleven months, September 1st, 1920, to July 30th, 1921, amounted to $7,471.26, indicating a total amount collected for dues from the membership of $37,356.30. If we divide this sum by eleven months dues, we have 9,703 paid-up members. The secretary reports that the greatest number of dues paid in any one month was in June, 1921, indicating 15,262 members as a maximum. From these figures it seems certain that the membership of this movement was considerably less than 100,000 nominal members in 1921, and somewhere between ten and twenty thousand active members.

The second annual convention was held in New York, August, 1921. Mr. Garvey announced: "50,000 delegates will participate." Noah D. Thompson, one of the delegates, asserted that there were less than 300 accredited delegates in attendance and that most of those were from New York.

The third convention met in New York in August, 1922. Mr. Garvey promised "the greatest event in the history of the Negro race—100,000 deputies and delegates to take part, representatives coming from Africa, Asia, Europe, Australia, South and Central America, Canada, United States, and the West Indies."

A record of balloting by delegates showed less than 200 delegates present including the New York delegates. The financial reports submitted were ordered printed by these delegates and we take pleasure in obeying their wishes:

UNIVERSAL NEGRO IMPROVEMENT ASSOCIATION
FINANCIAL REPORT—YEAR ENDING JULY 31ST, 1922

Receipts	General Funds
Balance in Bank Aug. 1st, 1921	$10,913.67
Membership Fees	3,662.03
Sales of supplies to Branches	10,328.59
Death tax	28,723.30
20% dues from Branches	14,722.59
Convention Funds	10,484.21
Sale of Almanacs and Pictures, etc.	3,522.75
Assessment Tax	20,543.17

Fees for Charters	5,192.05
Contributions (voluntary)	34,165.25
Loans (Schedule)	6,987.50
Refunds	592.52
Redeposit checks	3,247.18
Exchange checks	580.71
General Check (Schedule)	10,254.49
	$163,920.01
Construction Loan Notes	23,633.54
	$187,633.54

Disbursements

Light and Heat	$870.06
Telephone, telegraph, and cables	2,553.23
Postage and expressage	4,512.30
Minor repairs	351.98
Furniture and Fixtures	1,368.85
Salaries of officers	42,394.56
Salaries of employees	39,929.90
Salaries of men in Liberia	2,678.50
Salaries of B.S.L. Band	1,675.68
Travelling Expenses	8,735.72
Printing	11,263.88
Stationery and Office Supplies	2,141.22
Loans	1,668.00
Death benefits	4,439.64
Real Estate and Mortgages	25,384.75
Pay't to B.S.L. lease 54–56	3,000.00
Advance to B.S.L. a/c lease	3,668.98
Pay't to N.Y. Local a/c purchase N. World	1,300.00
General	17,192.38
	$175,129.63
Construction Notes Rec'd	10,962.68
Interest on same	828.85
	$186,921.16
Receipts	$187,633.54
Disbursements	186,921.16
Balance	$712.38

From this report it appears that death taxes of $28,723.30 were paid this year, representing payments on $68,664.80 due and unpaid last year and the payments for this year. This indicates less than 21,000 paid up members, only a part of whom belong to this year. Twenty percent of the membership dues amount to $14,722.59. In a membership of 17,500. We may conclude therefore that the U.N.I.A. has at present less than 18,000 active members.

This membership has paid in as dues, taxes and fees, $72,843.14. In addition to this, it has paid $13,851.34 in supplies, a total of $86,694.48, or nearly $5 per member. In addition to this these members and other persons have given and loaned to the organization during the year, $62,600.64; this makes total cash receipts of $149,292.12. We are not including among these receipts construction loan notes given but not yet paid. This money is reported to have been expended as follows:

Office expenses	$11,796.64—	6.5 percent
Salaries	86,678.64—	51.0 percent
Loans and Interest	33,721.73—	20.0 percent
Printing and Travelling	21,299.60—	12.5 percent
Unspecified General Exp.	17,192.38—	10.0 percent

Total $170,688.99

By counting in their loan notes and other bookkeeping items, the association reports a balance of $712.38

A balance sheet, condensed from the original, gives the following figures:

Resources

Cash, in various Funds	$20,881.24
Furniture and Fixtures	6,335.35
Machinery	23,963.42
Real Estate	18,400.00
Stock in Black Star Line & Factories Inc.	37,460.00
Good Will in Negro World	60,000.00
Accts. Receivable, principally from Branches	93,707.83
Notes Receivable	13,628.94
Inventory	4,222.55
Leases and Deposits	7,118.98
Total	$285,718.31

Liabilities

Notes Payable	$184,177.47
Mortgages Payable	5,500.44
Loans and Accounts Payable	37,050.48
Salaries and Death Claims	34,141.99
Total	$260,870.38

Printed in *Crisis* 25, no. 3 (January 1923): 120–122.

1. In a letter to W.A. Domingo dated 18 January 1923, Du Bois stated that he, too, agreed that "in the attack on Garvey, the object should be the opinions of the man and not the man himself or his birthplace." Du Bois, pointing out that he was himself of West Indian descent, reiterated

his opposition to deportation as punishment for Garvey (Herbert Aptheker, ed., *The Correspondence of W.E.B. Du Bois, 1920–1929* [Amherst: University of Massachusetts Press, 1973], pp. 263–264).

Perry W. Howard to William J. Burns

Washington. February 3, 1923

In the matter of the informal charges preferred against Marcus Garvey and his movement by Du Bois, Johnson and Pickens, representing the National Association for the Advancement of Colored People, and others, I beg to most respectfully advise in the interest of the Department of Justice that you be not guided by the bare allegations of these particular persons and that you make your independent investigations[1] to ascertain the truth or falsity of the same for the following reasons, to-wit:

1. Garvey's organization and the National Association for the Advancement of Colored People are rival organizations among the Negroes of this country, and their rivalry is very tense.

2. While Garvey has a vision that is impossible of realization, the National Association for the Advancement of Colored People is equally as visionary.

3. While the proponents of these charges allege that Garvey is stirring up race friction, it is true on the other hand that the N.A.A.C.P., as directed by Du Bois, Johnson and Pickens, has done more to create race friction in this country than any other agency I know.

4. The Garvey movement is not political, while the N.A.A.C.P. turns up in every campaign, in which we engage for the election of Republican candidates, as dyed-in-the-wool Democrats.[2]

5. The National Association for the Advancement of Colored People operates The Crisis through Dr. Du Bois, and I am attaching hereto a copy of the last issue, which is about as Bolshevistic as the propaganda by Haywood,[3] et al., and I would like for you to read particularly the references to the administration and some of our outstanding Senators.

6. That the allegations as to Garveyism taking on the aspects of Ku Kluxism, all their statements are as to attempts, etc. In other words, it is a case of my being a Methodist and assailing the other fellow for being a Baptist, and he resents it with the result that there is a near fight. That is about the sum total of their allegations.

7. Robert S. Abbott, representing The Defender and one of the proponents of these charges, is my very intimate and personal friend; but in looking well to the interest of the Department, especially that justice may be done, it is well to take into consideration that there has been considerable litigation obtaining between The Chicago Defender and the Marcus Garvey movement; this being in the nature of a libel suit, which gained wide publicity

and was in the courts for quite a few years.

8. It is of special note that all the allegations made against the Garvey movement, if true would only be offenses punishable by state jurisdictions, and I see nothing of which any Federal jurisdiction has any right or reason to take cognizance.

9. It reduces itself to a cannibalistic scheme of one rival getting rid of the other by annihilation or otherwise.

Concluding[,] I beg to suggest that I hold no brief for Garvey and I am not even personally acquainted with him, but I do not want to see the Department in the ridiculous attitude of throwing its strong arm of activities into a sweeping investigation of charges that are preferred by his rivals, many of whom are doing more damage to the general welfare of the Nation than his movement.[4] Respectfully

PERRY W. HOWARD

DJ-FBI, file 61. TMS, recipient's copy.

1. According to a report in the *Washington Star* of 3 February 1923, the U.S. Department of Justice claimed that its agents "have not undertaken any investigation of the Universal Negro Improvement Association and Marcus Garvey, its president, on allegations that it is fostering propaganda looking to creating dissensions between the white and black races in this country."

2. Howard had long insisted that the NAACP favored the Democratic party. In a letter written on 23 November 1922 to T. Coleman du Pont, an unsuccessful Republican candidate for senator in Delaware, Howard said, "I confess to you that I have blood in my eyes for the National Association for the Advancement of Colored People. . . . The purpose of this letter is to call attention of you and other outstanding statesmen to the fact that the National Association for the Advancement of Colored People is purely a Negro Democratic organization and has always been found on the side of the Democrats in the final analysis" (quoted in the *Crisis* 25, no. 3 [January 1923]: 104).

3. A reference to Harry Haywood (b. 1898), journalist, political theorist, and Communist party activist (Harry Haywood, *Black Bolshevik: Autobiography of an Afro-American Communist* [Chicago: Liberator Press, 1978]).

4. William Burns answered Howard's letter on 15 February, declaring, "I have read your memorandum of the 3rd inst., and will be guided by same" (DJ-FBI, file 61).

Confidential Informant Capt. J.W. Jones to William J. Burns

123 Roman St. c/o Turner,
New Orleans, La., Feb. 4, 1923

Sir:

In continuance of my investigation undercover I interviewed Dyer and Shakespe[a]re in the Parish prison today. These men talked very freely to me, and discussed their case with me from beginning to end. They denied their guilt as I expected, and said that Ramus said that he was down here to organize the police force in the New Orleans division by the orders of Mr. Garvey, but had never discussed with him the murdering of Eason. Dyer said that Ramus had left town the night he was arrested and had not been seen since, and his wife had done everything possible to locate him but had failed. I have talked with Mrs. Dyer, and she believes that if Ramus is arrested her husband will be released. I have encouraged this idea, and Mrs. Dyer has done everything possible to locate Ramus. I am convinced that no one here knew of Ramus' real mission here in New Orleans. I have had several interviews with Anderson, Garvey's representative that was sent here fro[m] New York to look after this case, and he says that this man Ramus was a nuisance around the office in New York and that Garvey just sent him down here to get rid of him. I am of the opinion that when Ramus is apprehended he will come across with the necessary information to indict Garvey.

Under the present circumstances I think there is very little more tha[t] I could accomplish here.

I am to have a conference with agent Gulley this afternoon but he seems to be of the same opinion as myself.

I will attend the meeting of the association this afternoon and all other meetings while here. Respectfully

J. W. JONES

DJ-FBI, file 61. TLS, recipient's copy.

Speech by Marcus Garvey

[[LIBERTY HALL, New York, February 4, 1923]]

In appreciation of the services rendered by the delegates to the League of Nations I must officially announce from Liberty Hall—even though I mentioned it in the Negro World of last week—that the French mandatory government has abolished slavery in West Africa and in Togoland following the British[,] who abolished slavery in German East Africa just a few weeks ago—all through the influence and representation of the representatives of the Universal Negro Improvement Association at the League of Nations at Geneva, Switzerland.[1] (Applause.) You and the rest of the race and all the world will hardly ever be able to appreciate the wonderful influence wielded by this Association at this time in Europe, and the great changes that are being brought about by the pressure of this organization upon international statesmen. In the days to come you will be better able to appreciate the service that you yourselves through being members of this organization have rendered to your race and the service that you have contributed to modern civilization.

AN ANSWER TO THE ATTACKS ON THE U.N.I.A.

I desire to speak to you tonight from the spirit of devotion and loyalty to the cause that you have sponsored. For quite a while the Universal Negro Improvement Association has been attacked from all sides and angles. The Executive leadership of the Association remained practically quiet during that period of attack for the purpose of testing the strength of the membership and the seriousness of the people who make up this organization. No general can go to battle without being able to rely on his soldiers. Negroes have been so wavering for the last hundred years that anyone who does not desire to spoil his career and his reputation has first of all to be sure of the ground before he leaps out too deep into the ocean, at least leading a people who need to be led.

On a wave of sentiment or a wave of war enthusiasm, the program of the Universal Negro Improvement Association swept the Negro off his feet and he threw his hat up into the air; but it was all war excitement and those who knew the Negro before the war calculated that there was no seriousness behind the enthusiasm and that there would be only a few who would stick by the enthusiasm and push it forward for what it was worth. Such a period of test came after the war excitement and we have passed through it and no more severely than in 1922—testing that backbone, testing that spirit and character that is to make the African program a reality by men and women sticking by it even to the extreme everywhere where they profess the doctrine of faith of this organization. Such a test we have had and some of our enemies mistook the period of test for weakness on our part. Some of our enemies mistook the period of test for a setting back of the program of the organization, not knowing that it is the way of all sensible, intelligent leadership to bring about that test before the great day dawns. And now the enemies thought they had the whole wa[y] of it; the enemies thought they had the right of way.

WAGE AN UNPRECEDENTED CAMPAIGN

It is for me to announce in Liberty Hall tonight that from tomorrow night for six months continuously throughout the length and breadth of America the Universal Negro Improvement Association will wage a campaign never seen and experienced by men before. (Applause.) This time it is not going to be a campaign reiterating the program of the Association, but it is going to be a campaign of cleaning house within the race to get men of stability and character that will lead us to the victory that we desire, as 400,000,000 people. (Applause.) There comes a time in the history of all nations when sometimes they have civil misunderstanding. We had a civil misunderstanding in America which brought about the Union and the time has come now that we are forced by a civil misunderstanding within the race to bring about a union that is necessary to bring emancipation to this race throughout the world. Du Bois, Weldon Johnson, Pickens, Randolph and Owen and the gang that have scattered themselves all over the country have invited this civil misunderstanding and the Universal Negro Improvement Association shall take up the gauntlet and carry on the fight to the bitter end. They have done their worst, thinking the Universal Negro Improvement Association was weakening; they will realize that there is no weakening within the ranks of this organization and when it comes to the test they will find that instead of our being five millions there will be at least ten million organized Negroes around this Western world. We are going to give them the race and fight of their lives. (Applause.) Du Bois made out that this movement was sponsored by West Indian Negroes,[2] but I challenge Du Bois to go into any American city from Maine to California and I will charge an admission fee of $1.50 and for every hundred people I have to hear me, he would not have ten. Du Bois knows that because he has spoken in some of the cities I have spoken and where he had 50 people, Garvey went there and spoke to 2,000 and 4,000 and 5,000 people at a dollar a seat and 50 cents a seat. That does not indicate that the movement is West Indian, does it? They have played the game long enough; they said that the Universal Negro Improvement Association is not in politics. Well, the Universal Negro Improvement Association is going into politics, if for nothing more than to clean up the National Association for the Advancement of Certain People. So from tonight the U.N.I.A. is in politics and we are going to make our politics so felt throughout this nation that not only Du Bois but all his gang will have to change their minds before 1924 arrives. It has always been the policy of the Universal Negro Improvement Association not to antagonize any Negro individual because our desire is to unite the race, but it is forced upon us now to clean house to save this race of ours. It is now a division of opinions; it is now two different classes fighting for the preservation of the Negro on the one hand and the extermination of the Negro on the other hand. Du Bois and the National Association for the Advancement of Colored People have lied for 14 years; they are as great Negro haters as the Southern crackers are, for the simple reason their program is race assimilation which will in another hundred years wipe out this Negro race and make a new race which will not be Negro in any degree. They have been lying to the race and they fight the Universal Negro Improvement Association simply because the Universal Negro Improvement Association has come with a determined program to solve the race problem on the pride of the race itself.

We are appealing to the membership of New York and to the membership throughout this country to stand fast for at least six months and you will see whether the Universal Negro Improvement Association has triumphed or not. I want to announce that from tomorrow night there will be a revival in Liberty Hall, and this revival will continue for at least two or three weeks every night. We want each and every one to come out and bring in a stranger with you so that we can go out for this program and let people know what must be done if we are to save this race and if this problem is to be truly solved. I have to thank you for carrying the Association up to where it is. It is unfortunate that we should have been encumbered and encompassed with all these difficulties, but now that they have transferred the fight from those who have been our common enemies back to ourselves, then it is for us to make a cleaning up until we have brought back the union of spirit that is necessary to put over the program we have engaged in. (Applause).

Printed in *NW*, 10 February 1923. Original headlines omitted.

1. The British mandate for the former German East Africa and the French mandates for Togoland and the Cameroons were passed by the League of Nations on 20 July 1922. The mandates'

provisions on slavery were identical. They outlawed the slave trade as demanded by the league covenant, and called for the "eventual emancipation of all slaves"; but both also contained provisions for the continuation of forced labor for public works and services in return for remuneration (*League of Nations Official Journal*, August 1922, pp. 865–868, 887; George Louis Beer, *African Questions at the Paris Peace Conference* [1923; rep. ed., London: Dawsons of Pall Mall, 1968], pp. 521–522).

2. In *Century Magazine* of February 1923, Du Bois said that West Indians composed the bulk of the UNIA membership and that "its main and moving nucleus has been a knot of Jamaican peasants resident in America." Du Bois argued that, because of the substantial West Indian membership, the Garvey movement paid little attention to the issues Du Bois felt were most important to American blacks, which were the right to vote, the antilynching movement, and the struggle for racial equality. The "American v. West Indian" theme also cropped up throughout the "Garvey Must Go" campaign of Randolph, Owen, Pickens, and Bagnall. It became particularly virulent in the *Messenger*, especially with the publication of an editorial entitled "A Supreme Negro Jamaican Jackass" (*Messenger* 5, no. 1 [January 1923]: 561) and Bagnall's article "The Madness of Marcus Garvey" (*Messenger* 5, no. 3 [March 1923]: 638, 648). W. A. Domingo, a strong Garvey critic as well as a Jamaican, pointed out the pejorative use of the term "West Indian" in the *Messenger*'s anti-Garvey campaign and took Owen to task in an open letter printed in March 1923. Owen evaded the substance of Domingo's charges, and Domingo in turn left the *Messenger*'s staff ("Back to Africa," *Century Magazine* 105 [February 1923]: 539–548; "Open Forum," *Messenger* 5, no. 3 [March 1923]: 639–645; Theodore Kornweibel, Jr., *No Crystal Stair: Black Life and the "Messenger,"* *1917–1928* [Westport, Conn.: Greenwood Press, 1975], pp. 133–175).

Marcus Garvey to Harry M. Daugherty

New York, U.S.A. February 4, 1923

HONORABLE SIR:—

It has been brought to my attention, through the return to me by a newspaper associate, of a copy of a letter forwarded to you by a group of Negroes in New York, forming themselves into a Committee of which one Chandler Owen is Secretary, that representations have been made to you and your Department as to lead you to believe that the Universal Negro Improvement Association and myself, are fomenting race strife and preaching race antagonism in the United States of America, and that my Organization is guilty of many criminal acts in violation of the Constitution of the United States of America. I hereby beg to inform you that there is absolutely no truth in the statements made in the thirty paragraphs of the letter herein referred to.

The eight persons who signed the letter and who have described themselves, are among a group that is being prosecuted by me and by the Universal Negro Improvement Association for criminal and civil libels, and many other charges.[1] They have been avowed enemies of mine for a long while through jealousy in Organization and rivalry in business. The majority of them are Socialists and Bolshevists, whose patriotism is more questionable than that of the Universal Negro Improvement Association, in that my Organization stands for loyalty and obedience to the American Constitution and there can be cited no instance where we have ever done anything inimical to the interest of the Nation.

The authors of the letter have for a long while been making the effort through rival Organizations, to outdo the Universal Negro Improvement

Association in its standing among the colored people, in that we have successfully developed a movement that has been helpful in bringing the Negro to a consciousness of himself much to the dismay of others who have been trying for a long while in the same direction and have failed, because of their insincerity and inability to impress. Having failed among themselves to injure the Universal Negro Improvement Association, they have resorted to misrepresenting to you and to other Departments of the Government, the Universal Negro Improvement Association, to the end that you or others of the Government would use your high offices in embarrassing the Organization.

The authors of the letter represent no one but themselves, whilst the Universal Negro Improvement Association represent[s] over two and a half million colored people in the United States of America, and three millions abroad, scattered in different countries. The objects of the Association are to improve the industrial, social, religious, educational, and political conditions of the race, and to help in building in Africa, a Government for the Negro peoples of the world.

There is absolutely nothing in the Constitution or in the make up of the Organization that suggests disloyalty of any kind to the United States Government, or any Government in the world, and all that has been said and done by the signatories of the letter em[a]nate from the spirit of jealousy and rivalry which they have so often manifested.

It is felt that you will not use your high office on the prompting of a few irresponsible persons to handicap and thwart the high aims and objects of an Association that is endeavouring to improve the condition of a struggling and suffering race.[2]

This matter is brought to your attention in fear that you may be disposed to believe in the statements made in the thirty paragraphs of the letter written to you by the individuals herein referred to.

The names signed to the letter as forwarded to you under date January 15th 1923, from 2305—7th Avenue, New York City are:—

Harry H. Pace—2289—7th Avenue, New York City.
Robert S. Abbott—3425 Indiana Avenue, Chicago[,] Ill.
John E. Nail—145 W. 135th Street, New York City.
Julia P. Coleman—118 W. 130th Street, New York City.
William Pickens—70—5th Avenue, New York City.
Chandler Owen—2305—7th Avenue, New York City.
Robert W. Bagnall—70—5th Avenue, New York City.
George W. Harris—135 West 135th Street, New York City.

I have the honor to be, Your Obedient Servant
MARCUS GARVEY
President-General
Universal Negro Improvement Association

DNA, RG 60, file 198940-285. TLS on UNIA letterhead, recipient's copy.

1. On 23 August 1922 Garvey had filed libel suits totaling $750,000 against the *New York Times*, the *New York Call*, the *New York Amsterdam News*, the *New York News*, Robert W. Bagnall, Chandler Owen, William Pickens, and A. Philip Randolph. Garvey charged that the *New York Times* and the *New York Call* had published defamatory statements by Bagnall and Randolph accusing him of "robbing ignorant Negroes" and "seeking an alliance with the Ku Klux Klan" (*Baltimore Afro-American*, 25 August 1922).

2. The Department of Justice replied to Garvey on 7 February 1923, promising to give his letter "appropriate attention" (John W. H. Crim, assistant attorney general, to Marcus Garvey, 7 February 1923, DNA, RG 60, file 198940-285).

C.B. Smith, Chief, Office of Extension Work, States Relations Service, Department of Agriculture, to Luther N. Duncan, Director of Extension Service, Alabama Polytechnic Institute

Washington, D.C. February 5, 1923

Dear Director Duncan:[1]

RE: BACK TO AFRICA MOVEMENT

T.M. Campbell,[2] who is now here reading the negro county agents' reports, has found some indications of propaganda among the negroes on the "Back to Africa Movement." One report in particular, from which we are quoting, indicates that this propaganda is in some degree affecting the extension work among the negro farmers. The quotation follows:

> "Back to Africa Movement" got into the four organizations which ceased to exist. This movement brought a great setback to these communities, as many of the farmers did nothing but walk around and talk about going to Africa and made no effort to progress as farmers. Not one of these farmers ever left, but they lost the year talking about it.

The above quotation is in answer to "How many community farmers' clubs have ceased to exist during the year?"

One of the Washington local papers carried a full column article concerning the activities of one Marcus Garvey, who seems to be heading this movement in New York City. It seems that a payment of money is required from the negro people to help defray the expense of transportation back to Africa. It is reported that the vessel on which they are to return never sails. It has been thought that this "Back to Africa" propaganda movement may be a matter which you desire to give some consideration and it is with that thought that it is being called to your attention. Very truly yours,

[C. B. SMITH, CHIEF
Office of Extension Work]

DNA, RG 16, general correspondence. TL on letterhead, carbon copy.

1. Luther N. Duncan (1865–1947) was an Alabama-born educator and agriculturalist; he graduated in 1900 from the Alabama Polytechnic Institute, Auburn, Ala., which he would later come to head in 1935. He was active in 4-H Club work and experimental farming from 1909 to 1920. Between 1920 and 1937 he served as the director of the extension service for Alabama Polytechnic Institute (*NYT*, 27 July 1947).

2. Thomas Monroe Campbell (1883–1956), the son of an Elbert County, Ga., tenant farmer, graduated from Tuskegee Institute in 1906. He became one of two agents of the Office of Extension Work, States Relations Service, U.S. Department of Agriculture, in charge of Negro agricultural work. In July 1931 he was sent to Tallapoosa County, Alabama, following the riot between members of the black sharecroppers' union and white law officers in Camp Hill. Campbell collected information on both the union and the Communist party organizers in the county for the Department of Agriculture. He was appointed to many government commissions and in 1944–1945 traveled to West Africa for the church missions of North America, Great Britain, and Ireland to study and report on rural conditions in several West African countries. He left the Department of Agriculture in 1953 (U.S. Agricultural Dept., *List of Workers in Subjects Pertaining to Agriculture* [Washington, D.C.: GPO, 1922], p. 48; Allen W. Jones, "Thomas M. Campbell: Black Agricultural Leader of the New South," *Agricultural History* 53, no. 1 [January 1979]: 42–59).

Editorial Letter by Marcus Garvey

New York, 6 February 1923

FELLOW MEN OF THE NEGRO RACE, Greeting:

I have to bring to your attention this week the greatest bit of treachery and wickedness that any group of Negroes could be capable of. This thing is so shocking, so vicious and murderous as to make it impossible for any self-respecting person to imagine that any one, other than a culprit of the meanest kind, could be responsible for its authorship.

HONOR AMONG THIEVES

It is said that there is honor even among thieves, but it is apparent that ther[e] is no honor and self-respect among certain Negroes in that they would resort to the meanest and lowest methods possible, not only to pilfer the pockets of their brothers but to rob one of his fair name. Stealing a man's money is, as Shakespeare says, trash, but to injure a man's reputation, to tarnish his character, is a crime of the lowest kind which not even ordinary thieves would indulge in.[1] To further imagine that a group of colored men could be responsible for writing to the Attorney General of the United States of America and to the white people at large in endeavoring to prejudice them against fellow Negroes whose only crime has been that of making an effort to improve the condition of the race is beyond the conception of the most fertile imagination; nevertheless, the thing has been done by a group of New York Negroes who have written their names down everlastingly as enemies of their own race by maliciously, wickedly and treacherously endeavoring to so misrepresent their race which represents the minority group in a majority civilization as to cause that majority to unwillingly, and not of its own accord, impose such punishment upon the race as to make it harder for us to survive in the country of our common adoption.

WRITING TO U. S. ATTORNEY GENERAL

The following vicious and wicked letter was written by a group of men whose names are appended hereto and directed to the Honorable Attorney General of the [U]nited States of America. My comment will continue at the end of the communication. . . .[2]

CONSIDERING THE LETTER

Let us consider the above [which] was written by these wicked Negroes and sent to the Attorney General of the United States of America and to the white press of the nation.

In the first paragraph of the above communication the writers, being Negroes, made use of the following statement, speaking to the Attorney General. They say:

> As chief law enforcement officer of the nation, we wish to call your attention to A HERETOFORE UNCONSIDERED MENACE TO HARMONIOUS RACE RELATIONSHIP. THERE ARE IN OUR MIDST CERTAIN NEGRO CRIMINAL AND POTENTIAL MURDERERS, BOTH FOREIGN AND AMERICAN-BORN, WHO ARE MOVED AND ACTUATED BY INTENSE HATRED AGAINST THE WHITE RACE. THESE UNDESIRABLES CONTINUALLY PROCLAIM THAT ALL WHITE PEOPLE ARE ENEMIES TO THE NEGRO.

GOOD OLD DARKIES

To imagine that any group of Negroes could be so base as to attempt to impress upon not only the Attorney General of the United States of America but the white people at large that members of their own race, although this is untrue, are desirous of murdering members of the white race and of maintaining a hatred against them, knowing well the position of the Negro in America and his relationship to his white brother, is more than any one would expect at this time in the struggle for race uplift. Everyone knows that the statement is false and only manufactured by these wicked and malicious individuals for the purpose of directing the hatred of the Attorney General and the white people of America against the Universal Negro Improvement Association and Marcus Garvey; nevertheless, the statement reveals in these Negro men the lowest possible trait. Like the good old darkey, they believe they have some news to tell and they are telling it for all it is worth—the liars and fabricators that they are, for everyone who knows the Universal Negro Improvement Association and Marcus Garvey, white or black, knows well that there is absolutely no desire on their part to murder anybody, and that as far as criminals are concerned, more are to be found probably among those who signed the letter than could be found in the extensive membership of the Universal Negro Improvement Association.

NO HATRED FOR WHITE PEOPLE

In paragraph 2 they stated that "the President-General of the Universal Negro Improvement Association is Marcus Garvey, an unscrupulous demagogue who has ceaselessly and assiduously sought to spread among Negroes distrust and hatred among all white people."

About being unscrupulous and a demagogue, we need pay no attention because the very villains who wrote such a letter are better able to interpret unscrupulousness and demagogy than anyone else, in that they seem to know more about it, but when it comes to the point of "Marcus Garvey assiduously seeking to spread among Negroes distrust and hatred for all white people," it is time for the white and black races to realize the truth about the Universal Negro Improvement Association and its President. At no time has the President of the Universal Negro Improvement Association preached hatred of the white people. That in itself is a violation of the constitution of the organization, which teaches all its members to love and respect the rights of [the] races, believing that by so doing, others will in turn love and respect our rights.

NO ILL FEELING BETWEEN RACES

In paragraph 3 they try to make out that The Negro World, sedulously and continually, seeks to arouse ill-feeling between the races, yet in the same breath they further try to make out that there is an alliance between Garvey and the Ku Klux Klan. If these men were in the possession of their senses, and were actuated by truth rather than by a desire to do harm and injury, they would have realized that the Ku Klux Klan is a white organization and stands for white supremacy, so that Garvey would be illogical and foolish if on the one hand he preached ill feeling and hatred between the two races and then went back upon all this and allied himself with the Ku Klux Klan.

WICKED MALIGNERS

These wicked maligners, above the protest of Marcus Garvey and the Universal Negro Improvement Association for over one hundred times, are still endeavoring to make it appear as if there is some understanding between the President of this organization and the Ku Klux Klan.[3]

"BUNCH" OF SELFISH GRAFTERS

In paragraph 4 these men state that: "An erroneous conception held by many is that Negroes try to cloak and hide their criminals; the truth is that the great majority of Negroes are bitterly opposed to all criminals and especially to those of their own race because they know that such criminals will cause increased discrimination against themselves." And here we have the high and lofty(?) purposes of these so-called race leaders and race reformers. Other races try to reform and improve their criminals whilst [these] splendid(?) Negro leaders of ours avow that they are bitterly opposed to them simply because they know that such criminals will cause increased discrimination against them. The selfish dogs that they are! It is not a question of i[mpr]oving the condition of the race; it is a question of how much they [can] benefit by being members of the race, and if there is a criminal [in] the Negro race it is preferable that he die rather than he should even exist to be improved, because in so doing he may cause a discrimination against these selfish individuals. We will prove that these men are just what they state themselves to be in these paragraphs—a "bunch" of selfish grafters who have been living off the blood of the race and who feel that the Universal Negro Improvement Association has come upon the scene to so change and improve conditions as to make it impossible for them to continue to suck the last drop of blood out of our people under the guise of race business men and race leaders.

PRIMITIVE NEGROES

In paragraph 5 they further state that "the Universal Negro Improvement Association is composed chiefly of the most primitive and ignorant element of West Indian and American Negroes."

Now we come to the crux of the matter. These fellows represent a small group of men led by Du Bois, who believe that the race problem is to be solved by assimilation and that the best program for the Negro is to make himself the best imitation of the white man and approach him as fast as possible with the hope of jumping over the fence into the white race and be completely lost in another one hundred years; therefore they hate everything Negro and they haven't sense enough to hide it. Now, what do they mean by "the most primitive and ignorant element of West Indian and American Negroes"?

We will all remember that in the slave days the Negroes of America and the West Indies were taken from Africa, and that they then represented their tribal primitiveness. The emancipation, both in America and the West Indies, has brought us up to the present state, with the majority of our people still bearing the resemblance of this tribal primitiveness, whilst a few have endeavored to make themselves Caucasianized. These men regard it as a crime to be as nature made us, and for us to be as nature made us is to be ignorant; this shows how much love these would-be Negroes have for the motherhood of our race. The paragraph stating that "The respectable element identified with the movement are largely professional men without calling," and that "the organization is composed of Negro sharks and ignorant Negro fanatics,["] again reveal to us the prejudice of these so-called business and professional scoundrels in that they endeavor to make it appear that only professional men are respectable, and that the [their?] organization has no white sharks or ignorant fanatics in it. Were it not for the ignorant element of Negroes, these very fellows would have starved long ago, because all of them earn their living either by selling out the race under the guise of leadership or by exploiting the race in business. We only hope that the so-called ignorant Negroes of America will get to know these fellows as they are and let them pay the price through their pocketbooks for insulting so large a number of people who are proud of their race and color.

FORCED COMPANIONSHIP BETWEEN RACES

These nonentities show us in paragraph 5 that they do not believe in or cannot tolerate any organization that is not made up of either respectable white people or white sharks and ignorant fanatics. These are the fellows who foment lynching by always endeavoring to encourage forced companionship between the two races.

In paragraph 6 they make Marcus Garvey as being intolerant of free speech, when, in fact, he has always advocated freedom of a universal kind. Again, in that paragraph they state that "The laws of the Universal Negro Improvement Association encourage violence." That is a lie. In many of the succeeding paragraphs they further endeavor to make out that the Garveyites or members of the Universal Negro Improvement Association have on several occasions disturbed the peace of public meetings and individuals organized to speak against Garvey and the movement.

The persons cited in the paragraphs who were alleged to be disturbed at the respective meetings are, with one exception, all members of the gang who have produced the letter now under criticism. They were all organized for the purpose of injuring the Universal Negro Improvement Association and Marcus Garvey. Nevertheless, at no time has the association or Mr. Garvey ever made any effort to check or embarrass them. Their own unworthiness created in their meetings, no doubt, the displeasure of the people who attended them, and now they try to label the Association and Garvey for it.

COLORED CASTE PREJUDICE

It is strange that whenever anything is referred to derogatory to the race, the gentlemen use the term "Negro," but whenever they want to impress either the Attorney-General or the white people [on] the standing of any member of the race they refer to him as "colored," such as paragraph 7, where reference was made to W. Ashbie Hawkins as one of the most distinguished colored attorneys in America, and to Noah D. Thompson as a distinguished colored citizen of Los Angeles, being employed, as he is[,] in the editorial department of the white Los Angeles Daily Express. This reveals again the hidden motive of intention of these plotters who are endeavoring to [set up] social caste as distinct from Negro, which they claim to be primitive and ignorant. There is much more in this than will be discussed at the present moment, but a return will be made to the subject in another article in The Negro World of next week in treating on the subject of "W. E. B. Du Bois as a Hater of Dark People."

SOCIALIST JUDGE AS PROPAGANDIST

In paragraph 25 the writers state that Judge Jacob Panken of the New York Municipal Court made certain derogatory remarks against Marcus Garvey and the Universal Negro Improvement Association in a case brought before him. They hadn't the honesty to tell the public and the Attorney-General in their letter that Judge Jacob Panken is a Socialist and that the writers of the letter are nearly all Socialists and that at the time the case was being tried the Socialist group of Negroes in Harlem, New York, looked upon it as a splendid opportunity to get back at Marcus Garvey and the Universal Negro Improvement Association, who had been against Socialism, to have the Socialist judge take advantage of the situation while hearing a case of Garvey by making use of such remarks as would be used by the Socialist group as propaganda against Marcus Garvey and the Universal Negro Improvement Association.

Now they are making use of the Statement of Panken, as they had hoped he would use certain remarks for propaganda purposes, and they still believe that all Negroes are foolish enough to follow the advice of a Socialist judge against whom, as a Socialist, Marcus Garvey and the Universal Negro Improvement Association stand out. Hundreds of other cases have been heard before other judges of New York, and no one has ever used the remark of Panken, hence everyone knows it was made for propaganda purposes. Negro voters will take keen notice of it.

U.N.I.A. CONTROLS THOUSANDS OF VOTES

In paragraph 27 they infer that "the Garvey followers are for the most part voteless." This is another lie, because the Universal Negro Improvement Association can marshal twenty times as many voters of the United States of America as all other Negro organizations put together, and that will be proved in a short while for the good of the race. About the "exaggerated membership" of the organization, any reader of the letter has but to take for granted that some of the things said about the organization in different parts of the country were true; but even if they were only partly true they would at least reveal a membership in three or four sections larger than they claim it to be all over the world. No one will ever know accurately the membership of the Universal Negro Improvement Association, because every second Negro you meet, if not an actual mem[b]er, is one in spirit.

A BARBER SHOP PHILOSOPHER

In reference to W. A. Domingo as an "intelligent" West Indian Negro of Jamaica who made an analysis of the Garvey membership, all those acquainted with the Universal Negro Improvement Association know that Domingo was a dismissed employe of the association and that he represents no one but himself.

He is what commonly is called a "barber shop rat," who talks the kind of philosophy indulged in by frequenters of the tonsorial artist. He also is a Socialist who has a desperate grudge against work and who has the dreamer's vision that one day all the rich people of the world will divide up their wealth with the loafer, thereby bringing into existence the true reign of Socialism.

CRUSADER MAGAZINE OUT OF BUSINESS

The magazine (Crusader) referred to also will be remembered as the mouthpiece of Cyril Briggs, who collected donations from colored and white people to support the paper some years ago, and who up to nine months ago published that he had received $5,000 for the purpose of starting another weekly paper called the Liberator, and that colored people were to subscribe $5,000 more. It is for me to state that the Crusader has long been out of business and the Liberator has never appeared.[4] What has become of the $5,000 acknowledged and the subscriptions taken for the publication of the Crusader no one knows.

W.E.B. Du Bois is a colored man who hates the drop of Negro blood in his veins, and he is as much against the Universal Negro Improvement Association from a prejudiced viewpoint as the Devil is against Holy Water.

The demolition of the Universal Negro Improvement Association is asked for by the writers of the letter. In paragraph 27 they state that the organization is as objectionable and even more dangerous than the Ku Klux Klan. Take it for granted that the Ku Klux Klan sought white supremacy and the Universal Negro Improvement Association sought black supremacy. If there was any such program these Negroes would prefer the exist[e]nce of the Ku Klux Klan to the Universal Negro Improvement Association, because to have the Universal Negro Improvement Association is more dangerous. This shows they are illogical, foolish, wicked and malicious. They seek to destroy the Universal Negro Improvement Association as a Negro organization, not knowing that a precedent will be set for the destruction of all Negro organizations that seek in any way to improve the condition of the Negro race. These bigots believe they own the United States of America. They have no more right in America than other colored men, so that they will be very much disappointed if they believe that the Department of Justice and the Attorney-General would, for the purpose of pleasing eight Negroes, defeat the ends of the Constitution of the United States of America. But who are these Negroes? They themselves have told us what they are in their relationship to business.

GROUP OF UNKNOWN PERSONS

To take them as they are, one is a business exploiter who endeavors to appeal to the patriotism of the race by selling us commodities at a higher rate than are charged in the ordinary and open markets.[5] Another is a race defamer of Chicago[6] who publishes in his newspaper week after week the grossest scandals against the race, showing up the crime and vices of our people. He was the man who published in his newspaper for over one year a full page advertisement showing the pictures of two women, a black woman and a very light woman, with the advice under the photograph of the black woman to "lighten your black skin."[7] The other is a real estate shark who delights, under the guise of race patriotism, to raise the rent of poor colored people even beyond that of white landlords, who are generally more considerate, knowing the economic condition of the colored race.[8] Another is a hair straightener and face bleacher whose loyalty to race is to get the race to be dissatisfied with itself.[9] Still we have another as a turn coat and lackey who has not enough manhood to stand up and defend his own cause in his relationship to others, but who was so mean and low down as to have approached Marcus Garvey for a job about nine months ago, representing to him that he was unfairly dealt with because of his color, and after he was offered a berth he took that as an opportunity of going back to his old employers to get them to raise his salary, which he never would have gotten raised but for the fact that he had secured new employment in a rival organization.[10] Then we have the grafter Socialist who started so many enterprises among colored people, such as the Elevator Men's Union, and has not been able to a[cc]ount for the funds.[11] We have still another who maintained a Blue Vein Society Church in Detroit, Mich.,[12] and who was subsequently relieved of his charge because of alleged immorality, and another unscrupulous politician whom everyone knows to be a man who has lost the respect of the ordinary members of the community.[13] These are the angels and "respectable" citizens who have written this infamous letter to the Attorney-General of the United States of America against Marcus Garvey and the Universal Negro Improvement Association.

SINNERS TO PURGE THEIR SOULS

It is hoped that these sinners will purge their souls of the crime they have committed against their race, for surely in the accusation of their own consciences they shall surely not see salvation.

Let me implore all members, divisions and friends of the Universal Negro Improvement Association to now make every effort to push forth the cause of our great movement. Now is the time for every man and woman to stand loyally by this organization. Whatsoever might have been the difference of opinions in local divisons of your dissatisfaction, you must stand unitedly as millions of members throughout the world, for the enemy within our own race is now knocking at the door. It is for us unitedly to stand together and meet the foe. The greatest weapon we can use at this time is stronger organization.

Let all members come together more than ever everywhere and prove to the world that not by misrepresentation, but by fair play and justice shall the great problem of race be settled.

It is hoped that the white people of America and of the world will take no cognizance of the vicious lies and misrepresentations of these wicked Negroes. Everyone will realize that the Universal Negro Improvement Association preaches the doctrine of human brotherhood and the love of all mankind.

227

All divisions are requested to send in their support immediately to the parent body and help to push the fight for the triumph of the Universal Negro Improvement Association over its enemies.

With very best wishes I have the honor to be Your obedient servant,

MARCUS GARVEY
President-General
Universal Negro Improvement Association

DJ-FBI, file 61. PD.[14]

1. A paraphrase of Shakespeare's *Othello*, act 3, sc. 3, lines 155–161.

2. Transcript of this letter has been omitted.

3. A reference to Garvey's meeting with Klan leader Edward Young Clarke in June 1922. An unidentified newspaper reported that on 7 February 1923 Clarke testified to a grand jury that he had met secretly with Garvey in October 1922. Clarke promised to produce papers that would "throw light on overtures made by Garvey" to the Klan in connection with the Black Star Line. Garvey denied the charge, stating that "the oft repeated allegation that I had sought the assistance of the Klan for the Black Star Line is base and unfounded. Mr. Clark [*sic*] and I never discussed the Black Star Line." (two unidentified newspaper clippings of 8 February 1923, found in DJ-FBI, file 61).

4. In what appears to be its final issue, the *Crusader* reported in its January–February 1922 issue on the progress of its fund drive for the publication of a new journal, the *Liberator*. Sponsored by the African Blood Brotherhood, the fund drive had a goal of $10,000, and by January 1922 the ABB's membership had already raised $5,100. The advertisement for contributors and subscribers called on readers of the *Crusader* to help the ABB to "better serve the Negro race, defend its honor and protect it from selfish, opportunist and craven leaders by the publication in the near future of a weekly newspaper known as The Liberator." Readers were called upon to "Remember Tulsa!" Subscriptions sold for $1.50.

5. Harry Pace was president of the Black Swan Phonograph Co., Inc., which produced classical music by black musicians (*Crisis* 25, no. 3 [January 1923]: 139).

6. A reference to Robert Abbott, editor of the *Chicago Defender*.

7. By November 1923 the *Negro World* would itself commence carrying advertisements for face bleaches and hair straighteners. The *Chicago Whip* noted that Garvey "has been quite successful in cluttering up his paper, the *Negro World*, with hair straightening advertisements and face bleaches" (*Chicago Whip*, n.d., quoted in a Bureau of Investigation report, ca. 23 November 1923, DJ-FBI).

8. A reference to John E. Nail.

9. A reference to Julia Coleman.

10. A reference to William Pickens.

11. A reference to Chandler Owen.

12. A reference to Robert Bagnall.

13. A reference to George W. Harris.

14. This letter was published as a booklet and was reprinted in the *Philosophy and Opinions of Marcus Garvey* (2: 294–308). Along with the letter the following postscript was appended:

> The signers of the letter to the Attorney-General are nearly all Octoroons and Quadroons. Two are black Negroes, who have married Octoroons. One is a Mulatto and Socialist, a self-styled Negro leader, who had expressed his intention of marrying a white woman but was subsequently prevented from doing so by the criticism of the U.N.I.A. With this lone exception all of the others are married to Octoroons. (*P&O*, 2: 308.)

There was also a *nota bene* following the letter which stated, "Since the signing of the letter to the Attorney General, George Harris has been twice defeated for election as Alderman" (ibid.).

Report by Special Employee Andrew M. Battle

New York, N.Y. [*11 February 1923*]

MARCUS GARVEY

Continuing the above matter, tonight the writer attended a meeting of the U.N.I.A. at Liberty Hall. The attendance was about 2500, two thirds male and one third female. The speakers for the evening were WM. SHERRILL, R.L. POSTUM [*Poston*] AND MARCUS GARVEY.

In MR. SHERRILL's address he pointed out facts to substantiate his suspicion that WM. PICKENS, HARRY H. PACE, ROBERT S. ABBOTT, JOHN E. N[A]IL, JULIA P. COLEMAN, CHANDLER OWEN, ROBERT W. BAGNALL, and GEORGE HARRIS were all traitors to the negro race and that they were telling the white race that GARVEY's teaching to the negro was to hate the white race. The speaker further stated that if the negroes did hate the white race, the white man had no one to blame but himself for his mistreatment of the negro and that after the world war and even up to the present time, GARVEY was showing the negro the real facts as to the negroes' rights and that the above mentioned men were betraying this great man GARVEY into the hands of his enemies.

The next speaker, was R.L. POSTUM, an officer of the U.N.I.A., but his talk was simply to corroborate the things pointed out by MR. SHERRILL.

GARVEY then spoke and the first words he uttered was a request for $500., stating that he wanted this sum for real work in Liberia and saying that he could not tell the audience just what the work was because PICKENS would go immediately and tell the white people.

Immediately after GARVEY's talk a collection was taken up at the conclusion of which GARVEY again spoke, and among other things said that if the negro intended to command respect he must first establish power and to have power he must get guns and plenty of ammunition, gas, submarines and every other thing that is used to command respect by the white people and that after they got them, they must be used properly, as there is no other method whereby respect for the colored race can be more quickly enforced. He then asked a question, addressing the audience, "Why did those eight men [*not?*] write to the Government and complain to the Government about the KU KLUX KLAN in the South, as it is common gossip that they got together and sent a complaint to Washington about me (GARVEY)[,] warning this race of mine what they might expect if they did not get together and do something for themselves, and I want everybody in this hall to attend the big meeting to be held at Carnegie Hall on the 23rd of February (this month) at which time we will tell the white people the aim and object of the U.N.I.A. and then, after my case is over, I will start on my tour of the world.["]

The writer observed that practically the entire audience was West Indian and everything said by the speakers caused an outburst of applause. There will be nightly meetings at Liberty Hall until the big meeting of February 23rd, at Carnegie Hall.

ANDREW M. BATTLE

DJ-FBI, file 61. TD.

Report by Special Agents James E. Amos and Mortimer J. Davis

New York, N.Y. Feb. 13, 1923

Referring to past reports rendered by Agents regarding the investigation of the killing of DR. EASON, the following information is respectfully submitted:

CHANDLER OWEN, former negro radical[and author, and ROBERT W. BAGNALL of the N.A.A.C.P. called at the Bureau office this morning and advised as follows:

On Wednesday last, J. AUSTIN NORRIS[,] a prominent colored attorney of the city of Philadelphia, located at 1508 Lombard St., came to New York to see OWEN. NORRIS is and has been for some time attorney for the Philadelphia Division of the U.N.I.A. Although it is known that he is not in sympathy with the movement, he was a very close friend of EASON and was known to sympathi[z]e with EASON in his stand against GARVEY although he did not come out in the open as EASON did. Therefore, through his continued connection with the U.N.I.A., he has been able to obtain what is believed to be incriminating evidence against MARCUS GARVEY and ESAU RAMUS. He advised OWEN that RAMUS' wife is at the present time residing at 2112 Catherine St., Philadelphia[,] Pa., under the names of MRS. HENRY PRINCE and MRS. WM. HENRY PRINCE, and that her husband, RAMUS, who is now in Detroit, is corresponding with her regularly. Also, RAMUS is corresponding with J.B. DILLARD, 1808 South Street, Philadelphia. NORRIS has, through private channels, been able to obtain such letters as have been sent by RAMUS to these persons and has them now in his possession. In these letters we are informed, RAMUS talks freely of his having shot EASON and also of the fact that he was inspired to do it and paid by GARVEY. In one of the letters we are told, RAMUS advises his wife that he would like to come to Philadelphia, but his wife replied that it would not be safe for him to do so. In another letter he tells of GARVEY's having visited him on January 31st in Detroit. It will be recalled that two weeks ago GARVEY left New York on what was supposed to be a speaking tour. We knew that he was in Buffalo on Wednesday of that week and was supposed to have been back in New York by Thursday. We are now informed that the purpose of this trip was to visit RAMUS in Detroit and Ramus wrote to his wife that he had a conference there with GARVEY, during which GARVEY told him to keep quiet and that as soon as the EASON matter blew over he would send him to Liberia, Africa. This [was] partly verified by Agent Battle of our office, who, on Sunday, February 11th, attended a meeting at Liberty Hall, N.Y., where GARVEY spoke, at which GARVEY spoke to his audience of a $500. collection for "immediate work in Liberia." GARVEY stated he would not tell his audience the exact reason for this money because certain colored traitors would immediately inform the whites if they knew.

NORRIS was also informed by MRS. RAMUS that Garvey had given her husband letters of introduction to one SMYER, who is supposed to be High Commissioner of the U.N.I.A. for the State of Louisiana, and who, with RAMUS, organized the police department of that society. SMYER, according to our information, is in Philadelphia today (February 13th). At the present time RAMUS is said to be active in the Detroit Division of the U.N.I.A. His description has been forwarded to the Detroit office by telegram last week.

OWEN and WM. PICKENS returned this afternoon and were taken to the office of Asst. U.S. Attorney MATTUCK where the above information was gone over again. A long distance call was immediately made to NORRIS, who stated that he would come to New York tomorrow morning, bearing the letters from RAMUS to his wife, as well as other documents. NORRIS also advised us over the telephone that he has now secured the correct address at which RAMUS is living in Detroit. Our idea of handling the matter is as follows:

Instead of having RAMUS picked up in Detroit on the murder charge in New Orleans, it would seem better to have him arrested on the charge of jumping his bail in Philadelphia and brought back to the latter city.[2] There, NORRIS would naturally act as his attorney and NORRIS has offered, if this transpires, to have RAMUS make statements to him regarding the orders he received from GARVEY in connection with the killing of EASON, so that the New Orleans authorities and the Government as well, may use same. RAMUS is known to be very stubborn and will probably, on being arrested on the New Orleans charge, say nothing. However, this matter will be gone over thoroughly tomorrow with MR. MATTUCK, at which time a plan of action will be laid out.

It is urgently suggested that the Philadelphia and Detroit offices take no action on this report until further advi[c]e is received by letter or wire from this office.

JAMES E. AMOS
MORTIMER J. DAVIS

DJ-FBI, file 61. TD.

1. By 1923 Owen had become disillusioned with socialist radicalism. In the mid-twenties he moved to Chicago and became involved in Republican party politics (Theodore Kornweibel, Jr., *"No Crystal Stair": Black Life and the Messenger, 1917–1928* [Westport, Conn.: Greenwood Press, 1975]; *DANB*).

2. On 20 February 1923 Ramus was, in fact, arrested in Detroit by the Bureau of Investigation for the murder of Eason (report of Agent Wilcox, 21 February 1923, DJ-FBI, file 61).

J. Edgar Hoover to William J. Burns

Washington, D.C. February 13, [*1923*]

MEMORANDUM FOR MR. BURNS.

Special Agent Jones, who has been in New Orleans on an under cover investigation incident to the killing of Dr. Eason, principal witness against Marcus Garvey in the government's case against Garvey, returned to Washington on Monday, February 12th, and I directed him to proceed to New York in line with certain leads he has developed in the east.

From the investigation it is quite evident that Eason was killed at the instance of Ramus, one of Garvey's police lieutenants[,] and the defense of the two negroes in custody in New Orleans will be based on the grounds that Ramus actually killed Eason and not the two men now held.

Ramus was one of Garvey's closest friends and confidants and is believed to be in or about New York. It is very likely that Ramus, if located and apprehended, will involve Garvey in this case, which would result in Garvey's being included as an accessory before the fact. Respectfully,

J. E[DGAR]. H[OOVER].

DJ-FBI, file 61. TNI, recipient's copy.

Editorial Letter by Marcus Garvey

[[New York, February 13, 1923]]

FELLOW MEN OF THE NEGRO RACE, Greeting:

W.E. Burghardt Du Bois, the Negro "misleader," who is editor of the "Crisis," the official organ of the National Association for the Advancement of "certain" Colored People, situated at 70 Fifth Avenue, New York City, has again appeared in print. This time he appears as author of an article in the February "Century" Magazine under the caption, "Back to Africa," in which he makes the effort to criticize Marcus Garvey, the Universal Negro Improvement Association and the Black Star Line. This "unfortunate mulatto," who bewails every day the drop of Negro blood in his veins, being sorry that he is not Dutch or French, has taken upon himself the responsibility of criticizing and condemning other people while holding himself up as the social "unapproachable" and the great "I AM" of the Negro race. But we will see who Mr. Du Bois is, in that he invites his own characterization. So we will, therefore, let him see himself as others see him.

"FAT, BLACK, UGLY MAN"

In describing Marcus Garvey in the article before mentioned, he referred to him as a "little, fat black man; ugly, but with intelligent eyes and a big head." Now, what does Du Bois mean by ugly? This so-called professor of Harvard and Berlin ought to know by now that the standard of beauty within a race is not arrived at by comparison with another race; as, for instance, if we were to desire to find out the standard of beauty among the Japanese people we would not judge them from the Anglo-Saxon viewpoint, but from the Japanese. How he arrives at his conclusion that Marcus Garvey is ugly, being a Negro, is impossible to determine, in that if there is any ugliness in the Negro race it would be reflected more through Du Bois than Marcus Garvey, in that he himself tells us that he is a little Dutch, a little French, and a dozen other things.[1] Why, in fact, the man is a monstrosity. So, if there is any ugliness it is on the part of Du Bois and not on the part of the "little fat, black man with the big head," because all this description is typical of the African. But this only goes to show how much hate Du Bois has for the black blood in his veins. Anything that is black, to him, is ugly, is hideous, is monstrous, and this is why in 1917 he had but the lightest of colored people in his office, when one could hardly tell whether it was a white show or a colored vaudeville he was running at Fifth Avenue. It was only after the Universal Negro Improvement Association started to pounce upon him and his National Association for the Advancement of Colored People that they admitted that colored element into the association that could be distinguished as Negro, and it was during that period of time that Weldon Johnson and Pickens got a look-in. But even Pickens must have been "ugly" for Du Bois, for they made it so warm for him up to a few months ago that he had to go a-hunting for another job, the time when Marcus Garvey was willing to welcome him into the Universal Negro Improvement Association.

DU BOIS AND WHITE COMPANY

It is no wonder that Du Bois seeks the company of white people, because he hates blacks as being ugly. That is why he likes to dance with white people and dine with them and sometimes sleep with them, because from his way of seeing things all that is black is ugly, and all that is white is beautiful. Yet this professor, who sees ugliness in being black, essays to be a leader of the Negro people and has been trying for over fourteen years to deceive them through his connection with the National Association for the Advancement of Colored People. Now what does he mean by advancing colored people if he hates black so much? In what direction must we expect his advancement? We can conclude in no other way than that it is in the direction of losing our black identity and becoming, as nearly as possible, the lowest whites by assimilation and miscegenation.

This probably is accountable for the bleaching processes and the hair straightening escapades of some of the people who are identified with the

National Association for the Advancement of Colored People in their mad desire of approach to the white race, in which they see beauty as advocated by the professor from Harvard and Berlin. It is no wonder some of these individuals use the lip stick, and it is no wonder that the erudite Doctor keeps a French beard. Surely that is not typical of Africa; it is typical of that blood which he loves so well and which he bewails in not having more in his veins—French.

LAZY AND DEPENDENT

In referring to the effort of Marcus Garvey and the Universal Negro Improvement Association to establish a building in Harlem, he says in the article: "There was a long, low, unfinished church basement roofed over. It was designed as the beginning of a church long ago, but abandoned. Marcus Garvey roofed it over, and out of this squat and dirty old Liberty Hall he screams his propaganda. As compared with the homes, the business and church, Garvey's basement represents nothing in accomplishment and only waste in attempt."

Here we have this "lazy dependent mulatto" condemning the honest effort of his race to create out of nothing something which could be attributed to their ownership, in that the "dirty old Liberty Hall" he speaks of is the property of Negroes, while in another section of his article he praises the "beautiful and luxurious buildings" he claims to be occupied by other black folk, making it appear that these buildings were really the property of these people referred to, such as, according to his own description, "a brick block on Seventh Avenue stretching low and beautiful from the Y.W.C.A. with a moving picture house of the better class and a colored 5 and 10 cent store, built and owned by black folks." Du Bois knows he lies when he says that the premises herein referred to were built and are owned by black folks. They are the property of industrious Jews who have sought an outlet for their surplus cash in the colored district. The Y.W.C.A. is a donation from the good white people; but he continues by saying "down beyond on One Hundred and Thirty-Eighth Street the sun burns the rising spire of an Abyssinian Church, a fine structure built by Negroes who for one hundred years have supported the organization, and are now moving to their luxurious home of soft carpets, stained windows and swelling organ."[2] He also knows that this building has been subscribed to by the Church Extension Society, which is white, and therefore the building is not entirely owned by the members of the Abyssinian Church.[3] Finally, he says[,] "the dying rays hit a low, rambling basement of brick and rough stone." This in reference to Liberty Hall.

INDEPENDENT NEGRO EFFORT

Liberty Hall represents the only independent Negro structure referred to in the classification of Du Bois about buildings up in Harlem, but he calls this independent effort "dirty and old," but that which has been contributed by white people he refers to in the highest terms. This shows the character of the man—he has absolutely no respect and regard for independent Negro effort but that which is supported by white charity and philanthropy, and why so? Because he himself was educated by charity and kept by philanthropy. He got his education by charity, and now he is occupying a position in the National Association for the Advancement of Colored People, and it is felt that his salary is also paid by the funds that are gathered in from the charity and philanthropy of white people. This "soft carpet" idea is going to be the undoing of W. E. B. Du Bois. He likes too much the luxurious home and soft carpets, and that is why he is naturally attracted to white folks, because they have a lot of this; but if he were in Georgia or Alabama he would now be stepping on the carpets of Paradise; but that is not all of the man, as far as that is concerned. He ridicules the idea that the Universal Negro Improvement Association should hold a social function in Liberty Hall on the 10th of August, 1922, at which certain social honors were bestowed upon a number of colored gentlemen, such as Knighthood and the creation of the Peerage.

SOCIAL HONORS FOR NEGROES

In referring to the matter, he says in the article: "Many American Negroes and some others were scandalized by something which they could but regard as a simple child's play. It seemed to them sinister. This enthronement of a demagogue, a blatant boaster, who with monkey-shines was deluding the people, and taking their hard-earned dollars; and in high Harlem there arose an insistent cry, 'Garvey must go!'" Indeed Du Bois was scandalized by the creation of a Peerage and Knighthood by Negroes, and in truth the person who is responsible for the creation of such a thing should go, because Du Bois and those who think like him can see and regard honor conferred only by their white masters. If Du Bois was created a Knight Commander of the Bath by the British King, or awarded a similar honor by some white Poten[t]ate, he would have advertised it from cover to cover of the "Crisis," and he would have written a book and told us how he was recognized above his fellows by such a Poten[t]ate, but it was not done that way. This was an enthronement of Negroes, in which Du Bois could see nothing worthwhile. He was behind the "Garvey must go!" program started in Harlem immediately after the enthronement, because he realized that Garvey and the Universal Negro Improvement Association were usurping the right he had arrogated to himself as being the highest social dignitary, not only in Harlem but throughout the country.

MARCUS GARVEY AND HIS BIRTH AND DU BOIS

In the seventh paragraph of his article Du Bois has the following to say: "Let us note the facts. Marcus Garvey was born on the northern coast of Jamaica in 1887. He was a poor black boy, his father dying in the almshouse. He received a little training in the Church of England Grammar School, and then learned the trade of printing, working for years as foreman of a printing plant. Then he went to Europe and wandered about England and France working and observing until he finally returned to Jamaica. He found himself facing a stone wall. He was poor, he was black, he had no chance for a university education, he had no likely chance for preferment in any line, but could work as an artisan at small wage for the rest of his life."

Now let us consider Marcus Garvey in comparison with Du Bois. W. E. B. Du Bois was born in Great Barrington, Mass., in 1868. Some wealthy white people became interested in him and assisted in his education. They sent him to Fisk University, from Fisk to Harvard, where he graduated as a commencement orator.[4] He raised part of the money for his later education by giving recitals in white summer hotels. Where he was born—that is, in Great Barrington, Mass.—he had early association with white surroundings. He was brought up with white boys and girls of the better type and more aristocratic class as found in rural towns. He had no love for the poor, even the poor whites in his neighborhood, although he was but a poor, penniless and humble Negro. As proof of that he wrote the following on the tenth page of his book known as "Dark Water": "I greatly despised the poor Irish and South Germans who slaved in the mills (that is, the mills of the town in which he was born), and I annexed myself with the rich and well-to-do as my natural companions."[5] Marcus Garvey's father, who was also named Marcus Garvey, was one of the best known men in the parish in which he was born, St. Ann, Jamaica. For a number of years he held prominent positions in the parish and was regarded as one of the most independent black men on the island, owning property that ran into thousands of pounds. Through his own recklessness he lost his property and became poor. His poverty did not in any way affect Marcus Garvey, Jr., in that the mother of the latter assumed the responsibility that the father failed to assume, and he therefore got an early education, not through charity, as did Du Bois, but through the support of a loving mother. Marcus Garvey, Jr., never knew the consideration of a father, because at the time when he was born his father had already lost all he had, and had shifted his obligation to his children to the shoulders of their mother. With the assistance Marcus Garvey got from his mother he educated himself, not only in Jamaica but traveled throughout South and Central America, the West Indies and Europe, where for several years he studied in completing the education that he had already laid the foundation for in his native home. All that was not done by the charity of any one, but by Marcus Garvey himself and the support he got from his mother. While, on the other hand, Du Bois, starting even from the elementary stage of his education up to his graduation from Harvard and his passing through Berlin, got all that through the charity and philanthropy of good white people. Admitting that Marcus Garvey was born poor, he never encouraged a hatred for the people of his kind or class, but to the contrary devoted his life to the improvement and higher development of that class within the race which has been struggling under the disadvantage that Du Bois himself portrays in his article.

COMPARISON BETWEEN TWO MEN

Marcus Garvey was born in 1887; Du Bois was born in 1868. That shows that Du Bois is old enough to be Marcus Garvey's father. But what has happened? With the fifty-five years of Du Bois' life we find him still living on the patronage of good white people, and with the thirty-six years of Marcus Garvey (who was born poor and whose father, according to Du Bois, died in a poor house) he is able to at least pass over the charity of white people and develop an independent program originally financed by himself to the extent of thousands of dollars, now taken up by the Negro peoples themselves. Now which of the two is poorer in character and in manhood? The older man, who had all these opportunities and still elects to be a parasite, living off the good will of another race, or the younger man, who had sufficient self-respect to make an effort to do for himself, even though in his effort he constructs a "dirty brick building" from which he can send out his propaganda on race and self-reliance and self-respect.

MOTIVE OF DU BOIS

To go back to the motive of Du Bois in the advocacy of the National Association for the Advancement of Colored People is to expose him for what he is. The National Association for the Advancement of Colored People executives have not been honest enough to explain to the people of the Negro race their real solution for the Negro problem, because they are afraid that they would be turned down in their intention. They would make it appear as if they are interested in the advancement of the Negro people of America, when, in truth, they are but interested in the subjugation of certain types of the Negro race and the assimilation of as many of the race as possible into the white race.

THE NEGRO PROBLEM

As proof of the intention underlying the National Association for the Advancement of Colored People we will quote from Du Bois himself. He states in his article:

> We think of our problem here as THE Negro problem, but we know more or less clearly that the problem of the American Negro is very different from the problem of the South African Negro or the problem of the Nigerian Negro or the problem of the South American Negro. We have not hitherto been so clear as to the way in which the problem of the Negro in the United States differs from the problem of the Negro in the West Indies.
>
> For a long time we have been told, and we have believed, that the race problem in the West Indies, and particularly in Jamaica, has virtually been settled.

Now Du Bois speaks of this settlement of the problem of the race in the West Indies and Jamaica with a great deal of satisfaction. What kind of a settlement is it? Du Bois knows well, but he is not honest enough to admit it, because he himself visited Jamaica and saw the situation there, wherein an arrangement has been effected whereby the white man is elevated to the highest social and economic heights, and between him is socially and economically elevated the mulatto type of Du Bois, and beneath them both is the black man, who is crushed to the very bottom socially and economically.

SETTLEMENT OF THE PROBLEM

Du Bois regards this as a settlement of the problem in the West Indies and Jamaica. Now this is the kind of a settlement that he and the National Association for the Advancement of Colored People want in America, and they have not been honest enough to come out and tell us so, that we might act accordingly. This is why Du Bois bewails the black blood in his veins. This is why he regards Marcus Garvey and the Universal Negro Improvement Association as impossible. This is why he calls Marcus Garvey "black and ugly." But while this settlement in Jamaica and the West Indies satisfies Du Bois and probably would satisfy him in America, he must realize that the fifteen million colored people in the United States of America do not desire such a settlement; that outside of himself and a half-dozen men of his school of thought, who make up the Executive[s] of the National Association for the Advancement of Colored People, the majority of Negroes are not studying him and his solution of the problem, but all of us colored people of whatsoever hue are going to fight together for the general upbuilding of the Negro race, so that in the days to come we may be able to look back upon our effort with great pride, even as others worse positioned than ourselves have struggled upward to their present social, economic and political standing among races and nations.

DECEPTION AND HYPOCRISY

To show the deception and hypocrisy of Du Bois, he pretends, in the above-quoted paragraph from his article, as if he were not thoroughly acquainted with the problem in the West Indies, when, in another paragraph, he states the following:

This is the West Indian solution of the Negro problem:

The mulattoes are virtually regarded and treated as whites, with the assumption that they will, by continued white intermarriage, bleach out their color as soon as possible. There survive, therefore, few white Colonials save newcomers, who are not of Negro descent in some more or less remote ancestor. Mulattoes intermarry, then, largely with the whites, and the so-called disappearance of the color line is the disappearance of the line between the whites and mulattoes and not between the whites and the blacks or even between the mulattoes and the blacks.

Thus the privileged and exploiting group in the West Indies is composed of whites and mulattoes, while the poorly paid and ignorant proletariats are the blacks, forming a peasantry vastly in the majority, but socially, politically and economically helpless and nearly voiceless. This peasantry, moreover, has been systematically deprived of its natural leadership, because the black boy who showed initiative or who accidentally gained wealth or education soon gained the recognition of the white-mulatto group and might be incorporated with them, particularly if he married one of them. Thus his interest and efforts were identified with the mulatto-white group.

This is the kind of settlement that Du Bois speaks of; and this is the kind of settlement that he wants in the United States of America. Du Bois, you shall not have it!

Garvey Challenges Du Bois

Du Bois says that "Garvey had no thorough education and a very hazy idea of the technique of civilization." Du Bois forgets that Garvey has challenged him over a dozen times to intellectual combat, and he has for as many times failed to appear. Garvey will back his education against that of Du Bois at any time in the day from early morning to midnight, and whether it be in the classroom or on the public platform, will make him look like a dead duck on a frozen lake.

Is Du Bois Educated[?]

Du Bois seems to believe that the monopoly of education is acquired by being a graduate of Fisk, Harvard and Berlin. Education is not so much the school that one has passed through, but the use one makes of that which he has learned.

If Du Bois' education fits him for no better service than being a lackey for good white people, then it were better that Negroes were not educated. Du Bois forgets that the reason so much noise was made over him and his education was because he was among the first "experiments" made by white people on colored men along the lines of higher education. No one experimented with Marcus Garvey, so no one has to look upon him with surprise that he was able to master the classics and graduate from a university.

Du Bois is a surprise and wonder to the good white people who experimented with him, but to us moderns he is just an ordinary intelligent Negro, one of those who does not know what he wants.

The Man Who Lies

Du Bois is such a liar when it comes to anything relating to the Universal

Negro Improvement Association and Black Star Line and Marcus Garvey that we will not consider his attacks on the Black Star Line seriously. He lied before in reference to this corporation and had to swallow his vomit.[6] He has lied again, and we think a statement is quite enough to dispose of him in this matter.

This envious, narrow-minded man has tried in every way to surround the Universal Negro Improvement Association and Marcus Garvey with suspicion. He has been for a long time harping on the membership of the Universal Negro Improvement Association as to whether we have millions of members or thousands. He is interested because he wants to know whether these members are all paying dues or not, in that he will become very interested in the financial end of it, as there would be a lot of money available. Du Bois does not know that whether the Universal Negro Improvement Association had money or not he wouldn't have the chance of laying his hands on it, in that there are very few "leaders" that we can trust with a dollar and get the proper change. This is the kind of leadership that the Universal Negro Improvement Association is about to destroy for the building up of that which is self-sacrificing; the kind of leadership that will not hate poor people because they are poor, as Du Bois himself tells us he does, but a kind of leadership that will make itself poor and keep itself poor so as to be better able to interpret the poor in their desire for general uplift. He hates the poor. Now, what kind of a leader is he? Negroes are all poor black folk. They are not rich. They are not white; hence they are despised by the great professor. What do you think about this logic, this reasoning, professor? You have been to Berlin, Harvard and Fisk; you are educated and you have the "technique of civilization."

The Failure of a Critic

Du Bois harps upon the failure of other Negroes, but he fails to inform the public of his own failures. In his fifty-five years Du Bois has made success of nothing personal. In all his journalistic, personal and other business efforts he has failed, and were it not for Mary White Ovington, Moorefield Storey, Oswald Garrison Villard and [Joel] Spingarn, Du Bois, no doubt, would be eating his pork chops from the counter of the cheapest restaurant in Harlem like many other Negro graduates of Harvard and Fisk.

Test of Education and Ability

When it comes to education and ability, Garvey would like to be fair to Du Bois in every respect. Suppose for the proof of the better education and ability Garvey and Du Bois were to dismantle and put aside all they possess and were placed in the same environment to start life over afresh for the test of the better man? What would you say about this, doctor? Marcus Garvey is willing now because he is conceited enough to believe that in the space of two years he would make you look like a tramp in the competitive rivalry for a higher place in the social, economic world.

Let not our hearts be further troubled over Du Bois, but let fifteen million Negroes of the United States of America and the millions of the West Indies, South and Central America and Africa work toward the glorious end of an emancipated race and a redeemed motherland.

IGNORING FREEDOM

Du Bois cares not for an Empire for Negroes, but contents himself with being a secondary part of white civilization. We of the Universal Negro Improvement Association feel that the greatest service the Negro can render to the world and himself at this time is to make his independent contribution to civilization. For this the millions of members of the Universal Negro Improvement Association are working, and it is only a question of time when colored men and women everywhere will hearken to the voice in the wilderness, even though a Du Bois impugns the idea of Negro liberation.

SUPPORT FOR MOVEMENT

Let all members, divisions and friends of the Universal Negro Improvement Association organize the more to support this great cause morally and financially. If this is done, and whole-heartedly, we need not fear the result even though a thousand Du Boises rave.

With the very best wishes for your success, I have the honor to be Your obedient servant,

MARCUS GARVEY
President-General
Universal Negro Improvement Association

Printed in *NW*, 17 February 1923. Original headlines omitted; reprinted in *P&O*, 2: 310–320.

1. Du Bois wrote that he was of African, Dutch, and French ancestry. From his mother's family, the Burghardts, he inherited West African, "Dutch and perhaps Indian blood" (W.E..B. Du Bois, *The Autobiography of W.E.B. Du Bois* [New York: International Publishers, 1971], pp. 62–69, 64). His father, Alfred Du Bois, was descended in part from French Huguenots who settled in the Bahamas (idem., *Darkwater: Voices from Within the Veil* [New York: Harcourt, Brace & Howe, 1920], pp. 5–9).

2. Du Bois had written:

> There was a long, low unfinished church basement, roofed over. A little, fat black man, ugly but with intelligent eyes and big head, was seated on a plank platform beside a "throne.". . . It was designed as the beginning of a church long ago, but abandoned. Marcus Garvey roofed it over and out of this squat and dirty "Liberty Hall" he screams his propaganda. As compared with the homes, the business, the church, Garvey's basement represents nothing in accomplishment and only waste in attempt. Yet it has a right to be. It represents something spiritual, however poor and futile today. (W.E.B. Du Bois, "Back to Africa," *Century Magazine* 105 [February 1923]: 539–548)

3. There is no record of the Church Extension Society subscribing money to the Abyssinian Baptist Church. The Abyssinian Church belonged to the Southern New York Baptist Association and the New York City Baptist Mission Society, both of which had a mostly white membership; the mission society paid the salaries for three employees of the Abyssinian Church. Rev. Adam Clayton Powell, Sr., noted that both "colored and white manifested their spiritual and financial interest" in the construction of the church (Adam Clayton Powell, Sr., *Against the Tide* [New York: Richard R. Smith, 1938], p. 72). There was, however, a Harlem Baptist Church on E. 123rd St., which was heavily supported by the Church Extension Society and the Mission Society (Susan

M. Eltscher, director of the Library for the American Baptist Historical Society, to Robert A. Hill, 29 August 1984; Baptist Church Extension Society of Brooklyn and Queens, *Annual Reports*, April 1921–May 1923; Southern New York Baptist Association, *Annual Report*, 1921, p. 25; 1922, p. 25; 1923–1924, p. 30; Adam Clayton Powell, Sr., *Upon This Rock* [New York: Abyssinian Baptist Church, 1949], pp. 16–25; Adam Clayton Powell, Sr., *Against the Tide*, pp. 67–86; *New York Age*, 23 June 1923; *NYT*, 18 June 1923).

4. Du Bois did receive some financial help from whites in his education. In elementary and high schools, the mother of a fellow student supplied his books. As the time for college approached, Du Bois's high school principal and two ministers formed a scholarship fund to raise money from the local Congregational churches of Great Barrington, Mass., to send Du Bois to Fisk University, Nashville. After graduating from Fisk, Du Bois was supported at Harvard in part by scholarships, grants, and loans. Starting in 1892 Du Bois studied at the University of Berlin for two years, supported by a grant, which was half gift and half loan, from the Slater Foundation, headed by former U.S. President Rutherford B. Hayes (W.E.B. Du Bois, *Darkwater*, pp. 13–15; idem., *The Autobiography*, pp. 86–87, 101–103, 147; Francis L. Broderick, *W.E.B. Du Bois: Negro Leader in a Time of Crisis* [Stanford, Calif.: Stanford University Press, 1959], p. 26; Arnold Rampersad, *The Art and Imagination of W.E.B. Du Bois* [Cambridge: Harvard University Press, 1976], pp. 12, 41–42).

5. Du Bois's version is slightly different. He wrote, "I cordially despised the poor Irish and South Germans, who slaved in the mills, and annexed with the rich and well-to-do as my natural companions. Of such is the kingdom of snobs!" (W.E.B. Du Bois, *Darkwater*, p. 10).

6. See *Garvey Papers* 3: 172–173.

Confidential Informant Capt. J.W. Jones
to William J. Burns

2303 7th Ave., New York City, Feb. 14, 1923

In continuance of my investigation undercover I interviewed Marcus Garvey. I first learned that Garvey knew of my presence in New Orleans and it was necessary for me to use the same story that I had used down there. I have every reason to believe that he believes my story as he talked very freely with me for more than an hour. I find that Garvey is very much afraid that he will get into serious trouble over the murder of Eason. He said to me that he knew that the gover[n]ment agents were working on the case and he was afraid that some lying negroes would get him mixed up in the case. He went on to say that I knew him well enough to know that he wouldn't do anything like the plan[n]ing of Eason's death. Of course I agreed with him. I then interviewed Harold Saltus, Garvey's right hand man. I learned from him that Esau Ramus had been in town but had left town after being here for a day or two. As near as he could remember it was about one week after the murder of Eason. Saltus said that he didn't know where Ramus had gone after he left New York. It seems that not many of the officials here knew that Ramus was in town, or that they didn't know what part Ramus had pla[yed] . . . [*lines multilated*] Until such time as is necessary for the apprehension of Ramus in Detroit I thought it best not to see Mary Prince. In case that Ramus is not arrested in Detroit I will then see this woman. In the meantime I will keep in touch with what is going on at Garvey's office and at the same keep in touch with Agent Davis, but away from the office here. Respectfully,

J.W. JONES

DJ-FBI, file 61. TLS, recipient's copy.

Report by Special Agent Mortimer J. Davis

New York City Feb. 14, 1923

Reference is made to my report of yesterday's date outlining the data secured through CHANDLER OWEN from attorney Norris of Philadelphia:

This morning Norris came to New York and, with Owens, William Pickens, Agent Amos and the writer, was taken to the office of Asst. U.S. Attorney Mattuck.

Norris advised that Esau Ramus, whose correct name is JOHN JEFFRIES, is at present in hiding at 1516 Russell Street, Detroit, Michigan.[1] This address he secured from a letter sent by Ramus to Mary Prince in Philadelphia a few days ago.

Norris also brought with him sample of Ramus' handwriting, consisting of a letter written by the latter to Elie Garcia (a defendant in the present case), signed "Esau Ramus—J.J." This letter is printed by pen and ink, and is, I am informed, the only way Ramus can write. Norris brought this specimen in order to show, by comparison, that Ramus is undoubtedly the person who wrote the anonymous letter to the Chicago "Defender" which was published in that paper on Feb. 3rd last, which letter purports to have been written by the murderer of EASON.[2] There is no question but that the two handwritings are identical.

Norris also brought to us a large photograph of Ramus in his uniform of the U.N.I.A. police—the photo is a group, all in uniform and shows Ramus off to good effect. Norris failed, however, to produce the letters between Ramus and his wife, which I was led to believe were in his possession, and which, from his conversations, he has undoubtedly seen. The material which he handed us has been photostated and will be sent to New Or[le]ans for the use of the city authorities there.

Norris' information was practically the same as that given us through Chandler Owens yesterday. However, he also advised us that Ramus is wanted by the New York Police on several charges, under the name of John Jeffries.

With Mr. Mattuck, plans for the arrest of Ramus were laid and it was decided that inasmuch as Ramus was wanted in New York, we have the police here request his arrest, bring him to New York, and when here use the various means at our disposal to connect Marcus Garvey with the shooting affair in New Orleans. Therefore, Agent Amos and the writer went to Police Headquarters and talked the matter over with Lieut. Gegan and Inspector Coughlan. The latter advised us that Ramus (or Jeffries) was indicted in New York County during April, 1921[,] for Attempted Larceny in the 1st degree, Assault, 1st degree, and for carrying a concealed weapon (Sullivan Law);[3] that he had entered a furniture store in the negro section at the time[,] attempted to hold up the proprietor, assaulted him, attempted to escape but was captured in the cellar of the place. He claimed to have dislocated his hip, however, and was removed to Harlem Hospital. While confined there he made his escape and has not been seen since. Inspector Coughlan considered the matter of such importance that he ordered Lieut. Gegan to have the arresting officer (Detective Donohue, 38th Prec.) leave for Detroit at once to arrest Jeffries, suggesting that when this was done Mr. Mattuck could make the necessary arrangements with the State District Attorney to send Jeffries to New Orleans from here. However, when Donohue was located he did not see[m] very anxious to make the trip, and claimed that his recollection of the prisoner was so poor that he doubted if he could pick him up at this time. Inspector Coughlan then ordered Lieut. Gegan to communicate with the Detroit police and have them pick Jeffries up on the New York charge and held for extradition.

Agents were of the opinion that the sending of the New York detective to Detroit would have been a safe procedure, but after the second suggestion was made came to the conclusion that if the subject were apprehended in Detroit merely on a New York request, he would ask a hearing, obtain bail and again escape. The Detroit authorities of course would not know the importance of holding the man without bail. Certainly Marcus Garvey would make every effort to prevent the return of Jeffries to New York and Agents felt that he would raise any bail demanded. We decided, therefore, to have Lieut. Gegan send to the Detroit police the warrant which the former had in his possession from New Orleans, asking that he be arrested on that. Accompanying this warrant was subject's full description and his fingerprints. Simultaneously, Agents sent the following wire to the Detroit office:

> Refer telegram 7th regarding Esau Ramus alias John Jeffries alias Prince wanted New Orleans for murder. Correct address this man is fifteen sixteen Russell Street, Detroit. New York Police have today mailed New Orleans warrant to Chief Police Detroit with full particulars asking his immediate arrest. Suggest you communicate police your city and when subject is apprehended wire Shanton, New Orleans and this office. Department very much interested this matter and arrest very important in connection with case against Marcus Garvey now pending Federal court here.

I do not believe it is necessary to remind the Detroit office that this subject is in hiding and will try to evade arrest; that he is in Detroit for the reason that a jump over the border to Canada is easy from there and that, if apprehended, his freedom on bail will mean his escape for good. I doubt if he will make any statement but should he do so, the New Orleans office should be supplied with it immediately.

Late today Agent received a telephone call from confidential employe 800, who has been working on this case undercover in New Orleans, and subsequently met him. He was advised of the progress of the matter and will probably now await the outcome of the Detroit lead.

One Dixon, who has been assisting agents, also came to the office today and confidentially advised us that Eli[e] Garcia told him that before Ramus left New York for New Orleans in the Fall he was given $100 by Garvey; the latter, as a matter of course, sent him to Garcia to receive the order for the money. Five days after Eason's shooting Garcia states that Ramus again came to the office and Garvey gave him an order for $60 which Garcia O.K.'d. For the information of the New Or[le]ans office, Garcia, who is a co-defendant with Garvey, has since split from him, having been arrested on Garvey's complaint that he stole a sum of money from him. I feel that he is telling the truth, in fact have reason to believe that before the case against him comes to trial he will enter a plea of guilty and turn state's evidence.

On this date also agent received from the Post Office department tracing of a letter (envelope) addressed to Mary Prince at 1807—3rd Ave[.,] this city. The letter was postmarked at Detroit Feb. 12th. There appear to be two Mary Prince's in this case, which I think [is] explained by the fact that Ramus had a "wife" in almost every city.

MORTIMER J. DAVIS

DJ-FBI, file 61. TD.

1. This was the address of UNIA's Liberty Hall in Detroit.

2. Bureau of Investigation Agent T. L. Jefferson obtained the original letter on 17 February from the city editor of the *Chicago Defender*, which printed it in its 3 February 1923 issue. The anonymous writer of the letter claimed, "I killed Eason and wroat [*sic*] a letter to the Mayor of New Orleans and Chief of Police Wher [*sic*] I was." The letter was forwarded to the New Orleans bureau office for handwriting comparison with letters received by the mayor and chief of police of New Orleans (report of 20 February 1923, DJ-FBI, file 61). A copy of the letter was also sent to Agent F. H. Hessler in Detroit, who was instructed to exchange reports on the search for Ramus with the bureau's offices in New York, Philadelphia, New Orleans, and Chicago (20 February 1923, DJ-FBI, file 61-50-237).

3. A reference to New York State Penal Law of 1916, allowing for the felony arrest of persons carrying concealed dangerous weapons (*New York Consolidated Laws Service Annotated Statutes with Forms*, 23A [New York: Lawyers' Cooperative Publishing Co., 1977]: 479).

Carl Murphy, Editor, *Baltimore Afro-American*, to Harry M. Daugherty

628 North Eutaw Street, Baltimore, Maryland
February 16, 1923

Sir:

Sometime ago[1] we asked if any action was intended against Marcus Garvey and his Association as requested in a document signed by six persons from New York. To date we have received no reply. Very truly yours,

THE AFRO-AMERICAN
CARL MURPHY[2]
Editor

DNA, RG 60, file 198940-286. TLS on *Baltimore Afro-American* letterhead, recipient's copy.

1. Carl Murphy originally wrote to Daugherty on 30 January 1923 (DNA, RG 60, file 198940-286).

2. Carl J. Murphy (b. 1889), editor and publisher of the *Baltimore Afro-American*, graduated from Howard University in 1911. He received his master's degree from Harvard University in 1913, subsequently returning to Howard, where he became assistant professor of German. In 1918 he left the university to become editor of the weekly *Afro-American* (*WWCA*, 1930, 1931, and 1932).

Confidential Informant Capt. J.W. Jones
to William J. Burns

2307 7th Ave., New York City, Feb. 18, 1923

Sir:

In continuance of my investigation undercover I find that Garvey will hold a large mass meeting at Carnegie Hall on the 23rd of February. This meeting[,] he says, is for the purpose of explaining to the public the aims and objects of the Universal Negro Improvement Association. The real purpose of this meeting is to create sympathy for his coming trial. In order to do this he has had printed about five thousand letters in the for[m]s of invitation which he is sending to all Judges, Lawyers, Court Attendants and to any one that he thinks their sympathies will do him good in his trial. I had heard that he had a list of the jury panel and was sending them a copy but, upon checking on this information I found that it wasn't true. I secured a copy of this letter and turned it over to Agent Davis, as he said that he wanted to turn it over to the District Attorney. I learned that Garvey had contemplated sending a copy of this letter to the jurymen but afterwards changed his mind.

I am keeping in touch with Garvey's office and am waiting to see what effect the arrest of Ramus will have on him. I am sure that Ramus is in Detroit as all information I have gotten leads to that city.

I would suggest that as soon as Ramus is arrested in Detroit' a search warrant be secured for the house of Mary Ramus in Philadelphia and all letters in her possession be taken as Ramus['s] possession, but that the letters refer[r]ed to in my previous report are in the possession of Mary Ramus in Philadelphia.

Will continue my investigation for any new developments. Respectfully,

J.W. JONES

DJ-FBI, file 61. TLS, recipient's copy.

1. Esau Ramus was apprehended in Detroit on 20 February 1923 by Agent Dupis of the Detroit office of the Bureau of Investigation. Ramus was scheduled to be returned to the Louisiana state authorities in New Orleans (Agent Wilcox to William J. Burns, 21 February 1923, DJ-FBI, file 61).

Speech by Marcus Garvey

[[Carnegie Hall, 23 February 1923]]

Mr. Chairman and Fellow Citizens: I am here tonight as the President-General of the Universal Negro Improvement Association to explain the aims and objects of this organization and to defend its principles. Over five years ago the Universal Negro Improvement Association placed itself before the world as the movement through which the new and rising Negro would give expression of his feelings. This association adopts an attitude not of hostility to other races and peoples of the world, but an attitude of self-respect of manhood rights on behalf of 400,000,000 Negroes of the world.

MUCH MISUNDERSTANDING ABOUT THE U.N.I.A.

In advocating the principles of this association we find we have been very much misunderstood and very much misrepresented by men from within our own race, as well as others from without. Any reform movement that seeks to bring about changes for the benefit of humanity is bound to be misrepresented by those who have always taken it upon themselves to administer to, and to lead the unfortunate—to lead and to direct those who may be placed under temporary disadvantages. It has been so in all other movements whether it is social or political; hence those of us in the Universal Negro Improvement Association who lead do not feel in any way embarrassed about this misrepresentation, about this misunderstanding as far as the Aims and Objects of the Universal Negro Improvement Association go. But those who probably would have taken kindly notice of this great movement have been led to believe that this movement seeks not to develop the good within the race, but to give expression to that which is most destructive and most harmful to society and to government.

A DENIAL OF THE MISREPRESENTATIONS

I am here tonight to deny that misrepresentation. I am here to remove the misunderstanding that has been created in the minds of the millions of people throughout the world in their relationship to the Universal Negro Improvement Association.

WHAT THE U.N.I.A. STANDS FOR

The Universal Negro Improvement Association stands for the bigger brotherhood; the Universal Negro Improvement Association stands for human rights, not only for Negroes, but for all races. The Universal Negro Improvement Association believes in the rights of not only the black race, but the white race, the yellow race and the brown race. (Applause). The

Universal Negro Improvement Association believes that the white man has as much right to be considered, the yellow man has as much right to be considered, the brown man has as much right to be considered as well as the black man of Africa. In view of the fact that the black man of Africa has contributed as much to the world as the white man of Europe, and the brown and yellow man of Asia, we of the Universal Negro Improvement Association demand that the white, yellow and brown races give to the black man his place in the civilization of the world. We ask for nothing more than the rights of 400,000,000 Negroes. We are not seeking, as I said before, to destroy or disrupt the society or the government of other races, but we are determined that 400,000,000 of us shall unite ourselves to free our motherland from the grasp of the invader. (Applause). We of the Universal Negro Improvement Association are determined to unite 400,000,000 Negroes for their own industrial, political, social and religious emancipation.

We of the Universal Negro Improvement Association are determined to unite the 400,000,000 Negroes of the world to give expression to their own feeling; we are determined to unite the 400,000,000 Negroes of the world for the purpose of building a civilization of their own. (Applause). And in that desire, we desire to bring together the 15,000,000 of the United States, the 180,000,000 in the West Indies and Central and South America, and the 200,000,000 in Africa. We are looking toward political freedom on the continent of Africa, the land of our fathers. (Applause).

NOT SEEKING A GOVERNMENT
WITHIN A GOVERNMENT

The Universal Negro Improvement Association is not seeking to build up another government within the bounds or borders of the United States of America. The Universal Negro Improvement Association is not seeking to disrupt any organized system of government, but the association is determined to bring Negroes together for the building up of a nation of their own. And why? Because we have been forced to it. We have been forced to it throughout the world, not only in America, not only in Europe, not only in the British Empire, but wheresovever the black man happens to find himself, he has been forced to do for himself.

THE DIFFERENCE BETWEEN THE U.N.I.A.
AND OTHER ORGANIZATIONS

The difference between the Universal Negro Improvement Association and the other movements of this country and probably the world is that the Universal Negro Improvement Association seeks independence of government, while the other organizations seek to make the Negro a secondary part of existing governments. We differ from the organizations in America like the National Association for the Advancement of Colored People because they seek to subordinate the Negro as a secondary consideration in great civilization. The N.A.A.C.P. knows that in America the Negro will never reach his highest ambition; it knows that the Negro in America will never get all his constitutional rights. All those organizations which are fostering the improvement of Negroes in the British Empire know that the Negro in the British Empire will never reach the height of his constitutional rights. What do I mean by constitutional rights in America? If the black man is to reach the height of his ambition in this country—if the black man is to get all his constitutional rights in America—then the black man should have the same chance in the nation as any other man to become president of the nation or a street cleaner in New York. If the black man in the British Empire would have all his constitutional rights it means that the Negro in the British Empire should at least have the same right to become premier of Great Britain as he has to be a street cleaner in the city of London. Are they prepared to give us such political equality? We are not asking the National association to answer that question for us; we can answer it for ourselves. You and I can live in the United States of America for 100 more years and our generations may live for 200 years or for 5,000 years and so long as there is a black and white population, when the majority is on the side of the white race, you and I will never get political justice or get political equality in this country. Then why should a black man with rising ambition after preparing himself in every possible way to give expression to that highest ambition allow himself to be kept down by racial prejudice within a country? If I am as educated as the next man, if I am as prepared as the next man, if I have passed through the best schools and colleges and universities as the other fellow, why should I not have a fair chance to compete with the other fellow for the biggest position in the nation? That is where the Universal Negro Improvement Association differs from the National Association for the Advancement of Colored People. That association knows well that the Negro will never occupy anything else but a secondary position within the United States. The time will never come for the black man to be president of the United States. The time will never come for the black man to be secretary of state to the nation, nor to be attorney-general of the United States. Why then should I limit my ambition to be street cleaner while the other fellow is president of the United States? I have feelings, I have blood, I have senses like the other fellow; I have ambition, I have hope. Why should he, because of some racial prejudice, keep me down and why should I concede to him the right to rise above me and to establish himself as my permanent master? God never created any master for the human race but Himself. God created all men equal, whether they be black, yellow, white or brown.

THE NEGRO TAKING A PART IN READJUSTMENT

And now that the world is readjusting itself politically, now that the world is readjusting itself socially, the U.N.I.A. calls upon 400,000,000 Negroes throughout the world to take a part in this readjustment. The readjustment that we seek is not that which will keep the Negro a lackey, a peon, a serf or a slave, but the readjustment that we are going to take a part in is that which will lift the colored man to a standard with all other races throughout the world. I refuse to stultify my ambition, and every true Negro refuses to stultify his ambition to suit any one, and there the U.N.I.A. decides if America is not big enough for two presidents, if France is not big enough for two presidents, if England is not big enough for two kings, then we are not going to quarrel over the matter; we will leave one president in America, we will leave one king in England, we will leave one president in France, and we will have one president in Africa. Hence, the Universal Negro Improvement Association does not seek to interfere with the social or political systems of America; the U.N.I.A. does not seek to interfere with the social and political systems of France, but by the arrangements of things today the U.N.I.A. refuses to recognize any political or social system in Africa except that which we are about to establish for ourselves.

They call me an anarchist; they call me a Bolshevist. If anarchy means to free Africa and drive out of Africa those who have no right there, if Bolshevism means to drive out of Africa those who have no right there, then I am a Bolshevist and an anarchist and a radical all rolled in one.

No Apology for Program

I have no apology to offer for the program of the Universal Negro Improvement Association. The program of the U.N.I.A. was the program of the man whose anniversary we celebrated yesterday [22 *February*]. The program of the U.N.I.A. for freedom and independence of Africa was the program of George Washington 146 [145?] years ago.[1] I am satisfied to be a part of the same political party of George Washington. If he was a radical[,] then I am a radical; if he was an anarchist, then I am an anarchist; if he was an anything else other than what we knew him to be, then I am that also. Because what Washington desired for America over 140 years ago is just what the U.N.I.A. desires for Africa now.

Not Afraid of Work

The difference between the Universal Negro Improvement Association and the other so-called Negro movements is this: That the U.N.I.A. is not afraid of work and its workers are not afraid of work. The difference between these organizations is that one is made up of a group of workers and the other is made up of a group of lazy men. They criticize Marcus Garvey and the U.N.I.A.; they criticize the African liberation program because they know it is a big job, and it is a man's job, and they are not prepared for a man's job. You cannot go about liberating a race—you cannot go about freeing a country and establishing a nation with silk stockings on. You talk about music and art and literature, as such men like Du Bois and Weldon Johnson take pride in doing. A nation was not founded first of all on literature or on writing books;

it is first founded upon the effort of real workers, and that is where we differ from the N.A.A.C.P.

They call us crude, ignorant and illiterate and they hold themselves up as leading lights, calling themselves graduates from colleges and universities, and gentlemen. Why, it surprises me to know that we have so many Negro gentlemen nowadays. The term "gentlemen" is a mark of distinction; it is not a thing that is assumed; it is a thing that is merited. They call us ignorant; they call us common people. Who made them different from us? Do you know where the difference comes in between peoples and between classes? Let us take the order of society. The man who is regarded as an aristocrat is the one who has merited it by service to his race or to his country. It is not a thing that you can assume. I want Du Bois and Weldon Johnson to understand that aristocracy and [n]obility are not things that can be assumed, otherwise all of us would be aristocrats, all of us would be gentlemen and nobles; but in the order of society the one class is uplifted above the other because of its service to humanity. What contribution have these fellows made to the advancement of this race of ours as to cause them to be different from us? (Cries of "None! None!")

The Opportunity for Service

The opportunity for service is now, not another fifty years, not another hundred years, not another two hundred years. When the historians of our race will write of the race's achievements and we can find a black Napoleon, whose picture we can hang in the Hall of Fame in Africa, when we can find a Bismarck, whose picture we can hang in the Museum of Art in Africa, when we can find a hundred years from now the grandson of some Negro of the present day who by sacrifice or service and by martyrdom contributed to this race, then we will talk about aristocracy and nobility. Dr. Du Bois, I want you to understand the time for service to your race is now, not to imitate the great white race, not to ask for social equality with the white race, because even that reflects the lowest in the Negro. The Negro is too proud to desire any other than the company of his own. Therefore we of the U.N.I.A. talk nothing about social equality with the white race, because we believe that a man has the right to associate with whomsoever he wants to, and really I do not want to associate with anybody except those who look like me, except in business and in those necessary associations that we may carry out not only for the good of the race but for the good of the nation.

Let me tell Dr. Du Bois and all those who are here tonight that the highest type of Negro is not the Negro who seeks or hankers after social equality with other people, but that the highest type of Negro is the one who is satisfied with himself (applause); not the Negro who would want to go to the white man's club and dance with the white man's daughter, as Du Bois wants to do; but the Negro who is satisfied with his own club and with his own women, who believes that all that is beautiful is reflected in this race of ours. If there is any aristocracy it must be found among the group of people who feel that way. The U.N.I.A. takes that stand because we believe that the time is opportune and if we lose this moment we lose everything.

NOT PREACHING HATE

I trust that everybody will understand that we are not preaching a propaganda of hate against anybody. We love the white man; we love all humanity, because we feel that we cannot live without the other. The white man is as necessary to the existence of the Negro as the Negro is necessary to his existence. There is a common relationship that we cannot escape. Africa has certain things that Europe wants and Europe has certain things that Africa wants, and if a fair and square deal must bring white and black with each other[,] it is impossible for us to escape it. Africa has oil, diamonds, copper, gold and rubber and all the minerals that Europe wants, and there must be some kind of relationship between Africa and Europe for a fair exchange, so we cannot afford to hate anybody.

. We want certain things that Europe has and Europe wants certain things that we have. We are not preaching hate at all, because if we are going to build up a nation we must have association with others. Later on it will be seen how much we love the white man in that we are going to form an alliance with him. That is the reason that I love America as I do. I love America because it is liberal enough to give the Negro an opportunity to give expression to his feelings and to his soul-throbs.

THE GOVERNMENT NOT FIGHTING THE U.N.I.A.

The fight against the U.N.I.A. is not made by the Government, it is made by a group of small-minded Negroes who realize that their occupations are going—a small group of Negroes who have sold us to the white man for over fifty years by misrepresenting us to the white man. The white man is not to be blamed because he was told about us. In their preachings, these so-called leaders of our[s] told them that we were satisfied with all that they were prepared to give, and the white man was satisfied to circumscribe us according to his own desire and feelings. He has been paying for that over fifty years ago and these fellows have been receiving the pay. Now that they realize that the U.N.I.A. has come upon the scene to give a true interpretation to the spirit of the Negro that is not in keeping with what they said before, they are fighting the Universal Negro Improvement Association so as to prevent the white man from hearing what the U.N.I.A. stands for. But the U.N.I.A. had made enough noise to let the whole world know that the Negro is only asking for an opportunity to show of what mettle and stuff he is made. We proved of what stuff we are made in France and Flanders and we are going to prove it more on the battlefields of Africa one of these fine days.

You may think me a radical; you may think me strange, but what do you think, what do you expect?

LIBERTY NOT WON BY BEGGING

Liberty is not won by begging; it is not won by praying for it; it is won by fighting and sometimes dying. That is how we differ again from the other organizations; they believe in petitions and mass meetings, we believe in solid organization when everybody is ready to make one big, long march. Instead of dissipating and wasting our energies here and there as fifteen millions in America, twelve millions in the West Indies, ten millions in Central and South America, that we come together as four hundred million Negroes and then demand the things that we want. That is the job that is too much for these fellows. It does not mean that the leaders of such a movement as this [are] going to get their reward in the present day and the present age, and these fellows want all that is coming to them now. That is just the difference. Marcus Garvey could be in an organization like the N.A.A.C.P. if he was satisfied to get a check from any philanthropist every six months or once a year, or get a salary of $5,000 a year, and live the best among Negroes and call himself a "dicty" aristocrat. That is what is called an easy job, but Marcus Garvey does not want an easy job. The job of Marcus Garvey means that sometimes he must be in jail and probably sometimes out of jail; that sometimes Marcus Garvey is not only in jail, but he must die prematurely for the cause that needs assistance. The jail is nothing to Marcus Garvey and those who lead the cause of Negro freedom. If they had caught George Washington 145 [146?] years ago he would not only have been in jail, but he would not have died at the time he did, but he got away with it and became the greatest American. If they had caught Lenin and Trotsky before they turned the trick they would not have been talking and writing about socialism; they would have been buried in the ground several years ago, but they got away with it.

Roger Casement, of Ireland, did not get away with it; he lost his head, M[a]cSwiney died in prison. Gandhi of India did get away with it. The men of the N.A.A.C.P., who criticize the U.N.I.A., there is none of them from its president down to its secretary who has ever taken the chance of being ten miles near the jail. Some leaders, fighting for the liberty of the people, people oppressed, martyred and massacred all over the world, and the leaders feel that the nearest they must go is in a parlor of carpet and cushions. Yet Du Bois thinks himself an aristocrat because he has a wrong idea of leadership. Before a race is established or makes itself a nation, there is no aristocracy within that race or among that people, because aristocracy is not based upon assumption, it is built upon service. What service has Du Bois rendered to the race? What service has Weldon Johnson rendered to the race[?] Take Du Bois, and if he did not get his six or seven thousand dollars a year from the N.A.A.C.P.[,] I feel sure he would have left long, long ago. If Weldon Johnson did not get his check for his service every month[,] I feel sure he would have looked for a job long, long ago, and I base my assumption upon the act of Pickens. Pickens at one time was not in good standing with the N.A.A.C.P.; he wanted more pay and they would not give it to him. He thought that the U.N.I.A. would have paid him more than he was getting; he went back and told them how much we would give him and they raised his salary to more than what we offered him. That is the kind of leaders we have in other organizations. Those who lead the U.N.I.A. on the Executive Council today sometimes go for a year without any salary, but we have worked honestly and faithfully because of the conviction we have and the faith we have in this race of ours.

AN ASSOCIATION OF SACRIFICE

The difference between the N.A.A.C.P. and the U.N.I.A. is the one is an association of sacrifice, an association wherein its leaders are prepared not only to live, but to die, for the accomplishments of its Aims and Objects. I am supposed to be different from Du Bois because I am prepared to go the limit. I have absolutely no cause to fear going to jail, or to fear arrest by the government. There is no government in the world that can say Marcus Garvey had anything in his private life to cause the police to come ten miles near his door; the only trouble that I am supposed to be in came from my services to the U.N.I.A. and my services to the race.

These men are not appreciative of services; the only regard they have for a man who has paid a price is to criticize and condemn him. Men who suffer and die for humanity are not treated that way. All those who have enough intelligence, not even education, see the truth. Any emancipation comes not through the avenue of ease, not on a bed of roses; it comes from sacrifices, and for that those who lead the Universal Negro Improvement Association are prepared.

I thank you for your presence here tonight, and for the support that you have given this organization at all times, and I feel this[,] that when judgment is to be passed finally by black and white, you will find that the U.N.I.A. through its leaders at the present time did its duty and did it well. (Loud and prolonged applause.)

Printed in *NW*, 3 March 1923. Original headlines omitted.

1. A possible reference to George Washington's role in the Continental Congress of 1776.

Article in *Norfolk Journal and Guide*

[24 February 1923]

TEMPER OF THE GARVEYITES

Commenting upon the well-known disposition of the Marcus Garvey followers to be intolerant of criticism, or news that is not favorable to them, the *National Herald* (Norfolk) says:

We deplore with much regret the arising misunderstanding of some people with respect to news matter and the opinion of the editor, as recent press notices published in our local contemporary regarding the Garvey Movement, have occasioned.

Threats of suits and dire happenings may occasion serious consequences and be harmful to any movement, for when bulldozing, assassination, thugism and similar methods are employed to make other people, ignorant and intelligent alike, swallow their isms, then Virginia is not the place for such a colony and it should be made plain that no such license is issued here.

We have tried to reason with the Garvey people, but we have found ourselves unable to do so. We have tried to point out to some of their local leaders the difference between news and editorial opinion but they still look the same to a Garvey disciple. An article printed on the front page might as well be printed in the editorial columns, so far as a Garveyite is concerned. The editor is, in their opinion, the author of and sponsor for it. So we have become weary of trying to reason with them. We have decided to go on and print the news, when it is favorable to the Garvey movement, and when it is not. They are going to fume and fuss and slander all who do not agree with them anyhow. That has been not only our experience, but the experience of every Negro newspaper that has tried to publish both sides of the Garvey question.

It is interesting in this connection to note that an increasing number of race papers are putting their condemnation upon the bullying, threatening tactics of the Garvey klan. The *Newport News Star* recently had the following to say:

> When people get to the point where they cannot tolerate honest difference they ought to be suppressed. A great deal of the trouble the Negro is having in this country is brought on by such irresponsible demagogues and blatherskites as Marcus Garvey has gathered together in his schemes to filch money from the pockets of his unsophisticated followers and sympathizers, and anyone who dares differ or oppose their schemes is roundly cursed and marked.

Outspoken disapproval of attempts to subsidize or muzzle the press like the above expression by Editor Lewis is bound to carry considerable weight with thinking people. There are still a few newspapers that lend encouragement to such methods as are complained of by the *Herald* and the *Star*. Such newspapers, not able, perhaps, to win public favor on their merits, find it to their commercial advantage to pander to the Garvey movement. But no paper worth the name will encourage lawlessness, the suppression of free speech and free thinking. No paper can do so and remain in public confidence and favor.

Printed in *Norfolk Journal and Guide*, 24 February 1923.

William J. Burns to Carl Murphy

[*Washington, D.C.*] February 24, 1923

Dear Si[r:]

The Attorney General has referred to me your letter addressed to him on the 1[6]th Instant, making inquiry with regard to Marcus Garvey.

Marcus Garvey is now under indictment in the Federal Court for the Southern District of New York for misusing the mails in a scheme to defraud. His case will come up for trial within a few days. Very truly yours,

WM. J. BURNS
Director
[Bureau of Investigation]

DJ-FBI, file 61. TLS, carbon copy.

NOW OFF THE PRESS

The Pamphlet

"EIGHT 'UNCLE TOM' NEGROES"

The Seven Men and One Woman of the Negro Race Who Wrote the "Infamous Letter" to the Honorable Attorney-General

—AND—

"W. S. BURGHARDT DUBOIS AS A HATER OF DARK PEOPLE"

BY

MARCUS GARVEY

Wholesale 10 cents per copy; retail 15 cents. Send in your order with cash for bundles of 10, 20, 25, 50 or 100. Quick sellers. Make some money in your spare time selling the pamphlets.

Write Book Department, Universal Negro Improvement Association, 56 West 135th Street.

Members, Friends. Divisions and Chapters should send in for bundles of these pamphlets to sell. Cash with all orders.

(*Source*: *NW*, 24 February 1923)

Speech by Marcus Garvey

[[Liberty Hall, New York, February 25, 1923]]

My subject tonight is "The Doctrine of White Supremacy." Everybody in America knows of William Jennings Bryan. He was thrice the Democratic candidate for the presidency of the United States of America. Mr. Bryan, besides being a politician or a statesmen, is also a Christian gentleman. He is regarded as a preacher, a social uplift worker, and a social reformer. A better Christian than Mr. Bryan I hardly believe you could find in any part of the world. He has converted thousands of men to Christianity and for over 30 years he has been prominently before the people of America (black and white). During that period of time he impressed not only those of his race but those of the Negro race, that he was a liberal-minded Christian and one who stood for the larger brotherhood—the brotherhood of man and the fatherhood of God. I came in contact with Mr. William Jennings Bryan about seven or eight years ago, when he visited the Panama Canal and some of the West Indian islands.[1] I heard him speak, and in one speech he made somewhere in Cristobal, Colón, he left an abiding impression on my mind: certain things he said I will never forget. "I have reached," he said, "the stage of life when I must make every minute count for something done, something accomplished." I never forgot that. I always had a good liking for Mr. Bryan, but I always believed him to be just like all other white folks, and he has not surprised me. A couple of days ago this thrice candidate for the presidency of the United States of America came out in Washington and said that he stands absolutely for white supremacy.[2] He was speaking of America and when he was questioned, he said: "I am absolutely converted to it now, but I have been thinking that way for twenty years." Yet this is a man who could have been three times president of the United States of America.

When I interviewed the Ku Klux Klan last July [*June*] some people purposely tried to form a wrong opinion and got the wrong idea of my intentions. My statements on the Ku Klux Klan were wickedly and maliciously misrepresented and misquoted by those who did not desire to speak the truth and see the truth as it is. Those of you who have paid careful attention to what I have said—those of you who have followed me carefully and minutely in all my expressions and in all my writings—will recall my saying that the Ku Klux Klan was not only an organization, but the Ku Klux Klan was the spirit of greater America. Some could not understand me in my expression, but this I hope will convince them that the Ku Klux Klan is not an organization: the Ku Klux Klan is a spirit that has its existence in the souls and in the hearts and the breasts of 99 per cent of white America. William Jennings Bryan is not a member of the Ku Klux Klan, but we find him standing for the principles of the Ku Klux Klan. He could have been the Imperial Wizard in the Klan, for that matter; he could have been the Imperial Giant or Cyclop or what-not in the Klan, because the Klan's program is not beyond the statement of Mr. Bryan, who could have been thrice president of the United States of America.

THE POSITION OF THE U.N.I.A.

Now, the position of the Universal Negro Improvement Association is this: To correctly interpret as far as possible the present and future relationship between the black and white peoples not only of any one country—not only of America, but of the world; and the Universal Negro Improvement Association feels this: That every other race group believes in its own absolute existence and its absolute ascendancy and supremacy over others; and it is for that reason that we cannot see any possible relationship between black and white politically, socially or economically that will make the black man the equal of the white man by the established standards of present-day civilization.

NO HOPE FOR JUSTICE OR EQUALITY

Now what can the American Negro expect out of America for justice, for equality, for constitutional rights when even your candidates for President believe in white supremacy? Now this is not Mr. Edward Young Clark [*Clarke*], Ku Klux Klan agent, speaking; it is not Colonel Simmons, the Imperial Wizard, speaking; this is one of the representative statesmen of America, one of the recognized statesmen of the world, William Jennings Bryan—not an ordinary politician, but a philosopher and a world recognized leader. Mr. Bryan is honest and I appreciate him for that and I love him more now than before because he has convinced me and Du Bois and Weldon Johnson and the National Association crowd that there is absolutely no hope of equality, politically, socially and economically, within the bounds of the United States of America so long as there is one white man alive.

Now what can fifteen million people do in a commonwealth, in a nation, in a country surrounded by a majority of another race that stands (through its greatest statesman) for the supremacy of their race? What faces us but absolute chaos and absolute defeat in political, social and economic competition with the stronger and dominant race? Hence it is plain for even a child to see that the Negro's future in America is fraught with great difficulties—is fraught with disappointment between now and eternity. Our position in America will be relatively between black and white, the same because the highest statesmanship in the country is not going to admit this minority group to rise that is not a group of creators, that is not a group of producers, to dominate the country or even to share the domination of the country with them equally.

We may talk religion; that sounds all right morally and ethically, but you cannot live religion in the twentieth century, otherwise you go foodless and shelterless. The man who attempts to live religion in this age of materialism is the fellow who won't take long to [be] hungry and shelterless. Let John D. Rockefeller with all his billions try to live religion, and in twenty-four hours he will be begging bread around New York. It is all well to preach and talk religion, but you cannot live it. The only place you can live religion is in heaven, and the fifteen hundred million souls that now populate the world are a long way from heaven. (Laughter.) The distance is long and the time is long; it may take another million years to get there. So while we talk religion down here we cannot very well live religion because of the sinfulness of the age in which we live. The only thing you can live down here is power and strength. And that is the only thing that is going to solve this Negro problem, not only in America but in all parts of the world. When the Negro develops not his spiritual muscles but his physical muscles strong enough to exert them in his own defense, then not only William Jennings Bryan, not only the Ku Klux Klan, but the "red shirts" and the "gray shirts" of Italy[3] and England[4] will change their mind about white supremacy and the inferiority of the darker peoples of the world.[5] (Applause.)

There is no white supremacy beyond the power and the strength of the white man to hold himself against others. The supremacy of any race is not permanent; it is a thing only of the time in which the race finds itself to be powerful. It is well for William Jennings Bryan to talk this way, because the thing gives inspiration and courage to men and women like those who make up the Universal Negro Improvement Association to fight stronger for the establishment of a government of our own on the continent of Africa.

THE COLORED MAN'S POSITION INSECURE

More and more we are coming to find in America that the colored man's position is insecure, and when I talk about the Ku Klux Klan I do so not because I have any interest in the Ku Klux Klan, but because I admire the Ku Klux Klan for its honesty of intention in expressing to the people what it means; and I have more regard for the Ku Klux Klan, and I have more regard for Mr. Bryan than all the other white people in America, because they feel the same way but are not honest enough to tell us what they mean. The man who is going to give you a licking and who prepares you for that licking is a better friend of yours than the fellow who is going to give you a licking that you know nothing about until he gives it to you.

I have the highest regard for Mr. Bryan and the Ku Klux Klan for telling me openly and telling 15,000,000 of us openly: "Negroes, we stand for white supremacy. We are not going to give you a chance to be our social, political or economic equals. If you have sense you will go out and look out for yourselves." So I have not fallen out with Mr. Bryan. I have nothing to do with the Ku Klux Klan more than thanking them for the information that they have given to me, because as they in their part of the world stand for white supremacy, so will 400,000,000 Negroes, under the leadership of the Red, the Black and the Green, stand in their part of the world for black supremacy. (Great applause.) Knowing the intention of the Ku Klux Klan, knowing the intention of William Jennings Bryan, let me tell you this: All this noise about suppressing the Ku Klux Klan and putting them out of business is all a farce; it is a lie; it is hypocrisy. They do not mean it at all. It is only a free advertisement that they are giving to the program of the Ku Klux Klan, so that all other folks who never thought that way will get to thinking about it.

But they are not manly enough to tell the people at large because they boast of a great democracy; they boast of liberalism in the country; they boast of humanity, and they could not very well go back on the program of Wilson—the program of democracy for all weaker peoples—by openly espousing the cause of the Ku Klux Klan, so they make it appear that they oppose the Ku Klux Klan. But at heart they are for the Ku Klux Klan and for the doctrine of white supremacy, not only in America, but throughout the world. They will fool everybody else except Marcus Garvey.

I repeat, I admire Mr. Bryan because of his honesty, and if we live long enough[,] not only will Mr. Bryan come out and say so, but other men in higher positions and higher places than Mr. Bryan will later make the confession that they believe in white supremacy for the people in America. (Applause.) . . .

Printed in *NW*, 3 March 1923. Original headlines omitted.

1. Bryan was a candidate for the presidency in 1896, 1900, and 1908. Garvey most likely would have heard him speak in Cristobal, Colón, Panama, on 12 December 1911, when Bryan presented a lecture entitled "Signs of the Times" (*NYT*, 12 December and 15 December 1911; *The Daily Star and Herald*, 13 December, 14 December and 15 December 1911; *WBD*).

2. Bryan delivered an address on the "negro question" on 20 September 1922 before the Southern Society of Washington. In a later article that amplified the points made in his speech, Bryan wrote: "the question is, which race shall control the Government and make the laws under which both shall live? The more advanced race will always control as a matter of self-preservation, not only for the benefit of the advanced race, but for the benefit of the backward race also. . . . Any one who will look at the subject without prejudice will know that white supremacy promotes the highest welfare of both races" (*NYT*, 18 March 1923). Bryan also expressed the opinion that slavery in America had been "an improvement over freedom in Africa" because servitude exposed blacks to white civilization. Bryan's sympathy for southern racial mores increased toward the end of his life, but his views were basically consistent throughout his political career. In 1901 he had defended disfranchisement as "absolutely essential to the welfare of the South" (Willard H. Smith, "William Jennings Bryan and Racism," *Journal of Negro History* 54, no. 1 [January 1969]: 127–149, 138). Similarly, during the public furor over President Theodore Roosevelt's invitation to Booker T. Washington to dine at the White House, Bryan denounced both for allegedly intending "to wipe out race lines" (Louis T. Harlan, *Booker T. Washington: The Wizard of Tuskegee*, 2 [New York: Oxford University Press, 1983], p. 4). As one biographer stated, Bryan's attitude toward blacks by the end of his life was "worthy of any Klan member" (Lawrence W. Levine, *Defender of the Faith: William Jennings Bryan: The Last Decade, 1915–1925* [New York: Oxford University Press, 1965], p. 257).

3. Garvey's reference to "red shirts" was obviously a misnomer for the armed bands of Fascist Blackshirts (*squadristi*). Garvey might have gotten them confused with Giuseppe Garibaldi's volunteer Red Shirts (*Garibaldini*), symbols of the military organization of a political cause that still captured, in Garvey's day, the popular imagination; thus, for example, in an editorial that same year, the *Negro World* commented that Mussolini's fascists "have the same dare-and-do way of doing things that made Garibaldi and his Red Shirt liberators of Italy so terrible to their enemies" ("Mussolini Says Americans Are Barbarians," *NW*, 8 December 1923; for historical accounts of the Red Shirts, see George W. Martin, *The Red Shirt and the Cross of Savoy: The Story of Italy's Risorgimento, 1748–1871* [New York: Dodd, Mead, 1969], and Andrea Viotti, *Garibaldi: The Revolutionary and His Men* [Poole, England: Blandford Press, 1979]). The Blackshirts were the principal force behind the political success of Italian fascism between 1920 and 1922 (Adrian Lyttelton, *The Seizure of Power: Fascism in Italy, 1919–1929* [New York: Scribner's, 1973]; Denis Mack Smith, *Mussolini* [New York: Alfred A. Knopf, 1982]; for early perceptions of Mussolini and Italian fascism in the United States, see John P. Diggins, *Mussolini and Fascism: The View from America* [Princeton, N.J.: Princeton University Press, 1972]; for the official view, see David F. Schmitz, "'A Fine Young Revolution': The United States and the Fascist Revolution in Italy,

1919–1925," *Radical History Review* 33 [1985]: 117–138, and "United States Foreign Policy Toward Fascist Italy, 1922–1940," [Ph.D. diss., Rutgers University, 1985]).

4. The first paramilitary uniform worn by British Fascists was the blue shirt, but it did not make its appearance until 1927. It was soon superseded when the British Union of Fascists (BUF), founded in 1932 by Sir Oswald Mosley (1896–1980), adopted the blackshirt as its official uniform. The name was also used for the official BUF organ, *The Blackshirt*, published 1933–1939 (Robert Benewick, *The Fascist Movement in Britain*, rev. ed. [London: Allen Lane/ The Penguin Press, 1972], pp. 27, 31, 139–140; R. B. D. Blakeney, "British Fascism," *Nineteenth Century* 97, no. 575 [January 1925]: 132–141; Sir Oswald Mosley, "Why We Wear the Blackshirts," *Sunday Dispatch*, 12 January 1934, and *Blackshirt Policy* [London: British Union of Fascists Publications, 1935]).

5. Racism did not become the official policy of Italian fascism until the adoption in July 1938 of the "Charter of Race" (also known as the *Manifesto of Fascist Racism*) which proclaimed that Italians were of Aryan racial origin and biologically separate from Africans and Jews, who were defined as belonging to "extra-European" races (Philip V. Cannistraro, ed., *Historical Dictionary of Fascist Italy* [Westport, Conn.: Greenwood Press, 1982], p. 28). In the early 1920s anthropologist Lidio Cipriani, a celebrated supporter of Mussolini, argued that racial doctrines were implicit in fascism and stressed the biological inferiority of Africans. The adoption of the Fascist race policy was greatly facilitated, however, by the heightened sense of Italian imperial consciousness that followed the conquest of Ethiopia in 1935–1936. In April 1937 the Italian regime promulgated racial decree-law no. 880 making it an offense, with a penalty of from one to five years imprisonment, for Italian citizens to establish conjugal relations with the subjects of Italy's African colonies (Ethiopia, Eritrea, Somaliland) or with foreigners who shared the same cultural make-up of the peoples of Italian East Africa. The law penalized only Italians and not their African conjugal partners. The turn toward racism also converged with the Fascist regime's adoption of anti-Semitism as its official policy (Arnaldo Cortesi, "The Tide That Swept Italy's Fascists to Power," *Current History* 17, no. 4 [January 1923]: 567–574; Gene Bernardini, "The Origins and Development of Racial Anti-Semitism in Fascist Italy," *Journal of Modern History* 49 [September 1977]: 431–453; Smith, *Mussolini*, pp. 220–220; Luigi Preti, "Fascist Imperialism and Racism," in Roland Santo, ed., *The Ax Within: Italian Fascism in Action* [New York: Franklin Watts, 1974], pp. 188–207). In the case of Britain, it was Mosley's rival, Arnold Leese, leader of the Imperial Fascist League, who adopted the theory of the "Racial Fascist Corporate State," as both the basis and the official name of the league's program (Benewick, *The Fascist Movement in Britain*, p. 46). Benewick denies that Mosley espoused any racial theory.

Worthy of note in connection with the history of racial supremacy in the United States is the earlier phenomenon of Red Shirts in the American South during the period of Reconstruction. "Even after the Klan and the Knights had disbanded," writes William Gillette, "their political purpose and terrorist tactics survived and became even more effective in such new, more highly disciplined organizations as the rifle clubs and Red Shirts of South Carolina, the White Liners of Mississippi, the White Man's Party in Alabama, and the White Leaguers of Louisiana" (*Retreat from Reconstruction, 1869–1879* [Baton Rouge: Louisiana State University Press, 1979], p. 43). In the case of the South Carolina Red Shirts, Gillette states: "Such men constituted a party that resembled an army . . . They had organized almost three hundred rifle clubs, sporting red uniforms that hinted at bloodshed. Making their presence and strength known by means of frequent, large, and well organized public parades, the Red Shirts counted on an overawing display of white strength to frighten the blacks out of their voting majority in the state and to demoralize the ineffective black state militia" (ibid., p. 316).

Chandler Owen to John W.H. Crim, Assistant Attorney General

New York City Feb. 26, 1923

Dear Sir:

We appreciate the prompt attention given to the petition recently sent you in re Marcus Garvey. The signers to that petition represent the most distinguished and responsible businessmen, educators and publicists among the colored people of the United States. Have you seen the editorial endorsing the petition in the Philadelphia Public Ledger (Feb. 5)?[1] For the purposes of your files I will forward same to you. Respectfully yours,

CHANDLER OWEN

DNA, RG 60, file 198940-287. TLS on *Messenger* letterhead, recipient's copy.

1. The editorial, which compared Garveyism "among the Negro populations" with the Ku Klux Klan "among the white people," stated that the "formal protest" to the attorney general would "be read everywhere with approval and sympathy by order-loving and humane people of whatever color" (*Philadelphia Public Ledger*, 5 February 1923).

Reports by Special Employee Andrew M. Battle

New York, N.Y. Feb. 28th, 1923

Continuing the above matter, WM. FERRIS, Editor of the "Negro World[,]" called on the writer [*18 February*] and stated that GARVEY had sent out 300 invitations to white people to attend the meeting of the U.N.I.A. to be held at Carnegie Hall on February 23rd, but did not invite any of the leading colored men or women because they were never in favor of the U.N.I.A.[1]

FERRIS also said that GARVEY was foolish to become mixed up in the killing of DR. EASON, especially at this time, because the colored people of this country did not lean any too strongly toward the U.N.I.A. movement and it was generally believed by them that the U.N.I.A. was mostly composed of West Indian non-citizens and without vote, and the Government was familiar with this condition, which opened a route for the reported acquaintance between GARVEY and men high up in the prosecuting attorney's office and also permitted GARVEY to arrange for the setting aside of his case, and by the spending of a little money they were able to get things pretty well fixed up in GARVEY's favor, but after GARVEY became foolish and had DR. EASON killed, the colored people of America were only too willing to assist the prosecuting attorney in fulfilling his duty against the man (GARVEY) responsible for EASON's death and the different statements made by GARVEY before and after the death of DR. EASON were sufficient to indict him before a grand jury and in the event they should get the third man hired to kill EASON, it would be "goodbye" to GARVEY, as that third party would tell all he knew.

The writer attended a meeting at Liberty Hall at 8:00 P.M., at which there were about 1500 present. MARCUS GARVEY spoke, and during his discourse said that the only thing that would make the white race respect the colored was for the colored race to get together and secure power and by power he meant plenty of arms and ammunition, guns and other implements of war, and when they once had them, they must be used and it would also be necessary to train the military branch of the U.N.I.A. so that when the critical moment came, they would be ready to act. GARVEY said, "By this method you can command as much respect as desired and any member who starts out with the U.N.I.A. and turns back again should be treated as a soldier is treated, who, in the fac[e] of battle, on his own initiative, retreats. As you well know, it is policy for the soldier seeing this condition to immediately shoot the retreating traitor and that will perhaps become necessary in this organization before it can actually become a proven power to its own people, the black race, and believe me, if I am captain when that time comes, I will see that such orders are carried out. I want you all to know that the military branch is being trained daily and they are becoming efficient."[2]

ANDREW M. BATTLE

DJ-FBI, file 61. TD.

1. According to the *Amsterdam News*, approximately twenty whites attended the Carnegie Hall meeting of over twelve hundred to fifteen hundred persons (*Amsterdam News*, 28 February 1923).

2. A Bureau of Investigation report by Special Employee Battle on 13 February disclosed, "[Arnold J.] Ford stated that they [all divisions of the UNIA] were training men regularly and had supplied them with arms and ammunition, and that they were doing it within the law" (28 February 1923, DJ-FBI, file 61).

New York, N.Y. Feb. 28, 1923

The writer interviewed ARNOLD J. FORD, Music Director of the U.N.I.A., 38 W. 131st Street [*24 February*]. The writer asked FORD what he thought about the statement made by GARVEY at Carnegie Hall, to the effect that he was prepared to go to jail and to be killed if necessary. FORD said the statement was a dead give-away for GARVEY, as it only goes to show that GARVEY has done enough to go to jail or be killed, the climax of his activities being the death of [D]R. EASON. FORD said, "I will warn MR. GARVEY not to make such a statement again, as it plainly shows that GARVEY has violated the law of this State and Government, as he knows that the arrest of RAMUS will cause GARVEY's imprisonment and death. They have told at New Orleans that RAMUS did the killing, and RAMUS came right back to GARVEY after he shot EASON, then GARVEY gave him the money to get away, which is all very bad for GARVEY."

The writer interviewed CAPT. [E]. GAIN[E]S, 314 West 137th Street. Among other things he said that MR. GARVEY was very foolish to make the statement he made at Carnegie Hall last night about his being prepared to die or go to jail. GAIN[E]S said, "If GARVEY had not done enough against this state to die or go to jail, why was he prepared to do either[?]" The writer told GAIN[E]s he was very glad he (GAIN[E]s) took notice of the statement.

The writer called at the U.N.I.A. office at which place he met W.H. TOOKS of 1043 Colorado Street, Philadelphia, Pa. The writer learned that TOOKS knew RAMUS at Philadelphia, but as MR. TOOKS had to catch a train back to Philadelphia, the writer did not have time to get what he wanted. The writer would advise that TOOKS be interviewed in Philadelphia. He came here to attend the meeting at Carnegie Hall.

At 8:00 P.M. WILLIAM FERRIS, Editor of the "Negro World[,]" called at 72 W. 131st Street to see me. Among other things he said that RAMUS, the man who shot DR. EASON, in New Orleans, left New Orleans the day after the crime, came to New York, saw MR. GARVEY and GARVEY gave him more money and told him to keep out of the way. RAMUS then went to Philadelphia, saw Counsellor Norris about handling his case and then proceeded to Detroit, Mich. FERRIS also said that when GARVEY went to DETROIT, Mich. without telling anyone where he was, he was trying to get away, but could not. Also that GARVEY gave himself away at Carnegie Hall on February 23rd when he said he was prepared to die or go to jail. FERRIS said, "It was hard for me to believe at first that GARVEY would advocate the death of [D]R. EASON, but now I don't have to believe it,—I know it. You see, MR. BATTLE, GARVEY was so wo[rri]ed that he could not deliver his address at Carnegie Hall on the 23rd. He can't get out of being implicated in the death of DR. EASON, because GARVEY gave RAMUS the money and a letter to go to New Orleans, instructing him to stay there until EASON was killed. RAMUS then came back to New York and then GARVEY gave RAMUS money to get out of the way, and now GARVEY is confessing every time he opens his mouth, one way or the other, that he was implicated in the killing of DR. EASON. You see RAMUS sent the telegram to GARVEY stating that he had killed EASON." The writer then said to FERRIS, "Is it not true that G. AMOS [*Emonei*] CARTER received the telegram[?]" FERRIS said that one or the other got the telegram, but anyway GARVEY received the message. "From what I know there is no way for GARVEY to get out of this charge of helping to kill DR. EASON. RAMUS had sent DR. EASON a letter warning him not to go to New Orleans, because DR. EASON had blocked GARVEY from ever speaking in New Orleans again. EASON told GARVEY on the steps of the [']Negro World['] office that he had blocked him from ever doing business in New Orleans again."

ANDREW M. BATTLE

DJ-FBI, file 61. TD.

[*New York*] March 1st, 1923

The writer had another interview with S[Y]DNEY DE BOURG, and he said that CLIFFORD S. BAUM [*Bourne*], A. [*James B.*] YEARWOOD, FRED A. TOOTE and MRS. V.H. [H.V.] DAVIS of the U.N.I.A. are all waiting for the Government to call them so they can give such evidence as will convict MARCUS GARVEY. The reason they do not come out in the open is that they are afraid if they come out too soon, GARVEY will put them all out of office before he is convicted, in which event they will not be reelected, because after the death of GARVEY they expect to carry on the U.N.I.A.

CLIFFORD S. BAUM has the checks that GARVEY drew for RAMUS when he went to New Orleans for the purpose of killing DR. EASON and BAUM also has the check that GARVEY gave to RAMUS when he went to Detroit (Amount, $60.00). BAUM is ready to turn all information over to the Government, and YEARWOOD, if called on, will tell all about GARVEY trying to go to Mexico, which he did not succeed in doing, as he was watched too closely. DE BOURG said that YEARWOOD was afraid to tell what he knew as most of the Garveyites would not believe it and they might try to put YEARWOOD out of the way.

ANDREW M. BATTLE

DJ-FBI, file 61. TD.

[*New York*] March 1st, 1923

. . . The writer attended a meeting at Liberty Hall [*21 February*], 138th Street & Lenox Ave., at 8:00 P.M., where there was a crowning of seven queens of Ethiopia by CAPT. [E]. GAIN[E]s of the U.N.I.A. and a bust of MARCUS GARVEY was unveiled by WM. SHERRILL. S. BAUM [*Bourne*], the High Chancellor of the U.N.I.A., in his address, said he expected to see GARVEY King of Liberia very soon, and the money raised by charging a fee of 50¢ admission tonight was to be used in the erection of a new hall.

There were 800 present at this meeting.

ANDREW M. BATTLE

DJ-FBI, file 61. TD.

Speech by Marcus Garvey

[[New York, March 4, 1923]]

My subject for tonight is "The Handwriting on the Wall." I hold in my hand a New York newspaper with a press report of something that has happened in another part of the country, just in keeping with the prophecy of the Universal Negro Improvement Association of five years ago; just in keeping with the propaganda of this organization to let Negroes know that their future in America is one of racial insecurity for the fifteen million Negroes and their offspring.

The difference between the Universal Negro Improvement Association and other organizations is, that we are endeavoring to peer through the future; to look down the future and try thereby to regulate ourselves for the good and well being of the race. Others look at things just as they are—only for the present. It is said somewhere, "Where there is no vision the people perish."[1] The Universal Negro Improvement Association is endeavoring through its vision to bring to the people of this country and to this Western World a picture of the future, just what conditions are going to be, and just how we will fare under these conditions. We have been criticized severely and brutally for endeavoring to hold up this vision before the people, but at times certain things happen that call not so much for our impressing upon the people this vision, but through which the people themselves see the thing that we are endeavoring to point them to.

The news I am going to read:

MISSOURI WHITES DRIVE OUT NEGRO LABOR

WORKERS FORCED TO LEAVE COTTON FIELDS BY HOODED BANDS

CARUTHERSVILLE, Mo. March 3—A carefully organized campaign of intimidation has driven more than 2,000 Negro workers from the cotton fields of Southeastern Missouri[2] within the last thirty days, according to complaints made to local officials here today. Negro leaders charged that threats and warnings were sent to the Negroes by white laborers fearful of losing their jobs by the influx of Negroes into the recently reclaimed sections. Ambrose Young, Negro, appealed for protection after he had received several warnings. "Nigger, get to hell out of here. This is a white man's country," was one notice delivered by five hooded men, Young said. "The next night I found another note on my front porch, weighted down with a cartridge box. It said: 'Nigger, if you can't read, run. If you can't run, you're as good as dead.'"

This bit of news is not broadcast; it is copied from one of the papers in New York. It is a significant bit of news. In thirty days 2,000 Negroes were driven out of a certain section of the country. These Negroes were driven out because the white laborers were fearful that those Negroes were going to take their jobs. That is not a State Senator's job; that is not a Congressman's job; that is not a lawyer's job; that is not a doctor's job; that is not a group of people wanting to be clerks in department stores; those are laborers. Now, according to the arrangement of society, the laborer is supposed to be the lowest citizen within the nation. These men were not driven out because they wanted President Harding's job, they were not driven out because they wanted a cabinet position; they were driven out because the white farm laborers in a cotton field section of the country—the lowest type of laborers in the country—feared that the black farm laborers were going to take their jobs. You see what is before us.

We are reaching the point in American life where the white man no longer holds himself up as the master as during the slave days, and was satisfied to be master and let the Negro do the menial work; we have reached the point where the white man is not satisfied to be the capitalist of the nation, to be the industrial head, to be foreman of the gang and foreman of the workshop, but we are reaching the point in American life where the white man is competing with the colored man for the lowest and most menial job in the nation. The position that you and I occupied for 250 years in slavery, and for 58 years in freedom is now coveted by the white man who was once our master. I trust you will see the change of attitude and change of condition.

THE CHANGE OF CONDITION

Once upon a time the Negro would have been welcome to do farm work because no white man wanted that job, but now we are gradually reaching the point where even the most menial job the white man finds that he has to do it, and is going to do it with a vengeance in preference to allowing the Negro to have it. Now if the Negro cannot even get the farm hand's job, what is he going to get later on?

THE VISION OF THE U.N.I.A

That is the vision of the Universal Negro Improvement Association. We have been preaching for the last five years that the time is going to come in the history of men, whether it is going to be 10, 25, 50 or 100 years from now, when America is not going to be large enough to accomodate two competitive races; when we are going to have a surplus white population in this country[,] more than enough to take care of all the jobs from the Presidency down to the farm hand's job. And we are gradually approaching that time. That was the thing that we were called crazy for—for prophesying that the time is coming when the colored man in America will be between hell and the powder house economically; that he will be forced out to starve and die or take his exit somewhere else. When conditions become bad in any section of the world, the people living in that section move to other sections. Some Negroes like Du Bois and Weldon Johnson and the group of the National Association for the Advancement of Colored People say that Negroes have no further place to go than America. Let me tell you that in 24 hours the fifteen million Negroes can be moved as the 2,000 Negroes were moved out of that Missouri town in 30 days.

PARTY AFFILIATIONS WON'T COUNT

What do they say? "This is a white man's country, nigger; move. If you won't move, run; if you can't run, you are as good as dead." Now, listen, that warning did not come from the Republicans or from the Democrats; that warning comes from Social Labor Unionists. Understand that—people who make up the backbone of the country—the workers, the unionists—the so-called Socialists who are more liberal to other people than anybody else; and this is their message to 2,000 farm hands in America. These Socialists[,] whom we are told believe in equality for everybody. Hence when we say that political parties do not count where the Negro is concerned, you will see our point— that whether the Negro is a Socialist or a Republican or Democrat is not going to matter when moving day comes. The moment the Negro threatens the economic existence of the white man, whether he is Socialist, Republican or Democrat, he feels the same way toward you. Now, as far as the Republican and Democrat crowds go, we know their attitude towards us. This is a Socialist class of people—people who belong to the Socialist group, and their attitude toward the Negro is that when he competes with the white man for his job he must move, and if he can't move quickly enough he is as good as dead. It is the language of the Ku Klux Klan; it is the language of Williams Jennings Bryan. Just last week William Jennings Bryan, one of the great statesmen of this country, said he believed in white supremacy. Standing on the pinnacle of American politics and American statesmanship, he said that, and this week the lowest element in American life has demonstrated its attitude towards the Negro race.

MOVING DAY COMING

Now, what are we going to do? That moving day is coming as sure as we are sitting in Liberty Hall tonight. It is only a question of time, and that it has not been heard before is simply because we had a war in 1914 to 1918, simply because the world has taken so long to return to normal. That is why many of us hold jobs around New York—because the world took so long after the war of 1918 to return to normal. Your opportunity and mine is now and is through organization toward that one alternative—a country of our own, living under our own vine and fig-tree. (Applause.)

What has happened in this Missouri town is going to happen all over America as seen through the vision and through the philosophy and through the teaching of the Universal Negro Improvement Association. I see that as clearly as I see you in Liberty Hall now. And that is why I have been wasting my time— that is why I have been giving my strength and my little intelligence to the program of the Universal Negro Improvement Association, because it will be a sad day when the Negro has nowhere to lay his head, and that day is coming—coming as sure as night follows day; coming as surely as you breathe now the breath of life; that day is coming in all countries, not only in America—in all countries where the Negro lives in the majority population of white people.

The world, as I have often said, is not becoming larger, but countries are becoming overcrowded and overpopulated with their own people. It was the overcrowding of certain sections of Europe that brought into existence the American nation. It is the overcrowding of other sections of Europe that is bringing about an African commonwealth for white people if Negroes do not look out now. And what is happening in that Missouri town is what is going to happen in Africa 200 years from now if Negroes do not look out. Two hundred years from now, after the white man gets his foothold in Africa, starting out as he is doing now, we will have the same conditions in certain sections of Africa as we are having in America now. Once upon a time America was the country of the Indian. The white man came all the way from Europe and in 300 years he tells everybody to clear out; this is a white man's country. The white man has set out now for Africa and in another 200 years, if he has built up Africa even as he has built up America, he will have the same message for the remnan[ts] of Negroes left there who come in competition with him for existence in the new country that he has built.

SOLUTION OF THE PROBLEM FOR THIS AGE

Therefore, the solution of the Negro problem is not for another age; the solution of the Negro problem is not for the age past; the solution of the problem is for this age in which we live, and the Universal Negro Improvement Association is endeavoring to solve that problem through universal organization of the 400,000,000 Negroes of the world. Caring not what others say, but with the vision we have followed, with the philosophy that we have expounded, with the doctrine that we have taught to the millions of people throughout the world, we are inspired the more to fight on until victory perches on the banner that we love so well—the banner of the Red, the Black and the Green.

I am not disappointed; I am not disturbed one bit about what those white laborers did in that Missouri town, because I knew long ago that would happen. I am only surprised it is not happening on a larger scale. I know it is because of the abnormality of conditions now, but we are going to hear much more of this later on in twenty-five or fifty years from now when the world will have returned to normal. The Negro's opportunity is now that the world is in confusion. Your opportunity and mine comes when the world is in confusion and the thing we pray for is that the world keeps itself in confusion. Out of the destruction of the systems already laid down will come your and my salvation and will come the salvation of our children. And I pray and every Negro should pray that France will continue to provoke Germany; that England will keep up the provocation of Turkey and Kemal Pasha, because the only hope for the Negro is the destruction of Europe.

We have nothing to hide in that respect for the simple reason that the world, as far as the Negro is concerned, is cold and indifferent. Whether it is Africa, or America or Europe, the world is cold and indifferent to the Negro, whether he is a black Frenchman or a black American or a black Englishman, the world is cold and disinterested in his future. Therefore, the only attitude we can adopt is that of racial self-interest, self-preservation. I do not care what they say about me, there is one thing I stand for and that is the interest of 400,000,000 and I will die for that. (Applause.) I do not care how much they say I hate anybody else, the time has come for Negroes to love themselves. (Applause.) And we live in the age of active statesmanship. All these flowery speeches of our so-called white friends in America, in England and France mean absolutely nothing. There is no speech that any so-called friend of mine can make to convince me otherwise than that the future holds just what this paper reveals to us now for us as a race of people; and I was very much amused this afternoon when I came into the hall; someone who came from South Africa said to me in conversation that the South Africans are putting up new buildings and some of them who had the vision of the future to such an extent made a joke on their friends and said, "You are putting up these buildings for that Garvey crowd to come over and get them." (Laughter.) They seem to have a true consciousness of the future; a true conviction of what is going to happen.

Up to the Present Generation

Let me tell you that the salvation of the Negro rests with the present generation—rests with the Negro who will think enough and see far enough to work now in his own interests and in the interest of the posterity of this race of ours. The Universal Negro Improvement Association, therefore, comes forward with the program of Africa for Africans, those at home and those abroad. We are not going to give up this program one bit, because it is the only solution of the problem, because, as I said a while ago, as sure as night follows day, life in America for the black man will be insecure; life will be miserable for any colored man in this country because this country is not going to be large enough and productive enough to accommodate two rival peoples—two competitive races.

Just imagine with all your intelligence, with all your education, with all the years of living in the country[,] in thirty days another group of your fellow countrymen can move you out of town against your will and nothing is said about it. The Government does not send you back to the same town; the Government that should protect us does not send us back to the same town; it does not even care where we go until the next news is out that they have moved another bundle of Negroes from somewhere else. They will be moving from one section of the country to another later on until they have moved us into the sea-front, but I suppose by that time the Black Star Line will be ready. (Laughter and applause.)

Garvey's Ambition

Let me tell you: Some fellows like Randolph and Owen and that Du Bois bunch think that my greatest ambition is to be where I am. They mistake the man. I wish you had not kept me here so long. They by their jealousy and maliciousness seem to think that Marcus Garvey feels that he has reached the height of his ambition. I knew when I started, I knew when I came here and I know now that the Negro cannot accomplish anything in a white man's civilization, surrounded by the white man's environment, and it is a waste of time for Marcus Garvey to live within the British Empire or the French Empire or within the American commonwealth. So the height of Marcus Garvey's ambition is not to be a successful Britisher or a successful Frenchman or a successful American. The height of Marcus Garvey's ambition is to settle down in Africa, among millions of other Negroes (applause) and in conjunction with them build up a civilization as our contribution to the world, as our contribution to the human race. Marcus Garvey feels that two years hence the Universal Negro Improvement Association's program will be so developed that we won't have to be wasting time around here with such insignificant Negroes as Du Bois and that bunch. The white folks will take care of them. Marcus Garvey knows that neither the Universal Negro Improvement Association nor any other Negro association can get anywhere in the white man's civilization. So long as the white man sits there as President, so long as he sits there as Governor, so long as he sits there as Mayor, so long as he sits there as Police Commissioner, so long as he sits there as Judge of the Municipal Court and the Supreme Court, so long will Negroes never accomplish anything in a white people's country. Therefore, Marcus Garvey realizes for the Negro to accomplish anything he must have a government of his own, that he must have his own President, his own Governor, his own Mayor, his own Police Commissioner, his own Municipal and Supreme Court Judges, and even his own jail to put unruly Negroes in. (Laughter.) So long as you build up a white man's country so long will he, directly or indirectly, destroy your progress. So long as he is to correct the evils within your race for the possibility of your success so long will they remain uncorrected. If you are waiting on the white man to give you protection for the possibility of your development, you and I will wait until eternity.

Therefore, the Universal Negro Improvement Association and Marcus Garvey and those of us who lead feel that the only solution of the Negro problem is to create a government of our own, where Negroes will rule Negroes; where Negroes will be compelled to be honest and true to Negroes because of the correction that will be enforced upon them by the laws made by Negroes for their own racial development. (Applause.) When you can make laws to punish unruly and treacherous Negroes as the Russians did when they were making the Russian Empire and as the British did when they were making the British Empire and as the fathers of this country did when they were making the American nation, then and only then will this race of ours go forward and enjoy the things that we have mapped out for the program of the Universal Negro Improvement Association. Fooling around with Negroes under white people's civilization will never get you or anybody anywhere. But the time is coming when through the efforts of the Universal Negro Improvement

Association we will establish a system of government by which we will be able to correct our own evils and give an inspiration to those who desire to follow in the right way for the development of this race of ours.

Printed in *NW*, 10 March 1923. Original headlines omitted.

1. A reference to Prov. 29:18.

2. In 1923 white workers in southeastern Missouri led an organized campaign to drive out black workers who were displacing them in the cotton fields. The two-month campaign, which reportedly drove out twenty-five hundred blacks, had its origins in the changing agricultural economy of the area as well as in the racism of whites. In the early 1920s cotton growers from the South moved into the reclaimed delta lands along the Mississippi River. Within a few years the agricultural base shifted from corn and grain to cotton farmed on large land holdings by sharecroppers. While local whites initially provided labor, black sharecroppers from depressed areas of the south began to migrate to the area, and landowners began to import black sharecroppers. According to the local press, blacks would work for less and were brought in to "take the place of white labor" (*Missouri Herald*, [Hayti, Mo.], 16 March 1923). There is some suggestion that white workers were demanding more pay and that growers imported blacks in response. The migration of hundreds of blacks to an area that had been predominantly white brought racial hostility to the surface. Some white workers formed local committees to drive out black sharecroppers: imitating the Ku Klux Klan, they posted notices warning blacks to leave town; night riders wearing white hoods shot at black homes; blacks were attacked and flogged, and hundreds fled into neighboring Arkansas and Tennessee. The local Klan, of which many landowners were members, denounced the white vigilantes as a "lawless element" of "ignorant, indolent, irresponsible white men" (*St. Louis Star*, 4 March 1923). The Klan hired detectives to locate leaders and wrote them letters stating that unless they stopped the attacks within twenty-four hours, they would be driven out of the state. Southeast Missouri, the Klan letter read, "needs Negro labor. It does not need men of your stamp" (ibid.). The attacks subsequently stopped.

Social tension continued in southeastern Missouri, however. During the Depression, the cotton areas of southeastern Missouri and the adjoining area of northeastern Arkansas became the organizing base for the Southern Tenant Farmers Union (STFU). In January 1939, after planters evicted thousands of sharecroppers, seventeen hundred black and white sharecropper families under the leadership of the STFU staged a nationally publicized sit-down strike on the highways of southeastern Missouri (*St. Louis Star*, 4 March 1923; *Caruthersville Democrat-Argus*, 16 March 1923; *Missouri Herald* [Hayti, Mo.], 16 March 1923; *Daily Globe-Democrat*, 3 March 1923; Thad Snow, *From Missouri* [Boston: Houghton Mifflin, 1954], pp. 154–165; H. L. Mitchell, *Mean Things Happening in This Land* [Montclair, N. J.: Allanheld, Osmun and Co., 1979], pp. 171–182; Milton D. Rafferty, *Missouri* [Boulder, Colo.: Westview Press, 1983], pp. 235–241).

Report by Special Employee Andrew M. Battle

New York, N.Y. March 15/23

Continuing the above matter, the writer attended a trial of ELI[E] GARCIA at the Washington Heights Court, N.Y. City. Among other things, GARVEY tried to prove that GARCIA had forged five checks against the U.N.I.A. amounting to $175.00, but having failed to establish the charge, the case against GARCIA was dismissed. However, GARCIA will be tried on Wednesday, March 14th, 1923, in Special Sessions Court, Part One, on a charge of forgery brought by GARVEY.

The writer interviewed H. VINTON PLUMMER, Bureau of Publicity of the U.N.I.A.[,] and PLUMMER advised that he was leaving the U.N.I.A.

today as he and AMY [*Enid*] LAMOS (GARVEY's secretary) could not get along. PLUMMER said he knew all about the crooked transactions of GARVEY regarding the U.N.I.A. and the BLACK STAR LINE, and could do GARVEY grave harm if he so desired.

On March 13th the writer attended the 7th District Court[,] 320 West 125th Street, GARCIA having entered suit against the U.N.I.A. for an $800. membership loan to the U.N.I.A. and a $500. note. The membership loan was to run for one year with interest, with the privilege of the lender of the money to demand the amount loaned to the U.N.I.A. fifteen days after the expiration of the year. GARCIA testified that this membership loan to the U.N.I.A. really covered GARCIA's salary, as the U.N.I.A. was not able to pay the salaried men, therefore GARVEY called this past due salary a membership loan to the U.N.I.A.

GARCIA also stated that the minutes of the nights from January 15th to 19th, 1922[,] of the U.N.I.A. had been destroyed; that YEARWOOD, 2nd Asst. Secretary took these minutes, which would show that each lender of money was to lend same to the U.N.I.A. for as long a period as they could spare it, and GARCIA loaned his $800. for one year. GARCIA further said that VIRGIL [*Vernal*] WILLIAMS, counsellor of the U.N.I.A.[,] caused him (GARCIA) to read the minutes of the meeting recorded on January 19th, 1922, looking for a way to evade paying DR. EASON the $500. the U.N.I.A. had received from DR. EASON, but those minutes were out of the minute book today, so it could not be proved that the money in question was due.

MARCUS GARVEY said that ELI[E] GARCIA had loaned the $800. for five years; that he (GARVEY) signed the books in blank form and when any lender of money came to the office to lend money, GARCIA would fill in the time when the money was loaned to the U.N.I.A. and that every officer loaned money to the U.N.I.A. as a membership loan for five years. However, the court then found that some of the officers had membership loans which did not state how long the money was to be loaned to the U.N.I.A., which proved that GARVEY was lying. The court then asked GARVEY if that was the reckless way he did business—signing notes and bonds by the hundreds before they were filled out. GARVEY answered that his office was a very busy one and he signed the notes and loans that way to save time. The Judge then asked GARVEY if he thought he was saving time by signing papers that way, as, after all, he would have to sign them, and it would not take any more time to sign a paper after it was made out. GARVEY did not reply to this. The Judge then asked VIRGIL WILLIAMS, if GARCIA got judgment, if there was any chance to collect. WILLIAMS said, "That is a question."

GARVEY had FRED A. TOOT[E] swear that GARCIA's loan was for five years and that there were no minutes taken by the U.N.I.A. from the 15th of January to the 19th. POLSUM [*Poston*] also swore to the above[.] MRS. H.V. DAVIS said she was out of town at the time of the above mentioned meetings, and [E].L. GAIN[E]S said he also was out of town at that time. GARVEY denied that he was provisional president of Africa or that he had veto power in the

U.N.I.A. However, he said that he directed the length of time for the officers to loan money to the U.N.I.A.

YEARWOOD said that he did record the minutes for January 15th to the 19th, 1922, in which it was stated that everyone who loaned money to the U.N.I.A. could collect it at any time after the expiration of the fifteen days, and that some of the loans were from one to five years.

WILLIAM FERRIS told the writer that GARVEY came to him this morning and told FERRIS not to tell how [long] his membership loan was to run, also that FERRIS should not appear in court this afternoon. FERRIS said that YEARWOOD would lose his job after telling the court that he did make the minutes of January 15th, which proved GARVEY a liar. The Judge reserved decision for ten days.

GARCIA told the writer if he gets judgment against the U.N.I.A. he will not go to the U.N.I.A. office to collect, but he knows where they have the money[,] which is the reason GARVEY is afraid of him.

GARVEY has another case against GARCIA in the Criminal Court, Special Sessions, Part One[,] on Wednesday, March 14th. The writer will attend the trial.

ANDREW M. BATTLE

DJ-FBI, file 61. TD.

Report by Special Agent James E. Amos

New York, N.Y. Mar. 15, 1923

Continuing the above matter, Agent interviewed [*14 March*] CHARLES E. WALCOTT,[1] former manager of groceries and restaurants for MARCUS GARVEY. WALCOTT resides at 32 West 136th Street, business address 552 Lenox Avenue. He was manager from August 1st, 1922[,] to November 15th, 1922, and informed Agent that the groceries and restaurants were never paying propositions and it was a matter of impossibility to collect salaries for the employees from GARVEY; that the only way he could collect his own salary was to buy one of the grocery stores and deduct his back salary, which amounted to $1500., from the purchase price of the store. WALCOTT further stated that he was willing to help the Government in any way possible and would give a statement to the United States Attorney at any time same was requested.

Agent attended the trial of ELI[E] GARCIA at Special Session Court today, GARCIA having been charged with stealing $47.00 from the U.N.I.A. and putting a forged check in its place. He was convicted and is to be sentenced on March 29th, 1923. GARCIA's attorney[,] however, was permitted to make an appeal for a new trial. GARCIA was convicted on circumstantial evidence, although Agent believes him guilty, but it has been customary in the past for employees of the U.N.I.A. for salaries, to draw a check for any amount up to $100., turn it over to the Treasurer and receive the money, and these checks held against the employee until he paid it back. (The check GARCIA is charged with forging was drawn in this manner.)

Agent also interviewed J.B. YEARWOOD, who was 1st Asst. Secretary General of the U.N.I.A. and who was discharged on March 13th, 1923, by GARVEY because YEARWOOD refused to go to court and perjure himself on the witness stand in regard to GARCIA. YEARWOOD has promised Agent that he will give another statement any time Agent calls on him for same.

JAMES E. AMOS

DJ-FBI, file 61. TD.

1. Charles Walcott later testified on Garcia's behalf at his trial for petty larceny (*NW*, 24 March 1923).

William J. Burns to Edward J. Brennan, Special Agent in Charge, New York Office, Bureau of Investigation

[*Washington, D.C.*] March 16, 1923

Dear Sir:

I have followed with considerable interest the reports recently submitted on the MARCUS GARVEY case and especially covering the meetings recently held at Liberty Hall in which there has been open advocation of the use of arms and ammunition by the Negro in enforcing his rights, which it is alleged are generally denied him by the white man. From an examination of these reports it certainly seems that the New York Police Department should be interested in the matter and I am calling it to your attention so that if you agree on the subject, it might be taken up with the local authorities in order to develop some very interesting points. Very truly yours,

W. J. B[URNS].
Director

DJ-FBI, file 61. TLI, carbon copy.

Speech by Marcus Garvey

[[LIBERTY HALL, NEW YORK, March 18, 1923]]

My subject for tonight is "The Confession of a Great White Man and Leader." Some Sunday nights ago you heard me speak of the speech made by William Jennings Bryan in Washington at a dinner where he was entertained by a large group of his own people. We commented on Mr. Bryan's speech in Liberty Hall, as well as through my front page article in the Negro World. Other Negro newspapers commented on the speech of Mr. Bryan, and these various comments led the daily "Times" of New York (I speak of the white "Times") to request of Mr. Bryan to write an article expressing his further opinion on the matter and explain himself for what he said at the dinner in Washington. Mr. Bryan repeated everything he said this morning in his article in the daily "New York Times" and adds even more.[1] In concluding the article he said this: "My views upon the race question do not depend upon my present residence in the South;[2] they were formed long before I ever thought of living in the South; they were expressed as the occasion required, and so far as I know do not differ from the views of other white men who have had occasion to express themselves on the fundamental principles involved when these principles would apply to themselves and to their own families."

In this article of today we have Mr. Bryan repeating himself what he said in his talk in Washington a few weeks ago and adding more as expressing his attitude on the race question. He held to his idea of white supremacy and his belief that government should only be in the hands of the white man because white men are best able to interpret the needs of humanity. He concludes this article by saying that his views, he feels sure, are the views and opinion of other white people when called upon to give an opinion upon the subject. The statement of Mr. Bryan confirms the opinion and attitude of the Universal Negro Improvement Assn. of five years and confirms my stand in the matter of the Ku Klux Klan and the misrepresentation that other Negroes tried to make of my interview with that organization and the statement I made after that interview—that all white men in America feel like the Ku Klux Klan, but the only difference is that the Klan is honest enough to give expression to its opinion and carry out its attitude in defiance of any other opposition whilst others are not honest enough to give expression but feel the same way. Mr. Bryan comes out and says as a leader and statesman that his feeling and his opinion on the race question is that there should be white supremacy and that government should be in the hands of the white race because the white race can best interpret the needs of humanity; that such is the feeling of other white men when called upon to give an opinion on the same subject. This should convince us now that the majority of white people in this country feel as the Ku Klux Klan feels and Mr. Bryan feels, and that is that the power of government should rest not with the Negro race in this country, but should rest with the white men. For that they intend to fight and for that they intend to die.

Now admitting that is so, and as we know it is so, what is the alternative for the Negro? The alternative is to follow in the cause of the Universal Negro Improvement Assn., that of the Negro building for himself. Hence the Universal Negro Improvement Assn. wastes no time in trying to explain itself. We do not need men like Mr. Bryan or Tillman and Vardaman to tell us that; we understand that well; we know that so long as this difference in numbers between the two opposite races that live in this country exists, the white man is going to carry out a program of white supremacy, and there will be absolutely no chance or opportunity between now and eternity for the colored man in America to take an equal place socially, politically and economically with the race that dominates. The one alternative is for the Negro not to waste his time and energy and ability in contributing to that which will make the other man great, but to use his energy and ability in contributing to build for himself. And that is where the Universal Negro Improvement Assn. differs from all the other movements in this country, in that we feel that whatsoever they do, whatsoever they say in trying to bring about a condition where colored men will co-operate side by side with the white man, at the best they are contributing to the white man's civilization, the white man's power, and are therefore wasting their energy and their ability that they should use in building for themselves.

PROGRAM OF THE U.N.I.A. CLEAN CUT

The Program of the Universal Negro Improvement Assn. is clean cut as far as our destiny in America and in other parts of the world goes, and when it comes to the carrying out of the program of the Universal Negro Improvement Assn. we need not fear the result or the consequences. This recent propaganda against us ha[s] done a great deal of good, for the simple reason that without invitation, without our request, we have brought to our support more and more a large number of men not of our race in this country who have held the view and opinion of the Universal Negro Improvemnt Assn. probably even before the Universal Negro Improvement Assn. came into being, and it brings to those of us who are leaders of the movement the fact that when the time comes for the Universal Negro Improvement Assn. to draw the line we will draw it with a great deal of support behind us in helping us to put the program over.

I am not going to blame Mr. Bryan for saying this, for the simple reason he is only speaking the truth as he sees it, and is only speaking the truth as the Universal Negro Improvement Association knows it. I have a better regard and appreciation of Mr. Bryan than the men who would try to deceive us into believing that all will be well in the future when they know that the future holds nothing but darkness t[o]ward this race of ours. By our being able to understand American political psychology, by our being able to understand the intentions of the political leaders of this country, we will be placed in a better position to prepare for ourselves and to act for ourselves. We have lived under this camouflage for over fifty years, so much so that there are many of the other organizations of the race coming forth and telling us they are working towards the time when justice and equality will be meted out to the Negro in this country. Such a time will never come as far as the Negro is concerned if the Negro relies upon the mere question of humanity to solve this great problem of race. Humanity has never settled any great political program between races and nations. The appeal to humanity is a thing that has fallen flat even from the time of Jesus to the present hour. The appeal to humanity will not solve the great human problem. The only appeal that will solve the great human problem is the appeal to power, to force. The Universal Negro Improvement Association, therefore, will not waste its time advancing a purely humanitarian cause, believing that one day the dominant race will become so converted in its attitude toward the oppressed that it will hand to the oppressed and weaker peoples of the world that which we call justice and real liberty and freedom and democracy. It has never been in the ages past and will never be in the ages to come. There has been but one resort for those who are oppressed and that was the resort to power, to force, and that is where the Universal Negro Improvement Association is striking 400,000,000 Negroes of the world, endeavoring to accumulate that physical power, that mental power, that political power out of which we will be able to convince the world of our ability to protect ourselves not only in one spot but throughout the world.

Therefore I trust that you have tonight, if not before, a true conception of the program of the Universal Negro Improvement Association as far as it affects us in our American life and in our American attitude. We believe in the eternal existence of man; we believe that in the end of time only the fittest of this great human race will survive. We believe also that at the present time humanity everywhere is preparing itself for a condition through which it will live into eternity; but in this regulation of human affairs we find all peoples heretofore oppressed clamoring for a chance, clamoring for an opportunity to make their impress upon the world, to make their contribution to the world, so as to convince others of their fitness to live, of their fitness to survive, and we can do nothing less than to make some contribution to the civilization of this age. The race or the nation that is to be recognized must be the race or nation which is capable of doing for itself. Dependent races and dependent nations will be ignored, will be pushed aside, will be weeded out, will be exterminated. It is only a question of time, and here we have it. As far as America is concerned, the great statesmen of the nation say that in the regulation of things the white man is the fittest individual to control government and to dominate government, because he is better able to interpret human needs. During the time that he has been interpreting human needs and the time that he has been regulating human society, what has he done? In that time he has brought us from freedom in our own native country to slavery, and kept us there for 250 years. That is his interpretation of the regulation of human society. Who can tell but that may be his interpretation in the next fifty years or the next hundred years? Can you, therefore, trust yourselves to his interpretation? (Cries of "No! No!") Can you, therefore, place your destiny in his hand?

(Cries of "No! No!") Therefore, the only alternative for the Universal Negro Improvement Association and all sober minded Negroes is for them to draw the line and strike out for themselves, because no one can better interpret your needs than you can yourselves.

I trust, therefore, those of you who doubted that America's attitude toward the Negro is that of white supremacy—that of Government in the hand[s] of the majority group will now be convinced by the utterances of Mr. William Jennings Bryan; and it pains me sometimes when I hear these little insignificant Negroes talking about what the white man can not do and saying that what Mr. Bryan has said is all bosh. They say what Mr. Bryan is saying is bosh and can not be done, and all the time it is being done. It is all right for you to write in your papers saying it can not be done, but what are you doing if they are doing it and not asking leave or license to do it? You must decide at the present time between propaganda and idle sentiment and facts. It is a fact that you have an organized strength in the country made manifest in the Ku Klux Klan and you have in conjunction with that the utterances of Mr. Bryan. Mr. Bryan when he speaks carries more weight in what he says than all the Negroes of the United States of America speaking at one time. Whatsoever Mr. Bryan says, whether he says it in Washington or Florida, carrie[s] more weight with the people of this country and the Government of the country than all our newspapers, magazines and books put together. Therefore, when a man like this talks we can not afford to say it is idle bosh. And what has happened? I told you in regard to this Ku Klux business that these newspapers and those local politicians who talk about putting the Ku Klux Klan out of business were only playing with you and were only adopting a clever method of advertising the Klan. This morning's papers brought out that the Klan is now stronger in the Northern States than they are in the South States; that there are more Klansmen in the State of New York than there are in Texas, that there are more Klansmen in Jersey than there are in Alabama, that there are more Klansmen in Illinois than there are in Mississippi.[3] And what has happened? Last Sunday fifty Klansmen put on their robes and the leader of them occupied the pulpit of a large church in Newark,[4] and all the other Klansmen had the front seats; and in New York they were so bold and were given the right of way that one of their members died and they paraded and attended the funeral all of them in their regalia, and the New York World tries to deceive and fool us that they are going to crush the Klan.[5] What has happened? The great noise that Governor Parker in Louisiana was making that he was going to lead all the governors of the States into a great organization to crush the Klan in every State and he was going to start crushing the Klan in the State of Louisiana and when they got hold of ten of the Klansmen an[d] accused them of killing two men in one of the towns of that State and they were making a great noise how they were going to convict them, the District Attorney of that State closed the case and said there was nothing against the Klan and has given the Klan a clean slate in the State of Louisiana.[6] It is nothing else but a skillful game of these men to advertise the Klan by showing the merit of the organization to those who never thought of it before.

So when these ignorant Negro papers talk about doing this and doing that, you will understand that when any group of white men get together in this country and talk about doing something, you had better get busy and look out for yourselves and don't think that appeal to humanity or any appeal to their Christian conduct is going to help you: it is not going to do it.

William Jennings Bryan is as big a Klansman as the Imperial Wizard himself, and not only Mr. Bryan but men bigger than William Jennings Bryan are deep down in the Ku Klux Klan and they are going to put over that program of white supremacy as sure as there is a God; and the only thing you can do is to get busy and get a country of your own and build up there so strong that not even hell and the Klan will be able to move you in the future. (Applause.)

So that my message to you tonight in Liberty Hall is to pay more and serious attention to what is going on, because within another fifty, another hundred years, especially when the world returns to its normal attitude and all these different nations are able to give more attention to their own domestic affairs, you and I will be confronted with a condition in this country, economically, that will end in nothing else but disaster for those of us who will live here at that time. I want you to understand that when the time comes for the white man to carry out his program of white supremacy for the purpose of eliminating the Negro as a political, social and industrial competitor he will not have to shoot you down, he will not have to lynch you and burn you to get rid of you. The Negro problem in America is such that economically he will grind us and push us to the wall, and in the space of two or three years he will solve the Negro problem without the Negro even realizing that the problem is already solved. The white man has laid the plan of economically forcing the Negro to the wall in another few years.

I am going back now to the bread-and-butter question. Do you know that every Negro in Liberty Hall tonight can die out by the end of this month without anybody poisoning you, without anybody putting a rope around your neck, without anybody shooting you or without anybody doing any bodily harm to you? Do you know? By starving. There is not a man in this building tonight who, if denied food for thirty days, would be able to resist death by starvation. What do I mean by that? I mean this: that we are so careless of ourselves, so careless of our future, that tonight 15,000,000 of us in America are dependent upon the white man for our daily existence, our daily sustenance and our daily bread. If the white man should say in another twenty-four hours that "I will not employ any more Negroes in my industry, on my farms or in my business,["] what would happen? Fifteen million Negroes would be jobless in the United States of America. And if you were kept jobless for a day or a week and rendered unable to go to the grocer to buy your provisions or to pay your rent to your landlord on the 1st or the 15th of the month and you were kept jobless for two weeks, everyone of us would have to leave our homes in Harlem and go out into the streets, unable to go to the grocer, and every one of us would be dying on the streets of New York, and I feel sure the white man would not have any objection to supplying the coffins to bury us by the hundreds, because it will be in keeping with his plan to get rid of us. Such a condition of unemployment would rid this country of 15,000,000 people just as the North American Indian was exterminated. And that was the white man's plan to get rid of the Negro problem in America up to 1913. But God Almighty sent the war and created a breach. We are still in that breach and if the 15,000,000 Negroes of America remain without action for another five or ten years and allow this country to return to normal to carry out their pre-war program, it is only a question of fifty or 100 years more when you and I will be weeded out from this Western civilization.

So the Universal Negro Improvement Association is pointing the way to destiny. There is only one relief, which is: While the world is readjusting itself now, while the world is reorganizing itself, while political boundaries are being adjusted, to pitch in and establish some political stronghold of your own. And there is no more logical place than Africa. (Applause.) The selfishness of the present-day Negro leader causes him to see only that in his lifetime he can get all that he wants and accumulate all he wants. Fellows like Du Bois will not think of the future, because they can get all they want. They have so much love for the Negro that if it comes to moving they can move to Brazil or Cuba; and as they do not like the Negro race already, it will be splendid for them to identify themselves with another race; they can be South Americans and Cubans. But you, the common people, who have nowhere to go, who have to struggle for your daily existence, you are the ones to be considered at that time, and you should see this danger that confronts us.

I trust you understand what the Universal Negro Improvement Association is driving at when we say that the time is now that we are to endeavor to create a nation of our own, and I thank God we are gradually creeping toward the realization of that dream. The strength of this movement is being admitted by the South Africans themselves[7] and the white men who have gone to Africa; they admit that the Universal Negro Improvement Association is pressing them to the wall. The best thing you can do is to get behind the Universal Negro Improvement Association, and as they are pressing us to the wall in this Western world, let us unitedly press them to the wall in Africa. If you give to this organization for another five years the moral and financial support that we need I feel sure that we will have a new tale to give to the world and the world will have a new history to write out of the achievement of the twentieth century negro. (Applause.)

Printed in *NW*, 24 March 1923. Original headlines omitted.

1. The article, which appeared on 18 March 1923, was an amplification of Bryan's earlier address to the Southern Society of Washington on 20 February 1923 (*NYT*, 18 March 1923).

2. In 1916 Bryan and his wife, Mamie, moved to Miami. By 1923 he maintained residences in both Miami and Lincoln, Nebr. (Charles Morrow Wilson, *The Commoner: William Jennings Bryan* [New York: Doubleday, 1970], pp. 357–358; *WWWA*, 1922–1923).

3. No official records have been found of Klan membership and probably none ever existed. Estimates of Klan membership fluctuated widely; in 1923 membership figures ranged from 1.5

million to 4.5 million (*NYT*, 14 February 1923; Kenneth T. Jackson, *The Ku Klux Klan in the City, 1915–1930* [New York: Oxford University Press, 1967], p. 235). The Klan itself rarely boasted of over 2 million members. In the early 1920s the Klan's strength had increased markedly, especially in the Midwest and the East. By 1925 New York was estimated to have 300,420 members and Texas 450,000; New Jersey boasted 720,000 members and Alabama 115,910; Illinois was said to have had 300,324 and Mississippi 93,040 (*NYT*, 14 February 1923; Jackson, *The Ku Klux Klan in the City*, pp. 10–12, 235–238, 289).

4. On Sunday, 11 March 1922, forty hooded Klansmen marched into the Grace Methodist Episcopal Church in Newark, N.J. The pastor of the church, who had arranged the event, then introduced the Klan leader as "the Exalted Cyclops" and permitted him to deliver a speech on the need for white Protestant supremacy. The pastor followed the address with a sermon on "Americanism" (*NYT*, 13 March 1923).

5. Probably a reference to the series of articles that appeared in the *New York World* attacking the Klan. In 1921 the *World* had run a three-week exposé of the Klan which was picked up by other national newspapers and helped lead to the federal investigation of the organization. The *World* continued to publish articles on the Klan throughout the 1920s (Jackson, *The Ku Klux Klan in the City*, pp. 11–13; David M. Chalmers, *Hooded Americanism: The History of the Ku Klux Klan* [New York: Franklin Watts, 1981], pp. 42, 227, 294).

6. In September 1922 Gov. John M. Parker of Louisiana condemned the Klan for the kidnapping of five men in the small town of Mer Rouge and stated his intention to fight the Klan "to the finish" (*New York Age*, 16 September 1922). In November Parker informed federal authorities that the administration of state law had come to a virtual halt in Louisiana and that U.S. government administration of law in certain portions of the state might be necessary. The governor also instructed the attorney general to use "the full power of the State, civil and military" in an investigation of the torture and murder of two of the five kidnapped men (*New York Age*, 25 November 1922). At the annual governors' conference in December, Parker again denounced the Klan and called for federal legislation requiring the registration of secret organizations with the Department of Justice. He also requested that the governors put themselves on record against the Klan's usurpation of the judicial process (*NYT*, 15 December 1922). No federal intervention was forthcoming, however, and in March 1923 a special grand jury, many of whose members were known Klansmen, failed to return a single indictment against forty-six suspects (*NYT*, 16 March 1923). Despite this failure, Governor Parker's crusade against the Klan proved successful, and by 1924 the Louisiana Klan was in rapid decline (Jackson, *The Ku Klux Klan in the City*, p. 87).

7. A South African newspaper, *Cape Argus*, carried an article on 29 January 1923 which reported that the Garvey propaganda "among the natives of South Africa . . . is having an unsettling effect, and is beginning to cause anxiety among the white people, who have worked for the good of the natives, and among the educated natives, who foresee danger in the present situation" (*Cape Argus* [Cape Town], 29 January 1923).

Article in the *Negro World*

[24 March 1923]

ELI[E] GARCIA, AUDITOR-GENERAL
U.N.I.A., CONVICTED FOR LARCENY OF
FUNDS OF THE ORGANIZATION

Eli[e] Garcia, dismissed auditor-general of the Universal Negro Improvement Association[,][1] was March [1]4 found guilty of forging a cheque[,] the property of the parent body of the U.N.I.A., before Justices John J. Fresch[i],[2] H.W. Herbert,[3] [and] J. O'Keefe in Special Session and remanded for sentence to the 23d inst.

The prisoner entered a plea of not guilty when arraigned and was represented by counsel. The prosecution was directed by a member of the district attorney's staff, who after outlining his case called on the Hon. Marcus Garvey, president-general of the association to depone.

Mr. Garvey's evidence was to the effect that on January 8, Garcia, who had surreptitiously removed a blank cheque from an old cheque book that was kept in the treasurer's drawer, filled it up for the amount of $40 and signed a ficti[ti]ous name—James Moore—to it. The cheque was on the Crown Savings Bank of Newport, Virginia,[+] a banking institution with which the organization kept an account a long time ago and which was closed as far back as 1920.

Garcia[,] after filling up the cheque for $40 and putting the name of James Moore to it, went into the office of the chancellor, Hon. Clifford Bourne, where he found that officer engaged in making up the money for the day[']s lodgment to be sent to the bank to the credit of the organization. Garcia engaged Mr. Bourne in conversation and[,] it is said, extracted $40 in cash from the money and slipped the bogus cheque in to make the total right.

The little game would have worked all right, but it happened that Mr. Marcus Garvey dropped into the chancellor[']s office just before the clerk left for the bank and he looked to see the amount being lodged and how it was made up.

The fictitious cheque caught his eye. He knew that the association had no account any longer with the Crown Savings Bank of Newport, and he wanted to know who James Moore was. It soon transpired how the cheque crept into the lodgment, who extracted the $40 in cash for the "scrap of paper" and Mr. Garcia, the auditor-general[,] found himself enmeshed in the toils of the law.

Mr. Garvey told how Garcia clandestinely slipped the bogus che[que] into an amount of currency of $40 that was lying on the Chancellor's desk and helped himself to the amount the che[que] represented in bills.

Other witnesses for the prosecution were the Hons. Clifford Bourne, on whom the game was played, and R. L. Poston, Secretary-General.

The prisoner called two witnesses, one Anderson, a beef vendor, and Charlie Walcott, to testify as to his previous good character. His lawyer also endeavored to establish a defense, but the forged cheque was in evidence, bearing silent testimony. Then the learned Justices in their desire to give him the benefit of the doubt (if there was any) had called on him to write what was written on the forged cheque. Both were identical, and after short consultation the Court adjudged him guilty.

Mr. Garcia's arrest and appearance in court was the source of a great deal of surprise and speculation as to the amount of defalcations against the association, in which he held such a prominent position, and also in which he had the confidence of his co-workers as well as the head of the organization.

Mr. Garcia has handled thousands of dollars of the association's moneys, and it is understood that an examination of his books is being made to find out the extent of misappropriations for which there is ground for belief. This will be done without prejudice to Mr. Garcia in order that the association may be safeguarded in the interests he so long had charge of.

Printed in *NW*, 24 March 1923. Original headlines abbreviated.

1. In an interview with Special Employee Andrew M. Battle, Garcia claimed he had had the city marshal attach all the office furniture of the UNIA, including that at Liberty Hall, as well as the sawmill purchased from the UNIA's Liberian venture (report by Special Employee Andrew M. Battle, 2 April 1923, DJ-FBI).

2. John J. Freschi (1877–1944), a prominent New York jurist, was also a leader of Italian-American causes. A graduate of New York Law School in 1895, Freschi began his judicial career in 1910 when he was appointed a magistrate. From 1915 until 1925 he served as justice in the Court of Special Sessions in New York. In May 1931 he was appointed to the New York State Court of General Sessions by Gov. Franklin D. Roosevelt (*NYT*, 30 July 1944).

3. Henry W. Herbert (1871–1937) served on the bench of the Court of Special Sessions for twenty-six years. Educated at Queens College, Dublin, Herbert was active in various Catholic and Democratic organizations (*NYT*, 25 December 1937).

4. The Crown Savings Bank of Newport News, Va., was a black-owned bank founded in 1905 by John H. Ridley, E. C. Brown, and others. It survived until 1965 (*Virginia Pilot*, 2 August and 7 August 1965).

Reports by Special Agent Mortimer J. Davis

New York, N. Y. 3/27/23

Some time ago while Expert Bank Accountant Merril[e]es and the writer were going over the facts in this case, it appeared that a violation of the Internal Revenue Laws had been committed by both the Black Star Line and Marcus Garvey personally, the former by submitting a fraudulent return for the year 1921 and the latter by falsifying his income for the same period.

Agents at that time took the matter up unofficially with representatives of Hugh McQuillan, Special Agent in Charge, Intelligence Unit, Federal Building, New York, who advised that ever since the arrest and indictment of Garvey, et al, they had been considering taking up the matter of the income tax returns of both the corporation and the individual officers but had been deferring same until the accountants of this department could release the books. Upon being advised that our accountants were practically through with their examination, Agents Seib and Schwartz of the Intelligence Unit took the matter up.

On the 26th instant Agent was called to the office of Assistant U.S. Attorney Mattuck and was there informed that a complaint had been filed against Marcus Garvey by the Internal Revenue Department on the basis of his 1921 return and that it was Mr. Mattuck's intention to arrest Garvey on the 27th.

On Tuesday, March 27th, Agent in company with Agent J.E. Amos appeared at Mr. Mattuck's office at 2:00 P.M.[,] at which time Garvey, accompanied by C.W. McDougall[1] and Vernal J. Williams, his attorneys[,] voluntarily surrendered himself.

Garvey's return for 1921 shows a total (both gross and net) income of $4,000, from which he deducted $1,400, claiming the support of a wife and disabled sister. Checks which are in our possession for the year 1921 issued to Garvey by the U.N.I.A., and plainly marked "Salary" on each show that he received something above $7,900 during that period. This does not include monies which he received from the Black Star Line during that period for expenses or monies paid him by the U.N.I.A. for similar reasons, none of which he reports in his 1921 return. Questioned regarding his return today in presence of his lawyers, Garvey stated his only plea is "ignorance of the law," in that he spent about five months of 1921 out of the U.S. and it was his interpretation of the law that persons could deduct from their income monies received by them from sources in the United States while they were temporarily residing outside the boundaries of the country. Garvey admitted that during the period of 1921 his wife was not living with him and that his sister for whom he claims support was over 18 and in addition was employed part of the time.

Garvey's attorneys admitted that an incorrect return had been filed and stated they were willing to have their client, Garvey, settle the matter by paying his tax or making some other sort of compromise financially for what is due the government, which of course, was declined by Mr. Mattuck.

Garvey was placed under $500.00 bond and hearing was set for April 27th at 2:00 P.M.

MORTIMER J. DAVIS

DJ-FBI, file 61. TD.

1. Cornelius W. McDougald was a prominent black lawyer in New York during the 1920s. Born on 1 May 1879 in Whiteville, N. C., he graduated from Lincoln University in Pennsylvania in 1904, received a further degree from New York University School of Law in 1907, and was admitted to the New York Bar the following year. He later served for five years as assistant district attorney for the County of New York and in 1923 became special assistant attorney general for the state; he was the first black person to occupy that position. In 1934, McDougald was involved in a public scandal involving William L. Sherrill, a former high UNIA official. Sherrill accused McDougald of having defrauded him during the course of a loan transaction, and the Appellate Division of the New York Supreme Court upheld the charge. While the court censured McDougald for unprofessional conduct, it did not disbar him, apparently in view of his prior good record. McDougald practiced law until his retirement and died in New York City on 5 October 1978 at the age of ninety-nine (*WWCA*; Cornelius McDougald, Jr., to Robert A. Hill, 7 May 1985; *New York Age*, 24 February, and 22 December 1934).

New York City 4-5-23

It will be noted in reports recently submitted by Andrew Battle, who is working undercover in this city among the Negroes, that he has reported rumors of various kinds throughout the Colored section, to the effect that certain Government officials have been "reached" and "bribed" in order to prevent the prosecution of the present case against Garvey and others.

When Battle first reported these rumors to the writer and also to Agent Amos, he was instructed to follow them closely and if possible trace them to their source.[1]

The writer has also previously called this situation to the attention of Assistant United States Attorney Mattuck, and while at first no attention was paid to same by either agents working on this case or Mr. Mattuck, the reports and rumors became so persistent that after a conference with Mr. Mattuck on April 2d, it was decided to subpoena to his office such persons as we believed were in possession of information regarding the alleged bribery, etc.

Today the following persons came to Mr. Mattuck's office under subpoena: S[y]dney de Bourg, J. B. Yearwood, Arnold J. Ford and Dr. [*Charles H.*] Duvall. These are persons named by Agent Battle who are alleged regarding the alleged bribery, or who have information regarding it. Duvall particularly was mentioned by Agent Battle as having stated after an interview with Agent Amos and Davis, that "he believed they had been bribed not to prosecute Garvey."

All of the witnesses examined today by Mr. Mattuck, in the writer's presence, admitted that for quite some time there have been rumors current in the colored section that Garvey would never be tried. None, however, could state where the rumors had originated or what they were based on. De Bourg, for instance, stated that a grocery dealer in Harlem told him some time ago that a friend of a friend of his said that he knew the District Attorney and that the District Attorney had stated to someone else that he did not intend to prosecute Garvey; Dr. Duvall on the other hand stated he had heard somewhere in Harlem that because Garvey was a British subject the United States Government was afraid to prosecute him; Ford had a different conception and stated that the general word passed around was that the various delays and postponements of the case indicated the fact that the Government did not have a case, and anyway Garvey was too powerful for them to prosecute. Dr. Duvall[,] of course, denied any assertions charged to him by Agent Battle, particularly a statement of his in which he is alleged to have charged that the writer and Agent Amos received $1,000 each.

Another witness subpoenaed, William Ferris, editor of the "Negro World," did not put in an appearance. Ferris, according to our information, has been spreading rumors such as outlined above[,] which are believed to have emanated direct[ly] from Garvey.

There is no question in Agent's mind but that there are rumors among the colored population regarding alleged laxity on the part of the Government in this case, but as the Bureau is fully acquainted with, none of these have any basis in fact.

This phase of the case is considered closed.

MORTIMER J. DAVIS

DJ-FBI, file 61. TD.

1. In an interview with Special Employee Andrew M. Battle, both Elie Garcia and Arnold J. Ford reported that Garvey had "bribed the officers in charge of his Government case, and the officers of the U.N.I.A. were afraid to go too far in telling what they knew" (report by Special Employee Andrew M. Battle, 2 April 1923, DJ-FBI, file 61).

Report by Bureau Agent Rocco C. Novario

Cleveland, Ohio 4/9/1923

ALLEGED COMMUNISTIC ACTIVITIES AMONG THE COLORED RACE OF CLEVELAND, OHIO

Acting under instructions from Agent-in-Charge J.V. Ryan, Agent proceeded along Central and Scovil Avenues, from 14th Street to East 55th Street (Colored belt), making undercover inquiries in all the confectionery and news stores where newspapers are sold. In all the stores Agent inquired [i]f they had for sale any copies of the "Solidarity" or "The Worker" and in every place was informed that the storekeeper had never heard of such newspapers. Agent observed that in all the stores there were on sale copies of the two local colored newspapers, namely: The Cleveland Gazette,—and the Cleveland Call, and the following out of town Colored papers:

Negro World,—published in New York City.

Indianapolis Ledger[1],—published in Indianapolis, Ind.

The Pittsburg[h] Courier,—published in Pittsburgh, Pa.

The Freeman,[2]—published in Indianapolis, Ind.

Agent also made inquiries if there were any radical agitators or organizers among the colored people, and from several sources was informed that there is a colored organization known as: "The Universal Negro Improvement Association" headed by Marcus Garvey, self-styled Provisional President of Africa (who is now indicted in New York City for embezzling funds) and about a year ago had several thousand followers in Cleveland; at the present time meetings are held Sunday afternoons at 5:00 P.M. at East 59th Street and Central Avenue, and several of the most enthusia[s]tic followers of Garvey are very bitter toward the Government officials in not suppressing the Ku Klux Klan, and in allowing the K.K.K. to antagonize the colored people.[3] There has been no agitation against our present form of Government or radicalism along the methods that are preached by the I.W.W. or the Communists.

The most radical members of the U.N.I.A., or Garvey Organization[,] is Roy Davis, who holds some office or title in the Garvey Organization, and a man named Jones, who was formerly organiz[e]r for the Colored Union of Meat Cutters, and a man named Bishop Lennox.

Roy Davis can be hired to make any kind of a speech. Jones is described as ignorant, and Bishop Lennox is very bitter against the Government in not suppressing the K.K.K. . . .

R.C. NOVARIO

DJ-FBI, file 61-391-112. TD.

1. The *Indianapolis Ledger* was published between 1913 and 1922 (Armstead Scott Pride, "A Register and History of Negro Newspapers in the United States, 1827–1950" [Ph.D. diss., Northwestern University, 1973], p. 239).

2. The *Freeman*, "a national illustrated colored newspaper" edited by George L. Knox, was published between 1888 and 1924 (*Freeman*, 8 January 1916; Pride, "A Register and History of Negro Newspapers," p. 239).

3. By 1923 the Ohio Ku Klux Klan was the second largest in the nation. It was strongest in the cities, where the hostility of white Americans toward the large numbers of blacks and eastern Europeans who had migrated to the urban areas of Ohio seeking work in the mills and foundries increased racial tensions and contributed to the Klan's growth. The industrial city of Akron, for example, southeast of Cleveland, had a Klan with over 50,000 members. Yet in Cleveland, where native white Protestants formed only one-fourth of the population, the Klan was smaller than in other Ohio areas, with an estimated membership of two thousand. There were, nevertheless, incidents of threatening letters, harassment, and violence against blacks. The municipal government, as in some other Ohio cities, took a public stand against the Klan. By 1921 the mayor had ordered the police to "suppress the Klan," Klan parades were forbidden, and in 1923 the city council voted unanimously to condemn the Klan and urged Congress to take immediate action to suppress the organization. Despite this, the Klan remained active in Cleveland (David M. Chalmers, *Hooded Americanism: The History of the Ku Klux Klan*, pp. 175–182; Kenneth T. Jackson, *The Ku Klux Klan in the City*, pp. 164–169, 236–253; Kenneth L. Kusmer, *A Ghetto Takes Shape: Black Cleveland, 1870–1930* [Urbana: University of Illinois Press, 1976], pp. 174–177; Russell H. Davis, *Black Americans in Cleveland* [Washington, D.C.: Associated Publishers, 1972], pp. 226–227).

Speech by Marcus Garvey

[[New York, April 13, 1923]]

My subject for tonight will be a restatement of the aims and objects of the Universal Negro Improvement Association. I have spoken so often to the New York local that I believe every member of this division and every visitor to Liberty Hall ought to be well grounded in the aims and objects and principles of this association. It is said that I speak better away of late from Liberty Hall than in Liberty Hall, simply because when speaking to people in other parts of the country I have to speak of the association as it is. I have to speak of the principles, the aims and objects of the association as they are; but you in Liberty Hall are so accustomed to hear me restate those aims and objects and principles that my speech here must naturally be different from the speech I deliver outside. But some of us fall by the wayside, or some of us are so hard-headed and some of us forget so easily that it becomes necessary at times to restate the aims and objects of this great movement.

Some people imagine that all the things that the Universal Negro Improvement Association aims at can be realized in a day. We never promised that. No one in his sober senses ever told you that—that the aims and objects of the Universal Negro Improvement Association can be realized in a day. The things we aim at are of such consequence as to make it impossible for us to measure time for their accomplishment. What we are endeavoring to do is even much more than what the Roman attempted to do for Rome, and Rome was not built in a day. In the founding and building of Rome things were much easier than today in the effort of the Universal Negro Improvement Association to found and build and establish a government in Africa. The world has changed to the point where, if anything is to be done, you must do it facing opposition, facing barriers and difficulties of all kinds. There is no age fraught with more difficulties and hardships and embarrassments and encumbrances for putting over any program or for advocating any reformation movement than the age of the twentieth century, and we of the Universal Negro Improvement Association have undertaken in the twentieth century to do something in the midst of a heartless materialism. We are endeavoring to improve the economic, including the industrial and commercial, the social, educational, religious and political conditions of Negroes, not only in one country, but in all parts of the world. We are endeavoring to lift them out of the condition of dependence and reliance on others—from serfdom into an atmosphere of independence and self-reliance; into a condition where they will be able to do for themselves. Indeed, we are endeavoring to carry out a physician [*physical?*] reformation among 400,000,000 Negroes.

Yet the program does not stop there. The program of the Universal Negro Improvement Association goes further, to the extent of saying that the time has come for these scattered millions of people of our race to reassemble themselves into a government—into a country of their own. Now everybody knows that it is impossible to accomplish such a program in a day, and every sane person knows that in advancing and carrying through such a program it is almost necessary for us to meet opposition of all kinds—opposition from without as well as opposition from within. Yet some of us who have heard the principles enunciated—who have heard these objects restated time and time again—become disheartened and despondent and lose faith because of some disappointment or because of some setback. How far do you expect to get— whether you are critics or whether you are member[s] of the association— without disappointment before accomplishment of the ideal you have in mind? In the pursuit of our Christian life and faith we have between the cradle and the grave to encounter hundreds and thousands of disappointments—spiritual disappointments—before we ultimately succeed in finding solace in that blessed and splendid religion we profess. Even as in religion, so it is in things temporal and things material.

No better evidence than the Universal Negro Improvement Association exists at this time, where so many of us started out buoyant in our hopes, enthusiastic in our exclamations about the aims and objects of the association, and after a month, after six months, twelve months, because something fortunate or unfortunate happens, we lose faith and fall by the wayside. Losing faith in the religion or the thing you profess will take you nowhere. It was because of lack of faith in the children of Israel that they were held up for so long in the wilderness and why so many of them died without seeing the Promised Land. That same lack of faith will be the downfall of many of us.

WILL TAKE TIME TO ACCOMPLISH

This thing of African redemption; this thing of improving the condition of the race, cannot be accomplished in a day or a month or a year. It is going to take time more than we can measure, probably more than we can calculate. There is no difference in the efforts of this association towards the liberation of the race than in the efforts of other races and other peoples. We have a splendid example in the perseverence exhibited by the Irish people in fighting for a cause such as ours for 750 years, laboring for, suffering for and dying for the achievement of their ideal of Irish freedom, and up to now they are only partially free; they have only received a modicum of that freedom for which they have fought for 750 years, and we of this association have seen more in five years by way of accomplishment of our program than the Irish have seen for hundreds of years after they started their program of national independence. Yet some of us are dissatisfied. What do you expect? You are expecting more of your organization than others have expected of world organizations struggling for the same purpose and the same ideal you are striving for.

Some of you have faltered because of the temporary mishap to the Black Star Line; because you have $5, or $25, or $500, invested in the Black Star Line, and you did not immediately get the dividends or your money back, you thought you should contribute no more to the Universal Negro Improvement Association. Let us place ourselves in a relative position to other peoples and of other governments. The United States Shipping Board during the war and immediately after the war invested hundreds of millions of dollars in shipping, and during that period of [time it lost] three hundred million dollars—not three million dollars; but it lost three hundred million dollars in shipping.[1] Now, suppose the people who made up the United States Government were as some of the people who make up the Universal Negro Improvement Association, which really is a government in embryo—suppose they were like us and had withdrawn their support from the United States Government, refusing to pay their taxes and refusing to pay their obligations to the Government, what do you think would become of the United States Government? The United States Government would have lost its prestige and financial standing and would be no longer able to maintain itself as a first-rate power among the other nations and governments of the world. The white American people did not draw away from the American Government. This money that the Government used in investing in ships and which the Government lost was the money of the people paid to the Government in taxes, but the people who pay taxes and for whom the Government lost three hundred million dollars did not withdraw from the government and did not refuse to pay any more taxes; they did not leave the country and go elsewhere as some of us have left the Universal Negro Improvement Association after the embarrassment to the Black Star Line. The American people did not leave the country and go to England because the Government threw away three hundred million dollars, but the people remained, knowing that those things are necessary—are essential in the life and existence of the nation; that it was necessary to invest money in ships at that time whether they made money or not and the people were willing to continue to subscribe to the Government to regain that loss of three hundred million dollars.

That is the attitude of sensible people and sensible races all over the world. Not so, however, with our race; we are prone to take one disappointment as an everlasting argument that everything will turn out the same way. With such a feeling and such a belief you will never get anywhere, and that is why our race has gotten nowhere. Take the great white race, take the Wall Street journals, and you will read that day after day, week after week, month after month, hundreds of billions of dollars are lost in Wall Street and other great financial centers in this country by white capitalists, but that does not put an end to the activities of Wall Street and Chicago and Los Angeles, but only act[s] as an inspiration and guide to [other] business institutions to be more careful in whatsoever they do. That ought to be a splendid example for Negroes who are endeavoring to lift themselves economically and politically in the same way as other races.

As I have said more than once, so long as the Universal Negro Improvement Association exists nothing connected with it can fail because the Universal Negro Improvement Association is a spiritual force—is a spiritual movement that moves from one age to the next. I do not look upon anything that happened to the Black Star Line as a failure so long as the Universal Negro Improvement Association exists. I look upon it only as a temporary setback to be adjusted a little later and therefore there is absolutely no reason for anyone to think that because of that the Universal Negro Improvement Association will fail. When the Association has failed then you have argument enough to say that you have failed, but so long as the U.N.I.A. exists—and from what I know it is going to exist forever—there is absolutely no reason for anybody to doubt anything. . . .

Printed in *NW*, 19 May 1923. Original headlines omitted.

1. The actual financial losses suffered by the U.S. Shipping Board are difficult to determine. According to the government's own reports, prior to July 1921 the books of the USSB were kept in such a fashion that "it is impossible to give accurate yearly operating statements showing profit and loss up to that time." In 1922 and 1923 the operating losses were $51,636,625.45 and $44,091,150.41, respectively (Darrell Hevenor Smith and Paul V. Betters, *The United States Shipping Board: Its History, Activities, and Organization* [Washington, D.C.: Brookings Institution, 1931], p. 81).

Report by Special Employee Andrew M. Battle

New York, N.Y. Apr. 27th, 1923

. . . On April 21st, the writer had a talk with MRS. MILDRED MILLER of 57 West 139th Street, who stated that she has more than $1000. worth of shares in the BLACK STAR LINE and that she also gave money to purchase linen for the "PHYLLIS WHEATLEY."

Attended a meeting at Liberty Hall, speakers, VERGIL [*Vernal*] WILLIAMS and MARCUS GARVEY. WILLIAMS said that this Government had tried to overthrow the aims and objects of the U.N.I.A. MARCUS GARVEY said that the U.N.I.A. has meant everything it has said and done—that the U.N.I.A. is a government itself and nothing can stop it. He said, "We have finished half of our work in Africa and in ten more years will complete it." There were 1400 at this meeting, nearly all West Indians.

In a conversation with PERCIVAL L. BURROW[S],[1] Commissioner of the U.N.I.A. from Trinidad, West Indies, he said, "I have well organized the U.N.I.A. in Trinidad. MR. GARVEY knows what he is about. We will have to keep the white folks fooled until we can rise up and demand a place. All of the other powers are at swords' points the U.S. is keeping out of the fight as long as it can. When the U.S. starts in, they will settle the fight in a year, but the U.S. will not be able to fight again for a long time—and we will rise up and demand our place with the other powers. You see, we will be on the safe side joining the other powers, because they are the darker races. The U.N.I.A. is very glad that the U.S. is keeping out of the fight until the last moment. We will not have to do very much fighting as individuals—Japan and the other powers will be at our backs, and we have got to keep this country fooled until that time comes."

The writer interviewed MRS. DOROTHY LAWSON, 2092 Madison Avenue, who said, "I was one of the first ones to give money to help buy oil for the 'PHYLLIS WHEATLEY'—$750.00 was raised for oil for that ship and given to MR. THOMPSON. I gave money for linen to be purchased for the 'PHYLLIS WHEATLEY' and MR. GARVEY made many promises to the members, saying that the 'PHYLLIS WHEATLEY' [wo]uld be ready to sail for Liberia, and he sold many tickets to the West Indies. He also advertised a good many times that the BLACK STAR LINE had bought a ship by the name of 'PHYLLIS WHEATLEY,' but no ship has ever been seen.["]

In a conversation with MRS. T. PARRIS, 117 West 142nd Street, New York City, she said that she was one of the first to buy stock in the BLACK STAR LINE. She also gave $45. to help raise enough money to buy the "PHYLLIS WHEATLEY," and also gave money to buy the oil and linen for this ship, and had packed up all her furniture to go to Africa. She said she would willingly tell everything she knew about GARVEY. MRS. PARRIS said she was one of the committee who signed the petition last year to the effect that they had no fault to find with MARCUS GARVEY, as at that time she did not believe that he was crooked, but she said that she is now convinced of it.[2] She said that nearly everyone who signed that petition last year is against GARVEY now. Continued.

ANDREW M. BATTLE

DJ-FBI, file 61. TD.

1. Percival L. Burrows (b. 1879), born in Barbados, immigrated to the United States in 1904. Described by the *Negro World* as a self-made man (*NW*, 3 November 1923), Burrows rose quickly through the UNIA ranks after he became a member of Buffalo's Division 79 on 16 December 1920. He established a small newspaper, *The Voice of Buffalo*, as the organ of Division 79, possibly to counter anti-Garvey material that was being published in the *Buffalo American*, the city's leading black newspaper. The Buffalo UNIA sent Burrows as one of its delegates to the 1921 UNIA convention, and there he caught the notice of Garvey and the national leadership. Burrows became high commissioner for the islands of Trinidad, Tobago, St. Vincent, and Grenada, as well as for Brazil and Venezuela (*NW*, 18 November 1922). Under his leadership, the UNIA established twenty-one new divisions in the region. Garvey promoted Burrows to first assistant secretary-general of the UNIA parent body to replace Thomas W. Anderson in August 1923 (*NW*, 3 November 1923).

2. A reference to the open letter from the New York UNIA local, written on 15 January 1922, and printed in *Garvey Papers* 4: 371–372. For information on Mrs. Paris, see *Garvey Papers* 4: 441–442.

Report by Bureau Agent W.L. Buchanan

Buffalo N.Y. 4/30/23

MARCUS GARVEY, President General of the Universal Negro Improvement Association, addressed a large audience of Buffalo negroes at Miller's Hall, Genesee Street, on April 29th.[1] His talk was along the same lines as those given by him in Buffalo on previous occasions, and when he praised the negroes in comparison with whites he was greeted with great applause by those present. He stated that Africa will become the United States of Negroes, and that it was richer than one hundred Americas put together; that Europe has just discovered this and wants to recoup its losses by exploiting Africa, the home country of negroes. He attacked Lord Robert Cecil,[2] who[m] he charged with making propaganda in this country, to draw America into the [L]eague of [N]ations, and he termed the league a league of destruction, adding that when such a league got to Africa they would find 400,000,000 negroes there using their hands and feet, and there is no white man whom a negro cannot match in letters, athletics or war. He further states that if President Harding weakens in his stand on the League of Nations, he will have to reckon with the negro vote in 1924.

W.L. BUCHANAN

DJ-FBI, file 61-184-80. TD.

1. Garvey's speaking tour included Washington, D.C., 18 April, and Cleveland, 30 April. In Washington, Agent A.L. Brent estimated the audience at about three hundred, "nearly half of whom were West Indians," who, according to Brent, displayed much greater enthusiasm than did the American blacks (21 April 1921, DJ-FBI, file 61). Garvey spoke in Cleveland before an audience of about eight hundred and apparently "blamed the negroes for not using their brains." In his report of the speech, Agent Rocco C. Novario noted that Garvey "did not say anything that could be construed as radical" (2 May 1923, DJ-FBI, file 61). Nevertheless, after hearing that while on

tour, Garvey continued to collect money from his audiences, U.S. Attorney Mattuck made it known that he would not allow him to leave the city again until the trial was over (report by Special Agent James E. Amos, 21 April 1923, DJ-FBI, file 61).

2. Lord Robert Cecil, viscount of Chelwood (1864–1958), British aristocrat and statesman, became a leading proponent of the concept of a league of nations while serving as minister of blockade in the wartime cabinet. In 1917 Cecil called for the establishment of an Anglo-American committee to study the league idea, and following his resignation from the government in November 1918, he was appointed to head the League of Nations section of the Foreign Office. In this capacity he drafted the so-called "Cecil plan," and in early 1919 he met with President Wilson, Colonel House, Jan Smuts, and others to negotiate a covenant for the League of Nations. Further negotiations and revisions worked out by Cecil and Wilson resulted in the final draft covenant of the league, which was adopted in June 1920 (*Times* [London], 25 November 1958; George W. Egerton, *Great Britain and the Creation of the League of Nations* [Chapel Hill: University of North Carolina Press, 1978], pp. 24–171). In the following years, Cecil, who was greatly disappointed by the United States' decision to remain outside of the league, took on the role of propagandist for the world body. In March–April 1923, he began a lengthy speaking tour of the United States, sponsored by the Foreign Policy Association. Although he refused "to dictate to America or to suggest what America shall do," Cecil, in a speech delivered in New York on 2 April, called on "all important" nations to participate in the League of Nations (*NYT*, 3 April 1923).

Agreement Between the UNIA, Marcus Garvey, and Amy Jacques Garvey

[*New York*] 5th day of May 1923

THIS AGREEMENT made this *5th* day of May, 1923, by and between the Universal Negro Improvement Association, Inc., a domestic corporation, with its principal place of business located at 56 West 135th Street, in the Borough of Manhattan, City of New York, the African Communities['] League, Inc., also a domestic corporation, with its principal place of business located at 56 West 135th Street, in the Borough of Manhattan, City of New York, parties of the first part, and Amy Jacques Garvey residing at 13[3] West 129th Street[,] party of the second part, and Marcus M. Garvey residing at 133 West 129th Street, party of the third part.

WHEREAS, Marcus M. Garvey, the husband of the party of the second part, is the author or subject of certain books, pamphlets or pictures already published or are to be published by the Universal Printing Shop under the auspices of the Universal Negro Improvement Association, Inc. or the African Communities['] League, Inc. parties of the first part, and,

WHEREAS, Amy Jacques Garvey, party of the second part[,] is the author or subject of certain books, pamphlets and pictures already published or are to be published by the said Universal Printing Shop under the auspices of the Universal Negro Improvement Association, Inc. or the African Communities['] League, Inc., parties of the first part and,

WHEREAS, the Universal Negro Improvement Association, Inc. has financed the printing and publication of the aforesaid books, pamphlets and pictures and,

WHEREAS, the Universal Negro Improvement Association, Inc. is to finance the printing and publication of the same,

NOW THEREFORE, THIS AGREEMENT WITNESSETH that for and in consideration of the mutual promises jointly and severally made by and between the respective parties hereto, for and in consideration of the premises herein and of the sum of One ($1.00) Dollar by each party to the other in hand respectively paid, the receipt whereof is hereby acknowledged, the parties hereto covenant and agree as follows:

FIRST: The Universal Negro Improvement Association, Inc. and the African Communities['] League, Inc. parties of the first part[,] and Marcus M. Garvey, party of the third part[,] agree that Amy Jacques Garvey, party of the second part, the wife of Marcus M. Garvey[,] party of the third part[,] shall receive one third of /all/ the gross receipts resulting from the sale of all books, pamphlets and pictures published by the Universal Printing Shop under the auspices of the Universal Negro Improvement Association, Inc., of which books, pamphlets and pictures Marcus M. Garvey[,] party of the third part, the husband of the said Amy Jacques Garvey, party of the second part[,] is the author or subject.

SECOND: The Universal Negro Improvement Association, Inc. and the African Communities['] League, Inc. parties of the first part[,] and Marcus M. Garvey[,] party of the third part[,] agree that the said Amy Jacques Garvey[,] party of the second part, the wife of Marcus M. Garvey, party of the third part[,] shall receive one third of all the gross receipts resulting from the sale of all books, pamphlets and pictures published by the Universal Printing Shop under the auspices of the African Communities['] League, Inc., of which books, pamphlets and pictures Marcus M. Garvey, party of the third part, the husband of the said Amy Jacques Garvey, party of the second part[,] is the author or subject.

THIRD: The Universal Negro Improvement Association, Inc. and the African Communities['] League, Inc.[,] parties of the first part[,] and Marcus M. Garvey[,] party of the third part[,] agree that the said Amy Jacques Garvey, party of the second part, the wife of Marcus M. Garvey, party of the third part[,] shall receive one third of all the gross receipts resulting from the sale of all books, pamphlets and pictures published by the Universal Printing Shop under the auspices of the Universal Negro Improvement Association, Inc., of which books, pamphlets and pictures Amy Jacques Garvey[,] party of the second part, the wife of the said Marcus M. Garvey[,] party of the third part[,] is the author or subject.

FOURTH: The Universal Negro Improvement Association, Inc. and the African Communities['] League, Inc.[,] parties of the first part[,] and Marcus M. Garvey[,] party of the third part[,] agree that the said Amy Jacques Garvey, party of the second part, the wife of Marcus M. Garvey, party of the third part[,] shall receive one third of all the gross receipts resulting from the sale of books, pamphlets and pictures published by the Universal Printing Shop under the auspices of the African Communities' League, Inc., of which books, pamphlets and pictures Amy Jacques Garvey, party of the second part, the wife of the said Marcus M. Garvey, party of the third part, is the author or subject.

FIFTH: The parties hereto jointly and severally agree that the Universal Negro Improvement Association, Inc. shall receive the remaining two thirds of all the gross receipts resulting from the sale of all the said books, pamphlets and pictures herein before mentioned and described and of which Marcus M. Garvey, the party of the third part[,] and Amy Jacques Garvey, party of the second part[,] are the authors or subjects.

SIXTH: It is understood and agreed by and between all the parties hereto that proper records and books of account shall be kept by the Universal Negro Improvement Association, Inc. of all the transactions herein provided for, for and on behalf of all the contracting parties herein.

SEVENTH: It is also understood and agreed that a proper and accurate financial report of all the transactions herein provided for, shall be made and a true copy thereof submitted to Amy Jacques Garvey, the party of the second part[,] once each month at the end of each and every month; and that at the time of delivery of such report the Universal Negro Improvement Association, Inc. shall contemporaneously therewith pay over to the said Amy Jacques Garvey, the party of the second part[,] her exact portion of the gross receipts as herein provided for to wit: One third of the same.

EIGHTH: It is further understood and agreed that the said Amy Jacques Garvey, the party of the second part[,] or her duly authorized agent or agents[,] shall have the right and privilege to inspect, audit and investigate at any and all times the records and books of account kept by the Universal Negro Improvement Association, Inc., one of the parties of the first part[,] concerning the transactions herein as provided for in the paragraph designated "Sixth" herein.

It is further understood and agreed that this agreement shall be effective as of the first day of January, 1923 and all the books, pamphlets and pictures, of which Marcus M. Garvey, party of the third part[,] and Amy Jacques Garvey, party of the second part[,] are the authors and subjects, published or printed prior to the date hereof and subsequent of the first day of January, 1923, shall be considered the subject matter of this agreement on a parity with /the/ books, pamphlets and pictures to be published or printed in the future.

> Universal Negro Improvement Ass'n. Inc.
> BY C. H. BOURNE
> Chancellor
> African Communities['] League, Inc.
> BY ROBT. L. POSTON
> MARCUS GARVEY
> A. JACQUES GARVEY

In the presence of: as to the Universal Negro Improvement Association, Inc. and African Communities['] League, Inc. /and/ as to Amy Jacques Garvey and Marcus M. Garvey.

> WITNESS: VERNAL J. WILLIAMS

TNF, MGMC, box 5, folder 1. TD. Notarized by H. Vinton Plummer; signatures attested by Thomas W. Anderson.

Report by Special Agent Mortimer J. Davis

New York City 5-10-23

Reference is made to Agent's previous report of April 27, 1923, in which it was stated that ESAU RAMUS, alias JAMES JEFFRIES, had pleaded guilty to First Degree Assault.[1] It will be noted therein also that he was apparently very anxious to talk, and a Writ of Habeus Corpus was therefore issued for him in the Southern District of New York.

He subsequently appeared in the office of Assistant United States Attorney Mattuck on this writ, and in the presence of Mr. Mattuck, Agent Amos and the writer, made a detailed statement. Jeffries is willing and anxious to testify against GARVEY but wants a Promise of a suspended sentence. Mr. Mattuck advised him that while he can promise nothing he will be glad to make representations to Judge Talley in Part 1, General Sessions, where Jeffries is to be sentenced, to the effect that he has assisted the Government. Jeffries thereupon agreed to have his sentence postponed until the Black Star Line Case comes up in the United States Courts. Agent, on the 3d instant, appeared before Judge Talley, upon request of Mr. Mattuck, and obtained postponement of the case.

In addition to the interview with Jeffries at Mr. Mattuck's office, Agent and Agent Amos again interviewed him at the Tombs Prison on the 7th instant.

In effect, Jeffries states that while in Philadelphia last year he received a letter from Garvey stating that EASON was to speak there and that "his meeting must be broken up or he must not return to New York alive," (meaning Eason). Jeffries states he and members of the African Legion succeeded in breaking up the meeting, which was held at one of the Philadelphia churches, but Eason was left unharmed. Subsequently Jeffries was informed that the New York Police were looking for him, so he came to New York and saw Garvey, who advised him to proceed to New Orleans and change his name. Garvey gave him $100 from the treasury of the U.N.I.A. for the trip. In New Orleans, states Jeffries, he was informed by a letter over Garvey's personal signature, that Eason was to speak there on a certain date and instructing Jeffries that "Eason had turned State's evidence against him, (Garvey) and must not be allowed to return to New York alive." This letter Jeffries states he showed to SHAKESPEARE and DYER, the two men now convicted for Eason's death.[2] It was also shown to other members of the African Legion, but, states Jeffries, these two men were to do the killing. Questioned further on May 7th by Agent Amos and the writer, Jeffries states that Dyer is the man who did the shooting[;] that Shakespeare was with him and while he did not shoot Eason, assisted in every other way possible in the act.

Jeffries states that he has destroyed the letter from Garvey, as suggested by Garvey in the letter itself. However, he states that if he can now locate MARY PRINCE, (formerly of 1807 Third Avenue, New York, but who has now disappeared), he will be able to prove everything. This leads to the belief that the letter and other papers are still in existence, probably in the possession of

Mary Prince, who[m] we are at present trying to locate.

Jeffries further states that if he gains his freedom he will willingly accompany Government Agents to various large cities and point out to them where large quantities of guns and ammunition have been stored by the branches of the African Legion.[3] He mentions particularly New York, Philadelphia and Washington, D.C. He himself, he states, made many of the purchases and states that in New York he was accompanied on these trips by VERNAL J. WILLIAMS, Garvey's attorney, and VINTON PLUMMER, Publicity Agent for the U.N.I.A. With these men he states he went to an Army Supply Store on 42nd Street, New York, between 7th and 8th Avenue, uptown side, where ammunition was purchased. He also made purchases of ammunition at a sporting goods store at Madison Avenue and 48th Street; also from a concern at 5th Avenue and 40th Street, (over Woolworth's Store), New York City. In Philadelphia he states that he was negotiating for the purchase of bombs from an ammunition concern at 5th and Market Streets, but that prices were too high. These negotiations were made either in the name of RAMUS or JEFFRIES. At this same place he also purchased quantities of ammunition. The plan, in general, was to make small purchases in various places and send them to the U.N.I.A. Headquarters. They were then split up and divided among trusted members of the Legion, who, after taking a solemn oath of fidelity, removed the ammunition to his home. If at any time circumstances made the removal of these goods [*necessary?*], other members were entrusted with them. The purpose of these purchases, states Jeffries, was to have a supply of guns and ammunition on hand in case of race riots. Garvey, he states, personally supervised many of these transactions and was always kept informed of same. In fact, much of the money for the purchases came direct from his office. In Philadelphia, states Jeffries, DR. FRANCIS and MAZIE KING have full information of such work. In New York a fellow named PHILLIP (last name) is in charge and Jeffries states he has seen large quantities of ammunition in his home; in Detroit a man named [*F. Levi*] LORD is the one in charge.

Jeffries refused to sign any statements, in fact will not talk when notes are made of his remarks. He states, however, that he will take the witness stand against Garvey if there is any assurance of his receiving a light sentence in the State Courts. Also, he is worried over the fact that many of his admissions may lead to his arrest in various cities.

The officers of the U.N.I.A. in New York have learned of Jeffries' appearance in the United States Attorney's office here, and our undercover man has reported a move on foot to bribe him into silence. Jeffries has stated to us, however, that he will refuse such advances. He showed me upon my last visit, a letter from DR. FRANCIS of Philadelphia, urging him not to testify against Garvey and promising him aid after he goes to prison.

Upon suggestion of Mr. Mattuck this office wired New Orleans asking whether there was any possibility of DYER or SHAKESPEARE talking at this time, but was in turn advised that their appeal will be heard on the 16th instant and that it was inadvisable to interview them until after the result is known.

Since writing this report Agent Amos has received from Jeffries, the following letter:

May 9/23

Hon. J. E. Amos, Dept. of Justice
Dear Sir:

This is to notify you of the locations where the goods was purchased which is as follows.

Winchester Sporting Goods Co.	40th St. & 5th Ave.
Army & Navy Store	42d St. bet. 7 & 8 Ave.
Amberc[r]ombie & Fitch	46th St. and Madison Ave.
Sporting Goods Store	48th St. & Madison Av.
Sporting Goods Supplies	5 & Market St. Phila. Pa.
Sporting Goods Supplies	Bet. 5 & 6 St. On Market. Phila.
Sporting Goods Supplies	Bet 10 & 11 on Chestnut Phila.
Pawn Shop	22 St. & South Phila, Pa.
Pawn Shop	12th & Bainbridge St. Phila.
Pawn Shop	9 & South St. Phila.
Hardware Shop	12 & 13 on South Phila. Pa.

We removed some ammunition from premises, 604 So. 17th St. Phila. about half hour before the Police came to New York by Dr. Francis and man named Simpson. In case you don't locate these remember I can. Awaiting your reply,

JOHN JEFFERIES

These are some of the addresses at which ammunition for the U.N.I.A. is supposed to have been purchased by Jeffries.

MORTIMER J. DAVIS

DJ-FBI, file 61. TD.

1. After Ramus was extradicted to New York on 6 April, he was incarcerated in Tombs Prison. UNIA attorney Vernal J. Williams represented Ramus and instructed him to plead guilty to attempted assault in the first degree. Interviewed by Agent Mortimer J. Davis, Ramus apparently stated that Williams had urged him to plead guilty because the judge, witnesses, and prosecuting attorney were white people and thus certain to convict him. While awaiting trial, the bureau contacted the Labor Department with a view to possible deportation of Ramus, who first entered the United States from St. Kitts in 1910 (reports by Special Agent Mortimer J. Davis, 11 April and 27 April 1923, DJ-FBI, file 61).

2. On 22 March 1923 Shakespeare and Dyer were found guilty of manslaughter in the death of J. W. H. Eason and each was later sentenced to the Louisiana State Penitentiary for a term of eighteen to twenty years (report of Special Agent H. D. Gulley, 10 April 1923, DJ-FBI, file 61). After a new trial in 1924, however, Shakespeare and Dyer were found innocent and freed.

3. Special Employee Andrew M. Battle once submitted a report on the UNIA, wherein he claimed "there were 800 present at the meeting tonight [19 March] and it is the writer's opinion that half of the men present carried guns or knives" (W. J. Burns to Edward J. Brennan, 4 April 1923, DJ-FBI, file 61, quoting Special Employee Battle's report of 20 March 1923).

Report by Special Agent Joseph G. Tucker

New York MAY 12, 1923

Marcus Garvey made a statement on the 9th inst. that the Fourth Annual Convention of the Universal Negro Improvement Association will be held next year in Liberia instead of this year in August in New York as originally planned.[1]

Garvey's plans include leaving for Africa with a boat load of negroes from the United States and South America.

Garvey's trial is set for the 16 inst.[2] before Judge Julian Mack.[3] . . .

JOSEPH G. TUCKER

DJ-FBI, file 61-228. TD.

1. The Fourth Annual Convention was held, as customary, in New York in August 1924.
2. The trial began on 18 May 1923.
3. Julian William Mack (1866–1943) was educated at Harvard University Law School, where he was one of the founders of the *Harvard Law Review*. He later taught law at Northwestern University and at the University of Chicago. In 1911 Mack was appointed a judge of the U.S. Circuit Court of Appeals, a position he held until his retirement. During his career on the bench, Judge Mack tried a number of famous cases, among them the 1926 trial of Harry M. Daugherty, former U.S. attorney general. In addition to carrying out his professional duties, Judge Mack was also early on engaged in social-welfare work during the Progressive era, work that later merged with the aspirations of the Zionist movement in the late teens. Becoming eventually second only to Louis Brandeis in the American Zionist movement, Mack was elected president of the Zionist Organization of America in 1918 and, a year later, to the presidency of the newly founded American Jewish Congress. As an official representative of the Zionist movement, he served as the first chairman of the committee of Jewish delegations attending the Paris Peace Conference in 1919. According to Mack's biographer, Julian Mack participated with Roger Baldwin, Stephen S. Wise, and Jane Addams in meetings "that led to the formation of the National Association for the Advancement of Colored People." He reportedly later presided over an early NAACP meeting at which Du Bois spoke (Harry Barnard, *The Forging of an American Jew* [New York: Herzl Press, 1974], pp. 77, 113). Yet no corroborating evidence of these claims has been found elsewhere, and no records have been located which would indicate that Julian Mack was ever an official member of the NAACP (*NCAB*, 32: 73–74; *DAB*; Melvin I. Urofsky, *American Zionism from Herzl to the Holocaust* [New York: Doubleday, 1975], pp. 134–135, 279–294; Walter Laqueur, *A History of Zionism* [New York: Schocken Books, 1976]; Peter Grose, *Israel in the Mind of America* [New York: Random House, 1983], p. 53).

Petition of Marcus Garvey to U.S. District Court

New York 14th day of May, 1923

The Petition of Marcus Garvey to Honorable Julian W. Mack, Respectfully Requesting his Retirement as Trial Judge in the Above Entitled Case.

UNITED STATES DISTRICT COURT, SOUTHERN DISTRICT OF N.Y.

UNITED STATES
AGAINST
MARCUS GARVEY, ELIE GARCIA, GEORGE TOBIAS AND ORLANDO M. THOMPSON, DEFENDANTS.

State of New York,
City and County of New York, ss:

Marcus Garvey, being duly sworn, deposes and says:

That he is one of the defendants in the above entitled case, which is an indictment found by the Grand Jury of the Federal Court in and for the Southern District of New York, charging a violation of Section 215 U.S.C.C., set for trial May 16, 1923, with Honorable Julian W. Mack designated as Trial Judge.

Petitioner verily believes that your Honor is disqualified from sitting in the trial of the above case because of your Honor's membership in and affiliation with the National Association for the Advancement of Colored People, which, through its responsible officials, has openly and viciously attacked not only the work of the petitioner in his several business ventures, but which has attacked him personally, and has only recently, to wit: on or about January 15, 1923, addressed a communication to the Attorney General of the United States concerning petitioner. . . .[1]

It will be noticed that this petition addressed directly to the Attorney General makes specific reference to the charge upon which the defendant is to be brought to trial, and that the bitter feeling against petitioner throughout is so evident that comment is unnecessary.

Petitioner does wish, however, to call attention of your Honor to the name of William Pickens, one of the signers of the petition, who describes himself as field secretary of the N.A.A.C.P., which is one of the most responsible offices. This man was formerly dean of a colored school, and is paid a high salary by the N.A.A.C.P.

Attention is also called to Robert W. Bagnall, another signer of the petitioner [petition], who is a director of branches of the N.A.A.C.P., a responsible position, a high salaried officer, and who, before coming to the N.A.A.C.P., was a clergyman.

Harry H. Pace, another signer of the petition, is also a director of the N.A.A.C.P.[2]

John E. Nail, another signer of the petition, is also a director of the N.A.A.C.P., and brother-in-law of James Weldon Johnson, the executive secretary of the N.A.A.C.P.

"The Crisis," a monthly magazine, the official organ of the N.A.A.C.P., is an open opponent of the petitioner and his work, in which have frequently appeared articles written by W.E.B. Du Bois, editor-in-chief of the "Crisis" and director of research in the N.A.A.C.P., criticising him adversely and condemning his work.

The attention of your Honor is called to an article appearing in the January, 1921, "Crisis," in which W.E.B. Du Bois deals with the Black Star Line, the corporation out of whose business transactions the indictment in part grew, upon which the defendant is to be brought to trial before your Honor, an excerpt from which follows:

> When it comes to Mr. Garvey's industrial and commercial enterprises there is more ground for doubt and misgiving than in the matter of his character. First of all, his enterprises are incorporated in Delaware, where the corporation laws are loose and where no financial statements are required. So far as I can find, and I have searched with care, Mr. Garvey has never published a complete statement of the income and expenditures of the Negro Improvement Association or of the Black Star Line or of any of his enterprises, which really revealed his financial situation. A courteous letter of inquiry sent to him July 22, 1920, asking for such financial data as he was willing for the public to know, remains to this day unacknowledged and unanswered.[3]

In an article appearing in the December, 1920, "Crisis," W.E.B. Du Bois, referring to the petitioner, says: "He has very serious defects of temperament and training: he is dictatorial, domineering, inordinately vain and very suspicious."[4] The N.A.A.C.P. and its officers were not content to attack your petitioner in their official organ, but during the month of July, 1922, and the month of August, 1922, during a month's session of the annual convention of the Universal Negro Improvement Association, of which petitioner is the president and organizer, public meetings, advertised in the press and by the distribution of circulars, were held each Sunday afternoon, at which the said William Pickens and the said Robert W. Bagnall spoke, presided or took prominent parts; and at which the slogan was: "Garvey must go, and he's going."

Your Honor, who is chosen to preside at the said trial of the petitioner, is a member of and contributor to the N.A.A.C.P., aforesaid; a reader of and subscriber to the "Crisis" aforesaid. Petitioner respectfully submits that in his honest belief, your Honor would be unconsciously swayed to the side of the Government against this petitioner in this trial, for, as a reader of the "Crisis," it is fair to assume that your Honor has read the bitter and unfavorable criticisms of the petitioner and his work, the very issues of which will come before your Honor in this trial. Petitioner feels deeply grieved that he should be tried before your Honor as presiding Judge, who has given financial support to the N.A.A.C.P., and thus indirectly assisted them in paying their officers to attack, hold up to ridicule and undertake to destroy this Petitioner and his work; and who, by subscribing to the "Crisis," assisted in the circulation of matter adverse to petitioner and his work; all of which involved the very issues which will be tried in this case.

The said W.E.B. Du Bois, the said William Pickens and the said Robert W. Bagnall are to this very day holding their said positions with the N.A.A.C.P., and the attacks referred to are known to the N.A.A.C.P., and if the N.A.A.C.P. did not approve of the said attacks upon this defendant and his work, by its direction the said W.E.B. Du Bois, the said William Pickens and the said Robert W. Bagnall would have been requested to discontinue these attacks.

In truth, it seems unconscionable to petitioner that a member of the N.A.A.C.P. should have any voice in a trial, either as a judge or a jury, in which petitioner's honor, his liberty are at stake. It is just as unseemly to petitioner for a member of the N.A.A.C.P. to sit as a Trial Judge when petitioner is seeking a fair and impartial trial, as it would be for a member of the Universal Negro Improvement Association or the Black Star Line to sit as a Trial Judge when W.E.B. Du Bois or some member of the N.A.A.C.P. would be tried on a similar offense, in which the life of their work, their honor and liberty were at stake.

In any question in which the facts or the law balanced evenly between the organizations representing petitioner's work, to which your Honor does not belong, lend his influence or assist in any way, and the N.A.A.C.P., petitioner feels that your Honor might unconsciously lean on the other side. Petitioner is forced to this conclusion because it is reasonable to assume that if your Honor did not approve of the work of the N.A.A.C.P.[,] that your Honor's support, influence and affiliation would be discontinued.

The petitioner is of the opinion that when your Honor was designated, if designated, by the Judge making assignment, the said Judge was not fully advised of all the facts and circumstances; and if your Honor were chosen at the instance of the United States Attorney, he was aware at the time of his suggestion, or request, that your Honor sit as Trial Judge in this case of your Honor's affiliation with the N.A.A.C.P.

It might be of interest to your Honor to know that on May 7th, when this case was called for trial, Moorefield Storey, a Boston attorney, and one of the highest officials of the N.A.A.C.P., was seen in the United States Attorney's office in and for this district. May not the petitioner respectfully inquire of your Honor, if it should be that your Honor were charged with a similar offense, would your Honor in these circumstances wish to be brought to trial before a Judge identified, as your Honor is, with the subject matter of this case?

Petitioner knows of no instance in which a single word of opposition has come from a member of the N.A.A.C.P. of its bitter attacks against defendant and his work. All of the members of the N.A.A.C.P. have apparently not only acquiesced in, but approved of the course pursued by it. As your Honor is a member of the N.A.A.C.P., petitioner must assume that your Honor knew of these attacks.

Petitioner further submits that he can find no basis for these attacks, except that the N.A.A.C.P., which seeks to be recognized as the dominant organization of the Negro race, and W.E.B. Du Bois, one of its organizers and moving spirits, who aspires to be recognized as a leader of the Negro race, are envious of the institutions of which the petitioner was organizer, and of the petitioner because he and his institutions are recognized as a worldwide force among negroes, alongside of which the N.A.A.C.P. and W.E.B. Du Bois sink into insignificance.

Petitioner believes that the N.A.A.C.P. in its attacks upon him is actuated by cruel, corrupt and sinister motives.

Petitioner is not seeking to impute to your Honor any intention to do him an injustice, but if an injustice is in point of fact done, the intention is not material[.] Petitioner is not seeking to choose a judge to try his case, but feels that a judge should sit who would not be a supporter to petitioner as a defendant, nor to any institution or influence which would assist the prosecution against him.

Petitioner respectfully submits that in his honest belief your Honor is disqualified, both in law and in propriety from sitting as Trial Judge in the above entitled case. This application was not made 10 days prior to the term because petitioner did not know who was designated as Judge.

Wherefore, petitioner prays that your Honor will retire as the Trial Judge in this case.

MARCUS GARVEY

Marcus Garvey v. *United States*, no. 8317, Ct. App., 2d Cir., 2 February 1925. PD. Notarized by H. Vinton Plummer.

1. Transcript of the letter to the attorney general has been omitted.
2. The letterhead on NAACP stationery in 1923 listed Harry E. Pace as a member of the board of directors (press release, 18 May 1923, DLC, NAACP).
3. W.E.B. Du Bois, "Marcus Garvey," *Crisis* 21, 3 [January 1921]: 112.
4. Du Bois, "Marcus Garvey," *Crisis* 21, 2 [December 1920]: 60.

James Weldon Johnson to Judge Julian W. Mack

70 Fifth Avenue[,] [*New York*] May 17, 1923

My dear Judge Mack:

The morning papers[1] carry an account which states that Mr. C.W. McDougald, counsel for Marcus Garvey, read a long printed document from this Association addressed to the Attorney General of the United States, in which attacks are made against Garvey and his associates.

I wish to say that the National Association for the Advancement of Colored People had nothing whatever to do with the document addressed to Attorney General Daugherty. Yours very truly,

JAMES WELDON JOHNSON
Secretary

DLC, NAACP. TD on NAACP letterhead. On 18 May the NAACP revealed the text of this letter as a press release.

1. The *Baltimore Afro-American* reported that C.W. McDougald's affidavit to disqualify Judge Julian Mack included a letter from the NAACP attacking Garvey and the UNIA. Johnson is referring to the letter to Attorney General Daugherty of 15 January 1923, printed above. Although Johnson disavowed any connection between the letter and the NAACP, a copy of the letter itself was located in the organization's files (*Baltimore Afro-American*, 18 May 1923; DLC, NAACP).

Report of the Opening Address
of Assistant U.S. Attorney Maxwell S. Mattuck

[*New York, 18 May 1923*]

PROSECUTOR TRIES TO MAKE IT APPEAR
THAT HE IS NOT AGAINST
U.N.I.A., BUT GARVEY! GARVEY!

District [*Assistant U.S.*] Attorney Mattuck th[e]n proceeded to outline his case for the government. "Gentlemen of the jury," he said, "as it is already indicated, these defendants stand indicted for a scheme to defraud. These defendants are officers of the Black Star Line and they are charged with misrepresenting by inference and in fact that they were the owners of several steamships which they would operate as passenger ships trading between this country and Africa and this country and the West Indies, and also as excursion boats, and that by reason of the false and fraudulent pretenses they induced large numbers of poor persons to part with their money and invest in the stock." He desired to make it clear from the very outset of the case that the government was not interested in anybody's dreams. It was not interested in anything about the formation of a government for the supposed betterment of anyone. All the government was interested in were the inducements offered by which people were victimized into investing their money. There was no law against a man doing anything for the betterment of his race or his people. There was no law to prevent a man endeavoring to crystallize his ideas or his beliefs into what he considered something for the betterment of his people. But there was a law against a man fooling, against a man scheming and obtaining money by false representations. The government, and the prosecutor in particular, respected the efforts of any people to better their condition, and he wanted it very clearly understood that in so far as the scheme for a social and political betterment of the people was concerned they had no quarrel. The trial was not against a class of persons who were honestly striving to uplift themselves or whose ideas of betterment took the form that was outlined in their plan. All the government was interested in was the methods that were employed in operating the Black Star Line and marketing its stock.

In the course of the case there would be a great deal of talk about other organizations connected with and subsidiaries of the concern other than the Black Star Line. They would hear about the U.N.I.A. and the African Communities' League. That was a corporation that was organized to do business which it was found the U.N.I.A. could not do. They first started out as the New York Local, then the Parent Body, and then they established branches all over the country. There was The Negro World, a newspaper used for propaganda purposes, which was first owned by the New York Local and then by the U.N.I.A.¹ There was also the Liberian Construction Loan and the African Redemption Fund, and a great many other subsidiaries. Funds from these were used and manipulated in various ways that will be told you. But what he wanted to bring home to them was, the Black Star Line was not a membership corporation. It was a business concern, not a social uplift venture, and one purely for the furtherance of the business of the organization. The Black Star Line was a corporation organized in the State of Delaware with a capital stock at the beginning of $500,000, divided into 100,000 shares of the par value of $5 each, which was increased six months later to $10,000,000, divided into 2,000,000 shares of the par value of $5 each. It was with the sale of the stock of that corporation they were interested, and nothing else. The Government w[as] going to prove that that investment of $800,000 additional in the Black Star Line was today represented by nothing. They were not interested in the U.N.I.A. as a corporation, but they would prove that the monies collected for the U.N.I.A. found its way into the treasury of the Black Star Line. They would prove that the monies of all the subsidiary organizations found its way into the treasury of the Black Star Line. So they were not interested in anything else but the people who were made the victims and who were made to believe that the stock of this corporation was and would be worth the price it was being sold and offered for sale.

He did not propose to go into details of the testimony that would be presented. But he proposed to show very briefly what became of the money. He further proposed to show the medium by which the money was collected. First it was through the medium of advertisement in the Negro World and by speeches and articles written by Garvey in the Negro World and supported by circulars and other literature sent through the mails. The[r]e would arise during the course of the trial many terms they may not readily understand. If at any time there was a doubt as to the meaning of anything he would be only too glad to explain it to the jury. The Black Star Line, as he told them, was incorporated in June or July, 1919, in the State of Delaware. The first boat bought by them was the "Yarmouth" and she made two or three trips abroad. The second was the "Shadyside," which had also made two or three trips; then the third boat, the "Kanaw[h]a," which made one trip to the West Indies. Then they bought or contemplated buying the "Phyllis Wheatley," which, they represented, was to take passengers to Africa, but which boat they never had delivery of. The moneys for the purchase of these boats were obtained from the investments of poor people. The Black Star Line today was defunct and was represented by less than nothing, and by that he meant the corporation had more debts against it than it had assets.

He asked the jury to [dismiss] from their minds everything except a purely business consideration. He felt sure there was not one of them who would quarrel with the defendants for trying to help their people bettering their conditions, but the government contended they had not benefited their people but had used the social side of it to "bucket"[2] their investments, which was wrong. Forty thousand people were today worse off for this concern[;] Garvey was the moving spirit of it.

Tobias was the treasurer, Garcia the secretary and Thompson was the vice-president. But they should not forget that Garvey himself was the guiding spirit. The case would be a complicated one, but he would remind them there was a big difference between an honest endeavor for the betterment of a people and victimizing them of their hard earned money. He would put his witnesses before them in groups and he anticipated they would have a difficult job, but he would be ready to explain everything that they could not understand. All they had to do was to ask and he would enlighten them on any point.

The jury were asked not to discuss the case and the court adjourned until 10.30 Monday [*21 May*].

Printed in *NW*, 26 May 1923. Original headlines omitted.

1. The *Negro World* was originally the property of the African Communities League.
2. A reference to the sale of worthless or highly speculative stocks (*The Pocket Dictionary of American Slang*, ed. and comp. Harold Wentworth and Stuart Berg Flexner [New York: Pocket Books, 1969], p. 43).

Speech by Marcus Garvey

[[LIBERTY HALL, New York, May 20, 1923]]

My case started last Friday and will continue from tomorrow. It may last for about five or six weeks. As I said before, it is the biggest case that is to be tried in the United States Court, not only in New York, but all over the country. It is a case that involves not Marcus Garvey but the existence of the Universal Negro Improvement Association. The ideals of the Universal Negro Improvement Association are on trial and those of you who are interested in the Universal Negro Improvement Association will naturally be able to weigh the situation in the next few weeks.

GARVEY IS NOT CONCERNED

Now understand that Marcus Garvey is not concerned a bit about the trial. As far as I am concerned it does not affect me as far as my work goes; that is cut out; my work cannot be destroyed; my work will live through the ages. (Applause.) Those who think that they can destroy Marcus Garvey are making a tremendous mistake if they think that by using all the available human physical forces that they can intimidate and destroy Marcus Garvey. Marcus Garvey, as I have often said, did not organize the Universal Negro Improvement Association without calculating its cost—the cost of ingratitude of those whom we are serving; the cost of uncharitableness on the part of those whom he suffers most for. All that does not concern him; their ingratitude does not concern him one bit; so Garvey will not be disappointed about anything in the trial. Nothing can disappoint me; my work is cut out; I have done it and I am still doing it and it will last forever, and those who think that they are getting even with Garvey are only laying the foundation that will destroy themselves in a short while. Let me say this: that Marcus Garvey is not afraid of hell itself, because Marcus Garvey has one conviction, and that is: until the Negro lays a foundation for his own freedom he will never have it and that there is only one way that it can be laid, and it must be laid through sacrifice, through death, through suffering (applause) and Marcus Garvey is prepared to go the whole length, and as far as he personally is concerned, it does not matter. I am saying to those who think they are getting even with Garvey, when Garvey dies a million other Garveys will rise up, not in America or not in the West Indies, for where the Negro has lived under the white man's civilization you can hardly make any use of him in this generation, but Marcus Garvey is satisfied that he has stirred Africa from corner to corner and Africa will take care of herself. (Applause.) Garvey goes to court like a man. Garvey had no cause to be in court for Garvey; Garvey could be one of the mos[t] successful and prosperous Negroes of the twentieth century. I am not going to court because of Garvey, but because of service to the people. Garvey calculated for that and is not surprised.

So don't be disturbed and don't be afraid about Garvey; Garvey knew the consequences and, like a man, he is going to face it. Marcus Garvey has been the target, believing that they can destroy Garvey they can subsequently destroy the Universal Negro Improvement Association. They may destroy the Universal Negro Improvement Association in America; they may destroy the Universal Negro Improvement Association in the West Indies. If Garvey should die or if Garvey should be imprisoned, let them know it will be only the beginning of the work in Africa. The Negro is in no mood to be tampered with now. The Negro who died on Flanders field—the Negro who died in Mesopotamia, is the same who is willing to do his part towards his race if it means dying in the attempt to put the program over.

So I want the whole world to understand that, like Robert Emmet, Garvey faces the worst; like Roger Casement, Garvey will face the arrows of "hell" for the principles of the Universal Negro Improvement Association. (Applause.) You who skin the teeth of ingratitude do not disappoint me one bit; you cannot harm Marcus Garvey; do your worst and Garvey is not affected, nor is he concerned about you; Garvey is concerned about the principles— the sacred principles for which men have died in the past and for which real men will die in the future and for which 400,000,000 Negroes are prepared to die. (Applause.) We do not go pussyfooting about this program; we do not go camouflaging and compromising and apologizing. The Universal Negro Improvement Association has not started its real work yet; we have only touched the surface of the great work of the Universal Negro Improvement Association, and any few Negroes or white men who think that they can destroy the great principles of a rising race are flattering themselves and making the greatest mistake and blunder of the age. Those who try to endanger and imperil and harass the work of the Universal Negro Improvement Association, they know not what they do for the simple reason they are but piling up sorrows for themselves and for their children, because long after some of us are passed away the principles of the Universal Negro Improvement Association shall live and live on forever. What are you going to do? Can you kill the souls of men? You can destroy the physical body but you cannot destroy the souls of men; you cannot even destroy the mind of man. Now how can they destroy Garvey when they cannot close Garvey's mouth? Garvey has already spoken to the world and is still speaking to the world and will speak to the world until he reaches the last moment in life, and even then Garvey will just have started to speak to the world. What Garvey cannot do in prison we are going to do otherwise, and as I said, we are not counting so much on the western world because the Negro in contact with the white man's civilization is practically useless and helpless; he has imbibed the poison of the white man's civilization and he is practically half dead. If my work had not gone beyond the borders of the western world, then I would have been disturbed, but, thank God, all Africa is awake—East Africa, North Africa, South Africa, West Africa—thank God, they have all caught the principles and propaganda of the Universal Negro Improvement Association; therefore our work of five years has not been in vain.

The National Association for the Advancement of Colored People, the cheap Negro politicians in Harlem and the brainy white men who have sense enough to know what they want and how to get it, who have combined to fight the Universal Negro Improvement Association, are going to be disappointed, because they cannot harm Garvey. They may waste all their money trying to put me in jail, and hang me and all of that, but you cannot harm Garvey; what you think will harm Garvey has not hurt him in the least, because Garvey knows what he is doing; Garvey knows that the Negro will have to suffer and fight before he gets what he wants. All we want is for the members of the U.N.I.A. to realize and understand what they are up against.

Marcus Garvey is afraid of nobody nor anything at all in the world except God. My father was fearful[;] my grandfather was fearful, but I did not inherit their fear, because we are living in a new age and in a new world. So that the case is on, and I am not going to talk about it because it may not be proper to discuss it, because I do not want to be misunderstood. Marcus Garvey calculated for all the consequences in a great movement like this; he calculated for the traitors within and the traitors without, so that when they appear he is not in any way surprised.

Marcus Garvey is prepared for the ingratitude of the people whom he serves. Marcus Garvey is prepared for everything, because Garvey was in his sober senses when he founded and started the Universal Negro Improvement Association. I suppose the Kaiser was in his sober senses when he started the war in 1914; therefore, he was satisfied to take what he got. Garvey started to seek the emancipation of 400,000,000 Negroes and the redemption of their country, and anything he gets in the way he is prepared for it, but it is going to react on somebody someday, if not today at some other time, but remember this, that the principles of the Universal Negro Improvement Association will live forever.

The history of the movement is now being written. Do you know what history means? History is the guide post of a race; is the inspiration for succeeding generations either to go forward or to stand still; either to revenge or be revenged. Marcus Garvey when he dies will not die alone; when Marcus Garvey dies for the principles of the Universal Negro Improvement Association, mark well. Before Garvey goes[,] Garvey shall have laid a foundation for other Garveys who will be more deadly in their sting than the one who passes off.

So the enemies and traitors are crazy if they think they can damage the Universal Negro Improvement Association. I am speaking to you as the man who founded and organized the Universal Negro Improvement Association, as the man who sacrificed and suffered to bring into existence the Universal Negro Improvement Association. I had a motive and a purpose; it was not the money, because I could have gotten that for myself and be satisfied; it was not position because I could have got that for myself. What is it? It was the crying voice from the grave that said "Garvey, we have suffered for 250 years for your day and for your time; we expect something of you at this hour." Let the world understand that Garvey hears the wail and the cry of millions of our forebears crying from the grave, for what? I will not tell you; probably another Garvey will tell you. So let those who fight the U.N.I.A. beware for some day they will have to reckon with 400,000,000 Negroes, for Garvey is but laying the cornerstone for the incoming of the New Africa—the new Ethiopia that shall stretch forth her hands unto God; the new day when princes shall come out of Egypt.

So you who understand the work of the Universal Negro Improvement Association be not disturbed; keep your peace; keep your minds in good order because this is only the starting point of the great battle that is to be waged for African redemption, and understand it is not Marcus Garvey on trial; it is not a question of money on trial; it is the principles of a race fighting for liberty on trial. When you attack Garvey you do not awaken anything in Garvey, but when you attack the principles of the Universal Negro Improvement Association Garvey goes to war and shall remain on the firing line until he passes away or until victory perches on the banner.

So you will understand that for the first time probably in the history of the Negro you will see a real Negro fight, a real battle for racial liberation. (Applause.) . . .

Printed in *NW*, 26 May 1923. Original headlines omitted.

Editorial Letter by Marcus Garvey

[[New York, May 22, 1923]]

Fellow Men of the Negro Race, Greeting:

There comes a time in the history of every race and nation when the supreme effort must be made to save that race or nation from its enemies, those within as well as those without. Such a time has come in the history of the Universal Negro Improvement Association in the fight for Negro liberty and African redemption.

ENEMIES AND THEIR PLANS

For over three years the enemies of Negro progress laid their plans by which they hoped they would ultimately destroy the new effort on the part of Negroes for the realization of a freer, economic, social, educational and political life.

THE FOUNDATION OF THE OPPOSITION

When the Universal Negro Improvement Association aggressively started its program in America five years ago, following up its activities in the West Indies four years prior, the enemies of Negro freedom within the race, as well as without the race, started to lay the foundation of an opposition which they calculated they could have used for successfully destroying the great program of this organization and dash back forever the hopes of a rising race. They calculated that out of the activities of this great organization they would have been able to so undermine our efforts as to make them appear as failures, and thereby strike back at the movement with what they would think to be irrefutable arguments of the organization's unworthiness. They tried many schemes, among them the laying of plans by which the Black Star Line Steamship Corporation would fail and other business activities connected with the Universal Negro Improvement Association, so that in their argument to the people who make up the Negro race, they would say: "We told you so; we told you so. It could not be done!" The enemies have counted without their hosts. Now is the time for the four hundred million Negroes of the world to stand together firmer than ever before, because, in truth, "the enemies shall not pass."

THE BLACK STAR LINE

The so-called business failure of the Black Star Line was but a trap set to destroy the Universal Negro Improvement Association. But how silly and simple these small-minded enemies are. Do they believe that they can destroy a spiritual movement in this kind of way? Can they believe in themselves that the Universal Negro Improvement Associat[i]on can die because of the failure of any business enterprise? The idea of the Black Star Line has not failed, can never fail, because four hundred million Negroes are determined that out of Africa shall spring one of the greatest governments of the world, and with the rise of a mighty nation and a great people will come all that contributes to human effort and human endeavors. There shall be a greater Black Star Line; there shall be a Black Star Line that shall belt the world with the industries of black men. So let us think not of failure in the sense that the enemies have laid the trap for it to be.

THE CALIBRE OF THE ENEMIES

Smart, brilliant, great and intellectual though you enemies believe yourselves to be, but, gentlemen, you are yet school boys in your conceptions. Real men laugh at opposition; real men smile when enemies appear. If you believe you can intimidate and destroy the courage of a race through the destruction of a business enterprise, or by the persecution of an individual, you are crazy, you are foolish, you are mistaken. It might have been so easy with the old Negro, but not with the new. Behind the Universal Negro Improvement Association stands a spiritual force that can never die; no power in the world can destroy it. It is the spirit of liberty, it is the spirit that faces death and smiles. We welcome the opposition of the world, because we are determined to see the battle through. Africa's battle-cry is not yet heard.

AFRICA'S DAY

What of the day, gentlemen, when Africa shall indeed unfurl her banner of liberty? The persecutions and the sufferings of the past shall be but our breast plates and shields and armour to fight until victory perches upon the banner of Negro liberty. We who are sober in our minds, and our vision, and our outlook, laugh at these children who believe that they can tear to pieces and destroy the principles underlying the Universal Negro Improvement Association as embodied in a Black Star Line, or any other business operation thereto connected.

We have not yet started the battle for liberty, gentlemen; we have just been talking about it. It is a fight that will continue down the ages; it is a fight that is confined to no one generation, but succeeding generations shall fight, the more especially when we write in the present for them a history of injustice and persecution, a history of sufferings as we now undergo them.

GARVEY AND PERSECUTION

What does Marcus Garvey care about persecution by the enemies? If the enemy could only know that Marcus Garvey is but a John the Baptist in the wilderness, that a greater and more dangerous Marcus Garvey is yet to appear, the Garvey with whom you will have to reckon for the injustice of the present generation.

THE SWORDS OF THE ENEMY

Gentlemen, you may as well sharpen your swords, because it is going to be a bloody conflict. History has been the inspiration of generations past, and what we record shall be the inspiration of black generations yet unborn. Marcus Garvey of the present shall so write a history that Negroes one hundred, two hundred years from now shall not forget, shall not forget, shall not forget.

Gentlemen, remember you are dealing with a serious [*man who is?*] living in a serious time. Marcus Garvey does not give a snap [of his fingers] for anything human but justice, and that which is based upon righteousness.

With all your trickery, with all your plots, you are just like "chaff before the wind,"[1] which shall in a while be blown to atoms. Previous generations have flirted with and fooled with Negroes' liberty. Today it is going to be a battle to the finish. We have no apologies, we have no compromises, we are not begging the issue; we are just determined we are going to live free men or die free men. So let the whole world of Negroes realize that the hour is approaching when black men shall be called upon to take their stand, to play their part, and play it well.

THE HOUR HAS COME

Let the members of the Universal Negro Improvement Association all over the world realize that now is the hour for the manifestation of loyalty and devotion to the cause that we love so well. The enemies think that they are at our door; some of us feel that they are there; now let us get ready to dislodge them. The enemies are not so much from without as from within the race. In the final reckoning, when Ethiopia shall have written her name on the new scroll of empires, when Princes shall come out of Egypt and Africa take[s] her stand in a new civilization, we will then reckon with the generations of vipers whose names and their children's shall go down to undying posterity.

A BATTLE OF THE CENTURIES

Fight on, enemies, fight on; it is a battle of the centuries. It is not of Garvey today; it shall be of all times. How long, how long, how long! Answer that for yourselves.

Some men believe themselves smart, some believe themselves wonderfully keen. But, ah! there is no sage who hath not a master! You who think that your small schemes and your secret propaganda to destroy the Universal Negro Improvement Association through its own members can be accomplished make a big mistake. We see that your ambition is to get Garvey out of the way and everything will follow. You said: "We will get Garvey out of the way if we destroy the Black Star Line." Well, Garvey did not go then. "We will get Garvey another way; we will undermine all his business ent[e]rprises, and try to make them failures and then tell the people, 'Oh! you see what has happened,' then Garvey is bound to go after that." Well, Garvey did not go. "Well," they said, "what is the matter? Let us attack him in person, then let our slogan be, 'Garvey must go.[']" But Garvey did not go. "Well, we will try to get him otherwise, because this Universal Negro Improvement Association idea must be throttled." Ah, but Garvey is here, and both of them shall go down the ages. If Garvey dies, Garvey lives; if the Universal Negro Improvement Association is embarrassed, a greater Universal Negro Improvement Association arises. Gentlemen, what are you going to do? You must first destroy the souls of black men before you can destroy Garvey, and destroy the Universal Negro Improvement Association, and you will have a h—— of a time doing that. Garvey cannot die, the Universal Negro Improvement Association cannot die, because, gentlemen, the thing is not only physical, the individual is not only physical, but there is a spiritual motive, there is a spiritual force back of it that cannot be destroyed.

GREAT IDEALS

Great ideals, great principles, great truths never die. Individuals die, the Christ died, Mohammed died; but you did not destroy Christianity or Mohammedanism. Garvey in the flesh can die, and he is ready to die at any time; but, gentlemen, the greater force will live on; one, I repeat, that will [g]o down the ages to tell the story, tell the story of the traitors, tell the story of those who stood in the way of a glorious redemption for Negroes; tell the story of those who tried to block the passage of the rising Ethiopia, of the new Africa. What shall be your defense before the bar of African redemption, gentlemen? Will you plead innocence; will you plead not knowing better? Ah, ignorance will be no excuse. Our history of the traitors shall go down the ages and shall be written in the black book of time, and even the Angel of Eternity shall lay it before the judgment seat of God.

THE TRAITORS AT THEIR WORST

The traitors are working hard, the enemies are doing their worst; but we smile in their faces. There are combinations of forces working against the Universal Negro Improvement Association, against which it is written by these enemies, "That association and Garvey must be destroyed." They have been using men once placed in positions of trust in this association to help destroy the movement. These traitors we have had to dismiss. Today they, with the rest of our enemies, are determined to tear down the structure that we have built. They have all entered into a conspiracy to sue and embarrass the Universal Negro Improvement Associat[i]on so as to make it . . . [*several words mutilated*] the fools, they know no better. Survive we must, [g]o forward we must so long as there is a God, so long as there is a world, so long as there is a human race. But, members, I repeat, these traitors are endeavoring to embarrass us before the courts, suing us for salaries, trying to force judgments upon us at a time when we are supposed to be fighting the common enemy, so that they could glory in the downfall of the movement. They also are mistaken.

Members and friends, let us pay these traitors, let us pay them off in their bits of silver. Therefore, I appeal to each and every member of the Universal Negro Improvement Association to do this bit of service now; send to the Parent Body whatsoever financial support you can give to help us pay off these traitors who are endeavoring to sue us. Let us dispose of them that way, and then let us continue the fight against the common enemy. These "bits of silver" shall bring them tears in the years to come. Let us hand them over now, the thirty pieces of silver. That which Judas received did not help him very long; he was willing to return it, but nobody would receive it. These enemies, these traitors, may yet rue the day when they turned their backs upon the Universal Negro Improvement Association, the organization that made them. Did we not make them?

MAKING MEN

We picked some of them up from the lowest and poorest of the race and made gentlemen of them, because we believed that by their sufferings they would be able to appreciate the service to which they were called. It takes a slave to appreciate liberty; it takes a man who suffers to understand freedom, and that was why we thought that in taking these men and making them gentlemen that we were rendering a service to the race. We made a terrible mistake. It is true all of us make mistakes. Some of these Negroes who never earned more than $25.00 per week[,] because of their intelligence we thought we could give them a chance to make good and make something of themselves. We gave them grand and noble positions. We tried to make statesmen of them, but they fell by the wayside. Yes, you know that, and you will see them drift back to the condition they were in before they came into the Universal Negro Improvement Association. Our generation and posterity may yet smile in their faces, but let us pay them. And you can do it now by sending your contribution to the "Bit of Silver Fund" to the Secretary-General, Universal Negro Improvement Association, 56 West 135th Street, New York City, U.S.A. With very best wishes, I have the honor to be, Your obedient servant,

MARCUS GARVEY
President-General
Universal Negro Improvement Association

Printed in *NW*, 26 May 1923. Original headlines omitted.

1. A reference to Ps. 35:5.

Report by Special Agent Mortimer J. Davis

New York, N.Y. 5/25/23

Since the trial of the defendants in this case opened before Judge Mack on the 21st instant, there have been a number of anonymous threats made against the various government witnesses. Agent Amos, Special Employee Battle and the writer, upon request of Assistant U.S. Attorney Mattuck, have been cooperating with the U.S. Marshals in endeavoring to run down some of these threats and afford protection to the persons under subpoena.

On the 23rd instant, after Capt. Joshua Cockburn had testified for the government he reported to agents that a colored man had approached him in the Federal Building and threatened to kill him for testifying against Marcus Garvey. We endeavored to have Cockburn identify this man but he had apparently left the Federal Building immediately. On this same date, Richard E. Warner, who testified on the 21st instant and who is a Special Agent attached to the Prohibition Department in New York, advised agents that he was informed by his wife, that on the night of May 22nd, during Warner's absence from home, two Garveyites had been hanging around his house and had stated to someone on the street that they were there to "get" Warner.

At the noon recess on the 24th instant, the writer was told by Hugh Mulzac, who is here under government subpoena from Baltimore, Md. that he and S[y]dney de Bourg, also a government witness, had been threatened. Mulzac stated he could identify the man who made the threat. Agent immediately secured the assistance of Deputy U.S. Marshal Hyer and Special Agent James E. Amos. Mulzac, without hesitation pointed out one, Linous Charles, whom the deputy marshal placed under arrest. When Judge Mack returned to court, he excused the jury and heard the charges against Charles. Mulzac and de Bourg stated that he had threatened that if they testified against Garvey he would "get them" if it took the rest of his life. Charles denied having made the threat. He admitted that he is a member of the U.N.I.A., also a member of the African Legion and a regular attendant at the Garvey meetings in Liberty Hall. He resides at 209 West 63rd Street, New York; is married; has second papers; born in the West Indies; states he served in the American Army; was wounded five times and gassed; is employed as a porter by the Interboro Rapid Transit Company.

Judge Mack found Charles guilty of criminal contempt and stated that if it were not for his war service record he would give him a very severe penalty. He then sentenced him to six months in prison but upon Charles' plea that his wife was in a delicate condition, the sentence was reduced to two months. Judge Mack set bail at $10,000 and directed that Charles be held for the Grand Jury on charges of intimidating government witnesses and obstructing justice.

There have been many rumors that Garvey sympathizers have been carrying weapons while attending the trial and it is the intention of Assistant U.S. Attorney Mattuck to have the various known Garvey sympathizers searched before being permitted to attend the trial.

MORTIMER J. DAVIS

DJ-FBI, file 61. TD.

Government Exhibit from Marcus Garvey's Trial

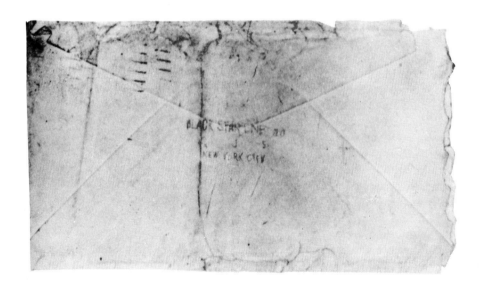

(*Source*: Marcus Garvey v. U.S.A., no. 8317, Ct. App., 2d Cir., 2 February 1925, Government Exhibit 112.)

Anonymous Letter to William J. Burns

[*New York?*] Friday, June 1, 1923

Gentleman—

Just a word to lead you along in regards to the deathog the Smith who committed suicide in your house,¹ for it is done mysteriously by an oniptoetent power of Garvey people in New York.

You must remember two years ago there were some people droppeddead in Washington when his case was on before.

He haz people working mystic power in Trinidad who working on the people's spirit so that you people cannot condemn him and sendhim away to Atalnta prison, just where he does belong.

The "BIG BLACK BULL" has cheated so many poor working ignorant class colored people out of their hard toil earnings, and some of themhad life time savings aged people at there. I mean striking aroudn sixty and seventy years of age. It is a shame the way hse has robbed them and told them lies, had them fooled up about Universal Improvement Association helpoing people when they got sick, and was going to give them sick benefit. They never has received one penny, but waer driven out of his office just like dogs.

It has been already said that he is going to win out and that he will never see atlanta prison, already so if you let him win out he will always have the Whip Hand of you. HE needs to go there and work out the amount of The $3,500,000 that he stoled from the people yat the rate of a dollar a day with the ball and chain on his foot. He is very selfish, will not hire any American Colored people in his place, but want the American people help him and in the American People's country. HE used to say that the people were nothing and that he was all. But when the cold winter came in 1922 and 21, he bought house in the Harelm ~~purt~~ part of New York in 135th Street put eh American C olored people out on the side walk with their familes in the bitter cold and put in his Westindian people. . Do you call that right? That man is nothing but a Brute.

He better not go back to Jamaica WAESTIndies from whence he came because his/d head will be taken off and he know s that too. He has not taken out any Citizen ship papaers out in this country, heis a British Subject, that is why he does as he likes, and he knowws that you cannot do anything with him. YOU make him takeout his Citizen ship papers and you will see what he can do then. Y/o/u will have the advantage of hiM.

Montreal Canada ought to me made given the money back, from the bank in which he put it in. That is a British country, and not United United Stestes. YOU all have him so hold him do not let him get away from you. He he has much brags going. You want to do him just like Joab [B]anton² is Doing the WALL STREET AND FULLER SCANDAL.³ Keep him.

But he has wichers working on you all trying to influence you all not [*to*] do anything . he is a slick Magician if you /~~en~~/ do anything with hinyou are a good won. YOUknow the NEgro is a liear and thief just put him away like you doo all the rest of them. he has hulled the black . . . [*words mutilated*] out, strutted far and wide all over this country, him and . . . [*line mutilated*].

He is a black . . . [*word mutilated*] Street, folloing the Negroes. Put him away in a good strong jail. [N]o TOmbes in New YOrk nor Sing Sing, But in Atalant Prison.

The sooner he gets there the better. H/i/m and his conventions are all hot air.

I would also like to acquaint you that in a place called Hackensack New Jersey, much Whiskey and Stills are in full blast, and also tru LITTLE Ferry New Jersey. Send your man over.

The Italaians and other Foreign nations are reaping a harvest.

I happend to read the ltem in the LAst evening's New York Journal concerning the Death of your freidn Mr Smith is what caused me to write you.

I AM READER OF THE NEW YORK JOURNAL.

DJ-FBI, file 61-50. TL, recipient's copy.

1. Jesse W. Smith committed suicide in the hotel suite of his close companion Attorney General Daugherty, not that of William J. Burns, who was summoned to the scene from his suite directly below. Smith, a personal friend of President Harding, had been active in the Ohio Republican party and had strong ties to organized crime. His death came during a period when charges of corruption were being leveled at members of Harding's cabinet and their associates (James N. Giglio, *H.M. Daugherty and the Politics of Expediency* [Kent, Ohio: Kent State University Press, 1978]; *NYT*, 31 May 1923).
2. Joab H. Banton (1869–1949), noted trial lawyer, was district attorney for New York County from 1922 to 1929. Banton vigorously prosecuted graft, commercial fraud, and "bucketing," a crime prevalent during Wall Street's boom. In 1929 he returned to private practice (*NYT*, 21 July 1949).
3. E.M. Fuller and Co., a brokerage firm partnered by Edward M. Fuller and W. Frank McGee, was placed in receivership in April 1923, having failed, with losses of over $5 million. A year earlier the company had been indicted by a grand jury on thirteen counts of "bucketing." Although a jury subsequently failed to convict Fuller, on 13 June the two partners agreed to plead guilty on one count and as a result received the minimum sentence of fifteen months. Since they were entitled to 120 days' commutation for good behavior, the sentence amounted to less than one year in jail (*NYT*, 19 April, 14 June, and 20 June 1923).

Editorial Letter by Marcus Garvey

[[NEW YORK, June 11, 1923]]

EXPECTED CONVENTION OF NEGRO PEOPLES
OF THE WORLD IN AFRICA 1924

FELLOW MEN OF THE NEGRO RACE, Greeting:

I write to inform you that the Universal Negro Improvement Association in another couple of weeks will prepare its program for its African Convention of 1924. There will be no international convention of the association in New York this year, but each and every Division of the association throughout the world will hold local conventions during the month of August, and each and every Division and all members of the association, as well as members of the race, will prepare to work toward the effort of making the 1924 convention in Africa the success that it should be.

PLANS FOR 1924

We hope to get our industrial plans under way in 1924 for the rehabilitation of our homeland. A great deal has been said about the failure of the Black Star Line, but now more than ever the Universal Negro Improvement Association will make its effort to have ready for the convention of 1924 the shipping facilities that will enable the delegates and emigrants who desire to go to Africa to be conveyed thereto without let or hindrance. . . .

REASSEMBLING OF AFRICA

Let us, therefore, look toward the reassembling of Africa's sons and daughters in our next international convention not in America, not in the West Indies, but in Africa. That shall be in August, 1924. All Divisions and Chapters of the Universal Negro Improvement Association will, therefore, be instructed to arrange for local divisional conventions for August, 1923, as there will be no international convention in New York for this year. All literature, statements and information needed for the guidance of local conventions from the Parent Body can be obtained by writing to the Secretary-General of the Universal Negro Improvement Association, 56 West 135th Street, New York City, N.Y. All local Divisions are entitled to copies of the kinds of reports that would have been made by the executive officers at headquarters if the convention were held for the present year. Same can be had on request at the office of the Secretary-General after the first of July. . . .

MARCUS GARVEY
President-General
Universal Negro Improvement Association

Printed in *NW*, 16 June 1923. Original headlines abbreviated.

Report of Angus Fletcher, British Library of Information, on His American Tour

[*n.p.*] June 12, 1923

. . . At Tuskegee, Alabama, I visited the Institute established by Booker T. Washington, now the largest and most important negro educational institution in the United States. I was received by the President, Dr. Moton, and was given every opportunity to meet the staff and many of the students. I spent some time in the Library and found the Librarian[1] most anxious to secure from us all documents relating to our Colonial administration and to educational methods. I heard here, as elsewhere, that anti-British literature, emanating from Irish sources, was constantly being poured into their library. The opportunity to secure authentic information from official sources was welcomed accordingly. At both Hampton and Tuskegee I learned that Marcus Garvey's influence is [s]till considerable among the negroes in spite of the frequent exposures of his rascality (one of which is now proceeding in New York). Marcus Garvey, it will be recalled, is the apostle of the "Africa for the Africans" movement. He publishes a paper in which he attacks Great Britain with a malignity reminiscent of the "Irish World."[2] . . .

ANGUS FLETCHER[3]

PRO, FO 395/389. TD.

1. A reference to Monroe N. Work (1866–1945), director of records and research at Tuskegee Institute from 1908 to 1938. Ordained as an AME minister, Work graduated from Chicago Theological Seminary in 1898, but instead of joining the ministry, he entered the University of Chicago, where he received an M.A. degree in sociology in 1903. Until 1907, Work taught at Georgia State Industrial College in Savannah, where he began research on African and Afro-American life. In 1908, at the request of Booker T. Washington, he joined Tuskegee, where he was to serve for thirty years. A prolific writer, Work founded and edited nine editions of the *Negro Year Book*, a compendium of information about black Americans. He instituted and directed the Tuskegee lynching records which were used by government officials, the press, and educators. Work also edited and compiled *A Bibliography of the Negro in Africa and America* (1928) and more than fifty-nine other articles on all aspects of black life in the United States (*WWCA*; *DANB*; Jessie P. Guzman, "Monroe Nathan Work and His Contributions," *JNH* 34, no. 4 [October 1949]: 428–461; Linda O. McMurray, *Recorder of the Black Experience: A Biography of Monroe Nathan Work* [Baton Rouge: Louisiana State University Press, 1984]).

2. Founded in 1870 in New York City by the Irish-American propagandist and anglophobe Patrick Ford (1837–1913), the *Irish World* was, along with the *Gaelic American*, for nearly fifty years the source from which a majority of Irish-Americans took their political lead. The newspaper's title was expanded in 1878 to become the *Irish World and American Industrial Liberator*, a name probably influenced by the circumstance of Ford's having learned printing in William Lloyd Garrison's *Liberator* office in Boston. The paper continued under this name until 1928, when it reverted to its original, shorter title.

The Irish leader Michael Davitt, who for a time served as a writer for the *Irish World*, expressed the widely shared view that the paper was "the most powerful support on the American continent of the struggle in Ireland" (Henry Boylan, *A Dictionary of Irish Biography* [Dublin: Gill and Macmillan, 1978], p. 114). The success of the *Irish World* as the major fundraising vehicle in America for successive Irish movements, beginning in the 1880s with the Irish Land League, is demonstrated by its having raised an estimated half a million dollars for an assortment of such organizations.

When Patrick Ford died in Brooklyn on 23 September 1913, his death received widespread publicity in Britain, to which Marcus Garvey, then residing in London, would have been exposed. At Patrick Ford's death, the editorship of the *Irish World* passed to his son, Robert Ford, who continued his father's tradition of active propaganda on behalf of the Irish national cause. (After Garvey came to America, he invited Robert Ford to a UNIA mass meeting in New York in 1918, but Ford was unable to attend [*Garvey Papers* 1: 287]. At the outbreak of the First World War, the paper broke with the Irish Nationalist party in Ireland and with its leader, John Redmond, when Redmond threw his support behind Britain and acquiesced in the suspension of Irish home rule legislation for the duration of the conflict. One result of the withdrawal of the newspaper's support was the immediate collapse of the hitherto-successful United Irish League (UIL) of America. At the time of its founding in America in 1900–1901 by John Redmond, the most powerful voice of the UIL was the *Irish World*, the elder Ford having now publicly rejected his previous advocacy of violence and the revolutionary Clan na Gael.

During the war, the *Irish World* became the chief mouthpiece in America for the Irish nationalist organization Sinn Féin. The paper was eventually banned from the U.S. mails and denied second-class mailing privileges because of its strident attacks on America's ally Britain, and for its openly pro-German stance; in this stance it took with it the rest of the Irish press. During the Russo-Japanese War of 1904–1905, the *Irish World* had similarly sided with Russia against Japan, since Japan was a British ally. (Alan J. Ward, *Ireland and Anglo-American Relations, 1899–1921* [Toronto: University of Toronto Press, 1969]; Dennis R. Gwynn, *The Life of John Redmond* [London: Harrap, 1932], pp. 417–418; *A Dictionary of Irish Biography* [Dublin: Gill and Macmillan, 1978]; *Times* [London], 25 September 1913).

3. Sir Angus Somerville Fletcher (1882?–1960), South African-born British government official, served in Africa and France during World War I. He first came to the United States in 1918 with the British War Mission, and after serving on the National Industrial Conference Board from 1919 to 1922, he joined the British Library of Information in New York. In 1928 he was appointed director of the library, a position he held until 1941. He later served as chairman of the United Nations Headquarters Commission (*NYT*, 8 August 1960; *Times* [London], 9 August 1960).

Report of Closing Address to the Jury by Henry Lincoln Johnson

[*New York, ca. 14 June 1923*]

MR. JOHNSON'S ADDRESS ON BEHALF OF GARCIA

Opening his address to the jury, Mr. Johnson said he felt mighty good at that hour. He had never felt better in his life. After four weeks of patience and devotion to the spirit of American laws and institutions, they had arrived at the point where an American jury, like Siam or Ancient Troy, was called upon to adjudicate without discrimination, for in an American court[,] citizen and alien should be treated alike. He did not want to test their patience further. This was a case all mixed up and tangled up. But it might as well be admitted at the outset Mr. Garcia had nothing to do with it.

FOR THE WANT OF A—

Plunging into the negotiations for the purchase of the Phyllis Wheatley, Mr. Johnson said: "Everybody agrees that if the Phyllis Wheatley had materialized, you would never have had this case. If the Phyllis Wheatley ever had materialized nobody would have been here. There never would have been a complaint. It has been a storm center about which all agitation has circled and still circles, as you have heard from the testimony of Mr. Garvey. Something like this must have been in the mind of the man who wrote that nursery pleasantry: 'For the want of a nail a shoe was lost, for the want of a shoe a foot was lost, for the want of a foot a horse was lost, for the want of a horse a rider was lost, for the want of a rider a battle was lost—all for the want of a horseshoe nail.'[1] (Laughter.) And the Black Star Line owed its ills to the want of a Phyllis Wheatley. But for the loss of the Phyllis Wheatley Negroes would have been now captains of the sea. There would certainly have been no trouble between Cockburn and Garvey. They would have been in faraway Africa enjoying the tropical breezes." (Laughter.) . . .

HAD NOTHING TO DO WITH IT

Continuing, Mr. Johnson said: "To sum up the whole of the Phyllis Wheatley business, Garvey had nothing to do with it. That is admitted all around. He was trying to get money to send back over here. And he got five or six thousand dollars, if the Court pleases. It was sorely needed. Garcia and the rest of them were here and they knew that a hard taskmaster was in the West Indies and he would return. And when they heard he was on his way they would say one to the other, 'You better have ships.' And they decided to tell him nothing about it but to make a great effort on their own. I can see the colored corporation saying, 'We are in trouble.' What is the matter? The [S.S.] Tennyson is on the discard and our hard taskmaster is coming! Get another ship. They called an executive council together and in six days $21,000 was raised.[2] Now, gentlemen, that is some kind of response on the part of a poor people—a people, gentlemen, whose past is pitiful to contemplate, but whose sun is rising, not the setting sun, whose day for everlasting memory among men is yet to come, but has not come. And why call it Phyllis Wheatley? Would you not call a daughter of yours Elizabeth Browning?[3] You would, for she is the poet laureate of your womanhood. And so Phyllis Wheatley stands like the bright morning star, beckoning to us from the hilltops and proclaiming the moment of our opportunity. That is why we call this ship Phyllis Wheatley. She stands to us like Elizabeth Browning does to you. And so we would name our ships Toussaint L'Ouverture and Booker Washington. Toussaint L'Ouverture, who put under his feet the proud army of Bonaparte, the best on earth, for which the black island, gentlemen, lives in our hearts, and his memory is cherished in our souls."

THE SHADYSIDE

Mr. Johnson paused, took up a copy of the indictment, paid a swift compliment to the prosecutor for his shrewdness and the ability with which he had sought to bolster up the indictment, then in satiric vein bade the jury understand that everything named in the indictment, every one of the troubles of the Black Star Line had been deliberately planned by the defendants. "The Sunnyside," no, the "Shadyside sank," he instanced. "We planned it. We planned that it sink. That ships were going to be broken down, that cylinders would blow off; we planned it. That is a fair interpretation of this case. We planned everything. That is right in keeping with the indictment. Gentlemen, it is hard to answer. That each one of these defendants, all of them married, every one of them, entered into an original plot, and planned and devised a scheme to defraud by the use of the mails, and pursued all of these propositions. That is the claim of this indictment. Any man that ever got mixed up in a conspiracy charge knows it is the worst charge. The government has unlimited latitude."

What Did He Get?

"And when," he continued, "did Elie Garcia have anything to do with this? The only reason why I produced those checks of Elie Garcia was for the sake of frankness. It is mightly seldom that a man at a time like this can give an account of stewardship. But Elie Garcia was able to do that. And whatever salary he drew he earned it. He was worth more than anybody in that corporation. He was the most intelligent. And how much did he get? It has been proven by the books that he got $25 for five weeks, and that is every dollar of Black Star Line that ever went into Elie Garcia's hands.[4] And it was not until October 11, 1920, that Garcia succeeded [C.B.] Curley as secretary. What happened before that? The Shadyside—bought, rammed and sunk. The Kanawha—bought, mortgaged, repaired, and in for a last repair, all before we got there. The Yarmouth—bought, yes bought, got a bill of sale and if the Court pleases, and I believe the jury will see as a matter of law, given a bill of title." Mr. Johnson then reviewed the transactions leading up to the purchase of the Yarmouth, submitting that the boat clearly belonged to the Black Star Line.

Cockb[u]rn, Lord of the Seas

Returning to Mr. Garcia's advent as an officer of the corporation, he said: "Before Garcia was ever born, take it that way, all these things happened. Shadyside come and gone. Garcia is not born yet. And the Yarmouth. Captain Cockb[u]rn, lord of the seas. Beautiful sea captain, the man that goes and sees a ship is old, a rotten vessel, and then comes and shamelessly swears to you under oath that the more the ship brings the more commission he gets.[5] Now, Dr. Jekyll and Mr. Hyde, a modern edition, with apologies to both and to Mr. Charles Dickens especially.[6] Nobody in the world could believe Cockb[u]rn in anything he said bearing on this case. The charge was that we proposed to go and buy worthless ships and pay fabulous sums with an arrangement that we get a comeback. But nothing was got from the Shadyside, unless [Thaddeus S.] Smith perjured himself. And it is the duty of this jury to reconcile the testimony without imputing perjury to anyone. Now Garcia was not born when they flashed the famous signal, 'We are sinking, we are drinking[,]'[7] and possibly both. Garcia is not born yet. Not at all."

Watkis True to His Trade

Asking the jury to bear with him while he digressed a moment, Mr. Johnson said if he had been given five days for each time he had committed contempt of court during the trial, he would be serving fifty years in jail. But they must forget that. They promise to keep on the mail line when they were empanelled. But who contemplated [Harry R.] Watkis, unmoved; Watkis the man who was a notary public by profession. Never in his life had he met a man whose sole occupation was a notary public, and nobody but a continuous law student could do so. Watkis had just a bad disposition. He was so full of love for Marcus Garvey that some of it overflowed on Garcia. But Garcia had not arrived yet. The only time he really arrived was with the Phyllis Wheatley. He was present on the 19th of December, 1920, when Mr. Morse was at the office and went over the contract for repairing the Kanawha. And that contract started in November.

WHERE IS SILVERSTON?

"There is one thing I do not understand," Mr. Johnson suddenly broke forth. "Why is not Silverston here? Why is not Smith-Green here? Why is not Powell here? Why, most of all, is not the good Dr. Silverston here? Explain Caesar with Caesar left out. The absence of Dr. Silverston is awful, awful. And still it seems to touch the tender sensibilities of even my good friend the bright, brilliant, shrewd, resourceful, able, distinguished District Attorney, for every time I mentioned Dr. Silverston's name he sang a song to me: 'Take him up tenderly, lift him with care, Silverston!['] If you could put your hands on Silverston you would put your hands on the one man that caused all these hot days of deliberation. He got $25,000, and then look at this bunch of telegrams from Silverston to Washington, to the Shipping Board. The things we suffered! Oh, gentlemen, you can have no idea what it means to be a Negro in a day like this—the ignominy of it. Hemmed in and surrounded, victimized in this and that, and still going on and respecting and obeying the laws and looking for a brighter and better day, trying to fashion ourselves for the glory of the civilization in which we live. We know that we lost every dime; but, gentlemen, if not only the members of the Universal Negro Improvement Association, but every black man, lost every dime that he had; if every black man had taken his all and dropped it into the sea, with the belief that it would make him somebody, the consciousness that he is somebody, the consciousness that he means something to somebody, the exchange would be well and good. It would be money well spent. There is no one in this group of people but believe, deep down in his heart, that there is need for a broad industrial [o]pportunity for his children. The black man does not live whose heart is not praying that some day, somehow, the hideous curtain of hell and hate and of oppression and of a lack of opportunity will some day be lifted from the vision of his children. I am praying for mine. Every black man hopes the same. And that is what he is trying to do.

["]Gentlemen, a little reflection on the history of this country will disclose the fact that the great Pennsylvania Railroad, that connects the capital of the greatest country on earth with the greatest metropolis on earth—the men who bought the first stock in this great Pennsylvania Railroad lost every dollar.[8] Somebody had to make a sacrifice. And if you put everybody in jail that has lost money in the last ten years there would be some very distinguished persons in the land of Georgia. The Shipping Board would be there itself, the great Shipping Board with the treasure of great America behind it. The Shipping Board lost millions of dollars running ships. And talk about propaganda, the six-day joy ride of the Leviathan pales us into insignificance.[9] The very fact that Congress has introduced a bill, which we call the ship subsidy bill,[10] is an admission that with all our money, with all our Drexels,[11] Vanderbilts[12] and Rockefellers, we cannot successfully run ships unless the government gives us a helping hand, and you expect these men to perform miracles, when the greatest civilization on earth has failed. Do you expect from your black brethren more than you can do? The Black Star Line is a failure so far as money is concerned, but very successful on other lines."

THOMPSON FELL AMONG THIEVES

Continuing, Mr. Johnson said the position seemed to him quite clear. Mr. Garvey went away and left the Board of Directors in charge. The Board of Directors reposed their trust in Mr. Thompson. Mr. Thompson went out and fell among thieves. He reposed his trust in Silverston and Nolan and Barnett[13] and [E.H.] Duff.[14] Why was not Silverston brought to that court? Because of frauds perpetrated on the Black Star Line[,] the Phyllis Wheatley was not obtained. Who was the fraud? Certainly not Garcia. There was no doubt that Thompson was duped by Silverston.

Mr. Johnson next dealt with the financial report of the 20th of July, 1920, which, with the matter of the Phyllis Wheatley, were the two high spots in the case. Garcia, he submitted, had nothing to do with it. Thompson was employed as an expert bookkeeper. Mr. Thompson testified that he worked on the books two days, then called in a firm of expert accountants, finding the books too much for him. That firm prepared a report, which was presented to the convention. The district attorney had that statement in his possession for a year and a half. Why did he not bring the accountants to the court? To convict Garcia the district attorney would have to show that, though that report was made on the 20th of July, 1920[,] Garcia knew about it from the foundation of the world, from the beginning of the . . . [line mutilated] was incorporated. It was not practical. When that report was being prepared Garcia was helping America win the war. The truth is there is no such thing as any conspiracy. If the indictment had been framed against defendants for discourtesy, mismanagement or display of bad judgment they would have pleaded guilty. But this is not the charge. Personally, he had followed the testimony very carefully, and he only made that statement in so far as the innocence of one would affect the innocence of all and there was not one dime lost that could be traced back to Mr. Garvey. He was very sorry that things had not been otherwise. He was sorry that the defendant Garvey had not been more civil in the court that gave him so much liberty. He could wish that Mr. Garvey had shown more appreciation of the unexampled patience which the court had shown him in the trial of the case. But that did not mean that Mr. Garvey was guilty of the charge. The indictment charged must be proved.

NO WRONG PROVED

Concluding, Mr. Johnson said: "Out of the great big scheme devised by

the defendants, as the Government declared, Garcia got only $130, six weeks[']
salary.[15] And if," he continued, "you believe that we have done one act or deed
charged in the bill, and if you feel that even Garcia has tried to take one dime,
we do not ask for freedom. We will take our medicine like men[,] we will go
and serve the time and we will come back and try to live down the handicap and
try to prove to you in years to come that, though sent down, we will yet come
again. Though we have fallen we shall not die. We have got a feeling we have
done no wrong. The Government has proved no wrong. The Government
has proved the boiling up of the hearts, of the souls of black people. The
Government has proved that the black man is tired of wearing clothes and
never making them. The Government has disclosed the fact that the aspiring
black man is tired of eating food and never selling it. The Government has
proved that the black man is tired of listening to the music of Mendelssohn
and the songs of Handel and not taking the centre of the stage sometimes.
The Government has proved that the black man is tired laboring in the bowels
of ships and not keeping watch on the bridge. The Government has proved
that we are tired of viewing Paderewski's[16] nimble fingers. We want to do
a little thumping of our own. We don't always want to hear the songs of
Caruso.[17] We want to put a singer on the stage ourselves. We don't want to
live in the glory of another race. We are trying to do a little something on
our own, and if you will not help us, don't hamper us. We know you will not
discourage us. This is our Court, our Judge, our jury, thank God for that. It
is all dear to us as the apple of our eye. We need your help. O God, give us
a chance to sail the seas, give us a chance to step with you. When we want
to take a trip, we realize the ships are yours and we must take second place.
Give us a chance to get ours. Let us get something ourselves. Go and get Dr.
Silverston, grab him by the nape of the neck, and say to him, 'Come here, you
have wronged these colored people; you wrecked their hopes and aspirations.'
For, sometimes in a business, you may have $100,000, but the lack of $150 in
cash will throw you into receivership, into ruin. That was what happened to
us. When we thought we had $22,500, we had $9,000. And what we now
have at the Shipping Board, Silverston is trying to take that from us. But so
long as the Shipping Board lasts, neither Silverston nor Duff nor Nolan nor
Barnett will get that money. Uncle Sam has got hold of that money and it is
going to be given to those it belongs to."

Printed in *NW*, 30 June 1923. Original headlines omitted.

1. A paraphrase of a passage from *The Temple* (1633), written by George Herbert (1593–1633).
Benjamin Franklin expressed a similar sentiment in his 1758 work, *The Courteous Reader* (*BFQ*).

2. Garcia testified that while the BSL had located a replacement for the *Tennyson*, the line needed
money for the down payment. Garcia referred to a BSL directors' meeting in which they agreed to
ask presidents of various UNIA branches to raise the money. In a short time they raised $20,000
needed for the payment on the *Hong Kheng*, due on 16 April 1921 (*Marcus Garvey v. United States*,
no. 8317, Ct. App., 2d cir., 2 February 1925, pp. 2,044–2,046).

3. Elizabeth Barrett Browning (1806–1861), English poet, was best known for her volume *Sonnets*

from the Portuguese, published in 1850 (*WBD*).

4. Garcia's testimony on this point is supported by Thomas Merrilees's assertion that "the books do not show that Garcia ever got a penny of salary" from the BSL (*Marcus Garvey* v. *United States*, pp. 1,061, 2,099).

5. Under Garvey's cross-examination, Cockburn testified that he had, unbeknownst to Garvey at the time, received a "commission" of "about $1,600" from the sellers of the *Yarmouth* for his part in the deal with the BSL (ibid., pp. 370–371, 375–378, 380, 404).

6. Robert Louis Stevenson, not Dickens, wrote *The Strange Case of Dr. Jekyll and Mr. Hyde* (1886).

7. A reference to the famous "whiskey cargo," the second voyage of the *Yarmouth*, which occurred in January 1920.

8. In 1905 the Pennsylvania Railroad was investigated by the Interstate Commerce Commission on charges of graft, illegal rebates, collusion with coal interests, and discrimination in allowing railway cars to coal companies in which the Pennsylvania Railroad had no interest. Alexander J. Cassatt (1839–1906) was its president during this time. The Pennsylvania Railroad later merged with its archrival, the New York Central, to form the Pennsylvania Central Railroad. The combined railroad later went bankrupt (Patricia T. Davis, *End of the Line: Alexander J. Cassatt and the Pennsylvania Railroad* [New York: Neale Watson Academic Publications, 1978], pp. 183–198).

9. Albert Lasker, chairman of the USSB, caused a stir in the spring of 1923 when it became known that he planned a trip for the refurbished steamship *Leviathan*, supposedly to test its new machinery and publicize the seaworthiness of the USSB's merchant ships in order to facilitate their sale to private interests. This trip was to consist of a six-day cruise to the Bahamas with six hundred hand-picked guests, and its estimated cost was $600,000. New York representative Fiorello La Guardia denounced it as a "joyride" and said that if Lasker needed to test the ship, he could take sick and wounded servicemen instead of the "wealthy persons invited as special guests" (*NYT*, 7 June 1923). Republican representatives, concerned about the unfavorable publicity, met to ask President Harding to stop the voyage. The Democratic National Committee condemned the trip and threatened to make it a campaign issue. Nevertheless, the S.S. *Leviathan* and its invited notables from the political, business, film, and literary worlds sailed on 18 June without incident (*NYT*, 25 March, 6 June, 10 June, 12 June, 13 June, 16 June, 20 June, and 23 June 1923).

10. The ship subsidy bill was introduced in February 1922 by President Harding. Written by the USSB, the bill proposed that Congress subsidize the Shipping Board in order to facilitate the sale of the merchant ships that it owned and to reduce government operating costs. The subsidy was estimated at around $30 million. Congress held hearings on the bill, yet even with a Republican majority in the House and the support of President Harding, the bill passed by only a small margin, and by February 1923 it had failed to come to a vote in the Senate (Paul Maxwell Zeis, *American Shipping Policy* [Princeton, N.J.: Princeton University Press, 1938], pp. 125–141; James M. Morris, *Our Maritime Heritage* [Washington, D.C.: University Press of America, 1979], pp. 212–217; *NYT*, 7 January, 20 January, and 18 February 1922, 25 February, 26 February, and 27 February 1923).

11. The Drexels were a family of Philadelphia bankers, including Francis (1792–1863) and his son Anthony Joseph (1826–1893) (*WBD*).

12. A reference to the prominent Vanderbilt family, whose fortune was made in the transportation and finance industries. Cornelius Vanderbilt (1794–1877) founded the family fortune, which included a controlling interest in the New York Central Railroad (*WBD*).

13. Charles M. Barnett (1885–1940) was president of the Clinchfield Navigation Corp., a firm of ship brokers. In 1921 the Black Star Line transferred power of attorney from Rudolph Silverston to Barnett (*NYT*, 27 April 1940; *Garvey Papers* 3: 497, 708).

14. E.H. Duff was an associate of the ship broker A. Rudolph Silverston (E. David Cronon, *Black Moses* [Madison: University of Wisconsin Press, 1969], p. 98).

15. There is no indication in the trial testimony of Garcia receiving a salary.

16. Ignacy Paderewski (1860–1941) world-renowned Polish pianist, composer, and statesman, made a triumphant comeback tour of the United States in 1923, following eight years in retirement. The tour raised a record $500,000, most of which was given to the "cause of Poland" (*WBD*; *NYT*, 29 April 1923).

17. Enrico Caruso (1873–1921), Italian tenor, had been the leading opera singer at New York's Metropolitan Opera (*WBD*).

Closing Address to the Jury by Marcus Garvey

[*New York, 15 June 1923*]

GARVEY'S BRILLIANT SPEECH

May it please Your Honor and Gentlemen of the Jury:

I stand before you indicted by the United States Government for conspiring with others to defraud certain persons of their moneys through the use of the United States mails. You have heard the testimony both on the part of the prosecution and the defense.

I feel sure that you have absolutely no doubt in your mind about the innocence of the defendant who now appears before you. We are charged jointly or separately of conspiring and scheming together to defraud the people mentioned in the indictment. We have Louis Schench[1] of Washington; G. Simon Scott[2] of Stamford, Conn.; [Mrs.] [[Mr.]] Smith[3] of Indianapolis, Ind.; Annie Still[4] of Philadelphia, Pa.; [Edgar Sayers[5] of British Guiana; and Parris[6] of British Guiana to testify, and Dancy.[7]] Others did not appear.[8]

The prosecution claims that we connived a scheme and conspired to do certain things. What were the things they said we did?—That we bought the Shadyside with the intention of wrecking her. That we bought the Yarmouth for the purpose of laying her in drydock and having her sold for $1,600, as they allege; that we absolutely connived never to have bought the Orion, but to have taken the stockholders' money and give[[n]] it to someone, whether it be Silverstone[[, the Jew,]] or anyone else. These are the things that they allege that we have done, and years ago, when the Black Star Line was incorporated, that we had in our minds the doing of these things. For what purpose? For the purpose of getting commissions and so on. Gentlemen, no one has testified here on the part of the government that one individual officer of the Black Star Line who started this corporation along with the rest of people who are interested, ever collected one nickel for commission or for profit. They talk about salary; every man is worthy of his hire. If a treasurer gives his time to the service of the corporation from eight to twelve hours per day, don't you expect that he must be paid? If the president gives his time, all his time, in that they say I speak all over the country, I travel all over the country, giving all my time day and night, don't you believe that such a servant is worthy of his hire? If the secretary gives his time, do you not believe his service is also worthy to be rewarded some kind of way? The very prosecutor of this case, Mr. Mattuck himself, draws a salary from the government for the service he renders to the government, and if he did not get that money he would probably sue the government or give up his job. If he is worthy of his pay, so is the treasurer of the Black Star Line, and the secretary, and the president worthy of whatsoever salary they get. And how much did they get?—Mr. Merrile[e]s, an expert accountant, taking his figures to be correct, said that Marcus Garvey got $5,000 as president of the Black Star Line for the time that the Black Star Line was in existence, from its incorporation, from the 27th of June, 1919, to the present time; and all he got by [the] testimony of their experts was $5,000.[9] And how much did we take in? Nearly $1,000,000. Now, gentlemen, let us reason if anyone wanted to defraud, to take the people's money, and to conspire, as charged by the government, would they [get] [[have taken]] only $5,000 salary during that period of time, when they said that about $800,000 or nearly $1,000,000 was taken in? How much the treasurer got has been produced in testimony. Tobias got $50 per week for being treasurer of a big steamship company, and they said we took in nearly one million dollars. Gentlemen, you are businessmen. I feel confident that you have judged this case; you have watched this case carefully, and that you will allow no prejudice, no sentiment, no machinations on the part of anyone who desires a conviction, to carry out any feeling of his to swerve you from the course of justice.

LAW AND JUSTICE.

Justice, gentlemen, as I have said before, is greater and above the law; if justice was not included in the law, then the law would be of no use to us as human beings. The law is supposed to be the expression of justice, and caring not how technical the charge may be, if there is no justice, the law counts for naught. It is true that I am not a lawyer, but I feel sure that His Honor and the district attorney meant no offense when they said that Marcus Garvey was not a lawyer. It does not mean that every man who is [[brought]] before the bar of American justice must [be] [[appear by]] a lawyer, otherwise we would be living under peculiar circumstances. The Constitution allows every man the privilege to defend himself, to so prove his innocence before an American court of justice, and I decided to do so,[10] irrespective of being a lawyer, because, gentlemen, it is not the law that I am concerned so much about, it is the truth.

If I have committed any offense in truth, and it is a violation of the law, I say your duty is to find me guilty and let me have the fullest extent of the law. I ask no mercy. I ask no sympathy. I ask but for justice based upon the testimony [passed] [[given]] in this court.

THE LAW ON FRAUD.

They brought several persons here to testify on this complaint of fraud. I will read you what the highest judgment in law of this country says about fraud as His Honor will direct at the proper time.

The Supreme Court of the United States in the case of Southern Development Co. vs. Silva[11] lays down the following rules for the detection of fraud:

1. That the defendant must make a representation in regard to a material fact.

2. That such representation must be false.

3. That such representation must be actually believed by the [defendant]

[[complainant]] on reasonable grounds to be true.

4. That it must be made with intent that it should be acted on.

5. That it must be acted on by complainant to his damage, and

6. That in so acting on it, the complainant must be ignorant of its falsity and reasonably believe it to be true.

That is laid down as His Honor will direct, as the interpretation of fraud by the highest tribunal in law in this great country [in] America.

Gentlemen, did any of the officers of the Black Star Line who were part of the organization of this company make any statement, any material fact that they did not believe to be true? What evidence, if any, have they brought here to prove that Marcus Garvey made any statement that he at any time did not believe was true? The only matter of doubt was the matter of the purchase of the S.S. Orion to be named the Phyllis Wheatley. You have heard testimony, whose fault was it [[that the Phyllis Wheatley was not obtained]]? Everybody believed that there was going to be a Phyllis Wheatley, every officer in the office believed it. Garcia believed that there was going to be a Phyllis Wheatley, [Garvey believed that there was going to be a Phyllis Wheatley,] all the directors believed it, and all the members of the executive council of the Universal Negro Improvement Association believed that there was going to be a Phyllis Wheatley, according to what they were told [[by Thompson]], as I will bring to you [again later, in my address to you] gentlemen.

You have heard the statements of the respective persons. You have watched them, [you heard them,] and I feel sure you will have absolutely no difficulty in centering your minds once more on the individual, and individuals in the chair. Before I go into details, however, I desire to assure you that in the beginning of the case I had absolutely no desire or intention to delay the activities of this court;[12] my one desire was to [get] justice, and to so have my case laid before you gentlemen, who are to be my judges, that there would be absolutely no mistake, in that a man's liberty is at stake. Liberty is man's dearest possession, and I feel sure that you appreciate your liberty, and [will] do everything in your power to secure it. You will, therefore, place yourselves in my position. I will leave no stone unturned to protect my liberty, and life, and see that justice is done.

I have to apologize to His Honor and the Court, if, in their opinion, I have committed any breach. It was not my intention, and whatsoever happened otherwise in this court, you will realize that it was done by a man who desired to give himself the fullest opportunity to prove his innocence, and one who was compelled to take the floor, if I might so term it, on his own account. I felt that no one could interpret to you, gentlemen of the jury, the circumstances surrounding the activities of the Black Star Line and its auxiliaries as I could do it, in that it would have taken two or three years to explain to anyone the circumstances surrounding the activities of these organizations.

First of all, the person had to enter into the spirit of the movement. It was not purely a professional job [by] someone to do some work, it was a position that I was placed in where I had to interpret my soul to someone who probably could not appreciate the interpretation of that soul. Hence my appearance on my own behalf as my attorney. So [that,] gentlemen, if anything should be said by the prosecutor [that caused me to take my own defense,] you will understand and appreciate my position in the matter.

THE DIGNITY OF THE RACE

Now, you have heard the indignities hurled at my race by the district attorney when questions were asked of certain witnesses as to whether they were dukes or ladies, which was offensive to me, because the Negro has as much right as any other race to dignify the person or individual[[s]] whom they believe worthy of honor, and, therefore, gentlemen, you will not believe that I meant any insult to any race or any one when I made certain retorts.

THE TYPE OF WITNESSES

Now, whom did the government bring to testify? The government brought in Edgar Gray, and, gentlemen, that was where Garvey and his attorney came to the parting of the ways. Garvey did not know whom the government relied on to support its charges against him, and when Garvey came into the court and saw the scoundrel, Edgar Gray, he wanted the opportunity to produce sufficient evidence of the character of Edgar Gray. Garvey asked his attorney to keep Edgar Gray over until he was able to search for the records. His attorney[[s]] rushed three [defendants] [[witnesses]] off the stand in one day, which were Edgar Gray, Richard Warner and Kilroe, the principal offensive characters of this charge, whom Garvey never knew would be here, and whom he desired to place under cross-examination to bring out the truth for this court. And when Garvey found that his liberty was at stake, he had to ask the attorney to retire to protect his own liberty.

AN ANALYSIS OF GRAY

Who is Edgar Gray? You saw him on the stand—a reckless, irresponsible man, full of talk, representing nothing, a great politician who has no office, a great know-all who has nothing in all his years, who is still a messenger at probably a meagre $18 per week. That is the man with a superabundance of intelligence; that is the man who up to now has not told us his real birthplace, who says he was born in Sierra Leone, [and was never known in Sierra Leone, West Africa. He] [[West Africa, when he]] was born in Antigua as testified [[to]] by witness for the defense. Edgar Gray, everybody knows came from the West Indies. He was born in Antigua. Can you believe the testimony of such a man as Edgar Gray, who left the Black Star Line, who left the Universal Negro Improvement Association when he was called [[upon]] to account for the funds of these organizations, [that] [[which funds]] he handled during the absence of Garvey, Davis, Tobias and Ashwood in Virginia? Gray, who disappeared from the office with the funds of the organization and for whom a warrant was to be sworn out in the [*Washington*] Heights Court by Garvey and his attorney, James Watson, which was postponed by the discretion of the judge, [[no doubt for the convenience of Kilroe,]] and a few hours after Garvey met Gray and Warner at the office of the District Attorney [there as a friend of the District Attorney] Kilroe. Gentlemen, can you see the situation?

WARNER DESCRIBED

Who is Warner? A man who testified that he would say anything that the District Attorney told him to say.[13] If the District Attorney said so, it was so. Would you call Warner a man? If Warner is a man, then God save the world of men. The rubber-stamp man without any character, who will be willing to say anything anybody else says, can you vouch for the testimony of such a man? Can you convict another man on the testimony of such a man? Remember, gentlemen, you are to be judged one day; you will therefore appreciate what it is to judge, to take away one's life[[, one's liberty]]. There is but one great Judge, and that Judge will judge all mankind at the right time [and] the opportune time, and you at this hour are placed in the position of this great High Judge to dispense justice to another, as you would expect Him to dispense justice to you. Would you condemn a man, take away the liberty of a man, of four men, on the testimony of Gray, on the testimony of Warner? Would the great God condemn a Christian soul on the testimony of the devil? Gentlemen, I appeal to your sense of reason, I appeal to your higher sense of justice. Warner, who said that the Black Star Line funds were used for the restaurant of the Universal Negro Improvement Association and the African Communities League while he was secretary; Warner, not remembering that he signed a statement showing what he did with some of the funds that he could not account for, not showing that which he could not account for which he received from the Universal Negro Improvement Association. I will show you Warner's statement, which disclosed that he received certain amounts of money and disbursed [it] [[same]] for the Universal Negro Improvement Association[:] [[,and not the Black Star Line's money, as he testified to.]][14]

Hon. Marcus Garvey,
56–58 West 135th Street,
New York City

Dear Sir:

Below is an itemized account as to how the $275 credited to House, Grossman and Vorhaus, lawyers for the Black Star Line, Inc., which money, when borrowed from the Universal Negro Improvement Association, was finally disbursed for the Universal.

June 30, salaries to the office employes by checks as follows: W.A. Domingo, $20; Edgar M. Gray, $18; A.G. Coombs, $15; Mrs. Leadett, $11; Mrs. Whittingham, $9; [H] [[R]].E. Warner, $20.

Salaries to restaurant employes by checks as follows: Two

waiters, $12 each, $24; one cook, $12. June 30, check to printer for paper issued to Mr. Gray, $150. Total, $279. It is believed your check book will verify said amounts, all of which you are well acquainted with.

R. E. WARNER[15]

Thus you will see, gentlemen, that it was the funds of the Universal Negro Improvement Association that were being used, and not the funds of the Black Star Line, as this gentleman Warner tried to make you understand. This Warner, who was such a businessman, he had such great business ability he could advise Garvey, and what is he now? As a businessman, where is his business? What benefit has he derived out of his great business ability? But for the Government he no doubt would have been a tramp, as we know him in [[the]] Harlem District.

AND NOW FOR KILROE

Watch the testimony of Kilroe. I am sorry to speak of an officer of the State government in this way. I regret it because I may be misinterpreted in this respect, because I have the highest respect for all American institutions.

I revere this great country and its great flag. I look to this country as the greatest democracy in the world, as the greatest government in the world. No other country in the world affords the opportunity for human liberty as this great American government, as this great American republic, but, gentlemen, nothing is at fault with the government. A government cannot commit any wrong, because governments do not administer themselves. It is the individual[s] who administer[[s]] government that sometimes bring ignominy upon the honor [[and integrity]] of the government.

KILROE CHARACTERIZED

Kilroe, the man who harbored Warner and Gray after he was told of their characters, had them sitting up in his office as if they were presidents of nations or governors of states, treating them with the greatest courtesy and respect, after he was told of the crimes they had committed against an American corporation. But not only one, but two American corporations. And he evinced no more interest in finding out if it was true, as far as the crime went, than to prosecute Garvey because he had some animus against Garvey, because Garvey could not politically at that time assist him, and these men were politicians who no doubt held out great promises as to what they could do for him at the next election. Kilroe, who tormented Garvey, who tormented the Universal Negro Improvement Association on over [five] [[nine]] occasions, having nothing to say, nothing to do; up to now Garvey and the Universal Negro Improvement Assn. [and the Black Star Line were never indicted by Kilroe. Kilroe, the man of vengeance, if he had Garvey and the Universal Negro Improvement Association] [[would have remained]] in his grip as an officer of the machinery of the government[,] [[.]] Garvey would have been prosecuted to the fullest extent, Garvey probably would have rotted in jail [[If Kilroe had a case against him]]; but for nine times, after calling Garvey and having nothing to say, [expecting] [[he expected]] Garvey to be docile! Gentlemen, as businessmen, busy in attending to your own affairs, how would you feel if someone unfortunately [attacked you at] [[attached to]] the District Attorney's office, [and] sent [[for]] you at your busiest hours, having nothing to say, using your [enemies against you, wasting your] time, humiliating you[[?]] How would you feel about it? Would you smile about it? And would you expect that Marcus Garvey, a human being, would smile at the attacks of Kilroe? Kilroe testified that he advised Garvey to do this and to do that. He knew he was not speaking the truth, but Garvey had not the opportunity to question Kilroe. And who is Kilroe? You, gentlemen, must have observed what happened in court—something about Mr. Kilroe that was not very pleasant. I will not go into it because it was not brought to your knowledge, but I will only ask you, gentlemen, to remember what happened for the few minutes when Mr. Johnson got on the floor and interrogated Kilroe about certain things. Imagine what these certain things were, who Kilroe was, and then you will have the character of the man. . . .[16]

MR. HEALEY

And now we come to our friend Mr. Healey. I am sorry to have to say anything about Mr. Healey, because I respect him. I had regarded him as a friend. The very morning when he came to testify here I met him on the outside. I shook his hand, and we were good friends then, as we were before. I never knew Healey was to be here as a witness testifying against me, and I was surprised to hear the things Mr. Healey said, but we will not take Mr. Healey seriously. He was only talking, I suppose, in the same character, in the same way Mr. Kilroe made a joke of Garvey being indicted. They come in contact with crime so often, and sending people to jail so often, for short and long terms, that they can smile about it. It is nothing surprising if a man goes to jail for twenty years. They smile over the matter. But, gentlemen, you are the judge[[s]]. You will not smile over such a matter. Once he said that Garvey was a good gentleman, impressed him as being honest and upright; then later on he said Garvey was a bad man. He called Garvey a bad man because he did not pay him the bills for the Black Star Line. Now Garvey is not the Black Star Line. We were not asking him his opinion of the Black Star Line; we were asking his opinion about Garvey, and because Garvey did not pay him what the Black Star Line owed Harris McGill or the North American Steamship Company,[17] of which he was attorney, then Mr. Garvey became a bad man, and he had a different opinion about Mr. Garvey, and he talked to Mr. Mattuck about it.

He said they talked it over, and he told Mr. Mattuck that Garvey was a bad man. But let us see if Mr. Healey was really serious. Mr. Healey, a member of the bar, [not a loose, irresponsible gentleman. Mr. Healey, a member of the bar,] and I asked him if he was a member of the Bar Association, and he said yes, and he was qualified as an assistant district attorney in the County of Brooklyn, and Mr. Healey knew about certain laws that went into effect in this country at a certain time, especially the prohibition law, and he testified that he wanted some whisky off the Yarmouth, and he was willing to buy it or get it anyhow, after prohibition had gone into effect. A member of the bar, remember; a district attorney of the County of Brooklyn, wanted to buy or get whisky after the prohibition law went into effect. But not only in that did Mr. Healey joke with us, but Mr. Healey said he wanted this money from the Black Star Line, and if he got the money he would keep it. He was only attorney for the North American Steamship Company. He was not even the treasurer of the North American Steamship Company, but if he received the money, that balance of $35,000, he would keep it. He did not know where the directors were, he did not care to know where Harris, the president, was; and I asked him what he would do with it, and he said he would frame it. Now Mr. Healey was jolly and was not serious, because Mr. Healey, as attorney, an intelligent man, knows that if he was treasurer or attorney of a corporation, and received $35,000 for that corporation, his duty would be to report it to the office of the corporation, especially the president of the corporation, and give a proper account of it, that it would have to pass through the books of that corporation. Did Mr. Healey mean to suggest that he would commit a fraud, and even while he was assistant district attorney in the County of Brooklyn? Surely we could not believe that. We know Mr. Healey was only playing with the court and the gentlemen of the jury, and smiling away the liberty of Marcus Garvey. He told us all about the contracts between [Morris] [[Harris]] McGill, Mr. Harris[s] and the Black Star Line, and [Mr.] [[Marcus]] Garvey; did he tell us the truth about it? I feel sure you gentlemen of the jury know that he was not telling the truth, but only joking; he was only trying to carry out his promise to the district attorney.

He told us that contracts were signed. He acted as the attorney for the North American Steamship Company. Mr. Healey knew that there was an oral understanding between the Black Star Line and Mr. W. Harris of the North American Steamship Company, that whether a bill of sale was actually passed in document or through legal process, that the Black Star Line was to be the owners of the Steamship Yarmouth. Mr. Healey knew that Mr. Harris was retiring from business, and going to Europe; he said he had no further use for the ship, and that he was willing then to sell his ship to the Black Star Line at that time, under any contract. And Mr. Healey drew these contracts, and kept that away from the court. Gentlemen, if you read the contracts, the many contracts that were subsequently signed, you will find that there must have been some understanding why there were so many contracts, because good business men know that an original contract which involved the forfeit of money must be lived up to by the party of the [first] [[second]] part, that they were not going to amend so many contracts for the convenience of the person who failed, they would have seized the [money] [[ship]] on the first contract, and let the forfeit go. Did they do that? At no time did they compel the Black Star Line to forfeit the contract. Why, because there was a common understanding. So everybody knows Mr. Healey did not tell the truth. [True business men like Mr. Healey, true] [[True and keen]] business men like Mr. Harris, do not do things that way. They wanted to sell us a Canadian boat, they wanted to sell an American corporation a Canadian boat, and they could not immediately give a bill of sale, that is why Healey was sent to Ottawa to see if they could [give us immediately a bill of sale. They found that they could not] do it, and they made these supplementary contracts, and then advised that we incorporate in Canada, the Black Star Line Steamship of Canada[,] so as to take over the bill of sale in the legal way under these circumstances. They were the geniuses of the whole affair, Healey and Harris were the men who engineered the way how [he] [[we]] could get the ship, because we knew nothing, we were innocent men trying to do the best for our people, and did not know all about the intricacies of business, and the ways we could get in and out. Healey knew it, and Harris himself knew it, and [he] [[they]] showed us the way, that is how we have a Canadian Black Star Line. We never dreamt of it. But they told us about the Canadian Black Star Line as the easiest way of getting the legal title, and that there was an oral title passed between us when we signed the first contract.

Healey himself told us that he got insurance for the ship Yarmouth on the first voyage. Admitting that that be true, why should he get insurance on the Yarmouth if they were not interested in the sale of the Yarmouth? Why didn't they make the Black Star Line live up to its contract after they signed the contract? You will find that there is something beneath the whole affair that Healey did not tell in that chair.

Healey said that he is a church brother of mine, that is true. That he is a friend of mine, that is true. But when it comes to justice, you cannot play with people's liberty that way. He became offended when I asked him if his brother was a colored man, he knew I meant no offen[s]e, I was trying out his [[logic in a]] previous statement he made, when he said that Mr. Garvey was there with certain gentlemen of his race when he said certain things, and when I asked him [[again]] he said his brother only [[was there]]. I asked him if his brother was a colored man, in that sense, and he became offended, but I did not mean any offense to Mr. Healey, because when it comes to a matter of race, I have absolutely no feeling about the matter. I think every race should stand on its own [tub] [[bottom]], whether it be [the] white race, black race, yellow race, or the brown race, each race should paddle its own canoe. I believe that the white man should look out for the white man, the black man should look out for the black man, and the yellow man should also look out for the yellow man. Mr. Healey said that he was of the belief that I was a member of the Ku Klux Klan. He knows that there is no black man in the Klan. How could I be a member of the Ku Klux Klan? For what reason? He wanted to be nasty to me, I suppose. If I [was a member of his church and the Klan is against members of his church] [[were of his denomination]], how could I be a member of the Ku Klux Klan? So you know, gentlemen, that Mr. Healey is not to be taken seriously in whatever he said on the witness stand.

We next had the real estate man Pilkington,[18] who said that he sold Amy Ashwood some property in October, 1919. Under cross-examination and under direct examination we asked him if he ever sold Marcus Garvey any property, he said no; we asked him if he ever knew Marcus Garvey, he said no. Why he was brought here I cannot tell. Why Pilkington was brought here to testify I cannot tell. I never saw the man before, never knew the man, never bought any property from the man, it was only a waste of the court's time.

They also brought one Whitfield,[19] who said that he purchased property from one Amy Ashwood, whom subsequently I married as Amy Ashwood Garvey, and divorced six weeks later because of her crookedness. She was supposed to have sold [[property]] to this Whitfield. I knew nothing about it. The first time I saw Whitfield was on that witness stand. I could not tell what the man was going to testify about, until I heard the question of property and Amy Ashwood; then I realized that there was something they were trying to connect me with Amy Ashwood before she became Amy Ashwood Garvey. That, gentlemen, I will touch again, but whatsoever explanation I gave I feel sure will stand, and if you believe that I got a penny out of that $500 that Amy Ashwood got, that I would look upon the struggles of a people to rob them of a penny, I should die, and not only before man, but to be sent to the farthest depths of hell by my God.

CAPTAIN COCKBURN

We have the testimony of the man Cockburn—Cockburn the swindler—Cockburn, who admitted to the hearing of the president of the Black Star Line in this court for the first time, and before this honorable court and these gentlemen of the jury, that he got $1,600 as his part [of] [[for]] selling the Yarmouth to the Black Star Line, and that five others got a like amount of money. The crook Cockburn, taking $1,600 out of the coffers of the Black Star Line, out of the dimes and nickles of poor people at that time when we were struggling to get a boat, who pretended that he was a member of the race and wanted to help. The very first boat we could not even pay enough money at the first time [[for]], which was only $16,500, and these crooks got $8,000 out of it, and had the nerve to go and sit in the chair as witnesses for the prosecution. That is the character of the witnesses we had from the government, crooks and sharks and men who know how to change up figures and amounts. All of them were not here, because some got scared and kept away. Where was Smith-Green? [The District Attorney told me] when I asked Cockburn: "I can get him for you if you want." Why didn't he produce Smith-Green here? Why didn't he indict Smith-Green on the investigation of the books of the Black Star Line for nearly two years? Did he not know the name of Smith-Green? In the second indictment they produced two letters signed by Edward Smith-Green,[20] and yet they did not produce the author of the letter[[s]], although they knew his name and his address and his whereabouts.

It did not suit [you] [[them]] at that time to bring Smith-Green, but we are going to find Smith-Green. If the District Attorney won't get Smith-Green, after you, gentlemen of the jury, have disposed of this case, we will get Smith-Green and we will present him before the bar of American justice.

Cockburn told [us] [[you]] how the Yarmouth was no good, after he had told us to buy the Yarmouth as a splendid boat. It is all in the record[s], gentlemen, what this man Cockburn said, and what he subsequently said under [direct examination and what he subsequently contradicted under] cross-examination. Cockburn the drunkard, when asked about his sober condition, stood before you and said: "It is my business." [If he was not a drunkard, wouldn't he answer, "No"? Why "It is my business"?] Because, no doubt, he knew he was a drunkard, a drunkard on the high seas, sailing the ships of the Black Star Line. And didn't you hear the testimony, gentlemen, that on the first trip from New York to Cuba the ship Yarmouth struck a reef? Didn't you hear the man Hercules[21] testify for the defense (he was very talkative)? And another engineer testified that the ship would have been a total wreck under the command of Cockburn the drunkard, [Cockburn the crook, who took $1,600 because $16,500 was the first payment, and if he got $1,600 out of that first payment] [[for himself]], [God knows how much he got out of the balance of $125,000 that was subsequently paid into the coffers of Harris, McGill & Co., that we bought the boat from] under the instructions of Cockburn.

Did Cockburn return after that first trip when he got the $1,600 for commission?—He returned to make the second trip, and when he came he found it was a cargo of whiskey, and he said, "Now is the time for me to get what is coming to me," and he said the ship could not go [[to]] sea, but when he found out he was getting $2,000 to split between himself and Smith-Green,[22] the ship went to sea at quick speed. Nothing was wrong with the ship [[then]]. And, gentlemen, was it only $2,000 that was split between himself and Smith-Green, which Mr. Healey knew about, and he did not want to tell facts [of it?] [[.]] After the ship sailed, and they got $2,000, it went only [out here] [[a short way out]], a [cable] [[radio]] was sent, "We are drunk, we are sinking," and immediately 500 cases of Green River Whiskey and champagne were thrown overboard, and tugboats were around. What were these tugboats doing there? Who got the money for the cargo? Didn't Hercules tell you on the witness stand that he was ordered by the captain to put so many cases of whiskey in a lighter? Who got the money for that whiskey?

Cockburn said that he bought property in his wife's name after he came back from his trip to [[make it]] appear that it was one bit of property;[23] we were not allowed the privilege to search and bring the testimony here; the search has been made, but the testimony could not be produced.

He tells us now that he is a real estate broker. Do you wonder that Cockburn is a real estate broker after that historic trip of the Yarmouth with that cargo of whiskey? Gentlemen, it is for you to think the matter over and see the characters of the men who were placed here to testify against the defense.

Men who got $25 for a few weeks, men who got $50 a week for about one and a half years, men who got $100 a week for just a year, while Cockburn got at one time what the president got for all the time he was president of the corporation. And Cockburn was getting how much? $400 per month, the same amount of money that the president was supposed to get [[as salary]]. At times the president was only getting $50 per week; Cockburn was not only getting [more than $50] [[$100]] per week, but $10 a day allowance, according to his [[own]] statement that a captain gets daily allowances outside of his salary. How much did Cockburn get? He got all the money of the Black Star Line and the [. . . ?] [[rest.]] It is no wonder that he became so haughty and demonstrated so much viciousness on the witness stand.

These are the characters of the witnesses who were brought here by the District Attorney to represent this great government, [to] convict a man. Gentlemen, do you think that is the spirit of this great government, the spirit of justice, honesty and truth? When that great father of our country, George Washington, brought into existence this great Republic, did he contemplate that the name of America would have been besmirched by [. . .] [[such rascals]] as demonstrated here by these witnesses, who were brought by the District Attorney to convict four men, and take away their liberty[?]

Gentlemen, as American citizens, I feel sure you will save the name of America from a scandal and from shame that is becoming worldwide, because the case of the Black Star Line is not a local matter, it is a case [where] [[which]] 400,000,000 Negroes of the world are watching [it] with an eagle eye to test America's justice, and you gentlemen have in your hands at this hour the name of America where black men are concerned, and I feel sure you will not pollute the fair name of this nation to please anyone, who has vengeance [[in his heart]] against someone [they desire] [[he desires]] to get even with, as Kilroe desires to get even with Garvey. Kilroe, who sent Tyler to shoot Garvey, and when Tyler shot four times and Garvey was only wounded and did not die, Tyler was taken to the jail and the next morning was said to [be a] [[commit]] suicide, was found dead on the first floor, [said] [[supposed]] to have dropped from the sixth floor [to] [[of]] the jail house.

Gentlemen, I feel sure you understand the situation as presented to you. I have no desire to hide anything. Did I hide anything about the character of Marcus Garvey? Didn't I ask them to tell what they knew of Marcus Garvey, and did not they tell the limit of what they knew, and afterwards when they knew no more, didn't they lie, and say, yes, there is more? [[the liars that they are.]]

We will pass from Cockburn, because it pains me to linger so long with a crook and a scoundrel. We come to Adrian Richardson, the master of 1919 and 1920 without a master's license, who so lied on the witness stand that he had a master's ticket when he came to the Black Star Line, and met me in 1919 in Boston[[.]] [, and when he came to the Black Star Line in 1920, with] Captain Swift, the man for whom he worked in the latter part of 1920, testified that he it was who tried to get a ticket for the man Richardson [[as a master]]. We subpoenaed the records of the Shipping authorities of New York, the records were brought that showed the same thing that Captain Swift testified to, but the defense was not permitted to question on the record,[24] and I excused the shipping master.

CAPTAIN RICHARDSON

[[The shipping]] master came with certain papers, and I was not allowed to question him in that the matter of Richardson was then closed, and it was not within the legal procedure. This man Richardson, another crooked captain, said he was not anxious to get into the service of the Black Star Line.

Who would believe a Negro like Richardson sitting [down] there, saying that he was not anxious to get into the service of the Black Star Line? Gentlemen, he said he met me in Boston. Now, I must be some great magician to know that the man is captain just by way of looking at him. He says he saw me in a public meeting. Now, is it reasonable to expect a man whom you never met before that you could just pick out as a captain and start to talk to him? [Would it] [[Does it not]] suggest that the person would speak to the man he knew was head of a steamship company, and say that he was a captain and tell him something about himself? It is reasonable that Richardson would beg for a job in the Black Star Line, would come to the Black Star Line with the idea of seeing if he could get what Cockburn got.

It is no wonder he advised [[us]] not to buy the Kanawha, even though the Kanawha was bought before he came, because he probably wanted to buy another boat to get his $1,600 out of the split of the brokers. Do you wonder, gentlemen, why Captain Richardson and Captain Mulzac were grieved? They are grieved because they did not get the chance like Cockburn had to make theirs, and become [a] real estate broker[[s]] afterwards; but Mulzac afterward became president of a steamship company, so he was in search for his, anyhow, but did not get it in buying the Yarmouth, so thought he would be president himself of some other steamship company. Richardson, the man who is supposed to have spent his thousands for the Black Star Line, when you could have seen that that Negro did not have a thousand cents. Thousands of dollars that he paid for crews' wages. Well, we were trying to get the book in evidence, but it was [then late] [[denied]], and we could not put it in, so you could see how this Richardson manipulated figures; how he put down his receipts and disbursements, [to show you] how he made one thousand dollars look like two, and charged the balance up to himself.

As to Silverston[[e, the Jew,]] I did not know the man Silverston[[e]] any more than I saw him once or twice, and I do not want to see him again unless when he returns the $25,000, we will see that the Black Star Line gets it back to pay its liabilities, also the [lost] [[last]] $11,000.

This Richardson who was dismissed in Jamaica, this Richardson, the man whom Thompson sent out with that beautiful ship the Kanawha, because, gentlemen, indeed that ship was beautiful. It was the yacht of that great millionaire Rogers. The Kanawha was the name of some interest he had;

it was a palace, but the government took it over one time and used it as an auxiliary cruiser, and when we refitted her she was nearly as [she was] [[perfect as]] when Rogers had it. The boat was a twin screw boat, its machinery was intricate and instead of placing [[a]] competent crew to manage such a boat, we had a captain without a license, a captain who got a license afterward, either by his [[fraternal]] signs or his political pull [to handle such a boat], a captain who gambled on the deck, a captain who was drunk [even] with his engineers, a captain who had not enough discipline to see that his engineers were in the engine room while the ship was at sea. Think of it, a ship at sea with nobody in the engine room, no engineer. Do you wonder the cylinder covers blew off and piston rods were broken? Do you wonder that the Kanawha became a wreck so many times?

I did not tell you about Cockburn and the bills he made, the repair bills for which they got commission. Do you know why the ship balked so many times, because commissions were paid for her repairs. Bills for $11,000 probably meant a commission of 15 [[or 20]] percent to the master, and no wonder our ships foundered so many times. [These crooked masters, because] [[Because]] we had made a statement that we were going to show that Negroes could run ships and because they were the responsible officers of the corporation, they took the opportunity of [blackballing the officers] [[blackmailing us,]] because they knew that we had to keep our word. We [had to make] [[made]] a mistake in a way, but, gentlemen, who do not make mistakes? Didn't the Pilgrims make mistakes when [we] [[they]] found[ed] this great country? Did we indict the Pilgrims for making an American Republic [[through mistakes]]? Indict us for trying to show the world that black men are capable, but you will not destroy the sentiment of the Negro for business [[and progress]]. Send Marcus Garvey to prison for what Silverston[[e]] has done. I am satisfied to go to jail even though I say so, for fraud, for money that some [one other than a Negro] [[white man]] received. [I] am satisfied, but I feel sure that the sense of American justice will secure fair play to me. Now for the circular advertising [about] the sailing of the Phyllis Wheatley.

Somebody might have suggested to the District Attorney [that they suggested to him] [[what]] the question[s] and the answer[[s shall]] [was to] be, [it is] [[to excuse]] Garcia and Thompson so the two [can] [[may]] get Garvey under indictment. And that [is why I] [[was why Hunt the printer]] was so eager to say Garcia and Thompson gave me this and Garcia gave me [this and, gentlemen], [[that. Gentlemen]] you [heard him] yourselves [[heard Hunt]] admit that any printing [[one printer does can be duplicated by]] another printer [can duplicate the printing] and that they can slip in words that were not [there] in the [copy] [[original]]. You can slip in a libelous word and a fraudulent word, and produce it as original, but Garvey denies that he wrote circulars identical[ly like those] [[to those submitted]]. Garvey never writes any circulars in his own handwriting. Why didn't they produce the handwriting of Garvey instead of the printed circular? You can take it to the printing shop and get the whole Bible printed for that matter. So, gentlemen, you will not convict a man on a printed slip that can be duplicated by any printer?

This Hunt[25] was getting $250 a week and sometimes $400 a week [and then] [[in printing, but when]] the Universal Negro Improvement Association [was getting] [[suddenly acquired]] a printing [house. He tried to get us bad anyhow] [[plant, he became sore and was willing to do anything to damage Garvey for the loss of business]].

THE NEGRO WORLD

I would like to [see] [[draw to your attention]] the Negro World of March [12] [[13]], 1921, [to place] in evidence. These Negro Worlds, government exhibits, are too long for me to go through all of them, but they are in evidence and you will see them. Garvey admits writing some of the articles in the Negro World. Garvey denies some of those articles in the Negro World. At times Garvey would be away and his articles would not get to New York in time and someone could write [[the]] articles and stick Garvey's name [on] them. I knew the phraseology was not mine, but the district attorney seized upon it as a valuable bit of evidence [upon] [[against]] Garvey. Garvey does not hold himself responsible. If you gentlemen desire to convict Garvey, Garvey is satisfied. When Garvey's conscience and soul is clear before man and God, he does not care what man does with his body. He may condemn the body but not the soul and conscience of the man.

In one of these Negro Worlds appears a ship that was supposed to be [[re-]]named the Phyllis Wheatley [afterward].[26] You will see that when you go to the jury room. Garvey knows about that ship; he knew the time the photograph was [put there] [[got out]]. He read the words under that ship. The district attorney did not read [it]. He read only that part which he believed would incriminate [us] [[me]]. Why didn't the district attorney [not] read the entire sentence and all the words beneath the photograph? I would not believe the honorable district attorney desired to deceive the court and the gentlemen of the jury. Surely, the government would not deceive itself. The government is too honorable for deceit. So, I will not impute any motive [of] the honorable district attorney for not reading entirely and completely all the words appearing on that page. What did it say? If you will subscribe enough money, we will have the ship. You will find that whenever [he sees] [[you see]] anything about any ship, it was always "If you give enough money you will have this," because I knew the people would not be crazy enough to expect us to give them something without money, and they knew that the officers had no money. We were not buying ships for ourselves but for the race. For what? For the industrial and commercial development of the race. That race was paying a price. Garvey, as a member of that race, contributes his part, and with the exception of a few who thought more of salary than of service, those of us who were officers of the Black Star Line did not remember [[anything]] about salary. When there was no salary, Garvey did not squeal; [Garcia did not squeal; and] Tobias did not squeal; but Thompson squealed, [where] [[when]] there was no salary. He disappeared when he couldn't get that $50 per week, and we never found Thompson until a month ago. Yes, gentlemen, we assumed responsibilit[ies], at least, Marcus Garvey assumes the responsibility for the photograph which Thompson gave [[him]] and which Thompson advised to be put in the Negro World, because Thompson was negotiating on the behalf of the Black Star Line for the purchase of the Tennyson which was to become the Phyllis Wheatley. He brought the photograph and gave it to Garvey and we all decided what to do.

Mr. Mattuck: I object as there was no testimony that Thompson gave him the photograph.

Judge: I do not remember hearing him testify to—

Mr. Garvey: But it was in evidence.

Judge: But not as Thompson gave it to you.

Mr. Garvey: All right, I withdraw it.

Mr. Garvey continues his address:

The photograph that the district attorney held up to the Court and the gentlemen of the jury with the words underneath, but he didn't read you the [represented] [[entire]] truth. We were, I testified, negotiating for the Tennyson, [which was] in continuation [when] [[of which]] Marcus Garvey went to the West Indies, South and Central America to raise money. [It was] $30,000 [[had]] to be raised in order to get the ship within twenty (20) days after Garvey left [to take over the Tennyson] as per arrangements explained here in testimony. The others were to raise so much and Garvey was to raise so much. In six (6) weeks Garvey raised $17,000 for the Black Star Line [or $19,000,] [[and]] as Jacques' [checks testified to.] [[books proved,]] Amy Jacques, for the Universal Negro Improvement Association, raised $13,000 or $14,000 in six weeks. We had over $30,000 from Garvey's side alone. Then they had raised over 20,000 odd dollars in America. If Thompson had not sent Richardson down with the dirty crew and Garvey did not have to spend the Black Star Line and Universal Negro Improvement Association money on the Kanawha [[repairs, all of]] the $30,000 would have been cabled to New York [[instead of only a part,]] and they would have had [over $60,000 with what they had] in New York [to meet] the payment on the ship. And, gentlemen, as business men, you know that if you don't use good judgment in business, whether the Standard Oil Company, even with its millions of capital, it will go out of business. If you take $30,000 here and so many thousand dollars [from] there, even the Standard Oil Company will go to pieces, and J. D. Rockefeller and Carnegie would look as tramps, as frauds and no good. What could Garvey do with such a crew [[bent on mischief in the West Indies]]?

We will [pass] [[go]] over these exhibits. Now we have the testimony of William Boody,[27] the man from Rogowski's, the printer. The man who knew nothing; who could say nothing, only what he heard [by hearsay]. Gentlemen, will you condemn a man on hearsay? He was brought in to testify about the [making] [[mailing]] of the Negro World. Did he tell [what part] the Negro World went to? Did he say he posted the Negro World to Washington, to

Connecticut, to Indiana? He said he got copies from the foreman. Where did the foreman get [it] [[them]]? I believe from the Negro World, was his answer. How do you know? I saw some one from the Negro World handling copies. Did some one from the Negro World hand[le] copies to the foreman? Yes. Can you remember who he was? No.

Gentlemen, can you convict anyone on such a testimony? He never received a mailing list from the Negro World. [Well] [[Yet]], he came in to testify. Why didn't the district attorney bring in the foreman from Rogowski's to tell from where he received the copies?

Gentlemen, surely, you shall discount the testimony of William Boody.

CARGIL[L], [[T]]HE LITTLE BOY

Now we come to [Gargill] [[Cargil]],[28] a little boy who spilt the beans [of] [[on]] the district attorney. [Gargill], the little fellow of about 20 years, who was placed there and said such beautiful things as the district attorney arranged with him to [do] [[say]]. When we asked him the question, "Who told you to [do] [[say]] those things; to identify those circulars." He answered: ["]the district attorney,["] and for the first time in the case we had the district attorney hanging his head down. We had got him [there] [[then]]. When we asked where he was born we could not get it out of him, because if we did we would have proved something. Who can tell if there was a [Gargill] in the employ of the Black Star Line? Let us see the pay roll book of the Black Star Line. The boy testified that he was working with the Black Star Line from 1919 to 1921. We will see how much he got for all that period of time in the cash book.

Gentlemen of the jury, you have heard the little boy, [Gargill], if that was his name, testify that he was employed with the Black Star Line from 1919 to 1921. In the [records] [[books]] you will not find [such a testimony w] [[any record. W]]hen you come to look on the treasurer's book [(he said he got his pay from George Tobias)], you will find there was one [Gargill] working only from July 2, 1920, to November 5, 1920, so when he testified he posted circulars in 1919 to 1921, was [Gargill] was [[not]] telling the truth? Where did that [Gargill] come from[?] We have not found out his first name yet. Such a [Gargill] never worked with the Black Star Line from 1919 to 1921, and the treasurer's book of the Black Star Line will tell the tale.

We have Mr. B. O'Shannon,[29] the mail foreman in the post office, bringing here a mass of figures about the Negro World's being sent out. From where to where? If these people were supposed to buy stock at certain points, why didn't they [specify] [[testify]] to what points the mail went, so as to establish the truth in their case and why didn't they show the signature of some representative from the Negro World to [show] [[prove]] that such a delivery was made to the postoffice? Oh, we can make up anything we want to suit our convenience when we wish. Gentlemen, will you take away some one's liberty on such things, just a mass of figures, dates, etc., to where?—to anywhere, some probably went to Limbo and Saturn for that matter because aeroplanes carry [money] [[the mails nowadays]].

OTHER WITNESSES

We come to Mrs. [Dorson] [[Lawson]],[30] another one who spilled the beans on our good friend, the District Attorney. When we placed her under cross-examination, we asked her to show [any] [[her]] subpoena. She fumbled around and looked at the District Attorney and bowed her head awaiting [for] [[his]] approval. Garvey saw it. You must have seen it, too. The lady with the dark glasses, [[who wore them]] so that you could not follow the movements of her eyes and the [movement of her face.] [[lines of her stare]]. Oh, a lot of things are hidden behind some [[dark]] glasses. The movement of the eyes tell when we are speaking the truth and when we are not going to speak the truth we hide our vision from the public [[for deception]]. She could not help bowing and waiting approval from the District Attorney. Gentlemen, you will surely not pay any attention to Mrs. [Dor]son. She said she bought stock in 1917, when the Black Star Line never sold stock in 1917[[, it was not in existence then]]. A woman who told such an untruth to testify away the liberty of other people. She was sick, she said, and wanted money, but you remember how her sickness coincided with the sickness of Mrs. Harrison[31] from Philadelphia and the other lady, Mrs. Carington?[32] They were all sick. It was the arrangement to be all sick, so as to appeal to the finer sympathy of you gentlemen. Their money was taken by Marcus Garvey, the arch villain, the arch thief. The actions of that woman on the bench showed that she could get $30 in five minutes, the woman was such a bully. She read an advertisement in the Negro World and bought her shares. That is what she said; then she went back and said she heard Garvey speak and bought her shares then. When did she buy her shares? When she read the advertisement in the Negro World or when Garvey spoke—which time? Surely you will not believe a character like that and take away anybody's liberty, not even a dog's liberty on such a testimony? She, who said that Garcia told her the company was bankrupt, but she didn't remember [since] [[the time,]] but wanted so badly to say that Garvey said the same thing. I suppose[[d]] she didn't remember the arrangement so as to hold Mr. Garvey for selling stock in a company after he said it was bankrupt. She placed it on Garcia, not on Garvey, in her testimony.

Then we come to Edward Orr,[33] [[the yellow man]] from the West Indies, who pretend[s][[ed]] that there is no prejudice between [black and brown] [[yellow, brown and black]] people in his part of the world. He sued Garvey before for [$805] [[$305]] for stock bought in the Black Star Line. He didn't buy stock in Garvey. Garvey was not [a] [[the]] corporation by himself. He bought stock in the Black Star Line, but sued Garvey to get back [$805] [[$305]]. Now, didn't that show [the] malice? Why didn't he sue the Black Star Line? He testified that Garvey never sold stock, but the secretary did, and he got his stock from the secretary of the Black Star Line [but when he sued, he sued Garvey and not the Black Star Line]. The malice of the man is enough evidence to satisfy you, the gentlemen of the jury, that you could not take away the liberty of anyone on the testimony of such a man.

Then we have Mr. Schenck. This Mr. Schenck from Washington. He couldn't remember or identify anything until he reached the point where he had to. The District Attorney made him identify something, and then he said he treated it as trash, threw it away. A man who treated something like trash is really not the man [to be] [[who is]] defrauded. But he testified he bought his stock at the meeting where Garvey spoke at a Baptist Church in Washington and not through the mail. From an agent at a meeting at Washington, where Garvey spoke. Where, then, can you establish that the mail was used to defraud in Washington? If he received literature in the mail after he bought his stock, he treated it as trash; therefore, it had absolutely no influence on him. There was no fraud. But he is an employe of the Government Printing Office [[in Washington]], and he thought he was doing a wonderful thing to [get some money] [[testify]], not knowing the spirit of our great government, which does not support anyone in falsehoods, untruths, and lies. Could a government support a man like Warner in [the American Government] [[in his lies]]? The whole world looks to this country for justice. Can we allow men like Warner [[to]] represent the [Mexican] Government? It is a shame, a disgrace, that they should link up [their names with our] [[these discredited persons for the]] government. [He] [[Schenck]] never bought stock through the mails. Now we will go to Mrs. [Anistry] [[Annie Still]]. You remember, she was very still when she came in. She was still because she was sick. She was [beyond] [[ever so]] still. Remember [the] sick lady from Philadelphia, who was so sick she could hardly talk? But when she found out she was [[cornered]] telling an untruth and we noticed it, she was as loud and as boisterous as anyone here, and I believe I [was] [[am]] the loudest one here.

So, you won't convict and take away one's liberty on this testimony. Her testimony was so confused we could not understand it. When the District Attorney asked her "Where did you get this letter?" she answered, "In New York." Can you convict anyone on such testimony? The testimony itself was not clear. She said she got some circulars and could not identify them. How flimsy this [report] [[testimony]] for this charge for which we are indicted and are to be condemned. She testified that she bought her stock at a meeting when Fred A. Toote was president in Philadelphia, where Garvey spoke. Surely, there is no harm in Garvey speaking to sell stock? So that testimony is not worth the time consumed in giving it. Whether Garvey sold stock in Liberty Hall, a church in Washington or Philadelphia, does not enter into this case, as the judge will charge you at the proper time.

Now we come to Benny [Danson] [[Dancy]], one of the [men] [[witnesses]] of the second count. Mr. Dan[son] knew nothing. When the District Attorney pounded at him, then he admitted that "[It] [[He]] went to my address in Brooklyn." Then he said: "I cannot remember." Then he said: "Did you read anything about a ship in Africa?" Then the man got sore and said: "Yes." Then I cross-examined him and his next move he said: "Yes. I read something about going to Africa." Can you convict a man on testimony like that? He said no first and yes afterwards. So, gentlemen, these persons that the District Attorney will tell you about, these poor washer women, these poor men who have not a dime[. Now listen to this] [[; now remember their]] testimony well. If you had an office and a woman came into it in [that] [[the]] attitude [[of Mrs. Lawson]], you would throw her out. I didn't do that. I asked her to leave. She acted the same way in my office only two years ago and went out with threats, [and] [[as she did on the stand,]] then I suppose she went to the District Attorney, who is the collecting agent for people who want to spite [[and get even with]] others. When some employees are dissatisfied, when someone believes they are taken advantage of, they go to him. She told the District Attorney, who takes away your books and holds you up many days and makes your business go to pieces, because someone wants to get even with [Garcia and] Garvey and somebody else, and the only way to do it is to go to the District Attorney, who is representing the government. Surely the government is not a collecting agent for people who want to spite others.

Now we come to Mr. Smith of Indianapolis, Ind. He also could not identify anything about envelopes. Couldn't say what came in [it] [[them]]. Could not remember that he signed a questionnaire[[;]] that [[he]] went to the post office and made it out, but after a while Mr. Smith was forced to say that this is the circular and that circular came through the mail. Surely you will not convict anyone on the memory of Smith, which failed [him,] to recognize anything but the envelope. And he had to recognize that somehow. The paper had no name when it was shown, and he could not remember until the District Attorney in his masterly manner got him to say "Yes, I think this kind of a circular came," and then he admitted he made out a questionnaire. Will you convict and take away one's liberty on the testimony of such people? I feel [surely] [[you will]] not.

Before I close, let's go to de Bourg, the aged man—I respect him for his years [[, but for nothing else]]—the man who has lost the spirit of truth [[, the man who has sent his soul to hell]].

Now we come to the other man from Stamford, Conn. He could not remember anything until from mere exhaustion he said, "I think I remember seeing this circular." So those testimonies on these counts are the ones on which you are supposed to convict four men, indicted before you for fraud.

[Harry] Watkis, the [[white]] wife kicker, Watkis, the man who talked about spending 60 percent of the Black Star Line [[money]] in a trip. Who told him to do that? When Garvey found out, didn't Garvey get him arrested? Did not Garvey get him indicted and up before the grand jury? And then he [came to talk] [[talked]] about the $300 [[he spent to get out of trouble]]. You remember I made several efforts to put in the letter of the police commissioner of Youngstown and I was not permitted to do so? Gentlemen, imagine what is in that letter. Imagine who got that $300. [Not, it is stated, that] Watkis got the $300 and [[split with]] Brooks. There is absolutely no testimony [[to convict]]. Could the jury convict a man on [that?] [[Watkis' testimony.]]

This innocent[[?]] Watkis, this crooked Watkis, is another star witness for the District Attorney, and Watkis was held in the Heights court before the grand jury of the county of New York, [where] [[when]] Kilroe was [once] Assistant District Attorney. Do you wonder that Watkis was not indicted? [by the grand jury?] That he went free?

MRS. FOLEY VS. POWELL

We pass from Watkis to [*Fred*] Powell. Look at Powell and you could see that there was something about him that you yourself would not trust[[. A man who looked like him convicts himself]] [a man who looked like him]. Would you trust him with your cash? A man who said he was always broke, looking [[anxious]] like that for [over 48] years and a student of law? Gentlemen, surely you do not pay any attention to what Powell said to you. Look at the man, the fellow who said Garvey put the cold hand [down] on him. Yes, I did, because he didn't [give up the back cash] [[look right and would not allow him to handle the cash]], and that is why he has it in for Garvey.

[Once Powell] [[He said he]] gave Garvey money for stock that Garvey never turned over. [Did Garvey—b] [[B]]ut Garvey came to his office and got Mrs. Foley,[34] his secretary, to make up the stock. He leaves an honest impression in your minds. After he said that, Garvey sent a telegram to Mrs. Foley, [to] [[at]] Atlanta, Ga., [[to be here]] at the expense of over $200, and you heard Mrs. Foley on that witness stand, during which time I searched the office of the Black Star Line and found the receipt, which you saw in evidence—the receipt signed by Powell himself in getting the money. Mrs. Foley surely impressed you as an honest woman. She had absolutely no cause to tell a lie, because the very morning she came in is the very morning she testified. This is the receipt, gentlemen, with Powell's name on it.

Then we will go [[back]] to Mr. [LeBourg] [[DeBourg]]. I am sorry to speak of that man and the things that [man] [[he]] told me, and said on the witness stand [[to the contrary, for the government]]. I tried to get in certain papers with Mr. [LeBourg]'s handwriting for him to identify, but I could not get them in. If I could have, [in his own handwriting, it] [[they]] would tell a different tale to what he said in that box. But it is too late. I am sorry for the man; I am sorry for his soul, and I need not say more about him. [[I leave him to his God.]]

And now the witnesses for the defense. I need not say one word about them. You have had your impression. You have seen them, and I feel sure you are impressed with what they said. You heard Miss Davis, the woman who lived [with me] [[at my house]] for years, the woman who said things that could have been misunderstood in many ways, the woman who was in Jamaica with me and lived in my house for over three years. Her testimony was such that you could not very well understand the situation. I asked her if I had money, if I went to the races. If I had been the kind of man the District Attorney painted me to be, Garvey could have fixed up Miss Davis and she could have given a testimony that would have sent me to heaven, but

Garvey never talked to her. Garvey doesn't even talk to his wife about this case, outside of what goes on, as far as his liberty is concerned. Garvey desires the world to tell the truth. I did not fix up any testimony with Henrietta Vinton Davis. She told what she knew.

We have Carrie Leadett, the black girl, who was [his] [[Garvey's]] first secretary, who told the truth as she knew it, and believed it to be, and whom the District Attorney tried to trip. Gentlemen, in the name of the government the District Attorney tried to trip her, and when he could not get her to tell lies, he left her in disgust. Surely, it is not the purpose of the great government to charge the jury under lies.

We have Mr. J.M. Certain, the man who testified what he knew, what he could remember. I believe as vice-president he tried to save himself and didn't want to tell all that he knew. I sympathize with him. But he told you what he knew about Garvey. I would not save myself at the expense of anyone else.

We have [Janie] [[Jennie]] Jenkins. You saw that woman was telling the truth. You understood that she was one of the first directors of the Black Star Line. She was assistant treasurer of the Black Star Line.

Next, Alice O'Gara,[35] another woman, a brown-skinned woman, who told the truth.

Gwen Campbel[[l]], the girl I asked if she was a friend of Garcia and Thompson. The girl who was my private secretary and desk clerk in my office during my absence in the West Indies, and who signed all the orders in my absence and placed my name on them. You saw her. You heard what she had to say, [you saw her.] I wanted her to speak the truth. She told some of the things she knew and kept back some things she should have said because, I suppose, she didn't want to hurt [anybody] [[her friends Thompson and Garcia]]. She was a government witness [[first]]. I suppose they could not use her in the way they wanted. Nevertheless, she testified for me.

We had Jas. Hercules, the man who sailed with Captain Cockburn. Look at his face. Decide for yourself whether he spoke the truth or not. You have Amy Jacques Garvey as witness. I will not go over the testimony of Amy Jacques Garvey. You formed your own impression of what she said.

You have John Garrett, the engineer man who testified twice. The last time he testified that he recommended many ships for the purchase by the Black Star line to be named the Phyllis Wheatley.

You had Mr. Morton,[36] who carried out the management for [*James M.*] Briggs in [sailing] [[selling]] the Kanawha [for] [[to]] the Black Star Line. He testified he knew no commission was given to Garvey.

We have Balfour Williams,[37] the man from Boston, whom the District Attorney tried to make lie. Enid Lamos, who told all the methods used in Garvey's office and his methods when he went to speak when she was with him. That she [took up] [[received]] the money[,] when she was with Garvey, and other secretaries did the same [things].

Did Garvey, who could speak at these meetings for 50 cents and 75 cents admission, bringing in $300 and $500 a night and turning it all over, have to send a letter through the mail to get $5.00 when he could speak at a meeting and collect $600? [When] Garvey can speak and collect $2,000 or $3,000 and Garvey gets but a meagre [$1,000] [[salary]] a year, is that the way men defraud?

You have the testimony of Clifford Bourne, who told of the trouble Garvey had in getting back [and] [[to this country. He]] he had to cable Secretary Hughes and the President of the United States in order to get back, because of others who tried [to keep him out. They tried] to throw the Black Star Line [in] [[into]] bankruptcy and keep Garvey in the West Indies, and say he stole the money[,] [and we have another company]. You see the connection between the Black Star Line of New Jersey and the Black Star Line, Inc.[,] of Delaware. You heard the testimony of William Ware, president of one of the large divisions. You have the testimony of all the other presidents from respective parts of this country, representing six million members of the Universal Negro Improvement Association, [[part]] of whom [part of them] are stockholders in the Black Star Line. Will such men lie? Could Garvey live if Garvey had defrauded so many people? Garvey, they testified, spoke at all their meetings. Garvey went to Detroit, they said, Cincinnati, Philadelphia, wherever stockholders are supposed to be. He spoke to 30,000 members of the organization in New York, and Garvey is in his body and his flesh [[safe]]; yet Garvey has defrauded the poor people according to the District Attorney.

WILFORD SMITH

I need not go over the [[testimony of the]] fifty-odd witnesses. It would take away from the time allotted to me. I will now touch upon this Orion vessel, but before [that] [[doing so]] I want to remind you about this power of attorney of Wilford Smith. You will find that there was never any power of attorney given him. It was only a matter of [properly] understanding that Mr. Smith would protect the signature and name of Marcus Garvey wheresoever it was used. That didn't mean that Smith was constituted president of the Black Star Line, or president-general of the Universal Negro Improvement Association, because these were corporate bodies and [[its officers]] could only be elected by the Board of Directors, and not by the president, especially when there was a vice-president. I had to protect my name because of the system used in the office, because they used my name and made me the scapegoat. They talk about Thompson being a scapegoat. Garvey is [a] [[the]] scapegoat when Garvey is about three or four thousand miles away [when] [[and]] his name is being used. He had to try some kind of protection to save [him] [[himself]] from things of this kind. Smith was a director. He was the attorney of the company. To whom better could I go than to such a man, an aged man of good reputation in the community, and especially when the vice-president had no financial interest in the company? He was sore [[(Thompson)]], according to what he said, but suppose Smith had not done that, not only would $25,000 been gone, but the whole company would have [gone] [[been stolen]]. That is what they are sore about, because Smith [would have to get] [[had to keep]] some kind of a check on the use of Garvey's name. They didn't [mind] [[want]] that. They wanted to get the use of Garvey's name, a free license to use Garvey's name. Then when anything went wrong, they would resign and poor Garvey would be in a [mess] [[fix]].

Garvey used the mails to find some folks, and could not get them. Let's take down that letter of Ware's written by Thompson, that Thompson[,] on the stand, denied that he wrote.[38] Will you turn to the back of that letter, and do you not observe the [sinister] [[symmetry of]] impression[?] [At] [[On]] the back of the letter you have the same impression above and below the man's signature. If one was typed before the other, the impression would not be the same. That man looked at the letter and denied it. Now consider the supposed Hong Kaeng. Hong Kong were the original names they are typed in. But when this man Garcia sent that cablegram about the Hong Kong, which was only a 400-ton boat, they said no, it is the Hong Kaeng, not the Hong Kong, and they slipped the "ae" in instead of the "o."

THE BLACK STAR LINE

Gentlemen, we come to the point where this Black Star Line was said to be bankrupt. Bankruptcy [[papers]] was never filed against the Black Star Line. The [[papers]] Black Star Line had times when it might not have been in the best financial condition, but no one had filed any papers for bankruptcy. We had liabilities and assets not only in money, not only in property, but the good will of the people, which was the greatest asset, and if somebody had not taken the funds and dissatisfied the people about that boat, we would have been a success.

Where did the Black Star Line get money to buy the Yarmouth? From the same people who would have been willing to buy [[the other boats]]. When we bought the Yarmouth we had no assets other than the good will of the people, and they subscribed the money to buy the Yarmouth, and the Kanawha and the Shady Side. If the people did that, then would not they have done more? They would have given one-half [of what] [[more if]] they had to acquire that African ship, but they were told the ship would be here tomorrow. Tomorrow never came, and the people who were the assets became doubtful and we could have no ships.

When Garvey was in the West Indies over $30,000 was wasted. If the management had signed [under] a proper contract with Morse we probably would have had the ship Kanawha [properly carried out] [[in different condition]]. It was not so much the money, but intelligence and brain. We started the organization with only 13 members, and today we have an organization of six million members throughout the world with 900 branches.

We had no other [money commission] [[monetary considerations]] or reward [[before us]], but [for] the good we could do for our race, for this and succeeding generations. Those of us who started [[the work]] did not think about salary of $50 a week. We thought of giving what we could in body and soul for the emancipation of a race and for our country. I hardly believe you understand the situation. You will say it was bad business. But, gentlemen, there is something spiritual beside business. You will say that we sold $800,000, in stock. They ought to have good ships. Did we get all that money at the same time? And during the time we were gathering this money we had to invest and carry on and show good faith. We had to pay in parts on the Kanawha and Shady Side. If we had [[all]] the money at the [same] [[one]] time we could have bought one of the best ships in this country.

When we made our purchase [[the tonnage on]] ships [were] [[was]] high. When we were supposed to [buy] [[have bought]] the Phyllis Wheatley [and the Yarmouth] tonnage had fallen,[39] ships were going practically for nothing. If we were able to get ships during the war we would have gotten ships; when shipping had fallen in this country, as far as the price went. The Shipping Board had numbers of ships. The failure of the Black Star Line was only a drop in the bucket. You had numbers of failures among your own race, gentlemen. You experts, you failed by the hundreds and during the period the Black Star Line had the difficulties the Shipping Board of the United States lost $300,000,000.[40] Was there fraud on the part of the Shipping Board in the use of the millions? The taxes of your money and my money, were converted into ships and the ships failed. Did we indict our great President for the use of the millions? Sometimes to fail is but stepping stones to greater things.

The Universal Negro Improvement Association and the Black Star Line employs thousands of black girls and black boys. Girls who could only be washerwomen in your homes, [gentlemen. Kitchen hands in your homes,] we made clerks and stenographers of them in the Black Star Line offices. You will see that from the start we tried to dignify our race. If I am to be condemned for that I am satisfied.

I am a Negro. I make absolutely no apology for being a Negro because my God created me to be what I am, and as I am so will I return to my God, for He knows just why He created me as He did. So, gentlemen, you will understand that behind the whole business proposition lies the spirit of the movement. I have no time to go into the work of the Universal Negro Improvement Association, but I say this: I know there are certain people who do not like me because I am black; they didn't like me because I am not born here through no fault of mine. I didn't bring myself into this western world. You know the history of my race. I was brought here; I was sold to some slave master in the island of Jamaica. Some Irish slave master who subsequently gave my great-grandfather his name. Garvey is not an African name; it is an Irish name, as Johnston is not an African name, Garcia is not an African name, Thompson and Tobias are not African names. Where did we get those names from? We inherited them from our own slave masters, English, French, Irish or Scotch. So, if I was born in Jamaica, it was no fault of mine. It was because that slave ship which took me to Jamaica did not come to American ports. [That is how Garvey was not born in America, and that] [[That]] is how some Negroes of America were not born in the West Indies.

We did not come here of our own [[free]] will. We were brought here, and so the question of birth does not enter into the question of the Negro. It was a matter of accident. Will you blame me for the accident of being a Jamaica Negro and not an American Negro? Surely you will not. But there is a bigger question involved. It is a question of race. What are you going to do with this question of race? You may sit quietly by, but it is going to be serious later on, and that is why the Universal Negro Improvement Association is endeavoring to assist you in solving the Negro problem by helping the Negro to become enterprising, independent politically, and by having a country of his own. If you follow me down the ages you will see within a hundred years you are going to have a terrible race problem in America, when you will have increased and the country will become overpopulated. It will be a fight for existence between two opposite races. The weak will have to go down in defeat before the strong. In the riots of Washington, East St. Louis, Chicago, Tulsa, study the race question and you will find that some serious thinking must be done now to solve this problem; otherwise our children will be confronted with it. Do you know when you want bread and the other fellow wants it, when there is only one loaf—[you know] what is going to happen? Enmity and pressure is going to spring up and a fight is going to ensue. That is why the Universal Negro Improvement Association has started this proposition to redeem Africa and build up a country of our own, so as not to molest you in the country your fathers founded hundreds of years ago.

Some Negroes believe in social equality. They want to intermarry with the white women of this country, and it is going to cause trouble later on. Some Negroes want the same jobs you have. They want to be [President] [[presidents]] of the nation. What is going to be the outcome? Study the race question and you will find that the program of the Universal Negro Improvement Association and the Black Star Line is the solution of the problem which confronts us, not only in this country, but throughout the world.

Folks try to misrepresent me and say I don't like white people. That is not true. Some of the best friends I have are white men. The bishop[41] who testified here has been [a] [[my]] friend from a youth. He said other things that some of us did not understand. I asked him, Do you know Marcus Garvey?—he said yes. What is your opinion of him? He said doubtful. Now probably you didn't understand what he meant. Garvey was a public man. Opinions differ. He was a priest and he had to tell the truth. Surely some men are doubtful of Marcus Garvey, and there are some who are not doubtful. He didn't say that Garvey was doubtful. He gives it as it was, when I asked him about his personal opinion I was not allowed because it was not the proper question [in court] [[, the court ruled]]. He said, however, Garvey was a worthy man, so I trust you will not have the wrong impression.

A HEART UNTAINTED[42]

. . . I stand before you and the honorable court for your judgment and I do not regret what I have done for the Universal Negro Improvement Association; for the Negro race, because I did it from the fullness of my soul. I did it with the fear of my God, believing that I was doing the right thing. I am still firm in my belief that I served my race, people, conscience and God. I further make no apology for what I have done. I ask for no mercy. If you say I am guilty, I go to my God as I feel, a clear conscience and a clean soul, knowing I have not wronged even a child of my race or any member of my family. I love all mankind. I love Jew, Gentile, I love white and black.

I have respect for every race. I believe the Irish should be free; they should have a country. I believe the Jew should be free and the Egyptian should be free, the Indian and the Poles. I believe also that the black man should be free. I would fight for the freedom of the Jew, the Irish, the Poles; I would fight and die for the liberation of 400,000,000 Negroes. I expect from the world for Negroes what the world expects from them.

I thank you for your patience, gentlemen, and his Honor for the patience he has exhibited also. There has been some differences[.] [[, but]] I have great respect [for his Honor and] for [all] this court. I respect the constitution of this great country, the most liberal constitution in the world. This great government, the most liberal in the world. Could I go to Washington [to pay] [[without paying]] my homage and respect to that hero, George Washington, and Abraham Lincoln, the emancipator of our million slaves? Then, how dare anyone accuse me of being disrespectful to the United States or the courts— I feel that my rights are infringed upon. If I differed from the judge, it is but human. I know you are businessmen just as I am. My business has been going to pieces and I know how much yours is going to pieces, but if you were to be tried and I were a [juryman] [[juror]] I would give you the same consideration as you have given me, therefore, I leave myself to you, feeling that you should judge me as your God shall judge you, not for friendship, not for satisfying the whims of someone, but because of truth and justice.

The district attorney will tell you it is Garvey, Garvey, Garvey. Garvey is the master mind, Garvey is the genius; Garvey is but a man. Garvey is but human. But Garvey must be destroyed, but in destroying the physical in Garvey, you cannot destroy the soul and I feel you gentlemen will not do anything except that which is prompted by justice, truth and the law, [but] [[as]] you know the law is but an expression of truth, of justice, and of thought. The law demands truth and justice so that justice can be done.

I leave myself to you. I have not denied anything that I know of [[and have done]].

Printed in *NW*, 23 June 1923. Reprinted in *P&O*, 2: 184–216.

1. Louis A. Schenck was a laborer for twenty years at the Government Printing Office in Washington, D.C. As a government witness at the trial, he testified that he bought stock in the BSL while attending a speech by Garvey at the Carmel Baptist Church (*Marcus Garvey* v. *United States*, no. 8317, Ct. App., 2d Cir., 2 February 1925, pp. 770–782).

2. John Smith Scott, a government witness, was from Stamford, Conn. Garvey referred to him as G. Simon, or George Scott, because that was the name printed on Scott's stock certificate. He testified that he bought BSL stock and had attended BSL and UNIA meetings but that he had

never read Garvey's writings (ibid., p. 894).

3. Thaddeus S. Smith, a government witness, testified that he bought BSL stock in March 1920 after reading about it in the *Negro World*, which he claimed he had received for several months prior to making his purchase. The stock certificate listed his name as T.I. Smith (ibid., pp. 852–860).

4. Actually Addie L. Still. Garvey called her Annie Still, and on the stock certificate her name appeared as Annie Smith. She testified that she and her niece bought three BSL shares after attending a meeting at which Garvey spoke in Philadelphia. She received her stock certificate in the mail after making the purchase and began receiving the *Negro World* and other UNIA information. During his cross-examination of the witness, Garvey attempted to link Still's disillusionment with the BSL with her illness. Still maintained, however, that she had joined the UNIA for the death benefits but had begun to fear violence at the meetings, particularly one at the Mother Bethel Hall, located at 6th and Lombard, where gunfire was actually exchanged (ibid., pp. 833–852).

5. Edgar Sayers was not a witness, but is mentioned in Garvey's cross-examination of postal inspector Alvin Williamson. Williamson testified that the Post Office unsuccessfully attempted to deliver mail from the UNIA to Sayers's home at 55 Broad Street, Georgetown, Demerara, British Guiana (now Guyana) (ibid., p. 906).

6. Fritz C. Herbert Parris, who lived in British Guiana, was one of the people to whom the Post Office attempted to deliver mail from the UNIA. Neither Sayers nor Parris was ever called as a witness, and in the final defense motion, it was alleged that they did not exist and that therefore all charges of fraud on these two counts should be dropped (ibid., pp. 906, 2,388–2,389).

7. Benny Dancy, a government witness, worked at Pennsylvania Station in New York. He bought fifty-three BSL shares and in return received letters from the UNIA, BSL, and Negro Factories Corp. He had heard Garvey speak, read the *Negro World*, and stated that he had received circulars and other BSL solicitation for investments in ships. At the trial Dancy identified an envelope marked "Black Star Line" as having been mailed to him at his Brooklyn residence. Dancy testified that at government request he had turned over his mail concerning the BSL to be used as evidence (ibid., pp. 860–865).

8. This transcription draws on versions printed in the *Negro World* and in *Philosophy and Opinions*. Most text is identical in the two versions. Text appearing only in the *Negro World* version is enclosed in square brackets [ ]. Significantly altered text in *Philosophy and Opinions* is enclosed in double square brackets [[ ]].

9. Thomas Merrilees testified that he calculated Garvey's salary as president of the BSL during the period 12 August to 22 December 1919 as $1,175; during 1920 it was $5,168.84. Garvey received no salary in 1921 (ibid., p. 1,053). Overall stock sales reached $765,130 (ibid., p. 1,057).

10. Garvey began conducting his own defense on 22 May 1923, the second day of the trial. He asked his lawyer, Cornelius McDougald, to remain in an advisory capacity. McDougald refused (ibid., pp. 184–185). He is reported later to have called Garvey a "damned fool" who had turned the trial into a circus (ibid., pp. 184–185; Cornelius McDougald, Jr., to Robert A. Hill, 7 May 1985).

11. In this case, which was settled by the U.S. Supreme Court in 1888, Silva, a private citizen of California, sued the Nevada-based Southern Development Co., a silver mining corporation, for misrepresentation of a mine purchased by Silva. The court decided against the complainant (*United States Report: Cases Adjudged in the Supreme Court*, 125, October term, 1887 [New York: Banks & Brothers Law Publishers, 1888]: pp. 247–259).

12. Judge Julian Mack's summation to the jury noted the trial's delays in the following words: "in my judgment, the case has been prolonged by reason of fact that the defendant Garvey has acted as his own attorney. I do not believe that in acting as his own attorney he had any intention thereby to prolong the trial, and, after a careful consideration of the entire case, I do not believe that he purposely or intentionally did prolong the trial" (ibid., p. 2,396).

13. While Richard Warner, former BSL secretary, testified that he frequently met with District Attorney Edwin Kilroe, he never admitted that Kilroe told him what to say (ibid., p. 175).

14. Warner testified that he kept no separate accounts for BSL monies, which at times he used to pay bills for the *Negro World*, the UNIA restaurant, and UNIA salaries (ibid., pp. 160, 180).

15. According to Garvey, the letter "shows the disposition of certain monies which Warner received in my [Garvey's] absence in Virginia, but it does not show the entire transactions of the Black Star Line" (ibid., p. 2,204).

16. This is a reference to the cross-examination of Edwin Kilroe by Henry Lincoln Johnson, Garcia's lawyer. In his questioning Johnson alluded to Kilroe's March 1921 conviction for conspiracy to obstruct justice in a bigamy case (*NYT*, 31 March 1921). Kilroe was forced to resign from the

district attorney's office in April 1921, but he was later reinstated when his conviction was overturned in December 1922. The court declared Johnson's line of questioning—designed to show Kilroe's bias—inadmissible (ibid., pp. 126–130). The next paragraph in the *Negro World*, which repeats the previous 170 words, has been omitted.

17. The North American Steamship Co. was formed by the North German Lloyd Line and the Baltimore and Ohio Railroad Co. in 1867 (N.R.P. Bonsor, *North Atlantic Seaway* [Prescot, England: T. Stephenson & Sons, 1955], p. 168).

18. George Pilkington, a government witness, was a real estate agent who arranged the sale of a house to Amy Ashwood on 15 October 1919 in New York. At the trial he stated that he had accepted a $500 check from the BSL, signed by Garvey, and $500 payment in cash for the purchase of the house, with the remainder to be paid in later installments (ibid., pp. 186–190).

19. Louis C. Whitfield, a government witness, was a real estate agent from 1907 to 1919. Whitfield worked for the Direct Leasing Corp., which in 1919 purchased Amy Ashwood's property at 125 West 131st Street. Whitfield stated that he dealt with Ashwood through a broker, Benjamin W. Smith (ibid., pp. 191–196).

20. Smith-Green was not called as a witness at the trial. The second indictment does not contain letters by Smith-Green; however, counts one and two of the first indictment contained Smith-Green's letter to Lelia Rogers and his letter to Marcus Evelyn-Graham as part of the indictment (ibid., pp. 8–10).

21. James Hercules testified in Garvey's defense. He had been employed as a boatswain on the Yarmouth in 1920 and testified that Captain Cockburn was corrupt (ibid., pp. 1,340–1,347).

22. While being cross-examined by Marcus Garvey, Cockburn admitted to receiving $2,000 from a Mr. George Nagi of the Green River Distilling Co. as a "consideration, as a present for the extra amount of energy that I put into getting this cargo off the dock" (ibid., p. 385). Cockburn denied that Smith-Green received any of this money.

23. Under Garvey's cross-examination, Cockburn admitted to buying considerable property after 1919. However, Judge Julian Mack declared Garvey's question about whether or not the property was purchased in Cockburn's wife's name as immaterial (ibid., pp. 414–415).

24. Adrian Richardson testified that he could not remember when his mariner's license was issued. Garvey attempted to reiterate this line of questioning, but Judge Mack ruled it immaterial (ibid., pp. 457–473).

25. Prosecution witness Lawrence J. Hunt testified that he regularly printed circulars for the BSL and that he received up to $350 a week in payment (ibid., pp. 671–675).

26. These advertisements appeared weekly in the *Negro World* from 19 March until 10 December 1921.

27. Actually William Cooney, a government witness who worked as a mailer for the *Negro World* printer, Henry Rogowski. Rogowski's printing shop was located at 444 Pearl Street, where Cooney was the foreman of the mail room; from November 1920 he was involved in mailing the newspaper (ibid., pp. 679–682).

28. Schuyler Cargill was a nineteen-year-old who had worked as an office boy for the BSL and was employed as a solution maker for the National Chemical Co. at the time of the trial. He gave contradictory testimony, stating at first that he worked at mailing, filing, and posting letters for the BSL from 1919 to 1921; later he changed his testimony by stating that he worked only in 1921. Cargill lived with his parents in Roselle, N.J. (ibid., pp. 683–704).

29. Actually Thomas J. O'Shaunnessey, employed as a foreman in the auditing department of the Post Office; he testified for the government on Post Office regulations and the location of various post offices in New York (ibid., pp. 705–708).

30. Dorothy Lawson, government witness, was a dressmaker; she lived with her husband at 1592 Madison Avenue near 131st Street. She stated that she bought stock in the BSL on 14 April 1919 because she wanted to help blacks and that she invested her entire savings of $100 in the BSL. Shortly after purchasing the stock she and her husband traveled to Cuba to promote commerce among blacks. In 1922 she visited the ships and became discontented with the BSL, at which time she confronted Garvey at his office and attempted to retrieve her investment. Her testimony was punctuated at various points with remarks about her illness, including comments that she needed to wear glasses as a result of her various illnesses (ibid., pp. 709–733).

31. No evidence of the identity of Mrs. Harrison has been uncovered.

32. Annie Carrington was a Trinidad-born government witness who lived in New York. She worked as a finisher. She stated that she spoke to Garvey personally in October or November 1921

and asked for the return of her $55 investment, but that she did not receive any money. Despite Garvey's allegation there is no mention in her testimony about her illness (ibid., p. 953).

33. Edward Orr, a government witness, was employed as a composer of music in New York. Born in St. John's, Antigua, he had lived in the U.S. for twenty-three years. He stated that he bought $105 worth of stock in the BSL (twenty-one shares) in December 1919. He was a reader of the *Negro World*, which he purchased from the newsstands near his home at 290 West 137th Street. Orr had brought Garvey to court earlier in an attempt to regain money invested both in the BSL and in the Liberian Construction Loan. Garvey accused Orr of being a Socialist and friend of Domingo, Randolph, Owen, and Judge Panken (ibid., pp. 733–770).

34. Mrs. Ella M. Foley, a defense witness, worked for the BSL in the office of the secretary, E.D. Smith-Green. She identified Powell's handwriting on the receipt, submitted as defendant's exhibit no. 22 in the trial (ibid., pp. 1,993–1,994).

35. Alice O'Gara testified that she bought stock in the BSL and was happy with the purchase. She was questioned about the supposed conspiracy among Garvey's associates to discredit him, but most of her testimony was stricken from the record (ibid., pp. 1,275–1,278).

36. Actually James A. Martin of the New York firm of Foley & Martin. Martin was a lawyer for James M. Briggs, who sold the *Kanawha* to the BSL. He was the intermediary between Briggs and Joseph Nolan, the attorney for the BSL, and Captain Swift, who was directly representing the BSL in the transaction (ibid., pp. 1,664–1,688).

37. Balfour J. Williams was a witness for Garvey. He was an accounting student and was made executive secretary for the Boston division of the UNIA. In 1920 he worked for the BSL in New York as a stock salesman under the supervision of E.D. Smith-Green, the BSL general accountant for stock sales. He was also employed as a steward on the *Shadyside* excursion boat, which traveled up and down the Hudson River three or four times a week during the summer of 1920. He was purser on the *Yarmouth* on its voyages from New York to Havana, Port-au-Prince, Haiti, and back to New York (ibid., p. 1,636).

38. A reference to a letter from O.M. Thompson to William Ware dated 24 June 1921, which Garvey entered as an exhibit (ibid., p. 2,721). Thompson admitted he wrote the original letter, but he denied writing the postscript, which claimed that "the Phyllis Wheatley had at last been acquired," and the BSL would be in possession of the ship (ibid., pp. 2,084–2,087).

39. See *Garvey Papers* 3: 232–233.

40. USSB operating losses reached a peak of $52 million in fiscal year 1922 (Paul Maxwell Zeis, *American Shipping Policy*, p. 138).

41. A reference to the Roman Catholic Bishop John J. Collins, who testified as a character witness for Garvey. He stated that he had known Garvey as a schoolboy in Jamaica and that he had received letters from him during Garvey's stay in England. Although he admitted to assisting him financially during his early years in Jamaica and England, Bishop Collins denied any direct knowledge of Garvey's activities since that time (ibid., pp. 2,020–2,021).

42. A reference to Shakespeare's *Henry VI*, act 3, sc. 2, lines 232ff. (*BFQ*).

Speech by Marcus Garvey

[[New York, June 17, 1923]]

Among the many names by which I have been called, I was dubbed by another name a couple of days ago. The District Attorney, with whom I have been contesting the case for my liberty and for the existence of the Universal Negro Improvement Association, in his fervid appeal—in his passionate appeal to the gentlemen of the jury last Friday—said: "Gentlemen, will you let the tiger loose?"[1] (Laughter.) So my subject for tonight is: "Will you let the tiger loose?"

The Tiger Let Loose

The tiger is already loose, and he has been at large for so long that it is no longer one tiger but there are many tigers. The spirit of the Universal Negro Improvement Association has, fortunately for us, made a circuit of the world, to the extent that harm or injury done to anyone will in no way affect the great membership of this association or retard its great program. The world is ignorant of the purpose of this association. The world is ignorant of the scope of this great movement when it thinks that by laying low any one individual it can permanently silence this great spiritual wave that has taken hold of the souls and the hearts and minds of 400,000,000 Negroes throughout the world. We have only started; we are just on our way; we have just made the first lap in the great race for existence and for a place in the political and economic sun of men.

Those of you who have been observing events for the last four or five weeks with keen eyes and keen perceptions will come to no other conclusion than that through the effort to strangle the Universal Negro Improvement Association—through the effort to silence Marcus Garvey—there is a mad desire, there is a great plan to permanently lay the Negro low in this civilization and in future civilizations. But the world is sadly mistaken. No longer can the Negro be laid low; in laying the Negro low you but lay civilization low; in laying the Negro low you but bring down the pillars of creation, because 400,000,000 Negroes are determined to a man to take a place in the world and hold that place. (Applause.) The world is sadly mistaken and rudely shocked at the same time. They thought that the New Negro would bend; they thought that the New Negro was only bluffing and would exhibit the characteristic of the old Negro when pushed to the corner or pushed to the wall. If you want to see the New Negro fight, force him to the wall, and the nearer he approaches the wall the more he fights, and when he gets to the wall he is even more desperate.

What does the world think—that we are going back to sixty years ago in America—going back to eighty-five years ago in the West Indies—going back to 300 years ago in Africa? The world is crazy if they indulge that thought. We are not going back. We are going forward—forward to the emancipation of 400,000,000 oppressed souls; forward to the redemption of a great country and the re-establishment of a greater government. (Applause.)

Garvey has just started to fight; Garvey has not given his first exhibition of his fighting prowess yet. Men, we want you to understand that this is the age of men, not of pigmies, not of serfs and peons and dogs, but men, and we who make up the membership of the Universal Negro Improvement Association reflect the new manhood of the Negro. No fear, no intimidation, no nothing can daunt the courage of the Negro who once affiliates himself with the Universal Negro Improvement Association. The Universal Negro Improvement Association is light, and we have entered into light and shall not go back into darkness. (Applause.) We have entered into the light of a new day; we have seen the light of a new creation; we have seen the light of a new civilization, and we shall follow where that light leads.

RIDICULES PRETENSE OF LOVE FOR NEGROES.

I was amused when my friend, the district attorney, said that he was more interested in Negroes than Marcus Garvey. (Laughter.) They are so accustomed to the old camouflage that they believe that they can plead it everywhere to the satisfaction of every Negro and to every one who comes in contact with them. That is the old camouflage that made them our missionaries sixty years ago; it is the same camouflage that made them our leaders since emancipation; but it is the camouflage that will not stand today. It is impossible for a Negro to be more interested in a Jew than a Jew is interested in himself. It is impossible for an Englishman to be more interested in an Irishman than an Irishman is in himself. It is a lie for any Jew to say he is more interested in Negroes than Negroes are in themselves. It is an unnatural lie to talk about one race being more interested in another race than that race is interested in itself. But that only shows how desperate they are. Sometimes we have to beware of Greeks bearing gifts. Unfortunately I did not have the last word and therefore I was silenced after I placed my defense in; but nevertheless, the world will know to-morrow the outcome of this case wherein Marcus Garvey and the Universal Negro Improvement Association is involved. One way or the other, the world will not be disappointed; one way or the other more than all, Marcus Garvey will not be disappointed. There is no verdict that would disappoint me. I tell you this: that there is to be no disappointment; if they were to give any other verdict than guilty, Marcus Garvey will be very much disappointed; Marcus Garvey knows them so well that Marcus Garvey will expect anything from them; so whether they give a verdict of guilty or not guilty it is immaterial to Marcus Garvey; the fight will just then be starting.

NOT FIGHTING THE GOVERNMENT

Now understand, this is a fight to the finish. We are not fighting this great government, because all Negroes in America—all Negroes over the world know that the greatest democracy in the world is the American democracy; the greatest government in the world is the American republic. We are not fighting America; we are not fighting this great government; we are fighting hypocrisy and lies, and these we are going to fight to the bitter end. Now understand me well—Marcus Garvey has entered the fight for the emancipation of a race; Marcus Garvey has entered the fight for the redemption of a country from the graves of millions of my forebears. At this hour I hear the cry and I am going to answer it even though hell is cut loose before Marcus Garvey. From the silent graves of millions who went down to make me what I am, I shall make for their memory this fight that shall leave a bloody page in the history of man.

They do not know what they doing. They brought 40,000,000 black men from Africa who never disturbed the peace of the world and black men shall put up a fight that shall write a page upon the history of human affairs that shall never be effaced until the day of judgment. I did not bring myself here; they brought me from my silent repose in Africa 300 years ago and this is only the first Marcus Garvey. They have thought that they could for 300 years brutalize a race. They have thought that they could for 200 years steep the soul of a race and let it go at that. They make a terrible mistake. Marcus Garvey shall revenge the blood of his sires. So don't be afraid of Marcus Garvey. When Marcus Garvey goes to jail the world of Negroes will be let loose. They have come at the wrong time.

I appreciate the splendid way in which you have behaved and conducted yourselves during the trial. We shall observe to the letter the laws of this great country, but Africa shall tell the tale. Marcus Garvey has no fear about going to jail. Like MacSwiney or like Carson,[2] like Roger Casement, like those who have led the fight for Irish freedom, so Marcus Garvey shall lead the fight for African freedom.

I repeat that if they think they can stamp out the souls of 400,000,000 black men, they make a tremendous and terrible mistake. We are no longer dogs; we are no longer peons, we are no longer serfs, we are men. Mattuck knew what he was saying about letting the tiger loose. The tiger is already out and the tiger is going to "raise cain." The spirit that actuated George Washington in founding this great republic—the spirit that actuated the fathers of this great republic is the spirit that actuates 6,000,000 black men who are the present-time members of the Universal Negro Improvement Association; it is the spirit that is to actuate 400,000,000 Negroes in the redemption of their motherland Africa. Tell us about fear; we were not born with fear. Intimidation does not drive fear into the soul of Marcus Garvey. There is no fear but the fear of God. Man cannot drive fear into the heart of man because man is but the equal of man. The world is crazy and foolish if they think that they can destroy the principles, the ideals of the Universal Negro Improvement Association. (Applause.)

Printed in *NW*, 23 June 1923. Original headlines omitted.

1. The district attorney's address has not survived. The trial transcript merely indicates that Mattuck delivered a summation to the jury (*Marcus Garvey* v. *United States*, no. 8317, Ct. App., 2d. Cir., 2 February 1925, p. 2,395).

2. Sir Edward Henry Carson (1854–1935), Dublin barrister and chief spokesman for the Irish Unionist cause during the Ulster crisis over home rule, has been termed "the spellbinding rhetorician of the movement" (Karl S. Bottigheimer, *Ireland and the Irish: A Short History* [New York: Columbia University Press, 1982], p. 220). In 1914 Carson spoke openly of leading armed resistance against the British government in order to block the granting of Irish home rule; in 1912 he had informed the signatories of the Ulster Covenant of Resistance, "Don't be afraid of illegalities" (*Dictionary of Irish Biography*, p. 52). Carson was also a leading force in the formation of the Irish Volunteers, a fifty-thousand member paramilitary force organized to resist home rule by force if necessary (guns were actually landed, in April 1914, at Larne in the north of Ireland). Carson abandoned his previous intransigence, however, with the passage of the Government of Ireland Act of 1920; he counseled Unionists to support the setting up under the act of a parliament for Northern Ireland as their only feasible option (H. M. Montgomery Hyde, *Carson: The Life of Sir Edward Carson, Lord Carson of Duncairn* [London: Heinemann, 1953]; F. S. L. Lyons, *Ireland Since the Famine* (London: Widenfeld and Nicolson, 1971), pp. 299–310, and *passim*).

Composite of Headlines from the *Negro Times* and the *Negro World*

THE Negro Times

SPECIAL EDITION | SPECIAL EDITION

VOL. 1 NO 149   DAILY   NEW YORK MONDAY, JUNE 18, 1923   FIVE CENTS

Garvey, Man of Destiny, Calmly Awaits Verdict

Judge Mack Charges The Jury In an Able and Impartial Way

JURY AT HALF PAST FIVE WAS STILL OUT CONSIDERING THEIR VERDICT

THE HEARING OF THE HISTORIC CASE AGAINST MARCUS GARVEY AND HIS CO DEFENDANTS HAS COME TO AN END

THE CONCENSUS OF OPINION UP TO THE TIME OF GOING TO PRESS WAS AN ACQUITTAL OR JURY NOT AGREEING

THE Negro World

The Indispensible Weekly | Reaching the Mass of Negroes
The Voice of the Awaked Negro | The Best Advertising Medium

A Newspaper Devoted Solely to the Interests of the Negro Race

VOL. XI. No. 24   NEW YORK, SATURDAY, JANUARY 28, 1922   PRICE FIVE CENTS IN GREATER NEW YORK SEVEN CENTS ELSEWHERE IN THE U.S.A. TEN CENTS IN FOREIGN COUNTRY

JUDAS ISCARIOTS WAGE COWARDLY WARFARE AGAINST LEADER OF U. N. I. A.

Like Martin Luther, George Washington and Eamon De Valera, Hon. Marcus Garvey Is a "Rebel," Willing to Die, if Need Be, for the Vindication of Ethiopia's Cause

---

THE Negro World

The Indispensable Weekly | Guaranteed Circulation 50,000
The Voice of the Awakened Negro—The Peerless Paper | Reaching the Mass of Negroes Throughout the World

ONE GOD! ONE AIM! ONE DESTINY

A Newspaper Devoted Solely to the Interests of the Negro Race

VOL. IX. No. 1   NEW YORK, SATURDAY, AUGUST 21, 1920   PRICE: THREE CENTS IN GREATER NEW YORK FIVE CENTS ELSEWHERE IN THE U.S.A. TEN CENTS IN FOREIGN COUNTRIES

THE DECLARATION OF RIGHTS READ IN LIBERTY HALL BEFORE THOUSANDS AMIDST TUMULTUOUS APPLAUSE

CRACKERS BEGIN WORK IN LIBERIA

Commissioner - General Introduces Georgia and Texas Methods in the African Republic.

NEGROES SHOULD ENFORCE THE PRINCIPLE OF AFRICA FOR AFRICANS AT HOME AND ABROAD

(*Source*: E. D. Cronon, *Black Moses*, p. 121.)

Article in the *New York Evening Post*

[19 June 1923]

JUDGE GUARDED AT GARVEY TRIAL

It might have been a Southern camp meeting that gathered to-day in the corridors of the Federal Building, while Judge Julian W. Mack charged the jury which has been sitting for many weeks in the trial o[f] Marcus Garvey and his three associates of the Black Star Line.

It was a calm enough looking crowd, with fans fluttering through the tobacco-laden air, gentle voices talking and here and there the flash of white teeth in a dark smile. But two detectives waited to conduct Judge Mack from the bench to his chambers in the Woolworth Building, and some of the ten marshals under Chief Deputy Alfred E. Bunner, who were on duty in the passage[,] said that people had sidled up to them and threatened to "get" them and the jury, too.[1]

That was why Lieut. James J. Gegan, with six members of the bomb squad and several special patrolmen, was also on duty in the corridor, and perhaps the reason why the crowd of dark faces was moved out of the building shortly before 1 o'clock, to congregate again in little groups along the sidewalk.

Since early morning the crowd had waited outside the closed doors of the courtroom. Many a vivid red or green hat shone out in the dim light of the corridor. There were white calicoes with black polka dots and there were the most modern chiffon with white silk stockings and black shoes. Many a necklace of imitation pearls shone out against a swarthy neck, and there were dangling earrings and jingling bangles. There were Panama hats and walking sticks among the men, too, to say nothing of checked suits and boutonnieres of red roses. People walked up and down and chatted with their friends, members of the "You and I" association, of which Garvey is the president.

Tiny picaninnies waited there, their pigtails sticking up straight in regular picaninny fashion, big eyes rolling back and forth in solemn faces. Near them one old woman fanned herself gently, recalling the days when she had lived south in St. Augustine.

"Yas'm," she said, "I believe in de unitin' of de negro race. That's what Marcus Garvey believes i[n]. We all willin' to stay in dis country long as we get our rights. We all belongs here. My father and mother, they belonged to old Abraham du Pont down in St. Augustine.[2] He lef' us to his son, Cornelius du Pont,[3] and he tol' him never to sell us, but jes' hire us out. My father, he fought all trou de Civil War, an' when it was over he got a pension and a lot of lan', and he an' my mother was de han' and foot of old Mr. Cornelius du Pont.

"Yes, mam, Mr. Du Pont, he didn't have nothin' after de Civil War and my father took him and his children to lib' with us, an' bought food for 'em, and hepped him to take care of de children. His wife was dead, his wife named Fanny. Dat's my name, after de ole' mistress, Fanny. . . ."

Judge Mack told the jury that Garvey had had the right to conduct his own case, and that the undue prolongation of the trial resulted, he believed, through ignorance of the practice of the law and not from intent. He asked the jury not to hold this against the defendant in their consideration of the case.

The question to be determined by the jury was, Judge Mack said, whether the money raised by the directors of the Black Star Line for the purchase of ships and the payment of salaries had been illegally used, and whether there was a conspiracy to defraud investors through misuse of the mails. He gave the jury an exposition of the law governing the credibility of witnesses.[4]

Printed in the *New York Evening Post*, 19 June 1923. Original headlines abbreviated.

1. According to Special Employee Andrew M. Battle, his interview with William Grant, an African Legion member, revealed Grant's threat to "kill Amos, Davis, Warren [*sic*], Edgar Gray [*sic*], Sidney de Bourg, Thompson, and everyone who had anything to do with convicting Mr. Garvey" (report by Special Employee Andrew M. Battle, 17–18 June 1923, DJ-FBI, file 61).
2. Abraham Dupont (1768?–1857) was born in South Carolina; in 1829 he settled at Matanzas, Fla., twenty-five miles south of St. Augustine, on part of the 1,850-acre land grant that his father had received from the Spanish government. In time, the French-speaking Dupont became a large and successful sugar planter. By 1852 he owned a house in St. Augustine, three plantations, and thirty-seven slaves. Upon his death, his property and slaves were divided among his nine children, among them Cornelius Dupont. While he did request in his will that slave families be kept intact, he did not stipulate that they were not to be sold (Judith Conlin, St. Augustine Historical Society, to Robert A. Hill, 23 August 1984; last will and testament of Abraham Dupont, 17 June 1852, St. Augustine Historical Society; diary of Mrs. J. A. Rowand, née Mamie Dupont, 14 October 1937, St. Augustine Historical Society; Wanton S. Webb, *Historical, Industrial and Biographical Florida* [New York: W. A. Webb & Co., 1885], p. 97; "Florida Slaves," *1850 State of Florida Census* [St. Augustine Historical Society], p. 32; Matanzas Cemetery Records, Matanzas, St. John's, Fla., St. Augustine Historical Society).
3. Cornelius Dupont (1824–1877), son of Abraham Dupont, was born in South Carolina, grew up in Matanzas and St. Augustine, Fla., and was educated in New York. He was married twice, the second time to Frances Solano, whom he married in 1854. Cornelius Dupont inherited 140 acres of land from his father, and by 1860 he owned a plantation near Federal Point on the St. John's River and had eleven slaves. He fought with the Confederate troops during the Civil War, but disappears from the historical record following the war (Andrew Dupont, Jr., to Robert A. Hill, 10 September 1984; Conlin to Hill, 23 August 1984; diary of Mrs. J. A. Rowand, 14 October 1937, St. Augustine Historical Society; "Florida Slaves, 22nd Division, St. John's County, Florida," *1860 State of Florida Census* [St. Augustine Historical Society], p. 407).
4. In his charge to the jury at the trial's end, Judge Mack cautioned the jury about the guidelines for determining the credibility and biases of witnesses (*Marcus Garvey v. United States*, no. 8317, Ct. App., 2d Cir., 2 February 1925, pp. 2,398–2,403).

Message from Marcus Garvey

Tombs Prison, New York City, U.S.A.
June 19, 1923

I am satisfied to be a victim of an international "frame-up," a conspiracy, not only engaged in by members of the opposite race, but including selfish and jealous members of my own.[1]

It has taken my enemies more than ordinary effort to injure my fair name. They have tried to rob me of the precious treasure, but that cannot soil my soul and conscience.

I am sorry that the name of the United States should be drawn into a "frame-up" and conspiracy to "get me," but the Government is not at fault. We have and must expect misrepresentations in Government, as well as in other human activities, hence I shall not entirely blame the Government for my present position.

In the trial of the case, I have had occasion to observe the ferocious attacks and unfair methods of Assistant District Attorney Maxwell Mattuck, and his hirelings. If he were a typical representative of our Government, then I should have no hope for America, but I feel sure that we have men of honor in this Government, and this great country who will jealously guard its fair name.

Mattuck through his agents, used the press to stir up white public opinion against me during the trial. They made a cowardly noise about the African Legion which they know to be untrue.[2] To imagine that Mattuck would be afraid of Negroes in an overwhelming population of a well prepared race. The thing is shameful and a disgrace to white bravery. I will dismiss the evil thought for what it is worth. It shows however how scared some people are. I know I have been sacrificed by the jury to bolster up the reputation of Mattuck. I am no lawyer, but in the face of evidence and the conduct of the case, Mattuck had easily lost to the defense. His handling of the case was a mean job and low down, it lacked dignity even though he was assisted by the shrewd and able jurist, Judge Julian Mack.

The peculiar and outstanding feature of the whole case is that I am being punished for the crime of the Jew Silverston, who during my absence in the West Indies took $36,000 of the Black Star money, without being able to account for it, and which has caused the ruin of the company.

I was prosecuted in this by Maxwell Mattuck, another Jew, and I am to be sentenced by Judge Julian Mack the eminent Jewish Jurist.[3] Truly I may say "I was going down to Jeric[h]o and fell among friends."[4]

The Jury remained out for eleven hours after being directed twice by a skillful Judge.[5] After the verdict, there was not one member of the Jury who could look me in the face. I am sorry for these twelve men, for the innocence of my soul shall rest with them, and haunt their consciences through the coming years.

My work is just begun, and as I lay down my life for the cause of my people, so do I feel that succeeding generations shall be inspired by the sacrifice that I made for the rehabilitation of our race. Christ died to make men free, I shall die to give courage and inspiration to my race.

[MARCUS GARVEY]

Printed in *P&O*, 1: 217–18. Original headlines omitted.

1. Agent Joseph Tucker later reported that Garvey blamed his downfall on mulattos and on the jealousy felt by other black politicians who "resented his leadership" (report by Special Agent

Joseph G. Tucker, 30 June 1923, DJ-FBI, file 61).

2. Agent Mortimer Davis reported that U.S. Attorney Mattuck attempted to introduce testimony concerning the purchase of guns and ammunition by Garvey's followers, but Judge Mack refused to hear such testimony, since it had little influence upon his sentencing of Garvey (report by Special Agent Mortimer J. Davis, 21 June 1923, DJ-FBI, file 61).

3. A series of articles in the *Kansas City Call* mentioned Garvey's outburst after the jury had returned its verdict, especially when he learned that he would be remanded to jail without bail (*Kansas City Call*, 22 June 1923). Garvey later told Joel A. Rogers in an interview in London:

> I am going to say now what I have refrained from saying in America because of the harm it might have done in places like Harlem. I wish to say, emphatically, that the Negro must beware of the Jew. The Jew is no friend of the Negro, though the Negro has been taught to believe that. It is not Rosenwald that is giving all that money to build schools, but it is the Jews who are clubbing their money and giving it to him to give Negroes. Just a clever form of advertisement. The Elders of Zion teach that a harm done by a Jew to a Gentile is no harm at all, and the Negro is a Gentile.
>
> When they wanted to get me, they had a Jewish judge to try me, and a Jewish prosecutor (Mattucks). I would have been freed but two Jews on the jury held out against me ten hours and succeeded in convicting me, whereupon the Jewish judge gave me the maximum penalty. (*Philadelphia Tribune*, 27 September 1928; quoted in J.A. Rogers, "Additional Facts on Marcus Garvey and His Trial for Using the Mails to Defraud," Negroes of New York Writers Program, New York, 1939, NN-Sc)

4. A sardonic paraphrase from Luke 10:30; "A certain man went down from Jerusalem to Jericho, and fell among thieves."

5. After Judge Mack's first charge to the jury, they retired at 12:22 P.M. The jury returned at 9:31 P.M. and received a second set of directions. The jury retired again at 9:45 P.M. and returned with a guilty verdict at 10:30 P.M. (*Marcus Garvey* v. *United States*, no. 8317, Ct. App., 2d Cir., 2 February 1925, pp. 2,414–2,417).

Rev. E. Ethelred Brown to the *New York World*

[[New York, June 20, 1923]]

To the Editor of The World:

I was specially impressed by the two following paragraphs which formed part of a news article which appeared in this morning's World under the title, "Garvey's Adherents Under Eye of Law":

1. "American Negroes in Harlem were elated yesterday over Garvey's conviction."

2. "Federal authorities say nine-tenths of Garvey's army are West Indian Negroes who have not been naturalized."

I hope No. 1 does not correctly describe the feelings of American Negroes. To be elated over the conviction of any man is, to say the least, not creditable. I have my doubts as to the correctness of No. 2.

But what impressed me was the clear intention of the writer in putting these two paragraphs one after the other. He intended to convey the idea that only American Negroes are on the side of justice and therefore approve the conviction, and that the majority of West Indians were and are in sympathy with the aims and methods of Garvey.

Nothing is further from the truth. West Indians were in the forefront of those who opposed both the aims and methods of this fallen man. Among them were many Jamaicans. They opposed the aims because they considered them impracticable and likely to divert attention from more urgent needs; they opposed the methods because when they were not crude they were mischievous. Many of these West Indians fought on principle and without any personal feelings, and I am sure that now that the end which they foresaw and endeavored to prevent has come upon Garvey and his efforts, they have no feeling of elation and cannot rejoice over the fall and degradation of a man who had so unique an opportunity to serve his race, but whose colossal conceit and remarkable pigheadedness neutralized to his ruin the many good qualities he possessed. The end, in view of the possibilities, is too tragic for spiteful glee or fiendish satisfaction.

E. ETHELRED BROWN
Minister[,] Harlem Community Church

Printed in the *New York World*, 22 June 1923.

Marcus Garvey to the Members
and Friends of the UNIA

Tombs Prison, New York City, U.S.A.
June 20, 1923

To the Members and Friends of the Universal Negro Improvement Association:

I take this opportunity to return thanks to you for the splendid interest you have manifested in me during the trial of my case.[1]

I bear with me the kindliest feelings toward you, I commend to your care and attention, my wife, who has been my helpmate and inspiration for years. She has suffered with me in the cause of service to my race, and if I have any sorrow, it is only on her account, that I cannot be alongside of her at all times to protect her from the evil designs of the enemy, but I commend her to your care and keeping and feel that you will do for her as much as you have done for me.

Her tale of woe has not been told, but in my belief that truth will triumph over wrong, I feel sure that a day will come when the whole world will know the story of her noble sacrifice for the cause that I love so much. With very best wishes, I have the honor to be, Your obedient Servant,

MARCUS GARVEY
President-General
Universal Negro Improvement Association

Printed in *P&O*, 1: 218.

1. The *Times-Picayune* reported that at the end of the trial:
> A crowd of negroes assembled about the federal building raised a wailing and a lamentation that it is believed was heard for blocks as Garvey approached. As he entered the building women shrieked and men groaned. Some tried to break through police lines to reach him but he waved them back with a sweep of the arm. None but counsel and relatives were allowed in the courtroom. More than 100 negroes, mostly women, pursued the patrol wagon as Garvey was taken from the court. As the wagon disappeared one woman fell on her knees and prayed that Garvey might be saved. A woman with a baby in her arms slapped her in the face. Spectators prevented further hostilities. Extra police were called to disperse the crowd. (*New Orleans Times-Picayune*, 22 June 1923)

Last Will and Testament of Marcus Garvey

[*New York*] June 20, 1923

I[,] MARCUS GARVEY, being of sound and disposing mind and memory, considering the uncertainty of this life, do make public and declare, this to be my LAST WILL AND TESTAMENT as follows, hereby revoking all other and former wills or codicils by me at any time made.

FIRST, after my lawful debts are paid, I give, and bequeath all my personal, real, and mixed properties including household effects, and chattels at 133 West 129th Street, New York City, New York, also all Bonds in the Universal Negro Improvement Association, and all wages that may be due me by the said Universal Negro Improvement Association for services up to the date of the termination officially of my service, and further all increments thereto appertaining to an Insurance Policy in the New York Life Insurance Company of New York, made payable to my estate, to my wife Amy Jacques Garvey, and said wife Amy Jacques Garvey is to be the only Beneficiary under this will and testament.

SECOND, that my wife AMY JACQUES GARVEY shall have all and exclusive rights to all the writings and speeches of MARCUS GARVEY and shall couple them and use same to her desire to the exclusion of all others.

THIRD, all my financial interest in all books, pictures, and pamphlets shall be included in this my bequest to AMY JACQUES GARVEY. She shall receive all monies, gifts, and considerations intended for me, and hold same as her own personal property.

On my death, the said AMY JACQUES GARVEY shall bury me out of the funds of my Insurance Policy as by her discretion, and all gifts at such funeral by the Universal Negro Improvement Association shall be accepted by AMY JACQUES GARVEY to be disposed of to her discretion.

FOURTH, I hereby appoint AMY JACQUES GARVEY to be Executrix of this[,] my last will and Testament.

IN WITNESS WHEREOF, I have hereunto subscribed my name and affixed my seal, the 20th day of June, in the year of Our Lord One thousand nine hundred and twenty three.

MARCUS GARVEY
Testator

WITNESSES

John E. Bruce, Florence A. Bruce, H. Vinton Plummer.

Subscribed by MARCUS GARVEY, the Testator named in the foregoing Will, in the presence of each of us, and at the time of making such subscription, the above Instrument was declared by the said Testator to be his LAST WILL AND TESTAMENT, and each of us, at the request of the said Testator, and in the presence of each other, and in his presence, signed our names as witnesses thereto.

Name	Residing
John E. Bruce	258 W. 139th Street, N.Y.C.
Florence A. Bruce	258 W. 139th Street, N.Y.C.
H. Vinton Plummer	56 West 135th Street
	243 West 136th Street

Printed in Amy Jacques Garvey, *Garvey and Garveyism* [Kingston: United Printers, 1963], pp. 115–117.

Salary Accounts of Marcus Garvey

[*New York*] June 21, 1923

SALARY RECEIVED
1922

Jan. 15 Prom. Note no. 1801 for	$2,043.29
Jan. 23 Check no. 1925	120.00
Feb. 6 Check no. 2026	150.00
Feb. 16 Check no. 2082	458.40
Feb. 23 Check no. 2117	50.00
Mar. 4 Check no. 2149	100.00
Mar. 13 Check no. 2160	150.00
Mar. 17 Check no. 2200	50.00
Apr. 5 Check no. 2357	200.00
Apr. 12 Check no. 2384	150.00
May 6 Check no. 2505	250.00
May 8 Check no. 2553	30.00
May 15 Check no. 2589	50.00
June 6 Check no. 2672	150.00
June 10 Check no. 2680	50.00
June 19 Check no. 2697	100.00
July 11 To Phila. (Report no. 1)	1,200.00
July 21 Check no. 2868	200.00
July 31 Check no. 2940	130.00
Aug. 16 Check no. 3077	130.00

Sept. 7 Check no. 3180 . . . . 150.00
Sept. 18 Check no. 3247 . . . . 75.00
Sept. 23 Check no. 3260 . . . . 100.00
Oct. 4 Check no. 3344 . . . . 100.00
Oct. 10 Check no. 3370 . . . . 40.00
Oct. 16 Check no. 3373 . . . . 60.00
Oct. 23 Check no. 3443 . . . . 70.00
Oct. 31 Check no. 3470 . . . . 60.00
Nov. 4 Check no. 3498 . . . . 100.00
Nov. 9 Check no. 3526 . . . . 40.00
Nov. 27 Check no. 170 . . . . 30.00
Nov. 28 Check no. 173 . . . . 50.00
Dec. 11 Western Trip (Report no. 2) 450.00

1923

Jan. 7 To Phila. (Report no. 3) 10.00
Jan. 8 Check no. 2690 . . . . 100.00
Jan. 17 Check no. 2733 . . . . 50.00
Jan. 20 Check no. 2749 . . . . 87.50
Jan. 29 Check no. 2787 . . . . 87.50
[F]eb. 3 Check no. 2797 . . . . 175.00
Feb. 19 Check no. 2892 . . . . 175.00
Mar. 5 Check no. 2988 . . . . 100.00
Mar. 12 Check no. 3029 . . . . 50.00
Mar. 19 Check no. 3075 . . . . 75.00
Mar. 24 Check no. 2975 . . . . 75.00
April 6 Check no. 102 . . . . 100.00
April 23 Check no. 202 . . . . 50.00
May 4 Check no. 242 . . . . 50.00
[Line mutilated] 75.00
[Line mutilated] 75.00
[Line mutilated] 150.00
[B]ooks and [Acco]unt Dept. $8,066.79
June 15 Balance due 6,893.08

———————

14,959.87

SALARY EARNED
1922

Jan. 15 Balance due and secured by Promissory Note (see Contra[)]$2,043.29
Jan. 21 1/2 Month Salary 333.33
Feb. 28 1 Month's Salary 666.66
Mar. 31 Month's Salary 666.66
Apr. 30 Month's Salary 666.66

May 31 Month's Salary 666.66
June 30 Month's Salary 666.66
July 31 Mo[nt]h's Salary 666.66
Aug. 31 Month's Salary 666.66
Sept. 30 Month's Salary 833.33
Oct. 31 Month's Salary 833.33
Nov. 31 Month's Salary 833.33
Dec. 31 Month's Salary 833.33

1923

Jan. 31 Month's Salary 833.33
Feb. 28 Month's Salary 833.33
Mar. 31 Month's Salary 833.33
Apr. 30 Month's Salary 833.33
May 31 Month's Salary 833.33
June 15 1/2 Month Salary 416.67

Total Earned   14,959.87
June 15 Balance d[ue]   6,893.08

I hereby certify that the above is a correct statement as shown by the book of and report filed in the Accounting Department, but which does not include [the] missing report.

LOUIS S. RAWLIN
Accounting Depart[me]nt

[*Endorsement*] OK C. S. Bourne

TNF, MGMC. TDS. Handwritten endorsement.

Negro World Notice

```
┌─────────────────────────────────────────────────────────┐
```

THE MARCUS GARVEY APPEAL AND DEFENSE FUND

The Expected First Blow Has Been Struck at the Race's Liberty

Everybody Must Subscribe Now to Test Whether the Black Man Can Obtain Justice

As was to be expected. Marcus Garvey has been found guilty by a jury of white men of using the United States mails to defraud.

Many believe that the charge was only a sham to get Garvey with the hope of destroying his work. The whole thing seems to be made up of an international plot which will shortly expose itself Several Negro men and organizations have been parties to what some regard as a "frame-up," but Truth shall have a hearing.

An appeal must be taken to the highest courts of the land to further test justice: therefore, every Negro of loyalty and manhood is asked to subscribe to this fund

The fight for Africa's liberty is just begun: let us all help.

Send in your subscription addressed to the Secretary. Marcus Garvey Release Committee. 56 West 135th Street, New York City, N. Y. ───────────

I, MARCUS GARVEY, have appointed Mrs. Amy Jacques-Garvey, Mr. William Sherrill and Mr. Clifford Bourne. as a committee to receive and disburse all moneys for my Appeal and Defense Fund. (Signed) MARCUS GARVEY,

June 21, 1923 (The Tombs.)

```
└─────────────────────────────────────────────────────────┘
```

(*Source*: *NW*, 30 June 1923.)

Article in the *Kansas City Call*

[[New York, N.Y., June 21, 1923]]

After a sensational trial which lasted twenty-seven days, Marcus Garvey, Provisional President of Africa and President of the Universal Negro Improvement Association, was found guilty in Federal Court here Tuesday [*19 June*] of using the mails for the purpose of selling stock in the Black Star Line, which the United States Government labeled a fraudulent proposition. His bond of $5,000 was discontinued[,] and he was remanded to the Tombs, pending sentence by Judge Mack.

The Garvey indictment and trial has been the sensation of New York City, and has been full of highlights. Ever since the indictment was returned, more than a year ago, various incidents have happened to cause postpon[e]ments of the trial date time after time, all of which served to create interest in the case.

Meanwhile, the foremost of the three [*four*] defendants, Mr. Garvey was constantly in the public eye by reason of the numerous civil suits against him by disgruntled stockholders in his various enterprises. Witnesses were subpoen[a]ed from all over the country, one of whom, Dr. Eason, was murdered in New Orleans by two alleged members of the Garvey organization. The coincidence of this crime and the fact that its perpetrators were Garveyites, was all used in an endeavor to show to what extremes the defense was prepared to go. Dr. Eason was preparing at the time of his death to go to New York, presumably to testify. As Eason had formerly been high in the ranks of Garvey counsellors, his testimony was supposed to have been of great assistance to the prosecution, and his death was made much of.

GARVEY GOES TO TRIAL.

Finally, however, the case was called for trial before Judge Mack, of the United [*States*] District Court. The defendants, Marcus Garvey, president of the company, George Tobias, treasurer, Elie Garcia, alleged to have been Garvey's chief aide in the enterprise, and Orlando Thompson, a sea-captain, who is alleged to have negotiated the purchase of the steamers for the company, elected to be tried jointly, though each retained separate counsel. Henry Lincoln Johnson, Republican National Committeeman, looked after the interests of Garvey throughout the trial.

BECOMES OWN ATTORNEY.

Shortly after the proceedings started, Garvey, who was the first to be called, dispensed with the services of his attorneys, and took his defense upon himself. His conduct was severely criti[ci]zed by Judge Mack. The irregularity of his examination of witnesses, his attire, his shortness of temper, all were the cause of remarks of disapproval from the bench, and for humorous stories in the daily press. It was early conjectured that the trial would be lengthy.

Witnesses called by Mr. Garvey to prove some minor point in the defe[ns]e, were allowed to talk at random on the entire history of the Black Star Line, with no attempt at intervention by him. Lady Vinton Davis proved a far better witness for the prosecution than for the defense, who called her. Mrs. Garvey, nervous and ill at ease under the barrage of questions hurled at her by her husband, disclosed facts that the prosecution were anxious to have presented to the jury, but were unable to devise a means of doing so.

The whole defense was based on the fact that the Black Star Line and Marcus Garvey were the innocent victims of two things—the financial depression which struck the country immediately following the war and the conspiracies hatched by his associates to discredit him, and enrich themselves.

Mr. Garvey, in the examination of his co-defendant, Mr. Tobias, attempted to prove [that] he, Mr. Tobias, was a party to a conspiracy against him. The answers he received caused even the Judge to smile broadly. In short, the defense put up by Marcus Garvey for himself was frail in that it was poorly executed and did not hold to the charge in the indictment. Instead of trying to prove he was innocent of fraud, he seemingly was taking this opportunity for exploitation of the U.N.I.A.

The prosecution was brief. It consisted only of a summing up of the evidence disclosed by defense witnesses, and a closing speech to the jury. Mr. Garvey consumed three hours in his clos[in]g speech for the defense and the case was given to the jury.

JURY CLOSELY GUARDED.

Closely guarded by U.S. marshals, the jurors retired for deliberation at 12:30 Monday afternoon [*18 June*].

Crowds of Negroes remained outside the Federal Building and special squads of policemen and detectives of the Bomb Squad were assigned to keep watch in the vic[in]ity. Some of the officers, as well as marshals, were stationed in the corrido[r]s outside of the jury room.

When the jury went out to dinner, six marshals accompanied them. They did not leave the building until a policeman had reported the south exit was clear.

Marcus Garvey and his co-defendants remained in the court room or corridors as hour after hour passed without word from the jury. The only message sent out by the jury was a request at 3:15 o'clock, for the Government's balance sheet of the Black Star Steamship Line's account and some of the firm's account books.

GARVEY APPEARED NERVOUS.

During the long wait Garvey sat at the counsel table or walked up and down, mopping his face with his handkerchief and fanning himself intermittently. His wife remained with him. The other defendants occasionally walked from the court room to the corridor, but Garvey did not leave the room.

Judge Mack completed his charge to the jury at 12:30 o'clock Monday afternoon. He reminded the jurors that Garvey was not to be blamed for prolongation of the trial, which lasted four weeks, and that they must not hold him responsible for the delay. He also cautioned the jury to ignore squabbles that marked the trial.

The jury also was advised to disregard racial antagonism and reminded that any inspirational aims Garvey might have had in or[ga]nizing the steamship line were immaterial.

"If Garvey has been foolish, you can't convict him for being a fool," said Judge Mack. He told the jurors they must determine whether Garvey undertook the organization of the Black Star Line as an honorable enterprise, or simply to advance his personal ambitions. The defendant had a right to buy ships and pay salaries, but not to make false financial statements, said Judge Mack.

The jury announced that they had arrived at a verdict Monday night at 10:30 o'clock and were escorted in.

The verdict was opened and read by the court. It found Marcus Garvey guilty and his co-defendants not guilty. Mr. Garvey immediately burst into a storm of rage and denunciation against the verdict, which was increased in force when Assistant District Attorney Maxwell S. Mattuck recommended that the defendant be remanded to jail without bond, pending sentence by the court.

"I have evidence to support my claim that funds of the U.N.I.A., with Garvey as president, were used to purchase arms and ammunition," said Mr. Mattuck. "Garvey is a dangerous man and should be held without bond."

Mr. Garvey has been free on $5,000 bond. He intervened at this point with his bitter denunciation of Mr. Mattuck, for wh[o]m he said he had nothing but contempt.

"I am satisfied to go before the world," he shouted to Judge Mack, "and let them say whether I am innocent or not. I am certainly surprised at the credence given the testimony of witnesses by jurors, in this plot to ruin me."

Detectives from the Bomb Squad were scattered all through the crowd in the court room as a precautionary measure, and Mr. Garvey was escorted to the elevator leading to the Tombs, by eighteen U.S. marshals, through a crowd of sobbing s[y]mpathizers.

The trial lasted twenty-seven days. After the prisoner had been removed Judge Mack thanked the jury for its patience, and excused them from Federal jury duty for four years.

No request for a new trial was made by Mr. Garvey, and no preparations towards perfecting an appeal.

He will remain in the Tombs until called up for sentence some time next week.

Printed in the *Kansas City Call*, 22 June 1923. Original headlines omitted.

Article in the *Pittsburgh Courier*

[23 June 1923]

GARVEY FOUND GUILTY

Among the members of the legal profession there is a piece of philosophy which runs: "The man who acts as his own lawyer has a fool for a client." Perhaps Garvey knew little or nothing of this very true saying, and, in his haste to demonstrate his native "smartness," he dismissed his counsel and took personal charge of the conduct of his case. The jury convicted him. At least, he has no criticism of his "lawyer," nor can he say he was not given the widest opportunity to "put in" his case. Perhaps, the legal fraternity is the better paid that Garvey and his followers have no lawyers to "blame" for the verdict.

Now that the verdict of guilty has been reached, and after Garvey had been given ample opportunity to offer everything he had in his own behalf, some comment on the "system" may be opportune.

If Garvey conducted his business as he did his trial, there is little wonder that it failed. He showed all through the trial that he was simply consumed with his own importance. This native big-headedness spelled the ruin of his gigantic scheme. There was too much Garvey, with little or no respect for the opinions of others. He was the supreme head of all thought, every idea, and every suggestion. It was Garvey's scheme, Garvey's system of operation, Garvey's supreme domination of every phase of the program; it was Garvey's crime, Garvey's case, Garvey's counsel during the trial, and Garvey's conviction.

Surely, Mr. Garvey has no complaint that he and his scheme were embarrassed by the ideas or counsel of any outsider. It was all Garvey at the beginning; and the end has come with Garvey still at the undisputed head of the Garvey Spasm.

And the money, did you say? The answer is simply—Garvey.

Printed in the *Pittsburgh Courier*, 23 June 1923.

Editorial by George W. Harris

[*New York News*, 23 June 1923]

When Marcus Garvey was convicted Monday of using the mails to defraud, the truth of an old adage was again exemplified. Ignorance of the law is no excuse for its violation. This we feel is stating the case more than fairly for the half zealot and half faker, who, able to play upon the prejudice and imagination of the black masses of the Western world and parts of Africa, had seduced from them hundreds of thousands of dollars and squandered it upon self-glorification and visionary projects. He accordingly acquired an obsession, if not a monomania, but these do not permit nor justify a despotic dreamer in the pursuit of his wild and dangerous schemes. These do not make his ruthless and riotous movements any less a menace to his people and this country. The expression heard upon every Harlem corner when his conviction was announced[,] that Harlem would not have been safe if Garvey had been acquitted, sums up the situation. His purposes may have been good, but his methods were bad. He was not only bankrupting his race but he was fast leading it to untimely bloodshed and suicide. That he made tens of thousands of his people think and read to some extent was the great thing that he did. It will be most unfortunate if the Universal Negro Improvement Association is not saved and, in sane and stalwart hands, pointed in the right direction. Garvey was a discordant factor, arraying the native born against the foreign born, the black against the yellow, the black against the white and vice versa. Africa must be eventually for the Africans. To that end all peoples of African extraction have been groping and working. That movement Garvey promoted. But he violated the laws. He pauperized unnumbered thousands of hard-working colored people. (For that he has been convicted. There was no other just and rightful solution of the problem he created. His counsel, including Attorney Henry Lincoln Johnson, William C. Mat[t]hews, [J.P.] Ifil[l] and McDouga[l]d, did wonders for Garvey's race and for Garvey in presenting his cause to the court and the public. The good that he did must be conserved. The evil that he wrought must be condemned. His case should be an example to all those agitating black demagogues who seek to serve themselves first and their race afterwards. His removal should enable all those whom he divided to get together to fight the common enemies of the black race. Marcus Garvey was a menace. His race will now be the better off for his removal.[2]

Printed in the *New York News*, 23 June 1923.

1. Ifill represented Orlando Thompson (*Marcus Garvey* v. *United States*, no. 8317, Ct. App., 2d Cir., 2 February 1925; *Garvey Papers* 3: 121 n. 1).

2. Using Harris's editorial in the *New York News* as evidence, Agent Tucker, in his weekly report, concluded "that the conservative element of the Negro Race is against Garvey and his methods and in favor of his recent conviction" (report by Special Agent Joseph G. Tucker, 30 June 1923, DJ-FBI, file 61-235).

Jean-Jules Jusserand, French Ambassador,[1] to the President of the Council, French Ministry of Foreign Affairs

Washington, D.C. 24 June 1923

RE: CONVICTION OF MARCUS GARVEY

The Department has had, on more than one occasion, to occupy itself with the "Pan-Negro" movement, organized by a black West Indian, Marcus Garvey, who has awarded himself the titles, "Provisional President of Africa," and President of the "Universal Negro Improvement Association"; he has organized propaganda fervently hostile to countries having African possessions, and has founded a steamship line "The Black Star Line" with nominal capital of $10 million, to operate between the coast of Africa and other parts of the world.

Appealing to the feelings of members of his race—he claims that 400 million of them exist in the world—he had succeeded in amassing subscriptions amounting to about $1 million. With this sum he has bought for his line, ships incapable of sailing, and led the sort of life suited to a Provisional President of such vast populations. He had founded a periodical "The Negro World" to celebrate his merits and the beauty of his undertakings. He made himself a present of the title "Knight Commander of the Sublime Order of the Nile" and gave equally shining titles to his colleagues; this, moreover, could be done without cost.

Complaints against his administration have just brought him to justice. He was sentenced principally for having continued to sell his shares of the Black Star Line, when he knew the company was indebted and the shares worthless; the jury declared him guilty and the judge gave him 5 years in prison on the 21st of this month.

[JEAN-JULES JUSSERAND]

AMAE, serie K, carton 4, dossier 1, 27. TL, carbon copy (translated from French).

1. Jean-Jules Jusserand (1855–1932), French author and diplomat, served as France's ambassador to the United States from 1902 until 1925 (*WBD*; U.S. Department of State, *Register*, 1924 [Washington, D.C.: GPO, 1924], p. 248).

Report by Special Employee Andrew M. Battle

New York City [24–26 June 1923]

June 24th.

Attended a patriotic mass meeting held at the Renaissance Casino, 138th Street and 7th Street [*Avenue*], where about 150 were present. William Ferris, editor of the "Negro World[,]" and Fred A. Toot[e], once Field Organizer for the U.N.I.A.[,] were the speakers. Ferris stated that the spirit of Garvey will never die, and that Garvey was the greatest leader the world has ever known. Toot[e] stated that Garvey has suffered disgrace in having to be handcuffed to a low white man and brought into a court room.

After the meeting I had a talk with Ferris, who stated that Garvey recommended that Captain Gaines, Mrs. Henrietta Vinton Davis, [and] Rudolph Smith be discharged as far as salary was concerned, but if they wanted to go in the field and raise money for the U.N.I.A. they could take 15 per cent of all the money they raised. He also recommended that Gaines be let go, so that white folks would be fooled, and no suspicion would be attached to the African Legion, as they could not then find the leader. Garvey wants to get rid of all the Americans, stating they cannot be trusted.

This evening attended a meeting at Liberty Hall, 120 West 138th Street, where about 3000 persons were present, and $700 was raised for the Garvey Defense Fund.[1] The speakers were R.L. Poston, First Secretary, William Sher[r]ill, First Assistant President of the U.N.I.A[.,] and Rudolph Smith.

Sher[r]ill stated that every direction of Garvey's will be carried out to the letter. He stated they were willing to shed blood for Garvey, and they would do all they could to have Garvey released.

June 25th.

Today spoke with Captain [E].L. Gaines, of the U.N.I.A. who stated that last Friday the officers came to search the U.N.I.A. Building, and asked him if he bought any guns, and he stated he had not. He further stated there is a big fight on between the officers, and that Garvey has directed Mrs.

Davis, G.O. Mark[e], Rudolph Smith and Gain[e]s be dropped from the pay roll. Gaines said he is going to resign before something else happens, as the U.N.I.A. is not using the money right, and another arrest might come soon.

While speaking to Mrs. Boyington, 122 West 134th Street, she said she was a member of the U.N.I.A. and the white folks need not think they have done anything by putting Garvey in jail, and that the Legion and the Motor Corps can get their guns and shoot ever[y] one up, and will do it when ever they get the word. She made this statement in the presence of Mrs. J. Battle and Miss Hannah Battle, 238 West 127th Street.

I then spoke with G. Gads[b]y, 28 West 131st Street, a member of the UNIA and president of the Panama Division until August, 1922, and he stated he could not understand how Garvey could say the African Legion didn't have guns, for the U.N.I.A. of Panama had just bought guns for the African Legion before the August convention. He said the African Legion are in every branch of the U.N.I.A. of this country, and every division has guns.

June 26th.

Today talked with Rudolph Smith, 2301–7th Avenue, who stated that Captain Gaines, G.O. Mark[e], Mrs. Vinton Davis and himself had received word their salary had stop[ped] from last Saturday, and when they received their letters they would split the U.N.I.A. and call a convention as soon as they could of all the presidents of the different branches of the U.N.I.A. so they could vote against Garvey managing the organization while in prison.

Gain[e]s is afraid the Government will take him for training the African Legion. J.B. Yearwood also stated he hoped Garvey would not secure bail, and would be kept in prison, in which event he would do all he could for the U.N.I.A. I then spoke with Arnold J. Ford, Musical Director of the U.N.I.A.[,] who stated a convention must be called so the management could be changed, and that the Legion will have to disband for a while, or else they would be subject to arrest. The Legion has been advised to get rid of the guns.

ANDREW M. BATTLE

DJ-FBI, file 61-50-395. TD.

1. Garvey appointed his wife, Amy Jacques Garvey, Clifford S. Bourne, and William L. Sherrill as a committee "to receive and disburse funds for his appeal and defense" (*NW*, 30 June 1923).

Report by Bureau Agent Harry D. Gulley

New Orleans, La. [*25 June 1923*]

ATTENTION MR. HOOVER

Reference is made to former reports on above subject, [*U.S. v. Marcus Garvey, et al.*] and particularly to report of Special Agent Mortimer J. Davis of the New York office, dated 6/21/23.

WILLIAM SHAKESPEARE and C.F. DWYER [*Dyer*] lost their appeal to the Supreme Court by decision rendered June 16, 1923, and will, within a few days, be taken to the State Penitentiary at Baton Rouge, La.

This agent endeavored to obtain statement from each of them, to ascertain if they had any knowledge of whether or not JOHN JEFFRIES, alias ESAU RAMUS, had been sent by MARCUS GARVEY to New Orleans for the purpose of murdering or effecting the death of Dr. Eason.

C.F. DWYER stated that he had full knowledge that his appeal had failed, and that he desired to tell absolutely the truth, but that as far as he knew RAMUS had never told him directly that he had been sent by GARVEY to New Orleans for the purpose of getting rid of EASON, but that RAMUS, from the first time that he met him, always stated that he was going to get DR. EASON. He would not change any of his statement with reference to the murder of EASON, or his (Ramus') connection with same, except as stated herein.

WILLIAM SHAKESPEARE denied that RAMUS ever made any statement that he was "going to get Eason", and denied that he had ever seen any letters or heard RAMUS make any statement that he had been sent here to murder EASON. He also would not change any statement made with reference to the killing of EASON January 1st, 1923.

Every effort was made to obtain information desired' without result as stated. . . .

HARRY D. GULLEY

DJ-FBI, file 61. TD.

1. Agent Gulley received his orders, on the suggestion of Assistant U.S. Attorney Mattuck, to interrogate Dyer and Shakespeare in this matter of Garvey's part in the Eason murder (report by Special Agent Mortimer J. Davis, 21 June 1923, DJ-FBI, file 61).

Report by Special Agent Mortimer J. Davis

New York City 6/25–26–27/23

Continuing Agent's investigation and report of June 21st[,] which reported that Garvey had been sentenced by Judge Mack and held without bail.

On the 25th inst. Garvey's attorneys, Armin Kohn,[1] Henry L. Johnson and William C. Matthews,[2] appeared before Judge Rogers[3] of the Circuit Court of Appeals to request that he permit Garvey bail. Agent James E. Amos and the writer were present at this hearing with Asst. U.S. Attorney Mattuck. Garvey's attorneys attacked the count upon which Garvey was found guilty, i.e., count three of the second indictment known as the "Dancy count," charging that this count was defective and, in fact, the weakest of any in either of the two indictments.[4] Asst. U.S. Attorney Mattuck was asked what bail he thought that Garvey should be allowed, upon which he stated the reasons why he believed Garvey should be permitted no bail, exhibiting to the Judge various threatening letters received during the past and one received by Mr. Mattuck on the 25th inst. Judge Rogers stated he would take the matter under consideration. On the 26th inst. Judge Rogers informed Garvey's attorneys that after going over the facts he could not see his way clear to permit Garvey bail, but added, that in turning down their request he was doing so "without prejudice." This phrase was not explained by Judge Rogers, but is presumed to mean that his denial in no way interferes with their making a similar request to other appeal judges in this district, and I am informed that Garvey's attorneys intend to apply to every such judge here.

With regard to the Universal Negro Improvement Association, Agent Amos and the writer have made visits to the Harlem section and have been informed that business is practically at a standstill due to Garvey's absence. There is a strong rumor of a factional split and, also, it is intimated that they may lose one of their main means of propaganda, i.e., Liberty Hall, mortgages upon which will soon become due, the meeting of which mortgages will mean that same will be foreclosed and the building lost to the Association. Without Liberty Hall the U.N.I.A. and its various branches will be without a meeting place and will be forced to hire such as are available in the city at considerable expense.

Agent Amos and the writer are also continuing efforts in cooperation with the City police to run down the various rumors regarding the purchase and storage of guns and ammunition, but up to the present time have not verified same, and it is believed that if such material was in possession of any of the Garvey adherents, it has now been either destroyed or removed, due to the great amount of publicity given this feature by the New York newspapers.[5]

MORTIMER J. DAVIS

DJ-FBI, file 61. TD.

1. Armin Kohn (1878–1940) was a member of the firm of Kohn and Nagler; he later joined the firm of J.E. Cohen and Fuchsberg. In addition to becoming Garvey's lawyer, he was legal counsel as well for David Lamar, known as "the Wolf of Wall Street" (*NYT*, 9 October 1940).

2. William C. Matthews (1877–1928), noted black lawyer, was born in Montgomery, Ala. He attended Tuskegee Institute and the Phillips Andover Academy before entering Harvard University Law School in 1905. Matthews, active in UNIA affairs since 1920, was among the most prominent black lawyers of his day; he later served as special assistant to the attorney general (*NYT*, 11 April 1928).

3. Henry Wade Rogers (1853–1926), New York-born judge, graduated from the University of Michigan Law School in 1877, later serving as dean of the school. In 1890 he was appointed president of Northwestern University, resigning in 1900 to take a position at Yale Law School. In 1913 President Wilson appointed him a judge of the Second Judicial Circuit, a position he held until his death (*NYT*, 17 August 1926).

4. The court convicted Garvey, in fact, on the third count of the first indictment. The prosecution charged that the Black Star Line mailed prospective stockholders circulars advertising the sale of shares in a ship that the BSL did not technically own. The prosecution presented as evidence of mail fraud a circular, identical to one supposedly sent to Benny Dancy, featuring a doctored photograph of a ship on which the name *Phyllis Wheatley* was superimposed over the ship's original name, *Orion*. The BSL was at that time still negotiating with the USSB for the purchase of the ship.

The prosecution's main piece of evidence was an empty BSL envelope addressed to Benny Dancy, which had allegedly contained the BSL flyer. It was postmarked at College Station on 21 December 1920. Though Lawrence Hunt testified that he printed the flyer, and Schuyler Cargill, a former mail boy for the BSL, stated that he mailed it from College Station, evidence directly linking the circular with the envelope Dancy received was fragmentary. In fact, Benny Dancy, in testimony that was fraught with confusion and contradictions, was unable to remember the contents of the envelope.

Acting as his own lawyer, Garvey badgered the witnesses but failed to question the many discrepancies in the prosecution's case. For example, the prosecution never established a direct link between Garvey and the circular. In fact, Garvey was out of the country when the flyer was mailed, and Orlando Thompson and Elie Garcia, the only defendants connected directly with the circular, were found not guilty. In addition, the prosecution failed to link the circular with Benny Dancy directly. No date was established for the mailing of the circulars, and Dancy could not remember what he received in the envelope. Finally, according to Bureau of Investigation documents, the bill for the doctored photograph on the flyer was signed by Orlando Thompson for work done in May 1921, five months after the 21 December 1920 postmark on the envelope used to convict Garvey (statement by Orlando M. Thompson, 12 January 1922, DJ-FBI, file 61; report by Special Agent Mortimer J. Davis, 8 March 1922, DJ-FBI, file 61; *Marcus Garvey* v. *United States*, no. 8317, Ct. App., 2d Cir., 2 February 1925, pp. 668–679, 860–865, 2,259–2,563, 2,626–2,627).

5. Reports of the assistant U.S. attorney's accusation that Garvey's African Legion had stockpiled guns and ammunition appeared in the *New York World*, 22 June and 24 June 1923. No report of the accusation appeared in the *New York Times*.

Report by Special Employee Andrew M. Battle

New York City [27–28 June 1923]

IN RE: NEGRO RADICAL ACTIVITIES.

Today [27 June] interviewed Mrs. E. James, 101 W. 132d Street, a member of the U.N.I.A. and a shareholder of the Black Star Line, who stated trouble has just started in the U.N.I.A. because Garvey has caused a big fight among the officers by directing the discharge of Gain[e]s, Rudolph Smith, Mrs. Henrietta V. Davis, and G.O. Mark[e]. She also said they are afraid Gain[e]s will tell about the guns and everything he knows about the U.N.I.A. Mrs. Davis lives in the home of Garvey and she knows all about the arms and the secrets of Garvey, for it was Garvey who had the guns bought for Gain[e]s. Captain Gain[e]s has been directed to get rid of all the guns by Garvey.

I had a talk with Captain Gaines, who stated he received a letter from Curby [*Kirby?*], President of the Chicago Division of the U.N.I.A.[,] telling him to attend a meeting of the U.N.I.A. to be held in Chicago on July 8th, at which all the presidents will attend.[1] Marke will call a convention for the U.N.I.A. after the Chicago meeting on July 8th.

William Ferris called to see me, and said he had to resign as Editor of the "Negro World" because he had changed some articles sent to him by Garvey, which were insults to Judge Mack, Mr. Mattuck and the court, and therefore Garvey not liking the stand taken by Ferris, changed the editor.[2]

June 28th.

This evening attended meeting at Liberty Hall, where Amus [*G. Emonei*] Carter said things are very discouraging, and the expenses of the U.N.I.A. are rapidly rising, with nothing to meet them, and only $700 has been raised for expenses of the U.N.I.A.[3]

It was also learned that the Chicago convention is being called without the knowledge of Garvey.

ANDREW M. BATTLE

DJ-FBI, file 61. TD.

1. The Bureau of Investigation investigated rumors of a meeting of dissident UNIA leaders to be held in Chicago on 7 July 1923. After interviewing informants, the bureau concluded that no such meeting would be held (10 July 1923, DJ-FBI, file 61, no. B-1091).

2. William H. Ferris remained on the *Negro World* staff through much of the summer that Garvey was incarcerated in the Tombs. Ferris was moved from his job as literary editor to contributing editor in the 7 July 1923 issue of the *Negro World*; William A. Stephenson joined the staff as assistant managing editor in the same issue, and the literary editor position was dropped altogether. Ferris's last appearance on the *Negro World* masthead occurred on 8 September 1923; the veteran black journalist T. Thomas Fortune, who joined the paper as of 6 October 1923, became the new assistant managing editor, replacing Stephenson.

3. Agent Tucker's report mentioned that the New York local had raised $750 of a necessary $1,500 for the defense fund (report by Special Agent Joseph G. Tucker, 30 June 1923, DJ-FBI, file 61).

William J. Burns to W.W. Husband, Commissoner General of Immigration[1]

[*Washington, D.C.*] June 28, 1923

My dear Mr. Husband:—

On the 21st instant MARCUS GARVEY was sentenced to a term of five years in the Federal penitentiary and a fine in the sum of $1,000 imposed following his conviction of a violation of Section 215 of the U.S. Criminal Code.

This subject is an alien and while he has previously been in the United States left this country early in 1921 and re-entered the United States at the port of New Orleans on or about July 9, 1921.

I am calling the matter to your attention for consideration of action under Section 19 of the Act of February 5, 1917.[2] Very truly yours,

W.J. B[URNS].
Director

DJ-FBI, file 61. TLI, carbon copy.

1. Walter W. Husband (1872?–1942) was appointed commissioner of immigration in 1921. He was later appointed second assistant secretary of labor by President Coolidge, a position he held until 1933 (*NYT*, 1 August 1942).

2. This section of the act of 5 February 1917 empowered the government of the United States to exclude aliens that were found at any time after entry into the United States guilty of teaching anarchy, the unlawful destruction of property, the violent overthrow of the government of the United States, or the assassination of public officials (U.S. Congress, *The Statutes at Large of the United States of America from December 1915 to March 1917*, 64th Cong., 2d sess. [Washington, D.C.: GPO, 1917, 39, pt. 1: 874–898).

Article in the *Kansas City Call*

[[New York, N.Y., June 28, 1923]]

Despite the activities of United States Marshals, Department of Justice agents and city policemen and detectives, followers of Marcus Garvey staged a demonstration as their leader was being removed from the Federal Building to the Tombs, after he had been sentenced to serve five years in a Federal penitentiary and pay a fine of $1,000 for using the mails to defraud in connection with the Black Star Line.

Failing to gain entrance to the Federal Building to hear sentence imposed, nearly 300 men and women followers of Garvey gathered about the "Black Maria" which was waiting at the north side of the building to carry Garvey back to the Tombs. The prison van had been parked among the mail trucks,[1] in the hope that it would not be noticed.

When Garvey, handcuffed, was led from the building at noon and entered the prison van, some of the women began wailing and the others surged about the car. Pedestrians from nearby streets, attracted by the cries of the women, swelled the crowd to approximately 1,000 persons.

WOMEN TRAIL AFTER CAR.

Traffic difficulties made it impossible for the prison van to be driven away for several minutes. When the way finally was cleared and the car moved up Park Row, several women ran a short distance in its wake, wailing and weeping.

Garvey sat at the front end of the prison van, handcuffed to a Deputy United States Marshal. Five or six other marshals were between him and the door at the rear. Garvey had been held in the Marshal's office in the hope the crowd would disperse. Only a few persons, holding permits, had been allowed to enter the building to hear sentence imposed.

Deputy Marshals, Department of Justice men, uniformed policemen and detectives of the Bomb Squad were stationed in the courtroom, the corridors and outside the building. Detectives accompanied Judge Mack into the courtroom.

The sentence was the maximum. Judge Mack said Garvey would be allowed the privilege of requesting that he serve his time in the Leavenworth Penitentiary instead of at Atlanta. Garvey prefers the Kansas prison.

Assistant United States Attorney. Mattuck offered to put on the stand a witness bearing out his statements that part of the money collected in Garvey's Negro movement was used to buy arms and ammunition. Judge Mack declined, however, to hear the witness, explaining that such testimony had no bearing on the sentencing of Garvey. The witness is a Negro now serving a term in Sing Sing. He was in the courtroom.

EXPLAINS MAXIMUM SENTENCE.

"Under American laws no man has the right to make misrepresentations of facts, no matter how great his hope may be as to the success of the enterprise," said Judge Mack in imposing sentence. "It is the enormous extent to which it was done, it is the financial character of the great mass of people who were induced to put their money into this hopeless undertaking that leads me to impose the maximum sentence in this case."

Mr. Mattuck agreed to permit Garvey to remain in the Tombs pending appeal, "provided he does not write any inflammatory ar[ti]cles for his Negro newspaper." One such article has appeared, the prosecutor charged.

Garvey said he would not bind himself not to write his "opinions as a man." When he was asked if he had any statement to make before being sentenced, Garvey said:

"The statement about the arms and ammunition is unfounded. I regard America as the greatest national friend of the Negro. It would be foolish and suicidal to do anything in the nature of armed activities. I am sorry for any interpretation that might have been put on my conduct in this court. I feel that the dawn of the Negro race will come and my children and people will appreciate my sacrifice. I am satisfied to serve any sentence the court may impose."

Armin Kohn, counsel for Garvey during the latter part of the trial, asked that his client be released on bail, but this was denied. Mr. Kohn said meetings of the Universal Negro Improvement Association, of which Garvey was President-General, have been held, at which the leaders have exhorted the members to live by the law. The lawyer then asked that Garvey should not be sent to prison until action had been taken on his appeal.

Printed in the *Kansas City Call*, 29 June 1923. Original headlines omitted.

1. The federal district court and circuit court of appeals were housed at 450 Post Office Building, 8th Avenue and 31st–32nd Streets, Manhattan (*New York City Directory, 1920–1921*).

Article in the *Financial World*

[*New York*, 30 June 1923]

Striking contrast is drawn by the difference in punishment meted out in two notable cases of fraud recently concluded in New York City. Certain defects in our statutes which could well be remedied are indicated. Otherwise, their tendency would be to encourage crime instead of to curb it, as is the intention of punitive laws.

Here we have FULLER & MCGEE, the plundering brokers, who succeeded in getting away with more than $6,000,000 through their crooked bucketshop, receiving a sentence of less than a year, after pleading guilty in the state court.

Over in the Federal Court MARCUS GARVEY, an intellectual negro, did not fare so well. He was sentenced to Leavenworth for five years, after a jury found him guilty of using the mails to defraud his colored brethren in connection with the sale of stock of the Black Star Steamship Line.

These disproportionate sentences almost make a comedy out of the serious crime of fraud. In the one case the loot amounted to $6,000,000. In the other, it did not come to more than $1,000,000. Yet it would appear as if, in the eyes of the law, that the greater the loot the less severe is the penalty upon conviction. At least this is how the victims of these frauds will feel.

In the same degree would appear the tolerance shown for the mentality behind fraud. The more stupid its nature the softer is the hand of justice. To lead people to believe he would establish a new Republic for them in Africa, as GARVEY proposed, was more difficult than inducing people to buy stocks through them as did FULLER and MCGEE. In this respect the black culprit's mentality was superior to that of the white rogues in Ludlow Street jail. Yet he gets five years while they receive less than a year.

As GARVEY thinks this over he may conclude it was an evil star instead of a black star which enmeshed him in the Federal statu[t]es.

Printed in *Financial World* 39, no. 26 (30 June 1923): 817. Original headlines omitted.

Negro World Notice

GENERAL NOTICE TO MEMBERS
OF
UNIVERSAL NEGRO IMPROVEMENT ASSOCIATION

Without Prejudice, This Is to Inform One and All That

MR. ELIE GARCIA
Is No Longer Officially Connected with the Universal Negro Improvement Association

All persons to whom Mr. Garcia has issued construction loan bonds or receipts or conversed with for the Universal Negro Improvement Association are requested to communicate at once with Complaint Department, Universal Negro Improvement Association, 56 West 135th Street, New York.

(*Source*: *NW*, 30 June 1923.)

Message from Marcus Garvey

The Tombs Prison, New York, July 1, 1923

Members and Friends of the Negro Race—

I have been informed of your effort on my behalf, that of holding a protest meeting to draw to the attention of the public of our great country the injustice that has been done me in the name of our great government.[1]

I appreciate very highly the step you have taken to arouse public opinion. I have an abiding faith in the justice of the people, and believe that when the truth is brought home to them they will not be slow to register their protest against any and all acts of injustice.

I need not repeat that I have been "framed up" and sacrificed because of prejudice and the political and organization designs of my enemies.

I believe that when my cause is properly presented to the higher and responsible officials of our government they will see that justice is done, and that they will not hesitate in upholding the sacred principles of the Constitution. America is founded upon truth, liberty and justice, and these, I feel sure, will not be denied the lowest of her citizens.

I desire that you be peaceful and loyal in your assembly and that you be mindful of the fact that I am always willing to suffer for the cause of my race and the general uplift of humanity.

Be cheerful, be loyal, be firm, be men, is the prayer of your humble and obedient servant,

MARCUS GARVEY
President-General
Universal Negro Improvement Association

DNA, RG 60, file 198940. TL, carbon copy. Also printed in P&O, 2: 219–220.

1. The UNIA held a mass protest meeting on 1 July 1923 at Liberty Hall. The meeting was covered by Special Employee Andrew M. Battle, who reported an attendance of about two thousand, "about two-thirds of whom were West Indian Negroes." At this meeting, a message of cheer from Garvey was read. Speakers included Poston, Tobias, Plummer, Sherrill, Rev. W. W. Brown, Charles Wright, and "Prince Imah Devount of Abyssinia." A petition asking the president to free Garvey was circulated, but apparently only West Indians signed it. On the following day Battle talked with Rev. W. W. Brown, J. B. Yearwood, Alonzo Pettiford, Henrietta Vinton Davis, and Arnold J. Ford. Battle reported that Davis and Ford criticized Garvey's Negro World editorials which, according to Davis, were insulting to the government and harmful to the UNIA (reports by Special Employee Andrew M. Battle, 3 July and 5 July 1923, DJ-FBI, file 61).

Editorial Letter by Marcus Garvey

[[Tombs Prison, New York, July 3, 1923]]

FELLOW MEN OF THE NEGRO RACE, GREETING: . . .

ENEMIES STILL AT WORK TO DISCOURAGE YOU

I understand that our enemies are still trying to discourage you, and now that I am imprisoned they are endeavoring to use several of our disloyal presidents and officers at different points of the country to disobey the orders of the Parent Body at New York and build up little organizations of their own by which they locally could exploit the people. Fellow members of the Universal Negro Improvement Association and fellow Negroes, watch carefully and guard your organization against local self-seeking presidents or officers. Remember the purpose for which you have been organized. It was not for supporting selfish men at your expense and to your loss, but for our coming together as one great body to do together what we could not do separately. . . .

SCHEMING IN CHICAGO

Information has been supplied me that a few disloyal presidents of certain divisions have been sending out requests to other presidents to meet them in Chicago in keeping with a plan of the enemy at this time to destroy the organization. If this information is true, I now take the opportunity of warning all loyal presidents and officers of the Universal Negro Improvement Association to ignore such communications and forward same to the Complaint Department of the Association in New York.

ONE OR TWO DAY CONVENTION THIS YEAR

Each division of the Association will hold a one or two day local convention this year and prepare for the big International Convention next year. There will be no State convention, but local divisional conventions. Members, be careful and watch the self-seekers who have done more harm to our great cause than good. Watch out for disloyalty and do not fail to act in removing the individual from office. . . .

MARCUS GARVEY
President-General
Universal Negro Improvement Association

Printed in *NW*, 7 July 1923. Original headlines omitted.

The Marcus Garvey Committee on Justice to Henry C. Wallace,[1] Secretary of Agriculture

New York, July 5, 1923

HONORABLE AND DEAR SIR:—

We, the undersigned, beg to inform you that we have been delegated as a Committee representing millions of citizens of the United States, to present to His Excellency the President of the United States, a petition of facts on behalf of Marcus Garvey[,] President-General of the Universal Negro Improvement Association[,] the largest Negro uplift movement in the world.

Because of your high and honorable place in the life of our Nation, and because of your undisputed reputation for justice, and especially to weaker peoples, make us feel obliged to lay before you a copy of the document, praying your co-operation and help in seeing that justice is done to the subject of the petition.

We know that you stand for the highest ideals in our American institutions, and that the people can always depend upon you to see that justice is done even to the most humble.

Millions of other people are now signing the petition,[2] whose names will be forwarded to you as an appendix to this document.

We ask that you be good enough as to acknowledge the receipt of this document through the Secretary of the Committee.[3] With profoundest regards and respect, We beg to remain, Your humble and obedient servants,

The Marcus Garvey Committee on Justice
DAVID E. TOBIAS
Chairman
WM. L. SHERRILL
ROBT. L. POSTON
Secretary

DNA, RG 16, general correspondence. TLS on UNIA letterhead, recipient's copy.

1. Henry Cantwell Wallace (1866–1924) served as secretary of agriculture in the cabinets of Presidents Harding and Coolidge (*WWW*).
2. A delegation led by Henry Lincoln Johnson tried to deliver the same petition to the attorney general (Mr. Martin to J. W. H. Crim, 6 July 1923, DNA, RG 60, file 198940-293).
3. The letter was acknowledged by Wallace's office on 7 July 1923 (W. A. Jump to Robert L. Poston, 7 July 1923, DNA, RG 16).

Enclosure

[*New York, ca. 5 July 1923*]

PETITION TO THE PRESIDENT OF THE UNITED STATES OF AMERICA FOR JUSTICE

"LET JUSTICE BE DONE
THOUGH THE HEAVENS FALL"

RE: CASE OF HON. MARCUS GARVEY,
PRESIDENT-GENERAL OF THE UNIVERSAL
NEGRO IMPROVEMENT ASSOCIATION, UNDER SECTION
215 OF THE U.S. POSTAL LAWS.

CONVICTED THROUGH PREJUDICE ON THE PROSECUTION
OF MR. MAXWELL S. MATTUCK, ASSISTANT
DISTRICT ATTORNEY OF THE SOUTHERN DISTRICT
OF NEW YORK, AND TRIED BEFORE
HIS HONOR JUDGE JULIAN MACK,
AND DENIED BAIL ON APPEAL THROUGH FURTHER
PERSECUTION OF SAID
ASSISTANT DISTRICT ATTORNEY.

THE FACTS

His Excellency, Hon. Warren G. Harding,
President of the United States, Washington, D.C.
Honorable and Dear Sir:

We, the undersigned petitioners, citizens and residents of the United States, beg to draw to Your Excellency's attention the following statements of injustice inflicted upon a fellow member and leader of the Negro race in the name of the great Government of our country:

Marcus Garvey (President-General of the Universal Negro Improvement Association, an organization of over six million members, scattered all over the world, with approximately two million five hundred thousand in these United States, and President of the Black Star Line, a Negro steamship corporation), through the machinations of political and organization enemies within and without the race, was indicted under Section 215 of the Postal Laws, namely, conspiracy to use the mails to defraud. This we commonly, jointly, separately and distinctly believe to be a frame-up charge against the said Marcus Garvey by his enemies.

For years (because of his success in organizing the Negro race, more than any other Negro had done) plots were laid through his enemies by which he could be discredited in his work of Race uplift.

The effort of the Black Star Line was but an auxiliary movement of the Universal Negro Improvement Association in the industrial advancement of the race. In fact, the Black Star Line bore a relationship to the Universal Negro Improvement Association such as the Shipping Board bears to our great Government. The project of the Black Star Line was engaged in during the period of the war, when shipping was high. Unfortunately, the promoters, one of whom was Mr. Garvey, fell into the hands of white and colored commercial sharks, who advised and represented them. With enemies operating against Mr. Garvey as leader of the greatest Negro Movement in the world, and sharpers seeking to exploit the Corporation of the Black Star Line, and with employees edged on to disloyalty and dishonesty inside the Corporation, without the Corporation being able to get proper redress before the law, a state of failure was forced upon the Black Star Line, and all for the purpose of discrediting the subject of their enmity.

For the good of the Universal Negro Improvement Association and for the good of the Black Star Line Mr. Garvey undertook a trip to the West Indies and Central America in February of 1921 to represent the interests of the concerns for about six weeks. His enemies then seized upon the opportunity of further exploiting the Black Star Line through disloyal officers and employees, to the extent that $25,000 was taken from the Corporation's treasury in May of 1921 to purchase a ship from the United States Shipping Board for the Black Star Line. A Jewish gentleman in New York by the name of Silverston got the money, representing himself as a broker. He made contracts with the Black Star Line through its Vice President to secure for the Company a ship in May of 1921. He failed to do so. He never lodged the $25,000 with the Shipping Board, as he promised to do. He kept and spent the money himself.

When Mr. Garvey made efforts to return to America from the West Indies and Central America after the expiration of his six weeks' stay he was debarred from securing a vis[a] for his passport at all points. His enemies had planned to ruin the Corporation in his absence, debar him from returning to the country, and then discredit him before the eyes of the world. For such reasons false representations were made against Mr. Garvey by his Negro enemies to the Department of Justice, the State and Immigration Departments, believing which, no doubt, the departments originally acted against Mr. Garvey on the matter of his return to the country.

Through the higher sense of justice, however, of the State Department, Mr. Garvey, after much trouble and difficulty, was permitted to re-enter the United States. He arrived in New York from New Orleans on the 15th of July, 1921.

He was led to believe whilst in the West Indies and Central America that the particular ship to be secured had been actually bought. He was surprised on his return to find that his belief was unfounded.

Being President-General of the Universal Negro Improvement Association, a big international movement, and being unavoidably away from headquarters for so long, and owing to the fact that the first of August of the said year was the opening of the second international convention of the Negro peoples of the world, in session for the entire month, day and night, under the auspices of the Universal Negro Improvement Association, and over which he had to pr[es]ide continuously as Speaker, he was forced to accept the excuses of the Vice President of the Black Star Line Corporation for the delay in the delivery of said ship.

Positive assurances were made to him as late as December of 1921 that the boat would be forthcoming, but as he discovered by inquiries from the Shipping Board through correspondence and otherwise that the money which should have been deposited since May was not wholly or substantially or partly lodged until December, and, then, $11,000 more of the Black Star Line's assets was pledged as an additional amount realized through the said Black Star Line by the said Silverston, with the knowledge of the Vice President, and said amount used to cover up and add to a smaller partial deposit with the Shipping Board, to the credit of the Black Star Line, so as to further deceive Mr. Garvey after he had started his investigation to trace the original $25,000 of the Black Star Line funds.

During the process of this investigation he was indicted on the charge herein complained of, and on which he has been convicted through frame-up and prejudice.

We hereby beg to bring to the attention of Your Excellency that during the trial of Marcus Garvey and the other defendant officers of the Corporation, namely, the Vice President, Treasurer and Secretary, it was plainly visible that the Prosecutor was maliciously arrayed against Garvey. The burden of his entire venom was leveled at Garvey, and he practically, during examination and summation, defended the Vice President,[1] even though the acts of the man were laid plain and open before the court, as the minutes will prove.

The conviction of Garvey through the efforts of his enemies, in combination and through prejudice, to us is a blot on the fair record of our great Government, and is especially so because he has been denied the Constitutional right of bail pending appeal.

The fact that the belief prevails that the prosecution has used manufactured evidence in prosecuting the case and in opposing bail for Garvey is reason for us, your petitioners, to request the interest of Your Excellency in the case, and to pray that Your Excellency will cause an immediate investigation to be made into the entire trial and subsequent movements on the part of the Prosecutor, so as to save the name of our great Government from what is fast becoming an international scandal, and the facts of which have surprised the Negro peoples of the world.

We do solemnly and humbly pray that Your Excellency will take cognizance of this petition for justice.

Marcus Garvey is honored and revered by millions of well-thinking Negroes in this country and all over the world, and we feel keenly the humiliation that has been heaped upon him by his enemies, which humiliation has affected terribly the entire Negro race.

We, your humble petitioners, love our country, and we trust that no such act as denying Marcus Garvey bail pending an appeal, a consideration that is granted even one accused of second degree murder, will be permitted to stand and cause us, who have served her in peace and war, to doubt her fair play even to the humblest of her citizens. We beg to remain,

YOUR EXCELLENCY'S HUMBLE PETITIONERS

DNA, RG 16, general correspondence. PD.

1. Mattuck's summation does not appear in the trial transcript. While Orlando Thompson's testimony occupied a good deal of the trial, it is difficult to assess whether Mattuck displayed undue bias toward Thompson, as the petitioners claim.

Aaron P. Prioleau, UNIA National Political Director General, to Harry M. Daugherty

326-G-St., N.W. Washington D.C.
July 7, 1923

My Most Esteemed Sir:

Knowing how vital and important that the New York State and the National Election will be in 1924, and that from the defeat of many candidates of the Republican Party in the last election of 1922 in your state and the Nation /which/ was primarily on account of the Afro-American Negro Voters that left the Republican Party.[1]

Thereupon feeling how great the necessity of the party doing everything in there power to consolidate the large number of Negro Voters of America, for the great fight of the Republican Party in the election of 1924[,] I, having been vested with the power of National Political Director General of the Universal Negro Improvement Association, of the United States of America[,] with headquarters at the capital, I, herein appeal in the name of the Negro Voters and Citizens of America to the leaders of the Republican in power in your state to see that the President, Marcus Garvey of the said Association petition for a writ of Hab[ea]s Corpus in the court of the state of New York [to] get before a friendly judge that will grant him bail.

This, I assure /can/ be done through your assistance, and in view of the fact that the colored people of America are Republicans and if the Republican party in power protect their civil and political rights they will be loyal and true to the party as they always have been and in 1920 /National election,/ all of which matter and things in the premises I have assured to this association /members/ will be done by their full support in the future for /the Republican/ party /Election 1924/. Thanking you for your due consideration by the use of your good office I am Sir, yours most sincerely

AARON P. PRIOLEAU[2]
National Political Director General
U.N.I.A., U.S.A.

DNA, RG 60, file 198940-291. TLS, recipient's copy.

1. The Democrats narrowly missed winning both houses of Congress in the off-year election of 1922. The movement of black voters toward the Democratic party was evident in 1922, and

the trend grew, until by 1928 half of the urban black voters voted for Al Smith, the Democratic candidate in the presidential election. In 1932 the Democrats were able to attract the majority of black votes for the first time (Arthur Link et al., *The American People: A History*, pp. 708–710).

2. Aaron P. Prioleau was also a member of the East Washington (D.C.) division of the UNIA (*NW*, 17 November 1923).

Meeting Announcement

AN

"APPEAL TO CAESAR"

A SPECIAL SERMON

IN BEHALF OF

MARCUS GARVEY

AND THE

REDEMPTION OF AFRICA

By Rev. W. H. Moses, D. D.

Pastor of

National Baptist Church

and

Field Secretary of the National Baptist Convention
of the U. S. A.

Representing 3,500,000 Constituents

SUNDAY, JULY 8th, 1923, 11 A. M. and 8 P. M.

AT

New York National Baptist Church

125th Street and Madison Avenue

(*Source*: NNC, Alexander Gumby Collection.)

W.E.B. Du Bois to Ida May Reynolds

[*New York*] July 10, 1923

My dear Madam:

Answering your letter of July 5th,[1] I beg to say I have never written any letters to the District Attorney or Judge Mack or anyone else in authority with regard to Marcus Garvey, nor have I had anything whatsoever to do with the prosecution of the case against him. Very sincerely yours,

W.E.B. DU BOIS

Reprinted from Herbert Aptheker, ed., *The Correspondence of W.E.B. Du Bois, 1920-1929* (Amherst: University of Massachusetts Press, 1973), 1: 272. Used by permission.

1. Reynolds's letter castigated the *Crisis* for "trying to wreck" the UNIA by "writing letters to the District Attorney, Judge Mack and others who were in authority." These "cowardly" methods, Reynolds claimed, would cause "everlasting enmity between the West Indian and the American negroes" (Ida May Reynolds to W.E.B. Du Bois, 5 July 1923, in Herbert Aptheker, ed., *The Correspondence of W.E.B. Du Bois,* 1: 271–272; see also *The Papers of W.E.B. Du Bois* [New York: Microfilming Corp. of America, 1981], reel 15, frame 515).

John E. Bruce to George B. Christian, Jr., Secretary to President Warren G. Harding

Manhattan Eye, Ear and Throat Hospital,
New York City, N.Y. July 10, 1923

Dear Mr[.] Secy[.]:

A very grave injustice is being done to Marcus Garvey, recently tried and convicted here on a charge of ["]using the mails to defraud," by the refusal of the U.S[.] Dist[.] Attorney to consent to his giving bail which his followers[,] to the number of 6[,]000,000 Negroes scattered throughout the country, are prepared to give in any amount required by the Court. Recently a Committee from the Universal Negro Improvement Association visited Washington with a petition asking the President to cause an investigation of this case, and to see to it that Marcus Garvey receives fair play. I am writing to you to supplement that request, and to ask you to bring this matter to the attention of the President, to the end that the truth about this trial and its *queer outcome* may be made plain and clear to the public who are convinced that Mr[.] Garvey has been framed in the interest of a *rival Negro organization* to which the judge who sentenced him is a cash contributor[.] There are several thousand voters in the Universal Negro Improvement Association of which Mr[.] Garvey is president, and they feel that a great wrong has been done its president, and that he and his organization should have an opportunity to expose the plotters, and vindicate themselves.

I trust sir that you will bring the matter to the attention of his excellency the president, whom we all want to see reelected, and whom we believe does not wish to alienate any clan of voters by consenting to the palpable wrongs inflicted on their leaders by those who have the power to use their authority unfairly and unjustly[.] *Vengeance is not justice.* All we ask for is justice! Respectfully

> JOHN E. BRUCE
> Editor Negro World
> Staff Cor. Kansas City Call, Kan. City, Mo.
> Richmond Planet, Richmond, Va.
> Lagos Record, Lagos, Nigeria, W.C.A.

DNA, RG 60, file 198940-300. ALS, recipient's copy. Emphasis in original.

Report by Bureau Agent Adrian L. Potter

Springfield, Mass. July 10–16, 1923

NEGRO AFFAIRS:

"Protest Meetings" held under auspices of various Negro radical organizations have been held at Springfield, Westfield, Worcester, Pittsfield, Holyoke, Leominster, Northampton and Great Barrington, re conviction in Federal Court of Marcus Garvey. Telegrams and letters have been forwarded to prominent newspapers[1] and also to Department heads at Washington. A.N. Service, field secretary, U.N.I.A.[2] is responsible for holding of "protest meetings" in this District of the Bureau, and publicity given to same would indicate general protest of negroes which is not a fact as meetings in no case were attended by more than a score of negroes, majority of whom are not citizens of this Country.

ADRIAN L. POTTER

DJ-FBI, file 61-120-99. TD.

1. The *New York Evening Post* reported that "scores of telegrams" were received by the Washington office of the Associated Press from Garvey's supporters (*New York Evening Post,* 16 July 1923).
2. A.Newton Service was listed in the 1920 and 1925 city directories of Springfield, Mass. as a real estate agent (Ed Lonergan, Genealogy/Local History Dept., Springfield City Library, to Robert A. Hill, 1 June 1983).

Vernal J. Williams to the UNIA Executive Council

[*New York, 15 July 1923*]

Dear Sirs and Madam:

I do not feel that under the present circumstances and the uncertain condition under which the Association is now proceeding, prudence will permit

me, as an attorney, to remain an officer of the Association and a member of
the Council. I therefore beg leave to tender my resignation herein, the same
to take effect immediately. Very truly yours.

VERNAL J. WILLIAMS
Asst. Counsel General

UNIA v. *Vernal J. Williams*, no. 32717, New York State Supreme Court, 1923, record
on appeal, p. 6.

Robert L. Poston to Vernal J. Williams

New York, U.S.A., July 16th 1923

My dear Mr. Williams:—

We have before us your resignation, of present date to take effect
immediately. We regret very much this step taken by you, and hope that you
will see your way clear to reconsider the matter, and meanwhile give us a little
time also to take the matter up with you personally.

At all events the Chancellor, Mr. Bourne, is absent and we deem it expe-
dient that it be delayed until we can meet you in a body.

We trust that if you are determined at any rate we may yet be able to
retain your services as Attorney, if not as an Officer. Trusting that you will
give this your careful consideration, believe us to be Yours Fraternally,

ROBERT L. POSTON

UNIA v. *Vernal J. Williams*, no. 32717, New York State Supreme Court, 1923, record
on appeal, p. 44.

Amy Jacques Garvey to the *Negro World*

[*New York*] [[July 16, 1923]]

MRS. MARCUS GARVEY REPLIES TO
ARTICLE IN NEGRO WORLD

DEFENDS HERSELF AGAINST REFERENCE
TO HER BEING HELPLESS

Editor The Negro World:

Please be good enough to publish the following re your editorial "Look
Out for Mud," which appeared in last week's issue of The Negro World.

In referring to a news item circulated by the Crusader Service in several

Negro newspapers to the effect that my husband "had turned over the organization" to me, you stated that "it is beneath the dignity of common decency to attempt to drag the name of an innocent and helpless woman into an arena where she cannot properly defend herself."

I desire to state that the article was shown to me, but, knowing that every division, branch and chapter of the Universal Negro Improvement Association in the world had been officially notified of the appointment of a Committee of Management to direct the affairs of the organization with the advice and instructions of my husband (such committee comprising Messrs. Sherrill, Poston and Bourne, officers of the organization), and that your paper carries a half-page notice to that effect[,] I ignored the article, because the news in itself is such a clumsy, unvarnished lie that it is worthy of the source from which it came, and did not in the least disturb the divisions, branches and chapters of the Universal Negro Improvement Association. I was certainly surprised to see your valuable paper giving such news almost a column of editorial space.

You have characterized me as "innocent and helpless." I am innocent of the honor of having the Universal Negro Improvement Association "turned over" to me by my husband, but I am not innocent of the depths to which colored men can stoop to further their petty personal schemes, even at the expense of a downtrodden race such as ours.

I am not "innocent" of the tactics employed by men of my race to get easy money from alien individuals, groups and sometimes nations.

I am not "innocent" of the undermining influences used by local individuals and rival organizations to destroy my husband and the Universal Negro Improvement Association; because such individuals and rival organizations fear the power and strength of our organization and have not the ability to create anything like unto it.

I am not "innocent" of all this, and, more, I am not "innocent" of individual psychology and know how, when, and where to treat with some men. My four and a half years of active service in the Universal Negro Improvement Association under the personal direction of Marcus Garvey has given me a fair knowledge of men and the methods they employ in the organization and out of it.

With my unusual general knowledge and experiences for a young woman, may I not ask if the word "helpless" is not misapplied?

If the editorial was written in my defense, I have to thank you for same, and hope that if ever I am in need of a protector (not to draw his sword in my defense, but to flash his quill), you, sir, will as on this occasion, unsolicited, spill as much ink as will prove my "innocence" and protect me as a "helpless" woman. I beg to remain. Yours truly,

AMY JACQUES GARVEY

Printed in *NW*, 21 July 1923.

William Hayward to Judge Martin Manton

[*New York, ca. 17 July 1923*]

Dear Judge Manton[1]:—

I am enclosing herewith the Government's memorandum on Garvey's application for bail, an affidavit of my Assistant, Mr. Mattuck[,] who is in charge of the prosecution, an affidavit of James E. Amos, Special Agent of the Department of Justice, a copy (in part) of the "Negro World"[2] which is typical of the defendant's recently published utterances and a copy of the indictment on which he was convicted.

In respect to the Government's position in opposing Garvey's application, it is perhaps unnecessary to state that it has been prompted solely by the Government's view as to how the best interests of the community will be served. Mr. Mattuck has been in contact with Garvey and the Garvey case for one year and a half and he feels that to let Garvey out before judgment has been rendered on his appeal is to let loose upon the public an extremely dangerous force. Judge Mack and Judge Rogers probably felt the same way; and the Attorney General[,] to whom a petition seems to have been made, also refused to take any action. In fact, it is the universal opinion of all who know the defendant and have observed him that his release on bail is bound to be followed by dreadful results and it would not at all surprise Mr. Mattuck if [i]t is followed by bloodshed. We urge upon your Honor a very careful consideration of all the facts and the circumstances before ordering the defendant's release. Certainly, the threats upon the lives of the prosecutor and the trial judge should give pause for careful consideration. . . .

And, neither will Garvey ever be put behind the bars once he gets out. The man is a shrewd propagandist whose idea of negro uplift, if such an idea really exists [i]n his mind, is second to his personal ambitions of self-glorification. He is president of everything in sight, including Africa[,] and to attain his selfish purpose, he has little worry or scruples about the means.

Garvey is indeed a menace and it is the hope of this office that his petition will be denied.[3] . . .

WM. HAYWARD
United States Attorney

DNA, RG 60, file 198940. TL, carbon copy.

1. Martin T. Manton (1880–1946) graduated from Columbia University Law School in 1901 and practiced privately until his appointment in 1916 to the U.S. Circuit Court. He was promoted in 1918 to the U.S. Court of Appeals and later became the senior judge of the court, a position in the federal judiciary second only to that of the nine members of the Supreme Court. He was convicted in 1939 of having sold his office to litigants for $186,146, and eventually served nineteen months in jail (*NYT*, 18 November 1946).

2. Not retained.

3. Judge Manton refused Garvey's application for bail on 16 July 1923 (report of Special Agent James E. Amos, 27 July 1923, DJ-FBI, file 61).

Enclosure

[*New York, 17*] July 1923

AFFIDAVIT OF MAXWELL S. MATTUCK
UNITED STATES OF AMERICA VS.
MARCUS GARVEY

. . . The trial of the said Garvey began on May 18, 1923, and continued until June 18, 1923. During the course of that trial repeated requests were made to your deponent by witnesses for protection against threatened bodily injury because of the fact that they might possibly be witnesses against the defendant. In fact, during the trial your deponent prosecuted one Linous Charles, a member of the so-called African Legion, an organization subsidiary to the Universal Negro Improvement Association of which Marcus Garvey was President, for intimidating in the presence of the Court two witnesses, Sidney de Bourg and Hugh Mulzac. Throughout the trial repeated anonymous written threats were made upon the life of your deponent as prosecutor and Judge Mack. Some of these letters are still in possession of your deponent. In fact, a few such letters have been received since the trial; and upon the very night the jury returned a verdict, an attempt was made by one clearly an adherent of the defendant to reach your deponent while leaving the Court House for the [p]urpose of inflicting bodily injury. In fact your deponent is informed and believes that the defendant himself, when being taken from the Court Room on the night that the jury returned its verdict, was heard to say, referring to the Prosecutor, "I'll get you."

Since his conviction and despite his incarceration at the Tombs, the defendant has carried on a campaign of preaching hatred against not only the Prosecutor but against negroes w[h]o he thinks instituted the prosecution; and those speeches and articles which have been printed in his "Negro World" are of an extremely inflam[m]atory nature and are but mild examples of the type of utterances which can be expected from the defendant if he is admitted to bail. A copy of the "Negro World" in part, dated June 30, 1923, is attached hereto as an example of Garvey's utterances while in jail.[1] The speeches which have been made by his followers in Liberty Hall during his absence are of a similar hate breeding character but the refusal on the part of the managers of those meetings to permit any one to take minutes of those meetings renders it impossible to state exactly what those speeches have been.

Moreover, your deponent feels and believes that if Garvey is admitted to bail he will never serve his sentence. He is not a citizen and though he did declare his intention in 1921 of becoming a citizen, your deponent is informed and believes that his reason for declaring such intention is the difficulty which he had in returning to this country in 1921. He has been a resident since 1916. His bail money, if bail is to be fixed, will be money which has been and is being collected from benighted followers for the purpose of using it as a defense or an appeal fund. The money ostensibly is not his and he has little to lose by forfeiting a bond which is costing him personally nothing. His "doubtful reputation" which was testified to by Bishop Collins, whom he himself called to the stand as a character witness, more than lends color to my belief that if the defendant is admitted to bail he will never serve. Deponent therefore respectfully prays that the petition of said defendant for admission to bail should be denied.

[MAXWELL S. MATTUCK]

Sworn to before me this [*17?*] day of July, 1923.

DNA, RG 60, file 198940. TD, carbon copy.

1. This is probably a reference to the editorial letter by Garvey published in the *Negro World* of 30 June. In it he referred to Mattuck as

> The Jewish District Attorney, who cried for my body, represented not the soul of great America and our grand and noble government, but the sinister elements of malice, jealousy, hatred and mob violence, when he cried out to the jury, "Gentlemen, will you let the Tiger loose?" This, as we know, is the language of the sinister and hypocritical National Association for the Advancement of Colored People, the so-imagined political whip behind the District Attorney to "get and deliver Garvey." (*NW*, 30 June 1923).

Enclosure

[*New York*] 17th day of July, 1923

AFFIDAVIT OF JAMES E. AMOS

. . . Prior to the trial of this action and on January 1, 1923, in the City of New Orleans, the Reverend [J].W. Eason, who was then and there under subpoena as a witness in the case pending against Garvey in the Federal Court for the Southern District of New York, was shot and killed by two negroes named Dyer and Shakespeare, who were members of the so-called "African Legion," a subsidiary of the Universal Negro Improvement Association, and members of a so-called Secret Police attached to that organization.

Your deponent is informed and verily believes that the said Eason was killed because of the fact that he had in his possession evidence which would help the Government in the prosecution of the said Garvey, and was in fact shot by the direction of and with the knowledge of the said Garvey.

The source of your deponent's information and the grounds for his belief are admissions and statements made to him by a third member of the so-called Secret Police, who was in the city of New Orleans at the time of the said murder and who escaped therefrom and was later apprehended in the City of Detroit, Michigan. The same person has also informed your deponent that he has bought arms and ammunition at the direction of the defendant Garvey, to be used by the said Legion and Secret Police as the use of the said ammunition became necessary, for the purchase of which he procured money from the said

Garvey. Your deponent's informant has been identified in his presence by a salesman of the Winchester Arms and Rifle Company, as being a person who came to him for purchasing ammunition.

Your deponent, upon investigation, has obtained information tending to corroborate the above facts.

Moreover, prior to the trial, during the trial and since the trial, other witnesses have been threatened and are even now in fear of bodily injury. Joshua Cockburn, a witness for the Government, was threatened both before and after taking the stand. A co-defendant, O.M. Thompson, has informed your deponent that he has been threatened since the trial and has appealed for protection. A witness Sidney de Bourg has informed your deponent of numerous threats both before and after the trial, and has repeatedly requested protection. Anna Carrington, another witness, has been threatened after the trial. In fact, one Linous Charles is now serving a sentence of imprisonment at the Essex County Jail for threatening in the corridor of the Post Office Building, two witnesses for the Government, de Bourg and one Hugh Mulzac. The janitor of Liberty Hall, the place of meeting for Garvey's activities, has been sentenced and is now serving time in a penitentiary of having threatened the life of Miss Lawson, who thereafter was a witness for the Government.

Your deponent honestly believes and has sufficient corroborative information to base the honest belief that, despite protestations to the contrary, insid[i]ous underground propaganda of inspiring fear into the hearts and minds of all who have dared to testify against Garvey, has been carried on by Garvey's followers.

As a further reason which your deponent urges that Garvey be denied bail pending his appeal, is Garvey's threat, as your deponent remembers it, in the "Negro World,"—Garvey's official publication—that he would never serve a day of imprisonment and if he were imprisoned he would not stay in jail.[1] This threat on Garvey's part, has been communicated to your deponent from numerous other sources, and in fact, on the night before Garvey was actually found guilty by a jury, he made a speech in Liberty Hall, advising in effect, that he would never go to jail.[2] Amongst the numerous reasons, as your deponent is informed, that [w]ere given why Garvey would not serve any time, was the bribery of all Government officials and agents.

Your deponent verily believes that in the event of Garvey's admission to bail in any amount, that he will never serve his sentence.

JAMES E. AMOS

Sworn to before me this 17th day of July, 1923.
Carl Bucher, Notary Public

DNA, RG 60, file 198940. TD, carbon copy.

1. This statement has not been confirmed by a search of the *Negro World*.
2. Garvey's speech does not contain such an assertion.

Report by Bureau Agent Adrian L. Potter

Springfield, Mass. July 17–23, 1923

NEGRO AFFAIRS:

A. N. Service, self-styled secretary of the U. N. I. A. of Springfield, Mass., commenting on conviction in the Federal Court of Marcus Garvey, stated as follows:

"The conviction of Garvey cannot operate to check the movement for the establishment of a Negro republic in Africa. Even though he were sent to prison, he could direct the movement from behind his prison bars, and he would have the co-operation of many of the foremost leaders of the race in all parts of the world. There are 1000 organizations with a total membership of nearly 3,000,000 Negroes enlisted in the movement.

"Our hope is to establish a Negro republic in Africa, not through a vast colonization scheme which would drain America of its Negro workers, but rather by educational methods. Educated Negroes from every country in the world are expected to volunteer their services in starting the machinery of government in the proposed Negro republic. Already there are hundreds of capable European Negroes in Africa, who are preparing the ground for those who will come after. The native Africans generally are in cordial sympathy with the movement and are at this moment cooperating in certain parts of Africa with the leaders of the race who are already on the ground."

ADRIAN L. POTTER

DJ-FBI, file 61-120-100. TD.

Affidavit of Marcus Garvey

[*New York*] 19th day of July, 1923

MARCUS GARVEY, PLAINTIFF-IN-ERROR,
AGAINST UNITED STATES OF AMERICA,
DEFENDANT-IN-ERROR.

. . . I have read the affidavit of Maxwell S. Mattuck and the affidavit of James E. Amos. I have also read the memorandum and letter written by Mr. Mattuck to Honorable Martin T. Manton, all submitted by the Government in opposition to the application made by me to be admitted to bail pending a decision of this Court of my appeal from the judgement of the lower court.

With respect to the affidavit of Mr. Mattuck I beg to state that it is drawn and framed with the sole view and object of prejudicing me in the eyes of this Court. It will be noted that Mr. Mattuck does not charge me personally with having sent threatening letters to him or to Judge Mack or with intimidating witnesses, but Mr. Mattuck insinuates or attempts to insinuate that I am responsibl[e] for the sending of such letters, and for such intimidation. He has made these insinuations, as I stated above, for the purpose of placing me in an unfavorable light before this Honorable court, and to make the Court believe that I am a dangerous person, and that it would not serve the best interests of the Community to admit me to bail.

This method of attacking me i[s] unfair and unAmerican, and is in line with the means pursued by Mr. Mattuck throughout the trial of the case. Mr. Mattuck, for some reason unknown to me, has taken a personal dislike to me, and seems to bear great animosity against me. He has more than once gone out of his way as a public prosec[u]tor to injure me and has vowed to do everything in his power to keep me in jail and thereby satisfy his personal hatred against me. He is apparently being inspired and supported in his attacks upon me, by persons who have been dismissed from the organization of which I am President. These persons have been willing to make false statements to hurt me in my reputation and good name, and these persons have boasted of their protection by the Government in their persecution of me.

Among such persons is James E. Amos, to whom reference will hereafter be more fully made.

While I have a host of friends and a large following, I naturally also have a number of enemies who would not stop at anything to destroy my life's work and to discredit me in the eyes of the public.

I have for years labored unceasingly to improve and better the conditions of my race, and in those labors I naturally came in contact with some persons who opposed me, and in their opposition to my work, these persons were ready to resort to any methods that would hinder me in my work and nullify the good results that I was able to accomplish for my race.

I solemnly swear that I at no time sent any letters, threatening or otherwise, to the Prosecutor or Judge Mack, and I further solemnly swear that I never, directly or indirectly, intimidated or caused to be intimidated any witnesses called by the Government in my case, and I deny that I at any time made the statement referring to the Prosecutor "I'll get you," as stated in Mr. Mattuck's affidavit.

It is my firm belief and opinion that the above mentioned Amos and other enemies of mine and members of rival organizations, inspired the writing of the anonymous letters to the Prosecutor and to Judge Mack, as part of their plan to convict me. I myself have recieved threatening letters, and received one in the Tombs as late as June 26th, 1923. This letter, together with the envelope in which it came is hereto annnexed.[1]

I deny that I at any time made a statement in Liberty Hall or elsewhere that I would never serve a jail sentence or words to that effect. Such a statement is false and unfounded.

I deny that I at any time made inflam[m]atory speeches or statements tending to arouse race prejudice or race hatred. On the contrary, I have always preached to my race, obedience to law and order, and to be tolerant and to work for their improvement and to be self-reliant.

As proof of my state of mind and utterances for the general improvement of my race, I respectfully beg leave to call the Court's attention to a book which I published long before the trial of this action took place, entitled "Philosophy and Opinion[s] of Marcus Garvey."[2] I respectfully invite the Court's attention to this book which I beg leave to submit with this affidavit, and particularly draw the Court's attention to the Preamble to the Constitution of the Universal Negro Improvement Association, written by me in the year 1914, and appearing on page 102 of that book.

I also beg to append hereto and to make part of this affidavit, a statement made by me and published in the Negro World, under date of July 10th, 1923. I have dedicated my life to and have for years worked for the uplift and improvement of my race. Every speech that I made and every statement that I issued, was in part for the purpose of directing the attention of the members of my race to the necessity of education, tolerance and square dealing, without any intended offense to any other race.

During my trial, the District Attorney and the agent Amos made sure that all my friends and sympathizers were not admitted to the courtroom. No one favorable to me was allowed in the building, while those that were opposed to me and who were anxious to see me convicted, were admitted. It is untrue that since my incarceration I have carried on a campaign against the Prosecutor. I have no personal feeling against the Assistant District Attorney who tried the case against me, and I am not interested in him but for the cause of justice in my case. All I seek is to have justice accorded me, but it seems to be the desire of the Prosecutor to deny me justice and to alienate my friends and to close my mouth and right of free speech, so that voice cannot be given to my cry for justice.

I have been writing for the Negro World, the paper of the Universal Negro Improvement Association, for five years, and at no time during that period have my articles inflamed the public mind against the peace of the Community. I am of course, not responsible for speeches made by others in my absence. Of course I have had no control over the meetings conducted at Liberty Hall since my conviction. I feel that Mr. Mattuck is unfair in the manner in which he opposes my application for bail. He seems to be bent in keeping me in jail irrespective of whether or not there is a strong likelihood of the judgement of conviction being reversed. If I am adjudged guilty by the Appellate Court, there is no other recourse for me but to serve the sentence imposed upon me, but until such judgement by the Appellate Court, I feel that in fairness and in justice, I am entitled to be admitted to bail.

Mr. Mattuck's reference to my not being a full citizen, as a further reason for my not serving a prison sentence if I am admitted to bail, is nonsensical. My not being a full citizen has of course nothing to do with my serving any sentence imposed on me by a Court of Justice, and the suggestion that I would not serve such a sentence is unfair and unfounded, especially so in face of the stand that I have always taken in the movement for race uplift and the possible fate that may at any time befall a Leader in such movement. On page 101 of my book, to which reference has already been made, is found the following—

CLOSING REGRET.

> There has never been a Movement where the Leader has not suffered for the Cause, and not received the ingratitude of the people. I, like the rest, am prepared for the consequence.

The further reason advanced by the Prosecutor that any money that may be put up for my bail will not be my own money, and therefore I will not have any hesitation in forfeiting the same, is baseless and without foundation whatsoever. My reputation and standing in the Community and in the Nation and all over the World is far beyond the limit of any amount of money subscribed to my defense, so that even without the fixed amount of a bail bond, my manhood would dictate to me no other course than that of answering at all times to the call of justice. I maintain a home with my wife whom I love with deep affection, and my business relations are of such a character as to make the thought of forfeiting a bond beneath me.

The District Attorney takes undue advantage of the word "Doubtful" used by Bishop J.J. Collins, a character witness. The Bishop explained that he never meant to use the word "doubtful" as the District Attorney seeks to apply it. The Bishop testified that I am a worthy man and that he has known me for 25 years. I, being a layman, who tried my own case, did not know the technical way of framing the question to be put to a character witness. I made a blunder in the manner in which I asked the question and the Bishop must have misunderstood me. When I later tried to clarify the question, I was denied the privilege of so doing. There were four character witnesses besides Bishop Collins. Each of these testified to my good character, reputation and honesty in the highest terms, as the record will show.

I am informed that an effort was made by my attorneys to reach Bishop Collins on the telephone for the purpose of obtaining a statement from him so as to clarify this matter, but my attorneys were informed that the Bishop is now in Kentucky and will not return for some time.

Mr. Mattuck in his prejudice against me, is apparently unable to grasp and appreciate human ideals. He seems to judge the cause of human uplift from the sordid and selfish angle of monetary gain, which was furthest from my mind at any time during my connection with the Black Star Line.

It is certainly illogical and inconsistent for the District Attorney to argue in one breath that I am a dangerous person and that my being admitted to bail would cause bloodshed, and in the other, to state that if I am released on bail I would forfeit my bail and flee from the jurisdiction of the court.

I have been a resident of Harlem in the City of New York for upwards of five years up to the time of my imprisonment, and none of the dreadful fears expressed by the District Attorney ever materialized.

I have always known and know now that I am not above the law, and that I must conduct myself in an orderly and lawful manner.

Mr. Mattuck states that money is being collected from benighted followers. The members of the organization of which I am President are not benighted, but highly intelligent people who cannot be swayed by prejudice and injustice, as their attitude must attest even in the face of propaganda to call them fools, ignorant, etc.

Mr. Mattuck has no real or substantial reason for opposing my application for bail, but has resorted to his methods of opposition solely out of hatred for me and to satisfy his personal animosity.

I hereby beg to submit the article of June 30, 1923, in the Negro World, in full, to which Mr. Mattuck has made reference, and also the statements issued by me from the prison to the members of the Universal Negro Improvement Association, in which I have advised loyalty and obedience. Certainly these articles do not warrant the interpretation placed thereon by Mr. Mattuck.

With respect to the affidavit of James E. Amos, I desire emphatically to deny the statements therein contained, which[,] in substance or in effect, charge that J.W. Eason[,] in said affidavit named, was shot by my direction or with my knowledge. This charge of the said James E. Amos is absolutely false and untrue and a most malicious attack upon me. I know absolutely nothing of the killing of the said J.W. Eason, except what I read in the newspapers. I have also read in the newspapers that the conviction of Dyer and Shakespeare[,] mentioned in Amos' affidavit, for the killing of the said J.W. Eason was reversed by the Court on appeal.[3] I do not know and never met either Dyer or Shakespeare. I did not know that the said Eason was to be a witness for the Government.

I do not know to whom Amos refers as the "third member of the so-called Secret Police." I do not know what information this "third member" gave to the said Amos but I do emphatically and solemnly deny that I at any time bought or instructed anyone to buy arms and ammuniton to be used by the "Legion and Secret Police" as mentioned in Amos' affidavit.

There is no "Secret Police" attached to the Universal Negro Improvement Association, so far as I know. I know nothing at all about the threats made to Joshua Cockburn and O.M. Thompson, and the other persons mentioned in Amos' affidavit. I emphatically deny that I at any time threatened the above named persons or any other persons and I solemnly swear before this Court that I at no time threatened said persons or any other persons, and I further swear that I at no time directed or requested anybody to make threats to said persons or to any other persons, or to use violence.

I emphatically deny the statement contained in Amos' affidavit that I said that I would not serve a day in prison. I deny that on the night before my conviction, I made a speech in Liberty Hall to the effect that I would never go to jail, as stated in the said Amos' affidavit. Amos does not say that he was present at that meeting. He does not give the source of his information. I know for a fact that he was not at such a meeting, but he apparently has no great regard for an oath, because he seems to be willing to swear to anything that will help keep me in jail. This man Amos is a friend of members of an organization opposed to the objects of my Society, and Amos uses and has been using his office in and connection with the Department of Justice to injure me and to promote the organization of his friends, of which organization I believe he is also a member.

For Mr. Amos to swear that I stated that if I were put in prison, I would not stay there, is on its face, ridiculous. There would be no way for me to get out of prison, except by process of law.

I further deny that I at any time directed any person or persons to purchase arms or ammunition, or that I furnished any money for such purchase. The assertion that I did so is not only prepostorous, but vicious and is made for the purpose of injuring me and to prejudice me in my effort to obtain bail.

I have never, directly or indirectly, purchased arms or carried a revolver. I am law-abiding and would not do or commit any act that would be or tend to be a breach of the peace.

To my personal knowledge, [t]he said Amos has followed me all over New York over a year. He has in many ways tried to interfere with my business activities and to spread disloyalty among my employees. He canvasse[d] stockholders of the Black Star Line and inspired them and dismissed employees of mine to testify against me. It is my firm belief that he is in the employ of in the confidence of a rival Negro organization, which seeks to smash the movement in which I have been engaged for years.

The said Amos, during the progress of the trial[,] stated to me in Court— "I will get you or throw away my gun and badge." I am informed that he bragged among his friends in the colored district in Harlem that he would send me to prison and keep me there.

I know nothing about the janitor of Liberty Hall being in prison for threatening any one. The vague reference in Amos' affidavit to bribery of Government officials and agents, is preposterous and shows the extent to which he will go to injure one whom he has singled out as a victim for persecution.

I desire to state further that throughout my trial, Amos manifested ardent desire to see me convicted. He sat close to Mr. Mattuck and along with him demonstrated his malice and hatred toward me. At the time the jury rendered its verdict, they both exhibited expressions of joy and gladness. They are now co-operating to keep me in jail and gloat over the fact that they have thus far succeeded in their unholy methods.

I desire once again to refer to Mr. Mattuck, and to respectfully call this honorable court's attention to the letter of Mr. Mattuck to Honorable Martin T. Manton, accompanying the papers submitted by him in opposition to my application. I beg to emphasize the fact that the copyletter submitted to me bears no date and purports to be written by Mr. Hayward. It is common knowledge that Mr. Hayward is at the present time in Europe and was in Europe at the time this letter was written.[4] In the second paragraph of that letter is contained a statement that the Government's purpose in opposing bail is prompted by the desire to serve the best interests of the Community, and that my admission to bail will be dangerous.

It is interesting to state in answer to the foregoing assertion that I have lived in Harlem for upwards of five years up to the time of my conviction and have never during that period caused any disturbance or unrest in the Community. On the contrary, as the hand of a large organization with a local membership of about 30,000 persons in the District,[5] I have always maintained peace and order, and some times under severe provocation. Therefore I submit that it is unfair to assume that I would cause any unpleasantness now, were I restored to liberty. Certainly if in five years I created no disturbance in the Community, it does not suggest fairness to charge that I might be a disturbing factor if admitted to bail especially so in view of the fact that there is absolutely no proof to that effect.

If[,] as Mr. Mattuck claims, Judge Mack and Judge Rogers shared in his opinion, it was because of the undue advantage taken by Mr. Mattuck in making statements without any evidence to support them. Furthermore, Judge Mack denied the motion with leave to apply to the Circuit Court, and Judge Rogers denied the motion without prejudice. His order entered in this Court under date of July 2nd, 1923, reads as follows—

ORDERED that said motion be and hereby is denied without prejudice.

H.N.R.

Mr. Mattuck would also make it appear that the whole District Attorney's office is opposed to my release on bail. This is absolutely unfounded. Mr. Mattuck is the only one[,] to my knowledge, who opposes my admission to bail.

I did not send any petition to the Attorney General, but friends of mine have sent a petition to the President, and as a matter of courtesy have left a copy of such petition with the Attorney General. Of course, it is known that the President is at the present time away from Washington. Thousands of persons have signed the petition asking for my admission to bail, and I am informed that over three hundred telegrams were received in Washington from the different divisions of the Universal Negro Improvement Association in the various States of the Union, respectfully asking my admission to bail.

In conclusion I respectfully beg to assure this Court that if I am admitted to bail, which I fervently pray, I will not commit any act to disturb the peace and harmony of the Community, because I always have been and now am a law-abiding and peace-loving person.

I attach hereto the affidavits[6] of VERNAL J. WILLIAMS, ALONZO D. PETTIFORD,[7] CLIFFORD S. BOURNE, ROBERT L. POSTON, THOMAS W. ANDERSON, WILLIAM SHER[R]ILL AND GEORGE E. CARTER.

I therefore respectfully pray that my application for admission to bail be granted.

MARCUS GARVEY

Sworn to before me this 19th day of July, 1923
John F. Burns, Commissioner of Deeds N.Y. County.

DNA, RG 60, file 198940. TD, carbon copy.

1. Not retained.

2. *Philosophy and Opinions of Marcus Garvey* was published in the period between December 1922 and January 1923 and was edited in part by Garvey's wife, Amy Jacques Garvey. According to her account, she began gathering Garvey's sayings for her personal record and decided "to enlarge on them and give the public an opportunity of reading some of his thoughts written in a simple and condensed style." Her greatest wish was to "help to counteract many of the misquoted statements attributed to my husband" (*NW*, 17 March 1923). Garvey, too, recognized the propaganda value of the volume. In a speech entitled "Propaganda and Service," Garvey declared "This book . . . is being read largely by the white people of this country, and it is surprising that they are knowing more about what we are doing and saying than our group of people" (*NW*, 24 November 1923).

3. Constance Dyer and William Shakespeare appealed their conviction for the murder of J . W . H. Eason, but their appeal was turned down on 16 June 1923. The Supreme Court of Louisiana, however, remanded the case to Judge Frank T. Echezabal in New Orleans for retrial. On 8 August 1924, after a five-day trial, the jury unanimously acquitted both men (*NW*, 9 August 1924; *Chicago Defender*, 16 August 1924).

4. Mentions of William Hayward appeared in United States newspaper reports up to 1 July and after 6 August. Thus it is possible that he was in Europe in July 1923, although no reference has been found to this effect. A letter purportedly written by Hayward in July bears a signature markedly different from that of other letters, raising the possibility that someone signed documents for him in his absence (*NYT*, 1 July and 6 August 1923; William Hayward to Harry Daugherty, 10 July 1923, DNA, RG 60, file 198940).

5. In 1920 73,000 blacks lived in Harlem, representing the largest concentration of the 109,000 blacks who lived in Manhattan. The area was growing rapidly, and by 1930 the population more than doubled, reaching 165,000 (Ira Katznelson, *Black Men, White Cities*, pp 63–65)

6. These affidavits have been omitted.

7. Alonzo D. Pettiford, born in Spaulding, Ohio, studied chemistry in Jamestown, Ohio, before establishing the Pettiford Chemical Co., with branches in Detroit, Columbus, Ohio, and Cincinnati. Pettiford became a resident of Detroit around 1910 and obtained a law degree from the Detroit College of Law. An active lawyer in the city, he ran unsuccessfully for Michigan's Wayne County Circuit Court in 1924. He was a member of the Bethel AME Church in Detroit and was active in the United Civic League and the Afro-American Council. He was listed in the Detroit City Directory until 1953 (Alice C. Dalligan, chief, Burton Historical Collection, Detroit Public Library, to Robert A. Hill, 8 March 1984).

Marcus Garvey to Vernal J. Williams

[*New York, ca. 19 July 1923*]

Dear Sir:

I received yesterday a copy of your resignation forwarded to the Board of Management of the Association asking that said resignation take effect on the 15th inst.[1]

I am surprised that you should expect us to accept a resignation immediately, the very day it was written, without giving the Association sufficient time for you to properly turn over your work and your office to your successor, or our legal representative. You know well that your office has handled dozens of important cases on matters dealing with the Association, and within the last eight months the methods of your office have been so slack, and the protection given us has been so loose that it is impossible for any reasonable attorney to expect that he could send in a notice of resignation in one day, and have it acted on immediately.

I am personally willing to advise the acceptance of your resignation provided you will bring your work that you have not properly attended to all during the time you have been there, for the last eight months, up to date, so that there will be no difficulty for us to know exactly our legal standing before any courts, with our different cases.[2]

When you have properly catalogued the cases, properly explained their standings in the courts, the likely time of their being called, the different arrangements that have been entered into with all such legal advice that should have been given during the period of your employ, then after such has been properly done in making up for the improprieties of the past prior to the date that you sent your resignation, then we shall be pleased to accept same. For that reason I am advising the Board of Management to request you to do as above requested.

I have asked Mr. Pettiford to receive from you in the presence of Mr. Plummer, Mr. Sherrill, Miss Green (your stenographer) and the other two members of the Board of Management, all documents and explanation of the cases herein above referred to, so that there can be a proper knowledge and understanding of our legal status in all cases now in your office, for and against the Association, its auxiliaries, its officers etc.

This I feel sure you will do without any feeling of ill will in that there is no need for same, and I shall be pleased that whatsoever statements you make bearing on the cases, and I trust they will be written, you will hand a copy of same over to my private secretary, Miss Lamos, who will also be present at the time when you are meeting the other individuals above mentioned.

I would advise that you make a minute and detail[ed] report of the standing of each case, what papers are in connection with them, those that have been tried, mention what disposition was made at the trial etc., and those to be tried, with all the history connected thereto, and all papers necessary. This you should have done before you sent in your resignation, then your work would have been complete, but that you did not do so, we feel sure that you will make up for the time that we were entitled to have same done in. I have the honor to be, Your obedient servant,

MARCUS GARVEY
President-General
Universal Negro Improvement Association

UNIA v. *Vernal J. Williams*, no. 32717, New York State Supreme Court, 1923, record on appeal, pp. 7–9.

1. Williams had stated, in fact, his willingness "to furnish all the pending cases begun by me and get into proper shape the legal affairs of the Association" (Vernal J. Williams to Marcus Garvey, 15 July 1923, *UNIA* v. *Vernal J. Williams*, records on appeal, p. 7).

2. On 22 July, Sherrill, Poston, and Bourne replied to Williams, stating that after conferring with Garvey they had agreed to accept his resignation provided that "you bring the work of your office up to date" (*UNIA* v. *Vernal J. Williams*, records on appeal, p. 198). In 1927 Garvey claimed Williams had acted without his authority in a libel suit Garvey had brought against the Workingman's Cooperative Publishing Co. in 1922. Garvey sought the court's protection, declaring, "he was not represented by counsel" (*Pittsburgh Courier*, 3 December 1927).

Editorial Letter by Marcus Garvey

[[Tombs Prison, Centre Street, New York,
August 1, 1923]]

ONE MILLION NEGROES TO VOTE TOGETHER, SAYS POWERFUL NEGRO ORGANIZATION

FELLOW MEN OF THE NEGRO RACE, Greeting:

The time is approaching in domestic politics when every man and woman who professes the faith of the Universal Negro Improvement Association— freedom, liberty, justice—must stand together as one man for what is equitable and just. Except in State and city elections we have never, to any organized extent, taken sides for the common good. Because of our quietude in this direction some people, and especially a few uninformed persons, thought we were ignorant of the force and power of the Universal Negro Improvement Association in politics.

EACH NEGRO WORKING IN HIS COMMUNITY

The time has come when every member of the Universal Negro Improvement Association, from Maine to California, must be an active worker in his or her community for the side that we shall nationally espouse for right and justice to Negroes. We shall, for the first time in the history of America, prove that one million Negroes can vote and stand together for a cause and on a principle.

REGISTERING AS A VOTER EVERYWHERE

Every officer, member and supporter is now asked to make preparation for registering as a voter for 1923–24. The greatest service and duty we can render and perform for the Universal Negro Improvement Association is to register and vote during the forthcoming political campaigns. Every division, chapter and branch of our great association shall work in unison with the Parent Body to put over the program that will be outlined for the good of the race.

WE SHALL ALL PULL TOGETHER

Negroes, we shall all pull together, and in the effort we shall make sure that the old distractors and camoufleurs be not allowed to blow off their annual and periodic camouflage and deception. Our campaign literature shall be scattered from State to State, city to city, town to town, district to district, hamlet to hamlet, home to home and door to door. This will be a period of work and sacrifice for each and every member, and we ask that you prepare yourselves for the work of love and duty.

ACTION AT LOCAL CONVENTIONS

At your local conventions this month you are requested to form your local political committees under the direction of your President and await instructions from the Parent Body. We have humored and smiled with our opponents, playing foolish and ignorant of our strength, but the hour has struck for the Universal Negro Improvement Association to stand together and be as one man. They have tried to misrepresent us and make out that we have no voting strength, the liars that they are. We have won many an election in New York, Cincinnati, Detroit, Cleveland, Los Angeles, Chicago, Philadelphia, etc., by silently lending our help without any desire to take credit for anything done. They attributed our silence to ignorance, but even the fool has an awakening, and so we shall now stand together as never Negroes did before.

THE AWAKENED VOICE

The call of the Universal Negro Improvement Association is the awakened voice of every Negro. We are fighting for an ideal that must appeal to the manhood and womanhood of the race. We want justice, liberty and political and industrial equality. We demand the rights of men. For this we have worked and are still working; therefore, we claim the sympathy, support and co-operation of one and all. Co-operation and determination must be our bulwarks of strength for the period ahead of us. We must remember that it is only by our own effort that we can put over our program and advance our cause.

GETTING TOGETHER POLITICALLY

This appeal for us to get together politically is made because we have reached the danger period where unworthy and unscrupulous individuals have been making efforts to undermine and destroy us; people who, in truth, manifest nothing in common with the race, but who insult us at times, and especially after they have benefited by our help and service. When it suits them they call us ignorant, illiterate and "benighted." Well, one million illiterate and "benighted" Negroes will now stand together and show to the world that they are capable to taking care of themselves politically and socially.

HAVE BECOME INTERESTED IN POLITICS

We have become interested in the politics of our respective communities, because it is that science of government that protects those human rights that are not protected by law. When justice fails you, there is but one reasonable and rational resort, and that is to the political readjustment of the community in which you live and a reorganization of the machinery that deprives the community of that justice. The medium for exercising your political opinion is the ballot box; hence, it becomes necessary for every Negro to make up his mind and do the right thing by himself during the approaching changes.

IMAGINE EVERY NEGRO TOGETHER

Let us imagine every Negro voting together on all public questions, and then you will have the program and attitude of the Universal Negro Improvement Association for 1923–24. Start now and line up your section of the big job.

YOU MUST REGISTER WHERE YOU ARE

Every Negro in the voting States must register at the proper time, and the best work that the members of our association can do just now is to go from house to house and prepare the people of their community for this civic duty. If there are any members of our association who are not naturalized, I advise that you take immediate steps to become so, that you may be better able to throw in your strength with the great majority and carry the day for the Universal Negro Improvement Association.

RETURNING THANKS

I take this medium of returning thanks to the many preachers and Negro newspapers who have, for the sake of justice, joined in the protest against my imprisonment and detention without bail. I am glad that they realize it is not a question of Marcus Garvey, but it is a penalty reserved for every Negro who dares to step out and make an honest effort for real race uplift and independence. I may be first, but under the system the door is opened for thousands more. It is only a question of time when "these dear friends of the colored people" will get at us one by one, under the guise of pleasing the race, and destroy the buoyant hopes we have encouraged for race redemption and salvation. Negroes, watch your steps, and beware of "Greeks bearing gifts." To imagine that some one can be more interested in the Negro than he is in himself is to suggest that the rats have taken up common residence with cats and there is to be a general holiday for the good of all. Oh, what hypocrisy! Yet for the sake of condemning Garvey we are told that it was done for the "good of the colored people." Surely, it is done for the good of the colored people to further close their eyes until the plan of race extermination is completed; until the plan of economic starvation is completely arranged, until the political strength of the race is destroyed; until the race has been weakened and scattered with divided interests; until the greater and more progressive races have properly adjusted themselves; until Africa has been completely made safe for the European; until England, France and Italy have succeeded in carrying out their design to "keep Africa white."

IMPRISONMENT CAN HELP

If my imprisonment can help to open the eyes of the sleeping Negro world to the danger ahead of us, then I shall be satisfied. Do not flatter ourselves about our temporary success in politics, industry and society, for a day of reaction is approaching, and when it arrives there will be universal racial chaos. That is why we ask you not to pay much attention to the individual politician who gobbles up everything for himself in the search for office. He will go no further than his day. He serves himself in the name of the race, yet we are no better off for destiny and a permanent place in the affairs of men; hence, we ask that our present political effort be a united one with a common program and purpose.

SUPPORT YOUR ORGANIZATION

Surely we shall rally together and stand together as never before. Give every help and encouragement to your association. Send in your support to the Parent Body and help the Committee of Management to put over the program for 1923–24. With best wishes for your success, I have the honor to be Your obedient servant,

MARCUS GARVEY
President-General
Universal Negro Improvement Association

Printed in *NW*, 4 August 1923. Original headlines abbreviated.

Marcus Garvey to Mrs. Warren G. Harding

[*New York* 2 August 1923]

TELEGRAPHED MESSAGE OF CONDOLENCE SENT TO MRS. HARDING ON DEATH OF PRESIDENT HARDING[2]

Madam—The world has lost one of its greatest advocates of peace and justice, and America one of her truest and noblest sons. Not only the nation, but the world of grateful, peace-loving humanity mourns the loss of your illustrious husband, and shall never forget the courage, manhood and character of Warren Gamaliel Harding. Four hundred million Negroes of the world and fifteen million of America, in particular, will ever remember your dear husband as a true and sincere friend of our race. His speech and advice to our race at Birmingham, Ala.,[3] is a classic in the utterances of American statesmen on the race problem.

We believe he was true and honest in his desire to see the Negro elevated to the standard of man; therefore, how could we do other than mourn with you from our deepest feeling of sorrow and regret in losing a true friend who was your loving and devoted husband, the like of whom the world may never see again.

In the history of our race your beloved husband, as a friend and well-wisher of our progress, shall have a place, and our children shall be taught and they shall remember that amidst all the horrors of prejudice and injustice to the Negro in the civilization of the twentieth century they had one, in the person of your husband, who was always kind and considerate and who never failed to lend a helping hand.

Be assured, dear Madam, that the world of Negroes at this hour mourn with you and pray for the entrance of the President's soul into the realms of Paradise.

> MARCUS GARVEY
> President-General
> Universal Negro Improvement Association and
> Provisional President of Africa

Printed in *NW*, 11 August 1923. Reprinted in *P&O*, 2: 54.

1. Florence Kling Harding (1850–1924) married Warren G. Harding in 1901. She campaigned at her husband's side during his races in Ohio State politics, as well as during his presidential bid (*NYT*, 22 November 1924).

2. President Warren G. Harding died suddenly of a stroke on 2 August 1923. Harding was on a speaking tour in San Francisco at the time of his death (*NYT*, 3 August and 8 August 1923).

3. Speech delivered in Birmingham, Ala., in October 1921 (see *Garvey Papers* 4. 141–149, 205).

Editorial Letter by Marcus Garvey

[[The Tombs, Centre St., New York,
August 4, 1923]]

WE ARE ALL THE CREATURES OF
OUR ENVIRONMENT

Members and Friends,
Universal Negro Improvement Association,
Liberty Hall:

We were severely shocked a couple of days ago on learning of the death of President Harding.

The Nation's Chief Executive, of himself, was a friend of our cause, and I believe that he, as a man, felt a deep interest in the struggle of our race to reach the top. He was only [a] man, and therefore had unfortunately, no doubt, to yield his desire of recognition of and service to a cause to the environments that generally hinder us at times from doing just that which we ourselves believe to be right. President Harding, with all that can be said, was indeed a great man and a liberal soul.

We should mourn his loss, and I ask that our Liberty Hall remain in mourning for the entire month of August, as a small token of our bereavement and sorrow in losing so great a friend to the cause of humanity.

We should believe that the President's work was not finished; that he intended more than he did; but that he was only a steward who had to give account of his stewardship, and he was hurri[e]dly called. Pray for the repose of his soul and, as you rise, may I not ask also that you chant a psalm of life for the entry of the spirit of our friend into the realm of eternal bliss?

Keep up your good work and hold fast to the ideal of your choice, is the prayer of Your humble servant,

MARCUS GARVEY
President-General
Universal Negro Improvement Association

Printed in *NW*, 11 August 1923.

President Calvin Coolidge to Rudolph E.B. Smith, 3rd Asst. President General, UNIA

[[White House, Washington August 6, 1923]]

My dear Mr. Smith:

I am indebted to you for transmitting the message informing me of the expression of sympathy adopted at the memorial assembly held by your association yesterday.

Messages like these are not only consoling, but are helpful in meeting the new responsibilities. Very truly yours,

CALVIN COOLIDGE[1]

[*Address*] Mr. Rudolph Smith, 3rd Asst.
President-General, Pittsburgh Division of
the Universal Negro Improvement Association,
Pittsburgh, Pa.

Printed in *NW*, 25 August 1923. Original headlines omitted.

1. Calvin Coolidge (1872–1933) completed Harding's term as president and was elected for his own term, which he served from 1925 until 1929 (*WBD*).

Marcus Garvey to Vernal J. Williams

New York August 6, 1923

My Dear Sir:

Your attitude of ingratitude is in no way surprising.

It is customary for me to be bitten by those whom I have tried to help. If I hadn't helped you when you were a Law Student and could not make it, by finding work for you, and if I hadn't helped you and your wife when you were both fully apart, and her acts in attempting to take you before the courts would have cut short your legal career, if I hadn't gone out of my way to find a place for you to keep you out of harm's way, you would not have been able [to,] at this minute when you think I am in trouble, be trying to do me the harm you desire.

I have a full line up on all your activities to injure me, and though I go to Atlanta or elsewhere, that will not prevent me coming back to have you before the Bar Association, if you do not do what is right by the Universal Negro Improvement Association even as I requested you to do by letter several weeks ago.

You are mistaken if you think that you and your friends who have been working to detain me in jail, and make my conviction as it is, will go unpunished before the law for the improper acts that you are continuing.

I am satisfied to go to Atlanta, but the voice of American truth will bring you all to Justice in the continuance of your designs.

I sympathize with your wife, because she is related to a friend of mine who nursed me when I was sick in Cuba, and would therefore not like to do anything in bringing you to justice that would affect her, but if you are a sensible man, you would be advised to halt your silly efforts to injure me and the Universal Negro Improvement Association, that have helped you in your distress.

I am still awaiting the time immediately, when you will in a proper manner turn over your office and all papers, documents, and cases to our Legal representative.

You will understand that until then, the Association refuses to make any payment to you on past services. When you have properly turned over your work, then we will adjust and satisfy you on the matter of back salary. Yours truly,

MARCUS GARVEY
President-General, per Sec'y
Universal Negro Improvement Association

New York August 6, 1923

Sir:

I write to warn and inform you again that the Universal Negro Improvement Association is waiting to receive from you all papers, documents, and cases in the office of the Attorney of the Association which office you represented for some time.

I brought Mr. Pettiford here at the cost of $150.00 and other legal expenses to have you turn over your office to him. You dodged the responsibility until he had left town, when you again started your trick to blackmail and hold up the Association.

I shall have another Attorney ready on Thursday afternoon the 9th instant to receive from you all the documents, papers, cases, etc., and if you fail to appear and turn over at our office all such papers, documents, cases, etc., we shall take immediate legal steps in the matter.

I now designate Mr. Maurice Nagler[1] to take over from you all papers for the Intertype Corporation's[2] case of the 9th, although you tried to deceive us as to the belief of the 6th.

If we owe you back salary, you know perfectly well how to adjust same after you have completed your duties for which you have been fully paid. This is my final and last notice to you. Yours truly,

MARCUS GARVEY
President-General, per Sec'y
Universal Negro Improvement Association

P.S. You and your friends may think that you won New York City, and the Courts, but be assured that there is justice in New York as anywhere else, and the Bar Association, and the Judges, are not all under your influence. You are not the only one with friends to see that Justice is done. I may be going to Atlanta, but that is not so far from Justice.

M[ARCUS]. G[ARVEY].

UNIA v. *Vernal J. Williams*, no. 32717, New York State Supreme Court, 1923, record on appeal, pp. 23–26.

1. Maurice Nagler (1879–1961), a New York lawyer associated with the firm of Kohn and Nagler, represented Garvey in many legal actions, culminating in his appeal in 1925 (*NYT*, 12 July 1961).

2. A reference to a legal case of Intertype Corp., a concern that held a chattel mortgage on a typecasting machine for the ACL, which published the *Negro World*. In May 1923, Justice John Ford of the New York Supreme Court ordered the Intertype Corp. to seize its typesetting equipment from the ACL in order to foreclose a lien of $3,675 (which represented the unpaid principal) against the ACL (plaintiff's exhibit E, *UNIA* v. *Vernal J. Williams*, records on appeal, pp. 200–201). On 9 August 1923 the New York State Supreme Court was scheduled to hear Intertype Corp.'s plea for judgment against the ACL (plaintiff's exhibit F, records on appeal, p. 212). In September 1923, Judge Isidor Wasservogel ordered that the plaintiff, the Intertype Corp., recover its judgment for foreclosure of the lien against the ACL. The judge ordered that the material be sold at auction and that the plaintiff bear the costs of this auction (*Intertype Corp.* v. *ACL*, New York State Supreme Court, 19 September 1923, NNHR). The machines were sold at public auction on 1 October 1923, and the court-appointed referee on the sale filed his report on 9 October 1923 (*Intertype Corp.* v. *ACL*, affidavit of E. Raymond Shephard, 29 April 1924, NNHR).

Vernal J. Williams to the
UNIA Committee of Management

[*New York*] August 6th, 1923

Gentlemen:

There are two cases on the Court calendars for Thursday [*9 August*] of this week against the Association. One is de Petrie against U.N.I.A.[1] and the other is Intertype Corporation against A.C.L. I hereby notify the Association through you that I shall not handle these cases, and hereby demand that you get other counsel to handle the same. I have under my control the papers in these cases, and will be glad to have any attorney you may name substituted in my place upon receipt of a substantial payment of my salary to date.

I may advise you that it is imperative that you obtain other counsel, for unless you do so, judgment will be obtained against the Association by default. Very truly yours,[2]

VERNAL J. WILLIAMS

UNIA v. Vernal J. Williams, no. 32717, New York State Supreme Court, 1923, record on appeal, p. 28.

1. A reference to the case of Arnold de Petrie, a former employee of Garvey's short-lived *Daily Negro Times* newspaper, who sued the UNIA for back wages of $30.00 (see *de Petrie v. UNIA*, Municipal Court of New York, Seventh District, 10 July 1923; *New York Age*, 21 October 1922).

2. Williams sent Garvey a similar letter on 6 August 1923 (*UNIA v. Vernal J. Williams*, records on appeal, p. 29).

Vernal J. Williams to Marcus Garvey

[*New York*] August 9, 1923

My dear Mr. Garvey:

I have received your three latest letters; two dated August 6th and one dated August 7th, 1923.[1]

In your first letter of August 6th you discussed the help which you claimed you gave me when I was a law student. You are mistaken. You did not know me when I was a law student. I left law school in June, 1919, and did not join your association until 1920.

You have gone into a rather minute discussion of my domestic affairs; but as it is not relevant to the issue between us I hardly think i[t] is necessary for me to discuss the subject with you.

I do not understand what you mean when you say that you "have a full line up of all my activities to injure" you. I would be the last person in the world to add to your present miserable predicament, Mr. Garvey.

Neither do I understand what you mean, when you say that I and my friends "have been working to detain you in jail and make your conviction as it is." In the first place I know of no friends of mine who sought to have you convicted. I know personally that all my friends had always hoped that you would have been acquitted[.] As for me, in spite of outrageous mistreatment at your hands, I did whatever I could to assist in the case of the Government against you, until by word and conduct you made me feel that my usefulness to you had ended as one of the attorneys in that case.

In your second letter of August 6th, you mentioned the fact that you brought Mr. Pettiford here at the cost of $150 and "other" legal expenses to have me turn over my office to him. You have evidently forgotten the circumstances under which Mr. Pettiford came here, Mr. Garvey. Don't you remember that you called Mr. Pettiford to New York two days before I sent in my resignation? Don't you remember that the primary reason for Mr. Pettiford's coming to New York was to make an affidavit concerning his conversation with Esau Ramus in Detroit, which you were to submit on your last application for appeal? You accuse me of "Black Mailing" and "Holding Up" the association. If seeking to obtain my pay for what I feel to be honest services, makes me a "Blackmailer," Mr. Garvey, then I shall have to content myself with remaining so.

I held on to the papers because of the attitude exhibited by you in your letter in response to my letter of resignation and because of the fact that experience had convinced me that had I simply withdrawn, without exercising my rights as attorney, I would never receive the back salary that is due me.

You have precipitated a strained relation between us that was hardly necessary. I cannot see the reason for your attitude, especially after our last three interviews in the Tombs. The facts in the case are very simple.

On July 15th, I tendered my resignation to the association because for some time prior to that date, I felt that the manner in which the work was progressing was not such as would permit me as an attorney to remain an officer. I did not think that we could stand the light of legal investigation. I felt more and more convinced that day by day we were conducting the affairs of the association in a manner that could in no way receive the sanction of law. For these reasons therefor[e,] I asked that I be relieved of my services as an officer. At the same time I assured the officers, and you, orally and in writing, upon proper terms and arrangements, I would continue only the legal work of the association until such time as you would obtain other counsel. In response to that, you wrote me a letter in which you claimed that I did not give the association the proper legal protection. This question may have to be passed upon by someone more competent than you; therefore I will not discuss that here but will leave the consideration of that phase of the matter for another time when the records will speak for themselves, and when reputable members of the Bar of this State, whom I have opposed in cases for the association, and judges before whom I have appeared in its behalf, will bear testimony as to the quality of service that I have rendered. I am sorry, Mr. Garvey, that you took the attitude you have taken. I never expected that. The whole situation is entirely uncalled for, and I shall be very glad if you will adjust the differences.

In the meantime I shal[l] have to assert what I feel to be my right in exercising a lien on the papers, because having given up my entire time to the legal work of the association with perhaps few exceptions, I am now at a point where I am practically impoverished.

If the Courts adjudicate that I am wholly in the wrong and that I must return them to the association, whether or not I am paid, I shall gladly do so.[2]

I hardly think it is necessary for you to try to intimidate and threaten me, Mr. Garvey. Your threats can hardly take the place of righteousness.

If you will make arrangements to pay me the unpaid salary that is due me up to the 4th day of August, 1923, when I actually left the association, simultaneously, with suitable arrangements, I shall return the papers.

Concerning the Intertype case, I have obtained an adjournment of one week, pending disposition of our matter, and for all purposes. When I first wrote to you about this case I had not the papers with me, and made a mistake as to the date. You will note, however, that I later corrected the error. I instructed Mr. Plummer this morning how to handle the de Petrie case. Yours truly,

VERNAL J. WILLIAMS

UNIA v. Vernal J. Williams, no. 32717, New York State Supreme Court, 1923, records on appeal, pp. 30–33.

1. Garvey sent a letter to Williams on 7 August 1923 concerning the appointment of Maurice Nagler as the UNIA's lawyer for the Intertype Corp. case (UNIA v. Vernal J. Williams, no. 32717, New York State Supreme Court, 1923, records on appeal, p. 27).

2. On 27 October 1923 a New York court awarded Williams a judgment of $2,010.66 in back pay and legal costs incurred in his suit against the UNIA. The UNIA appealed the decision to the New York County Supreme Court (UNIA v. Vernal J. Williams, 12 November 1923).

Sermon by Rev. E. Ethelred Brown

[New York] 12th Aug[.] 1923

GARVEY-ISTIC DEVOTION

Whether we wish to admit /it/ or not, Marcus Garvey is today an international figure. I /however/ hesitated to make him or his Association or his followers the subject of another address from this platform for fear it should be charged against me that I am paying more attention to the man than he deserves. But realising as I do that whether he deserves attention or not he is receiving it on all sides, I decided that the pretence of ignoring him would be futile and perhaps unwise and in a sense—a very important ethical sense—he deserves attention[,] the attention which means an impartial[,] unprejudiced study and appraisement of the man and his work.

I find myself /in undertaking this task/ between two fires. My friends are on either sides of the line, and I stand somewhat in the mid part—neither a fanatic defender of Garvey nor a bitter enemy. This man has /indeed/ divided this little church;[1] and I regret to say that there is in discussing Garvey—his activities and his downfall—an amazing exhibition of intolerance and an unnecessary expenditure of passion and heat, which is tending to create enmities among the members of this church. I take /therefore/ this opportunity of appealing to our members to be liberal to the limit of their liberality. This is[,] as far as our church is concerned[,] an extraneous matter. We are attempting to do a unique work, the accomplishing of which demands the best in the best of us, and should not therefore be halted by any such matter as the discussion of Garveyism. There is room[,] abundant room[,] for a difference of opinion, and as you have and forcibly express your views on the differing phase of this question, without accenting unworthy moti[ves,] permit others to hold and forcibly to express their views even though they be opposed to yours. Let not Garvey destroy the harmony of this little family. As for me, I do hope no attempt directly or indirectly will be made to influence me to express here or elsewhere any opinion but my own. It would /indeed/ be surprising that a church which permits me to be my own self, and to utter fearlessly my views on political, social, theological and philosophical questions—to speak as I am persuaded of Marx and Debs, of Moses and Paul, of Bud[d]ha and Jesus[—]should /now/ deprive me of that right as the leader of this liberal religious movement /simply because/ the topic of discussion is Marcus Garvey and the U.N.I.A. Silence /at this time/ would be cowardice on my part, and compromise would be almost criminal. With regard to the public at large I am not /at all/ appealing to the gallery. I have no inducement so to do. As to the membership of this church I recognise two well marked groups— the one strong on the side of Garvey, the other strong against him. There may be a few with me steering a medium course, neither fanatical supporters nor bitter denouncers. To all I ask you once again, permit me to be myself, and knowing as you must do how much I desire[,] apart from the personal friendship existing between you and me—the support of all of you—Garveyites or anti-Garveyites, in the carrying on of this unique and supremely important work of religious emancipation, that you will uphold the sacred principle of this church—freedom in pulpit and in pew—and concede to me the right to express on this[,] as on every other matter[,] my own well considered judgment. Let us differ about Garvey if we must, but let us be as one in the aim and purpose of this liberal church.

This introductory appeal is I believe in the light of events fully justified. And now to the point. We are to study again tonight what I have called "Garveyistic devotion."

We are the witnesses of an unusual phenomenon. Marcus Garvey, the founder of the Universal Negro Improvement Association has been convicted by a jury of the serious offence of using the United States mail to defraud. He has been sentenced to serve a sentence of 5 years in a Federal prison, and now lies in the Tombs awaiting the determining of his appeal. A conviction of this kind means that the man convicted deliberately /set out to deceive/ by printed or written matter /sent/ through the mail with intent to defraud the person or persons addressed. To be particular, Garvey as the President of the Black Star Line Corporation /is claimed to have/ given out misleading statements[,] in fact, absolutely false statements concerning the corporation, for instance that the Corporation had in its possession a palatial vessel named the Phyllis Wheatley which would in a short time be ready to take passengers and cargo to Africa, when in truth and fact at the time of the representation and subsequently thereto, the Corporation did not own such a ship; and further after the Corporation was bankrupt and had ceased to function having not a ship on the ocean, Garvey used the mails as the means of carrying over the country papers and circulars inducing prospective shareholders to invest money in what was represented as a /live/ and growing corporation when in fact and truth at the time of such inducement the corporation was to all practical intents and purposes non-existent. On these general charges—epitomised in one specific count—Garvey was found guilty and sentenced. In plain language he lies in the Tombs tonight a convicted deceiver of his confiding followers. Apart from the legal aspect—the technical terminologies—the specific charge on which conviction was based and sentence pronounced[,] it is generally known by impartial observers that the Black Star Line was criminally mismanaged—that is to say, in these among other ways—a business proposition and a delicate and highly specialised business proposition at that—was /turned from the purpose/ in hand into a propaganda agency, resulting in waste of time and consequently heavy loss of money—the salaries paid were extravagant and wholly out of proportion to the services rendered and surely out of proportion to the /profits/ earned, the spirit of gambling was too evident as also was the desire to dazzle the eyes and set on fire the imagination of credulous supporters,—speculation went mad in the purchase of old rotten boats one after the other, and more and ever more money was placed on the gambling table in a vain effort to recover the losses which were dragging the Corporation down to bankruptcy. Garvey—a coward President and a stubborn man—because of his cowardice to admit failure when failure was obvious, because of his remarkable stubbornness to /attempt to/ carry through a scheme doomed for obvious reasons to failure from the /very/ start, is beyond doubt responsible for the cruel wilful waste of thousands and thousands of dollars cast into the very depths of the sea.

Ponzi[2] had his day of popularity, but his end came; and his victims knew him /then/ for what he was and wasted on him neither pity, nor sympathy. Horatio Bottomley[3] for years played his part as the champion of the rights of England's poor. He became bold & bolder in success, but he walked the slippery path once too often, and now lies in an English prison at the eventide of life dishonoured and disgraced. The English people were stunned at the revelations of his dishonesty. They were shocked at the /surprise of the/ fall of their idol—the fearless uncompromising Editor of "John Bull." Stunned and shocked, /yet/ they let him pass into the darkness of his cell to reap the reward of his despicable conduct. The hero was slain and no attempt was made to rescue him. But Marcus Garvey, a prisoner in the Tombs, is still the idol of his people, and enjoys today even in greater measure than in the days of his freedom, their loyal affection and undim[in]ished devotion. He is their martyred saint, their crucified Saviour. This is the fact we face. This is the unique phenomenon we are to consider. The victims of his waste /remain/ his loyal friends! the dupes of his ill considered schemes are his passionate defenders! victims and dupes his sincere worshippers! How explains this unique, this unparall[el]ed[,] this Garveyistic devotion?

Let me say at once that in spite of every consideration there is an instinctive feeling of approval for such a remarkable display of devotion to a fallen leader. This standing by a man in the hour of his humiliation and degradation appeals at once to the imagination as to [the] heart. Would that faithfulness of this kind were always shown to those who beyond doubt have merited it more.

But let us not forget in seeking for an explanation of this Garveyistic devotion that the majority of those devoted followers do not believe that Garvey has committed any offence worthy of punishment. To them he is no criminal; he is a victim. As I have already said he is their martyred saint, their crucified saviour. They have heard of frame-up, & of international plots. They have heard that it is because Garvey has stirred up the manhood of the race, and has vowed to lead a militant and awakened band of negroes into a redeemed Africa that the principal nations of the world have conspired together to rid the world of this menace to white superiority and ha[ve] made the court of the United States a willing tool to fulfil their nefarious purpose. They have heard all these things and they believe them, and believing them they feel that Garvey is now suffering in their behalf[,] suffering because he dared to declare them to be men, and dared to believe in the possibility of a Negro Empire in Africa redeemed. He is suffering for them! How else must they act, unless they be ungrateful dogs, than to cheer him in his cell with the news of their love[,] affection and devotion? It is, I repeat, a moving spectacle[,] this crowd of devoted followers standing to a man true to their leader and in spite of everything retaining unshaken their confidence in his honesty of aim and action. Moving, unique[,] remarkable!

It may be that all are not wholly of this frame of mind. Some have sensed the wrong he did, but for the sake of the good he intended to do are ready to forgive. He did a little wrong in his attempt to do a great good[.] Over his errors they have drawn the mantle of forgiveness. Here again is a fine spirit. It is noble to be able to rise to the height of a great forgiveness. It is a hopeful sign when negroes who have lost heavily are able to say of the man held responsible for their losses:—"He meant well; we bear him no ill will, nay more[,] we wish him well, and are ready and willing to help him with our money and at his call to make further investments. We are not victims as has been alleged, we are co-partners in misfortune."

Whether or not I have suggested the reasons actuating the Garveyites it is beyond doubt as you view it on the surface and from their point of view a splendid inspiring exhibition of devotion and loyalty to a leader in the hour of darkness and the day of humiliation. I have permitted myself at times thus to view it, and I have been convinced that all men are not ungrateful; all men do not easily forget him who champions their cause, all men do not desert their friend in the hour of his need. This Garvey-istic devotion is a reproof— a reproof needed by many—and a challenge to us all to be true to our ideals, and to remain loyal and steadfast to the cause we espouse.

But, and at this but is for me the parting of the ways, this Garvey-istic devotion when examined below the surface presents other aspects, not only not inspiring[,] but from the racial point of view[,] painfully discouraging and fraught with all manner of evil consequences. It is the fruit of ill-considered[,] one-sided judgment—it is affection for a person gone stark staring mad, it is the blind love which in its refusal to see wrong encourages wrong and blocks the way to repentance and amendment. These devotees of every shade of intelligence are fairly chargeable with inexcusable prejudice. They simply close their eyes to the unwelcome facts which stare them in the face.

As I proceed to this deeper examination let me preface our exploration of the situation by stating a few irrefutable propositions—

1) Negroes are under no racial obligation whatever to defend or protect or apologise for a crook or a swindler simply because he is a Negro. 2) The fact that the victims of a swindler are contented to be swindled is no reason why the arm of the law should not be invoked to punish the swindler and to protect the victims. 3) The fact that the motives of the prosecutor are mixed or wholly bad is not proof of the innocence of the accused. These propositions are axiomatic and universal. I may refer to them as I proceed.

I admit at once that Marcus Garvey is a good propagandist. If we are thinking straight and deep we shall perceive that my admission is not necessarily a commendation, for it depends on the nature of the propaganda. I am however prepared to go further and admit that Garvey got the ears of the crowd because he struck a responsive chord in their souls. He did, he was not the first who did it or the only Negro who did it, but he did awaken the Negro to a realization of the fact that he was a Man,—a Man with all the potentialities, the aspirations and the rights of a man, and that old oft repeated truth seemed to have been served in a remarkably effective way by him and marked him at once as the man with a message[,] the man of the hour. But as /impartial/ investigators we must find on the facts that the crowd was more so drawn and undoubtedly more so kept by other slogans. If the bombastic promise of leading the Negroes from the Egypt of their European masters into the Canaan of a redeemed Africa—an Africa for Africans—an Africa completely and forever rid of every vestige of white domination—an Africa ruled by Negroes for the benefit of Negroes—not as later modified in the far distant /future/ but in the near tomorrow. This fired the imagination and touched the hearts of Negroes all over the world. A Moses had appeared. The day of redemption is at hand. Add to this the other equally well-thought-out proposition involved in the promise—a fleet of ships on the high seas owned by Negroes and manned by Negroes from the pantry boy to the Captain /and you have the secret of the crowd!/ The critics of Garvey have suggested that he would have crowned himself with everlasting honor and /no less/ helped the race if he had used his large following and his rich Treasury to remedy the wrongs we suffer here, and, if instead of investing in ships he had invested in houses. But these critics forget that same proposition of the kind suggested would get him neither the crowd nor the money. The crowd and the money came because of the very boldness and audaciousness and insanity of the schemes. But let us inquire further as impartial investigators and appraisers. What did Garvey do when he got his crowd and got the crowd's money? Did he, as a fact, do anything else but get the crowd and collect and spend the money? These questions are harsh and unpleasant but they are necessary. What is the honest impartial answer? Nothing—absolutely nothing. The Back to Africa scheme was not conceived in seriousness and therefore was not worked out in seriousness. It is either by invasion or by peaceful occupation that the Negroes will have Africa. The former need /ships &/ soldiers and guns and ammunition, and the latter presupposes the consent of the Powers /now/ in control. Both require money.

Has there I ask been any serious preparation to accomplish this loudly heralded purpose of redeeming Africa? Were the people inspired to prepare themselves for the great sacrifice? They were ready, they were willing, and they *did* give thousands and thousands of dollars for the reconstruction of Liberia, of which practically every cent was spent in New York—spent in helping the Negro World to function, in buying shares in a dead corporation, in paying salaries and travelling allowance to officers already well paid—spent every cent with the exception of a comparative paltry sum—in every other cause but that for which it was subscribed[,] namely the building up of Liberia. And that is all that has been attempted with regard to the Back [to] Africa scheme. And as to the fleet of ships! This scheme was conceived in iniquity and born in sin. Graft! graft! graft! It had to fail. It was run not as a business proposition but as a propaganda agency and a joy ride facility. It provided fat salaries and used up in running expenses every cent of the subscribed capital. It was beyond doubt a criminally mismanaged venture the responsibility for which must in all fairness be laid on the shoulders of the man who was more anxious to /try to/ save his own face than to protect the money of the stockholders. Tell me in the face of these things if the good done in getting the crowd together has not been completely wiped out by the waste, and the disappointment, and the reaction that is yet to come.

And now to Garvey's trial and conviction. I have written that it is my opinion that he should be granted bail pending the hearing of his appeal and that if possible his sentence should be reduced. I have no reason in either case to change my opinion. But I am not at all with those who are talking of frame-up and making themselves ridiculous by suggesting international conspiracy. I do not consider it worthwhile to refer further to this absurd suggestion of an international conspiracy. But let me examine the charge of a frame-up. This word is being very loosely used. To frame up a man is deliberately to charge him falsely and to prove him guilty of your false charge by putting in the witness box perjured witnesses. Does anybody really believe that this is what happened in Garvey's case? Let us admit that his Back-to-Africa idea, his white-hating speeches, and his whole attitude in behalf of his race has created for him enemies among the white people, and especially among the officers of the law.

Let us admit also that his success as it appeared on the surface—the number of his followers and his popularity and his marked personal financial superiority may have created jealousy in the hearts of other Negroes. And /let us admit/ that no[n?] white and colored enemies united in the desire to have him removed out of the way launched this prosecution which ended in his conviction. Let us admit as a consequence of our former admissions that the motive of the prosecution was bad—that it originated not in a high sense of public duty, not in any desire to avenge the alleged victims of this alleged spoiler for the injustice did them, but that it was based on jealousy and hate— let us go the very limit and for the purpose of the argument admit all this, and then I ask you how does our admission help Marcus Garvey? His innocence is not proved thereby. The question still remains to be answered—Did he or did he not do the things set forth in the several counts of the indictment? If he did not, then not only did the witnesses lie but documents were forged. If he did, then the motive of the prosecution is of no account, and he has only himself to blame for affording them the chance by reason of his wrong doing to bring down on his head the punishment due to such wrong doing. Did he for instance offer shares to the public in a defunct or bankrupt corporation? Did he in order to induce people to invest misrepresent the status of the concern and make promises as to profits which on the facts known to him were false? In a word did he as charged use the mail of the United States of America to defraud? Did he? Defenders and friends of Garvey[,] answer without passion[—] did he? And if by these false representations persons invested[,] it is no answer to the charge to say that the investors are reconciled to the loss. If one single investor of the thousands of investors complained that he was fooled and invoked the law to punish his deceiver, the law is justified[,] if the complaint of this single investor is sustained, to punish the offender regardless of the rantings of the host of others genuinely or pretendedly reconciled to their exploitation. To my mind Garvey had a fair trial, as fair a trial as he would have in Jamaica, and he was given more latitude than would have been given him by any English Judge presiding over a Colonial Court. And, in my opinion, although I consider that under all the circumstances the maximum sentence is too severe, the verdict of guilty was justified by the evidence. All talk therefore of plots and frame-up are so much unmeaningless talk excusable in the case of the illiterate and emotional but [discreditable?] when indulged in by the educated and thoughtful.

And now just a few remarks as to Mr. Garvey as a great leader—some of my friendly critics have prophesied that in the future when the heat and passion and prejudice shall have passed away, Marcus Garvey will be generally appraised a great leader. I differ. When the present fanaticism shall have been drowned in the facts of the situation Garvey will be revealed as he is—and the revelation will I am assured not portray him as a great leader. A leader works for the accomplishment of a great overmastering purpose—works—not talks of it. To what great purpose has Marcus Garvey *worked*? Like Napoleon he seems to have been saying: "I must dazzle and astonish. A great reputation is a great noise; the more there is made, the farther off it is heard. Laws, institutions, monuments, nations all fall, but the *noise* continues." Yes, it continues; but at length it ceases, and is not even heard in the rumbling of the distance. But apart from this Marcus Garvey as a man has been unfortunately equipped to be a leader.

In the first place he is bombastic, conceited and arrogant. These qualities are too painfully obvious to call for further comment. Secondly, he has no regard whatever for exactness of statement and cares nothing for the character and reputation of other men. He lives in an atmosphere of exaggerations and falsehoods. He tells you of 50[,]ooo delegates at a Convention attended by 200, and he makes it impossible by his exaggeration /for anyone/ to know when his figures are true or near true or absolutely false. As to the reputation and character of men, almost every man who has left his association has been branded a thief and a liar and worse. He has prostituted the high uses of a newspaper to his own unscrupulous ends. And he has not changed. Even the silence of a cell has not cured him of these terrible faults. From the [T]ombs he stretches the long arm of the Negro World to bedaub with mud the men he hates, and even from the place of confinement he sends out to the public an uncalled for personal article punctuated with exaggerations[,] falsehoods and insinuations. Thirdly, Marcus Garvey cannot work with men. He gets on splendidly with tools but any man who dares to be a man becomes his enemy and is forthwith dismissed from his presence. On two succeeding conventions he has brought about the dismissal of men whom he himself at the preceding convention presented for election as efficient[,] loyal and honorable. They were too efficient[,] too loyal[,] too honorable to continue to be his tools, his phonograph—and they went.

Fourthly—he is a mean shifter of responsibilities. He claims all the honor and disowns all the blame. No more disgusting contradiction of his claim to greatness could be found than in the ignoble attempt at his trial to obtain his acquittal at the cost of the conviction of his co-defendants. He would have sent . . . [*page missing*].

I am not attempting to [*turn?*] the devoted followers of Marcus Garvey [*away?*] from their fallen leader. Let him have [*peace?*] awhile[,] this comfort of consolation[,] if it [*were?*] not neutralised by his own consciousness that such loyalty[,] such devotion is undeserved. I plead for no revengeful treatment. All I intend to do to-night and I believe I have carried out my intention is to prove that away from the atmosphere of fanaticism and passion there is no justification at any rate for denouncing those of us who have not been infected by this Garvey-istic devotion—this devotion characteristic[,] unique[,] unparall[el]ed[,] remarkable—unwarranted.

We shall not jeer at his humiliation[,] we shall not give way to the expressions of revengeful satisfaction[,] not indulge in the laugh of fiendish joy, we shall not stamp our feet upon his upturned face, but neither shall we adorn him with the garland [of a] hero, mourn him as a saint or worship him as a Saviour.

The salvation of the Negro race is of . . . [*Remainder mutilated*].

NN-Sc, E. Ethelred Brown Papers. AMS.

1. The Harlem Community Church was pastored by Rev. E. Ethelred Brown, who formed the church with a group of fellow Jamaicans upon arriving in Harlem in 1920. Most members of the small Unitarian congregation were young West Indians who gravitated to the progressive political and intellectual forum that the church provided. Among its charter members were Garveyites and prominent black Socialists or Socialist sympathizers, such as Richard Moore, Grace Campbell, Frank Crosswaith, and W. A. Domingo. Yet the political and intellectual focus that made the church unique led as well to splits and divisions among the congregation. Almost from its inception, church members were sharply divided over the Garvey movement. In his 1923 sermon, Brown admonished the congregation not to allow the issue of Garvey to divide the church. By 1928, however, Brown declared in a Sunday sermon, "While I do not approve of deportation as such, I heartily approve of Marcus Garvey's deportation, which was better for America in general and the Negro in particular." An African member of the congregation who belonged to the UNIA responded with a vigorous defense of Garvey. This precipitated a heated denunciation of Brown and culminated in an attack on the pastor by one of the pro-Garvey parishioners (Mark D. Morrison-Reed, *Black Pioneers in a White Denomination* [Boston: Beacon Press, 1980], pp. 31–113; *Garvey Papers* 1: 527–531).

2. Garvey was frequently compared to Charles Ponzi (1878–1949), the Italian-born swindler of the 1920s who established his financial career in Boston and promised his investors that he would "double their money in 90 days." He claimed his business, which was a variation on the pyramid scheme, was based on profits from favorable exchange rates for the purchase of International Postal Union coupons. Ponzi paid his early investors, but soon federal authorities began an investigation that revealed Ponzi's bankrupt condition, with liabilities $3 million in excess of his assets. Indicted for larceny by the state of Massachusetts, he received a seven-year sentence but was freed on bail. While on bail he tried to recoup his losses in a Florida land scheme for which he was again convicted, this time for fraud. He jumped bail and was captured in New Orleans and extradited to Massachusetts to serve his original jail term. Federal authorities deported Ponzi to Italy following his release from prison in 1934. He left Italy for Brazil prior to World War II and died destitute in a Brazil charity hospital (*NYT*, 19 January 1949; Donald H. Dunn, *Ponzi!* [New York: McGraw-Hill, 1975]).

3. Horatio William Bottomley (1860–1933), English newspaper editor and folk hero, was the founder of the influential weekly *John Bull*. He served as an M.P. from 1906 to 1912 and from 1918 to 1922, winning a reputation during World War I as a rabid nationalist and patriot. Bottomley's fame faded in the years following his 1922 conviction for fraud (*WBD*; *NYT*, 27 May 1933; Alan Hyman, *The Rise and Fall of Horatio Bottomley* [London: Cassell and Co., 1972]; Julian Symons, *Horatio Bottomley* [London: Cresset Press, 1955]).

Marcus Garvey to Sir Eric Drummond

NEW YORK, U.S.A. Aug. 14th, 1923

Dear Sir:

I am instructed by the Universal Negro Improvement Association, representing the Negro peoples of the world, to inform you that the Hon. Jean Joseph Adam has been re-elected as a delegate to attend the 1923 September session of the League of Nations Assembly at Geneva to further represent the race's interest in the subject matter of the petition as submitted to your Assembly last year.[1]

It is hoped that the League will deal with the subject of the petition at the forthcoming session.

I am also instructed to ask that you be good enough to reserve a seat for Mr. Adam at the opening of the session. Mr. Adam will leave New York in time to be present and in attendance at the session,[2] and will call on you to present his credentials.[3]

It is the desire of the Association as representatives of the Negro peoples of the world, that you bring the subject matter of the petition of last year before the assembly of 1923. With best wishes, I have the honor to be, Your obedient Servant,

MARCUS GARVEY
President-General
Universal Negro Improvement Association

LNA, file 1/30405/21159. TLS on UNIA letterhead, recipient's copy.

1. Garvey's message concerning the role of Jean Joseph Adam as the UNIA's representative to the league was read at a series of Liberty Hall meetings held between 9 and 19 August (report by Special Agent Joseph G. Tucker, 20 August 1923, DJ-FBI, file 61; *P&O*, 2: 225).

2. Adam left New York on 22 August 1923, according to the British Embassy in New York (Gloster Armstrong to Henry G. Chilton, 24 August 1923, PRO, FO 371/8513).

3. Adam's credentials, co-signed by Garvey as the UNIA's president general and by Percival L. Burrows as the assistant secretary-general, described him as "a permanent Delegate to the League of Nations" as well as the association's representative in France (Marcus Garvey to League of Nations, 20 August 1923, in *Jean Joseph Adam* v. *UNIA*, no. 6966, 1926, NNHR).

Marcus Garvey to Henry E. Manghum,[1] Commerce Counsel, United States Shipping Board

[*Tombs Prison, ca. 17 August 1923*]

The company has on lodgment with you Twenty-two Thousand[,] Five Hundred ($22,500.00) Dollars on the purchase of a ship and we are asking that you continue to hold the amount to the credit of the company until you have been approached by mandate of the stockholders to dispose of same.[2]

It is the desire of the stockholders of the Company that the amount be applied on the purchase of a ship from you as soon as an adjustment can take place. This request supercedes all other requests.

There has been an attempt by several "broker sharks" to deprive the Black Star Line of the money now lodged with you, but we feel sure that the Government will not lend its aid or assistance to the depriving of poor Negroes of that which they have sacrificed and suffered for.

[MARCUS GARVEY]

DNA, RG 32, file 605-1-653. TMS on BSL letterhead, recipient's copy.

1. Henry E. Manghum was a USSB examiner (*Seventh Annual Report of the United States Shipping Board* [Washington, D.C.: GPO, 1923], p. 3).

2. On 18 August, Manghum wrote his fellow commissioners a memorandum concerning Garvey's letter, wherein Manghum asked if further action was necessary. Commissioners Fred Thompson and Edward Plummer both felt that "no disbursements of these BSL funds or any disposition be made unless and until the list of stockholders who bought it should be refunded" (Fred Thompson to Henry E. Manghum, n.d., quoted in Carl Kremer to S.H.E. Freund, 29 August 1923, DNA, RG 32, file 605-1-653). The whole matter was referred to the USSB's legal department for final disposition.

Marcus Garvey to President Calvin Coolidge

[*Negro World*, 18 August 1923]

Having laid our deceased and lamented President to rest amidst the honor due him as one of America's truest and most devoted sons, the two and a half million members of the Universal Negro Improvement Association in America, and the millions in other parts of the world who joined in sympathy and condolence, beg of you to accept their best wishes on your assumption of the Presidency. As citizens we pledge you our loyal support in upholding the principles of our glorious Constitution, and we shall pray God's blessing upon you so that you may ever see the right in directing the affairs of state. The other millions of . . . [*line mutilated*] for your success and hope that your vision on international matters will be so clear as to lead you to be just and fair to all mankind.

The world still awaits a champion for the cause of humanity, irrespective of race or color, and we pray God to find such in you, who have been called to lead our nation and point the world to a sober adjustment of our human ills.[1]

Long live President Coolidge! Long live America! is the prayer of the Universal Negro Improvement Association.

[MARCUS GARVEY]

Printed in *NW*, 18 August 1923. Original headlines and preface omitted.

1. Two days after the telegram was sent, the UNIA Press Service released an article expressing the "surprise and shock" of blacks throughout the country at the appointment by President Coolidge of C. Bascom Slemp as private secretary to the president. Slemp, a former congressman from

Virginia, had won a reputation as an outspoken segregationist, and had consistently sought to bar blacks from the Republican party in the state (report of Special Agent Joseph G. Tucker, 25 August 1923, DJ-FBI, file 61; *Washington Eagle*, 18 August 1923).

G. Emonei Carter, First Vice President, New York Division, UNIA, to President Calvin Coolidge

NEW YORK, U.S.A. August 21st, 1923

Honored Sir:—

Humanity is so constituted that the element of self is ever seeking to obtrude itself. Very often this selfish expression works a detriment, sometimes it proves of mutual good.

It is this mutual good that I am seeking to establish, which prompts this writing. When I had the pleasure to serve you and your excellent family in Palm Beach, Fla., as check-writer in the Royal Poinciana,[1] I did not think at that time I would be now addressing you as President of these great United States; but this goes to prove what a great country is ours, and how every man can rise to the highest office within the gift of the people.

May I convey to you the gratification, which is mine to know, that I have in the White House, a President which I had personally contacted even in a most casual manner, one whom I have stood and admired, as he came in and went out as Governor of the great Commonwealth of Mass.

I am now engaged in the work of serving my people. The hotel work was a means to an end. I strove to do my best while in it; and I am determined to do my best here.

I have an excellent chance to serve my fellow citizens; and knowing your peculiar fitness in doing things constructive at the crucial moment,[2] you may call on me at any time to serve you in any capacity however small.

Praying for a closer cultivation of an acquaintance with our President, I am, Very sincerely,

G. EMONEI CARTER
1st Vice Pres. of New York Local Div.
of The Universal Negro Improvement Association

DLC, CC. TLS on UNIA New York division letterhead, recipient's copy.

1. The Royal Poinciana was the largest resort hotel in the world when it opened in 1894. The hotel, which was frequented by the white elite and staffed by "gentlemen of color," was built by black workers, who continued to live along Sunrise Avenue in Palm Beach until the early 1900s, when their community was burned in a fire which was reportedly "set by the town fathers" (J. Wadsworth Travers, *History of Beautiful Palm Beach* [Palm Beach: Author's Pub., 1928], p. 25; John Ney, *Palm Beach* [Boston: Little, Brown, & Co., 1966], p. 98ff).

2. Other UNIA members also contacted Coolidge. After a local convention in August, Washington, D.C. division members Joseph H. Steward, Lionel L. Oxley, Russell Morris, and Walter S. James wrote to Coolidge about the UNIA's aims and objects, hoping to lay the

groundwork for the "proper time . . . to make an appeal to you on behalf of our President General Marcus Garvey" (Washington, D.C., UNIA division to President Coolidge, ca. 7 September 1923, DLC, CC).

Article in the *Dawn of Tomorrow*

[25 August 1923]

The U.N.I.A. Convention at Montreal

The Sundays, August 19 and 26 are to be devoted to Convention matters, when very important questions of interest to the Colored community will be discussed. These questions will include Education, Politics, Society, etc., discussions on which will be thrown open to the public[,] without, however[,] voting on the several questions. This local convention was inaugurated because of the fact that the usual annual convention at headquarters, New York, will not be held this year owing to the recent imprisonment of their leader, the Hon. Marcus Garvey, which drawback however, does not in any way serve to impede the progress of the U.N.I.A. in Montreal, but, on the contrary, and not unlike other divisions, would seem to have added zest, zeal, enthusiasm and increased determination to stand by the U.N.I.A. and uphold its principles of unified race consciousness and a redeemed Africa.

Just recently this division also held two very successful social ventures, both numerically and financially. The first was a steamer excursion on the evening of July 19th, sailing up the St. Lawrence on the steamer Empress. Nearly three hundred joined in the moonlight frolic. Space will not permit a detailed report of the trip, but on the whole everybody seemed to have enjoyed themselves immensely, particularly if we are to judge from the fact that refreshments were sold and consumed to the last drop, insomuch that the steamer's Purser came to the rescue, with half a gross additional bottles of cold drinks but even this was insufficient to satisfy the demands of the thirsty excursionists. Dancing of course was indulged in, the music being supplied by Karl Gale and Co.

Their second venture took the form of a day[']s outing by train to Otterburn Park, about fifty miles from Montreal for which a special train was chartered and which carried about five hundred of Montreal's excursionists, nearly one fifth of the Colored population, so popular was the outing.

The foregoing shows that the U.N.I.A. in Montreal is aiming at great gains and doing great things in an endeavor to supply popular and innocent amusement for the Colored community to say nothing of its other unceasing activities in trying to ameliorate conditions to the benefit of a down-trodden race who are so slow to show their good qualities when given the opportunity. At the present time the Montreal division is not making a noise but is nevertheless steadfastly plodding its way successfully, even though quietly.

And by the way we must not omit to mention that the August celebration will wind up with a dance on Thursday the 30th, when there will be another big muster of adherents and friends to the U.N.I.A.

Printed in the Montreal *Dawn of Tomorrow*, 25 August 1923.

Robert L. Poston to the *Negro World*

[*New York*] [[August 29, 1923]]

APOSTLE OF NEW THOUGHT AMONG THE NEGROES
TELLS STORY

Sir:—

I have just completed reading a very interesting article in the September "Current History" by the Hon. Marcus Garvey, which should be read by Negroes throughout the world who desire inside information about this man of destiny.[1]

This article, written by Mr. Garvey, in prison, casts new light upon the character of the most talked of Negro in the world. In his characteristic way he tells of his early struggles to get an education, and of the things which eventually led him to devote his energies to the work which has caused him his imprisonment.

After reading this article one can fully realize why this man is willing to suffer so readily for a downtrodden race. As he sets forth in the article[,] such talent as he possesses could have been utilized to a great advantage in accumulating personal wealth had he elected to so use his talents. But the thoughts of his early struggles and the experiences with what he calls "whites," "near whites," and "blacks" compel him to forget self, in interest of the race with which he is identified.

The story itself is simply told, maintaining interest throughout, and leaves one to wonder why, before the time of this great man others did not see the deplorable condition of the Negroes of the world, and did not dedicate themselves to the task of establishing the race in the land of its nativity, Africa.

The article should be read and read again, until the truth of it sinks deeply into the heart of the reader and enwrap[s] him with the vision of the man who is truly the apostle of new thought among Negroes. Very truly yours,

ROBERT L. POSTON

Printed in *NW*, 8 September 1923.

1. "The Negro's Greatest Enemy," Garvey's most extensive autobiographical account written for the American public, was published in the September 1923 issue of *Current History*. The same account first appeared in the 5 August 1923 edition of the *New York World* under the headline "I made everyone respect me, says Marcus Garvey in the Tombs Prison" (See *Garvey Papers* 1: 3–12 for the complete text).

Editorial Letter by Marcus Garvey

[[The Tombs, August 31, 1923]]

MOTIVE OF N.A.A.C.P. EXPOSED

FELLOW MEN OF THE NEGRO RACE, Greeting:

The policy of the Universal Negro Improvement Association is so clean-cut, and my personal views are so well known, that no one, for even one moment, could reasonably accuse us of having any other desire than that of working for a united Negro race.

Some of us make the mistake to state in America, the West Indies and Africa that the nearer we approach the white man in color the greater our social standing and privilege, and that we should build up an "aristocracy" based upon caste of color and not achievement in race. It is well known, although no one is honest enough to admit it, that we have been, for the past thirty years at least, but more so now than ever, grading ourselves for social honor and distinction on the basis of color. That the average success in the race has been regulated by color and not by ability and merit; that we have been trying to get away from the pride of race into the atmosphere of color worship, to the damaging extent that the whole world has made us its laughing stock.

There is no doubt that a race that doesn't respect itself forfeits the respect of others, and we are in the moral-social position now of losing the respect of the whole world.

There is a subtle and underhand propaganda fostered by a few men of color in America, the West Indies and Africa to destroy the self-respect and pride of the Negro race by building up what is commonly known to us as a "blue vein" aristocracy and to foster same as the social and moral standard of the race. The success of this effort is very much marked in the West Indies, and coming into immediate recognition in South Africa, and is now gaining much headway in America under the skillful leadership of the National Association for the Advancement of "Colored" People and their silent but scattered agents.

The observant members of our race must have noticed within recent years a great hostility between the National Association for the Advancement of "Colored" People and the Universal "Negro" Improvement Association, and must have wondered why Du Bois writes so bitterly against Garvey and *vice versa*. Well, the reason is plainly to be seen after the following explanation:

Du Bois represents a group that hates the Negro blood in their veins, and has been working subtly to build up a caste aristocracy that would socially divide the race into two groups: One the superior because of color caste, and the other the inferior, hence the pretentious work of the National Association for the Advancement of "Colored" People. The program of deception was well arranged and under way for success when Marcus Garvey arrived in America, and he, after understudying the artful doctor and the group he represented, fired a "bomb" into the camp by organizing the Universal "Negro"

Improvement Association to cut off the wicked attempt of race deception and distinction, and to in truth build up a race united in spirit and ideal with the honest desire of adjusting itself to its own moral-social pride and national self-respect. When Garvey arrived in America and visited the office of the National Association for the Advancement of "Colored" People to interview Du Bois, who was regarded as a leader of the Negro people and who had recently visited the West Indies, he was dum[b]founded when, on approach to the office but for Mr. Dill[1] and Dr. Du Bois himself and the office boy, he could not tell whether he was in a white office or that of the National Association for the Advancement of "Colored" People. The whole staff was either white or very near white, and thus Garvey got his first shock of the advancement hypocrisy. There was no representation of the race there that anyone could recognize. The advancement meant that you had to be as near white as possible, otherwise there was no place for you as stenographer, clerk or attendant in the office of the National Association for the Advancement of "Colored" People. After a short talk with Du Bois,[2] Garvey became so disgusted with the man and his principles that the thought he never contemplated entered his m[i]nd—that of remaining in America to teach Du Bois and his group what real race pride meant.

When Garvey left the office of the National Association for the Advancement of "Colored" People, to travel through and study the social life of Negro America, he found that the policy of the association was well observed in business and professional life as well as in the drawing room, etc., all over the country. In restaurants, drug stores and offices all over the nation where our people were engaged in business it was discoverable that those employed were the very "lightest" members of the race—as waitresses, clerks and stenographers. Garvey asked, "What's the matter? Why were not black, brown-skin and mulatto girls employed?" And he was told it was "for the good of the trade." That to have trade it was necessary and incumbent to have "light" faces, as near white as possible. But the shock did not stop there. In New York, Boston, Washington and Detroit, Garvey further discovered the activities of the "Blue Vein Society"[3] and the "Colonial Club."[4] In New York we had both organizations going. The West Indian "lights" had the "Colonial Club" and the American "lights" had the "Blue Vein Society." The "Colonial Club" would give annual balls outside of its regular weekly or monthly soiree and no one less than a quadroon would be admitted; and gentlemen below that complexion were only admitted if they were lawyers, doctors or very successful business men with plenty of "cash," who were known to uphold the caste aristocracy. At St. Phillip's Church, New York, where the Very Rev. Dr. Daniels held sway and dominion, the "society" had things so arranged that even though this man was a brown-skin clergyman, and his rector a very near white gentleman, he had to draw the line and give the best seats in the church and the places of honor to the "Blue Veins" and the others would have a "look in" when they, by fawning before and "humbling" themselves and by giving lavishly to the church, admitted the superiority of caste. By the way, Dr.

Daniels was also an executive officer or director of the National Association for the Advancement of "Colored" People. In Washington one or two of the church[es] did the same thing, but in Detroit the Very Rev. "Bob" Bagnall, now director of branches of the National Association for the Advancement of "Colored" People held sway. In his church no dark person could have a seat in the front, and, to test the truthfulness of it after being told, Garvey, *in cog.*, one Sunday night attempted to occupy one of the empty seats, not so very near the front, and the effort nearly spoiled the whole service, as Brother Bob, who was then ascending the pulpit, nearly lost his "balance" to see such a face so near the "holy of holies." Brother Bob was also an officer of the National Association for the Advancement of "Colored" People. On Garvey's return to New York he made (*in cog.*) a similar test at St. Phillip's Church one Sunday, and the Rev. Daniels was nearly ready to fight.

Now, what does all this mean? It is to relate the hidden program and motive of the National Association for the Advancement of "Colored" People and to warn Negro America of not being deceived by a group of men who have as much love for the Negro blood in their veins as the devil has for holy water.

The National Association for the Advancement of "Colored" People is a scheme to destroy the Negro Race, and the leaders of it hate Marcus Garvey because he has discovered them at their game and because the Universal Negro Improvement Association, without any prejudice to color or caste, is making headway in bringing all the people together for their common good. They hate Garvey because the Universal Negro Improvement Association and the Black Star Line employed every shade of color in the race, according to ability and merit, and put the N.A.A.C.P. to shame for employing only the "lightest" of the race. They hate Garvey because he forced them to fill Shil[l]ady's place with a Negro.[5] They hate Garvey because they had to employ "black" Pickens to cover up their scheme after Garvey had discovered it; they hate Garvey because they have had to employ brown-skin "Bob" Bagnall to make a showing to the people that they were doing the "right" thing by them; they hate Garvey because he has broken up the "Pink Tea Set"; they hate Garvey because they have been forced to recognize mulatto, brown and black talent in the association equally with the lighter element; they hate Garvey because he is teaching the unity of race, without color superiority or prejudice. The gang thought that they would have been able to build up in America a buffer class between the white and the Negro, and thus in another fifty years join with the powerful race and crush the blood of their mothers, as is being done in South Africa and the West Indies.

The imprisonment of Garvey is more than appears on the surface, and the National Association for the Advancement of Colored People knows it. Du Bois and those who lead the Association are skillful enough to be using the old method of getting the "other fellow" to destroy himself, hence the activities of "brown-skin" Bagnall and "black" Pickens. Walter White, whom we can hardly tell from a Southern gentleman and who lives with a white family in

Brooklyn, is kept in the background, but dark Bagnall, Pickens and Du Bois are pushed to the front to make the attack, so that there would be no suspicion of the motive. They are to drive hard and hot, and then the silent influence would bring up the rear, hence the slogan, "Garvey must go!" and the vicious attacks in the different magazines by Pickens, Du Bois and Bagnall.

Gentlemen, you are very smart, but Garvey has caught your tune. The conspiracy to destroy the Negro race, is so well organized that the moment anything interferes with their program there springs up a simultaneous action on the part of the leaders. It will be observed that in the September issue of the "Crisis" is published on the very last page of its news section what purports to be the opinion of a Jamaica[n] paper about Marcus Garvey and his case. The skillful editor of the "Crisis," Dr. Du Bois, reproduces that part of the article that would tend to show the opinion about Garvey in his own country taken from a paper called the "Gleaner" (edited by one Herbert George De Lesser) and not the property of Negroes.[6]

The article in the original was clipped from the "Gleaner" when it appeared, and was sent by a friend to Garvey, so that he knew all that appeared in it. In it the editor extolled the leadership and virtues of Dr. Du Bois, and said it was the right kind of leadership for the American Negro people, and bitterly denounced Garvey. Du Bois published that part that denounced Garvey, but suppressed the part that gave him the right of leadership; and he failed to enlighten his readers that the editor of the "Gleaner" is a very light man, who hates the Negro blood of his mother and who is part of the international scheme to foster the Blue Vein Society scheme. Dr. Du Bois failed to further enlighten his readers that he visited Jamaica and was part of the "Colonial Society" scheme; he also failed to state that in the plan De Lisser is to "hold down" the West Indian end of the "caste scheme" and he and others to "hold down" the American end, and their agents "hold down" the South African section.

But now we have reached the point where the entire race must get together and stop these schemers at their game. Whether we are light, yellow, black or what not, there is but one thing for us to do, and that is to get together and build up a race. God made us in His own image and He had some purpose when He thus created us. Then why should we seek to destroy ourselves? If a few Du Boises and De Lissers do not want their progeny to remain of our race, why not be satisfied to abide their time and take their peaceful exit? But why try in this subtle manner to humiliate and destroy our race?

We as a people, have a great future before us. Ethiopia shall once more see the day of her glory, then why destroy the chance and opportunity simply to be someone else?

Let us work and wait patiently, for our day of racial triumph will come. Let us not divide ourselves into castes, but let us all work together for the common good. Let us remember the sorrow of our mothers. Let us forget not that it is our duty to remedy any wrong that has already been done, and not of ourselves perpetuate the evil of race destruction. To change our race is no credit. The Anglo-Saxon doesn't want to be a Japanese; the Japanese doesn't want to be a Negro. Then, in the name of God and all that is holy, why should we want to be somebody else?

Let the National Association for the Advancement of Colored People stop its hypocrisy and settle down to real race uplift.

If Du Bois, Johnson, Pickens and Bagnall do not know, let me tell them that they are only being used to weaken the race, so that in another fifty or a hundred years the race can easily be wiped out as a social, economic and political force or "menace." The people who are directing the affairs of the National Association for the Advancement of "Colored" People are keen observers and wise leaders.[7] It takes more than ordinary intelligence to penetrate their motive, hence you are now warned.

All the "gas" about anti-lynching and "social equality" will not amount to a row of pins; in fact, it is only a ruse to raise money to capitalize the scheme and hide the real motive. Negroes, watch your step and save yourselves from deception and subsequent extermination. With best wishes for your success, I havae the honor to be, Your obedient servant,

MARCUS GARVEY
President General
Universal Negro Improvement Association

P.S.—This is the first of a series of articles to be written occasionally to expose the motive of the so-called National Association for the Advancement of Certain People. It is also desired to point out that Cyril Briggs, of the so-called African Blood Brotherhood and the Crusader Service, who fought against the Black Star Line, the Universal Negro Improvement Association and Marcus Garvey to destroy them, belongs to the American-West Indian African group, so near white that it is impossible to tell his race. He is from the West Indies and has been most vicious in his attacks upon Marcus Garvey in promoting the Universal Negro Improvement Association. It is alleged that Briggs, like others, believes that the darker element of Negroes should be led and not allowed to lead.

M.G.

Printed in *NW*, 8 September 1923. Reprinted in *P&O*, 2: 55–61. Original subheads omitted.

1. Augustus Granville Dill (1881–1956) was born in Portsmouth, Ohio, and educated at Atlanta University and at Harvard, where he graduated in 1908. Dill subsequently replaced W.E.B. Du Bois as professor of sociology at Atlanta University. In 1913 Du Bois persuaded him to come to New York and become the business manager of the *Crisis*, where he remained for fifteen years (*WWCR*; Charles Flint Kellogg, *The NAACP*, pp. 96, 151; *NYT*, 10 March 1956).

2. It is not certain whether Garvey did meet with Du Bois on Du Bois's visit to Jamaica in 1915 (see *Garvey Papers* 1: 120).

3. Charles Waddell Chesnutt (1858–1932), the well-known satirist of middle-class mulatto social standards, described the activities of a fictional "Blue Vein Society" in his stories "The Wife of His Youth" and "A Matter of Principle." Chesnutt described the organization as a "little society of colored people, more white than black," whose skin was white enough to show blue veins. He apparently based his satirical account on the group known as the Cleveland Social Circle, an

organization of the "better educated people of color" of Cleveland to which Chesnutt and his wife belonged in 1880. There is evidence that the term was used among Caribbean immigrants as well, namely, the All Blue Club in New York, a coalition of social organizations that sponsored annual coronation parties (Ira De A. Reid, *The Negro Immigrant: His Background, Characteristics, and Social Adjustment, 1899–1937* [New York: Columbia University Press, 1937], pp. 156–161; Sylvia Lyons Render, *Charles W. Chesnutt* [Boston: Twayne Publishers, 1980], pp. 37–38; William L. Andrews, *The Literary Career of Charles W. Chesnutt* [Baton Rouge: Louisiana State University Press, 1980], pp. 109–116; Frances Richardson Keller, *An American Crusade: The Life of Charles Waddell Chesnutt* [Provo, Utah: Brigham Young University Press, 1978], pp. 153–154).

4. Although it is unclear whether actual West Indian social organizations existed under the name of Colonial Clubs, numerous social organizations based on color and class flourished in the West Indian communities of the United States. Clubs that were probably limited to light-skinned members, such as the Club Aristocrat, Astor Social and Literary Club, and the Cosmopolitan Tennis Club, gave soirees and balls and helped to solidify ties among its members (Ira De A. Reid, *The Negro Immigrant*, pp. 156–161).

5. John R. Shillady (1875–1943), a young white social worker from Canton, N.Y., was secretary of the NAACP from 1918 to 1920. He was succeeded by James Weldon Johnson. After leaving the NAACP, he became executive director of the National Consumer League and later became general director of the National Association of Travelers Aid Societies (*NYT*, 7 September 1943).

6. The editorial that appeared in the September 1923 issue of the *Crisis* was culled from an editorial in the *Daily Gleaner* of Jamaica that was published on 26 June 1923. While Du Bois edited the article for the *Crisis*, the substance remained the same: a vehement denunciation of Garvey, Garveyism, and the UNIA. The *Gleaner* editorial, written at the end of Garvey's trial, called the trial fair and said that Garvey's conviction "sounds the death knell of Garveyism." The editorial called Garvey an "unblushing imposter" and "transparent charlatan" responsible for duping people out of money for the ill-fated Black Star Line. The editorial briefly and unfavorably contrasted Garvey to black leaders Booker T. Washington, W.E.B. Du Bois, and Dr. Edward Wilmot Blyden whom, it said, believe "only education of mind and character can elevate the race" rather than "hatred and the accumulation of money" ("In His Own Country," *Crisis*, September 1923; "Garvey Convicted," *Daily Gleaner*, 26 June 1923).

7. In the *Negro World* of 8 September 1923, the text read, "Keen observers and wise leaders."

Marcus Garvey to Emperor Yoshihito of Japan[1]

[*New York, 6 September 1923*]

Emperor of Japan,

Please accept the deep sorrow and sympathy of the four hundred million Negroes of the world and the Universal Negro Improvement Association over the catastrophy that has befallen your empire.[2] The Negro peoples looked to Japan as a friend in the cause of racial justice and we at this hour mourn with you in the sad national affliction that has visited the empire unawares.

MARCUS GARVEY
Provisional President of Africa and
President-General, Universal Negro
Improvement Association

[*Address*] Imperial Palace, Tokio, Japan

Printed in *NW*, 15 September 1923. Original headlines omitted.

1. Emperor Yoshihito (1879–1926) began his fifteen-year reign in 1912 (*WBD*).
2. A reference to the disastrous earthquake of 1 September 1923 that killed over 200,000 people and destroyed Tokyo. At the UNIA meeting of 13 September, William Sherrill made an appeal

for funds to aid the Japanese relief effort, and on 22 September the *Negro World* printed a cabled reply from the "Minister Imperial Household" of Japan expressing deep gratification for Garvey's "sympathetic message" (*Current History* 19, no. 1 [October 1923]: 384–385; *NW*, 22 December 1923).

Report by Special Agent Joseph G. Tucker

[*New York*] SEPT. 8, 1923

UNIVERSAL NEGRO IMPROVEMENT ASSOCIATION

The New York Local of the above organization held a 3-day convention beginning on August 29th and ending August 31st, during which afternoon and evening sessions were held.

Among the subjects discussed were the following:

"Our part in the redemption of Africa—how best can our local gain prestige and should the U.N.I.A. send missionaries to Africa to assist in establishing missionary schools to meet the needs of the African people?"

A telegram was sent to Marcus Garvey at the Tombs Prison in which the local renewed its assurances of loyalty to Garvey as President and to the programme of the U.N.I.A.

Among the subjects taken up at the convention were the need for a new Liberty Hall, work on which it was thought should begin in 1924 and the need for another steamship line to take the place of the defunct Black Star Line. It was also suggested that the New York Local would be making a wise step if they called for volunteers to dwell among the Africans in order to become better acquainted with and influence the native Africans.

Mrs. I[*rena*] M[*oorman*] Blackstone, who was one of the speakers at the convention, pointed out to those present the advantages that might be gained by boycotting the white businessmen in the Harlem District, where the Negro population predominates. She told her audience that if they would put the boycott into effect they would find Black businesses on the avenues where white ones now thrive.[1] Further on in the course of her remarks, according to the Negro World of September 8th, Mrs. Blackstone said that there are Negro women waiting on white women who are the white women's superiors and also added that if the Negro women only realized it, the white women envied them their strength and physique just as much as they envied them the physique of their men and that this was at the bottom of many of the lynchings down in Georgia. Continuing, she said:

"I want you to understand that Americans are not mad because you are Black. They are not Jim-Crowing you because you are inferior. They are not ignoring you because you are ignorant. They are not hating you because you have not got anything. They are clever propagandists and they are keeping before the World the issue that you are Negroes and don't deserve anything. They want you to think that, but they don't think so. I will tell you why they don't think so. If a colored man or woman does anything, you will find it in the headlines of the newspapers. The reason why they do this is because they want you yourself to feel that you are savages. I want you to understand you are the superior race, because the superior race fears you in your inferiority. You never saw a boy throw stones at a tree with no apples on it.["]

The usual Sunday evening meeting was held at Liberty Hall on the 2nd instant and one of the speakers was Tobitt, who stated that he had called on Garvey at the Tombs and that he had never felt more highly honored than when the keys of the Tombs were turned upon him and he found himself in the presence of Garvey. He closed by saying:

"My friends, I want to tell you, let men crave to be in the presence of Kings, let them crave to be in the presence of Presidents and other great men of this World, I choose no greater position than to be at the feet of so great a man than the Honorable Marcus Garvey."

JOSEPH G. TUCKER

DJ-FBI, file 61-245. TD.

1. Although no evidence has been found that this boycott was put into effect, former Garveyites did play a major role in the 1934 Harlem boycott against white-owned businesses that did not hire blacks in white-collar jobs. The boycott, launched in June 1934 during the Depression, was organized by the Citizen's League for Fair Play, an umbrella organization embracing sixty-two social, religious, and business groups. The driving force behind the boycott came from the radical wing of the organization, led by Sufi Abdul Hamid, Ira Kemp, and Arthur Reed. Kemp and Reed, both former Garveyites, had earlier organized the African Patriotic Committee, another offshoot of the Garvey movement. As William Muraskin notes, "Most of the radicals, whether a part of the Citizen's League for Fair Play, Sufi's Negro Industrial and Clerical Alliance, the African Patriotic League, the Rebel Picketing Committee, or the Harlem Labor Union, were followers or ex-followers of Marcus Garvey. In fact the reason for their interest in self-help movements was the spirit of Negro nationalism which Garvey had instilled in them" (William Muraskin, "The Harlem Boycott of 1934: Black Nationalism and the Rise of Labor-Union Consciousness," *Labor History* 13 [summer 1972]: 371). By September the boycott effectively forced Blumstein's, the target store, to capitulate and hire black saleswomen. But when the fifteen women hired turned out to be so light-skinned as to seem Caucasian, the league split apart. Kemp and Reed, who attacked the league for discriminating against dark-skinned blacks, resigned from the league and formed the Rebel Picketing Committee, which by 1936 coalesced into the Harlem Labor Union (Robert A. Hill, Introduction to *The Black Man: A Monthly Magazine of Negro Thought and Opinion*, ed. and comp. Robert A. Hill, pp. 28–29; Claude McKay, *Harlem: Negro Metropolis* [New York: E.P. Dutton and Co., 1940], pp. 180–262; Gunnar Myrdal, *An American Dilemma* [New York: Harper and Row, 1962], pp. 313–314; William Muraskin, "The Harlem Boycott of 1934," pp. 361–373).

Negro World Notice

NOTICE
Extraordinary!

To the Members and Friends of the Universal Negro Improvement Association.

It has come to our knowledge that unscrupulous persons have been circulating among our membership application blanks to subscribe to stock in an alleged Liberian Development or Exploration movement. Please be warned that we know nothing about the matter, and that it is apparent that a list of the membership of our organization has been stolen from the office.

Look out for all new circulars and letters sent by persons asking you to buy stock in such enterprises as Exploration Companies and steamship enterprises.

By order

UNIVERSAL NEGRO IMPROVEMENT ASSOCIATION

(*Source*: NW, 8 September 1923.)

Statement by Marcus Garvey

[*New York*] Sept. 10, 1923

STATEMENT TO PRESS ON RELEASE ON BAIL
PENDING APPEAL

My detention in jail pending the appeal of my case has in no way affected my vision of justice. To those who are conscious of themselves there can be no incrimination from without, it must be from within. When a man's conscience convicts him then there is no appeal: Thank Goodness I am not convicted.

I am not peeved at what has been done to me; it is natural and to be expected, that in an effort like mine to serve humanity—and black humanity at that—that powerful enemies will be encountered. The enemies I have are chiefly of my own race, and they have worked hard and long to discredit and destroy me.

They have only succeeded however in arousing the fighting spirit of millions of black men all over the world. There is nothing to fire a people to action like injustice, and I feel sure that time will tell the good that has been done to my cause, by the injustice meted out to me within the last three months.

The experience I have had, will help me greatly in the determination and conduct of the work that is ahead of me. A large number of people only looked at and enjoyed what to them seemed the humorous side of my program. There is no more humor in it than we find in all the other serious reform movements started for the uplift of humanity. The newspapers will, however, make the people laugh as a recreation, and a break in the monotony of a life of economic drudgery and social discord. If I afforded some amusement, I hope that the public will not blame me for it, for I am the direct opposite of the clown. I am serious, I have but one purpose, and that is the uplift and betterment of my race.

My detention in jail[,] after my application for bail pending appeal, was but a reflex of the state of mind of Mr. Maxwell S. Mattuck, the Assistant District Attorney who tried my case for the Government.

I am not blaming the Government for my conviction and detention in jail. The Government cannot represent itself. If at times we meet disappointments in the representation of Government, we must reason that all men do not think and act alike. Some persons are worthy of, and dignify[,] any position that they hold, others on the other hand, at their best are but libels to decency and propriety.

The methods that have been used to prejudice the court and the public against me, are of such as to make me shiver in fear that probably hundreds of thousands of innocent persons have lingered and died in prisons from the practise of such a system by unfair and unworthy representatives of Governments.

I shall make a fight to bring to the attention of the people and the government of this great country the evil methods used to railroad me to prison, to rob me of my name, to destroy my work for the pleasure of rival organizations, and the attempt to prevent me from speaking to the great American conscience by a suppression of free speech, and a muzzling of the press.

I am glad, and feel proud, we have worthy representatives in Government to outbalance any singular attempt at misrepresentation and injustice. Our institutions and country shall live forever, so long as the people have such worthy men as representatives to whom we can always appeal from the doings and machinations of the unjust.

I love America for her laws, constitution and her higher sense of fair play and justice. One can always find justice in America.

I have to thank my white friends and the members of my organization, as also the large number of liberal minded colored citizens who raised their voice in protest, and who helped generally in my being admitted to bail. I have to thank the Judge[1] and all those who had to do with my being liberated.

The few unfair white persons who have acted against us were misinformed, therefore I have no blame for them. They, like the great majority, do not understand the Negro, but I hope they will now make a closer study of the talebearers of our race who fabricate against their own for special favors.

My imprisonment of nearly three months has but steeled me for greater service to the people I love so much and who love me. I had no money before I was indicted. I had none when I was tried, and none when I was convicted and sentenced, because I gave all to the movement, but the people whom I served, and who know me, did not desert me. They stuck by me and paid for my defense, and subscribed for my bail.[2] These are the people whom my enemies accuse me of defrauding. [*Those who?*] hounded me haven't lost a penny in the ventures of our organization. They never placed a penny in it, yet they are so aggrieved. I feel sure that white America will, when properly informed, agree with us that the only solution of the Negro problem is to give the Negro a country of his own in Africa and for this I am working without any apologies.

I was kindly treated by the Warden and prison officials. I shall ever remember the kindly and sympathetic attitude of those worthy representatives of our Government. I am also glad to state that not one of my white fellow prisoners believed me guilty of the crime charged against me. It is amazing, but the prisoners seem to keep a tab on all that is going on in the courts. My case was well known to them, so that when I arrived at the jail, they were all surprised and disgusted at the results. They had a kind word of sympathy for me.

Some of the prisoners I met were honest enough to admit their guilt for whatever crimes they were charged, but I believe that there are others who are also innocent victims of circumstances.

Several liberal minded white friends visited me in jail, and did their best for me in the cause of justice. I am not asking for mercy or sympathy, I am asking for justice, and I have confidence in our constitution to know that it will not be denied me.

[MARCUS GARVEY]

447

Printed in *P&O*, 2: 228–230.

1. A reference to Federal Judge Martin Manton, who eventually granted Garvey's bail (*New York Age*, 8 September 1923).

2. Garvey's bail, originally set at $25,000, was later reduced to $15,000 (*NW*, 15 September 1923).

Speech by Marcus Garvey

[[Liberty Hall, New York, 13 September 1923]]

Ladies and Gentlemen:—

It is needless for me to say that [the] pleasure of meeting you in Liberty Hall, the shrine of Negro inspiration, after an enforced absence of three months, is beyond my ability to express.

The news of the trial of the celebrated case of fraud and my so-called conviction, have made the circuit of the world, and black humanity everywhere, even to the remotest parts of our homeland Africa, have formed their opinion of Western twentieth century civilization and justice, as controlled and administered by the white man.

My absence from you did not leave me despondent, nor desolate, for in the daily silence of the passing hours in my cell I thought of you, the warriors of true liberty, who were working for the consummation of our ideal—a free and redeemed Africa, and my meditations led me into greater f[l]ights of hope that shall strengthen me for the nobler work of self-sacrifice for the cause that we represent.

THE TRIAL

The amusing part of my trial is that I was indicted along with others for conspiracy to use the United States mails to defraud in the promotion of the Black Star Line Steamship Company, yet my conviction was void of conspiracy, in that I alone was convicted, and if I understand my conviction clearly, I was convicted for selling stock in the Black Star Line after I knew it to be insolvent. The difference between us and the trial court is that they wanted a conviction, caring not how it came about, and they had it to suit themselves, to the extent that all the others, who had more to do with the actual selling of stock than I, went free, because they were not wanted, while I received the fullest penalty that the law could impose—five years in the penitentiary, the maximum fine of one thousand dollars as provided by law, and the entire cost of the case, a condition not generally imposed but, maybe, once in twenty-five years.

THE NEGRO'S POINT OF VIEW

Our point of view is that we cannot defraud ourselves in the sense of promoting the Black Star Line, for the idea of a line of steamships operated by Negroes for the promotion of their industrial, commercial, fraternal and material well-being can never be insolvent or bankrupt (applause); for, as long as the race lasts and as long as humanity indulges in the pursuit of progress and achievements, the new Negro will be found doing his part to hold a place in the affairs of the world. It is true that we have been defrauded, but it was done, not by those of us who love our work and our race, but by disloyal and dishonest ones, whom we thought had the same feeling as we do, and by crooked white men, who were not even ashamed of hiding their crookedness. One white man said in court that he sold us a ship when he knew it was not worth the money paid for it.[1] Another took $25,000, and an additional $11,000 to buy the Phyllis Wheatley to go to Africa, which never materialized, and which money was never returned, the reason of which supplied the legal cause for my indictment. And yet it is said in the law of those who tried me that there was fraud and I should pay the penalty.

THE BLACK STAR LINE

The Black Star Line, as we all know, was but a small attempt, or experiment, of the race to fit and prepare ourselves for the bigger effort in the direction of racial self-reliance and self-determination. (Hear, hear.) To say that we have failed, because a few black and white unscrupulous persons deceived and robbed us, is to admit that the colonization scheme of America failed because a few Pilgram Fathers died at Plymouth, and that the fight of the Allies to save the world to a new civilization failed because the Crown Prince met with early success at Verdun.[2] The Black Star Line was only part of an honest effort on the part of real Negroes to re-establish themselves as a worthy people among the other races and nations of the earth, and but a small contribution in the plan of a free and redeemed African nation for the Negro peoples of the world. The idea of a Black Steamship Line, therefore, can only fall when the Negro race has completely passed away, and that means eternity. (Applause.)

THE REASON WHY

I was convicted, not because any one was defrauded in the temporary failure of the Black Star Line brought about by others, but because I represented, even as I do now, a movement for the real emancipation of my race. (Cries of 'Yes.') I was convicted because I talked about Africa and about its redemption for Negroes. (Renewed cries.) I was convicted because an atmosphere of hostility was created around me. I was convicted because wicked enemies, malicious and jealous members of my own race, misrepresented me to those in authority for the purpose of discrediting and destroying me.

I would not blame the few white persons who contributed to my conviction, neither would I blame the Government and the illiberal of the white race who had prejudices against me. They knew no better than the information they received from treacherous, malicious and jealous Negroes who, for the sake of position and privilege, will sell their own mothers.

I feel, however, that these white persons and the Government have now the opportunity of learning the truth, not only about my case and my conviction, but about the differences in the Negro race, that set one against the other.

APPEALING THE CASE

I have no fear of the ultimate outcome of my case. I shall take it to the highest courts in the land, and from there to the bar of international public opinion, and, even though I go to jail because of prejudice, I will have left behind for our generations a record of injustice that will be our guide in the future rise of Ethiopia's glory. (Applause.) Nevertheless, I believe that the higher courts of this country will not mingle prejudice with justice and condemn a man simply because he is black and attempts to do good for his race and his fellowmen.

"THE JAIL HAS NO TERRORS"

Whatsoever happens, the world may know that the jail or penitentiary has no terrors for me. Guilty men are afraid of jail, but I am as much at home in jail for the cause of human rights as I am in my drawing room (laughter), the only difference being that I have not my good wife's company even as I know how glad she would have been to share my lot, but hers must be a life of sacrifice also, painful though it be. When my life is fully given for the cause, and she is left behind, I trust that you will give her the consideration that is due a faithful and devoted wife, who gave up her husband for the cause of human service. During my trial cowards tried to blemish her character, but it is an accepted truth that character is not blemished from without; it is from within, and the noblest souls that ever peopled this world were those maligned and outraged by the vile and wicked.

Service to my race is an undying passion with me, so the greater the persecution, the greater my determination to serve. (Loud applause.)

AMERICA FRIEND OF NEGROES

As leader of the Universal Negro Improvement Association, of which the Black Star Line was an auxiliary, I must state that the millions of our members in this country and abroad look to America as a national friend, and citizens and residents as we are, we are jealous of her fair name among the other nations of the world and zealous in the effort to be to her loyal and true. (Applause.)

The Universal Negro Improvement Association seeks to do for Africa similarly what the Pilgrims, and later, George Washington, sought to do for America. We Negroes want a government of our own in Africa, so that we can be nationally, if not industrially and commercially, removed from competition in race, a condition that will make both races better friends, with malice toward none, but respect and appreciation for each.

Our greatest trouble, however, is with our own people. There are some of the race who are not in sympathy with an independent Negro nation. To them "they have lost nothing in Africa." They believe in the amalgamation of races for the production of new racial and national types; hence, their doctrine of social equality and the creating of a new American race. Feeling as they do divides us into two separate and distinct schools of thought, and, apparently, we are now at war with each other, and they have gained the first victory in having me, through their misrepresentation, indicted and convicted for the purpose of rendering me hors de combat.

We who believe in race purity are going to fight the issue out for the salvation of both races, and this can only be satisfactorily done when we have established for the Negro a nation of his own. We believe that the white race should protect itself against racial contamination, and the Negro should do the same. Nature intended us morally (and may I not say socially?) apart, otherwise there never could have been this difference. Our sins will not make the world better; hence, to us of the Universal Negro Improvement Association the time has come to rebuild our ancient and proud race.

PERSONAL SUFFERING

My personal suffering for the program of the Universal Negro Improvement Association is but a drop in the bucket of sacrifice. To correct the evils surrounding our racial existence is to undertake a task as pretentious and difficult as dividing the sea or uprooting the Rock of Gibraltar; but, with the grace of God, all things are possible, for in truth there is prophecy that "Ethiopia shall stretch forth her hand" and "Princes shall come out of Egypt." (Applause.)

We are expecting the co-operation and support of liberal White America in the promulgation of the ideal of race purity, and the founding of a nation for Negroes in Africa, so that those who, after proper industrial and other adjustments, desire to return to their original native homeland can do so in peace and security.

Now that the world is readjusting itself and political changes and distributions are being made of the earth's surface, there is absolutely no reason why certain parts of Africa should not be set aside absolutely for the Negro race as our claim and heritage. If this is not done, then we may as well look forward to eternal confusion among the races.

SUPERSTATE FOR NEGROES

Negro men will never always feel satisfied with being ruled, governed and dictated to by other races. As in my case, I would never feel satisfied with being absolutely tried and judged by a white judge, district attorney and jury, for it is impossible for them to correctly interpret the real feelings of my race and appreciate my effort in their behalf; hence, the prejudice from which I suffer. A white man before a black district attorney, judge and jury would feel the same way, and thus we have the great problem that can only be solved by giving the Negro a government of his own. (Loud and prolonged applause.) The Black Star Line was an effort in this direction and bore a relationship to the Universal Negro Improvement Association as the Shipping Board does to the Government. My effort was not correctly understood, and that is why some people have become prejudiced toward me. Yet in the final presentation of truth the fairminded is bound to come to the conclusion that the program of the Universal Negro Improvement Association is reasonable and proper for the solution of the vexed question of races.

Africa at this time affords a splendid opportunity for the creation of a super Negro State, notwithstanding the machinations of France, Italy, England, Belgium and Portugal. The peace of Europe and of the human race will only be settled on a proper adjustment of the African situation, and selfish European nations should not be allowed to transfer the theatre of war and human butchery from Europe to Africa, for if their present plans and schemes are carried out without check or hindrance it will mean that in another fifty years another Napoleon or William II will be attempting to create out of Africa another European empire at the cost of countless millions of lives. (Hear, hear).

I have but briefly outlined some of the things in my mind, but I must assure you that my imprisonment for three months has not left me sore. I am not vexed with anybody. I calculated that my own people would be against me for serving them, but I also feel satisfied that the masses are with me, and that it is with their support that I find that it is possible to be here tonight. But for the constant illness of my wife I would have had no sorrow.

RETURNING THANKS

At this juncture I want specially to return thanks to you, the members of Liberty Hall, who stuck by the principles of the Universal Negro Improvement Association when your leader was removed from you. I can understand and appreciate the struggles that were undergone by you while I remained in the Tombs. You had, for the purpose of dragging me from behind bars, to fight the lip service and insincerity of those who pretended that they wanted me to be free yet were working to keep me in jail. But for you, the people, and a few of those who associated themselves with me as members of the council, I would not only have remained in the Tombs, but I would have been sent to Atlanta.

THE PART MRS. GARVEY PLAYED

I publicly have to thank my wife for the sacrifice that she made along with Mr. Bourne, Mr. Poston and Mr. Sherrill, of the Executive Committee, and Mr. D.E. Tobias, to secure my release[,] to fight the battle to the end. When she started to present my case to America and to the world several of those who should have stood behind me, who pledged they would have stood behind the principles of the Universal Negro Improvement Association, attempted to deter that poor, little woman, to strike fear and terror into her heart and told her she was doing the wrong thing. But, obedient wife as she is and loyal as she has been to me and the Universal Negro Improvement Association, she carried out the instructions I gave her,[3] and tonight, with your assistance and the assistance of the other members of the Universal Negro Improvement Association, I am able to be with you in Liberty Hall. (Applause.) When she started the fight and this little woman took my commands to carry them out, several of the men got weak-kneed and said we could not afford to fight the government. We will fight hell. (Uproarious applause.) We were not fighting the United States Government. We were not fighting the Government, but we were fighting injustice, and we shall fight injustice to the gates of hell. (Applause.)

COUNTED THE COST

Who tells them, whether they be leaders or followers of the Universal Negro Improvement Association, that we will stop at anything when we started the fight of African redemption? Who tells them that anything in the world besides God can strike terror and fear in the hearts of twentieth century black men? Who tells them that Garvey is afraid of jail? Who tells them that Garvey is afraid of five, twenty or thirty years in Atlanta? Garvey is as ready to go back as he was ready to go in the first instance. The jail has no terrors for me. As I said before, I am as much at home in the Tombs as in my drawing room and but for the pale face of my wife and the suffering depicted in her countenance every morning as she came to see me I would have been as happy there sending out the messages of inspiration and hope to 400,000,000 black souls as speaking from the platform of Liberty Hall. As I told you more than once, I counted the cost of being identifed with the Universal Negro Improvement Association as one of its leaders before I started. And, therefore, I have no sorrow, I have no tears. I have no regrets for what has happened to me and for what may happen to me in the future. To hell with the jail! (Applause.) The jail was not made for me, but if [I] get in jail, my brain can be as resourceful in jail as out of jail. And the three months they kept me in jail supplied me with new ideas—(laughter and applause)—and with a new program. And if they want to give me five years' rest[,] then I will have edited an encyclopedia of ideas, and if I become too old to execute them I will pass them on, one by one, to others who I know are working as assiduously as I have done and I am doing for this great cause of ours. (Applause.)

"WHY I TRIED MY OWN CASE."

Some of you have heard many things; you have heard many discussions during my trial and during my confinement. Some of you said I should not have tried my own case. If I had not tried my own case, at this time I would be facing a sentence of thirty years. I would have been found guilty on six or seven counts, would have been given five years on each count out of the twelve on which I was indicted. But I was not such a fool to let any Negro put me in jail for thirty years without opening my mouth. So on the second day I took over my own case and got five years where I would have gotten thirty years.

Now I am not going to discuss the case. It is not proper. It is not within the law. But I tried the case, not because I wanted to go free, because the best legal minds said at a certain time: "Garvey, we can get you free by fighting this thing only on the law. It is purely a commercial case, and we can do this and we can do that, and there is no offense committed by you against the law." But it meant this: If I had tried my case with probably the best attorney in this country, Marcus Garvey would have gone free and the Universal Negro Improvement Association would have been smashed up. Now you must understand that we had a complicated affair. We were before a law court and not before a public gathering. I was indicted for using the United States mails to defraud in the promotion of the Black Star Line, not in the promotion of the Universal Negro Improvement Association.

It was purely a commercial case from the viewpoint of the law. If I had gone to trial on only the viewpoint of the law as some lawyers wanted to do, I probably would have been acquitted with the other men, because no wrong was committed. We did the best we could but for those who tried to rob and pilfer us. But in the law all things said about the Universal Negro Improvement Association would have been irrelevant. No lawyer could have introduced them, because no court would have tolerated it. And, therefore, being a layman and the president of the Universal Negro Improvement Association, my duty was to save the Universal Negro Improvement Association and save the ideals of the people even at the cost of imprisonment for five years. So that there was much more to be considered than the case on the surface. I feel sure that every honest-minded person knows no wrong has been done in the promotion of the Black Star Line. We are satisfied now to carry the case to the highest court of appeal in this country and hire the best lawyers to protect my interests.

GOOD NEWS FROM AFRICA

I come back to you feeling happy, feeling glad, feeling satisfied you have done nobly. You have done well. I remained in jail long enough to get the news. Do you know what news I got? I got the news that West Africa was on fire. On the twenty-eighth [*twenty-ninth*] of August the Chicago "Tribune," the second largest daily paper in this country, published a three-column article,[+] a special radio dispatch from West Africa, stating that the blacks of West Africa and of the Soudan and of the Southeast of Africa were agitating and clamoring for a black African republic (applause)—because they were incensed over the imprisonment of Marcus Garvey. So if to remain for three months is to get the Africans in one section declaring for a republic, I am willing to remain five years to get all Africa. (Applause.)

Now I am not going to keep you longer, because I want to meet those of you who are my friends one by one and shake your hands. I have to thank those of you who subscribed so liberally and freely from your meagre means to assist in securing bond for me. Every effort made to secure bond was blocked. When we complied with one thing the bonding companies wanted another. Our enemies were at work to block every effort to free me, and when the last resort was to get $25,000 in cash you got it in twenty-four hours, between New York and Detroit, noble Detroit. You in New York in the space of twelve hours subscribed $12,500. Detroit in the space of twenty-four hours subscribed $7,000. Between New York and Detroit and Cincinnati and Philadelphia, $25,000 or $27,000 were subscribed in forty-eight hours, and when we had the $25,000 it was reduced to $15,000.

STICK BY THE PRINCIPLES

Now again let me publicly thank those of you who subscribed to help lift the bond. Again must I thank those of you who did not subscribe but who would have subscribed if you had the money. Let me thank you again for holding together, because morally we won our victory by your sticking together. (Applause.) They thought that the Universal Negro Improvement Association would have gone down with Garvey in jail, and then I would have died a disappointed man. But I lived a hopeful man and slept in jail a happy and peaceful man. When I read of the splendid meetings you were holding in Liberty Hall on Sunday nights; when I read some of the beautiful speeches made in Liberty Hall, some true and some lip service—and I am very glad that you were so educated that you can tell your man at a glance, and that you adopt the policy of hearing men but doing as you feel you should do—I felt very glad indeed. Keep up that policy and we are bound to win. When the other fellow thinks he is deceiving you he is deceiving himself. Let everybody talk, but stick by the principles of the Universal Negro Improvement Association. God is with us. I know God is with me and I am with God, and I know God is with the Universal Negro Improvement Association and the Universal Negro Improvement Association is with God. Let us continue our faith in God. Let us continue to accept Jesus Christ on this side of Christiandom as our leader. Others who are Mohammedans believe in the same God, the God [of n]ature, who inspired the prophecy, "Ethiopia shall stretch forth her hand unto God."

And methinks at this hour, looking at this vast assembly,[5] that I see Negroes assembled not only in New York, but in other parts of the world. As I go along I shall see vast throngs in Philadelphia, in Detroit, in Cincinnati, in Kansas and on the way out West, where I hope to spend a few weeks' holiday. I am going to stop off at Leavenworth[6] and tell the boys, "I will soon be there." (Laughter.) May God bless you. (Loud and prolonged applause.) . . .[7]

Printed in *NW*, 22 September 1923. Original headlines omitted.

1. Leo Healy, attorney for ship broker William Harriss, admitted that when the Black Star Line "offered us such a lucrative price, the business acumen for which Mr. Harris [*Harriss*] is well known in business naturally asserted itself and he made a bargain" (*Marcus Garvey* v. *United States*, no. 8317, Ct. App., 2d Cir., 2 February 1925, p. 255).

2. A reference to the Battle of Verdun, where German troops, led by Crown Prince William, took the French sector of Fort Douaumont on 25 February 1916. The Germans made further gains in the region, with June victories at Fort Vaux and Fort Thiaumont. Led by Gen. Charles Mangin, French forces counterattacked at Verdun, recapturing Fort Douaumont and Fort Vaux by November 1916 (*EWH*, p. 959).

3. Amy Jacques Garvey's efforts on Garvey's behalf were eulogized by George Alexander Mc-Guire in his journal, *The Negro Churchman*. Called "this little Joan of Arc," she was praised for her selfless devotion to the cause during Garvey's imprisonment (*Negro Churchman* 1, nos. 9–10 [September–October 1923]: 11).

4. On 29 August 1923 the *Chicago Tribune* published an article by Floyd Gibbons, dispatched from Senegal. "The name of Marcus Garvey," the article read, ". . . who recently was sentenced by a New York judge . . . and reports of fabulous financial backing by American Negroes, are being used in an attempt to foment an uprising among the blacks of northern Nigeria. . . . Garvey's proclamations, translated in Arabic, have been circulated throughout Nigeria, and are being used to urge the natives to revolt against the British authorities in the northern provinces. In the southern provinces, where thousands of Negroes have become English speaking, the propaganda is reported to be even more widespread, due to the awakening desire among the partially educated blacks to possess more of the white man's liberty and culture" (*Chicago Tribune*, 29 August 1923).

5. The meeting was reportedly attended by about five thousand, most of whom paid fifty cents to seventy-five cents for admission. Garvey, who wore a "cocked hat" with "a plume of red and white feathers," was given a five-minute ovation before he rose to speak (*NYT*, 14 September 1923).

6. Judge Mack requested that because of Garvey's race, Leavenworth might be a better place for imprisonment than Atlanta. On 22 June 1923 U.S. Attorney William Hayward wrote to Attorney General Harry M. Daugherty requesting that authorization be given to imprison Garvey in Leavenworth (Hayward to Daugherty, 22 June 1923 and 10 July 1923, DNA, RG 60, file 198940-289).

7. The omitted portion of the speech is devoted to paying tribute to David E. Tobias for his efforts in securing Garvey's release.

Speech by Marcus Garvey

[[LIBERTY HALL, New York, September 16, 1923]]

My subject for tonight is "The Sign by Which We Conquer." Perseverance and determination on the part of any people lead ultimately to the goal which they seek. That you are here this evening and hundreds of thousands and millions probably of Negroes are so assembled in different parts of the world in mass meetings tonight carrying out the exercises of the Universal Negro Improvement Association, is proof that perseverance and determination will ultimately bring about success for any people.

A CHANGED ATTITUDE TOWARDS THE U.N.I.A.

When we started our movement a few years ago with just a few, the world of other men spurned us, laughed at us, and said that we were wasting time because we could not impress the world. Today that opinion has changed. It has been changed because of the perseverance of the few and the determination of the few. They persevered long enough until they were able to impress not

UNIA delegation to the League of Nations

Joel A. Rogers

S.V. Robertson

John Jeffries elias Esau Ramus

This picture taken at the time SUBJECT was Chief of
Secret Service for the Garvey organization.

Esau Ramus

James A. Amos

Julian W. Mack

Garveyites, New York, 1924

J. J. Dossen

UNIA delegation to Liberia in Lisbon

UNIA delegation to Liberia, 1924

JAMES N. WALCOTT
Ship Carpenter and Builder

JAMES C. ROBERTS
Electrical Engineer

REGINALD HURLEY
Carpenter and Builder (now in Africa)

WILLIAM W. STRANGE
Supervising and Directing Civil and Mining Engineer

J. NICHOLLS
Mechanical Engineer

RUPERT CHRISTIAN
Executive Secretary and Paymaster

UNIA delegation of technical experts
to Liberia

Marcus Garvey and Amy Jacques Garvey

HON. MARCUS GARVEY
In Uniform of Commander-in-Chief of
the African Legion

Marcus Garvey in Universal African Legion uniform

George O. Marke, Kojo Tovalou-Houénou, and Marcus Garvey

Marcus Garvey in academic robes

Marcus Garvey and UNIA officials on viewing stand, convention parade, 1924

UNIA marching band, 1924

Marchers in UNIA convention parade, 1924
(front pair, Lawson of New York and J.A. Craigen of Detroit;
Rev. Van Richards of Liberia, third row right)

UNIA Juvenile division

Marcus Garvey in regalia, 1924

Booker T. Washington University, 1924

Funeral of John E. Bruce, 1924
(Florence Bruce, Marcus Garvey, Arthur Schomburg, far right)

Crowd at the 1924 UNIA convention

Marcus Garvey at Liberty Hall, 1924

Marcus Garvey and UNIA Officers reviewing the convention parade

only their immediate community but attract the entire world. And tonight the organization that a few founded four and a half years or five years ago has become the talk of the world and has made such an impress on the world that statesmen everywhere, not only in America but throughout civilization, are worried as to the outcome. We are conscious of ourselves what the outcome will be. The outcome for us will be nothing more and nothing less than an independent government for Negroes. (Applause.)

It was that vision that attracted us five years ago when just thirteen or a few more of us founded this organization; it is the same vision that attracts us now that we are six million organized; it is the same vision that will attract us until we have completely brought into the fold—if not in active labor, with sentiment and sympathy—the 400,000,000 Negroes of our race. (Applause.)

THE EFFECT OF HIS IMPRISONMENT

My imprisonment for three months was one of the avenues through which we would get our program presented to the world; and I was not sorry one bit to contribute in that direction to at least impress the world some more about the seriousness of the Universal Negro Improvement Association. That impression of seriousness—the compliment of it is for you, not for me, in that I was placed in a position that I could not help myself more than to write to the world; but that could not move men. The impress that was made upon the world for the last three months was made by you—by your perseverance and by your determination.

The world knows that human achievements and human movements are carried on not by everybody but by the direction of those who lead, and the strategy of a few people has always sought to remove the leaders of movements and if successfully cornered they calculate they would destroy the movement.

EXPERIMENTING WITH GARVEY

Well: they were experimenting with me. They put me in jail to try out if they could destroy the Universal Negro Improvement Association and then they found a greater Universal Negro Improvement Association. (Applause.) Now I suppose they will change their tactics; nevertheless the three months has convinced me everywhere that the new Negro is here. Now what they did to me for three months with the intention of destroying the movement represented by me would have succeeded in another age, and another time prior to this. Ten years ago—twenty-five years ago if anyone attempted to start a movement as big probably as the Universal Negro Improvement Association and they did what they did to me, naturally as from the attitude of the Negro himself they would have destroyed the movement; but that was the time of the old Negro. They had the plan all right, but they worked the plan in the wrong time. If they had worked that plan ten years ago or fifteen years ago they would have succeeded, but they cannot crush the rising spirit of the Negro in the twentieth century by sending him to jail. They cannot crush the rising spirit of the Negro of the twentieth century by holding a club over his head; you cannot crush the rising spirit of the twentieth century Negro by drawing his blood. The more you do these things the more he will fight. (Applause.)

THE UNIVERSAL NOT STARTED YET

And the Universal Negro Improvement Association has not started yet. Now I am one of those in the Association that know what we are doing, because I happen to be one of the leaders, and we have not started anything yet; we have not done anything yet. Up to now we are just good Sabbath school children; and if acting like good Sabbath school children we create an unrest among other folks, what will happen when we start to behave like men? (Laughter and applause.)

There is no doubt about it that the man who is doing right is never fearful of anything. I do not see why the world should be worried about the Universal Negro Improvement Association and worried about Marcus Garvey. If the world has not done anything to Negroes why should it be worried about the activity of Negroes. The world must know that we as a people are not seeking to create any disturbance—to affect the peace of communities and the harmony of races. We are not disposed that way. We are too appreciative of other people's rights to go out of our way to offend them. We are too considerate of other people's happiness to go out of our way to create disturbance; therefore the world of honest people need not be afraid of us; but if there are any dishonest people in the world who have held or are holding what is belonging to other folks—if they have anything belonging to Negroes naturally they will be disturbed because Negroes are going after those things.

We are living in America, but I am speaking not only to you who live in America. As I speak from Liberty Hall I am speaking to Negroes all over the world. America claims she has nothing for us; and England says she has nothing for us; France says so, and the different European governments say they have nothing for us, and we hear some talk now that they have nothing for us in these parts; but we have decided that we have something for ourselves—that we possess something of ourselves, and we have understood that somebody has been keeping it for us. Now we are just about thanking them for being so good in keeping that which was belonging to us, and we are just asking them to cease their kindness for a while and hand over to us what is belonging to us. If somebody gave you something to keep for me and you are honest, when I approach you you will give it to me. They said we were heathens; we were pagans; we were savages and did not know how to take care of ourselves; that we did not have any religion; we did not have any culture; we did not have any civilization for all those centuries, and that is why they had to be our guardians. Well, we are satisfied that they were our guardians for all this while, because we did not have the civilization; we did not have the culture; we did not have the Christianity. But thank God we have them all now, as we are asking that you hand back to us our own civilization—hand back to us that country which you have robbed and exploited us of in the name of God and Christianity for the last 500 years. We are asking England to hand it back; we are asking France to hand it back; we are asking Italy to hand it back; we are asking Belgium to hand it back; we are asking Portugal to hand it back; we are asking Spain to hand it back, and by God, the Moroccans made them hand it back.[1] (Great applause.) And if you will not hear the voice of a friend crying out in the wilderness to hand back those things, then, remember, one day you will find, marching down the avenue of time, 400,000,000 black men and women ready to give up, even the last drop of their blood, for the redemption of their motherland, Africa. (Great applause.) If you don't want us in Johnstown, Pa.;[2] if you don't want us in Tulsa; if you don't want us in East St. Louis, we want ourselves where we want to be, and we are not going to remain here and create any trouble longer than is necessary. We are not going to leave now. All of us didn't come at the same time and, therefore, all of us won't leave at the same time. (Laughter.) They took time bringing us here; so we will take time going there. Some of us have to take our clothes out of pawn (laughter); some of us have to sell our property before we can go. So naturally, we cannot all go at the same time; and then the Black Star Line has not sufficient ships yet. (Applause.)

THE BLACK STAR LINE

You know they have a peculiar, a queer notion about the Black Star Line. Some people say the Black Star Line has failed. Now, stars don't fall every day. (Laughter.) Like the sun, sometimes they go into eclipse, but they come out again, don't they? And sometimes they shine more brilliantly than at other times. And when the Black Star Line comes back she is going to shine for ever more. (Deafening applause.) The Black Star Line is the rising hope of a race. And we have placed that star in the firmament of stars. And the Black Star Line shall only fall when the great firmament of stars has passed away. Don't be discouraged. We have been temporarily embarrassed because we did not know ourselves. Believe me, I did not know the Negro when I started to work with the Negro. I had a mistaken notion of the Negro. I believed all Negroes felt like me. What I suffered from the other fellow, what I went through at the hands of the other fellow I thought every Negro went through the same suffering and hardship and felt like me. But all Negroes did not feel like us. We have to sort ourselves. And the big mistake we made in the Black Star Line was that we believed when we started everybody felt like us. But we now know we have a lot of sorting to do, and once bitten we shall be twice shy. So that those of us who are stockholders in the Black Star Line, you need not lose heart. And I trust none of you will tear up your stock certificates or give them away, because these very stock certificates you think little of now will turn up like the German mark twenty years from now.[3] You cannot keep a good thing down. You cannot destroy a good thought. You cannot destroy great minds, great characters. The whole world laughs at Germany now because the mark is low, but the German mind is not low. The whole world of curious, foolish people laughed at the Black Star Line, but the mind of the black man is still active and idealistic. Before you can successfully destroy the Black Star Line, even as before you can successfully destroy German activities, you must destroy the minds of men. Imprisonment cannot destroy that. You cannot destroy the mind. You can only imprison the body. The mind is ever active.

GOTTEN AWAY

It is impossible at this time to tell any person in the world to hold the minds of the twentieth century Negro. They may as well keep us out of jail as in jail. The thing has gotten away from them. You know we told them, "The more you look, the less you see," and they were looking in one direction and not in the other. They thought Garvey was the whole show. (Laughter.) But they did not seem to know that we have some Garveys scattered all around, and all of them are not in America either. The most of them are now in Africa and raising hell down there. (Loud applause.) The thing has gotten away from them, and even if Garvey wanted to call it back it cannot come back. (Laughter.) Can't come back. It has gone too far.

A FRANK STATEMENT

But, men, remember this. You at this time can only be destroyed by yourselves, from within and not from without. You have reached the point where the victory is to be won from within and can only be lost from within. The time has come when we have, as I said a while ago, to sort ourselves. I have been placed recently in a very embarrassing position. I have no secrets to keep from you or anybody. I like frankness, honesty of expression of thought and deed. I calculated when I started this movement that we would have worked together and kept our own counsel as a race of people without mixing much with other folks, without going to other folks, and I was successful in keeping to that policy up to three months ago. I calculated that not until the proper time had we to approach the other fellow and tell him what we wanted. That time naturally would come. We could not do everything on this side of the Atlantic without ultimately telling the white man what we want. But I believed the time had not come yet. I do not believe in doing anything prematurely, and I calculated we would have just worked among ourselves until we were ready and then gone to the other fellow and said, "We are ready, and we are asking you to let us come to terms and get this thing done." But, apparently, some of our folks are forcing us to talk with the other fellow before the time comes.

THE U.N.I.A. NEW ATTITUDE

You know we are in a white man's country, not a black man's country. That is our disadvantage, and you can't very well move around the other fellow's country without telling him what you are doing. He becomes suspicious. And we have been moving around for all these years not even paying the other fellow the compliment of letting him know what we are doing. And, because of that, others went and lied and told what we were not doing and got me into a pickle and you in a bad fix. Every fellow believed he was doing a great deed when he started to talk and tell. Well, there are two sides to a story. They told and they thought by telling they would have done us a great deal of harm. They caused me to be sent to jail for five years and caused you to have to put up $25,000 to get me out. But they alone are not going to do the talking. We are going to do some of the talking, too. It is going to be tell for tell. You understand what I mean. Our people are so wicked to themselves, that they are not satisfied until they are telling the enemy something about themselves. And because they have resorted—the N.A.A.C.P., the African Blood Brotherhood, the Friends of Negro Freedom—because they have resorted to telling the white man what they do not know about the Universal Negro Improvement Association for the purpose of destroying us, we are not fools to keep our mouths closed, but we are not going to tell about them as they told about us. We are only forced to approach the white man quicker than we anticipated. We were only going to approach him when we were fully organized, but we cannot wait until that time, because, if we do, the enemy will destroy us. So if you see me talking to white folks now, you will know what for.

POLITICS TO COUNT

I am not going to let Du Bois, Weldon Johnson, or Pickens, or Randolph or Owen lie the Universal Negro Improvement Association out of its purpose of emancipating a race, redeeming a motherland. That means, we are going to play politics, too. And I am going to ask something of you. I did not intend to ask you so early, because I felt the time had not come yet. I was hoping in two, three, four, five or six years, politically, we would go to the President of the nation and to the different parties, the Republican and the Democratic and say, "Our program is six million of us want to go back to Africa . We want you to make it a plank in your platform." We wanted to do that in six years' time. But they are forcing it on us now. I am saying to you now: "Get registered wherever you are." If you are not citizens, for your own convenience and for the convenience of carrying on the program you must get naturalized. It won't do you any harm. It will do you a great deal of good, because when the final time comes, we are not going to beg this question, we are going to force it. And if the N.A.A.C.P. feels they can play politics with 200,000, we can play politics with 2,000,000. If they can get one man in jail with 200,000, we can get a dozen men in jail with 2,000,000. So now you quite understand if you see us talking to white folks and bringing them here, you know what we are up to. It is because the other fellow is trying to undermine the cause. And, remember, we are in a white man's country. That is why we have to play this game. We are hoping the time will come when we will be able to deal with our folks other than through the white man. I may not be living then, but my son may be a judge. (Laughter.) My son may be a warden of the Tombs some day and he may lock the Tombs and throw away the key. (Laughter.)

A FIGHT FOR ALL TIME

I thank you for this good humor and I have to thank you for your deep and sincere interest in me. I have no doubt about that . . . [*words mutilated*] for little service that I had rendered, and I was in no way doubtful during the three months I remained in the Tombs, because you expressed that interest in me day by day. I must thank you for the loans you made to raise my bail bond so that I could be with you tonight and will be with you always. We are still in the fight. Be satisfied, however, that if one general goes down in the fight, other generals will rise. It is a fight that must be carried on, not for a day, not for a limited time, but for all time, and I feel sure that you appreciate the suffering of those who give themselves up for the cause that all of us do love. I thank you all, and I trust we will better understand ourselves and continue the great work for the good of the Universal Negro Improvement Association. (Loud applause.)

Printed in *NW*, 22 September 1923. Original headlines omitted.

1. By the fall of 1923 the Rif of northern Morocco were on the verge of expelling the Spanish and establishing their own republic. The Rif had begun their fight for independence in 1920, and the three-year struggle climaxed in June 1923 when the Spanish army suffered a catastrophic defeat at their hands. Under the command of Abd el-Krim, three thousand Rif defeated nineteen thousand Spanish troops, captured large amounts of arms and ammunition, and drove the Spanish back to the ports. By the end of 1923 the Rif began a new campaign into Tangier and began to organize the Republic of the Rif with a president, legislature, and plans for a constitution. While Abd el-Krim was captured in 1926 by a joint expedition of French and Spanish troops, the Rif were not defeated until 1934 (David S. Woolman, *Rebels in the Rif: Abd El-Krim and the Rif Rebellion* [Stanford, Calif.: Stanford University Press, 1968]; S. Fleming, "Primo de Rivera and Abd El-Krim: The Struggle in Spanish Morocco, 1923–1927" [Ph.D. diss., University of Wisconsin, 1974]; Douglas E. Ashford, *Political Change in Morocco* [Princeton: Princeton University Press, 1961], pp. 25–31; *Baltimore Afro-American*, 15 June 1923).

2. Following the murder on 31 August 1923 of three Johnston, Pa., policemen and two detectives by a "drink-crazed negro," Mayor Joseph Cauffiel of Johnstown ordered all blacks and Mexicans with less than seven years residence in the city to leave the Johnstown area immediately. The initial shooting of the officers took place when police rushed to the site of a riot in the small black and Mexican ghetto of Rosedale, located adjacent to the Cambria plant of the Bethlehem Steel Corp. Most of the blacks and Mexicans ordered to leave by Cauffiel were new arrivals brought to the city by Bethlehem. Under the mayor's order, all assemblages of blacks and Mexicans were prohibited, and by 14 September over two thousand Rosedale residents were reported to be ready to leave. Protest letters against Cauffiel's action were sent by the NAACP and the National Equal Rights League to both Gov. Gifford Pinchot of Pennsylvania and President Coolidge, and on 20 September Cauffiel denied that he had issued a formal order of deportation. Cauffiel did claim, however, that "about 2,000 negroes have gone within the last three weeks" and that "newly arrived negro citizens" were being ordered to leave town (*NYT*, 1, 15, 20 and 21 September 1923).

3. A reference to the massive deflation of the German mark in the summer of 1923. The old mark was replaced on 15 November 1923 by new Rentenbank notes at a rate of one trillion to one (*EWH*, p. 1,006).

Report by Special Agent Mortimer J. Davis

New York City 9–29–23

On September 25th, during my absence, Inspector Zucker from Ellis Island called at the Bureau Office and informed Agent Scully that he has instructions from his department in Washington to prepare a deportation case against Marcus Garvey based upon alleged radical speeches which the subject has made during the past.

On the 28th instant agent interviewed Inspector Zucker and was informed by him that it is the wish of his department to prepare the case based on radical statements so that should Garvey's appeal from his recent conviction on a mail fraud charge be successful the charge of radicalism can be placed against him.

After going over the matter with Inspector Zucker it was agreed that agent would endeavor to locate from the Bureau records and otherwise, copies of speeches made by Garvey during the past, which would in turn be furnished to the Immigration authorities for their use in this matter, and agent was engaged on the 28th and 29th locating such material. Continued.

MORTIMER J. DAVIS

DJ-FBI, file 61. TD.

Article by Rev. George Alexander McGuire

[*Negro Churchman*] September 1923

. . . By invitation of the President General we were present, and occupied a seat on the platform in Liberty Hall, on Thursday evening, September 13th, to witness the enthusiastic demonstration which the members of the New York Division of the Universal Negro Improvement Association gave in honor of their returned leader. It was reminiscent of the conquering hero of ancient times making his triumphal entry into the imperial city. The clash of musical instruments, the stentorian efforts of the robed choir, the spontaneous cheers and loud hurrahs were all simultaneously and involuntarily mixed, while many of the older and more restrained group who had for three months prayed to Almighty God for the deliverance of this man, wept silently, interceding still that Garvey may be permanently released and exonerated.

Outsiders will never understand the psychology of those they call "Garveyites." We doubt, if we who are thus nicknamed, understand it ourselves. The binding spell, the indefinable charm which Mr. Garvey exercises over us beggars description. But we find the reason for it in our conviction that no man has spoken to us like this man, inculcating pride and nobility of race, and clearly pointing out the Star of Hope to a discouraged and downtrodden people. We have reason to believe that his enforced solitude has clarified his vision. From Horeb[1] and Sinai Moses came back to Israel with new revelations, even as subsequently St. John the Divine came back to the Christian Church from his exile on the lonely isle of Patmos.[2] We venture to predict that Marcus Garvey who left "The Tombs" on Monday, Sept. 10th, will rise and ascend to higher leadership, and that Negroes everywhere will be the beneficiaries of the NEW IDEAS, which he tells us he has gained during his vacation.

Printed in the *Negro Churchman* 1, nos. 9–10 (September–October 1923): 11.

1. In Horeb, Moses struck the rock and water came forth as predicted by the Lord (Exod. 17:6).
2. John "was in the isle that is called Patmos, for the word of God, and for the testimony of Jesus Christ" (Rev. 1:9).

Speech by Marcus Garvey

[*Youngstown, Ohio*] October 2, 1923

AN APPEAL TO THE SOUL OF WHITE AMERICA

Surely the soul of liberal, philanthropic, liberty-loving, white America is not dead.

It is true that the glamour of materialism, has, to a great degree, destroyed the innocence and purity of the national conscience, but, still, beyond our politics, beyond our soulless industrialism, there is a deep feeling of human sympathy that touches the soul of white America upon which the unfortunate and sorrowful can always depend for sympathy, help, and action.

It is to that feeling that I appeal at this time for four hundred million Negroes of the world, and fifteen million of America in particular.

There is no real white man in America, who does not desire a solution of the Negro problem. Each thoughtful citizen has probably his own ideas of how the vexed question of races should be settled. To some the Negro could be gotten rid of by wholesale butchery, by lynching, economic starvation, by a return to slavery and legalized oppression; while others would have the problem solved by seeing the race all herded together and kept somewhere among themselves, but a few—those in whom they have an interest—should be allowed to live around as the wards of a mistaken philanthrophy; yet, none so generous as to desire to see the Negro elevated to a standard of real progress, and prosperity, welded into a homogeneous whole, creating of themselves a mighty nation with proper systems of government, civilization, and culture, to mark them admissable to the fraternities of nations and races without any disadvantage.

I do not desire to offend the finer feelings and sensibilities of those white friends of the race who really believe that they are kind and considerate to us as a people; but I feel it my duty to make a real appeal to conscience and not belief. Conscience is solid, convicting and permanently demonstrative;

belief, is only a matter of opinion, changeable by superior reasoning. Once the belief was that it was fit and proper to hold the Negro as a slave and in this the Bishop, Priest and layman agreed. Later on they changed their belief or opinion, but at all times the conscience of certain people dictated to them that it was wrong and inhuman to hold human beings as slaves. It is to such a conscience in white America that I am addressing myself.

Negroes are human beings—the peculiar and strange opinions of writers, ethnologists, philosophers, scientists and anthropologists notwithstanding—they have feelings, souls, passions, ambitions, desires, just as other men, hence they should be considered.

Has white America really considered the Negro in the light of permanent human progress? The answer is NO.

Men and women of the white race, do you know what is going to happen if you do not think and act now? One of two things. You are either going to deceive and keep the Negro in your midst until you have perfectly completed your wonderful American civilization with its progress of art, science, industry and politics, and then, jealous of your own success and achievements in those directions, and with the greater jealousy of seeing your race pure and unmixed, cast him off to die in the whirlpool of economic starvation, thus, getting rid of another race that was not intelligent enough to live, or, you simply mean by the largeness of your hearts to assimilate fifteen million Negroes into the social fraternity of an American race that will neither be white nor black. Don't be alarmed! We must prevent both consequences. No real race loving white man wants to destroy the purity of his race, and no real Negro conscious of himself wants to die[,] hence there is room for an understanding and an adjustment, and that is just what we seek.

Let white and black stop deceiving themselves. Let the white race stop thinking that all black men are dogs and not to be considered as human beings. Let foolish Negro agitators and so-called reformers, encouraged by deceptive and unthinking white associates, stop preaching and advocating the doctrine of "social equality," meaning thereby the social intermingling of both races, intermarriages, and general social co-relationship. The two extremes will get us nowhere, other than breeding hate and encouraging discord, which will eventually end disastrously to the weaker race.

Some Negroes in the quest of position, and honor, have been admitted to the full enjoyment of their constitutional rights, thus we have some of our men filling high and responsible Government positions, others on their own account, have established themselves in the professions, commerce and industry. This the casual onlooker, and even the men themselves, will say carries a guarantee and hope of social equality, and permanent racial progress. But this is the mistake. There is no progress of the Negro in America that is permanent, so long as we have with us the monster evil prejudice.

Prejudice we shall always have between black and white, so long as the latter believes that the former is intruding upon their rights. So long as white laborers believe that black laborers are taking and holding their jobs[;] so long as white artisans believe that black artisans are performing the work that they should do; so long as white men and women believe that black men and women are filling the positions that they covet; so long as white political leaders and statesmen believe that black politicians and statesmen are seeking the same positions in the Nation's Government; so long as white men believe that black men want to associate with and marry white women, then we will have prejudice and not only prejudice, but riots, lynchings, burnings, and God to tell what next and to follow!

It is this danger that drives me mad. It must be prevented. We cannot allow white and black to drift along unthinkingly toward this great gulf and danger, that is nationally ahead of us. It is because of this, that I speak, and now call upon the soul of great white America to help.

It is no use putting off, the work must be done, and it must be started now.

Some people have misunderstood me. Some don't want to understand me. But I must explain myself for the good of America, and for the good of the world and humanity.

Those of the Negro race who preach social equality, and who are working for an American race that will in complexion be neither white nor black, have tried to misinterpret me to the white public, and create prejudice against my work. The white public, not stopping to analyze and question the motive behind criticisms and attacks, aimed against new leaders and their movements, condemn without even giving a chance to the criticised to be heard. Those who oppose me in my own race, because I refuse to endorse their program of social arrogance and social equality, gloat over the fact that by their misrepresentation and underhand methods, they were able to have me convicted for a frame up crime which they calculate will so discredit me as to destroy the movement that I represent, in opposition to their program of a new American race; but we will not now consider the opposition to a program or a movement, but state the facts as they are, and let deep souled white America pass its own judgment.

In another one hundred years white America will have doubled its population, in another one hundred years it will have trebled itself. The keen student must realize that the centuries ahead will bring us an overcrowded and over populated country; opportunities, as the population grows larger[,] will be fewer; the competition for bread between the people of their own class will become keener, and so much more so will there be no room for two competitive races, the one strong and the other weak. To imagine Negroes as District Attorneys, Judges, Senators, Congressmen, Assemblymen, Aldermen, Government Clerks, and Officials[,] Artisans and laborers at work while millions of white men starve, is to have before you the bloody picture of wholesale mob violence, that I fear, and against which I am working.

No preaching, no praying, no presidential edict will control the passion of hungry unreasoning men of prejudice when the hour comes. It will not come I pray in our generation, but it is of the future that I think and for which I work.

A generation of ambitious Negro men and women, out from the best Colleges, Universities, Institutions, capable of filling the highest and best positions in the nation, in industry, commerce, society and politics! Can you keep them back? If you do so they will agitate and throw your constitution in your faces. Can you stand before civilization and deny the truth of your constitution? What are you going to do then? You who are just will open up the door of opportunity and say to all and sundry "Enter in." But ladies and gentlemen, what about the mob, that starving crowd of your own race? Will they stand by, suffer and starve, and allow an opposite competitive race to prosper in the midst of their distress? If you can conjure these things up in your mind, then you have the vision of the race problem of the future in America.

There is but one solution, and that is to provide an outlet for Negro energy, ambition, and passion, away from the attraction of white opportunity and surround the race with opportunities of its own. If this is not done, and if the foundation for same is not laid now, then the consequences will be sorrowful for the weaker race, and be disgraceful to white ideals of justice, and shocking to white civilization.

The Negro must have a country, and a nation of his own. If you laugh at the idea, then you are selfish and wicked, for you and your children do not intend that the Negro shall discom[m]ode you in yours. If you do not want him to have a country and a nation of his own; if you do not intend to give him equal opportunities in yours; then it is plain to see that you mean that he must die even as the Indian to make room for another race.

Why should the Negro die? Has he not served America and the world? Has he not borne the burden of civilization in this Western world for three hundred years? Has he not contributed of his best to America? Surely all this stands to his credit, but there will not be enough room and the one answer is "find a place." We have found a place, it is Africa and as black men for three centuries have helped white men build America, surely generous and grateful white men and women will help black men build Africa.

And why shouldn't Africa and America travel down the ages as protectors of human rights and guardians of democracy[?] Why shouldn't black men help white men secure and establish universal peace? We can only have peace when we are just to all mankind; and for that peace, and for the reign of universal love I now appeal to the soul of white America. Let the Negroes have a Government of their own. Don't encourage them to believe that they will become social equals and leaders of the whites in America, without first on their own account proving to the world that they are capable of evolving a civilization of their own. The white race can best help the Negro by telling him the truth, and not by flattering him into believing that he is as good as any white man without first proving the racial, national[,] constructive metal of which he is made.

Stop flattering the Negro about social equality, and tell him to go to work and build for himself. Help him in the direction of doing for himself, and let him know that self progress brings its own reward.

I appeal to the considerate and thoughtful conscience of white America not to condemn the cry of the Universal Negro Improvement Association for a nation in Africa for Negroes, but to give us a chance to explain ourselves to the world. White America is too big and when informed and touched, too liberal to turn down the cry of the awakened Negro for "a place in the sun."

DNA, RG 59, file 000-612. Printed pamphlet (New York: UNIA Publications, 1924). Published also in *NW*, 6 October 1923, and *P&O*, 2: 1–7.

Marcus Garvey to Harry M. Daugherty

NEW YORK, U.S.A. October 3, 1923

Honorable Sir:

I am charged with the duty and responsibility of writing to you on a subject which I feel that you are interested in, because of your high and elevated position in the Nation, and because of your humanitarianism, which is felt to be beyond question. The subject is that of the Negro problem as it confronts us, not only in America, but in the world.

There is a deep and earnest desire on the part of some of the world's most forward looking statesmen to make an immediate effort for the settlement of the perplexing and grievous question of race. We in America should not delay the settlement of this great question, because it cannot settle itself.

The Universal Negro Improvement Association, an organization of six million scattered members of which I am President-General, is working for a solution of the problem through the founding and establishing in Africa of a nation for Negroes, where the race will be given the fullest opportunity to develop itself such as we may not expect in countries where we form but a minority in a majority Government of other races.

There is no doubt that the 20th century Negro in America is different from the Negro of the last century. To-day he is forward looking and ambitious. He is the product of our best schools, colleges and universities. With his training, he is not prepared to be satisfied as a secondary consideration in the social, economic and political life of the nation. By his ambition, he is aspiring to the highest in political office, and industrial position. This under the Constitution cannot be reasonably denied him; but in the midst of a majority race that is not inclined to allow the minority to enjoy the benefits of the best that the nation affords, we have the great problem that must be solved.

It is not the humanitarians of the white race that the Negro fears, nor those who are broadminded enough to consider the rights of man regardless of color, but it is for the great mass that does not think in the higher terms of humanity, but who are guided purely and simply by their economic, social and political relationship to others.

We of the Universal Negro Improvement Association, after having taken into consideration the impossibility of the liberal and humanitarian few to successfully curb the passion of the great mass, are endeavoring to so create sentiment among the fifteen million Negroes of America and other parts of the world, as to lead them to see that the only and best solution for the race problem is for us to have a nation of our own in Africa, whereby we would not be regarded in countries like America as competitors of the white race for the common positions in politics, industry and society, but that we would be regarded as a people striving in our own country to present to the world a civilization and culture of our own. Knowing that you must have some feeling on a question like this led the Universal Negro Improvement Association to direct me to write to you, asking for a frank and open opinion of our program. The opinion that you give will be kept private if you so desire, or may be used if you so feel inclined. Your wishes on this matter shall be respected in every particular.

The following symposium is therefore submitted to you most respectfully asking that you be good enough to answer each question in conjunction with this communication, so that we may be able to judge how much sympathy there is among the leaders of the white race in this country, as touching the effort we are making for the solution of the vexed problem of race that confronts us in America.

SYMPOSIUM

1. Do you believe the Negro to be a human being?

2. Do you believe the Negro entitled to all the rights of humanity?

3. Do you believe that the Negro should be encouraged to develop a society of his own, that is for social intercourse, and marrying within his own race?

4. Do you believe the Negro should be taught not to aspire to be the best imitation of the white man, but the best product of himself?

5. Do you believe that the Negro should be taught not to aspire to the highest political positions in Governments of the white race but to such positions among his own race in a Government of his own?

6. Do you believe that the Negro should have a Government of his own in Africa?

7. Would you help morally or otherwise to bring about such a possibility?

8. Do you believe that the Negro should be encouraged to aspire to the highest industrial and commercial positions in the countries of the white man in competition with him, and to his exclusion[?]

9. Do you believe that the Negro should be encouraged to create positions of his own in industry and commerce in a country of his own with the privilege of trading with the other races of the world?

10. Do you believe that the Negro should be encouraged to regard and respect the rights of all other races in the same manner as other races would respect the rights of the Negro?

11. Should five or six million or any large number of Negroes in the United States of America desire a repatriation to Africa in the peaceful building up of a country of their own, or in the settlement of such countries as are established among Negroes without any serious handicap to the industries of America, would you assist in this direction?

It is felt that you will give deep consideration to this communication, and receive it in the spirit in which it is written—that of a desire to amicably settle a vexed question.

I am forwarding you along with this letter, a copy of the book "Philosophy and Opinions of Marcus Garvey," and a copy of the September 1923 Number of the Magazine "Current His[to]ry," in which appears three articles on the Negro question in America, and one written by the writer of this letter.[1]

In the book "Philosophy and Opinions of Marcus Garvey," you will also find attached a reprint of a magazine article under the caption "An appeal to the soul of White America."[2] I am asking that you read the book and the articles, not with the eye of prejudice, but with the feeling of justice, in that the articles were written by a Negro from the viewpoint of a Negro, as he feels, on a question that deeply affects him.

Knowing your broadness of vision, and your liberality of soul, leads me to feel that you will judge the subject matter of the book with fairness to the race. With very best wishes, and hoping for an immediate reply, I have the honor to be, Your humble and obedient servant,

MARCUS GARVEY
President-General
Universal Negro Improvement Association

DNA, RG 60, file 198940-379. TLS on UNIA letterhead, recipient's copy. Garvey sent identical letters to selected senators, representatives, and cabinet officers.

1. The three articles on black-related topics in the September issue of *Current History* were "The Negro's Greatest Enemy," by Marcus Garvey, "Should the Color Line Go?," by Robert Watson Winston, and "The Negro Exodus from the South," by Eric D. Walrond (*Current History* 18, no. 6 [September 1923]). The UNIA later reprinted these three articles as a pamphlet.

2. Later reprinted as the first item in *Philosophy and Opinions*, vol. 2 (1925): 1–6.

Negro World Front Page

(*Source*: NW, 6 October 1923.)

Account of the Black Star Line by Capt. Hugh Mulzac in the *Cleveland Gazette*

[Baltimore, Md., ca. 6 October–3 November 1923]

WHY THE BLACK STAR LINE FAILED!

(Forwarded by Universal Service Bureau) There have been so many conflicting reports, giving various reasons for the failure of the Black Star Line that I have decided, as one of the officers of the company,[1] to publish the truth.

First: The management in the New York office was incompetent.

Second: The ships were worthless.

Third: They were used mostly for propaganda.

The office at 56 W. 135th St., New York City, consisted of the following officers to manage the B.S.L. Steamship Corporation:

Mr. Marcus Garvey, pres.; M. Jer[e]mia[h] Certain, vice-pres.; Henrietta Vinton Davis, second vice-pres., George Tobias, treas.; Smith Green, gen. mgr.; L. Johnson, traffic mgr. Not one of these persons knew the first thing about a ship or the management of shipping business. Mr. Garvey, a great organizer and the founder of the greatest Negro movement on earth, has no knowledge of ships or of the shipping business. The first vice president is a cigarmaker. The second is a reader and elocutionist. Messrs. Green, Johnson and the other officers were not at all familiar with the business. I had just returned from Europe as chief officer of the Steamship "Pasadena"[2] of the U.S. Shipping Board when a letter came to my home from Mr. Garvey asking me to come to New York City to take charge of the "Yarmouth," as chief officer. I heard of his great plans and I was very much enthused. Therefore, I immediately resigned my position with the U.S. Shipping Board and went to New York City. On my arrival, I bought five shares of the Black Star Line stock and also became a member of the U.N.I.A. From that time I was an ardent supporter of Mr. Garvey and believe[d] in him, but I never believed in the business methods of the Black Star Line and my only reason for sticking was that I thought Mr. Garvey, recognizing his inability to handle the shipping business, would eventually turn it over into the hands of experienced men before failure would come. I knew little of him at that time and did not think that he would be the man he has proven to be.

However, on Jan. 23, 1920, I boarded the Yarmouth as chief officer as she was lying at anchor outside the [S]tatue of Liberty laden with whiskey. I did not like the condition of things, for the ship had just returned from distress off Cape May and was partly water-logged. The condition of the passengers, numbering thirty-five, was pitiful. They had to sleep in cold, wet, filthy rooms and were partly frozen. I thought at that time that I was between the devil and the deep sea for I had just given up a decent position for the sake of race pride. However, I decided to fight it out and make the ship as seaworthy as possible. Captain Cockburn was master in charge at that time and I questioned him concerning the conditions. He told me that he did not intend to make the trip for Mr. Garvey and that Mr. Smith Green had drawn up the most ridiculous contract he had ever seen. Therefore, he had refused to take the ship out of New York. The cargo was worth one million dollars and the ship was chartered the day before prohibition went into effect and she had to be loaded away from the port before midnight or the cargo would be confiscated. Therefore, the freight was valued at $100,000 which the owners of the whiskey would have been glad to pay in order to get it out of New York. The Black Star Line's president and the general manager drew up a contract for $11,000 without consulting the captain. That amount would not even be enough to pay the expenses of the ship to its destination. Then again, the cargo was not even assigned to anyone and had to be put in bond in Cuba. For these reasons, Captain Cockburn refused to sail. Thereupon, the owners of the cargo approached him and offered him $2,000 to take the ship out. He accepted and sailed but unfortunately the whiskey was thrown into the ship's hold in such a hurry that the cargo shifted off Cape May as a result of bad weather, causing the ship to have a heavy list. She got water-logged and part of the cargo had to be thrown overboard, so the ship had to return to New York. The Yarmouth was built in 1885 [*1887*] in Scotland and she was a very good ship in her day but her condition at the time she was purchased by the Black Star Line was very poor. Her boiler crowns were entirely gone and had to be patched up at every port. Her hull was practically worn out and her passenger accommodations were "fierce." She was used for hauling coal during the war and was not in any shape for carrying passengers. I valued her, at the time I joined her, at about $25,000 but I learned later that they had paid $165,000 for her. We eventually sailed again for Cuba after I had succeeded in making her seaworthy and got to Cuba on March 3, 1920.

[13 October 1923]

THE "YARMOUTH" PURCHASED FOR $165,000,
SOLD FOR $6,000

. . . On the Yarmouth's arrival in Havana we were greeted by thousands of Negroes and boats of all descriptions laden with spectators hovered around the ship. I had refused to allow anyone to come aboard until I had completed cleaning and painting. This took five days. However, after that, spectators crowded her from stern to stern. The cargo was assigned to no one. Therefore, we had to lay out in the stream for two weeks before we could secure a dock in hope of getting the cargo ashore in bond. At that time there was a strike of longshoremen; it took another two weeks before we finally discharged the cargo. We were in Cuba thirty days. When the charter party for the whisky was drawn no demurrage clause was entered, the Black Star Line's manager knowing nothing of the shipping business. This caused the ship to lose the thirty days. The Yarmouth lost $500 a day for that period as a result of the delay. If a demurrage clause is entered in the charter party, it p[r]ovides that three days after the ship has arrived and is ready to discharge, it is entitled to claim any demurrage, the earning value of the ship, day by day, Sunday included. We had on board thirty-five passengers from New York bound for Jamaica and Colón, who had to be fed and kept during this time. Foodstuff in Havana was extremely high and it cost thousands of dollars for the ship's up-keep with passengers on board. However, in spite of all the trouble of the Black Star Line, there was a future for it that no other steamship had had in Cuba. The wealthy Cubans were so enthused that they were willing to give concessions, they were willing to secure the trade, if the Black Star Line would secure proper ships. They did not think much of the Yarmouth as a commercial prospect, but they were enthused over the intelligent body of officers who manned the ship, and thought of a greater future prospect for the race. After our cargo was out, we left Havana with passengers only and two days later were in Jamaica. The ship's boilers were in very bad shape and had to be welded in every port.

Our chief engineer, John O. Garrett, was one of our most intelligent young engineers and no one could have handled that ship with better skill. After our boilers had been repaired, the ship coaled and provisioned, we were ordered to Colón. There were only a few passengers on board. On our arrival, we were again greeted by thousands of Negroes who had made elaborate preparations for us. We spent three days in Colón while the captain arranged to take 500 immigrants to Cuba since the ship had no cargo. I had to build accommodations in the ship's hole for them. From Cuba, we were ordered to Bocas Del [T]oro, then A[l]m[i]rant[e] (Republic of Panama), where we loaded 100 tons of cocoanuts. Thence to Port [L]imón (Republic of Costa Rica). We had been ordered to these ports as propaganda and the U.N.I.A. gained thousands of new members as a result. The prospect of trade was very good. We then sailed to Santiago, Cuba, where we landed our immigrants and sailed for Jamaica again. On our arrival there, we arranged for a load of cocoanuts, coaled the ship, had the boilers repaired and started to load the cocoanuts when we received a telegram, signed by Mr. Garvey, ordering the ship to sail immediately for Boston, cargo or no cargo. However, we got seven hundred tons of cocoanuts on board and sailed. We could not get enough provisions in Jamaica to take the ship to Boston as it was just after the war and the British government still had its war restrictions in effect. Therefore the captain decided to call at Nassau where a little more provisions were secured. We left Nassau and made for the gulf stream, but when off Cape Hatteras, we found we would not have enough coal (or provisions) to reach Boston as the ship was burning twenty-five tons of coal daily on account of leaky boilers. We then decided to call at Norfolk, Va., to coal and provision.

On our arrival, we had orders from Mr. Garvey to proceed to Philadelphia. We had 700 tons of cocoanuts on board, assigned to New York, and they were perishable. However, we had to obey orders and proceed to Philadelphia. After carrying thru the regular program of the U.N.I.A. there, we were again ordered to Boston. After staying there two days, we were ordered to New York where we discharged the cocoanuts, partly rotten. Finally, the owners of the cocoanuts filed suit against the Black Star Line for damages. At the end of this trip, Captain Cockburn was discharged by Mr. Garvey and a white man (Captain Discon)[3] was sent to take command of the ship. O.M. Thompson, a graduate in commercial law, was then employed as general manager. The Yarmouth was again chartered to load fertilizer for Cuba. I did not know what was paid for this charter but the freight rate at that time was $22 a ton from New York to Havana, for that kind of a cargo. We were loaded with 900 tons and sailed. After five days of pleasant weather, we arrived in Cuba and landed our cargo in five days. We were then ordered to Port au Prince, Haiti. On our arrival, we found no cargo and were running out of coal and provisions, neither of which could be had there at that time. Therefore, after three days, and with our few passengers from New York to Jamaica on board, I advised the captain to leave immediately. Seeing the danger of being stranded in Haiti, he cleared at once for Jamaica. On our arrival, we had to have our boilers repaired again. At this time, a Japanese ship called the Kayo Maro was ashore on the S[er]rana Banks, 300 miles south of Jamaica, and wanted a ship to salvage part of her cargo. Mr. Wilson, a building contractor, was agent for the Black Star Line in Jamaica and, like the officers of the Line in New York, knew nothing of the shipping business. He, too, was disinclined to be advised. This was a salvage cargo, freight valued from three to five times as much as an ordinary cargo. And yet Mr. Wilson drew up a contract to take the cargo. at the same rate per ton and per cubic measurements as an ordinary cargo. It consisted of cotton, iron, glass, wire, etc., and after it was put into the ship's hole Mr. Wilson's charge was only about $12,000 when it should have been at least $40,000.

The Kayo Maro had been lying on the rocks for two weeks trying to get some ship to relieve her of part of her cargo so that the wrecking tugs would be able to pull her off, but no ship would take the risk. After a conference between the captain and myself, I advised Mr. Wilson to charter the ship's space (her hole) for $45,000, which the owners of the cargo would have been glad to pay, but Mr. Wilson would have his own way and the Black Star Line lost the difference between twelve and $45,000. The captain (white) was not interested, as this was a Negro's concern and he was only there for what he could get out of it in the way of salary. However, we sailed for the S[er]rana Banks with fifty-two passengers on board. We succeeded in getting alongside the Japanese ship, loaded in two days, with the assistance of the Japanese crew, and then proceeded to New York. On our way, we had boiler troubles again and our coal was giving out. Therefore, we had to put in at Charleston, S.C., to coal and provision again. Then concluded our trip to New York. On our arrival, I submitted a plan of the cargo to O.M. Thompson, general manager. This plan also contained its weight and cubic measurements. I drew it the two days and nights we were loading. I did not get ten minutes rest during that time so great was my anxiety to secure the Black Star Line proper pay for carrying the freight on board the ship. We had a super-cargo and a purser on board the ship (Mr. Garvey's relatives). However, when the cargo was to be checked off in New York, the Black Star Line had no one in the office who could measure it so as to check up with the owners. Therefore, they had to accept the figures submitted to them by the owners of the cargo. This was the last trip of the Yarmouth because she was unseaworthy and the boilers were bad. Finally she was taken to Morse's dry dock in Staten Island where she lay until she was sold at auction by Mr. Morse for $6,000 for wharfage.

In my next article, I will write about the Kanawa and Shadyside, the Black Star Line's other two boats. Then I will make even clearer, the cause of the failure of the B.S.L.

[20 October 1923]

THE KANAWHA LIKE THE YARMOUTH ONLY WORSE

. . . The two other boats, in addition to the Yarmouth, were the Kanawha and the Shadyside. The Kanawha was a yacht built by Seabury's Shipbuilding Company for some millionaire in 1907. During the war she was commandeered by the U.S. government for use in the navy and wartime use had practically put her boilers and engine out of commission. She was a very valuable piece of property in her day, but at the time she was purchased by the Black Star Line Company she was worth but very little and to put her in shape again would cost thousands of dollars. However, the company had paid $65,000 for her which was $55,000 more than she was worth. The Kanawha was of no material value, was no good for commercial purpose and could not even be used successfully in the West Indian Intercolonial trades. She had been very speedy, and consumed more coal than would clear her expenses. She was equipped with Seabury water-tube boilers and the most delicate and high powered piece of machinery any ship could have. At the time she was bought by the Black Star Line her boiler tubes had been practically burnt out and her machinery condensers and evaporators were all out of commission. I failed to see why such a ship was bought. She had no cargo space and could only accommodate thirty-five passengers. The Kanawha made several vain attempts to sail from New York for the West Indies.

The first was made by a white captain (Captain Swift), the very man from whom they had bought the ship and who recommended her as a first-class ship. This man could not take the ship any further than the Jersey coast and had to put in at Philadelphia. He left her there because the ship was not seaworthy. She was towed back to New York and after lying there, a few months, Mr. Garvey decided to make his excursion tour of the West Indies and Central America in his yacht, the Kanawha. He there upon contracted with the Morse [D]ry [D]ock in Staten Island to repair the ship for $25,000 and, after a wait of about two months, he had to leave for the West Indies without the Kanawha. Not knowing any better, O.M. Thompson, vice president and general manager of the Black Star Line, extended President Garvey's contract with the Morse Dry Dock Co. from $25,000 to $45,000 for the contemplated repairs on the Kanawha. When the Dry Dock Co. announced the completion of the repairs, I warned him that the ship was NOT completed and that she would never reach the West Indies, adding: "If she happens to get there, she will never return." I knew the work on the water-tube boilers was not done as it should have been. However, my advice was ignored, as usual, and the ship sailed; this time under Captain Richardson, a member of the race. As soon as the ship got outside of New York harbor, she broke down and had to return for repairs. After putting in some more tubes in her boilers, she sailed again. This time she reached Norfolk, Va.[,] then limped to Florida and Havana. It took the Kanawha 25 days to get to Cuba. A ship in good condition could make the run in three days, but as I said before she was lucky to get there at all. After some extensive repairs in Havana, she managed to get to Santiago, Cuba, and from there to Kingston, Jamaica, but crippled for fair. They tried to proceed to Colón, but could not make it. However, after Mr. Garvey spent $10,000 more on her in Jamaica she succeeded in reaching Antilla, Cuba[,] where she is still lying at anchor, if the Cuban government has not sold her for harbor dues. This was the end of $65,000 paid to Morse Dry Dock and other companies for repairs. In addition there were numerous other expenses incurred in the effort to run the ship. The Kanawha must have cost about $200,000, in all, of the Black Star Line Co.'s money and, in return, never turned in to it one cent.

I have shown how very expensive and unseaworthy was the boat Yarmouth in article 1. In article 2, I have covered the expensive and also unseaworthy Kanawha, the second of the Black Star Line's three boats. In my next and last article, I will cover the third boat's experiences, etc., and explain the "mystery ship," the Phyllis W[he]atley, and explain the status of the Orion deal which never went thru.

[27 October 1923]

THIRD BOAT LEFT TO SINK!

. . . The third, the Shadyside, was only an excursion boat built of wood. The Black Star Line Co. paid $35,000 for her. How she ever passed the steamboat inspectors, I do not know, but I do know people took desperate chances of their lives to sail in her. At no time did the boat clear its expenses, as was stated by Captain Wise (white)[,] who ran her. She made a few trips up and down the Hudson river and then was left to sink somewhere in the river. That was the last of that $35,000. The Yarmouth's cost and repair charges totaled over $200,000 as was true in the case of the Kanawha, making a total of at least $435,000, nearly a half million dollars literally squandered for the three unseaworthy and almost worthless boats.

Now about "the mystery ship," or the promised boat, the Phyllis Wheatley. There never was any ship by that name, nor was there any by the name of Frederick Douglass or Antonio Maceo. The hulks, Yarmouth, Kanawha and Shadyside, were all the boats the Black Star Line Co. ever owned,

477

and it is almost a libel of the word "boat" to call any one of them that. A loyal member of the U.N.I.A. and a stockholder in the Black Star Line Co., it made my heart ache to note the waste of money sunk in the Yarmouth, Kanawha and Shadyside.

After President Marcus Garvey sailed for the West Indies, Vice Pres. O.M. Thompson, general manager of the Black Star Line Co., started the purchase of an ex-German ship, named the Orion, and still owned by the U.S. Shipping Board. It was to be named the Phyllis Wheatley and it was claimed that $25,000 had been paid the U.S.S.B. on a bid for it. I got the ship's specifications and found that her great consumption of coal and her low rate of speed would make her an expensive boat, too. It was indeed fortunate that the Orion was not delivered to the Black Star Line Co., for she would surely have been another "white elephant" on its hands. She would have caused the loss of many more thousands of dollars of poor people's money which had been literally "thrown into the sea." Only the $25,000, which is still held by the shipping board, and which it claims as forfeit of contract, was lost on the contemplated purchase of the Orion. I had been appointed captain of the "Phyllis Wheatley" but they never got the ship, Orion, to rename it such. Thus ended the Black Star Line ships history and much of its money, up to the time of Mr. Garvey's trial.

The Black Star Line failed because its officers were totally ignorant of the shipping business and would not listen to the advice of those who were experienced in the business. They refused absolutely to employ on their office-staff any person of practical experience to assist in managing the business. Here is a lesson for our people, generally, that should not be lost.

HUGH MULZAC

Printed in the *Cleveland Gazette*, 6–27 October 1923. Original headlines abbreviated throughout.

1. Although Mulzac was employed by the BSL, there is no evidence that he was an officer of the stock-selling company.

2. In 1918, after having passed his master's license, Hugh Mulzac sailed as chief mate on the S.S. *Pasadena*. The ship sailed to Finland to deliver grain and returned to New York in 1919. With the postwar decline in shipping, however, Mulzac like other blacks, was unable to find a job with the USSB. In 1920, shortly after he returned from Europe, Garvey sent Mulzac a telegram offering him a job with the BSL (Hugh Mulzac, *A Star to Steer By* [New York: International Publishers, 1963], pp. 63–86; *Garvey Papers* 3: 48; David C. Hanson, chief, Documentation and Records Branch, U.S. Coast Guard, to Robert A. Hill, 22 October 1984).

3. When he wrote of the same event in his memoirs, Mulzac said "a Captain Dixon, a white Canadian with English papers, was hired as master" (Hugh Mulzac, *A Star to Steer By*, p. 83).

Godfrey E.P. Hertslet, British Consul, St. Louis, to Sir Henry Getty Chilton,[1] British Embassy

British Consulate, St. Louis, Mo.
8th. October, 1923

Sir,

I have the honour to transmit extract from the St. Louis "Star," giving an account of a meeting held here on Friday last, October 5th, under the auspices of the St. Louis Division of the Universal Negro Improvement Association, the President of which is S. R. WHEAT.[2]

The Meeting was addressed by MARCUS GARVEY, President-General of the Universal Negro Improvement Association, Provisional President of the Republic of Africa, etc., who appears to be conducting an active campaign.

The heading in the St. Louis "Times," which gives a shorter account of the proceedings at this Meeting, is "WAR FOR NEGRO RIGHTS IS FORESEEN BY GARVEY—We Mean to Fight to Gates of Hell, African Republic Head says."

Copy of this despatch has been forwarded to the British Passport Control Officer at New York, who has asked to be kept informed of any trace of the activities of Marcus Garvey and his associates. I am, Sir, Your obedient, humble Servant,

GODFREY E.P. HERTSLET[3]
H.B.M. Consul

PRO, FO 371/8513. TL, carbon copy.

1. Sir Henry Getty Chilton (1887–1954) served in the British Embassy in Washington, D.C., from 1918 to 1920 and again from 1921 to 1928, the last four years as minister. In subsequent years Chilton represented Britain in Santiago and Buenos Aires, as well as in Madrid during the Spanish Civil War. During World War II he returned from retirement to serve at the Ministries of Economic Warfare and Information (*Times* [London], 22 November 1954).

2. Samuel R. Wheat was a coal merchant and a partner in the firm of Green and Wheat. His partner, William M. Green, was also the treasurer of the St. Louis UNIA. In July 1923 Wheat and Green, in their capacities as officers of the UNIA local, sent a telegram to Harry M. Daugherty protesting the imprisonment of Marcus Garvey and the denial of bail (Leland Hilligoss, St. Louis Public Library, to Robert A. Hill, 25 July 1984; *Gould's St. Louis City Directory* [St. Louis: Polk-Gould Directory Co., 1923], p. 2, 580; telegram from S.R. Wheat et al., to Harry M. Daugherty, 15 July 1923, DNA, RG 60, file 198940-304).

3. Godfrey Edward Proctor Hertslet served as Great Britain's consul for the district of Arkansas, Colorado, Kansas, Kentucky, Missouri, Oklahoma, and Tennessee beginning in March 1922 (U.S. Department of State, *Register*, 1924 [Washington, D.C.: GPO, 1924], p. 268).

Enclosure

[*St. Louis Star*, 6 October 1923]

GARVEY IS HAILED AS ANOTHER CHRIST
BY NEGROES HERE

BACK-TO-AFRICA LEADER TELLS 500
HE'LL 'FIGHT LIKE HELL' TO GET THERE.

The American flag, with its forty-eight "eyes[,]" and the red, black and green flag of his projected United States of Africa, are the symbols, which when united, the world will have to look forward to for its salvation, according to Marcus Garvey, self-styled "Honorable," president of the Negro Factories Corporation, president-general of the Universal Negro Improvement Association and African Communities['] League and provisional president of the Republic of Africa, and a lot of other things, who addressed approximately 500 negroes at a meeting in Douglass Hall, Beaumont street and Lawton avenue, last night.

The meeting was sponsored by the St. Louis division of the Universal Negro Improvement Association.

Garvey is out on bond pending an appeal from a five-year sentence in the federal prison at Atlanta, which was imposed in the federal court in New York following his conviction on a charge of using the mails to defraud. He was alleged to have fleeced a number of persons through the sale of stock in the Black Star Steamship Line, which was to have been owned and operated entirely by negroes.

FLAGS USED TOGETHER.

Garvey entered the hall at the head of a column of Black Cross nurses and Knights of the Black Cross Legion, marching between the folds of the Red, White and Blue, and the Red, Black and Green, while a choir sang "God Bless Our President."

Following a prayer in which gratitude was offered God "for keeping His hand on the throttle and the train on the tracks to lead Garvey here," and "that He would keep His hands on the throttle and keep the wheels on the rails when he left," Garvey was introduced as another Christ, destined to lead the forces of the world, a martyr of his race, the morning star of negro co-operation and the Blue Knight of his race. This was followed by prolonged applause and ejaculations of "amen," and "yes, it's true," from his audience.

WEARS TUXEDO AND MUSTACHE.

Garvey, a coal black Jamaican, small and heavy set, of prepossessing appearance, wearing a Tuxedo, a mustache and indications of a beard, immediately fell into the enthusiasm of his speech.

He spoke of the world being surprised at their action and that an old estimate was held of the negroes, insofar as "that by striking the shepherd the sheep would flee." He was referring to his own incarceration in a New York jail. Garvey said it was a mistake and his listeners indorsed the remark by shouting: "A big one, too."

"We mean to fight our way to the gates of hell," continued Garvey, "for the cause of human rights and the emancipation of the black race. We are determined to get what we want, and what it takes to get it we have got. The time for action is drawing near. We will fight for a new Africa out of which will come a restored Ethiopia for the black people of the world. If the world is hard [of] hearing we will not be responsible for what happens. We love our Father's children, but of all His children, we love ourselves the best. We can't win by sitting in the parlor with silk stockings on.

HEAVEN LONG TIME OFF.

"We expect a great deal of God, but that will come when we get to heaven, and that's a long time off. Gabriel will probably blow his horn before any of us can expect to be presidents, governors or mayors.

"Congressman Dyer,[1] in whose district I understand I'm in, has failed to say anything about a civil rights bill for his district. I was not allowed to be served a chocolate sundae in a drug store this morning because I was black. They'll keep on fooling you as long as you can be fooled. Measures that are advocated for the advancement of the negro you can take with a grain of salt.

"In 200 years we will be faced with the survival of the fittest and that's what we are preparing for now. Once upon a time only two people owned the world. Look how many Adams and Eves there are now. Next time, before we go to war, we will ask for a division of the political sport, the spoils of war. White philosophers—Darwin[,] Locke, Newton and the rest—forgot that the monkey would change to a man, his tail would drop off and he would demand his share. We want our share of apples, peaches and bananas, even though there be no bananas today."[2]

Indignation was expressed by his audience as he described the seizure of his great-great-grandfather as a slave and he declared that "he was brought here against his will and he (the great-great-grandson) would fight like hell till he got back."

It was said that the proceeds of the admittance charge of 50 cents would go toward defraying Garvey's traveling expenses and that he also would get a "bonus."

Printed in the *St. Louis Star*, 6 October 1923. Found in PRO, FO 371/8513.

1. Leonidas C. Dyer (1871–1957) served in the U.S. Congress from 1911 to 1913 and from 1915 to 1933 (*WWWA*).
2. "Yes, We Have No Bananas," by Frank Silver and Irvin Cohen, was a hit song of 1923. Introduced by Eddie Cantor in a revue entitled "Make It Snappy," the song caught on quickly. Garvey's reference parodies the song's lyrics (David Ewen, *American Popular Songs* [New York: Random House, 1966], pp. 453–454; Nat Shapiro, *Popular Music* [New York: Adrian Press, 1969], p. 113).

Report by Special Agent James E. Amos

New York, N.Y. Oct. 19/23

RE: U.S. VS. MARCUS GARVEY, ET AL.

In connection with the above entitled matter, from a confidential source Agent learned that MARCUS GARVEY's brother-in-law, CLEVELAND JACQUES, has arrived in the United States from JAMAICA, W.I., for the purpose of assisting GARVEY in making his escape from America.[1] GARVEY is reported to be in Los Angeles, Calif., at the present time.[2] However, informant has promised Agent that just as soon as he gets anything definite regarding the attempt to escape he will communicate with Agent at once.

Agent is keeping in close touch with the situation and will notify the Bureau immediately on receipt of further information. CONTINUED.

JAMES E. AMOS

DJ-FBI, file 61. TD.

1. Jacques arrived in Philadelphia on 19 September 1923. The United States consul in Kingston, Jamaica, monitored his departure from Jamaica and reported to the State Department, which noted that Jacques "is considered undesirable and a racial agitator." The department did not attempt to prevent him from being given a visa, however (R.C. Bannerman to W.W. Husband, 18 September 1923, DNA, RG 59, file 000-612).

2. On 16 October Garvey cabled an editorial from Los Angeles to the *Negro World* (*NW*, 20 October 1923).

Sen. William E. Borah to Marcus Garvey

[*Washington, D.C.*] October 19, 1923

My dear Mr. Garvey:

I have your letter of the 8th which I have gone over carefully.

I should certainly like to be helpful to the negro race. I have, in common with thousands of others, thought much over the perplexing problem of what is best for the colored race. I have never been in favor of the African colonization or proposition. It has never seemed to me either practicable or in the last analysis humane. I do not believe the negroes would to any marked degree accept of any such proposition.

But nevertheless, I am quite willing to be convinced and I shall be glad to consider any literature which you may send me. If I should come to the conclusion I am in error, I should frankly say so. I only want to know what is best for the colored people and I shall undertake to work along that line after I have ascertained that fact. Very respectfully,

[WILLIAM E. BORAH][1]

DLC, W.E. Borah Papers, general office file, box 133. TL, carbon copy.

1. William E. Borah (1865–1940) served as a U.S. senator from Idaho from 1907 until 1940. Borah was a well-known isolationist who opposed the U.S. entrance into the League of Nations and the World Court (*WBD*; Marion McKenna, *Borah* [Ann Arbor: University of Michigan Press, 1961]; Robert James Maddox, *William E. Borah and American Foreign Policy* [Baton Rouge: Louisiana State University Press, 1969]).

Henry C. Wallace to Marcus Garvey

[*Washington, D.C.*] October 20, 1923

Dear Mr. Garvey:

Your letter of October 4 came while I was absent on a western trip and has just now come up to me. There are so many things clamoring for my attention now that I do not have time to give your letter the consideration it seems to merit. Also I want to read your book and the magazine article. I am sure I shall find them interesting. Very sincerely,

HENRY C. WALLACE

DNA, RG 16, general correspondence. TL, carbon copy.

John W.H. Crim to Marcus Garvey

[*Washington, D.C.*] October 23rd., 1923

Sir:

This Department acknowledges receipt of your letter of the 3rd instant, relative to the Negro Problem of the World, in which you request that certain questions set out therein regarding the race to be answered.

In reply I regret to inform you that the Attorney General is not authorized to render opinions or furnish advice to others than the President or the heads of the several executive Departments, and in view of this ruling it would be impracticable to comply with your request.

The publications which accompanied your letter are being returned to you under separate cover. Respectfully, For the Attorney General:

JOHN W.H. CRIM
Assistant Attorney General

DNA, RG 60, file 198940-379. TL, carbon copy.

Marcus Garvey to R. R. Moton

Oakland, California October 23rd, 1923

Dear Doctor Moton:—

I am on a trip that will take me through the South. I expect to be in Birmingham on the 30th inst. My wife is travelling with me and I would like to show her Tuskegee and some of the work of the late Dr. Washington. With this in view I am arranging to visit your Institution on the 31st inst., to the 1st prox. I am asking therefore, if you could be good enough to provide lodgings of two rooms at the Institute for us on the occasion. My party includes a lady secretary [*Enid Lamos*], my wife and self.

Thanking you in anticipation. With best wishes. Yours truly,

MARCUS GARVEY

ATT, RRM, general correspondence, 1923. TLS on UNIA letterhead, recipient's copy.

Editorial Letter by Marcus Garvey

[[Oakland, Cal. October 23, 1923]]

THE WONDERS OF THE WHITE MAN IN BUILDING AMERICA

Fellow Men of the Negro Race, Greeting:

Away out on the Pacific Coast of America I view with alarm, yet with hope, the future of our race.

I have reached this section of America through a trip of several weeks from New York on the East, and in my travels everywhere I saw before me the wonders wrought by the white man's skill, daring and perseverance. On every hand I came in contact with his rising civilization—that for which he will die, holding it as sacred to his generation and to posterity.

THE KU KLUX KLAN

I have traveled through and am now in the stronghold of the Ku Klux Klan, that mighty white organization that faces America with a program that is supported by every second man in the nation, whether he wants to confess it or not.

The Klan has captured the South, the West, the Northwest and the Middle West, and it is only a question of time when that organization will in truth be the most powerful weapon of the white race in prosecuting their ideal of white supremacy in America.

No Time to Waste

The Universal Negro Improvement Association has never fought the Klan as an organization, and does not intend to do so in America, for it will be useless and non-availing, except to the point when all will unite against us for supremacy—namely, Jew, Catholic and Klan.

The Universal Negro Improvement Association knows America will always be a white man's country, including all elements of that race. Then why waste time in attempting the impossible and in allowing others to make fools of us?

Responsibility of Saving the Negro

The responsibility of saving the race rests upon our leaders of today, and it is for us to realize that any wholesale antagonism of a group of people who are in a position to enforce their likes and dislikes will but redound to the disadvantage of the unfortunate minority, such as we are, and surrounded as we are by a 90 per cent. Klan spirit, unspoken though it be. Ninety per cent. of white America is sympathetically Klan and would be untrue to itself if it were not. Our relationship, therefore, is like that of the sheep to the lion; the former, then, must be very careful not to be devoured by the latter; and thus we warn the race to be careful in the handling of propaganda against the Knights of the Ku Klux Klan, for the majority of those who seemingly are opposed to the Klan, and who have been inviting Negroes to fight with them against the Klan, are greater and more heartless Klansmen than the Knights themselves. It is purely a question of "NEGROES, WATCH YOUR STEPS AND YOUR (?) FRIENDS."

The Solution of the Problem

There is but one solution of this great problem, and that is for the Negro to look toward building for himself, for neither the Klan nor any other group of white men intend to hand over to Negroes the civilization and materialism of America, which they have spent their strength and blood to create. If the Klan and the white race want to make America a white man's country, as they ultimately will, then why not 400,000,000 Negroes unite and make Africa a black man's country, and thus save a conflict of ideals and aspirations that is bound to end disastrously to the weaker race?

America, the country with the program of the greatest good for the greatest number, will always be that of the white man, for he is in the majority. 'Tis hard, 'tis woefully hard, for a Du Bois or a Weldon Johnson to admit this, but how can one wisely "kick against the pricks?"[1]

Get Busy and Build Nation

Negroes, get busy building a nation of your own, for neither Europe nor America will tolerate us as competitors in another half century. Let's get busy now, and, like the Ku Klux Klan and Knights of Columbus,[2] fight for those ideals that are possible—not to ever see a black President, Governor, Cabinet Officer or Mayor in the country or state where the white man forms the majority population, but of ourselves to build up Africa, where our race will have the opportunity to rise to the highest positions in society, industry and government.

DON'T BE DECEIVED

I appeal to the black race of America not to allow itself to be deceived by the professions of a Dyer with his antilynching bill, or a Morefield Storey, Spingarn or Mary White Ovington with their oily tongues of hypocrisy and deception. There is no white man in the world who could afford, at this time of the fight for the survival of the fittest, to be more interested in another race than his own. He would either be a traitor or a fool. If the ideals of black and white clash in America, how is it possible for these persons to better serve the black race through the National Association for the Advancement of Colored People than their own? These people tell us to fight the Ku Klux Klan, because they know well that if any one is to suffer for so doing it will not be the advisers, but the doers. They tell us that we must fight against the methods of the President, or the programs of the Republican or Democratic parties; but if any one is to suffer for so doing it is Negroes, and not the "PHILANTHROPISTS."

DYER AND HIS ANTI-LYNCHING BILL

Dyer is so sincere in opposing the Klan for Negroes and in carrying an anti-lynching bill in Congress to protect Negroes that in his own State and in his own Congressional District in St. Louis a Negro cannot drink a soda in a white drug store or eat a sandwich in a white restaurant for the want of a civil rights bill! Yet he flies around the nation telling us about the anti-lynching bill, which, if passed, would mean nothing more than other laws already on the statutes, but ineffective in their application to the Negro.

Dyer's bill is not to stop the mob; it is to punish the mob. But the deed is already done. Who will be the judge and jury to punish the mob but the brother and cousins of the violators of the law? And yet Dyer and his gang think they can fool all of the people for all of the time.

CATCHING THE NEGRO

Once upon a time the Negro was caught by the brandishing of the red kerchief; then, later, by the beating of the drum, and now in the twentieth century our good friends try to catch us with high-sounding words and promises; but some of us have come from Missouri, Mr. Dyer's own State, and you have to "show us."[3] Dyer gloried in the conviction of Garvey in his speeches for the National Association for the Advancement of Colored People, because he knew that Garvey was one of the Negroes he could not fool for all of the time. If Dyer does not know, let me tell him that I was in his Congressional District in St. Louis two weeks ago and could not get a soda served even by a dirty Greek, who kept his so-called white soda fountain in a Negro section, the section represented by the "famous" anti-lynching advocate. Oh! the hypocrisy of this world! Here do I leave my untidy home, crusading for the cause of having others clean up that which I failed to do in my own house!

CONGREGATION OF ANIMALS

I was traveling down the street and came upon a great congregation of animals of all kinds. There I saw lions, tigers, elephants, bears, foxes, sheep, goats, dogs, cats, rats and fowls. I observed that every species kept to itself; the tigers were afraid of the company of the lions; the elephants were not uniting with the tigers; the foxes tried to escape the bears; the rats were running away from the cats, and even the fowls were just nervous about the appearance of the foxes, and therefore I learned a great lesson. The fox hobnobbing with the fowl can have but one object, and that is in some way to steal a chicken. And then do I see that the presence of any opposite animal, human or otherwise, in the midst of others means that some stealing is to be done, either in ideals, character, pride, vision or life.

TELLING THE NEGRO THE TRUTH

Those who tell the Negro what they mean are the Negro's greatest friends. Those who hide their intention under the guise of fellowship, philanthropy and Christianity are our greatest enemy. If I were to decide between the Ku Klux Klan and Dyer as friends of the Negro I would choose the Ku Klux Klan, because they are honest enough to tell me what they mean—"white supremacy"—and thereby give me a chance to save myself, rather than the other fellow, who tries to tell me it is daylight when, indeed, he knows that night is approaching. Does Dyer stand for white supremacy or black ascendancy? He dares not answer in favor of the latter, and be a man and a Christian, even as his colleagues are unable to answer. Then they are to us as much members of the Invisible Empire as any outspoken Klansman, who is not afraid nor ashamed to tell America and the world what he means.

HOW THE NEGRO IS TO RISE

If the Negro is to rise he must look to himself and to those of the white race who are honest enough to tell him his faults and help him to be the best of himself and not expect to be the nearest imitation of a white man.

ROOM FOR EVERYBODY

There is room in the world for white and black, both having their eye set upon ideals of their own without deception or hypocrisy. There is room enough in America for the white man and there is room enough in Africa for the black man. Then let us strive after those things that are possible and not be deceived. With best wishes for your success, I have the honor to be Your obedient servant,

MARCUS GARVEY
President-General
Universal Negro Improvement Association

Printed in *NW*, 27 October 1923. Original headlines abbreviated.

1. A reference to Acts 9:5, "I am Jesus whom thou persecutest: it is hard for thee to kick against the pricks."

2. The Knights of Columbus, an organization of Roman Catholic laymen, was chartered in 1882 as a mutual benefit society. The Knights established councils within the United States and abroad. Primarily a social organization, the Knights opposed communism and other movements it considered contrary to the interests of Catholicism. The organization was bitterly opposed to the Ku Klux Klan which, in turn, charged the Knights of Columbus with being the armed and subversive agents of the Pope (*Collier's Encyclopedia* [New York: Macmillan, 1980], 14: 120; Kenneth T. Jackson, *The Ku Klux Klan in the City: 1915–1930*, pp. 12, 38, 179).

3. Missouri is known as the "show me" state (Federal Writers' Project, *Missouri: A Guide to the "Show Me" State* [1941; reprint ed., St. Clair Shores, Mich.: Somerset Publishers, 1973]).

Robert L. Vann to James Weldon Johnson

518 Fourth Avenue Pittsburgh, Pennsylvania
Oct. 27, 1923

Dear Sir:

The enclosed is a verified copy[1] of a letter sent by Marcus Garvey to a certain United States Senator. I am sending you the letter in full. Read it, contemplate its contents and make any use of it you care to make. Do not disclose your source of information. I have my personal reason for making this request.

It is the opinion of the writer that this letter has been prepared by Garvey and sent out to many United States Senators for the purpose of seeking through them some medium of escaping from the Federal Prison. Without disclosing my source of information, I expect to make bold use of it in THE PITTSBURGH COURIER. The letter was sent under date of October 22, 1923 on official stationery of the U.N.I.A. Yours truly,

The Pittsburgh Courier Pub. Co.
R.L. VANN
Editor

DLC, NAACP. TLS on *Pittsburgh Courier* letterhead, recipient's copy.

1. This letter was the same as the one sent by Garvey to Attorney General Harry M. Daugherty, on 3 October 1923 (see *Garvey Papers* 5: 468–470).

James Weldon Johnson to Robert L. Vann

[*New York*] October 30, 1923

Dear Mr. Vann:

I have your letter of the 27th with the enclosed copy of a letter which has been prepared by Garvey to be sent out to certain United States senators. I am very glad you let us see this and we will decide on the very best use we can make out of it. I am particularly glad to know that so widely read and influential a paper as the *Pittsburgh Courier* is going to give this communication the sort of publicity that it deserves. The letter is a very insidious appeal to the egotism which is dormant, if not active, in ninety-nine out of every hundred white men. Yours very truly,

[JAMES WELDON JOHNSON]
Secretary

DLC, NAACP. TL, carbon copy.

Robert L. Vann to James Weldon Johnson

518 Fourth Avenue Pittsburgh, Pennsylvania
Oct. 31, 1923

Dear Mr. Johnson:

I have your letter of October 30 acknowledging my enclosure to you under date of October 27. I note that you are under the impression that the letter is "to be sent out." You are mistaken, it has been sent out and the letter forwarded to me by a senator whose confidence I happen to enjoy. I suspect a similar letter has been sent to all senators. The attitude of southern senators can be anticipated with almost mathematical accuracy.

Personally I have never exercised myself over Garvey and his nonsense but when his propaganda takes the insidious form so apparent in the letter sent to senators, I feel that I should make my little contribution toward whatever opposition can be created against such a malicious program. Yours truly,

The Pittsburgh Courier Pub. Co.
R. L. VANN
Editor

DLC, NAACP. TLS on *Pittsburgh Courier* letterhead, recipient's copy.

Address by Marcus Garvey

Chapel [*Tuskegee Institute*] Nov. 1, 1923

Dr. Moton, The Faculty and Students and Friends of Tuskegee:

It affords me a great deal of pleasure to find myself among you and to say a few words bearing on the struggle of a race for a place in the world.

First of all I must pay my respects to the great man, Dr. Washington. To me, Dr. Washington stands out as the greatest man of America—yea, the greatest man in the Western world; all that he has created he has given to the world. He has created a philos[o]phy that has changed the destiny of another race. I am only sorry we hadn't Mr. Washington 50, 30, 20 or even 10 years ago.[1]

The founder of Tuskegee has been brutally criticised, condemned on the one hand; on the other he has been praised. But he hasn't received the reward merited for the work he did to uplift this struggling race of ours. They condemned him because he taught industrial education and the dignity of labor. Dr. Washington taught us the dignity of labor. Had he not fostered his program of industrial education we today in this country could not boast of the wealth that we now possess and the clean homes which we have and the clean lives that we live. I have traveled throughout the nation, from coast to coast. I am just returning from such a trip that took me out to California from New York and I have come in contact with the living work of Dr. Washington out in California[,] out in the Northwest and out in the Middle West where there is a greater amount of prosperity. We find our people building homes— not the old log cabin homes but beautiful homes and when you strike such cities as Los Angeles and Portland[2] and Kansas as a stranger you could not tell in some parts beautiful homes that the Negroes have built. This is the work of 5, 10 or 20 years—the work of this great man, the son of Tuskegee.

It is true, Dr. Washington did not represent all within the race. It[']s impossible for any one man to represent the people[,] you know. Dr. Washington was not a politician or a professional statesman; he was essentially an industrial leader and as such he stands out not only in America but all over the world as the greatest of them all. Because in the beginning he taught his people to take nothing and make something, not only in his country but throughout the whole world. The whole world looks to Tuskegee and great men and great women visit Tuskegee in person; they want to see Tuskegee and its work as fostered by the great man whose death all of us lament.

As I have said, Dr. Washington has left to mankind a name to be proud of for all time by this race of ours; and because out of Tuskegee, out of his work, out of his philosophy great things have come and you who are here tonight and you who are staying at Tuskegee are the ones that we will be looking forward to [to] create some of this great influence in the future.

I hope that among you as a student body we have many more Washingtons; because not only America but the entire Negro world is in need of such characters. As I said before, if we had Mr. Washington a quarter of a century ago we would have been better off but nevertheless, through the inspiration and the teachings of his successor and those who are supporting him we feel sure that this institution will continue to give inspiration to the race. All of us cannot be engaged in the same occupation; some of us are not industrial leaders in the proper sense of it; some of us are preachers; some of us are public men; some of us are endeavoring to be politicians and statesmen, and the world needs such men. No nation is made up exclusively of any one class of men but the nation is made up of men of different callings, the great American nation of which we are citizens and of which some of us are a part in spirit and a part in feeling and a part in sympathy.

This nation is made up, I say, of men in different walks. We have heard and seen[,] some of us; men like Roosevelt; a great statesman Roosevelt was. We are still reading of him; we are still reading of men like William Jennings Bryan, Woodrow Wilson, Warren Harding and of the great and present President Coolidge. These men stand out as leaders of the people; leaders of the nation; we call them statesmen. We call some of them politicians. Upon them rests the responsibility of leading the people; and of directing the affairs of the government. Yet in the great change that is coming over the world there will yet be just government; and I feel sure you will one day be called upon in this nation of America or in some other nation—probably a nation of your own race of people—to play your part and surely all of us will not be industrial leaders; all of us will not be politicians; all of us will not be statesmen; but each and every one will have his or her work to do to make up the great order of society. At the present time some of us are more hopeful for the race, although there are some who have their heads down, hopeless, visionless; have no faith and confidence in this. There are some of us who have more faith and confidence in the future; confidence in ourselves, in our Creator; that confidence and that faith bid us look forward to brighter things, to a greater day when some of us will fit ourselves into the affairs of government; fit ourselves into the affairs of the nation and be real men and real women. I believe such was part of the inspiration of the great man of Tuskegee, Dr. Washington. I believe he had it in his mind; he had visions of brighter things than he accomplished all of the time. He had a time and a place for everything and I believe today his . . . [*words mutilated*].

Out of Tuskegee will come great men and women of the future and I have no doubt that such of them are found among you now in the making. There is a chance for you young men and women. Our forefathers were environed differently; they were slaves; they had no will of their own; they had no purpose of their own; they did not know themselves; but the environments of today give us a freedom of action and a freedom of thought so that it is possible for you to rise to the highest position possible that you desire to create for yourselves. Now, that is the thought that I want to leave with you, the student body of Tuskegee; that you cannot rise higher than yourselves. As high as you desire to rise in the world that is your limit. The Great Creator has placed a limitation on man; He has placed a limitation on the angels, creating both naturally. He has placed certain limits to which we can rise, ascend; and in the limited place, by God, you and I and all of us can rise to the highest in our thoughts and actions. If you remain down you have no one to blame but yourselves; blame it not on God. Blame it not on your fellow citizen; blame it not on any other race. Some people say that the white man keeps the Negro down. No one can keep you down; and I trust the students of Tuskegee do not have that belief and do not voice that opinion that we are kept down because of the white man or we are kept down because of somebody else. We are kept down because of ourselves! If you feel your insignificance and believe that you can be nothing yourself but a serf and a slave, that shall you be. If you regard yourself as a human being, if you believe yourself to be a man created by the same source or by whatsoever name you call the Great One who has brought this old universe into existence, just so much shall we find our place in the world. If you have the conviction that you cannot be as successful, as prosperous as the other fellow, then surely you shall not be as successful and as prosperous.

We look at the world and we see the great white man. I call him great because indeed he is great; he has imagination and understanding. He has mastered the understanding of himself to the point where he has a full control of all things material and temporal, by his keen study of nature, by his keen study of God and by his keen study and knowledge of himself. From this he has become the master of the world and of the material situation that concerns us, and our failure in the past to rise has been due to the fact that we fail to conceive our God as He is, who loves all His creatures. He has no particular place for you in the world, so far as our occupations go. He didn't make a man to be a street-cleaner; or a shoe shine or a porter and then make another man especially to be a banker, a senator or a congressman or a president of a nation. God made all men; gave them the same physical being and extended to all the same opportunity in nature, to enjoy nature, to enjoy His greatest purpose and plan and if you can't find no better position or better place in the world than being just a shoe shine or a bell hop or a porter then you will blame it not to God. You will blame it to no one around you. You will blame it to yourself as feeling that you are not fit for the highest calling.

Now, the difference between the great white race and the black race is this. That every white boy and girl has the ambition, has the feeling that he or she can rise to the highest and "I will rise to the highest and I will push myself to the highest." Now, that is the boy who will do for himself and not others do for him. That's the difference between the great white race and the black race. The white race does for itself. The black race depends upon others to do. I trust that the Tuskegee spirit that you have will make you realize that your place in the world will be cut out by yourselves, will be made by yourselves and not by others. Repeating myself, no one can keep you down but yourself[.]

The new doctrine that some of us are preaching is of that kind, and we are endeavoring to inspire this present generation to look forward to the highest in society, in industry, in politics. We say that whatever other peoples have been able to do we also are able to do by application. And that is the point that I trust you will take from me tonight; that you must assiduously work out your own salvation. When you leave Tuskegee, when you go out into the larger world to grapple with men and human affairs you must do it with the feeling and conviction of men believing that your place is there; that God has placed no limit on you and that you are just going to rise to the place that you have got in mind.

Now, as I have said before, we are not all going to be industrialists; we are not all going to wear out the plow. Some of us will have to work there. We are not all going to work in the garden; some of us will have to be porters. Some are looking for the larger opportunities, to indulge in the larger life. For that no one will blame you. No one can work successfully to keep you back.

Perhaps I have been represented to you or come to your knowledge anyhow as being one who is not favorable to the white race. I trust that I may here now hope that you will not indulge in such further belief. I love all humanity personally but I believe that each group in this great human family has its own problem and should produce its own leaders to solve that problem. The great white race has its own problem. It desires to be the supreme race in the world. I do not blame them. If I were a white man and a member of the white race my duty would be to keep my race ahead, to [m]ake it the most progressive and prosperous race in the world and to control things; control the whole world if possible; the whole universe. That would [b]e [m]y highest ambition. And if I were belonging to the Yellow Asiatic race I would feel in similar manner. I am a member of the Negro race and therefore my supreme duty in life is to help advance the interests of my race, respecting the rights of others. I believe that the real white man of America respects the rights of the Negro and of other races. Such white men as have helped our lamented founder to build this great institution and such other men as will ultimately save the world—the world is so wrought up today; it has become so malignant; one race against the other that but for the good ones in every race we would be looking forward to a terrible holocaust that would destroy the whole entire human race; but with such white men as have helped the founder of Tuskegee to make this institution, with good men of the yellow and black races we look forward to a solution of this great human problem. It may be a thousand years from now but I feel that the spirit of such men will triumph ultimately. But we are in the making; we are in the reign of racial selfishness and it seems to me that might has become right; unfortunately might had become right; the might of the nation rules the world; the strength and might of the race rules the people and it would appear that we have practically to meet power with power and might with might and that is why the yellow peoples of Asia are looking forward to the building of great imperialisms to match the imperialisms of Europe, where we have a powerful Anglo-Saxon nation like the British and where we have a powerful race like the French and a powerful race like the Italian. The Yellow peoples are endeavoring to build up a similar power among themselves and it would appear that is the only way we are going to bring about this compromise and thus come back to our broader sense in the desire to be one great family; and therefore some of us of the black race are looking forward to the time when this race of ours will be able to advance to the terms of government, in the terms of nation-[*hood?*]. I mean by that that one of these days some of us are to be that.

There is a great British Government; there is a great French Government, a great Chines[e] Government or Japanese Government; some day there will also be a great black government where the black peoples of the world—fifteen millions of Americans, say—and the millions of these from the western world and the millions of Americans will have come together of themselves and create a great nation where it happens to dwell or find itself; as we in America find that we are surrounded with terrible environment; environment that we ourselves did not create but which our great brother has created and he controls by his major power and it is well that we understand ourselves and our relationship with that brother; it is well that we know that he has in his heart the belief and the determination that he shall rule this great country. And that minority groups, such as we are[,] shall but play a second part that has been laid out for us. We well realize it and by knowing it we will be able to so direct and guide ourselves as to save ourselves from harm or trouble or conflict that may happen and come about because of not knowing better. We know that we have certain limits foist upon us; that the fullest of our ambitions and toil cannot be realized; that we will never have the opportunity—none of us—to be president of a nation or a senator or a congressman representing a senatorial district of the South or North. Yet we have the ambition to be the best and God has not limited us beyond that ambition and I feel that is the desire and that is the reason why some of us are looking out for larger opportunities and I know well that the great white man in this country when the time comes and you present a proper program through unity will at least do something to satisfy that ambition that has been put in us. The thing that the American white man needs is a program from the Negro—Booker Washington gave an industrial program that was reasonable, was clear. There were white men of the nation ready to come to the rescue and come to the assistance and I believe in other departments, social and political, when we can through unity of purpose present a program to the great white man of America he will have to hear because a nation of fifteen million must be felt.

And before I close, as I am about to now, I want to pay my respects to the Southern white man. Now, I have some particular notions and beliefs as a man and as a thinker; and this is my opinion of the Southern white man: I believe that the Southern white man has done more within recent times to help the Negro than any other white man in this country or in the world; not only helped the Negro of America but he has helped the Negro of the world. Now, that's strange and I am mindful of the terrible institutions that still exist here, the outrages that we cry out against. It is strange probably for a man from the North to say that; but I have said that because I am convinced that if there is any progress that is worth while in America today, if there is industrial progress, commercial progress and social progress and even religious progress and if there is anything like race conscienciousness in America today; if [there is] anything like race consciousness in the western world and in the entire world among Negroes it is due to the prejudice of the Southern white man who doesn't deny the fact that he has his prejudices and that he has placed a social and other limits to this race of ours by making us to understand that there is a difference between the two races socially and otherwise. The Southern white man has given us a conscience and I feel there is going to be a solution of this great race problem and is going to be the making of this race of ours.

I tell you this, if I have any race pride at all, if I have any love for race at all, I didn't get it from anybody else but from the Southern white man; and if I ever rise to be anything in the world by way of helping my race or to find a better place for the race in the world I will ever give the glory and credit of it to the Southern white man for driving home to me the conscience of pride and of race. When I realize that this difference exists and that we can go so far and no farther, it gives me the courage to do for myself, such courage as has been given to the hundreds and thousands of men who are making good of our race throughout this country. When we think of your fine doctors, your lawyers and your ministers and your great industrial magnates that we are producing now, when we think of all of that, you will have to give credit to the Southern white man for giving us that pride and conscience.

There is going to be a better understanding. Great things are ahead of us and greater opportunities are ahead of us but with good leaders to gather the people and direct the thoughts of the world; and I cannot but th[a]nk Dr. Moton and the faculty for the wonderful insight they are giving you into this problem of race and of the future, and the inspiration that they are giving you for fitting you to help solve it. This problem must be solved. We cannot hide ourselves from it. We cannot ignore it. All the races—kings of the world are presenting their men and leaders to solve these problems. England is presenting David Lloyd George; France is presenting Poincaré and Clemenceau and Italy is presenting its Orlando and Mussolini[3] and the great America is presenting its William Jennings Bryan, its Woodrow Wilson and our Coolidge and our Harding. And it is our duty in America as part of the great American common wealth, as part of the great American citizenry to find our own leaders and push them forward, get behind them and stand behind them.

I am pleased with the manner in which you have unitedly stood behind your leader, Dr. Moton, so as to give him confidence and courage to go through the country and speak not only to us but to speak to the white race; speak to the nation and the world. We must find such leaders; we must morally and financially support them and I hope the time will come when we will have a greater Tuskegee, a Tuskegee not only assisted and supported by the contributions of philanthropic, Christian, liberal-minded white men but a Tuskegee supported by some of you students who will become men and women in the future; a Tuskegee that will be supported by our successful business men so that the larger Tuskegee can take on the larger vision which Dr. Washington dreamed. Because I still believe, I still hold the opinion Dr. Washington had in his mind greater things; many great things that he hoped to accomplish during his life time and I trust that the vision of the great man will not perish; and I hope that some of you will go out and that yet from those things will claim an even larger and greater attention. (Applause).

ATT, general files. TD, stenciled copy.

1. Booker T. Washington became the first principal of Tuskegee forty-two years before Garvey's speech. The Tuskegee Normal and Industrial Institute was established by the Alabama general assembly in February 1881, officially opening in July 1881. Washington was appointed to head Tuskegee after General Samuel C. Armstrong (president of Hampton Institute, where Washington was an instructor) recommended him to Tuskegee trustees, telling them that he was "the best man we ever had here." Washington held the position until his death in November 1915 (Louis R. Harlan, ed., *Booker T. Washington Papers*, 2: 107–109, 127, 137).
2. Garvey visited Portland, Oreg., 11–13 October on his trip west (*NW*, 10 November 1923).
3. Benito Mussolini (1883–1945), leader of the Italian Fascist movement, came to power at the end of October 1922 (*WBD*; Dennis Mack Smith, *Mussolini* [New York: Alfred A. Knopf, 1982]).

Marcus Garvey to R. R. Moton

At Tuskegee. Ala. November 2, 1923

Dear Sir;—

Please accept my thanks for the accommodation afforded me during my stay at your institution.

I must state that I am very much impressed with the wonderful work that is being done for the uplift of the race.

Language fails me to express my high appreciation for the service Dr. Washington has rendered to us as a people.

You will find herein enclosed a small donation to the institution of $50.00[.] You may count on me as one of your annual supporters. With very best wishes. Yours truly,

MARCUS GARVEY

ATT, RRM, general correspondence, 1923. TLS, recipient's copy.

Sen. Frank B. Willis to Marcus Garvey

Columbus, Ohio 21 Federal Building
November 5, 1923

Dear Mr. Garvey:

I have your letter relative to the movement in which your Association is interested. I have not yet had time to examine the literature which has come to me on this question. I do not mind saying, however, that my own view has always been that the negro, having been here in America about as long as the white people have been here and having been a part of its history and development, should work out his destiny here.

This statement is made as explanatory of my general views of the question and is not to be taken as prejudicial against propositions which may be set forth in the literature which I shall read with interest. Very truly,

[FRANK B. WILLIS][1]

OC-HS, collection 325, box 16, folder 68. TL, carbon copy.

1. Frank B. Willis (1874–1928), a Republican lawyer, served as Ohio's senator from 1921 until 1927. Willis's prior career included service as a member of the Ohio legislature (1900–1904), as a U.S. congressman (1911–1915), and as Ohio's governor (1915–1917) (*WWW*).

R. R. Moton to Marcus Garvey

[*Tuskegee Institute, Alabama*] November 6, 1923

My dear Mr. Garvey:—

I was very much gratified to have your contribution of Fifty Dollars towards the support of the work of the Tuskegee Institute, and I wish to take this opportunity to thank you for having come to see the work of Tuskegee Institute and to give Mrs. Garvey the opportunity of seeing it also. Our students and teachers alike were most appreciative of the address which you delivered in the Institute Chapel. I know that your sentiments of race pride will be an inspiration to our young people here.

Our Treasurer's receipt for the amount of your contribution is herewith enclosed. Yours very truly,

[R. R. MOTON] PRINCIPAL

ATT, RRM, general correspondence, 1923. TL, carbon copy.

James Weldon Johnson to Robert L. Vann

[*New York*] November 9, 1923

Dear Mr. Vann:

I was glad to get your letter of October 31.

You are entirely right about the effect that the Garvey correspondence will have upon certain senators. In your letter you say Southern senators, but I believe his letter will have the effect which you anticipate upon nine-tenths of all the men in the Senate. It is the sort of insidious propaganda that appeals to the in[n]ate egotism of the white man. We shall take steps to oppose and counteract the program involved in Garvey's letter. Yours very truly,

[JAMES WELDON JOHNSON]
Secretary

DLC, NAACP. TL, carbon copy.

Editorial by Robert L. Vann

[*Pittsburgh Courier*, 10 November 1923]

Heretofore, the Pittsburgh Courier has not taken any par[ticular] position with respect to the Garvey and anti-Garvey controversy. We have contented ourselves with publishing what [both] factions had to say merely as a matter of news value. As [lon]g as Garvey confines his activity to interesting Negroes in [wan]ting to go to Africa at their own expense, we have nothing [to] say. Since some Negroes just delight to be fleeced, we are as [con]tent to see Garvey fleece them as any one else.

But when Garvey seeks to interest the United States Government in the expatriation of Negroes whose blood has long [since] bought their right to a peaceful residence in this country, the Pittsburgh Courier revolts at the idea, and views it as [insi]dious. The letter published below[1] was sent to a United States Senator by Garvey himself. It bears Garvey's signature. [We] publish it as a disclosure to the world of the dangerous ex[tre]mes to which Garvey will resort to continue his impractica[ble] program at the expense of gullible Negroes; and at the same [time] induce the Federal Government to underwrite his preach[men]ts. He may be trying to interest Senators in a pardon, and [he] may be "selling his whole race for a pardon," but the Pittsburgh Courier can inform Mr. Garvey that his letter will never [earn] for him a pardon, nor for his impracticable scheme any [fe]deral sanction. The Pittsburgh Courier vouches for the gen[uine]ness of the letter.

[ROBERT L. VANN]
The Editor

Printed in the *Pittsburgh Courier*, 10 November 1923. Original headlines omitted.

1. See above, pp. 468–470.

Speech by Marcus Garvey

[[LIBERTY HALL, NEW YORK, NOV. 11, 1923]]

We are living in a material world, a world of human beings where man lives with the function of two lives, the life spiritual and the life physical. To God we owe the obligation of our spiritual lives; to ourselves we owe the obligation of our physical lives.

The understanding of man of himself has been the puzzle of the age. The difference of conditions between races and peoples is the difference in understanding one's self. That is to say, the difference between, probably, the white race and the black race is because of the difference of understanding of self by each and every one of those two races. Apparently, and I do not doubt it, the white man seems to have a complete knowledge and understanding of himself. Apparently, and I do not doubt it from my observation[,] the Negro has failed to understand himself and to know himself, and to that is due the difference in conditions between the two peoples. The one realizes that it owes as a race a spiritual obedience to the great Creator in the things that are spiritual, in the things that are God's, as well as realizing that it owes to itself a physical duty, a physical obligation, with which they do not fail to comply. The Negro from my study and observation of him has made but one life of himself and seems to subordinate all things to that one life. The Negro lives apparently with only the spiritual life, and with that spiritual activity he seems to look to the source of the spiritual existence for all things, not realizing that the source of spiritual life has detached [H]imself from the physical life which He makes man responsible for to himself.

The Spiritual and the Physical

Now if you get to understand me in what I am saying, you will get the whole race problem. The Negro up to the present time has failed to realize that he has two lives, the spiritual which he shall give to God, and the physical which he shall take care of for himself and by himself, and that to God he goes for spiritual grace and spiritual strength, and on himself he relies for all the physical needs. This is the understanding that the white man has gotten out of life. While as a Christian he has the same hopes as the Negro of one day enjoying the beauties of heaven that we in our great religion speak and talk of and pray about, he, realizing his physical responsibility to himself, works to so create conditions around him in this life as to insure the happiness that he needs while he moves around this creation that God has given to man and of which He has made him lord.

God's Disgust

Until the Negro gets to understand himself more and gets to know that, as far as the material things of life go, these things are his responsibility and shoulders them, until then will he ever be the underdog of the world, until then will he ever be the despised and rejected of men and even the despised and rejected of God, in that the great God has laid out certain duties and obligations that man must fulfill. God created this world not with the intention of taking care of it Himself in its physical, material development, but He created His masterpiece, man, to take care of this physical world for Him, and out of it all to give Him that spiritual obedience that he exacts from all within His creation. I mean by that that God has given the universe. God has given the great world in which we live and all the other worlds to the creatures created therein. We see no other creatures but ourselves as human beings. We do not know the other creatures that live in Jupiter and Mars and Saturn. We take it for granted they are creatures too of God. But in this great universal creation of worlds of which we form a part God creates His creatures to function, to do certain work, to carry out certain duties, and when His creatures fail to live up to these responsibilities He despises them. He rejects them now even as He did in the past. And you know your Scriptures. You know that God has rejected humanity more than once, and at one time he was so disgusted with the people whom He created because they were not living up to His expectations at that time He was about to destroy the world, and someone of Himself said, "I will save them," and He said, "If you can, try."

WHITE MAN HAS MEASURED UP

But God in His creative plan expects certain things of his creatures, and if you have gotten to the understanding or the knowledge that you are the creatures of God, then understand God is expecting something of you, and what God is expecting of you is not only to black shoes and plant potatoes, but God is expecting you to rise to the highest in the possibilities of His created creatures. And the admiration that the white man is held in is the admiration that every sane and sober mind must give to him, because he has not failed one bit in measuring up to the expectations of God in the things physical, in the things temporal and the things material.

There are some of us who flatter ourselves into believing that the white man is off the track of the spiritual purpose of God. I am not so crazy as to believe that the white man is off. I believe up to now the white man is the elect of God's people. You know why? Because the white man up to now is the only creature created by God living up to the fullest of his opportunities as a human being, and all this talk about white folks going to hell because they are too material is fool talk. If there is anybody going to heaven, it is the fellow who can get the best satisfaction out of this life so that he can be comfortable and happy and spiritually serve his God without molestation. (Applause.) And if anybody is going to hell, it is that race that is so poor that it can't take care of itself and is always miserable. No miserable, hungry man can go to heaven in these days. (Laughter.) Understand me.

MISTAKEN IDEAS

I want you Negroes to change your ideas about the white man going to hell and the white man is not pleasing God because the white man has the wealth of the world. How can you blame the white man for having the wealth of the world when God Almighty gave the wealth of the world to man? If God did not intend this, He would never have creat[ed] a world and its wealth. But the very fact that God created the world with all its wealth, the great mineral wealth, the great resources that you see, that men are clamoring for, the very fact that God created them in the world meant that man should possess himself of them, and the man who possesses himself of them is the man who is pleasing God, and the fool who rejects them and does not appreciate them is the fool who does not appreciate the creation of God. Whom do you think God Almighty created the beautiful peaches and apples and pears and bananas for? Whom do you think? (Laughter.) Whom do you think God Almighty created the beautiful vineyards for? For the tiger and the lion, the donkey and the rat? God Almighty created nature for the pleasures of man, and therefore man shows appreciation [for] the creation of God when man holds on to these things and enjoys himself with them. And any fool who says he does not want any possessions down here, and any happiness down here, he is not going to have any happiness at all anywhere. (Applause.) You are going to have hell with you always. You are going to have hell down here, and you are going to have hell when you reach. (Laughter.)

What God Intends

So we want Negroes to stop this foolish talk about not wanting anything down here because Jesus and the good angels are preparing beautiful homes for them somewhere else. Indeed Jesus is preparing a beautiful home for us, but Jesus, the angels and God intend we should enjoy ourselves the best we can down here, not forgetting them, not forgetting God. The world was given to us for the beauties of it, for the pleasures that we can get out of it without forgetting God, to whom we should give thanks and praise and honor. And that is the philosophy of the Universal Negro Improvement Association—teaching the Negro of today that it is not only a spiritual life which must bow in obedience to God, but a physical life, which, of himself, he must take of for himself.

But there are some of us Negroes who expect God Almighty, as I have often said, to do everything for us, from giving us spiritual strength to giving us a job, as if God was some big employment agent whose only duty it is to sit at a switchboard or a desk and when some Negro wants a job and rings Him through prayer for Him to answer him and say—(Laughter and applause.) You have the wrong idea of life if you think that God's duty is to find a job for you. You have the wrong idea of life if you think that God's duty is to give you the chance and opportunity to get the best out of the world. That is not God's duty. His duty and obligation is to give you spiritual strength and spiritual grace, but it is your duty to get the best out of life. If you want a job, go and hunt for it. If you want a good home like that of your neighbors, do not be malicious about her or him having it; do not be envious. Go out and work for yours. (Applause.) Do not expect that God, by your prayer, is going to take the neighbor's house and give it to you. You have a long prayer before you expecting such. That is what some expect—that by our prayers God is going to take away the goods of the world from the white man and give it to the black man. Brother, you have a long, long prayer before you, I say, because God is not thinking of you in that direction; otherwise He would be an unfair God if through your prayers He were to take away from the other fellow and give to you when the other fellow is also praying to Him for more. (Laughter.) God has made man a free agent and [l]ord of creation and the architect of his own physical destiny, and whatsoever man wants in creation man can have, not for the praying about it, but for the going about getting it. There is nothing that you want that you cannot get, so long as you do not aspire to interfere in the province of God.

SEEK AND FIND

Now, understand me. There is nothing that you want that you cannot get which is possible to man except attempting to interfere in the province of God. Therefore no one is responsible for your condition. If you are poor, if you are a beggar, if you are a shoe black, if you are but a farm hand picking cotton, nobody is responsible for your condition and your job; but the best job you want you will get as long as you want it. And God is not going to change that job for you [*not*] because He cannot, but because that is not His prerogative, that is not His function, that is not His duty. If you are dissatisfied with your condition, if you are dissatisfied with your job, it is your duty to go about improving your condition and getting a better job. And don't worry God about getting that job, either; and don't worry anybody, saying somebody is keeping you from getting the job you want, because nobody can keep you down but yourself. God Almighty, the One we worship and adore, is a God of justice and love, and, as I have often said, no respecter of persons. He never made the banker for the bank; He never made the railroad president for the railroad; He never made the industrial captain for the big commercial downtown or the commercial mart; He never made the cotton picker to pick cotton; He never made the shoe black to black shoes. He made man, and man chooses the job he wants, and God has nothing to do with it. Therefore it simply means this: That if you want to be the banker, if you want to be the railroad president; if you want to be the next Congressman or Senator; if you want to be the President of the nation, it is your business to go and seek the job that you want and not to worry anybody else about it.

DESTROYING THE OLD EDUCATION

Now, if you get the thought that I am trying to convey to you then you will have before you the program of the Universal Negro Improvement Association. God is not going to give us better opportunities; God is not going to give us a country of our own. If we want these things we must reach out and get these things and pray to God to give us grace and strength to go through with the job. I say this so that I can impart to you the philosophy of this movement. Before we can properly help the people we have to destroy the old education of the people, the old education that teaches them that somebody is keeping them back and that God has forgotten them and that they can't rise because of their color. That old education leading in that direction must be destroyed before we can build a new Ethiopia. We can only build the new Ethiopia with confidence, with faith in ourselves and with self reliance, believing in our own possibilities, that we can rise to the highest in God's creation, to the highest limit placed upon man by the great Creator. And you know God Almighty has given man a large and a liberal leeway and headway to climb as high as he wants. As I said, the only limit that God Almighty has placed upon man is that he does not interfere in His divine province, as when man attempted, after he had all the glories of the world and the wonders of his own perfection, when he attempted to build the Tower of Babel to reach up to the clouds and to see God's holy face and wonders. Then God stopped him and confused his tongue.[1] So long as you do not interfere in the province of God you can rise to the highest. That is the teaching of the Universal Negro Improvement Association. And if you are down it is because you want to be down. If you want to be up, then you will ascend to the highest pinnacle yet ascended by man, whether white, yellow or red. And that is the work and that is the ambition of the Universal Negro Improvement Association not to stop below, but to climb to the top, to the top of human progress, to the top of human achievement. And that is why we say that the problem, the race problem, will only be solved when the Negro has completely measured up to the standard of man.

The Standard of Man

Now, what did I say? To the standard of man. Whom did God create? God created the animals, the lesser animals, the lower animals, and above them all He created the greater animal, the masterpiece man. Man has established a standard. There is no doubt about it that the standard of man is the white man. He is the standard man because he has snatched from the rest of the people, created in the image of God, the power and control of the world, and he has become so conceited, he has become so arrogant, that he boasts of the fact that he is the standard of man. But he is not alone going to be the standard man. The yellow man of the East, looking at him, observing him in every particular, has decided that he also shall measure up to the standard of man. And if you were to survey the world today you will find there is no standard the white man has achieved that the yellow man cannot boast of a similar. The standard of man is established. The reign of man is also established.

What is the Negro?

Now the white man is a man. What is the Negro? That is the speculation of the age. If the white man is a man and not a demi-god and not a god and not an angel, if he is but man, then what are we? Well, the human answer is that we are men. Well, if we are men compare ourselves with other men and you will find without my telling you how far below we fall in the comparison and the established standard of other men. It is no wonder then that the white man says he is a superior man and that we are an inferior race. And the white man shall continue to hold that opinion so long as he monopolizes the standard of man and so long as we keep ourselves below the common standard. Our duty, therefore, to establish our right as men is to lift ourselves to the common standard of men, and that is what the Universal Negro Improvement Association is endeavoring to do with four hundred million Negroes throughout the world—to establish the standard of man. So long as you make the other man the creator in the material progress of the world; so long as you depend upon the other man, through the environments created by the other man, for your comfort, for your happiness and for your pleasure, so long will the other man despise you and look down upon you as an inferior creature. But when you by your own creation have lifted yourself to the common standard of man in the common progress that he has made, in that very hour there is no inferior man, there is no superior man—there will be but man. Until the hour comes the Southern white man is going to jim-crow the Negro, the Southern white man is going to lynch the Negro, until that time comes the Northern white man is going to socially segregate and industrially jim-crow the Negro and the white world is going to look down upon the black man as an inferior creature.

A NEW SPIRIT

But thank God the spirit has been driven into us, the vision has been given unto us and we are seeing the light of a new day and by this vision we are determined to lift ourselves to the common standard of man, saying thereby, whatever man has done we must do. What did I say? Whatsoever man has done we must do. What has man done? Man has changed God's wilderness into a world of beautiful nations and beautiful cities, built up a wonderful and amazing civilization. That is what man has done to God's world. God's vast wilderness. God's vast virgin forests in Europe. The white man has changed the wilderness into the beautiful nations of England and France and Germany and Italy and Spain and Russia and Austria and Hungary. On this American continent man has changed God's wilderness and virgin forests into the beautiful and wonderful nation of the United States of America, into the beautiful and wonderful nations of Mexico, of Canada, of Brazil, of the Argentine, of Colombia, of Costa Rica and of Panama, and the rest that you know. That is what man has done with God's created world—made it not only to the satisfaction of himself as man, but to the satisfaction of God the Divine.

RENDERING AN ACCOUNT

Now, what have you done with your part of the world that God has placed under your charge and your care? You have kept it just so long until the other fellow is ready to take it away from you and show to God what he has been able to do with the talent of the lazy servant who was too lazy to use it, according to the direction and the will of the Master. Negroes, are you going to remain here and allow God Almighty to damn and curse us for our lethargy and our laziness? Remember the parable of the servants.[2] That parable stands out now as it stood out in the day of the Master who uttered that parable. God Almighty is expecting of you as much as He expected of the servants to whom He distributed the talents when He was going on that long journey. Negroes, God Almighty is expecting something of you. God Almighty did not create you to be dogs, God Almighty did not create you to be cats, otherwise he would have made you creeping, running about things. He created you men, and God Almighty is expecting you to function as men. Function by yourselves, because God Almighty did not make a mistake when he created you by yourselves. God must have had some special purpose to make this mark of distinction, when he made some men black and made some white and made some yellow. He must have had some idea that He was going to take account of these people and He did not want any mixing up so that he could know them and see them by their works. And therefore when God made you black He must have set out some purpose for you in Heaven. Negroes, find that purpose, live up to that purpose and do not merit the curse of God, your Father and Creator. As a parent would expect some kind of progress from his children, so God expects some kind of progress and some kind of action from His children. As a parent would expect Jimmy, whom he did everything for, to turn out a good boy, to become an eminent barrister, an eminent doctor and reflect credit on the family so that the neighbors can say, "Mrs. So-and-So has good children, they are making good," so God desires to hear a good word of the work of the black man, because the devil is going to question God about His creation, and God would like to know His creation is so perfect the devil would have nothing on Him. And therefore since God Almighty created the black man as one of His children, and the red man and the white man, God the Father is going to expect some kind of a good report of them.

An Illustration

Now put yourselves in the position of God as parents. Suppose you had three sons and you did everything possible for these three sons. You gave them a common education, a common distribution of your wealth and said "Go out and do for yourselves." And two went out and became eminent men, prosperous, so prosperous that they glorified the parent who gave them a start in life. And the other fellow[,] all he accomplished was being a bum and a hobo, a good-for-nothing, a menace to society, always in jail, always drunk and good-for-nothing, and always dirty. Tell me, would you have as much appreciation for that boy as for the other two who made good and reflected honor and credit on your name[?]

That is the comparison the human race bears to its Creator; and Negroes[,] you had better get busy before the great Gabriel blows his horn so that you can have some account to give to your Creator for the stewardship he entrusted to you in this life since he created man. As far as I understand myself, and as far as I know myself in relationship to the great God, I shall do my best to measure up so that when Peter opens the gate he can say "Garvey, pass in!" (Laughter and applause.)

I say before I conclude, that the responsiblity of life is yours, and not the white man's and not even God's. The only responsibility of God, is, as I said, that of spirtually helping us and directing us when we find ourselves spiritually weak; but physically we depend upon ourselves, and if we are down it is because of ourselves; if we are up, it is because of our highest ambition—the ambition that the Universal Negro Improvement Association is endeavoring to implant in every Negro throughout the world. (Applause.)

Printed in *NW*, 17 November 1923. Original headlines omitted.

1. A reference to Gen. 11: 4–9.
2. A reference to Matt. 25: 14–30.

Marcus Garvey to Sen. Frank B. Willis

NEW YORK, U.S.A. November 15, 1923

My Dear Senator Willis:—

This serves to acknowledge your letter of the 5th inst., in reply to the communication I sent you, asking your views on certain questions affecting the Negro race.

I have to thank you for your frank and friendly opinion. I trust however that you will read through the literature sent you, so that you can better form an opinion after studying what the Negro himself is thinking.

It is true that the Negro has been in America for a long while, and even as long as that of his white fellow citizen, but in view of the fact that he is hopelessly outnumbered, and his chance of developing on equal lines with his fellow citizens is more remote through the prejudice that exists, he feels that the best that he can do at the present time, is to strike out on his own account with whatsoever assistance can be given him, by his friends, and it is with that spirit that the forward looking Negroes are working for the establishment of a Government of their own in Africa.

It is also true that there are Negroes in the country, who are not disposed to go to Africa or anywhere else, but who feel that they should remain here, and agitate for their higher rights, but in the face of opposition the thoughtful of us realise that the attempt would be futile. The group that is satisfied, represents a small minority who of themselves are succeeding, and to the disadvantage of the great mass of our people. This selfish group will adduce arguments against the emigration of the race to Africa to build up a Government of their own with the help of their friends, but the organization that I represent, is not thinking of that group, because it has no voice other than its own, and does not truly represent the mass feeling of our people. Our organization has over five hundred branches throughout the United States, and we have a full knowledge of the feeling and wants of the people, and as soon as plans for repatriation [are] ready, which we are working out, there is no doubt but that millions will embrace it.

We do not want to do this without the knowledge and sympathy of such friends as you. It was for that reason that the letter was written. Our Organization has strong branches in your State, and in Cincinnati we have a membership of about fifteen thousand, in Cleveland about twenty thousand, in Columbus about ten thousand, in Youngstown and vicinity about three thousand, in Dayton about four thousand, in Hamilton about one thousand, and in Akron about two thousand, and thousands more in other parts of the State.

If there is anything that we can do in your support at any future time, we shall be pleased to be at your command. With very best wishes, and hoping that you will find time to read the literature sent you.[1] I have the honor to be, Your obedient servant

MARCUS GARVEY
President-General
Universal Negro Improvement Assoc.

[*Endorsement*] R.S.—Just file.

OC-HS, collection 325, box 16, folder 68. TLS on UNIA letterhead, recipient's copy. Handwritten endorsement.

1. Garvey enclosed a speech delivered by Tristam Burges of Rhode Island to the 21st U.S. Congress on 10 May 1830 entitled "Claims of Africa." Burges declared that "Africa, like a bereaved mother, holds out her hands to America, and implores you to send back her exiled children" (OC-HS, collection 325, box 16, folder 68, *Register of Debates in Congress*, vol. 6, part 2 [Washington, D.C.: Gales and Seaton, 1830], p. 941). Burges (1770–1853) was a member of Congress from 1825 to 1935 (*Biographical Dictionary of the American Congress* [Washington, D.C.: GPO, 1971], p. 668).

Marcus Garvey to President C.D.B. King of Liberia

New York City, N.Y. December 5, 1923

MAY IT PLEASE YOUR EXCELLENCY:—

That this letter serves to introduce to you HON. ROBERT L. POSTON, Secretary-General of the Universal Negro Improvement Association, ATTORNEY J. MILTON VAN LOWE[1] of Detroit, Mich., and LADY HENRIETTA VINTON DAVIS, 4th Assistant President-General of the Universal Negro Improvement Association, who have been sent[2] as a delegation from the Universal Negro Improvement Association to interview you and your good government, in continuation of the proposition undertaken with you in 1921 for the furtherance of the plan to assist in the development of Liberia, industrially, and commercially, by the settlement in some parts of the country of a large number of American and West Indian Colonists who desire repatriation to their native land, Africa, for the establishment of permanent homes.

The spirit of kinship has ever lingered with us on this side, and now, more than ever, millions of people are looking homeward, as the only solution of their grave problem and condition.

Mr. Poston is Chairman of the Delegation, and Mr. Van Lowe its Secretary. They are charged by the Universal Negro Improvement Association, representing six million Negroes, to confer with you for the purpose of arriving at some amicable arrangement by which the Association and the people at this end, can help in the settlement of industrial groups in Liberia, for the, as above stated[,] commercial and industrial development of the country, and for the advancement of their own peace and happiness.

Your visit to America has brought you [in] close touch with the race problem, which presses greatly upon our people causing a great dissatisfaction, which leads large numbers of them to feel that the only place where they could have permanent happiness and peace is Africa, their Fatherland. There are thousands of families now awaiting the word from you and your good Government that they will be welcomed, to settle in some part of the country to help in its building. These families that are ready for settlement as soon as arrangements are reached, will go out not as charges, but as persons of independent means. In this respect we can guarantee the repatriation to any part of the country that you may designate according to previous talks with you in 1921[3] between twenty and thirty thousand families in the first two years, starting, say[,] from September 1924. The worth of each family would be roughly estimated at $1,500.00 each, the multiplication of which would make such Colonists more helpful to the country in revenue, and through other resources.

It is felt that our intention has been grossly misrepresented to you by our enemies and outsiders, who have sought on so many occasions to embarrass us in our good intention toward you and Liberia, but as you must realize, reform movements like that of the Universal Negro Improvement Association, will always be misrepresented, and no one more than you could better appreciate the difficulties such movements have to undergo in the beginning. We have had to spend the last five years organizing sentiment in the West Indies and America toward the appreciation of the plan of economic and industrial interest in Africa by Negroes, in that for a long while the Negro has been trained at this end to absorb and become entirely a part of the civilization around him, and to ignore the creation of an independent existence that would lend honor and prestige to the race. Because of that, we have had an up-hill fight for the last five years, which has caused us to have encountered many bitter enemies, who, no doubt, have tried to influence you and your good Government in prejudice against us, but you know well the situation, and can, as above stated, appreciate our trying position.

As you know, Mr. King, the race has been practically divided against itself through color and other prejudices. In America and the West Indies we have had a tremendous fight of the lighter element against the darker ones, and that is accountable to a great extent for some of the bitterness that exists against the Universal Negro Improvement Association at this time, but when it is considered that we can only succeed by being a united people, you will further appreciate our effort to bring about such a result.

Our earlier work in Liberia was handicapped, because of misunderstanding and bad representation. The men, Crichlow and Garcia, whom we sent out did a great deal of harm with their indiscretions, which caused us to have delayed, and in other words suspended, the efforts we started to make in the carrying out of our industrial program in Liberia. The setback was chiefly due also to certain unforeseen circumstances, but it is felt that no prejudice will be harbored against us in Liberia because of that, in that you can all well appreciate the difficulties we had to encounter. We are now starting in real earnest with the backing and support of a stalwart membership and if your good government will help as you promised to do in 1921 by the grant of lands in certain parts, and especially around the region of the River Scess,[4] or any other part that you may designate to the delegation, we feel sure that in another twelve months from the first settlement, that we will be able to show wonderful improvement in helping in the development of the country.

The people at this end are uncertain of their future, and large numbers of them who are fairly independent are desirous of permanent home settlement, and these people are now anxiously awaiting word from you that would satisfy them in making up their minds to make Liberia their future home. We can see nothing else but a bright future for Liberia in this direction, and if you will enter into the spirit with which we are desirous of helping, there is no reason why you and your government could not become in a few years the Saviour of our wandering people.

It is for us to state that our program for the industrial development of Liberia and its settlement by Negroes from this part is supported by a large number of influential friends, who will be willing to do anything to help us along, with what we are able to do ourselves, but there must be an assurance that there is appreciation for what we are endeavoring to do from your side, which could be made manifest in the granting to us of the accommodation for the people who are desirous of settling.

We need not discuss with you in this letter the many evil and wicked misrepresentations that have been made against us, but suffice it to say that the heart of every real member of the Universal Negro Improvement Association is with Liberia in its higher industrial and commercial development.

We would like to see Liberia become one of the first powers of the world, and anything that we can do economically and industrially shall be done unstintingly.

As you know, the Black Star Line, one of our early ventures, was temporarily suspended because of disloyalty and dishonesty on the part of some of the people we engaged in our earlier venture, but on a favorable report from the delegation, the Association intends to have two large ships equipped between September and December, 1924, for permanent trade between Liberia and America. We are now laying plans for the carrying out of this project.

Our bigger work is still ahead of us, and if we are given a fair chance and opportunity, we shall be able to carry out more successfully to the good and betterment of Liberia and those concerned.

We are therefore asking you to give the delegation, as our representatives, the consideration necessary, so as to enable us to make the kind of report by which the people will be encouraged to take advantage of settling in the country for its development.

Anticipating a favorable understanding, we shall work assiduously to bring about an era of prosperity for Liberia and our people, starting in the year 1924. With very best wishes for a successful administration and for the

THE MARCUS GARVEY AND UNIA PAPERS

progress of your country, I have the honor to be, your obedient servant,

[MARCUS GARVEY]
President-General
Universal Negro Improvement Association

DNA, RG 59, file 882.5511/15. Transcript.

1. J. Milton Van Lowe was attorney for the Detroit division of the UNIA. Born in the British West Indies, Lowe studied at the University of California and the University of Pennsylvania before receiving a law degree from the Detroit College of Law. He addressed the UNIA convention in 1924. He was also a member of the Bethel AME church in Detroit (*NW*, 25 September 1926; Alice C. Dalligan, chief, Burton Historical Collection, Detroit Public Library, to Robert A. Hill, 8 March 1984).

2. The UNIA's delegation to Liberia did not sail from New York until 11 December 1923, aboard the Fabre Line steamship S.S. *Britannia*. During the previous evening, Garvey presided over a farewell mass meeting for the delegates at Liberty Hall (report of Special Agent Joseph G. Tucker, 22 December 1923, DJ-FBI, file 61-267).

3. King visited the United States in March 1921. UNIA officials met with him in New York on 7 March 1921 (see *Garvey Papers* 3: 243 n.1).

4. River Cess is a town located in Grand Bassa County, Liberia, at the mouth of the Sestus River. During a meeting of 22 March 1921 between the Liberian cabinet and UNIA commissioners, UNIA potentate Gabriel M. Johnson expressed his interest in a River Cess site as an area for future UNIA settlement. Liberian acting president Edwin Barclay replied that he did not suppose that the government would have any objection to this, as the Liberian legislature had already zoned a River Cess settlement for occupation by immigrants (interview with the Liberian cabinet, 22 March 1921, Archives of the Department of State, Ministry of Foreign Affairs, Monrovia, Liberia).

Dr. Theodore M. Kakaza to
Rep. Clarence MacGregor[1]

191 William Street, Buffalo, N.Y.
Dec[.] 7th '23

Dear Congressman,

We, the undersigned voters and residents of your district, hereby petition your influence in Congress or the Senate, to secure an investigation of the case of Marcus Garvey of New York City, who, as a Leader of the Negro race, has been discriminated against and convicted on an alleged charge of using the mails to defraud, and sent to the Federal Penitentiary at Atlanta, for five (5) years and to be deported upon the expiration of his sentence.

We, the people of your community, know the entire proceeding is nothing short of a frame[-]up to discredit the leadership of this man whom we know and acknowledge as a Peerless Leader of the race.

We, your constituents, therefor[e] respec[t]fully ask that you insti[tu]te immediately, an inquiry into the entire proceedings and that you further use your good influence to have Marcus Garvey liberated from prison. Awaiting the result of your action in this behalf, we beg to remain your constituents and petitioners.

THEODORE M. KAKAZA[,] M.D.[2]
Secretary of Petitioners

DNA, RG 233. TLS, recipient's copy. The letter includes a list of 345 signatures of petitioners.

1. Clarence MacGregor (1872–1952) served in the New York State Assembly from 1908 to 1912 before his election to Congress. He completed four terms in the House of Representatives, resigning in 1928 to serve as a justice on the New York State Supreme Court (*Biographical Directory of the American Congress* [Washington, D.C.: GPO, 1971], p. 1,321).

2. Dr. Theodore M. Kakaza was the South African-born president of Buffalo's Division 79 of the UNIA (*NW*, 3 November 1923).

Marcus Garvey to Nicholas Murray Butler

NEW YORK, U.S.A. December 18, 1923

My dear Dr. Butler:

I am instructed by the membership of the New York Division of the Universal Negro Improvement Association, to write to you asking if you will be good enough to address one of the series of meetings that will be held in Liberty Hall[,] 120 West 138th Street[,] during the months of December 1923 and January 1924.

The New York Division of the Universal Negro Improvement Association, has a membership of 30,000. From time to time, they invite some of our most prominent citizens to speak to them on timely topics.

It is in continuation of this policy, that they request me to ask if you will be good enough to speak before them. They desire this, because they regard you, as one of the best friends of our Race.

I therefore ask if it will be possible for you to speak to them either on Monday night December 31st 1923, or Wednesday night January 2nd 1924[,] at 9 o'clock.

Our Association is striving for the ideal of building in Africa an independent Government for Negroes, as well as to improve the economic, social and educational condition of Negroes everywhere.

We will be glad to have you speak on the subject of: "The Educational development of America" or some similar theme. Trusting you will be able to help us in this matter,[1] I have the honor to be, Your obedient Servant,

MARCUS GARVEY
President-General
Universal Negro Improvement Ass'n

NNC, NMB. TLS on UNIA letterhead, recipient's copy.

1. Butler declined Garvey's invitation on the grounds of "the pressure that is upon me this winter both at the University and elsewhere" (Nicholas Murray Butler to Marcus Garvey, 20 December 1923, NNC, NMB).

Editorial Letter by Marcus Garvey

[*New York*] January 1, 1924

WHAT WE BELIEVE

The Universal Negro Improvement Association advocates the uniting and blending of all Negroes into one strong healthy race. It is against miscegenation and race suicide.

It believes that the Negro race is as good as any other, and therefore should be as proud of itself as others are.

It believes in the purity of the Negro race and the purity of the white race.

It is against rich blacks marrying poor whites.

It is against rich or poor whites taking advantage of Negro women.

It believes in the spiritual Fatherhood of God and the Brotherhood of Man.

It believes in the social and political physical separation of all people to the extent that they promote their own ideals and civilization, with the privilege of trading and doing business with each other. It believes in the promotion of a strong and powerful Negro nation.

It believes in the rights of all men.

Universal Negro Improvement Assn.
MARCUS GARVEY
President-General

Printed in *NW*, 12 January 1924.

Negro World Notice

[[1 January 1924]]

NOTICE TO MEMBERS OF
UNIVERSAL NEGRO IMPROVEMENT ASSOCIATION

Please be loyal and true and pay up your Annual Dollar Tax immediately.[1] All Secretaries of Divisions will collect this tax from each member and forward to Parent Body. This tax is due on the 1st January, 1924. By order,

The Parent Body
Universal Negro Improvement Association

Printed in *NW*, 12 January 1924.

1. Special Agent Joseph G. Tucker noted on 5 January that "the finances of the organization are evidently in an unhealthy condition, as Garvey is taking advantage of every opportunity to impress upon the members of all divisions and branches, the importance of . . . paying the dues of the organization up to date" (report of Special Agent Joseph G. Tucker, 5 January 1924, DJ-FBI, file 61).

John E. Bruce to Florence Bruce

[*New York*] 1/2/24

Dear Florence,

Tell Mr. G. to send this Cable to [*J.E. Casely*] Hayford, I will tell him, Hayford, what to do to break the force of Du Bois' influence in Gold Coast and I . . . [*remainder missing*].

[JOHN E. BRUCE]

NN-Sc, JEB, MSL 33-4. TN, carbon copy.

Enclosure

[*New York*] Jany. 2/24

Dear Chief,

If you think it worthwhile, (I think it is) you may Cable in my name the following to Hayford at once: Du Bois—Crisis—on trip to Africa,[1] bent on mischief, due to failure of his 'Pan African Congress.'[2] Financed by Joel Spingarn, a Jew, and other interests (white) inimical to African Independence. Watch him. Letter follows. Make no commit[t]als. Yours,

BRUCE-GRIT

NN-Sc, JEB, MSL 33-4. TL, carbon copy.

1. In December 1923 President Calvin Coolidge appointed W. E. B. Du Bois U. S. representative to Liberian President C. D. B. King's inauguration in 1924. See Garvey's reaction in "Exposing the Game of Race Destruction among False Leaders," *NW*, 29 December 1923.

2. Du Bois convened the Third Pan-African Congress in London and Lisbon in November 1923 (Imanuel Geiss, *The Pan-African Movement*, trans. Ann Kemp [New York: Africana Publishing Co., 1974], pp. 251–256).

Speech by Marcus Garvey

[[LIBERTY HALL, NEW YORK, January 6, 1924]]

My subject for tonight is "The Struggle for Power." The world is an eternal battleground where men engage themselves in conflict with one another for the survival of the fittest human group. This struggle continues through the centuries right down to the last minute of our existence. Wheresoever you find humanity you will find this eternal conflict—this eternal struggle. We have reached the point of our human history where we have divided ourselves up into groups, having group interests and group desires. These group interests and group desires prevent the one group from being directly or even indirectly interested in the other. Twentieth century civilization has brought us face to face with a materialism so exacting that each group feels that its supreme duty is to protect its own interests as against the interests of others.

HUMAN FRIENDSHIP AND FELLOWSHIP

When we talk about human friendship and human fellowship they must not be interpreted to mean a friendship or fellowship of the race for the other. It must be interpreted to mean friendship and fellowship within that race and for the members thereof. Any other interpretation placed upon friendship and fellowship is wrong in twentieth century civilization and twentieth century materialism.

It provokes me as part of the Negro group when other members of my race try to impress me that other people are so interested in us as to leave their business undone to attend completely and thoroughly to ours. We have had so many of those professions in the face of the material instinct. To repeat myself, every race is charged with the absolute responsibility of looking after itself, and when members of another race try to impress the world that they are as much interested in the activities of another race as their own, it is only to be interpreted as one of the means and methods used by that race to deceive the other portions of the world.

DECEIVING OTHERS THROUGH CHRISTIANITY

In the struggle for power man resorts to subterfuges of all kinds and practices of all kinds to outdo his neighbor or his brother. These subterfuges sometimes find expression in noble and lofty sentiments emanating from the individual race that desires to deceive others to whom they make those wonderful and beautiful statements. Among the many agencies used to convey these beautiful sentiments to the world has been Christianity. Christianity has been one of the most abused morals in the world. For hundreds of years certain people resorted to the beautiful moral and ethical truths of the Christian religion and used them to deceive the other portion of the world and the rest of mankind. When the other fellow wants to deceive you he tells you about Jesus; he tells you about heaven; he tells you about the beautiful things of the Christian religion, which he himself will preach to you but will never practice himself. He preaches them to you because he believes it is the easiest way to reach your emotion and appeal to your sentiment, and deprive you of that which he wants. Such a subterfuge the white man used in Africa. Such a subterfuge the white man has endeavored to use on all the unfortunate peoples of the world. He sends out his priest, his bishop and his missionary to foreign lands to foster the desire that he has—that of colonial dominion or exploitation of native peoples and their lands. In the modern analysis of things we regard that as a subterfuge—the subterfuge by which one race is able to deceive others and ride into power.

That is responsible for the ascendancy of certain races over others at the present time. The race that wants to get somewhere to the disadvantage of the other will adopt subterfuge by which it will deceive other races, thereby acquiring the benefits that it desires to derive.

Loyalty to Ourselves

Such a subterfuge is being practiced up to the very minute and in our very midst. We of the Universal Negro Improvement Association, as we have often said and declared, love all humanity. We hate none in the great creation of God, but we realize that our first and supreme duty is loyalty to ourselves. In the prosecution of this duty we become, therefore, very jealous of what is said and done to affect our existence. We do not hate the white man. We regard and respect the white man as we respect and regard all humanity, but we have reached the point where we are not going to allow any white man, or yellow man, or red man, to fool us, as they have done for hundreds of years, and make us their footstool. We have reached that conclusion because we have discovered ourselves in a soulless, heartless, material world.

Dyer and His Anti-Lynching Bill

I understand that Congressman Dyer was around this neighborhood in New York today[1] talking about his Dyer Anti-Lynching bill under the auspices of the National Association for the Advancement of Colored People. I want to say this frankly and openly that any measure that would render assistance and protection to the Negro is heartily indorsed and supported by the scattered world-wide membership of the Universal Negro Improvement Association. We are for every measure that seeks to bestow benefit or advantage upon this race of ours, but we are against hypocrisy whether it comes from the public or any liar moving around trying to deceive the Negro race. Mr. Dyer knows that he does not mean anything about the Dyer Anti-Lynching bill. He does not mean it anymore than the devil means to make it comfortable for all sinners when they come to his region. (Laughter.) Mr. Dyer knows that he is but playing the trick his race has played for centuries—trying to introduce to the same camouflage, the same hypocrisy, the same subterfuge as Livingston[e] conveyed to Africa—as the missionaries took to Africa and India and to Asia. He is but spreading this propaganda of the Dyer Anti-Lynching bill in the same way the white man has spread Christianity in heathen lands for the last 1,900 years—a lie, a fraud and hypocrisy.

I love the straightforward, honest, white man, and that is why I have great respect for the members of the Ku Klux Klan. You understand me. I regard and respect an honest white man; but I hate a liar in whatsoever color he comes. (Applause.) Here is a white man, a member of the Ku Klux Klan, [f]or what he is. He is honest enough and tells me: "Look here, Nigger, you shall never have social equality with me; you shall never have political equality with me; you shall never have justice with me. Nigger, if you have sense you will go and look about your own business." There is an honest man I respect and honor for his honesty. Here is another man who feels the same way; he feels with that man who says, "Nigger, you shall never have social equality and you shall never have political equality," but in his hypocrisy he comes and tells me, "Negro, I love you so; you are my friend." If I must hate I would hate the man who deceives me, and if I must love I would revere and honor and respect the man who tells me the truth and prepares me for my course in life. I have lost complete interest in Mr. Dyer, and I want that to be conveyed to him. I have lost complete interest in him because I know he does not mean what he says in his presentation of the so-called Dyer Anti-Lynching bill. How could he mean it in the face of conditions and circumstances and environments that hem him in[?] He is but a white man like the rest of the white people of this country.

His supreme interests must be that of the white race, and if he tells me to the contrary I will tell him to his face that he is mistaken. Every white man in this country that is conscious of himself is bound by laws morally, legally and in every way to think of himself first before he thinks of others. Otherwise he would be a rebel and a traitor to his race. And when Mr. Dyer comes and tells me and tells fifteen million Negro people of the United States of America that his intention is to pass a bill that will permanently and forevermore stop the abuses to Negroes in the South and other parts of the country, I tell him that he is a camofleur and a deceiver. He wants probably to pass the Dyer Anti-Lynching bill, true; I wouldn't doubt him in that. I believe Mr. Dyer wants to pass the bill, but before Mr. Dyer presented that bill Mr. Dyer made cocksure before he drew that bill that the bill would mean nothing to the Negro if passed. Mr. Dyer had already contrived this as a method of fooling Negroes: "Pass the bill and let them believe that that will settle the question, and we will adopt some other method to fool these Negroes." There are many ways of killing a dog without putting a rope around the dog's neck. Some say it is inhuman to hang the dog and great agitation is being made about hanging the dog with a rope. My supreme desire is to kill the dog anyhow, but public sentiment is against my hanging this dog. Well, I will stop hanging the dog, but I will get some poison for the dog; I will set a trap for the dog, the dog will die anyhow and those who did not want the dog to die with ropes around its neck will have been satisfied because I passed the anti-rope bill. (Laughter.)

NEW NEGRO CANNOT BE FOOLED

If Mr. Dyer thinks he has sense enough to fool all Negroes he makes a mistake. There are those Negroes of the Universal Negro Improvement Association who it will take hell and all the world to fool. We did not go to school for nothing. My great-great-grandparents did not get those lashes on their backs for 250 years for nothing to give me this intelligence that I have now to make other men fool me in the twentieth century. They will have to come cleaner and better than that. They have to deliver the real goods and do not come with all this camouflage, beating their breasts and turning red and throwing their hands up to heaven and talking about how "we love the good colored folks." Let me tell you there was never a white man in the world who ever truly loved colored folks.

No Supreme Love for the Negro

Now I am saying that, and I am saying that with the authority of hundreds of years of information and knowledge behind that. Victoria[,] who signed the emancipation proclamation that set at liberty hundreds of thousands of West Indian Negroes, never had any supreme love for the Negro. Abraham Lincoln, who signed the emancipation proclamation in the United States of America that set free four million Negroes, never had any supreme love for the Negro. Your Lovejoys,[2] your Wilberforces, Clarksons, your Buxtons, your Garrisons never had any supreme love for the Negroes. On the public platform they make beautiful statements, beautiful speeches against the injustice of slavery, the iniquity of slavery. It is true; and their agitation freed the slave. It is true, but if you go into the private lives of each and every one of those men you will find them saying things that will prove they never had any supreme love for the Negro. One of the greatest philanthropists, one of the greatest emancipators was approached in his study one day by a friend, another white man, and the friend said to him, "What ails you, Bill? You look very ruffled in your manner today." And he says, "I am disturbed. A horrible thing happened to me. A black just came in sight of me." That man was an abolitionist. He was working for the freedom of the slaves, and he was ruffled and spoiled in the spirit of the day because a black came across him. Yet he goes down in history as a great lover of colored folks. And there is not one of them that comes on the platform and professes their love who does not feel the same way in their drawing rooms and in their private chamber. If you doubt it, you, Mr. Negro, dress yourself up, put on the best Sunday clothes you have and call at Mr. Dyer's home and ask to see somebody.

Can't Serve Two Masters

I hate this hypocrisy. I hate this hypocrisy; I hate this lie. You can't serve two masters. You can't serve the white race and the black race at the same time. Therefore, what does Mr. Dyer mean? Is he serving the white race or the black race? That is how I get at my friends. I want to know your motive, your reason and purpose for coming around me. Now, if you love your race more than mine, what are you doing among mine? Any time you see a fox around a coop he is looking for a chicken, believe me. With all the profession of Brother Fox, "How I love the chickens![,]" whenever you see [B]rother Fox get out of his company and come around the chickens he is looking for a chicken. Understand that. And, as I said, I admire the beautiful sentiments of Mr. Dyer, his desire for a Dyer Anti-Lynching bill. It is a beautiful thing. But how can we accept him[?] . . .

From Caesar to Caesar

They will never be able to pass the Dyer Anti-Lynching bill with the result they talk about, and they don't mean it anyhow. What bill can we pass in the United States that is going to help Negroes when white folks are the persons against whom this legislation is passed? It is like appealing from Caesar to Caesar. The thing looks foolish and ignorant and illogical, notwithstanding the great so-called intellectual leadership of the N.A.A.C.P., with its Harvard professors and its Berlin graduates. Have they not enough sense to know it is an appeal from Caesar to Caesar? Could not Du Bois sit down and drag his intelligence for a few minutes to realize and see this, that you can't curb human prejudice by law? There is no law in the world, Divine, moral or legal; physical or human; that can curb the prejudice of man toward man. It is only the direct interference of God Himself that can regulate that. If I hate that woman and refuse to take her to my heart as my wife and love her as such, there is no law between heaven and earth to make me love her. If I hate you, if I hate that man, there is no law in the land to compel me to love him. You can pass a million laws, I will knock him down every time I see him. Therefore, Dyer knows well that the Dyer Anti-Lynching bill means nothing. As Mr. Smith[3] said a while ago, it is not necessary to pass more laws to protect the Negro. The Constitution of the United States is enough to protect all its citizens. It is not the law.

IT IS THE MOB

The mob is the law. Strange philosophy. But it is the truth. The mob is the law. Wherever you find a majority group of people and that majority group has certain desires, those desires are the law of the land irrespective of how many laws are on the statute books. Government gets its existence from the people. Modern democracy says that the majority rules. Therefore, Government is at the mercy of the majority in a democracy. And if a majority hates a minority there is no law in that community to compel that majority to respect the rights and wishes of that minority. Tell Du Bois to go and reason that out. Tell Weldon Johnson to go and reason that out, and they will find they are wasting time asking for laws to be made in Congress or anywhere else to curb the mob spirit of a race that is prejudiced against another.

"JUSTICE IS STRENGTH"

There is only one protection for the individual who suffers from the prejudice of another, and that is power, that is strength. There is no justice but strength. There is no law but power.

Another strange philosophy, nevertheless it is true. If you are strong you have justice on your side. If you are weak you are at the mercy of the dispenser of justice. Haiti is weak and America has overrun her shores with American marines because she keeps up little troubles in the Caribbean and violates the principles of the Monroe Doctrine, she says. France is at large in Europe menacing not only the peace of the Caribbean, but France to-day is a menace to civilization and to humanity. France, by her inhuman conduct to Germany, is fomenting the greatest war ever contemplated. But America winks at it, because France is reputed to have several thousand modern airships. France is reputed to have a standing army well equipped and immediately available. And

America and England wink at France's outrage and threat against civilization because France is strong. But because Haiti is weak, everybody says, "Go into Haiti and settle that dispute and keep them quiet."

GET POWER

I repeat what I said a while ago, there is no justice but strength; there is no justice but power. Negroes, if you have sense and want justice, get power, get it quick, get it anyhow. (Applause.) When you shall have gotten power on your side there will be no more need for Dyer to come to Harlem or go anywhere else and talk about a Dyer Anti-Lynching bill. Your aeroplanes hovering over cities will talk for you. Your submarines sailing under the seas will deliver your messages. When you get to think in terms of modern thought, which is based upon racial consciousness, racial self-preservation and racial self-protection, then you will be on the right track to redeeming yourselves, redeeming your race and redeeming your country. (Applause.)

YOURSELF YOUR OWN FRIEND

It is my desire to warn the Negroes of America and of the world of threatening dangers. I again warn you against the professions of certain men who talk about being the friends of Negroes. There can be no friend as true as yourself. If you want a friend look to yourself. If you must accept a friend from the outside accept him in the same manner as the outside accepts their friends. The Japanese accept their friends with caution. The English accept their friends with caution. The Italians accept their friends with caution. The Anglo-Americans accept their friends with caution. Negroes all over the world, I am warning you to accept your friends with caution. The only friend I know is God, outside of myself and my race. I expect to see Him the second time, either in the spirit or the person when He comes. If he comes looking like anybody else I will doubt His friendship. (Laughter.) Now you don't blame me for it. This experience I have gotten out of the world for the last five, ten, twenty thousand years, the history of the world is the same throughout the ages. The strong will always rule and oppress the weak. The weak will always be serfs and slaves of the strong. If you perpetuate this confidence you have in others, if you continue to follow the leadership of others, your position will be fixed eternally in the affairs of a material world. Our position was fixed once. Some accident changed it. Human promise is frail. Human goodwill is insecure. If your neighbor across the street promises to loan you one hundred dollars next week do not be too sure about it until you get it in your hands, because that neighbor may change his mind about it just one second before he puts it in your hand. Brother, there is no permanent fixture in civilization. I promise you good will today; I change my mind tomorrow.

MAY CHANGE HIS MIND

The white men once had the Negroes as slaves. He said, "I will change my mind about it. I will give them their freedom." In the same way he changed his mind from having you as slaves to be as free men, one of these days, fifty or one hundred days from now he may change his mind about your being free men. Mark the warning for the Universal Negro Improvement Association. There is no justice but strength. There is no justice but power. And that is why Great Britain seeks power. That is why France seeks power. That is why Japan seeks power. That is why Anglo-America seeks power. Negro, if you have sense, in the name of God you will seek power for the preservation of your race. (Applause.) Not the kind of power that will cause us to be beggars depending on others to do things for us, but the kind of power that will put initiative in our hands, initiative to do for ourselves or die in the attempt. Those are the principles of the Universal Negro Improvement Association as we teach them from Liberty Hall Sunday night after Sunday night. We send out these principles to the four corners of the world, hoping that four hundred millions of the people will come in contact with the message of truth, with the message of racial love and racial patriotism. (Loud applause.)

Printed in *NW*, 12 January 1924. Original headlines omitted.

1. The *New York Age* reported that Congressman Dyer addressed a capacity crowd on 6 January at one of the most successful NAACP meetings of the time in New York. At the meeting, Representative Dyer announced that the anti-lynching bill would appear before the judiciary committee the following week and that he was certain of its passage by the House of Representatives. Among those speaking at the meeting in support of the bill was the assistant secretary of the navy, Col. Theodore Roosevelt, Jr. (1887–1944) (*New York Age*, 12 January 1924).

2. Elijah Paris Lovejoy (1811–1837), printer and editor of the *St. Louis Observer* and later of the *Alton* (Illinois) *Observer*, publicly advocated the immediate emancipation of slaves. Although his press was destroyed three times by anti-abolitionists, he continued to print articles denouncing slavery. In 1837, shortly after founding the Illinois branch of the American Anti-Slavery Society, Lovejoy was killed by a mob attempting to destroy his press (Louis Filler, *The Crusade Against Slavery, 1830–1860* [New York: Harper & Bros., 1960], pp. 78–81; Merton L. Dillon, *Elijah P. Lovejoy, Abolitionist Editor* [Urbana: University of Illinois Press, 1961]; *WWWA*, pp. 392–393).

3. Third Assistant President-General Rudolph Smith, whose speech has been omitted, claimed that the Constitution was "strong enough to give protection to every man irrespective of race, creed or color" and therefore did not advocate the passage of the Dyer anti-lynching bill (*NW*, 12 January 1924).

Speech by Marcus Garvey

[[Washington, D.C., January 15, 1924]]

My subject for tonight is "The New Education." The U.N.I.A., the organization that I have the honor to represent, is engaged in promulgating among the Negro peoples of the world the new education. I am selected to be one of the spokesmen of this New Education. It is no easy task to educate. It takes a youth a number of years before he completely gets education fitting him for his place in life. The teacher, the schoolmaster, the professor has to exhibit patience through the years of tuition. Some refuse to imbibe all that is taught. We have been teaching the New Education among the Negroes for six years, and we have been able to educate six million. We are still in the process of educating, and we hope one day that we will succeed in educating four hundred million Negroes of the world.

That is why I come to Washington so often, and go to other places, so as to reach those who have not yet come into the classroom. The U.N.I.A. is seeking to destroy the old education, and to import the new. The old education separates [*us?*] from our own racial vision, our own racial outlook[,] and causes us to see things only through the spectacles of the other fellow—this must be destroyed (applause). And the education that will enable the Negro to see through his own spectacles, that will enable him to take on his own vision[,] must be promulgated.

ALSO AN IDEALIST

I am a Negro idealist just as white teachers, philosophers and leaders are white idealists; just as Asiatic, yellow teachers and philosophers are yellow idealists. We stand for the ideals of the Negro race, even as other races stand for their own respective ideals. We have no quarrel with anyone in this respect as we respect the ideals of all peoples. We accord to all people the right to have their own set ideals; to fight for them, to struggle toward them and to die for them if they care. A similar right we demand. The U.N.I.A., therefore, is not advancing the programme of hatred among the races, as I have recently emphatically stated; but we are endeavoring to bring about a union of sentiment, a union of ideals, among the four hundred million Negroes of the world, that will enable [*them*] to lift themselves to a common standard of humanity, to the plane of human progress, and there to be recognized as men co-equa[l] with the other men of the other races and nations in the world.

In America, as in countries where we form minorities, unfortunately we have been badly educated because the other fellow thinks it is his duty to give us the kind of education that will make us what he wants us to be, and, therefore, he is not to be blamed.

As I said on my last visit here, if I were a white man, I would give to Negroes and all other peoples who do not look like me, the kind of education that would keep them down. Now, I mean that. If I were a white man I would study every possible ways and means to keep other folks down. Now, I am plain in that. Therefore, I am not expecting anything other than what is reasonable from the white man, or other people who are not identified with my race.

It has become a law of human nature. The individual races or nations must look out for themselves, and the other race or nation that thinks that the other race should look out for them, has the wrong concept of humanity and of life. (Applause.) I have ceased long ago to believe that it is the white man's duty to prepare a place for me in life; except that which he wants to fix me in. It is his duty to fix me just as he wants me. It is my duty to fix myself up as I want myself. (Applause.)

He fixed my grandfather, he fixed my great grandfather; he fixed my father, and he is still determined to fix me; but I am not going to give him a chance to fix me, brothers. (Applause.)

THE FIXING PERIOD

We are in the fixing period now. Everybody is trying to fix the other. The European is trying to fix the Asiatic; the Asiatic is trying to fix the other people surrounding them, and everybody seems to be trying to fix the Negro. If you allow the other fellow to fix you, you will stay fixed and be in a hell of a fix. Here is one organization that is not going to allow anybody to fix the New Negro, but the Negro himself, and we want to be fixed in a position of industrial freedom, of political freedom, of social freedom, and of national freedom. That is the kind of fixing we are fighting for, and that is the kind of freedom that some of us will die trying to get.

There is nothing offensive in the program of the U.N.I.A., except to the man who wants to fix the Negro in the position that he does not want to be in. There is no offense to the liberal mind and soul because of what the U.N.I.A. seeks to do, which is to elevate the race. Is there anything whatsoever about that that is dangerous, to elevate the race? It is the desire of all peoples to elevate themselves. The white man has had thousands of years doing it at the expense of others. He has gotten away with it, and it is his good luck. But we have reached the stage of civilization where all the people have enough sense to see about their own affairs, whether they be Irish, Jew or Gentile, or Egyptian, Hindoo. All these people are looking towards improving themselves, strengthening themselves and advancing their own causes. We can do nothing else if we are men, and we are now conscious of this fact that we are men.

FIGHTING FOR NATIONHOOD

The U.N.I.A. is fighting towards the ideal of nationhood; the highest ideal among peoples at the present time. In America we have argued that there is no need for a separate and distinct nation for Negroes; within the British Empire, those who are British have argued similarly. They [*say we are?*] all citizens and we are all subjects, but we have to realize that we are citizens without rights, and subjects without consideration. Now, we are tired with this kind of thing. If a thing is worth while having, it is worth while having well. I am satisfied to be a subject of the king, if I am going to have the same privileges like all other subjects, but you are not going to give certain subjects special privileges and deny them to me. If I am a citizen, I want the same rights and privileges, and opportunities like the other citizens.

Now, the Negro, as he faces the world, realizes that so far as his rights under these governments go they are limited, whether they be British, French, Italian or American Negroes, and we must face these facts. I have come back to Washington to speak to you in a rational and reasonable manner of these things, because the fault is going to be ours and not the white man's if we do not adjust ourselves immediately for the danger that is ahead. I am not in a position to blame anyone but the Negro for his present condition, in that I am of opinion that no one can keep you down but yourselves. I have not seen the man yet who can permanently keep me down. I reason and argue the same way that if each and every individual would exert himself, no one can keep you down and make you what you do not want to be. As it is to the individual, so it is to the race. If a race is down, it is because that race is satisfied to be so. That race will rise from its position and condition when it makes up its mind. That is what we are endeavoring to do now. But to get the Negroes to make up their minds and lift themselves from the condition in which they are, and not expecting God or the white man to do it, as they are not going to do it, is our duty and not theirs.

Survival of the Fittest

The white man in America, as in other parts of the world, has his own affairs and his own racial business to attend to, and when he goes out of his way to assist others it is charity, it is philanthropy and it is sympathy. That sympathy, charity and philanthropy cannot be kept up for long because of the great changes that are now affecting the human race as a whole. The time is coming, and very shortly, when the white man will have to fight for his own existence, because we are nearing a period of the survival of the fittest, when every man will have to fight for his own existence, whether he be yellow or red, white or black. There is no doubt about it, and that is why the white race, whether in America or elsewhere, is now seeing about themselves and are not showing that philanthropy and sympathy for other peoples. It is the law of self-preservation, and the common understanding and interpretation of such a law has caused the U.N.I.A. not to expect them to do for us what we ought to do for ourselves.

The world has reached a point where there is bound to be a conflict in ideals which may lead to disaster on the part of those who are not strong enough to hold their own. We are living in a world of economics, a world of bread and butter. That is what life really devolves itself into—a problem of bread and butter. With all the high-sounding philosophies and ethical principles initiated from pulpits and schoolrooms, etc., life is purely a question of bread and butter—your three square meals a day—and it has reached the point now where there is going to be a desperate scramble for these three square meals. There is not going to be enough for everybody to get an equal portion. The strong [weak?] fellow is going to go hungry, and later die.

That is the problem that confronts us now. There are going to be many conflicts and wars. If you Negroes sit down here; if you stay in America and the world, and allow Europeans to grab Africa and parcel it out, in another twenty-five or fifty years, if you have nowhere to lay your heads, do not blame it on the white man, do not blame it on God, but blame it on your own indolence, your own laziness, and your own lack of vision.

Africa the Only Salvation

That is why the U.N.I.A. presents the African program to the Negroes in America, the West Indies, and the world, at this time. Africa is going to be the only salvation of the Negro. It will not be Asia, but Africa that is going to be the salvation of the black man, if he has sense enough to act in time. There are some of us who do not like Africa. We have peculiar ideas and notions about Africa. We have imagined hideous and horrible things about Africa, as we are harboring in our imaginations about hell. Africa is like hell to us—a place to which we do not want to go. But let me just leave this one statement with you: If Africa was such a hell, England would not want to go there; and if it was such a hell and place to be despised, France would not be endeavoring to grab every square inch of land; and Italy, Belgium, Portugal and Spain would not be making such desperate efforts to colonize there. This suggests, therefore, that there is something worth while about Africa. It is this something that the world is going after. That something worth while in Africa at present is oil, rubber, gold, copper, coal, and various other minerals. If you believe these things are useful to the world, if you believe they are valuable to our present civilization, then let me tell you that these are the things that interest England and France, and Italy, Belgium and Portugal, which cause them to be going into Africa. They are not going after fever, as some of us think we will get when we go there. They are not going after elephants and tigers and lions that will eat them up, but they are going after the oil, the rubber, the diamonds and coal, etc.

Getting What You Want

. . . [*Line mutilated*] necessary to his existence and comfort. They contribute to his wealth, and wheresoever these things are, if they are in hell, he will go after them. (Applause.) It is not the place, but what is there. For instance, which of you, having gotten private information that there is ten billion dollars across the river, located in a certain spot, and all that is necessary is to swim or get across the river anyhow, before anybody else, would not devise some means of getting there. It is not the river, but what is beyond the river. If you know what is beyond the river, and you have to swim, you must expose yourself to the danger of drowning; so, therefore, if you want these things, you must go after them. The white man in Europe, hundreds of years ago, heard about this new land, that was discovered by Columbus; heard that it was virgin and valuable, and worth while and he came in search of it and found it. You see what he has got out of it. He has got a new civilization; he had built up a new nation in wealth and imperialism, and he is going to hold it until "Thy Kingdom Come."

Negro Must Look to Himself

And any Negro who thinks the white man is foolish enough to turn that over to him—wait on, brother! Wait on! If you want what is worthwhile, go in search of it yourself, and risk the same dangers. You are crazy if you think the other fellow is going to risk his life for the beautiful and for the valuable resources of nature, and, after he has risked his life and been successful, to hand that to you. You know you are not reasonable. There is only one Being in the world who risked His life for something and then gave it entirely away to somebody else, that person is Jesus. And He came to the world but once. He promised to come a second time, but they made it so hot the first time that two thousand years have passed and He had not come back yet. You do not find people like that nowadays, people who are willing to risk their all, and give it away freely to somebody else, without consideration for themselves. How often have you met such people? Brothers, they are not here, they are in Heaven, and when we get there we will associate with them, but while we are down here we are in a world of sin, a world of materialism, and you have to face that world of sin and materialism and treat it as it treats you. Therefore, do not expect more than is humanly reasonable in a world like this. Do not expect the white man to take his soul and give it to you, because they have need of their own souls. I have said this to show that the Negro's future is dependent upon himself. If he has no vision today he is lost. It is that vision that we are endeavoring to give to all peoples of the world.

I love all mankind; I love all governments; I believe in the system of government; I believe in the regulation of human society. Without order you cannot do anything. I believe that there should be a great American government for the American people; that there should be a great English government for the English; a French government for the French, but I, under the interpretation of democracy, when it is said that the majority must rule, believe that the majority must rule, and wheresoever minorities find themselves existing or living under the governments of majorities, they must expect all the time to be always agitating and fighting and begging for their rights, because they will never get them.

THE MAJORITY MUST RULE

The majority will always monopolize the government; it is human nature, because of sin. If I have a family of ten, and there is my neighbor with a family of two, I am going to look after my family first, according to the constitution, although it is written for the twelve of us. We shall always interpret that constitution to the interests of the ten, and what is left we will give to the two. It is human nature. You cannot get away from it so long as the other fellow is in the majority. Whether white or black, that majority is going to rule, if it has any sense.

The work of the U.N.I.A. is to educate the black majorities so that they will have the same privilege of ruling as the white and yellow majority. That is our purpose in organizing the four hundred million Negroes of the world in one great social, educational, and political movement. Are we organizing for fighting to take from the white man America? Are we fighting for larger opportunities in Europe? Or are we fighting the Asiatic to take away his country? No; we are fighting, we are demanding the black man's right, which is Africa. (Applause.)

THE PROBLEM OF TODAY

We believe in human justice and in human rights. We can only prosper and live peacefully when we give to the other fellow what is his, and expect him to give what is ours. Now, let us come to a common sense expression of this American problem. We are in troubled waters. Later on, somebody is going to drown, somebody is going under. There was a calm, and there is a storm coming on. If the storm does not stop immediately, somebody is going overboard and be drowned. We are in troubled waters. What do I mean? We in America have evolved into a new state, a new mental state. Here we have fifteen million people, the product of four million slaves of sixty years ago, people who could not decipher their own names, who could not conjugate a verb, who knew nothing of the science of the language they spoke; who had no outlook on life; who were mainly satisfied to be serfs and peons and slaves, believing that to be their fixed position in life by the dispensation of the Great God who created them. Here we are[,] an improvement on such people, and such thoughts. We are now higher in culture and in civilization, in education, we are capable of holding our own against all comers. It is a fixed law that you cannot educate a man and keep him down. If I am ignorant I will be satisfied to go around probably half-clad, living in a log cabin and sleeping on a rough bed or walk[ing] for ten or fifteen miles to perform my daily task; but after you have educated me and brought me within reach of culture and civilization, I must have good clothes and board; I must live in good surroundings; my home must be comfortable, my furniture good, and if I have to go to my employment fifteen miles away I should be able to take the street car to go there or drive in my automobile. That is what education has done for me; and I look around and see the other fellow has not more education than I have, and I see him becoming President. Therefore, I ask why should I not be President also. That is what education has done for me, and for the fifteen million of our race today.

Brothers, we are in troubled waters; we are in the fixed mood and mind, to demand justice, because we are educated to the appreciation of democracy, liberty and equality in all things. Now, this education of ours cannot be destroyed. To do so you would have to destroy the entire Negro race, because the mind is the thing that fixes a man's outlook. To destroy that outlook, you have to destroy the man.

NEED FOR DIPLOMACY

Here we have the New Negro as courageous, as bold, as self-assertive, as self-conscious as any man Almighty God ever created. Now, what are you going to do with him? Trample him and keep him down? If you attempt that, you are looking for trouble. (Applause.) The result is, you must either give him the opportunity to rise or expect trouble. Now, all of us are determined to rise; but our environment is not so favorable to our rising from where we are to the higher things without encountering great trouble. The trouble is the overwhelming prejudice with which we have to compete. Common sense, common judgment, will dictate to you that even if your ca[u]se is right and just, if you should win your complaint, reason will dictate to you that you had better be careful as to how you present your complaint against the majority, otherwise they may fix your position. Now, we all know we are deprived of certain rights; we all know that we are being suppressed in our ambitions. But what can we do? Reason dictates that at this time there is great need for diplomacy on the part of the Negro; there is great need for keen leadership on the part of the race. If there is a race that needs good diplomacy and leadership in the world, it is the Negro race; because we are in a devil of a fix. We have our hands in the lion's mouth, and reason should dictate to us how we should take it out. If you disturb the lion, you may miss the sunlight, but if you can gradually move out that hand without arousing the suspicion of the lion, then you are safe.

That is the position fixed for the Negro in America. We are confronted with a keen, active race in opposition to our ambition. Those who think that the white man is asleep, I advise for their own good to change that belief and attitude. If the white man is even half-drunk, he is still thinking about his supremacy in the world; and he could be half dead, and he would still try to maintain it. There is no white man in the world who does not feel the call of race, and therefore, whether he is American or English, or French, his own supreme thought is to hold himself supreme in the affairs of men. He is not going to let you get his place; and the power of the white man stands beyond question. He is on top. If he has to use keen diplomacy to keep him on top, how much more has the fellow down below to lift himself to the position of the white man by kee[n]er diplomacy[?]

INDUSTRY BEFORE POLITICS

These are things that the Negro politicians in America do not realize. They do not realize that industry and politics are important counterparts in the progress of a race or nation; that you must have industry before politics. Any man can be a successful politician if he gets three square meals per day. Therefore, my duty is to insure three square meals a day, and afterwards talk politics if I want. Until you can feed yourself, you cannot talk politics. I have said that to bring home to you the fact that I do not like to talk politics foolishly or to talk on popular subjects just for talking. Before I talk about anything[,] I try to find out to what extent it is going to benefit the people in whom I am interested. It does not take very much to become popular. But the person or individual who has an outlook or purpose in life, analyses all things whether popular or not, and then discusses them afterwards. It has been popular to talk about the Ku Klux Klan, and talk about fighting them. But we must remember, that our hands are in the lion's mouth. We all know the lion is an animal we should always try to kill, but we should not let the lion know that we are going to kill him. Rather than tell him, it is better to go right ahead and do it.

No Permanent Progress

There is no permanent progress for the Negro in America. When that progress threatens the power of the white man he at once brings the Negro back to [the position he has fixed?] for him. Therefore, it calls for a high degree of statesmanship to lead the Negro at this time.(Applause.)

Where the Negro is in the minority in a majority civilization, and under a majority government, until we get good statesmanship, we will, in spite of anti-this or anti-that bills, be always in the same position. I am not criticizing Congressman Dyer's bill, nor am I saying that the bill will serve [h]is purpose. Mr. Dyer knows that he is playing the same game with us as the missionary plays and has played with us in Africa for the last 2,000 [y]ears. It is the same thing over and [o]ver again. The strong will always [t]ake advantage of the weak; the intelligent will always take advantage of the fool.

Now, what more can the anti-lynching bill do than the laws now in force against vagrancy or stealing? There is the law on the legal and moral statutes; laid down by God himself through Moses and adopted by men, "Thou Shalt Not Steal," yet men [s]teal every day (laughter). There is [a] law about taking another's life, yet [p]eople commit murder everyday.

No Law but Power

There is no law, there is no justice but Power. So it is left to us to get strength and power as quickly as we can. (Applause.) If France was not powerful today, she would not have ventured to keep herself in Germany [so] long against international sentiment. She would not have invaded Germany at the time, and remained in the coal regions as she has done. It was wrong. It was in violation of the principles of the peace that all the nations had fought for; and that England and America desired. But France represents power and that is right. If it is wrong, it is still right. France today is the greatest disturber of the world, and she is allowed to continue her unreasonable and inhuman attitude toward Germany, which she knows will lead to another bloody world war, because it is impossible for sensible men to think that they can keep down 60,000,000 intellectual people like the Germans, people of science and industry. You can keep a fool down because he does not know how to protect his rights, but you cannot keep people down who know how to mix deadly gases, etc.

France is foolish to think she can keep the Germans down. The French statesmen and historians know that they are laying the foundations of another war as Germany laid when she levied her unreasonable indemnity on France after the Franco-Prussian war of 1870.[1] France's attitude is based on that of Germany's in 1870. England and America know that France is laying the foundation of great world-wide con[fli]ct and that she is a menace to the peace of the world. But they know that France is well equipped with many thousands of airplanes and that she can [ho]ver over their cities and drop certain [thi]ngs not pleasant to their populations. [The]refore, whatsoever France does is [rig]ht. There is no justice but power; [the]re is no right but strength.

THE CASE OF HAITI

Because Haiti, little Haiti, has had her little political troubles, like every [othe]r nation, America says to her: "You [are] violating the Monroe Doctrine; you [are] disturbing the peace of the Caribbean." Therefore our army and navy proceeds to invade the little country and [est]ablish jurisdiction over it. But [Fr]ance, which troubles the peace of the [wo]rld, is allowed to do as she pleases. [Ho]w? Because France represents pow[er.] France represents strength, while [Hai]ti represents nothing. The last [Hai]tian gunboat lies under the Carib[bean.]

The French airplanes guarantee [Fra]nce against interference of any [pow]er in the world that seeks to carry [out] the law. You therefore realize that [ther]e is no law but strength and power, [that] it is foolish for Negroes to sit here [and] believe they can pray this question [away.] Brothers, if you have lungs strong [enou]gh, pray on. Pray on. But our [pray]ers will not help us with this [prob]lem. Let the whole 15,000,000 Ne[groe]s of the country decide to pray for [one] week straight and keep on praying, ["Lo]rd keep this man from kicking me," [but] they will still kick on. But if all [of] us were organized and represented [st]rength and a powerful government[, we] would not have to pray about being [ki]cked, because no one would kick us.

TRUE POSITION OF THE NEGRO

I am endeavoring to bring to you the [tr]ue position of the Negro, not merely [in] America, because America is the most [ho]nest country in the world today [to]ward the Negro. And the most honest [pa]rt of America is the South. It is the [be]st part of America, because it tells us [the] truth. I like a man who tells the [tru]th. The South says: "Negro, thus [far] and no farther. Do not let the sun [go d]own on you here." I like that hon[esty] and frankness, because I am then [bett]er able to look about myself. And [tha]t is why I like America better than England and France and other white [gove]rnments of the world.

[A]merica says: "Negro, you are lim[ited and] you shall not rise above this limit." [If] you want to do otherwise it is your [priv]ilege. Some of us think that that [att]itude will change. Were it not for that attitude we would have been deceived in America as we have been in England and France, and would be the lowest elements in the community. We cannot say we are the lowest here, because some of us represent prosperity and culture and wealth because of that honesty.

Do you know that were it not for this honesty of America there would be no black doctors, preachers, lawyers or anybody worth while? Negroes here would follow the line of least resistance and let white preachers preach to them "because they are sent from God," or let white dentists pull their teeth, or let the white doctor give them medicine, because the black doctor's medicine is hoodoo.

If today we represent anything of the prosperity and wealth of America, we have to thank the honest American white man for it. If we get the race consciousness that we are getting now we have to thank America for it. When I want inspiration, I go south from New York to New Orleans, and get jimcrowed and find myself unable to get a soda from a white soda fountain. Then I get courage and inspiration to strike out more boldly for Negroes.

"How Many More?"

Again I emphasize that you and I are crazy if we think that the white man is going to yield up to us without a fight this beautiful environment that he has created for himself. Now, if you have ever traveled between any points in a Pullman car, you will have observed what I have often seen. The moment a colored man enters the car, the other persons in the car will look at you and look at each other until you take your seat. The average man will not say anything, but, beneath those looks, is the question: "How many more? How many more?"

Our prosperity will bring us in closer contact with the white race in every way, and, as that prosperity shows itself, so much the more will pressure of race be brought to bear upon us. That is the future that I see. Even though every Negro in America should become prosperous overnight, that would not ensure the safety of the Negro in America, for the simple reason that the Negro cannot permanently prosper, or any minority race in the community, when the majority or part of the majority is starving. The spirit that drives the successful Negro dentist or farmer from the Southern town by the power of the white mob is the same that will make it hellish for the Negro when he aspires for industrial and economic prosperity in the surroundings of a majority race, who are faced with hard industrial and economic problems. So that in every instance there is nothing but gloom ahead of us, and darkness. There is no prosperity, no success, no law, no justice but strength and power. (Applause.) We need industrial strength and political and industrial power.

Human Nature

You know two bulls cannot live in the same pen, and you either have to separate them or the weaker one dies. I trust that I have conveyed to you what is in my mind. Contemplate the matter in all seriousness and you will see that there is no solution for the Negro problem than to build a nation of your own in a country of your own, because our economic, industrial and political positions are fixed in all communities where we form the minority group.

It is human nature, and that is why I have stopped abusing the white man. The more I study the question the more I understand his position. Reverse the position of the races in this country, and let there be 95,000,000 blacks and 15,000,000 white men, and you will have the same outrages committed upon the whites in Mississippi, Texas and Georgia as we have been having for the last fifty years. It is hard to believe, but you cannot get away from it. Power will always abuse its strength. That is the cause of sin.

Take your mind back, centuries ago, and you find the same thing when the white man was subject to that great Negro civilization on the banks of the Nile. In those days the Egyptians kept down the Israelites without mercy, and God had to turn back the Red Sea so as to allow the Israelites to escape. It has been human nature in all the ages, so do not expect more from the white man than you gave when you were in the position he is in now. Therefore, do not abuse God or the white man for the present condition, because this will go on so long . . . as there is sin in the world and as long as we have not the strength and power to hold our own. . . .

Do as the White Man Did

If the white man had sense to know that he would need the fish that is in the sea, and so got hold of it, that is his advantage. The white man knew that he would have to organize a system of society, so that they could unite with each other and get hold of the land. He had sense enough to know that if he wanted automobiles, he should look for oil. He knew that the pleasures of society, and the vanities of women would entail his having to get diamonds for her, so he grabbed the diamond mines that were our own. The white man has a sense of the future; he knew what he wanted, and he grabbed them all. If the Negro had no sense to know that he would want all these things and sit down, and allow them to take it away from him, then he should stay where he is; and that is where he has been for hundreds of years. He had no appreciation for the beauties of nature and God's wonderful creation, and so he has none of it. But through the U.N.I.A. he is beginning to appreciate the value of coal, oil and diamonds; and so we are going to have our share of it (applause). And we are fair about it, too; we are merely going to take our portion, and leave the white and yellow man to have theirs.

If Asia is good for the Asiatics, if Europe is good for the Europeans, and America for the Americans, we are going to have ours in Africa, and we are going to fight and die for it, if you please. (Applause.)

But the Negro does not want to fight and die, because he loves peace and humanity too well, and that is why the U.N.I.A. takes the program of peace and good will to all mankind.

How to Proceed

Reason tells us in twentieth-century civilization that if your neighbor has something that is yours, do not burn your neighbor out, but go and inform him that he has something that belongs to you, and ask him kindly to return it. The neighbor may be a little sore about this, but prove to him that it is yours, and that you want it, then, when you prove successfully that the thing is yours, and the neighbor does not want to give it up, then you move your hand out of your right hand pocket and say: "Look here, this thing is mine, please give it to me." Do not knock him down. Then, if he refuses, draw back and say: "Give it to me, or I will give it to you." (Applause.)

The U.N.I.A. does not contemplate the third stage; we do not even contemplate the second stage. We believe the world will be reasonable enough, when arguments are produced, to acquiesce to our demands and requests to give Africa to the Africans, to whom it justly belongs.

That is why we feel sure that when the appeal is made to the liberal-minded white people in America and the world, to restore the Negroes to their possessions, they will by justice and reason do so. I do not believe in provoking a man, but I am saying this emphatically to the world, as a friend of the world, that the Negro is in this attitude. If you place him in a corner where he must eventually die, he can equally die here.

If the Negro realizes that the world desires to take from him these things that would make him comfortable, and he realizes that sooner or later he will die, then he will decide to die like a man, fighting for something worth while.

AROUSING AFRICA

And that is why I would not like to see England or France arouse the sleeping passion of Africa, because I like peace and humanity too well. I am only endeavoring to interpret to the nations of the world the position of the sleeping Negro.

England and France know it better than anybody else that if the Negro is determined, he can do pretty well whatever he chooses, and that he will go through the gates of hell without shrinking as he went through the Marne and Verdun, over the heights of Mesopotamia, as he fought on the battlefields of Flanders, because of the sentiment of Democracy, and because of the vision of Democracy. For that only he made those sacrifices. If he made such great sacrifices, only for the interpretation of a sentiment, how much will he not sacrifice for the vision of his liberty and manhood, and the freedom of his own soul? (Applause.)

Therefore, let us be as human beings, reasonable. It is impossible for us to have peace in the world so long as one part of the world keeps the other down.

I am going to take up another phase of this subject tomorrow, and I trust those of you who are interested in this question will come out and bring your friends so that we can intelligently go into the discussion of this problem. It is one that we must discuss from a sympathetic viewpoint. We must be as sympathetic to the white as he should be to us. With sympathy on both sides, the problem will be solved. The question may start in America, but will not end here. There are millions of our people all over the world. Sixty years ago our people were satisfied to be taken from four o'clock in the morning until night to work in the cotton fields, but we are living in a different world now. India and China and Africa will have changed conditions. It may be tomorrow, five, ten, or a hundred years from now, but there is bound to be a change affecting humanity as a whole that will bring about a leveling of the things that affect the human race. So while we are in this period, let there be a friendly adjustment, otherwise we are going back to the same thing that is affecting Germany now, and will affect France in the future, namely, revenge.

If we do not come to a sympathic settlement of this human question now, I repeat, that war and rumors of war will repeat themselves until the doom of the world and the wreck of all matter.

And the U.N.I.A. desires that adjustment that will establish peace on all sides. It is no use of ex-President Wilson talking about the League of Nations, or of Clemenceau or any other politician. There can be no League so long as part of the world seeks to keep down the other.

AFTER BURGLARY—A POLICEMAN

Brother, you think you can come to my house, put me out, take all my clothes and money, and then talk to me about peace and justice, after you have beaten me and robbed me and knocked me down, talk to me about a League of Nations for peace? All the burglars get together after robbing the community and then say "Let us have peace." No, the policeman is hunting for the burglar, and the burglar will never be safe until he is lodged in jail. There is not going to be peace until the world returns the stolen goods that they have robbed. They have plundered Africa these five hundred years, as England has plundered India, and, until that ceases, there will be no peace in the world, notwithstanding all the plans of Wilson, Clemenceau and David Lloyd George.

We have reached the point where there must be some sympathetic and intelligent adjustment of this question. I am appealing to the intelligence and culture of Washington to think this thing over. You college students, teachers and professors; you ordinary men who are living in this community, think this question over, and then you will realize what Marcus Garvey and the U.N.I.A. are talking over. (Applause.)[2]

Printed in *NW*, 26 January 1924. Original headlines omitted.

1. The Franco-Prussian War broke out in 1870 when Napoleon III declared war on Germany. The French, rapidly overwhelmed by Germany's military power, were defeated within six months. Under the humiliating peace terms, the French were obliged to pay five billion francs to Germany (an unprecedented sum at the time) to sustain German occupying troops, as well as to cede the largely French-speaking border area of Alsace-Lorraine, rich in coal, iron, and textile production. French bitterness over the peace terms—especially the loss of Alsace-Lorraine—contributed to the Franco-Russian alliance of 1894 and to the hostilities that ultimately led to World War I (R.R. Palmer, *A History of the Modern World* [New York: Alfred A. Knopf, 1978], pp. 513–519, 664–665; A.J. Ryder, *Twentieth Century Germany: From Bismarck to Brandt*, pp. 81–88, 140–146).

2. The paraphrased conclusion of Garvey's speech relates how he urged the audience to sign a petition he intended to submit to President Coolidge, as well as sign similar ones to the king of England and the president of France, concerning "the rights of the Negro" (*NW*, 26 January 1924).

Editorial Letter by Marcus Garvey

[[Washington, D.C., January 16, 1924]]

Fellow Men of the Negro Race, Greeting: . . .

THE PEOPLING OF THE WORLD

The fight of the Negro of the present is to prevent the European from making Africa his new home. The European has already peopled Europe, America and Australia. He made a strong bid for the peopling and dominating of Asia, but he failed, thanks to the activity and alertness of the Asiatic.

DOOMED FOREVER

If Negroes sit supinely by and allow the European to prosecute his desires in the direction of Africa, then it simply means that we are doomed forever. The European has his plan of world conquest and domination. It is not likely that he will take the Negro into his confidence. It is for us to discover his purpose, and, as far as it affects us, to see to it that we are protected. This is the work of the Universal Negro Improvement Association.

PROTECTING INTEREST OF RACE

We feel it our duty to at all times protect the interest of the Negro race, and with such responsiblity resting upon our shoulders we go forward advancing the banner of the Red, the Black and the Green, with the object of creating out of our united efforts the idea of African imperial redemption. The thing that we desire is to see a great and powerful African commonwealth where Negroes will have the same opportunity and privilege to rise to power and glory as the white man has in America, Europe and Australia. We are asking for the whole-hearted co-operation of the Negro peoples of the world for the accomplishment of the program of the Universal Negro Improvement Association. Let us do everything possible to develop industrially and commercially the now existing Negro nations by strengthening their hands with our western intelligence and helping in their growth to political power.

RESPECT OF OTHER RACES

We must place ourselves in a position where the other races and nations of the world will not fail in their respect for us as a people. We want to stir the Negroes of America and the West Indies to the realization and the fact that Africa affords just at this time a glorious opportunity for colonization, and as the white man for centuries went from Europe to colonize and people America and Canada, so should the Negro from the West Indies and America turn toward the colonization of Africa.

OUR WESTERN EDUCATION

We should convey to Africa all that we have imbibed by the way of education and culture from the contact of three hundred years with western civilization. Africa needs scientists, mechanics, engineers and tradesmen of all kinds. Yes, she needs doctors, teachers, business men and captains of industry. America and the West Indies have been splendid training grounds for the Negro for the last three-quarters of a century. We have learned from the best universities of Europe, Canada and America, and we can now apply that knowledge for the development of our Motherland. Surely all thoughtful Negroes of America and the West Indies will dedicate themselves to the work of Africa's development.

PREPARING OURSELVES

Those of you who are preparing yourselves in the banking and other financial institutions of America be assured that we shall expect you to become the great financial magnates of Africa in directing the banking systems of the Mother Country. You who are in the insurance business of the United States of America, surely we are expecting you to preside over the "Metropolitan" and "New York" African insurance companies and corporations of the future. You men and women who are engaged in your little industrial enterprises, surely you are training yourselves to become the presidents and managers of department stores and other corporate enterprises of Africa. Surely you lawyers and other professional men who are experimenting in the United States and the West Indies are but getting ready for the bigger field of practice in the great Commonwealth of Africa, where you shall become leaders in statesmanship and in society. And you men and women who have had to labor by your hands, surely you are preparing yourselves to undertake the bigger task of building for your own race and laying the foundation for your own commonwealth. The contact and civilization that we have had in the western world will surely fit us for undertaking the big task of African redemption. Let us, therefore, focus our attention upon African colonization in 1924.

REPATRIATION BOOM

Let us save our dimes and dollars and accumulate them so as to be ready when the great boom starts in repatriation. The Universal Negro Improvement Association hopes that in 1924 several hundred thousand families from America and the West Indies will be repatriated to Africa to work in its development.

DUTY OF MEMBERS OF ORGANIZATION

Members of the Universal Negro Improvement Association everywhere should redouble their energies and determination and push forward the program of the organization for this new year. As we labored six years to make this our movement the greatest organization in the world, so we should continue during 1924 and 1925 to see that a great part of the program is accomplished. With very best wishes for your success, I have the honor to be, Your obedient servant,

MARCUS GARVEY
President-General
Universal Negro Improvement Association

Printed in *NW*, 19 January 1924. Original headlines omitted.

Speech by Marcus Garvey

[[LIBERTY HALL, New York, January 20, 1924]]

The progress of man is marked by what he has accomplished. The world judges races and nations by what they have done. Modern civilization is very exacting. It divides races and nations into groups. The progressive groups they honor and revere and respect; the non-progressive groups are despised, ignored and in many cases rejected. Among the despised and rejected groups of humanity we have the Negro standing out prominently; probably he is the most rejected of all the despised and rejected groups. The question is, why? And the world answers, because the Negro has done nothing, has accomplished nothing.

It is all well for a race to flatter itself into believing in the broad love of humanity, but when we come to a serious study of the human problem in the materialism of today we realize that brotherhood is not regarded and respected and admitted except that brotherhood represents progress. To repeat in other words what I said a while ago, why the Negro is kicked and tossed about in all parts of the world is because he represents nothing progressive, he represents nothing that he has of himself contributed to modern civilization. Now I am making this positive statement so that my stand and the stand of the Universal Negro Improvement Association cannot be mistaken.

NO PERMANENT CONTRIBUTION

We of the Universal Negro Improvement Association[,] I of myself, admit that the Negro has made no independent contribution to modern civilization, and it is because of that that he has become the pariah of the world, that he has become the despised creature of all races and nations. Tell me what progress we represent that is permanent. Tell me what progress we represent that is entirely and completely ours. I dare any Negro in the world to show me in twentieth century civilization any progress that he has made that is permanent, from his own contribution and from his own efforts. That is the cause of the judgment passed upon us by the great races and nations of the world. Until the Negro makes such an independent contribution, until the Negro makes such an independent progress which stands out purely demonstrative, he will never be able to lift himself in the appreciation of the world higher than where he is at the present time.

And that is why the Universal Negro Improvement Association struggles forward for this higher accomplishment. That is why the Universal Negro Improvement Association adopts the high ideal of the founding and the establishing of a nation for the Negro race out of which they will build a structure and contribute a civilization of their own. The vainglorious Negro will tell you, "I am educated, I represent the highest in modern intelligence; I am a graduate of the best schools and colleges and universities of America, of Europe and other parts of the world. How dare you say that I have made no progress?" The conceited financier of the Negro race will say, "How dare you say I have made no progress when I represent in the banking institutions of my race so many millions of dollars, when the race represents so much property?" The average Negro will say, "How dare you say we have made no progress, we have made no contribution, when I have my home, when I have reared my family, when I am worth certain money which I have in the bank? How dare you say I have made no progress?" And the answer of the Universal Negro Improvement Association is to the Negro that there is no progress that you have made, there is no state or condition you are in at the present time, that cannot be denied you and taken away from you in twenty-four hours by those who have made it possible for you to represent such a state or such a condition or such a progress.

LIVING ON BORROWED GOODS

The Negro is living on borrowed goods. The Negro is but consuming and using that which someone else has contributed to the world for his own comfort, for his own happiness and to satisfy his own desires. So long as you wear the clothes of your neighbor, you are still exposed to nakedness, because that neighbor may ask you at any time to return that which you borrowed. The Negro at the present time is wearing the garment of civilization of the other fellow, and so long as the other fellow is disposed to allow you to wear that garment you may be able to demonstrate your progress, but when that fellow calls upon you to restore that garment you stand as naked in the world as you ever were. It is that nakedness of achievement that causes the white race and the other races of the world to despise the Negro at this time. It is not because of your color, it is not because we are black, it is not because we are of this varied hue that the world despises us. The world despises the Negro because the world knows that the Negro has made absolutely no independent contribution to civilization and to the world. The world knows that the Negro is a pariah and a consumer in another man's civilization. And if I give you my clothes to wear, if I loan you my clothes to wear, you will not expect that I will have as much respect for you as if you had on your own garment. (Applause.)

DO NOT APE

So long, so long as we continue to ape this white man in this white man's civilization—and he is intelligent enough to know what he has contributed to the world, he has contributed everything we use here, everything we consume. And you doubt it? Let Edison turn off his electric light and we are in darkness in Liberty Hall in two minutes. Let the white architect, out of whose mind modern white architecture was created, tear down Liberty Hall and say, it is the creation of the white man's mind, it is the white man's contribution of architecture of the world, and you and I will be exposed to God's heaven. Let the white man come to the door and call Garvey's bluff because he talks too much about the success and progress of the Negro, and in a few minutes the white man will have Marcus Garvey naked even as he came into the world, will have every Negro in here naked. He will say, "Garvey, I have contributed to the world the system or the pattern of clothes that you wear. Garvey, you have on a dress coat; take it off. The pattern is mine." And I will have to take it off, because I could find no reason to keep it on. "Also, Garvey, you have a vest. It is the style of my dress; take it off. Say, Garvey, you wear a shirt, it is the style of my garb which I contributed to my civilization. Take it off. Garvey, you have on pants that are my contribution to civilization. Take them off." And in a few minutes every Negro man and woman in this building would stand naked before the white man's civilization as God Almighty created you from the time of Adam and Eve up to present. You and I will be in the same position of that ancient grandparent of ours who was picked up in Africa three hundred years ago with a naked body and brought across the Atlantic to work as a slave in the Western World for three hundred years. You and I have made absolutely no improvement upon ourselves as a race since the first slave was brought into the Western World three hundred years ago. That is how the Negro stands now in comparison with other races and nations.

SEGREGATING THE NEGRO IN THE NORTH

Every race has a culture of its own, has its own civilization, whether it be China, whether it be Japan, whether it be the countries of Europe or the countries of Asia. Every one of them has its own contribution to civilization, its culture and customs, and each and every one of them feels happy over their own ideas. The Easterner feels happy with his turban, his fez and his flowing garment. The white man feels satisfied and proud with the garb in which we are now clothed, which we have borrowed from him. The Negro will be proud of his nakedness. That is our condition in the world today. And why? The white man kicks the Negro around in the South, the white man jimcrows the Negro in the South, and the white man is now seeking to segregate the Negro in the North. There is now an organized campaign of segregation all over the North that is sweeping to the Northwest right through Maryland. There is now an agitation going on in Maryland to further segregate the Negroes of Maryland and to keep them out of close proximity to the white man's settlements and white sections of the community.[1] The same thing is now being started in New York. There is a conference to be held between the Northern real estate man to jimcrow and segregate the Negroes in the North[2] just as they are doing in the South, because they claim that wheresoever the Negro moves there is created a depreciation in property value, and because of that no white community in the North is going to further tolerate the living of Negroes in white districts.

The Negro's Poverty

Do you know what that is? I say not because of your color, but because of your poverty. Because of your poverty in civilization, in your contribution to civilization. Even the Jew has contributed something to civilization. He has the power of the money bag. He has contributed something that the world wants, you are a poor thing in the world. The world does not think of people who have nothing. The world does not count people who have nothing. The Jew has something—money. The Italian has government and power. The Anglo-Saxon has government and power. The Chinese represent government and power. The Japanese represent government and power. Everybody remembers these people. The Negro represents nothing and nobody remembers the Negro until he comes in contact with somebody. Listen! The white man does not see a Jew before he thinks of and remembers him. The white man only wants to think of money and the Jew comes up to him. When the white man wants money he is bound to know the Jew lives, because the Jew has the money bag. Therefore, the white man cannot think of money without thinking of the Jew. The white man, if he thinks of world conquest, cannot think of it without taking into consideration the great powers that rule the world. Therefore, he thinks of the Englishman, the Frenchman, the Italian.

The white man cannot think of traveling East without thinking of Japan, because the Japanese race stands as guardians of the East. But nobody needs to think of the Negro, because the Negro has nothing that anybody wants. We have not a culture that the other people want, we have not a civilization that the other people want, nothing material the other people want except our cheap labor. When the white man thinks of somebody that can be exploited and robbed, that is the only time he thinks of the Negro, somebody to trample on, to kick around. When anyone wants to show their superiority in the world, they think of the Negro, the footstool, on which they rise. So long as we remain in that condition, so long as we remain in that state, so long will we be jimcrowed and segregated, kicked and tossed about, not only by America, but by all the other nations and races of the world.

Build an Empire

Hence the Universal Negro Improvement Association says the time has come for the Negro to make his independent contribution. We are going to make our contribution, not through singing and praying, but we are going to make our contribution through the building up of one of the greatest nations and empires in the world. (Applause.) That is what the Universal Negro

Improvement Association is endeavoring to do. And when you have laid successfully the foundation of government, when you have built successfully the pillars of empire, there will [be] no more segregation ordinances, there will be no more jimcrowing among Negroes, there will be no more disrespect shown to us because of our race or because of our color. The white man jimcrows us on the railroad that runs from New Orleans to New York because he knows that all the railroad systems in the world belong to him and the yellow man. And, therefore, brother, you don't think I am going to give you the kind of accommodation in my house that is going to make you over-comfortable all the time, if you can't return the compliment to me some of the time at least. I may accommodate you once, but if you come too often I am going to slam the door in your face, except you can return the compliment, except you can invite me to your house and treat me in like manner. You don't expect that you will come to my house from January to December and get away with it like that. I am no fool to be always accommodating you, always giving you cushioned seats and nice things to eat and drink, and you will not return the compliment. You are crazy if you think I am such a fool. And you are crazy if you think the white man is such a fool to accommodate the Negro all the time when he knows the Negro has nothing to give in return. The white man accommodates the other white men, the Englishman, the Frenchman and the Italian because he knows they can return the compliment. The white man is even willing to be most hospitable to the yellow man of Asia because he knows the yellow man can return the compliment. But the white man knows the Negro has no compliment to return, therefore he does not care how he treats the Negro. When you and I represent a civilization with all the comforts, with all those things that are necessary for human comfort as the other races do, at that very hour the other races and nations of the world will change their attitude and disposition towards us.

LAST HAPPY EXPERIENCE

That is the appeal that the Universal Negro Improvement Association is making to the world of Negroes to get up and do. Depending on the white man for another century, we are but depending on our doom. I am only sorry time will not permit me to elaborate, because I desire to give some of my time to the Ambassador to England,[3] but I would like to draw a picture of America in another short while, because in another short while America and the Western world and the white world will be a hard place for Negroes to find existence in. We are now undergoing our last happy experience in America. In another ten or twenty years that condition that we have been existing under will have passed away for a new condition. We are facing economic starvation in America, in another five, ten, twenty or thirty years. The readjustment of the world, as I have often said, is going to bring about an economic, industrial stagnation in America that is going to reduce the Negro to his last position in this nation.

WHAT A FRANK WHITE MAN SAYS

I have in my possession a letter, one out of hundreds, written by one of the biggest men in this country, a white man, in answer to certain frank questions I asked him on the Negro question in America and the world. To me such a man is one of the Negro's best friends. But some Negroes would not agree with me in that. They would regard him as they regard the Ku Klux Klan. I regard any man who is honest enough to tell me the truth not only as my friend, but as a person to be respected. I respect and honor the man who tells the truth. As I said before, I hate and despise the liar, whether he comes in white or black. This white man was honest enough to tell me this in answer to certain queries I placed before him: "Yes, the Negro may find an existence alongside of the white man in America for another generation or two, providing he keeps his place." He went on to say what he meant by "keeping his place." We are willing, he said, to tolerate the Negro as a laborer, and we will even allow him to be a member of the trades. He may be a bricklayer, he may be a mason, he may be a carpenter, if he belongs to disorganized labor. He may be a teacher, a doctor, he may be a preacher among his own people so long as he does not put on airs. So long as he will confine himself in these positions and as outlined and will continue to be meek, humble and servile without any desire to take part in politics and become a part of government he will even have the protection of the white man for another generation or two. But if he attempts to put on airs and to desire a place in government, it is going to end in a bloody conflict to his detriment.

A WEARY WAIT

Now, this is not Marcus Garvey speaking, but one of the biggest white men in this country who has written that to me as explaining the attitude of the class of people he represents in their attitude toward the Negro problem in America. You hear what he said. He did not say, "Beyond two generations." If we are satisfied to be meek and humble, to be laborers and all that, our position will be all right for a generation or two. Now, he must have had something in his mind after two. (Laughter.) He meant this: That after the second generation we will all be dead. You know some black folks are waiting for white folks to go out on the highways and tell them what is in their minds. You are waiting until Jesus comes. The white man is not going to tell you his plans from the public platforms. He is not going to tell you from his newspapers. He is going to work out his plans, and if his plan is going to operate against you[,] you must have sense enough to find that out before he succeeds and before it affects you. And that is what the Universal Negro Improvement Association found out five years ago when it organized the association in America for the purpose of building a government for the Negro peoples of the world.

And this white man said this also: "Because of my love for humanity and because of my love for the black people—because I was born among them and grew up among them—I would advise them to follow and support a program like yours. (Applause.) And surely because of my love for humanity and your race I would do anything to help in that direction, but I know all the people of your race will not take kindly to the thing you talk about, but I have this to say to you by advice. Those who will seek a government of their own and help to establish it let them go and live there. Those who prefer to live among the white people shall eventually pass away." Here we have the program of the honest white man in a nutshell.

THE MIGRATION FROM THE SOUTH

Negroes, do you know what is happening now? Do you not know that that terrible migration from the South the other day was no chance work, was an organized effort of certain Southern and Northern white leaders to create an industrial stampede to the North so as to arouse the sleeping passion of the Northern white man and open his eyes to the danger of the Negro overrunning his community? The white man, from the days of the Civil War and immediately after Abraham Lincoln signed the emancipation proclamation, had his plan for further dealing with the Negro. The white man of the South told the white man of the North, "You are foolish, you are ignorant to fight against [for?] the Negro, and you have done that because you don't understand the Negro. You have done that because you have not a Negro problem on your hands. But if you were to have a Negro problem on your hands, you would treat the Negro as we do down South. We understand the Negro because we live alongside of him."

The recent migration from the South to the North was an organized effort among certain Southern leaders and Northern leaders who have been inoculated with the Southern doctrine to push up North sufficient Negroes to create a problem in Northern communities so that the North could have a better appreciation of the condition of the South. And after there were riots in certain Northern sections where Negroes flocked from the South, certain propaganda was made in the North to draw the Northern white man's attention to the danger of the Negro problem North such as you have in the South. The result was after certain industrial leaders were consulted they said, "We will not, therefore, give these Negroes employment to harbor them North; we will refuse to employ them so that they will go back South where they will be regulated by the Southerner who understands them.["]

No longer ago than last week an industrial committee met somewhere in Philadelphia consisting of Northern employers of labor and Southern farmers,[4] and it was decided among them that they would discourage the employment of Negroes in the North so that they could be returned South to be exposed, as you know, to the actions of the white man in the working out of the white man's plan in his relationship to the Negro. You see how helpless the position is.

An Understanding Between Southern and Northern Leaders

There is fast becoming an understanding between the Southern leaders and the Northern leaders, and in another ten years, if not earlier, the Negro in the North is going to be in the same hellish position as the Negro in the South. And some of our Negro politicians are contributing also to the hastening of this day. These Negro politicians, who are crying out for a Negro in Congress, and for a Negro in the Senate,⁵ if they knew what they were doing they would go about what they want in a more diplomatic and quiet way, because if they continue to antagonize the white man politically, and to show him what we mean, the ballot will be taken from us in the North, as God lives, as it was taken from us in the South during the days of the reconstruction. The white man is no fool. The white man wouldn't give up this country even to Jesus Christ, much less to the Negro. (Laughter.)

Do you know what the white man has done? The white man has killed the Indian so as to get this country. Negroes, do you think he loves you better than he loves the Indian? If he killed the Indian, what will he do to us? He will send us to Hell, and further than Hell, if we come in competition with him for his country, which he has shed his blood for, and which he has sacrificed and died for.

The Need for Able Leadership

This time, more than ever, the Negro in America needs able leadership and statesmanship. May God bless us with such a leadership at this hour. I am sorry I haven't time to develop this theme, but I will continue it tomorrow night in this hall, and I hope you will come out and bring your friends. Suffice it to say the Universal Negro Improvement Association is on the side of all that suggest progress for the Negro. We want a Negro in the Senate and a Negro in the House as bad as any other Negro wants it, but we realize sometimes when you have your hand in the lion's mouth it is good sense to easily and quietly take it out. You may want to kill the lion, but the best time to kill the lion is when the lion is fast asleep. If you attempt to kill the lion any other time you may see the stars for the last time. (Laughter.)

Therefore, you will understand what I mean—that it takes diplomacy and keen statesmanship to lead the Negro in America at this time as a minority group competing with a great majority whole that rules the nation through prejudice. The majority in a modern democracy will always rule. America is a democracy. America, therefore, accepts the established rule of democracy— that the majority must rule. The minority, therefore, can only agitate, and will forever agitate, and will get no further than agitation, so long as the majority rules. That sums up the hopeless position of the Negro in America. As a minority group, prejudice against him by the majority will never be able to improve our position from now until eternity. Now take that away, if nothing more.

THE PLATFORM OF THE U.N.I.A.

That was the platform of the Universal Negro Improvement Association all the time. I talked on that and emphasized that for five years and the last week I was up in Washington. Speaking along the line I stopped off in Washington to address the Washington Division of our Association for two nights; and on Wednesday [16 *January*] I went to the House of Representatives just to look in and I also went into the Senate, and as I stopped in the gallery of the House of Representatives there was a member of Congress from one of the Western States who was speaking on some bill that was before the House for about three or five days, and th[e]se were some of the words that emanated from him at the time I got in there: "It is all ignorance to countenance the agitation of a minority; whenever a majority has ruled, the law must be upheld. Gentlemen, except you are going to stand for minority rule—which would be against the constitution of the United States of America; which would be against the constitution of a modern democracy—except you are going to do that you cannot tolerate the agitation of the minority in altering the laws laid down by the majority. So long as I am an American citizen," he said, "so long as we live under a constitution of the majority, we, in this Congress, shall allow no minority to influence a majority opinion of the people of this nation."[6]

He was a Congressman. Now, analyze that and apply that to our agitation and to our race and you will find out that between now and eternity the Negro has no right to get under the constitution, because the constitution is interpreted by the majority for the good of the majority and not for the good of the minority. I trust you quite understand that. Those are the things that force the Universal Negro Improvement Association to the one declaration and the one conclusion, that the Negro can only hold his own in the world when he is able to build up a majority government of his own. (Applause.) The Negro, being a minority in America, the Negro being a minority in a scattered world outside of Africa, and realizing that minorities have no voice, so to speak, constitutional rights in the governments of majorities, we say the best thing we can do is to link up these minorities into one great majority whole and thus lay down the pillars—lay down the foundation of a great African empire. (Applause.) Take that and think it out; but let me warn the politician—the Negro politician—let me warn Robert Abbott, of Chicago[,] let me warn [*James*] Weldon Johnson, of the National Association for the Advancement of Colored People, that they are trifling with the destiny and the future of the American Negro by their senseless, rabid agitation for a Negro in the Senate and a Negro in the Cabinet and flaunting that in the face of the white man. It is like dazzling a red rag before a bull. If you want to kill a bull, don't . . . [*words mutilated*] a red rag and expose it before him; he will gore you to death. If you want to get the bull, wait until the bull has eaten—wait until the bull is masticating its food—wait until the bull has laid down to sleep and when you are sure that the bull is fast asleep, then you can carry out your intention of strangling the bull. Now, I cannot make it plainer than that.

I cannot give better advice to Weldon Johnson and Robert Abbott than that.

Diplomacy Must Be Used

Surely, I repeat, the Universal Negro Improvement Association would like to see a Negro Senator and Congressman, but there are many ways to kill a dog, as I said before, than by rope around the dog's neck. Diplomacy is the medium through which intelligent people work towards the accomplishment of what they want. The Negro in America must be more diplomatic than he is, because he is a minority fighting against a majority, endeavoring to compete politically and industrially with the majority. We are at the mercy of the majority. Before a race of people can talk politics they must first lay a foundation of industry. You do not talk politics first; you have your meals first (laughter); then you talk politics afterwards. Until the Negro can insure his meals—until the Negro can guarantee his meals, he has to be very careful in America how he threatens the white man politically.

Do you know what politics is? Politics is the science of government that protects those human rights that are not protected by law. If you are thinking that the white man is contemplating Negroes governing them, you wait on for the realization of it. When the Negro starts to talk politics he means to indulge in government. And now we are talking about putting a Negro in the Senate—putting a Negro in Congress. That is what the white man will never tolerate and especially when the Negro's existence depends on him to make it possible for such a Negro to talk politics and make law. If we want to go to the Senate—if we want to go to Congress, the first thing Robert Abbott and Weldon Johnson—those two fools—should do is to guarantee the bread and butter of the black men whom they want to vote for them. The man who feeds you calls your politics; and that is the danger I want to point out to Robert Abbott and to Weldon Johnson of the National Association. Here we are in New York 150,000 Negroes. Here we are in Chicago, where Robert Abbott lives, probably 150,000 or 200,000. It is true that we are strong enough in a Negro Senatorial or Congressional district to unitedly vote to send a Negro to Congress.[7] Let it be so that we are strong enough in our Senatorial district to vote and send a Senator to the Senate; and the same way in Chicago.

Just as a matter of race appeal, Marcus Garvey, a mob psychologist[,] comes before you and says "150,000 of us here in Harlem constitute ourselves the strongest voters in this Senatorial district; we shall have a black man represent us in the Senate." All right you follow my advice and elect Garvey. I am elected to a job of $7500, and the little rakings down that I can get, and for the term my riches are insured. I have a good job; but you don't know the problem Marcus Garvey has left behind him in Harlem. Yes; we elect Robert Abbott from Chicago to the same position as Garvey, but Abbott does not know the position he has left behind him in Chicago—putting black men in the Senate, which arouses the ire of every other Senator and arouses the indignation of the country that they represent. It would not be more than 24 hours before every Negro in Harlem and every Negro in Chicago would feel the pinch and experience the reaction of sending Marcus Garvey, only by mob sentiment, to the Senate or to the House. White people are not fools. We are not dealing with Negroes now; we are dealing with white people with set plans and set progress. After Garvey appears in Congress, to the resentment of the other members of Congress and to the humiliation of the white man whom Garvey defeated in the Negro congressional district, do you know what will happen? All the leaders of the great parties will say "we will have to take steps to remedy this thing right here. How came Garvey to be here as a representative of New York?" They take up the political map of New York and the industrial map of New York.

They also take the political map and the industrial map of Chicago and they sit down in committee meeting and examine these two maps and they have discovered in truth that 150,000 Negroes really live up in Harlem. That by the residence there of 150,000 Negroes it becomes possible for them to elect a Negro Congressman and a Negro Senator. They say "we never saw this danger before; now we must go about this thing and rearrange it." And so the Congressional Committee comes down to New York with its industrial map. The first man they go to is John Wanamaker, and they say: "Mr. Wanamaker, how many Negroes [do] you employ in your business down here?" "Two thousand." "Do you know what has happened in New York in the last two months?" "No; what is it?" "Well, a Negro has been elected Senator or Congressman from the Senatorial or Congressional district in Harlem." "Is that so?" "You have been in New York and don't know that?" "Well, Wanamaker, here you are a good Democrat or Republican; here you had a representative of your own race representing your industrial and commercial interests in Congress for the last ten years, and you sit down here and allow these Negroes up here to defeat your own interests and do not know it." John Wanamaker scratches his head and says, "Is that so?" "Well, you know what you have to do? Let those Negroes go tomorrow morning." They leave Wanamaker's and they go to Gimbel Brothers. "Say, Gimbel, how many Negroes have you employed here?" "Five hundred." And they repeat the same instructions, and they make a tour of every employer in the city of New York who employs Negro labor, and they find out where the 150,000 Negroes are employed. By next week every Negro has got his "walking papers" and every place puts up the sign "No colored wanted." You know what will happen in the space of thirty days, when all the Negroes in Harlem are out of employment. Nearly every Negro in Harlem will have to pack his little bag and move to some near-by city—to Detroit, to Philadelphia, to Pittsburgh, or to somewhere else to look for a new job. Where 150,000 Negroes lived forming this voting power in a Congressional district last week, next week you will find only 3,000 Negroes there—not even enough to elect a rat to a cat's convention. (Laughter.)

So long as the Negro is employed by the other man, so long must the Negro be ruled by the prejudice of his political masters. The white man is regarded as the master because he represents the government. Therefore my advice to Robert Abbott and to Weldon Johnson of the National Association for the Advancement of Colored People [is] to be careful how you tamper with the Negro's future in the United States of America. It calls for statesmanship; it calls for diplomacy; it calls for keen leadership, and I trust God will bless us with it at this time. (Applause.)

Printed in *NW*, 26 January 1924. Original headlines omitted.

1. As large numbers of blacks migrated from rural to urban areas, white real estate agents and property owners employed both legal and sub-rosa methods to establish and maintain urban segregation. Laws passed in the South to legalize segregation had been struck down in a 1913 Supreme Court ruling that declared segregation laws unconstitutional under the Fourteenth Amendment. In 1924, however, the issue of legal segregation was raised again in Baltimore. In a ruling on commercial zoning, Judge Heuisler of the Maryland Supreme Court stated that if restrictive commercial zoning were constitutional, so were laws segregating whites from blacks. At the same time, the Baltimore real estate board pressured the zoning board for authorization to segregate blacks into specific sections of the city. The result was that while efforts to legalize segregation failed, restrictive covenants were used effectively to maintain segregation, and, as the *Baltimore Afro-American* reported, "every section of the city is being organized to prevent what is termed a 'Negro invasion'" (*Baltimore Afro-American*, 4 January, 18 January, 1 February and 28 February 1924; August Meier and Elliott Rudwick, *From Plantation to Ghetto* [New York: Hill and Wang, 1966], p. 198).

2. Evidence of this meeting has not been discovered.

3. On 22 January 1924 Rev. Richard Hilton Tobitt was formally appointed the UNIA's ambassador to England and given the title, Sir Knight Commander of the Sublime Order of the Nile, "as a mark of honor and appreciation for exemplary services rendered to the Negro race" (*NW*, 2 February 1924; see also *Garvey Papers* 2: 496–497).

4. Evidence of such a meeting has not been discovered.

5. No black representatives served in the U.S. Congress between the retirement of George H. White of North Carolina in 1901 and the election of Oscar De Priest of Illinois in 1928. After 1890 disfranchisement deprived the mass of southern blacks of suffrage, and only with the vast migration northward during World War I did representation again become a realistic possibility. During the early twenties, various race leaders demanded that blacks receive major party nominations to run for Congress. For example, at the National Colored Republican Conference of 1924, party spokesman George H. Cannon recommended an "aggressive campaign" to elect blacks to federal office (*Pittsburgh Courier*, 12 July 1924). Disappointment with the Republican party over this issue lead to considerable agitation in the burgeoning urban ghettoes of the north (*NYT*, 12 March, 6 July, and 13 July 1924; *Baltimore Afro-American*, 15 August 1924; Harry A. Polski and Roscoe C. Brown, eds., *The Negro Almanac* [New York: Bellwether Publishing Co., 1967], pp. 463, 466–467).

6. This quotation is similar to arguments presented in debate over House Resolution 146, introduced on 14 January 1924, to amend the rules of the House of Representatives. Republican representative Walter F. Lineberger of California argued:

> Our great Federal system, founded with the three branches of government . . . is the pillar of the American scheme of government. . . . It was said at the time that any other system carried within it the seeds of its own dissolution. So I believe that whenever you substitute minority government for majority government, whether it be on the floor of this House for the purpose of calling up a bill, whether it be in committee or whether it be in party caucus, such substitution carries with it the seeds of dissolution of American traditions. (*Congressional Record*, 68th Cong., 1st sess. [3 December 1923–15 January 1924], 1: 943–944)

7. Blacks were in fact increasing in electoral strength, but still no black was elected to the Senate or Congress until 1928, when Chicago politician Oscar De Priest was elected to Congress (Ira Katznelson, *Black Men, White Cities*, p. 95).

Report by Bureau Agent H.J. Lenon

Pittsburgh, Pa. January 22nd, 1924

. . . Just recently Agent engaged a well known negro in conversation as to radicalism among the negroes, and naturally the name of GARVEY was quickly suggested by this man. Among other things he said that he felt that GARVEY understood mob psychology better than other men in the lime-light of the world at the present time. He said that money had turned GARVEY's head, and when he turned crooked and was caught[,] it hurt his pride, and now he is bitter and more dangerous than ever before, and advised that we keep close tab on GARVEY.

He further stated that he, GARVEY, will begin anew perhaps on the old lines somewhat altered. He will "prove" that he was "framed" and that big business feared him and his eleven million black friends and sought to destroy his usefulness by Court proceedings and "mark what I tell you GARVEY will make 99% of the negroes believe his story. He will re-organize a new movement and he will play politics with his enemies, why[,] he will even convince smart men like Chandler Owen. He will take a man from every faction that opposed him and give them a place in his cabinet or on his many committees. Then watch GARVEY go, and right here let me give you a tip, GARVEY will never let that cabinet dominate the movement, he will have his inner circle paired with every one of his enemies. Another thing I would watch, ["] suggested my colored friend, ["]keep your eye on the white men he meets and corresponds with, he may hook up with the Communists.". . .

H.J. LENON

DJ-FBI, file 61-3006-181. TD.

Marcus Garvey to J.H. Thomas, British Colonial Secretary

NEW YORK U.S.A. January 25, 1924

My Dear Mr. Thomas[1]:—

This letter introduces to you Honorable Richard Hilton Tobitt, High Commissioner and Minister Plenipotentiary to His Britan[n]ic Majesty's Government, representing the interest of the four hundred million Negroes of the world, under the auspices of the Universal Negro Improvement Association, an organization of six million active members, with sovereign power to represent the aspirations and destiny of the Negro peoples of the world.

Honorable Richard Hilton Tobitt is accredited by the Universal Negro Improvement Association to interest himself in all matters affecting the interest of the Negro race within Great Britain.

His credentials have been submitted to His Majesty's Prime Minister and Foreign Secretary, and it is hoped that His Majesty's Government will accord to him such courtesies as are extended to other representatives of independent races and sovereign peoples. Wishing you and your party continued success,[2] we beg to remain, Your obedient servants,

> Universal Negro Improvement Association
> MARCUS GARVEY
> President General
> P.L. BURROWS
> Asst. Secretary-General

For identification Hon. Richard Hilton Tobitt's signature appears below. Signature:—R.H. Tobitt

PRO, CO 554/64/7535. TLS, on UNIA letterhead, recipient's copy.

1. James Henry Thomas (1874–1949) served as colonial secretary in the first Labour government that came to power in January 1924. A railway worker, Thomas began his political career as president of the Amalgamated Society of Railway Servants. In 1910 he was elected on the Labour ticket to represent Derby in the House of Commons, a seat he held until 1936. As president of the Railway Union, Thomas led the dissolution of the "Triple Alliance" of coal miners, railwaymen, and transport workers during the miners' strike of 1921, which led to the defeat of the miners. In 1931 he followed Ramsay MacDonald into the National government, precipitating his dismissal from the union. He later retired from political life, afterward becoming chairman of British Amalgamated Transport, Ltd. (*NYT*, 22 January 1949; Gregory Blaxland, *J.H. Thomas: A Life for Unity* [London; Frederick Muller, 1964]).

2. Garvey is referring to the first Labour government, formed by Ramsay MacDonald on 22 January 1924, after liberals swung their support to Labour and defeated the Conservative government of Prime Minister Stanley Baldwin. The uneasy alliance between Liberal and Labour was short-lived. By October 1924 the Labour government was at loggerheads with the House of Commons and called a general election. By then the Liberal party had withdrawn its support, especially on the issue of Anglo-Soviet treaties. Only days before the election, the press printed a letter allegedly written by Grigori Zinoviev, president of the Communist International, urging British Communists to support the treaties and inviting working-class rebellion. Although the authenticity of the letter has never been established, it was instrumental in the defeat of the Labour party. The defection of Liberals and local pacts between Liberals and Conservatives contributed to a Conservative victory at the polls. MacDonald resigned his post as prime minister on 4 November 1924, thus ending the first Labour government in Britain (Carl F. Brand, *The British Labour Party* [Stanford, Calif.: Hoover Institution Press, 1974], pp. 94–116; Maurice Cowling, *The Impact of Labour, 1920–1924* [Cambridge: Cambridge University Press, 1971]).

Speech by Marcus Garvey

[[LIBERTY HALL, New York, Jan. 27, 1924]]

Somewhere in Moscow today was lowered into a grave the body, the mortal remains, of one of Russia's greatest men, one of the world's greatest characters and probably the greatest man in the world between 1917 and the hour of 1924 when he breathed his last and took his flight from this world. Some people, the privileged class and their representatives, speak of Lenin in terms not very complimentary. They call him names not calculated to enhance his standing among the unthinking peoples of the world. But they say these mean things of Lenin because he was a reformer. They say these things of him as they said them of Christ who came nearly two thousand years ago to spiritually reform the world. It was Lenin who in disguise about five years ago marched up to a certain building in Russia, even though they were looking for him and searching for him—this man whom they regarded as a traitor, as a disrupter of the peace and a revolutionist, marched into a gathering of his compatriots and in a few words declared for the freedom of the new Russia.[1] And at that hour the revolution that we read of took out of the hands of the privileged class the destiny of Russia's government, the destiny of Russia's people. For over five years Lenin and Trotsky were able to hold the Russian peasantry together and established for the first time in modern days a social democratic government, a government wherein the people ruled.

OPINION DIVIDED

Opinion is divided in the world about Lenin. Some think him a great man, a great benefactor, a great reformer, a great leader, and a great teacher. Others look upon him with hatred, with scorn, with contempt. The class that has been kept down, the class that has been exploited and robbed looked to Lenin as a savior. The class of the exploiter and robber looked upon him as a revolutionist and a menace to society. That class is glad that Lenin is dead. But as they rejoice over the death of this great man, so the millions of the peasantry of Russia and the millions of the oppressed of the world bow their heads in solemn reverence, in sorrow and condolence over the loss of this great man. It is cold in Russia, very, very cold, much colder than it is in New York tonight, and you know how cold it is. It has been so in Russia for several days, and the Russian people think so highly of Lenin that for days they uncovered their heads, stood out in the open streets and took their turn, millions of them, one by one, for the privilege of entering into that building in order and in discipline to look for the last time upon the face of their savior, their leader and their emancipator. When millions of people will do that, you realize that they fully appreciate the cause to which the man gave his life and appreciated the man for the sacrifice made.

LEADER OF THE PEOPLE

It is impossible to expect that all the people will think kindly of any one individual in the world, because there is a division of interests in the world; all peoples are not interested in the same thing. That is why we are divided into classes; that is why society is divided into different orders. Each class has its own representatives. Each class has its own leaders. If it were the King of England who was to be buried today, the aristocracy and the nobility of the world would mourn, because he was their representative, he was one of their number. If it were the President of France that was to be lowered into his grave this afternoon, the middle class of society would mourn and weep and express their sorrow because one of their number was taken away. But the class represented by an aristocratic king, the class represented by the so-called middle-class people, are not the classes affected in the leadership of Lenin, because he was a leader of the common people, he was a leader of the peasantry, and there are so many of them.

EMANCIPATING THE SOULS OF MEN

Therefore Lenin stands out greater than all because he was the representative of a larger number of people. Not only the peasantry of Russia mourn for Lenin at this hour, but the peasantry of all Europe, the peasantry of the whole world mourn for Lenin, because he was their leader. And we also, as Negroes, mourn for Lenin. Not one but the four hundred millions of us should mourn over the death of this great man, because Russia promised great hope not only to Negroes but to the weaker peoples of the world. Russia through her social democratic system promised a revolution to the world that would truly and indeed emancipate the souls of men everywhere. Negroes have not yet gotten to realize the effect of certain world changes. We of the Universal Negro Improvement Association who lead have studied carefully and keenly the activities of Lenin and Trotsky. We have never before committed ourselves to any public opinion as touching the system of government now existing in Russia, because we did not believe it politic, we did not believe it wise. The social democratic Soviet government of Russia is not yet recognized by all the other governments of the world. Only a few recognized governments have recognized Russia. The governments of the capitalist class, the governments of the privileged class have refused to recognize Russia as a government. They are still seeking and hoping that another revolution will be enacted in Russia that will take the power and control of government out of the hands of the peasantry and pass it back into the hands of the privileged class. At that hour all the other governments not yet recognizing Russia will recognize her government. But we of the Universal Negro Improvement Association, as I said, had our own opinion, had our own idea in the matter of the new government of Russia. And it is without any hesitancy, without any reserve, we could not but favor the existence of a social democratic government in Russia or in any other part of the world, because we are of the class that rules in Russia and naturally our sympathy should be with the people who feel with us, who suffer with us.

EXPECTING THE IMPOSSIBLE

The Russian Socialist government is still an experiment. The outer world judges it without sympathy. They expect that in five years Lenin and Trotsky could have made their government so perfect as to justify its existence. It is impossible. During the reign of the czar, the masses, the peasantry of Russia, were kept in such ignorance that they were not cognizant of their existence.

It is this untutored, unwieldly mass that Lenin and Trotsky took and made a government of, made a nation of. It is impossible, therefore, to expect that such people who lived for ages under the most crude systems of civilization, the crudest systems of twentieth century culture[,] could have demonstrated the worthiness of their government as a social democracy in five years. It was impossible for the world to expect them to reach a state of perfection when they, the privileged class, who controlled for centur[i]es[,] have yet to demonstrate that perfection, and it is because of that lack of perfection among them that we have had wars and rumors of wars between 1914 and 1918.

TIME WILL INDORSE RUSSIA

I believe, in time, that the whole world will take on the social democratic system of government now existing in Russia. It is only a question of time, I say. England is the first to have reached out for this perfect state of social democratic control among its peoples. What England is doing tonight is what Russia taught them to do through the revolution of Lenin and Trotsky. The British people are better appreciated in their social democratic government as led by the British Labor Party because the British people have had a better system of training, they have had a better system of education. The average Englishman is an educated man, an intelligent man, and that is why they are able today to reach out in a social democratic government without arousing in any way the suspicion of the world. But what Lenin and Trotsky attempted to do for Russia is just what Ramsay MacDonald[2] is about to do for the British people, and that is, make the majority rule through labor. The laboring man in England, I said, is a more intelligent man than the laboring man in Russia.

THE LATE CZAR'S RUTHLESSNESS

The czar was so exacting, so inhuman[,] that he kept away from the average Russian the light of civilization, the higher learning that would make the Russian peasant a competent and an able citizen. The English people were able to force better consideration in that respect and because of that they are better able to rule now, and I feel sure that Ramsay MacDonald and his government will demonstrate to the other monarchical governments of Europe that the best government after all is a social democracy. And I feel that when time has flown and passed away that Lenin and Trotsky will get their proper and due place in history.

U.N.I.A. SENT MESSAGE OF SYMPATHY

We mourn with Russia over the death of this great man. We mourn with the proletariat of the world for the demise of the world's greatest leader. And, as it is customary with us, we did not fail at the hour to pay our tribute to the All-Soviet Congress when the news was flashed to the world of the death of Lenin. Immediately we cabled the All-Soviet Congress expressing the sorrow and condolence of the 400,000,000 Negroes of the world. Unfortunately, we have not yet sent an ambassador to Russia, but I feel sure that our message is conveyed and I feel sure that our message is received with as much respect and as much honor as the message of any other peoples or governments in the world.

TROTSKY'S GREATNESS

So that we want you to take interest in these world events. The death of a man sometimes means a great deal to the world and to civilization. If some man dies the wheels of progress for certain peoples turn back probably for a century or a half. We trust it will not be so with Russia because Lenin was indeed the greatest of Russians. He brought Russia to a higher state of progress than any other Russian for hundreds and thousands of years. We trust, we do hope, that they will not destroy the work of this man and send Russia back to the ages of the past. As I said the death of a man sometimes means so much to a people, so much to a nation, because sometimes his ideals die with him. I trust and hope that the plan of a greater Russia[,] a greater Russia for a majority of Russians[,] has not died with Lenin, has not been buried with him. Unfortunately, immediately before his death there had sprung up among the Soviets such misunderstanding as to have divided them into factions. Trotsky, who was as important in the revolution as Lenin, was ostracized from the party. I also regard Trotsky with great respect, with great reverence. I believe him to be a great leader and a great patriot and I hope[,] as I understand that it is most likely, that the death of Lenin will bring about a reconciliation between the factions and the parties of the Soviets,[3] so that unitedly they can go on perpetuating the social democracy for which they fought and for which they bled and for which Lenin has died.

LENIN RISKED ALL

It is painful to those of us who can appreciate ideals to see lofty ideals die which would help in saving a people or in redeeming a race. I feel that the ideals of Lenin were high and lofty, and that there are no better ideals in Russia today than those for which he stood, and I hope Russia will not fall back into the hands of the monarchists. I trust Russia will not fall back into the hands of the privileged class, but that the peasantry of that great country will continue to perpetuate the government for which this great man struggled, for which he risked his all. Lenin, when he started the revolution that seized the government from the privileged class and turned it over to the peasantry, risked everything he had. He was sought for on every hand. They were looking for him everywhere, and he was in their midst, and in their very midst he declared the revolution that brought about the change. A man of such courage, a man of such loyalty, of such patriotism to his class, is worthy of honor, is worthy of respect, and in his death he is worthy of the sorrow, of the condolence of all, not only of his class, but of all mankind.

LESSONS TO BE LEARNT

We also will have days of sorrow as we march on from one condition to the other. We will also have to lose our great men. We will be better able to appreciate them when they die, when they pass out of this world, by being able to appreciate the sacrifices of leaders of other races, appreciate them for the sacrifice they make for their own people. We are not Russians. We are Negroes. But we can learn lessons from this. It is the lesson that Russia teaches that interests me, the lesson wherein a majority of the people are able to rule, to establish a government. All majorities should rule. It is the law of modern democracy. All majorities should rule. And that is why we suffer so in this country, because the majority rule. The majority will always rule. The majority should always rule. And it is because we realize our impotence as minorities scattered here and there that we are endeavoring to link these minorities into a great majority, that we also may rule. I trust that you will therefore appreciate the situation. I trust that when you read things said about Lenin you will be able to have your own opinion and form your own conclusion. The average Negro is led away by what he reads, he is led away by what he hears. You do not always read the best of the individual. You do not always hear the best of individuals, and it is rather unsafe for any one to form an opinion just by what he has read or just by what he has seen or heard. Opinion should be formed only after most careful examination of the truth. And I trust that will be the attitude of the members of the Universal Negro Improvement Association at all times. You are not to form your opinion about men and about measures just by what you read or by what you hear, but you must place yourself in the position mentally where you are able to discriminate until you have found the truth, then you will go and pass your opinion on the truth.

THE CASE OF LLOYD GEORGE

A lot of unkind things will be said of Lenin. A lot of unkind things are said of the world's greatest leaders and benefactors. But if we were to form our opinion about leaders and individuals who are probably before the public on the strength of just what is written and what is said, we today would have very few leaders, because very few men would be bold enough to be leaders. But very few men accept the censure of the privileged class, whose interests they do not represent in advocacy of right for the greatest number. Take the case of Lloyd George of England. David Lloyd George sprang from the common people. At one time he was just a so-called British subject or English citizen. He sprang from one of the poorest families of Wales and when he was struggling up with his ideal of service to the larger number of his countrymen[,] when he was struggling upward with the desire of service to humanity, the privileged class attacked him; they called him a demagogue, a rebel; they called him all manner of names. They said he was a re[v]olutionist, a Socialist; they practically called him names that would hurt the soul of the devil. But David Lloyd George had those of his class who believed in him, who knew he was giving expression to their feelings and representing their desires. Whilst the one class denounced David Lloyd George, whilst the one class hounded him down, whilst the one class called him all manner of names, the class he represented stood behind him and gradually he came into power, until he himself became one of the privileged class, one of the privileged leaders of his country, and after a while he became leader of the Empire because his class had sufficient confidence in him to support him and back him until he was able to give expression to their feelings. Lloyd George was a Liberal, but he won his spurs to such an extent that the nobility of England and the aristocracy of the Empire had to reverence and respect Lloyd George in the expressions he gave vent to on behalf of the people he represented. .

FORM YOUR OWN JUDGMENT

And so you will find in history past and history that is being made by the world leaders, you will not expect the best things to be said about them. The best things are not said about Christ. It took time before men started to pay homage and respect to the name of Christ. In Christ's day they said as vile and wicked and hurtful things about him as they said about Lenin during his lifetime, as they said about Lloyd George, as they said about all reformers. So I am advising the members of the Universal Negro Improvement Association to get yourselves in a frame of mind to discriminate between what is written and said and form your own opinions only on the truth. Lenin to us was a great man. Lenin to us was a savior of his people or a savior of his country. Lenin to us has pointed the way where the majority of the people will rule, and Lenin has pointed the way for a better system of government through which humanity, will, I hope, have peace and perfect peace. (Applause.)

Printed in *NW*, 2 February 1924. Original headlines omitted.

1. In April 1917 Vladimir Ilich Lenin (1870–1924) secretly slipped back into Russia from his exile in Zurich. After traveling across Germany hidden in a sealed train, he was given a warm and tumultuous welcome by workers, soldiers, and members of the Soviet leadership, who were waiting for him at the Finland Station in Petrograd. Days later, at a joint meeting of the Mensheviks and Bolsheviks, Lenin demanded that the Bolsheviks split from the provisional government then in power and urged that, in alliance with Russian workers, they transform the bourgeois democratic revolution into a proletarian socialist revolution. Although Lenin initially faced opposition even within his own party, by the end of April, the Bolshevik leadership was won over (Alexander Rabinowitch, *The Bolsheviks Come to Power: The Revolution of 1917 in Petrograd* [New York: W.W. Norton, 1978], pp. xvi–xxxiii; Edward H. Carr, *The Russian Revolution: From Lenin to Stalin* [1st American ed., New York: The Free Press, 1979]).

2. James Ramsay MacDonald (1866–1937), the first Labour prime minister of England, was born in Lossiemouth and Branderburgh, Scotland, the son of a laborer. He joined the Labour party in 1894, serving as secretary from 1900 to 1912 and as treasurer from 1912 to 1924. MacDonald was a member of Parliament from 1906 to 1918 and leader of the Labour party from 1911 to 1914. He opposed Britain's entry into the First World War, and because of the unpopularity of his pacifist views, he lost the party's leadership in 1914 and his Parliament seat in 1918. By 1922, however, he was again elected to Parliament, and shortly thereafter he assumed the Labour party leadership. In October 1924, only nine months after becoming prime minister, MacDonald was defeated in the elections called by the Labour government in response to a dispute within the House of Commons. He became prime minister again in 1929, but in 1931 he accepted the dissolution of the Labour government and became prime minister of the coalition National government, a position he held

until 1935 (Carl F. Brand, *The British Labour Party*, 112–115; David Marquand, *Ramsay MacDonald* [Totowa, N.J.: Rowman and Littlefield, 1977]).

3. By late 1922 Lenin voiced fears of increasing party instability caused in part by signs of an impending split between Leon Trotsky (1879–1940) and Joseph Stalin (1879–1953). At the twelfth party congress in April 1923, preliminary skirmishes over party leadership had begun between Trotsky and Zinoviev, who was supported by Kamenev and Stalin; both factions were nevertheless still in agreement as to the need to maintain party unity. But by October 1923, Trotsky openly denounced the central committee. Stalin led the counterattack. By the time of the thirteenth party congress, beginning on 16 January 1924—only a few days before Lenin died—Stalin led an open attack against Trotsky. Although reconciliation may have seemed possible during the mourning period for Lenin, factional fighting intensified after Lenin's death (Isaac Deutscher, *The Prophet Unarmed* [New York: Oxford University Press, 1963]).

Report by Special Agent Joseph G. Tucker

NEW YORK, N.Y. FEB. 2, 1924

UNIVERSAL NEGRO IMPROVEMENT ASSOCIATION

Marcus Garvey sent the following cablegrams to Ramsay MacDonald, British Premier[,] and Phillip Snowden,[1] Chancellor of the Exchequer, complimenting them on their elevation to their new positions. He also sent a cablegram to Russia upon the death of Lenin which reads as follows:

[*ca. 24 January 1924*]

Hon. Ramsay Macdonald, British Premier,
10 Downing Street, London:

The Universal Negro Improvement Associaton, representing the four hundred million Negroes of the world[,] sends you greeting on the triumph of labor in Great Britain and on your elevation to the Premiership of the nation. As Negroes fighting for our independence and a nation of our own in our motherland Africa, we shall look to your meritorious party for help and consideration. May you live long to administer the affairs of your country.

> MARCUS GARVEY,
> President-General,
> Universal Negro Improvement Association
> and Provisional President of Africa

January 24th, 1924

Phillip Snowden, Chancellor of the Exchequer,
10 Downing Street, London

Please accept the congratulations of the four hundred million Negroes of the world for the triumph of labor in England and your elevation to the Exchequer as Chancellor. The Universal Negro Improvement Association looks to you and your party as friends of the Negro race in their fight for national independence in Africa. Long live the new chancellor.

MARCUS GARVEY

January 25th, 1924

All Soviet Congress,
Moscow:

Please accept the deep sorrow and condolence of the four hundred million Negroes of the world over the death of Nikolai Lenin, and the irreparable loss of the Russian people. To us Lenin was one of the world's greatest benefactors. Long life to the Soviet Government of Russia.

MARCUS GARVEY

JOSEPH G. TUCKER

DJ-FBI, file 61-23-273. TD. The telegrams quoted in the report were also printed in *NW*, 2 February 1924. Tucker's summary of Garvey's speech of 27 January 1924 is omitted.

1. Philip Snowden (1864–1937) was a British viscount and Socialist politician. He served as chancellor of the exchequer in the Labour government of 1924 and again from 1929 to 1931 (*Times* [London], 17 May 1937; Colin Cross, *Philip Snowden* [London: Barrie and Rockliff, 1966]).

Workers Party Resolutions for the Negro Sanhedrin[1]

[*Chicago, ca. 12 February 1924*]

. . . UNIVERSAL NEGRO IMPROVEMENT ASSOCIATION

Whereas the Negro population of this country is at best a minority of little more than one out of ten, and to win its freedom requires the solidarity and united efforts of all Negroes, and

Whereas the Universal Negro Improvement Association is not represented in this conference, its leaders having seen fit to decline the invitation, and

Whereas the Universal Negro Improvement Association, no matter what faults it may have, is of special significance because it is the largest mass organization of Negroes; therefore

Be it resolved that the leaders of the Universal Negro Improvement Association assumed a grave responsibility in refusing to meet with other organization[s] to plan a common program; and those responsible for the refusal did not act in the best interests of their followers or the Race; and

Be it further resolved that this conference, declaring for the principle of

557

the United Negro Front, immediately sends a telegram repeating its invitation to the Universal Negro Improvement Association to be represented here; and

Be it further resolved that this conference elect fraternal delegates to attend the International Congress of the Universal Negro Improvement Association to be held next August, fraternal delegates to be elected upon nomination made by such of the present delegation as may care to nominate.[2]

NNC, RM, box B, folder "Negro Sanhedrin." TD; a similar version of the resolution also appears in DJ-FBI, "Radical Negro Activities, Chicago, Illinois."

1. A conference of the Negro Sanhedrin, or All-Race Assembly, was held at the Wabash Avenue branch of the YMCA in Chicago, 11–18 February 1924. Organized by a coalition of six black organizations, the Negro Sanhedrin attracted delegates from 41 pre-registered groups, ranging from the Workers Party of America to the AME Church.

The planning for the Negro Sanhedrin began in New York in March 1923 at a meeting of the newly-formed United Negro Front Conference organized by Cyril Briggs of the ABB. The statement of purpose drafted at that initial meeting stressed close cooperation "among all the agencies working for the civil and citizenship rights of Negro Americans" and implored that "we should not allow any differences, either of opinions or methods, to blind us to the fact that we are all striving for one great common goal." This statement was signed by W. A. Domingo of the ABB, George S. Schuyler of the Friends of Negro Freedom, James Weldon Johnson of the NAACP, William Monroe Trotter of the National Equal Rights League, Kelly Miller of the National Race Congress, and D. N. E. Campbell of the International Uplift League ("Toward Realization of a United Negro Front: Concordat Signed by Six Leading Civil Rights Organizations," New York, 23–24 March 1923, DLC, NAACP, c-232). Dean Kelly Miller of Howard University, Washington, D. C., was appointed chair of the Committee of Arrangements for the Sanhedrin, which was originally scheduled for November. Dr. M. A. N. Shaw of Boston became president, with Briggs in the position of secretary of the United Front's main administrative body or central committee. The executive functions of the new coalition were thus divided geographically among three northeastern cities. Disparate organizational affiliations led to a rivalry of sorts between Miller and Briggs, especially as the Sanhedrin began to be referred to as "Kelly Miller's All-Race Conference" in the popular press (Atlanta Independent, 28 June 1923; "Minutes of Third Assembly of the Permanent United Front Conference," 16 June 1923; Cyril V. Briggs to the editor, the Pittsburgh Courier, 28 June 1923; Cyril V. Briggs to James Weldon Johnson, 3 July 1923 and 12 July 1923; Kelly Miller to Cyril Briggs, 22 July 1923; DLC, NAACP, c-232).

Invitations for delegates were issued to a variety of black organizations, including the UNIA. Garvey apparently declined the invitation. An article on the Sanhedrin published in the Daily Worker confirmed that "no representatives will be present from the Garvey movement," and attributed the absence of Garveyites to the idea that "the UNIA holds to its African nationalistic policy and refuses to take part in a movement that is concerned primarily with winning rights for Negroes where they live" ("Great All-Race Negro Congress Opening Today," Daily Worker, 11 February 1924).

In a letter written to Briggs in July, Miller reported that "Mr. Garvey has launched an attack in the Negro World" (Kelly Miller to the Members of the United Front Conference, 28 July 1923, DLC, NAACP, c-232). Garvey's editorials, along with other articles published in the Negro World in the summer of 1923, indicate that he regarded the Sanhedrin as a direct threat to the UNIA and part of a larger scheme planned by his opposition to imprison him and strip him of his authority and following. In a front-page editorial on race leadership in the Negro World, written in the Tombs prison and published on 28 July 1923, Garvey referred to Cyril Briggs as a "Bolshevik agent," accused Kelly Miller of glorying "in the conviction of Garvey," and compared the Sanhedrin to "that ancient cabal that plotted against Christ."

The name "Sanhedrin" was taken by the organizers from the Hebrew word for "council," a reference to the supreme council of the Jews, first mentioned in the bible in the Maccabean period (1 Macc. 11:23; 12:6). During New Testament times, the Hebrew Sanhedrin was comprised of elders, high priests and scribes, many of whom were members of the Pharisee sect. The supreme council exercised both religious and civil authority over the Jewish communities of the diaspora. The Negro Sanhedrin was thus similar in intent, as it was envisaged as a centralized forum for coordinating race leadership and policy-making among disparate black associations. The analogy

Garvey drew to the historic Sanhedrin was a reference to its involvement in issuing orders for the apprehension of Christians (Acts 9:2, 22:5, 26:12), in the trial of Jesus, and the interrogation and imprisonment of Peter and John (John L. McKenzie, *Dictionary of the Bible* [Milwaukee: Bruce Publishing Co., 1965], pp. 152–153).

Despite Briggs's hopes that the United Front Conference would continue to function as a permanent umbrella organization following the February assembly of the Negro Sanhedrin in Chicago, the coalition declined rapidly and dissolved by the spring of 1924 (DLC, NAACP, c-232).

2. While there is no direct evidence of a delegation from the Negro Sanhedrin attending the August 1924 UNIA convention, there was at least one delegate present from the Workers party. The delegate was Olivia Whiteman, who participated on a committee that drafted a statement of confidence in Garvey's leadership, and who spoke from the floor of the convention on behalf of black women's rights and social equality (Robert Minor, "All Africa in Rebellion, Is Garvey Report," *Daily Worker*, 19 August 1924; Robert Minor, "Race Problem Answer Can't Satisfy All," *Daily Worker*, 15 August 1924).

Other resolutions proposed by the Workers Party of America at the Negro Sanhedrin addressed the following topics: lynching; violations of the 14th and 15th amendments; the Ku Klux Klan; black representation on juries trying black defendants; the independence of Haiti, Santo Domingo (now known as the Dominican Republic), the Virgin Islands, Hawaii and Puerto Rico; an alliance between black and white workers and the formation of interracial labor unions; election of a delegation from the Sanhedrin to study post revolutionary Soviet society, and the official recognition of the Soviet Union; the planning of an All-World Negro conference to take place in 1924; the election of delegates to a Farmer-Labor convention in St. Paul, Minnesota; the end to segregated housing; the declaration of the League of Nations as null and void; the abolition of laws forbidding racial intermarriage; the abolition of jim-crow policies within the U.S. army and navy and in southern schools; the protection of the rights of tenant farmers and sharecroppers; freedom of speech and assembly for the poorer classes; the appointment of black people to political jobs; the public ownership of railroads; and support for agitation in favor of the independence of French African colonies (report on "Radical Negro Activities," Chicago, Ill., 14 February 1924, DJ-FBI).

A.L. Woodley, Marcus Garvey Release Committee, to J.R. Ralph Casimir

NEW YORK CITY, N.Y. February 28th, 1924

My Dear Mr. Casimir;

We beg to acknowledge with thanks the receipt of your kind favor of February 21st, in which you enclosed the amount of $6.10 for the "MARCUS GARVEY APPEAL AND DEFENSE FUND." The names of, and the amounts contributed by each of the several contributors will be published in the "NEGRO WORLD" and will credited as follows:

Roseau Division. $6.10

Through the kind contributions from our members and numerous friends, we have succeeded in engaging a very prominent Attorney[1] who will lead the fight on the "Marcus Garvey Appeal." Already his work has borne fruit, and our self-sacrificing and indomitable Leader is once more with us, having been released on bail. God grant that he will be victorious. Again thinking you for your kind contributions, we are, with best wishes, Fraternally yours,

PER A. L. WOODLEY
Marcus Garvey Release Committee

JRRC. TLS, recipient's copy.

1. A possible reference to George Gordon Battle.

British Colonial Office Report on the UNIA

Colonial Office [*London*] Feb. 1924

THE UNIVERSAL NEGRO IMPROVEMENT ASSOCIATION
AND AFRICAN COMMUNITIES LEAGUE

Mr. R.H. Tobitt asks for interviews with the Prime Minister and the Secretary of State, in order to deliver to them "credentials"[1] from the Universal Negro Improvement Association and African Communities League. This Association was formed ostensibly to establish a great Negro State in Africa. A beginning was to be made in Liberia (which has, however, officially repudiated any knowledge or interest in the movement)[2] and the white man was later to be expelled from Africa.

The Association has occupied itself for some years in propaganda among the negroes in the United States, the West Indies and (to a slight extent) West Africa, with the object of inculcating among them a sense of "nationality" and of sowing the seeds of discontent and revolt against their existing conditions of life. The movement deliberately attempts to foment racial antagonism and has assumed a seditious and revolutionary aspect, which finds expression in the organ of the Association, a newspaper known as the "Negro World" with a considerable circulation in the West Indies, though its importation is prohibited in Nigeria, the Gold Coast and the Gambia.[3]

A prominent place in the utterances of speakers on behalf of the Association was a few years ago given to appeals for the investment of money in the "Black Star Line," which was a Steamship Company with a nominal capital equal to £2,000,000, registered in the United States. The object of this Company was to provide the means for transporting negroes from other parts of the world to Africa and for laying the foundations of the commerce of the Negro State. So far as is known, it never owned more than two or three small vessels and never made any appreciable headway. The chief leader in the movement is Marcus Garvey, the self-styled "Provisional President of the Republic of Africa"; he was arrested some time ago in the United States on a charge of using the mails with intent to defraud (in connection with the flotation of the Black Star Line) and was sentenced last year by a Federal Court to five years' imprisonment. Our most recent information about him is that in October last he was out on bail, pending an appeal against this sentence.

The movement has made little headway in the British West African Colonies, though we have evidence that natives of those Colonies have been victims of Garvey's fraud; but in 1923, after consulting the Governors of the British West African Colonies, the Duke of Devonshire[4] asked the Foreign

Office to issue instructions that, if after his term of imprisonment Garvey applied for a visa to visit any of those colonies, it should not be granted.[5]

The Governors of the various West Indies were asked whether Garvey should be allowed to land there; and with the exceptions of Bermuda and Trinidad, they agreed that his landing should not be prohibited.

To turn to Mr. Tobitt himself,—in November 1920, the Governor of Bermuda reported that the Reverend R.H. Tobitt, a coloured clergyman of that Colony, had been elected "Leader of the West Indies (Eastern Province)" under the auspices of the Universal Negro Improvement Association, and had signed a document described as a Declaration of Independence, which contained many clauses antagonistic to the existing Order. He was later disavowed by the African Methodist Episcopal Church there and withdrew from his vows under that Body.

Later, he attempted to land in Trinidad; but was refused permission because of his connection with this Association. He petitioned Mr. Churchill, then Secretary of State, against this treatment; but was informed that the Secretary of State saw no reason to intervene in the matter.

PRO, CO 554/64/7535. TD. Handwritten corrections.

1. Tobitt presented his credentials (signed by Percival L. Burrows) to the Colonial Office on 19 February. On 20 February he wrote to Colonial Secretary Thomas asking for an interview for the purpose of "laying before you certain matters seriously affecting the welfare of loyal Negro subjects in various colonies of the British Empire, with a view of bringing about a more satisfactory state of affairs for the good—not only of the people I represent—but for the good of the Empire of which we are citizens." The Colonial Office replied on 8 March, regretting that it could not grant the interview (PRO, CO 565/64/XLM02252). The UNIA branch in London gave a warm welcome to Tobitt at a meeting in east London on 17 February. Although membership had declined and finances had dwindled on account of recent unemployment and strikes, Tobitt's visit, they reported, "marked a new epoch in progress" for the UNIA in England (*NW*, 5 April 1924).

2. President C.D.B. King repudiated the UNIA in 1921 (see *Garvey Papers* 3: 342–343).

3. Both French and British colonial authorities were concerned about the circulation of the *Negro World* among Africans and by 1922 they had banned the paper. In Nigeria the paper was banned in June 1922, and in December it was banned in the Gold Coast (Ghana), where copies of the newspaper were confiscated by local post offices. It was banned in Gambia the same year (*New York World*, 15 September 1922; *NW*, 21 April 1923, 19 September 1925; *Chicago Tribune*, 29 August 1923; DJ-FBI, special report, 16 September 1922; John R. Thomas, Jr., military attaché, Belgium, to assistant chief of staff, G-2, War Department, Washington, D.C., 15 September 1922, DNA, RG 165, file 10218-439; C.R.M. Workman, governor deputy of Gambia, to duke of Devonshire, 29 May 1923, Public Record Office, The Gambia, confidential 727).

4. Victor Christian William Cavendish (1868–1938) came from one of Britain's oldest families and was one of the wealthiest of British landowners. In 1908 he became the ninth duke of Devonshire upon the death of his father. Following World War I, he served from 1916 to 1921 as the governor-general of Canada. From 1922 to 1924 he was secretary of state for the colonies (*NYT*, 7 May 1938; *Times* [London], 7 May 1938).

5. The under secretary of state, Foreign Office, wrote British consular officials in the United States on 14 September 1923, "I am directed by the Duke of Devonshire to state . . . that if, after his terms of imprisonment, Garvey applies for a visa to visit any of the British West African Colonies in connection with his proposed world tour, he should not be granted it." Messages to this effect were also sent to British colonies in Africa (under secretary of state, Foreign Office, London, 14 September 1923, PRO, FO 371/8513; O.T. Davis, secretary, Office of the High Commissioner for the Union of South Africa, 16 June 1923, South African Government Archives, 29824/23).

Report by Special Agent Joseph G. Tucker

[*New York*] MARCH 1, 1924

UNIVERSAL NEGRO IMPROVEMENT ASSOCIATION

Robert Lincoln Poston, Henrietta Vinton Davis and Milton Van Lowe, the three delegates who were sent to Africa by the Universal Negro Improvement Association[,] were expected to return to this country on the 14th of the present month and to be the chief figures at the mass meeting which is to be held on the afternoon and evening of March 15th at Madison Square Garden.

At the usual Sunday night meeting of the Association held at Liberty Hall on February 24th, Marcus Garvey was the chief speaker. His subject was "The Battle of Wits," and he told his audience that the only way for the Negro to eventually win a place for himself was to organize and fool the rest of the World. In one part of his speech he said:

"I go before the world with a plain and blunt expression of truth. I am interested only in the development of 400,000,000 Negroes; the rest of the world can go to hell. That is what the rest of the world means toward me and those who look like me, but they cover it up with the prayer book and the Bible. The Pope and the Archbishop of Canterbury tell us that we are all brothers related to one common father and when the brother pleads for help they kick you out in the open snow. That sort of farce can hold the world no longer; that kind of lie cannot take any longer, and that is why the Universal Negro Improvement Association is making this positive declaration. The hour has come for Negroes to get together and stick together and live together, and if we must die, to die together." The rest of Garvey's speech was along practically the same lines, and he lost no opportunity to stir up race feeling.

In another part of his speech he said:

"Whilst our own America is telling us about peace, they are endeavoring to sell the Philip[p]ines, to sell Porto Rico, to sell Haiti, to sell Cuba, to sell everything they can put their hands on."

JOSEPH G. TUCKER

DJ-FBI, file 61-23-277. TD.

Speech by Marcus Garvey

New York, March 16, 1924

SPEECH OF MARCUS GARVEY BEFORE NEGRO CITIZENS
OF NEW YORK, AT MADISON SQUARE GARDEN,
SUNDAY, MARCH 16, 1924, AT 4 O'CLOCK

Fellow Citizens:

The coming together, all over this country, of fully six million people of Negro blood, to work for the creation of a nation of their own in their motherland, Africa, is no joke.

There is now a world revival of thought and action which is causing peoples everywhere to bestir themselves towards their own security, through which we hear the cry of Ireland for the Irish, Palestine for the Jew, Egypt for the Egyptian, Asia for the Asiatic, and thus we Negroes raise the cry of Africa for the Africans, those at home and those abroad.

Some people are not disposed to give us credit for having feelings, passions, ambitions and desires like other races; they are satisfied to relegate us to the back heap of human aspirations; but this is a mistake. The Almighty Creator made us men, not unlike others, but in His own image; hence[,] as a race, we feel that we, too, are entitled to the rights that are common to humanity.

CRY FOR LIBERTY

The cry and desire for liberty is justifiable, and is made holy everywhere. It is sacred and holy to the Anglo-Saxon, Teuton and Latin; to the Anglo-American it precedes that of all religions, and now come the Irish, the Jew, the Egyptian, the Hindoo, and, last but not least, the Negro, clamoring for their share as well as their right to be free.

All men should be free—free to work out their own salvation. Free to create their own destinies. Free to nationally build by themselves for the upbringing and rearing of a culture and civilization of their own. Jewish culture is different from Irish culture. Anglo-Saxon culture is unlike Teutonic culture. Asiatic culture differs greatly from European culture; and, in the same way, the world should be liberal enough to allow the Negro latitude to develop a culture of his own. Why should the Negro be lost among the other races and nations of the world and to himself? Did nature not make of him a son of the soil? Did the Creator not fashion him out of the dust of the earth?—out of that rich soil to which he bears such a wonderful resemblance?—a resemblance that changes not, even though the ages have flown? No, the Ethiopian cannot change his skin; and so we appeal to the conscience of the white world to yield us a place of national freedom among the creatures of present-day temporal materialism.

Not Asking for Europe or America

We Negroes are not asking the white man to turn Europe and America over to us. We are not asking the Asiatic to turn Asia over for the accommodation of the blacks. But we are asking a just and righteous world to restore Africa to her scattered and abused children.

We believe in justice and human love. If our rights are to be respected, then, we, too, must respect the rights of all mankind; hence, we are ever ready and willing to yield to the white man the things that are his, and we feel that he, too, when his conscience is touched, will yield to us the things that are ours.

We should like to see a peaceful, prosperous and progressive white race in America and Europe; a peaceful, prosperous and progressive yellow race in Asia, and, in like manner, we want, and we demand, a peaceful, prosperous and progressive black race in Africa. Is that asking too much? Surely not. Humanity, without any immediate human hope of racial oneness, has drifted apart, and is now divided into separate and distinct groups, each with its own ideals and aspirations. Thus, we cannot expect any one race to hold a monopoly of creation and be able to keep the rest satisfied.

Distinct Racial Group Idealism

From our distinct racial group idealism we feel that no black man is good enough to govern the white man, and no white man good enough to rule the black man; and so of all races and peoples. No one feels that the other, alien in race, is good enough to govern or rule to the exclusion of native racial rights. We may as well, therefore, face the question of superior and inferior races. In twentieth century civilization there are no inferior and superior races. There are backward peoples, but that does not make them inferior. As far as humanity goes, all men are equal, and especially where peoples are intelligent enough to know what they want. At this time all peoples know what they want—it is liberty. When a people have sense enough to know that they ought to be free, then they naturally become the equal of all in the higher calling of man to know and direct himself. It is true that economically and scientifically certain races are more progressive than others; but that does not imply superiority. For the Anglo-Saxon to say that he is superior because he introduced gunpowder to destroy life, or the Teuton because he compounded liquid gas to outdo in the art of killing, and that the Negro is inferior because he is backward in that direction is to leave one's self open to the retort of "Thou shalt not kill" as being the divine law that sets the moral standard of the real man. There is no superiority in the one race economically monopolizing and holding all that would tend to the sustenance of life, and thus cause unhappiness and distress to others; for our highest purpose should be to love and care for each other and share with each other the things that our Heavenly Father has placed at our common disposal; and even in this the African is unsurpassed, in that he feeds his brother and shares with him the product of the land. The idea of race superiority is questionable; nevertheless, we must admit that, from the white man's standard, he is far superior to the rest of us, but that kind of superiority is too inhuman and dangerous to be permanently helpful. Such a superiority was shared and indulged in by other races before, and even by our own, when we boasted of a wonderful civilization on the banks of the Nile, when others were still groping in darkness; but because of our unrighteousness it failed, as all such will. Civilization can only last when we have reached the point where we will be our brother's keeper. That is to say, when we feel it righteous to live and let live.

No Exclusive Right to the World

Let no black man feel that he has the exclusive right to the world and other men none, and let no white man feel that way, either. The world is the property of all mankind, and each and every group is entitled to a portion. The black man now wants his, and in terms uncompromising he is asking for it.

The Universal Negro Improvement Association represents the hopes and aspirations of the awakened Negro. Our desire is for a place in the world; not to disturb the tranquillity of other men, but to lay down our burden and rest our weary backs and feet by the banks of the Niger, and sing our songs and chant our hymns to the God of Ethiopia. Yes, we want rest from the toil of the centuries, rest of political freedom, rest of economic and industrial liberty, rest to be socially free and unmolested, rest from lynching and burning, rest from discrimination of all kinds.

Race Out of Slavery

Out of slavery we have come with our tears and sorrows, and we now lay them at the feet of American white civilization. We cry to the considerate white people for help, because in their midst we can scarce help ourselves. We are strangers in a strange land. We cannot sing, we cannot play on our harps, for our hearts are sad.[1] We are sad because of the tears of our mothers and the cry of our fathers. Have you not heard the plaintive wail? It is your father and my father burning at [the] stake; but, thank God, there is a larger humanity growing among the good and considerate white people of this country, and they are going to help. They will help us to find and know ourselves. They will help us to recover our souls.

As children of captivity we look forward to a new day and a new, yet ever old, land of our fathers, the land of refuge, the land of the Prophets, the land of the Saints, and the land of God's crowning glory. We shall gather together our children, our treasures and our loved ones, and, as the children of Israel, by the command of God, face the promised land, so in time we shall also stretch forth our hands and bless our country.

America Knows Story

Good and dear America that has succored us for three hundred years knows our story. We have watered her vegetation with our tears for two hundred and fifty years. We have buil[t] her cities and laid the foundation of her imperialism with the mortar of our blood and bones for three centuries, and now we cry to her for help. Help us, America, as we helped you. We helped you in the Revolutionary War. We helped you in the Civil War, and, although Lincoln helped us, the price is not half paid. We helped you in the Spanish-American War. We died nobly and courageously in Mexico, and did not we leave behind us on the stained battlefields of France and Flanders our rich blood to mark the poppies' bloom, and to bring back to you the glory of the flag that never touched the dust? We have no regrets in service to America for three hundred years, but we pray that America will help us for another fifty, until we have solved the troublesome problem that now confronts us. We know and realize that two ambitious and competitive races cannot live permanently side by side, without friction and trouble, and it is for that that the white race wants a white America and the black race wants and demands a black Africa.

Let white America help us for fifty years honestly as we have helped her for three hundred years, and before the expiration of many decades there shall be no more race problem. Help us to gradually go home, America[.] Help us as you have helped the Jews. Help us as you have helped the Irish. Help us as you have helped the Poles, Russians, Germans and Armenians.

The Universal Negro Improvement Association proposes a friendly co-operation with all honest movements seeking intelligently to solve the race problem. We are not seeking social equality; we do not seek intermarriage, nor do we hanker after the impossible. We want the right to have a country of our own, and there foster and re-establish a culture and civilization exclusively ours. Don't say it can't be done. The Pilgrims and colonists did it for America, and the new Negro, with sympathetic help, can do it for Africa.

Back to Africa

The thoughtful and industrious of our race want to go back to Africa, because we realize it will be our only hope of permanent existence. We cannot all go in a day or year, ten or twenty. It will take time under the rule of modern economics to entirely or largely depopulate a country of a people who have been its residents for centuries, but we feel that, with proper help for fifty years, the problem can be solved. We do not want all the Negroes in Africa. Some are no good here, and naturally will be no good there. The no-good Negro will naturally die in fifty years. The Negro who is wrangling about and fighting for social equality will naturally pass away in fifty years, and yield his place to the progressive Negro who wants a society and country of his own.

Negroes are divided into two groups, the industrious and adventurous, and the lazy and dependent. The industrious and adventurous believe that whatsoever others have done [they] can do. The Universal Negro Improvement Association belongs to this group, and so you find us working, six million strong, to the goal of an independent nationality. Who will not help? Only the mean and despicable "whomever to himself hath said, this is my own, my native land."[2] Africa is the legitimate, moral and righteous home of all Negroes, and now that the time is coming for all to assemble under their own vine and fig tree, we feel it our duty to arouse every Negro to a consciousness of himself.

RESPECTING EACH OTHER

White and black will learn to respect each other when they cease to be active competitors in the same countries for the same things in politics and society. Let them have countries of their own, wherein to aspire and climb without rancor. The races can be friendly and helpful to each other, but the laws of nature separate us to the extreme of each and every one developing by itself.

OWN ATMOSPHERE

We want an atmosphere all our own. We would like to govern and rule ourselves and not be encumbered and restrained. We feel now just as the white race would feel if they were governed and ruled by the Chinese. If we live in our own districts, let us rule and govern those districts. If we have a majority in our communities, let us run those communities. We form a majority in Africa and we should naturally govern ourselves there. No man can govern another's house as well as himself. Let us have fair play. Let us have justice. This is the appeal we make to white America.[3]

DNA, RG 16, general correspondence. Printed pamphlet.

1. A paraphrase of Ps. 137:1–4.
2. This is taken from Sir Walter Scott's poem "The Lay of the Last Minstrel" (1805), pt. 6, st. 1 (*BFQ*).
3. In his weekly report, Special Agent Tucker described Garvey's speech as "a very temperate speech in which at times he eulogized the generosity of the White Race." Tucker also noted that Garvey's eight-page pamphlet "An Appeal to the Soul of White America" was distributed at the meeting (report by Special Agent Joseph G. Tucker, 24 March 1924, DJ-FBI, file 61-280).

Special Agent Frank C. Higgins
to Robert S. Sharp

[*New York*] March 18, 1924

Sir:

In accordance with your instructions, I attended the Mass Meeting of the UNIVERSAL NEGRO IMPROVEMENT ASSOCIATION and AFRICAN COMMUNITIES LEAGUE held at Madison Sq. Garden on the evening of Sunday, March 16, 1924, under the Chairmanship of the West Indian Negro Agitator MARCUS GARVEY, designated as "President-General" of the foregoing and now out on bail while a 5-year sentence for fraud through the U.S. Mails is being appealed from by his attorneys.

There were really two of these meetings: one of which occupied the afternoon[;][1] the greater occasion being held at 8 o'clock on the same day.[2]

I append to this report a copy of an article which appeared in Monday's "New York World,"[3] which is substantially correct and also copies of propaganda literature which seems to have been generally circulated among New York businessmen about a week or ten days previously, the recipient in this case being Mr. Oliver H. Sawyer, a former Special Agent of this Department.[4] . . .

I also append the official program of the evening's proceedings.

In answer to my specific instructions, I would say that there was a notable absence of the white elements which I have observed at many other radical meetings in this city, Irish, Jewish, Bolshevik, etc. The whole affair seemed to be exclusively negro-managed—at least that was the surface appearance. The one white speaker of the evening was Surrogate John P. O'Brien[.][5] The most significant part of the whole show seemed to be an attempt on the part of GARVEY to demonstrate that he had already formed a political junta which assumed to be a provisional government of the African Continent merely awaiting opportunity to proceed thither and take possession of what was now being already mapped out and allotted for future political development. His attitude differing very little from that assumed by Eamon de Valera when he was posing as the President of an Irish Republic while collecting funds in the United States.

Garvey was attended not only by his First and Second Assistants-President-General but his recently returned "Ambassadors" from Ethiopia and Japan,[6] while it was one of the distressful episodes of the meeting when he announced the sudden death on S.S. George Washington, while hurrying to the meeting, of his Secretary-General, "Sir" R.L. Poston, K.C.O.N.[,][7] who was "Ambassador" to the League of Nations and had just secured an important concession of African territory from the Portuguese Government,[8] which was to be the entering wedge of the GARVEY COLONIZATION SCHEME.

The spectacular part of the performance consisted in the drilling, marching and counter-marching around the Garden of units representative of Garvey's future Army and Navy, consisting of various commissioned officers in resplendent blue and gold uniforms with the a[i]guil[l]ettes denoting that they were military aides-de-camp, also an "Impi"[9] of khaki-clad youths with shrapnel helmets and wooden guns, a cohort of Boy Scouts, and one of Girl Scouts arrayed in navy blouses, and sailor caps[,] who elicited the observation from a colored wit in my vicinity that if this was the crew of the Black Star Line, he was going to stay in a lifeboat all the way over.

Finally there was a squad of opulent Black Cross Nurses, most of whom looked as if they had just stepped out of the familiar "Aunt Jemima Pancake" poster.[10]

The colored guard of this military array carried three flags, the Red, Green and Black tri-color of the proposed GARVEY AFRICAN EMPIRE, the American flag and the Garvey personal standard, which was another tri-color bearing a central escutcheon of some nondescript figures which were not easily discernible. These colors having been saluted, with flourishes from the sabres of the Garvey Aides, were several times carried at a respectful dip before the throne of the dusky potentate himself in the second tier of boxes.

The only conspicuous white man in the Garden was an elderly gentleman in military uniform who seemed to be acting in the combined capacity of Drill-Master to the Garvey Army and Navy, and Toastmaster to his diplomatic corps with whom he was seated on the dais with Garvey.

Garvey wore evening dress over which was draped an elaborate gown of some heavy material in the red, black and green of his organization, looking very much like a colored edition of President Nicholas Butler of Columbia University, about to confer a degree on a foreign dign[i]tary, both men being about the same in girth, weight and contour.

The principal speakers besides Garvey and Surrogate O'Brien, were Assistant-President-General Sir Wm. L. Sherrill, K.C.D.S.O.E.[,] and a stentorian-voiced colored parson, Rev. Dr. W.M. Moses, D.D., Pastor of the New York National Baptist Church.

Both of these two last named gentlemen were much more inflammatory in their utterances than Garvey himself, giving it to be distinctly understood that they had the absolute control of 6,000,000 in the U.S. who had sworn to achieve their end or take the consequences, being prepared to shed their blood to the last drop and 100,000,000 negroes in Africa and the British West Indian possessions who are going to do the same thing as soon as the Garvey forces lead the way, to victory.

These utterances might be largely taken as a joke when it is considered that the achievement of such a purpose would mean numerous negro rebellions in all of the European colonies in Africa, especially Cape Colony,[11] which was specifically mentioned, but it was confidently asserted that all of these localities were "swinging into line one after the other."

It was asserted that all the colored clergy throughout the world were working for Free Africa and that they had "Ambassadors" located in every important section. Sir Wm. Sherrill evoked the greatest applause of the evening by his description of how ignorant serfs of Russ[i]a had within the present generation overthrown the tyran[n]y under which they labored and were now masters of their old oppressors. There was also [a] feeling response to references to the recent Irish Rebellion against England.

I was able to observe from the tone of the meeting that the whole movement is essentially a black man's movement; that the more prognathous and ebony-hued gentlemen in the audience happened to be, the more they enthused and contributed when the plates were passed. The yellow or mulatto conti[n]gent seemed rather half-hearted, giving full color to Garvey's own contention that the yellow negroes of America have been contaminated with white blood until they are no longer any use as negroes.

Mr. Garvey as the orator of the evening unfortunately did not get the floor until pretty late, when the audience had started to leave; there had been too much military manoeuvring and too many musical numbers from the excellent negro band in the center of the Garden and the chorus of colored vestals in the robes and caps of Doctors of Music, who surrounded the Presidential Throne, and trilled when occasion required.

The text of Mr. Garvey's own speech was very largely based upon an expression which he claimed to have found in the Constitution of the United States to the effect that this Commonwealth was formed to procure the greatest good to the greatest number, and he pathetically inquired as to what was going to be left for the negro after the white man had "cut the cake." He also announced he was helping the United States out of a great difficulty because he said that in 100 years the population of the United States would be double what it is now and the negro would be in every respect the intellectual and physical equal of the white race on this continent, in which case there would be a terrible struggle for the mastery if the U.S. did not grasp the splendid opportunity they had 'of getting rid of the negro while he was still in the minority by assisting his proposed Exodus to the Conquest of Africa, which he compared to the assistance rendered by Great Britain to the Jews to repopulate Palestine. It was the only solution, he thought, of the race problem.

Mr. Garvey also had a great deal to say about the negro now having his back to the wall and it was a matter of liberty or death.

There is no doubt that the utterances of all the speakers conveyed calm but positive assurances that they were going to get what they wanted or somebody was going to get hurt.

Mr. Garvey concluded by inviting all sympathizers to attend the nightly meeting at "Liberty Hall," 120 West 138th St., New York City, which is the headquarters of his movement.

I roughly estimate that the afternoon and evening meetings took in[,] in ticket-sales alone, at least $7,000 or $8,000 while subscriptions must have brought the sum up to pretty near $10,000 which must have netted[,] less the cost of the Garden, a very handsome sum.

Garvey is absolutely nobody's fool and by no means to be considered a mere trifler. Sunday's meetings which brought out a combined attendance of seven or eight thousand negroes[,] all of whom were willing to pay for the excitement, shows that Garvey has pulling power and his speech is that of a man educated among and thoroughly at home among white people. My apprehension as to this Garvey Movement is not based nearly so much upon the carrying out of Garvey's expressed dream of conquering Africa as upon the fact that he is already at the head of a very large mass of dissatisfied negroes whom he is teaching that they have got to either get certain "rights" from the whites peaceably if they can, but forcibly if they must, as they cannot possibly carry out their schemes without such opposition from this and foreign governments as will absolutely nullify them. It therefore only remains for Garvey to eventually cast his lot with any such militant radical development as will seem to promise to these negroes the autonomy to which they aspire. In this respect he is an extremely dangerous character. Respectfully submitted.

FRANK C. HIGGINS
Special Agent

DNA, RG 59, file 000-612. TLS, recipient's copy.

1. A copy of the speech Garvey delivered in the afternoon, "In Honor of the Return to America of the Delegation Sent to Europe and Africa by the Universal Negro Improvement Association to Negotiate for the Repatriation of Negroes to a Homeland of Their Own in Africa," was later sent to Secretary of Agriculture Henry Wallace (DNA, RG 16, general correspondence, 28 March 1924); it is printed above.

2. Garvey's evening speech, "The Negro and the Future," has not been preserved (program, 16 March 1924, Alexander Gumby Collection, NNC). There are no extant *Negro World* issues for the period 16 February to 22 March 1924, and all other newspaper accounts of the speeches (*NYT*, 17 March 1924; *New York World*, 17 March 1924; *Philadelphia Tribune*, 22 March 1924) refer to Garvey's two speeches but do not print them.

3. "Garvey Proclaims Negroes' Right to Self Government," *New York World*, 17 March 1924, printed below.

4. Oliver Sawyer (1877–1931) was a prominent paper manufacturer's agent in New York. During World War I he worked in the Treasury Department Secret Service and later in the Bureau of Special Agents of the State Department (it is unclear how long Sawyer continued to work with the Department of State). Garvey's letter to Sawyer, found in the records of the Department of State, was a variation on the letter containing the eleven-point symposium printed above, pp. 468–470 (*NYT*, 11 April 1931; Marcus Garvey to Oliver Sawyer, 4 March 1924, DNA, RG 59, file 000-612).

5. John Patrick O'Brien (1873–1951) Massachusetts-born lawyer, served as a corporation counsel of New York City from 1901 to 1922, just before his election in 1922 to the position of surrogate of New York County. In 1932 he was elected mayor of New York to fill the unexpired term of James J. Walker, but a year later he lost the Democratic party nomination for mayor to Fiorello La Guardia (*NCAB*).

6. On 9 December 1922 Garvey had announced plans to send an ambassador to Japan and a representative to the Abyssinian court (*NW*, 9 December 1922).

7. Poston died of lobar pneumonia while at sea aboard the S.S. *President Grant* on 16 March 1924. At a Liberty Hall meeting Garvey conferred upon him the posthumous title "prince of Africa" (special report by Joseph Tucker, 29 March 1924, DJ-FBI, file 61-281; *NW*, 29 March 1929). Contrary to this report, Poston was not a delegate to the League of Nations. The league delegates were James O'Meally, Jean Joseph Adam, G.O. Marke, and William L. Sherrill.

8. On their way to Liberia, UNIA representatives Robert L. Poston, J. Milton Van Lowe, Henrietta Vinton Davis, and J.J. Adams met with representatives of the Liga Africana in Lisbon (*NW*, 21 June 1924).

9. The original impis were formations within the Zulu army developed in the early nineteenth century by Shaka (1787–1828), the famed Zulu leader. The discipline and organization of the Impis combined with the use of new military tactics, most notably there placement of the throwing javelin with the short stabbing spear, were crucial to the Zulu military campaigns of 1817 to 1828, and to

later Zulu resistance against the British in South Africa in the Zulu War of 1879 (Monica Wilson and Leonard Thompson, eds., *The Oxford History of South Africa* [Oxford: Oxford University Press, 1971], 2: 251-253, 262-267; Michael Barthorp, *The Zulu War* [Poole: Blandford Press, 1980], p. 20).

10. The stereotypical figure of the black mammy, Aunt Jemima was depicted as a large woman with a perennially broad smile, wearing an apron over a long dress, a shawl, and a kerchief on her head. The brand image, first introduced in 1893 by R.T. Davis Milling Co. to promote a ready-mix pancake flour, derived its name from two blackface comedians who, dressed as southern "mammys," performed to the tune of "Aunt Jemima." Davis conducted an extensive marketing campaign, hiring a woman to portray Aunt Jemima at promotional demonstrations and selling Aunt Jemima rag dolls. In 1910 a new campaign featured Aunt Jemima advertisements in magazines and posters, making the racial stereotype of the southern black mammy a national symbol for the pancake mix (Augustus Low and Virgil Clift, *Encyclopedia of Black America*, p. 144; Molly Wade McGrath, *Top Sellers, USA* [New York: William Morrow and Co., 1983], pp. 77-79).

11. Garvey's slogan of "Africa for the Africans" had widespread appeal among the colored and African communities of Cape Province, but there is no evidence to suggest that rebellious action was ever planned. James Thaele, the outspoken and influential South African Garveyite and president of the Western Cape Province African National Congress, advocated organized resistance to "European oppression" using tactics of noncooperation, including a boycott by African labor of the South African mines (*Umteteli wa Bantu*, 11 October 1924).

Enclosure

[*New York World*, 17 March 1924]

GARVEY PROCLAIMS NEGROES' RIGHT TO SELF GOVERNMENT

The sweep of the "Hallelujah Chorus," the clank of sabres and the rhythmical military tread of his legion, his Black Cross nurses, his motor corps and his juvenile soldiers-to-be ushered in the public reappearance of Marcus Garvey, President-General of the Universal Negro Improvement Association yesterday. Garvey, before 6,000 persons, mostly Negroes,[1] spoke in Madison Square Garden, again demanding Africa for the Negroes and the right of the "black man to anything, any time, that anybody else has."

Garvey is at liberty upon appeal in the Federal Courts with a sentence of five years hanging over him, following his conviction last year of using the mails to defraud.

REVIVAL OF ACTION NOW

Yesterday afternoon as he stood on a platform twenty-five feet high in the Garden to speak, his voice, when he raised it, echoed to the corners of the big hall. After reading a set speech and then breaking into extemporaneous passion, the same thought and practically the same words brought forth cheers.

"There is now a world revival of thought and action," he said, "which is causing people everywhere to bestir themselves toward their own security, through which we hear the cry of Ireland for the Irish, Palestine for the Jew— and thus we Negroes raise the cry of Africa for the Africans.

"We feel that no black man is good enough to govern the white man, and no white man good enough to rule the black man."

Garvey passionately denied the alleged superiority of the whites, and to a tremendous chorus of "That's so," "Listen," "You're right, you're right," insisted that the Negro, instead of being inferior, was only backward.

The President-General claimed his association numbers 6,000,000 members over the globe—3,500,000 in America and 30,000 in New York. His assistant, Sir William L. Sher[r]ill, K.C.D.S.O.E., said, amid intense excitement:

"Sink or swim, survive or perish, we are determined to go on in the face of lies, plots and traitors."

BLACKS TO RESCUE AMERICA

He prophesied a time when America would be rescued by airplanes carrying black armies to these shores for the succor of this Nation against its enemies.

Surrogate O'Brien, as the guest speaker, praised the Negro for his ideals and in particular he applauded Garvey for his leadership.

Garvey later said his commission to obtain concessions of African land from the Portuguese Government and the Liberian Government had been successful and that this commission was expected to report as soon as the steamship Roosevelt, due here to-day, discharges her passengers. The commission left for Europe Dec. 13, and consisted of Robert L. Poston, Chairman, Henrietta Davis and J. Milton Van Lowe, Secretary.

Garvey was in the middle of his speech at a second meeting in the Garden last night when he received a radiogram from the Roosevelt announcing the death at 5 o'clock yesterday morning of Poston. His reading of the message caused many in the audience to weep.

A repatriation petition to President Coolidge was circulated amongst the audience and a collection made.

Printed in the *New York World*, 17 March 1924. Original headlines abbreviated.

1. Following the Madison Square Garden meeting, the Belgian ambassador to Washington, Baron Emile de Cartier de Marchienne, sent copies of the *New York World* to the minister of foreign affairs, noting that "his [Garvey's] stay in Prison does not seem to have dampened his enthusiasm. Last Sunday in a meeting he held in Madison Square, New York, he proclaimed once more 'Africa for the Africans'" (Baron de Cartier de Marchienne to Paul Hymans, 19 March 1924, SAMAE, file 1440/204).

Black Cross Navigation and Trading Certificate

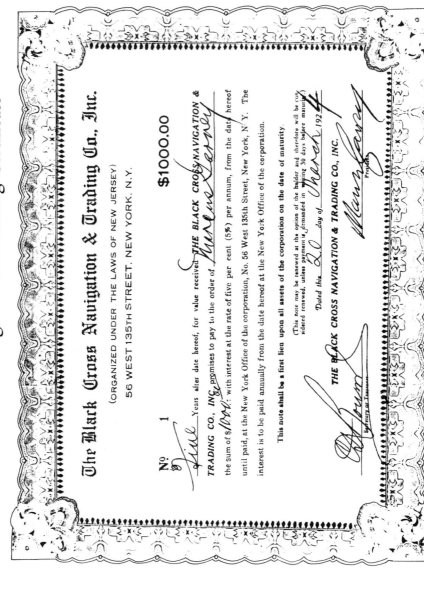

The Black Cross Navigation & Trading Co., Inc.

(ORGANIZED UNDER THE LAWS OF NEW JERSEY)

56 WEST 135TH STREET. NEW YORK. N.Y.

$1000.00

No. 1

_____ Years after date hereof, for value received THE BLACK CROSS NAVIGATION & TRADING CO., INC., promises to pay to the order of _____ the sum of $1000 with interest at the rate of five per cent (5%) per annum, from the date hereof until paid, at the New York Office of the corporation, No. 56 West 135th Street, New York, N.Y. The interest is to be paid annually from the date hereof at the New York Office of the corporation.

This note shall be a first lien upon all assets of the corporation on the date of maturity.

(This note may be renewed at the option of the holder and therefore will be considered renewed, unless payment is demanded in writing 30 days before maturity.)

Dated this 20 day of _____ 192_

THE BLACK CROSS NAVIGATION & TRADING CO., INC.

President

Secretary & Treasurer

Source: TNF, MGMC.)

Negro World Announcement

[*Negro World*, 22 March 1924]

In keeping with the desires of the Third International Convention of the Negro Peoples of the World, held under the auspices of the Universal Negro Improvement Association in New York from August 1st to August 31, 1922, the Universal Negro Improvement Association has incorporated the steamship line known as the "Black Cross Navigation and Trading Co." for the purpose of carrying out the shipping plans of the organization in continuation of the activities started by the defunct Black Star Line Steamship Corporation.[1]

The "Black Cross Navigation and Trading Company" will enter into the shipping business for the main purpose of carrying out the present plans of the Universal Negro Improvement Association, of developing a trade relationship between Negroes of Africa, the United States of America, the West Indies and South and Central America. This new steamship corporation will profit by the failure of the old Black Star Line. No stock will be sold in this new company, but all interest will be held by the Universal Negro Improvement Association and its members.

An effort is now being made, with the help of the association and its members, to place the first ship on the ocean by September 1 of the present year. Following the close of our convention on August 31, in New York, it is expected that this ship will sail on September 1, carrying the first organized group of colonists to Liberia.

The Universal Negro Improvement Association is now about to bend all its effort, with its members, to make it a possibility. All members of the association in America, Canada, the West Indies, South and Central America are requested, therefore, to get in immediate communication with the parent body of the Universal Negro Improvement Association at 56 West 135th Street, for further information for the further carrying out of our shipping plans.

All members of the Universal Negro Improvement Association who are desirous of going to Africa are advised to communicate with the Universal Negro Improvement Association at headquarters before any step is taken. No member of the association should undertake upon himself or herself to leave for Africa without first getting the approval and advice of the association. The association will not be ready to ship out its first contingent before September 1st. All those who desire to go will, therefore, act accordingly. The association will not hold itself responsible for anyone who goes without the proper protection of the organization. Proper discipline and accom[m]odation and arrangements will be made before any one undertakes to leave for Africa. In another week or two an approved program will be submitted through the columns of the Negro World to the entire membership of the association. All are requested to observe these orders.

Printed in *NW*, 22 March 1924. Found in DJ-FBI, file 61-280.

1. The formation of the Black Cross Navigation and Trading Co. was officially announced on 20 March 1924 at a mass meeting at Liberty Hall (*NW*, 29 March 1924).

Application for Transportation to Liberia

Form—1E

"LET'S PUT IT OVER"

Universal Negro Improvement Association

56 WEST. 135th STREET
NEW YORK. U.S.A.

APPLICATION FORM FOR TRANSPORTATION TO LIBERIA, WEST AFRICA UNDER THE AUSPICES OF THE UNIVERSAL NEGRO IMPROVEMENT ASSOCIATION

1. Name in Full ....

2. Address: { Street ....
{ City or Town .... Country ....

3. Age .... 4. Occupation ....

5. How many years experience ....

6. Married? .... 7. Single? .... 8. How many children? ....

9. Age of child or children ....

10. Name of wife .... 11. Address ....

12. State briefly why you want to go to Liberia ....
....
....
....

13. Is it your purpose only to seek employment? ....

14. Is it your purpose to work on your trade? ....

15. Is it your purpose to do business? ....

16. What business do you want to engage in? ....

17. Are you a Farmer?............ 18. How many years experience have you in farming? ....

19. Do you intend to become a citizen of Liberia? ....

20. Do you intend to live there on your own responsibility? ....

21. Are you a Member of the U. N. I. A. ?................

22. Are you financial? ....

23. What Division of the U. N. I. A. are you a member of? ....

24. Have you paid your annual Tax to the Association? ....

25. Are you a bond holder in the Black Cross Navigation and Trading Co.? ....

26. What amount of Bond do you hold? $...............

27. Are you willing and able to subscribe to a Bond? ....

28. How much? $.............

29. Have you money to defray your expenses to Liberia? ....

30. How much after you have paid your expenses can you land in Liberia with? $.............

31. Will you be a good citizen in Liberia? ....

32. Will you respect the law? ,..................

33. Are you healthy? ....

34. Are all of your family healthy? ....

35. Are you willing to work hard to help in the bulding up of a Negro nation? ....

36. When do you want to sail for Liberia? ....

37. Do you want to sail aboard the ships of the Black Cross Navigation and Trading Co.? ....

38. Will you respect and always obey the advices of the U. N. I. A·? ....

39. Who is your nearest relative? ....

40. Address ....

41. Of what country are you a citizen? ....

42. Have you ever secured a passport before? ....

43. When you leave for Liberia will you be leaving any property behind? ....

44. Who will care it or attend to it for you? ....

45. Name .... 46. Address ....

(*Source*: DJ-FBI.)

UNIA Registration Card

PRINT
NAME _____

ADDRESS—STREET_____

CITY OR TOWN_____ STATE OR COUNTRY_____

SINGLE	MARRIED	WIDOWER	AGE	WEIGHT	OCCUPATION

How many children?_____:_____Boys_____Girls_____

Age of Children_____

NATIONALITY	DATE NATURALIZED	MEMBER OF WHAT DIVISION?

Name and Address of nearest relative or interested person_____

Regular profession or trade_____

PLEASE TURN OVER

Ever lived or worked in tropical country if so, when and where?

Have you money to defray your expenses to Liberia?_____

How much?_____Do you hold Bond in the Black

Cross Navigation & Trading Co.,_____How much_____

REMARKS Do not write in space below!

(*Source*: DJ-FBI.)

James Weldon Johnson to John Mitchell, Jr., Editor, *Richmond Planet*

[*New York*] April 3, 1924

Dear Sir:

Your editorial of March 29 contains a misapprehension which I am sure you will give me the privilege of correcting for readers of the Richmond *Planet*; that is, that the N.A.A.C.P. set out to attack Marcus Garvey.[1]

If you had published the extracts from Marcus Garvey's literature which the N.A.A.C.P. sent out, your readers would have had opportunity to see for themselves that the N.A.A.C.P. was merely informing colored citizens of the sort of propaganda which Mr. Garvey is sending out to white people.[2] This propaganda includes agitation of the "social equality" bogey and attacks upon other groups, incidentally the N.A.A.C.P. which Mr. Garvey accuses of "advocating" race intermarriage.

Furthermore, the documents Marcus Garvey is writing and sending out to white people represent large groups of American Negroes as being willing to forfeit their citizenship rights in favor of an African state which exists only in Mr. Garvey's imagination. We have no objection to Mr. Garvey's going to Africa if he can get there and taking as many people as care to accompany him. But there is the most emphatic objection to his spreading the impression among white people that any considerable body of American colored people would be willing to abdicate their constitutional rights and privileges in favor of his migration scheme. Certainly this propaganda of Mr. Garvey cannot by any stretch of the imagination be taken as "encouraging race pride." Rather, it humiliates colored people in that it encourages white people in America to believe that large numbers of Negroes willingly will endure discrimination and disabilities since they are only a temporary element in the citizenry.

In calling the nature of Mr. Garvey's propaganda among white people to the attention of colored editors and readers, the N.A.A.C.P. was merely doing what it conceived to be its duty in protecting colored Americans from misrepresentation of their opinions, beliefs and ideals. In the documents of Mr. Garvey written for and sent to white people, from which the N.A.A.C.P. published quotations after many protests had been received from colored people, Mr. Garvey not only urged a migration of colored people to Africa, but he justified that migration to white people and urged them to support it on the ground that the white people would thereby be relieved from the necessity of according colored people their constitutional rights and privileges in the United States.

Under the circumstances the N.A.A.C.P. felt itself in duty bound not to "let Marcus Garvey alone." Yours very truly,

[James Weldon Johnson]
Secretary

DLC, NAACP. TL, carbon copy.

1. An editorial entitled "Again Attacking Garvey" appeared in the *Richmond Planet* of 29 March 1924. The editorial decried the mutual hostility between the Garveyites and the NAACP and admonished each to cease making vituperative remarks: "To the Duboisites, we say, 'Let Garvey and his followers alone; they are joined to their Africa!' To the Garveyites we say, 'Let the Duboisites alone; they are joined to the Constitution of the United States and the guarantee to all men, black as well as white, thereunder.'"

2. On 21 March 1924 the NAACP sent out a press release under the following headlines: "Marcus Garvey Advocates Abdication of Constitutional Rights by American Negro," "Uses 'Social Equality' as Bogey to Alarm Whites," and "Extracts Made Public from Documents Addressed to White People." The extract was prefaced by a statement by James Weldon Johnson, secretary of the NAACP, which said in part:

> Mr. Garvey, who is not an American citizen, has taken it upon himself to go before the white people of this country advocating that the American Negro abdicate his Constitutional rights, quit this country and go to Africa. Mr. Garvey apparently does not know that the American Negro considers himself, and is, as much an American as anyone in the nation and that the American colored people have not the slightest intention of leaving their country or surrendering their share in it. . . . Mr. Garvey makes most insidious and dangerous use of "social equality" as a bugbear to work on the prejudices and fears of white people.

The document then included extracts from Garvey's "An Appeal to the Soul of White America" (press release, NAACP, 21 March 1924, DLC, NAACP).

Eunice Lewis to Amy Jacques Garvey, Associate Editor, *Negro World*

[[3223 Indiana Avenue, Chicago, Ill.]]
[*ca. 19 April 1924*]

To the Women's Department:[1]

There are many people who think that a woman's place is only in the home—to raise children, cook, wash, and attend to the domestic affairs of the house. This idea, however, does not hold true with the New Negro Woman. The true type of the New Negro Woman is bent on tackling those problems confronting the race. She knows that in order to be a regular help to her race, it is necessary to learn all of the essentials of leadership. She is conscious of the value of pure womanhood that has the power to win and conquer the beastly side of man. Here are a few of the important places which the New Negro Woman desires to take in the rebirth of Africa, at home and abroad:

1. To work on par with men in the office as well as on the platform.

2. To practice actual economy and thrift.

3. To teach practical and constructive race doctrine to the children.

4. To demand absolute respect from men of all races.

5. To teach the young the moral dangers of social diseases, and to love their race first.

In a word, the New Negro Woman is revolutionizing the old type of male leadership.

We are determined to have the Negro race represented and respected by every Negro leader.

We are women of the newer type,

Striving to make our Race sublime—

Conscious that the time is ripe,

To put our men on the firing line!

EUNICE LEWIS

Printed in *NW*, 19 April 1924. Original headlines omitted.

1. Amy Jacques Garvey edited the *Negro World*'s women's page, which was formally instituted on 2 February 1924 and entitled, "Our Women and What They Think." Her editorial mandate was a comprehensive one. She sought a readership "not by any means limited to the membership of the Universal Negro Improvement Association, but [one that would] include the womanhood of the race." "We earnestly desire," she continued, "that all shall feel free to send us contributions on phases of race conditions in the places where they are as they affect our women, on phases of child and woman uplift work, and original contributions of prose or verse" (*NW*, 7 June 1924).

"LET'S PUT IT OVER"

A Home In Africa

NOTICE TO
Members of Universal Negro Improvement Association

All members of the Universal Negro Improvement Association who desire to go to Liberia, West Africa, to settle to help in the industrial, commercial and cultural development of the country, and who intend sailing September, October, December, 1924, or January, February, March, April or May, 1925, are requested to send in for application form to be filled out.

Address

UNIVERSAL NEGRO IMPROVEMENT ASSN., DEPT. E

56 West 135th Street
NEW YORK CITY, U. S. A.

(*Source*: *NW*, 10 May 1924.)

BIG SEND-OFF OF

ENGINEERING AND MECHANICAL EXPERTS

TO LIBERIA

TO PREPARE FOR COLONISTS

Who will sail in September

AT

LIBERTY HALL

120 W. 138th Street, New York

WEDNESDAY NIGHT

JUNE 4, 1924, AT 8:15 O'CLOCK

Come and see the Vanguards of Liberty and Democracy

These experts will sail in a few days
They will start building houses, laying out farms,
streets, roads, etc., for the colonists

BIG PROGRAM

HON. MARCUS GARVEY IN THE CHAIR

ADMISSION 50 CENTS

BE EARLY TO GET SEATS

(*Source*: *NW*, 31 May 1924.)

Article by W.E.B. Du Bois

[*Crisis*, May 1924]

A LUNATIC OR A TRAITOR

In its endeavor to avoid any injustice toward Marcus Garvey and his followers, THE CRISIS has almost leaned backward. Notwithstanding his wanton squandering of hundreds of thousands of dollars we have refused to assume that he was a common thief. In spite of his monumental and persistent lying we have discussed only the larger and truer aspects of his propaganda. We have refrained from all comment on his trial and conviction for fraud. We have done this too in spite of his personal vituperation of the editor of THE CRISIS and persistent and unremitting repetition of falsehood after falsehood as to the editor's beliefs and acts and as to the program of the N.A.A.C.P.

In the face, however, of the unbelievable depths of debasement and humiliation to which this demagog has descended in order to keep himself out of jail, it is our duty to say openly and clearly:

Marcus Garvey is, without doubt, the most dangerous enemy of the Negro race in America and in the world. He is either a lunatic or a traitor. He is sending all over this country tons of letters and pamphlets appealing to Congressmen, businessmen, philanthropists and educators to join him on a platform whose half concealed planks may be interpreted as follows:

That no person of Negro descent can ever hope to become an American citizen.

That forcible separation of the races and the banishment of Negroes to Africa is the only solution of the Negro problem.

That race war is sure to follow any attempt to realize the program of the N.A.A.C.P.

We would have refused to believe that any man of Negro descent could have fathered such a propaganda if the evidence did not lie before us in black and white signed by this man. Here is a letter and part of a symposium sent to one of the most prominent businessmen of America and turned over to us; we select but a few phrases. . . .[1]

The pamphlets include one of the worst articles recently written by a Southern white man advocating the deportation of American Negroes to Liberia and several articles by Garvey and his friends.[2] From one of Garvey's articles we abstract one phrase:

THE WHITE RACE CAN BEST HELP THE NEGRO BY TELLING HIM THE TRUTH, AND NOT BY FLATTERING HIM INTO BELIEVING THAT HE IS AS GOOD AS ANY WHITE MAN.

Not even Tom Dixon or Ben Tillman or the hateful[l]est enemies of the Negro have ever stooped to a more vicious campaign tha[n] Marcus Garvey, sane or insane, is carrying on. He is not attacking white prejudice, he is grovelling before it and applauding it; his only attack is on men of his own race who are striving for freedom; his only contempt is for Negroes; his only threats are for black blood. And this leads us to a few plain words:

1. No Negro in America ever had a fairer and more patient trial than Marcus Garvey. He convicted himself by his own admissions, his swaggering monkey-shines in the court room with monocle and long tailed coat and his insults to the judge and prosecuting attorney.

2. Marcus Garvey was long refused bail, not because of his color, but because of the repeated threats and cold blooded assaults charged against his organization. He himself openly threatened to "get" the District Attorney. His followers had repeatedly to be warned from intimidating witnesses and one was sent to jail therefor. One of his former trusted officials after being put out of the Garvey organization brought the long concealed cash account of the organization to this office and we published it.[3] Within two weeks the man was shot in the back in New Orleans and killed. We know nothing of Garvey's personal connection with these cases but we do know that today his former representative lies in jail in Liberia sentenced to death for murder.[4] The District Attorney believed that Garvey's "army" had arms and ammunition and was prepared to "shoot up" colored Harlem if he was released. For these and no other reasons Garvey was held in the Tombs so long without bail and until he had made abject promises, apologizing to the judge and withdrawing his threats against the District Attorney. Since his release he has not dared to print a single word against white folk. All his vituperation has been heaped on his own race.

Everybody, including the writer, who has dared to make the slightest criticism of Garvey has been intimidated by threats and threatened with libel suits. Over fifty court cases have been brought by Garvey in ten years. After my first and favorable article on Garvey, I was not only threatened with death by men declaring themselves his followers, but received letters of such unbelievable filth that they were absolutely unprintable. When I landed in this country from my trip to Africa,[5] I learned with disgust that my friends stirred by Garvey's threats had actually felt compelled to have secret police protection for me on the dock!

Friends have even begged me not to publish this editorial lest I be assassinated. To such depths have we dropped in free black America! I have been exposing white traitors for a quarter century. If the day has come when I cannot tell the truth about black traitors it is high time that I died.

The American Negroes have endured this wretch all too long with fine restraint and every effort at cooperation and understanding. But the end has come. Every man who apologizes for or defends Marcus Garvey from this day forth writes himself down as unworthy of the countenance of decent Americans. As for Garvey himself, this open ally of the Ku Klux Klan should be locked up or sent home.[6]

Printed in the *Crisis* 27, no. 7 (May 1924): 8–9.

1. The symposium appears in a letter printed above; see pp. 468–470.

2. This may be a reference to an article by Robert W. Winston entitled "Should the Color Line Go?" which appeared in *Current History* (18, no. 6 [September 1923]: 945–951). In it he advocated the colonization of Liberia by American blacks. The article was later reprinted in an undated UNIA pamphlet (Alexander Gumby Collection, NNC).

3. The *Crisis* published the financial report in the January 1923 edition. While the UNIA claimed a balance of $712.38, according to the figures obtained by the *Crisis*, the organization had a balance of $24,827.

4. Du Bois was referring to Milton J. Marshall, a black American UNIA organizer and president of the Brewerville division in Liberia, who was convicted in August 1922 of killing his business partner, Joseph Edmunds. Marshall's conviction was appealed to the supreme court of Liberia; on 21 January 1924 the supreme court upheld the lower court's conviction of Marshall (*Liberia Law Reports* [New York: Cornell University Press, 1960], 2 [January 1908–November 1926]: 455–461).

5. In March 1924 Du Bois returned from an extensive journey in Europe and Africa. He initiated the trip to attend the Third Pan-African Congress. He also met in Portugal with the Liga Africana, a group of African organizations from Portuguese Africa. From Portugal he traveled to Africa, where he visited Sierra Leone and Senegal. He spent over a month in Liberia, where he attended the second inauguration of President King, acting at that event as official representative of President Calvin Coolidge (Elliot M. Rudwick, *W.E.B. Du Bois* [New York: Atheneum, 1969], pp. 231–233; *New York Age*, 22 March 1924; *Philadelphia Tribune*, 29 March 1924).

6. Du Bois's attack on Garvey prompted critical response from the black press. While most did not support Garvey, they questioned the vehemence of Du Bois's attack on the UNIA leader. The *Richmond Planet*, for example, criticized Du Bois for his "outburst of temper" and noted that a "mere statement of the facts . . . would . . . bring around Mr. Garvey's undoing among loyal citizens who have the brains and ability to think for themselves" (*Richmond Planet*, 3 May 1924). The *Chicago Whip* supported Du Bois, attacking Garvey as "a menace to all American citizens of black skins" (*Chicago Whip*, 24 May 1924). The *St. Luke Herald* of Richmond, contending that there were grounds for "sane criticism" of both Du Bois and Garvey, editorialized: "Again, we pin as much faith to the wisdom and ultimate success of Mister Garvey's efforts in Africa as we do to the wisdom and ultimate success of Doctor Du Bois. But why should we grow too serious-minded about nothing? Why should we curse and raise black hell because Doctor Du Bois returns from Europe and Africa in a quizzical frame of mind?" (*St. Luke Herald*, 17 May 1924).

Marcus Garvey to Thomas V. O'Connor,[1] Chairman, United States Shipping Board

56 West 135th St. NEW YORK CITY,
3 June 1924

I AM ASKING FOR APPOINTMENT TO SEE YOU IN WASHINGTON ON FRIDAY 6TH JUNE RE SHIPS PRESIDENTS ARTHUR AND FIL[L]MORE AND POTOMAC[.][2]

MARCUS GARVEY
President
Black Cross Navigation and Trading Co.

DNA, RG 32, file 605-1-653. TG, recipient's copy.

1. Thomas Ventry O'Connor (1870–1939) served as chairman of the USSB from 1924 until his resignation in 1933. The son of a brush maker from Ireland, O'Connor, a marine engineer, became active in the International Longshoremen's Association, rising to president of the organization in 1908. As president, he refused to sanction strikes by union members, among them the 1920 strike of three thousand Irish longshoremen in New York and Boston, a strike that had garnered much black support. He resigned the presidency of the union in 1921 to become vice-chairman of the USSB. O'Connor also served as chairman of the board of trustees and president of the Merchant Fleet Corp. (*Marine Review* 51, no. 8 [August 1921]: 346; *NYT*, 18 October 1939; for information on Garvey and the 1920 strike, see *Garvey Papers* 3: 13–14).

2. O'Connor responded to Garvey's telegram on 5 June, saying he would be in New York on Friday, 6 June, and suggesting that Garvey defer his visit until the following week (T. V. O'Connor to Marcus Garvey, 5 June 1924, DNA, RG 32, file 605-1-653).

Speech by Marcus Garvey

[[Liberty Hall, New York, June 4, 1924]]

We are making history tonight. It is the brightest chapter in the history of the Universal Negro Improvement Association. Tonight we finally send away to Africa a serious and well prepared group of men.[1] To do what? To visit Africa? No. This group of men go to the historic country of Liberia, a country founded a little over one hundred years ago by another serious and responsible group of people, for the purpose of encouraging a work just like this.

It was in the minds of the people who constituted the American Colonization Society over one hundred years ago that this hour would come in the history of the black people[,] in the development of the black people in this country, why they established that little country called Liberia that is now the only independent nation on the West Coast of Africa. The people who live in Liberia today are blood of our blood and flesh of our flesh, especially the ruling element, the Americo-West Indian Liberians. They represent in Liberia today the offspring of an earlier generation of Negroes who went from this country and from the West Indies 100 years ago, 80 years ago, 50 years ago, one-quarter of a century ago to make it possible to find and have freedom, a freedom that would, indeed, be worthwhile not only for themselves, but for the rest of their kind. And the hour has come.

ALERTNESS OF LIBERIA'S FOUNDERS

Years ago a small group of Negroes left this country. Some went from Maryland, some from the Carolinas, to found that new home that they call Liberia, the Liberia that is now attracting us. They got together there and they made laws among themselves, imitative of the laws of this great republic, for the purpose of insuring and perpetuating their society. Coming down the ages they have developed it to the extent that today Liberia is one of the recognized nations of the world. Her constitution is as liberal and as modern as that of any other nation, only that in that constitution and in the laws they made, because they had an eye to the future, an eye to this hour, they saw to it that the constitution was so made and the law was so constructed that that country would be preserved not only for them, but their children and for succeeding generations of Negroes exclusively. So much so, that because of these protecting laws they were able to keep out alien intruders, alien self-seekers who desired to have robbed them of their country years ago under the guise of friendship and diplomacy.[2] But because of the keenness of our fathers who founded the Liberian Republic and because of their loyalty to their race and to their native land, Africa, they held that country even against odds, tremendous difficulties, insomuch that the world seems to misunderstand them to the extent of saying that for one hundred years they have done nothing.

But if they have done nothing, they had a method in not doing anything. There was a method in their madness. If they had attempted to do anything, the something that the outer world desired, there would have been no Liberia today, and there would have been no free country on the continent of Africa. But we are satisfied with what our fathers did, what the rulers and directors of Liberia have done for the one hundred years they have occupied the country. They have been able to arouse the sleeping consciousness of the four hundred million Negroes of the world to go to the rescue, to help build Liberia and make her one of the greatest nations of the world.

And we are going to do it. The answer of the six million active members of the Universal Negro Improvement Association in the Western world, the answer of the four hundred million Negroes who have got the vision of the Universal Negro Improvement Association is that, "Yes, we are going to do it." And I feel sure that with the men we are sending out as forerunners in practical work, in practical achievement, give us 25 years and we will compel the world to change its opinion about the backwardness of Liberia and the inability of the Negro to demonstrate the ability of government.

A FAIR CHANCE WANTED

We are asking the world for a fair chance. That is all we ask for. We are asking the world for a fair chance to assist the people of Liberia in developing that country, as the world is giving the Jew a fair chance to develop Palestine. And, if they do not give us a fair chance, we are going to raise hell. (Applause.) The world will have to make room for us or we will realize the world has no sympathy for us, and if we must die we may as well die fighting with our backs to the wall. But I feel sure a sensible world will not inflict that much upon us because the world ought to know that the Negro, like everybody else, is entitled to just, liberal and fair consideration. That is all we ask. We ask that of liberal America. We ask America to help us in this enterprise. As they have helped different countries of Europe, Russia, France, Belgium, Serbia, so do we ask the liberal white man of America to help the Universal Negro Improvement Association put over this program for the development of a country of our own in Africa. We ask the liberal minds of Europe for the same consideration that they have shown to other people seeking self-development.

We are going there on a peaceful mission, a mission for the industrial, agricultural, commercial and cultural development of that country. We want to prove our worth. And, surely, men, we are going to prove it. We have already demonstrated our worth in helping others to climb the ladder of success. We have splendidly helped America for 300 years to her position in the world today. We have splendidly helped the British Empire for over 300 years to her position. We have for nearly 300-odd years helped France build the French Empire, and we are asking them for nothing more than for their friendly encouragement and consideration in this program of self-help.

The Negro Makes His Call

We want to help ourselves, and we feel sure that when the appeal is made to the conscience of America, America will respond to us as we responded to the call of America. We have never failed America in any circumstances. From the revolutionary period to this we have been willing and ready to answer the call of America, the adopted home of 15,000,000 of us. We have never failed the British when they called. From the time of the Ashanti war,[3] from the time of the Zulu war[4] to the war of 1918[,] British Negroes, millions of them, never failed the British and their call to service and to help. The Negroes have never failed the French. From the first days of French colonizing in Africa to the guard on the Rhine the French Negro never failed to hearken to the call of France. And, now, we are making a similar appeal, a similar call for help to these great peoples and these great nations. If they hear us not it is because they have lost the sense of humanity, it is because they have lost the sense of justice and fair play. And if their souls [are] so dead, surely we will not be responsible for the consequences in dealing with dead souls.

What Do the Critics Mean?

We are a serious group of people just at this time. We want a chance to live because we know that if we do not exert ourselves to live we are bound to die, and we are not going to allow anybody to kill us before our time. We know the consequences if we do not start out on our own initiative and our own account. And that is why we do not understand our critics and those who seem to condemn us. What do they mean? Do they mean we must sit down and prepare ourselves to die as the world intends weak and inactive people to do? They cannot be our friends if they do not want us to be active and up and doing. But we count our friends by the million[,] outside even of this race of ours because the world must be sober enough to understand in an age like this you cannot keep so many people down, four hundred millions of them. Some of us at least are alive to this, and the Universal Negro Improvement Association is thinking for the race, and we are presenting the program for the Negro, the program of self-development and initiative. We are going to try it, at least, if nothing more. I feel sure, men and women, that as these men go away from us in a few days they will take with them our best wishes and our united determination to stand by them to the last. So long as I am President-General, they shall be in want of nothing in their desire to carry out the program of the Universal Negro Improvement Association. (Applause.)

VANGUARD OF EXPERTS

They are going, I say, to do serious work. They are going to prepare for the group of those of us who will sail from this country in another few months. As you know we are preparing that the first group of colonists sail from New York in September. They will arrive in Liberia around the first week in October. By the time these men sail and land and by the time you get there these men are supposed to have ready for you certain accommodations. You are not going to Africa like the Pilgrim Fathers came to America. Nobody invited them to America. They came of their own accord and they did not know where they were going, and the storm drove them around the New England coast, and they got off the boats and made the trees their home, and they lived in and under those trees for a long while. Now we have been invited home. We have been requested to come home,' and then we have been told how to get ready to come home, and the sending of these experts is a part of the arrangements under which we are to go home. We are not going home to live under trees. We are going home, and when we get off the boat these men are going to have ready for us temporary homes in which we will live until we build permanently for ourselves. And please leave your native laziness behind. (Laughter.) Don't think these men will furnish you with homes. You will get busy and build permanent homes of your own. Negroes like to pay too much rent anyhow. We will introduce a new system. We are going to pay so much rent. This engineer of ours is going to lay out plans whereby every industrious man and woman can have a home of his own when you get there. As I said before, we do not want any bums to go to Africa now. And if I have any friends who are bums take my advice and stay where you are, because we will put you in jail. If you look up the engineer's plans you will find one of the first buildings to be erected is a jail. (Laughter.) The fellow who has a grudge or a spite against the other fellow's goods, please stay in Harlem, in America, and make the best you can with the Irish cop.

Leave that part of the white man's civilization in New York, in Harlem, in America, because we have a new civilization for Africa.

We have made arrangements whereby every industrious family going to Liberia will have twenty-five acres of land which you can develop agriculturally or industrially, and in addition to that you will get a free house lot in the city to build your home, and after you have built your house on it the government will give you a free title in fee simple for the occupation of the land. If you are single you will get fifteen acres of land. If you are a woman you will get ten acres for industrial or agricultural development and a free house lot. You will get five acres for every child you have. We have a list of thousands of people who want to go this year and next year. We want all to get busy. Work hard so that you can land in Liberia with at least two or three hundred dollars to start with, because a bum in Liberia is just as bad as a bum in Harlem. Society has no use for such a character at this time. (Loud applause.)

Printed in *NW*, 14 June 1924. Original headlines omitted.

1. On 7 June 1924 the *Negro World* announced that the UNIA would shortly send a team of technicians to Liberia. Rupert Christian, executive secretary, Reginald Hurley, carpenter and builder, J. Nicholls (also spelled Nicholas), mechanical engineer, and James Walcott, ship carpenter and builder, set out on 20 June 1924. James O'Meally, commissioner, and William W. Strange, supervising and directing civil and mining engineer, set sail the following day. On 25 July only three members of the original team arrived in Monrovia; they were immediately put under police guard by Liberian authorities and deported on the next ship bound for Hamburg, the intermediate port from whence they had come (*NW*, 14 June 1924; *P&O*, 2: 388–389).

2. Under the Liberian constitution, only "men of color" were eligible for citizenship, and whites were not allowed to own land. Whites were allowed, however, to hold land in the form of lease concessions, a practice first utilized on a significant scale during the presidency of Arthur Barclay (1904–1912). The Liberians also legislated a protectionist trade policy with the 1849 Act Regulating Navigation, Commerce, and Revenue, which attempted to establish monopolistic control over coastal trade by restricting the activities of foreign traders to specified ports and by requiring that Liberians act as their intermediaries in local trade (*African World* [London], 7 June 1921; Nathaniel R. Richardson, *Liberia's Past and Present* [London: Diplomatic Press and Publishing Co., 1959], p. 249; Tom W. Shick, *Behold the Promised Land: A History of Afro-American Settler Society in Nineteenth-Century Liberia* [Baltimore: Johns Hopkins University Press, 1980], pp. 103–104).

3. The West India Regiment, first formed in 1795, served in British West Africa throughout the nineteenth century and saw service in the Ashanti War of 1873–1874 Abioseh Nicol, "West Indians in West Africa," *Sierra Leone Studies* 4 [June 1960]: 14–23; Aba Karama, "The Origin of the West Indies Regiments," *Science and Society* 35 [spring 1971]: 58–62).

4. African troops were used by the British against the Zulu in 1879, 1906, and 1907. In 1906 African combatants composed over half of the British fighting force against the Zulu (Michael Barthorp, *The Zulu War*, [Poole, England: Blandford Press, 1980, pp. 18, 33–35; T. R. H. Davenport, *South Africa: A Modern History* [London: Macmillan, 1977], pp. 110–112, 152).

5. There is no evidence suggesting that the UNIA had been officially invited to Liberia. Indeed, Liberian president C. D. B. King was reluctant to meet with the three UNIA commissioners, Henrietta Vinton Davis, Robert L. Poston, and Milton Van Lowe, who had been sent by the UNIA to Monrovia to negotiate a settlement agreement with the Liberian government. Bowing to pressures applied by a group of wealthy and prominent Liberians, King nonetheless consented to an unofficial meeting with the UNIA delegation. Three days prior to the 11 February meeting, King issued a statement declaring that he had declined an official interview and that all discussions were to be informal and between private individuals. He also rejected "any proposal for the settling of 3,000 immigrants to Liberia." In doing so, according to King, he was "keeping his mind on the

Obligation of Liberia to the Great Powers, and as such to the maintenance of the Independence of the Republic." During the informal discussions King approved of the idea of establishing an advisory committee consisting of Arthur Barclay, D.E. Howard, J.J. Dossen, W.F. Dennis, Dixon B. Brown, D.C. Carranda, and H.T. Wesley, for the purposes of proposing a plan under which UNIA-sponsored immigration to Liberia might take place. A document reported to be the recommendations of the private advisory committee was published in the second volume of *Philosophy and Opinions*; it established guidelines for the type and numbers of immigrants desired, the conditions and localities of settlement, and the provisions and equipment that would be needed by the immigrants. There is no indication that President King ever approved of the plan (British Foreign Office to the Dominions Office, 5 September 1924, PRO, FO 371/9553; PRO, CO 532/289; *African World* [London], August–September 1924; *NW*, 19 April, 6 September and 15 September 1924; *Baltimore Afro-American*, 20 June 1924; *P&O*, 2: 371–372).

Esme Howard, British Embassy, Washington, D.C., to Ramsay MacDonald, Prime Minister of Great Britain

WASHINGTON. June 6th, 1924

Sir,

In his despatch No. 808 of June 27th, 1923, Mr. Chilton reported that Marcus Garvey, head of the Universal Negro Improvement Association and self-styled "President of the African Republic" had been found guilty of using the mails to defraud investors in the Black Star Steamship Line, of which he was a promot[e]r, and had been sentenced to five years' imprisonment and to pay a fine of one thousand dollars. Garvey subsequently appealed against this sentence, and still remains at liberty on bail pending a final decision by the Courts.

I now have the honour to inform you that notwithstanding his previous unfortunate experience in dealing with shipping, Garvey is again engaged in the organisation of a steamship company entitled the Black Cross Navigation and Trading Company (incorporated under the laws of New Jersey), and in this connection I enclose herein copy of an advertisement published in the "Negro World" on the 24th ultimo, from which it will be seen that Garvey now aims at the development of Liberia.[1]

Of late there has been a certain revival in the activities of the individual above-mentioned. In April and May he visited Philadelphia, Pittsburgh, Cleveland, Detroit, Gary, Cincinnati and Boston, in order to address meetings on behalf of the Universal Negro Improvement Association, and in March articles appearing in his newspaper "The Negro World" drew attention to the discontent existing among the negro populations of the British West Indies. Garvey, however, does not confine his attentions to the British Empire alone but champions the causes of all "subject" peoples. He is a warm supporter of Philippine Independence.[2] I have, etc.,

ESME HOWARD[3]

JA, 1 B/5, dispatches, no. 961. TL, carbon copy.

1. The advertisement reads, "All members of the Universal Negro Improvement Association who desire to go to Liberia, West Africa, to settle, to help in the industrial, commercial and cultural development of the country, and who intend sailing September, October, December, 1924 or January, February, March, April or May, 1925 are requested to send in for application form to be filled out" (*NW*, 24 May 1924).

2. In the 1920s Filipino demands for independence increased as it became clear that the United States would not abide by a 1916 agreement to grant self-rule. In 1924 President Coolidge firmly opposed independence on the grounds that Filipinos were "by no means equipped, either in wealth or experience, to undertake the heavy burden which would be imposed upon them with political independence." Nevertheless, in the elections of 1923 leaders of the Philippines' Coalition party favoring independence won. In May 1924 Manuel Quezon, president of the Filipino legislature and leader of the independence movement, arrived in Washington, D.C., to lobby for independence. The *Negro World* carried news sympathetic to Filipino independence in both its Spanish and English-language sections (*NW*, 15 April 1924; *NYT*, 12 June 1924; Walter Robb, "Filipinos' Demand for Independence," *Current History* 19, no. 2 [November 1923]: 281–288).

In the British Foreign Office's minutes referring to Howard's dispatch on Garvey, there is a handwritten notation that reads, "It's a pity the cannibals do not get hold of this man!" (PRO, FO 371/9633, British Foreign Office minute, 17 June 1924).

3. Esme William Howard (1863–1939) served as British ambassador to the United States from 1924 until his retirement in 1930. In 1930 he became Baron Howard of Penrith and served in the House of Lords until his death in 1939 (*Who's Who*, 1925 [London: A. and C. Black, 1926], p. 1,420; *DNB*, 454–455).

Report by Special Agent Joseph G. Tucker

[*New York*] June 7, 1924

The following is the program for the convention of the Universal Negro Improvement Association, which is to be held at Liberty Hall, from August 1st to 31st, inclusive:

RELIGIOUS

1. Discussing the Deification of Jesus as a black Man of Sorrows.

2. The canonization of the Virgin Mary as a Negress.

3. The Idealization of God as a Holy Spirit, without physical form, but a Creature of imaginary semblance of the black race, being of like image and likeness.

POLITICAL

1. Discussing the formation of the Negro Political Union.

2. The educating of Negroes in communities where they form the majority population to rise to the responsibility of self-government.

3. Conferring with the white nations and with the League of Nations for an amicable adjustment of the race issue and for a rearrangement of the system

under which Negroes are governed.

4. Presentation of petition of four million American Negroes on the 6th of August to his Excellency the President of the United States for his consideration of their desire to peaceably build up a country of their own in their motherland, Africa.

5. Presentation of a similar petition to the Senate and House of Representatives at their next session.

6. Presentation of a similar petition of two million West Indian Negroes in the British Isles to His Majesty King George V and the Parliament and the House of Lords of Great Britain.

INDUSTRIAL

1. Discussing the development of Liberia, Abyssinia and Haiti as independent black nations, and other countries where Negroes form a majority of the population, i.e., Jamaica, Barbados, Trinidad, British Guiana, British Honduras and other islands of the West Indies and Africa.

2. Ways and means of adjusting the race problem of the Southern States of the United States of America to the satisfaction of all concerned.

3. Ways and means of correctly educating white public opinion to the needs and desires of the Negro race.

SOCIAL

1. Discussing the educating of the Negro race as to the real meaning of society, and laying down the principles that should guide those who are desirous of becoming socially distinctive.

2. Creating an atmosphere of purity around the young generation of the race, to better prepare them for a higher social life.

COMMERCIAL

1. Discussing the linking up of all Negro communities in a trade and commercial relationship.

2. Promotion of exchange business enterprises in all Negro communities.

3. Encouraging travel among and between Negroes of commercial and industrial professions.

EDUCATIONAL

1. Discussing the formulation of a code of education especially for Negroes.

2. The censoring of all literature placed in the hands of Negroes.

3. The educating of the race to discriminate in the reading of all literature placed in its hands.

4. The promotion of an independent Negro literature and culture.

Propaganda

1. The tabooing of all alien propaganda inspired to destroy the ideals of and the enslaving of the minds of the Negro.

2. The disseminating of education among the race for the promotion of its own ideals.

Constitutional

1. Amending the constitution of the Universal Negro Improvement Association as found necessary.

2. Discussing the annual business of the Universal Negro Improvement Association.

Humanity

1. Discussing the promotion of a closer bond of fellowship between the black and white races of the world.

2. Discussing, without prejudice, the aims and objects of the Ku Klux Klan.

3. Discussing the intra-racial problems of the white race, as they affect the Negro.

4. Discussing the program of a white Canada, a white America, a white Europe and a white Australia, as enunciated by white leaders.

5. Discussing the sincerity of the League of Nations as a clearing house for the ills of the world.

6. Discussing France's policy toward the Negro.

7. Discussing England's policy toward the Negro.

8. Discussing America's policy toward the Negro.

9. Discussing the Negro's share of the spoils of war of 1914–1918.

10. Discussing the new German demand for the return of certain colonies in Africa that were robbed from the natives and taken from the Germans during the last war.[1]

11. Discussing the honesty of diplomacy in its dealing with the lands, liberties and rights of weaker peoples.

12. Discussing the forwarding of an appeal to His Holiness the Pope of Rome, His Grace the Archbishop of Canterbury and the heads of the American

churches, as leaders of Christianity, for an honest and human settlement of the problems of humanity, especially as such problems affect the Negro.

13. An appeal to the Kings of England, Italy, Spain and Belgium and their parliaments for a square deal for Negroes in Africa and the colonies.

14. An appeal to the Presidents of America, France and Portugal for a square deal for Negroes in Africa, America and the colonies.

15. Discussing the Negro's attitude in the next great war.

16. Discussing the petition of appeal of the Negro Peoples of the World to the League of Nations for the turning over to them of certain mandatories in Africa now being exercised by alien peoples over the natives.

JOSEPH G. TUCKER

DJ-FBI, file 61-290. TD.

1. A reference to the German Colonial League's demand in April 1924 for the return of German colonies taken by the Treaty of Versailles, an issue taken up primarily by colonial societies and organizations. In 1924 the German Colonial League appealed to the general public by organizing a convocation, the Continental Congress, to mark the fortieth anniversary of the beginning of the German colonial empire. Newspapers carried articles declaring Germany's right to the colonies. By December, Foreign Secretary Gustav Streseman made the return of German colonies a precondition for Germany's entrance into the League of Nations. The issue was to become increasingly important in the 1930s under the Third Reich (*NYT*, 25 April, 18 September, 23 September, and 28 September 1924; Wolfe W. Schmokel, *Dream of Empire: German Colonialism, 1919–1945* [New Haven: Yale University Press, 1964]; Rayford W. Logan, *The African Mandates in World Politics* [Washington, D.C.: Public Affairs Press, 1948], pp. 26–110; Mary E. Townsend, "The Contemporary Colonial Movement in Germany," *Political Science Quarterly* 43, no. 1 [March 1928]: 64–75).

Articles in the *Negro World*

[7 June 1924]

THE COLONIZATION PROGRAMME FOR LIBERIA

UNIVERSAL NEGRO IMPROVEMENT ASSOCIATION RAISING FUND OF TWO MILLION DOLLARS FOR BUILDING FIRST COLONY IN LIBERIA

The Universal Negro Improvement Association is now starting to carry out its colonization plans for helping in the cultural, industrial, agricultural, economic, educational and social development of the black republic of Liberia, west coast Africa, as a permanent home for scattered Negroes of the world who desire to live in a country of their own where they may enjoy the benefits of real freedom, liberty and democracy.

The good people of Liberia anxiously welcome to their country, their hearts and their ideals the soberminded, industrious, law-abiding, ambitious Negroes of America, West Indies, South and Central America and Canada who desire to settle among them and become a part of a peaceful, growing black nation. The Universal Negro Improvement Association is now helping in this direction as the Jews are helping to build and restore Palestine.

The Association has undertaken to develop four colonies in Liberia, the first to be built on the Cavalla River,[1] to which the first group of colonists is expected to sail in September of 1924 from New York and regularly thereafter.

The Association is to spend two million ($2,000,000) dollars on the development of each colony for public works and other utilities.

They are now raising the first two million ($2,000,000) dollars for the building of the Cavalla colony.

The following plans are to be carried out for the building of each and every one of the four colonies, all government buildings, however, to be under the direction of the Liberian Government and all persons shall observe the laws of the Republic of Liberia accordingly.

BUILDING PLANS

GOVERNMENT

1. Court House and Post Office
2. Town Hall

    a.   Public Safety

        1.   Police Station

        2.   Fire Protection

        3.   Hospital

COMMUNITY INTEREST AND ENTERTAINMENT

1. National Theatre
2. Churches (2)
3. Large Public Hall
4. Public Park

PUBLIC EDUCATION

1. Public Library
2. Public Schools (2)
3. Public High School (1)
4. College of Arts and Sciences

5. Trade School and Engineering Works

PUBLIC UTILITIES

1. Electric Light and Power Plant
2. Water Filtration Plant
3. Sewerage System and Sewage Disposal Plant

    a. Transportation Facilities

       1. Roads, Street and Pavements

       2. Wharf and Dock and Water Front Improvement

       3. Railroad 4-15 miles

    b. Commissaries (2)

    c. Dormitories (2)

All those who desire to help the Negro under the auspices of the Universal Negro Improvement Association in developing himself are asked to subscribe to the fund of two million ($2,000,000) dollars now being raised for the promotion of the Cavalla Colony.

The first group of engineers will sail in a few days to start construction work for the accommodation of the first group of colonists who will leave in September.

Please help this fund with a substantial donation.[2] Address your donation to the "Colonization Fund, Universal Negro Improvement Association, 56 West 135th Street, New York, U.S.A."

All substantial donations will be acknowledged by letter and by publication in the Negro World. Small donations will be acknowledged in the Negro World weekly.

THE FUND

Marcus Garvey	$100.00
Mrs. Marcus Garvey	50.00
William C. Ritter[3]	25.00

Printed in *NW*, 7 June 1924. Original headlines abbreviated. Reprinted in the *New York World*, 25 June 1924.

1. The Cavalla, or Cavally, River runs along the border between Liberia and Ivory Coast.

2. On 14 June 1924 Agent Tucker reported that the UNIA had already received $663.95 toward the fund (special report by Joseph G. Tucker, 14 June 1924, DJ-FBI, file 61).

3. Possibly William C. Ritter (1872–1934), Hungarian-born Brooklyn banker, philanthropist, and communal worker. Ritter was the founder of the Congregation Sons of Israel and vice-president of the Jewish Community House of Bensonhurst from 1926 to 1934. He was a member of the board of directors of the Israel Zion Hospital, the Brooklyn Federation of Jewish Charities, and, from 1914 to 1927, the Young Men's Hebrew Association. Ritter was also a Mason and an honorary member of the Grand Army of the Republic (*NYT*, 8 May 1934; *Jewish Daily Bulletin*, 9 May

1934; Philip J. Cohen, executive director, Jewish Community House of Bensonhurst, Brooklyn, to Robert A. Hill, 16 November 1983).

[7 June 1924]

WHEN THE LION AND THE LIZARD MET
IN A CINCINNATI HOTEL

(From the Cleveland Gazette)[1] CINCINNATI, O.—Last week Monday morning [*19 May*], Prof. "Alphabe[tic]al" (W.E.B.) Du Bois, editor of The Crisis magazine, was in this city and had 10 A.M. breakfast at Hotel Sterling with Prof. W.P. Dabney,[2] editor of our local publication, The Union. But let the latter tell about it:

"As I (Dabney) journeyed to the hotel,[3] I thought of how Du Bois in The Crisis, only last month, had assailed the doctrines of Marcus Garvey, and personally called him 'everything he was big enough to call him'; in short, things the reverse of complimentary. We were saddened, for we knew Garvey's foreign blood (West Indian) and fiery temper. We prayed that the two would never meet, unless surrounded by minions of the law. We entered the Hotel Sterling office, found Du Bois, and, as we were early, the time was agreeably spent in a tête-a-tête. * * *[4]

["]Fragrant odors wafted from realms below told that a feast fit for the gods was in process of preparation or materialization. To the elevator we went. Waiting a moment, the door was suddenly thrown open, out stepped a guard of honor, consisting of several ladies splendidly costumed, and a stout dark gentleman, gorgeously apparelled in military costume! Ye gods! 'Twas Garvey. He saw me, a smile of recognition, then a glance at Du Bois. His eyes flew wide open. Stepping aside, he stared; turning around, he stared, while Du Bois, looking straight forward, head uplifted, nostrils quivering, marched into the elevator, seemingly 'all the world forgetting,' but not by all the world forgot for Garvey was still gazing, petrified, as though uncertain whether 'twas really his arch foe who had been so near and yet was getting farther away every second. A sigh of relief escaped me as we entered the club. Immediately, I remarked, 'I must compliment you upon your wonderful nerve, your coolness, your poise. The only sign I saw of nervousness was the quivering of your nostrils.'

" 'What are you talking about?' said [he].

" 'Why, about your meeting with Garvey, just now. I expected him to attack you at once.'

" 'Are you crazy? Garvey? Where is Garvey?'

" 'Why, he stepped out of the elevator as we entered.'

" 'Stepped out of elevator? Garvey? Why[,] I did not know it. I saw a man in uniform, but paid no attention. I was deeply thinking about something.'

" 'Well, if you did not know it was Garvey, why was your nose twitching so?'

" 'That was caused by thought. You see, I smelled the breakfast, and was wondering how soon we would reach the table.'

"We ate, he chuckling with laughter as he thought of the meeting, and I a little serious at the thought of what might have happened. But 'All's well that ends.' " [5]

DABNEY

Printed in *NW*, 7 June 1924. Original headlines abbreviated. Reprinted from the *Cleveland Gazette*, 31 May 1924; original article in the *Cincinnati Union*, 24 May 1924.

1. The *Gazette* headlines read: Du Bois & Garvey Meet!/No Blood Is Shed!/The Quivering of Du Bois' Nostrils/ The Only Casualty/Garvey Stared at Du Bois—the Latter Pretended He Did/ Not See Him—Some Tense Moments in the/Lobby of Hotel Sterling, Says/Editor Dabney.

2. Wendell Phillips Dabney (1865–1953) owned, edited, and managed the *Union*, a black weekly in Cincinnati, from 1905 until his death. Dabney, the son of a Virginia slave, attended Oberlin College from 1885 to 1886 and taught school in Richmond for eight years before moving to Cincinnati to take over management of his uncle's hotel, the Dumas House. Dabney quickly became involved in black Republican politics in the city, and the Dumas House served as a center for Republican political rallies. In 1896 Dabney was instrumental in taking over the Douglass League, a black Republican organization, making the league a secret organization and becoming its president. Yet rather than stay within the folds of the Republican party, which Dabney termed a new form of slavery, the league joined the Fusion movement of 1896, which brought together Democrats and Independent Republicans. In response to black demand for more political power within the government of Cincinnati, a number of blacks were appointed to political office; Dabney was appointed the first black assistant paymaster in 1898 and then head city paymaster, the highest political position held by a black in Cincinnati. He served from 1898 to 1900, then was returned to the post, serving from 1907 until 1923.

Dabney was an accomplished musician. He taught music, wrote six books on musical method, and composed several songs and musical works. He was also president of the Dabney Publishing Co. and the author of *Cincinnati's Colored Citizens* (1926), president of the Royal Union Improvement Co., and a member of the Masons and the Shriners (*WWCA*; *WWCR*; *NYT*, 5 June 1953; *Cincinnati Times-Star*, 3 November 1945; Wendell P. Dabney, *Cincinnati's Colored Citizens* [Dabney Publishing Co., 1926]; Langston Hughes, "America's Most Unique Newspaper," *Negro Digest* 3, no. 2 [October 1945]: 23–24).

3. The *Cincinnati Union* article reads:
As we journeyed to the hotel, before us arose visions of the immense banquet for the most distinguished white and colored citizens given in New York recently on the arrival of the doctor from Europe and Africa. Thought of what a wonderful thing it was that the colored people who contemplated remaining in this country, were establishing inter-racial relations on terms of equality that would be so beneficial to coming generations.
This banquet to honor Du Bois occurred on 12 April 1924 at New York's Café Savarin (*Philadelphia Tribune*, 26 April 1924).

4. The asterisks replace the following passage from the *Union*:
that embraced, lovely tales of the wonders of Africa, our magnificent-looking relatives in that country; choice bonmots gathered here and there, sketches of Europe in its many phases and forms, prospects for the next Pan-African conference, the present itinerary of many cities on a lecture tour, the coming great gathering of the N.A.A.C.P. in Philadelphia next month.

5. The *Negro World* omits the final word, "well."

J. Harry Philbin, Manager, Ship Sales Division, United States Shipping Board, to General Counsel

[*Washington, D.C.*] June 11th, 1924

SUBJECT: BLACK CROSS NAVIGATION &
TRADING CO., INC.

This concern has submitted a firm offer to purchase the SUSQUEHANNA, intending to complete payment of the proposed purchase price, $140,000.00 by August 30th, 1924. The offer was not quite clear as to whether or not title is to rest in the Government until completion of payment, and I am having this point cleared up before presenting the matter to the Shipping Board.

The Company above named is headed by Marcus Garvey, who you will recall was President of the Black Star Line. I think the Board has a deposit of $22,500.00 from the Black Star Line, arising out of negotiations with that Company for the sale of a vessel in 1921. Such negotiations were not consummated and subsequently I testified in the New York District in a case brought against Garvey.[1]

The present venture is an undertaking of the Universal Negro Improvement Association, of which Garvey is the head and I understand the moving factor. The Black Star Line was also a subsidiary of this Association.

The offer which we now have from Black Cross Navigation and Trading Company, Incorporated[,] does not associate negotiations with any heretofore conducted with the Black Star Line, but I thought that the matter should be called to your attention, if for any reason the present status of the case against Garvey should be invited to the attention of the Shipping Board. Will you kindly advise me on the matter.[2]

J. HARRY PHILBIN
Manager
Department of Ship Sales

DNA, RG 32, file 605-1-653. TLS, recipient's copy.

1. On 9 June 1923 Joseph Harry Philbin testified at Garvey's trial regarding the $22,500 deposit that had been made by the BSL to purchase the ship *Orion*. As a result of the disputes over claims to the deposit money, Philbin said, the board continued to hold the deposit. On 11 February 1924 Philbin wrote General Counsel Parker, requesting an investigation into the *Orion* case and seeking advice as to whether the board was now free to dispose of the ship as it saw fit. By March, Parker had replied affirmatively (*Marcus Garvey* v. *United States*, no. 8317, Ct. App., 2d Cir., 2 February 1925, pp. 1,875–2,192; J. Harry Philbin to General Counsel Parker, 11 February 1924, DNA, RG 32, file 605-1-653; Chauncey G. Parker to J. Harry Philbin, 31 March 1924, DNA, RG 32, USSB, file 1091-1250, p. 3).

2. Stephen Barker, assistant to the general counsel, responded on 13 June, advising Philbin to bring the matter to the attention of the USSB (Stephen Barker to J. Harry Philbin, 5 June 1924 DNA, RG 32, file 605-1-653).

Speech by Marcus Garvey

[[Liberty Hall, New York, June 15, 1924]]

Gradually the world is reforming itself. In the reformation each and every one has a part to play. If you were to take stock and pay careful attention to the activities of the different peoples of the world at this time you will find that the Universal Negro Improvement Association is not so much composed of dreamers after all because, indeed, things are coming to pass.

Years ago, when we started this great movement, those of us of vision prophesied that there would be world changes; that in the midst of these changes would come the opportunity, the chance that we desire. They have not all come yet, but they are gradually coming, and we are on our way. Great Britain has changed within the last five years. France has changed within the last forty-eight hours. The whole world is changing and is traveling our way. On Tuesday by 12 o'clock midnight South Africa will have changed even as England and France have changed.[1] South Africa will pass from being one of the strong outposts of the great British Empire, and will be on the way toward an independent republicanism which will ultimately spell the ruin of that section of the Empire.

WORLD CHANGE AND THE NEGRO

All that we had in our minds six, seven, eight years ago when we organized the Universal Negro Improvement Association. It is only a question of patience and organization and preparedness and we are bound to get where we want to go. As the world has changed within the last five years, so will the world change in another ten years, so will the world change in another twenty years, so will the world change in another fifty years. And those peoples, especially the oppressed, who have vision and foresight enough and who have organization, will ultimately walk into those changes that they have dreamed about, that they have organized for, that they have worked for, and with very little resistance.

PREPARES FOR THE SCRAMBLE

The greatest instrument today for world control is organization. And I am glad that the Universal Negro Improvement Association has not faltered on the way, but year by year we have been building up a stronger organization to meet the exigencies of the times. Let me tell you, men and women of Liberty Hall, let me tell you, Negro men and women the world over, the hour is drawing near for Africa's redemption, even without the Negro striking a blow in that direction. It is not even so much force of arms that will redeem Africa; it is not so much gunpowder that will redeem Africa; it is organization among Negroes that will redeem Africa. And that is the organization that we are endeavoring to build up among the Negro peoples of the world, because Africa, certain parts of Africa, will be going a-begging one of these days, belonging to nobody. Anybody can occupy because everybody will be engaged.

I have a vision, and you may call it that of a lunatic, but I have a vision that in another fifty years the West Indies and Africa, as far as colonial possessions are concerned, are not going to belong to anybody; it will be a scramble for anybody that wants it. And that is why we are getting ready for the scramble, because we are going to be in it. We don't want to kill anybody, to fight anybody. Get ready, keep ready, get organized, and you will pick up something one of these days.

WHAT JAPAN SAYS

If I understand the papers correctly, Japan is all up in the air now. And Japan is talking loud, so loud that they have to be organizing a proper system of suppression, suppressing the newspapers because they are talking too much.[2] You know what Japan has said within the last fortnight? Japan has said openly in the press of Tokio that the time has come for Japan to line up Asia and call in all Africa.[3] (Applause.) And Marcus Garvey did not say that. The press of Japan said that this very week. Last week they said that. Marcus Garvey did not say that, but Marcus Garvey foresaw that six years ago. And that is why he brought into line the Universal Negro Improvement Association. (Applause.)

Something is going to happen. You are not going to start it, but you are going to finish it. We are not troubling anybody. We are too helpless and too weak and too poor to interfere with anybody or start anything, but we know the world is getting ready to start something that only four hundred million Negroes can finish. Look out, France has gone into the hands of the socialists. England has gone into the hands of the socialists. England has gone into the hands of the workingman. Germany is already in the hands of the socialists.[4] You know what that is going to lead to? It will lead to a world upheaval, a world upheaval between capital and labor, between socialism on the one hand and the plutocracy on the other, and when all these rogues start to fight you look out and get your share, that is all. Don't start anything, but keep ready to pick up what is going by. And if you keep ready there will be lots to pick up down in Africa and in the West Indies, too. Uncle Sam is going to keep his hands off, and so long as fifteen millions of us are still here we are going to play that politics that will see that Uncle Sam keeps his hands off. If anything is going a-begging in the West Indies, Uncle Sam will help us pick it up anyhow.

ANOTHER TEN YEARS

Something is on the air. Don't be discouraged, boys. Another few years will tell the tale, will tell the tale of a free and independent India, will tell the tale of a free and independent Canada, will tell the tale of a free and independent Australia, will tell the tale of a free and independent South Africa. Everybody is going to scramble for himself and you get ready wheresoever you are to scramble for the things you want. And I am not going to tell you what you want; you know it more than I do. All you have to do is to keep in good form, keep organized.

What we are doing today as an organization was not made possible by Marcus Garvey and two or three people, but is made possible because we are a powerful organization in this country. There are things we can get today, ears that we can reach today, that, if it were for Marcus Garvey alone, never could have been gotten, never could have been reached. But because of the tremendous motive power of this organization, of six million men and women who are dedicated to one purpose, one supreme object, that is why the Universal Negro Improvement Association is being talked about not only in America, but in Europe.

U.N.I.A. STILL A PUZZLE

Continental Europe talks and thinks more about the Universal Negro Improvement Association than you think about it. Not the Internationale,[5] not the Socialist movement, not even the non-co-operationist movement of India, but the movement of the Universal Negro Improvement Association is the coming movement of the world. They have reckoned with Socialism already; they have reckoned with the Internationale already; they have reckoned with the non-co-operationist already, but they do not know yet to what extent they have to reckon with the coming movement of the Universal Negro Improvement Association that is backed up by four hundred million black men and women the world over. (Applause.)

We are having now the ear of Europe and we are going to have it more. We are having the ear of this country and we will have it more, because we have not yet given our platform and presented our program entirely to those who should know about it. We will do it this year. August of this year will be the biggest month and year in the history of the Universal Negro Improvement Association. This year we are going to change world opinion.

The editor of the New York World[6] the other day, in commenting on one or two items that we gave out to be discussed at the convention, said among other things, that the Negro was always willing to accept everything as it is and never attempted any originality, and it is surprising now to see they are contemplating discussing the idealization of a God of their own race.[7] That is a big thing. You hardly imagine how far around the world that thought has gone.

The white man knows the gravity of it. He feels and understands the meaning of it. And we are going to discuss a programme in Liberty Hall in August that is going to revolutionize the thought of the whole world as far as the Negro goes. In this very hall we are going to deify a Man of Sorrows looking like ourselves. You know what that means. It means this: That we are going to make Jesus look like us. It simply means that the Universal Negro Improvement Association has led the Negro to the point now where he has created his own ideal and refuses to accept the ideal of others. That is going to create a world revolution that was impossible five years ago. But it is not impossible now because of the authority and strength of the Universal Negro Improvement Association.

A RIGHT TO LEAD

The Universal Negro Improvement Association leads and has a right to lead at this time because it represents a larger group of thinking Negroes than any other movement in the world. We are bound to lead, and lead in a manner and way of giving directions to the rest of those who must follow, and we have been followers and nothing more for the last 300 years and without the proper leadership. We started out after emancipation to follow a false leadership that had ideals that were not of our own making, and church and State and all of us followed in that direction for long years until we have reached this point where we have become the laughingstock of the world. But the Universal Negro Improvement Association assumes the authority, the sovereignty to redirect the mind, the vision, and the ideal of the Negro, and as white men have misled us for fifty years since emancipation in America, for eighty odd years since emancipation in the West Indies, for 300 years in this western world, the Universal Negro Improvement Association is going to take a decided and definite stand in seeing that the Negro is properly led for the rest of eternity. (Applause.)

Call it presumption, call it what you may, it is as much the right and authority of the Universal Negro Improvement Association to give a system and a code to the Negro race as it was the right of the white people in days of yore to give a system to their race and to give to their race a code by which they should be guided and led. It was not God Almighty who directed, in all things, the affairs of men. It is not God Almighty who has built up all these human ideals. The ideals that men worship today and foster today, these ideals that lead the world, that direct the human race, were created and built up by men in ages past, and we have as much right now in the twentieth century to build our own ideals as they did in ages past.

CUTS BOTH WAYS

The critic asks why Garvey wears a red robe. Marcus Garvey flings back the retort, "Why does the Pope wear a red robe?" "Why does the King of England wear purple robes?" The same authority that made them wear robes indicative of the spirit of their movement is the same authority that leads Marcus Garvey and the Universal Negro Improvement Association. (Applause.) Man's authority in things temporal reaches no higher than man, and since man is the creator of human ideals, and white men have created such ideals for the guidance and leadership of their own people, we as Negroes have as much right to create such ideals within the twentieth century, if not earlier. Man has taken upon himself the right and the prerogative to idealize a god in his own s[e]mblance, and since man has taken upon himself the right to idealize a man of sorrows in his own physique, countenance and semblance, and since we did not know better when we started the religion and made the mistake, now, that we know better, we will correct the mistake. (Applause.)

GOD IS A SPIRIT

The editor of the New York World is crazy if he thinks that after all this schooling we have had on this side of the Atlantic and which we paid for so dearly, he is going to tell us that we must continue to worship the idea of a white God and white Jesus, since they have made them so. The books we have studied from did not tell us Jesus was a white man. The books we have studied from did not tell us God was a white man. They said God was a spirit, a divine, mighty, omnipotent spirit. But since whites are seeing him through the eyes of whiteness, we are going to see him through the eyes of blackness. (Uproarious applause.)

And any white man who thinks Marcus Garvey should not do that, he had better go drown himself in the Hudson River, because Garvey is not going to change his mind, until they change their minds. God is with us, as with all peoples. God is love. The white can have the white part. We will have the black part. God is as much black as he is white. He is divided up into many parts. (Loud applause.)

Printed in *NW*, 21 June 1924. Original headlines omitted.

1. The day before Garvey's speech, Édouard Herriot, leader of the Radical Socialist party in the French assembly, was appointed prime minister, paving the way for the *de jure* recognition of Soviet Russia in October 1924 (*NYT*, 15 June 1924). Garvey spoke in anticipation of a National party victory in South Africa. Within this party there were strong elements that supported South Africa's secession from the British Empire and the establishment of an independent republic. On 17 June 1924 a coalition of the Labour and National parties, led by James Hertzog, defeated Jan Smuts's South African party. During the elections Hertzog agreed to put aside the secession issue in exchange for Labour party support, but there was speculation that secessionists within the National party would eventually force a new election and reintroduce the issue of an independent republic. South Africa, however, did not become a republic until 1961 (*Current History* 20, no. 4 [July 1924]: 713–717; *EWH*, pp. 1,083–1,084, 1,277; *Times* [London], 21 June 1924; *NYT*, 19 June 1924).

2. Japan had a long tradition of press censorship, and a series of press laws passed in the late nineteenth century gave a legal framework to governmental suppression of the news. These laws sharply restricted what was to be reported and deemed newspapers that reported political dissent responsible for inciting the population; if such reports resulted in any social unrest, the newspapers were found as guilty as the actual demonstrators themselves. The Japanese government also frequently suspended or prohibited the distribution of newspapers and arrested journalists. The ever-present threat of government action worked to encourage the self-censorship of newspapers. In the 1920s press censorship concentrated on coverage of the growing labor and communist movements in Japan. In September 1923 authorities used the chaotic aftermath of the Tokyo earthquake to enact press censorship ordinances aimed at suppressing the communist left (Richard H. Mitchell, *Censorship in Imperial Japan* [Princeton, N.J.: Princeton University Press, 1983], pp. 190–195; Kisaburo Kawabe, *The Press and Politics in Japan* [Chicago: University of Chicago Press, 1920], pp. 136–168; George Oakley Totten III, *The Social Democratic Movement in Prewar Japan* [New Haven, Conn.: Yale University Press, 1966], pp. 39–66; Harry Emerson Wildes, "Press Freedom in Japan," *American Journal of Sociology* 32 [January–May 1927]: 601–614; Richard H. Mitchell, *Thought Control in Prewar Japan* [Ithaca, N.Y.: Cornell University Press, 1976]).

3. At the time, the Japanese press and public were reacting with outrage to the passage on 26 May of the United States Immigration Act of 1924, which excluded Japanese immigration. The *New York World* quoted one paper, the *Yorodzu*, as saying: "Racial conflict is destined to come sooner or later, and America is now going to precipitate it. All the colored people must be up

in arms. Nay, even among the European countries there are some who are on the *qui vive* for an opportunity to deal America a hard blow." The *World*, summarizing the press reports, declared: "The only form of retaliation hinted at is an effort to draw the Asiatic races together, and possibly the Africans with them for united resistance to American 'imperialism' " (*New York World*, 15 June 1924; *NW*, 7 June and 5 July 1924; *Kodansha Encyclopedia of Japan* [Tokyo: Kodansha, 1983], pp. 18–19; Roger Daniels, *The Politics of Prejudice* [Berkeley and Los Angeles: University of California Press, 1962], pp. 65–107).

4. Garvey was probably referring to the German elections of May 1924, when a Centrist government was formed in Germany by a coalition composed of the People's party, the Centrists, the Democrats, and the Socialists. The Socialists remained the largest party in the Reichstag, but they lost over seventy seats in the elections, with almost all of the Socialist votes going to the Communist party, which quadrupled its representation in the governing body. The right-wing Nationalists made a stronger showing than in earlier years, but internal party divisions, opposition to the government-supported Dawes Report, and lower voter support than anticipated excluded them from the government coalition. The new coalition, headed by Centrist Wilhelm Marx, included the Socialists and commanded a two-thirds majority in the Reichstag (*NYT*, 4 May, 5 May, 20 May, and 27 May 1924; Michael Sturmer, "Parliamentary Government in Weimer Germany, 1924–1928," in Anthony Nicholls, ed., *German Democracy and the Triumph of Hitler* [London: George Allen and Unwin, 1971], pp. 59–78).

5. A reference to the Third Communist International.

6. The editor of the *New York World* was Ralph Pulitzer (1879–1939), the eldest son of newspaperman and publisher Joseph Pulitzer (*NYT*, 15 June 1939; *WWWA*, 1924–1925).

7. The *Negro World*, noting that the first published comment on the religious aspects of the convention program came from the *New York World*, reprinted the *New York World*'s report in its entirety, noting that "The New York World hates Marcus Garvey—but the truth overcometh." The *New York World*'s editorial of 5 June stated that while this is "occasion for . . . amusement, the greatest necessity of a downtrodden race is a belief in itself, its history, its prophets, its character and destiny. Tacitly the Negroes are charged with never having achieved much of a civilization. Mr. Garvey counters the assertion. . . . There is courage in this for the Negroes who have faith in it." Noting that warring nations and factions create gods in their own images, the editorial remarked that "there has been much making of gods in local images in the last ten years. There are few who, laughing at Garvey's heavenly hierarchy, can be sure they are not laughing at themselves" (*NW*, 14 June 1924).

Memorandum by J. Harry Philbin

[*Washington, D.C.*] June 16th, 1924

An offer has been received from the Black Cross Navigation & Trading Co. Inc., New York, to purchase the combination ex-enemy cargo and passenger vessel SUSQUEHANNA for $140,000.00, payable 10% on acceptance of bid, $26,000 on June 30th, 1924, $40,000 July 30th, 1924 and the balance $60,000 on August 30th, 1924.

The SUSQUEHANNA is a twin screw combination vessel of 11,650 DWT, and [9]959 gross tons, with three decks. She is equipped with two quadruple expansion engines and 4 Scotch boilers, designed to steam about 14 knots on a consumption of about ninety-five tons of coal a day. As presently arranged, she is outfitted to carry sixty-six first class passengers, one hundred and seventy-nine third class and six hundred and fifty-three steerage. She was built in 1899 and after being withdrawn from operation on the North Atlantic run, was over-hauled for operation between the West Coast of the United States and the East Coast of South America. She proved uneconomical in this trade and was withdrawn last summer, being now tied up at Seattle. She is reported to be in fairly good condition, requiring an expenditure of about $20,000 to be placed in commission.

The Black Cross Navigation and Trading Company, Inc. is a negro enterprise, fostered by the Universal Negro Improvement Association, Marcus Garvey being the head of both organizations and apparently the moving spirit. In 1921, the Black Star Line, a similar project of the Universal Negro Improvement Association, negotiated with the Board for the purchase of the ORION, a smaller ex-enemy vessel, and deposited $22,500 on the proposed purchase price of $225,000. The purchase was not completed and the Legal Department advise[d] that on June 18th, 1923, Garvey was convicted in the Southern District of New York on a charge of defrauding investors in the capit[a]l stock of Black Star Line, and was on that day remanded to the Tombs for sentence. He is at liberty at the present time, but the status of the case at this time has not been ascertained. The deposit of $22,500 has not been returned because of the failure of the Black Star Line to properly establish to whom it should be remitted.

The Credit Department reports that the present undertaking, the Black Cross Navigation & Trading Co., Inc., having the same officials as the Universal Negro Improvement Association, has about $20,000 in its Treasury. The Company has indicated that it hopes to have the vessel awarded and then to complete the payment of the purchase price before taking title and delivery, although wishing to start any necessary reconditioning following the award.

The Company has outlined in connection with its offer that the acquisition of the SUSQUEHANNA is part of a project to develop repatriation of negroes to Liberia, West Africa[,] and to assist in bringing about agricultural and industrial development and trading with the colored race in that Country and in the United States. Apparently the completion of the purchase price would be accomplished by subscriptions from members of the Association.

Mr. Garvey, referring to the previous unsuccessful negotiations of the Black Star Line[,] alleges that they were exploited and robbed by a group of New York brokers who had been engaged to handle negotiations with the Board. We are unable to corroborate any information in this connection, although the records do show that the Black Star Line became involved with several brokers in their negotiations.

The SUSQUEHANNA was valued at $150,000.00 in the valuation of the Fleet at June 30th, 1923, when she was in operation and considering the necessity of usual overhauling, the price of $140,000.00 would be recommended as an acceptable figure at which to sell the vessel. Assuming that the efforts to establish a line permitting repatriation of negro[e]s were a sincere one, and even one bearing some prospect of material success, it would appear that the embryonic nature of the Black Cross Navigation & Trading Co., Inc., would hardly warrant the extension of any exceptional consideration because of the proposed establishment of a trade route; therefore, the offer could best be considered in the light of the value actually to be received for the vessel.

The Company in its affidavit avers that it is 90% American and if $140,000.00 in cash could be realized, this Department would be prepared to recommend the sale of the vessel. Having in mind, however, the result of the efforts of the Black Star Line[,] in which case it appeared that after the award of the Shipping Board, the Company used this as a persuasive argument for stock subscriptions, it would seem to be highly advisable to avoid making any award of the SUSQUEHANNA under conditions which would permit of a repetition of such a stock-selling scheme. The Company has filed firm offer with the usual deposit and doubtless could complete the payment of 10%, but would likely depend upon further stock subscriptions for the payment of the balance and if these were unsuccessful or fraudulent[,] criticism might be directed at the Shipping Board.

I would recommend that the Company be notified that the Shipping Board has considered its offer and is prepared to dispose of the vessel at about the price proposed to a responsible American Company which can pay cash; and, that if the Company will furnish evidence satisfactory to our financial officers that the purchase price would be paid in cash in the event of an award, the matter will be placed under further deliberation.[1]

J. HARRY PHILBIN
Manager
Department of Ship Sales

DNA, RG 32, file 605-1-653. TM, carbon copy.

1. Philbin's memorandum was later submitted by Leigh C. Palmer (1873–1933), the president of the USSB's Emergency Fleet Corp., and to the entire Shipping Board. In his judgment, Palmer agreed with Philbin's findings and wrote "that no definite decision be made on this offer until the Company [Black Cross Navigation and Trading Co.] is prepared to show its financial ability to complete the transaction in case of award" (memorandum of L. C. Palmer to the USSB, 16 June 1924, DNA, RG 32, file 605-1-653). At a subsequent meeting of the Shipping Board on 19 June 1924, board members considered Palmer's memorandum and approved his recommendation that no definite decision be made on the offer of the Black Cross Navigation and Trading Co. for the *Susquehanna* (Carl P. Kremer to L. C. Palmer, 19 June 1924, DNA, RG 32, file 605-1-653).

Letter of Introduction for James O'Meally

New York June 23, 1924

TO WHOM IT MAY CONCERN:

This communication serves to introduce the Hon. Sir James O'Meally, High Commissioner General of the Universal Negro Improvement Association, who is on a special mission to the Court of Liberia, West Africa. Sir James O'Meally will spend several months in Africa and Europe. Any courtesies shown him will be highly appreciated by the Universal Negro Improvement Association representing the interest of the Negro race throughout the world. Thanking you in anticipation of such courtesies, We have the honor to be, Your obedient Servants,

Universal Negro Improvement Association
G. O. MARKE
Supreme Deputy Potentate
MARCUS GARVEY
President-General
P. L. BURROWS
Secretary-General

George O. Marke v. *UNIA*, no. 38300, New York Court of Special Sessions, December 1926. TLS, recipient's copy.

Livingston, Paperne and Wachtell, Accountants and Industrial Engineers, to Marcus Garvey

35 West 43rd Street, New York, June 23, 1924

Dear Sir:

In connection with an engagement to make an audit of the books of your company and issue our certificate certifying to the cor[re]ctness of the same, we beg to state that after a partial examination of your books and records which you desire us to audit, our accountants report to us a rather discouraging state of affairs.

They report to us that you have not adopted our previous suggestions for a better control of the incoming funds, nor a proper control of the note certificates and receipt books in the hands of your agents.

Under these conditions we shall be unable to certify to the correctness of your financial position, and in view of the circumstances must therefore decline to make the audit. We her[e]with enclose our check for $30.00 refunding the unused portion of the retainer fee which you paid us in advance.

Thanking you for past courtesies, and assuring you of our regret that we are unable to proceed with the work, we are, Very truly yours,

LIVINGSTON, PAPERNE AND WACHTELL

Printed in the *New York Age*, 16 August 1932. Original headlines omitted.

New York World Advertisement

[New York, 25 June 1924]

Colonization of Africa by Negroes as Solution of Race Problem

Universal Negro Improvement Association Working to Develop Colonies in Liberia as Peaceful Homes for Negroes —Similar to Homeland in Palestine for Jews

Over a hundred years ago the white friends of the Negro in America, known as the American Colonization Society, helped establish the Black Republic of Liberia with the hope that it might become the home of those Negroes who wanted a home among themselves. After great sacrifice and with much difficulty the early settlers of the republic have perpetuated the government until it stands out to-day as the most serious attempt of the race to help itself.

The Universal Negro Improvement Association, organized under the laws of the State of New York, aims at assuming the responsibility of helping to develop Liberia as a natural home for Negroes. Toward this end several missions have been sent to Liberia for the purpose of arranging for the repatriation of as many Negroes as desire to go to that country to settle and to help in her industrial, agricultural and cultural development.

The following plans have been decided on by the Universal Negro Improvement Association: That the Association is to build four colonies in the Republic, the first on the Cavalla River, for which a group of civil and mechanical engineers have been sent to start preparatory work for the accommodation of the first batch of colonists who will sail from New York during the Fall of the present year and following years.

The Association is raising a fund of $2,000,000 to bear the cost of constructing and establishing the first colony. The building plan for each colony is as follows (all Government buildings to be under the control of the Liberian Government): . . .¹

This Is the Best Solution of the Negro Problem

All those who desire to help the Negro under the auspices of the Universal Negro Improvement Association in developing himself, are asked to subscribe to the fund of two million ($2,000,000) dollars now being raised for the promotion of the Cavalla Colony.

Address your donation to the "Treasurer, Colonization Fund, Universal Negro Improvement Association, 56 West 135th Street, New York, U.S.A."

Bankers: Chelsea Exchange Bank, Harlem Branch, 135th Street and Seventh Avenue. . . .[2]

Universal Negro Improvement Association
Marcus Garvey, President
William Sherrill, 2nd Vice-President
Rudolph Smith, 3rd Vice-President
Henrietta Vinton Davis, 4th Vice-President
G. Emoni Carter, Secretary
Clifford Bourne, Treasurer
Levi F. Lord, Auditor
G. O. Marke
Thomas W. Anderson
Pervical L. Burrows
James O'Meally
Norton G. Thomas

Printed in *New York World*, 25 June 1924.[3]

1. The plans are printed above on pp. 596–597.
2. Omitted here is a list of 74 persons who contributed a total of $4,086.20 to the fund.
3. This advertisement appeared the day after the Democratic party opened its national convention in Madison Square Garden.

Press Release by Ernest Lyon

826 N. Carey Street, Baltimore, Md.
July 10, 1924

My dear Mr. Editor

For the benefit and information of American Citizens or for that matter any person or persons who may be interested by attractive offers and promises by the Garvey movement with Liberia as their objective point[,] as Liberian Consul Genl. in the U.S. I am authorized to say that no person or persons leaving the U.S. under the auspices of the Garvey movement in the U.S., will be allowed to land in the Republic of Liberia. All Liberian Consuls in the U.S. are instructed and directed not to visa the passport of any persons leaving the U.S. for Liberia under the direction of that movement.

It is due the public in order to save future trouble and embarrassment to uninformed person[s], who may leave the U.S. under the auspices of the Garvey movement for the Republic of Liberia, that this information be widely circulated.[1] Yours truly

ERNEST LYON
Liberian Consul Genl. in the U.S.

DJ-FBI, file 61. TL, transcript. This letter also appeared in a report of Special Agent James E. Amos, 7 August 1924, DJ-FBI, file 61.

1. The press release was given wide circulation in the black community (*Chicago Defender*, 19 July 1924; *Baltimore Afro-American*, 18 July 1924; *New York Age*, 19 July 1924).

ROSE DAY

TUESDAY
JULY 15, 1924

IN

NEW YORK CITY

Celebrated by the Ladies of the Colonization
Fund, Universal Negro Improvement Associa-
tion, to raise funds for the Association's work in
Africa.

On this day the Ladies of the Association will
sell flowers and roses all over New York City.

You may purchase a rose or a bouquet. Buy
a rose for 10c, 25c, 50c, $1, $2, $3 $4, $5. Buy a
bouquet for $1, $5, $10, $20, $50, $100, and help
the work of colonization

A Big Day of
Music and Pleasure

BIG CONCERT

IN

LIBERTY HALL

AT NIGHT

Celebrated Artists to Help in Program

FLOWERS AND ROSES ON SALE BY THE LADIES FROM
8 A. M. TO 12 P. M.

LET EVERYBODY HELP

Buy a Rose   *Buy a Bouquet*

(*Source*: *NW*, 12 July 1924.)

Otey J. Porter, M.D., to Robert Watson Winston[1]

806 S. Garden St., Columbia, Tenn. July 20[,] 1924

My Dear Sir:—

While on a recent trip to N Y City—I called at the Headquarters of the Universal Negro Improvement Association—56 W. 135 st. I met and talked with the leading officers of this organization. I presume you are familiar with the purposes of this Association.

Among other documents I procured there is your—"Should the Color Line Go." Its reading greatly interested me and impressed me with the near identity of our ideas and conclusions. I send with this a booklet written in 1920.[2]

There *must* be many, many men of the South—(and of the North, West and East) who think as we do. We surely ought to get together. We should get behind Garvey and see to it tha[t] his plans do not miscarry.

It matters not whether Garvey is a great man and leader or an adventurer. He is the only capable Negro who is proposing the only possibly correct course.

The whites, who visualize what must come to our country if present conditions continue, should seize, with avidity, the opportunity of getting behind Garvey and, if possible supplying him with a whole hearted, honest aid in the way of white men and money to help him (and our race).

The "Negro Problem" is not complicated. It is as plain as the midheaven sun.

Cannot we start an organization to cooperate? Write me your thoughts on this. Sincerely

O. J. PORTER[3]

NCU, Robert Watson Winston Papers, file 2369-70. ALS, recipient's copy.

1. Robert Watson Winston (1860–1944) came from an old North Carolina family and, according to the *New York Times*, "personified the traditional 'southern colonel.'" He served in the state senate in 1885 and as a judge of the Superior Court of North Carolina from 1889 to 1895. Winston spent most of his life fighting to preserve white supremacy, although in his later years he advocated equal educational opportunity for blacks. He published an autobiography in which he outlined his support of voluntary repatriation of blacks to Africa (*It's a Far Cry* [New York: Holt and Co., 1937] pp. 339–340, 375–379). He was well known for his biographies, *Andrew Johnson: Plebian and Patriot* (New York: Holt and Co., 1928); *High Stakes and Hair Trigger: The Life of Jefferson Davis* (New York: Holt and Co., 1930); and *Robert E. Lee, a Biography* (New York: W. Morrow and Co., 1934); as well as for such articles as "Should the Color Line Go?" (*Current History* 18, no. 6 [September 1923]: 945–951; *NYT*, 15 October 1944; *WWWA*, 2: 587).

2. Probably a reference to the pamphlet by O.J. Porter entitled "Haiti, the United States, the Negro," written around 1920 (private publication, n.d.) Although the pamphlet emphatically stated he was "not a negro hater," Porter doubted the capacity of blacks for self-government. In the pamphlet he advocated segregation and the repatriation of blacks to Haiti, Santo Domingo, or Liberia (Cheairs M. Porter, Columbia, Tenn., to Robert A. Hill, 9 February 1984).

3. Dr. Otey Porter (1867–1946) was born in Williamsport, Tenn., graduated from Vanderbilt University School of Medicine, Nashville, in 1894, and opened a practice in Columbia, Tenn., in 1898. He was noted as an outstanding physician in the treatment of smallpox and pellagra, and he studied diseases in Haiti. He also organized and managed the Citizens Telephone Co. of Columbia, Tenn., and was an extensive landholder in the area (Cheairs M. Porter, Columbia, Tenn., to Robert A. Hill, 9 February 1984; *Nashville Tennessean*, 17 January 1946).

UNIA Membership Loan Booklet

Universal Negro Improvement
Association

No. 1801

MEMBERSHIP LOAN BOOK

per
le b. Acco

He

56 WEST   ＾ STREET
NEW YORK CITY

Parent Body .... Division

Marcus Garvey
Name of Member

133 W. 129 St
Address

Universal Negro Improvement Association

56 WEST 135th STREET   NEW YORK CITY

No. 1801

Nominal Value of Loan $ 5,000 00

First Payment on Loan $ 2,043 59

Name of Division...... Chalent Barry U.X.Ia

Name of Ex. Sec'y.... Fred. A. Toote

THE UNIVERSAL NEGRO IMPROVEMENT ASS'N promises to pay to the order of

Marcus Garvey

133 West 129th st

ADDRESS

a member of this Association, all amounts appearing on account here attached. 10 years after date with interest at 5% per annum payable at the office of the Association, 56 West 135th Street, New York City, or at the place of issue.

For use in the furtherance of the Industrial, Commercial and Agricultural purposes of the Association in its Construction Plans in the interest of the race.

This day of.... 15th of January, 19..

Universal Negro Improvement Association

Secretary General   President General

SPECIAL—This note must not be detached from this book. This note is subject to the terms printed on the back

---

Loans will be accepted from members of the Universal Negro Improvement Association only.

Universal Negro Improvement Ass'n

Head Office: 56 W. 135th Street, N. Y.

THIS Book must be presented to the Executive Secretary of the Division of Issue any time a loan is made to the Association or when loan is to be redeemed by the Association.

UNIVERSAL NEGRO IMPROVEMENT ASSOCIATION

THIS BOOK CONTAINS 9 FOLIOS OR 18 PAGES.

Report on the UNIA Convention Opening

[*New York, 1 August 1924*]

THOUSANDS THRONG LIBERTY HALL
AS FOURTH INTERNATIONAL OPENS
WITH IMPRESSIVE SERVICE

At 10 o'clock, precisely, divine service started. The U.N.I.A. band, under the direction of Bandmaster Arnold J. Ford, struck up the well-known air, "O Africa, Awaken," and the procession wended its way, slowly but solemnly, toward the platform. The order of the procession was as follows: Members of the African Legion, Black Cross Nurses, the U.N.I.A. choir, two Acolytes carrying chandeliers, the Crucifer, the Torchbearer, Rev. J.C. Millington, curate of the Church of the Good Shepherd, bishop's Chaplain; Archdeacon George S. Brooks, African Orthodox Church; His Grace Archbishop McGuire, Celebrant.

Next came the high officials of the association, as follows: Mrs. A.J. Robertson, First Assistant Lady President of the New York Division; Hon. Geo. Weston, First Vice-President, New York Local; Hon. [F.W.] Elligor [Ellegor], Intoner; Hon. R. Van Richards; Hon. Percy L. Burrows, Assistant Secretary-General; Hon. T. Anderson, Minister of Labor; Hon. Levi Lord,[1] Auditor-General; Hon. C.S. Bourne, High Chancellor; Hon. Marcus Garvey, President-General and Provisional President of Africa.

Arrived on the platform, the choir and congregation sang the hymn, "Shine On, Eternal Light" after which the opening prayers of the service were recited by Rev. Mr. Elligor, the various units having been reviewed and seated. The congregation responded devoutly and heartily to all the exercises and there was evident a feeling that all realized the solemnity of the occasion. Psalm 30, "Exaltabo De Domine,"[2] was sung by the choir, assisted by the congregation, who were provided with a detailed program of the service. Hon. George Weston read a lesson from the Holy Scriptures, which was very appropriate for the day's exercises. "Jubilate Deo" ("Oh, be joyful in the Lord," etc.) was next sung by the Celebrant, Archibishop McGuire, the responses being made by the choir. In this, special reference was made to the aims and objects of the association, and in the Litany prayers were recited for the President-General, the Potentate, the Honorable Executive Council and [all] others who were assisting in the work of the organization. The Universal Negro Ritual was also recited and this part of the service was concluded by the further recital of special prayers suitable for the occasion and the object of the gathering by Chaplain Elligor.

A sacred item by the Harmony Four was next announced, and after this was executed, Mrs. Weston[3] sang a solo with most telling effect.

His Grace Archbishop McGuire, of the African Orthodox Church, then delivered a sermon.

At its conclusion the choir rendered an anthem.

The President-General then announced the lifting of the collection. This was done while the band struck up a martial air.

This concluded, and a special thank[s] offering having been made, the President-General declared that His Highness the Supreme Deputy and Acting Potentate Hon. G.O. Mark[e] will solemnly declare the Fourth International Convention of the Negro Peoples of the World formally opened.

DECLARING THE CONVENTION OPEN

The Acting Potentate then ascended the rostrum and said: "As you are aware, in the absence of the Potentate, it falls to my lot, as Supreme Deputy, to do what he would have done on this occasion. On the program you will find that an address should be delivered by the Potentate, but owing to the lateness of the hour we are obliged to postpone that address until Monday.[4] I therefore declare officially opened the Fourth International Convention of the Negro Peoples of the World."

The President-General then made several announcements as to the afternoon's program, which included the parade.

The Universal Ethiopian Anthem was next sung by the convention, accompanied by the band. The procession retreated from the platform and marched, while the congregation remained seated, to the robing rooms, to the tune of the hymn, "God Bless Our President."

The service, which was memorable in several features, was concluded at about 12 noon.

DR. McGUIRE'S SERMON

Bishop McGuire said: I take my text from Exod. IV, 2: "And the Lord said unto him, What is that in thine hand? And he said, A rod."

The cry of a people held in bondage for centuries had reached the throne of Justice and Mercy, and He that sat thereon remembered His promise to their forefathers that He would make of their posterity a great nation. The time for fulfilment had come, and the man to act the role of deliverer has for eighty years been under going training unknown even to himself. He is at this time a refugee, serving as the chief shepherd of the flocks of an Ethiopian patriarch in whose employ he had been for forty years, and one of whose beautiful daughters he had married.[5] One day, as this man, Moses, is feeding Jethro's sheep on the slopes of Mt. Horeb, there comes to him a most convincing call to a divine commission. Out of a burning acacia bush, the leaves of which remained unscorched, the Voice of the Eternal addresses him, saying, "Behold, the cry of the children of Israel is come unto me, and I have seen the oppression where with the Egyptians oppress them. Come, now, therefore, and I will send thee unto Pharaoh that thou mayest bring forth My people out of Egypt into a land flowing with milk and honey. Go and gather the elders of Israel and tell them that I, the God of Abraham, Isaac and Jacob, have sent you to deliver them."

WHAT IS THAT IN THINE HAND?

Moses accepts the commission, but he asks for credentials—some evidence of his power and authority, for, says he, without this "they will not believe me, nor hearken unto my voice, for they will say, 'The Lord hath not appeared unto thee.'" "What is that in thine hand?" is the question which Jehovah puts to him. "What is that in thine hand?" Moses answers, "A rod." "Cast it on the ground," commands Jehovah[.] Moses obeys, and instantly the rod becomes a wriggling serpent, and Moses flees from it. "Put forth thy hand and take it by the tail," is the next command, and again Moses obeys. He seizes the reptile, which immediately is converted into a rod. For long years Moses had carried that shepherd's rod to perform the ordinary duties of his office. But that stick of polished desert wood has now, by supernatural endowment, become possessed of a mysterious potentiality. "Take this rod in thine hand, wherewith thou shalt do signs and wonders." So commands Jehovah. Henceforth this shepherd's rod is transformed into a rod of authority and freighted with mysterious forces that would cause even the forces of Nature to halt in their established course. It has now become a thing divine, an instrument consecrated by Deity and placed in the hands of humanity to solve the crucial problems and simplify the difficult situations of a people seeking liberty, life, peace and happiness in a land and government of their own.

SUN OF SPIRITUAL POWER

Returning to Egypt, Moses carries his rod, which he now styles "the rod of God," and in all his conferences with the elders of Israel and interviews with King Pharaoh he bears in his hand this outward and visible sign of his inward and spiritual power. Let us note the use of this rod on two important occasions in the career of Moses. Let us in imagination be distant spectators of that acute and critical situation in which the Hebrews found themselves following the Exodus. A mountain to the right of them! A mountain to the left of them! The Red Sea before them, and the Egyptian army thundering onward behind them. Escape is impossible. Each speeding moment brings the enemy nearer—the whirling chariots, the flying cavalry. Destruction imminent, the Hebrews are seized with panic and hurl at Moses the shafts of piercing sarcasm. "You God-sent leader, were there not graves enough in Egypt that you should bring us here to be massacred, our bodies to decay and our bones to whiten in this desert? Fine leader you are!"

Impervious to taunt and ridicule, this natural leader of men, in sublime tranquility, stands before them with his rod in one hand, while he raises the other and with commanding gesture silences the cowardly mob. "Fear not," says he; "stand still and see the salvation of God. These Egyptians which ye see today ye shall see no more forever. Hold our peace. Jehovah shall fight for you. Stand still and see." Immediately Moses gets into communication with God. Prayer is his one asset, and inaudibly he sends up his appeal. Quicker than by radio, the answer comes flashing back through the immense expanse of ether. "Moses, wherefore criest thou unto me? What is that in thine hand? Have you forgotten so soon its powers? Speak unto the children of Israel that they go forward. Point your rod over the sea and divide the waters." The sequel of this narrative we are all familiar with.

BLAMING THE LEADER

Let us note another occasion as the people encamp at Rephidim to discover in great consternation that there is no drinking water in the district.[6] As usual, the leader is to be blamed for all vicissitudes even though they be "acts of God." Perishing from thirst, the people assail Moses, becoming violent and threatening his life. "Find us water at once that we may drink. Hast thou brought us out of Egypt to kill us, our children and our cattle with thirst? Find us water or we shall kill thee first." As they approach him menancingly with stones, Moses, rod in hand, falls upon his knees. "O Lord God," he cries, "what shall I do unto this people? They be almost ready to stone me." "Moses, arise; stand on your feet," is the answer. "What is that in thine hand? Is it not the rod that divided the sea? Proceed at once to Horeb, smite the rock there, and the water shall come forth as a river to quench the thirst of man and beast."

CONTEMPT FOR THE SCOFFERS

Fellowmen of the Negro Race, pursuant to the call of the President-General of the Universal Negro Improvement Association and African Communities League, you have assembled in this historical edifice for conference during the thirty-one days of this month of August on vital matters pertaining to our blood-kin everywhere. With calm determination and firm resolution you face today the task. But in this throng all are not friends and sympathizers. Scoffers are here. Doubting Thomases are here. Calamity howlers are here. These groups I shall treat with the contempt of silence. Let this sermon be a buttress to the confidence of the overwhelming majority, whose hope in the ultimate success of this movement remains unshaken. Let me summon, as it were, four such stalwart ones and as each stands before you put to him the question of the text, ["]Negro, what is that in thine hand?" The first replies, "The Rod of Political Destiny." Negro, what is that in thine hand? The second replies, "The Rod of Industrial and Commercial Achievement." Negro, what is that in thine hand? The third replies, "The Rod of Financial Acquisition." Negro, what is that in thine hand? And the fourth replies, "The Rod of Spiritual Freedom." They are correct. Within their hands they hold the dynamic combination by means of which the aims and hopes and aspirations of this noble Race are to be realized. May we not with profit consider each of these answers—each of these factors in the multiple? Negro, what is that in thine hand?

THE ROD OF POLITICAL DESTINY

Destiny does not imply a blind fate. Destiny is that which is so well expressed in the well-known lines, "There's a Divinity that shapes our ends, rough-hew them how we will."[7] It is destined by Divinity that in a nation and government of his own, in his motherland, Africa, the Negro shall enjoy liberty and happiness with a civilization and religious worship of his own, without hindrance from any other race or government. Whence came this doctrine, this political faith which has seized the people of our group during the last seven years? It came from the brain and heart of him who called into existence the Universal Negro Improvement Association. Some claim that Marcus Garvey was not the original thinker of the idea of "Africa for Africans." As for that, none but the Omniscient knows who was the first thinker along this line,[8] but all the world knows that the original doer is the man under whose leadership we are gathered, and who has won a thousand times more converts and followers than any other Negro leader. Read the constitution which this man put into effect in July, 1918, and which the First International Convention of 1920 approved and ratified.

READ THE CONSTITUTION

Among the aims and objects, what do we find touching the political destiny of this race? "To establish an universal confraternity among the race; to promote the spirit of pride and love; to assist in civilizing the backward tribes of Africa; to assist in the development of independent Negro nations and communities; to establish commissionaries and agencies in the principal countries and cities of the world for the representation and protection of all Negroes irrespective of nationality." My fellow men, I suggest to you that the mind which evolved that political program is the mind of a genius. I suggest to you that the hand that wrote it is the hand of a master. Render unto Caesar the things that are Caesar's.[9] We come today not to bury Caesar, nor to magnify his faults but pay tribute to Caesar for what he has planned and for what he has done for Rome and Romans.[10] When in August, 1920, we accepted that constitution we officially notified the world we had taken in our hand the Rod of our Political Destiny. But we did not rest our case upon our statements in the constitution.

DECLARATION OF RIGHTS

During that same convention, in this hall, which then and there became our "Cradle of Liberty," we issued our Declaration of Rights to be henceforth our Magna Charta, our Declaration of Independence. In that immortal document we declared all men, women and children of our race free—free denizens of the countries they inhabit, and cojointly free citizens of Africa, their motherland. On the principle of Europe for Europeans, Asia for Asiatics, we demanded Africa for Africans at home and abroad. We further declared it to be the inherent right and duty of the Negro to seek the restoration and repossession of Africa, and that such right and duty should not be considered an infringement upon any right or claim by any other race or nation. We condemned the cupidity of those who have seized the territories and natural wealth of Africa, and placed on record our solemn determination to reclaim the ownership of our ancestral continent. We stressed the principle of self-determination for all peoples, including the Negro race, and what is important just at this time, we demanded the right of free emigration of Negroes to any country or State without molestation or discrimination, especially when they pay equal fare with travelers of other races. In this declaration of rights we assumed, my fellow men, a large political order, but with unwavering confidence in the rectitude of our cause, and with implicit trust in our fathers' God, we signed our Magna Charta with the ink of our tears and pledged each other to defend and maintain it with our lives, our fortunes, and our sacred honor. Four years have passed since that day when strong men and earnest women shed tears of deep emotion.

AN UNFORGETTABLE MOMENT

We who were fortunate to witness or participate in that drama will never forget the solemn awe which swept this building. It was as though we were standing at the foot of Sinai when the Decalogue was pronounced,[11] or in the upper room in Jerusalem when the Holy Spirit descended on the Day of Pentecost. Four years have rolled away since then.

Negro, what is that in thine hand, that Constitution, that Declaration of Rights? It is the rod of your Political Destiny. Nationhood has been the greatest stimulus to any people, and Africanism, or Garveyism as some prefer to term it, has won to its banner an ever-increasing number of new Negroes in both hemispheres. As sure as God lives and holds in the hollow of His hands the destinies of empires, kingdoms and nations, in the fulness of time Africanism shall be triumphant. After seven centuries of struggle for nationhood the Irish people are rejoicing in the Free State of Ireland. After ages of almost forlorn hope the Jews are rejoicing in the triumphs of Zionism and the repossession of the land of their forefathers. Their fulness of time has come. So will ours, for, in the Eternal Volume of Truth it is predicted that "Princes shall come out of Egypt."

Ethiopia, what is that in thine hand? It is the Rod of Thine own political rehabilitation and renaissance. Stretch forth thine hands unto God for the day of thy redemption draweth nigh. The mills of God grind slowly, but surely, and exceeding fine.[12] One day with Him is as a thousand years, and a thousand years as one day. What if your eyes and mine behold not that day, that land, that government? We now and here dedicate all that we are and all that we have to the "Cause Afric." Our lamented brother, Sir Robert Poston, of blessed memory, saw the land and had hoped to be here in person to report to this convention that our political destiny will assuredly be realized. He is not here in the flesh, but his spirit broods over us. That tired body sleeps in its narrow grave in his old Kentuck[y] home, but his unconquered soul goes marching on with us to our motherland. Let the heathen rage and imagine their vain things.[13] No power or foe, no vile strategy of cowards, nor schemes of hell can deter us, for the Rod of our Political Destiny is in our hands, wherewith we shall divide the Red Sea before us, and in the morning of victory again employ it for the confounding of our helpless pursuers. Again, I ask, Negro, what is that in thine hand?

THE ROD OF INDUSTRIAL AND COMMERCIAL ACHIEVEMENT

Among the aims and objects of this association as outlined in the constitution you will discover this, "To conduct a world-wide commercial and industrial intercourse for the good of the Negro people." That was the reason why our founder organized and incorporated the African Communities League, which should foster our commercial and industrial interests, in conjunction with the Universal Negro Improvement Association, a social, benevolent and educational society for the general uplift of the Negro peoples of the world. That was the reason for the Negro Factories Corporation. That was the reason for a Ministry of Labor and Industry. And for our commercial development a mercantile marine is an indispensable and vital factor. We must have ships, and more ships. If one venture fails, we must, from the lessons gained by experience, struggle on until the Negro shall place upon the high seas and lanes of international traffic a navigation and trading company, not only to link in commerce our scattered groups, but to win our share of the marine business of the world.

THE PRIDE OF NATIONS

Ships are the pride of every nation. They are [the] bulwark of Britain and the protector of America and Japan. No scheme of colonization planned by this organization can become effective without ships. And in connection with the establishment of independent African communities and colonies, the task is one for which the Negro from the West Indies is peculiarly talented. He it was who supplied the brawn and much of the brain in the construction of the Panama Canal. He it was who, in Cuba and Central America, in the employ of the United Fruit Company converted the howling wilderness and dismal swamps into thriving towns, central factories and fertile fields of sugar cane, oranges and bananas. What he has done for others he can do for himself, and we look forward to the time when public buildings, theatres, churches, institutions of learning, docks, bridges, tunnels and railroads will be erected by him in our own African communities and colonies. There is no engineering or architectural work needed which you Negroes cannot perform, and I bid you hold yourselves in readiness for future service. Meanwhile, it is our bounden duty to lay secure foundations at our central seat of operations.

STRENGTHEN OUR STAKES

The great British Empire, upon whose flag the sun never sets, and whose drumbeat is heard around the globe, has fortified England, the center, the mart and metropolis, the seat of government of her worldwide possessions and interests. While "Africa for Africans" is both our hope and inspiration, we must strengthen our stakes so as to lengthen our cords. Our Association must drive firmly its commercial and industrial stakes here at headquarters, here in Harlem, here in the United States, and then lengthen its cords to Haiti and to African communities in the Motherland.

Negro, what is that in thine hand? The Rod of Commercial and Industrial Achievement. Stretch it forth, and like a magic wand you will bring cities out of deserts, cover the seas with ships, and dot the plains with factories. I submit once again the question, Negro, what is that in thine hand?

THE ROD OF FINANCIAL ACQUISITION

It is evident, my fellowmen, that our political destiny and our commercial enterprises require an accumulation of capital, and, as the number of our money barons and captains of finance is almost negligible, it is to the great mass of our people that those intrusted with the execution of our program must turn so that by welding into one gigantic whole, the innumerable small gifts, loans and investments, they may hereby capitalize and operate the several departments. In this polyglot nation there is no group which, in proportion, wastes such tremendous sums of money as those which Negroes squander in luxury, frivolity, speculation and unsound investments. The waste is well-nigh criminal. The Universal Negro Improvement Association has been advocating the conservation of our funds for racial progress, and for the solution by ourselves of the problems which confront us, and in this way millions of dollars have been raised and expended in preliminary work and costly experience. During this period, Negro business men of Harlem have prospered. Operators of real estate and holding corporations in this city openly acknowledge that their success during the last five years has been largely due to the successful stimulus given by its organization. Such are not the men who seek its destruction, for they possess enough business acumen to capitalize its spirit of race consciousness and convert it into an asset.

WHO ARE THEY?

Our would-be destroyers are those demagogues who receive their 30 shekels of silver for the commercializing of racial discriminations and misfortunes[,] who perceive their means of livelihood, somewhat like that of Demetrius, the Ephesian silversmith, threatened by the success of this movement,[14] and, therefore, declare war to the bitter end, employing every implement at their command, however foul or diabolic. While much has been done to conserve Negro money for Negro enterprises, this is but the beginning. Think of the large sums of money which Negroes put annually into life insurance controlled by the other race! Think of the enormous deposits made by them in the white banks of New York to be loaned to white business, while Negro business is almost consistently refused loans from the deposits of the race!

LINK YOUR DIMES

Fellowmen, link up your savings. Link your dime with every other Negro dime, link your dollar with every other Negro dollar, even as our Jewish friends do. You have in your hand the Rod of Financial Acquisition. Astor, Carnegie and Rockefeller used that rod, starting out with less wages and a smaller income than many of you, yet they amassed fortunes and built up great enterprises. Down in British Honduras a black man, a deceased and honored member of this Association, Sir Isaiah Morter, proved beyond semblance of doubt that even outside the United States it is possible for humble Negroes to attain financial distinction by making use of the opportunities of their environment. Morter, like Moses, had a rod which he skilfully polished and used with powerful effect, leaving behind him a fortune reputed to be about half a million dollars. All honor to Isaiah Morter, and still greater honor in that in his last will and testament he bequeathed the bulk of his estate to the Universal Negro Improvement Association. When an individual of his cool, calculating type, a man unmoved by passing sentiment or wild emotion, deliberately wills thus the major part of the earnings of an eventful life, it is evidence that the movement has taken a firm grip upon the new Negro, who sees in it the only solution by which the full salvation of this race is to be procured. At this solemn movement [moment?], when we revere the memory of Sir Isaiah Morter, I most earnestly urge you, one and all, to emulate his illustrious example. Donate, lend, invest during your lifetime, but see to it that in your last will and testament you provide, to the extent of your ability, a legacy for this movement, or, what is equally good, take out an insurance policy making the Universal Negro Improvement Association the beneficiary. "Negro money for Negro development,"—note that well, mark it, learn it and inwardly digest it. And now I shall present my text in its last phase. Negro, what is that in thine hand?

THE ROD OF SPIRITUAL FREEDOM

This was the original rod in the Negro's hand, and for a long time following his emancipation he held on to it as though it were his peculiar monopoly. It had served him as a prop during the period of enforced servitude to the white man. A slave in body, he nevertheless felt free in soul, since none could deny him the solace of religion. More religious by nature than other races, Negroes neglected their political, industrial and financial progress, content to sing "It is well, it is well with my soul." They lulled themselves into tranquil slumber with the opiate of religious expectation, and in their spirituals and melodies chanted of heaven,—"I want to go to heaven when I die to hear Jordan roll." [15]

SHUN EXTREMES

It has taken the race a half century to discover its error. But in endeavoring to correct it we have failed to remember that two wrongs never can make one right. Instead of striking the golden mean between the two extremes, we have allowed the pendulum to swing to the limit in the contrary direction, proclaiming religion to be a menace and stumbling block to the Negro. Yet many who thus presumptiously and perniciously advocate the abandonment of Negro churches and Negro ministers, are foremost in seeking the use of these same churches and the co-operation of these same ministers. Let it be understood, once and for all, that no constructive program for the Negro can be effective which underestimates the hold his religious institutions have upon him. The material without the spiritual is as bad as, nay, worse than the spiritual without the material. We must have the anchor of religion, but we must make certain that it is what we consider conscientious for us as Negroes. That is what is meant by that object in our constitution, which reads,—"to promote a conscientious spiritual worship among the native tribes of Africa," implying, of course, that we shall first promote it among ourselves. That is what is meant when in our Declaration of Rights we demand "freedom of religious worship." This means freedom in our theology, freedom in our ritual and freedom in the control of our ecclesiastical organizations. We demand the exercise of a conscientious, spiritual freedom for the reason that spiritual freedom is the basis of all other freedoms. "Ye shall know the truth, and the truth shall make you free." [16] And in the exercise of this freedom we claim the right to set forth theology as we understand it.

WHY IS GOD WHITE?

If God be our Father, and we bear His image and likeness, why should we not teach our children that their Father in Heaven resembles them even as they do Him? Why should we permit the Caucasians to constantly and indelibly impress upon their youthful minds that God is white? Why should not this race, which bore the Cross of the Man of Sorrows up Mount Calvary and has borne it ever since, not claim Him as their own, since He carried in His veins the blood of Ham as well as the blood of them? It is on record that at least two of His ancestors were of Hamitic descent. One of these was Tamar, mother of Pharez, the son of Judah,[17] and the other Rahab, mother of Boaz, the great grandfather of David.[18] Pharez and Boaz both had Ham's children as mothers and Jesus was a lineal descendant of both. If the Man of Sorrows lived today in Dixie with his pedigree known as it is, the color line would be drawn against Him. Why may we not write the facts down in our theology? And what is true of Our Lord is true also of His mother, for she also was descended from these two daughters of Ham. When, therefore, our Negro artists, with brush, chisel and otherwise, portray the Madonna for their race, let them be loyal to truth, and present us the Blessed Virgin Mother and her Most Holy Child in such manner as to reveal both the Hamitic and Semitic blends. No longer must we permit white religious "pastors and masters" to hold us in spiritual serfdom and tutelage. Their regime has remained unmolested far too long.

Artillery to Dominate

As the emissaries of their government and their capitalists, white missionaries have employed Christianity as propaganda to subjugate, and artillery to dominate, our race in Africa and the West Indies. They have defiled the religion of Jesus Christ and made it the harlot of their lust, avarice and ambition, and the time has now come when we must stand squarely in their pathway and call, "halt." Negro, what is that in thine hand? It is the rod of your spiritual freedom. Refuse to have your children taught any longer the white man's catechism which requires them to "submit myself to all my betters, and to order myself lowly and reverently." Fellow men, if you did not realize it before, realize it now, that only Negro pastors and bishops can be true Shepherds of Negroes. Some white ministers pretend and some few try to be, but they just simply cannot.

In our convention of 1921 this association passed a resolution indorsing all religious bodies under Negro control,[19] and I trust that all our loyal members will govern themselves accordingly. The Universal Negro Improvement Association has never, and will never, indorse churches under white control. Whether we be Methodists, Baptist, Episcopalians, Romanists, Jews or Mohammedans, we must see to it that Negroes are in control and set up for ourselves.

Because, through this association I have a new perspective, white Episcopalians whom I served for a quarter of a century have written up in their periodicals [that] the religious organization of which I am the leader is a by-product of that queer movement among Negroes known as Garveyism, and have execrated me, to continue in their own words, for "leading away his race from the church";[20] that is, the Anglo-Saxon Church. And my colored brethren whom I have left behind, not having yet seen the light, have heaped ridicule upon me, conferring upon me the mock title of "High Priest of Garveyism." To all of which I simply say, "Amen, so let it be."

Spiritual Slaves, Never!

George Alexander McGuire, what is that in thine hand? It is the Rod of Spiritual Freedom divinely given to me with a commission, and while I have breath I shall continue to urge Negroes never, never to be spiritual slaves. The member of the Universal Negro Improvement Association who is still a spiritual slave has not yet caught its spirit, for this movement is preeminently "a spiritual movement." I take no credit for this description. The phraseology is that of the founder himself. In making his masterful defense in the District Court of the United States, June, 1923,[21] pleading not so much for his personal liberty, but with fervid and inspired eloquence, advocating that his race be given the opportunity to work out its own salvation—advocating with that earnestness which marked Abraham's plea for Sodom and Gomorrah, Moses' plea for Israel when Jehovah would have destroyed them, or Esther's plea to Ahasuerus when Haman planned the extinction of her race—in making that defense the Hon. Marcus Garvey not once, nor twice, but several times, declared that the Universal Negro Improvement Association is a "spiritual movement." [22]

GARVEY BEFORE THE JURY

As I sat and listened for three hours, thrilled by the sublime effort of the superman, I discovered a few Negroes whose cynical smiles proved them unworthy to be numbered among this race, smiling at such a moment and occasion, and in silent wonder I wept at their effrontery as much so as at the touching words of the orator. That scene, that appeal, and that man as I saw him then, shall never fade from memory's page. But of the tens of thousands of words which the speaker uttered, this is the sentence which has since echoed and re-echoed in my ears, "Gentlemen of the jury, this is a spiritual movement."

Negro men and women, either this is true, or not true. Do you believe with the founder, that the Universal Negro Improvement Association is and should be, a spiritual movement, not only in verbal characterization but in actual operation? If you do, say so now as emphatically as he has done and endeavor in this convention to spiritualize it more and more. The Jews made of Zionism a spiritual movement and today the goal is achieved, the fact accomplished. Africanism must become a universal spiritual movement among Negroes.

NO TIME FOR MATERIAL FORCE

Let those who will continue to advocate force as the solution and to preach that force can be offset only by force. It smacks of courage, but if it means more than idle words intended for the gallery, it is that blind courage which caused the wild bull of the Western plains to charge fiercely the speeding railway engine that had recently penetrated his undisputed domain. He pitted his physical force against the force of steel and steam and was annihilated.

Blind courage is not good strategy. Speaking recently with an official of a Negro college in the Southland, where I had been invited to deliver the commencement address, he informed me that his beloved wife, knowing his courageous instincts, had frequently requested him, that in the event of her being offered insult by men of the other race in that section, not to be in a hurry to die for her as she much rather preferred him to live for her. This is no time for preaching material force. Possibly our trials and setbacks are God's plan to bring us to realize that this is a spiritual movement, and can survive only as a spiritual force. "Not by might, nor by power, but by My spirit, saith the Lord of hosts." [23] "Except the Lord build the house, their labor is but lost that build it; except the Lord keep the city, the watchmen waketh but in vain." [24]

THE CAUSE IS ALL

This is a spiritual movement and that is why our adversaries fail to fathom its hold upon us, and style us fools and fanatics of Garvey. They think only of the man and never of the cause. Philosophical as many of them profess to be, they have not yet discovered that the spirit of this movement which he has fanned into flame finds its habitat in the heart yearnings of millions of Negroes, that this movement possesses an immortal germ, and because immortal, spiritual. The founder himself by no act of his, can destroy this movement, and long after he shall have passed from labor to reward the work begun by him shall continue into fruition and maturity. On the day that Moses stood before the burning bush to receive his divine commission he held in his hand the shepherd's rod which he himself had made. That rod was to bring deliverance to his people and discomfiture to their foes, but not until he had cast it down to be consecrated and energized by God. Until that day he had used that shepherd's rod in the care of Jethro's flocks. Henceforth it becomes the medium of wonderful achievements for his race.

THE ROD OF THE U.N.I.A.

Before the burning bush our leader stands today, and from the unsinged foliage comes to him a voice, the voice of the God of his forefathers, the God of Ham, and Cush,[25] and Nimrod;[26] the God of Zerah[27] and Ebedmelech,[28] and Endich of Ethiopia,[29] thus interrogating[,] "Marcus Garvey, what is that in thine hand?" Reverently he answers, "A rod—the rod of the Universal Negro Improvement Association." Then comes the divine mandate: "Cast it down, Garvey, on the ground before me that I may consecrate it. Then put forth thy hand and take it again unto thee, no longer thy rod, but Jehovah's rod, and go forward to perform with it mighty things for the redemption of thy race." God grant that he may hear the divine voice, and hearing may comply. Negro, in your hand you have carried the rod of several years, but only to a limited extent has it been of service. Cast it down today at the feet of the Omnipotent, and see! See how the seemingly inanimate and inert thing becomes instantaneously a creature pregnant with life and energy and motion! Cast down before the King Immortal and Invisible this organization to be baptized with the new birth, and in joyful wonder and glad surprise you shall witness the glorious and victorious achievements of all its aims and objects.

"O God, the protector of all who trust in Thee, without whom nothing is strong, nothing is holy, increase and multiply upon this association thy mercy that Thou being our ruler and guide, we may so pass through things temporal, that we finally lose not the things eternal." And for our leader we add our earnest prayer. "Out of many dangers hast Thou safely brought him. Continue unto the end Thy fatherly and protecting care."

"Endow him, Lord, with faith and grace
And courage to endure,

The wrongs he suffers here apace,

And Bless him evermore."—Amen.

Printed in *NW*, 9 August 1924. Original headlines abbreviated.

    1. Ferrara Levi Mitchinson Lord was born in the parish of St. Philip, Barbados, on 25 October 1890 and baptized on 6 December of the same year at Holy Trinity Church, also in St. Philip. His parents were Samuel Francis Lord, a fisherman, and his wife Georgiana (née Ward) of Sea View in St. Philip. Levi Lord was trained as a schoolteacher and was also taught the craft of shoemaking by his father. After working as a policeman in Barbados for several months, in 1918 he migrated to the United States, settling in Brooklyn, where he found work in a shoe factory. Hearing about Marcus Garvey and other black radicals, Lord visited Harlem, heard Garvey speak, and joined the movement. Proficient in shorthand, he became a transcriber of Garvey's speeches for the *Negro World*. In the fall of 1923, together with Alonzo Pettiford, president of the Detroit division, Lord was awarded the order of Knight Commander of the Cross of African Redemption. He had assumed the role of auditor general of the UNIA before being appointed chancellor in 1923. Lord later helped to found the Paragon Credit Union in Brooklyn, of which he was a treasurer and manager. He resigned from the UNIA in October 1927 (*NW*, 22 September 1923, 11 September 1926, 26 March and 15 October 1927; letter to Levi Lord, 1 August 1922, NN-Sc, UNIA Central Division records, box 2; Ferrara Levi Lord, interview with Robert A. Hill, June–July 1978).

    2. Ps. 30, "I will extol thee, O Lord."

    3. The wife of George A. Weston.

    4. From *Negro World* accounts of the convention, it does not appear that this speech was ever delivered.

    5. During the forty years Moses spent in the Midian Desert, where he sought refuge from the Egyptians, he tended the flocks of Jethro, the pagan priest into whose family he married. Moses' period in the wilderness is regarded as his second period of preparation, the first being his training as a scribe in the palace of his adopted mother, Hatshepsut, daughter of Thutmose I. In the course of the flight of the Israelites through the wilderness, Moses was challenged by Aaron and Miriam—"And Miriam and Aaron spoke against Moses because of the Cushite woman whom he had married; for he had married a woman of Cush" (Num. 12:1). The jealous complaint resulted in divine judgment against Miriam, who "became leprous, white as snow" (Num. 12:10). The woman referred to may have been Zipporah, Jethro's daughter, who was a Midianite (Exod. 18:1–2). Midian and Cush are linked in the Bible, e.g., in Hab. 3:7.

    In the Afro-American tradition of biblical interpretation, which stresses the role of blacks in sacred history, Jethro is characterized as an "Ethiopian Priest [who] was the divinely appointed religious preceptor of Moses" (Alonzo Potter Burgess Holly, *God and the Negro: Synopsis of God and the Negro or the Biblical Record of the Race of Ham* [Nashville: National Baptist Publishing Board, 1937], p. 56). Similar examples of Ethiopianist readings of the Bible are found in Joseph E. Hayne, *The Negro in Sacred History, or Ham and His Immediate Descendants* (Charleston, S.C.: Walker, Evans, Cogwell, 1887); Rufus Lewis Perry, *The Cushites, or the Descendants of Ham as Found in Sacred Scripture* (Springfield, Mass.: Wiley and Co., 1893); and Benjamin Tucker Tanner, *The Negro in Holy Writ* (Philadelphia: n.p., 1900). For the tradition of Ethiopianism in Afro-American thought and its applications, see J.G. St. Clair Drake, *The Redemption of Africa and Black Religion* (Chicago: Third World Press, 1970); William R. Scott, "'And Ethiopia Shall Stretch Forth Its Hands': The Origins of Ethiopianism in Afro-American Thought, 1767-1896," *Umoja* II (spring 1978): 1–14; and Albert J. Raboteau, "*Ethiopia Shall Soon Stretch Forth Her Hands*": Black Destiny in Nineteenth-Century America (Tempe: Department of Religious Studies, Arizona State University, University Lecture in Religion, 27 January 1983).

    6. Exod. 17:1.

    7. Shakespeare's *Hamlet*, act 5, sc. 2, line 10.

    8. See *Garvey Papers* 4: 66, n. 4.

    9. A paraphrase of Matt. 22:21.

    10. A paraphrased reversal of Mark Antony's eulogy in Shakespeare's *Julius Caesar*, act 3, sc. 2, lines 79–80.

    11. A reference to the Ten Commandments; see Exod. 20:3–17.

    12. Friedrich von Logau's "Retribution," *Poetic Aphorisms* (1654): "Though the mills of God grind slowly, yet they grind exceedingly small"(*BFQ*).

    13. A paraphrase of Ps. 2:1.

14. Acts 19:24: "For a certain man named Demetrius, a silversmith, which made silver shrines for Diana, brought no small gain unto the craftsman." Demetrius led a riot against Saint Paul's conversions in Ephesus, which threatened Demetrius's business.

15. A possible allusion to the black spiritual "Roll, Jordan, Roll" (W. F. Allen et al., *Slave Songs of the United States* [New York, 1871]).

16. John 8:32.

17. Ruth 4:12; Matt. 1:3.

18. Matt. 1:5.

19. See *Garvey Papers* 3: 647.

20. Bishop McGuire was referring to an editorial in the Episcopal church organ, *The Living Church*, one of several religious periodicals published by the Morehouse Publishing Co. of Milwaukee, Wis. Entitled "'Garveyism' Among the Negroes," the text of the editorial read:

> We learn with some concern of a negro movement that has resulted in an "Independent Episcopal Church", which is said to have three congregations in Greater New York. It is a product of that strange movement among negroes known as Garveyism. At its head, according to the *Negro World*, is "the Most Rev." George Alexander McGuire, who is called "Chaplain General of the Universal Negro Improvement Association and Titular Archbishop of Ethiopia", and who is referred to throughout the article as "His Grace." "Called of God, elected by Negro Deputies from all over the world, and approved by the ministers of the Independent Episcopal Church of Ethiopia, Archbishop McGuire feels himself fully equipped and authorized for the large work entrusted to his care and supervision, and hopes to prove himself truly an Episcopus or overseer of the Church for which Negroes everywhere are looking. When Dr. McGuire left the Church of England in 1919 he left behind him the fragile theory and doctrine of Apostolic Sucession." Accordingly he is described in the same article as ordaining a man to be a "presbyter."
>
> We regret to say that this McGuire is, or was until recently, one of our clergy. He was ordained by the Bishop of Southern Ohio and for a time, beginning in 1911, was a field agent of the American Church Institute for Negroes, being at that time canonically resident in the diocese of Massachusetts, where he had previously had work in Cambridge. In 1914 he was transferred by the Bishop of Massachusetts to the diocese of Antigua, in the West Indies, and was dropped from the American clergy list. His name appears in *Crockford* thereafter as rector of St. Paul's, Antigua, until the volume of 1920, when his name was dropped.
>
> We regret that one who had thus received the Church's orders and the confidence of Churchmen should now take the initiative in leading men of his race away from the Church.
>
> "The Negroes of the world," says the *Negro World*, "in convention assembled made the Most Rev. Dr. G.A. McGuire the first Prince of the Church Ethiopic. We understand that plans are under way of his enthronement at the coming convention in August next."
>
> Apparently this has been his undoing. (*The Living Church*, 11 June 1924, p. 168)

21. A reference to Garvey's closing address to the jury in the mail fraud trial. See *Garvey Papers* 5: 330–356.

22. See *Garvey Papers* 4: 364–366.

23. Zech. 4:6.

24. A paraphrase of Ps. 127:1.

25. Gen. 10:6.

26. Gen. 10:8; 1 Chron. 1:10.

27. Gen. 36:13.

28. Jer. 39:16.

29. In his account of blacks in sacred history, Alonzo Holly states that, Endich "as tradition names him, was the Ethiopian Eunuch, whom St. Philip, the deacon of Jewish ancestry[,] converted and baptized" (*God and the Negro*, p. 102). Holly goes on to note: "Philip would have continued with Endich from Asia Minor into Ethiopia but it was not in accordance with the Divine Purpose, hence the Spirit caught him away to return to his work among his own people and fellow Asiatics. The man of dark hue 'went on His way rejoicing' [Acts 8:39] to be a missionary to his own, the first Christian missionary, laying foundations which have survived until today" (ibid.). Philip was one of the seven Hellenistic Jews whom the apostles had appointed officers to handle works of public charity. The Ethiopian eunuch was the treasurer to the court of the queen of Ethiopia. The story of the Ethiopian chamberlain's conversion, which took place on the Gaza road from Jerusalem, is told in Acts 8:26–40.

This passage gives an account of the early expansion of Christianity from Samaria into ancient Nubia. The seminary of Rev. George A. McGuire's African Orthodox Church bore the name Endich Theological Seminary (*Negro Churchman* 2 [November 1924]: 7; its formal curriculum appeared in the *Negro Churchman* 3 [February 1925]: 7–8; see also Edward W. Blyden, "Philip and the Eunuch," in *Christianity, Islam and the Negro Race* 2nd ed. [London: W. B. Whittingham and Co., 1888], pp. 174–199).

Speech by Marcus Garvey

New York, August 1, 1924

SPEECH OF MARCUS GARVEY BEFORE DELEGATES AND DEPUTIES TO 4TH ANNUAL INTERNATIONAL CONVENTION OF NEGRO PEOPLES OF THE WORLD AND WHITE AND NEGRO CITIZENS AT CARNEGIE HALL, NEW YORK, AUGUST 1, 1924, 8:30 P.M.

Delegates to the Fourth International Convention
of the Negro Peoples of the World,
Ladies and Gentlemen:–

The pleasure of addressing you at this hour is great. You have re-assembled yourselves in New York, coming from all parts of the world to this Annual Convention, because you believe that by unity you can alleviate the unfortunate condition in which racially we find ourselves.

We are glad to meet as Negroes, notwithstanding the stigma that is placed upon us by a soulless and conscienceless world because of our backwardness.

As usual, I am not here to flatter you, I am not here to tell you how happy and prosperous we are as a people, because that is all false. The Negro is not happy, but, to the contrary, is extremely miserable. He is miserable because the world is closing fast around him, and if he does not strike out now for his own preservation, it is only a question of a few more decades when he will be completely outdone in a world of strenuous competition for a place among the fittest of God's creation.

NEGRO DYING OUT

The Negro is dying out, and he is going to die faster and more rapidly in the next fifty years than he has in the past three hundred years. There is only one thing to save the Negro, and that is an immediate realization of his own responsibilities. Unfortunately we are the most careless and indifferent people in the world! We are shiftless and irresponsible, and that is why we find ourselves the wards of an inherited materialism that has lost its soul and its conscience. It is strange to hear a Negro leader speak in this strain, as the usual course is flattery, but I would not flatter you to save my own life and that of my own family. There is no value in flattery. Flattery of the Negro for another quarter of a century will mean hell and damnation to the race. How can any

Negro leader flatter us about progress and the rest of it, when the world is preparing more than ever to bury the entire race? Must I flatter you when England, France, Italy, Belgium and Spain are all concentrating on robbing every square inch of African territory, the land of our fathers? Must I flatter you when the cry is being loudly raised for a white America, Canada, Australia and Europe, and a yellow and brown Asia?[1] Must I flatter you when I find all other peoples preparing themselves for the struggle to survive, and you still smiling, eating, dancing, drinking and sleeping away your time, as if yesterday were the beginning of the age of pleasure? I would rather be dead than be a member of your race without thought of the mor[ro]w, for it portends evil to him that thinketh not.[2] Because I cannot flatter you I am here to tell you, and emphatically, that if we do not seriously reorganize ourselves as a people and face the world with a program of African nationalism our days in civilization are numbered, and it will be only a question of time when the Negro will be as completely and complacently dead as the North American Indian, or the Australian Bushman.

PROGRESS ON SAND

You talk about the progress we have made in America and elsewhere among the people of our acquaintance, but what progress is it? A progress that can be snatched away from you in forty-eight hours, because it has been built upon sand.

You must thank God for the last two generations of whites in our western civilization; thank God that they were not made of sterner stuff, and character and a disposition to see all races their rivals and competitors in the struggle to hold and possess the world, otherwise, like the Indian, we would have nearly all been dead.

The progress of the Negro in our civilization was tolerated because of indifference, but that indifference exists no longer. Our whole civilization is becoming intolerant, and because of that the whole world of races has started to think.

DOES NOT BLAME THE WHITE MAN

Can you blame the white man for thinking, when red and yellow men are knocking at his door? Can you blame the tiger for being on the defensive when the lion approaches? And thus we find that generations ago when the Negro was not given a thought as a world competitor he is now regarded as an encumbrance in a civilization to which he has materially contributed little. Men do not build for others, they build for themselves. The age and our religion demand it. What are you going to expect, that white men are going to build up in America and elsewhere and hand it over to us? If we are expecting that we are crazy, we have lost our reason.

If you were white, you would see the rest in hell before you would deprive your children of bread to give it to others. You would give that which you did not want, but not that which is to be the sustenance of your family, and so the world thinks; yet a Du Bois and the National Association for the Advancement of Colored People will tell us by flattery that the day is coming when a white President of the United States of America will get out of the White House and give the position to a Negro, that the day is coming when a Mr. Hughes will desert the Secretaryship of State and give it to the Negro, James Weldon Johnson; that the time is just around the corner of constitutional rights when the next Ambassador to the Court of Saint James will be a black man from Mississippi or from North Carolina. Do you think that white men who have suffered, bled and died to make America and the world what it is, are going to hand over to a parcel of lazy Negroes the things that they prize most?

Stop flattering yourselves, fellowmen, and let us go to work. Do you hear me? Go to work, go to work in the morn of a new creation and strike not because of the noonday sun, but plod on and on, until you have succeeded in climbing the hills of opposition and reached the height of self-progress, and from that pinnacle bestow upon the world a civilization of your own, and hand down to your children and posterity of your own a worthy contribution to the age of human materialism.

FAIR AND JUST

We of the Universal Negro Improvement Association are fair and just. We do not expect the white man to rob himself and to deprive himself for our racial benefit. How could you reasonably expect that in an age like this, when men have divided themselves into racial and national groups, when the one group has its own interest to protect as against that of the other?

The laws of self-preservation force every human group to look after itself and protect its own interest, hence so long as the American white man or any other white man, for that matter, realizes his responsibility, he is bound to struggle to protect that which is his and his own, and I feel that the Negro today who has been led by the unscrupulous of our race has been grossly misguided in the direction of expecting too much from the civilization of others.

THE CARPET-BAGGER

Immediately after emancipation, we were improperly led in the South by this same group and ultimately lost our vote and voice. The carpet-bagger and the thoughtless, selfish Negro politic[i]an and leader sold the race back into slavery. And the same attempt is now being made in the North by that original group prompted by the dishonest white political boss and the unscrupulous Negro politician. The time has come for both races to seriously adjust their differences and settle the future of our respective peoples. The selfish of both races will not stop to think and act, but the responsibility becomes more so ours, who have the vision of the future.

CRIMINALS OUT OF JAIL

Because of my attempt to lead my race into the only solution that I see would benefit both groups, I was and have been maliciously and wickedly maligned, and by members of our own race. I have been plotted against, framed up, indicted and convicted, the story which you so well know. That was responsible for our not having a Convention last year. I thank you, however, for the tribute you paid me during that period in postponing the Convention through respect to my enforced absence. Last August I spent the entire month in the Tombs in New York, but I was as happy then as I am now. I was sent there by the evil forces that have always fought and opposed reform movements, but I am as ready now to go back to the Tombs or elsewhere as I was when I was forced to leave you. The jail does not make a criminal, the criminal makes himself. There are more criminals out of jail than in jail, the only difference is that the majority of those who are out are such skilful criminals that they know how to keep themselves out. They have tried to smear my name so as to prevent me doing the good that I desire to do in the interest of the race. It amuses me sometimes to hear the biggest crooks in the Negro Race referring to me as a criminal. As I have said before, Negro race leaders are the biggest crooks in the world. It is because of their crookedness that we have not made more progress. If you think I am not telling the truth in this direction you may quiz or query any of the white political bosses, and those who will tell the truth will reveal a tale most shocking as far as our Negro leaders are concerned. This is true of the group of fellows of our race that lead universally as well as nationally. They will sell the souls of their mothers and their country into perdition. That is why the Universal Negro Improvement Association has to make such a fight, and that is why the opposition is as hard and marked. You can pay the Negro leader to hang his race and block every effort of self-help. This is not commonly so among other races. We must give credit to the great white race, to the extent that they will fight among themselves, that they will cheat each other in business, but when it approaches the future and destiny of the race, a halt is immediately called. Not so with the Negro, he does not know when and where to stop in hurting himself.

REORGANIZING THE RACE

I repeat that we must reorganize ourselves as a people if we are to go forward, and I take this opportunity as you assemble yourselves here from all parts of the world to sound the warning note.

To review the work of our Association for the past two years is to recount the exploits of a continuous struggle to reach the top. Our organization has been tested during the past two years beyond that of any other period in the history of Negro movements. I am glad to say, however, that we have survived all the intrigues, barriers and all the handicaps placed in the way. Some of our enemies thought that they would have been able to crush our movement when I was convicted and sentenced to prison. They had depended upon that as the trump card in their effort to crush the new spirit of freedom among

Negroes, but like all such efforts, it was doomed to failure. I will bring to your memory a similar effort made a little over nineteen hundred years ago when on Calvary's mount the Jews[,] after inspiring the Romans, attempted to crucify the man, Christ, the leader of the Christian religion. They thought that after the crucifixion, after he was buried, that they would have silenced the principles of Christianity forever, but how successful they were is made manifest today when we find hundreds of millions of souls the world over professing the principles for which the man died on Calvary's cross. As in the rise of Christianity, so do we have the spiritual rise of the Universal Negro Improvement Association throughout the world. They tried to crucify it in America, and it has arisen in Africa a thousand fold. They tried to crucify it in the American continent, and it is now sweeping the whole world. You cannot crucify a principle; you cannot nail the souls of men to a cross; you cannot imprison it; you cannot bury it. It will rise like the spirit of the Great Redeemer and take its flight down the ages, until men far and near have taken up the cry for which the principle was crucified.

Unbroken in Spirit

We of the Universal Negro Improvement Association are stronger today than we ever were before. We are strong in spirit, strong in determination; we are unbroken in every direction; we stand firm facing the world, determined to carve out and find a place for the four hundred millions of our suffering people. We call upon humanity everywhere to listen to the cry of the new Negro. We ask the human heart for a response, because Africa's sun cannot be downed. Africa's sun is rising, gradually rising, and soon he shall take his place among the brilliant constellations of nations. The Negro wants a nation, nothing less, nothing more; and why shouldn't we be nationally free, nationally independent, nationally unfettered? We want a similar nationality to that of the English, the French, the Italian, the German, to that of the white American, to that of the yellow Japanese; we want nationality and government. We can realize that the American nation in a short while will not be large enough to accommodate two competitive rivals, one black and the other white.

Black Man's Aspirations

There is no doubt about it that the black man of America today aspires to the White House, to the Cabinet, and to the Senate, and the House. He aspires to be head of State and municipal governments. What are you going to do with him? He cannot be satisfied in the midst of a majority group that seeks to protect its interest at all hazards; then the only alternative is to give the Negro a place of his own. That is why we appeal to the sober white minds of America, and not the selfish ones. The selfish ones will see nothing more than the immediate present, but the deep thinking white man will see the result of another fifty or one hundred years, when these two peoples will be brought together in closer contact of rivalry. As races we practically represent a similar intelligence today. We have graduated out of, and passed through, the same schools, colleges and universities. What can you do with men who are equally and competently fitted in mind but give them an equal chance, and if there is no chance of equality, there must be dissatisfaction on the one hand. That dissatisfaction we have in our midst now. We have it manifested by W.E.B. Du Bois, by James Weldon Johnson; we have it manifested by the organization known as the National Association for the Advancement of Colored People, that seeks to bring about social equality, and political equality, and industrial equality, things that are guaranteed us under the Constitution, but which, in the face of a majority race, we cannot demand, because of the terrible odds against us. In the midst of this, then, what can we do but seek an outlet of our own, unless we intend to fight a losing game. Reason will dictate that there is no benefit to be derived from fighting always a losing game. We will lose until we have completely lost our stand in America.

THE PERIOD OF SELF-PROTECTION

To repeat myself, we talk about progress. What progress have we made when everything we do is done through the good will and grace of the liberal white man of the present day? But can he always afford to be liberal? Do you not realize that in another few decades he will have on his hands a problem of his own—a problem to feed his own children, to take care of his own flesh and blood? In the midst of that crisis, when he finds not even enough to feed himself, what will become of the Negro? The Negro naturally must die to give way and make room for others who are better prepared to live. That is the danger, men; and that is why we have the Universal Negro Improvement Association. The condition that I have referred to will not only be true of America and of continental Europe; it will be true wherever the great white race lives. There will not be room enough for them and for others who seek with them to compete, and that is why we hear the cry of Egypt for the Egyptians, India for the Indians, Asia for the Asiatics, and we raise the cry of Africa for the Africans[,] those at home and those abroad. That is why we ask England to be fair, to be just and considerate; that is why we ask France and Italy, Spain and Belgium to be fair, just and considerate; that is why we ask them to let the black man restore himself to his own country; and that is why we are determined to see it done. No camouflage and no promise of good will will solve the problem. What guarantee have we, what lease have we on the future that the man who treats us kindly today will perpetuate it through his son or his grandson tomorrow?

ABILITY TO PROTECT SELF

Races and peoples are only safeguarded when they are strong enough to protect themselves, and that is why we appeal to the four hundred million Negroes of the world to come together for self-protection and self-preservation. We do not want what belongs to the great white race, or the yellow race. We want only those things that belong to the black race. Africa is ours. To win Africa we will give up America, we will give up our claim in all other parts of the world; but we must have Africa. We will give up the vain desire of having a seat in the White House in America, of having a seat in the House of Lords in England, of being President of France, for the chance and opportunity of filling these positions in a country of our own.

That is how the Universal Negro Improvement Association differs from other organizations. Other organizations, especially in America, are fighting for a political equality which they will never get, and never win, in the face of a majority opposition. We win so much today and lose so much tomorrow. We will lose our political strength in the North in another few years, as we lost it in the South during reconstruction. We fill one position today, but lose two tomorrow, and so we will drift on and on until we have been completely obliterated from western civilization.

CHANGES AMONG NEGROES

You may ask me what good has the Universal Negro Improvement Association done, what has it accomplished within the last six years? We will point to you the great changes that have taken place in Africa, the West Indies and America. In the West Indies, black men have been elevated to high positions by the British Government, so as to offset and counteract the sweeping influence of the Universal Negro Improvement Association.[3] Several of the Colonies have been given larger constitutional rights. In Africa, the entire West Coast has been benefited. Self-government has been given to several of the African Colonies, and native Africans have been elevated to higher positions, so as to offset the sweeping spirit of the Universal Negro Improvement Association throughout the Continent of Africa. In America, several of our men have been given prominent positions; Negro commissions have been appointed to attend to affairs of state; Negro Consuls have also been appointed. Things that happened in America within the last six years to advance the political status, the social and industrial status of the Negro were never experienced before. All that is traceable to the Universal Negro Improvement Association within the last six years. In the great game of politics you do not see the immediate results at your door, but those who are observant will be able to trace the good that is being done from the many directions whence it comes. If you were to take a survey of the whole world today of Negroes you will find that we are more highly thought of in 1924 than we were in 1914. England, France and the European and Colonial powers regard the Universal Negro Improvement Association with a certain amount of suspicion because they believe that we are antagonistic. But we are not. We are not antagonistic to France, to England or Italy, nor any of the white Powers in Europe. We are only demanding a square deal for our race. Did we not fight to help them? Did we not sacrifice our blood, give up our all, to save England, to save France, Italy and America during the last war? Then why shouldn't we expect some consideration for the service rendered? That is all we ask; and we are now pressing that claim to the throne of white justice. We are told that God's throne is white, although we believe it to be black. But if it is white, we are placing our plea before that throne of God, asking Him to so touch the hearts of our fellow men as to let them yield to us the things that are ours, as it was right to yield to Caesar the things that were Caesar's.[4]

LET US BE FAIR

As we deliberate on the many problems confronting us during the month of August, let us not lose control of ourselves; let us not forget that we are the guardians of four hundred millions; let us not forget that it is our duty to so act and legislate as to help humanity everywhere, whether it be black or white. We shall be called upon during this month to take up certain matters that are grave, but dispassionately we shall discuss them; and whenever the interest of the different race groups clash, let it be our duty to take the other fellow's feelings into our consideration. If we must be justly treated, then we ourselves must treat all men similarly. So, let no prejudice cause us to say or do anything against the interest of the white man, or the yellow man; let us realize that the white man has the right to live, the yellow man has the right to live, and all that we desire to do is to impress them with the fact that we also have the right to live.

DNA, RG 16, general correspondence. PD.

1. In the 1920s the growth of Chinese and Japanese nationalism was increasingly recognized in the West. In China, Sun Yat-sen and his supporters overthrew the rule of the Manchurians in 1912 and established a republic. Internal conflict followed, but by January 1924, only months before Garvey was speaking, the first Koumintang National Congress was held at Canton. Organized by Sun Yat-sen, the congress opened itself to the newly formed Chinese Communist party, along with the party's Soviet advisers. Upon the death of Sun Yat-sen in 1925, Chiang Kai-shek, who was trained in Japan and headed a team of Russian and German instructors in the new Whampoa Military Academy, became the focal point of nationalist loyalties within China, in opposition to the growing Communist movement.

Since the nineteenth century, Japanese nationalism had been directed against the incursion of Western powers throughout Asia. In 1905 the Japanese defeated the Russian empire in a drive to expel Russian interests from the Far East. The victory of 1905 marked Japan's ascendance as a world power, but this ascendance was viewed not only as a Japanese victory but as a victory of Asia against the West. The 1920s saw the emergence of Japanese ultranationalist groups opposed to Western-style politics and to the more liberal government that was then in power. These groups also supported the return of militarism which was to become the basis for official Japanese policy in the 1930s.

Within each country secret nationalistic societies played key roles. While some worked primarily within each country, there was also cooperation between countries in a self-conscious drive toward Pan-Asian unity, a concept that had its roots in nineteenth-century opposition to Western imperialism. Secret societies in Japan as well as in China, for instance, were instrumental in helping Sun Yat-sen's revolution. By the late 1920s members from among these Pan-Asian societies recognized the common aspirations of their movements and Garvey's UNIA (Immanuel C. Y. Hsu, *The Rise of Modern China* [New York: Oxford University Press, 1983], pp. 355–540; Harold Hakwon Sunoo, *Japanese Militarism* [Chicago: Nelson Hall, 1975], pp. 9–43; F. Gilbert Chan and Thomas H. Etzold, eds., *China in the 1920s* [New York: Franklin Watts, 1976]; Delmar M. Brown, *Nationalism in Japan* [Berkeley and Los Angeles: University of California Press, 1955], pp. 113–200).

2. A paraphrase of "Take therefore no thought for the morrow: for the morrow shall take thought for the things of itself. Sufficient unto the day is the evil thereof" (Matt. 6:34).

3. In the 1920s UNIA branches and agencies of the BSL were established in Nigeria, the Gold Coast, Senegal, and Sierra Leone. Most of these organizations were short-lived, but the ideas of radical African nationalism that Garvey espoused were disseminated throughout most of West Africa. The *Negro World* as well as UNIA tracts written in English, French, and Arabic were distributed, while UNIA emissaries were sent to organize on behalf of the association. British and French colonial authorities, alarmed by the rising agitation, banned these UNIA publications, though the publications continued to be smuggled into the colonies.

The UNIA was not the only political group advocating a program of African nationalism. Influenced by the idea of African self-government and by the example of the Indian National Congress, African delegates from the Gold Coast, Sierra Leone, Nigeria, and Gambia assembled in Accra in 1920 to form the National Congress of British West Africa (NCBWA). Among other things, the NCBWA program called for legislative representation for Africans. Under increasing African pressure, the British Colonial Office eventually moved to establish a system of limited African representation in its West African colonies. In 1922 Nigeria became the first British West African colony to be given a new constitution; under its provisions four Africans were elected to the legislative council. In 1924 Sierra Leone received a similar constitution, and in 1925 a new constitution was introduced in the Gold Coast, although it did not take effect until 1927 (Michael Crowder, *West Africa under Colonial Rule* [London: Hutchinson of London, 1968], pp. 454–456; James S. Coleman, *Nigeria: Background to Nationalism* [1958; rep. ed. Berkeley, Los Angeles, London: University of California Press, 1971], pp. 187–196; Okoi Arikpo, *The Development of Modern Nigeria* [London: Penguin Books, 1967], pp. 39–47; J. Ayo Langley, *Pan-Africanism and Nationalism in West Africa, 1900–1945* [Oxford: Clarendon Press, 1978], pp. 107–134; *New York World*, 15 September 1922; *NYT*, 7 April 1923).

4. Matt. 22.21, Mark 12:17.

Editorial in the *New York Evening Bulletin*[1]

[2 August 1924]

It has been the favorite sport of some New York newspapers to make fun of Marcus Garvey, the Negro leader, because he is prone to adapt long and high-sounding titles and voice extravagant claims, and because some of his enterprises have come to grief. Despite all this, has any other man of his race in the past century succeeded in assembling a more representative gathering of his people? Men and women from many countries and from almost every state have met in New York at Garvey's call; they are willing to follow his leadership. And even the worst enemy of Garvey must admit that there was logic and truth in the statements he made to the convention. Here are a few of his sentences which merit consideration:

> There is no value in flattery. I wouldn't flatter you to save my life. And unfortunately we are the most careless and indifferent people in the world. Must I flatter you when England, France, Italy, Belgium and Spain are all concentrating on robbing every square inch of African territory, the land of our fathers?
>
> Must I flatter you when the cry is being loudly raised for a white America, Canada, Australia and Europe, and a yellow and

brown Asia? I find all other peoples preparing themselves for the struggle to survive, and you, still smiling, eating, drinking, dancing and sleeping away your lives, as if yesterday were the beginning of the age of pleasure.

Printed in the *New York Evening Bulletin*, 2 August 1924. Reprinted in Amy Jacques Garvey, *Garvey and Garveyism* (Kingston, Jamaica: United Printers, 1963), pp. 159–160.

1. Amy Jacques Garvey prefaced the editorial with the remark, "The white editor of the *New York Evening Bulletin*, August 2, 1924, chided those who ridicule Garvey, and challenged colored men to equal his achievement" (*Garvey and Garveyism*, p. 159).

Marcus Garvey to President Calvin Coolidge

[*New York, 3 August 1924*]

Will your Excellency please accept the best wishes of the 400,000,000 Negroes of the world through us, their representatives, assembled in international convention? We mourn with you the loss of your son,[1] but pray that you will be strengthened to carry on the great work of leading the American nation that now confronts you. We thank you and your race for the friendship you have shown that portion of our people that forms a part of the nation, and hope that we may speedily arrive at some solution by which the two races may continue to live in peace with each other and become the guardians of liberty, human rights and real democracy.

Fourth Annual International Convention
Negro Peoples of the World
MARCUS GARVEY
Chairman

Printed in *NW*, 9 August 1924.

1. Calvin Coolidge, Jr., died of blood poisoning on 7 July 1924 at the age of sixteen (*NYT*, 8 July 1924).

Marcus Garvey to Ramsay MacDonald

[*New York, 3 August 1924*]

The 400,000,000 Negroes of the world send you greetings through our convention. We pray that you and your country will adopt a fair and honest attitude toward Africa and the Negro race. The Negro, like the Indian and Irish, desire unfettered nationhood, and we hope your government will realize that the time for African colonial exploitation has come to an end and a new era of justice to all men ushered in. We ask that you and your countrymen be fair and reasonable to the black race.

Fourth Annual International Convention
Negro Peoples of the World
MARCUS GARVEY
Chairman

Printed in *NW*, 9 August 1924.

Marcus Garvey to Sir Eric Drummond

[*New York, 3 August 1924*]

We beg to draw to your attention our petition of two years before the League and the League Council asking for the turning over to us of the late German colonies, to be developed as independent Negro nations. We ask for immediate action on the matter.

Fourth Annual International Convention
Negro Peoples of the World
MARCUS GARVEY
Chairman

Printed in *NW*, 9 August 1924.

Marcus Garvey to Premier Édouard Herriot[1] of France

[*New York, 3 August 1924*]

The 400,000,000 Negroes of the world, through our convention, appeal to you and your people for justice. Will France not consider that the time has come to let Africa govern herself? We ask for the freedom of the blacks under your control, and that you be generous enough to help them toward real self-government and not exploitation.

> Fourth Annual International Convention
> Negro Peoples of the World
> MARCUS GARVEY
> Chairman

Printed in *NW*, 9 August 1924.

1. Édouard Herriot (1872–1957), French statesman, scholar, and leader of the Radical Socialist party, served on three occasions as premier of France. He first became premier in 1924, but his coalition government fell a year later. In subsequent years he held a variety of ministerial positions, including minister of state and president of the Chamber of Deputies; in 1932 he again held the premiership briefly. Herriot was arrested and imprisoned by the Nazis in 1942 but returned to politics in 1945. A year later he was elected president of the National Assembly, a position he held until his retirement in 1954 (*WBD*; *NYT*, 27 March 1957).

Marcus Garvey to Premier Zaghlul Pasha of Egypt

[*New York, 3 August 1924*]

Greetings from Fourth Annual International Convention of Negro Peoples of the World, now sitting in New York. We glory in your victory and success.[1]

> MARCUS GARVEY
> Chairman

Printed in *NW*, 9 August 1924.

1. A reference to the victory of Saad Zaghlul Pasha's Nationalist party, the Wafd, in the Egyptian elections of late 1923, and to Zaghlul's appointment as premier in January 1924 (*EWH*).

Marcus Garvey to President Louis Borno[1] of Haiti

[*New York, 3 August 1924*]

We are in deep sympathy with the indignation of the people of Haiti in the matter of the rape of the country through a forcible occupation by an alien race.[2] We shall work along with the patriots of Haiti to free her from the yoke of exploitation. Long live free and independent Haiti, the pride of the black race of the Western world. Our convention sends greetings to you and the people of Haiti.

> Fourth Annual International Convention
> of the Negro Peoples of the World
> MARCUS GARVEY
> Chairman

Printed in *NW*, 9 August 1924.

1. Louis E.A.F.J. Borno (1865–1942), Haitian lawyer and politician, served two terms as president of Haiti from 1922–1930. An advocate of U.S. intervention in Haiti in 1915, Borno was frequently accused of being a tool of American interests. In 1930 he accepted the recommendation of the Hoover Investigating Committee that American marines be withdrawn gradually and that popular elections be held (*NYT*, 30 July 1942).

2. The United States occupied Haiti in 1915 and remained there until 1934. The Haitians revolted against the military occupation in 1918, but the revolt was suppressed by 1919. International pressure to remove the marines increased by the mid-1920s. In July 1924, at a meeting of the Congress of the International Federation of League of Nations Societies in Paris, Dantès Bellegarde, former Haitian minister to France, raised the question of the military occupation of his country. His resolution demanding the immediate withdrawal of American marines was defeated, and a watered-down version was substituted. This version put the league on record as sympathizing with the Haitian people and encouraging that troops be withdrawn as soon as possible. In the election year of 1924, the issue was taken up by blacks and progressives in the United States. In Atlantic City the National Colored Republican Conference passed a resolution, which they sent to presidential candidate Calvin Coolidge condemning U.S.–Haitian policy generally and the military occupation in particular. Sen. Robert La Follette, running for president on the Progressive ticket, joined in condemning the occupation of Haiti and the Dominican Republic and warned of the "financial imperialism" that had fostered this occupation and that would, he felt, precipitate more in the future (Robert I. Rotberg, *Haiti: The Politics of Squalor* [Boston: Houghton Mifflin, 1971], pp. 25–146; Kethly Millet, *Les paysans Haitiens et l'occupation americaine, 1915–1930* [Quebec: Collectif Paroles, 1978]; Arthur Millspaugh, *Haiti under American Control, 1915–1930* [Boston: World Peace Foundation, 1931]; Brenda Gayle Plummer, "The Afro-American Response to the Occupation of Haiti, 1915–1934," *Phylon* 43, no. 2 [summer 1982]: 125–143; Leon D. Pamphile, "The NAACP and the American Occupation of Haiti," *Phylon* 42, no. 1 [spring 1986]: 91–100; *NYT*, 30 June, 1 July, 3 July, 5 July, 16 August and 29 October 1924).

Marcus Garvey to Premier Benito Mussolini of Italy

[*New York, 3 August 1924*]

Please convey to His Majesty the King[1] and people of Italy our good-will and impress upon them that the 400,000,000 Negroes of the world through us are looking for a change of policy in your African colonial plans. We feel that the time has come for Italy to allow Africa to govern herself and be left alone and not be exploited by foreign races and nations. We trust that you will set a good example by setting your black colonies free.[2]

Fourth Annual International Convention
Negro Peoples of the World
MARCUS GARVEY
Chairman

Printed in *NW*, 9 August 1924.

1. Victor Emmanuel III (1869–1947) became king of Italy in 1900. Italy increased its territories under his active leadership in World War I. After Mussolini came to power, he at first maintained only distant relations with the new leader; but by 1923 had become only a titular figure and spokesman for the Fascist regime. He disagreed with Mussolini's decision to ally with Germany in the war, but under pressure from Mussolini he supported the alliance. Although he attempted

to maintain his position as king following the war, he was finally forced to abdicate, and, in a last-ditch effort to maintain the monarchy, he handed it over to his son, Umberto II, before he exiled himself to Portugal (*EB*; *Times* [London], 29 December 1947; *NYT*, 29 December 1947; Denis Mack Smith, *Mussolini*, pp. 16, 50–54, 145–146, 293–299).

2. Left with only the protectorates of Somaliland and Eritrea following its humiliating defeat in 1896 at the Battle of Adowa, Italy aspired to avenge itself in later decades. In 1924, along with France, Italy supported Ethiopia's entrance into the League of Nations, a maneuver that was designed to undercut British influence in the region. It is possible that Garvey mistook Mussolini's support of Ethiopia's petition to join the league as a sign of approval for African sovereignty. In fact, the Italian dictator was merely laying the groundwork for his eventual plan of conquest (Robert L. Hess, *Italian Colonialism in Somalia* [Chicago: University of Chicago Press, 1966], pp. 13–84; Daniel A. Sandford, "The Making of Modern Abyssinia," *Current History* 19, no. 5 [February 1924]: 800–801; Denis Mack Smith, *Mussolini*, pp. 188–203).

Marcus Garvey to Empress Zauditu of Ethiopia[1]

[*New York, 3 August 1924*]

Greetings from the 400,000,000 Negroes of the world through our convention now sitting in New York. We hope for you and your country a reign of progress and happiness. Our desire is to help you maintain the glory of Ethiopia. Your expression of goodwill toward us two years ago through your consul-general[2] is highly cherished and we are looking forward to the day when large numbers of us will become citizens of Ethiopia.

> Fourth Annual International Convention of
> Negro Peoples of the World
> MARCUS GARVEY
> Chairman

Printed in *NW*, 9 August 1924.

1. The reign of the Empress Zauditu of Ethiopia (1876–1930) was marked by instability and a gowing antagonism between the conservative proponents of the Ethiopian Orthodox church and an increasingly powerful westernizing party. She assumed the throne in 1910, but regents actually ruled the country until her death in 1930. She was succeeded by the prince regent, Ras Tafari, who was crowned emperor and given the official title of Haile Selassie I (*EWH*; *NYT*, 4 April 1930; Daniel A. Sandford, "The Making of Modern Abyssinia," pp. 793–801).

2. See *Garvey Papers* 4: 1,005–1,007.

Marcus Garvey to Pope Pius XI[1]

[*New York, 3 August 1924*]

Will Your Holiness please accept the greetings and best wishes of the Negro peoples of the world as expressed through their delegates and representatives attending the Fourth Annual International Convention of the race now assembled in New York. We pray that your vision of the future be so clear as to enable you to use your influence on a wounded world to treat decently and fairly, politically, socially, industrially and religiously the 400,000,000 members of our race scattered throughout Africa, Europe, Asia and the Americas.

> Fourth Annual International Convention of
> Negro Peoples of the World
> MARCUS GARVEY
> Chairman

Printed in *NW*, 9 August 1924.

1. Pope Pius XI (1857–1939), a cardinal from Milan, was elected pontiff in 1922. He signed the Lateran Treaty with Benito Mussolini in 1929; this treaty established Vatican City (*WBD*).

Marcus Garvey to Mahatma Gandhi

[*New York, 3 August 1924*]

The Negroes of the world through us send you greetings. Fight on for the freedom of your people and country. We are with you.[1]

> Fourth Annual International Convention
> Negro Peoples of the World
> MARCUS GARVEY
> Chairman

Printed in *NW*, 9 August 1924.

1. In 1924 the non-cooperation movement, under the leadership of Mahatma Gandhi, was continuing to press for self-government in India. Gandhi, who had been imprisoned by the British, was released in February 1924 because of his failing health (*EWH*, pp. 1,101–1,103).

UNIA to President C.D.B. King

[*New York, 3 August 1924*]

The thousands of delegates attending the opening of the Fourth Annual International Convention of Negro Peoples of the World, representing all sections of the Negro race, greet you as the head of the only independent black republic in Africa and trust that you will be so guided during your administration as to reflect the highest credit upon our people. We, the convention, view with alarm and surprise the statement that is circulated by internal and other enemies of our race and attributed to your Secretary of State as touching discriminatory emigration to Liberia. We could not believe that you, the head of a Negro State, could be responsible for doing anything that would tend to dampen the spirit of love that the people of the Universal Negro Improvement Association have for you and your country and the effort that they are making to assist in making your nation the pride of the race and a credit to o[u]r civilization[. Long may] you live to do the right by our race. God save you and your beloved country is the prayer of our convention.

UNIVERSAL NEGRO IMPROVEMENT ASSOCIATION

Printed in *NW*, 9 August 1924.

Convention Addresses by Marcus Garvey, J.J. Peters, and Bishop George A. McGuire

[*New York, 3 August 1924*]

HON. MARCUS GARVEY'S SPEECH

. . . MUST BE FAIR TO EACH OTHER

Who says God did not spare the Negro to teach man how to live? Who says that God did not have an intent behind the inspiration of the psalmist when he wrote, "Princes shall come out of Egypt, Ethiopia shall stretch forth her hands unto God." Ethiopia is stretching forth her hands at this hour telling white men and yellow men that you cannot continue to exist if you will do so selfishly, with a world of discontented men around you, otherwise there will be a repetition of the same thing we have had in history ever since God Almighty said let there be light. We can only prosper—white, black and yellow—when we are fair to each other, and the white and yellow men are crazy if they think they can keep 400,000,000 black men down forever. We have not forgotten to fight since 1914 and 1918. Black men have not forgotten how to die. We died nobly, gracefully and splendidly in the Revolutionary War, in the Civil War, in the Spanish-American War and on the battlefields of France and Flanders. We died to bless the world with human love, with a perpetuation of civilization and Christianity and with the reign of democracy. And after we shed our blood for such sacred principles and for such a noble cause, what did they say to us? You are black. Because of that you cannot rise higher than where you are. We were lynched in the very uniform in which we fought on Flanders field.

Wilson told us it was a fight for democracy, and we believed him, as we have believed his race ever since we came in contact with it. But we are a little doubtful now. And that is why we realize that things have not been so well. Even with our God, as taught to us by the other fellow. We have found out a lot of things since 1914. We have found out a lot of things, not only of our own choice, but because we were forced to. We were forced to analyze this God that we prayed to all the time.

Now, we were praying so long for help, sympathy and salvation, and every year the lynching record mounted. Every year more Negroes were killed and burned and discriminated against. And we searched ourselves and found out that we were worshiping false gods, because God Himself said, "You shall worship no God but me, the God of My image, of My likeness." And we were worshiping a God not of our likeness, and that is responsible for all our sins. We were committing idolatry. Because if man is created in the image of God, if man is created in the likeness of God and [I a]m the son of God, in the name of God, my mother being a black woman, how can I have a white father? (Laughter and applause.)

Well you may say it is in [the] physical. But our physical existence is only an imitation and a secondary part of the spiritual. We are all children of the same spiritual God, though spiritual. I stand before you a two-fold creature, a two-fold personality, a physical being and a spiritual being. Now I cannot reconcile how one part could be black and one part white. I cannot see it. It would be inconsistent with the purpose of the Divine to have me mixed up that way. So it is natural for me to believe that I am man, spiritual and physical, and God the Creator, my God[,] physical and spiritual, must look like me. And when we start to worship anything other than ourselves, in the image of our God, we only place ourselves worshiping a strange idealism.

Do you know there are millions of Negroes in America and the West Indies whom you could not tell that God is not a handsome, prepossessing white man with a flowing beard? That is the picture. I went up to Pittsburgh the other day to visit the Pittsburgh Division of the association and I stopped with one of our members there. She belonged to the same faith as I, the Catholic faith, and when I was about to leave the house I noticed a picture on the wall. I looked at the picture and called upon one of my secretaries to explain the nature of the picture. What was it? There was a high elevated seat and there was something like a judge's desk, and sitting before this desk was a handsome, prepossessing white man, and his hands rested on the desk like this. On either side of him were two beautiful white women with wings. Below this desk was a white woman, a little child in the middle, a white woman on the right and a white woman to the left, and there was a kind of halo around the head of the little child. I said to my secretary, "Explain this picture." And she explained it as the artist intended. The white man sitting at the desk was God. The two white women on either side were white angels; the woman on the right side was the Virgin Mary, the child below was the Son of God, Jesus Christ. The man to the left was Joseph, the foster father. And that was a colored woman's house. I looked and said, ["]where is the other picture?["] I turned to the other side of of the wall, but the other picture was not there. But the idea was there. The idea was in that home. There was another picture of a hideous, monstrous creature that was the devil, and there were little imps around. Those were the angels of hell. But the artist did not hang that picture. That picture was created in the minds of all the Negroes all over the world and for hundreds of years. They encased that picture in their minds and kept it in their skulls.

What can you expect to accomplish; what can you hope to achieve when your ideal is that of another race? If you make your God a white man, angels white, Christ white, it means you will go to hell as a race created as you are and placed in the world without an idealism of your own. The hour has come for the Negro, like the Mongolian, like the Chinese and the Japanese and the Hindu to worship a God of their own. And the Universal Negro Improvement Association in this fourth International Convention is going to strike the keynote. We will reform the minds of Negroes everywhere. We will give a new religion, a new history and a new education to the four hundred million Negroes of the world. (Applause.)

Dr. J.J. Peters, president of the Chicago division, next addressed the convention. He said he had to present greetings from the Windy City, Chicago. The division was getting along splendidly and they were proud of the Universal Negro Improvement Association.

Reverting to the theme of Mr. Garvey's address, he said, "God is no respector of persons. Each man created the type of God that answered to his likeness. The Negro has been a compound ass. Personally, no religion appeals to me like my race. Unless you adapt yourself to the materialistic theory, you are doomed forever. I have no love for any country that does not protect, and the country that protects me I don't care who rules that country, whether God, Christ or Mohammed. I believe in justice to all men, but I'll be damned if I have any regard for any country that will not protect me and mine."

Continuing, he said: "I do not expect Weldon Johnson and that type of man to speak [for] black men. They are working against each . . . [*words mutilated*] support when they do that. But we know we can speak for ourselves because our leaders are supported by black men. We must determine our own affairs. White people do not undersand us as well as we understand ourselves. Du Bois, Johnson and Pickens! Pickens attempted recently to get a job with the La Follette group.[1] They would not notice him because they would not bother with the Ku Klux Klan issue because the Ku Klux Klan issue is a white man's issue. You talk about the Ku Klux Klan being opposed to the Jew[,] the Catholic and the Negro. Nonsense! The Negro has to fight the Catholic, the Jew and the American white man. When Pickens is trying to get a job he goes from one degree of grace to another. He does not believe in the potency of the Negro; he does not believe the Negro can do anything for himself. President Coolidge has told you, and I am glad he has, "Negroes, damn your souls forever, work for yourselves." (Applause.) You must recognize this one thing— this is a world of races. There is no brotherhood of man anywhere in this world. No such animal exists. This is a world where every race is trying to preserve its own virtue, and we have got to do the selfsame thing. And when you read your history you will see that any race that ever amounted to anything had to pay in blood, money and virtue. No prayer, no Jesus, no Mohammed. It was the will and the determination plus the faith within to crush and to die crushing."

"Some of you," the speaker concluded, "do not agree with me. I cannot expect you all to do so. But I want you to use your brains. I am wholly responsible for what I say. I want you to understand that the Negro has reached a point where he must forget his religious bugaboo and go forth like a man; go forth and do as the white man has done and is doing. Do not stop to think that Jesus will do all because your cause is just. We in Chicago are determined to put over the program. We are determined that Africa be redeemed by and for black men, and we will work for its salvation. Nothing is going to stop us. We will attempt to get it, and if we die in the attempt we will go to our graves and be free." (Applause.)

Bishop George A. McGuire next gained the floor. He said he was very grateful to the chairman for giving him the opportunity to address the assemblage for a few minutes. He did not propose to take issue with the last speaker but to say a few words for the other side.[2] Many present would remember his sermon on Friday morning when he showed that in the Negro's hands were the rod of his political destiny, the rod of his industrial and commercial achievement, the rod of financial acquisition and the rod of spiritual freedom. It would be remembered that he stated then that when the Negro was oppressed all he used was the rod of spiritual freedom—he relied on Jesus. Jesus had stood with him and brought him emancipation through the medium of Victoria and Abraham Lincoln. And the Negro could not now afford to throw Jesus overboard. One extreme was as bad as another.

"I stand here," the speaker continued, "to hold up the idealism of religious freedom—that we write our own theology. What is theology? The knowledge which men have of God, whether by revelation, whether by nature or by their own tuition. In the beginning there was polytheism, many gods, a god for rain, a god for lightning, a god for war, a god for agriculture. There was Ceres, the god of grain; Bacchus, the god of wine, and so on down the line. All men were polytheists. Every man had his own god. Afterwards came the idea of a god for every nation. . . . [*Words mutilated*] Moses came down the idea of a Universal God, a Father for all men and not a national God. But if the white man is going to emphasize his God and make Him a white God and impress Him indelibly upon the children of my race, if they are going to impress that everything black belongs to the devil and hell, I say, let us today and during this convention rewrite theology. (Cheers and applause.) We are not going to throw God overboard. If they will do it in the Windy City, we will hold on to God here." (Applause.)

Printed in *NW*, 9 August 1924. Original headlines omitted.

1. William Pickens, field secretary for the NAACP, served as that organization's representative to the 1924 Progressive party convention which nominated Robert M. La Follette for president. Pickens addressed the delegates, telling them that blacks "had been deceived by both old parties and were ready for independent action" (Belle Case La Follette and Fola La Follette, *Robert M. La Follette, June 14, 1855–June 18, 1925* [New York: Macmillan, 1953], 2: 1,114). Ironically, on the very day of Peters's speech accusing La Follette of ignoring the Ku Klux Klan because it was a "white man's issue," La Follette forthrightly stated his opposition to the Klan (*NYT*, 6 July 1924; David L. Waterhouse, "The Failure of Working Class Politics in America: The Case of the Progressive Movement of 1924" [Ph.D. diss., University of California, Los Angeles, 1982], p. 133).

2. *The Churchman*, a journal of the Episcopal church, reported the discussion of the black deity in the following manner:

A black Deity was discussed by three speakers at the meeting of the Universal Negro Improvement Association in Liberty Hall, New York City, on Aug. 3. The speakers were Marcus Garvey, Dr. J.J. Peters of Chicago, and Bishop George Alexander McGuire, head of the African Orthodox Church.

Garvey declared: "If we worship anyone not in our own image we are worshiping a false God."

Dr. Peters, in a burst of oratorical frenzy, shouted:

"My race comes first. Jesus and the rest come second.

That drew mild rebukes from Garvey and from Bishop McGuire.

"The Negro has always found solace in his religion," the bishop said. "He has been content to let the white man have the earth if he could have Jesus.

"We are not going to throw God overboard. We're going to hold on to Him—but a black God, not a white God. We must have religious freedom to write our own theology."

Several thousand Negroes filled the low, flat frame structure the Garveyites know as Liberty Hall. They were quiet and attentive, and occasionally responded with cheers or "Yeas" to the speakers' declarations. (*The Churchman*, 16 August 1924, p. 27)

Convention Report

[*New York, 4 August 1924*]

MONDAY MORNING SESSION, AUG. 4

The Fourth International Convention of the Negro peoples of the World began its business sessions at 11 a.m., when the Hon. President-General and Provisional President of Africa, declared the meeting open and announced the singing of the hymn, "From Greenland's Icy Mountains." This was followed by the usual prayer laid down in the ritual for the success of the convention.[1]

Hon. Marcus Garvey, presiding as Speaker in the convention, then said: We are unable to perfect our state of organization because of the fact that all the delegates have not yet registered, and I am suggesting, if it meet with the approval of the delegates, that we adjourn until 2 o'clock in order to allow all the delegates to register, so that we may go into the business of the convention.

Hon. S.J. Lee, of Chapter 87, Philadelphia, seconded by Hon. [F].E. Johnson, of Detroi[t], moved the motion for the adjournment until 2 o'clock, which was carried without any dissentient.

The Speaker in adjourning the convention announced that the agenda of the day will be reported from delegates and representatives.

AFTERNOON SESSION, AUG. 4

There was a considerably larger attendance of delegates at their places when the convention resumed at 2 p.m. The usual hymn and prayers were recited by the Hon. President-General.

The minutes of the previous sessions were read by Hon. N.G. Thomas, secretary of the convention, after which on the motion of Delegate W.A. Sampson, of Dayton, O., seconded by Hon. Freeman Martin, of St. Louis, they were confirmed with necessary corrections.

The Speaker then asked the delegates to rise and swore them in accordance with the constitution.

The Speaker stated that the order of the day was reports of delegates and deputies as touching conditions as they were charged to lay them before the convention for the purpose of remedy and legislation. He suggested that one delegate be elected spokesman for each delegation, and also the laying down of a time limit.

On the motion of Delegate Martin, of St. Louis, seconded by Hon. C.H. Bryant, of Panama, the time limit for speakers was fixed at five minutes. It was also decided that delegates speak from their places rather then from the platform in order to save time.

Hon. Dr. J.J. Peters, of Chicago, was the first speaker. He spoke of the progress that his division had been making under his administration. He had taken up the work of the division after a period of maladministration in spite of discouragements on the part of enemies of the organization, and at the . . . [words mutilated] much of the practice. They were progressing with the purchase of their property and had initiated educational and other schemes for the membership. They were proud also of the . . . [line mutilated] the auxiliaries that were exist[ent] in any other division, and that the membership was very much increased.

Hon. Jacob Chambers, of East St. Louis, said that under his management, which dated from March 29, last, the division had been progressing very satisfactorily. He had found after having been a member of various churches and organizations that the U.N.I.A. seemed to offer most for satisfying the needs and wants of the Negro.

He had brought with him a report of the state of his division, which showed that since the reorganization there had been a membership of over 300, the debts were all wiped out, and there was a substantial balance in the treasury.

Hon. R.H. Bachelor,[2] of Oriente, Cuba, said he represented several divisions in that republic, and the work was progressing, but the most urgent need there was the presence of a commissioner, who would be able to explain throughly the aims and objects of the association. The presence of such a man would do good, not only to the people themselves, but to the association in general, as there were many who are in a position to help the parent body financially and otherwise. He also complained of the quarantine system which prevails in Cuba, whereby there is discrimination shown against our colored men and women after landing in Cuba, the whites being allowed to go free while our people are detained, and are made to suffer untold hardships while in quarantine. At the same time, he stated that the Cuban Government is in sympathy with the movement so that a commissioner, competent to represent the association, would benefit the members financially, politically, religiously and otherwise.

Hon. Freeman Martin, of St. Louis, said at one time his division had boasted of some thousands of members, but among them were several professional and business men who proved to be self-seekers and grafters, the result was that there were splits and the division dwindled in numbers. Since he had taken over the administration things were progressing owing to the fact among other things that the financial system had been improved, and many of the grafters were no longer in the movement. An organization, called the Oriental Trading Company, purporting to be affiliated with the parent body, had done a great deal of mischief by taking away many of the members until the President-General had notified them that it had nothing to do with the Universal. He spoke of the housing problem, which was the most difficult they had to handle, there being many restrictions to the occupation of certain parts of the city by our people.[3] This, however, was being remedied.

Hon. H.C. Holland, of North Carolina, said conditions in the divisions which he represented are fine, the people of the little towns of Winston-Salem, living without any segregation, and there being no housing difficulty.[4] The people had taken well to the organization, and the membership was increasing satisfactorily.

Hon. R.H. McDowell, of Blytheville, Ark.,[5] said that the people, who were mostly farmers, were struggling with organization in face of the opposition of the preachers and others, among them some professional men. But the organization had had the sympathetic consideration of the town authorities so much so that when members of another Negro organization [fought?] [to prevent them meeting in the] town, complaining that the aims and objects of the association were not satisfactory, the mayor not only gave them permission but recommended the work as being very good for the race.

Hon. R.A. Martin,[6] of Camaguey, Cuba, said he indorsed many of the remarks [made by the delegate from] Oriente. He urged the sending of a commissioner to the island who could talk Spanish and French, as there were thousands of Spanish and French-speaking people in that island who were thirsting to learn more of the working of the organization. He also urged the distribution in those languages of more literature for the same purpose.[7]

Hon. J. B. Simmons, of Blytheville, Ark., said he came from the rural part of the country and his people had sent him to find out several things. He first wanted to know something of certain resolutions which they had sent up to the convention, and, secondly, they wanted some definite information concerning the ship that was expected to sail on September 1 next. Their division had had many setbacks, but still they were doing well. At a recent meeting the secretary said that he was 100 per cent Negro. Another member said he was 125 per cent Negro, and that was the opinion of lots of folks in his section of the country.

Hon. R. H. Crosgrove, of Natchez, Miss.,[8] said he pastored a little church of about 500 members, and every one was a member of the association, as he was of opinion that if he was to be a spiritual leader he should also be able to lead them in their temporal affairs. He attended the convention to see things for himself so that he could take back to the people who trusted him a true report of the work of the movement.

Hon. A. G. Ellengburg [Ellenberg], of Gary, Ind., said the people in Gary were in need of employment, the steel mills having closed down.[9] In some of the shops there notices were posted to the effect that the white traders catered only to white trade. That was a serious state of things. They also were encountering opposition from the professional men and pastors, but the work was progressing satisfactorily.

Miss Hattie Johnson, of Baltimore, spoke of her work in spite of opposition of those who, while acting as officials of the U.N.I.A., were also connected with the N.A.A.C.P. The result of this was that the division had lost a very large number of the members. She also complained of the treatment of our people at the hospitals and also the bad conditions at the homes of the people. She also complained of the stand taken by the pastors, but promised to continue the work in spite of all opposition.

Mr. M. Askernese, of Farrel[l], Pa., said that employment was scarce for the people in his district.[10] The preachers no longer openly fought the association there because they found that fighting gave it more strength. He had heard the remarks about the White Christ, and he had taken out the picture from its frame and was only awaiting the time when the proper pictures will be published to replace the white Christ by a black one. He related how a near riot was averted by the confidence the authorities had in the U.N.I.A. and its members.

Hon. A. Mills, of Newark, N.J.,[11] said that much of the success of his division was due to the fact that they had a very beautiful hall. They had lost some of their members, owing to dissensions in their ranks, and chiefly owing to the disobedience of an ex-secretary. They had difficulty in getting satisfactory treatment at the hands of the employment agents there and ha[d] as a result decided to open their own employment agency. He asked that some one from the parent body be sent to straighten out some of their difficulties.

Hon. J. Smith, of New York Division No. 1 spoke of the fact that his division was the parent and spoke of the [work that had been done in Liberty] Hall and by the auxiliaries.

Hon. M. Daniels, of Brooklyn, No. 2, complained of the neglect of that division by the parent body, and asked that more attention be paid to them.

. . . [*line mutilated*] Indianapolis, Ind., said that had it not been for dissensions in the division much more progress would have been recorded. He had, however, done much to improve the financial standing and the work in general. He had come to observe things and to take back a report which he [hoped wo]uld enable them to work even more for the redemption of Africa.

Hon. G.H. Logan, of Atlanta, Ga., said his people were all working towards the realization of the program of the association.

Delegate Walker, of Delaware, said that though their membership was small still they were all 125 per cent, as had been stated by a previous speaker.

Hon. W.L. Carter, of Norfolk, Va., said that the work had been hampered by the work of ex-officers who had sought to tea[r] them asunder and who had establi[sh]ed some organization bearing the same name, with an alleged charter from Richmond. He had, however, determined to stick to the association, in spite of all the efforts of the enemy.

Hon. E.B. Grant,[12] of Bermuda, reported on the progress of the division in that colony, spoke of the ruse he had to make in order to get to the convention, and then complained of the officials who had been drawing the moneys of the association without working for it or without any authority. He asked that someone be sent to Bermuda at the expense of that division to straighten out their affairs.

Rev. E.J. Smith, of Jersey City, N.J., explained the condition of the division in that city. He said the pastors were not opposed to it and the membership was satisfactory.

Hon. J.B. Salisbury, of Homestead, Pa., also spoke of being both a spiritual and temporal leader of his people. They were anxious to know more about the Black Cross Company, as many of them were prepared to go to Africa and establish industries there.

Hon. S.R. Weeks [Wheat], of Chicago Division, No. 313, said he had found the division in chaos, from which he had managed to bring it at the present time. The membership was growing, although they had difficulty with professional and other men who had entered the movement for the purpose of exploiting the people.

Hon. H. Clark, of Clarksburg, W. Va., said in his district there were about 20 divisions within an area of 50 miles, but many of them were between the hawk and the buzzard.[13] He came to ask for better supervision of the work of the association in that section of West Virginia.

Hon. Mrs. H[enrietta] Red[d], of Gary, Indiana, spoke of the large membership of h[er] division and of h[er] connection with the A.M.E. Church, the two organizations working satisfactorily together, although there were many members who sought to oppose the work and to take them away from allegiance to the parent body.

Hon. E. Alle[y]ne,[14] of Toronto, Canada, made an appeal to the convention to send officers more often to the division to help along the work. Officers were sent to Detroit and other nearby points, but did not cross the border.

Hon. Edward Allen, of Pittsburgh, Pa., said his division was getting along fine and they were doing good work among the auxiliaries. The preachers had been hard on the organization. The people of those parts were anxious to hear more about the association, as they did not well understand the aims and objects, and he was doing a great deal to help them. As to labor conditions, Mexicans were now being employed to replace the Negro,[15] and this had caused many fights, as the people did not understand Spanish.

The speaker at this stage suggested adjournment and the fixing of the time for the meetings.

On the motion of Hon. Freeman Martin, seconded by Hon. S.J. Lee, the hours fixed were from 10 a.m. to 12 noon and from 2 p.m. to 5 p.m. The evening sessions, from 8:30 to 11 p.m.

The adjournment was then taken at 5 p.m.

MONDAY EVENING, AUGUST 4

The convention assembled at 8:30 p.m., the speaker, Hon. Marcus Garvey, in the chair.

Prayers were said and then the minutes were read and confirmed, Hon. C.[H.] Bryant, of Costa Rica, and Hon S.J. Lee, of Philadelphia, moving and seconding the motion for confirmation.

The order of the day was then proceeded with.

Hon. C.H. Bryant, commissioner for Panama, Costa Rica and Nicaragua, then delivered his report, which dealt at length with conditions in his field. He detailed a number of vicissitudes through which several units in his field had passed, and announced that he had succeeded in overcoming all opposition and had placed the various branches and chapters in a position where they would be able to go forward successfully on their own account.

Hon. E.T. Winston, of the Highlands Heights Chapter,[16] said his was a small community, with only 500 Negroes, but the spirit existing there was 100 per cent for the cause.

Hon. M. Spencer, Cincinnati, dealt chiefly with the deplorable living conditions for Negroes in Cincinnati. It was time, she said, that Negro women exerted themselves on behalf of their children, who would be the U.N.I.A. of tomorrow. Women must take a leaf from white women's book and support their men with the ballot.

Hon. Maggie Scott,[17] Cincinnati, endorsed the Hon. Spencer's remarks.

Hon. Issac Kellum,[18] Columbus, Ohio, dealt with the internal affairs of the Columbus Division. Dissension was [rife, he said, and an effort should be] made speedily to straighten out affairs.

Hon. J.W. Ross, Fort Smith, Ark., told of the imprisonment of certain members of the division on lying testimony of jealous and wicked Negroes.[19] He was glad to be able to say that the men had been freed and exonerated by the court, and influential white people in Arkansas had endorsed the U.N.I.A. and its principles.

Hon. Wm. H. Wood, Hartford, Conn., declared that Hartford and the other communities in Connecticut needed a commissioner, a real worker, to supervise the work of the association.

Hon. W.O. Sampson, Dayton, said the Dayton Division was progressing splendidly. He asked the hearty cooperation of the parent body.

Hon. J.B. Eaton, Berkeley, W.Va., said his community stood four-square behind the organization and was prepared to respond to every appeal of the parent body, especially in connection with the purchase of a ship by the Black Cross Navigation & Trading Company.

Hon. P.E. Johnson, Cleveland, spoke of internal affairs in the division. He appealed to the administration to hold up the hands of presidents, who according to the constitution, were supposed to exercise the same control as the president-general exercised over the movement.

Hon. H. Lowry, Portland [Hartford?], Conn., said Connecticut was in need of a strong man to supervise the divisions. The spirit was there and the finances were there. All that was needed was direction.

Hon. F.A. Toote, Philadelphia chapter, dealt with economic, industrial and social conditions in Philadelphia, which, he said, boded no good for the Negro. Georgia was moving up North, and day by day it was becoming clearer that the U.N.I.A. was the only salvation. Owing to disloyal officers the Philadelphia Division was temporarily at a standstill, but he was glad to report that under his leadership, which he exercised temporarily, the chapter had added over 500 members in two months. He condemned the attitude of divisions in expecting the parent body to set their house in order. They do it for themselves. By the same token Negroes should not sit supinely by and say when a ship was procured[,] support would be forthcoming. If the ship was to be procured support should be given now. The Philadelphia Chapter, he was glad to state, was giving its best in this direction.

Hon. H.B. Williams, Boston, gave an encouraging report of the progress of the work in his community.

Hon. G.M. Brown, Miami, Fla., said Miami was cursed with some nearsighted preachers who sought to embarrass the movement. But the mass of people in Miami stood 100 per cent. for the cause.

Hon. Amy Lawson, Chicago, told of the splendid work the juveniles were doing.

Hon. James A. Hassel[l],[20] Seattle, Wash., in a very informative address, stressed the absolute need of the association acquiring ships. Ships made every nation great. They made the Japanese great. The Japanese in 1876 borrowed $275,000 from France for this purpose, and when the note fell due, they borrowed a million from England to satisfy their obligation and to carry on.[21]

So they grew, Negroes must do likewise, never forgetting, however, that ships required money, and more money for their operation. Sixty-six years of age, he came from a family of seafarers, and his knowledge of ships and shipping had prompted the division to send him to New York City to impress upon the convention the importance of holding up the hands of the administration in the shipping project.

At this stage the adjournment was taken, the Speaker announcing after the delegates had all made their reports the convention would proceed to discuss the formation of a Negro political union.

Printed in *NW*, 16 August 1924. Original headlines abbreviated.

1. The usual prayer of the UNIA meetings, "Prayer for Opening of Meeting, Dedicated to the Universal Negro Improvement Association of the World," was written by John E. Bruce (*Garvey Papers* 1: 278).

2. Richard Hilton Bachelor was also the official reporter for UNIA Division 164 in Guantánamo, Cuba (*NW*, 5 September 1923).

3. When blacks began to migrate to St. Louis, this city, the largest in the southern border states, reacted quickly with restrictive covenants to enforce segregated housing, a move that was in fact begun in 1910, earlier than in most northern cities. In 1917 in a public referendum, the populace voted in favor of housing segregation, and by 1923 the St. Louis Real Estate Exchange passed a referendum that stipulated that none of its members would sell property to blacks outside of specified areas. Most of the arrangements were neighborhood covenants in which neighbors within a particular area agreed among themselves not to sell to blacks. The covenants were called the "St. Louis Real Estate Exchange Restriction," and the exchange was a trustee to the covenants established in the city. The number of covenants rose dramatically in the 1920s and continued to rise through the 1930s; they were not successfully defeated until the late 1940s (Leland Hilligoss, St. Louis Public Library, to Robert A. Hill, 2 October 1984; Herman H. Long, *People vs. Property: Race Restrictive Covenants in Housing* [Nashville: Fisk University Press, 1947]; Davis McEntire, *Residence and Race* [Berkeley and Los Angeles: University of California Press, 1960], p. 244; Clement E. Vose, *Caucasians Only: The Supreme Court, the NAACP, and the Restrictive Covenant Cases* [Berkeley and Los Angeles: University of California Press, 1959], pp. 10–11, 100–121; *Baltimore Afro-American*, 2 May 1924; James Neal Primm, *Lion of the Valley: St. Louis, Missouri* [Boulder, Colo.: Pruett Publishing Co., 1981], pp. 435–441).

4. Winston-Salem is a manufacturing city located in central North Carolina. In the 1920s it was a rapidly growing community of almost fifty thousand, with textiles and tobacco processing among its leading economic activities. The community's black population was large—twenty-one thousand in 1920—having more than doubled in the previous decade. Many blacks were employed in Winston-Salem as industrial workers. Integrated neighborhoods had long existed in the city, but in 1912 the city government tried to reverse the condition by enacting one of the nation's first residential segregation laws. During the First World War, racial tension escalated markedly with an influx of black migrants. In November 1918 an attempted lynching developed into a major riot; twenty-five people died during several days of violent conflict between blacks and whites.

Winston-Salem possessed the largest concentration of Garveyites in North Carolina. In 1925–1926 the parent body reported almost two hundred paid members, despite the hostility of what a local UNIA leader earlier described as "many Negroes, who like to imagine themselves as belonging to the aristocrats of the race" (*NW*, 10 November 1923). The Winston-Salem division was still sporadically active during the late 1930s (membership lists, 1925–1926, NN-Sc, UNIA Central Division records, box 2, a.16; Report by Samuel Haynes, ca. 1936, NN-Sc, UNIA Central Division records, box 9, d. 33; Bertha Hampton Miller, "Blacks in Winston-Salem, 1895–1920: Community Development in an Era of Benevolent Paternalism" [Ph.D. diss., Duke University, 1981], pp. 116, 118, 125, 131–135, 196–213, 276, 281).

5. In 1920 Blytheville, situated in the extreme northeastern tip of Arkansas, was a regional agricultural center having a population of nearly sixty-five hundred, of whom about one thousand were black. In the decade after 1910, the community experienced rapid growth, and during World War I, it enjoyed a cotton boom. During the early twenties, however, agricultural recession struck, and the arrival of the boll weevil in 1924 drove many sharecroppers from the area.

Little is known of UNIA activities in Blytheville, but it is possible that antiblack agitation in neighboring Caruthersville, Mo., which included night-riding and other forms of white violence, influenced growth of the town's Garveyite movement. Several black sharecroppers who had been driven out by these disturbances resided in Blytheville and may have have been a factor in encouraging racial militancy among blacks. Thus one Blytheville UNIA leader declared that the "policy of the white man was this. . .[,] we are only letting you stay here until we are ready to turn you out, when we no longer need you" (*NW*, 8 August 1924).

By 1926 the Blytheville division reported fewer than ten dues-paying members, but in spite of this decline, discontent continued to characterize the area's black population. Northeastern Arkansas and adjacent areas of Missouri became the organizing base for the Southern Tenant Farmers Union in the late 1930s. The union's vice-president, E. B. ("Britt") McKinney, came from nearby Tyronza, Ark. This tenant farmer turned preacher was himself a former Garveyite (membership lists, 1925–1926, NN-Sc, UNIA Central Division records, box 2, a.16; H. L. Mitchell, executive director, Southern Tenant Farmers Union, to Robert A. Hill, 13 April 1984; H. L. Mitchell, *Mean Things Happening in this Land* [Montclair, N. J.: Allanhead, Osmun and Co., 1979], pp. 17–27, 36, 158–161; Federal Writers' Project, Works Progress Administration, *Arkansas* [New York: Hastings House, 1941], pp. 131–135; Lee R. Dew, "The J. L. C. and E. R. R. and the Opening of the 'Sunk Lands' of Northeast Arkansas," *Arkansas Historical Quarterly* 27, no. 1 [spring 1968]: 33–39).

6. R. A. Martin was division president in Florida, Cuba, in 1923 (*NW*, 21 July 1923).

7. A reference to the thousands of Haitians who had emigrated to Cuba. Most had come originally as wage laborers to work in the sugar plantations of Oriente Province. By 1900 Oriente, whose primary crop was sugar, was dominated by United States capital investment and large landholdings; the United Fruit Co. alone owned 200,000 acres in the area. Following a brief but bitter insurrection by local blacks in 1912, the United Fruit Co. received government permission to import Haitian workers to work on its Oriente plantations. Cuban government restrictions on the importation of nonwhite labor were dropped, and between 1913 and 1925 large numbers of Haitians and other West Indians entered Cuba. Over 81,000 Haitians came to Cuba between 1913 and 1921.

Many Haitians were seasonal workers who returned home following the harvest, but others remained in Cuba. Some stayed in rural areas, but others moved to the cities, where they became part of Afro-Cuban culture. It was from the ranks of these Haitian workers that the French-speaking support of the UNIA in Cuba was drawn (Ramiro Guerra y Sanchez, *Sugar and Society in the Caribbean: An Economic History of Cuban Agriculture* [New Haven: Yale University Press, 1964], pp. 144–146; Hugh Thomas, *Cuba* [New York: Harper and Row, 1971], pp. 129, 131, 241, 523–526, 540, 684; Robert B. Hoernel, "Sugar and Social Change in Oriente Cuba," *Latin American Studies* 4, no. 6 [November 1976]: 215–249).

8. Natchez, Miss., is a small port and commercial center on the Mississippi river. During the antebellum period, Natchez was one of the South's richest boom towns, but after the Civil War, it entered into a long period of commercial decline, which was compounded by the arrival of the boll weevil in the early 1900s. Located in the midst of a plantation region, Natchez's economy depended on the cotton trade, but textile and lumber mills were also present by the First World War. In 1920 Natchez had a population of about 12,500, having grown little during the preceding years, about 7,000 of whom were black. Most of the Afro-American population of Natchez worked in the lumber mills or as domestics.

R. H. Crosgrove's account of the strength of the UNIA in Natchez is well substantiated. The city reported between 77 and 133 dues-paying UNIA members, making it the largest division in Mississippi. The UNIA's mass following was even larger: seven hundred blacks reportedly signed a petition for Garvey's release from prison in 1927. In the words of a Garveyite leader in the mid-1930s, Natchez had one of the "most loyal divisions in America" (Report by Samuel Haynes, ca. 1936, NN-Sc, UNIA Central Division records, box 9, d.33).

As late as 1941 a sociological study of Natchez reported that "a few lower-class individuals still maintain a rapidly dying branch of the Universal Negro Improvement Association and speak with nostalgia of Marcus Garvey. This organization is not conceived as a threat to the caste structure, however" (Allison Davis et al., *Deep South; A Social Anthropological Study of Caste and Class* [Chicago: University of Chicago Press, 1941], p. 249; membership lists, 1925–1926, NN-Sc, UNIA Central Division records, box 2, a.13; Natchez UNIA Division 704 to Calvin Coolidge, 23 May 1927, WNRC, RG 204, file 42-793; Jill Tempest, Natchez Public Library, to Robert A. Hill, 6 September 1984; U. S. Bureau of the Census, *Fourteenth Census of the United States, 1920* (Washington, D. C.: GPO, 1921), 1: 243, 3: 541).

9. A severe depression hit the steel industry in the spring of 1924, and by June, United States output had fallen to about 45 percent of capacity, the lowest level since 1921 (*NYT*, 22 June 1924).

10. In the early 1920s, Farrell, Pa., situated in the northwest corner of the state, was a small industrial city of almost sixteen thousand. Dominated by a United States Steel factory which employed nearly half the population, Farrell underwent significant growth during the period. By 1940 it contained a large number of southern European immigrants. Farrell's UNIA division undertook a variety of economic enterprises. For example, like other divisions it provided burial benefits to its members, making this a focus of fundraising efforts. The local UNIA also pursued cultural endeavors, soliciting funds for a piano in order to stage musical programs. The division proved more enduring than most, as it was still operating as late as 1936.

The local body's delegate to the 1924 convention, Michael Askernese, also served as president of the division. Little is known of his leadership save for his occasional complaints of neglect by national officials. He once wrote to the *Negro World*: "We would like to have some of the representatives of the parent body visit us a little oftener" (NW, 31 March 1923). No UNIA speakers had been to Farrell for the preceding six months, he noted (report by Samuel Haynes, ca. 1936, NN-Sc, UNIA Central Division records, box 9, d.33; U.S. Bureau of the Census, *Fourteenth Census*, 1: 287; Federal Writers' Project, Works Progress Administration, *Pennsylvania* [New York: Oxford University Press, 1940], p. 577).

11. By the early twentieth century, Newark, N.J., had already emerged as a major industrial city. It was a manufacturing center with a diversified economic base, and its leading industries included leather goods, electrical machinery, and other machine-shop products. In the twenties it was the fifteenth-largest city in the United States, having over 400,000 inhabitants. Southern and eastern European immigrants represented the bulk of the population, and in 1925 two-thirds of Newark's residents were either first- or second-generation Americans.

Newark's black community numbered about 17,000 in 1920; its numbers increased rapidly during the teens and twenties, but it still represented a relatively small minority. Though no major riots occurred immediately after the First World War, blacks in Newark experienced the same prejudicial treatment in housing and employment reported elsewhere. As Newark Garveyite A.J. Mann stated at the 1920 national convention, "conditions in the North are practically the same as in the South, as far as discrimination against the colored people is concerned" (*Garvey Papers* 2: 533).

In 1924 the Newark UNIA occupied part of a building at 8 Lackawanna Avenue. Because of the city's proximity to Harlem, Newark became an early focus of UNIA activity. Garvey visited repeatedly on behalf of the organization, and Newark sent full delegations to most of the UNIA international conventions and meetings. In 1925–1926, there were three chapters and one division in Newark, with an aggregate paid membership of as many as two hundred. This made it one of the stronger centers of Garveyite support, and the movement remained significant well into the 1930s. According to a leader writing about 1936, the Newark UNIA withstood "many efforts of the Father Divine Cult and the Japanese Movement to destroy the division" (report by Samuel Haynes, ca. 1936, NN-Sc, UNIA Central Division records, box 9, d.33). Despite this claim, however, Father Divine did attract many of the members of the UNIA (membership lists, 1925–1926, NN-Sc, UNIA Central Division records, box 2, a.16; *BM* 2, no. 3, [September–October 1935]: 10–12; U.S. Bureau of the Census, *Fourteenth Census*, 1: 76, 9: 927–928; John T. Cunningham, *Newark* [Newark: New Jersey Historical Society, 1966], pp. 272, 278, 282; Clement Alexander Price, "The Afro-American Community of Newark, 1917–1947: A Social History" [Ph.D. diss., Rutgers University, 1975], pp. 34, 96).

12. Rev. E.B. Grant headed the Bermuda division of the UNIA. He also attended the 1922 convention as a delegate (*NW*, 28 July 1923).

13. Located in the northern portion of West Virginia, Clarksburg was a booming mining and manufacturing city in the early 1920s. Its population was almost twenty-eight thousand in 1920, having tripled in the previous decade. The city's black community of about twelve hundred was relatively small, but the black community was larger in the surrounding coal mining district. In 1924 Clarksburg acquired a degree of national prominence as the home of John W. Davis (1873–1955), the Democratic nominee for president of that year.

The assessment of the strength of the Garvey movement in the area is well documented. In 1922 a Garveyite leader referred to the "Negro miners in West Virginia, a large number of whom were members of the U.N.I.A." (*Garvey Papers* 4: 861). By mid-decade West Virginia boasted forty-four UNIA divisions and chapters, with at least twenty-two in the Monongahela Valley adjacent to Clarksburg.

This concentration of UNIA strength probably owed a great deal to changes in mine management in the area. Blacks had long been employed in the southern reaches of West Virginia, but in the northern part of the state the heavily unionized white miners had largely excluded blacks until the 1920s, when black laborers from the deep South entered the region in increasing numbers.

"In 1923 there were not more than 2,600 Negro miners in the entire Fairmont District, but by 1926 there were 3,359 Negro miners there" (Darold T. Barnum, *The Negro in the Bituminous Coal Mining Industry* [Philadelphia: University of Pennsylvania Press, 1970], p. 21). Blacks generally were employed as strikebreakers during the "major strikes" which characterized the decade, particularly the important strike which occurred in 1925 in the northern West Virginia mines (*ibid.*, p. 21). The racial tension which resulted probably contributed both to substantial Ku Klux Klan strength in the area and to Garveyite agitation as well. In the words of a contemporary observer, "In some places in the northern counties where racial animosity of the Ku Klux Klan was highest there was a corresponding growth of Garveyism" (James Tamplin Laing, "The Negro Miner in West Virginia" [Ph.D. diss., Ohio State University, 1933], p. 488).

Little is known about specific UNIA activities in the community. Although in 1925 three hundred local residents reportedly signed a petition for the pardon of Marcus Garvey, in the following year the parent body reported only eleven dues-paying members in the city. As late as 1936 Garveyite agitation continued in the general region, with several divisions reported active (El Angelo Heilprin and Louis Heilprin, eds., *Lippincott's New Gazetteer of the World* [London and Philadelphia: Lippincott, 1905], pp. 422–423; U.S. Bureau of the Census, *Fourteenth Census*, 1: 313, 2: 359, 3: 1110; *Baltimore Afro-American*, 15 August 1924; report by Samuel Haynes, ca. 1936, NN-Sc, UNIA Central Division records, box 9, d.33; E.B. Lovelace, vice-president, Clarksburg division, UNIA, to the attorney general, 5 November 1925, WNRC, RG 204, file 42-793).

14. E. Alleyne of Toronto was his division's reporter to the *Negro World* (*NW*, 26 January 1924).

15. In April 1923 the Bethlehem Steel Corp. of Pennsylvania, in cooperation with the Mexican consulate of San Antonio, Tex., contracted with Texan employment agencies to recruit about one thousand Mexican laborers for unskilled work in the plant. Following the onset of the depression in the steel industry in 1924, however, many of these Mexican workers left Bethlehem or took other employment in the city (Paul S. Taylor, *Mexican Labor in the United States* [Berkeley and Los Angeles: University of California Press, 1932], 2: 1–24).

16. The location of the Highland Heights UNIA chapter (No. 76) remains unclear. According to UNIA membership lists, it was found in Bedford, just south of Cleveland; but the *Negro World* on one occasion refers to it as in Columbus, halfway across the state from Bedford. Little is known of the activities of the Highland Heights chapter. In 1924 it reportedly forwarded funds to the parent body, and the chapter still functioned in 1930. Garveyite activities continued in the Cleveland area into the late thirties (*NW*, 14 June 1924, 3 May 1930; report of Samuel Haynes, ca. 1936, NN-Sc, UNIA Central Division records, box 9, d.33; Heilprin and Heilprin, eds., *Lippincott's New Gazetteer of the World*, p. 185).

17. Maggie Scott was the lady president of the Cincinnati UNIA division (*NW*, 20 October 1923).

18. Isaac Kellum served as president of the Columbus, Ohio, division of the UNIA (*NW*, 20 October 1923).

19. In the early 1920s Fort Smith was a growing banking and manufacturing city and an economic center for the eastern portion of Arkansas. Located in the northern tip of the cotton belt, Fort Smith was a community of almost thirty thousand, of whom about thirty-six hundred were black. Many of the blacks were employed as factory hands and reportedly enjoyed a higher standard of living than those employed in cotton cultivation. There is some evidence that Fort Smith did not have a history of strict residential segregation.

Both the NAACP and the UNIA were represented in Fort Smith, the UNIA division being especially active. It functioned at least from 1923 to 1926, during which time repeated visits from Garveyite officials were made. The local division, unlike some others, found favor with certain community religious leaders, for its 1924 annual session was held in the African Methodist Episcopal church and was addressed by the pastor of the congregation.

No information has been discovered of the arrests of the UNIA members referred to here (*NW*, 29 September, 6 October and 29 December 1923, 3 April, 19 April, and 6 September 1924; membership lists, 1925–1926, NN-Sc, UNIA Central Division records, box 2, a. 16; Heilprin and Heilprin, eds., *Lippincott's New Gazetteer of the World*, p. 666; U.S. Bureau of the Census, *Fourteenth Census*, 1: 181, 2: 117, 3: 90; Federal Writers' Project, Works Progress Administration, *Arkansas*, p. 143; *Crisis* 20, no. 4 [August 1920]: 181).

20. James Hassell was a UNIA member and BSL representative in Seattle since 1920 (DNA, RG 65, file OG 185161, 16 March 1920).

21. In 1867 the Japanese Bakufu shogunate, with French capital and guidance, begain work

on the Yokosuka Iron Foundry and dockyards. The project was completed in 1871, despite the overthrow of the Bakufu in 1868. In 1870 the new Meiji government secured a $1-million loan from British banks for the construction of a railway line from Yokohama to Tokyo (E. H. Norman, *Origins of the Modern Japanese State* [New York: Pantheon Books, 1975], pp. 222–229).

Convention Report

[*New York, 5 August 1924*]

TUESDAY MORNING, AUGUST 5

The convention was called to order at 10 a.m. Hon. Marcus Garvey, speaker, occupied the chair.

Prayers having been read, the minutes of the previous session were read. On the motion of Hon. S. V. Robertson, seconded by Hon. J. J. Thomas, Pritchard, Ala.,[1] the minutes were confirmed.

The order of the day, the presentation of reports by the delegates was then proceeded with.

Hon. J. J. Thomas, Pritchard, Ala., said he represented Pritchard and Mobile, Ala. The divisions were making splendid progress, though he must say some preachers opposed their efforts.

Hon. A. R. Patesaul [Patespaul],[2] Alliance, Ohio, gave a very encouraging report on the conduct of the work in his community. Division 712, he said, though young, bowed to no branch of the association in its loyalty and contribution to the cause of Africa. Their units were all well organized, and the mainstay of the division. The preachers were the life and soul of the division.

Hon. William Ware, Cincinnati, said he represented the parent body of the West, the Cincinnati Division, of which he was president. He inveighed in strong terms against the tendency of members of the organization to ascribe all their ills to Du Bois, the preachers and the knockers. What was required, he said (and the convention cheered the statement) was attention to the efforts of rascally Negroes within the division who were the embodiment of faction and discord. Speaking of living conditions in Cincinnati, he described them as execrable. Negroes were forced to live in dog houses, and the economic situation was becoming grave—work was alarmingly scarce.

Hon. I. Curry, Monongah, W. Va.,[3] said she had no grievances to ventilate. She had been sent to the convention to ascertain exactly in what way and what measure her division could assist the parent body in the various projects it had embarked upon. They stood ready to give of their all to the furtherance and triumphant putting over of the program.

Hon. J. A. Craighen [Craigen],[4] Detroit, said he represented the second greatest division of the association, second only to New York. The economic situation there was better than in the average city, thanks to the Ford factories, in which Negroes were employed on equal terms with whites. It was true, however, that the foreman whom Ford employed did not carry out what Ford wills to the letter—they were victims of prejudice and discrimination.[5] The Detroit Division was on the upgrade and was determined to stand by the cause to the last man and to the last dollar.

Hon. D.H. Kyle, Laura Lee, W.Va.,[6] laid stress on the opposition the association encountered from certain quarters. This opposition was, however, being met successfully, and in time would be completely dissipated.

At this stage the speaker asked the delegates to confine their reports to the general situation in their communities. He further suggested that the presentation of reports be concluded with the close of the morning session, so as to permit during the afternoon session the discussion of the formation of a Negro political union.

Hon. S.J. Lee, Philadelphia, reported that his chapter was making splendid progress. The living conditions were bad, but, thanks to the U.N.I.A., there was a silver lining to the dark cloud.

Hon. W. Wallace, Chicago, in an address of much warmth and power, challenged the spirit exhibited by a couple of the members to underestimate the importance of intelligence as a pre-requisite of those who would guide the U.N.I.A. If the movement is to attain the maximum success it must have intelligent and educated men at the helm. It was silly and stupid to attack the preachers or any established institution. The duty of the U.N.I.A. was to win over established institutions. This could not be done by knocking. His experience was that the preachers were for the most [part?] antagonized in those communities where the U.N.I.A. stood in need of intelligent leadership. It was the old story of the U.N.I.A. being criticized and harassed through an imperfect presentation of its aims and objects. He was glad to relate that in Michigan and Illinois, during the course of his labors as a field representative of the association, he had witnessed the conversion of preachers and, indeed, all ranks of the community to the cause through the intelligent leadership of the men at the head of divisions.

Hon. F.E. Johnson, Detroit, next rose to speak.

Exception was taken to his gaining the floor in the order of the day on the ground that another delegate from Detroit had already spoken.

By motion, however, unanimously carried, he was accorded the special privilege of addressing the convention.

The Hon. Mr. Johnson prefaced his remarks by taking exception to the fact that a special motion had been necessary for him to gain the floor. He explained that though he was the President of the Detroit Division, he was also supervisor of the divisions in the suburbs and neighboring vicinity of Detroit, and in that capacity he had an indisputable right to speak. He had organized several divisions around Detroit.

He endorsed the remarks of the Hon. Craighen as to the economic conditions existing. He stated that the Detroit Division was now a power in Detroit. Realizing the power of politics and the ballot, the division, 7,000 strong, had registered, and politicians were now courting them, conscious of the power they wielded. To all those who approached him he had made it clear that the U.N.I.A. had no special candidate at present. Their votes would be cast for the man who would conserve and protect their interests. Detroit was ready to support the association, with all its resources.

Hon. Bryson Hall [Hale],[7] Milwaukee, said his community was in line, heart and soul.

Hon. K. Baxter, Jamaica, said Jamaica was a ripe field in which U.N.I.A. sentiment had been created. He asked the parent body to send out a strong man to reap the fruits for the association and the cause of Negro freedom. The people were strong for the acquisition of ships.

Hon. S.V. Robertson,[8] commissioner for Louisiana and Mississippi, said Louisiana was 100 per cent for the cause, and Mississippi was fast getting there. He had organized 16 divisions, and he found popular opinion solid for the U.N.I.A. The association had recently won a brilliant victory in New Orleans, La., where two members of the association accused of having slain Dr. Eason, were liberated by a jury and the name of the association cleared.

Hon. J.L. Simmons, Charleston, Mo.,[9] said his division was getting along nicely and becoming a power in the community.

At this stage Hon. Peters, Chicago, moved that after the morning session all reports of delegates be suspended, and the chair use its judgment from time to time in calling upon such delegates as may have a pressing report to present to make their reports.

Hon. Jackson, Georgia, seconded, and the motion was carried unanimously. The convention then adjourned until 2:30 by common consent.

TUESDAY AFTERNOON, AUG. 5

The convention resumed at 2:30 p.m. The Speaker, Hon. Marcus Garvey, in the chair.

After prayers the minutes of the previous session were read and confirmed.

The order of the day was then proceeded with—discussion of the formation of a Negro political union.

The Speaker outlined the administration's viewpoint. He emphasized that the Universal Negro Improvement Association was not a political organization, but, according to its constitution, the association had a right to organize under its jurisdiction such departments as would tend to help carry out the objects laid down. The association felt the time had come to play an important part in the politics of the world; the time had come when the American Negro, and Negroes throughout the world, should vote solidly to carry out the principles of the association. Politics was the science that protected those human rights not protected by law, and if there was a race whose rights were not protected by law, that race was the Negro race. The association intended to play an important part in the coming Presidential election. The votes of four million Negroes in the United States would be mobilized for that purpose.

Hon. Freeman L. Martin, St. Louis, said it was indisputable that such a union was necessary.

Hon. D.H. Kyle, Clarksburg, W.Va., said the formation of a political union would assuredly assist the association in putting over its program.

Hon. William Wallace, Illinois, said he considered this one of the most important steps the association was about to take. With such a union, Haiti, the Phillipines and Liberia could be helped in their fight for independence and expansion.

Hon. J.J. Peters, Chicago, warned that care must be taken to checkmate the political grafter.

Hon. J.B. Eaton, Norfolk, Va., said he trusted the administration had envisaged plans which would foil the self-seeking.

Hon. [V.] Wattley, New York, deprecated the distrust indicated by the previous two speakers.

Hon. Lowry, Hartford, Conn., asked if it was the intention of the parent body to control the proposed union.

The Speaker said if and when a motion was carried for the formation of the union the whole matter would be referred to a committee, which would report on the matter back to the convention.

Hon. Wm. Sherrill, 2nd Assistant President-General and titular leader of the American Negroes, said it was of vital importance that Negroes be taught and made to vote, not for any particular party, but in terms of their ultimate salvation. The U.N.I.A. did not propose to indulge in cheap politics, to get a job for an individual here and an individual there, to help those who would help the U.N.I.A. America was the base of operations, and the Negro vote here should be corral[l]ed and concentrated, the various committees being kept under control. The U.N.I.A. was playing for big stakes—nationhood for the Negro in Africa.

Bishop McGuire said the one thing necessary in the machinery of the organization was the proposal now before the convention. With the Negro it was no longer a matter of party, but men and measures. He was glad that the convention was about to endorse the proposal unanimously, and he would move the following motion:

> That it is the sense of the Fourth International Convention of the Negroes of the World, assembled in Liberty Hall, on this, the 5th day of August, 1924, that a Negro political union be formed to promote and secure all the aims and objects of the U.N.I.A. not only in this country but throughout the world where Negroes dwell, and to protect the entire Negro race under the auspices of the Universal Negro Improvement Association.

Hon. Brewster sec[on]ded and the motion was carried unanimously.

Hon. W.A. Wallace moved that a committee of eleven be appointed to draft the rules and regulations governing the Negro Political Union, the report to be submitted by Monday, August 11.

Hon. F.L. Martin seconded and the motion was carried.

The Speaker then named the following committee:

Sir William Sherrill, Hon. William Ware, Hon. F.E. Johnson, Hon. Bishop McGuire, Hon. Wm. Wallace, Hon. G.E. Carter, Hon. Dr. Peters, Hon. F. Martin, Hon. Hattie Johnson, Hon. Curry and Hon. Grant.

The convention then adjourned.

TUESDAY EVENING, AUGUST 5

The Convention resumed at 8:30, the Speaker, Hon. Marcus Garvey, in the chair.

Prayers were read, after which the minutes were read and, on motion of Hon. J.B. Eaton, seconded by Hon. Mary Massey, confirmed.

The order of the day was then proceeded with. The discussion of the deification of Jesus as a black Man of Sorrows; the canonization of the Virgin Mary as a Negress; the idealization of God as a Holy Spirit, without physical form but a Creature of imaginary semblance of the black race, being of like image and likeness.

The Speaker led off. He counselled the Convention to enter into the discussion with full reverence for the Creator. There was no doubt that the Man, Jesus, had been accepted by the Christian world as the Spiritual Redeemer of mankind. Negroes, with the rest, had accepted this great personality, this great character, as their Savior. There seemed, however, to be a great deal of misunderstanding as touching the personality, the race and origin of the man Christ. Different races had idealized Him as a Creator, representative of themselves. The Teutonic conception was different from the Anglo-Saxon. The Russian Christ did not appear to be the same as the Austrian Christ, and a glance at the various paintings and portraits of Jesus showed Him typified after the race to which the particular artist belonged. Negroes on this side of the [river had accepted Christ, while on] the other side, many of them, had accepted Mohammed. The administration was not endeavoring to bring Mohammed into the Western world. Mohammed was not in need of change. He was a colored man, anyhow. But . . . [*line mutilated*] Western world particularly [are] accepting the personality of someone who did not look like themselves. Christ was not black, Christ was not white, Christ was not completely red—Christ was the embodiment of all humanity. To be Christ he must have an equal part of all mankind in Him. The white people had claimed the white part and Negroes were claiming the black part.

The Speaker characterized this as the most important topic on the agenda. It sought to establish a great principle, he explained. It sought to give to the great Negro race and to generations yet unborn a real, racial inspiration, a real racial idealism. It sought to inculcate self-respect and pride in the Negro. How could the Negro expect to lift himself to the high pinnacle of human recognition and respect and achievement when his idealism was borrowed from others, an idealism completely out of tune.

The Negro had been told that God was a form. Reduce him to physical form, and he was made representative of white men by white men. Negroes now believed God was white. Jesus Christ, God, the Virgin Mary, were all depicted as white, and hell and Satan and his imps as black. The white man had given the black man a measure of emancipation from physical slavery and had accomplished his spiritual enslavement.

The Speaker warned his hearers not to be led away by criticism. Negroes had as much right to deliberate in this fashion on this vital subject in Convention as the Council of Trent[10] had. Let the world say what it cared. Negroes were now determined to think and act for themselves. If Negroes were not to have and worship a Jesus that looked like them, what kind of Jesus were they to have?

The Rt. Rev. Bishop [J.D.] Barber followed. He said he considered this one of the most important events in the history of the Negro peoples of the world. The subject was very far-reaching and destined to shape the destiny of unborn generations. He proceeded to show that the Virgin Mary was of Ethiopian extraction, descendant of Tamar and of Rahab. The genealogy of Jesus Christ included David, who had as his wife the widow of Urias,[11] the daughter of a Hittite, descendant of Ham. Solomon, son of David, was a black man. In his first book of songs, fifth verse, he said, "I am black."[12] The Man of Sorrows was a direct descendant from King Solomon. Being so, he must have had some black blood in his veins, and black blood was very strong blood, for it only required a few drops nowadays to take a man out of the white race. Even Moses, the speaker continued, was a black man, and recounted the incident where Moses was told to thrust his hand to his bosom.[13] On its being withdrawn it was found to be white. John the Baptist, the speaker showed[,] was also a black man, and John had announced Jesus as a black man, with hair like lambs wool, eyes like a flame of fire, feet like polished brass.[14]

The speaker closed with a discussion of the origin of the Bible, which he declared, written first in the Ethiopian language,[15] was incomplete and greatly [t]ampered with.

Rt. Rev. Dr. McGuire, Primate of the African Orthodox Church, followed[.] Our Lord and Saviour, he declared, if He came to New York today, could not dare live on Riverside Drive, but would be forced to dwell in Harlem, because He certainly was not white. He was of a reddish brown color. Negroes must know the truth, and the truth would set them free. They must throw away the religious shackles with which they were bound and write their own theology. Who dared con[d]emn the U.N.I.A. because the Madonna was carried through the streets of Harlem on August 1 pictured as a woman of the Negro race—he disliked the word Negress? If it were a Japanese procession, the Christ would be a little yellow man with almond eyes. The Roman Catholic Church on Corpus Christi Day carried pictures of Christ and the Madonna.

Dr. McGuire inquired who was responsible for the color scheme in religion? Who made the devil black? In Africa, he understood, the natives all thought the devil white. Satan, they were told, was cast down from Heaven.

If all those who dwelt in Heaven were white, then Satan must be white.

The Negro was tired of being taught by picture that one race was superior to another. As a race looked up to its own standard so would that race achieve. The Negro race was demanding new leadership and new ideas, and its great leader, Marcus Garvey, was supplying those ideas. The time had come when a day should be set apart for the burning in a bonfire of all pictures of a white Jesus, a white God, a white Madonna, now in the home of Negroes. A new start must be made. Prehistoric man, he showed, was a chocolate color and lived in subtropical regions. As he crossed to the Equator he became black. Other regions had other effects. The white man had lost something he had originally. It was all a matter of environment, distance from the Equator.

The last point made by the Bishop was in recalling the incident of Simon, the Cyrenian, being "compelled" to bear the cross of Jesus. The word "compelled" was significant. Simon was a black man. The white man, the Roman, persecuted Jesus and prodded him with spears; the Jew, the yellow man, then mocked him, and a man of Ethiopia offered him sympathy. He would always think of the Deity as a great patriarchal Negro, and the Negroes of the world could not do otherwise without stultifying themselves.

At this stage the convention adjourned.

Printed in *NW*, 16 August 1924. Original headlines omitted.

1. Prichard, Ala., is a small industrial community on the northern outskirts of Mobile. Before World War I it was only a village, but the creation of a shipbuilding plant brought an influx of laborers. In 1925 the town was incorporated with a population of just over three thousand. According to one study, incorporation was a response to the "undesirable citizens" brought in by the new industry; local residents decided that "something would have to be done to keep the community from becoming a haven for law violators" (Johnnie Andrews, Jr., and William David Higgins, *Prichard: The Formative Years* [n . p.: Bienville Historical Society, 1970], p. 33).

Just outside Prichard was a settlement called "Africky Town," with a population of several hundred. This community reportedly had been founded by the last boatload of slaves smuggled into the South: shortly before the Civil War broke out, Capt. Tim Meaher landed the *Clothilde* in the marshes along the Mobile River; he had difficulty disposing of his human cargo, and there, in the environs of Prichard, the Africans remained. As late as 1941 it was said that "the Negroes of Africky Town have remained pure Guinea stock and still have many customs and beliefs brought from Africa" (Federal Writers' Project, Works Progress Administration, *Alabama* [New York: Richard R. Smith, 1941], p. 359). Residents of Africky Town participated prominently in UNIA division affairs.

Prichard's division seems to have been organized by 1923, and for the next several years it was relatively active, sponsoring well-attended public functions. In 1926 it reported eleven dues-paying members, and Garveyites were still active as late as 1930. The delegate to the 1924 UNIA convention, Rev. J . J. Thomas, also served as president of the local division. Despite the fact that he himself was a clergyman, he often complained about religious leaders who were "keeping their members in darkness, preventing them from seeing the light of racial consciousness" (*NW*, 1 December 1923). Thomas acted as a field agent for the UNIA (*NW*, 24 November 1923, 2 February and 17 May 1924, 3 May and 23 August 1930; membership lists, 1925–1926, NN-Sc, UNIA Central Division records, box 2, a.16; Federal Writers' Project, Works Progress Administration, *Alabama*, p. 359; Andrews and Higgins, *Prichard: The Formative Years*, pp. 31–37).

2. Dr. A . R. Patespaul, a member of the Alliance, Ohio, UNIA Division 713 for three years, was better known as "old Dr. Patt." Patespaul, a linguist as well as a pharmaceutical specialist, was a member of the Greater Negro Medical, Inc., and represented the C . D. Holley Manufacturing Co., a drug and chemical concern, throughout the Ohio–western Pennsylvania area (*NW*, 14 June 1924).

3. Monongah is a coal-mining town situated on the Monongahela River in northern West Virginia; in 1920 it had a population of about two thousand. The community was the scene of a mining accident in 1907 in which 361 lives were lost. Little is known of the UNIA in Monongah, but the whole West Virginia mining region was an area of concentration of Garveyite strength. Several divisions existed in the surrounding communities, and UNIA activities continued in the area through the mid-1930s (*NW*, 30 May 1925; report of Samuel Haynes, ca. 1936, NN-Sc, UNIA Central Division records, box 9, d.33; Heilprin and Heilprin, eds., *Lippincott's New Gazetteer of the World*, p. 1,203; U.S. Bureau of the Census, *Fourteenth Census*, 1: 313).

4. Joseph A. Craigen served as general secretary of the Detroit division of the UNIA (*NW*, 5 April 1924).

5. The Ford Motor Co. was the main industrial employer of blacks in Detroit, with six thousand black workers (eleven percent of the work force) at the River Rouge plant and an estimated four thousand black workers at the Highland Park plant in the mid-1920s. As a part of his overall paternalistic philosophy, Henry Ford believed that blacks were entitled to full economic opportunity but that the races should be strictly segregated. Even though Ford Motor Co.'s reputation for hiring and promoting blacks was better than that of most other companies, the overwhelming majority of black workers was concentrated in the foundry and in unskilled jobs. Nevertheless, the company's hiring policy, its close working relationship with black community and church organizations, and Edsel Ford's frequent contributions to the NAACP fostered harmony between the company and Detroit's black community. The city's black leaders later opposed United Auto Workers' organizing drives at Ford plants, and the NAACP locally opposed trade union efforts in the auto industry until the 1940s, despite that organization's national policy in support of trade unions (August Meier and Elliott Rudwick, *Black Detroit and the Rise of the UAW* [New York: Oxford University Press, 1979], pp. 6–29; Sterling D. Spero and Abram L. Harris, *The Black Worker* [New York: Columbia University Press, 1931], pp. 154–157).

6. The Laura Lee division was located at Lumberport, W. Va., a small town nine miles northeast of Clarksburg. Lumberport had a population of 900 in 1920, having grown from about 120 recorded years earlier. The town was situated in the midst of a coal mining district with a substantial Afro-American population.

D. H. Kyle, the division's representative to the 1924 UNIA convention, is described elsewhere as residing in Clarksburg. Often referred to as Professor Kyle, he was a public schoolteacher by occupation. Kyle played a prominent role in the convention, and in 1925 he received appointment as state commissioner of the UNIA for West Virginia (*NW*, 28 March 1925; membership lists, 1925–1926, NN-Sc, UNIA Central Division records, box 2, a.13; Heilprin and Heilprin, eds., *Lippincott's New Gazetteer of the World*, pp. 422–423, 1,071).

7. Bryson Hale was president of the Milwaukee UNIA (*NW*, 5 January and 5 July 1924).

8. On 1 May 1923, S. V. Robertson was appointed as commissioner for Louisiana and Mississippi (*NW*, 5 May 1923).

9. Charleston, a small agricultural community in the southeast corner of Missouri, with a population in 1920 of about 3,400, was the commercial and banking center for the surrounding cotton district. After 1910 agitation began for restrictive covenants in housing, and in 1916 the electorate overwhelmingly passed a residential segregation ordinance. More telling was the 1924 lynching of a black man in the streets of Charleston. The victim, Roosevelt Grigsley, was "hanged in front of a grocery store; shots were fired through his body and later he was tied behind a car and dragged through the streets of the black section of the town" (Lorenzo J. Greene et al., *Missouri's Black Heritage* [St. Louis: Forum Press, 1980], p. 111). Charleston is in the same section of the state as Caruthersville, the scene of violent activity against black sharecroppers in the early 1920s.

The UNIA division had been formed by 1923, and in 1925–1926 the parent body reported as many as thirty-one dues-paying members in Charleston—a strong following for a division in such a small southern town. The president of the local UNIA, J. L. Simmons (also referred to as Dr. L. Simmons), was sent as a delegate to the national convention in 1924. Unlike many others, Charleston's division survived well into the 1930s. A UNIA source reveals that when a longtime Garveyite, Joseph Grey, met with the Charleston city council around 1936, he "presented the [Garvey] program so intelligently, that the Mayor and officials endorsed his work there with the U.N.I.A." (report of Samuel Haynes, ca. 1936, NN-Sc, UNIA Central Division records, box 9, d.33; *NW*, 15 December 1923, 19 July 1924; membership lists, 1925–1926, NN-Sc, UNIA Central Division records, box 2, a.16; Heilprin and Heilprin, eds., *Lippincott's New Gazetteer of the World*, p. 384; P. B. Clemens, State Historical Society of Missouri, to Robert A. Hill, 16 October 1984; U.S. Bureau of the Census, *Fourteenth Census*, 1: 245).

10. The Council of Trent met intermittently between 1545 and 1563, primarily in response to the threat posed to the Roman Catholic church by Martin Luther. Under Jesuit guidance, the council's doctrines were rigidly formulated in opposition to Reformation teaching. The council rejected Luther's teaching of free will and justification by faith, reaffirmed the validity of the seven sacraments, and reaffirmed the supremacy of the Pope against conciliar claims (*EWH*; David Maland, *Europe in the Sixteenth Century* [New York: Macmillan, 1973], pp. 724–728).

11. Bathsheba was the wife of David, a widow of Uriah, and the daughter of Eliam (2 Sam. 11:3, 12:24).

12. Song of Sol. 1:5: "I am black, but comely, O ye daughters of Jerusalem."

13. Exod. 4:6.

14. Rev. 1:14–15.

15. Rev. J. D. Barber's reference is to the First Book of Enoch, also known as the Ethiopic Enoch, the first of three books of ancient Jewish writings preserved under the name of the patriarch Enoch. The First Book of Enoch, a collection of diverse literary material from various periods and sources, is regarded as canonical by the Ethiopian Orthodox church. The version brought to Europe in 1773 was based not on the Semitic original, of which no copies remain, but on a Greek translation probably made around 400 A.D. The Book of Enoch is divided into five sections: the first predicts future judgment, a second contains the parables of Enoch, a third is devoted to astronomical movements, a fourth (usually compared to the the the Book of Daniel) contains dream visions that Enoch recounts and prophesied phases of history leading up to Judgment, and the fifth surveys human history, with exhortations and descriptions of miracles (Michael A. Knibb, *The Ethiopic Book of Enoch* [Oxford: Clarendon Press, 1978]; James H. Charlesworth, ed., *The Old Testament Pseudepigrapha* [Garden City, N.Y.: Doubleday & Co., 1983], 1: 5–89; *The Book of Enoch the Prophet*, trans. Richard Laurente [Minneapolis: Wizard Bookshelf, 1976]).

Convention Report

[*New York, 6 August 1924*]

WEDNESDAY MORNING, AUGUST 6

The convention reassembled at 10 a.m., the speaker, Hon. Marcus Garvey, in the chair.

Prayers were said, after which the minutes were read, and on the motion . . . [*line mutilated*] [seconded by Hon. F.L. Martin, St. Louis] were confirmed.

The order of the day was then proceeded with.

Continuing the discussion in regard to the deification of a Black Man of Sorrows, etc., initiated at the previous session.

Hon. Hannah Nichols [Nicholas],[1] New York, said this would be one of the greatest sources of inspiration brought to the black man. She had to confess that she herself believed subconsciously in a Caucasian God and Jesus, and full enlightenment had only come with the discussion of the subject in that convention.

Hon. R.A. [R.H]. Bachelor, Oriente, Cuba, emphasized that the various preachers present in convention should exercise the greatest care in explaining the doctrine in the respective communities.

Hon. J.J. Peters, Chicago, said this was the age of psychology. There were more psychologists produced in the last ten years than in the previous thousand years[.] The time was opportune for the proposed step.

Hon. A.G. Ellengurg [Ellenberg], Gary, Ind., quoted Scripture in support of his proposition that black men would only attain to full manhood status when they worshipped as was now proposed and when they returned to their native land, Africa. Up to the present time the Negro race was a race of idolators.

Hon. F. Johnson, Somerset, Va.,[2] supported the proposal.

Hon. T.[D].H. Kyle, Clarksburg, W.Va., contradicted the statement set forth in history by white men that the Hamites belonged to the Semitic family. He emphasized that care be taken that the delegates return to their constituencies with a correct version of the discussion.

Hon. Hattie Johnson, Baltimore, Md., expressed her impatience with long-drawn-out speeches and dissertations on the Bible in the discussion of a subject on which all must be agreed: One God, One Aim and One Destiny, and that God, a black God, was incontrovertible.

Hon. Gill,[3] Pittsburgh, said Pittsburgh was to a man behind the proposition.

Hon. Arnold Ford, New York, said he was not a Christian, though he believed in a Superior Being. Jesus was depicted as a black man, he said, until the time of the Renaissance in Europe, when a German, the burgomaster of Dresden, conceived the idea of having a white man substituted, and gave Europe and the white world a picture of himself, which it readily accepted to further its superiority propaganda.[4] He warned the convention that it should be remembered that the majority of black men dwelt in Africa, and they were not Christians, but Mohammedans. The great need of the moment for the black man is education.

Hon. G. Weston, New York, said it must not be overlooked that they were dealing with religion and not denominationalism. The convention was on safe ground.

At this stage Hon. J.J. Peters, Chicago, moved that the discussion be closed.

Hon. F.L. Martin seconded and the motion was carried.

Hon. F.L. Martin moved that it be the sense of the delegates assembled in the Fourth International Convention of Negroes that the deificiation of a Black Man of Sorrows be adopted as the ideal of the Negro race.

Hon. J.B. Eaton seconded and the motion was unanimously carried.

When the clause relating to the Virgin Mary was about to be adopted some discussion ensued as to the appropriateness of the word Negress. The chief objection voiced was that the word Negro was a Spanish word applied to the race by the white man and the feminine affix breathed contempt.

It was fully moved by Hon. Hannah Nicholls, New York, and seconded by Hon. [Carrie] Minous [Minus], New York, that the canonization of the Virgin Mary as a black woman be adopted a[s] the ideal of the Negro race.

The motion was unanimously carried.

Hon. Berber [Barber] moved that the idealization of God as a Holy Spirit, without physical form, but a Creature of imaginary semblance of the black race, being of like image and likeness be adopted.

Hon. Boyd seconded and the motion was carried unanimously.

Hon. Boyd moved that the picture of Jesus presented to the convention by the administration be immediately circulated among the Negro peoples of the world.

Hon. Wallace, Illinois, seconded and the motion was unanimously carried.

Hon. Hassell, Seattle, moved that the administration be empowered to take steps to have a crayon picture of the Madonna taken and submitted to it for pictures to be subsequently ordered and circulated among the Negroes of the world.

Hon. Bryant seconded and the motion was unanimously carried.

Hon. McGuire moved that a copyright be taken by the proper officers of the organization so as to protect the interests of the association.

Hon. Wallace seconded and the motion was unanimously carried.

The convention adjourned until 3 p.m., the time being 2 P.M.

WEDNESDAY AFTERNOON, AUG. 6

The convention resumed at 3 o'clock. Hon. F.L. Martin, St. Louis, reminded the chair of the suggestion of the Hon. Kyle during the morning session in regard to the preparation of a pamphlet in connection with the motions passed. The speaker informed the Hon. Delegate that he had ruled that such a motion would be acceptable under the item "Education."

The convention then proceeded with the order of the day, the discussion without prejudice of the aims and objects of the Ku Klux Klan.

Initiating the discussion, the speaker said the subject was a very delicate one. It was necessary for the association to take into deep consideration the practical side. The institution of the . . . [*line mutliated*] [would be seen] and felt. [It was not only] a name, it was not only an organization, it was a visible as well as an invisible institution, an institution promoted and supported by the majority group. Negroes formed the minority group, and it was, therefore, incumbent upon them to be very guarded in what they said. The Ku Klux Klan's activities were rampant in Georgia, Mississippi and Texas, and they would be felt in the North later on. The Ku Klux Klan was an institution made up of a group of people with an ideal of white supremacy. It was, therefore, the duty of this convention to direct its attention to the consideration of ways and means as to how it could get around it and escape its influence.

The speaker then read certain extracts from Klan literature which, he said, had been forwarded to him by a member of the U.N.I.A. This literature revealed the attitude of the Klan as contemptuous of the Negro, who, it held, having been a slave, should not be allowed to attain to a position approaching equality with a domin[a]nt race, the white race, his erstwhile master. If the Klan, the speaker concluded, could tie up a Democratic National

Convention,[5] impose silence on presidential candidates, then, he submitted, it was an institution that should be handled carefully, consideration being given to the precarious condition of the Negro in the United States at the present time.

Hon. Maguire [McGuire] expressed his complete approval of the stand taken by the speaker.

Hon. J. Hassell, Seattle, Wash., said 66 per cent of the American people was permeated by K.K.K. ideals. The only friend the Negro had at the present time was the capitalist, and the reason why he was the friend of the Negro, in a certain sense, was because he used the Negro to further his ends. The day was coming, he predicted, when the United States would be assailed by jealous white enemies, and on their treatment of the Negro at this hour hinged the coming of the Negro to their defense as heretofore.

Hon. H. Nicholas, New York, said the Ku Klux Klan had set out to conserve white supremacy. Negroes should go and do likewise.

Hon. J.J. Thomas, Mobile [Prichard], Ala., said the activities of the Ku Klux Klan had redounded to the benefit of the Universal Negro Improvement Association, when the intolerance of the Klan pressed hard on Negroes they realized the logic of the "Back-to-Africa" slogan.

Hon. J.J. Peters, of Chicago, said as the Jews were driven to nationhood by the Egyptians so would the Negro be driven to nationhood by the Klan. He emphasized the power of the Ku Klux Klan and giving an example, said the Klan could stop the Crisis Magazine from going into the South, could break up every branch of the N.A.A.C.P. in the South, could force them to move their headquarters from Fifth avenue. He inveig[h]ed against the attitude of the labor unions in refusing membership to black men.[6]

Hon. G.E. Brown, Miami, Fla. indorsed the last speaker's remarks in regard to the furtherance of the aims and objects of the Universal Negro Improvement Association by the activities of the Klan. He thought the best course the convention could pursue was to remain silent on this issue. He lived in Miami, and he knew. Hon. Johnson, of Detroit, said that while it was true that the Klan sought to take the law into their own hands, it was, at the same time true that they wielded a very great power in the nation. He was glad, however, to find that the Klan made Negroes think.

Hon. Cipriani,[7] Trinidad, Hon. Robertson, New York, and Hon. Crossgrove, Natchez, Miss., spoke, advocating the necessity for the Negro peoples of these United States doing nothing that would antagonize the Klan.

Hon. M.E. Boyd, New York, assailed the point of view of [the] previous speaker, who, she said, had spoken as if the Klan were a friend of the Negro. However true it might be that the activities of the Klan increased the membership of the U.N.I.A., it was cowardly to acquiesce in the intolerance the Klan exhibited. Negro men must learn that their duty was to place their women in a state of independence. The race could not rise when women had to scrub the floors of white men for a living. No race rose higher than its women.

Hon. Sir Wm. Sherrill, second assistant president-general and titular leader of the American Negroes, said it was the duty of the association and of this convention to protest against, and to condemn, any cowardly acts by the Klan, but it was imperative that they do not lose sight of the fact that the Klan was strong and powerful. The Klan was no friend to the Negro, to say so would be to give the appearance of indorsement of the Klan's alleged lynching and burning of Negroes. He felt that the association should adopt a policy of neutral opportunism towards the Klan. They should be watchful and ready to take advantage of any opportunity that might present itself in the program of the Ku Klux Klan to assist the Negro in realizing his objective.

Hon. McGuire then introduced the following motion:

Aug. 6, 1924.

Resolved That the Fourth International Convention of the Negro Peoples of the World regard the alleged attitude of the Ku Klux Kan to the Negro as fairly representative of the feelings of the majority of the white race towards us, and places on record its conviction that the only solution of the crucial situation is that of the Universal Negro Improvement Association, namely, the securing for ourselves as speedily as possible a government of our own on African soil.

Hon. J.A. Hassell, of Seattle, seconded the motion and, after considerable discussion, during which a substitute motion by the Hon. Wallace, providing that the brutality and atrocities perpetrated upon members of the Negro race by members of the Klan be condemned, was defeated, the motion was carried. Hon. Wallace then moved, Hon. Plummer seconded and it was carried unanimously, that it shall be the policy of the Universal Negro Improvement Association to protest against the brutalities and atrocities alleged to be perpetrated upon members of the Negro race by the Ku Klux Klan or by any other organization. The convention then adjourned until 8.30 p.m.

WEDNESDAY EVENING SESSION, AUG. 6

The convention resumed at 8.30 p.m., the Speaker, Hon. Marcus Garvey, in the chair. Prayers were read, after which the minutes of the previous session were read and confirmed.

The convention then proceeded to discuss the following subject:

The forwarding of an appeal to His Holiness the Pope of Rome, His Grace the Archbishop of Canterbury, as leaders of Christianity, for an honest and human settlement of the problems of humanity, especially as such problems affect the Negro.

In answer to a question by the Hon. G.A. Weston, the Speaker announced that the convention was being guided by Roberts' Rules of procedure,[8] and by the custom established in convention.

Initiating the discussion, the Speaker said the Negro, living in a Christian dispensation and in a Christian civilization, desired to make to the great leaders of Christianity, an emphatic appeal, ethical and moral, for their assistance and help. The Negro had been turned down by the secular world and was still being abused. The church had a great influence on the life of the body politic, wielding great power and influence o[n] millions of men in Europe and America.

Hon. J.D. Barber felt that the appeal, if properly made, would have a splendid effect. The condition of the Negro race in Africa was vile, and the heads of the church should be made to realize that Negroes were alive to the suffering of their brethren throughout the world.

Hon. A.G. Ellenberg, of Gary, Ind., and Hon. J.J. Peters, of Chicago, followed, supporting the proposal, the latter emphasizing the value of appeal even though the benefits may not immediately accrue.

Hon. G.E. Carter, Secretary-General, said it would be a means of notifying the church that Negroes were watchful of the situation and that the exploitation of natives by missionaries who went to Africa with the Bible in one hand and diplomacy in the other, must cease. He suggested that the majority of churches in America be reached through the federated council.[9]

Hon. Mr. Lowry, of Hartford, Conn., said an appeal to local preachers bore good results, so would [an] appeal to the religious heads benefit the movement greatly.

Hon. H.C. Stokes, of Middletown, O., stressed the effect the appeal would have on destroying the false propaganda that the U.N.I.A. was bent upon destroying the church.

Hon. Rudolph Smith, Third Assistant President-General, and titular leader of the West Indies, then moved that the discussion be closed.

Hon. S.V. Robertson, Commissioner, Louisiana and Mississippi, seconded, and the motion was carried unanimously.

Hon. Rudolph Smith then moved that the chairman appoint a Committee of Seven to frame resolutions to be sent to the heads of the various churches, and that the committee report back to the convention on Wednesday, August 13.

Hon. F.L. Martin, of St. Louis, seconded, and the motion was carried unanimously.

The Speaker then nominated the following committee:

Hon. Rev. Barber[;] Hon. Kyle, West Virginia; Hon. G.E. Carter, Secretary-General; Hon. Bishop McGuire[;] Hon. A.G. Ellenberg, Gary, Ind.; Hon. H. Nichols, New York; and Hon. W.A. Wallace, Illinois.

Next before the house was the subject of an appeal to the Presidents of America, France and Portugal, for a square deal for Negroes in Africa, America and the Colonies and the forwarding of a petition to the President of the United States of America by the four million members of the U.N.I.A. on August 21, asking for his co-operation and help in the establishment of a nation in Africa for the Negroes of this country.

Hon. H.V. Plummer, New York, moved that discussion of the subject be suspended, and that a Committee of Seven be appoined to draft the appeal and report back to the convention.

Hon. J.J. Peters, Chicago, seconded, and the motion was carried unanimously.

The following committee was then nominated by the Speaker:

Sir William Sherrill[;] W.A. Wallace, Illinois; Hon. J.J. Peters, Chicago; Hon. Wm. Ware, Cincinnati; Hon. F. Johnson, Detroit; Hon. F.L. Martin, St. Louis; Hon. Wightman [Whiteman], Chicago.

The following committee of five was then appointed by the Speaker to take care of the drafting of the petition to the President of the United States:

Hon. G.E. Carter, Secretary-General; Hon. Rev. Barber, Hon. Prof. Kyle, W.Va.; Hon. H.V. Plummer, Hon. Hattie Johnson, Baltimore, Md.

The following delegation of seven to wait upon the President of the United States, on August 21, and present the petition, was then nominated by the Speaker:

Hon. Sir William Sherrill[;] Hon. G.E. Carter, Secretary-General; Hon. F.L. Martin, St. Louis; Hon. Kyle, W.Va.; Hon. Lady Henrietta V. Davis, Fourth Assistant President-General; Hon. Bishop McGuire, and Hon. W.A. Wallace, Illinois.

The convention then adjourned.

Printed in *NW*, 16 August 1924. Original headlines abbreviated.

1. One of the early members and incorporators of the UNIA, Hannah Nicholas held the office of assistant secretary to the New York division (*NW*, 25 August 1923).

2. Somerset is a small rural village located in north-central Virginia. In the early twentieth century it reported a population of one hundred. The Somerset UNIA division had seven dues-paying members in 1925–1926, but little else is known of Garveyite activities in the area (Heilprin and Heilprin, eds., *Lippincott's Gazetteer of the World*, p. 1,727; membership lists, 1925–1926, NN-Sc, UNIA Central Division records, box 2, a.16).

3. James Gill served as president of the Pittsburgh division in 1923 (*NW*, 25 August 1923).

4. No documentation has been found to support Ford's claim that Jesus was depicted in Europe as a black man until the time of the Renaissance. Over time, many paintings develop a darker hue, so it is possible that Ford may have thought that in these early depictions Jesus was originally painted as a black man. There were, however, black depictions of Jesus in Africa (Peter Mark, *The African in European Eyes: The Portrayal of the Black African in Fourteenth- and Fifteenth-Century Europe* [Syracuse, N.Y.: Maxwell School of Citizenship and Public Affairs, 1974]; J. Vercoutter et al., *The Image of the Black in Western Art*, vol. 1, and J. Devisse et al., *The Image of the Black in Western Art*, vol. 2, pts. 1 and 2 [New York: William Morrow and Co., 1976, 1979]; Paul Henry Daniel Kaplan, "Ruler, Saint, and Servant: Blacks in European Art," [Ph.D. diss., Boston University, 1983]; Arno Lehmann, *Christian Art in Africa and Asia* [St. Louis: Concordia Publishing House, 1969], pp. 44–52).

5. With two million members and having enjoyed a series of political gains, the KKK began to move into national politics at the party conventions of 1924. At the Democratic party's convention, however, a plank was proposed that condemned secret societies in general; at the same time a minority plank was proposed which named the Klan in particular. Two of the major Democratic presidential contenders, Al Smith and Oscar Underwood, publicly condemned the Klan and supported the minority plank, but the leading contender, William Gibbs McAdoo, hoping to avoid an open fight and to retain the support of the Klan which controlled a large slate of delegates, opposed it and supported instead a plank calling for enforcement of existing laws. There then ensued a heated and protracted fight among the convention delegates. As the debate wore on, a vote to name the Klan became associated with a vote against McAdoo, pushing reluctant McAdoo supporters to vote against the anti-Klan plank, which eventually lost by one vote. The bitterness over the Klan issue, the most controversial of the convention, carried over into the selection of the Democratic nominee. With the McAdoo, Smith, and Underwood forces locked in a stalemate, delegates were unable to agree upon any of the three. After a nine-day debate, a compromise

candidate, John W. Davis, was nominated. Ultimately, the acrimony engendered by the fight over the Klan plank lost McAdoo the nomination and, it is believed, lost the Democrats the presidential election (Kenneth T. Jackson, *The Ku Klux Klan in the City, 1915–1930*, pp. 248–249, 286; Arnold S. Rice, *The Ku Klux Klan in American Politics* [Washington, D.C.: Public Affairs Press, 1962], pp. 63–64, 76–89, 134–136; David M. Chalmers, *Hooded Americanism: The History of the Ku Klux Klan*, pp. 203–212, 220, 300; *NYT*, 20–23 June and 27–28 June 1924).

6. Most American labor unions had long refused blacks admission as members. Though some organizations welcomed them, such as the radical Industrial Workers of the World, the mainstream labor movement demonstrated little interest in enrolling black workers. The American Federation of Labor, under the leadership of Samuel Gompers (1850–1924), allowed its local affiliates to bar Afro-Americans.

The unions justified excluding blacks because of their extensive use as strikebreakers. Beginning in the mid-1870s, southern blacks figured in many northern labor disputes, first in mining and then in other industries. As black migration increased in the teens and twenties, this became a primary means of securing factory work, and race leaders, such as Booker T. Washington, urged their use in labor disputes for this purpose. The discriminatory policies of the unions caused resentment among black workers. This resentment, in turn, disposed them to act as strikebreakers.

In Chicago, labor strife of this kind exacerbated racial tensions that attended the arrival of large numbers of southern blacks. Attacks on strikebreakers frequently became generalized to include the entire black community. In 1905 large-scale violence grew out of one such incident, and similar causes contributed to the massive race riot during the "Red Summer" of 1919. As Allan Spear noted, nearly "every overt racial clash in the North in the early twentieth century involved conflict between blacks and working class whites. . . . In many instances labor disputes led directly to attacks on black workers by white strikers and their sympathizers" (Allan Spear, "The Origins of the Urban Ghetto, 1870–1915," in Nathan I. Huggins et al., eds., *Key Issues in the Afro-American Experience* [New York: Harcourt Brace Jovanovich, 1971], 2: 153–166).

During the early 1920s the AFL began to make tentative efforts to reach out to black laborers, urging that affiliate unions remove racial restrictions from membership provisions. Little resulted from this policy, however, and in 1930 only 4.3 percent of all blacks in American manufacturing were union members (William Tuttle, "Labor Conflict in Chicago, 1884–1919," in Milton Cantor, ed., *Black Labor in America* [Westport, Conn.: Negro Universities Press, 1969], pp. 86–111; Spero and Harris, *The Black Worker*, pp. 319–461; William H. Harris, *The Harder We Run: Black Workers Since the Civil War* [New York: Oxford University Press, 1982], pp. 5, 20–21, 42–45, 55).

7. I. Cipriani was probably a member of Trinidad's noted Cipriani family. One of the family members, Joseph Emmanuel Cipriani, was mayor of Port of Spain. Another, Arthur Andrew Cipriani was a captain in the British West India Regiment during the first World War and leader of the Trinidad Workingman's Association (C.L.R. James, *The Life of Captain Cipriani: An Account of British Government in the West Indies* [Nelson, England: Coulton and Co., 1932]).

8. *Robert's Rules of Order*, a manual on parliamentary procedure based on the British parliamentary tradition, was first compiled by Henry Martin Robert, an engineer in the U.S. Army in 1876. The manual, which modified the traditional rules to meet the needs of "ordinary societies," was revised in 1915 (Henry M. Robert, *Robert's Rules of Order*, comp. Rachel Wayman [New York: Jove Publications, 1967]).

9. Probably a reference to the Federal Council of the Churches of Christ, formed in 1908 to promote interdenominational cooperation among Protestant churches. Thirty denominations joined the organization, which was in large part inspired by the Social Gospel movement that attempted to apply the teachings of Christianity to society, economic life, and political structures, as well as to individuals. While the genesis of the council had come from earlier Christian cooperation movements, the Federal Council of Churches was the largest of these organizations (T.C. O'Brien, ed., *Corpus Dictionary of Western Churches* [Washington, D.C.: Corpus Publications, 1976], pp. 321–332; John A. Hutchison, *We Are Not Divided: A Critical and Historical Study of the Federal Council of the Churches of Christ in America* [New York: Round Table Press, 1941]; Ronald C. White and C. Howard Hopkins, *The Social Gospel* [Philadelphia: Temple University Press, 1976], pp. 200–290; Charles Howard Hopkins, *The Rise of the Social Gospel in American Protestantism, 1865–1915* [New Haven, Conn.: Yale University Press, 1940], pp. 302–320).

Convention Report

[*New York, 7 August 1924*]

THURSDAY MORNING, AUGUST 7

The convention resumed at 10 a.m., Marcus Garvey, Speaker, presided.

After the usual preliminaries, the convention proceeded to discuss the following: The French policy toward the Negro, the British policy toward the Negro, and the American policy toward the Negro.

The Speaker outlined the subject, giving his views on the different policies and suggesting the channels in which the discussions should run. He said that the British policy was skillful and hypocritical, harmful and dangerous; the French was better, and the American was more straightforward. However, it seemed that the French and Americans were gradually adopting the British policy. He called upon Bishop McGuire to address the house on the British policy.

Bishop McGuire explained that on account of the stand he had taken, whereas he had once been very popular, now he was in disfavor with his former government, the British. They thought that as the exponent of religious freedom for the Negro, he was striking at the very roots of the British religious system, which was part of the policy to subjugate and dominate the Black people. England had used the Anglican Church and other religious societies with telling effect in the scheme of conquest of the natives, and he predicted that she will become more concerned when she hears of the resolutions that had been passed with regard to the deification of the Black Man of Sorrows. The mainstay of Britain's policy was "Divide and rule." It was very effective, especially among Negroes.

Hon. W.A. Wallace, of Illinois, who was called by the speaker to speak on the policy of America, said that the political weapon was one of America's agencies. Negro preachers were easily secured for a consideration to preach to their congregations and get their support for a certain candidate. In that way an economical slavery was established. The doctrine of the South was a white supremacy, while the supporters in the North adopted the policy also of keeping the Negro in his place. The only solution of the problem facing the race in America was the building up of a nation in Africa which would be in a position to protect the interests of Negroes everywhere.

Hon. J.J. Peters, on invitation of the chair, outlined the policy of France toward the Negro. He claimed that that policy was the best of the three making comparisons as to the treatment of the people by the three different governments. He said the Negroes under the French were considered as citizens and were given high office. The French, however, exploited the people in the colonies in the same way as the British, and handicapped them in many directions, particularly in regard to nationhood. He also discanted on the shrewd, vicious and hypocritical policy of the British.

In the discussion that followed, Hon. J. Hassell, of Seattle, Wash., threw

677

much light on the various policies, showing that he had a world of information in regard to the present position of the Negroes in the three countries. He spoke of the impoverishment of the West Indies in regard to sugar as being due to the fact that the British preferred to help the German beet growers,[1] than to help the islands because many colored people owned plantations. As to the French, he said they were given many opportunities to rise, and instanced the fact that at the beginning of the war, General Dobs [*Dodds*], colored man, was adjutant general of the French forces, but had been retired because of the protests of the British and the French.[2] He next pointed out the effect of the American policy and instanced Hawaii, which was now under control of America, and which was now owned chiefly by the descendants of the original missionaries, who went to those islands, and who married among the princesses and wealthy natives.[3] After some further discussion, the morning session adjourned.

THURSDAY AFTERNOON, AUGUST 7

On the resumption, discussion of the British, French and American policy toward the Negro was continued.

Hon. C.H. Bryant, commissioner of Panama, Costa Rica and Nicaragua, referred to the conceit of the British, who, he said, were determined to maintain their domination of the Negro people, no means for doing so being too despicable. France's policy was one of expediency, Negroes being necessary for her protection. As for America, the stars were for America, and the stripes for Negroes.

Hon. D.H. Kyle, Clarksburg, W.Va., said he agreed with the previous speakers when they said that the British, French and Americans dominated through their system of education, the cult of white supremacy and white superiority. It was for Negroes through the U.N.I.A. to meet propaganda with propaganda.

Hon. M. Askerlese [Askernese], Penn., emphasized that religion was used to subjugate the Negro. The lesson of turning the other cheek had been well taught.

Hon. Arnold Ford, New York, said religion, education, the economic system, politics and the social order were the means by which the Negro was oppressed. Negroes must produce their own literature. It was a disgrace that they knew nothing of the principles that guided their fathers.

Hon. R.A.[H.] Bachelor, Oriente, Cuba, gave a vivid account of the oppressive tactics and methods of the British people in their dealings with Negroes. It seemed to him that it was not so much "policy" as "poison," with which the British inoculated their victims. He had seen Negroes starving, unable to provide themselves with shelter, unable to secure a day's work under British rule, and yet singing "God Save the King" with the greatest fervor.

Hon. H.E. [A.G.] Ellenberg, Gary, Ind., said that the American system, as far as the Negro was concerned, was physical bondage, then spiritual bondage, then intellectual bondage, all attended with a shocking inhumanity.

Hon. E.B. Grant, Bermuda, endorsed the remarks of the Hon. Bachelor. Hon. Edward Allen, Pittsburgh; Hon. Rogers, Newport News, Va.; Hon. H. Nicholas, New York[;] and Hon. Jackson, New Orleans, supported the point of view of the preceding speakers, stating that it was for the Negro to take steps to resist the propaganda of the white race with similar propaganda.

Hon. G.A. Weston, New York, showed that the British policy was very shrewd and insidious and instanced that within his knowledge, in pursuance of the system to divide and rule, the British had employed Turkish agents to preach Islamism to members of the Universal Negro Improvement Association.[4]

Hon. F. Johnson, Detroit, emphasized that America used one section of Negroes to oppress another.

Hon. J.D. Barber referred to the British and French policy of oppression in Somaliland and the Sudan respectively.[5] He suggested that the U.N.I.A. send out missionaries to counteract their propaganda. At this stage the convention adjourned until 8:30 p.m.

THURSDAY EVENING, AUGUST 7

The Convention was called to order at 9 p.m., the Hon. Rudolph Smith in the chair.

The Hon. Rudolph Smith informed the Convention that the Hon. Marcus Garvey was absent on very pressing business connected with the Universal Negro Improvement Association.

The discussion of the subject which engaged attention at the afternoon session—the British, French and American policy toward the Negro—was continued.

Hon. J.B. Eaton, Berkeley, Va., dealt with the American policy, which, he said, was one of oppression through denial of political rights.

Hon. Jacob Chambers, East St. Louis, said it was the settled determination of the white man to keep the Negro in a state of servitude. In East St. Louis a law had been passed excluding Negroes from the South,[6] and this attitude would in time become general, eventually approximating the attitude now adopted towards the Japanese.

Hon. Daniels, Brooklyn, agreed with previous speakers who showed that a system of repression through the medium of education was in general use by the white man everywhere.

Hon. Baxter, Jamaica, said the policy of the British as exemplified in Jamaica was destruction by starvation. He referred to the introduction of cheap labor from India against which the Negro could not compete.

Hon. F.L. Martin, St. Louis, said the policy of the white nations was based on the survival of the fittest. He was, however, not so much concerned with consideration of the policy of the white man toward the Negro as the plans the Negro [would] adopt to combat the policy of the white man.

Hon. Col. [Vincent] Wattley, New York[, said] all were agreed as to the policy of the British, French and the Americans toward the Negro. The policy the Negro could adopt to oppose this was the policy of the U.N.I.A.

Hon. J.R. Gill, Pittsburgh, said the Negro in America had no policy and proceeded to elaborate in this strain, when the Acting Speaker ruled him out of order. The honorable gentleman thereup[on] took his seat.

The Acting Speaker here vacated the chair to address the House, and Hon. Percival Burrows wielded the gavel.

Hon. Smith, in a lengthy address, referred to the tremendous hold which France and Great Britain had on Africa, and their determination, in their own interests, to maintain their grip. He referred to the policy of divide and rule which England had developed everywhere and said it was for the Negro to be educated to the meaning of this sinister instrument. He dwelt at length on the antagonism of black against light brown which the British had stirred among Negroes in the colonies. Propaganda was one of the chief weapons and he instanced how in Cuba, where the Association had a very large membership, one newspaper had declared that Marcus Garvey had been arrested as a bootlegger. He moved that the Chairman of the Convention, Hon. Marcus Garvey, on his arrival the next day, appoint a committee of seven to draw up plans providing for the remedying of those ills affecting Negroes which had been introduced by the policy of the British, French and Americans.

Hon. F.L. Martin, St. Louis, seconded.

Hon. J.J. Peters, Chicago, moved an amendment, and several rose to speak on unreadiness, whereupon a motion to adjourn was moved and carried.

Printed in *NW*, 16 August 1924. Original headlines abbreviated.

1. In the wake of the destruction of sugar beet factories in France and Belgium during World War I, the West Indian sugar industry boomed, augmented by increasing sales to the United States. In 1920, however, there was a disastrous sugar market crash, and international sugar investment began to shift. By 1924 there was a growing interest in the exploitation of the German sugar industry by British and American bankers expecting to benefit from the anticipated settlement of war reparations. British banks, aided by the Bank of England, played a major role in financing the German beet-sugar industry. In July 1924 a consortium of American banks, hoping to compete with the British, arranged a $4-million loan to Germany for raising, refining, and marketing the German sugar crop (*Times* [London], 7 May and 30 May 1924; *NYT*, 19 May, 29 July, and 31 July 1924; Sir Harold Mitchell, *Europe in the Caribbean* [London: W. and R. Chambers, 1963], pp. 17, 83, 170).

2. A reference to Gen. Alfred Amédée Dodds (1842–1922), a prominent French general during the period prior to the First World War. Born in St. Louis, Senegal, of African and European descent, he graduated from the St. Cyr military academy and then joined the marine infantry. He served in the Franco-Prussian war of 1870, during which he was decorated with the Legion of Honor for valor and promoted to captain. In 1872 he was assigned to West Africa where, aside from short periods of service in Southeast Asia (1878 and 1883), he spent twenty years in Senegal. In 1891 he returned to France to command the 8th Marine Infantry; the following year he was selected to command an expeditionary force to Dahomey. During the next two years he conquered that kingdom and annexed it and its hinterland region to the colonial empire of France. He returned to France as a hero and was awarded a second Legion of Honor. He commanded troops in China in 1896 and from 1900 to 1902. During the Boxer Rebellion of 1900 he was commander-in-chief of the allied forces of France, Britain, Germany, Japan and the United States. When he returned to France, he became inspector general of colonial troops and subsequently was appointed as a member of the Superior War Council in 1904. In 1907 he transferred to the reserves, and he retired from military service in 1912. He was recalled to duty in 1914 when he served briefly on the Supreme War Council. No evidence has been found to suggest that Dodds was forced to retire from this council. Following his death in 1922, he was accorded full military honors at his funeral (Joel A.

Rogers, *World's Great Men of Color* [New York: Collier Books, 1972], pp. 389–393; *Dictionnaire Bio-bibliographique du Dahomey* [Porto-Novo: Institut de Recherches Appliquées du Dahomey, 1969], pp. 68–71; Boniface I. Obichere, *West African States and European Expansion: The Dahomey-Niger Hinterland, 1885–1898* [New Haven, Conn.: Yale University Press, 1971], pp. 102–118; *EB*).

3. Missionary acquistion of land in Hawaii dated from the 1840s. When the missionaries first arrived, Hawaiian land was held by the king but used in common, since there was no concept of private ownership of land. In the 1840s the king invited some missionaries to participate in his government, in part to deal with the changes that were occurring because of increasing trade with foreigners. One of the missionaries, Dr. Gerit P. Judd, instigated a series of laws that changed landholding from traditional communal use to private ownership. Under the "Great Mahele," as the plan was called, thousands of Hawaiians lost access to land or sold off land to foreigners for low prices. The result was that the percentage of foreign-owned land increased dramatically: by 1862, for example, three-quarters of the land on the island of Oahu had passed over to foreign control. The missionaries and their descendants were major beneficiaries of the change, and many missionaries decided to leave their calling to become landowners. Thus, two former missionaries, Samuel N. Castle and Amos Cooke, formed the partnership Castle and Cooke, which was to become one of the largest landowning companies in Hawaii. More often, missionaries' children took advantage of the land law: another of the largest companies, Alexander and Baldwin, was founded by the offspring of missionary parents. These two companies long remained among the five largest landholding companies in Hawaii, owning more than 13 percent of the land.

Missionary-acquired land came primarily through the new landholding law, rather than by intermarriage with Hawaiian women. Intermarriage between missionaries and Hawaiians was opposed by the ministry, and the only missionary to marry a Hawaiian woman was expelled from office. The children of missionaries did, however, intermarry with Hawaiian women (Bradford Smith, *Yankees in Paradise* [Philadelphia: J. B. Lippincott Co., 1956], pp. 243–333; Graeme Kent, *Company of Heaven: Early Missionaries in the South Seas* [Sydney: A. H. & A. Reed and Co., 1972]; Ralph S. Kuykendall, *The Hawaiian Kingdom* [Honolulu: University of Hawaii Press, 1947]; Edward Joesting, *Hawaii* [New York: W. W. Norton and Co., 1972]; Marion Kelly, "Land Tenure in Hawaii," *Amerasia Journal* 7, no. 2 [fall/winter 1980]: 57–73).

4. An editorial in the 1 November 1924 issue of the *Negro World*, entitled "White Leadership of Islam a Delusion and a Snare," stated that both British colonialism and Turkish Islam were white forces alien to Africa and thus contrary to UNIA interests. The Mahdi defeat, the editorial in the *Negro World* argued, had thrown "the Mohammedan world back into the arms of the Turkish authorities who have always used it more in their own interest in dealing with European powers than in the interests of the African and Asiatic Moslems." The Mahdi revolt against the Anglo-Egyptian administration in the Sudan was defeated in 1898 at the Battle of Omdurman; this brought an end to the independent Mahdist state, which extended from the Red Sea to central Africa.

Weston's comments may have been influenced to some extent by the spread of the Moorish Science Temple in the United States, a movement formed in New Jersey in 1913 by Noble Drew Ali (the former Timothy Drew from North Carolina, 1886–1929). Temples were established in Newark, N. J., Pittsburgh, Detroit, and various places in the South, but the movement was strongest in Chicago, where there were at one point an estimated ten thousand members. Noble Drew Ali's teachings combined elements of the Koran, the Bible, and the teachings of Marcus Garvey, whom he eulogized as "the John the Baptist" of the Moorish movement. Although the movement claimed that American blacks were of Moorish descent and thus "Asiatics," not blacks, its appeal to racial pride and freedom from European domination may have attracted active or potential UNIA members. Whether the Moorish Science Temple undercut UNIA membership is, however, unclear. The Moorish Science Temple split into factions in 1929. Yet the legacy of the black Islamic movement in the United States persisted, and in 1932 one of the offshoots of the Moorish Science Temple founded the Temple of Islam, first in Detroit and then in Chicago, under the leadership of W. D. Fard and later under Elijah Mohammed (Robert A. Hill, ed. and comp., *The Black Man: A Monthly Magazine of Negro Thought and Opinion*, pp. 35–36; Arna Bontemps, *They Seek a City* [New York: Doubleday, 1945], pp. 174–185; Arthur Huff Fauset, *Black Gods of the Metropolis* [London: Oxford University Press, 1944], 3: 41–51; E. U. Essien-Udom, *Black Nationalism: A Search for an Identity in America* [Chicago: University of Chicago Press, 1962], pp. 33–62; Noble Drew Ali, *The Holy Koran* [Chicago: Moorish Science Temple of America, ca. 1927]; DJ-FBI, file 62-25889, sections 3–4, 11, 14; *Chicago Tribune*, 29 August 1923).

5. French, British, and Italian Somalilands were relatively quiet in the early 1920s, but British-ruled Sudan was feeling the first stirrings of modern nationalism. In May 1924 'Ali 'Abd al-Latif, a disgruntled ex-army officer, founded the White Flag League, dedicated to expelling the British

from the Nile valley. He was arrested after demonstrations in Omdurman and Khartoum in June. Even larger scale demonstrations followed in August (P.M. Holt, *A Modern History of the Sudan* [London: Weidenfeld and Nicolson, 1961], pp. 125–132; Robert O. Collins and Robert L. Tignor, *Egypt and the Sudan* [Englewood Cliffs, N.J.: Prentice-Hall, 1967], pp. 125–126).

6. While no law had been passed in East St. Louis that excluded blacks from the South, the mayor and city council formally asked the NAACP to help halt southern black migration by publicizing the overcrowded labor market and poor housing conditions in the city. The black population of East St. Louis had increased from six thousand in 1914 to eighteen thousand by 1924. With organized labor hostile to black labor, some city officials feared an influx of black migrants might precipitate a race riot similar to that of 1917 (*Chicago Defender*, 2 August 1924).

Report by Special Agent James E. Amos

New York City 8/7/24

Synopsis of Facts:

Marcus Garvey arrested on charge of Perjury and swearing falsely to Income Tax Return for year 1921.[1] Garvey pleaded not guilty and was held by Judge McClintic[2] under bail of $2500.

Details:

Agent was in Judge McClintic's Court when Garvey was brought in Court on a charge of Perjury and swearing falsely to Income Tax Return for year 1921. GARVEY pleaded not guilty and was held by JUDGE MCCLINTIC under bail of [$2]500[.] The New Amsterdam Casualty Company, 60 John Street, put up bail for Garvey.

Agent also interviewed Mr. Ilgen, Agent for Elder Demster S.S. Line[,][3] who informed Agent that he had instructions from his superior not to sell any tickets to Negroes going to Africa, and especially the Garvey crowd.

Agent also interviewed Mr. Sohm of the Bull S.S. Line,[4] who informed Agent that he had received the same instructions as Mr. Ilgen.

Mr. Sohm further stated that on July 25, 1924 that the Garveyites had shipped by his line lots of machinery, but he had been informed since that it would not be allowed to land.[5]

The Elder Demster and Bull Lines are the only steamship companies sailing from this port to Africa.

Agent also interviewed Mr. E.T. Merrill, who is the Liberian Consul, at 326 W. 19th Street, New York City. He gave Agent copy of letter sent to all papers in New York, and which copy is attached to this report. Mr. Merrill further stated that he had also received instructions from the Secretary of State of Liberia not to visa any passports for any Garveyite; he also stated that he had communicated with the British Consuls and advised them of the instructions he received as there were other ports Negroes could leave the United States by. Mr. Merrill further stated that he had been informed that Garvey had sent a cable to President King of Liberia, stating that he was greatly surprised at King's attitude toward him. He also sent a cable to the King of Abyssinia.

Attached to this report are clippings from New York daily papers.[6]
CONTINUED.

JAMES E. AMOS

DJ-FBI, file 61. TD.

1. The indictment was ultimately dismissed nolle prosequi on 31 May 1932 (NFRC, Marcus Garvey case file exhibits, C 38 771, 539461).

2. Probably George W. McClintic (1866–1942), who practiced law in Charlestown, W.Va., from 1888 to 1921, before President Warren G. Harding appointed him to a federal judgeship, in which position he served from 1921 to 1942. He was called to preside at a mail fraud case in New York in 1924 (*WWWA*; *NYT*, 26 September 1942).

3. The Elder Dempster Line was founded in 1890 by Alfred L. Jones (1845–1909) as a result of a reorganization of the British and African Steam Navigation Co., originally founded in 1869. Jones had risen within the ranks of the Elder Dempster Co. to become a junior partner and finally president. By the 1880s the company had established a virtual monopoly over trade and shipping to West African ports. In the 1890s Jones helped to establish a West African cotton industry, invested heavily in the exploitation of minerals, and in 1894 founded the Bank of British West Africa. Jones subsequently expanded his shipping and trading interests to the Canary Islands, developing the banana trade there. In 1901, he inaugurated a new steamship service to Jamaica, bought up hotels, and began to revive the flagging West Indian trade. Jones was also a philanthropist who felt that Africans were "a fine race," and, if fairly treated would "conscientiously serve their white employers." During the nineteenth century Jones had close ties with African leaders such as Edward Wilmot Blyden. He also promoted technical education for Africans and sponsored a number of industrial training schools in Africa. In the hopes of eradicating African malaria, Jones also helped to found the Liverpool School of Tropical Medicine, and in 1903 he became the chairman of the Liverpool Institute of Tropical Research (Peter Davies, *Trading in West Africa, 1840–1920* [London: Croom Helm, 1976], pp. 180–201; Hollis R. Lynch, *Edward Wilmot Blyden* [London: Oxford University Press, 1967], p. 209; *DNB*, 1901–1911, 23: 379–380; *WWW*).

4. The A. H. Bull Steamship Co., Inc., was a New York maritime firm owning dozens of steamships. During the early twenties the company ran regular service to West African ports for passengers and cargo (*The Dictionary of Shipowners, Shipbuilders and Marine Engineers* [London: Dictionary Publishing Co., 1935], pp. 107–108; *Marine Review* 52, no. 2 [February 1922]: 71).

5. The UNIA dispatched a shipment of goods from New York to Liberia on 25 July 1924 with a scheduled arrival date at Cape Palmas of 22 August. The vendor of the merchandise, H. D. Taylor Co., succeeded in having the Admiralty Law Division of the USSB stop delivery of the shipment upon its arrival at Cape Palmas, as Garvey's check for the purchase proved worthless. According to the vendor's attorney, the goods were then stored at a Cape Palmas customs warehouse. In mid-December 1924, the UNIA and the H. D. Taylor Co. adjusted between themselves the matter of the balance of the purchase price due on the goods, and on 21 December H. D. Taylor informed the shipping board that delivery of the goods need no longer be withheld. Liberian customs authorities, however, then threatened to sell the goods to pay for the cost of their storage. According to the vendor's attorney, no one representing the UNIA as consignee ever appeared with the bill of lading to claim the merchandise. Eventually the Liberian government confiscated the goods for the payment of storage charges. A *Negro World* article of 17 October 1924 presented a version of the disposition of the goods, consisting of "sawmills, engineering stores, medicinal stores, etc.," that was significantly at odds with that furnished by the vendor's attorney (*NW*, 17 October 1924; selected correspondence from December 1924 to 13 January 1930, DNA, RG 32, file 605-1-653).

6. The clippings were not retained.

Convention Report

[*New York, 8 August 1924*]

Friday Morning, August 8

The convention assembled at 10 a.m., the Speaker, Hon. Marcus Garvey, in the chair.

Prayers were read, after which the minutes of the previous session were read by the secretary.

Winding up the discussion of the previous session, Hon. Martin, St. Louis, moved that a committee of seven be appointed to draft a plan to determine the policy of the association with respect to the policy of France, England and America toward the Negro, the committee to report next Friday, August 15.

Hon. S.V. Robertson seconded and the motion was carried unanimously. The following committee was then appointed by the speaker:

Hon. W.A. Wallace, Illinois; Hon. F. Martin, St. Louis; Hon. S.V. Robertson, Louisiana; Hon J.D. Barber, Hon. P.L. Burrows, first assistant secretary-general; Hon. R.A.[H.] Bachelor, Oriente, Cuba; Hon. S.R. Wheat, West Chicago.

The convention then proceeded to discuss ways and means of adjusting the race problem of the Southern States of the United States of America to the satisfaction of all concerned.

Initiating the discussion, the speaker, Hon. Marcus Garvey, said the subject was a very important one. The South was the sore spot of the nation, but at the same time the South was the character-making center of Negroes. The South had given more character to the Negro than any other section of the world. It had made more real Negro men and women than had been made anywhere else, but, paradoxically, it was that part of the world where Negroes suffered most within the pale of civilization. It was, therefore, the duty of the convention to discuss how to educate the people in the South lands so as to render themselves best able to emancipate themselves. The highest purposes of the Universal Negro Improvement Association were liberty and freedom for the Negro, but there must be the backbone of education if liberty and freedom were to be obtained. He was not prepared to condemn the South wholesale or yet to uphold the South. Its people had shown themselves the most honest in their attitude toward the Negro American and African Negroes would become the finest Negroes in the world because of their contact with the brutally frank white residents in the South of America and in South Africa, a contact which inculcated in the Negro the spirit of self-reliance, self-respect and self-development. The South, it must not be forgotten, he concluded, was powerful in Republican no les[s] than in Democratic politics.[1]

Hon. Bishop McGuire, New York, drew a parallel between the relations of Negroes and Caucasians in the South and in America as a whole and th[o]se that existed between the descendants of Ham and the Hebrews when the latter sought refuge among the former.[2] So long as two distinct races, living side by side, had both made up their minds to preserve their racial identity and to remain pure, there would be a dominant race and a subject race. He had visited the South on many occasions and preferred living conditions there to the hive existence eked out in New York apartments. In Greensboro, North Carolina, he instanced, Negroes lived in palatial homes with every comfort and convenience and unmolested by the white residents, whose concern ended at segregation. Thank God for the South, he said; thank God for the opportunities Negroes enjoyed there, thank God for the limitations placed upon their enjoyment which made them think of their fathers' God and hold in mind the destiny of the race.

Hon. Jacob Chambers, East St. Louis, said he was born and reared in the South. Talking about conditions that existed there, he said, would not solve the problem that confronted the race there. The only way to solve the problem to the satisfaction of all concerned was by putting more energy, more money and giving more help to the Universal Negro Improvement Association and its leader. The people in the Mississippi Valley and in Tennessee were ready to embrace the tenets of the U.N.I.A. and a strenuous and well directed effort should be made to reach the Negroes in the South.

Hon. R. McDowell, Blytheville, Ark., said the South would be solid for the Universal Negro Improvement Association if proper measures were taken to spread the principles. The Negro of wealth in the South stood between the masses and their salvation. It was that class of men to whom the attentions of the U.N.I.A. should be directed. The policy of the white man was this, he told the Negro, prepare somewhere to go, for we are only letting you stay here until we are ready to turn you out, when we no longer need you.

Hon. C. Minus, New York, said it must be remembered that Negroes in the South were taught from the white man's books and literature. The U.N.I.A. must seek to correct this.

Hon. Henrietta V. Redd, Gary, Ind., said she was born in Mississippi, and lived there nearly all her life. She condemned in strong terms the unsympathetic treatment meted out to Negroes who migrated from the South by their Northern brothers—she referred particularly to the States of Indiana and Illinois.

Hon. L. Jones, Cincinnati, said he was born and reared in the Southern States. As he saw it the U.N.I.A. should concentrate its attention on the preachers and the teacher.

Hon. Haywood Hampton, Georgia, suggested that the heads of great fraternal bodies, such as the United Odd Fellows and the Masons, and certainly wealthy Negroes of influence should be brought together in conference.

Hon. D.D. Daniels, of New Madrid, Mo.,[3] said he was a native of Mississippi, and 76 years of age. The preachers and teachers, he agreed, were the greatest stumbling block in the way of a successful solution of the problem.

At this stage the adjournment was taken on the motion of Hon C. Minus, seconded by Hon. R.A.[H.] Bachelor.

Friday Afternoon, August 8

On the resumption at 2 o'clock the discussion which engaged attention at the morning session was continued.

Hon. C. Stokes, Middletown, Ohio; Hon. Col. Wattley, New York; Hon. A. R. Patesaul, Alliance, Ohio, and Hon. L. [J.] Simmons, Blytheville, Ark., spoke suggesting the use of literature and the press. Hon. J. D. Barber said the eyes of the preacher should be opened, he should not be fought, the preachers were not to blame for they were [in] the majority of cases mere creatures of a system. He said that one of the reasons why the south did not want to see the Negroes leave was because they wanted the company of Negro women and it would be an excellent thing if they lined up with the white women of the south, and thereby gaining the friendship of the latter, in fighting the relations of white men with black women.

Hon. B. Hale, Milwaukee, said if the masses were taught and converted, their leaders, the preachers would follow. Hon. Askernese, Farrel[l], Pa., was of the same opinion. If a house was on fire, he said, the tenants would not wait until the preachers told them to leave.

Hon. Wightman, Chicago, said courage was needed in dealing with the situation.

Hon. J. B. Eaton, strongly condemned the suggestion that the preachers be approached. Get the masses, he declared. It would be a waste of time and money to prepare literature for circulation among the preachers.

Hon. May [Mae] Boyd, New York, said it was economic stress that prevented Negroes of the north assisting Negroes of the south more than they did when they came north.

The Speaker, Hon. Marcus Garvey, said two important points had been made. The statement of the Hon. Henrietta Redd, in regard to the attitude of the Negro to his brother was true. The big Negro or the educated or privileged Negro cared nothing about the unfortunate Negro. The race as a whole was suffering from the same capitalistic, grafting bunch that the white people [were] suffering from and were now fighting. The fight was an internal one. The race had a group of professional Negroes who had no more consideration for their people than the Devil had for holy water, their one objective being exploiting the unfortunate of their own race. The average Negro preacher was a curse to the race.

Hon. Johnson, Hon. J. Richardson, Norfolk, Va.; Hon. A. G. Ellinburg, Gary, Ind.; Hon. Brown, Miami; Hon. W. [S. V.] Robertson, Hon. G. A. Weston, Hon. Allen, Toronto; Hon. Smith, Jersey City, also spoke, after which the discussion was closed.

Hon. F. Martin, St. Louis, moved that a committee of five be appointed by the speaker to formulate the suggestions as to the ways and means of adjusting the race problem in the south.

Hon. R. A. [H.] Bachelor, seconded and the motion was carried.

The following committee was appointed by the Speaker. Hon. Kyle, W. Va.; Hon. Robertson, Miss.; Hon. Henrietta Redd, Ind.; Hon. Mc-Dowell, Ark.; Hon. G. A. Logan, Atlanta, Ga. The meeting then proceeded to discuss ways and means of correctly educating white public opinion to the needs and desires of the Negro race. Hon. Kyle, W. Va., said one of the greatest hindrances to the movement was the misunderstanding on the part of the white race and suggested that this understanding be remedied by a system of propaganda put out through literature. The white man was cool, philosophical, logical and calculating and with literature in his hands informing him of the true principles of the association he would be able to appraise the statements of the enemy at their true value. The Negro World was a powerful instrument that should be used to the full.

Hon. Powell, Cincinnati; Hon. McDowell, W. Va. [Ark.]; Hon. Rudolph Smith, also spoke suggesting the dissemination of literature after which Hon. Smith moved that a committee of three be formed to formulate suggestions as to the needs and desires of the Negro race. Hon. Martin seconded and the motion was unanimously carried. The following committee was then appointed by the Speaker: Hon. F. Johnson, Detroit; Hon. Peters, Chicago; Hon. Nicholas, New York.

Hon. Weston moved that a committee be appointed to draft a resolution of condolence to be presented to the widow [Florence Bruce] of the late Sir John E. Bruce, and that the committee attend the funeral exercises Sunday,[+] and read the resolutions on behalf of the Fourth International Convention.

Hon. Rudolph Smith seconded and the motion was carried.

The Speaker appointed the following committee: Hon. Geo. Weston, Hon. Bishop Barber and Hon. Rudolph Smith.

The convention then adjourned until 3:30 p.m. Sunday, Aug. 10. . . .

Printed in *NW*, 16 August 1924. Original headlines abbreviated.

1. Following the defeat of Radical Reconstruction and the later disfranchisement of the black population, the southern electorate overwhelmingly supported the Democratic party. Despite this, as Garvey points out, the South maintained considerable political influence within the Republican party. The region possessed a large bloc of delegates at Republican conventions, with the result that the southern—largely black—leadership traditionally exercised an influence disproportionate to their small number of followers.

This situation changed in the early 1920s, when the Republican party made a concerted effort to capture southern votes. Under President Warren G. Harding, the national organization envisioned a new "lily-white" Republican party in the South; black leaders were excluded from party politics in several southern states, and some Republican candidates ran overtly racist campaigns. On the national level, Harding and the Republicans failed to take a strong stand either against lynching or the Ku Klux Klan. This Republican wooing of the white South, though unsuccessful, alienated many northern blacks. By 1923 many black leaders were threatening to quit the party, and in 1924 the NAACP recommended that blacks abandon the Republican party and cast independent ballots (Richard B. Sherman, *The Republican Party and Black America* [Charlottesville: University Press of Virginia, 1973], pp. 113–223; Ralph J. Bunche, *The Political Status of the Negro in the Age of FDR* [Chicago: University of Chicago Press, 1973], pp. 24–39; Numan V. Bartley and Hugh D. Graham, *Southern Politics and the Second Reconstruction* [Baltimore: Johns Hopkins University Press, 1975], pp. 1–24).

2. Ps. 105:23.

3. New Madrid is located in southeastern Missouri on the Mississippi River. Founded by the Spanish in 1783 for trading purposes, this port town grew slowly as American settlement proceeded. In the early twentieth century New Madrid had about two thousand inhabitants; it was a shipping point for cotton, grain, and livestock and also contained flour mills and cotton gins. Cotton cultivation increased significantly in the early 1920s, and many black sharecroppers, fleeing the boll weevil, arrived in the area from farther south. This influx may have encouraged growth of the Garvey movement; in 1926 New Madrid reported a strong UNIA membership of as many as fifty-one dues-paying persons. Four years later the division was still functioning (*NW*, 3 April 1926, 3 May 1930; Federal Writers' Project, Works Progress Administration, *Missouri* [New York: Duell, Sloan, and Pearce, 1941], p. 457; Thad Snow, *From Missouri* [Boston: Houghton Mifflin, 1954], pp. 154–161; Heilprin and Heilprin, eds., *Lippincott's Gazetteer of the World*, p. 1,962).

4. John E. Bruce was survived by his second wife, Florence Adelaide Bishop Bruce, and their daughter, Olive. Florence Bishop was born in Cleveland and married Bruce in September 1885. She worked with Bruce on his literary efforts and remained involved with the UNIA after Bruce's death: in 1930 she was listed as one of the directors of the newly incorporated Negro World Publishing Co. (*NW*, 16 August 1924; certificate of incorporation of the Negro World Publishing Co., 1 April 1930). Bruce died on 7 August 1924 at the age of sixty-seven. He was buried with full official ceremony. A cortege followed Bruce's casket from the funeral home down 7th Avenue to Liberty Hall, where it was met by clergy, units of the New York UNIA, and the UNIA choir. Inside Liberty Hall, the impressive funeral rites were attended by over five thousand members, many of whom were delegates to the Fourth UNIA International Convention. The ceremony was conducted in three parts: the first by Rev. Charles Martin of the Moravian church, of which Bruce had been a member; the second by Rev. G. Emonei Carter, secretary-general of the UNIA; and the third by the Prince Hall Masonic Society, to which Bruce had belonged. Marcus Garvey, William L. Sherrill, and Arthur Schomburg delivered eulogies, while resolutions in memory of Bruce were presented by the Fourth International Convention of the Negro Peoples of the World, the Negro Society for Historical Research (of which Bruce had been the co-founder), the American Negro Academy, the *Negro World* editorial staff, the Ladies of the Royal Court of Ethiopia, and divisions and auxiliaries of the UNIA (*WWCR*; *DANB*; *NYT*, 11 August 1924; *NW*, 16 August 1924; *Pittsburgh Courier*, 16 August 1924).

Report by Special Agent James E. Amos

New York City, 8/9/24

In an interview [*8 August*] Agent had with VERNAL WILLIAMS, one of Garvey's former Attorneys, whose office is at 145 W. 45th Street, New York City, Agent was informed by Williams that in 1921 he had pleaded with Garvey to make out his Income Tax Return correctly, Williams telling Garvey he would certainly get himself in serious trouble with the Government if he did not make out a correct statement, as there were so many people who knew just how much money he had received during the year. GARVEY told Williams to mind his own business and the Government could go to the devil as he did not care anything about the Government of the United States.

CONTINUED.

JAMES E. AMOS

DJ-FBI, file 61. TD.

Report by Special Agent Joseph G. Tucker

[*New York*] August 9th, 1924

UNIVERSAL NEGRO IMPROVEMENT ASSOCIATION

Marcus Garvey, President General of the above Association, was arrested on the 5th instant, charged with filing a fraudulent income tax return for the year 1921 and with perjury. He was arraigned before Federal Judge McClintic and after pleading not guilty, was released [o]n $2500. bail, which was furnished by a Bonding Company.

Garvey went directly from the Federal Building to Liberty Hall where the Convention of the Association is being held, and made the statement to his followers that politics was at the bottom of his most recent trouble; that at the last election when Smith was elected Governor and Hylan Mayor of New York, he swung the Negro vote to the Democrats, and as a result, the indictment was handed down.[1] He claimed that he had already been indicted in connection with his Income Tax Return for 1921 and the new indictment was merely being sprung at this time to hurt the Convention.

On the same day E.T. Merrill,[2] the Liberian Consul, stated that he had received word from Doctor Ernest Lyon, Liberian Consul General at Baltimore, instructing him to refuse to vis[é] passport for Garvey or any member of the Universal Negro Improvement Association movement to proceed to Liberia and that all Liberian Consuls in the United States had received instructions to the same effect.

This decision was set out due to a plea that Garvey's proposed African Republic would endeavor to supplant the constitutional regime of President King of Liberia.

Garvey admitted that the refusal of the Liberian Consul to allow entry to that country of his, Garvey's, followers gave him considerable concern. He stated that President Harding had appointed Solomon Porter Hood of New Jersey, a member of the National Association for the Advancement of Colored People (a conservative Negro organization)[,] Consul in Liberia[,][3] and W.E.B. Du Bois, also a member of the National Association for the Advancement of Colored People, as Special Representative of the United States at the Inauguration of President King in February last. Garvey said these two men had no doubt prevailed upon President King to oppose the Universal Negro Improvement Association.[4]

It is known that Garvey has tried to ship a portable saw mill and some agricultural implements to Africa via the Bull Steamship Line, but the Line has been notified not to deliver this merchandise in Africa, and it will be returned to this country and held until the shipper pays the full round trip freight, otherwise it will be sold at public auction.

Garvey, later in discussing the Liberian situation, stated that the

Association had intended to send three hundred colonists to Liberia in October and has a waiting list of twenty thousand (20,000) people eager to go, but would not send any boat until the present trouble is fixed up. . . .

JOSEPH G. TUCKER

DJ-FBI, file 61-299. TD.

1. Garvey's indictment was handed down by a Republican administration. Garvey did allow the Democratic mayoral candidate, John F. Hylan, to address a mass meeting at Liberty Hall prior to the election on 3 November 1921. Black voters supported Democratic candidates in the 1921 and 1922 elections, and in 1923 the *Baltimore Afro-American* reported that "thousands of colored voters, especially those living in the Harlem district . . . helped to swell up the big majority given former Governor Alfred E. Smith, Democrat" (*NW*, 5 November 1921, 26 August 1922; *Baltimore Afro-American*, 10 November 1922; DNA, RG 65, file BS 198940-229).

2. Probably a reference to Edward G. Merrill, the Liberian consul in New York from October 1906 (U.S. Department of State, *Register*, 1924 [Washington, D.C.: GPO, 1924], p. 276).

3. Solomon Porter Hood (b. 1853) was appointed resident minister and consul general to Liberia on 26 October 1921. Born in Lancaster, Pa., and educated at Lincoln University (Pa.), where he graduated in 1880, Hood joined the AME ministry in 1877. He later served as a missionary in Haiti, and during the Haitian revolution of 1890 he acted as under secretary of the American legation. Hood returned to the United States in 1892 and subsequently became the pastor of several churches in Pennsylvania and New Jersey, later accepting the position of literary editor of the AME Sunday School teachers' quarterly. No evidence of Hood's putative membership in the NAACP has been found (*WWCR*; *WWCA*).

4. At the suggestion of William Lewis, U.S. assistant attorney general, President Coolidge appointed Du Bois special minister plenipotentiary and envoy extraordinary to represent the president at the inauguration of President King of Liberia. Accusations emanated from several sources that Du Bois's appointment implied an alienation between the Liberian government and the UNIA, and it was suggested that Du Bois himself was at least partly responsible for this alienation. In 1932, in response to an inquiry from Ben Nnamdi Azikiwe, future founding-president of the Republic of Nigeria, Du Bois denied that he had played any part in the rift between Garvey and the Liberians. "I beg to say," Du Bois wrote, "that I had nothing to do at all with the relations of Garvey and the Republic of Liberia. Garvey's colonization scheme had already been rejected before I went there and before there was the slightest intimation of my appointment. . . . My relations to Liberia were purely formal and I did not mention Garvey to Mr. King or to any Liberian official during my stay there" (W.E.B. Du Bois, *The Autobiography of W.E.B. Du Bois*, p. 272; Ben N. Azikiwe to Du Bois, 6 November 1932; Du Bois to Azikiwe, 11 November 1932; Du Bois to C.D.B. King, 21 January and 29 July 1924; King to W.E.B. Du Bois, 30 June 1924, in Herbert Aptheker, ed., *The Correspondence of W.E.B Du Bois*, 1: 277–283, 464–465).

Address by Marcus Garvey

[[New York, August 11, 1924]]

IN MASTERLY REVIEW OF LAST TWO YEARS' WORK
HON. MARCUS GARVEY LAYS BARE THE DETAILS
OF THE STRENUOUS BATTLE WAGED BY THE
UNIVERSAL NEGRO IMPROVEMENT ASSN. AGAINST ENEMIES

. . . I have not made a written report because of the pressure of time and also because of the many things that I would like to incorporate. So the report is going to be oral.

Deputies and delegates of the Fourth International Convention of the Negro Peoples of the World and of the Universal Negro Improvement Association: It is my duty as President-General to make an annual report to you as touching the affairs of the organization as a whole under my supervision and administration. According to the constitutional designation, I am administrator of the affairs of the association.

Our convention adjourned in September of 1922 to meet again, as is customary, on the first of August, 1923. Unfortunately, we were unable to meet last year because of certain developments to which I shall refer later on. Officially, therefore, I had to announce through my office and through the executive council the postponement of the holding of the convention of 1923 to the holding of the convention this year. Naturally, you have been following the work of the organization during that period of time, and it is for me now to say that we have had a trying and a[rd]uous time, the hardest period of our association's existence was between 1922, after the adjournment of the convention, and the present time.

It was difficult because the association had taken on wide dimensions. It had practically introduced propaganda and its sentiments were scattered round the world, bringing into existence diversified agencies that were working for the suppression of this new expression on the part of the people for freedom and independence, as characterized by the ideals and aims of the organization. The world was more appreciative during these years of the real objective and purpose of the association, and it goes without saying that there are many and great agencies in the world that are opposed to the advancement and development of the Negro on certain lines. Those lines we husbanded most and tried to project for the good and welfare of the entire race, because organizations had sprung up here and there, and individuals and agencies of government here and there, to block and hinder the effort that was being made to carry out the aims and objects of the association.

EFFORTS TO HINDER GREW

During 1923 and the latter part of 1922, after the adjournment of the convention, the effort to suppress this organization and hinder and handicap it grew stronger than at any other period. Just about that time we had a tremendous amount of internal troubles and difficulties. The association had grown so large that it was impossible to centralize control. It was impossible to exercise the discipline that was necessary to bring the whole movement into one supple working institution. We had built up around us hundreds of branches of the association into which were individuals not in tune with the service, but who were looking for opportunities whereby they could create themselves local authorities and local forces and powers, and to use those forces and powers to their own personal benefit and direction. I mean by that that in 1922 and immediately after the convention we had succeeded in the years of work in building up an organization which had its agents and branches all over the world. Agencies and branches that were built to harness in obedience to the constitution of the association and centralize our authority[,] the rule[,] and which would mean immediate and unbounded success for the association. But immediately after the rising of the convention, the individuals who were at the head of these branches took up an attitude and authority to act contrary to the purpose and spirit of the constitution, thereby instead of giving whole-hearted support to the central body, started to build up LOCAL PRINCIPALITIES and local authorities to suit their own selfish purposes. As, for instance, one of our greatest strongholds was the City of Philadelphia. We had a tremendous division there and immediately after that convention the president, Lionel Francis, seemed to have got into his head that he should be president-general or should be at the head of the association. Instead of being loyal to the association he began to disintegrate it, and tried to localize it for himself. As is his case, so were others. So that between 1922 and 1923 we had such internal dissensions and internal disloyalty that it was impossible for us to even carry out half of the things decided upon in the convention of 1922. Nearly 80 per cent of these divisions made absolutely no reports from the rise of the convention even up to the present moment. The local division would collect moneys for dues, assessments, annual taxes, and from other sources and would expend every nickel, and we would hear nothing of their activities until probably someone died or something happened, when they would directly try to collect death grants, etc., from the parent body without sending in their reports.

INTERNAL TROUBLE

Such internal dissensions affected the parent body during that period of time. I am not speaking of the opposition that was outside, because we would have been better able to handle the opposition on the outside if we had the proper and efficient conduct of the organization internally. It is apparent, however, that there is absolutely no rule or law to lay down towards the Negro at the present as he is educated and now stands. There is absolutely no secular or civil rule to lay down to control him, because we have had fair examples of the disposition of the Negro to purposely disobey orders. They will not respect any law, if this law conflicts with their personal desires. And that is what we have been suffering from. It is not because we haven't a constitution. The constitution is clear and well defined in every detail, so that every officer and member and executive would know their relationship towards each other. It is just because the constitution has stood in the way of individuals doing what they wanted done. You who come from divisions know that if I had to attend to all the complaints that come to headquarters I would be unable to do anything else, and we would not have been here today had I to give all my time to the adjustment of these complaints. There was not five percent of the divisions that went without internal complaints, and of that five we did not hear about them at all, and that is why we had no complaints from them.

HOW TO DISCIPLINE THE NEGRO

So it brings us to the consideration as to how we can successfully discipline the Negro. It is a most gigantic task confronting the organization and the people. How can you discipline the Negro to get him to do what is right? This association is built upon righteousness and justice, charity and sympathy and love for our people. But it seems to me that very few of us who are officers seem to understand it that way. We have lost sympathy for the people that we are endeavoring to help in search of our immediate success, and this is one of the propositions that I want you to take out of my address and discuss at the close or during the time when we are going to adjust the affairs of the association, because it is very important that we devise ways and means to successfully conduct the affairs of our race dependent on individuals of the race to lead, as they must if we are to go anywhere.

I need not cite instances, because every one of you here almost have come from divisions where such internal differences have been manifest. If I think of Chicago, we have had hundreds and hundreds of complaints. We have had fights galore. If I think of Philadelphia it is the same. If I think of Cleveland it is the same. If I go as far as I can, to Los Angeles, it is the same condition, and if we go to the West Indies and Central America it is the same.

EATING THE SOUL

It is a canker that is eating the vitals and the heart and soul of the Negro who has no nationality. This thing is everywhere, not only in America. We have had the same thing and probably worse here. We have had men fighting each other; one group putting the other in jail and as that group gets out of jail they put the other group in jail. One group tries to get into power by saying that the other is dishonest, and as soon as they get into office they do the same thing they complained against.

Now I am nearly disgusted as to how to find men. One man would come and say that that president is doing wrong, and that very man is the one who, when he gets started and gets elected to the same office, would within three months have the same complaint made about him as he had made. That is the condition that we have in the East and West, North and South, in America, the West Indies, in South and Central America.

What are we to do with these Negroes? As I said before, their education is bad. The psychology under which we live is bad and we have to take that into serious consideration. I am sorry for the poor people and that is why my heart bleeds. The poor people do not know where to turn. They flocked to this organization when we organized it because they believed it was a relief from the old order of things. And, my good friends, it seems hard and almost impossible to destroy the old order of things. It is deepseated in the heart of the old Negro.

As to the new conditions, it seems almost hopeless. I do not know what to say and what to recommend. We have to discuss it and see what to do.

All the middle-aged, the old and the new men, all seem to be possessed of the same idea, and that is to get rich at the expense of the people who they believe cannot see and cannot understand and whom he leads nowhere, absolutely nowhere.

ALARMING ECONOMIC CONDITIONS

When we look at conditions as they confront us; when we review the general economic conditions as they have existed during the last two years, we see that they are alarming. I have to report to you that our people today are in a hopeless economic and industrial state and condition in this country and abroad. In the American states, I have come into contact with hundreds and thousands of unemployed, and the unemployed list is growing among us as a race, larger and larger everyday. There is no work. The same prophecy that we gave out during the war, of a terrible economic reaction[,] is being fulfilled. And if you want to go to the big cities, Detroit, Cleveland, Philadelphia, and even cosmopolitan New York, you will find that hundreds and thousands of our men are out on the streets, some of them not having been employed for 6, 12 or 18 months, and day by day we are losing our foothold [i]n the industries of the country and there is absolutely no provision being made to stem the tide except we attempt to go forward with the program of the U.N.I.A. for which we have suffered barriers and handicaps of all kinds and which we will endeavor to adjust during this sitting of the convention.

The situation industrially and economically in America and in the West Indies is alarming. In Cuba, we have cries and complaints from thousands of Negroes there who are suffering there and dying. From the other islands of the West Indies, it is the same. In Central America where a good condition existed up to [a] few years ago, it is the contrary now. The people are suffering here and there is absolutely no outlook except through a rigid industrial program on the part of the U.N.I.A.

ALLOWING OPPORTUNITIES TO SLIP

The pain is that day after day we are allowing the chance and opportunities to slip away which will not come again because day after day the race is becoming poorer as we grow older in this industrial and economic and commercial arrangement with the other people. In our communities the race is losing its financial hold day by day and in another few years we are going to be hopeless. And there is where the sorrowful part on the part of our leaders come[s] in. Our leaders have done more to dishearten our people than we could talk about. For the reason that where there is no confidence there is no support because the bulk of the people are not educated to the point of knowing and understanding the situation. The bulk of our people are not educated in the higher principles and purposes of life. They drift and flow according to arrangements and environment. They do not think for themselves. They have to be advised and when it is considered that these people have been advised to do this and that which they have been doing for the last 50 years without any result, it is time for the confidence of the people to be destroyed and broken. We now have to deal with this broken confidence on the part of the people who have become disgusted with the kind of leadership that we have had and the success of the association during the past five or six years was due to the fact that the people ran to us, rushed to us, because it would be a relief from the old order of things. Local officers and international officers have done more to set back the progress of the association than have the enemy, for the simple reason if you are whole and united together internally it is more than hard and difficult for the enemy on the outside who does not know your business and intentions to harass and handicap you. But when you are broken in spirit and absolutely divided it is easy for the enemy to fight you. I have no explanation of virtue to give or to apply on the part of any individual in the organization during that period, because there has been such reckless misuse of power and authority and misunderstanding of responsibility that as I have said before it bleeds my heart to calculate the consequences and I cannot imagine where we are going to find men and people who have charity for the people and who are prepared to do them service, because if there is any age demanding service to the Negro, it is this one. It is not only an age of service but of sacrifice.

NEED FOR SACRIFICE

We Negroes expect to get results too easily and quickly. We have to make sacrifice and render service unselfishly if we are to get anywhere. We generally desire to jump off in the desire to have everything in one day or in a few years. If we read our histories it will be found that the foundations of all great movements were laid on sacrifice and sweat and blood. I do not want to go outside of this country to get you to understand what I mean. The civilization that the people of this country enjoys today in the City of New York, was laid and buil[t] upon the foundation of blood, the blood of 400 years. When the Pilgrim Fathers came here they were not looking for big jobs, and big salaries, but they grouped themselves together by sacrifice to build and die and lay the foundations for succeeding generation[s] of their own.

That spirit we haven't got in the U.N.I.A. to any extent at this time, nor do we have it in the race, and that is why we are doomed until we can develop it. When I speak of the opposition and trials and troubles on the part of most of the leaders in the division, I will bring to your notice the provisions we made when we came before the first and second conventions, and even the last one, when we stood on this platform, dozens of us swore away our lives in the service of this organization. When I tell you that there are only two of such people of that old group who swore away their fortune, their lives and their all to this convention in 1920, and they are Lady Davis and your humble servant, you will understand. Succeeding groups did the same swearing, and as quickly as they swore and as quickly as they were placed in a position of trust and responsibility, as quickly were they willing to allow themselves to be used for the destruction of the organization and the exploitation of the people.

Now let me recount more in detail what I mean by that. There are some of us who respect our oaths; there are some people who because of their belief in God and the Creator swear in the presence of their God, and regard that oath as sacred. That is why, come weal, come woe, some of us are bound to be found at the helm of the U.N.I.A. because we respect our oaths to uphold the sacred trust of the 400,000,000 Negroes of the world.

At the first convention we made a tremendous mistake. Yet it was not a mistake. It was just an experiment for which we had to pay, and for which all people, starting out new ventures, naturally have to pay. We entered into the arrangement with a whole souledness and with self-consciousness, with race love and race pride, but we never calculated on the other human side and the evil side which is part of us all the time, which we tried to destroy, but which existed after we made our arrangement.

After our deliberations at the first convention, we voted large salaries to the different heads of departments and to the Executive Council. That was done because we desired then to remove our leaders from temptation. We wanted to surround them with such financial independence as to prevent them from doing anything as would injure or damage this race. We wanted to remove them from suspicion and bribery of all kinds. That was the intention behind the voting of large salaries. We did not want our men to be purchased or to sell out the interests of the association. But it was also understood at that convention that with the spirit that was sweeping over the world at that time, the men would dignify their offices, and would be so capable that they would have earned their salaries by loyal service. Unfortunately we over-calculated the men. No sooner had we voted their salaries than it was their disposition to sit down in the dignity of their office and get the salary from wherever it came.

We never calculated that any of those men would have been so mean and low and unracial to have put this association into a situation of embarrassment, knowing that they themselves failed to make those provisions. Let me give you an idea of what I mean, because some of you came into the association at a late period and do not know its history.

CO-PARTNERS IN SUFFERING

This association was founded on sacrifice and suffering, and torture of all kinds, because it was the personal and spontaneous desire of the individual to give birth to something that was not in existence, and present it to the people for what it was worth. That meant that there was no immediate remuneration or reward for the effort to start a thing of the kind, and it was just based upon the spirit of race love, race pride and the desire for sacrifice. It was for such a purpose that that convention was called. The reports then made demonstrated that there was suffering all over the world. Men who spoke from the platform as delegates and deputies revealed the hard and difficult conditions that confronted them, and from which they were seeking means of relief. They made us co-partners of the same suffering, fellows of the same desires and wants, and it was in this spirit that we elected the first group of officials in that convention to serve the people. Money was a secondary consideration, because the convention revealed that we had no money. I believe that we had just about $3,000. So when we elected them to the offices, with the big salaries, they knew very well that we had absolutely no resources to meet these salaries, but it was because we wanted an organization wherein the men who felt so much and suffered so much, according to their own expressions, would have had the opportunity and the privilege to serve their people, and in that service their people would have been willing to reward them according to their service.

CAPITALIZING THE WORK

And the people did according to their financial ability. When we adjourned that first convention in 1920, we had to devise ways and means to capitalize the organization and carry on its work and the program that had been laid out. That program for the year was an elaborate one. We had to go out and educate the world with the propaganda and link up the different communities. It called for the expenditure of large sums of money. We, therefore, got together and decided that we should float a loan immediately in order to capitalize the work of the organization so that we could scatter the principles and aims and objects all over the world. It was then decided, I believe, to borrow $200,000 or thereabouts, for the capitalization of the work. The money was to be paid back in periods of from one to five years. We borrowed this money on notes called construction notes in amounts from $50 to $1,000, believing in the honesty and confidence of those first group of men. That money, as I have already said, was for the immediate organization purposes to scatter and ramify and strengthen the association all over the country, and also to meet immediate demands. Some of those executive officers during the first year helped us to raise the money. Some did not do anything. Among those who were able to bring results were Dr. McGuire, I think; also Dr. Eason and myself. I believe, out of the whole group, these three were the only ones who raised any substantial part of that money. The rest went out, and some of them would not even bring back their railroad fare.

The next thing was when they started to say they were big officials and could not do this or that. The result was that in the first year we raised about $120,000 and capitalized the association. To show how loyal some of them were, it was to the extent of seeing that they got their salaries on every first and fifteenth out of the moneys that we raised. In the second year, when the time came for us to double up and spread, scatter and strengthen the work of the association in order to get results so as to reimburse those who had made loans for short periods, and they found they had to work and earn the salaries that were paid them, that a bunch of Negroes started to resign and sue the association for the balance of the big salaries supposed to be due them for the work they had not done.

DISHONEST OFFICIALS

That was how our first trials and troubles started after they had eaten up for salaries practically all the moneys we had borrowed to capitalize the work. They resigned today, and on the following day their lawyers sent letters to the effect as follows: "I am directed by Mr. So-and-So to inform you that the association is owing him so much for salary, and we ask for immediate payment." Men, you must have heard of the lawsuits we had. This is the explanation that I have to give. And now only Miss Davis and myself have been left to reimburse the people and pay the salaries of those men and to carry on the work of the organization up to this time.

Now, as to Mr. de Bourg. In the spirit of service, believing that man was capable, we elected him here at a salary of $6,000 per year. During his sixteen months' tenure of office, in the first year he did not report; otherwise we would have tried him, as we did Mr. Tobitt. He did not bring in $500 for his sixteen months' tenure of office; and, though it was decided that the salaries would be cut down proportionately because of the condition of the association, that man got a lawyer (at the time when I was on trial in New York) to file a suit against the association for $12,000 salary; toward which he had contributed only $200; and with the aid of officers who were in and those who were outside, and with their lawyers and our lawyers, they connived to keep back the proper defense of the association and allow immediate judgment to be given by default so that de Bourg would collect that amount.[1] The one inside helped the one outside so that he would get help when he put in his claim also. So it is, when a case was called, we would find one man helping the other to collect so that he in turn would be helped.

THREATENED WITH RECEIVERSHIP

This is the trouble we have had with the money we should have had to pay the people from whom we borrowed. We have had to pay all these damnable, soulless Negroes. Were it not through the grace of God, we would have had to close the doors of the association more than a year ago. These people did not only sue the association, but they even asked for receivers to come in and take charge of the affairs of the association and to put the association into bankruptcy. You can imagine what a fight we had to make. Sometimes I had to run here from Los Angeles, or from Detroit, in order to stop proceedings and to save the association from a receivership.

Then, outside of that, we had the dishonesty of the divisions which would make no reports, although we had these tremendous obligations to meet. It was no wonder we had to appeal to the people in the columns of the Negro World. I have had to leave New York, three weeks in every month, to go on the road to speak for the benefit of the association.

The[s]e were the difficulties between 1920 up to the present moment, but let me tell you men[,] that is not all. These very officers whom we elected[,] if we were to reveal all the things that they have done, and all the trouble that they have given in the Black Star Line case and in the tax case. When they found that the association did not die, and because it would not die, they would do something else to make it die. They went to the law officers and did everything to smash up the organization.

If we go before the court in New York, the court would start very good this morning, and you would be unable to tell on what side the case would go. Before mid-day, however, some Negro would tell judge and the jury that this association is Marcus Garvey's, who is trying to organize the Negro to kill all the white people. Naturally, this meant that we lost the decision before the case was tried.

THE BLACK STAR LINE CASE

The trial of my case in connection with the Black Star Line would have ended in my being exonerated because there was nothing against me. It was just prejudice. Those Negroes wrote letters to the judge and jurors saying that Garvey was organizing his people to kill them. These are the methods that these men inside of this organization, along with others outside, have used to handicap the U.N.I.A., and today, when you see the U.N.I.A., you can hardly imagine the struggle and fight we have had to keep it going. I feel sure that it is God's grace and spirit that it is alive today, because it is not for the lack of trials and tribulations. Why sometimes we arranged with courts to give a certain judgment at a certain time and, believing the association had no money, and in order to place it in embarrassment, they would proceed at once and bring receivers. But because of God's good spirit every time they turned one way we turned the other.

That group of men I will never forget, that first group of men who helped us to raise the money on the construction loans from the people, and when the time came to stick together and work and raise the money to pay them back, that bunch of vagabonds deserted and left the responsibility upon the shoulders of other men. I could never forget and pardon such men. When they thought that money was easy to get they were all willing to serve, but when they found out they were to work for it they resigned and got lawyers to sue. If these Negroes had a sense of responsibility they would not have been one of them with guts enough to go and sue this organization, because they would realize that they were suing themselves.

In this respect, among those who resigned for other reasons, there are about two men out of the whole group who never embarrassed us in a court. They were Doctor McGuire and Mr. Toote. They were the only two who resigned from the association because of certain explanations, who never took us to court, who never did anything to embarrass us, and who did everything to help us.

THANKS TO MR. TOOTE

I have personally to thank Mr. Toote even after he left the association for his determination to help and protect us against the other group of fellows.

To show how wicked and vicious these men were, when we could not pay these salaries we cut down by half and gave notes for the balance we could not pay. It was understood that these notes would be for five years or more in order to give the association time to pick up so that we could pay them. These men, especially the chancellor, and the auditor, made out certain notes for one year without the knowledge of the others, for themselves, while they made other notes for myself and others for ten years, showing that they had in mind that in one year they would desert the association and collect their money. All of these tricks they worked because we did not know what they did and only found out afterwards.

We never anticipated these things when we went before the court to adjust the matter. These very men who sat down and arranged certain things would swear before God that it was not so and among them the only m[a]n upon whom we could rely was Mr. Toote, who came and testified as to what really had taken place, but what could he do in the face of three or more others who agreed to support each other by making affidavits for each other and thus we found we were encumbered and handicapped during the period under report.

REALIZING THE RESPONSIBILITY

I cannot explain half of the troubles through which we have gone in order to carry on the work of the association. When they thought the association did not have any money they would try to go to the bank and tie up everything I had. Thank God I never had more than two or three hundred dollars. I got just what they got but I tried to economize, otherwise I would not have had anything. And every time the association would be in need I would go to the bank and draw out, as the chancellor would tell you, sometimes the whole amount to tide over the association. Every little money I would save I would lend the association. Sometimes I dared not even tell my wife the things I had to do for the association. Even at the time when I was arrested and convicted I only left her $50 to face the world. I realized the responsibility, and it is no wonder that I have now a sick and half-dying wife because of the sufferings that we have had to undergo. Had it not been for the kind consideration of those of you who came to my rescue I do not know what would have become of the woman, because of those devils who did everything in the world to embarras[s] us in the work.

And today I appeal to you. Let us, during this convention, seriously and soberly enter into the spirit of the movement and you, presidents, for God's sake, remember that this race of ours is not going to rise higher than its leaders will lead them in the right direction.

As to the white man, we won't talk about him any more. We all know what he is up to. As I can see it, the white man is determined to kill this race of ours. I know it, it is only a question of time, of another hundred years when this race of ours will be as dead as the Indian. The white man is not going to tell you everything, it is for you to find out. And no wonder they place obstacles. I, for one, would expect nothing otherwise, but the things that pain me are that our very people allow themselves to be used to carry out the intentions and desires of those who desire to kill this virile race of ours.

Let us realize this. There is a God Almighty who is not asleep. This situation that we leaders brought upon our own people, we leaders are going to pay for not only in this world, but if there is another world the sufferings will multiply themselves, because how can one intelligent man, seeing the situation, fail to act honestly, truthfully, and faithfully towards people who are willing to suffer for them.

TO GO THE LIMIT

And this is my responsibility and that is why I take so much risk. Why I am determined to go the limit. Because I realize the responsibility that something must be done and someone has to do it. It cannot be postponed. When I go from place to place in this country and come into contac[t] with the sufferings of the people, my heart bleeds within me and we haven't gone half the journey yet. If we are suffering now what will it be in ten, twenty-five, fifty or a hundred years hence. I have often told you that in another hundred years there will be an over-populated America for the white people. There is not going to be enough room and opportunity for the two races and the American white man, like the English, is preparing to kill the Negro and they will do so through starvation, they would not have to shoot, lynch, or burn. All they have to do is to turn him out of employment and when he has no employment he will have no money; then without money, no food, and if he hasn't food, he will have to starve, and if he starves he will die.

The white man every day is manoeuvring and creating new designs by which he can gain control. You read many things in the papers to which you pay no attention. You may have read about the death rays and such things. Do you know what is going on in the laboratories of the universities and museums of research? The white men day and night are working on scientific methods by which they could outdo the rest of civilization. We are living in a scientific age and let me tell you, if we do not look out, between science and industry, they will kill every Negro out within a hundred years.

WHEN THE WHITE MAN ENTERS AFRICA

Let us take Africa. Do you know that as soon as white people decide that certain parts of Africa are habitable for white men, when it is made possible by scientific achievement through schools of science, to travel and study the conditions of the tropics so as to adjust the white man to those conditions and enable him to live there, these men of science will inoculate certain germs and call it a peculiar disease of the natives and in five years where there was a teeming population there would hardly be any, and when asked what had become of them they would simply say that an epidemic had taken them away. Between the white scientist, the industrial capitalist and the statesman we do not know what is going to occur. Do you know why they crowd us here in Harlem? Do you know what is going to happen? Don't you know that the death rate of Negroes is over 50 per cent higher than that of the white and that the birth rate is tremendously lower? You read the papers and do not understand what it means. This is the white man's safeguard. So long as the death rate is higher than the birth rate he knows that he has us in the palm of his hand. Do you wonder we can hardly do anything but eat and sleep and go to work and die?

The economists of the white race have arranged it so that you get only enough for today and when you have paid for rent, food and clothes so that you can make a good appearance in the society they have established, there is absolutely no margin left out of the money you have earned. But the very white people get a margin after they have paid all of their expenses, they have left at least 25 per cent to store up for their children and for a rainy day.

NEGRO HERE ON SUFFRANCE

These arrangements the white man has had and made not only in New York and America, but all over the world. They keep us in their industries just because they haven't enough men to do all the work required to be done. You and I are in America and in the world because the white man has not enough men to do his menial work, and we have to do it until they get men of their own. And when this country trebles its population they will have more than enough men to do what they want, from sweeping the streets to occupying the presidency. What will become of the Negro? That is the danger. That is why we are fighting so and that is why I intend to give up my life fighting for the preservation of the race because I know what the other race is up to. I know the intentions of the other man. He will not tell you, but you will find it out for yourself. That is why I cannot compromise heartlessly with the leaders, with the men whom we elected, who joined with others to destroy us.

DISLOYAL EXECUTIVE OFFICERS

You will observe, as I said before, that last year we had no convention. We were unable to have this convention because we would not have had an organization and better judgment on my part caused me to postpone it. I thank you for the obedience you showed to the instructions I gave for the postponement of the convention until this year. The purpose was, if I have to say it, they believed that I am the moving spirit of the organization and they believed if they were able successfully to remove me, it would have been easy to destroy the whole organization. That was the white man's viewpoint. There were others who thought it would have been a splendid opportunity for them to get into power and when they got into power they would get the other man to get me out of the way and still look at me in the face and smile. You can hardly imagine the patience I have had to exercise to sit down with men that I know are trying to put a rope around my neck. I had to smile with them because of the good of the association because every one we turn out adds one more enemy that we have to fight. They do not leave the office one minute before they find the enemy somewhere and they decide what they will do on the morrow. Anything that is going to happen to me I know one month before hand. Even now we have men whom I look at and smile, I know what they are doing at night time, somewhere trying to fix up something so that they would get into power. I do not know how long they intend to remain in power. It simply shows how purchasable and wicked our race is when we try to kill each other for our self-advancement and for our ego.

There are very few of us who can stand responsibility and honor. They lose their heads as soon as they are honored. Nobody is just as good as they are. I have had to deal with so many of them because of the insults they have given to you members and because of those you have suffered from some of the executive officers who do not seem to realize that they are part of us and that we could not exist were it not for the spirit of the people of the organization and behind it.

I am speaking this morning—and that is why I have not made a written report—because I could not touch on all these things. I want you to realize the social responsibility which all of us owe to each other. I am not afraid of the consequences of what they are doing, but it is to what extent the doing of these things affect the ideals and objects that we have in view.

"Garvey Is Meddling"

You are intelligent people. You know. You have read. The U.N.I.A. is not the first reform movement formed to help the people. And though all those who have led know of the misrepresentations and sufferings of all kinds which such movements entail, I am willing still to do my part and to give my all for the success of the movement. And that is why I so jealously regard the success of the U.N.I.A. All kinds of propaganda and tricks have been used to thwart our efforts. When I try to do something they say Mr. Garvey is meddling and would not allow us to work. When I leave it to them the thing blows up. That is how the Black Star Line went down. When I tried to help, everybody said Mr. Garvey is doing everything. But it was not six months after I passed over the responsibility to them that the trouble came.

It is so difficult for us to realize what responsibility means. The average man wants to get rich overnight. They want a house and automobile overnight. Where could it come from if the thing of which you are a part is to succeed and continue? We have to devise ways and means during this convention to make these officers—presidents, secretaries and executive officers—true.

Truth About Captain Gaines

Let me tell you again, we are suffering from the germ of dishonesty, and if we can legislate to kill that germ we will have done a great deal of work. There is one man now abusing the U.N.I.A. Captain Gaines is saying all kinds of things about me. Suppose I tell you the truth about the things that he has done. I have on the Executive Council now men who are my personal enemies, but I do not think about that. So long as they can serve the organization, I am glad to let them stay there. I would be the last man to put a man out. We sent Captain Gaines to all parts of the country at the time when we wanted money and help, and we could not get one report from that man. He went to Chicago and took up hundreds and hundreds of dollars. He also went to Cleveland and the next thing was we heard the strange news that he was cabling money to his private banking account. Yet that man goes and says that he has not got his salary from the association.

When we sent him to Chicago for three months that man collected over $1,000 and never said one word to the Parent Body. When we got reports about him, I had him under surveillance for a long time to see if he would act better. The last time I went West, I learned that he left Chicago, where he was sent, and went to Gary and to Cincinnati and told the people there he had been sent by the Parent Body, and from Cincinnati he collected $190, and other sums from Gary and Chicago, and nobody here knew anything about it. We did not know that he went there and it took us six months to find this out. What can we do with such a man?

TAKING MONEY FROM TWO PARTIES

At Gary, during the political primaries, he took money from two different parties in the name of the U.N.I.A., telling them he would send it to the Parent Body, and that the association would assist them. He also told the colored people there that Marcus Garvey got into trouble through politics and he would take all the money he could get from the politicians. This he said although federal agents were present. He also advised the Negroes to get as much as they could out of politics.

He went to Chicago and did something, but still I gave him a chance. He continued and found it was time to end that. I telegraphed that I had appointed another President and that he must wind up the affairs and return to New York. He refused to carry out my instructions to induct the new president, and he would not leave Chicago. He would not come to face me in New York, and now he goes and says that I am bad. And he has started an organization with Francis, of Philadelphia. In the name of God Almighty, where can we go? And now this man has become my bitter enemy. Simply because we tried to make him straight. Recently I heard that he was in Washington trying to go to the Shipping Board with whom we were negotiating for a ship. That shows you what we have to incur.

Can you blame the white people for what they are doing? Here is a man who has been in the organization for five years. The people believed in him, and that is why we have had all this trouble with the people from the outside.

THE CROOKED GO

I have explained this to you so that you would be able to understand the true situation of affairs. Those men we put out of the association were put out because we could not do better. Whosoever goes out of the association goes because he is crooked. We do not want anybody out, but want everybody in. But when we cannot get on with people we must separate from them. [So] I trust you have no misguided opinions as to what has happened.

"WHY I TRIED MY OWN CASE"

You will ask me, why I tried my case. I tried my case in the matter of the Black Star Line in 1923, because I had to save the U.N.I.A. If I had not tried that case myself, I would have been sentenced to 30 years. The association would have been wound up, and the hope of the Negro would have been buried forever. There were plots on every hand. There were plots with the very men with whom I was indicted. They knew they were going to be discharged long before the case was tried. And they indicted me first. Then when they found out that we were not so foolish and that the thing looked so bad, that out of the Black Star Line directors they should only pick on me, they went and indicted the other three men just to show it was not only Garvey they were looking for. But the other men knew before hand that nothing would happen to them. It went so far that in the trial of the case, at a certain point, the very District Attorney who was prosecuting me, turned around and defended one of the other men.

The plan which I found out before we had gone two days in the case was that the Government would have two and a half weeks in prosecuting me, and my lawyer would only take half a week in my defense, so that the judge and jury would go away in three weeks as arranged. The government was to use 80 witnesses against me during that time, and I was to have half a week in defending myself. That was the arrangement made for me, and no one said anything about it for me.

Therefore, I decided that all the lawyers could go to hell. If I was to go to jail I would make the world know the true situation of affairs, the result of which you well know. They were to show that Garvey was a crook. Now, the politicians had arranged that. I had some "friends" among them. I had some friends who did not want to see Garvey go to prison, but who could not stand Garvey's rivalry. So they decided to fix up things so that the jury would say Garvey is guilty and they would go and beg that he be given a suspended sentence and pardon. But my career as a rival would be dead.

MONEY SPENT FREELY

That is the arrangement they made for me and that arrangement I was not prepared to fall into. The truth had to be told. How far we told the truth you know—those of you who were at the trial and those who read the Negro World. But half has not been told. Money was spent freely—spent by England, France, the N.A.A.C.P., etc.—and was used by the Negro politicians in Harlem and by those Negroes whom we had dismissed from the Association and from the Black Star Line.

It was a combination from which only God Almighty could come free. The best I could do was to stop the thing by fighting and avoiding the sentence of thirty years. It would have taken God Almighty to go there and get a verdict of acquittal from those men, because they had to convict Garvey; because, by convicting him, they would have been able to scatter, eradicate and destroy the work of the Association and England and France believed it would be all over.

BRITAIN BUSY

They did not know of the new Negro. Some of you do not know international problems. There is a great international problem today, and the U.N.I.A. is one of the organizations of the world that is giving them trouble and concern in their work. You don't know it. If Garvey was an insignificant man, if all of us were a bunch of fools[,] do you think all those things you read about in the papers would happen[?] The British have given instructions that nobody who belongs to the U.N.I.A. should be allowed to land in their possessions in Africa. Do you think the British would send out an order like that? Do you think the Negro World could be such an insignificant paper when they pass laws in Dahomey,[2] Nigeria, the Gold Coast and in the West Indies against its being circulated there?[3] Do you think they would call special sessions of the Legislature to pass laws to prevent the circulation of the Negro World if it was foolishness—in British Guiana, British Honduras, Trinidad, Grenada, the Leeward Islands and Jamaica?

Some of the governments in certain parts of Africa called special Council meetings. Smuts of South Africa sent a petition to London begging and praying the British Government to prevent the Negro World being circulated in certain parts of Africa.[4]

When you have the governments doing that[,] you are [d]oing some-[thing]. All you have to do is to keep on doing and wait for your chance, as we tell you. The chance is coming in five, ten or twenty years, and the only thing we must have is a solid and firm organization.

PROPOSED VISIT TO ENGLAND

They look upon Marcus Garvey as a bad man. They looked upon De Valera as a bad man, but when they found out how things were going they granted the Irish the Free State.[5] They would call me now were it not for those damnable Negro politicians who acted so that I could not get my final papers. Were it not for that damnable organization, the N.A.A.C.P., who understood that I was going on a world tour in 1923, England would have come to terms long ago. And France would have come to terms, because I would have carried the fight to the heart of England and France. I knew that I would not have returned here in 1923 without bringing concessions for the Negro.

Those devils tried to block it. The Englishman is no fool and we are not fools. We know what we want. When you want to get something from people you do not read Sunday school texts to them. When you want to have a thing you often have to ride roughshod. I knew that as soon as I was able to get out of this country, with the many things off my mind, and approach the British Government, especially the present Labor Government, I felt sure we would have had Southern Nigeria or somewhere else, and we would have had more land than we want to carry out the programme of the U.N.I.A.

NEGRO MUST BE A RADICAL

But those Negroes who do not know anything about diplomacy or the handling of the world's problems tried to embarrass us. They talk about Garvey being radical. How can a Negro be conservative? What has he to conserve? What have you but pain, suffering and hardship? It is time for the Negro to be radical and let the world know what he wants. If it takes a radical to tell that, then you cannot help being one.

All that[,] England is doing. To show you how Negroes are foolish and how the white man is different from our people, the Negroes said before I went to the West Indies in 1921 that the English would arrest me when I reached Jamaica and do all kinds of things to me. But when I left here the most courteous people I had to deal with were the British. When I went to get my passport the official greeted me with, "Oh, Mr. Garvey, what can we do for you? Can we do anything to help your people?" They gave me the passport. Then those Negroes said the British would send a battleship down to stop Mr. Garvey landing. After I left Cuba who was the first man to meet me at the pier but the Inspector-General of Police, who said he was glad to see me and that he had been detailed to see that nothing occurred. I never had any trouble with the British Government while I remained there.

AN EXCLUSIVE ORDER

The trouble started when I was about to come back when those bad Negroes went to Washington and asked the Government to prevent my return. The Government issued instructions to every American consular agent along the Atlantic seaboard not to issue any visas for me. That was the time those devils were trying to get money from the Black Star Line. I had not left 24 hours before they took $25,000 from the treasury and ruined the Black Star Line. Owing to their efforts in trying to prevent my return it took me nearly five months instead of thirty days, as was planned.

So don't mind what is being said. Hold steadfast to the program. There are many ways to kill a dog without putting a rope around his neck.

HOW IT WORKED

The great American Government said I was not to be admitted here. But, by the exercise of a little patience, and as soon as we get things, we will get results. I got my passport visa[ed] and I went to New Orleans instead of New York, because the Negroes were waiting there. I had to use a little stroke. When I reached the Mississippi breakwater the immigration officers were waiting for me. They had received instructions not to let Garvey in, as I would not have a passport. When the passengers were lined up and the man was cocksure that I had no passport, [h]e told me, "wait a while," and he sent to call another man, saying, "Garvey is here." The other man asked what I had there, and I showed him my passport. He was so surprised he said: "Good God, look at this." He turned red all of a sudden in the face. He said, "We cannot understand this." They thought they had the man, but I had them. To make sure of me they said, "Do not go, you have to wait on the quarantine ground for inspection." I understood the situation and saw they intended to work something new. The man at the quarantine station called me to the office and asked my business, etc., and I saw they were trying to get time to communicate with certain people here to see if they could not cancel my visa. I sized the situation, so I said: "I want you to send this telegram to the President," I said it loud enough for the man to hear. I wrote the telegram and the man took it to the office of the other men. Then I said: "I want you to send this telephone message to Secretary Hughes." That man turned red, and two minutes afterward he said: "All right, Mr. Garvey, you may go." They were trying to work up sentiment to block me, and I understood the situation, so I scared those fellows and they let me go.

THE LAST INDICTMENT

I have recited all this to show you the methods the enemy resorted to. They did not succe[ed]. Then they got me indicted. They timed it just before the convention. Why, in regard to the last indictment, I knew two weeks before it happened that the indictment would be made on that day.

Well, we have to grapple with the situation. All we want is the honesty and devotion of the people we are sending to take charge of the groups that we have. If we can do that we would be able to marshal all our forces under the red, black and green; then we will be sure of success.

We have to legislate graft and greed and dishonesty out of our hearts and systems, because the men who have tried it have found that dishonesty has taken them nowhere. Dishonesty cannot lead us anywhere, and if we do not adopt the program of honesty for ourselves we are doomed.

THE AFRICAN PROGRAM

I will now touch on the African program. As you know, we sent several commissions out to Africa. The first went in 1920. We sent two in 1921. Two in 1922, and the last one we sent under the direction of Sir Robert Lincoln Poston in 1923.[6] The previous commission of 1921 had gone so far as to have received certain concessions for the association from the Liberian Government. The government had chartered in the Republic of Liberia, the U.N.I.A. and A.C.L. Owing to the setbacks we had in the latter part of 1921, we were unable to carry out our Liberian program. Because of the failure of the Black Star

Line there was a tremendous financial reaction, and we were unable to develop and take advantage of the concessions that we had been offered.[7]

We laid the matter in abeyance until last year, when we sent out Sir Robert Poston, Lady Henrietta Davis and Hon. M. Van Lowe to discuss the taking up of the old concessions and the carrying out of the new program for the development of Liberia. They came back and gave us their report, which was most favorable. I do not know whether Mr. Van Lowe would like to discuss the matter or whether he would like to have it discussed when Lady Davis is here. I want to have them report to you the arrangements that were made in Liberia for the carrying out of the colonization plan. Lady Davis is expected here between now and the 20th from British Honduras, where she is on a tour on behalf of the Black Cross Navigation and Trading Company. I think it wise to allow them to make their own report. They were on the spot handling the situation and made all the arrangements, and I think it is due to them to make their own report.

We got the report and it caused us to start in real earnest to carry out our plans in Liberia for the colonization of that country. Everything had gone splendidly. Now, Mr. O'Mally [James O'Meally] is on his way, and we do not want to embarrass him. We sent him specially to find out the situation down there. It is a purely diplomatic matter and cannot be handled in the ordinary way. I do not want to say anything that will hurt our prospects and arrangements, but it is provoking in the midst of all that is said on the outside to keep our mouths closed.

Nevertheless, I feel that if we say anything now it might hurt our own cause, and whatsoever I say I have to be very careful and diplomatic, because there is much we can say and somebody is going to be hurt. It will not be the U.N.I.A. We have to be cautious, and I have to appeal to the patience of the convention until Lady Davis comes here, so that she and Mr. Van Lowe will make the report they made to us, and by that time we expect to have a communication from Mr. O'Mally, so that we will be able to fully discuss the matter.

BOUND TO BE REALIZED

But whatever happens the realization of the program of the association is bound to occur. You need not be afraid to get yourselves in readiness to carry out the instructions. As far as we have gone we have done everything to carry out the arrangements. On June 24 last we sent a shipment to Liberia. On July 25 we sent another consignment. We have done everything to keep faith with you and the people and to carry out the African program.

The most important matter is our ships. During the last few months we had arranged to have a ship in readiness for carrying out our program in Africa and elsewhere. It was purely, as I said to the New York members, a question of money. We could have had the ship ready a month ago, not only one ship but several ships. But, unfortunately, because of the poverty of the members and other causes we have only been able to collect part of the money. During that time we have had lots of trouble to get a ship for the money we have. When I left here recently we had a contract drawn up only to be signed. Unfortunately, it seemed that agencies are still at work to embarrass us. If we had all the money in hand we could have bought the ship all right and end the matter. But because we had only part of the money they want to impose certain conditions which are not easy to live up to. I had hoped up to yesterday to be able to tell you go and see your ship. It is right here in the river. It is only a question of money.

The fault is not ours. We cannot get other people's property unless you pay for it. And when they have to give concessions, as they do not like you, you have to be guarded, because every one wants to take advantage of you. You have to be careful as to the kind of contract you sign. Because we haven't the money we have to sign a contract and give terms which are very hard and difficult. Our dependence is on you, and the enemy knows that. That is why they carry on this propaganda to disunite us. That is part of the scheme, but as I feel sure that God is with us we will get through. Give us a little time and we will be ready.

I didn't want to ask you for money until you saw the ship. I wanted you to see the ship on Sunday. The ship we arranged for is one of the best ships afloat, and it would be a credit to the association. Nevertheless, we will carry out everything in detail.

I thank you for the patience you have exhibited, and I want you to realize that the program before us is one of legislation. We have an important period ahead of us, and we can do things in this convention that will help to bring about a quick relief in another twelve months. We will discuss that as part of the industrial program.

On the question of the executive officers. We have been having a terrible time to carry things along. If we had the complete support of all the members, we would have no difficulty. It is purely a matter of money. You can hardly imagine how much money it takes to carry on an organization like this. It is not a joke. The thing that we are trying to do is as big as any government. Yet we haven't the agencies at our hand to carry it on. It requires hundreds and thousands and millions of dollars to carry out successfully a proposition like this. About the Liberian situation. If we had money, you would at this moment be having everything you want in regard to Liberian development. You cannot blame certain people for their actions, because Liberia is obligated to England and France. Liberia owes them one and half million dollars. They must be careful how they act. If you owe me ten dollars, you have to be careful before you entertain my enemy, because I may take proceedings against you. This is but an idea to show you that these people who do not want us to carry out the program are going to embarrass the people with whom we are dealing. The only way we could have relieved the situation is if we had money. Unfortunately, everything we have to do we have to tell you before we are able to get a dime.

Getting Ships

Now, take that ship proposition. There are some of you who do not believe we will get a ship, and so you will not put up a dime. Thus we cannot get the ship. A ship does not cost $100 or $1,000. We can get ships right now in the harbor with everything equipped. All that there is to be done is to put in coal and send the ships to sea. But for the keeping back of some of you, we would have had the money to get that ship. I believe some of you would want to know the name of the ship and the parties with whom we are dealing before you subscribe; but if we tell you, the enemy would get the information and in five minutes the deal would be off.

We have been forced to tell you everything about Liberia and tell you what we intend to do, exposing our plan to the enemy simply because we are so difficult to get along with. And yet, I cannot blame our people. It is the fault of your leaders. I have placed the situation before you and I trust you will have the remedy.

I have to tell you about the salary proposition. I advise you against that. I am telling you now, I cannot afford to work for other people. I have practically worked myself a nervous wreck to pay those big salaries for which they have sued. I am sick and tired of all that. I cannot have a comfortable night's rest in my bed. I have to be leaving New York and my family practically three weeks in every month. I think the time has come when every man should bear his own burden. I think it is wicked to have to pay salaries that people cannot earn.

I think the time has come when every man should work and get results and when we come to the salary proposition we should put the officer in a position to earn it. We should adjust the salary proposition this year.

Voluntarily, on the suggestion I made to them, we arranged a salary basis. I have a good executive body now; some are hypocrites, but the majority of them are sincere and willing to help me. Some of them say one thing and two minutes afterwards say something else outside. But I think the group of men we have are willing and reasonable enough to adjust themselves to the situation of the association as it is.

Reduction of Salaries

The basis we arrived at was that whereas the maximum was so much, each person would accept the minimum. Unfortunately, we have been unable to pay even the minimum for the whole year. I think that for the next two years we should make it the minimum and do not promise any more so that when they leave they will not be able to make trouble. When we voted those big salaries conditions were different, people were earning more money. So, when we come to the question of the U.N.I.A. I suggest we adjust the salary proposition to the ability of the association to meet them.

Printed in *NW*, 23 August 1924. Original headlines abbreviated.

1. John Sydney de Bourg won a $9,781 judgment for back salary, interest, and court costs in October 1923 in his suit brought in the New York State Supreme Court against the UNIA (*Chicago Defender*, 20 October 1923).

2. The French banned the *Negro World* in Dahomey in 1922 (*New York World*, 15 September 1922; *NW*, 21 April 1923, 19 September 1925; *Chicago Tribune*, 29 August 1923).

3. Following the end of World War I, a growing quantity of black nationalist literature, most prominently the *Negro World*, poured into the West Indies from the United States. In response, West Indian governments began to pass legislation to ban the *Negro World* and other "seditious" literature. In January 1919 the acting governor of British Honduras banned the *Negro World*. By 1920 a series of legislative measures were passed to ban the paper in the Windward Islands, the Leeward Islands, Grenada, Trinidad, Jamaica, and British Guiana. This movement was not universal, however, since an attempt to ban the paper in Dominica failed. Despite legislation, the *Negro World* continued to be smuggled into the West Indies (*Daily Argosy*, 6 September and 12 September 1919; *NW*, 5 May 1920; *Times* [London], 30 October 1919, 13 August 1920; W. F. Elkins, "Suppression of the *Negro World* in the British West Indies," *Science and Society* 35, no. 3 [fall 1971]: 244–347).

4. No evidence has been found indicating that South African Prime Minister Jan Smuts petitioned the British government to ban the *Negro World* in South Africa. In any case, the issue of censorship would have been handled without any recourse to Great Britain. Indeed, in 1921 the South African government initiated an internal debate on the advisability of confiscating UNIA literature in the mails. The South African postmaster general had been notified in April 1920 by the secretary for the interior to keep watch for UNIA propaganda; as a result, the postmaster general made copies of the *Negro World* available to the secretary for the interior. The secretary for the interior considered it advisable that copies of the *Negro World* received in the mails be stopped in transit and forwarded to the Returned Letter Office for disposal. Yet the secretary for native affairs objected to such an action, on the grounds that the questionable *Negro World* articles, which were reprinted from the colored Cape Town paper *A.P.O.*, organ of the African Peoples' Organization, reflected "only what it is possible to regard as the legitimate aspirations of the natives and are innocent of any such incitement to violence or desire to embitter racial feeling as characterise some of the other native publications in the Union" (secretary for native affairs to the secretary for the interior, Pretoria, 14 January 1921, South African Government Archives, 18/168/74).

Once again, in June 1924, the issue of confiscating the *Negro World* in the mails emerged as a result of a report by the postmaster of Kimberley, South Africa, indicating that thousands of copies were being received there weekly. The Kimberley postmaster considered the paper to be a "great danger to the State in that it tends to embitter racial feeling." The acting postmaster general was also alarmed because the paper was distributed "among semi-civilized natives in districts where the Government has been obliged to suppress risings by force of arms" (acting postmaster general to the secretary for the interior, 12 June 1924, South African Government Archives, 31/168/74, no. 12472). In response to their expressed concerns, the secretary for the interior requested that a copy be removed from the postal consignments and sent to him, but the acting postmaster general refused the request with the argument that he possessed no legal authority to remove a copy. The secretary for the interior then turned to the justice department for an opinion on the legality of confiscating the *Negro World* under the provisions of sect. 23(c) of Act 9 of 1913. The legal advisers remarked that the *Negro World* did not qualify as an obscene or indecent print, painting, or engraving and therefore could not be confiscated under its provisions. Finally convinced that legal confiscation was not possible, the interior department placed its own subscription to the *Negro World*. Thereafter the South African government maintained a close watch over the newspaper, but there is no indication that it was ever prohibited (*NW*, 13 September 1924, 30 April 1926; South African Government Archives, 16/168/74).

5. On 6 December 1921 Irish representatives signed a treaty with the British government, granting Ireland dominion status as the Irish Free State (*EWH*, p. 984).

6. Only one UNIA commission was sent in 1921; none was sent in 1922.

7. There is no evidence that any concessions were granted by the Liberian government.

Convention Report

[New York, 11 August 1924]

MONDAY MORNING, AUGUST 11

The convention assembled at 10:30 a.m., the speaker, Hon. Marcus Garvey, in the chair.

After prayers, the minutes of the previous session were read and confirmed.

Hon. Marcus Garvey, president-general, then presented his annual report to the convention. . . .

Hon. Fred A. Toote, Philadelphia, moved that the report be adopted and that it be laid on the table for future reference.

Hon. Freeman L. Martin, St. Louis, seconded.

The motion was unanimously carried.

Hon. Freeman L. Martin, St. Louis, moved that a committee of five be appointed to draw up a resolution of confidence in the president-general, in which for this convention and for the world, would be expressed confidence in the honesty and conscientiousness of the president-general in managing the affairs of the organization and the conviction that he has acted in all respects for the best advantage of the organization and has not used any of its funds for his own purposes.

Hon. Bishop McGuire seconded and the motion was unanimously carried.

The following committee was appointed by Hon. G. E. Carter, who acted as speaker, while the report of the president-general was being dealt with:

Hon. Bishop McGuire, New York; Hon. Freeman L. Martin, St. Louis; Hon. F. A. Toote, Philadelphia; Hon. F. E. Johnson, Detroit, and Hon. Hattie Johnson, Baltimore, Md.

The following motion was then moved by Hon. F. E. Johnson, Detroit:

> Be it resolved that we, the delegates of the Fourth International Convention of Negroes, petition His Excellency the President of the United States for a Federal Grand Jury investigation of the acts of Hon. Maxwell Mattucks and of other federal agents of the district of New York who have allowed themselves to be used by Negro politicians and rival organizations of the Universal Negro Improvement Association to handicap and impede its efforts in working for a feasible and practical solution of Negro problems and, of the persecution of the Hon. Marcus Garvey in this direction, such investigation to be made immediately.

Hon. Freeman L. Martin, St. Louis, seconded, and the motion was unanimously carried.

Hon. F.A. Toote, Philadelphia, moved that Friday, Saturday, Sunday and Monday next be set aside as Black Cross Navigation and Trading Company Days, on which a special effort be made to secure additional funds for the purchase of a ship, the delegates issuing appeals immediately to their divisions and chapters toward this end.

Hon. J.J. Peters, Chicago, seconded, and the motion was unanimously carried.

At this stage the convention adjourned until 3 p.m.

MONDAY AFTERNOON, AUGUST 11, 1924

The convention assembled at 3 p.m., the speaker, Hon. Marcus Garvey, in the chair.

After prayers, the minutes of the previous meeting were read and confirmed.

It was moved by Hon. C.H. Bryant of Costa Rica that the President-General's report be taken from the table, given the proper characterization and handed over to the President-General to be properly scrutinized, printed and distributed among the delegates to be conveyed to the members of the organization. The motion was seconded by Hon. Johnson of Cleveland, Ohio, and unanimously carried.

Hon. R.A.[H.] Bachelor, Orient[e], Cuba, stated that the Cuban government had be[e]n very helpful to the divisions in Cuba and made the suggestion that a cable of thanks be sent to the president of Cuba.

Hon. P. Garrett, New York, seconded. The motion was carried unanimously.

He then moved that a cable be sent to President Zayas of Cuba bearing greetings from the U.N.I.A. and the convention as an expression of their thanks to him and his government for the protection and aid rendered by him to the divisions in Cuba.

Hon. C.H. Bryant, Costa Rica, moved that a similiar cable be sent to the president of Panama and Costa Rica, at his expense.

Hon. R.A. Martin, Florida, Cuba, seconded the motion which was unanimo[u]sly carried.

The President-General then called for the report of the secretary-general.

Hon. G.E. Carter, secretary-general, presented the report and, among other things, stated that he had been appointed to succeed the late Sir R.L. Poston, and that he was greatly indebted to the Hon. Percival L. Burrows, first assistant secretary-general, and Hon. Norton G. Thomas, second assistant secretary-general, and the office staff for their valuable assistance to him in the work. He further stated that the growth of the organization was surprising, and had surpassed their expectations. Nearly 100 new charters had been issued this year with 105 charters pending. There were now 1,400 branches, more than one-half of which were to be found in the United States. The growth of the association in the United States has been wonderful, especially in the South, and the outlook for doubling the strength of the organization was bright. He commended the presidents, officers and members for their loyalty during the incarceration of the President-General. He further stated that the death rate had been very small, less than 250 in the United States and fifty in the foreign field. The splendid growth of the organization was proof that the Universal Negro Improvement Association is the spiritual urge of this century that will usher men into the racial consciousness of a free and redeemed Africa. Great improvement, he said, was shown in the handling of the vast amount of mail that came through the department and he promised, further improvement in this respect. There were dictated and mailed from his office since August, last, to July 1, 1924, 50,000 letters and 4,000 parcels were mailed[;] in conclusion he stated that the race was to be lifted and the continent redeemed by the return of black men to the mastery of arts, literature and culture.

Hon. C.H. Bryant, Costa Rica, moved, and Hon. Carrie Minus, New York, seconded that the report be received and adopted.

Hon. P. Johnson, Indianapolis, moved as an amendment to the foregoing motion that the report be received and adopted after the secretary had submitted a detailed statement of the standing of the organization.

Hon. S.V. Robertson, Louisiana and Mississippi, moved that the amendment be tabled. The motion was unanimou[s]ly carried.

Hon. C.H. Bryant, Costa Rica, moved that the secretary's report be also printed and distributed among the delegates. The motion was lost for the want of a seconder.

The speaker then announced as the next item for discussion, "The Development of Liberia, Abyssinia and Haiti as independent black nations and other countries where Negroes form a majority population, namely, Jamaica, Barbados, Trinidad, British Guiana, British Honduras, and other islands of the West Indies and Africa."

At this point, the Hon. Rudolph Smith, third assistant President General, was granted permission to make his report as titular leader of the West Indies, South and Central America. He stated that the organization had a strenuous fight since August, 1922, which had not been thoroughly realized by the divisions. There had been internal and external fights. He related many attempts made by individuals within the organization to disrupt the movement. He was pleased to state, however, that, during all of their trials, the members held fast and that at present the work was going forward splendidly. After the trip to Cleveland, he was sent to Cincinnati, and found the division there making excellent progress under the able leadership of William Ware, and he commended the president for the splendid work done by him in the Cincinnati Division. He stated here that, in his opinion, the Ohio divisions were the best divisions and stood firmly behind the Universal Negro Improvement Association. He was then sent to West Virginia to visit the various divisions, and found that one Smith-Green, was misleading the members, stating his Liberian Steamship and Sawmill Company was a part of the Univeral Negro Improvement Association.[1] He exposed the man, Smith-Green, enlightened the members, and advised them to have nothing to do with the Liberian Steamship and Sawmill Company and left the divisions in high spirits with a renewed determination to carry on the work of the Universal Negro Improvement Association. He told how a Mr. Owens had visited some of the divisions, representing that he was connected with the movement, and then when allowed to speak tried to defeat the cause and advocated the supporting of the Socialist movement, but he was turned down by the membership and disregarded in these divisions. The Hon. Smith stated that he was then sent to Chicago and, to his great surprise, he found there an official and member of the Executive Council trying to induce the people to disregard the constitution of the organization and creating dissension in the divisions. He was trying to influence the members to engage in crooked politics. That this officer, Capt. E.L. Gaines, was trying to encourage the members to withdraw their support from the Parent Body and follow under his leadership. Fortunately, he was able to show the people the error of following Capt. Gaines and just as the division was on the point of disruption, he succeeded in keeping it together and with the assistance of Commissioner W.A. Wallace, installed, the Hon. J.J. Peters, as president. He was glad to report that the Chicago Division is now going forward with renewed faith and courage and doing well. And so, with the various divisions that he visited in Missouri, wherever he found them struggling and misguided by some internal or external enemy, he willingly did all within his power to assist them and left them rejuvenated and doing well. He further stated that Capt. Gaines had preceded him in Cleveland and Pittsburgh, trying to poison the minds of the people in the divisions, but without results. He was next sent to visit the divisions in Cuba, by the President-General. He stated that he was hospitably received in the various divisions and left them all doing well.

Upon motion by the Hon. Freeman L. Martin, of St. Louis, seconded by the Hon. F. Johnson, of Detroit, the report of the third Assistant President-General was unanimously adopted and a vote of thanks given him for his untiring efforts in behalf of the organization.

The Hon. C.H. Bryant, of Costa Rica, moved that the session be adjourned until 8:30 p.m.

The Hon. R.A. Martin, of Florida, Cuba, seconded, and the motion was unanimously carried.

MONDAY EVENING, AUGUST 1[1]

The convention resumed at 8:30 p.m., Hon. P.L. Burrows, First Assistant Secretary-General, in the chair.

The Acting Speaker said he had received a message from the Speaker and President-General stating that he would not be present, owing to business of pressing importance. He had requested him to open the convention in the usual way and, after the reading of the minutes, convert the session into a mass meeting.

The minutes of the previous session were read by the secretary and, on the motion of Hon. C.H. Bryant, Costa Rica, seconded by Hon. A. [J.] B. Salisbury, Homestead, were confirmed.

Hon. C.H. Bryant, Costa Rica, moved a suspension of the standing order, in accordance with the wishes of the President-General. . . .

Printed in *NW*, 23 August 1924. Original headlines abbreviated.

1. Edward Smith-Green had been a member of the UNIA in New York and secretary of the BSL. He resigned from both organizations in spring 1920, upon his return from the final voyage of the *Yarmouth* to Cuba. The following year it was reported that Smith-Green had organized the Liberian American Steam Ship Co., Inc., a corporation capitalized at $500,000. The organization was intended to engage in trade between the United States and Liberia, North Africa, the West Indies and Central America. In an effort to raise money, shares were sold at five dollars each. The company foundered after operating for a few years.

There is no indication that Smith-Green's corporation had any association with the Liberian Steamship and Sawmill Co., organized in 1919 by Dr. Lewis A. Jordan and Bishop W.H. Heard. Jordan had worked closely with the UNIA and had addressed UNIA meetings (*Brooklyn and Long Island Reformer*, 8 January 1921; *NW*, 25 April and 11 June 1920, 12 November 1921, 14 July 1923; see also *Garvey Papers* 1: 227; 2: 16).

Convention Report

[*New York, 12 August 1924*]

TUESDAY MORNING, AUGUST 12

The convention was called to order at 10:30, the delegates arriving late, owing to rain. The Speaker, Hon. Marcus Garvey, occupied the chair.

After prayers, the minutes of the previous session were read and confirmed.

Hon. P.L. Burrows moved that the order of the day—discussing the development of Liberia, Abyssinia and Haiti as independent Black nations, and other countries, where Negroes form a majority of the population, i.e.[,] Jamaica, Barbados, Trinidad, British Guiana, British Honduras and other islands of the West Indies and Africa—be suspended and that the next business be proceeded with.

Hon. S.R. Wheat, West Chicago, seconded, and the motion was carried unanimously.

The convention then proceeded to discuss the educating of the Negro race as to the real meaning of society and laying down the principles which should guide those who would become socially distinctive; also the creating of an atmosphere of purity around the young generation of the race to better prepare them for a higher social life.

Hon. G.A. Weston initiated the discussion. He said the race must become socially distinctive through unselfish service. The aristocracy must be formed of persons who had deserved well of the race through service. Purity must be inculcuated in the home, in the day school and in the church school and in street contact. There was no organization more prepared or fitted to educate the Negro along this line than the Universal Negro Improvement Association.

Hon. Bishop McGuire stressed the need for racial education. The young generation should be taught the history of the race, the part Negro men and women had played and were playing in the world. In regard to social education in the last analysis the matter reduced itself to one of disobedience. Obedience should be instilled in the child in the home. Nowadays, instead of parents' words being law to their children, the children ruled the home. This was true not only of the Negro race in this country but elsewhere. The lack of this training and the resultant evils were so marked that he wondered whether the time was ripe for unlimited democracy being placed in the hands of the Negro.

Hon. R.A. Martin, Florida, Cuba, said example was the great influence. Hon. P.L. Burrows said he felt sure that the question had been fully covered by those who had spoken, and moved that a committee be appointed and instructed to bring back to the convention a well arranged system by which the young could be prepared for the higher social life.

Hon. C.H. Bryant, Costa Rica, seconded.

Rising to unreadiness, Hon. W.A. Wallace, Illinois[,] explained he was unready because he wanted to join in the discussion and suggest that more attention be given to the Juvenile Department. Juveniles should not be made to pay dues as adults did. They should be admitted under more favorable conditions into the organization.

Hon. J.J. Peters, Chicago, said he also was unready. He could not agree that the preceding speakers had fully covered the subject.

Hon. J. Chambers, New Orleans, said he desired to suggest that a system be arranged by which the teachers of the young could be taught.

The Speaker suggested that the discussion be left unfinished and that the convention adjourn until the evening, giving the various committees an opportunity to formulate their reports and present them to the convention the next day. At the evening session the unfinished business would be dealt with, after which the convention would proceed with the discussion of the development of Liberia, Abyssinia and Haiti, as independent Black nations, and other countries where Negroes form a majority of the population.

Hon. Freeman L. Martin, St. Louis, moved that a committee of three be appointed to confer with the officers of the U.N.I.A. relative to the status of the negotiations in the procuring of a ship and report their findings to the convention.

Hon. S.R. Wheat, West Chicago, seconded, and the motion was unanimously carried.

On the motion of the Hon. Bishop McGuire, seconded by Hon. A.G. Ellenburg, the convention adjourned until 8:30 p.m.

TUESDAY EVENING, AUGUST 12

The Convention resumed at 8:30 p.m., the Speaker, Hon. Marcus Garvey, in the chair.

After prayers the minutes of the previous session were read and confirmed.

The Speaker granted permission to the Hon. Bishop McGuire to present two resolutions from the Committee, and vacated the chair, which was temporarily occupied by Hon. Rudolph Smith.

The first resolution expresses confidence in and appreciation of the leadership of the Hon. Marcus Garvey, President-General.

Hon. Bishop McGuire moved the adoption of the resolution by a rising vote and that a special copy of the same be prepared and signed by every delegate of the Convention, and by friends, visitors and members present.

Hon. C.L. [G.H.] Logan, Atlanta, Ga., seconded, and the motion was unanimously carried, a rising vote being given.

Hon. Bishop McGuire then moved the adoption of the second resolution conveying the Convention's thanks to Mrs. Amy Jacques-Garvey for the valuable assistance rendered her husband and wishing her a speedy restoration to health.

Hon. C.H. Bryant, Costa Rica, seconded, and the motion was carried unanimously, a rising vote being given.

Hon. Rudolph Smith then tendered to Mrs. Garvey, who was seated on the platform, an expression of the good will and appreciation of the Convention.

Hon. Marcus Garvey then returned to the chair.

In a felicitous speech he introduced to the Convention Dr. Marie Louise Montagu [Montague], President of the International Humanity League, a member of the white race, who, one of the leading spirits in the country, had demonstrated her friendship for the race and had assisted in the promulgation of the principles of the Universal Negro Improvement Association.

Dr. Marie Louise Montagu said it seemed to her that the esoteric idea in the scriptural cry, "I am black but beautiful," conveyed to the world that certain shades of color were not incompatible with pulchritude. Were she in a mood to preach she would take that passage as her text. Continuing, she said the most puzzling phenomenon in the world today was the almost universal condition of disorder existing in the world in face of the fact that the all-powerful Redeemer could change and adjust things in an instant. The primary and wonderful fact should not be overlooked, however, that God had bestowed upon the human race one of His own prerogatives, that of free will. That fearful and wonderful privilege of refusing to obey God's mandates was the secret of the disorders of today. She showed that Lucifer's disobedience of God's will brought about his fall and that of his followers, and Lucifer, she added, was not necessarily black. The only recorded example of the devil's appearance to humanity was in the form of a serpent, and serpents were generally green. The black man had no monopoly of disobedience. It was the white race that stood before heaven and earth responsible for present-day world disorder. Black men were not the transgressors. The black man's faith, his willingness to help and to serve, she thought, gave him priority over the other races, lighter in color, but selfish and useless, and she predicted the day would come when the black race would lead the other races. She congratulated the Convention and the race upon being one of the greatest assets in the world today, a fact which was exemplified in the recognition of the black race as voters and property holders in this country when the Oriental races were rejected.

Hon. Sir William L. Sherrill, Second Assistant President-General, moved that a vote of thanks be given Dr. Montagu for her excellent address, and for her sympathy with the work in which that convention was engaged.

Hon. C.H. Bryant, Costa Rica, seconded, and the motion was unanimously carried, a rising vote being given.

Hon. Marcus Garvey, Speaker, then tendered the thanks of the body to Dr. Montagu, who returned her thanks.

The order of the day was then proceeded with—the discussion of the educating of the Negro race as to the real meaning of society, and laying down the principles that should guide those of the race desiring to become socially distinctive; also creating an atmosphere of purity around the young generation of the race to better prepare them for a higher social life.

Hon. Hannah Nicholls, New York, said much had been said about the part that should be played in the home by the mother, especially, but it seemed to her that what was greatly needed and most essential was the practice of self-control and purity by the men. This would give the child health in body and mind.

Hon. J.J. Peters, Chicago, said something more sociologically valuable should be added to the oft-quoted statement, "A race can rise no higher than its women." It should rather be said, "The women can rise no higher than where the men put them." He referred to the social diseases so rampant,[2] and urged upon men and women, in the interest of the next generation, to banish prudery and mock modesty; be more frank in their relations, and give pr[o]creation more eugenic attention.[3]

Hon. Dr. Rawlins,[4] New York, said venereal disease had increased alarmingly among the members of the black race. This was due to concealment, the result of ignorance. It was not that the black race was more vicious than other races, but members of the white race, for instance, always saw to it that curative treatment was obtained early.

Hon. J.A. Hassell, Seattle, remarked that the disease mentioned by the two doctors was the legacy of the missionary white man. It was also due to the inclination on the part of men of the black race, who traveled[,] to regard women of other races as more beautiful and desirable than their own.

Hon. Prof. D.H. Kyle, Clarksburg, W.Va., emphasized that example, not so much precept, was the method by which the evils referred to would be remedied.

The Speaker hereupon remarked that there was a disposition to stray from the subject under discussion.

Hon. J.B. Eaton, Norfolk, Va., said the so-called intellectuals had a false conception of society. In many communities "society" was regarded as composed of those who went to church whenever the doors were thrown open.

Hon. Rudolph Smith, Third Assistant President-General, spoke on the lighthearted manner in which matrimony was entered into. There was too much imitation of the other fellow. He also dwelt on the false conception of the essentials for admission into "society." He advocated the dissemination of helpful literature by the U.N.I.A., and then moved that the discussion be closed and that a committee be appointed to prepare literature to be sent out to the divisions so that the boys and girls of the race might be better educated.

Hon. C. [G.] H. Logan, Atlanta, seconded.

Hon. H.V. Plummer, New York, suggested to the mover that he amend his motion to read, that the committee be appointed to formulate some concrete proposition under which the President-General could have the literature circulated.

The suggestion was accepted.

Rising to unreadiness, several delegates expressed the opinion that the subject had not been discussed from important angles. The social side had hardly been touched.

The motion was then put to the house and carried by a majority vote.

The Speaker then appointed the following Committee: Hon. P.L. Burrows, First Assistant Secretary-General; Hon. Dr. Rawlins, New York; Hon. Mrs. M. Boyd, New York; Hon. G.A. Weston, New York, and Hon. Rudolph Smith, Third Assistant President-General.

The Chair intimated that on resumption next day reports of committees would be received, after which the convention would proceed to discuss the development of Liberia, Abyssinia and Haiti as independent black nations, and other countries where Negroes form the majority of the population.

On the motion of Hon. R.A. Martin, Florida, Cuba, seconded by Hon. Carrie Minus, New York, the adjournment was taken.

Printed in *NW*, 23 August 1924. Original headlines abbreviated.

1. Marie Louise Montague, a native of West Virginia, was founder and president of the International Humanity League, a non-denominational but religiously inspired organization established in the hopes of creating "a solution to the vital problem of world harmony, as a prophylactic against future wars, and to inaugurate that unity for which Jesus stands." The league claimed to have an international following, with delegates from at least twenty-four countries in 1923. Stressing that dissension within Christianity stemmed from the early interweaving of church and state, the league urged the establishment of a universal brotherhood of man under the "Fatherhood of God"—a brotherhood that would supersede national, racial, and religious divisions.

In 1923 Montague worked closely with Bishop George Alexander McGuire of the African Orthodox church. She envisioned that blacks, under the leadership of the church, would eventually lead humanity back to "restore universally the Christian Gospel of Apostolic Days." Describing Marcus Garvey as "the Moses of the African people," she supported the plan for a black state in Africa that would "blaze a trail to freedom that will effectually enable Ethiopia to 'stretch forth her hands unto God.'" In 1928 Montague was active in New York State politics, and she ran for president on a platform endorsing the separation of church and state, enforcement of Prohibition, farm relief, high tariff, and establishment of a world court (*Negro Churchman* 1, no. 2 [February 1923]; 1, no. 3 [March 1923]; 1, nos. 9–10 [September–October 1923]; 1, no. 11 [December 1923]; 2, no. 2 [February 1924]; 2, no. 5 [May 1924]; 2, nos. 9–10 [September–October 1924]; *NYT*, 9 June 1928).

2. There was a long tradition of depicting venereal and other social diseases as symptomatic of general black racial decline. As early as the post–Civil War period, many southerners proclaimed that disease and dissipation would eliminate the freedmen, as had happened to the American Indians. The popularity of social Darwinist-inspired racial theories by the late nineteenth century reflected increasing public acceptance of such views. An influential study by insurance industry statistician Frederick L. Hoffman found the extinction of blacks to be probable. "All the facts prove," he wrote, "that a low standard of sexual morality is the main and underlying cause of the low and anti-social condition of the race at the present time" (*Race Traits and Tendencies of the American Negro* [New York: Macmillan, 1896], pp. 52, 55, 60, 95). W.E.B. Du Bois wrote that universal racial prejudice brought the "inevitable self-questioning, self-disparagement, and lowering of ideals which ever accompany repression and breed in an atmosphere of contempt and hate. Whisperings and portents came borne upon the four winds: Lo! we are diseased and dying, cried the dark hosts . . ." (*Souls of Black Folk* [Chicago: A.C. McClurg, 1903], p. 51).

After a dramatic increase during World War I, reported venereal disease declined throughout the 1920s, though it continued at a higher level than in prewar years. A significant change in outlook during the 1920s was the replacement of race-linked, pseudoscientific theories to explain the causes of venereal disease with the idea, among medical practitioners at least, that the disease spread in unhygienic and unsanitary living conditions, prompting social service agents and black medical practitioners to call for greater attention to cleanliness and hygiene among the black population (Mark J. White, "Report of the Committee on Venereal Diseases of the State and Provincial Health Authorities," *American Journal of Public Health* 13, no. 9 [September 1923]: 723–737; "The Prevalence of Venereal Disease," *American Journal of Public Health and the Nation's Health* 18, no. 5 [May 1928]: 632–634; James H. Jones, *Bad Blood: The Tuskegee Syphilis Experiment* [New York: Macmillan, 1981], pp. 30–44).

3. Garveyite concerns about "eugenic attention," race suicide, a declining black birthrate, and a desire to improve the race reflected the broad popularity of eugenics in the 1920s. Eugenics had its origins in the 1890s, following the discovery by Gregor Mendel of the phenomenon of inherited physical characteristics. This discovery provided a pseudoscientific basis for social Darwinists and eugenicists, who argued not only that genetics determine physical characteristics, which Mendel had proved, but also that they form the entire determinant of intelligence as well as other human qualities, which neither Mendel nor anyone else has shown to be true. The social Darwinists argued that the decline in the birthrate of the "nordic races" and the higher birthrate among immigrants, many from southern Europe, would eventually result in the "race suicide" of Nordic Americans. Cloaked in the garb of "race improvement," the eugenics program was often an aspect of the reformist urge in early twentieth-century America.

The eugenics movement gained further influence in the early 1920s when it became the ideological cornerstone of the movement to restrict immigration. Eugenicists used newly developed data, such as IQ tests, to support their argument that intelligence and ability were racially inherited. Books such as Madison Grant's *The Passing of the Great Race; or, the Racial Basis of European History* (1916; 4th rev. ed., New York: C. Scribner's Sons, 1921) and Theodore Lothrop Stoddard's *The Rising Tide of Color* (New York: Scribner, 1921), brought eugenicist arguments about racial "suicide" to a broader public and helped to lay the basis for support for immigration restriction. The actual debate over immigration in the early 1920s was infused with eugenicist arguments designed, in large part, to preserve the "distinct American" type. The 1924 bill provided a quota system that systematically reduced the number of immigrants from non-Nordic countries. An alliance of industrialists, the AFL, and the Ku Klux Klan supported the bill's passage (John Higham, *Strangers in the Land: Patterns of American Nativism, 1860–1925* [New York: Atheneum, 1970], pp. 234–330; Linda Gordon, *Woman's Body, Woman's Right* [New York: Penguin Books, 1977], pp. 116–158, 391–402; Robert A. Divine, *American Immigration Policy, 1924–1952* [New Haven, Conn.: Yale University Press, 1957], p. 1,052; Daniel J. Kevles, *In the Name of Eugenics: Genetics and the Uses of Human Heredity* [New York: Knopf, 1985]).

4. Dr. E. Eliott Rawlins occasionally wrote the "Health Talk" column in the *Negro World* (*NW*, 24 February 1923).

Enid Lamos to President Calvin Coolidge

NEW YORK, U.S.A. August 12, 1924

May it Please Your Excellency:—

I am instructed by the Hon. Marcus Garvey, President-General of the Universal Negro Improvement Association, to forward you a copy of the speech delivered by him before the delegates and Deputies to the Fourth Annual International Convention of the Negro Peoples of the World, at Carnegie Hall, on Friday night August 1st.[1] He hopes it will interest you. With very best wishes, Yours truly,

E. LAMOS
Secretary

DLC, CC. TLS on UNIA letterhead, recipient's copy.

1. See *Garvey Papers* 5: 631–638.

Resolution of Confidence Presented to Marcus Garvey

[*New York*] [[August 12, 1924]]

We, your undersigned committee, appointed to prepare an expression of confidence in and our appreciation of the leadership of the Honorable Marcus Garvey, president-general of the Universal Negro Improvement Association, following his report upon the condition of the association since the rise of the last convention, September, 1922, and his general review of the same for the four years last past, do hereby submit the following preamble and resolution:

Whereas, The Honorable Marcus Garvey had been handicapped in his administration by executive officers who were chosen to serve with high salaries, and that a large number of said executive officers resigned in succession and formed a combination to harass the president in the civil courts to recover salaries they could not or would not earn; and,

Whereas, Several of those who were chosen to succeed to these executive offices played false, pretending to be serving loyally their organization and its leader, but secretly conspiring with, and giving aid and comfort to the enemy that they might, in the event of the elimination of the president-general, assume leadership and management of the association, and that immediately following the rise of the convention of 1922, certain high officials of influence, and a large number of presidents of divisions entered upon a campaign to foster rebellion, disloyalty and non-support of the parent body and its head, and have continued this policy until this hour to the very point of disruption of the association and its impotency in achievement of its aims and objects, and that simultaneously with this state of internal subordination, there has been a supreme effort on the part of the enemies of the leader of the association to discredit him before the American public, and the Negro peoples of the world, these enemies being sordid politicians, jealous rival leaders and their sychophants, and also governmental agencies of European countries which maintain colonies in Africa;

Therefore, be it resolved. That this convention expresses its profound and sincere sympathy with the Honorable Marcus Garvey, in the many misfortunes that have befallen him in his untiring efforts to continue the threatened existence of the association, and places on record its appreciation of the unlimited personal sacrifices,—physical, financial and otherwise, which he endured during the trying period, further:

Be it resolved. That this convention give a rising and unanimous vote of confidence without reservation, in the sincerity of purpose, honesty in financial dealings, and unswerving determination of the president-general to employ every means in his power, and every talent of which he is possessed, to lead this organization to victory; further;

Be it resolved. That we believe that no cause of fault, failure or neglect for the misfortunes of the association can be attributed to the Honorable Marcus Garvey, who has been instant in season and out of season to promote its welfare, and finally

Be it resolved, That this convention ascribes to Divine Providence its deep sense of gratitude for His watchful care over the Universal Negro Improvement Association, and His loving protection of its leader, as without such Divine assistance both our organization and its President-General would have been destroyed by the mighty forces of evil arrayed against them.   Respectfully submitted.

BISHOP GEORGE A. McGUIRE
Chairman
FRED A. TOOTE
Secretary
FREEMAN L. MARTIN
HATTIE JOHNSON
FRED E. JOHNSON
OLIVIA WHITEMAN
Committee

Printed in *NW*, 23 August 1924. Original headlines abbreviated.

Editorial Letter by Marcus Garvey

[[New York City, August 1[3], 1924]]

Fellow Men of the Negro Race, Greeting:

My message to you this week is one of explanation, because I think it necessary for the better enlightenment of all concerned.   As President-General of the Universal Negro Improvement Association, the leading Negro organization in the world, it is my duty at all times to bring before you conditions as they do exist and affect us.

SU[RV]EY OF RACE CONDITIONS

After a thorough and careful survey of race conditions within the last five years, and especially that period immediately following the war, we discovered that in time, and shortly, there would have been a severe industrial and economic reaction in the United States of America and the Western world, to affect terribly the existence of our people. We realized that the abnormalities that existed industrially would gradually pass away, leaving the bulk of our people the greatest sufferers. Anticipating that, we were forced as leaders to devise ways and means by which the situation could be relieved and the anticipated suffering of the people be prevented, or at least alleviated. It was in that wise that we decided on the African colonization plan of helping to build up Liberia and other West African countries industrially as places where Negroes from the Western world could settle, finding their permanent homes and helping themselves to a greater industrial expansion. Having this in view the association organized its African expeditions and within the last twelve months more energy was put into the proposition to make it a success. To carry this out in a practical and business way, several missions were sent to Africa; one in 1920, two in 1921, and the third in 1923, at a cost of over $40,000. The missions were instructed to arrange for certain rights and concessions which could be used by the association for the carrying out of its industrial program in Africa. Such concessions were arranged and the association was advised to promote the plan above referred to.

CARRYING OUT A PROPOSITION

After due publicity was given to the proposition and the association undertook to spend large sums of money for the carrying out of the idea, the usual group of Negro obstructionists in this country, working in conjunction with other narrow-minded Negroes, started to undermine and block every effort in the direction of making the proposition a success.

Recently the association undertook to assist in building up the Republic of Liberia industrially as a natural homeland for the dissatisfied of the race and in this direction a proper organization was perfected. According to arrangements a group of expert engineers as well as consignments of materials were shipped away, costing the association over $30,000. In the face of this, the same group of Negro obstructionists who have always blocked every legitimate effort to assist the race, started to use their influence to prevent the plan going through to the extent that they have sought to misrepresent the association to the British, French and Liberian governments as to bring about a terrible situation that cannot be easily overcome. The group of obstructionists have been our leaders in public life for many decades. Their selfishness has been so marked as to leave them without credit for one real substantial act of benefit to the people. To the contrary, they have waxed fat and rich

725

at the expense of the poor masses and so now that the Universal Negro Improvement Association attempts to do something to benefit the entire [race], we find them making every effort and using their energy to thwart the plan.

HINDRANCES TO OUR RACE

It is sad to say, that the Negro leader, generally the big preacher, politician and professional man, is the greatest hindrance to the progress of his race. He refuses to do anything out of the ordinary course to assist his race and will not tolerate an effort on the part of anyone else. This narrow-mindedness and selfishness has caused us now to be in a condition bordering on our economic destruction, for there is no ignoring the fact that all over the country, especially in the big cities, you can now find hundreds of thousands of our people out of work, without any immediate hope of employment. The very churches that some of these preachers lead cannot be properly supported because of the non-employment of a large number of the members. The cry everywhere is, "No work among our people," and yet these so-called leaders will go out of their way to obstruct and destroy every effort that would seek to bring relief in this direction. When it is revealed that these so-called leaders have gone out of their way to send false and misrepresenting letters to the British and French governments and to the Liberian government asking them to block and prevent the carrying out of the plan of the Universal Negro Improvement Association in Africa, for the industrial development of these countries, you will easily see how vicious and wicked these men are. They have not only done that but they have tried to use and are using certain political connections with those unworthy white men in governmental office to handicap and destroy commercially the Universal Negro Improvement Association as evidenced in the infamous letter that was written to Harry Daugherty, late Attorney-General of the United States, asking to imprison Marcus Garvey and destroy the Universal Negro Improvement Association, and as written to the English and French colonial governments in the West Indies and Africa pointing out to them that it was the intention of the Universal Negro Improvement Association and Marcus Garvey to undermine and destroy the existing governments of those powers in the colonies and in Africa, communications for which the man Samuel Duncan was responsible, working in conjunction with the same group above referred to. The men who have done these things and are still doing them are the so-called leaders of the race, the intellectuals who claim to possess a superabundance of learning.

FALSE LEADERS

What can the common people expect when their so-called leaders and educated men will stoop to the performance of such acts as to embarrass the ent[ir]e race in their spite and desire to injure one whom they may be jealous or afraid of. Not only are these men wickedly inclined [in this] [direction?] but their dishonesty to their own race is so marked as to leave the impression upon other races that there is nothing good in us.

. . . [*Words mutilated*] [group] of political gangsters who prevented Liberia from getting the five million dollars that was sought from the United States some years ago. Not only was President Harding willing to let Liberia have the five million dollars, but the Senate was willing, until it was discovered that these political grafters would have collected 25 per cent. of the amount for commission and graft, discovery of which caused the Senate to refuse to sanction the loan. These are the men who hold themselves as patriots and leaders of the people; these men are the men who have been fighting the Universal Negro Improvement Association; these are the men who stand in the way of a higher development, and so today I think it no more than my duty to call upon the masses to bestir themselves and to be awake, for if we, the people, do not start out now to exercise the power that rests in our hands, that of repudiating these unscrupulous leaders, it will simply mean that in another decade our condition will be such as to prevent our further helping ourselves.

NEGRO OWN ENEMY

It is sad to admit it, but it is a fact that the Negro is his own greatest enemy.[2] These Negro politicians and preachers who have been opposing the Universal Negro Improvement Association are worse than any enemy that we could encounter anywhere. That we have been handicapped in carrying out our work is not directly traceable to the white man, but it is positively traceable to the enemies that we have in our own race. The idea of men calling themselves leaders[,] writing to foreign and powerful governments to take steps to block the development of their own race, and yet these so-called leaders will go back to the churches and preach to us about Heaven and God and the love they have for their people to get their support after they have already crucified them on the cross of industrial and economic . . . [*word mutilated*]. What other recourse is left but for us to advise the people to desert such leaders and let them starve and die by the wayside. Can we recommend the political leaders of our race? Can we recommend the many preachers of our race who have been so selfish and inconsiderate? It is impossible. We recommend men of character and purpose, with a love and devotion to their people but not such as we have referred to.

PEOPLE SHOULD OPEN THEIR EYES

It is time that the people open their eyes North, East, West and South, and see that the salvation of the race depends on themselves and not upon these unscrupulous leaders who have been in their way for nearly a half century. It is not that we fear these men that we recount these things, because ultimately the Universal Negro Improvement Association is bound to triumph, but it is the hindrance and unnecessary barriers placed in our way, because our work would have been much easier if we had not [had] such encounters. The Negro must realize that our leaders are selfish and wicked. If we must triumph, we must do so without their assistance. They haven't the soul of race consciousness as leaders of other races have; they haven't the patriotism of race as other leaders have. It is the selfish effort of our leaders to reach the top at the expense of others that has caused the race to suffer, and the poor unfortunate masses of our people must pay the price. If you doubt me, take a proper count of the men who lead you in your community and find out the difference between them and the people led. You will find that their leadership always results in their enrichment, while the poor people stagnate and in many cases go backward. Take your so-called big preachers all over the country. You will find them all rich men whilst the congregations remain poverty stricken without any hope of relief when bad conditions affect their community. Such are the men who are fighting from the pulpit and platform the effort of the Universal Negro Improvement Association to save the people. They fight us because they believe we are going to remove large numbers of people from the communities where they have waxed fat and rich to climes far beyond their reach where it will not be so easy for them to exploit them. It is that selfish purpose, it is that narrow-mindedness that has driven them to the extreme of doing what has been recounted. The Negro politician is no better in the same direction. He uses the people only for the convenience of what their voting strength is worth to him. Outside of that there is no interest and as the selfish preacher would resort to underhand[ed] and unscrupulous means to get rid of the Universal Negro Improvement Association, so does the politician.

These evils we have to fight and it is well that we know them. With all that has been done, however, the Universal Negro Improvement Association stands firm and determined to carry out its program and intends to fight to the bitter end to secure permanently and progressively this struggling and suffering race of ours. We can only emancipate ourselves after we [have] succeeded in laying a strong and solid economic foundation; hence we again appeal to every member of the organization and member of the race to help the organization to put over its industrial plans. We want ships and more ships to help us reach the different groups of our people around the world, to trade among them, to take their produce from one section to the next and to build up an international commercialism upon which we can successfully build ourselves as a race and people. Let us do this and do it now. The weapon of freedom is in our own hands as the masses, and if we get together as such, we can put over any kind of a program that we want. The program now is for ships. Let us have the help that is necessary. With very best wishes, I have the honor to be, Your obedient servant,

MARCUS GARVEY
President-General
Universal Negro Improvement Association

Printed in *NW*, 16 August 1924. Original headlines omitted.

1. President Coolidge requested Daugherty's resignation for reasons of misconduct on 27 March 1924 (James N. Giglio, *H.M. Daugherty and the Politics of Expediency* [Kent, Ohio: Kent State University Press, 1978], p. 172).

2. "The Negro's Greatest Enemy," an essay first published in *Current History*, is Garvey's most extensive autobiographical statement (see *Garvey Papers* 1: 3–12; *P&O*, 2: 124–134).

Convention Report

[*New York, 13 August 1924*]

WEDNESDAY MORNING, AUG. 13

The convention assembled at 10:15 a.m., the speaker, Hon. Marcus Garvey, in the chair.

After prayers, the minutes of the previous session were read and confirmed.

The speaker announced that from the 21st of the month the sessions would be devoted to discussing the business of the Universal Negro Improvement Association. He, therefore, appealed to the delegates and deputies to expedite the other business on the agenda.

Hon. Bishop McGuire moved that ten minutes be allowed each delegate or deputy for discussion of the business before the house and twenty minutes to such delegate or deputy as may be called upon by the speaker to make the keynote address.

At the suggestion of Hon. H.V. Plummer, New York, and Hon. F. Johnson, Detroit, the motion was altered to read five minutes for delegates and fifteen minutes for the keynoter.

The motion was unanimously carried.

Hon. P.L. Burrows, First Assistant Secretary-General, moved that the resolution read and adopted at the previous session expressing confidence in the leadership of the President-General be published over the names of those who subsequently signed it in the next issue of The Negro World.

Hon. C. Minus seconded, and the motion was unanimously carried.

Hon. W.A. Wallace intimated that the report of the committee in regard to formation of a political union was ready, though the chairman and secretary were absent on business.

It was agreed that the report be read by the chairman later.

Hon. J.D. Barber, as chairman, then read the report of the committee appointed to draft an appeal to His Holiness the Pope of Rome, His Grace the Archbishop of Canterbury, and the heads of the Christian churches, as leaders of Christianity, for an honest and human settlement of the problems of humanity, especially as such problems affect the Negro.

After some discussion of the report in committee it was decided, on motion of Hon. D. Daniels, Brooklyn, seconded by Hon. Jeffers, New York, that the report be re-committed to the committee to be re-drafted with the assistance of Bishop McGuire, the report to be presented on Friday next.

Hon. Prof. D.H. Kyle, Clarksburg, W. Va., as chairman, next presented the report of the committee appointed to formulate suggestions as to the ways and means of adjusting the race problem of the Southern States to the satisfaction of all concerned.

Hon. F.A. Toote, Philadelphia, moved, after a brief discussion, that the report be received and adopted as read.

Hon. R.A.[H]. Bachelor, Oriente, Cuba, seconded, and the motion was unanimously carried.

Hon. F. Johnson, Detroit, next presented the report of the committee appointed to draft an appeal to the Presidents of America, France and Portugal, and to the Kings of England, Italy, Spain and Belgium, and their parliaments, asking for a square deal for Negroes in Africa, America and the colonies.

After some discussion it was decided, on the motion of Hon. Bishop McGuire, seconded by Hon. F.A. Toote, Philadelphia, that the report be referred back to the committee, which shall confer with the proper officers of the U.N.I.A. with a view to certain changes of a diplomatic nature in the wording being made.

The convention then adjourned.

WEDNESDAY AFTERNOON, AUGUST 13

The convention resumed at 2:20 p.m., the speaker, Hon. Marcus Garvey, in the chair.

After prayers the minutes of the previous meeting were read and confirmed.

News items which appeared in the New York papers showing the unrest existing in the Sudan where the natives are agitating for autonomy' and a recent conquest by the Moroccans of the Spanish, were read to the convention at the direction of the speaker, the Hon. Marcus Garvey, who in a brief address referred to the sentiment the U.N.I.A. was creating throughout the world and especially in the motherland, Africa.

The order of the day was then proceeded with.

Hon. Freeman L. Martin, St. Louis, then read the report of the committee appointed to draft the regulations for a Negro political union.

Hon. Freeman L. Martin moved that the report be received.

Hon. H.V. Plummer, New York, seconded, and the motion was unanimously carried. The speaker, Hon. Marcus Garvey, congratulated the committee on their splendid report, remarking that it was a splendid document.

The convention then proceeded to discuss the report, section by section.

Each section was carefully discussed.

The report, in so far as it was amended, is as follows:

The name of the union shall be known as the Universal Negro Political Union.

OBJECTS

Art. I.—Sec. 1. To conserve the integrity and purity of the Negro electorate in the independent and untrammeled exercise of the elective franchise, and intelligently and systematically direct the use of such as will best serve the interests of the race.

Sec. 2. To marshal the entire vote of the membership of the Universal

Negro Improvement Association and of the entire Negro race locally, nationally and internationally.

MEMBERSHIP

Art. II.—All members of the Universal Negro Improvement Association shall be considered members of the Universal Negro Political Union without the payment of a further entrance fee, and all others shall be admitted on the payment of an entrance fee of 50 cents. A[n] annu[a]l fee of $1 shall be paid by such members.

ORGANIZATION

Art. III.—The Executive Council of the U.N.I.A. shall constitute the Directorate or Supreme Political Committee which shall be the governing body of the Universal Negro Political Union.

DUTIES

Art. IV.—Sec. 1. In all Local, Municipal, State, National and International questions, the Supreme Political Committee shall initiate and determine the program to be followed, and after the said committee has decided upon a program, locally, nationally, or internationally, the same shall be executed through the office of the leaders of the various sections as hereinafter set forth.

Sec. 2. The Universal Negro Political Union shall be an auxiliary of the Universal Negro Improvement Association, and shall be governed by the by-laws of the said Universal Negro Improvement Association and such other laws as are made by the Universal Negro Political Union, and no law shall be made by the Universal Negro Political Union in conflict with those of the Universal Negro Improvement Association.

Sec. 3. (a) The President of the Local Division of the Universal Negro Improvement Association shall be the official representative of the Universal Negro Political Union in that district and he shall, along with his executive officers, appoint, with the approval of the Supreme Political Committee, the President and other officers of the Universal Negro political Union, who shall act under his instructions at all times, in conformity with those received by him from the Supreme Political Committee.

At this stage the session was adjourned.

WEDNESDAY EVENING, AUG. 13

The convention resumed at 9 p.m., the speaker, the Hon. Marcus Garvey, in the chair.

After prayers the minutes of the previous sessions were read and confirmed.

The Hon. Marcus Garvey announced to the accompaniment of rounds of applause that the contract for a ship had that day been signed and arrangements were being made for its inspection by the delegates and the public at 3 o'clock on Sunday afternoon.

The convention then proceeded with the unfinished business of the afternoon—discussion of the report of the committee appointed to draft the regulations for the Universal Negro Political Union.

The article and sections as finally amended were as follows:

Art. IV., Sec. 3. (b) Where there is a commissioner or high officer of the Universal Negro Improvement Association stationed in that district such officer shall be the supervisor of the activities of the Universal Negro Political Union and he shall make a conscientious and true report at all times to the supreme political committee, under whose direction he shall operate.

Sec. 4. Each division of the U.N.I.A. shall have a local political committee and the officers of the division shall constitute the local political committee along with the president of the local division of the U.N.I.A. as its chairman, all members of the committee being bona fide members of the U.N.I.A.

This committee shall be the representatives of the Universal Negro Political Union and shall have authority to regulate the affairs of that city, town, parish, province or other minor political territorial division to which a charter has been issued; and where there is more than one charter of the U.N.I.A. all such chartered divisions or chapters shall affiliate with the Universal Negro Political Union of that district.

Sec. 5. In all political affairs local or municipal, the local committee shall conduct the political program in accordance with such general specific rules as are issued by the supreme political committee.

Sec. 6. All political agreements or arrangements must be made with a view of putting over the program of the U.N.I.A., thereby conserving every avenue of political influence for the purpose of forwarding the aims and objects of the U.N.I.A.

Sec. 7. The second Assistant President-General shall be the directing head of the Universal Negro Political Union, under the supervision of the administration.

Sec. 8. All local committees shall make a full report of all activities and transactions to the supreme political committee under the direction of the president of the local division of the U.N.I.A.

Sec. 9. All commissioners of the U.N.I.A. shall have a supervisory power over all local committees and shall see that they conform to the instructions issued by the supreme political committee, but they shall not in any way interfere with any of the arrangements that have already been entered into by the local committee with the approval of the supreme political committee.

At this stage the convention adjourned.

Printed in *NW*, 23 August 1924.

1. A reference to a mutiny of pro-Egyptian Sudanese cadets at the military school in Khartoum and a simultaneous anti-British demonstration of the Egyptian railway battalion at Atbara in the Sudan, on 9 August 1924. The protests were put down by British troops and by the Sudan Mounted Rifles who inflicted several casualties on the railway battalion. The anti-British actions by the Sudanese and Egyptians coincided with preliminary negotiations in preparation for a meeting between British prime minister Ramsay MacDonald and the Egyptian leader Saad Zaghlul Pasha; the leaders met to discuss the Egyptian claim to the Sudan in September and October 1924 (*NYT*, 12 August, 13 August, and 15 August 1924; Anthony Clyne, "Zaghlul Pasha, Egyptian Revolutionist and Premier," *Current History* 21, no. 2 [November 1924]: 234–240).

Convention Report

[*New York, 14 August 1924*]

[THURSDAY MORNING, AUGUST 14]

On the convention assembling, the discussion of the report of the committee appointed to draft regulations for the gover[n]ance of the Negro Political Union was resumed.

The articles and sections as amended were:

ARTICLE V.

Sec. 1. The revenue for the Universal Negro Political Union shall be derived from entrance fees, annual tax, gifts, and donations and by such other means as the supreme political committee may determine.

Sec. 2. All moneys intended for the Universal Negro Political Union shall be deposited in a bank in the union's name to be designated by the local committee of the said Universal Negro Political Union, with the approval of the supreme political committee, and shall be drawn only on the signatures of the president, secretary, and the treasurer, with the approval of the president of the Universal Negro Improvement Association of that district on the authority of a duly called meeting of the union, except in cases where there have been appropriations for required current expenses.

Sec. 3. The secretary of the Universal Negro Political Union shall receive all moneys intended for the union and pay over same to the treasurer and receive in return a proper receipt for same. He shall also make the proper entries on his books to show the receipt and disbursement of such moneys.

Sec. 4. The secretary shall not keep in his possession any moneys intended for the Universal Negro Political Union longer than 24 hours.

Sec. 5. The treasurer of the Universal Negro Political Union shall be bonded in such amount as shall be determined by the union, and he shall receive from the secretary all moneys collected and intended for the union, and he shall immediately on receipt of such moneys deposit same in the bank designated by the union. He shall not keep such moneys in his possession longer than 24 hours.

Sec. 6. The secretary of the union shall also be bonded in such amount as shall be determined by the union.

Sec. 7. Moneys shall only be paid out by the treasurer on the presentation of proper vouchers signed respectively by the secretary and president in conformity with the method of disbursement.

Sec. 8. The local committees of the Universal Negro Political Union shall not be allowed to dispose of their funds or assets in excess of their current and regular expenses without the approval of the Supreme Political Committee, and that wherever there is a desire on the part of the local committee to expend any moneys other than that which is provided for in these laws a proper application must be made to the Supreme Political Committee setting forth the object and purpose for said expenditure.

Sec. 9. Local divisions of the Universal Negro Political Union shall be privileged to expend from their funds with the approval of the Supreme Political Committee such amounts as would help them in supporting any local candidate for office upon whom they can depend for their protection or assistance in carrying out the aims and objects of the Universal Negro Improvement Association if elected to said office.

Sec. 10. The Supreme Political Committee shall have the right to request of any or all local divisions of the Universal Negro Political Union that they pay over to the general funds of the said Universal Negro Political Union such surplus amounts in their local treasury as to assist the said Supreme Political Committee in supporting any national, state, or municipal election that would tend to help and advance the aims and objects of the Universal Negro Improvement Association: and that the surplus so collected shall not be more than 50 per cent of the funds of the local divisions.

Sec. 11. That the annual tax of one dollar paid by each and every member of the Universal Negro Political Union in accordance with laws already laid down shall be remitted to the Supreme Political Committee at headquarters for the general fund of the committee to carry on the international work of the union.

Sec. 12. That the annual tax of one dollar shall be paid immediately upon entrance or within 30 days after and the secretary shall see to the collection of same.

Sec. 13. The annual tax shall be paid as from the 1st of January of each year and payment made in any other month of the said year shall be considered as payment for that year.

Sec. 14. That the secretary of each local committee of the Universal Negro Political Union shall make a monthly report and remit all moneys collected for annual tax to the secretary of the Supreme Political Committee at headquarters. He shall also make a regular monthly report of all the financial transactions of the division properly countersigned by the president of the union and the president of the local division of the Universal Negro Improvement Association.

Sec. 15. No local division of the Universal Negro Political Union or its officers or committees or sub-committees shall receive contributions, gifts, donations, presents or grants or campaign funds from two opposing candidates in the same district or in the same campaign and no contributions, gifts, etc. shall be accepted contrary to law.

Sec. 16. All campaign funds collected in the name of the Universal Negro Political Union by any officer, committee, sub-committee or member of the union for campaign purposes shall be immediately turned over to the financial officers of the union and a proper report made of same. And no funds shall be collected by such individuals or committees except on the proper authority of the Supreme Political Committee on the recommendation of the local committee.

Sec. 17. No officer or member of a local committee of the Universal Negro Political Union shall of himself negotiate for receiving any campaign funds from any individual without first securing the commission, endorsement and authority of the local political committee.

At this stage the co[n]vention adjourned.

THURSDAY AFTERNOON, AUG. 14

The convention resumed at 2:15 p.m., the speaker, Hon. Marcus Garvey, in the chair.

After prayers, the minutes of the previous session were read and confirmed.

Unfinished business was proceeded with the formulating of regulations governing the Universal Negro Political Union.

Article V, Section 18, was amended as follows:

The first and third Mondays of each month shall be the regular meeting nights of the Universal Negro Political Union.

Section 19: That the meetings of the Universal Negro Political Union shall be held at the same place used as a meeting place by the local division of the Universal Negro Improvement Association, wherever possible.

"COMPENSATION"

Article [VI]. The duly authorized officers and other persons who performed duties for the Universal Negro Political Union shall be compensated in proportion to such services rendered and that such compensation shall be voted by the general membership of the local union with the approval of the local executive officers, and the Supreme Political Committee.

Hon. H.V. Plummer moved that the report of the committee be received and adopted in its entirety with the corrections made.

Hon. Ellinberg, Gary, Ind., seconded and the motion was unanimously carried.

Hon. W.A. Wallace, Chicago, moved that a pamphlet, in printed form, of the resolutions and articles adopted be printed and circulated after the rising of convention.

Hon. Mae Boyd, seconded, and the motion was unanimously carried.

Hon. H.V. Plummer moved that the executive officers of the Universal Negro Improvement Association be authorized to incorporate, in the State of New York, the articles of incorporation of the Universal Negro Political Union.

Hon. Carrie Minus seconded, and the motion was unanimously carried.

Hon. C.S. Bourne, Chancellor, then presented his report.

Hon. Freeman L. Martin moved that the report be received and adopted and that a vote of thanks and confidence be given to the Chancellor.

Hon. H.V. Plummer seconded, and the motion was unanimously carried.

Hon. F.E. Johnson, Detroit, moved that copies of the report be printed and distributed among the delegates.

Hon. G. Brown, Miami, seconded, and the motion was carried unanimously.

Hon. Freeman L. Martin moved that the Auditor's report also be received and adopted and a vote of thanks be accorded him.

Hon. H.V. Plummer seconded, and the motion was unanimously carried.

Hon. G.E. Carter, as chairman, next presented the report of the committee appointed to draft a petition to the President of the United States in connection with the development of independent Negro nations as a means of helping to solve the race problem.

On the motion of Hon. A. Foulkes, seconded by Hon. Mr. Jeffries, the report was received and adopted without further addition or comment.

Hon. F.E. Johnson, Detroit, next presented the report of the committee appointed to draft an appeal to the Kings of England, Italy, Spain and Belgium and to the Presidents of America, France and Portugal, asking for a square deal for the Negro in Africa, America and the colonies.

The report was discussed paragraph by paragraph and slightly amended, after which, on the motion of the Hon. F.E. Johnson, seconded by the Hon.

R.A. Bachelor, it was adopted as amended. The convention then adjourned.

THURSDAY EVENING, AUGUST 14

The convention resumed at 8:30 p.m., the Speaker, Hon. Marcus Garvey, in the chair.

After prayers, the minutes of the previous session were read and confirmed on the motion of Hon. C.H. Bryant, Costa Rica, seconded by Hon. S.J. Lee, Philadelphia.

The subject on the agenda was the discussing of the development of Liberia, Abyssinia and Haiti as independent black nations, and other countries where Negros form the majority of the population, such as Jamaica, Barbados, Trinidad, British Guiana, British Honduras and other islands of the West Indies and Africa.

Hon. Marcus Garvey initiated the discussion in a speech of much eloquence and power. The time had come, he said, for the Negro to bestir himself industrially and commercially in laying a sound foundation upon which this and future generations will build. In a convincing manner he stated the case for the acquisition of ships by the Negro race, and, incidentally, made an effective reply to the oft-heard statement that the U.N.I.A. should buy apartment houses instead of ships. He showed how Captain Baker,[1] thirty years ago, with a single schooner began trading between Boston and Jamaica, B.W.I., transporting bananas produced solely by the black people of that island. From such a small beginning the project has grown into the great United Fruit Company with a surplus of six hundred million dollars and a capital of one billion dollars, and two hundred ships. He dwelt on the root of prejudice, which was merely an economic question. Prejudice against the Negro was due to condition.

Hon. R. Van Richards,[2] chaplain to the Senate of Liberia, said he was convinced of the sincerity of the Universal Negro Improvement Association and the fitness of those who composed it for citizenship in his mother country, Liberia. He was sure that the association had been misrepresented to his government by members of the race hostile to the movement through jealousy of the power and influence it wielded. He was confident, however, that the present difficulties would soon be ironed out. As soon as the Liberian government had been truly informed of the power, honesty and sincerity of the association and its leaders, all would be well. He assured the convention that in him it would have a friend at court; he would use all his influence in behalf of the organization. The possibilities and potentialities of Liberia were also portrayed by the speaker.

Hon. Bishop J.D. Barber, confining his attention to Abyssinia, spoke in a glowing manner of its riches and its prowess, its healthful climate and the sound sense of its people and rulers. He was confident that in the not distant future the Universal Negro Improvement Association would be working hand in hand with the great people of Abyssinia, increasing sensibly the greatness of that historic country.

At this stage the convention adjourned.

Printed in *NW*, 23 August 1924. Original headlines abbreviated.

1. Lorenzo Dow Baker (1840–1908) was a merchant and sea captain who pioneered the commercial importation of bananas into the United States. In 1870 Baker, on a return voyage to Boston from Venezuela, stopped in Jamaica and took on a cargo of bananas. The bananas sold well, and upon his subsequent return to Jamaica, Baker encouraged farmers, white and black, to plant the fruit, which had previously grown wild, for its sale. The rapid growth of the banana trade coincided with the decline in the Jamaican sugar industry, and bananas became a major agricultural crop. In 1885 Baker along with eight others formed the Boston Fruit Co. to market bananas. In time Baker became the president of the company. In 1897 the company absorbed its competitors to form the United Fruit Co., and Baker served as the managing director of the Jamaican division. The United Fruit Co. rapidly increased banana imports not only from Jamaica but also from other Latin American and Caribbean countries. By the turn of the century the United Fruit Co. owned land in over thirteen countries, as well as railways and steamships, and had begun to play a major role in the politics of the countries in which it had investments (Thomas P. McCann, *An American Company: The Tragedy of United Fruit* [New York: Crown Publishers, 1976], pp. 14–17; Frederick Upham Adams, *Conquest of the Tropics: The Story of the Creative Enterprises Conducted by the United Fruit Company* [New York: Doubleday, Page and Co., 1914]; Charles Morrow Wilson, *Empire in Green and Gold: The Story of the American Banana Trade* [New York: Henry Holt and Co., 1947], pp. 18–116; Eugene P. Lyle, Jr., "Captain Baker and Jamaica," *World's Work* 11, no. 5 [March 1906]: 7,295–7,308; *DAB*; *WBD*; *NYT*, 22 June 1908).

2. R. Van Richards was the son-in-law of the chief justice of Liberia, J.J. Dossen (*NW*, 6 September 1924).

Article by Robert Minor[1]

[[NEW YORK, Aug. 14, 1924]]

RACE PROBLEM ANSWER CAN'T SATISFY ALL

NEGRO CONCLAVE HEARS COMMUNIST DELEGATE

The question of "The Adjustment of the Race Problems of the Southern States to the Satisfaction of all Concerned" has aroused keen interest and lively debate at the fourth annual international convention of the Universal Negro Improvement Association, now in session here.

Mrs. Olivia Whitemen [Whiteman], a delegate of the Workers Party to this international Race congress, addressed the convention asking whether anyone seriously believed that the race problems of the Southern states would ever be solved "to the satisfaction of all concerned."

CAN'T SATISFY ALL.

Answering her own question, the Communist woman delegate assured the gathering that the race question in the South will be solved all right, "but the solution will not be to the satisfaction of all concerned." She undertook to show that there is no chance in the world that the self-respecting Negroes would ever accept any adjustment of the race problem that would be satisfactory to the white ruling class.

Mrs. Whiteman insisted that the Negroes in America must stand firm for the redemption of Africa from the imperialists who are oppressing it, but that in doing so they must not let themselves become a weak and submissive people here in this country. She continued:

"NEED BACKBONE IN FIGHT."

"I cannot see how men, millions strong, who will permit their rights to be deprived them and their initiative crushed, will ever survive long enough to protect the great wealth of Africa, whose wealth any country will put up a strong battle to hold. Don't ever think that Negro liberty can be redeemed by a submissive spirit. It is going to take men with experience and training in courage and backbone to claim their own."

Men who do not stand up for their rights here, she said, when they start off for Africa will find it "a little late for training." She continued, "In order to have an army of men worth while, it is necessary to have a first-class training camp. Train them here," she demanded, "in contending for their rights here. When such men go to Africa," she said, "they will be able to stand [on] their own whatever the storm may be."

Refer[r]ing to a tendency of some of the delegates to address their appeals to preachers instead of to the masses of Negro people, Mrs. Whiteman said:

SLAMS PREACHERS.

"The preachers are a group of persons who have always known the oppressed condition of the Negro, and to my mind they have always given their official blessing to slavery and have always supported the government which oppressed my people."

In regard to the deplorable condition of mistreatment which colored women are compelled to suffer, Mrs. Whiteman exclaimed, "Whether we be in Alabama, Mississippi, Illinois or New York, we must take a definite and independent stand against permitting Negro women to be deprived of their rights and proper respect."

Because of the threatened imprisonment of Marcus Garvey, which is interpreted as an effort of the federal government to deprive the Negro movement of an able leader, many speech[e]s are devoted to the matter of his leadership.

S.S. [R.] Wheat, a Chicago officer of the organization, described the hopeless condition the American Negroes found themselves in just after the end of the world war, a period in which they were unorganized and helpless while their rights were more and more disap[p]earing.

"And at last," he said, "out of the islands of the sea we heard the cry of Marcus Garvey. Hopes were gone, hopes were lost, when this giant came on the scene."

CHARGES JEALOUSY.

Claiming that Negro leaders who have themselves been unable to organize the Negro masses were jealous of the new leader, Mr. Wheat said, "But the old reactionary Negro, that old 'Uncle Tom' Negro, is a back number now." The jealousy of such men, he said, has caused them to encourage the federal officials to frame up indictments against Garvey. "But we have got to make enemies on the day that we step into this organization," said the speaker.

Mrs. Ada Hogues of Chicago told of the manner in which she had been stirred by the propaganda of the Garvey movement and her appreciation of its leader.

Chairman William Sherrill, describing the hardships and dangers of attempting any sort of organization of the Negroes in Alabama, Mississippi and Texas, then introduced S. B.[V.] Robinson, commissioner of the Universal Negro Improvement Association for Mississippi and Louisiana, who he said had done heroic work in "prizing up the southern part of the country."

Mr. Robinson told of the work "in the Southland, among men who have no regard for human life." He said the lethargy had been so great that "the only thing the Negroes wanted was Jesus—and let the white man have all the rest." He declared that the organizing work and propaganda of the U.N.I.A. were causing the Negroes of the most backward regions of the South to stop singing that old song.

Fred E. Johnson of Detroit said that yesterday the Negro was slumbering, but that such a time had passed away for the black man. He attributed the awakening in large measure to the work of the leader Garvey. He declared that the incarceration of Garvey would not succeed in stopping the organization. He referred to several Negro intellectual leaders as having had a hand in the indictment affair and asked his hearers to tell these men "to make this their last attack on Marcus Garvey. And tell Coolidge that, too!" he said. Pausing a moment, he then shouted, "And tell the Ku Klux Klan that, too!"

MAY RECONSIDER K.K.K.

The latter remark, coming after the evasive action that was taken on the Klan question, seemed to be meant as a hint that all that was to be said about the Klan question was not contained in the official resolutions. Later Johnson said, "If you have a gun in my face, I'll buy you an ice-cream soda. Yes, I'll smile and talk pleasant. But you had better not lay that gun down and turn your back on me. Marcus Garvey can't afford to say some things because of the position he is in."

The resolutions on the subject of the Ku Klux Klan passed by the convention a few days ago appear in their official form as follows:

> Resolved that the fourth international convention of the Negro Peoples of the World regards the alleged attitude of the Ku Klux Klan to the Negro as fairly representative of the feelings of the majority of the white race towards us and places on record its conviction that the only solution of the crucial situation is that of the Universal Negro Improvement Association, namely, the securing for ourselves as speedily as possible a government of our own on African soil.

> Moved, that it shall be the policy of the Universal Negro Improvement Association to protest against the brutalities and atrocities alleged to be perpetrated upon members of the Negro race by the Ku Klux Klan or by any other organization.

A passage of the original resolution, describing the Negro organization's position as being "neutral" toward the Klan was stricken out by amendment on the suggestion of President Garvey, who said that the Negro convention could not afford to be "neutral" on so vital a question. This is a fact which was overlooked in my first dispatch on the subject.[2]

Printed in the *Daily Worker*, 15 August 1924.

1. Robert Minor (1884–1952) was born in Texas; he worked as a war correspondent during World War I. In 1918 he traveled to the USSR, where he met with Lenin. He became an active member of the Communist party in 1920, upon his return to the United States from Europe. By 1921 he was elected a member of the central executive committee of the Workers party, and became an editor of the *Daily Worker*. He also worked as a political cartoonist for the *Masses*, the *Liberator*, and the *St. Louis Dispatch*.

From his earliest days in the Communist party, Minor and his wife, Lydia Gibson, were active in black issues; both played a major role in Chicago's South Side campaign against high rents. By 1925 Minor was a member of the party's central committee and was responsible for work in black communities. Minor was involved with the Negro Sanhedrin, helped launch the short-lived League for the Struggle for Negro Rights in 1930, and later was involved with the Scottsboro Boys' defense committee (report on the radical press, October 15–November 15 1924, DNA, RG 59, file 861.0-2417; "Death of a Program," *Workers Monthly*, April 1926; "After Garvey, What?" *Workers Monthly*, June 1926; Harry Haywood, *Black Bolshevik: Autobiography of an Afro-American Communist* [Chicago: Liberator Press, 1978], pp. 117, 131, 138–140, 361–362, 543–544; Joseph North, *Robert Minor: Artist and Crusader* [New York: International Publishers, 1956]).

2. In 1924 Minor wrote a number of articles in the *Liberator* and the *Daily Worker* on the Garvey movement; they were sharply critical of Garvey's ties with the KKK and his African colonization plan. Yet Minor stressed the importance of the UNIA, "the largest organization of negroes in the world [because it] is made up almost entirely of the working class," and praised the organization as vital to the development of black nationalism, both in the United States and abroad. By 1926 Minor became increasingly critical of the UNIA leadership, which he described as retreating into a "more and more fantastic opportunism" (*Daily Worker*, 29 July, 13 August, 18 August, 29 August, and 12 September 1924; "The Black Ten Millions," *Liberator*, February 1924; "The Negro Finds His Place and a Sword," *Liberator*, August 1924; "The Handkerchief on Garvey's Head," *Liberator*, October 1924).

Convention Report

[*New York, 15 August 1924*]

FRIDAY MORNING, AUGUST 15

The convention assembled at 10 a.m., the Speaker, Hon. Marcus Garvey, in the chair.

After prayers the minutes of the previous session were read and confirmed.

The order of the day was then proceeded with.

Speaking on the subject before the house, Hon. J. Milton Van Lowe, Detroit, stressed the importance of acquiring ships, showing how the possession of a mercantile marine had contributed to the greatness of nations, ancient and modern, and the lack of it had kept certain nations in obscurity.

Hon. Marcus Garvey, in an address delivered for the guidance of the house in the discussion, showed that the Universal Negro Improvement Association held in its hands the means of changing the entire industrial position in the Eastern and Western world. He demonstrated the fact that Negroes were in the main the producers and the white capitalists fattened on their produce, achieving commercial and industrial greatness for themselves and their nations. Ships were indispensable in promoting the commercial and industrial advancement of the Negro race. After Negro produce had been corral[l]ed, wherever no local market, through strenuous competition or some other cause[,] was available, ships would play their part in transporting to the best market. The Negro now had his last chance, and if he did not act now, starvation and stagnation and ultimately destruction would face him and his. In Africa, in the West Indies, in Central America, Negroes tilled the soil exclusively, and the harvest was reaped by the white man exclusively. It was the duty of Negroes of America to help members of the race domiciled in other parts, thereby helping themselves and preventing their own destruction. Co-operation on the part of Negroes abroad with Negroes here would operate in the same manner.

Hon. R.A.[H.] Batchelor, Oriente, Cuba, referred to the amazing fertility of the Haitian and Dominican soil, which, tilled and tended exclusively by Negroes who were adept, nine out of every ten of them, only enriched the white foreigner. He suggested emigration of Negroes to those countries where with small capital they could not only enrich themselves in a short time but help their brothers, the farmers, who were practically slaves in the hands of the white man. Haiti was all black in thought, one hundred per cent race conscious, and knew no nationality; it only mattered that you were black, and the blacker the better. He painted a harrowing picture of the system under which the foreigner enriched himself at the expense of the native farmer.

Hon. J.B. Eaton, Berkeley, Va., emphasized that it was practically useless for Negroes to start manufacturing establishments in the face of the keen competition to be found everywhere in the United States unless they owned steamships to permit them marketing their products abroad.

Hon. Marcus Garvey expressed his agreement with this point in view, stressing that it was their aim to build up industrially and commercially by getting the raw materials from Negro communities all over the world and bringing them to factories here and returning the finished article. He took the opportunity to assert once more that it was never the intention of the Universal Negro Improvement Association to gather up all Negroes everywhere and have them go back to Africa.

Hon. Smith,[1] Detroit, said it was his ambition to go to Africa and make a name as a captain of industry. It was foolish for Negroes to build up industrially here and invest all their money here, when there was no outlet.

Hon. H. Hampton, Ga., said he desired to go to Africa and utilize the specialized knowledge he possessed of mining and industry. That way the industrial progress of Negroes lay.

The convention then adjourned.

FRIDAY AFTERNOON, AUG. 15

The convention resumed at 2 p.m., the Speaker, Hon. Marcus Garvey, in the chair.

After prayers, the minutes of the previous session were read and confirmed on the motion of Hon. S.J. Lee, Philadelphia, seconded by the Hon. C.H. Bryant, Costa Rica.

A motion for the suspension of the order of the day having been adopted, reports of various committees were presented.

Hon. P.L. Burrows, as secretary, read the report of the Committee appointed to draft recommendations in regard to the policy which the Negro race should adopt in view of the policy of England and France and America towards the Negro.

After some discussion of the report it was decided that the report be referred back to the Committee to be revised and again presented to the convention.

Hon. P.L. Burrows, as Chairman, read a report from the Committee appointed to recommend ways and means of the educating of the Negro race as to the real meaning of society, and laying down the principles that should guide those who are desirous of becoming socially distinctive. Also the creation of an atmosphere of purity around the young generation of the race, to better prepare them for a higher social life.

It was decided that the report be returned to the Committee so that more specific recommendations may be made.

Hon. F.E. Johnson, Detroit, as Chairman, presented the report of the Committee appointed to recommend ways and means of correctly educating white public opinion to the needs and desires of the Negro race.

It was decided that the report be returned to the Committee for re-drafting and presentation again to the convention; also that Hon. Sir William Sherrill be added to the Committee.

Hon. W.A. Wallace, Chicago, presented the report of the Committee appointed to draft an appeal to the various religious heads for an honest and human settlement of the problems of humanity, especially as such problems affect the Negro.

The report was unanimously adopted as read on the motion of Hon. W.A. Wallace, seconded by Hon. J.U. Chambers, East St. Louis.

The order of the day was then proceeded with discussing the development of Liberia, Abyssinia and Haiti as independent black nations, and other countries, where Negroes form a majority of the population.

Hon. C.H. Bryant, Costa Rica, spoke on the economic and industrial condition existing in Panama, Costa Rica and Nicaragua, and suggested that agricultural loan banks be formed.

Hon. M. Askernese, Farrell, Pa., said basis of operation should be established, precedented to the undertaking of industrial enterprises on a larger scale.

Hon. J.J. Peters, Chicago, stressed the importance of developing the race industrially. It was his opinion that Liberia should be developed, and that that should be the first care of the association. He emphasized the need for money to put over the program.

Hon. J. Chambers, East St. Louis, said what was needed was labor, not so much money.

Hon. [A.] G. Ellenburg, Gary, Ind., said the association should concentrate its attention immediately upon building up a trade between the United States and the West Indies and Liberia. When settled trade relations had been established, it would be found that immigration would follow and be welcomed as a matter of course.

Hon. Mr. Smith, Detroit, made a plea for industrial and commercial development.

Hon. W.A. Wallace, Chicago, said the white man was looking for more markets for the things he produced. Connecting Liberia, Haiti and Abyssinia commercially with the United States on a big scale would be hailed by the white man as well.

Hon. H.E.[B.] Williams, Boston, stressed the needs for ships to alleviate the economic stress in the West Indian Islands.

Hon. Mills, Newark, pointed out that a splendid trade could be built up between this country, the West Indies and Africa, the association making a splendid profit, not only on produce brought here, but on produce shipped away.

Hon. I. Chambers,[2] New Orleans, suggested that agencies be formed, especially in the South, through which cotton and other produce of the Negro could be bought, thereby preventing white capitalists from obtaining this produce at a ridiculously low figure, as was the case at present to the undoing of the farmer.

The meeting then adjourned.

Friday Evening, August 15

The Convention resumed at 9 p.m., the Speaker, Hon. Marcus Garvey, in the chair. The minutes of the previous session having been read and confirmed, the discussion of the development of Liberia, Abyssinia and Haiti as independent black nations, and other countries where Negroes form the majority of the population, was continued.

Hon. M. Daniels, Brooklyn, spoke on the importance of commerce, industry and finance.

Hon. T.R. Daley, New York, suggested that a commissariat department be established.

Hon. S.V. Robertson, Louisiana and Mississippi, then moved that the discussion be closed and a committee be appointed to formulate recommendations and report back to the Convention.

Hon. C.H. Bryant, Costa Rica, seconded, and the motion was unanimously carried.

The following committee was then appointed by the Speaker: Hon. Sir William Sherrill, Hon. P.L. Burrows, Hon. C.H. Bryant, Hon. S.W. Robertson, Hon. I. Chambers, Hon. R.A. Bachelor, Hon. A.R. Patersaul.

Hon. F.E. Johnson, as chairman, then presented the report of the committee which was appointed to formulate ways and means of correctly educating white public opinion to the needs and desires of the Negro race.

The report was discussed section by section and adopted with slight corrections.

At this stage Hon. A. Newsum,[3] Mississippi, was permitted to make his district report. He spoke on the work he had done in Mississippi, along with Hon. S.V. Robertson, Commissioner, and stated that Bolivar County,[4] where he labored and where he pastored three churches, was ethusiastic for the cause. Mound Bayou,[5] a wholly Negro city, had been won over after initial opposition.

The Convention then discussed the following subject: "Encouraging Travel Among and Between Negroes of Commerical and Industrial Professions."

Hon. Sir William Sherrill in a keynote address said the American Negro had done little or no traveling, while of the West Indian the opposite was true. To this was perhaps due the fact that when the movement was started West Indians resident in New York were the first to follow.

Hon. Dr. J.J. Peters, Chicago, said ships would furnish encouragement.

Hon. Alleyne, Pittsburgh, spoke, after which Hon. Hassell, Seattle, made a plea for support of the shipping company. It must be remembered, he said, that a large sum of money was required to equip the ship for her first voyage.

Hon. Col. Harrigan, New York, advocated encouraging professional men to travel.

Hon. Smith, Detroit, said there was no need for thinking out plans by which the Negro should be encouraged. The Negro, owing to economic stress and his firm belief in the principles of the U.N.I.A., was ready to travel, and would do so readily when ships were secured.

At this stage the adjournment was taken until 2 p.m. Sunday.

Printed in *NW*, 23 August 1924. Original headlines abbreviated.

1. Leonard Smith was the first vice-president of the Detroit UNIA (*NW*, 15 December 1923).

2. Professor I. Chambers had made a fifty-dollar loan to the Black Cross Navigation and Trading Co. at a New Orleans UNIA division meeting (*NW*, 21 June 1924).

3. Rev. A. Newsum (also spelled Newson) represented the UNIA's Mississippi divisions. He resided in Cleveland, Miss. (*NW*, 9 August 1924).

4. In 1924 Bolivar County, Mississippi, was an economically depressed rural area located in Mississippi's Yazoo Delta. The county entered agricultural production in the 1850s and 1860s, when cotton planters drained the swamps to reveal topsoil of great natural fertility. Because of the expense of reclaiming the land, only wealthy planters could take full advantage of this opportunity, and the area became dominated by large plantations, with blacks making up most of the population. Even before the Civil War, slaves outnumbered whites in Bolivar County by nearly ten to one.

After emancipation, the region's planters continued to prosper, though conditions remained difficult for the work force. The vast majority of freedmen remained either sharecroppers or tenant farmers, and labor discipline in the delta was harsh, even by contemporary southern standards. The economy of Bolivar County remained based on cotton, although some corn and alfalfa were grown; local industry consisted mainly of cotton gins, cottonseed oil mills, and sawmills.

In the early 1920s agricultural recession and the boll weevil undermined the local economy. Cotton prices plummeted, land values fell, and many blacks who had acquired land lost their holdings. By 1925 over 90 percent of the farmers in the county were again tenants, and many blacks migrated from the distressed area. The UNIA had a relatively strong presence in Bolivar County. In 1925–1926, divisions existed around Boyle, Cleveland, Merigold, Mound Bayou, and Shelby; several local chapters also functioned in the area. These bodies reported an aggregate paid membership of at least seventy-nine (membership lists, 1925–1926, NN-Sc, UNIA Central Division records, box 2, a.16; Florence Warfield Sillers, comp., *History of Bolivar County, Mississippi* [Spartanburg, S.C.: Reprint Co. Publishers, 1976]; James W. Loewen and Charles Sallis, eds., *Mississippi: Conflict and Change* [New York: Pantheon Books, 1974], p. 207).

5. Mound Bayou, in Bolivar County, Mississippi, was one of several self-governing black communities founded in the late nineteenth century. In 1887 Isaiah Montgomery and Benjamin F. Green, two former slaves, set up an all-black colony in an uninhabited section of the rich Yazoo Delta. Many of the original settlers were former slaves of Confederate President Jefferson Davis (1808–1889) and of his relations, and had participated in a Reconstruction era attempt to purchase the Davis Bend plantations near Natchez. The Mound Bayou settlement prospered for several decades, and the town's population increased from about three hundred in 1900 to some eight hundred in 1920. The community's success inspired a good deal of pride among its residents, many of whom viewed it as validating their race's capacity for social progress.

The UNIA's stress on black economic activities must have seemed familiar in Mound Bayou, for the community had long fostered a variety of such racial endeavors. In 1904 local businessmen created a black-owned bank, and in 1910 the black-owned Mound Bayou Oil Mill and Manufacturing Co., financed largely by stock sales among local farmers, was established as well. Booker T. Washington assisted these community projects, publicizing them as working models of his program of economic uplift.

By the time the UNIA appeared in the early 1920s, Mound Bayou had entered a period of economic recession. Declining cotton prices led to the failure of the bank, and soon thereafter the mill closed. By 1923 some four thousand farmers in the area had lost their farms. The general ethos of racial pride and economic self-help may have encouraged receptivity to the UNIA, though the "initial opposition" referred to by the speaker may have reflected the conciliatory nature of the politics pursued by the town's black leaders (Janet Sharp Hermann, *The Pursuit of a Dream* [New York: Oxford University Press, 1981], pp. 219–245; Norman L. Crockett, *The Black Towns* [Lawrence, Kans.: Regents Press of Kansas, 1979], pp. 52–70, 124–134, 158–168; Federal Writers' Project, Works Progress Administration, *Mississippi* [Washington, D.C.: GPO, 1940], p. 320; Florence Warfield Sillers, comp., *History of Bolivar County, Mississippi*, pp. 337–339; *New York Age*, 29 April 1912; August Meier, "Booker T. Washington and the Town of Mound Bayou," in *Along the Color Line: Explorations of the Black Experience*, ed. by August Meier and Elliott Rudwick [Urbana: University of Illinois Press, 1976], pp. 217–224).

Convention Report

[New York, 18 August 1924]

MONDAY MORNING, AUGUST 18

The Convention assembled at 10.30 a.m., the Speaker, Hon. Marcus Garvey, in the chair.

After prayers, the minutes of the previous session were read and confirmed.

Hon. Marcus Garvey addressed the delegates in regard to the shipping project, expressing the hope that all were satisfied with the ship and that they would do all in their power to make it possible that more ships be acquired in the near future.

The discussion of the following subject, left unfinished at the previous session, was continued: "Encouraging travel among and between Negroes of commercial and industrial professions."

Hon. P.L. Burrows, First Asst. Secretary-General, spoke of the excellent education to be obtained through travel.

Hon. C.H. Bryant, Costa Rica, pointed out some of the benefits to be derived.

Hon. Dennis Washington, Louisiana, Hon. R.A. Martin, Florida, Cuba, and Hon. M. Daniels, Brooklyn, also spoke, whereupon the discussion was closed and the following committee appointed by the speaker to draft recommendations and report back to the Convention: Hon. J. Hassell, Seattle, Hon. R.H. Bachelor, Oriente, Cuba, and Hon. A.R. Patersaul, Alliance, Ohio.

The Convention then proceeded to discuss (1) the formulation of a code of education, especially for Negroes; (2) censoring of all literature placed in the hands of Negroes; (3) the educating of the race to discriminate in the reading of all literature placed in its hands; (4) the promotion of an independent Negro literature and culture.

Hon. Bishop McGuire, called upon to deliver the keynote address, stressed the importance of the subject and promised, with the approval of the chair, to do so during the afternoon session.

Hon. Prof. D.H. Kyle, Clarksburg, W.Va., in a very thoughtful address, in which he showed why certain songs and hymns should be condemned, recommended that every delegate and deputy make it his duty on returning to his or her community to see that their lodges and societies reverse the thought by which to "blackball" meant to reject and "whiteball" to elect. He stressed the need for the teaching of Negro history, suggesting that such a book be compiled by a committee designated by [the] U.N.I.A.

At this stage the convention adjourned.

Monday Afternoon, August 18

The Convention was called to order at 2.30 p.m. The discussion on education was continued from the morning, after the usual preliminaries.

Hon. Marcus Garvey, Speaker-in-Convention, was in the Chair.

Hon. Freeman Martin, of St. Louis, said that the Negro was suffering from a dreadful disease which he called "White man's Psychology." In order to eradicate it we must use educational methods by the publication of literature, books and periodicals. He referred to the text books and histories used in the schools at the present time which were quite unsuitable for the education of the Negro racially. He kept a good Negro library, and while he was teaching he used such books to much advantage.

Hon. W.J. Donald, of Arkansas, emphasized the keeping of pictures of Negro leaders and heroes and also the education of the children to useful manners and general conduct. Hon. J. Peters also stressed the psychological factor; the training of the young and the necessity of publishing literature to free the race from the mental enslavement of the white man. He urged the delegates to teach the children the love of race; teach them the ancient glories of the race, and above all pay attention to psychology, which was the science of today.

Hon. A.G. Ellengburg, of Gary, fell into the psychological trend, referring to the religious aspect, especially in the use of pictures in the homes, because of their influence on the minds of the children.

Hon. J.[I.] Chambers, of New Orleans, spoke of educational psychology.

Hon. Mrs. Brown, of Newark, spoke of the neglect of the men of the race to take their part of the responsibility of home training. As a result, while the poor woman was at work, the children received their training in the streets; and at nights father, instead of taking a hand in teaching the children, left the home and went elsewhere. The race could not improve under such conditions.

Hon. R.H. Bachelor, of Cuba, urged the adoption of an educational code in the same way that the white man has his code for the schools and universities.

He further suggested that efforts should be made to counteract the propaganda of the white missionaries who, in their endeavors to collect moneys for converting alleged savages[,] print many objectionable pictures and statements in their literature, tending to cause the Negro to despise his race.

Hon. R. [J. Milton] Van Lowe, Detroit, supported the last speaker in his suggestion that an educational code be instituted and suggested the indirect method of teaching, if frontal attacks were not successful. Especially, he urged, that attention be paid to the churches and schools.

Hon. Arnold Ford, of New York, said the Negro was suffering from "Leucomania" or white mentality. Suggested the publication of all kinds of literature for propaganda purposes to cure the terrible disease.

Hon. J.B. Eaton, of Virginia, agreed with those who urged the publication of literature.

Hon. G. A. Weston, New York, stressed the influence of environment in connection with the subject. He said it is not so much the environment as the environed that counts, because no matter what the environment is, the matter depended upon whether the environed accepts the thing or not. He said that the Negro should get rid of the alleged "curse" theory said to be found in the Bible.

Eventually, after further discussion, a committee consisting of Professors Kyle and Chambers; Hon. Lawyer Martin, Bishop McGuire and Hon. R. H. Bachelor was appointed to go into the matter.

Hon. Marcus Garvey said that a letter[1] had been sent to the convention by the Workers' party of America[2] protesting the attitude adopted by the convention in the matter of the Ku Klux Klan. The speaker said that they should give the letter courteous consideration as he had given to any other political party, but he said it was not to be denied that all white men felt they were different to the black man no matter how much they expressed themselves to the contrary. He realized that the working class people were being crushed by the capitalists, but said it was quite a different kind of crushing to that given to the Negroes.

Hon. Dr. J. Peters, Chicago, said it was clear to him that the white man did not well understand Negro psychology, judging from that letter and other facts.

The letter, which was a lengthy one, was received and read.

The Hon. Marcus Garvey again referred to the letter and said that problems of the white men of different classes were easily solved. Not so between white and black. The lynchings and burnings in the South attributed to the Klan paled into insignificance when compared to the wholesale killings and destruction caused by the working classes during the riots which took place at so many different places in the United States recently.[3] The Jews and Catholics can easily fight the Ku Klux Klan because they own their factories and other commercial places where they can get employment, but when the Negro starts to fight, his meal ticket is liable to be cut off, as he has no such establishments to give him employment. He therefore urged Negroes to watch their step.

Hon. W. Wallace of Chicago, agreed with the remarks of the speaker in general and reminded the convention that on one occasion when the black and white waiters in Chicago went on strike,[4] on settlement of the strike the blacks who had assisted in putting it over, were left on the streets, while the whites went back to work without giving any aid to the former. He also pointed out that the worker of today becomes the capitalist of tomorrow. This is not so with our people here.

Hon. F. Martin, of St. Louis, moved that the convention, while fully appreciating the proffer of counsel in the matter, and also the offer of co-operation in what they termed a common fight, begged to advise that the position taken by the convention fully represented the point of view best calculated to serve our interests.

This resolution was unanimously carried.

Convention adjourned at 5 p.m.

MONDAY EVENING

The convention resumed at 9 p.m., the Speaker, Hon. Marcus Garvey, in the chair.

After prayers, the minutes of the previous session were read and confirmed.

The Speaker announced that the Haitian delegation, through their spokesman, Hon. Theodore Stephens,[5] would be heard, and in a brief address paid a tribute to the great soldier-statesman-martyr, Toussaint L'Ouverture. He expressed the sympathy of the administration with the Haitians in their [f]ight for independence and true liberty.

Hon. Rev. Theodore Stephens then addressed the convention, making a stirring appeal to the United States Government and to American public opinion, through the convention, for the restoration of autonomy to Haiti.

At this stage the Speaker announced that His Royal Highness Prince Kojo Tovalou Houenou,[6] of Dahomey, who spoke French but very little English, would be introduced to the convention by Hon. Theodore Stephens. The Prince, who had just arrived from France, said the Speaker was the man responsible for the new spirit that is sweeping Colonial France at the present time. He had come to see the Universal Negro Improvement Association in its organized forces and activities.

Hon. Mr. Stephens then introduced the Prince, whom he described as an erudite scholar and great thinker, barrister-at-law of the Court of Appeals, Paris, doctor of medicine, editor, author and president of the Universal League for the defense of the black race. He was the nephew of the late King Behanzi[n], who was deported to Martinique after his kingdom was conquered by France, and who later returned from exile to die in Algeria.[7] The Prince journeyed to France in 1900, where he remained ever since pursuing his studies.

The Prince then came forward to address the convention and was given a rousing ovation. Speaking through an interpreter, Hon. Stephens, he paid a tribute to the Hon. Marcus Garvey, to the Universal Negro Improvement Association and to the convention. He lauded France's sense of justice while deprecating passionately the abuses of her agents committed in Africa. It was for the Negroes of the world, he said, under whatever flag they might be, in whatever organization[,] to unite their forces and go marching back to their motherland and wrest it from the common enemy.

The discussion of the Haitian appeal was then resumed.

Hon. J.A. Hassell, Seattle, referred to the brilliant exploits of Toussaint L'Ouverture in freeing his people.

Hon. Prof. D.H. Kyle, Clarksburg, W. Va., said the convention should go on record to use its influence in the various communities of America through their national representatives to secure Haitian freedom. The ballot was the weapon to be used.

At this stage the convention adjourned.

Printed in *NW*, 30 August 1924. Original headlines abbreviated.

1. This letter has not been located.

2. The Workers Party of America (WPA) was established in December 1921 by members of the Communist Party of America (CPA) in compliance with a directive of the Third Congress of the Communist International (the Comintern), which met in Moscow in June and July 1921. This directive was itself responsive to the disastrous condition of the CPA, whose illegality had driven it underground and whose leadership had been decimated by a series of arrests and deportations in the latter part of 1919. In an effort to move American communism from a clandestine position to one of open alliance and involvement with the general populace, a movement began among certain CPA members to form a legal party. Other members resisted the emergence of the party from underground, however. This factional dispute remained unsettled by the formation of the WPA and was finally submitted to Moscow for decision. With the support of Lenin and Trotsky, it was decided that the Communist movement in the United States should be placed in the hands of a legalized party. Nevertheless, some CPA members still held out for the continued separate organizational existence of the illegal party and voted in the CPA's central executive committee to resist obedience to the Comintern's instructions.

The issue was brought to a head when the leadership of the CPA was arrested at the party's 1922 convention, held at a secret meeting place in the woods near Bridgeman, Mich. As a result of further instructions from the Comintern's fourth congress, held early in December 1922, the CPA dissolved itself on 7 April 1923 and merged with the WPA, simultaneously authorizing the Workers party to use the name Communist Party of America whenever desirable.

The attitude of the Workers party toward Garvey was shaped in part by the party's position on blacks, which subordinated national and racial questions to those of class. "The Negro problem," as the party program of 1919 stated, "is a political and economic problem. The racial oppression of the Negro is simply the expression of his economic bondage and oppression, each intensifying the other. This complicates the Negro problem but does not alter its proletarian character." While trying to win Garvey over as well as to infiltrate the UNIA, it publicly attacked both, in keeping with its ideological subordination of the racial question to economic or class factors. But although the Communist party attacked Garvey for his African repatriation plans, it recognized the UNIA as the largest organization of black workers in the United States.

Robert Minor, the member of the Workers party's Central Executive Committee responsible for work among blacks, openly praised the UNIA in the *Daily Worker* as the "first and largest experience of the Negro masses in self organization." Reporting on the 1924 convention, Minor wrote glowingly of the international representation at the meeting and of the strength of the UNIA organization, which he credited with having frightened the imperialist powers of the world, but he made only small note of the Ku Klux Klan. "Garvey may destroy himself by fawning in the organization's name before the cowardly Ku Klux Klan, but with one set of leaders discredited and disgraced, the organization will go on nevertheless and will find leaders who are not afraid" (*Daily Worker*, 29 August 1924; U.S. Congress, *House Committee on Un-American Activities Rept. 1694*, 83d Congress, 2d sess., 28 May 1954, 69-79).

3. Between 94 and 115 blacks were killed in the riots that broke out in East St. Louis, Omaha, Chicago, and Tulsa between 1917 and 1921. Of these, 9 whites and approximately 39 blacks were killed in the East St. Louis riot of 2 July 1917. Precise figures on the number of blacks killed by the Ku Klux Klan are unavailable. According to reports of the killings in the press, 4 blacks were killed by the Klan in the years 1920 and 1921 (*New York World*, 19 September 1921). In addition, some 148 other acts of violence, including mutilations and floggings, were reported. The specter of the Klan provoked and encouraged a wave of violence that terrorized black communities and that is unquantifiable. From 1917 until 1921, some 225 blacks were lynched in the United States, and estimates of attacks on blacks in the 1920s were in the thousands (John Samuel Ezell, *The South Since 1865* [New York: Macmillan, 1963], p. 371; Elliott Rudwick, *Race Riot at East St. Louis, July 2, 1917* [1964; reprint, Urbana: University of Illinois Press, 1982], p. 4; *NYB*, 1921-1922, p. 75; *New York World*, 6 September and 19 September 1921; Harry A. Ploski and Roscoe C. Brown, eds., *The*

Negro Almanac, pp. 212–215).

4. According to the Chicago Commission on Race Relations, around 1905 "Negro waiters lost their positions in many of the first class hotels through circumstances in which they felt they had been 'double-crossed' by the unions, of which they then were members" (Chicago Commission on Race Relations, *The Negro in Chicago: A Study of Race Relations and a Race Riot* [Chicago: University of Chicago Press, 1922], pp. 418–419). Bitterness resulting from the episode damaged the labor movement in the hotel trade; in 1920 white waiters waged an unsuccessful strike because of the intervention of black strikebreakers (*Buffalo American*, 28 November 1923; Allan H. Spear, *Black Chicago: The Making of a Negro Ghetto, 1890–1920* [Chicago: University of Chicago Press, 1967], p. 165).

5. Theodore Stephens was the *Negro World*'s editor for its French section (*NW*, 5 April 1924).

6. Kojo Marc Tovalou-Houénou (1887–1936) was the son of a well-educated and wealthy Dahomey merchant, Joseph Padonou Tovalou Quenum (or Houénou), and claimed to be a nephew in the family of Behanzin, the king of Dahomey who was deposed and exiled by the French. Sent to Paris for his education at an early age, Tovalou-Houénou lived in France and elsewhere in Europe between 1890 and 1925. He read law at the University of Bordeaux, where he received his *licence*, and he subsequently set up legal practice in Paris. At the outbreak of World War I, he enlisted with the French army, and it is reported that he fought bravely at the battles of Douaumont and Verdun. In 1923 he was expelled from a cabaret in Montmartre by American tourists who were shocked at the presence of a black man in evening dress; thereafter, his political stance took a radical direction. He founded the *Ligue Universelle pour la Defense de la Race Noire* in July 1924, and in collaboration with Jean Fangeat and René Maran published an influential monthly journal, *Les Continents*. *Les Continents* provided extensive coverage of UNIA activities and published speeches of Marcus Garvey. French authorities as well as the *Baltimore Afro-American* came to label him the "Marcus Garvey of Europe" because of his stand on political autonomy for Africans. Following his appearance at the 1924 UNIA convention, Tovalou-Houénou appears to have fallen out with the UNIA, possibly over his association with the NAACP. On 6 June 1925 the *Negro World* accused him of having given a "back-handed blow in the face to the UNIA," supposedly in order "not to offend these Black Nordics," and as a result, the UNIA had "dropped him without shedding any tears." Yet by 1929 Tovalou-Houénou and the UNIA had evidently reached a rapprochement, as he was then described as the UNIA representative in Paris.

When his father was dying in late 1925, Tovalou-Houénou, as the eldest son, returned to Dahomey to assume leadership of the family of several hundred members and claim its fortune, but he lost out to his younger brother. The brother, Georges Tovalou Quénum (1887–1943), was a merchant who, while also politically active and critical of French government, benefited in this instance from administrative support. Tovalou-Houénou died in Dakar in 1936 (*NW*, 6 June 1925, 17 August 1929; *Baltimore Afro-American*, 9 May 1924; Iheanachor Egonu, "Les Continents and the Francophone Pan-Negro Movement," *Phylon* 42, no. 3 [fall 1981]: 245–254]; J. Ayodele Langley, *Pan-Africanism and Nationalism in West Africa, 1900–1945: A Study in Ideology and Social Classes* [Oxford: Clarendon Press, 1973], pp. 290–300).

7. King Behanzin (d. 1906), son of Glele, ruled the powerful centralized state of Dahomey. In 1889 Glele died, possibly by his own hand, thus avoiding negotiation with the French, who had taken the Dahomean port of Cotonou. Behanzin succeeded him and in 1890 began to mobilize popular resistance against French economic and political encroachment, precipitating a series of Franco-Dahomean wars. In fact, the dense population of Dahomey and the high degree of political and military organization of the Dahomean state made resistance against the French one of the most effective in all of Africa. Behanzin, using German mercenaries and equipped with modern military equipment, defeated the French in a series of battles. Yet in 1892 the French, under the leadership of Gen. Alfred-Amédée Dodds, decisively defeated Behanzin, who surrendered himself to Dodds in 1893 and was deported, first to Martinique and then to Algeria, where he died in 1906. Before his deportation Behanzin wrested from the French the concession that his brother Agoliagbo would succeed him, thus continuing the throne of Abomey, although under French colonial rule (Michael Crowder, *West Africa under Colonial Rule*, pp. 101–104; Prosser Gifford and William Louis, eds., *France and Britain in Africa*, pp. 483–485; Boniface I. Obichere, *West African States and European Expansion: The Dahomey-Niger Hinterland, 1885–1898*, pp. 51–118).

Article by Robert Minor

[[NEW YORK, August 18, 1924]]

ALL AFRICA IN REBELLION, IS GARVEY REPORT

FULL RIGHTS DEMANDED BY NEGRO COMMUNIST

A flash of light was thrown upon the international character and wide political interests claimed by the convention of Negro peoples of the world, now in session here, under the auspices of the Universal Negro Improvement Association, when Marcus Garvey, president of the organization, interrupted the proceedings to read to the delegates two dispatches, one telling of an uprising of natives of the Sudan in Africa and the other of the defeat of both the French and the Spanish troops by natives of Morocco.

The large Negro audience, composed of a thousand or more Harlem Negroes and also of delegates from many colonies of colored population, from the West Indies to the French and British possessions in Africa, shook the roof of Liberty Hall with their cheers and shouts of joy.

"Some of us may not know the tremendous import of this movement," said Garvey, his face beaming with delight. "Lack of knowledge of what we are doing accounts for a great deal of misunderstanding, as expressed by some of our critics.

"The international character of our movement and its determining purposes are so marked that we cannot but feel happy and glad when certain things happen which are in accord with the spirit in which we are working. Now and then things occur in which our movement is especially interested— especially things that are happening in Africa, for we must remember that our supreme purpose is to free and redeem the African continent for the colored people who are entitled to have it and to work out their destiny there.

"Now some things have been happening there which are of great interest and importance, and yet which some people do not pay much attention to because they do not realize the significance of them. Yet they are events which show the immense work that the association is doing. They show that we are dealing with a sentiment that cannot be destroyed—the growing and persistent sentiment for African freedom and redemption which is behind our organization.

"You should know that every section of Africa has stirred itself to this same sentiment, which grows and spreads thru all the colonies. Morocco is in rebellion, the Sudan, East Africa, West Africa—all of the peoples there are responding to this great urge for liberation. I have just received a letter from South Africa which states that the downfall of General Smuts in South Africa was absolutely due to the activities of the natives.[1]

"And the Moors. The Moors are beating Spain, and they have shattered her armies until they have practically upset the government of Spain[,] which is now in a precarious condition."[2]

After Mr. Garvey had read the two dispatches from two afternoon newspapers, and after the demonstration was quieted, the convention passed into consideration of a plan for the formation of the proposed "Universal Negro Political Union." It must be explained that the Negroes use the term "universal" in the sense of "international." The operations of the proposed union would, according to indications gathered from the speeches, be of an anti-imperialist nature thr[ough]out all colonial and semi-independent Negro countries, but as to their nature within the United States there is less clear indication as yet. There is some reason to think that the leaders intend to operate in the United States on the basis of selecting individual candidates on Republican and Democratic tickets who are supposed to be "good" to Negroes' interests—in short, the same plan which Gompers has so disastrously applied to the labor union movement.[3] But it is impossible as yet to make sure what the domestic policy of the Negro Political Union will be.

An attempt was made by Mrs. Olivia Whiteman, Communist delegate, to have the appeal to governors of southern states, which was passed the day before, reopened for reconsideration.

"I make this request," said Mrs. Whiteman, "because I notice for one thing that the resolution says that the Negroes do not seek social equality. Now I don't think there is a man or woman here who does not think that he or she is the social equal of any white person on earth—or at least I hope there is no such person here." While attempting to read her remarks, which she had written out, Mrs. Whiteman was ruled out of order. She then handed to the press table her statement, which reads in part:

"I for one intend to fight for the equality of my people—any kind of equality, and every kind of equality, everywhere—including social equality.

"I am not a republican, as so many Negroes are. And I am not a democrat. I am a Communist, a member of the Workers Party. And in that political party we believe in and practice the dignity of the Negro people as the equals of anybody. As a Communist I could not give my consent that the Negro should give up his demand for social equality, or to consent to any limitation of the equality of the Negro.

" 'Social equality'? Well, what is social inequality? That means Jim Crow! That means being kicked and cursed around as an inferior, and being exploited more and paid less than the white person, and lynched if we don't get off a sidewalk for some bully with a white face.

"I think we are obliged, for our own dignity, to reconsider this matter. I also think the resolution is mistaken in being addressed to the southern authorities instead of Negroes."

William A. Wallace, a Chicago leader of the Universal Negro Improvement Association, today told me that he believes I did him an injustice in reporting his actions in the convention during the debate on the Ku Klux Klan resolutions.[4]

"Facts are facts," said Mr. Wallace, "and you have a right to print them. I don't object to the facts you printed, but when you expressed your view of my amendment, that it completed the surrender of the Negro's manhood rights, you certainly were not fair. You should have taken into consideration what my purpose was. I intended in a diplomatic way to accomplish the very thing that you contend should be done—that is, to overcome the completely weak resolution of Bishop McGuire.

"When the objection was made to my amendment 'condemning' the Klan, it is true that I consented to change it to read 'we protest against the atrocities and brutalities alleged to be perpetrated,' etc., but this was only for the purpose of diplomatically doing something to strengthen the stand we were to take."

"But, Mr. Wallace," I said, "what I mainly referred to was the assurance you were giving that the Negroes would not demand 'social equality,' which I contend is a term behind which the white ruling class robs the Negro of any sort of right they desire to take away from him."

Mr. Wallace replied:

"Even tho he sees fit to use that term for the purpose you state, nevertheless I contend we do not have to accept his interpretation of the phrase, but rather concentrate our efforts on a social standard that is applicable to both, automatically creating an equality of social basis."

Printed in the *Daily Worker*, 19 August 1924. Original headlines omitted.

1. See R. J. Vidimande, Capetown, South Africa, to Marcus Garvey, July 1924, reprinted in "Claim Bantus Felled Premier Jan C. Smuts," *NW*, 9 August 1924. Black South Africans played no role in events leading to the Rand strike of white miners in 1922 which led to Smuts's defeat in the 1924 election and the establishment of a pact government of the Labour party and Hertzog's National party. The strike by white miners was precipitated by the decision of the South African Chamber of Mines to end the so-called *status quo* agreement that underpinned the color bar in mine employment. The resultant competition from black workers would have threatened the jobs of approximately four thousand white miners (Peter Walshe, *The Rise of African Nationalism in South Africa* [Berkeley and Los Angeles: University of California Press, 1971], pp. 75–76; H. J. Simons and R. E. Simons, *Class and Colour in South Africa 1850–1950* [Middlesex, England: Penguin Books, 1969], pp. 271–299). When the *Negro World* covered the transition in power in an editorial, the editors stated that "the natives . . . may gain but little" by the change, but that Smuts "has admitted that the natives no longer regard 'the whites as gods,' which is a great gain, and which many Negroes in the United States and the West Indies could learn to the common advantage" (*NW*, 5 July 1924).

2. In the early 1920s Spain suffered several humiliating defeats in Morocco at the hands of the Rif people. Popular outrage at home led to a government crisis which was resolved in September 1923, when Gen. Miguel Primo de Rivera led a military coup and proclaimed himself dictator (A. Ramon Oliveira, *Politics, Economics and Men of Modern Spain, 1808–1946* [London: Victor Gollancz, 1946], pp. 183–187; F. L. Carsten, *The Rise of Fascism* [1967; 2d. ed., Berkeley and Los Angeles: University of California Press, 1982], p. 195; *NW*, 9 August and 23 August 1924).

3. Samuel Gompers inaugurated a policy "to reward friends and punish enemies" in the congressional campaigns of 1906. This remained the dominant AFL electoral strategy throughout the 1920s (Joseph G. Rayback, *A History of American Labor* (1959; reprint ed., New York: Macmillan, 1966], p. 253).

4. See *Daily Worker*, 23 August 1924; *Garvey Papers* 5: 772.

Editorial Letter by Marcus Garvey

[[New York City, August 19, 1924]]

New Negro Steamship Company
Secures First Ship for Africa

Fellow Men of the Negro Race, Greeting:

Our convention during the past week discussed one of the most vital and important questions that demands the attention of our race—that of our industrial development. It was pleasing and satisfying to listen to the delegates and deputies, who threw their whole hearts and souls into the discussion. We were able to bring out information pointing to the fact that an ocean of possibilities lies before us as a people industrially. All that is necessary for us to do, and especially in America, is to mobilize our financial forces and through the Universal Negro Improvement Association, develop the untouched wealth at our race's command in the West Indies, South America, Central America, Africa and the United States, through which we will be able, in a short while, to build up a race so industrially and commercially firm as to bring to us all the things that we do clamor and agitate for at the present time, which there is no hope of getting except through the proper demonstration of our own ability to possess them. In the discussion, stress was laid on the need for ships and still more ships, and we are glad to say, this week, that we have secured the first ship of the Black Cross Navigation and Trading Company, the S.S. General G.W. Goethals,[1] of over 5,000 tons, for our passenger and cargo service. The first payment has been made on this ship and we now need $70,000.00 more before we come into complete possession of same. This money must be raised immediately and I now take the opportunity of appealing to every stalwart member and friend of the Universal Negro Improvement Association to send in his and her loan immediately to the Black Cross Navigation and Trading Company. This is no time to put off for another week or month. If we are to completely own and possess this ship, we must have the money immediately. Now is the time for you to loan your $50, $100, $200, $300, $500 or $1,000 to the corporation. Loan it for five or ten years, bearing an interest of 5%. If you will subscribe this money immediately to enable us to carry out all of our obligations on this ship, we will be able to put it in operation in another sixty days and start actively the business of the corporation. Help us now, men and women, to start the race off commercially and industrially.

Loads of Cargo Waiting

There are hundreds of shiploads of cargo waiting for us in Africa, in the West Indies, South and Central America to convey back to the United States of America. Millions can be made for the race in the conveying of raw materials from one part of the world to the other, and the return to them of our finished products. We want the Universal Negro Improvement Association, in a short while, to be in a position to employ millions of our own people in America, West Indies and Africa, thereby making our race industrially independent. This can be done if you will help us now to buy more ships. Let us, before the close of the year, have another ship, and let us, during 1925, add at least four more ships to the Black Cross Navigation and Trading Company, and surely, when that time comes, the Negro in America, West Indies and Africa will have no more need to be fearful of the future nor dependent upon the good will of others to exist, but we will be able to build ourselves up so industrially firm as to find employment for our dependent millions.

BEATING THE CRITICS

Don't you pay any attention to what the Negro critic is saying in his newspaper or pulpit. No one of them can hand you a loaf of bread. They have no provision for employing the people: they only take away from the people. The Universal Negro Improvement Association seeks to feed the people, employ the people and to make the people independent. We, the Universal Negro Improvement Association, as above stated, can build up, in a short while, a strong world movement that will be capable of accomplishing all the things that the race desires in the way of greater liberty, freedom and independence.

THE VICIOUS AND WICKED

The vicious and wicked of our own race have tried to handicap us at every turn. They have tried to thwart us in our African colonization plan, but let it be known that the Universal Negro Improvement Association cannot be successfully handicapped. Our program is too wide and large to submit to any permanent disability. Give us the opportunity, and we feel sure that our members will, and in a short while, we will show the enemies how strong our organization is and how futile is their opposition. These Negroes are only hurting themselves and do not know it. History shall write them down as the greatest traitors, villains and scoundrels the race has produced in the twentieth century and, when we write their names down, as we intend to do, it will reveal the vicious machinations of men of two continents, who have tried to stand in the way of the progress of their race. The old Negro leader, as we have said before, is no d— good. He is only fit for the scrap heap. He is crooked, he is raceless, he is conscienceless, he is but a selfish cur. Show him where he can make a "pile" and he will sell his mother, his family, his race, his country and his God. These men we will have to dislodge from leadership. We have to take them out of the pulpits, off the platforms and from the public places, and relegate them to the scrap heap of racial treachery. They have conspired for decades and are still conspiring to rob and exploit the masses. Because of the advantages of education that some of them have had, they are trying to use it to stultify the growth of the common people. It is because they hate the common people and fear the chance of the common people to elevate themselves that they are trying to block the program of the Universal Negro Improvement Association, but the common people shall make them bow down on their knees and beg for bread. We shall starve and press out these so-called leaders. Don't support them. Make them work as hard as you do, and when you, yourselves, start to correct this evil of leadership, the devils will change their tactics. They call us the common people. They say we are illiterate. Let us see if they can live without the common people. Let us see if they can live without the so-called illiterates. Let the philosophers live off their books and philosophies. As you know, there is not one of them who is willing to do a hard day's work, but they are all willing to scheme to exploit and rob those whom they call the "common people." Thank God that the common people are so many that we can help and protect ourselves and, when it comes to a showdown, we are going to do it through the Universal Negro Improvement Association. The so-called "big Negro" is no good. Dump him or else we will be laid into the jaws of Death and the bowels of Hell. With an organization like the Universal Negro Improvement Association, we are bound to triumph and solve the great problem that has confronted us for a half century. Not only have we found out the treachery of the so-called Negro leader, but the white leader has found him out. They know he cannot be trusted. He is dishonest: he is a liar: he is a misrepresentative of the truth: he is selfish, greedy and grafting, and that is why we get so little consideration from the leaders of the other race, because ours are so well known. The world is calling for new leadership among us. As I stated in my front page article last week, it is no wonder that Liberia did not get the loan of five million dollars. It was because of the graft and greed of the same type of politicians that America turned down the loan. It is that same group of selfish Negroes who are trying to hinder us from developing Liberia and save the race from the world-threatened danger.

MASSES WITH U.N.I.A.

We are glad, however, that the great masses of the people of Liberia are for the Universal Negro Improvement Association. The far-seeing and progressive leaders of that country and the people feel that the only salvation for Liberia is through the efforts of the Universal Negro Improvement Association. For this we feel glad and happy. The future is still bright for that great promising country, and as we develop our program, so will we inform the people what they should do in the direction of nation-building.

DON'T BE TRICKED

I appeal, however, to all the members of the Universal Negro Improvement Association and all members of the race, not to allow themselves to be tricked by any slick group of Negroes or by any of the old type leaders who are endeavoring to thwart the plans of the Universal Negro Improvement Association so as to be able to individually exploit those Negroes who desire to go to Liberia. No Negro should go to Liberia except advised by the Universal

Negro Improvement Association and under its auspices. If you attempt to do so, you will be robbed and exploited by that crafty group of Negroes, who have always planned to rob the innocent and uninformed. Wait until the Universal Negro Improvement Association gives you full information and instructions what to do. Do nothing until then. Let us, as requested above, concentrate on developing our steamship line. Let us start to trade with the different Negro countries of the world and, when we have successfully built up ourselves as a financial power, all of our ills will then be remedied and our cries will be no more. The enemies referred to have tried to block us even in the securing of our first ship, but, as has been stated, they will have a hard time keeping up with the Universal Negro Improvement Association. These villains, who call themselves leaders in the different communities, hate us, the common people, so that they will do everything to place stumbling blocks in the way and yet the devils cannot live without us, the common people. We again make an appeal to you, not to support them and not strengthen their hands to crush you. As the white working man and white common people have been fighting the white capitalist class, who are trying to crush them and crush their very blood, so must the common people of the Negro race fight the scoundrel group of leaders and race capitalists, who are trying for their destruction. They are soulless, heartless and raceless, and before the thing becomes too dangerous, we must nip it in the bud. Hence, we are again calling upon the four hundred million Negroes to call a halt against these men who have misrepresented us and tried to injure the cause of liberty among us. Remember, every member of the Universal Negro Improvement Association and every member of the race, do your duty by the Black Cross Navigation and Trading Company in helping us to pay for the first ship by sending in your loan. Address your communications to the Black Cross Navigation and Trading Company, 56 West 135th Street, New York City, U.S.A. With very best wishes, I have the honor to be, your obedient servant,

MARCUS GARVEY
President-General
Universal Negro Improvement Ass'n.

P.S. All members, branches, divisions and chapters of the Universal Negro Improvement Association are asked to send in immediately all Convention Collecting lists with all moneys in hand for the association. The Parent Body is in need of financial help, so all those who have reports and cash in hand are requested to send in same immediately.

M.G.

Printed in *NW*, 23 August 1924. Original headlines abbreviated.

1. According to the Bureau of Investigation reports, "The 'Gen. G.W. Goethals,' the ship he [Garvey] has acquired, was formerly a United States Shipping Board boat and it is Garvey's intention to change its name to 'Booker T. Washington.' It is a five-thousand-ton vessel, was formerly German owned before taken over by this Government after being interned here, and has accommodations for seventy-five first-class passengers and one hundred second-class" (DJ-FBI, file 61-301, 23 August 1924). The Black Cross Navigation and Trading Co., Inc., purchased the S.S. *General Goethals* on 20 October 1924 from the Panama Railroad Co. for $100,000. The company

paid $75,000 in three payments before taking over the ship in October 1924 but was not able to secure a bond guaranteeing the payment of the remaining $25,000. An agreement was later reached that provided for three payments of $8,500 each, to be made in November and December 1924 and January 1925 (vice president, Panama Rail Road Co., to Col. M. L. Walker, 29 October 1924, DNA, RG 41, file 61-H-2). The S. S. *General Goethals* was officially launched by the Black Cross Navigation and Trading Co. in January 1925 (*NW*, 17 January 1925).

Convention Report

[*New York, 19 August 1924*]

TUESDAY MORNING, AUGUST 19

The convention assembled at 10:30 a.m., the Speaker, Hon. Marcus Garvey, in the chair.

After prayers, the minutes of the previous session were read and confirmed on the motion of Hon. Rennis [Dennis] Washington, Maryland, seconded by Hon. R. A. Martin, Florida, Cuba.

The speaker called for reports, and the Hon. B. [P.] L. Burrows presented the report of the committee appointed to frame suggestions in regard to the "educating of the Negro race as to the real meaning of society, and laying down the principles that should guide those who are desirous of becoming socially distinctive"; "creating an atmosphere of purity around the young generation of the race, to better prepare them for a higher social life."

A minority report was presented by Hon. Mae Boyd, New York.

Both reports were received for discussion section by section.

The convention was still engaged in discussing and amending the majority report when the adjournment was taken until 8:30 p.m.

TUESDAY EVENING

The Convention reassembled at 8:30 p.m., the Speaker, Hon. Marcus Garvey, in the Chair.

The Convention concluded the discussion of the report of the Committee appointed to frame suggestions in regard to the educating of the Negro race as to the real meaning of society and laying down the principles that should guide those who are desirous of becoming socially distinctive; also creating an atmosphere of purity around the young generation of the race to better prepare them for a higher social life.

The report was then adopted on the motion of Hon. R. A. Bachelor, Oriente, Cuba, seconded by Hon. C. H. Bryant, Costa Rica.

Discussion of the minority report was deferred until the next session, Thursday morning, the Convention adjourning to be entertained with Negro moving pictures.[1]

Printed in *NW*, 30 August 1924. Original headlines abbreviated.

1. The idea of utilizing the "moving picture" as a tool to propagate a positive image of black America appeared as early as 1909. Following the release in 1915 of D. W. Griffith's landmark *The Birth of a Nation* (the first film to be screened in the White House) the idea of a black cinema gained currency, in part as an alternative to largely abortive attempts to ban showings of Griffith's production because of its negative racial stereotyping, and also as a tool to combat the standard Hollywood portrayal of blacks.

Among the most notable attempts prior to 1920 to launch a suitable black production was the one initiated by Booker T. Washington and carried out by his secretary, Emmett J. Scott. Griffith had originally called his offensive masterpiece *The Clansman*, after the novel and play by the South Carolina white supremacist Thomas Dixon, Jr., and the film premiered in Los Angeles under this title. When the picture, renamed at Dixon's suggestion, opened in New York and Boston, Washington, who had previously cooperated with documentaries about Tuskegee and who had been baited by Dixon for years, found his interest rekindled in creating what he called a "counter irritant." Emmett Scott was busily pursuing the sale of the film rights to the Tuskegee founder's autobiography, *Up from Slavery*, only a few days before Washington's death. Thereafter, Scott managed to produce a different film (*Birth of a Race*, 1919) after turning to white backers who diluted his intentions; it was an artistic and financial failure. An NAACP committee, whose original members included W. E. B. Du Bois, also tried to produce a cinematic response to Griffith, but its efforts proved fruitless.

A third, and more successful, black entry into the moving picture field was the Lincoln Motion Picture Co., founded at the same time. Begun in 1915 by Noble Johnson, a black actor from Universal Pictures, and his brother, George, the company produced its movies in Los Angeles and distributed them from Omaha, where George Johnson worked as a postman. On 4 July 1916 the company's first film, *The Realization of a Negro's Ambition*, a modest two-reeler that focused its efforts on attracting a black audience, not on improving the black image among whites, opened in Los Angeles.

The various attempts made at establishing a black cinema faced the formidable barriers of a shortage of capital, a lack of experience and expertise, and a paucity of distribution outlets. As a result, of the two dozen or so earliest entries, only the Lincoln Motion Picture Co. survived the decade as a significant motion picture producer, and by 1921, even it had collapsed—a victim of, in addition to structural factors, according to Thomas Cripps, the "postwar depression, coupled with a raging influenza epidemic" (Thomas Cripps, *Slow Fade to Black: The Negro in American Film, 1900–1942* [New York: Oxford University Press, 1977], p. 88). In the same decade, however, something of a miniature boom in black filmmaking began. For by then the World War I migration of blacks to northern cities had provided an urban audience, and the prosperity of the period yielded a small increase in the funds available for such ventures. Conversely, the growing demand for black motion pictures and the expansion of movie houses that screened them (perhaps seven hundred outlets were in existence by 1930) encouraged the growth of small companies. Nonetheless, a continuing shortage of capital, internal competition for black audiences, and the inferior technical quality and poor distribution of the product, together with a growing rivalry with the wider world of the Hollywood screen, meant that these companies seldom survived to produce more than a few offerings, and many made none at all.

An exception to this pattern of attrition was the success of independent producer Oscar Micheaux, a multitalented and persistent entrepreneur from the plains of South Dakota. Beginning in 1918 after leaving the Lincoln Motion Picture Co. and for nearly thirty years thereafter, working first in Chicago and then New York, Micheaux not only raised the necessary capital for his films but also wrote and directed them. With the exception of his work the contents of black motion pictures were, in effect, black versions of white cinematic plots that seldom varied significantly from their white models. Some films were black westerns, detective stories, or partook of other standard genres; many others proffered the image of a racially integrated society attended by the fulfilled personal aspirations of a black middle class, but in these films, poorer blacks were often portrayed as villainous.

Most probably the UNIA convention would have been shown films such as the Lincoln Motion Picture Co.'s *The Realization of a Negro's Ambition*, which in the Horatio Alger mold dramatized a hardworking man's successful rise in the oil fields of California as he overcame racial discrimination along the way, and *A Giant of His Race* (1921), which, although made by the white-owned North State Film Corp. of Winston-Salem, N. C., featured a nearly all-black cast and chronicled Afro-American history from its African roots to the aftermath of emancipation in 1865. Some years later, in 1932, Garvey's life was satirized in *The Black King* (Southland Pictures) (Thomas Cripps, *Slow Fade to Black*, pp. 41–89, 170–202; Louis R. Harlan, *Booker T. Washington: The Wizard of*

Tuskegee, 1901–1915 [New York: Oxford University Press, 1983], pp. 431–435; Fred Silva, ed., *Focus on the Birth of a Nation* [Englewood Cliffs, N.J.: Prentice-Hall, 1971], pp. 43, 111–124, and passim; John Hope Franklin, " 'Birth of a Nation'—Propaganda as History," *The Massachusetts Review* 20, no. 3 [autumn 1979]: 417–434; Brian Gallagher, "Racist Ideology and Black Abnormality in *The Birth of a Nation*," *Phylon* 43, no. 1 [spring 1982]: 68–76; "A Giant of His Race," n.d., file no. 1042, George P. Johnson Collection, University Research Library, University of California, Los Angeles).

Convention Report

[*New York, 20 August 1924*]

WEDNESDAY EVENING, AUG. 20

His Highness the Supreme Deputy, G.O. Marke, and the Executive Council received the deputies and delegates attending the Fourth Annual International Convention at the Third Court Reception held in the history of the Universal Negro Improvement Association. The function was a very brilliant one, surpassing in splendor both previous occasions. Liberty Hall was tastefully decorated and presented a gala appearance, the floral arrangements being especially effective. When at 8:15 P.M. the members of the Executive Council arrived, there was a large assembly of persons who evinced the keenest interest in the proceedings. The arrival of His Highness the Prince of Dahomey, guest of honor, created considerable stir, the vast assembly rising to its feet in an effort to get a full view of the distinguished guest.

The members of the Executive Council, the clergy, represented by Hon. Dr. George Alexander McGuire, Primate of the African Orthodox Church, and the Prince of Dahomey went in procession to the dais where, after an excellent musical programme was rendered, the house of delegates and deputies was received by His Highness the Supreme Deputy, on either side of whom sat His Excellency, Hon. Marcus Garvey, Provisional President of Africa, and His Highness the Prince of Dahomey. Presentation of the Ladies Pageant Court of Ethiopia followed, after which honors were bestowed on the following persons[1] by his Highness the Supreme Deputy, assisted by His Grace Primate of the African Orthodox Church.

A banquet followed, at the conclusion of which the health of His Highness the Prince of Dahomey was toasted by Hon. Marcus Garvey, the Prince acknowledging in a happy speech. The proceedings wound up with a State ball at which the Prince led off, his partner [in] the opening number, a waltz, being Miss Ida Jacques, sister-in-law of the President-General.

Printed in *NW*, 30 August 1924. Original headlines abbreviated.

1. The following persons received UNIA honors at the ceremony: George C. Reneau, Puerto Barrios, Guatemala; Dr. E. Elliott Rawlins, New York; Bishop George A. McGuire, New York; William Ware, Cincinnati; Isabella Lawrence, Belize, British Honduras; Charles Bryant, Port Limón, Costa Rica; Amelia Sayers, New York; Mark Burke, New York; Mrs. M. Sharperson Young, New York; Charles Jackson, New Orleans; S.V. Robertson, New Orleans; John Scott, Cleveland; Mrs. John Scott, Cleveland; Mrs. E.G. Headley, Boston, Mass.;

Mrs. Josephine Washington, Pittsburgh, Penn.; Ella Chase, Brooklyn, N.Y.; Mary J. Spence, New York; Col. Harrigan, New York; Col. V. Wattley, New York; William Duncan, Montclair, N.J.; Prof. D.H. Kyle, Clarksburg and Laura Lee, W.Va.; James Hassell, Seattle; Henrietta Redd, Gary, Ind.; Milton Van Lowe, Detroit, Mich.; F.E. Johnson, Detroit; Joseph Craigen, Detroit (*NW*, 30 August 1924).

Convention Report

[New York, 21 August 1924]

THURSDAY AFTERNOON, AUG. 21

The Convention resumed at 3 o'clock, the Hon. Marcus Garvey in the Chair. After the usual formalities, the delegates began the discussion of the minority report on "Educating the Negro race as to the real meaning of society and laying down the principles that should guide those who are desirous of becoming socially distinctive."

This report recommended among other things that a woman's department be established in every division with a training class for prospective mothers as well as a cradle roll and register; health certificates should be exchanged between the contracting parties before marriage; children should be taught morality based on the Ten Commandments; illiteracy should be discouraged; children should be taught thrift and to develop a spirit of independence, etc.

During the course of the discussion, Hon. Wm. Sherrill begged leave to introduce two gentlemen who came to visit them. They were Dr. J.W. Robinson, vice-president of the Douglas National Bank, of Chicago, and Pastor of St. Mark[']s Church of New York city and Dr. T.W.H. Walker[^] of Jacksonville, Fla. Of Dr. Robinson he said that that gentleman did not believe that his activities were limited to his church, but on the contrary he had identified himself with all the activities which tended to the progress and advancement of the race.

Dr. Robinson said he was primarily there to introduce Dr. Thomas W.H. Walker, of Jacksonville, Fla., who was pastor of the Simpson Memorial Episcopal Church. He explained that he very much admired Hon. Marcus Garvey and his work with the program of which he was in accord. He introduced Dr. Walker by saying that he was not only a pastor, a historian and a leader of the race, but because he had lived in Liberia, a country in which they were all interested.

Dr. Walker then delivered a very impressive and inspiring address, during which he urged his hearers to continue under the guidance of their leader because whatever they do they were sure to progress because such leadership must carry them somewhere. He drew a picture of Liberia and regretted that time did not permit him to enlarge on the subject.

A hearty vote of thanks was accorded to the distinguished visitors on the motion of Hon. F. Martin, seconded by Hon. S.V. Robertson.

The discussion was resumed and proved to be very lively and interesting. The items regarding the exchange of health certificates, and the adoption of the ten commandments evoked some controversy in which many of the delegates joined, including Hon. Peters, Bishop McGuire, Mrs. Boyd and several others.

Eventually on the motion of Bishop McGuire the report was adopted as read.

Another report was presented to the convention. It was that of the Committee on Education.

After consideration the meeting adopted the report.

The next item was the discussion of the appeal of the Haitian delegation to the convention to assist in bringing about independence. This discussion had been commenced during Monday's session and the Hon. Speaker refreshed the memories of the delegates of the salient points of the appeals as well as to what was expected from them. He stressed that Haiti was near by and was willing to accept all Negroes and those who did not desire to go all the way to Africa might think well of interesting themselves in the economic and industrial progress of Haiti even though they did not feel willing to go over there as colonists.[2] He also reminded them of the present position of Haiti.

Hon. H.D. [C.] Stokes, of Middletown[,] and Hon. I. Cipriani, of Trinidad, joined in the discussion which was adjourned till the evening session.

Hon. Bishop McGuire moved that the convention request the speaker in convention to convey to His Highness, the Supreme Deputy and to His Excellency, the President-General and also to the High Executive, their profound gratitude and appreciation of the deputies and delegates for the magnificent reception given them on the previous evening.

This was seconded by Hon. Carrie Minus and carried.

Convention adjourned until the evening.

THURSDAY EVENING

The convention reassembled at 9 p.m., Hon. P.L. Burrows in the chair.

After prayers a short concert program was rendered, the acting speaker announcing that he would occupy the chair until the arrival of the speaker.

Shortly after it was announced that the speaker was detained on pressing business and would not be present at that session.

The order of the day was suspended and the following delegates addressed the house at the invitation of the acting speaker: Hon. Joseph Craigen, Detroit; Hon. R.H. Batchelor, Oriente, Cuba; Hon. S.R. Wheat, Chicago; Hon. Charles Jackson, New Orleans; Hon. M. Daniels, Brooklyn, and Hon. Mrs. S.V. Robertson, New York.

The proceedings closed with the singing of the Ethiopian National Anthem, the adjournment being taken until the following morning.

Printed in *NW*, 30 August 1924. Original headlines abbreviated.

1. Dr. Thomas H. Walker (1873–1948) of Tallahassee, Fla., began to teach at the age of fifteen, to preach by the age of sixteen, and to build a church by the time he was nineteen. He attended the Cookman Institute in Daytona, Fla., while he continued to serve as a Methodist pastor and to teach school. From 1900 to 1903 he attended the Gammon Theological Seminary in Atlanta, where he edited the first major black magazine in the city, entitled the *Church and Society World*. Walker studied in Africa, receiving a doctor of divinity degree from the College of West Africa in 1907 and from the College of Liberia in 1926. He was the founder of the St. Joseph Aid Society, which by 1927 had a membership of over 150,000 in branches throughout the United States. Walker, a Republican, was also a member of the Masons, the Odd Fellows, and the Knights of Pythias. He served as pastor of the Simpson Memorial Episcopal Tabernacle in Jacksonville, Fla. Walker wrote a number of books that reflected his interest in Africa and black history, among them *Presidents of Liberia* (1915), *History of Liberia* (1915), and *Egyptology* (1906) (*WWCA*; *WWCR*).

2. In the nineteenth century Haiti had rivaled Africa as a possible site of Afro-American colonization. In 1824 the Haitian government, under President Jean Pierre Boyer (1776–1850), saw black immigration as a stimulant to the Haitian economy and sent agents to the United States to help facilitate immigration. Some potential emigrants who were disenchanted with African colonization turned to Haiti as an alternative. In New York, Loring Dewey organized the Society for Promoting the Emigration of Free Persons of Color to Hayti. Although in August 1824 thirty black families were sent from Philadelphia to Haiti, the project quickly collapsed. Fearing that the new colonists would be a source of possible unrest against his regime, President Boyer withdrew his support for the program. Differences of religion, language, and law, as well as the poverty they encountered, moved most of the emigrants to return to the United States.

Interest in Haiti as a site for colonization nevertheless persisted. At black conventions held in 1854 and 1856, delegates discussed the relative merits of emigration to Haiti and to Africa. At the 1854 National Emigration Convention, when James T. Holly assumed leadership, Haiti was again proposed as an emigration site. Haitian interest in Afro-American immigration also revived, and in 1858 Haiti once again invited black American immigrants. With the experience of the 1820s still remembered, however, leaders of the movement urged that no immigration take place before the Haitian government guaranteed the colonists freedom of religion, access to land, political privileges, and free passage to the island. By this time a number of emigration clubs had spread across the country. In New York, for example, blacks had formed a Haitian Agricultural Emigration Association. By June 1861 seven groups of colonists had been sent to Haiti, but they encountered several obstacles to their settling on the island. Spanish military incursions into Haiti prevented migration to areas of possible conflict, and while Haiti had offered colonization for farmers seeking a frontier life, a number of the colonists were not farmers and thus basically unsuited for the life they found. Finally, the Haitian government was unable to live up to its guarantees to protect the rights of the emigrants. Sickness and death also took their toll. An ill-conceived project in 1862 by Bernard Kock, an entrepreneur and swindler, to settle black emigrants on the island further soured the lure of Haiti for black migration. Furthermore, just at the moment that many of the American emigrants became disenchanted with their new home, events in the United States decreased the interest in migration: the Emancipation Proclamation, the peace that followed the end of the Civil War, and the rights guaranteed to blacks by the passage of the Fourteenth Amendment all increased the hopes of newly freed black men and women for a better life in the United States. Indeed, many black emigrants returned from Haiti; of the estimated two thousand who migrated to Haiti by the 1860s, fully two-thirds returned to the United States (James Theodore Holly and J. Dennis Harris, *Black Separatism and the Caribbean, 1860*, ed. Howard H. Bell [Ann Arbor: University of Michigan Press, 1970], pp. 1–14; Howard H. Bell, *A Survey of the Negro Convention Movement, 1839–1861* [New York: Arno Press and New York Times, 1969], pp. 245–274; Frederic Bancroft, "The Ile à Vache Experiment in Colonization," in Jacob E. Cooke, ed., *Frederic Bancroft, Historian* [Norman: University of Oklahoma Press, 1957], pp. 228–258; P. J. Staudenraus, *The African Colonization Movement, 1816–1865* [New York: Columbia University Press, 1961], pp. 82–87, 106–110, 244–250; Floyd J. Miller, *The Search for a Black Identity: Black Colonization and Emigration, 1787–1863* [Urbana: University of Illinois Press, 1975], pp. 232–249).

Convention Report

[New York, 22 August 1924]

FRIDAY MORNING, AUGUST 22

The Convention assembled at 10 a.m., the speaker, Hon. Marcus Garvey, in the chair.

After prayers, the minutes of the two previous sessions were read and confirmed.

The order of the day, consideration of the Haitian appeal, was proceeded with.

Hon. R.H. Bachelor, Oriente, Cuba; Hon. Freeman L. Martin, St. Louis; Hon. J. Milton Van Lowe, Detroit; Hon. Bishop McGuire, New York; Hon. Smith, New York; Hon. Dr. J.J. Peters, Chicago; Hon. J.B. Eaton, Norfolk, Va.; Hon. Prof. I. Chambers, New Orleans; Hon. J. Craigen, Detroit; Hon. Charles Jackson, New Orleans; Hon. R.A. Martin, Florida, Cuba; Hon. C.H. Bryant, Costa Rica; Hon. G. Brown, Miami, Fla.; Hon. M. Daniels, Brooklyn; Hon. Alleyne, Pittsburgh, Pa.; Hon. C. Green,[1] Jacksonville, Fla.; and Hon. W.A. Wallace, Illinois, spoke, expressing their conviction that the time had come when a wholehearted effort should be made by the Negroes of America, through the Universal Negro Improvement Association, to assist Haiti in regaining complete independence in terms of her appeal to the convention and the association.

The consensus of opinion was that the ballot in America should be used, through the Universal Negro Political Union, to force the United States Government to restore autonomy to Haiti, it being made known by presidents of divisions in their various communities to candidates for office, senators and congressmen that support of the Union was contingent upon their intention to support the nation-wide effort of Negroes to restore to the Haitians freedom and true independence.

At the conclusion of the debate, in the course of which there was a recital of the wrongs and abuses visited upon the Haitians and of the motives for the American occupation, the following committee was appointed by the speaker to draft recommendations as to the best means and methods of rendering to Haiti the assistance sought, the committee to report back to the convention during the afternoon session:

Hon. G.E. Carter, Secretary-General; Hon. Dr. J.J. Peters, Chicago; Hon. W.A. Wallace, Illinois; Hon. Freeman L. Martin, St. Louis; Hon. D.H. Kyle, Clarksburg, W.Va.; Hon. R.H. Bachelor, Oriente, Cuba, and Hon. J. Craigen, Detroit.

The convention then adjourned until 2 p.m.

FRIDAY AFTERNOON

The convention reassembled at 2 p.m., the speaker, Hon. Marcus Garvey, in the chair.

After prayers, the minutes of the previous session were read and confirmed. The convention then proceeded to discuss the program of a white Canada, a white America, a white Europe and a white Australia as enunciated by white leaders.

Hon. Bishop McGuire, New York, in the keynote address, referred to an article which appeared in the current issue of the Pittsburgh Courier attacking the association's program in regard to the redemption of the motherland and referring to America as "our country."[2] He declared this was merely a delusion; that it was the determination to make America a white man's country, the Negro being here only on suff[e]rance at the present time, and that the Negroes of the world had made up their minds to establish a government of their own in Africa. It seemed useless to appeal to the white man's conscience, which, apparently, was dead; and, therefore, Negroes were prepared to pray and to fight, to march with the sword and the Bible, until their goal was reached.

Hon. A. G. Ellenburg, Gary, Ind., kept the house in roars of laughter as he bade Negroes to purchase a ship, one for each Negro, so that they might all live on the high seas. This was, as he saw it, the only alternative to going back to Africa, the white man having made every other part of the earth his. If the white man had no conscience, he still had feelings, and Negroes were determined not to yield up Africa without a struggle. "Watch and pray," he said, was the Biblical injunction, "and be ye also ready."[3]

Hon. Dr. J. J. Peters reminded his hearers that the "Back to Africa" movement was regarded as the only solution for the problem of race by many great thinkers, and urged Negroes to regard the program of the U.N.I.A. as sacred and to act accordingly.

Hon. Smith, New York; Hon. J. J. Fenner, Richmond, Va.; Hon. Hattie Johnson, Baltimore, Md.; Hon. F. A. Toote, Philadelphia; Hon. Rogers, Norfolk, Va.; Hon. Mrs. Brown, Newark, N. J.; Hon. Mae Boyd, New York, and Hon. Mrs. Simmons, Bermuda, also spoke, after which the convention adjourned until 8:30 p.m.

FRIDAY EVENING

The convention resumed at 8:30 p.m., the speaker, Hon. Marcus Garvey, in the chair.

After prayers, the minutes of the previous session were read and confirmed.

Hon. C. H. Bryant, Costa Rica, as Secretary, then read the report of the committee appointed to draft recommendations in regard to the development of Liberia, Abyssinia, Haiti and other countries where Negroes form a majority of the population as independent Negro communities.

The report was discussed section by section and adopted with minor amendments. The full text appears in another column.

Hon. Freeman L. Martin, St. Louis, next read the report of the committee appointed to draft recommendations in regard to the appeal of the Haitians to the convention and to the Universal Negro Improvement Association for assistance in securing the restoration of autonomy.

The report was considered section by section and adopted with a slight amendment. The full text of this report appears in another column.

The convention then adjourned until 3:30 p.m. Sunday afternoon.

Printed in *NW*, 30 August 1924. Original headlines abbreviated.

1. Claude Green was president of the Jacksonville branch of the UNIA (*NW*, 27 December 1923).

2. An advance edition of the *Pittsburgh Courier* dated 23 August 1924 contained an article attacking Garvey for his endorsement of the Klan; it said that "Mr. Garvey's indorsement of the Klan is a logical sequence in his train of twisted reasoning. To begin with he admits that this is a white man's country and that the only home of the Negro is in Africa." For the black in the United States, "to run away now, after the battle of three centuries is almost won, would prove him the most ignoble coward that ever lived. And for these reasons he does not give this country up as 'white man's country.' It is OUR country, belonging to all citizens. We have faced worse odds than the Ku Klux Klan and won out, and we will win over the Klan, Mr. Garvey . . . notwithstanding."

3. A paraphrase of Mark 13:33.

Article by Robert Minor

[[NEW YORK, August 22, 1924]]

NEGROES WON'T FIGHT KU KLUX KLAN, GARVEY

COMMUNIST PROPOSALS DECLINED BY MEET

The convention of the Universal Negro Improvement Association here on Monday afternoon heard the reading of the official communication of the Workers Party of America on the question of the Ku Klux Klan, refused to table it, and decided to regard it as "a friendly communication to be answered in the same spirit."

Then after a discussion that threw a strange light upon the vast chasm of misconceptions, dangers and potentialites that divides the field of labor in the United States on the race question, the convention sent an answer to the Workers Party refusing to change its attitude toward the Klan.

GARVEY KLAN'S DEFENDER.

Notwithstanding any "friendly spirit" that may gloss over the surface of his remarks referring to the Communist Workers Party, the fact remains that Marcus Garvey thru this second act of restraining the Negro's hand from striking at the Klan, has taken upon himself the role of chief defender of the Klan, which the Workers Party fights and will fight to extermination. Mr. Garvey admitted in his speech that the Klan kills and terrorizes Negroes. Mr. Garvey, has read to the convention long articles published by the Klan sneering at the Negro as similar to "baboons and monkeys."

Mr. Garvey admits from one corner of his mouth that the Klan is a reactionary terror organization against the Negro, while with the other corner of his mouth he tells his followers that they cannot attack the Klan with even so much as words. Mr. Garvey says, "Don't let the Communists trick you."

WHO TRICKS NEGRO?

The Communists say, "War to extermination against the Klan," and Mr. Garvey says, "Don't fight the Klan." Pray, Mr. Garvey, who is tricking the Negro—the Communists or Mr. Garvey?

In announcing the receipt of the communication from the Workers Party, Mr. Garvey told the assembled thousand or more visitors and delegates that the association "has a very liberal platform" and has at all times been open to addresses from democrats, republicans and socialists, and is now addressed by Communists. "At our last convention," he said, "we were addressed by Mrs. Rose Pastor Stokes, a Communist, who sought to indoctrinate us with her views.[1] We gave Mrs. Stokes a hearing. Some people thought that we should not have done that because we are not interested in the philosophy of Communism. But I thought it was but right that we should have Mrs. Stokes present her views. Now we have a communication from the Workers Party criticising us for what we have done in the matter of the Ku Klux Klan and asking us to reconsider the resolutions that we passed.

"Altho the communication is rather long, I shall ask the secretary to read it to us.

NEGROES ARE UNDER DOGS.

"Let me say, however, that while we belong to the group of 'under dogs,' which includes the members of the Workers Party, still we are a group of peculiar 'under dogs' within that group. Even among 'under dogs' there is prejudice. Now you take no matter what group, and there is, thruout, that eternal question of difference. I say this irrespective of what class of people it may be.

"I dare any white man, be he worker, middle class or capitalist c[la]ss, to tell me that deep down in his heart he does not feel any different from the Negro. And if he tells me that he does not feel himself to be any different from the Negro, I will tell him that he is a damn liar. I say so irrespective of whether it is the right type or the wrong type of white man—he feels himself to be a little different from the Negro. Now I ask this organization not to be tricked by the capitalist class, or by the working class, or by the democrat or the republican, or the socialist or the Communists.

"SYMPATHIZE" WITH COMMUNISTS.

"We have sympathy for the Workers Party. But we belong to the Negro party, first, last and all the time. We will support every party that supports us, and we appreciate the attention the Workers Party has given us in sending this friendly communication. But the Communists have a long time ahead of them before they can do anything for themselves in this country. When they get there we will be for them. But meantime we are for ourselves.

"We, as a group that is crushed, have sympathy for the working man of the white race. But, brother, listen to me—he is crushed by his own brother, the capitalist of his own race. He is suffering from a different kind of crush from the kind we are getting.

"It is all right to have sympathy, but when anything happens, watch your step! You will find that the socialist white man is a cousin to the republican white man, and the republican, is a brother to the democrat. And I think you will find that the white Communist is a brother to them if anything happens. They will none of them stand by and see their own brother perish and die.

"You Are Negroes."

"But the white Communists claim that they have an interest in common with the Negro people. Very well, we are glad to see they are looking for the interest in common, but when the time comes and somebody has to get out of the way—Negroes, watch your step!

"You are Negroes, and I want you to remember that at all times."

After the reading of the Workers Party communication, which was listened to with breathless attention, Dr. Jay J. Peters of Chicago hastened to get the floor. He said that ever since his entrance into the organization he had been fighting first the philosophy of the socialists and then that of the Communists. He contended that neither one of these understood the psychology of the Negro, and that this communication of the Workers Party was "the same long-winded talk that has been handed out by all of them." Peters added that "now and then we find a white man who seems to have a different way of considering the Negro, but on the whole thruout the white race we find the self-same condition and point of view."

Motion to Table Lost.

A motion was then made to table the communication from the Workers Party. President Garvey immediately objected, saying:

"Now this is a communication that was sent to us, and it needs a cautious reply. It is a very important question that is dealt with here. I think we ought to consider it as a communication sent to us in a friendly manner. I think we must discuss it in a concrete and friendly manner and give it a reply in the same spirit in which it has been sent to us. I think we have to deal with it in that way."

The motion to table the communication having been withdrawn, Garvey proceeded:

"If I understand the communication correctly the people of the Workers Party want us to be more emphatic and positive in dealing with the Ku Klux

Klan. They want us to condemn the Klan for the crimes it commits on the Negro. Now I want to say that the mobs that kill and burn Negroes are members of the working class."

The speaker continued:

WORKERS IN MOBS.

"When you add up the total of killings of Negroes by the Ku Klux Klan in a whole year in Louisiana, Texas, Georgia, Alabama and Mississippi, you will find that the total number pales into insignificance when compared to the killings committed by the working class right in Omaha and Chicago and Tulsa and East St. Louis. Now we know that the people who are lynching in the South belong to the working class.

"We know that the lynching and the beating up and the running out of town everywhere is done, not by capitalists, but by people of the working class. Now we have to be careful what we do about this. We agree with the white workers that they are crushed and exploited and oppressed by the capitalists, but that is only the work of their own brothers.

"When the republicans go out of power and the democrats go in, we find that the two agree all the same on what to do to the Negro. And when the socialists succeed in destroying the democrats and the republicans we find that they are of the same blood, of the same flesh, of the same race, and that their attitude toward the black man is the same. And when the Communists shall have come into power and destroyed the democrats and republicans and the socialists, I think their attitude will be the same toward the black man. So we must be very careful how we handle this thing.

EVERYBODY IS OKAY.

"We are with everybody," said the speaker with a smile and gesture of irony that brought laughter. Then, sobering the crowd's mood with a grave expression, he added: "We can't afford to be against everybody in this whole country. That's the situation that we are in in regard to this Ku Klux Klan business. Let the Communists go to the Jew and the Catholic with their proposal to fight the Ku Klux Klan. The Jew can fight the Klan because the Jew can stand by himself, and nobody can cut off his meal ticket, because he has his own economic strength. The Jews and the Catholics have their own resources of employment, but the Negro has not.

"When you Negroes fight the Ku Klux Klan and then you go back, you find that you are cut off, and you can lie down and die and perish. That is why you don't fight the Klan. Let the Jew and the Catholic fight the Klan.

"I think it is all right to let the white groups fight among themselves. The more rogues fall out, the more the other people can get their dues. And therefore I would advise the Workers Party to send their communication to the Jews and the Catholics, and advise them to fight on, and fight on, and fight on."

OFFERS RESOLUTION.

Freeman L. Martin, an attorney of St. Louis, then offered the resolution addressed to the Workers Party of America, as follows:

"Resolved, that we appreciate your proffer of counsel in this matter and your offer of co-operation in what you term a common fight, but we beg to advise that the position taken by this convention represents the point of view best calculated to serve our interests."

Speaking on the resolution, William A. Wallace of Chicago said that a few months ago the Communist International had sent instructions to the Workers Party of America "to intensify the work among the Universal Negro Improvement Association," and that the communication from the Workers Party should be appreciated in the light of that alleged incident. He indicated that he did not find the attitude of the Workers Party objectionable on the question of the Negroes generally, but that the Party was carrying out instructions to "look for numbers."[2] He then cited one of the numerous high power propaganda slanders against Soviet Russia which appeared recently in the capitalist press in the form of a fake news report of a "Jewish exclusion act"[3] passed by the Russian government. Mr. Wallace swallowed this propaganda lie as tho it had been the truth, and reasoned from it that when the Communists get control of America, "they can say also to the black man, 'you can get out.'" He estimated that "the workers of today are the capitalists of tomorrow, and they are all white, and they all say to the Negro, 'you stay in your place.'"

WALLACE CONFUSED.

Mr. Wallace later in conversation with me said that he formerly thought that the Russian government was largely made up of Jews, but that the item in the newspapers saying that an exclusion act against the Jews had been passed by the Russian government convinced him that it was all a mistake about Jews having any power there.

There was no Communist delegate present when the Workers Party communication was brought up.

Printed in the *Daily Worker*, 23 August 1924.

1. Rose Pastor Stokes addressed the second UNIA convention on 19 August 1921; for the complete text of her speech, see *Garvey Papers* 3: 675–682.
2. On the Comintern and American blacks, see pp. 841–854, below.
3. No evidence of a published news item on a "Jewish exclusion act," fake or otherwise, has been located. There is no evidence that there was ever such an exclusion act (Lionel Kochan, ed., *The Jews in Soviet Russia Since 1917* [New York: Oxford University Press, 1972]; Aaron Breitbart, Simon Wiesenthal Center, Los Angeles, to Robert A. Hill, 10 February 1984).

William R. Castle, Jr., Chief, Division of Western European Affairs, Department of State, to Charles Evans Hughes

[*Washington, D.C.*] August 25, 1924

The Secretary:—

Mr. Ernest Lyon, Liberian Consul General in Baltimore, came to see me this morning to transmit a message from his Government relating to the activities of Marcus Garvey and his associates in this country. I took a copy of Mr. Lyon's official instructions, which he initialed.

He says that the Liberian Government is very much disturbed over the situation, that he has said everything he could and would be extremely grateful if a statement could be given out by this Department. The situation is really serious because it looks as though Mr. Garvey would try to take over several hundred emigrants to Liberia. If his scheme can be nipped in the bud by any statement we can make now it will save us an enormous amount of trouble in the end because we shall have to decide whether or not we shall give passports. Furthermore, if these people should actually get away and go to Liberia, the Liberian Government would not let them land.

In accord with the Consul General's request, I have prepared the draft of a statement hereto attached, which you might be willing to give out.

[WILLIAM R. CASTLE, JR.][1]

P.S. Since dictating the above I have had a talk with Hugh Wilson[2] about the matter. Of course, the main purpose of the Liberian Consul General in asking us to make a statement for the press was to get publicity. Mr. Wilson thinks that this could be accomplished equally well if I should have a talk with the representative of the Associated Press and of the United Press, giving them the background of the situation and telling them that the information was to be printed not as coming from the Department. If you prefer this method I should be glad to see these men.

W.R.C.

[*Endorsement*] O.K.'d by the Secretary & me
[W.R.C.?] Aug 26.

DNA, RG 59, file 811.108G 191/34. TL, recipient's copy.

1. William R. Castle, Jr. (1879–1963), graduated in 1900 from Harvard University, where he taught until appointed director of the Bureau of Communications of the American Red Cross in 1917. In 1919 he entered the State Department as special assistant, a position he held until promoted to chief of the Division of Western European Affairs in December 1921. In 1927 he became assistant secretary of state; in 1930 he was appointed under secretary of state in the Hoover administration. He strongly opposed recognition of the Soviet Union (*NYT*, 14 October 1963).

2. Hugh Robert Wilson (b. 1885) graduated from Yale University in 1906 and entered the State Department's diplomatic service in 1911. He subsequently served as secretary of the American legation in Guatemala (1912), Argentina (1914), Germany (1916), Austria (1917), Japan (1921), and Mexico (1923) (U.S. Department of State, *Register*, 1924, p. 206).

Enclosure

August 25, 1924

STATEMENT FOR THE PRESS.[1]

Mr. Ernest Lyon, Consul General at [of] Liberia, called at the Department of State on August 25 to deliver a message from the Government of Liberia. This message, Mr. Lyon said, was sent by the Liberian Secretary of State because of the concern of the Liberian Government at the widely advertised plans of Mr. Marcus Garvey to bring about the emigration of American negroes to Liberia. He stated that Liberian consuls had received instructions to refuse visas to any supporters of the Garvey movement and that four members of the Universal Negro Improvement Association, who had gone to Liberia before the arrival of the orders to refuse visas, had been deported on arrival.[2]

The message from the Secretary of State of Liberia is as follows:

> The Government of Liberia having noted with some concern the continued activities of Marcus Garvey, particularly in respect of his widely advertised plans for the emigration of American Negroes to Liberia, I have been directed by the President to instruct you to call at the Department of State, Washington D.C. and there make the following declaration:—

> The Government of Liberia, irrevocably opposed both in principle and in fact to the incendiary policy of the Univeral Negro Improvement Association headed by Marcus Garvey, and repudiating the improper implications of its widely advertised scheme for the immigration of American Negroes into the Republic under the auspices of this Association, which scheme, apart from not having the sanction of the Liberian Government, does not appear to be bona fide and has in addition a tendency adversely to affect the amicable relations of the Republic with friendly States possessing territories adjacent to Liberia, desire to place on record their protest against this propaganda so far as it relates to Liberia, and to express their confidence that the Government of the United States will neither facilitate nor permit the emigration under the auspices of the Universal Negro Improvement Association of Negroes from the United States with intent to proceed to Liberia. I have the honor to be, Sir, Your obedient Servant,

EDWIN BARCLAY
Secretary of State

DNA, RG 59, file 811.108G 191/34. TL, transcript.

1. The press release was published in the *New York World* on 26 August 1924 and in the *New York Times* on 27 August 1924; the *New York Times* headline reads "Liberia Sends a Protest: Tells Washington She is Opposed to Garvey's Negro Plans."

2. On 20 and 21 June 1924 five technicians set sail from New York to Liberia as part of an advance guard to establish a UNIA-sponsored colony in the Cavalla River region of Liberia. The Liberian government instructed its consuls on 3 July 1924 to make public declarations that would prevent the immigration of black Americans to Liberia under the auspices of the UNIA. These instructions seem to have been implemented by Ernest Lyon, Liberian consul general in Baltimore, only on 24 July 1924. On 25 July three members of the original five UNIA technicians reached Monrovia; they were immediately put under police guard by the Liberian authorities and deported on the next ship bound for Hamburg, the intermediate port from which they had come (*NW*, 14 June 1924; letters received, 1922–1925, Liberian Consulate General, Baltimore, 29 September 1924, ADSL; *P&O*, 2: 388–389; AMAE, DAPC, K-4-1).

Convention Report

[*New York, 25 August 1924*]

MONDAY MORNING, AUGUST 25

The convention assembled at 10 a.m. The Speaker, Hon. Marcus Garvey, in the chair.

After prayers, the minutes of the previous session were read and confirmed.

Amending the constitution was the order of the day.

The speaker-in-convention said he had a suggestion in regard to section 3a of Article VII of the constitution, which read as follows:

"All officials of the Universal Negro Improvement Association shall be paid their salaries at the minimum, which shall be half of the maximum, and each shall be allowed to earn the maximum by ability and fitness, which maximum shall be paid at the end of each month according to the record of such official."

He suggested that that section be struck out and a fixed scale of wages substituted. The time has come, he said, when the association has to effect retrenchment in the matter of salaries. It was not so much what the office was worth as what the association could afford to pay at the present time. The action of the convention of voting big salaries in the past had embarrassed the organization, owing to the disloyalty of certain officers who drew and sued for salaries which they did not earn, the administration being powerless to prevent this, as it could not dispense with services of officers elected by the convention. He suggested that the salaries of the various officers be fixed as follows:

President-General, $5,000.00.
First Assistant President-General, $3,000.00.
Deputy Supreme Potentate, $3,000.00.
Second Assistant President-General, $2,500.00.
Secretary-General, $2,250.00.
High Chancellor, $2,250.00.
Third Assistant President-General, $2,000.00.
Fourth Assistant President-General, $2,000.00.

High Commissioner-General, $2,000.00.
Auditor-General, $2,000.00.
Minister of Labor and Industry, $1,750.00.
Minister of Legions, $1,750.00.
First Assistant Secretary-General, $1,750.00.
Second Assistant Secretary-General, $1,750.00.

The convention proceeded to deal with the suggested list, taking each office separately.

After some discussion, in the course of which the view was expressed that the President-General and the Auditor-General's salaries be increased by $1,000 and $250, respectively[, t]he salaries of the Supreme Deputy Potentate, the President-General, the First Assistant President-General, Second Assistant President-General, Secretary-General, the Chancellor and the Auditor-General were fixed as suggested. Considerable discussion ensued when the salary of the Fourth Assistant President-General, the present holder of that office being Lady Henrietta Vinton Davis, was being fixed. Several thought the figure insufficient, but it was pointed out that it would be impossible to increase her salary without revising the whole scale.

The Speaker, stating that as President-General, he was somewhat embarrassed over the issue that had arisen, consigned the chair to the Hon. G.E. Carter, Secretary-General.

On motion by Hon. Joseph Craigen, Detroit, seconded by Hon. Dr. J.J. Peters, it was unanimously agreed that the list submitted by the Speaker be accepted in toto.

The convention then adjourned.

MONDAY AFTERNOON, AUG. 25

The afternoon session of the convention was devoted to the continuation of the consideration of a revised scale for the salaries of the high officials.

The Hon. Marcus Garvey, speaker, suggested that provision be made for the salaries of the consul general, surgeon-general, minister of education, chaplain general and the international organizer, the positions of which are not now filled, owing to the present financial position of the organization. He did not suggest the filling of the offices this year, but when conditions are more favorable.

A general discussion arose as to the desirability of the payment of such officers.

Hon. J.A. Hassell of Seattle moved that no more offices be filled than already agreed to and that such officers be given a 5 per cent bonus per annum, if they worked faithfully. The motion was declared to be out of order, as it referred to past legislation.

Hon. Dr. J.J. Peters of Chicago questioned the wisdom of making provision for the payment of the surgeon-general. He did not know what his function would be, but thought, as occurs in the divisions, that some doctor would rather pay for the honor of being so designated. Admitting payment was necessary, he thought the figure too small for a whole time officer.

In the ensuing discussion Hon. Freeman Martin of St. Louis; R.A. Martin and R. Bachelor of Cuba and Baxter of Jamaica spoke as to the fact that the activities of such an officer would be limited to New York, except he went on lecture tours, and thought he should not be paid. Hon. J. Eaton of Virginia also agreed with this. Hon. H.[M.] Boyd and Amelia Sayers of New York pointed out that such an officer was very necessary in connection with the Legions and the Black Cross Nurses.

Hon. Bishop McGuire did not think that the salaries suggested were sufficient for professional men to devote all their time and made the suggestion that such offices be titular or honorary.

Hon. F. Johnson of Detroit moved that the offices of surgeon-general, chaplain-general and international organizer be honorary.

Hon. Arnold J. Ford of New York seconded, and the motion was carried.

Some discussion arose as to the desirability of paying the consul-general, but the speaker pointed out, along with other members, that a permanent lawyer was necessary to advise on the many small and large matters that always crop up in an organization like this.

Hon. F. Johnson of Detroit moved that the salary be $3,000 per annum.

Hon. J. Peters did not think that officer should be paid, especially as another lawyer was usually employed whenever there was a case.

Eventually it was agreed to pay the amount proposed in the motion.

Another discussion arose as to the position of minister of education. The salary suggested by the speaker was $2,000. His work is to take charge of educational matters connected with the whole organization, including propaganda.

Hon. J. Craigin of Detroit moved that the minister of education be paid $2,000. Hon. A.J. Ellinburgh of Gary seconded, and the motion was carried.

A discussion took place as to the wisdom of incorporating the positions of minister of labor and that of first assistant president-general.

The speaker stated that those were two of the most important positions, as each had very responsible duties to perform.

The question then arose as to the paying of dual salaries.

Hon. Wallace of Illinois reminded the speaker that the last convention had legislated against such a thing.

The speaker said he remembered the fact, but unfortunately in revising the constitution somehow or other this law had been left out.

It was decided that the section should be re-enacted.

Eventually it was decided not to amalgamate the two offices.

The meeting adjourned until the evening.

MONDAY EVENING, AUGUST 25

The Convention resumed at 8:30 this evening, when the chair was occupied by Lady Henrietta Vinton Davis, Fourth Assistant President-General.

There was a large attendance, despite the fact that an admission of 25 cents was charged, a moving picture entertainment being staged after the meeting.

The minutes of the afternoon session were read and[,] on motion duly made and seconded[,] were adopted.

Lady Davis expressed her great pleasure at being in Liberty Hall again after her trip abroad in the West Indies and Central America, in the interests of the Universal Negro Improvement Assn. She extended a hearty welcome to all present and spoke encouragingly of the wholehearted co-operation the people in the places she had visited were giving to the work of the Association and their unbounded enthusiasm over the ship that had been acquired by the Black Cross Navigation and Trading Co. She called upon Dr. J.J. Peters of Chicago to be the first speaker for the evening. . . .

Printed in *NW*, 6 September 1924. Original headlines omitted.

Convention Report

[*New York, 26 August 1924*]

TUESDAY MORNING, AUGUST 26

The convention was called to order at 10:50 a.m., the delegates arriving late owing to rain. Hon. Marcus Garvey, Speaker, occupied the chair. After prayers the minutes of the two previous sessions were read and confirmed, with necessary corrections.

The Speaker said something had been said at a previous session on the subject of compensation for those officers that had done exceptionally well, and suggested that the convention deal with that question so that the salary matter may be definitely settled. He advised that the convention pause before placing any law as to special compensation in the Cons[titution]. Hon. C.H. Bryant, Costa Rica, was of opinion that the matter should rest with the salaries as fixed.

Hon. W.S. Vaughan, Youngstown, Ohio, suggested some scale of compensation for officers based on the amount of money raised in the field. Hon. Prof. D.H. Kyle, Clarksburg, W.Va., was of opinion that, inasmuch as the President-General was in a better position than any to judge the situation, his scale of salaries should stand as the only reward for service on the part of executives. He moved that no changes along the line of remuneration be made, but that the suggestion of the administration be followed.

Hon. C.H. Bryant, Costa Rica, seconded.

The motion was thrown open for discussion.

Hon. W.A. Wallace, Illinois, felt that the convention should not overlook the necessity for rewarding merit and service when such qualities were found. In regard to the compensation for officers on a basis of money raised in the field, he pointed out that some officers never went on the field and yet did as useful, if not more useful, work than some who went campaigning. The idea was also faulty, inasmuch as in order to get results beneficial in the first degree to the organization it might be necessary to forego monetary results. He suggested that the officers be made to report monthly and annually to the convention.

The Speaker pointed out that a system of daily reporting had been instituted by the administration with bad results, officers failing to report after a time.

Hon. Dennis Washington, Louisiana, spoke on the great loyalty of the Louisiana divisions and subscribed to the view that the President-General's suggestion in regard to compensation should be accepted. Hon. J. Craigen, Detroit, emphasized that sacrifice on the part of officers was necessary, referring to his personal sacrifice in refusing a $100 a week job to accept a third of that working for the Universal Negro Improvement Association. He moved the following motion, accepting amendments for indorsement by Hon. Mea Bowd [Mae Boyd], New York, and Hon. J. A. Hassell, Seattle:

> That all executive officers make a daily report in triplicate to the President-General, the Chancellor and the Secretary-General of their work in the field and at headquarters and of all financial transactions, so that same can be summarized in monthly reports and finally in annual reports to the convention, and upon failure to make such reports such officer or officers shall be considered not to have worked on and to have forfeited salaries for the days on which such reports were not made.

Hon. C. H. Bryant, Costa Rica, seconded.

Hon. J. B. Eaton drew applause as, speaking on the motion, he deprecated the idea that the salaries voted the various officers were insufficient. Which of them could earn such salaries in these strenuous times outside? he asked. These same strenuous economic conditions made it imperative that the poor people, who had to pay those salaries, sacrifice in order to meet their obligations.

At this stage Hon. Rudolph Smith, Third Assistant President-General, joined the discussion, making a plea ad misericordiam to the convention. He felt aggrieved, he said, that the services rendered by him to the organization had not received commensurate appreciation from the administration.

The Speaker challenged the Hon. gentleman to tell the convention what had been the result of his recent efforts on the field.

Hon. Smith did so, and after further discussion the motion was put to the house and unanimously carried.

Hon. Freeman L. Martin, St. Louis, said he had drawn up in proper form the amendments to the Constitution article VII, embodied in the motion passed in regard to salaries at a previous session. He had done so in the desire to have everything kept straight. The amendments were as follows:

Salaries of high officials—Article VII—Section 3-A. That the following annual salaries shall be paid to the following named officials of the High Executive Council of the Universal Negro Improvement Association and African Communities League.

To wit:	Per year
Supreme Deputy	$3,000
1st Asst. Pres. General	5,000
Counsel General	3,000
2nd Asst. Pres. General	2,500
Secretary General	2,250
Chancellor	2,250
3rd Asst. Pres. General	2,000
4th Asst. Pres. General	2,000
Minister of Education	2,000
Auditor General	2,000
High Commissioner General	2,000
1st Asst. Secretary General	1,750
Minister of Legions	1,750
Minister of Labor & Industry	1,750
2nd Asst. Secretary General	1,500

Sec. 3-B. That the offices of Surgeon General, Chaplain General and International Organizer shall be that of honorary without salary.

Sec. 3-C. That Sec. 3-A, Art. VII. and all other sections and parts of sections in conflict herewith, be, and the same are hereby repealed.

Sec. 3-D. That the schedule of salaries set forth above shall become effective and operative at the rising of this convention.

Sec. 3-E. That the aforesaid annual salaries shall be paid bi-monthly as of the 1st and 15th of each month.

Hon. J. Craigen, Detroit, described this action on the part of the honorary member from St. Louis as premature.

The Speaker differed, and upon motion for acceptance by Hon. Dr. J.J. Peters, Chicago, seconded by Hon. H. V. Plummer, New York, the amending draft was received.

The convention thereafter adjourned.

TUESDAY AFTERNOON, AUGUST 26

The convention resumed at 3 p.m.

Hon. Freeman L. Martin of St. Louis intr[od]uced amendments to the section of the Constitution governing the dismissal of officers. The amendments provided that the President-General be given power to peremptorily dismiss any officer or official of the High Executive for disloyalty, inefficiency or insubordination.

Considerable discussion ensued, most of the delegates objecting to the gran[ting] of such autocratic power to any official. It was thought to be not only unfair to the present administrator, in whom, it was true, every confidence was reposed, but was unfair to the association, because a probable successor to the President-General may take advantage of the situation to the detriment of the members.

The speaker said, in reply to a question, that he did not like the provision as it stood. He liked to give a man a fair trial, but, at the same time, there had been occasions when he found that members of the executive did not, in similar matters, act as they should to the best interests of the association, although his remarks did not apply to the present executive.

Eventually the following amendments were passed:

> Sec. 14a. The President-General shall have authority to dismiss peremptorily any officer or official of the High Executive Council for disloyalty, inefficiency or insubordination, and such officer or official's salary shall cease as from the day of dismissal.
>
> (b) The President-General shall have authority to fill the vacancy of all elected officers thus made until the next convention by appointment.
>
> (c) Before an elected officer is dismissed by the President-General and administrator, he shall first be given a hearing before the Privy Council of the organization and, if found guilty of the charges laid against him, be dealt with according to section "a" of this article. In the event of the accused being one or more members of the Privy Council, the President-General shall have power to appoint temporarily such other person or persons as he may desire.
>
> (d) The Privy Council shall consist of the administrator and three loyal bona fide members of the U.N.I.A. or members of the High Executive Council, to be appointed by the administrator.

The convention then adjourned until the evening.

TUESDAY EVENING, AUGUST 26

Tonight's session, which commenced at 9 o'clock, was devoted entirely to discussion on the amendments to the constitution.

Hon. Marcus Garvey, presiding as Speaker in Convention, announced that the convention would deal with that part of the constitution relating to the duties of officers. In this connection he drew attention to the fact that under the constitution as it existed there were some officers whose offices were not placed under any direct control. Because of that fact the association had lost suits in court brought by the last Speaker in Convention[1] and the last Surgeon General.[2] In those cases the court after reading the constitution ruled that there was no specific reference as to what these officers should do and under whose instructions they should [be, and] they were therefore privileged to do what they willed. In the case of the Speaker in Convention there was no provision as to what he should do except to receive amendments to the constitution during the rising of the convention and to preside over the convention, for which he was to receive $3,000 a year. He thought, therefore, it was necessary to amend the constitution in order to make these officers come under proper jurisdiction.

Another point was in reference to the office of First Assistant President General. He thought they should insist that the First Assi[stan]t President General be a competent business man and one of pronounced ability. The organization had been criticized for its business methods, yet at the same time it was a fact that of all the organizations, business institutions and corporations started in the last four years the Universal Negro Improvement Association was the only one surviving. He suggested that the following addition be made to the section dealing with the First Assistant President General:

"That he shall be a competent business man who shall by his experience and ability be able to constitute himself an asset to the organization; he shall be at his post of duty at all times and shall not be allowed to devote his time or service with any other organization or institution, but shall give his entire time to carrying out the orders given him for the good of the association."

The suggestion was embodied in a motion and moved by Hon. Wm. Sherrill, seconded by Hon. Mr. Johnson of Detroit. It was carried without dissent.

To carry out the suggestion of the President General in regard to placing jurisdiction or supervision over the other executive officers, Hon. Mr. Creagen of Detroit moved the adoption of the following clause as touching the First Assistant President General: "He shall be under the jurisdiction and supervision of the President General, who shall assign him his respective duties, and the failure of this officer to obey his command shall be considered as an act of insubordination and shall be dealt with as specified in Article 4, Section 14, a, b, and c, of the constitution."

Hon. Mr. Cipriani seconded the motion and a lengthy discussion ensued thereon. It was the opinion of some of the delegates that the duties of the First Assistant President General should be specifically designated and, to that end, Hon. Dr. J.J. Peters moved the adoption of the following clause:

"The First Assistant President General shall supervise all industrial and commercial enterprises owned and controlled by the Universal Negro Improvement Association and African Communities League and shall perform such other duties that may be assigned to him by the Administrator or President General."

The convention passed by a vote of 53 to 10 the motion of Hon. Mr. Craigen, but defeated the motion of Dr. Peters by a vote of 22 to 30.

Hon. Rudolph Smith moved that in [the] absence of the President-General, [the] First Assistant General shall supervise the activities of all departments of the organization at headquarters, and report his findings to the President-General each and every day.

The motion was seconded by Hon. Mr. William,[3] of Hamtramc, Mich., but was subsequently tabled on motion of Hon. Mr. Martin, St. Louis, seconded by Hon. F. Johnson, of Detroit.

The duties of the Second, Third and Fourth Assistant President-Generals were then taken up. The Speaker suggested the following addition to the sections governing their duties:

"They shall likewise perform those duties that are assigned to them by the President-General, and shall perform them with skill and ability. They shall be found at their post of duty at all times; and shall not be allowed to devote their time with any other organization or institution, but shall give their entire time for the good of the Universal Negro Improvement Association, or in carrying out the order of the association."

The amendment was adopted on motion of Hon. F. Johnson, of Detroit, seconded by Hon. F.L. Martin, St. Louis.

The following addition suggested by Hon. Col. Harrigan was also adopted: That in the absence of the First Assistant President-[General], the [Second] Assistant President-General shall perform the duties of said office, and shall be held responsible by the President-General, and in his absence the Third and Fourth Assistant President[s]-General shall, respectively, be held responsible.

The offices of Secretary-General and High Commissioner were then considered.

On motion of Hon. S.V. Robertson, of Mississippi, seconded by Hon. J.A. Hassell, Seattle, the following addition was adopted to Article 5, section 16: "And he shall carry out and perform those duties that are assigned to him by the President-General and Administrator to whom he shall be held responsible in office. That he shall see to it that all divisions, branches and chapters shall keep financial to the parent body."

The following addition to all sections regarding the duties of officers was adopted on the motion of Hon. F. Johnson, Detroit, seconded by Hon. Mr. Welch, Detroit: "And he shall work under the direction of the President-General and administrator."

The convention then adjourned till 10 a.m. next day.

Printed in *NW*, 6 September 1924. Original headlines omitted.

1. Adrian Johnson.
2. J.D. Gibson.
3. In 1923 George A. Williams served as executive secretary of the Hamtramck, Mich., UNIA (*NW*, 23 June 1923).

Convention Report

[*New York, 27 August 1924*]

[WEDNESDAY MORNING, AUGUST 27]

The convention was called to order at 11 o'clock, the speaker, Hon. Marcus Garvey, in the chair.

After prayers, the speaker announced the death, which took place suddenly on the 17th inst., of Chief Justice J.J. Dossen, of Liberia. Mr. Dossen, he said, had been sponsoring the work of the association in the Cavalla Colony, and his demise was a severe blow to the association. He suggested that the convention adjourn for five minutes as a token of esteem.

The convention then adjourned for five minutes on the motion of Hon. F.E. Johson, Detroit, seconded by Lady Henrietta Vinton Davis.

Hon. C.H. Bryant, Costa Rica, moved that expressions of sympathy and condolence be tendered to the relatives of the deceased through the deputy potentate in such manner as he may deem fit.

Hon. R.A. Martin, Cuba, seconded, and the motion was unanimously carried.

At the suggestion of the speaker, Hon. R.A. Martin, Florida, Cuba, moved that a memorial meeting in honor of the deceased be combined with the proceedings at next Sunday afternoon's meeting at Carnegie Hall when the work of the convention will be reviewed.

Hon. C.H. Bryant, Costa Rica, seconded, and the motion was unanimously carried.

The following communication from several lady delegates to the convention was then read by the secretary, and dealt with:

Aug. 27, 1924.

Honorable Speaker-in-Convention,
Honorable Delegates and Deputies to This Fourth International Convention of Negroes of the World:

In view of the fact that the women of the Universal Negro Improvement Association who possess moral integrity, ability and a burning desire to work at all times for the good of the U.N.I.A. and A.C.L., and being well known and respected in their various divisions and expressing to us through their lady presidents and delegates their desire to further benefit their association by a concerted effort among the other women of their various divisions:

We, the ladies whose names are appended, offer for the consideration of this august body at this time, the following:

Be it resolved that:

(a) The Ladies of the Royal Court of Ethiopia become an international auxiliary of the U.N.I.A. and be encouched as such in its constitution.

(b) Branches of the Ladies of the Royal Court of Ethiopia, to be known as the Daughters of Ethiopia, be established in each division.

(c) That the president-general and high executive council recommend a continuance and expansion of the work heretofore done by the Ladies of the Royal Court of Ethiopia along the lines formerly pursued and along such other lines as they may deem useful to the body at large.

After considerable discussion it was moved by Hon. Mrs. De Mena,[1] Chicago, seconded by Hon. Mrs. Curry, Monongah, W.Va., and unanimously carried, that the Daughters of Ethiopia shall be the name of an auxiliary that shall be encouched in the Constitution of the Universal Negro Improvement Association by this convention.

Hon. Dr. J.J. Peters, Chicago, moved that a committee be appointed, with Lady Henrietta Vinton Davis as chairman, to draft rules and regulations for the governing of the Daughters of Ethiopia Auxiliary.

Miss De Mena seconded, and the motion was unanimously carried.

The speaker then appointed the following committee: Lady Henrietta V. Davis, Mr. William Sherrill, Hon. Mrs. O'Brien, Montreal; Miss De Mena, Chicago; Hon. Mrs. Sharperson Young, with the speaker as ex-officio chairman.

Hon. J.A. Hassell as chairman then presented the report of the committee appointed to draft recommendations with a view to the encouragement of travel on the part of Negroes of the industrial and commercial professions.

On motion of Hon. Bishop McGuire, seconded by Hon. J.B. Eaton, the report was adopted as read.

Hon. Freeman L. Martin, St. Louis, moved that the secretary to the convention bring back to the convention four copies of all the amendments to the Constitution, one copy to be given to the President-General, one to the Secretary-General, one to the Chancellor and one for the press, so that a check could be kept on the faithful reproduction of these amendments when they were printed.

Hon. C.H. Bryant, Costa Rica, seconded, and the motion was unanimously carried.

The convention then proceeded to deal with the question of death grants. The discussion was initiated by Hon. W.A. Wallace, Chicago, who said that the time had come when the finances of the association must be conserved. Unpaid death claims had piled up, to the embarrassment of the parent body. He therefore moved that no one shall receive the death benefit of $75 unless such individual produces a physician's certificate as to good health within thirty days after entering the association; and on failure by such individual to produce such a certificate the secretary shall not collect from him any further death tax.

Hon. C.L. Logan, Atlanta, seconded, and the motion was carried.

Hon. W.A. Wallace then introduced the following amendment: That no one over the age of sixty years at time of joining shall be entitled to the death grant.

A lengthy discussion ensued, the convention adjourning with the matter undecided.

WED. AFTERNOON, AUG. 27

On Wednesday afternoon when the convention resumed, the Liberian situation was the subject for discussion.

The Hon. Marcus Garvey had promised that the two surviving members of the delegation which had been sent to Liberia this year would give the convention a report of what had actually transpired in that country. He called upon Hon. J. Milton Van Lowe to speak. . . .[2]

Printed in *NW*, 6 September 1924. Original headlines omitted.

1. By 1924 Maymie Leone Turpeau De Mena, born in San Carlos, Nicaragua, around 1892, was an active member of the Chicago division of the UNIA. She resided in the United States, first in 1913–1914 and again from 1917 on, living in Indianapolis and Chicago; she listed her occupations variously as stenographer, clerk, and clerk interpreter. Lively, articulate, and charismatic, De Mena was appointed the UNIA's assistant international organizer in 1926. By 1930 she was in charge of organizing additional American UNIA branches (Timothy Connelly, National Archives and Records Service, to Robert A. Hill, 25 February 1985).

2. A separate and complete version of this report is printed below.

Report of the UNIA Delegation to Liberia

[New York, 27 August 1924]

DELEGATION SENT TO LIBERIA 1923–1924
GIVES REPORT TO CONVENTION REPUDIATING
FALSE STATEMENT THAT THERE WAS
NO AGREEMENT WITH LIBERIAN GOVERNMENT
TO COLONIZE LIBERIA

The convention resumed at about 3:30 p.m.

Hon. Marcus Garvey, Speaker in Convention, presided.

The usual hymn was sung and the prayers recited.

The secretary read the minutes of the previous meeting, which were received and adopted on the motion of Hon. A.S. Askerless, seconded by Hon. C.H. Bryant.

Hon. Speaker: We promised to devote this afternoon to the report on the Liberian situation, and we will ask Lady Davis and Hon. J. Van Lowe, whom we sent as part of the delegation to make their report to this convention. They have already made their written report to the executive council on which we acted subsequently. They will make the report as they saw, understood and did things under the leadership of our late lamented Sir Robert Lincoln Poston. I want to say before they speak that we are handling an international situation, and I want you to understand the position of the administration.

We have been unable to say many things within the last month, even though a lot of propaganda has been published about our proposition simply because we did not want to complicate matters. You all know the seriousness of the U.N.I.A. in regard to its objective, which is the redemption of Africa. We have tremendous influences to fight against in carrying out our program. Untoward influences have been at work which more than ordinary minds have been unable to understand. International matters and complications have to be brought into this discussion, and I trust everybody here is broad enough in the understanding of international matters to understand certain things. It is more than on the surface. It is a deep question of diplomacy that calls for the exhibition of statesmanship. This has been the position of the administration all the time. There are things we wanted to say that we could not say because of policy and the results. But it has reached a point where we have to enlighten you and the public that desire information. Nevertheless, the situation remains just the same. It is a delicate political situation. We have Liberia on the one hand with whom we are dealing. It is a little black republic. On the other hand we have the powerful bolies [bullies?] known as England and France, who have held the club and said certain things to those who have not been manly enough to maintain their position. It is either that somebody must take a man's stand for what is right or play the part of a coward before the bully. The association has to protest its position and reputation, and we have to tell the public the whole truth. It may not be morally good for somebody when the truth is told, but nevertheless we are placed in a position where we have to tell the truth.

DOUBLE-CROSSING

A terrible amount of double-crossing and intrigue has been going on and somebody is to be the scapegoat, and I don't believe it should be the U.N.I.A. The truth ought to be told to you and the organization, so that you may know the situation. Those of us who read understand and know what I am saying, but the average man does not understand. There is nothing that can happen to disable the U.N.I.A., but, nevertheless, a great deal of injury has been done.

From 1921 we had an understanding with Liberia to colonize the country. In that year there was a written understanding signed by the very man whose name was published in the papers, that man Edwin Barclay. And that agreement was further supplemented by the visit of our delegates there in February last, and a lot has happened since. I have told you many things that some of you do not take kindly to. The Negro is peculiar and you have to tell him the same thing many times before he understands it, and during the time you tell him, somebody else gets the information. We told you that our work was purely a question of money and determination; to get that money we have had to bawl our souls out. What it took us more than a year to get prepared for other people have been able to obtain since our organization got those concessions. Somebody else went there, and because they have money to circulate they got away with murder and somebody wants to make us the scapegoat. The Firestone Rubber and Tire Company of Ohio went there and got one million acres of land to exploit for rubber and minerals.[1] That is where we will show you the hypocrisy and double-crossing of certain people. I will now ask Hon. Mr. Van Lowe to make his report.

Hon. J.M. Van Lowe said: The time has come when we as the remainder of the delegates that had been commissioned to go to Liberia to obtain certain concessions for the U.N.I.A. must tell you the whole truth and nothing but the truth, so help us God. Many of you who are from the different divisions and those of you who are members of the New York local have heard me say on many occasions that I detest a falsifier—I said, in plain words, that I hate a liar. And I would not lie when there is no cause. So I will tell you under oath that on February 1 of this year we arrived at Monrovia, Liberia. On arrival there we were met by a great number of members and friends of the U.N.I.A. They did not even allow us to land, but came on board our steamer and escorted us into the port of Monrovia, and when we landed we met thousands and thousands of the most enthusiastic people, members and friends of the U.N.I.A. I cannot recall a reception so cordial or enthusiastic, and I cannot recall a welcome so endearing as we had on our arrival.

A RECEPTION

We were taken to our different residences. Lady Davis resided at the Faulkner Hotel and we stayed at a place directly opposite at Mrs. Dunbar's. Our distinguished friend Re[v]. Van Richards knows Mrs. Dunbar very well. We have many persons of prominence to visit us and on February 5, a reception was tendered us. This reception was held in one of the biggest buildings in Liberia, the Methodist Church in Monrovia. That evening the place was thronged to its utmost capacity with friends of the association and a great number of members and many high officials of Liberia. Among those present were the distinguished and deceased Chief Justice Doss[en], of Liberia[,] ex-President Barclay and ex-President Howard, senators and several men high up in the government. That evening we had complete co-operation. We were so greatly applauded, kindly received and highly appreciated that we felt doubly rewarded for having gone there. And that night the late Chief Justice spoke from the fullness of his heart. He was the Charles Evans Hughes of Liberia[,] one of the most powerful and influential gentlemen of that republic. He said that Liberia needs new blood to be developed. "Others have refused to help us and there is absolutely no other agent in the world; there is at this time no hand nor friend in sight but that great intrepid leader of the U.N.I.A., Marcus Garvey." And he spoke in that strain and with such emotion that many an eye was wet with tears of joy, joy because there was a general demeanor and a feeling that we had come to apply to Liberia the assistance she longed for.

Ex-President Barclay voiced the same sentiments and others spoke and said that they had tried to do everything to obstruct the work of the U.N.I.A., but he was glad to say that in spite of the opposition the Hon. Marcus Garvey had acted so bravely that we had at last come to do the great thing for Liberia that she needed so much. After the reception we went to our homes escorted by many friends. I may say that among the ladies who were there and who spoke was Mrs. Howard[,] the wife of the ex-President.

INTERVIEW WITH THE PRESIDENT

She spoke so eloquently that if any one wanted inspiration he got it there. Other ladies of high rank and distinction also spoke.

We were to see President King about the fifth or seventh of the month, as he was not quite through with matters relative to his inauguration. It happened, unfortunately, that his A.D.C. [aide-de-camp] had died up the St. Paul's river, and he had to attend the funeral, so his absence from Monrovia prevented us having an immediate interview.

He returned on Feb. 10 and on the 11th we had our interview. At that interview was President King, the late Chief Justice [D]ossen, ex-President Barclay, Sir Robert L. Poston, Henrietta V. Davis and your humble servant. We disclosed our plans to President King, informing him that the concessions that were made to us previously, we were prepared to carry out, but there had been quite a lot of propaganda to the effect that we were not wanted there and that we would not be welcome. President King told us that we must not pay any attention to such assertions because, as a matter of law and according to the constitution it was impossible for such a thing as that to occur. Because the Constitution of Liberia, a copy of which he showed us and which we brought back and submitted to the President-General, provides in substance that Liberia shall be the home and refuge for the oppressed Negroes of the world, regardless of nationality. This is encouched in the Constitution of the Republic of Liberia.

Therefore, President King said it was impossible because we would be transgressing against our own Constitution and it would be treachery to our own race. And there, let me tell you, God being my judge, President King went on to discuss the working general possibilities and feasibilities of the plan of this organization. He discussed it with a zeal, enthusiasm and an appreciation that could not have been excelled by the Hon. Marcus Garvey himself.

Our hearts le[a]pt with joy as we received a reception and welcome that surpassed every dream or imagination. And there President King in all his zeal and apparent anxiety upon his own initiative set out to suggest and brought out plans by which we could successfully carry out our colonization scheme. He suggested that we first send material, artisans to lay out the land and build homes for those people, so that when they came they would have somewhere to go and would not be left to the mercy of others. He also suggested that places would be provided for them to develop the land and further that on the arrival of the colonists, instead of going to Monrovia, as the capital, they should proceed to places that he suggested, such as Cavalla, Sino, Cape Palmas, Cape Mount and Grand Bassa. That would prevent them a great deal of inconvenience and a long journey. He said those places were among the most fertile lands that Liberia possessed. In addition to that, fearing that we might have a failure or mishap to our plans, he suggested that a committee be appointed to assist, instruct and advise a system of preparing those homes and by which on arrival of the colonists some one would be on the spot to meet them and correctly direct them to their several places.

As a resul[t] of his own suggestion there, the committee was appointed which met that night. To prove the truth of my statement, do you think for a moment that the Vice-President of Liberia, who sits directly at the side of the President, would find himself on such a committee to prepare homes and provide places for the colonists when they came to establish themselves and develop the place[?] Do you think he would be there without some express or implied authority, so to speak, to carry out the plans of the President?

On that committee there was Vice-President Wesley, Chief Justice Dossen, ex-Presidents Barclay and Howard, Mr. Caranada, Mr. Dennis and Mr. Dickson Brown, Comptroller of Liberia.[2] All of these men were there.

The plans were drawn up and signed and are in the possession of our president-general. They were drawn in the most solemn manner apparently with blood and tears and when we discontinued, the venerable deceased chief justice said: "Thank God, the dawn of Liberia's glory, wealth and power has now come."

We departed that night and thereupon several letters were interchanged between President King and our delegates. All of that was done and one of the last expressions that President King told us was, "I have implicit confidence in this delegation, now I am satisfied that you are determined." He also said, upon my oath, that you will find the government of Liberia and the Liberians standing ready to co-operate with you.

Therefore on our leaving we received certain tokens of appreciation and we received such replies as to know that there was appreciation for the business relation that existed between us. President King further said, "You will find when you establish yourselves upon the Cavella river, that with proper working that alone would doubly repay you for all the ventures and sacrifices that you have made.["]

While we were there the news went around like wildfire all through Liberia. Men and women came from up the river, and from other places, twos, threes, dozens and more to see us, to bring us greeting and congratulations.

And I am here to tell you without prevarication that at least 95 per cent of the people are in sympathy with the organization and are wishing, encouraging and hoping that the association will be able to carry out its program. Anyone who is trying to interfere with our plans will have a subsequent reckoning to meet with the people. We are not making any threats but we are talking facts.

All through Liberia, wherever we went, one could not find a more hospitable and amiable people than the Liberians. I want to tell you, conscientiously and fearlessly, if our people in America particular[l]y and in the West Indies were just one third as amiable or hospitable it would be a great advantage for this organization, as we would have a practically perfect race, for I have traveled throughout the United States and in a great many islands in the West Indies and elsewhere, and I shall speak of that fact.

For these reasons I wish to say that these people showed that spirit of welcome, co-operation and enthusiasm for the U.N.I.A. which was no grandstand play, but absolutely genuine.

It was the assurance given by President King which caused us to bring back such glowing reports.

We have acted in accordance with the assurances that have been given us, and I cannot believe that gentlemen holding so distinguished a position before the eyes of the world can be guilty of any act of unfairness toward this organization and toward our race. I would not believe for a moment that President King is guilty of this propaganda that is so rampant in America and fostered by Ernest Lyon and the Negro press.

Hon. Speaker: Before we hear the second member of the committee I would ask the secretary to read a few communications and especially the signed suggestions brought back from Liberia by the delegation signed by members of the committee appointed by President King himself to draw up suggestions under which we should operate and support the colonies.

The secretary read the documents,[3] which were most convincing.

Hon. Speaker: [Referring to a communication,] I believe that is one of the last letters written by the judge. It was written on July 1,[4] and he died on July 17 [August 17]. We will now ask Lady Davis to make her report.

Lady Henrietta Vinton Davis said: I am deeply touched and deeply moved by the reading of the letters that have come from that wonderful leader of men, Chief Justice J.J. Dossen of the Republic of Liberia. I am proud to say that he was a friend of mine. A man of great soul—that you can see by his letters. A man who loved his race. A man who was ready to lay down his life for the Republic of Liberia and the preservation of the Negro peoples of the world. We have decorated this platform in mourning in honor of that great man. I wish to say that the report given by the secretary of the delegation, the Hon. J.M. Van Lowe, I heartily concur with and endorse every word that he has said. He has spoken in detail of our visit to the Republic of Liberia in the interest of the U.N.I.A. and the 400,000,000 members of our race. We left here on December 11 and went by way of Portugal to the beautiful city of Lisbon and from there went to the Canary Islands, transshipping at each place and arrived in the City of Monrovia on February 1, 1924.

We were welcomed as Mr. Van Lowe has told you. We were greeted by the very best people in the Republic. Reaching Liberia two weeks after the inauguration of President King, we found in Monrovia many who had come to that inauguration. We found many chieftains from the interior of Liberia and we were very glad, indeed, as they were, to meet them and talk over with them the coming of the U.N.I.A. colonists to the republic.

We not only had the assurance of the civilized people of the republic, but we have the assurance from the aborig[i]nes of Liberia that this great organization shall be welcomed whenever they come. In talking with the chieftains from the interior, discussing the plans for the emigration of our people, they hailed it with joy, and said they would [give?] every facility in their power for the entertainment and hospitality and welcome and keeping up our people in the republic. These are the sentiments of the so-called savage people, the aborigines of the republic as well as the sentiments of 98 per cent of the civilized people.

We had the interview with President King on February 11. We could not have been more courteously, more cordially, more enthusiastically received by any one than by the president of the republic. Chief Justice Dossen was there; the Hon. A. Barclay, ex-president, was also there, one sitting on either side of the president. The delegation sat facing them and, as Mr. Van Lowe has told you in the report, many suggestions as to the colonists' coming were brought forward by President King himself. He had this committee appointed, the advisory committee whose names you have heard and whose suggestions you have heard read. He it was who named them, and so we were so elated after our interview with the president that the late lamented Robert L. Poston went at once to the cable office and cabled the Hon. Marcus Garvey the one word, "Success." And the three of us went home feeling so happy that we had accomplished that for which we were sent and, as Robert Lincoln Poston said, "We have even gotten more than we asked for[,] Lady Davis." I said, "Yes, the good people of the republic of Liberia are generous."

President King assured us that we could have a colony at the Cavalla, at Sino and at Grand Bassa, and when I said to him, "Mr. President, I was so impressed with Cape Mount as our ship went into port," he said, "You can have land there also." And, therefore, we have four concessions set aside for the U.N.I.A. He said, "After the coming of the colonists we will arrange to give them all the land that they will desire." What more can be asked of anyone? What more can be expected of anyone? No wonder the soul of Robert L. Poston was elated. No wonder that he shook hands with the delegation all around and rejoiced that we had gotten what we had been sent for.

I can understand diplomacy. I am something of a diplomat myself. But among high officials who should maintain the honor of their country I cannot understand duplicity. I say this advisedly. I say it to show you the cordial treatment of this delegation. I tell you this because in contradistinction of the treatment we got and the concessions we obtained, there comes out in the "World" of yesterday afternoon an artic[l]e saying that this great organization is not welcome in the republic of Liberia, that passports will not be vised for members of the association who are going to Liberia.

The motto of Liberia is engraven on my heart. It met my eyes the moment I stepped in Liberia. That motto is, "Love of Liberty brought us here." The forefathers of Liberia knew well that the Negro of the Western world would cross the mighty Atlantic undaunted and undismayed because the love of liberty would bring him to the republic of Liberia. And so the love of liberty burns in every man's breast. It will bear all things and suffer all things and as Patrick Henry said: "Give me liberty or give me death."

And then for the door of liberty to be closed in the face of Negroes, such a thing cannot stand. (Cries of No!). Such a thing shall not stand. (Applause.)

I for one will knock at the door of liberty until I die, seeking for admission. It shall be opened. It must be opened. It is God's will that it must be opened and with our intrepid leader, Hon. Marcus Garvey at our head, we will break down all barriers, all doors and everything that shall be placed in the way of a race that loves liberty, so that our people might be free.

We love liberty because we have suffered slavery. We love liberty because we have worked as peons, and as slaves we are still so working in some parts of the world. But six years ago, Marcus Garvey sounded the clarion cry to the members of the U.N.I.A. that they should break off the shackles that bind them; that they should rise up as new Negroes and go forth to conquer and to victory.

Vice-President Wesley, of Liberia, who attended the meeting of the committee, is an aborigine of Africa, born of aboriginal parents, but civilized and educated. There are several men in the high official life in Liberia with such antecedents. He is a magnificent man, who is deeply interested in the project of the colonization of the republic. He was present and made suggestions along with the Hon. A. Barclay, the nestor of the bar of Liberia, an aged man, but a man of such learning, a man of such wonderful culture, a man of such keen ideas that I felt in having the Hon. Ex-President at the head of the committee that we had a man who would stand forever at the gate of Liberia, and that should any attempt be made to close the gate of Liberia against the U.N.I.A. he would stop it with his very body.

Chief Justice Dossen was an intellectual giant as well as a man of exemplary character and unimpeachable integrity. A man towering above ordinary men with a massive brain. I had the privilege of attending a session of the Supreme Court where he presided and heard him deliver his opinion and pronounce sentence of death upon a man named [Milton] Marshal, who had committed a crime. I have visited the Supreme Court of the United States of America in the city of Washington, and listened to the learned judges on the bench there. Never in my life have I seen a man more dignified; never more learned in the law and never in my life have I heard a judge deliver sentence in such a manner. I said to my comrades, "A magnificent man" is Chief Justice Dossen.

I did not know then that this great man was the great friend of the U.N.I.A. that he was. He was a tower of strength in the republic. But God has called him to his reward and to his rest. But I want to say here, that in the land of Africa there is a Samson lying sleeping who will soon awake, and with an avenging hand and in an unlooked for hour he shall rise in might and power. What dastard can his mighty strength withstand?

Hon. Rev. Van Richard of Liberia: My heart is paining me at this moment. I am deeply grieved at the news of the death of Chief Justice Dossen, who was my father-in-law. I did not believe the report when I first heard it. One of the greatest men of Liberia is surely dead. He was one of the ablest jurists the world has ever known. In his death Liberia has lost a noble character, one of her ablest sons. And who shall fill his place only God knows.

He was a warm and sincere friend of the U.N.I.A. and [I] did not know how great a friend he was or how deeply he was interested in it until I heard those letters read this afternoon. How his daughter will take the message only God knows. May God raise up in Liberia another J.J. Dossen, another stalwart son of Liberia, another who could champion its cause. The republic was never ashamed of him. He was one of the ablest jurists who ever presided over the Supreme Court of Liberia. You have lost a sincere friend. I will ask that you ask God to raise up another supporter, and I am sure that God will do it. Because your cause cannot die, no matter what obstacles are placed in your way. In God's own time they will and must be removed.

I enjoyed the report of the Hon. J. Van Lowe, his words sank into my heart, all that he said was so very true. There is but one exception I wish to take and that is President King, our great President[,] was born in Monrovia. His father[,] whom I knew well[,] was a British subject.[5] His mother was a Liberian. What he told you about the Liberian people, is what I have already told you. They are not like the people here, they are hospitable, generous, loving and kind and with no disdain. Their very smile bids you welcome to Liberia.

I admire the remarks of Lady Davis when she said she will knock until the doors of liberty are opened. Brothers[,] those doors are bound to be opened. The powers of hell cannot keep the doors of Liberia barred against black men and they shall be opened.

My being here was absolutely unknown to myself. I never thought I would be here at this time. But conditions over which I had no control have kept me here in New York and I think it is the hand of divine providence so that I will be able to go back to Liberia and tell my people that if the doors are barred against our people who want to go to Liberia it would be a most serious and damning mistake. You cannot send any man to tell those people what I will tell them and you may be assured that I will tell them all that they desire to know.

I have seen people who want to go to Liberia. I have been to their homes in Pennsylvania. Some of them have already sold their possessions and the[ir] homes, have packed up and are ready to go to Liberia, and it is a stinking shame that such a thing should happen. When I go home I will tell my people that the people who wish to come to Liberia are not the scum but some of the best people in America, who will be able to help us do what we cannot do for ourselves.

They have been telling you that the organization is not known in Liberia. Here is a copy of the Liberian News of July 17, with an article entitled, "The U.N.I.A. of Monrovia, Liberian Division."

(Reads article.)

July 17. The Mo[n]rovia division of the Universal Negro Improvement Association held a very interesting meeting and executed a very interesting program which had been staged for the occasion. At the proper hour the first vice-president, Dr. J.F. Lawrence, took the chair and called the meeting to order, in consequence of the recent illness of the president, Mr. W.F. Dennis, who is now convalescing. Mrs. A.J. George presided at the organ, while the division sung the usual opening song. The business part of the meeting was interspersed with beautiful recitations and solos, which was most pleasing to all present. There [were] also impromptu addresses by a few of the members which were loudly applauded.

This division without doubt is forging ahead rapidly, not-withstanding the criticisms and oppositions with which it has to undergo. Still, the members are determined to do their level best to help put the propaganda of the association over the top.

Previous to closing the meeting the vice-president, presiding, thanked the members for their kind and sympathetic attention. He also spoke in glowing terms of the manner in which all those who had taken such active part in the program of the evening. The members appear still cheerful and hopeful that in God's time they will be able to put their propaganda over the top.

It is clear from that the U.N.I.A. is known in Liberia and is very active. And when I go back, they will take to it more readily and they will take to it more strongly because I will tell them what I have seen and heard and witnessed at first hand. I have seen the steamer, I have been aboard it, so I can tell the people that I saw the ship.

Don't fear. You have a strong leader in the person of Hon. Marcus Garvey. Just recently the late Chief Justice Dossen, my father-in-law, wrote me a letter in which he said Mr. Garvey was a great man and a great planner for the redemption of Africa. Africa is to be redeemed by the African and not by the white man, and as sure as God sits on His eternal throne it shall be. Our forefathers did not plan Liberia for others, but for every black man.

Now I want to tell you the doors are not locked against you, nor are they barred. They are only shut and a small zephyr will blow them open and you will be able to enter Liberia as sure as God wills.

Hon. Marcus Garvey said: As I said in my opening remarks, the situation is purely a diplomatic one. I understand quite well what is going on, but I cannot tell you everything. You must imagine a part of it for yourselves. We of the U.N.I.A. work best when there is a fight in hand. Now I only hope that all the members of the association feel like men. I know all that has happened. Somebody has to play smart. Somebody has to sidetrack somebody. Somebody has to play the fool. You remember when we were sending our ambassador to England what I said about diplomacy. Diplomacy is "If everything is all right, I know you." If everything is not all right "I never saw you before." Now read between the lines. At the same time it is such a mix up that we have to explain a lot before our people can understand. Now I trust this will prove to you the importance of the U.N.I.A. Tell me the Negro organization in America or in the world that could have such a document to be sent out to the United States of America. That thing has lifted us to the status of international importance. The whole thing is pressure.

When the delegation was in Liberia, the English and French consuls danced around trying to find out what was going on. They had instructions. Ultimately they found out what we intended to do viz., to help to build up Liberia. So long as she remains undeveloped[,] Liberia supplies an argument for England and France and Italy and Spain that the Negro is incapable of self-government, therefore they must go there with their protectorates, mandatories and colonial domination and run the country until they have exploited all its wealth. England and France knew well that if a group of progressive Negroes coming from the Western World equipped with the best in science, in art and in literature went there[,] it will only be a question of time when all Africa will be on the march to progress for the black man[,] and they should not allow that to go on, so they had to put some obstruction in the way.

Therefore, they called upon little helpless Liberia, who has borrowed money from them. She owes England and France over a million dollars,[6] and they said to her, it is an unfriendly act to allow the U.N.I.A. to settle here. Now what are you going to do about it[?] Unfortunately we hadn't a J.J. Dossen as President of Liberia, who would have replied: "Go to hell," and let the black man redeem his country. It is purely a question of backbone and guts and the belief that we could not pay off the two million dollars. If we had that amount to give England and France we could put backbone into somebody. That is one side of the matter. A couple of weeks after our delegates left Liberia the Firestone Rubber and Tire Company of America went there when they heard that Negroes had been there.[7] They knew it was valuable, and what the land contained and what Negroes who had the aid of science would do. They said[,] look, here is money, give us some land. You know what money is. And one million of acres of land, nearly half of the country was given to that capitalist concern of Ohio to exploit for rubber and all minerals. That is the other side of it. Now, would the Firestone Company like going there with two million natives who are crude and whom they can employ in the rubber fields just as they did in Peru and in the Congo[?][8] Give them hardly anything but hash twice per day[?] Surely they should keep out the American Negroes, who know about the price of labor and of union labor and high wages. And the word was therefore passed to keep out the U.N.I.A. crowd. That is what they played up to, and it is there that the Negro proved that he is the greatest enemy and curse to the race. That man Du Bois is the greatest enemy of his race that God Almighty has ever made. He is the man who supplied the argument. Two years ago he wrote in the Crisis that it was the intention of the Garvey men to go into Africa and drive out all the whites from there.[9] That is the man who gave the argument to the English and French to tell President King.

Do you wonder why Du Bois was in Liberia part of this year? Go and find out among the capitalists' class who are paying Negroes to keep down Negroes. You would find out why Du Bois wrote over two years ago about the Garvey movement and why the Afro-American of Baltimore also wrote their recent articles.[10] It was wicked propaganda with the object of causing Negroes to fight against Negroes.

We are our greatest enemies. But men, you will realize this—that the Liberian Government is not all the Liberian people.

The things that they have published only show how weak England and France feel and how fearful they are of the U.N.I.A. If I have no fear of John Brown I would not try to prevent him going to his house. But because they are afraid of John Brown they seek to close the doors of his house against him in the hope that the snow shall fall and that he will be frozen and die. We know the strength of the U.N.I.A. and with the aid of the 400 million Negroes of the world[,] we are going to work on. The damned audacity of it. That a bunch of Anglo-Saxon rapers, villains, scoundrels and felons to stay in Europe and say that we must not go to Africa. Our people saw hell in the cause of France and England. In France and Flanders and in Mesopotamia we died. They saw a hell in the cause of America in the Spanish-American war, and we can see hell in our own cause. Yes, let England know that the 400,000,000 Negroes are determined to redeem Africa, and even though they can use little weak-kneed, fish-bone Presidents to block the cause of Negro freedom, the day is not done.

We are sorry that such a noble character like Chief Justice Dossen is dead. He was a real man. I appreciate a man who will live and die for a principle. Chief Justice Dossen would be alive today, I believe, but when he learned what the Negroes were doing in Monrovia I believe the poor man's heart failed. Because he had received materials already in Cape Palmas as had been arranged to start the colony.[11]

The skunks had not the decency to tell us what they were doing before they published the articles. I despise the man who has not enough decency and respect for his own manhood. You know what politics and government are. Coolidge is not the everlasting President of the United States, and King is not the everlasting president of Liberia.

The U.N.I.A. is going to fight until it helps save Liberia. So that when King passes away, Liberia will still be marching on. It is a fight to the finish. Brother, they were looking for me in 1914 and 1918 and they could not find me, but nobody has to look for me now. The U.N.I.A. can look for me any time the call comes. If these white folks think they can rob, murder and kill everybody and get away with it, they make a big mistake. They have taken advantage of the situation. It is a shame and a disgrace that Edwin Barclay should pen such a letter, after he himself penned the document in 1921 that welcomed the U.N.I.A. to Liberia.[12] And the lying skunk says he did not approve the thing. Coward! What could England do to Liberia in the face of world sentiment at the present time? Could England invade Liberia and live? So help me God, no! There would be more Englishmen dying in the West Indies and all over the world than have died for 1,000 years. It was only a matter of courage. Now I give it out again from Liberty Hall. You cannot fool with the U.N.I.A. It is not an organization; it is the spirit of four hundred million men. It is not a question of whether we are going to Liberia or not, although we are going. It is a question of when black men get ready to do something to win their freedom.

Africa will redeem herself when the time comes. Not from without, but from within. So do not be worried—just stick to your program. Six years ago Marcus Garvey was on the streets on a little soap box, pleading the cause of Africa, and was unknown. Now he has one Secretary of State writing to another begging to suppress the force of this mighty movement.

Please wait awhile. There is going to be some more change. We have the chancelleries of Europe working overtime. All you have to do is to keep up these things. The idea of sending all over the world now to the different consuls not to give passports to certain people. They had to disarrange the whole diplomatic service to carry out that order. Any Negroes who can do that show that they are stepping on the gas.

Keep your organization intact. World changes are going on and all you have to do, even without fighting, is to step on the gas. Where is Rome? She tried to stop the progress of the people. Buried and gone. Just a few years ago Germany could have dictated the policy of certain countries and peoples. Where is she now? Asking for an economic chance. So just keep your organization intact. When you find these things are happening it means that you are nearer the goal. With all the bluff of England and France, were it not for the bad Negroes we would have already had what we wanted. And no notes would have been sent. But wait until these troubles are clear, and I get to England and France. Then you will see something.

When all these things happen don't accuse the people for it. The people of England and France are not to be blamed; nor those of Liberia. It is that group of self-seekers and grafters who are placed to represent them. But when they arouse the sleeping conscience of the people those fellows have either to deliver the goods or get away. It is only a question of time. We are going on with the program, and we are determined to put it over.

We will give them a run for the money. Brother, somebody is crazy if he thinks he can plan to strangle the new Negro; to brutalize and enslave and kill him and leave him still smiling.

What does all this talk of preventing the Negro going to Africa mean? Is it friendship or fellowship? It means that somebody hates the Negro so bad that he does not want to give the Negro a chance to live. Would you call any man who tries to keep you from your home a friend? And when you find out his designs would you greet him with kid gloves? If I have to fight to the end, I would die to prevent his plan going through.

We are up against the survival of the fittest. That is why the late chief justice took his stand. I believe he was the greatest African patriot the world ever produced. But that man realized that the destiny of his country and the life of his race was at stake. You heard reference made by him to the pamphlet that he sent to be reproduced.[13] I thought I was a radical and I thought I loved Africa, and I thought I had something to say about African freedom. In his speech delivered in Liberia in 1915, you will find that nearly everything that we have been doing here was encouched in his remarks.

Such a man is a prince not only of his race, but of his country.

Gentlemen, if you want anything, in time you will win it. Going down on your knees will not win it. But stand your ground and strike back, and, by God, the Negro will strike back. Anyone who thinks that the U.N.I.A. is made up of cowards is mistaken. We have men here who are willing to die for the principles of right and justice and the liberation and emancipation of the 400,000,000 Negroes of the world.

Somebody is crazy. The audacity of these men. We were at our homes 300 years ago and never disturbed anybody. These men stole us away from our homes, kept us in chattel slavery and bondage for 300 years, raped or brutalized us, sapped our life's blood or milked us. And, now that we are ready to go home, they talk about keeping us out of our home. Brothers, we will fight, and, even if the devil in hell tries to prevent us, we will kick him out of hell, in keeping with the popular refrain of the "Blues"—"We are going home, going home." [14]

Three cheers were given for Liberia, and, with cries of ["]down with the traitors of the Negro race!["] the meeting adjourned.

Printed in *NW*, 6 September 1924. Original headlines abbreviated.

1. In April 1924 the Firestone Tire and Rubber Co., searching for new sources of rubber, secured a tentative agreement with the Liberian government to lease one million acres of land for a period of ninety-nine years. The final agreement, negotiated over the next few years, substantially increased Liberia's dependence on foreign-controlled investment. In exchange, Harvey Firestone guaranteed a loan of $5 million to Liberia from the Finance Corp. of America, a subsidiary of Firestone. At first Liberia balked at accepting the stringent loan terms from the Firestone-dominated company, but in 1926 the government agreed to the loan, partly to save the nation from bankruptcy and partly to secure its borders from French and British encroachment by encouraging U.S. investment. Under the terms of the agreement, the Liberian government agreed to grant Firestone the lease of the million acres of land at from five to ten cents per acre. (Frank Chalk, "The Anatomy of an Investment: Firestone's 1927 Loan to Liberia," *Canadian Journal of African Studies* 1, no. 1 [March 1967]: 12–32; Harvey Firestone, in collaboration with Samuel Crowther, *Men and Rubber* [Garden City, N.Y.: Doubleday, Page & Co., 1926], pp. 254–269; Charles Morrow Wilson, *Liberia: Black Africa in Microcosm* [New York: Harper and Row, 1971], pp. 128–139).

2. On 31 March 1924 Garvey wrote a letter to President C.D.B. King, in which he declared, "The other members of the delegation laid before us certain suggestions of the local committee, consisting of the Hons. Arthur Barclay, D. Howard, J.J. Dossen, Dixon Brown and Messrs. W.F. Dennis and D.G. Caranda, which fit in splendidly with the plans of our association, and which we are pleased to adopt, and to inform you of same" (DNA, RG 59, file 882.5511/15). The committee members were prominent Liberians.

3. Most probably these were documents later published in the *Philosophy and Opinions of Marcus Garvey* (pp. 367–380). They include: a letter of 5 December 1923 from Marcus Garvey to Liberian President King introducing the UNIA delegation that arrived in Monrovia on 30 January 1924; the suggestions of the local Liberian committee appointed by President King to advise him on UNIA-

sponsored settlement; the letter of 31 March 1924 to President King, containing Garvey's response to the suggestions of the local Liberian committee; and two letters from J.J. Dossen to Garvey. In the document authored by the local Liberian committee, it was suggested that the committee be empowered to direct and manage UNIA immigration to Liberia as well as to direct the general affairs of the UNIA in Liberia. It also established a nine-point plan to assure successful settlement of black Americans and West Indians in Liberia (*P&O*, 2: 367–380).

4. The only surviving letter that fits this description is Dossen's letter to Garvey of 2 May 1924, wherein Dossen agrees to Garvey's amendments to the plans of the Liberian committee (*P&O*, 2: 378–379).

5. According to a report later presented to the British Foreign Office, President C.D.B. King's father was a "West Indian Negro" who migrated to Sierra Leone and later to Liberia (PRO, FO 371/14658, 30 January 1930).

6. In July 1912 the governments of Germany, France, Great Britain, and the United States, in order to service payments on a loan of $1.7 million to the Liberian government, took legal charge of the Liberian customs receipts. With this 1912 loan, for which the National City Bank of New York was the fiscal agent, Liberia paid off an 1871 loan from British sources, as well as other indebtedness. Funds for the 1912 loan were raised through the floating of bonds. The large majority of these bonds were held in Great Britain, with a sizable block held in the Netherlands and France. Smaller amounts were held in the United States ($200,000) and Germany. Most of the bonds were owned by private holders, though a small amount was held by two banks. In 1922 the outstanding principal on the loan amounted to approximately $1.6 million (U.S. House of Representatives, *Credit for Government of Liberia* [Washington, D.C.: GPO, 1922], pp. 5–26).

7. Donald A. Ross, an employee of the Firestone Corp., arrived in Liberia in December 1923 to investigate the prospects of establishing a rubber plantation. The UNIA delegation, consisting of Henrietta Vinton Davis, Milton Van Lowe, and Robert Poston, did not reach the Liberian capital until 30 January 1924. Firestone was motivated by a new company policy of seeking direct control of its sources of organic rubber, and its particular interest in Liberia had been aroused following the company's failure to secure legislative reforms granting land tenure and labor immigration in the Philippines, matters considered by Firestone to be indispensable for profitable rubber production. Ross encountered an abandoned rubber plantation at Mt. Barclay which had been developed in 1910 by a British firm. The growth, yield, and latex quality of the abandoned trees convinced Ross that Liberia held out a rich potential for rubber production; accordingly, in April 1924 the Firestone Corp. sent out a delegation, including Ross, to begin negotiations with the Liberian government on the granting of extensive land concessions (Harvey S. Firestone in collaboration with Samuel Crowther, *Men and Rubber*, pp. 255–264; Alfred Lief, *The Firestone Story: A History of the Firestone Tire and Rubber Company* [New York: Whittlesey House, McGraw-Hill Book Co., 1951], pp. 150–156; Wayne Chatfield Taylor, *The Firestone Operations in Liberia*, case study 5, National Planning Association series of United States Business Performance Abroad [Washington, D.C.: National Planning Association, 1956], pp. 58–85).

8. The exposure of the brutal conditions of forced labor in the rubber-growing areas of the Congo (Zaire) and Peru by Roger Casement, a British consular official, caused an international scandal in the first decade of the twentieth century. Under the direction of King Leopold of Belgium, the Congo Free State had required Africans to pay a rubber tax, which was delivered each week to the local commissioner. The commissioners paid the chiefs a small amount in cloth and salt, but workers received no wages. Workers who refused to work had a hand or a foot cut off by the rubber sentries. Others were beaten. As supplies of rubber surrounding the villages became exhausted, Africans were forced to search further into the interior, where many died from exposure or starvation. The harsh conditions of the forced labor system resulted in a large number of deaths, which dramatically reduced the population in a number of Congo villages.

In 1909 similar conditions began to come to light in Peru. The rubber-rich area of Putamayo was under virtually complete control of Julio Cesar Arana and his Peruvian Amazon Co. The company had imported guards from Barbados to force Indians to harvest rubber. Indians became actual prisoners of the company, and some were chained together by their necks to prevent their running away. Casement uncovered incidents of Indians being tortured, decapitated, and murdered on the whim of Arana or the guards, while workers of all ages were systematically beaten. Casement's exposure of conditions in both the Congo and Peru was so damning that it was credited with destroying King Leopold's empire in the Congo and Arana's fiefdom in Peru (Brian Inglis, *Roger Casement* [London: Hodder and Stoughton, 1973], pp. 13–107, 169–219; B.L. Reid, *The Lives of Roger Casement* [New Haven, Conn.: Yale University Press, 1976], pp. 35–155).

9. In October 1922 the *Crisis* printed an article entitled "The Press and 'Back to Africa,'" a

series of short selections from press articles on Garvey's repatriation plans. It was not Du Bois who made the allegation but rather Charles Lawton of the *New York Sun*, who stated that the Garvey movement "not only involves the deportation, as it were, of 12,000,000 Negroes from the United States, but also implies the evacuation of Africa by all whites who now reside there" (*Crisis* 24, no. 6 [October 1922]: 273).

10. The *Baltimore Afro-American* printed several stories on the UNIA and Liberia in the weeks preceding the August 1924 convention. These featured increasingly explicit avowals by Liberian officials that UNIA delegations would no longer be received and that UNIA-sponsored immigrants were not welcome. Garvey actually sued the newspaper's agents over an article headlined "Liberia Bars Garvey" in the 20 June 1924 issue, but the court dismissed the suit (*Baltimore Afro-American*, 20 June, 27 June, 25 July, 8 August, and 24 August 1924).

11. There is no evidence indicating that Dossen received the consignment of UNIA goods prior to his death on 17 August 1924. To the contrary, they were due to arrive on 22 August, and in any case, no one representing the UNIA as consignee ever appeared with the bill of lading to claim the merchandise. Eventually the Liberian government confiscated the goods for the payment of custom-warehouse storage charges (*NW*, 20 September 1924; selected correspondence, December 1924 to 13 January 1930, DNA, RG 32, file 605-1-653).

12. No evidence has been found of a letter written in 1921 from Edwin Barclay to Garvey. However, Barclay did write a letter to Elie Garcia of the UNIA on 14 June 1920 which can be construed as a letter of welcome. See *Garvey Papers* 2: 347.

13. In Dossen's letter of 2 May 1924, he referred to his pamphlet "Origin, Rise, and Destiny of Liberia," which, he said, he wanted printed to "serve as a propaganda in your emigration enterprise" (*P&O*, 2: 378).

14. Garvey may have been referring to the chorus of a popular song, "West Indies Blues," written in 1923 by J. Edgar Dowell, Spencer Williams, and Clarence Williams. The song, which described the lament of the West Indian immigrant who wanted to return to his native Jamaica, contained such lyrics as "I'm gonna be a great big 'Mon'/Like my frien' Marcus Garvey" (Edgar Dowell, Spencer Williams, and Clarence Williams, "West Indies Blues," 1923, NNC, Alexander Gumby Collection). It ended with the following refrain:

Gwine home, won't be long

Gwine home, sure's you born,

I'm gwine home, won't be long

'Cause I've got no time to lose.

Gwine home, I can't wait

Gwine home, Mon, I'm late

I'm gwine home, I can't wait

'Cause I've got the West Indies Blues,

Got the West Indies Blues,

Got the West Indies Blues.

The metaphor "going home" was merely one of many examples of movement found in the lyrics of traditional black music and remained an important symbol. As Lawrence Levine notes, "the *idea* of emigration could be as important psychologically as the *fact* of emigration itself" (Lawrence W. Levine, *Black Culture and Black Consciousness* [New York: Oxford University Press, 1977], pp. 264, 261–270).

The songwriting team of Dowell and Williams (probably Clarence Williams, who was also involved in music publishing) composed another Garvey-related song, "The Black Star Line," which Rosa Henderson recorded on the Aeolian label of the Vocalion Co. in 1924. Henderson sings:

I done put my lastest dime

Down on this great steamship.

Lord, I hope that it won't sink,

I wanna take this trip.

These recordings represented a potent combination of talent. Rosa Henderson (1896–1968) was one of the most recorded black female vocalists of the 1920s (*Biographical Dictionary of Afro-American and African Musicians*, comp. Eileen Southern [Westport, Conn.: Greenwood Press, 1982], p. 177). J. Edgar Dowell, described in the *Crusader* as "the talented young colored composer," wrote music for the Mills Publishing House (*Crusader* 4, no. 1 [March 1921]: 23). Clarence Williams (1893–1965) was a prolific songwriter as well as a pianist who accompanied Bessie Smith on some of her Columbia Records blues recordings. Clarence Williams, whose company published "West Indies Blues," later left performing to concentrate on his music publishing business (*NW*, 16 June 1923; *NYT*, 9 November 1965; Leonard Feather, *The New Edition of the Encyclopedia of Jazz* [New York: Horizon Press, 1960], p. 462). Spencer Williams (1889–1965), no relation to Clarence, was a New Orleans-born composer of such noted blues numbers as "Basin Street Blues" and "I Ain't Got Nobody" (*NYT*, 17 July 1965; Feather, *New Edition of the Encyclopedia of Jazz*, p. 464).

Garvey and his enterprises had figured in black popular music prior to "West Indies Blues." In 1920 Andy Razafkeriefo, who as "Andy Razz" later went on to write lyrics for many of Fats Waller's songs, composed "Garvey! Hats off to Garvey" and "U.N.I.A." Razafkeriefo also wrote poetry which appeared in the columns of the *Negro World* and the *Crusader*, and his songs were occasionally featured at Garvey's meetings (*Garvey Papers* 2: 230, 237–238).

"West Indies Blues"

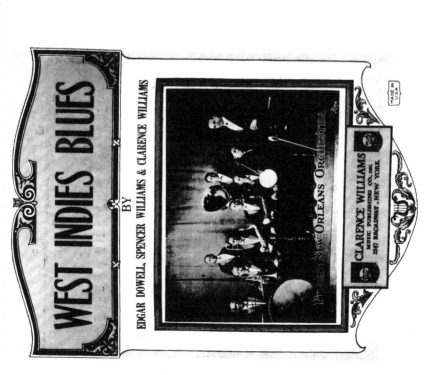

West Indies Blues
(A CALIPSO)

By EDGAR DOWELL
SPENCER WILLIAMS
CLARENCE WILLIAMS
Arranged by Eugene Platzman

Moderato

Got my grip and trunk all packed, Steamship I'm gwine to
Don' give up de best - es' job, A run-aid el - e -

take her, So good-bye good old New York Town, I'm gwine to Ja - mai-ca, When
va - tor, I told my boss Mon' I'd be back Some-time soon or la - ter, When

I git on de ud - der side, I'll hang a - round de wa - ters, I'll
I git back to dis great land, You bet - ter watch me Har - vey, 'Cause

(*Source:* NNC, Alexander Gumby Collection.)

Convention Report

[*New York, 28 August 1924*]

THURSDAY MORNING, AUG. 28

The Convention was called to order at 11 o'clock, the Speaker, Hon. Marcus Garvey, in the Chair. After prayers discussion of the Liberian situation was resumed. . . .[1]

Hon. Milton Van Lowe, adding to his report delivered the previous afternoon, as one of the delegation of three that visited Liberia last fall, stated that the delegation, after the interview with President King, has actually leased a building from the President's stepson to be used as a commissary as suggested by the President's Committee. This was, undoubtedly, with the President's knowledge, and made his subsequent reported acts all the more inexcusable, indefensible and high-handed. He also showed how Dr. Du Bois when visiting Liberia had influenced Mr. Solomon Porter Hood, American Consul at Monrovia, against the U.N.I.A. and, possibly, in favor of the Firestone Company.[2] Hon. Freeman L. Martin, St. Louis, Mo., expressed his conviction that the efforts of the enemy to embarrass the Universal Negro Improvement Association would prove of no avail. Dr. Du Bois, he said, was not a leader; he was "just out in front" in the same way as a dog kept "out in front" of its master though dependent on him for direction as to the road he should take. The world had begun to re[alize] that the U.N.I.A. and Marcus Garvey were no joke and . . . [*words multilated*] in real earnest. The Liberian colonization plans and the . . . [*words mutilated*] brough[t] that home to them. Therefore opposition was expected.

Hon. Dr. J.J. Peters, Chicago, said Negroes were in grim earnest today, and it was well that the world realized that they would allow nothing to stand in the way of their deliverance.

At this stage the Speaker counselled the delegates not to stray from the main point of the discussion, and, while naturally they felt aggrieved, they should be careful in their speech, and say nothing they did not mean or which would embarrass the organization.

Hon. Prof. D.H. Kyle, Clarksburg, W.Va., thought the time had come when a rule should be made that no member of the Universal Negro Improvement Association could at the same time be a member of the N.A.A.C.P. Sir William Sherrill pointed out that after all[,] those who were in control in Liberia were merely holding it in trust for the Negroes of the Western world, and he was confident that any effort on their part to violate that trust would surely lead to their downfall. The same America, which brought the little republic into being, would now see that the raison d'etre was not violated.

Hon. F.E. Johnson, Detroit, next spoke, condemning the attitude of Negroes who sought to oppose the progress of the race, and moved the following motion:

In view of the fact that W.E. Du Bois has continually attempted to obstruct the progress of the Universal Negro Improvement Association to the loss and detriment of the Negro race, and that he has on several occasion[s] gone out of his way to try to defeat the cause of Africa's redemption, that he be proclaimed as ostracized from the Negro race as far as the Universal Negro Improvement Association is concerned, and from henceforth be regarded as an enemy of the black people of the world.

Hon. S.A. Haynes, New York, seconded, and the motion was carried. The convention then adjourned until 3 p.m.

THURSDAY AFTERNOON, AUG. 28

The convention reassembled at 3 p.m., the Speaker, Hon. Marcus Garvey, in the chair.

After prayers, the minutes of the previous session were read and confirmed.

Hon. J. Craigen, Detroit, moved the following resolution:

Be it resolved: (1) That a petition be sent[3] to the Firestone Rubber Company of Akron, Ohio, requesting them not to take advantage of the Negro peoples of the world in accepting the one million acres of land of the republic of Liberia given to them by certain officials of that government, in that Negroes of this western hemisphere are desirous of building up themselves there economically and otherwise and thus show[ing] to the world they are capable of doing for themselves what other races have been able to do for themselves.

(2) Therefore, that this matter of the Liberian colonization be left entirely in the hands of the Administrator, and that the administration go forward diplomatically or in any way they may see fit to put the program over, remembering always that 400,000,000 Negroes stand behind them for the perpetuation of this noble race.

Hon. M. Boyd, New York, seconded, and the motion was unanimously carried.

The Speaker then called upon the Secretary-General, Hon. G.E. Carter, to read certain paragraphs from the constitution of Liberia. The paragraphs were as follows:

Section 12. No person shall be entitled to hold real estate in this republic unless he is a citizen of the same. Nevertheless this article shall not be construed to apply to colonization, missionary, education or other benevolent institutions, so long as the property or estate is applied to its legitimate purpose.

Section 13. The great object of forming these colonies being to provide a home for the dispersed and oppressed children of Africa, and to regenerate and enlighten, this benited continent, none but persons of color shall be admitted to citizenship in this republic.

Section 14. The purchase of any land by any citizen or citizens from the aborigines of this country for his or her own use or for the benefit of others, as estate or estates, in fee simple, shall be considered null and void to all intents and purposes.

Section 15. The improvement of the native tribes and their advancement in the art of agriculture and husbandry being a cherished object of this government, it shall be the duty of the president to appoint in each county some discreet person whose duty it shall be to make regular and periodical tours through the country, for the purpose of calling the attention of the natives to those wholesome branches of industry and of instructing them in the same, and the legislature shall, as soon as it can conveniently be done, ma[k]e provisions for these purposes by the appropriation of money.

Section 16. The existing regulations of the American Colonization Society, in the commonwealth, relative to immigrants, shall remain the same in the republic until regulated by compact between the society and the republic; nevertheless, the legislature shall make no law prohibiting emigration. And it shall be among the duties of the legislature to take measures to arrange the future relations between the American Colonization Society and this republic.

Hon. Fred A. Toote, Philadelphia, next spoke. He read extracts from an address delivered by President King of Liberia in 1920, where, speaking on immigration to Liberia, he pointed [out] the need for new blood from the Western world and stressed the desirability of adding to their population settlers from America who would help in building up the country.[4] He also pointed out that as America thrived by having the open door so must Liberia prosper also. The action of the government of Liberia today, commented the speaker, seemed to be in strange contrast to those dic[t]a. Hon. J.B. Eaton, Hon. S.A. Haynes, and Hon. C.H. Bryant, Costa Rica, also spoke, the last named moving the following motion, which was unanimously carried:

That a protest be sent to the Liberian Senate against the attitude of the government in discriminating in its emigration policy in violation of the spirit of the Constitution of the Republic.

That a petition be sent to the Congress of Liberia asking it not to grant the concessions sought by the Firestone Rubber and Tar [Tire] Company of Ohio, United States, as it is our belief that it would create a condition that would ultimately lead to the destruction of the autonomy of Liberia.

That an appeal be sent to the people of Liberia protesting against the action of the government in preventing the Universal Negro Improvement Association from carrying out its program for the good of the people and the country.

Hon. Bishop McGuire, New York, moved that the administration present a plan tomorrow to the Convention in regard to the situation.

The motion was unanimously carried.

THURSDAY EVENING, AUG. 28

The convention was called to order at 9 p.m., the Speaker, the Hon. Marcus Garvey, in the chair.

After prayers the minutes of the evening session were read and confirmed.

The business before the house was amending the constitution.

Hon. Freeman L. Martin introduced an amendment to section 29a, article 3, providing for a graduated scale of payment of death grants according to the length of membership.

A lengthy discussion ensued and the amendments were rejected on being put to the vote.

The following resolution introduced by Hon. Freeman L. Martin was carried unanimously:

In view of the fact of the multiplicity of suits against the Association and the large sums in judgment obtained against it by unscrupulous persons, and in view of the further fact that the Association has inaugurated a comprehensive and intensive program to realize the great and ultimate aims and objects of the Association and especially the commercial phase of it;

Be it resolved, that it is the sense of the delegates and deputies here assembled that the parent body of the Universal Negro Improvement Association be relieved of its obligations to pay all outstanding death grants to the various members in said Universal Negro Improvement Association by the local division assuming said obligation and adjusting said claim.

The following resolution suggested by the Speaker was unanimously adopted by the house:

That on the death of each member of a local divison an extra tax of 25 cents be levied on each member for the death grant of $75 and that the amount so collected in the local division shall constitute a part of the $75 to be paid by the parent body, and each division shall be taxed according to its last month's report for the return of 25 cents for each member in this local division; and in case it amounts to more than $75 the local division shall pay the death claim and the balance be added to its local treasury, and a report of same sent to the parent body.

Hon. Mary Massie [Massey], Chicago, introduced the following amendments under the heading of "Juveniles," which were unanimously carried.

All children from one to ten years of age may become members of the juvenile department on payment of 25 cents entrance fee and 10 cents per month dues. This shall not entitle a member of the juvenile department to the $75 death grant. This sum shall only be issued to those from 10 years up paying the regular required dues of the association.

No child or children between 1 and 10 years inclusive, shall be required to pay any special or annual tax.

Hon. G. A. Weston introduced a special legislative measure providing for the creation of a patriotic fund as a set budget for development work. The measure was referred to the administration for analysis.

A resolution introduced by Hon. Wilbur J. Roberson, Minister of Legions, providing for the creation of a speaking committee of five to broadcast the program of the U.N.I.A.[,] was unanimously referred to the Education Department.

The following motion amending by addition to Section 54, Article 3, made by Hon. S.A. Haynes, was unanimously carried: "And it shall be compulsory for large divisions, chapters and branches to purchase at least 100 copies and smaller divisions 50 copies of The Negro World weekly, discretionary power being vested in the administration.["]

Hon. W. A. Wallace, Indiana, moved the following motion[,] which was unanimously carried: "That wherever the words 'Black Star Line' occur in the Constitution, the words 'Black Cross Navigation and Trading Company' shall be substituted."

Hon. Col. Wattley, New York[,] introduced a resolution providing for the formation of a regiment to be known as the Universal African Royal Guard, to be stationed at the headquarters of the Universal Negro Improvement Association.

A spirited discussion took place on this measure, which was ultimately tabled on the motion of Hon. Col. Harrigan, by a vote of 67 to 5.

The convention then adjourned.

Printed in *NW*, 6 September 1924. Original headlines abbreviated.

1. The discussion contains a brief description of the geography of Liberia.
2. While Du Bois was in Liberia to attend the inauguration of President C. D. B. King, he accompanied U. S. Minister to Liberia Solomon Porter Hood, along with a rubber expert for the Firestone Rubber Co., on a journey to examine a forest area for possible Firestone investment. Du Bois enthusiastically supported the company's involvement in Liberia and wrote to President King in July 1924 encouraging the acceptance of American investment. In 1925, following the completion of the Firestone agreement with the Liberian government, Du Bois wrote to Firestone, expressing his support for the project. Du Bois said he hoped that Firestone would institute a system of

benevolent capitalism in Liberia and suggested that educated American and Liberian blacks be given prominent positions in the management of the operation.

Du Bois's support for the Firestone Co.'s Liberian role continued for some years. In March 1927 he argued in the *Crisis* that a pending loan by the Finance Corp. of America to Liberia did not involve Firestone; in fact, though, Firestone privately underwrote the agreement. By October of the same year, however, the *Crisis* noted that while it was pleased with Liberia's improved financial position, it was "alarmed at the increasing power and influence of the owners of the Firestone rubber concession," lest it encroach upon "the political independence of Liberia" (*Crisis* 34, no. 8 [October 1927]: 264).

There is no direct evidence that Du Bois influenced Hood's attitude toward the UNIA, but Du Bois's antipathy toward the Garvey movement was well known (Frank Chalk, "Du Bois and Garvey Confront Liberia," *Canadian Journal of African Studies* 1, no. 2 [November 1967]: 135–142; *Crisis* 27, no. 6 [April 1924]: 247–251; 34, no. 1 [March 1927]: 34; Du Bois to Harvey S. Firestone, 26 October 1925, in Herbert Aptheker, ed., *The Correspondence of W.E.B. Du Bois, 1920–1929,* 1: 320–323; see also pp. 260, 282–283; Nancy Kaye Forderhase, "The Plans That Failed: The United States and Liberia, 1920–1935" [Ph.D. diss., University of Missouri, 1971], pp. 55–73).

3. No evidence has been found that the UNIA sent this petition to Firestone.

4. In a portion of his 1920 inaugural address devoted to American immigration to Liberia, President C.D.B. King of Liberia declared:

> While immigration to our country should be carefully handled, so that we may not get an influx at any time of such large numbers of people as we would be unable to absorb into the body politic, yet there can be no doubt as to the desirability of adding to our Americo-Liberian population, settlers from America, who want to come here, and who, if carefully selected and properly aided would help us to build up the country. (C.D.B. King, "First Inaugural, 5 January 1920," in *The Inaugural Addresses of the Presidents of Liberia, From Joseph Jenkins Roberts to William Richard Tolbert, Jr., 1848 to 1976,* comp. and ed. Joseph Saye Guannu [Hicksville, N.Y.: Exposition Press, 1978], p. 252)

Speech by Marcus Garvey

[[*New York,* 28 August 1924]]

MARCUS GARVEY IN CLEAR SPEECH REVEALED THE MOTIVE BEHIND THE RAPE OF THE REPUBLIC OF LIBERIA

THE CONVENTION INFORMED OF THE TRICKS OF DIPLOMACY IN DEPRIVING LIBERIA OF HER FREEDOM

. . . The order of the day is discussing the report of the delegates from Liberia bearing on the arrangements with the Liberian Government and people to colonize that country. You heard the report yesterday from the secretary and from Lady Davis, a member of the delegation, as well as the report of the President-General and the statements of the Hon. Van Richards, chaplain to the Senate of Liberia. Now we are going to discuss it this morning. . . .[1]

The present government consists of a family arrangement. The President is brother-in-law to the Secretary of State, the Secretary of State is brother-in-law to the Attorney-General, the Attorney-General is brother-in-law to the other heads of departments, and so it is a family ring. While the common people of Liberia have been suffering for over one hundred years, nothing has been done to bring the great bulk of the native people, two millions of them, into the pale of Western civilization, which we are seeking to do through the work of the Universal Negro Improvement Association. And the position is this, when we publish, as we published in The Negro World some time in June,[2] our intention of building the first American city on the Cavalla River, the English saw we were in earnest, because the program that we laid out for building on the Cavalla River was on a modern American plan, and they knew well that when American Negroes and West Indian Negroes had gone to Liberia it would be a question of about 25 years when we would have a modern, first-class nation on the West Coast of Africa, proving the Negro's ability for self-government, a thing the great powers do not want.

THE ANGLE OF SELFISHNESS

That is the whole sum and substance of the situation from the international political angle. Then from the angle of selfishness. After we had incurred great expense, so the delegates from Liberia explained, after we had two arrangements with the Liberian officials, one in 1921 welcoming the association into Liberia and signing the document of welcome, the other in 1923, the President of Liberia himself outlining the manner, the method in which we should proceed, appointing his Vice-President as Chairman of the committee that was to perfect the arrangements[,] the Chief Justice of the country, and the Comptroller of Customs, a member of his own cabinet, with some of the most prominent men in the country, after they had outlined the plan under which we should work, they suggested the first group should reach in October, that prior to reaching there we should send out a group of expert men to build homes so that when the people get there they would have homes to live in. We sent away from here in June the first group of experts, six engineers under the direction of a licensed civil engineer of 25 years' experience, working for one of the biggest companies in this country out West. We sent out materials, two shipments of materials, one on the 25th of June and the last on the 25th of July. They accepted the landing of the materials, and then, after doing all that, without an official word to us, they decided to send through the Consul-General such a document to the American Government, as if there was absolutely no understanding.

TREACHERY EXTRAORDINARY

It is the greatest bit of treachery that has happened to the race and that has happened in diplomacy, and, as I said yesterday, the other phase of it is pure graft. You know the Firestone Company of Ohio sent out a group of men after we left there, and those Negroes, King and Barclay, arranged to give to these people one million acres of land. Understand, Liberia is only the size of Ohio, the only independent little country left to the blacks, and to give away, although they [the whites] have eleven and a half million square miles [of Africa] already, another million acres, it is worse than murder. This group of selfish Negroes gave away one million acres of land in violation of the constitution, as we will show you. The constitution of the Republic of Liberia reserves the land of the people of Liberia as a permanent home. The white people have all Europe, all the American continent. They have taken away nearly eleven and two-thirds million square miles of Africa, leaving only a speck of Liberia, and they want that. Where must the Negro live? Where must the Negro live but in the sea as a home?

APPEALING TO WHITE AMERICA

Now we appeal to the conscience of white America because we believe the millions of white people in America will stand behind the principles of the Universal Negro Improvement Association, and I think we should send a petition to Mr. Firestone asking him not to take adva[n]tage of the concessions that these selfish Negroes have given away constitutionally or otherwise, because it is the only hope of the Negroes of this country and of Africa to redeem themselves. And I feel that if we appeal to the conscience of Firestone he will not take advantage of the situation. It is only going to be another outrage like the outrage in Peru. Those poor natives that have not been brought into the pale of civilization and modern arrangements! Going there with a group of men with no intention but exploitation, they will exploit them and work them to death as they did in the Congo and in Peru, because their only purpose is to get the materials and the wealth of the country, and can we allow such a thing to be perpetrated on the race? (Cries of "No.") God Almighty would condemn us for allowing another outrage like the Congo and Peru. You know what King Leopold did in the Congo, and what happened in Peru, and we cannot sit here and allow this outrage to go on; and besides our petition to Coolidge that is to be presented on the 3rd, and to the Congress[,] asking for a thorough investigation of this matter[,] we should send a petition to the Firestone Rubber Company and ask him not to exploit that bit of Africa left [us as our only protection.] (Applause.)

Printed in *NW*, 6 September 1924. Original headlines abbreviated.

1. The omitted material deals with Liberia's history.
2. *NW*, 7 June 1924.

Convention Report

[*New York, 29 August 1924*]

FRIDAY MORNING, AUG. 29

The convention was called to order at 10:30 a.m., the speaker, Hon. Marcus Garvey, in the chair.

After prayers, the minutes of the previous session were read and confirmed.

Hon. W.A. Wallace, Illinois, moved that all financial transactions oc-cur[r]ing between any division and any person visiting that division collecting money therefrom shall be reported to the parent body during the week of said visit or financial transactions, and this shall include officials from headquarters, visiting speakers, or any one receiving money from the division after addressing that division, also that report blanks be made and sent to the local divisions and these report blanks be made out in triplicate, one to be sent to headquarters, one to be kept by the local and one to be given to the officer, and all to be sent by the person or persons receiving such moneys, such reports to be made daily at the close of each meeting.

Hon. J. Craigen, Detroit, seconded, and the motion was unanimously carried. Hon. D.H. Kyle, Clarksburg, W.Va., drew attention to the omission of the State of West Virginia in the list of districts in Sec. 56b, Art. III of the constitution and moved that District 3 be as follows: Maryland, Virginia, West Virginia, and the District of Columbia.

The motion was unanimously carried.

Hon. Mrs. Harvey,[1] Dayton, O., moved:

> Whereas, at present the divisions have no local auditors, and in view of the fact that certain officers of divisions may handle the finance of such divisions to the detriment of its success:

> Be it Resolved, That each local division in the Universal Negro Improvement Association elect an auditor from its membership whose duties it shall be to audit the books of said divisions each and every month and file a copy of this report with the auditor-general of the Universal Negro Improvement Association and a copy of same with the local division, and that such report be forwarded with the monthly report of the secretary of said division.

Hon. G.A. Weston, New York, seconded, and after some discussion the motion was carried. 61 for, 1 against.

Hon. G.A. Weston, New York, then moved the following resolution:

> In view of the fact that there has been coming before the convention from year to year ever since our first convention complaints of men who have gotten into our organization as officials without character, and even community standing, and in

many cases not even with the indorsement of their own divisions, and also causing men and women who have stood the test and paid the price for the cause Afric to be looked upon as dishonest by the delegates attending conventions through the general statements made of crooked men.

Therefore be it resolved, That all persons coming up for appointment and election shall before taking office get a two-thirds majority from his or her division that sent him or her to the convention as to his loyalty, honesty and character as well as his standing in the community, and should any charges be made against his or her honesty and loyalty as well as his character that an investigation be made by the President-General through a committee, and if found true the person be expelled if not those who make the accusati[o]n be in turn expelled from the association.

Hon. R.A. Martin, Florida, Cuba, seconded.
After some discussion the motion was unanimously carried.
Hon. Williams, Hamtramck, Mich., then introduced the following resolution:

Be it resolved, That hereafter no financial member of the N.A.A.C.P. be accepted as a member of the Universal Negro Improvement Association, and in the event of any person or persons joining the Universal Negro Improvement Association are found to be financial members of the N.A.A.C.P., they shall be asked to relinquish membership in the N.A.A.C.P., and in the event of refusal by such person or persons to do so they shall be expelled indefinitely.

After considerable discussion the motion was amended as follows by the Hon. W.S. Vaughn, Youngstown, Ohio, and unanimously carried:

That hereafter no officer of the N.A.A.C.P. shall be accepted as a member of the Universal Negro Improvement Association, and in the event of any such person who may join the Universal Negro Improvement Association being found to be or to have been an officer of the U.N.I.A. [N.A.A.C.P.?] after becoming a . . . [*line missing*] [ex]pelled indefinitely from the association.

The following motion by the Hon. G.E. Carter, Secretary-General, was also unanimously carried: If any member of the U.N.I.A. after becoming a member of the U.N.I.A. shall become a member of the N.A.A.C.P. he shall be expelled.

The following motion was then moved by Hon. Williams, Hamtramck, Mich., and unanimously carried: If any person or persons on joining the U.N.I.A. are found to be members of the N.A.A.C.P., they shall be asked to relinquish membership in the N.A.A.C.P., and upon refusing to do so shall be suspended.

Hon. F.E. Johnson, Detroit, moved that the Universal Negro Political Union be instructed to carry out an intensive campaign in the interests of the civil, political, industrial and social rights of the Negroes of the United States of America, and shall see to the passage of such legislation as shall at all times protect the rights of the race in the United States of America and its possessions.

Hon. Williams, Hamtramck, seconded, and the motion was unanimously carried. The adjourmen[t] was then taken.

FRI[D]AY AFTERNOON, AUGUST 29

The afternoon session began at 3 p.m., with the usual formalities. Hon. Marcus Garvey presided.

On the motion of Bishop McGuire, it was decided the legislative session be continued on Saturday morning in an effort to complete the work of the convention except the winding up meeting on Sunday afternoon.

Hon. Marcus Garvey said his purpose was to report to them his plan for dealing with the Liberian situation. He pointed out, however, that it being a matter of diplomacy, he could not tell them everything and they were to just wait and watch and exercise patience. Before going further, however, he referred to an editorial which appeared in the New York Evening Bulletin of that date,[2] which, written by white men, clearly confirmed his suspicions and the remarks he had made, and even went further. The editorial deserved their attention. It was as follows:

1. Liberia protests against Garvey to President Coolidge.

2. Harvey Firestone, rubber tire king, goes to Plymouth with Edison and Henry Ford and plays a part in the "Old Sap Bucket" drama, enjoying the President's hospitality on the "Colonel's" farm.[3]

3. Liberia grants Harvey Firestone a concession, which gives him absolute control of 1,000,000 acres of land where crude [rubber] is procurable.

This land is the most valuable rubber-growing territory available in the world: the British Empire controls practically all the rest.[4]

Now, get the combination: Liberia and Firestone; Firestone and Coolidge.

Perhaps the old sap bucket is going to be used to carry crude rubber from Liberia to the United States.

When Garvey says there is something rotten in the state of Liberia you should not dismiss his allegations. Perhaps he knows what he is talking about.

He thinks Liberia's rubber supply should belong to his race, not to Firestone.

Is there anything dangerous or menacing in that belief?

In his suggestions, after descanting on the efforts of Negroes to help the white man against Negroes, and after stating that they should have no fear of the future, he told the delegates when they returned to their divisions to advise the people not to lose hope. They were not to make any move before they got instructions from headquarters. Any one who desired to go to Liberia could do so individually at any time, because there was nothing to prevent them, but doing so would be playing into the hands of their enemies and they would be arriving in Liberia, if they went, without any protection, and would be at the mercy of those who did not mean them well. They would be liable to be fooled, robbed or inconvenienced. It was best to go under the protection of the U.N.I.A. and he had no doubt that the matter would be settled satisfactorily according to the program of the association.

In regard to his plans for dealing with the Liberian situation, he urged that their industrial program be pushed as strenuously as possible and that they should concentrate on the shipping proposition, as that would enable them to establish immediate business relations between the United States, the West Indies, Central America, and Africa. The business done and the presence of their ships in those places would considerably hearten the people, and Liberia would soon be willing to ask them to come in. The Negroes would also be urged to furnish their own cargoes and to handle them on arrival here.

At the conclusion, Hon. J. Craigin [Craigen] of Detroit moved that the program as outlined be adopted. This was agreed to.

The convention then went into ways and means of raising the required installments between September 1 and October 15, and it was decided that the members of the executive visit the various divisions and with the aid of the local executives inaugurated a Black Cross drive and so raise the money.

Quotas were decided upon for the various divisions. The President-General also again urged those who had taken out loans to complete their payments, and urged upon those who had not taken loans to do so.

Some of the members urged taxation of individual members and the taking of donations from those who were not able to subscribe for large amounts. While gifts were acceptable, it was decided that it was best to give the people something for their money rather than merely seeking gifts. Taxation would bring little result in the end.

After attention to several matters of minor importance the meeting was adjourned.

FRIDAY EVENING, AUGUST 29, 1924

The Convention resumed at 9 o'clock this evening[,] Hon. Marcus Garvey presiding as Speaker in Convention. After the usual preliminaries, the minutes of the morning and afternoon sessions were read and on motion duly made and seconded, were adopted.

The Chair announced as the order of the day the election of elective officers and appointing of appointive officers for the next four years administration of the Universal Negro Improvement Association. The elective positions, he stated, were: President-General and Administrator, First Assistant President-General, Second Assistant President-General, Third Assistant President-General and Fourth Assistant President-General. The appointive positions were: Secretary-General, Second Assistant Secretary-General, Minister of Education, Chaplain General, Surgeon General, Counsel General and International Organizer. He called attention to the fact that the Convention had decided at a previous session that the offices of Surgeon General, International Organizer, and Chaplain General would be honorary positions to be filled conveniently, and also that the positions of Minister of Education, and Counsel General should also be filled conveniently. The speaker pointed out the importance of the office of First Assistant President-General and added that this position had remained vacant since 1923 because of the desire of the Administration not to place there some one who do[es] the organization more injury than good. He warned the Convention against electing to that office any other than a most thoroughly competent and experienced man, inasmuch as the organization had reached the stage where there was a great deal at stake in money and property, and where they could not afford to experiment as they did in 1920, 1921 and 1923 [1922?]. He requested the most sober and careful thought in the selection of a choice for First Assistant President-General and an intelligent choice of persons for the other elective offices. He then declared the offices of the Executive Council of the Association vacant and threw the meeting open for nominations.

Hon. Dr. J.J. Peters, Chicago, expressed the feeling that the outgoing officers of the Executive Council were persons who were striving hard to make good in many instances. Their personality and character could not be questioned, and they had been tried and tested. He, therefore, moved that the entire personnel of the Executive Council be re-elected by acclamation.

Hon. S.V. Robertson, of Mississippi [Louisiana?], seconded the motion.

The constitutionality of Dr. Peters' motion was questioned, and on its being pointed out by the Speaker that such a re-election was contrary to the Constitution, Hon. Bishop McGuire moved that the Secretary cast one unanimous vote for Hon. Marcus Garvey as President-General for the ensuing term of four years.

The motion was seconded by Hon. Mr. Ellenburg [Ellenberg] and carried unanimously. The Secretary accordingly cast a unanimous vote and Hon. Marcus Garvey was re-elected President-General and Administrator amidst scenes of the greatest enthusiasm.

Mr. Garvey thanked the convention for the renewed responsibility they had imposed on him, and promised that he would continue, to the best of his ability, to serve in the future as he had served in the past.

The office of First Assistant President-General then engaged the attention of the convention. It was the unanimous feeling of the convention that the office should be left vacant until such time as the Administration found a capable man who would measure up in character, integrity and loyalty, to fill the position, and on the motion of Hon. V. Plummer, seconded by Hon. Mr. Johnson, Detroit, the office of First Assistant President-General was left vacant.

The convention then proceeded to elect officers for the remaining positions on the Executive Council, and the following were re-elected with acclamation by one unanimous vote cast by the Secretary: Hon. William Sherrill, Second Assistant President-General and Titular Leader of American Negroes; Hon. Rudolph E. Smith, Third Assistant President-General and Titular Leader of Negroes of the West Indies, South and Central America and Lady Henrietta Vinton Davis, Fourth Assistant President-General.

The newly-elected officers each returned thanks for the honor conferred on them and promised loyal and faithful service to the best of their ability.

The President-General then proceeded to make appointments to the appointive offices. In doing so he asked the approval of the convention of the persons selected by him. The following were appointed and unanimously approved by the convention:

Sir Clifford Bourne, Chancellor; Sir Levi Lord, Auditor General; Sir James O'Meally, High Commissioner General; Hon. G.E. Carter, Secretary-General; Hon. Percival Burrows, First Assistant Secretary-General; Hon. Wilmer [Wilbur] Roberson, Minister of Legions; Hon. N.G. Thomas, Second Assistant Secretary-General; Hon. Freeman L. Martin, Counsel General; Hon. James Hassell, Minister of Labor and Industry.

By unanimous vote the convention created the position of secretary to the President-General as one of the appointive positions and authorized the President-General to make the appointment at his convenience and to use his own discretion in fixing the salary.

On motion of Hon. William Sherrill, seconded by Hon. Mr. Jackson, of New Orleans, a rising vote of thanks was accorded to Hon. Bishop Geo. McGuire for the splendid services he had rendered the convention. Bishop McGuire, in an appropriate address, acknowledged the vote of thanks, which, he said, he appreciated more than if he had [been] given a certified check for $1,000. He alluded with regret to the one mistake he had made during the years that he had been a member of the organization—namely, getting mad and telling the President-General he was going to leave the organization—but that he had made amends eighteen months later, when the New York local sent him a notice as a member by paying up his arrears and assessments for two years.

Hon. Marcus Garvey at this stage made a public denial of the charge laid against Hon. Vinton Plummer by a former member of the organization of disloyalty to him. He took occasion to state that during his incarceration Mr. Plummer had rendered him loyal and faithful service, which he highly appreciated and for which he had always maintain[ed] a great deal of attachment and respect for him.

On motion of Hon. J. B. Yearwood, a rising vote of thanks was accorded to the New York local for the courtesies and hospitality extended the delegates and deputies to the convention during the month.

The vote of thanks was acknowledged by Bishop McGuire and Hon. Geo. Weston, First Vice-President of the New York local.

Hon. Bishop Geo. McGuire moved a rising vote of thanks to the speaker in convention for the faithful and indefatigable services rendered so earnestly and successfully during the thirty-one days of the convention, and also to the secretary, N. G. Thomas, for his excellent services in preparing and rendering the minutes of the sessions. The vote of thanks was passed with acclamation.

Hon. Marcus Garvey in returning thanks expressed his appreciation of the help and co-operation he had received from the delegates and deputies without which he could not have successfully presided over the convention. It was noteworthy, he said, that we were able to conduct a convention for 29 or 30 days without even finding it necessary to appoint a sergeant-at-arms or any one else to keep order, notwithstanding the fact that the delegates and deputies came from different parts of the world—the South meeting the East, the East meeting the West, the West meeting the North, the man from Barbados meeting the man from Jamaica. It showed that the Negro was getting there and if we can mob[i]lize the 400,000,000 of us all over the world after the example of our efforts here in the last 30 days, we will have one glorious victory for Africa and for the race.

Hon. N. G. Thomas suitably acknowledged the vote of thanks accorded him.

Hon. Marcus Garvey then afforded some of the delegates and deputies the opportunity to address the convention in view of the fact that their labors would close on the following day and they would be departing for their respective homes.

The following delegates and deputies made brief parting addresses: Hon. F. E. Johnson, Detroit; Hon. William Ware, Cincinnati; Hon. C. Jackson, New Orleans; Hon. J. B. Eaton, Virginia; Hon. J.[I.] Chambers, New Orleans; Hon. Mrs. De Mena, Chicago; Hon. W. S. Vaughn, Youngstown; Hon. Mr. Green, Jacksonville, Fla.; Hon. R. [H.] Bachelor, Cuba; Hon. Mrs. O'Brien, Montreal, Canada; Hon. A. G. Ellenb[e]rg, Gary, Ind.; Hon. J. Craigen, Detroit; Hon. Prof. D. H. Kyle, West Virginia.

They all spoke in a very happy vein, expressing their joy at the inspiration they had received during their whole month and the stimulus given them to return to their respective divisions filled with a greater love for the organization and with stronger determination to put over the program of the Universal Negro Improvement Association.

The convention then adjourned till 10 o'clock next day, Saturday, Aug. 30.

Printed in *NW*, 6 September 1924. Original headlines abbreviated.

1. Cecilia Harvey of Dayton, Ohio, was her chapter's first lady vice-president (*NW*, 2 June 1923).

2. The editorial referred to, dated 29 August 1924, is reprinted in Amy Jacques Garvey, *Garvey and Garveyism* [Kingston, Jamaica: United Printers, 1963], p. 155. No copies of the *New York Evening Bulletin* for that day have been located.

3. On 19 August 1924 President Coolidge entertained Henry Ford, Thomas A. Edison, and Harvey Firestone at his family's homestead in Plymouth, Vt. Coolidge gave Ford a gift, a maple sap bucket made about 1780 by the president's great-great-grandfather. Ford reportedly responded with the comment, "I never received anything since I got Mrs. Ford that I appreciated so much" (*NYT*, 20 August 1924). The textual reference to the "colonel" is to the president's father, John Coolidge, whose title was purely honorific. The white-owned *New York Evening Bulletin* was noted for its favorable treatment of Garvey. Its editorial remarks on Garvey's arrest in 1925 were said to be "the fairest and most sympathetic sentiment of them all" (*Spokesman* 1, no. 4 [March 1925]: 32). Amy Jacques Garvey also commented favorably on the paper's editorial policy in her memoirs (see *Garvey and Garveyism*, p. 159).

4. In 1922 the Federated Malay States and other British sources produced 67 percent of the world's crude rubber. To halt wildly fluctuating world rubber prices, the British government and planters inaugurated the Stevenson Plan as a means of raising the price of rubber artificially by reducing the quantity of rubber exported from the British colonies. The Stevenson Plan was very successful, but as a result, rubber producers in Java, Sumatra, and Borneo greatly expanded production. When the Stevenson Plan went into effect, the Dutch produced only 16 percent of the world's rubber supply, but in 1927 they were supplying 38 percent of the world market, while the British share had dropped to 52 percent. In these circumstances, the British terminated the Stevenson Plan at the end of 1928 (Frank Chalk, "The Anatomy of an Investment: Firestone's 1927 Loan to Liberia," *Canadian Journal of African Studies* 1, no. 1 [March 1967]: 13–15; Wayne Chatfield Taylor, *The Firestone Operations in Liberia*, case study 5, National Planning Association series, U.S. Business Performance Abroad [Washington, D.C.: National Planning Association, 1956], pp. 42–47).

Convention Announcement

THE END OF A PERFECT CONVENTION

SPECIAL DEMONSTRATION OF NEGRO UNITY WILL MARK THE CLOSING SCENE OF THE FOURTH ANNUAL INTERNATIONAL CONVENTION OF NEGRO PEOPLES OF THE WORLD

————AT————

CARNEGIE HALL

57th STREET and Seventh Avenue, NEW YORK

SUNDAY AFTERNOON, AUGUST 31

AT 3 O'CLOCK SHARP

Brilliant Array of Speakers

High Class Musical Program

Exhibition of Rolls of Petitions of Four Million Signatures of American Negroes Petitioning President Coolidge and Congress for Support to Establish a Government for Negroes.

Come and See the Delegation That Will Leave for Washington to Present the Petition

COME AND HEAR

MARCUS GARVEY

IN HIS GREATEST SPEECH

ADMISSION   FREE

(*Source*: *NW*, 30 August 1924.)

Convention Reports

[[CARNEGIE HALL, New York,
Sunday Afternoon, Aug. 31, 1924]]

. . . At the conclusion of the musical program, Hon. Marcus Garvey said: We are assembled here this afternoon for a two-fold purpose—to bring to a close the Fourth International Convention of Negroes of the World that has been in session for 31 days and nights. We are to officially say good-bye to you, the delegates and deputies representing the Negro peoples in the different parts of the world who were gathered together in this great City of New York to legislate for the future good of 400,000,000 Negroes. You have done your work well; you have written another chapter in the history of our race.

From all sides we have heard it said that this Fourth Convention has ecl[i]psed all the other conventions held by the Universal Negro Improvement Assn. It is said that we are about to separate to return to our respective places, but we are also glad because we will take back with us the new light which will guide Ethiopia on the way to destiny.

Then again, we are assembled to pay our respects to the memory of a stalwart son of Africa, a prince of Africa, who has fallen on the way in the person of the late Chief Justice of Liberia, Hon. J.J. Dossen, a member of our organization, a friend and co-worker, an advocate whom we could ill afford to lose just at this time; the man who was to receive our first group of colonists; the man who during the last two months has been making the greatest preparations possible for the welcoming to Liberia of the first group of colonists who should have sailed away from New York between September and October. Nevertheless, in spirit[,] Dossen of Liberia is not dead. We will hear something about him this afternoon from those who have come in close contact with him and from one who is closely related to him. He was the greatest man of Liberia of this time and of this age. He was a man of far vision; he was a man who dreamt of and who saw before him the redemption of Africa. So that the second part of this meeting will be turned into a memorial meeting in his honor.

COMPLIMENTING THE DELEGATES

I have to compliment you the delegates and deputies and members of the Universal Negro Improvement Association for the splendid work you have done, irrespective of race or of people. No race or any people could have conducted themselves with greater propriety than you had in your convention during the entire month of August. We have read of conventions; we have heard of conventions. We have read of the Republican Convention; we have read of the Socialist Convention; we have read of the Democratic Convention; we have read of conventions of different organizations and fraternities, like the Knights of Columbus, the Masons, and so forth; but in modern times I hardly believe that the convention you held during this month of August has any parallel because you were able, thousands of you, to conduct your affairs every day and every night of this month without even appointing in your midst a sergeant-at-arms to keep order—something the Democrat[s] couldn't do in their convention; something that the Republicans couldn't do, and for the whole month we never had to call the policeman or anyone else to restore order. It shows that the Negro is nearly where he should be—the leader of the world in decency, in character making, in decorum; and if the world give[s] us a chance we will show them how to run the world. (Applause.) We will show that men can live together without killing each other, without fighting each other and without being unfair. We never heard a complaint on the convention floor against any delegate or deputy, and we adjourned yesterday everybody feeling satisfied, everybody feeling that he was fairly dealt with; and that is an object lesson not only for Democrats, for Republicans and other white[s] and other races of the world to follow the lead of the Negro for decency. . . .

PRINCE OF DAHOMEY SPEAKS

Hon. Marcus Garvey then introduced as the next speaker His Highness Prince Kojo Tovalon Hobenou [Tovalou-Houénou], Prince of Dahomey. His Highness the Prince of Dahomey said: In appearing at the Fourth International Convention of the Negro Peoples of the World, under the auspices of the U.N.I.A., I brought you the greetings and salutations of Africa. Now, at its adjournment, I reiterate to you Africa's farewell.

The U.N.I.A. has one supreme object, and that is Africa and its redemption. I do not know in detail the proceedings of the convention, but I know sufficient of its work in its various sessions to make all hearts vibrate in unison and solidarize or consolidate our efforts for this great objective—the redemption of Africa.

The problem of the race in toto is not national, but international. At the meeting of the League of Nations in Geneva the late President Wilson forgot one thing, and that was to take into consideration the problem of the races. For him it was an acute problem, a gordi[a]n knot that could not be severed. At Geneva we also want and must have our place, so that we can seek to have our own, and Africa, the cradle of the black race, will in [the] course of time have her own government and the world at large will realize that Africans are capable of their own government and will be welcomed in the concert of nations.

You have chosen as your haven or port of landing that portion of Africa called Liberia. And, as its name indicates, it symbolizes and stands for liberty. And all other parts of Africa await you, and you shall be thither guided, not by a little star of night, but thither shall your path be guided by the great sun which illuminates all Africa.

What I have heard and seen I shall take back to my people, and next year, when I shall visit Liberia during my tours in Africa, I shall have the pleasure of saluting those of you who shall be in Liberia. Other parts of Africa are awaiting you to give you a favorable and warm welcome. You are the elite of this race of ours; you will bring to the shores of Africa, our motherland, your Western civilization; you will bring to your brothers in Africa the arts and industries of the world in which you are living; you will bring all the education and morality and all that you have learned and all that you now possess you will bring over, and there shall be a fusion and community of ideas and spirit in our great motherland, Africa.

Deputies and delegates, I charge you in returning home not to forget Africa—Africa that for thirty-one days you have had before you; and this convention shows how much you have always held Africa in high esteem. Therefore I urge that you forget her not on your return home.

In conclusion, I reiterate my thanks to you, and I thank you especially for all that I have seen, for all the great spectacles or manifestations that you have made. Today I wish you a sacred and solemn farewell, and tomorrow it will be in Africa. (Applause.)

PETITION TO THE PRESIDENT OF UNITED STATES

Hon. Marcus Garvey then said that one of the things done at the convention was to appoint a committee of seven citizens to interview the President of the United States of America and present to him and later to the Congress of the United States a petition signed by the 4,000,000 members of the Universal Negro Improvement Association in America, asking for their co-operation and help in assisting the association to establish for the Negroes in this country a nation of their own in Africa, and to ask him to send a message to the next Congress asking for the same thing. A petition is also to be presented to the next Congress of the United States. The members of the committee would take the petitions away on Monday to meet the President in Washington on the 3rd, and deliver the petition from the four million members of the Universal Negro Improvement Association in the United States of America. You will understand, said he, that the U.N.I.A. is not an organization on paper; it is an organization in fact; we are going to the President with the actual signatures of four million black men and women, citizens of the United States of America, asking for what they want. They are from every State of the union, and they give the lie to the National Association for the Advancement of Colored People, to Fred R. Moore and George Harris[,] that this organization is made up of West Indians. You haven't four million West Indians in America. Then we have another petition signed by seven million African and West Indian citizens to be sent to the Parliament and the King of England, and to the President and House [of] Deputies in France.

MEMORIAL TO THE LATE CHIEF JUSTICE DOSSEN

Hon. Marcus Garvey then announced that the remainder of the meeting would be devoted to a memorial for the late Chief Justice Dossen, of Liberia, who passed away on August 17. The memorial opened with the singing of the hymn "Nearer, My God, to Thee."

LADY DAVIS'S EULOGY

Lady Davis was called upon to deliver an eulogy on the late Chief Justice and said:

It is my painful duty this afternoon to speak of the death in Africa of a mighty man, Chief Justice J.J. Dossen. On the 17th day of August, 1924, at Cape Palmas in Liberia, on the Cavalla River, there passed away this giant intellect; this wonderful leader of men, this great influence in the U.N.I.A. in the Republic of Liberia. His loss was irreparable. In looking over the leaders of our race I can find no one that can fill the unique position that Chief Justice Dossen did. In reading Frederick Starr's book on Liberia one finds this narration from the American Consul Ellis concerning Chief Justice Dossen, of Vice President Dossen, and he was Vice President during the second term of President A. Barclay and Chief Justice of the Supreme Court. ["]He is a man of magnificent physique and splendid intellectual powers, aggressive and proud in spirit, ready and forcible in language, who has enjoyed a useful public record. For ten years he was associate justice of the Supreme Court and compiled the publication of the Supreme Court decisions. He served as envoy extraordinary to France and to the United States and now presides with becoming dignity over the deliberations of the Liber[i]an Senate. It was a matter of disappointment to us, that we were unable to meet J.J. Dossen in Liberia. He is certainly one of the best men in Liberia and in the public life of the country much is still expected of him."[1]

This was published in 1913 by an American white man, Frederick Starr,[2] who visited Liberia and has written this book upon Liberia.

During the recent visit of the delegation to Liberia in the interests of the U.N.I.A.[,] it was our great pleasure every day during our stay in Monrovia to be in the company of Chief Justice Dossen. It was a privilege, I assure you, to hear this man converse, and especially when it was upon the topic of Liberia and the freedom and redemption of Africa. It was Chief Justice Dossen who saw the vision not only of the redemption of Africa, but of the founding of a nation in Africa that should be known as the United States of Africa. A wonderful man[,] words fail me that I should praise him. As I have said, he was a giant among men. He stood as an outstanding character of all West Africa; for his great humanitarism, for his great love of race, and when we think of the National Anthem of Liberia as it was sung upon our reception in Liberia, [we think of?] Judge Dossen in the beautiful anthem whose words are:

All hail, Liberia hail! This glorious land of Liberty shall long be ours.
Though new her name, green be her fame and mighty be her powers.
In joy and gladness with our hearts united,

We'll shout the freedom of a race benighted.
Long live Liberia, happy land,
The home of glorious liberty by God's command.
All hail, Liberia, in union strong success is sure[,]
We cannot fail.
With God above our rights to prove, we will the world assail.
With heart and hand our country's cause defending,
We'll meet the foe with valor unpretending,
Long live Liberia, happy land,
The home of glorious liberty by God's command.

That was the spirit of the Chief Justice. And that which has gone before us is his spirit. His heart is with us this afternoon, I am sure. His spirit will guard and guide the purpose of the U.N.I.A. He passed away upon the natal day of our great and noble leader, Marcus Garvey. On August 17, God called J.J. Dossen from this world to the world above, but Marcus Garvey is here, vivified by the spirit of J.J. Dossen, and we look [t]o him to carry on the fight for the redemption of the Negro.

May the spirit of J.J. Dossen envelop and permeate the very soul of Marcus Garvey, that he too, a giant among the Negroes of the world, the leader of four hundred million Negroes, that ere he joins that innumerable caravan, he shall redeem Africa and establish the vision of J.J. Dossen for the United States of Africa, the greatest republic on the face of the globe.

All honor, all praise, all glory, to the life of J.J. Dossen.

Rev. J. Van Richards said: A prince and a great man has fallen in Liberia. There are but three persons in this great assembly that ever met and became acquainted with the Hon. J.J. Dossen. They are Hon. G.O. Mar[ke], Lady Davis and J. Van Lowe. Therefore you cannot enter so deeply into sympathy on this occasion, because you are not acquainted with the personality of this man.

But I want to repeat that a great man and a prince has fallen in Liberia. The Hon. J.J. Dossen was born in County Maryland about 1866, and he was educated in Liberia. He was a man of deep learning and an able scholar. He held many local positions in the County of Maryland, and by reason of his intellectual ability and love of race and country the government reached out for this noble son, and he was for a number of years a member of the national legislature. He was vice-president for eight years during the administration of President Barclay, was associate judge of the Supreme Court for ten years, and would have been president of Liberia but for political tricks.

For 13 years he was Chief Justice. A dignified man he was. A noble spirit, his height was about 7 feet, beautiful in stature, a beautiful gait and lofty look, yet not too proud. He filled the position of Chief Justice with honor and with credit to himself and the Republic of Liberia. In his death Liberia has lost one of its noblest sons; one of its greatest jurists, a lover of his race; a man of large vision and a man of great and noble spirit. He was not a man with narrow mind and small hearted, and he not only loved his country, but the black race and the U.N.I.A. Before I came to know Hon. Marcus Garvey, Chief Justice Dossen had often spoken to me of him, and on the morning I was leaving Monrovia for America he said to me to be sure to see Mr. Garvey because he is a great man. In a letter I recently received he said Garvey is a great man. That is one great man speaking of another.

The U.N.I.A. has lost in Liberia a sincere friend, a strong defender and a mighty champion. If he had been in Monrovia, what happened to the delegation would not have taken place. You heard the letters read which breathed the spirit of love for the U.N.I.A. They showed how great was his heart and how great was his zeal for the development of Liberia through this great movement. Overcome by human weakness you are led to ask why was this man, so learned, a man so useful to his country and to his family and friends, so zealous for the defense of his race, smitten down by the hand of death? But his life work was ended, his mission accomplished, and the Lord who gave was pleased to take him.

I recall the morning of March 26, when I left his home and shook his hands as he said bon voyage, it did not seem to me that I would never see him in life again. I have to give the Hon. Marcus Garvey praise for having given me the information, and I have written to his wife as to the news of his death and to the fact that Liberty Hall had been put in mourning and that there would be a memorial service held in his honor. I am sure that his wife will be glad of that. We were surprised when a cable sent to Cape [P]almas was not answered and was returned undelivered, and that when a cable was sent to Monrovia the reply came that the Chief Justice was dead. He did not live to see Marcus Garvey. I had the pleasure of seeing him. He did not attend the Convention, but I had the opportunity to do so. I can assure you, however, that God, who stands back of the association, will send some one to take the place of Dossen as sure as He liveth.

Printed in *NW*, 6 September 1924.

1. Frederick Starr, *Liberia* [Chicago: n.p., 1913], p. 99.
2. Frederick Starr (1858–1933), American anthropologist and author, was a professor at the University of Chicago, as well as curator of the University's Walker Museum. Starr did fieldwork in the Philippines, Japan, and Korea, as well as Liberia (*WWWA*; *NCAB*; *NYT*, 15 August 1933).

[[LIBERTY HALL, New York,
Sunday Night, Aug. 31, 1924]]

RELIGIOUS CEREMONY AT LIBERTY HALL
THAT CORRECTS MISTAKE OF CENTURIES
AND BRACES THE NEGRO

The curtain fell on the final scene of the Fourth International Convention of Negroes of the World with a unique ceremony in the form of divine service for the canonization of the Lord Jesus Christ as the Black Man of Sorrows, and also the canonization of the Blessed Virgin Mary as a black woman. The hall was crowded to capacity and the vast audience participated with reverence and devotion in the ceremonies which were solemn and impressive in character. His grace the most Rev. Sir George A. McGuire, K.C.O.N. [Knight Commander of the Nile], lord primate of the African Orthodox Church, was scheduled to officiate at the service, but while in the act of delivering a masterful sermon, fell ill, being overcome by the excessive heat and his place was taken by Father Holinseed, canon of St. Simon Church. . . .

Hon. Marcus Garvey said: The occasion on which we are assembled tonight is a sacred and holy one. In keeping with the commands of the Fourth International Convention of Negroes of the world, we have created to ourselves a new ideal and a new purpose, the ideal of realizing and knowing the truth. The truth that will set us free. The convention, believing that education is one of the greatest weapons that you can place in the hands of the people for their emancipation, for their freedom and emancipation, decided that we would convey to the 400,000,000 Negroes of the world a new program of self-consciousness; a new ideal by which they should lift themselves to a higher life and to a higher purpose, and in keeping with this most solemn declaration the convention is here assembled tonight in the act of the canonization of the Virgin mother as a woman of the Negro race, and the canonization of the Man of Sorrows, Jesus, the Christ, as a man of our race. I am only sorry that the Bishop, who had prepared a theological treatise on the matter, could not conclude because of the terrible taxation of the heat, but I felt sure that with what has been discussed before and the explanation that he has given and with the explanation of Bishop Barber, the canonization services that we have carried through mark a new epoch in the history of this great race of ours. We have been over 300 years in exile, been educated under false and misdirected leadership. Today we rise[,] a new people with a new ideal and with a new purpose. I feel sure that this service that we have celebrated here today will mark an eventful part in the history of the U.N.I.A. and of the Negroes of the world. Assembled as we are from different parts of the world we have come [in]to contact with different ideals and teachings, by different kinds of people, of different races and nations, we are glad indeed that we have come at this hour under an ideal of our own creation. You will understand that the U.N.I.A. in its convention has not as yet been repeated by those who criticize whatsoever we do, created a new God. There is but one God—God, the Father, God[,] the Son and God, the Holy Ghost. But as that God through his own spiritual inspiration has protected us, that through Him we see ourselves, we of the U.N.I.A. have elected to see God Almighty through our own creation. We believe that that great God shall be for all time the God of the children of Ethiopia. God, who had led us out of the tribulations, the trials and the troubles of all kinds, that God we have elected to be our leader, to lead us toward his own prophe[c]y that princes shall come out of Egypt and Ethiopia shall stretch forth her hands unto Him.

TAKE BACK THE RIGHT TEACHING

At this hour as we are about to return to our different places I feel sure that you will take back the inspiration and the right teaching and the right doctrines of the U.N.I.A., the doctrine of the Fatherhood of God and the Brotherhood of Man. Take back to your respective places the new ideal that you are to see God through the physical form of man; let your God be as your image in as much as he made you in his own likeness, and so tonight in our worship we bow to that Man of Sorrow who nearly two thousand years ago gave up his life on Calvary's cross for the spiritual redemption of the human race and as was so beautifully pointed out in the convention during the discussion that why the Man of Sorrow was crucified on Calvary and was not wanted, was simply because he was not of the race that looked for a Savior and a Messiah. It was because the Savior was a representative of this race of ours why the world rejected him, and up to now the true history of this matter is not known.

We are glad that we are privileged at this time to realize the oneness of this race of ours, for the defense of the Savior who died nearly 2,000 years ago on Calvary's cross. That same God, that same Christ[,] that same son of man who died for us, is the same son of man and Christ who leads the U.N.I.A. at this hour, to whom we bow in adoration[,] in worship and in sacred praise, for the manifold gifts and blessings bestowed upon this race of ours.

And as we honor the Son so we honor the mother. As the two bishops pointed out to you during the discussion in the convention, that there was a direct line between the Virgin Mary and this race of ours running back for hundreds and thousands of years, I am sorry that the good Bishop was unable to reach that point in his address tonight. But let us know the truth and let the truth stay with us as we are going forth with a new determination, with a new spirit to see the world as the world sees us.

And so when we worship le[t] us understand we are worshipping that one God, the everlasting God, the Father of all truth, the Father of all time, the Father of all ages, that Father who sent His only begotten Son to the world to redeem fallen mankind. That Savior whom the world, the world of other races, sought to dishonor, to despise, to disgrace and ultimately crucify, the Christ of our race who in His mortal agony in endeavoring to climb the heights of Calvary was spurned by all mankind, was spat upon by Jew and Roman, was spat upon by every other member of the human race, was ridiculed by every other member of the human race, until another brother of his race in the person of Simon, the Cyrenian, came to his rescue, took the cross and bore it up the heights. As Simon, the Cyrenian, bore the cross of Jesus up the height of Calvary, so at this hour 400,000,000 Negroes are still struggling under the other cross of Calvary, and as we helped our elder brother up the heights of Calvary, so that elder brother, who is now sitting at the right hand of God Almighty, God the Father, will come to our rescue as Simon did and help us to bear the cross up the heights of African redemption.

KINGDOM COMING NEW

So let us in all spiritual devotion and confidence bow before the Almighty God, that God of all races, that God of all men, God the Creator of the universe and all the worlds therein. Let us never forsake Him, let us never forget Him, and when we pray[,] do not forget to say, "Our Father, Who Art in heaven, hallowed be Thy name; Thy kingdom come." For indeed his Kingdom shall come. It is coming now. It is coming in the stretching out of Ethiopia's hand as He himself to the psalmist prophesied, and not even the legions of the darker world can stop the onward march of Ethiopia's children toward the point of destiny. God bless us, the Lord Jesus Christ be with us, the Virgin Mary be our suppliant at the footstool of God the Father, God the Son and God the Holy Ghost to pray for a safe passage for the children of Ethiopia in exile that they may one day safely under His wings return to their own vine and fig tree.

Africa is calling at this hour, calling from every quarter of the globe, calling from the East, calling from the West, calling from the North and calling from the South; and, gathered as we are in this Fourth International Convention of Negroes, so are we answering the call of Mother Africa: "We are coming, we are coming, 400,000,000 of us are coming, with Jesus Christ as our standard-bearer and God Almighty, God the eternal Father, God the creator of all, as our spiritual and divine Director. To Him we bow always in obedience and not to man.["]

Mistake not the purpose of this meeting. We are not canonizing an individual in physical form. We are not lifting to [the] height of a deity or sainthood any physical individual, but we are lifting to the height of sainthood and deity the spiri[t]ual individuals in the person of Mary, the mother of God, and Jesus the Christ, the Son of God. They are those whom others have seen fit to sanctify. The Catholic Church, through its right to apostolic succession, has lifted Him from the cross to the heights of heaven. Him the Christian world honors, whether Protestant or Catholic. Them we honor tonight in our own race, as others do honor to them in their race, seeing them through their own likeness and seeing them through their own image. And so we shall no longer make the mistake of worshipping false images and false idealisms. He Himself said: "Thou shalt not worship any other God but Me; thou shalt not bow down to graven images or any other likeness but Mine."[1] And when He Himself had declared that man was created in his own image and likeness, if you were to give your God and your spiritual master a form, He could have no other form but that in which you were created by Him.

NO NEW CREATION

Man is God's masterpiece; man is God's handiwork and if we are created in the likeness and image of our God, it is indisputable that our God in physical form must naturally look like us; but there is no God in the physical sense; there is a God in the spiritual sense, and every one is part of the spiritual God, that God who is no respector of persons whether they be white, yellow, red or black; that God who loves all mankind. Then why do we seek to see him as we desire? Because of the nature of the world in which we live; because of the claim of all races of mankind to the right of their own idealism. As the Anglo-Saxon claims the right to his own idealism; as the Teuton claims the right to his own idealism; as the Mongolian claims the right to his own idealism[;] so the African at home and abroad claims the right to his own idealism; and we show to you this evening the portrait of a Negro Christ. If you go to Germany you will see the painting there of a typical Teuton Christ; if you go to England you will see the painting of a typical Anglo-Saxon Christ; if you go to Austria you will see there a portrait of a typical Austrian Christ, and in the same idealism of humanity the 400,000,000 Negroes of the world presents a portrait of a Negro Christ—a Christ the brother of all mankind; the Christ who will come a second time to save the world; the Christ who will come as he came before, the embodiment of all humanity. And that is the point we want to make. It is not only modern, but it seems to be ancient. A certain class of people have always tried to discriminate against others. It is said in this country today that one-sixteenth of Negro blood makes a man a Negro.[2] It is no new creation of America; that prejudice is as old as the hills; that prejudice existed in the time of Christ, and that is why He was rejected by the Jews and the Romans. Because of the Negro blood in the veins of Christ[3] he was held as much a colored man 1,900 years ago as any other individual tonight having Negro blood in his veins is held a Negro in the United States of America.

And that was responsible for the crucifixion, because Christ was not of the pure Roman stock, because Christ was not of the pure Jewish stock, because he was the embodiment of humanity, and if that be so Christ had to be Jew, Roman, Caucasian, Negro, Mongolian and everything. Christ was a mixture of humanity and, because of the prejudice of the world, the German has taken out of the Christ the German blood of Christ, the Anglo-Saxon has taken out of the Christ the Anglo-Saxon blood of Christ, and tonight, since He must be a Negro, the Negro has taken out of Christ the Negro blood of Christ. He is the one Christ, the brother of mankind, and as he came to the world 1,900 years ago the embodiment of all humanity, so at his second coming he shall be the embodiment of all humanity; the world rejected Him once, but under the leadership of the Universal Negro Improvement Association we shall ever look for the Christ, and when He comes 400,000,000 Negroes shall not deny Him, because we have elected Him to be our standard bearer. We know indeed He has been with us always, for it was a black man, Simon the Cyrenian, who rendered Him service by bearing His cross to the Mount Calvary. He was with us in the days of slavery in the southern parts of this country; He was with us in the West Indian islands as we labored for 230 years under the yoke of alien masters.

We close in our worship in canonizing the black man of sorrows and canonizing the mother of that most holy Man, that holy personage, Mary the Virgin.

Now, it has been a taxing day. Those of you who are under our voices can hardly imagine the great strain under which we labor, having to speak more than once a day. May we not [now?] rise and sing our national anthem as a climax of this hot night?

The audience rose and sang lustily, "Ethiopia, Thou Land of Our Fathers," and this brought to a close the Fourth International Convention of the Negroes of the World.

Printed in *NW*, 6 September 1924. Original headlines abbreviated.

1. See Exod. 20:3–5, 23:24.

2. Legal and popular criteria for defining "race" have varied throughout American history. After the Revolution, for example, Virginia established one-quarter African ancestry as the legal definition of a "Negro," and this remained the state's standard over the next half-century. After emancipation Southern states moved toward increasingly narrow definitions of the fraction of African ancestry which made a person a Negro, and this trend gradually pervaded the national consciousness. In 1908 a legal scholar wrote that the "Code Committee of Alabama of 1903 substituted 'fifth' for 'third,' so that at present in that State one is a person of color who has had any Negro blood in his ancestry in five generations." According to this same scholar, Florida, Georgia, Indiana, Missouri, and South Carolina defined as "a person of color" anyone with as much as "one-eighth Negro blood," while Nebraska, Oregon, Virginia, and Michigan drew the line at one-quarter (Gilbert Thomas Stephenson, *Race Distinction in American Law* [New York and London: D. Appleton and Company, 1910], p. 15; Joel Williamson, *New People: Miscegenation and Mulattoes in the United States* [New York: Macmillan, 1970], p. 1).

3. Garvey paraphrases the title of W. L. Hunter's 1901 work, *Jesus Christ Had Negro Blood in His Veins: The Wonder of the Twentieth Century* (Brooklyn, N.Y.: Nolan Press). In 1924 the *Negro World* carried mail-order advertisements for Rev. James Webb's *The Black Man Was the Father of Civilization*, as well as "a picture of Jesus as a colored man with wooly hair" which used the headline "Jesus Was a Negro by Blood" (*NW*, 6 September 1924).

APPENDIX I

Delegates to the 1924 UNIA Convention

The following is a list of the delegates whose names appeared in accounts of the convention printed in the *Negro World*. In some cases, spellings of the names have been standardized.

Edward Allen
E. Alleyne
Michael S. Askernese
Richard Hilton Bachelor
Rev. Bishop J. D. Barber
K. Baxter
Clifford S. Bourne
Mae Boyd
Mr. Brewster
G. Brown
Mrs. Brown
C. H. Bryant
Percival L. Burrows
George Emonei Carter
W. L. Carter
I. Chambers
Jacob Chambers
I. Cipriani
H. Clark
Joseph A. Craigen
R. H. Crosgrove
Mrs. I. Curry
T. R. Daley
D. D. Daniels
M. Daniels
Henrietta Vinton Davis
Mrs. M. L. T. De Mena

W. J. Donald
J. B. Eaton
A. G. Ellenberg
J. J. Fenner
Arnold J. Ford
A. Foulkes
P. Garrett
Amy Jacques Garvey
Marcus Garvey
James R. Gill
E. B. Grant
Claude Green
Bryson Hale
Haywood Hampton
Ludwig Harrigan
Cecilia Harvey
James A. Hassell
Samuel A. Haynes
Ada Hogues
H. C. Holland
Charles Jackson
Mr. Jackson
Ida Jacques
Jeffers (Jefferies)
F. Johnson
Fred E. Johnson
Hattie Johnson

P. Johnson
P. E. Johnson
L. Jones
Isaac Kellum
D. H. Kyle
Amy Lawson
S. J. Lee
Mr. Logan
F. Levi Lord
H. Lowry
R. McDowell
George Alexander McGuire
G. O. Marke
Freeman Martin
R. A. Martin
Mary Massey
A. Mills
Carrie Minus
A. Newsum
Hannah Nicholas
Georgianna O'Brien
James O'Meally
A. R. Patespaul
Dr. J. J. Peters
H. Vinton Plummer
Mr. Powell
Dr. E. E. Rawlins
Henrietta Redd
R. Van Richards
J. Richardson
Wilbur J. Roberson
S. V. Robertson
Mr. Rogers
J. W. Ross
J. B. Salisbury

W. A. Sampson
Amelia Sayers
Maggie Scott
William LeVan Sherrill
J. B. Simmons
J. L. Simmons
Mrs. Simmons
J. Smith
Leonard Smith
Rev. E. J. Smith
Rudolph Smith
Mrs. M. Spencer
Theodore Stephens
H. C. Stokes
J. J. Thomas
Norton G. Thomas
Fred A. Toote
Kojo Tovalou-Houénou
J. Milton Van Lowe
W. S. Vaughn
Mr. Walker
William A. Wallace
William Ware
Dennis Washington
Vincent Wattley
M. Welch
George A. Weston
S. R. Wheat
Olivia Whiteman
George A. Williams
H. B. Williams
E. T. Winston
William H. Wood
James B. Yearwood
Mary Sharperson Young

APPENDIX II

Delegates to the 1924 Convention Listed by UNIA Division

ALABAMA DIVISION

Prichard

J.J. Thomas

ARKANSAS DIVISIONS

W.J. Donald

Blytheville

R. McDowell
J.B. Simmons

Fort Smith

J.W. Ross

CONNECTICUT DIVISION

Hartford

H. Lowry
William H. Wood

DELAWARE DIVISION

Mr. Walker

FLORIDA DIVISIONS

Jacksonville

Claude Green

Miami

G. Brown

GEORGIA DIVISIONS

Haywood Hampton
Mr. Jackson

Atlanta

Mr. Logan

ILLINOIS DIVISIONS

Chicago

Mrs. M.L.T. De Mena
Ada Hogues
Amy Lawson
Dr. J.J. Peters
William A. Wallace
S.R. Wheat
Olivia Whiteman

East St. Louis

Jacob Chambers

INDIANA DIVISIONS

Gary

A.G. Ellenberg
Henrietta Redd

Indianapolis

P. Johnson

KENTUCKY DIVISION

Highland Hts.

E.T. Winston

LOUISIANA DIVISIONS

Dennis Washington

New Orleans

I. Chambers
Charles Jackson
S.V. Robertson

MASSACHUSETTS DIVISION

Boston

H.B. Williams

MARYLAND DIVISION

Baltimore

Hattie Johnson

MICHIGAN DIVISIONS

Detroit

Joseph A. Craigen
Fred E. Johnson
Leonard Smith
J. Milton Van Lowe
M. Welch

Hamtramck

George A. Williams

MISSISSIPPI DIVISIONS

A. Newsum

Natchez

R.H. Crosgrove

MISSOURI DIVISIONS

Charleston

J.L. Simmons

New Madrid

D. D. Daniels

St. Louis

Freeman Martin

NEW JERSEY DIVISIONS

Jersey City

Rev. E. J. Smith

Newark

Mrs. Brown
A. Mills

NEW YORK DIVISIONS

Brooklyn

M. Daniels

New York

Clifford S. Bourne
Mae Boyd
Percival L. Burrows
George Emonei Carter
T.R. Daley
Henrietta Vinton Davis
Arnold J. Ford
P. Garrett
Amy Jacques Garvey
Marcus Garvey
Ludwig Harrigan
Samuel A. Haynes
Ida Jacques
F. Levi Lord
George Alexander McGuire
Carrie Minus
Hannah Nicholas
H. Vinton Plummer
Dr. E.E. Rawlins
Amelia Sayers
J. Smith
Rudolph Smith
Norton G. Thomas
Vincent Wattley
George A. Weston
James B. Yearwood
Mary Sharperson Young

NORTH CAROLINA DIVISIONS

Winston Salem

H.C. Holland

OHIO DIVISIONS

Alliance

A.R. Patespaul

Cincinnati

L. Jones
Mr. Powell
Maggie Scott
Mrs. M. Spencer
William Ware

Cleveland

P.E. Johnson
William LeVan Sherrill

Columbus

Isaac Kellum

Dayton

Cecilia Harvey
W.A. Sampson

Middleton

H.C. Stokes

Youngstown

W.S. Vaughn

PENNSYLVANIA DIVISIONS

Farrell

Michael S. Askernese

Homestead

J.B. Salisbury

Philadelphia

S.J. Lee
Fred A. Toote

Pittsburgh

Edward Allen
James R. Gill

VIRGINIA DIVISIONS

Newport News

Mr. Rogers

Norfolk

W.L. Carter
J. Richardson

Richmond

J.J. Fenner

Somerset

F. Johnson

WASHINGTON DIVISION

Seattle

James A. Hassell

WEST VIRGINIA DIVISIONS

Berkeley

J.B. Eaton

Clarksburg

H. Clark

Laura Lee

D.H. Kyle

Monongah

Mrs. I. Curry

WISCONSIN DIVISION

Milwaukee

Bryson Hale

FOREIGN DIVISIONS

Bermuda

E.B. Grant
Mrs. Simmons

Canada

E. Alleyne, Toronto
Georgiana O'Brien, Montreal

Cuba

Richard H. Bachelor, Florida
R.A. Martin, Cameguey

Dahomey

Kojo Tovalou-Houénou

APPENDIX II

Haiti	*Panama*
Theodore Stephens	C.H. Bryant
Jamaica	*Sierra Leone*
K. Baxter	George O. Marke
Liberia	*Trinidad*
R. Van Richards	I. Cipriani

APPENDIX III

The Comintern and American Blacks,
1919–1943

In the complex history of the Communist International (the Comintern), the Afro-American community occupies an important place. Founded in Moscow in 1919 to coordinate the activities of the international Communist movement, the Comintern set policies that guided each of its constituent parties across a wide range of political issues. Changes in Comintern policy toward blacks in the interwar years would influence the role that the American Communist party played in its conduct of agitation among black Americans. Consequently, the nature of this interrelationship forms a significant chapter in the overall history of black radicalism in the United States. The account of Comintern relations with American blacks which is presented here seeks to offer not merely a résumé of what is presently known, but by approaching the unfolding of the relationship from the perspective of the Afro-American community, it also lays stress on an aspect of the phenomenon that has been too often overlooked.

"The Negro question," as it was called, first came before the Communist International at its Second World Congress, held in Moscow in July 1920. During the course of the discussions that led to the adoption of the congress's Theses on National-Colonial Question, American delegate John Reed called on the Comintern to begin organizational work among blacks in the American South. Reed stressed, however, that American blacks were primarily concerned with winning equal rights as citizens within the United States, and he is reported to have argued that nationalist or "Back to Africa" movements had "no success among the negroes" (Harry Haywood, *Black Bolshevik: Autobiography of an Afro-American Communist* [Chicago: Liberator Press, 1978], p. 223). The timing of Reed's statement was ironic, since it came on the eve of Garvey's successful August 1920 First International Convention of the Negro Peoples of the World (Theodore Draper, *American Communism and Soviet Russia* [New York: Viking Press, 1960], pp. 319–322; Claude McKay, "Soviet Russia and the Negro," *Crisis* 27, no. 2 [December 1923]: 61–65).

Just before Reed's speech, a Stockholm-based agent for the U.S. Military Intelligence Division reported to his superiors that "a systematic plan" for "Bolshevik propaganda among Negroes" had been formulated by the Comintern, and that this propaganda would probably enter the United States from Mexico (DNA, RG 165, file 3057, 17 July 1920). In fact, the Comintern did not act upon Reed's appeals, and no evidence of serious American Communist interest in blacks was found to exist prior to June 1921, when the New York police arrested a white Communist for distributing leaflets protesting the Tulsa race riot and urging blacks to help establish "the Soviet Republic of America." Sometime in mid-1921, New York trade unionist Joseph Zack, formerly Communist organizer for Harlem, became liaison to the black community, apparently in response to a letter to the American Workers (Communist) party from Lenin questioning the American party's lack of interest in blacks. Finally, in October 1921 the party published its first major article discussing its role in "the Negro Struggle," arguing that American blacks were potential allies, though as yet untouched by Communist agitation (*Crusader* 4, no. 6 [August 1921]: 12; Theodore Draper, *American Communism and Soviet Russia*, pp. 321–322).

By the end of 1921, most of the newly formed Workers party's efforts to win support in the black community were limited to cooperating with the small African Blood Brotherhood (ABB), which in October 1921 had announced its intention to "establish contact with the Third Internationale and its millions of followers in all countries of the world" (*Crusader* 5, no. 2 [October 1921]: 18). The ABB further predicted "most of the [black] leaders and pioneers who will carry the message across the world will go forth" from the United States. In April 1922 the London-based *Communist Review* reprinted the ABB's revolutionary manifesto, thereby drawing attention to the rise of black radicalism in the United States. Yet despite the growing Communist interest in the ABB, the Workers party was unable to recruit more than a handful of black members, in part as a result of the prejudice and paternalism displayed toward blacks who attended Communist meetings and in part as a result of the party's near-exclusive stress on the issue of class over that of race. Indeed, the Chicago-based black Communist Otto Hall and others from the ABB actually urged blacks not to join the Workers party until either the American or the Soviet leadership took action against the party's internal racism (*Garvey Papers* 1: 524; Claude McKay, "Soviet Russia and the Negro," *Crisis* 27, no. 2 [December 1923]: p. 64; *Communist Review* 2 [April 1922]: 6; Harry Haywood, *Black Bolshevik*, pp. 121–122; "Negro: Otto Hall and Harry Haywood," box 51, Theodore Draper Papers, Robert W. Woodruff Library, Emory University, Atlanta [hereafter cited as Draper Papers]).

Other figures were effective in bringing the potentially explosive race issue in America to the attention of the Comintern. Coinciding with the ABB's shift toward the Workers party, symbolized by Cyril Briggs's attendance at the party's December 1921 convention, was the arrival in the Soviet Union that year of the Japanese revolutionary Sen Katayama. Katayama had lived for several years in the United States, where he had observed firsthand the divisive effects of racism on the American working class; he resurrected the Negro question before the Comintern. In the fall of 1922 the Workers party, reportedly at the urging of the Comintern, agreed to send a black delegate to the Fourth World Congress of the Comintern, held in November 1922. This delegate was the Surinamese Otto Huiswoud; in Moscow Huiswoud was joined by the black poet Claude McKay, who, although an ABB member, had traveled to the Soviet Union without Communist sponsorship or knowledge. McKay nevertheless received a warm welcome from Sen Katayama, whom he had known in the United States, as well as from other Comintern leaders, and he soon established himself as a spokesman for black America. Both McKay and Huiswoud addressed the Comintern's special session on the Negro question, with Huiswoud introducing the final theses that were adopted by the congress. In his speech Huiswoud (who took the name Billings) noted that the virulent racism of the white trade union movement permeated the Workers party, and he warned that black Americans, unless radicalized, would remain a potentially reactionary strikebreaking force for the capitalists (DNA, RG 59, file 811.01-48, December 1922, and file 861.00, 6 December 1922; Cyril Briggs to Theodore Draper, 24 March 1958, Draper Papers; *The International* [South Africa], 2 March 1923; *Fourth Congress of the Communist International: Abridged Report of Meetings Held at Petrograd and Moscow, November 7–December 3, 1922* [London: Communist Party of Great Britain, n.d.], pp. 257–263, hereafter cited as *Fourth Congress*).

In his various talks in Moscow Huiswoud identified the three major black American organizations as the NAACP, the UNIA, and the ABB; he noted that the Garvey movement possessed radical potential but was prevented from taking a progressive position "by its own leader" (*Fourth Congress*, p. 258). Huiswoud stated that of the three, only the ABB had a revolutionary outlook, and he reported that black Communists maintained close contact with the organization in preparation for future struggle. According to a U.S. State Department transcript of one Comintern committee meeting, Huiswood stated that racial conflict would ultimately be violent, adding that "streams of blood and heaps of bodies will cover our path to victory." He believed that blacks would be forced to establish their own fighting organizations for self-defense. These would be based on "committees of action," according to the report, made up of detachments of highly disciplined armed men. Funds for the committees, which were to be established in all states with large black populations, would be provided by the Workers party, and arms would be purchased in small shipments from Mexico. Prior to the armed struggle, the committees would "also try to establish close and friendly relations with the American Labor organizations and various Socialistic groups" and would "devote its energy to the struggle against prejudice and superstition" (DNA, RG 59, file 861.00, 22 December 1922).

Several of Huiswoud's suggestions were endorsed without argument by the Negro Commission of the congress, and at the end of the session the commission formally voted to apply the "Theses on the Colonial Question," drawn up at a previous congress, to the black American question. This in turn required the congress to support all anticapitalist black organizations, to fight for the economic and political equality of white and black, to pressure trade unions to admit black workers, and, finally, to take steps to convene a "Negro World Congress" (Jane Degas, ed., *The Communist International, 1919–1943* [London: Oxford University Press, 1956], 1: 398–401).

Similar addresses were made to the Moscow congress by white Communist Rose Pastor Stokes (under the pseudonym Sasha) and Claude McKay. Both gave lengthy interviews to *Izvestia*, in which they pointed out "the inequality existing between the white and negro races in America" but noted the discrimination of which labor unions and white workers were themselves guilty. In a brief discussion of the Back to Africa movement, McKay also declared that Garvey had "a negative influence as far as the revolutionary spirit of the negroes is concerned." Nevertheless, another *Izvestia* article, entitled "The Awakening Race" and featuring a Soviet commentator on the Comintern, U. Steklov, predicted that through the U.S. black population Communism would penetrate Africa. It was "precisely the negroes of America," he maintained, who "can and must create the Negro Communistic literature and press, the circles and societies of agitators, that will do the work, not only in the United States but also in Africa, by means of correspondence, and by sending their agitators to various places" (DNA, RG 59, file 861.00, 11 December 1922; *Izvestia*, 16 November and 18 November 1922).

News of the impact of the blacks who attended the Comintern congress was sensationalized in the American press, the *New York Herald*, for example, declaring that "Moscow has striven to incite the negro race here into rebellion" (12 December 1922). For its part, the Communist *Worker* (later renamed *Daily Worker*) carried a long article on the Negro question by Rose Pastor Stokes, the delegate to the congress responsible for preparing the final draft of the congress's theses on the Negro question. In this article she pointed out that while the issue had been raised briefly before, "Credit is due America for introducing the question of a [standing] Negro Commission" of the Comintern (*Worker*, 10 March 1923). Stokes proudly noted that a warm reception had been given the black American delegates and that one of them, Claude McKay, had been selected to remain in Moscow as head of the proposed Negro Bureau. In fact, McKay had become something of a celebrity in Moscow, meeting with leading Soviet artists and politicians, including Leon Trotsky, and reading his poetry before large crowds. Moreover, during their visit, McKay and Huiswoud were invited to visit the ailing Lenin, and in February 1923 *Pravda* even carried an official reply from Trotsky to a question posed by McKay on how to prevent the French from deploying black troops in Europe. This, Trotsky declared, could only be done by the blacks themselves, who should "refuse to give service to Imperialism" (Claude McKay, "Soviet Russia and the Negro," Part 2 *Crisis* 27, no. 3 [January 1924]: 114–118).

American race relations continued to attract considerable attention in Moscow after the Comintern's fourth congress concluded in December 1922. During the first months of the following year, McKay worked with Sen Katayama and other Comintern officials on plans for organization of a Negro

Bureau for Africa and America, and he helped draft a manifesto "to the oppressed Negro Peoples of the World" (DNA, RG 59, file 861.00/9909, 30 April 1923). Leon Trotsky supplemented this manifesto in May 1923, publishing suggestions in which he stressed the needs for a revolutionary cadre of "enlightened young, self-effacing negroes" and for radicalizing black troops used by "French and English capital" in Europe (*The International*, 25 May 1923, p. 1). Some weeks later, in June 1923, the British Communist Ivan Jones criticized the "religious and racial charlatanism" in the Garvey movement and dismissed Du Bois's faith in white philanthropists. By contrast, Jones argued, the "organization of negro Communists known as the African Blood Brotherhood" had achieved considerable progress and would undoubtedly "supply the leaders of negro emancipation" (Ivan Jones, "Africa's Awakening," *International Press Correspondence* 3, no. 43 [14 June 1923]: 4).

On his return to the United States early in 1923, Huiswoud, together with Cyril Briggs, helped bring the ABB into the Workers party, a process under way since Briggs's employment with the Workers party's "Friends of the Soviet Union" in March 1922. Although as late as July 1923, Briggs himself denied that the ABB was affiliated with the Workers party, the merger with the Communists was in fact almost complete and little further reference to the ABB was made by the Workers party after August 1923 (Philip S. Foner, "Cyril V. Briggs: From the African Blood Brotherhood to the Communist Party," paper presented at the Annual Conference of the Association for the Study of Negro Life and History, Los Angeles, 12–15 October 1978).

At the Comintern congress, Otto Huiswoud conceded that the Garvey movement and "its rebel rank and file element" had, despite its many flaws, influenced "the minds of the Negroes against imperialism" (*Fourth Congress*, p. 258). In keeping with this view, the ABB and other Communists repeatedly attempted to enter the UNIA and enlist it in an alliance with the Workers party. As early as mid-1920 Sen Katayama was in contact with the Garveyite leadership, and in 1921 Rose Pastor Stokes had addressed the UNIA annual convention; several Communist delegates were actually expelled from that gathering. The Communists also communicated with the 1924 UNIA convention, urging the delegates to abjure their connection with the Ku Klux Klan. As the possibility of alliance with Garvey dimmed, however, the Workers party turned against the UNIA leader and shifted its attention to other black political organizations, such as the NAACP and the short-lived Negro Sanhedrin (All-Race Assembly), organized in February 1924. Cyril Briggs's closeness to W.M. Trotter, one of the founders of the Sanhedrin, and also his own long-standing political interest in achieving a common front among black leaders, resulted in Briggs's informing the party in late 1923 of the ABB's support of the Sanhedrin. The party's Negro Commission agreed with this decision and sought to promote its views in its own name at that gathering (*Garvey Papers* 1: 675–682, 691–694, 2: 546–548; *Daily Worker*, 11 February, 12 February, and 23 August 1924; Roger E. Kanet, "The Comintern and the 'Negro Question': Communist Policy in the United States and Africa, 1921–

1941," *Survey* 19, no. 4 [autumn 1973]: 93–94).

Despite continuing friction with the UNIA, it was not until September 1924 that Garvey was openly denounced by the white Communist spokesman on the Negro question, Robert Minor. Indeed, as late as mid-August 1924, during the fourth UNIA convention, the *Daily Worker* reported encouragingly of Garvey's attack on "the capitalist class of Negroes" and dismissed his mail-fraud conviction as itself fraudulent. But it was Garvey's defense of his relationship with the Ku Klux Klan that finally ended the communist flirtation with the UNIA, and in October 1924 Minor compared Garvey to the "House negro," willing to betray his own people (Robert Minor, "The Handkerchief on Garvey's Head," *Liberator*, October 1924, pp. 17–25). Communist relations with the UNIA would remain poor for the next decade, with recurring episodes of mutual recrimination and worse; for example, a series of Harlem street fights culminated in 1930 with the death of Alfred Levy, a black Communist activist (Kanet, "The Comintern and the 'Negro Question,'" pp. 93–94; Theodore Draper, *American Communism and Soviet Russia*, p. 330; *Daily Worker*, 12 August, 13 August, 18 August 1924, and 30 June 1930; Mark Naison, *Communists in Harlem During the Depression* [Urbana: University of Illinois Press, 1983], pp. 39–40).

Although it condemned Garvey after 1924, the Workers party had by then accepted the significance of Garveyite black nationalism. Among those emphasizing the lessons of Garveyism for the Workers party was Lovett Fort-Whiteman, formerly contributing editor of the black socialist *Messenger* magazine, who had risen to become one of the leading black members of the Workers party and who, while undergoing political training in Moscow in 1924 and 1925, appealed for a greater attention to the racial dimension of black radicalism. Writing in February 1925, shortly before his return to the United States, Fort-Whiteman argued that Garveyism expressed all the pent-up hatred and discontent toward American institutions felt by blacks. Commenting on this article, the editors of the *Communist International* further noted that while the Back to Africa movement was escapist and utopian, the party "must energetically support . . . all negroes settled in definite territories in their aspirations for self-determination" (*The Communist International*, February 1925, p. 52). At the same time, however, it was necessary to struggle against the racism of white American workers which had led the black working-class to adopt "these dreams and illusions" (Lovett Fort-Whiteman, "The Negro in America," *The Communist International*, February 1925, p. 52; Theodore Draper, *American Communism and Soviet Russia*, p. 329; Homer Smith, *Black Man in Red Russia* [Chicago: Johnson Publishing Co., 1964], pp. 77–83).

Having failed in its efforts to penetrate the UNIA, the NAACP, and other black organizations, the Workers party announced the impending formation of its own American Negro Labor Congress (ANLC). The ANLC, whose founding conference was held in Chicago in October 1925, was led by Lovett Fort-Whiteman. Although a public rally on the eve of the gathering attracted over eight hundred, only forty delegates attended the meeting, and none of them were farmers or southerners. Small branches of the ANLC were formed in New York and Chicago, but the response—especially from the black community—was disappointing. The ANLC remained a relatively insignificant union body, hampered by the hostility of most white labor organizations, though it did undertake some organizing activity among coal miners in West Virginia and Pennsylvania, and in several other scattered areas. Among its more important activities was the intermittent publication of a periodical, *The Negro Champion* (Theodore Draper, *American Communism and Soviet Russia*, p. 331; Harry Haywood, *Black Bolshevik*, p. 143); Mark Solomon, "Red and Black: Negroes and Communism," [Ph.D. diss., Harvard University, 1972], pp. 594–596; *Daily Worker*, 27 April 1927, 12 January, and 7 May 1928).

One accomplishment of the ANLC was to send a group of ten American blacks, including Otto Hall and his brother Harry Haywood, to Moscow to attend the University of Toilers of the East and the Lenin School in 1925–1926. The clandestine departure of the black delegates was, like Lovett Fort-Whiteman's activities in general, closely monitored by the Department of Justice, and in January 1926 J. Edgar Hoover, in a letter to Alexander Kirk of the Department of State, stated that most of the travel money for the group had come from Robert Minor's wife (DJ-FBI, file 61-4960; DNA, RG 59-U-2, file 155).

Beginning in 1928, a sweeping revision of Comintern policy occurred; this affected Communist activities among blacks in the United States and throughout the world. It came during the Comintern's so-called third period, which lasted roughly until 1934. (The first period coincided with the radical "War Communism," until 1921–1922; the second with the period of Lenin's more moderate New Economic Policy, which followed.) During the third period, Moscow pushed for a revolutionary line on a variety of issues after severe political reverses had soured the Soviet leadership on the previous policy of seeking wider coalitions. Largely at the initiative of Stalin and growing in part out of his struggle with the "Right Opposition" of 1927–1929, this political shift in Comintern strategy resulted in an escalation of agitation among American blacks; it also encouraged a more strident anticolonial posture by the international Communist movement.

Joseph Stalin's personal role in determining the change in policy toward American blacks appears to have been significant, but its full extent cannot be ascertained from the available evidence. Prior to the Russian Revolution, he had been the Bolsheviks' leading theorist on "national minorities," and now he took an active interest in racial issues. In his *Marxism and the National Question* (1913), Stalin had described several attributes that rendered an oppressed ethnic group a distinct nation with the right to national self-determination. A nation, he wrote, was a "historically constituted, stable community, formed on the basis of a common language, territory, economic life, and psychological makeup manifested in a common culture" (Joseph Stalin, *Collected Works* [Moscow: Foreign Languages Publishing House, 1953], 2: 307). In 1927–1928 Stalin believed that blacks in the southern United States (along with those of South Africa) fit this definition, and he began sounding out Afro-American Communists present in Moscow on the issue of a separate black state. The blacks were initially resistant; for example, Harry Haywood, who eventually became a spokesman for the concept, initially thought it "farfetched" and "not consonant with American reality" (Harry Haywood, *Black Bolshevik*, p. 230; Smith, *Black Man in Red Russia*, pp. 79–80).

At the Sixth World Congress of the Comintern in early 1928, the American Negro question became a topic of protracted discussion. It would appear that the views of Stalin, who by now had consolidated his power, prevailed. Led by the Finnish delegate Ottomar Kuusinen, the Comintern was critical of the failure of the Communist Party of the United States of America (CPUSA) among Afro-Americans, and was struck with the appeal of Garvey's Back to Africa rhetoric; black nationalism, as delegate Haywood viewed it, was an "authentic trend" that needed to be addressed by the Communist movement (Harry Haywood, *Black Bolshevik*, p. 230). The Sixth World Congress passed resolutions endorsing "the right of Negroes to national self-determination in the Southern states, where the Negroes form a majority of the population" (Harvey Klehr, *The Heyday of American Communism: The Depression Decade* [New York: Basic Books, 1984], p. 325).

American Communist leaders greeted the self-determination concept with little enthusiasm. Many members of the party faction surrounding CPUSA leader Jay Lovestone remained lukewarm toward it, and only after Lovestone's removal as executive secretary did the party's press devote much attention to the issue. At times party documents suggested an actual separate state for blacks, while in other instances self-determination was presented as the right of the black majority in the deep South to *choose* separation. Uncertainty existed as to the appropriate formulation of this doctrine, a problem which the Comintern itself did little to rectify. For example, the Comintern endorsed the concept's limited use as a slogan in 1929, then modified its position the following year by proclaiming self-determination the party's central demand in the South. Nor were Afro-American Communists comfortable with the separate state idea; mostly integrationist by conviction, they tended to view it as a variant form of segregation. Indeed, Otto Huiswoud openly denounced the reigning idea in the Comintern, namely that there was no difference between "the National-colonial character of the Negro question in Africa and the West Indies and the racial character of this question in the United States" (Harvey Klehr, *The Heyday of American Communism*, p. 325).

But if black party members had reservations regarding the new theoretical formulation, most soon fell in line with the Comintern's wishes; indeed, many became enthusiastic about the new emphasis on the revolutionary potential of black America. West Indian-born Cyril V. Briggs recalled that blacks were then "preoccupied" with the struggle against racism in the party, and they therefore viewed the separate-nation issue within this context (Cyril V. Briggs to Theodore Draper, 24 March 1958, Draper Papers). Likewise, Communist vice-presidential candidate Benjamin Gitlow remarked that the "campaign for a Negro republic was tied up with a campaign in the party ranks against white chauvinism," and also with a desire to comply with the orders from Moscow (Roger E. Kanet, "The Comintern and the 'Negro Question,'" p. 104). The critical point, as Otto Hall told Stalin, was that "prejudice and discrimination were largely responsible for the lack of Negro membership in the party" (Otto Hall, interview with Theodore Draper, 28 November 1958, box 51, Draper Papers). Many blacks hoped that Comintern pressure would improve not only their standing but also party policy in the United States.

This expectation was borne out, for both the Comintern and the CPUSA escalated their agitation for black rights. One indication of the new interest of Moscow in blacks was the creation in 1930 of the International Trade Union Committee of Negro Workers at Hamburg. This gathering was held under the auspices of the Profitern (the Red International of Labor Unions) and was attended by the Trinidad-born George Padmore and also by James Ford, both soon to become important black communist leaders. This meeting represented one of the earliest attempts by the Comintern "to bring together black workers on a world scale," as Otto Huiswood put it (Harry Haywood, *Black Bolshevik*, p. 329).

In America, the Comintern's influence was particularly evident in the southern states. The Soviet leaders pushed for work among black tenant farmers, and in response the American party devoted considerable resources to the region. The Sharecroppers Union, whose membership in Alabama and elsewhere numbered several thousand in the 1930s, developed out of this organizing activity. Though social repression was too intense in the South for these efforts to result in lasting changes, they did enhance the party's standing among blacks outside the region. The celebrated 1931 Scottsboro, Alabama, rape case and the Angelo Herndon trial in Atlanta during the same year provided further favorable publicity for the Communists. In the words of party leader Earl Browder, "What Negro in America is there who does not know of the Scottsboro boys . . . [and] of what the Communists have done to save them?" (Earl Browder, *The People's Front* [New York: International Publishers, 1938], p. 47; Theodore Rosengarten, *All God's Dangers; The Life of Nate Shaw* [New York: Alfred A. Knopf, 1974], pp. 296–326; Nell Irwin Painter, *The Narrative of Hosea Hudson: His Life as a Negro Communist in the South* [Cambridge: Harvard University Press, 1979], pp. 75–126).

A related development indicating the increasing importance of blacks to the party was the emphasis of the Communist-led legal aid organization, the International Labor Defense (ILD), on assisting blacks on trial in the South and elsewhere. In 1928, one party leader said that the ILD had thus far "almost completely neglected work amongst the Negro masses" (John Pepper, *American Negro Problems* [New York: Workers Library Publishers, 1928], p. 14). This situation changed dramatically in the early 1930s, for the ILD became spectacularly involved in the Scottsboro case and a host of similar trials of interest to the black community. The ILD also provided small stipends to political prisoners and their families, and by 1936 some thirty percent of the aid dispensed to long-term prisoners was going for the support of black inmates. Such activities enhanced the party's reputation in the black community (Charles H. Martin, "The International Labor Defense and Black America," *Labor History* 26, no. 2 [spring 1985]: 177).

The main success of the Communist party among blacks occurred in the northern ghettoes. Demonstrations against the Scottsboro trial provided much of the initial impetus, but the party also espoused militant agitation on behalf of urban blacks. In Harlem, for example, the party responded to the depression by organizing councils of the unemployed and successfully pushing for larger city relief appropriations. Interracial defense squads were also formed to return the furniture of evicted tenants to their apartments. Such tactics "attracted broad support—and sometimes participation—from Harlem residents" (Mark Naison, *Communists in Harlem During the Depression*, p. 41). Similar activities in other cities earned the Communist party growing influence during the early years of the depression, though black membership actually remained at only a few thousand.

Shaped by the Comintern's militant Third-Period line, the American Negro Labor Congress was replaced in 1930 with the League of Struggle for Negro Rights (LSNR). Both these bodies shared similar limitations. They were explicitly revolutionary organizations that rejected alliance with more mainstream groups. "The Garvey movement and the NAACP," wrote Otto Huiswoud, "are classic examples of the reformist movements . . . betraying the Negro workers in their struggle against capitalist exploitation" ("World Aspects of the Negro Question," *Communist*, February 1930, p. 146). Rhetoric of a similar character toward more moderate organizations was common, and even the black churches came under attack in the *Daily Worker* and elsewhere (though at the grass roots level activists sometimes cooperated with religious groups). Because of this overall strategy, both the ANLC and the LSNR had only limited appeal; black Communist spokesman and vice-presidential candidate James W. Ford later described these bodies as "too narrow" and thus "completely isolated from the basic masses of the negro people" (James W. Ford, *The Negro and the Democratic Front* [New York: International Publishers, 1938], p. 82).

After several years of pursuing an ultramilitant approach, the Comintern began to moderate its policies in 1933. One of the first aspects of the Third-Period line to be downplayed was the idea of self-determination. In the words of Earl Browder, "it is clear that the Negro masses are not yet ready to carry through the revolution which would make possible the right to self-determination" (Earl Browder, *Build the United Peoples' Front* [New York: Workers Library Publications, 1936], p. 60). While in the United States this shift had little negative effect, in Africa it signaled a significant change. The Communists had attained some success in their anticolonial agitation, but now the Comintern deemphasized it. In response, the head of the Comintern's African Bureau, George Padmore, left his position and abandoned Communism for a Pan-African political orientation. Padmore argued that the

Comintern had "put a brake upon the anti-imperialist work of its affiliates" (James R. Hooker, *Black Revolutionary: George Padmore's Path from Communism to Pan-Africanism* [London: Pall Mall Press, 1967], p. 31). Padmore's claim that the African work had been sacrificed to the need of the Soviets to conciliate England and France had some validity. Those American blacks who agreed with Padmore that anticolonialism was a critical issue could only be disappointed with the Comintern's programmatic turn away from anticolonial agitation.

By 1935 the Comintern's reformulation of policy was in full swing. In response to the rise of Nazi Germany the Seventh World Congress of the Comintern dropped the organization's revolutionary line and inaugurated the Popular Front (or People's Front), calling for cooperation with liberals and progressives against the Fascist threat. As Georgi Dimitroff, a Comintern spokesman, noted, the Communists were ready "to arrange joint actions between the proletariat and the other toiling classes interested in the fight against fascism." The goal, he continued, was the creation of a "broad peoples' anti-fascist front" (Georgi Dimitroff, *Working-Class Unity: Bulwark Against Fascism* [New York: Workers Library Publishers, 1935], p. 38).

The Popular Front period, lasting until late 1939, signaled an alliance with middle-class and reformist black organizations and represented the historic high point of Communist agitation—and influence—in the black community. The Communists ceased denouncing the NAACP and the Urban League and instead looked for common ground for action. One consequence was that the party disbanded the radical League of Struggle of Negro Rights in the interest of broader racial unity. Now searching for diverse allies, the Communists cooperated with Father Divine's Peace Mission Movement; and spokesman James W. Ford commended approaching Garveyites "in a friendly manner" on issues emanating from the Italian invasion of Ethiopia; this represented an abrupt departure from the party's previous policy (James W. Ford, *The Negro and the Democratic Front*, p. 33). Thus, in December 1934 the Communists successfully worked with New York division leader A.L. King and other Garvey followers to establish the Provisional Committee for the Defense of Ethiopia. The formation of the National Negro Congress in 1936 represented the zenith of this strategy, with non-Communists like A. Philip Randolph and Ralph Bunche prominent in the organization. The party's deliberately limited influence in the body helped give the National Negro Congress substantial legitimacy as a civil rights organization (Lawrence S. Wittner, "The National Negro Congress: A Reassessment," *American Quarterly* 22, no. 4 [winter 1970]: 883–901).

The Popular Front's appeal to blacks was significantly reinforced by the dramatic events then transpiring in organized labor. In 1935, the body that would become the Congress of Industrial Organizations (CIO) split off from the American Federation of Labor and soon thereafter entered into a de facto alliance with the Communist party; the CIO unions proclaimed themselves forthrightly egalitarian on racial matters. As the CIO constitution stated, its goal was to "bring about the effective organization of the working men and women of America regardless of race, color, creed, or nationality" (Herbert R. Northrup, "Organized Labor and Negro Workers," in *The Negro in Depression and War: Prelude to Revolution, 1930–1945,* ed. Bernard Sternsher [Chicago: Quadrangle Books, 1969], p. 139). The CIO followed this pronouncement with aggressive efforts to recruit black members. This policy, combined with highly successful organizing drives in 1936 and 1937 in the steel and automobile industries, won the CIO a significant following in the black community, and the respect the organization thus gained also benefited the Communist party. In the words of one historian, "Responsible positions in the CIO gave Negro Communists a prestige in the black community which they would not have otherwise had; it provided them a platform . . . for the united front program among all sectors of the race" (Wilson Record, *The Negro and the Communist Party* [New York: Atheneum, 1971], p. 146).

World events also aided the success of the Popular Front during this period. Adolph Hitler's racist rhetoric troubled blacks, and the Communist party's strident anti-Fascist position found an enthusiastic response. Moreover, the Italo-Ethiopian War permitted Communists to portray antifascism and anticolonialism as logically interrelated. During the Popular Front period, the party's presence expanded in the black community, especially among black intellectuals, so that by 1939 the Communists could claim almost seven thousand black members, more than double the 1935 figure (Harvey Klehr, *The Heyday of American Communism,* p. 348).

The hard-won influence of the Communist party, however, began to decline in the late 1930s; one reason for the decline was the changing fortunes of the New Deal coalition. The economic recession which set in late in 1937 damaged President Roosevelt's capacity to pursue further welfare relief and social reform measures. The economic situation also markedly slowed CIO organizing activity. By 1938 these trends had cost the left some of its momentum, and the lessening capacity of the Communists to win substantial reforms compromised its credibility with blacks.

Such difficulties increased enormously after August 1939, with the signing of the Nazi-Soviet Non-aggression Pact and the subsequent outbreak of the Second World War. Following years of anti-Nazi propaganda, the Soviet agreement with Germany to partition Poland placed Communists on the defensive with blacks as well as with the American public at large. The Comintern insisted that the CPUSA drop its anti-Fascist line and, in the words of Earl Browder, denounce the war effort of Great Britain and France as "carried on to extend and perpetuate imperialist control over the world" (Harvey Klehr, *The Heyday of American Communism,* p. 390).

The new Comintern policy was to lead to the CPUSA's abandoning its Popular Front domestic alliance with Roosevelt and the New Deal liberals. While most committed black Communists appear to have stayed with the party after the pact, this shift wreaked havoc on the party's relations with other civil rights supporters; in particular, it left the party's black membership isolated and demoralized. For example, in Harlem the Rev. Adam Clayton Powell, a longtime ally of the party, denounced the Communists for abandoning the anti-Fascist struggle. "Fellow travellers must seek new companions," he observed, "and the united front must be born under new auspices" (*New York Amsterdam News*, 11 November 1939, quoted in Mark Naison, *Communists in Harlem during the Depression*, p. 292).

The decline of the National Negro Congress illustrated the dissension which the Nazi-Soviet Pact caused among left groups. The Communists insisted on resolutions from the National Negro Congress upholding an antiwar course; but while successful, this demand resulted in the departure of A. Philip Randolph from the organization's presidency, other black leaders following suit. As Roger E. Kanet has argued, "Membership in the Congress dropped radically, for many Negro organizations which had supported it were not willing to affiliate with an openly Communist front" ("The Comintern and the 'Negro Question,'" p. 119.) The party's new line toward reformists also led to self-exclusion from the March on Washington movement; because of the party's squabble with Randolph, the *Daily Worker* denounced the march's leaders as "agents of Wall Street imperialism" (ibid., p. 120). Thus the Communist party condemned the most successful civil rights activity of the decade; at that point the rupture of Popular Front cooperation from other black leaders and organizations was almost complete.

After Hitler's invasion of the Soviet Union in June 1941, the Comintern executed an immediate about-face. The Communists dropped their pacifism and became aggressively anti-Fascist once again. When America entered the war, the CPUSA enthusiastically supported the struggle against the Axis powers, thereby returning to its former policy of seeking alliances with liberals and progressives. Nevertheless, the party's credibility had been so compromised by these maneuvers, as well as by the criticism of the March on Washington movement, that its influence in the black community remained extremely restricted. This situation continued up to Stalin's order dissolving the Comintern in May 1943, in deference to his Western allies.

Throughout the evolution of the Comintern's thinking on the Negro question, an important consideration, especially during the 1920s, was the prevailing attitude of the Afro-American community toward black nationalism in general and the Garvey movement in particular. This interrelationship could be charted in the changing course of Comintern policy. The exemplary success achieved by Garveyism in mobilizing black support thus became a factor in the evolution of Communist strategy; it provided instances of both positive and negative aspects in one powerful mass movement. From the perspective of Afro-American history, this circumstance underscores once again the international repercussions of the Garvey phenomenon.

In summary, during the 1920s and 1930s, the Comintern exercised two antithetical influences on the radical movement among American blacks, both aiding and retarding it.

On the one hand, the Comintern encouraged Communists in the United

States (and in South Africa) to adopt a more aggressive position with respect to black rights; by 1928, with the implementation of the Third-Period line, this had become one of its major concerns, remaining so throughout the Popular Front period of the middle and late 1930s. Moscow directed the American party to increase agitation among blacks and to repress racist tendencies among its white members. While the Comintern's position calling for black self-determination in the deep South caused the CPUSA some embarrassment, Comintern prodding did move the American leadership toward a forthright espousal of full civil rights for blacks. The Communist party helped popularize the cause of black rights among liberal and radical whites in the labor movement and elsewhere, an infusion of considerable significance in the later development of the civil rights coalition in the United States. This, in turn, increased the party's appeal to those blacks who were receptive to the idea of an alliance with white leftists in their struggle against racial domination and European colonial rule.

The CPUSA's connection with the Comintern also provided certain direct benefits to members of the black radical movement. By bringing American black leaders to Moscow, the Comintern provided them international experience, which few of them could otherwise have obtained at the time. By the same token, blacks lent important legitimacy to the Comintern's espousal of the cause of "oppressed peoples," and Afro-American Communists also provided essential cadres for the transmission of Comintern directives concerning the form in which struggles were to be waged by the black community. In this dual sense, the Negro question existed both as a national and as an international political issue.

On the other hand, if the Comintern's policies were in some respects advantageous to the black radical movement, they also had a contrary influence. The international Communist movement was everywhere subordinated to the interests of the Soviet Union, and in the 1920s the Comintern fell victim to the internal struggles of the various Bolshevik factions. Thus, the "Black Belt Nation" concept was used by Stalin as a litmus test of loyalty to his leadership, in both the Soviet Union and the United States. Inevitably, the abrupt policy changes imposed by the Comintern, especially after the Nazi-Soviet Nonaggression Pact, cost the party much of whatever influence it had attained among blacks in the twenties and thirties.

MICHAEL W. FITZGERALD
MICHAEL FURMANOVSKY
ROBERT A. HILL

INDEX

A Note on the Index

An asterisk (*) precedes annotated biographical entries found in the text. A page number followed by an *n* with a digit indicates that the entry appears in the footnote cited. An entry that appears both in the text and in a footnote on the same page is indicated by the page number only, except in the case of an annotated entry. Bibliographical information can be found in the annotations that accompany the text.

When there are variant spellings of a name, the accepted spelling is used; in other instances, where there is no generally accepted usage, the spelling which seems most correct is given. Variants have not been indexed. Women are indexed under the name that first appears in the text; married names are indicated by parentheses, as, Ashwood, Amy (Garvey). Cross-references to both married and maiden names are supplied.

Government agencies are listed by name. Cross-references to the appropriate cabinet-level department are provided when necessary, as, United States Department of Justice, *See also* Bureau of Investigation.

Topics of speeches and writings are indexed using the actual phraseology of the document. No attempt is made to present topical information using ideological categories of a later period; thus, "black nationalism" is not an index entry.

Abbott, Robert S., xxxiv, 186, 187, 212, 218, 228 n. 6, 229; Garvey on, 226–227 (unnamed), 544, 545, 547

Abd al-Latif, Ali, 681–682 n. 5

Abd el-krim, 462 n. 1

Abolitionism, 517, 520 n. 2

Abraham, 626

Abyssinia (Ethiopia), 3, 388 n. 1, 683; Italy invades, 5–6 n. 2, 262 n. 5, 852; in League of Nations, 644 n. 2; UNIA ambassador to, 568; UNIA Convention on independence for, 593, 715, 737–738, 744, 745, 767. *See also* Ethiopia.

Abyssinian Church (New York City), 187 n. 2, 234

Adam, Jean Joseph, 28, 29; as UNIA delegate to League of Nations, liv, 18, 19, 432, 571 n. 7

Addams, Jane, 301 n. 3

Adowa, Battle of, 644 n. 2

Africa, 146, 274, 310, 454; for Africans, 271, 427, 531, 532, 533, 563, 572 n. 11, 573, 595, 620, 623, 636, 637; aroused, 306, 532; as black civilization, 272, 535, 536; black nation/black government in, 205, 250, 282, 294, 404, 426, 450–451, 452, 467, 468, 469, 470, 485, 486, 506, 507–508, 509, 511, 544, 544, 560, 563, 564, 566, 567, 589–590, 635, 674, 675, 741, 767, 823, 824; blacks' right to, 526; E.E. Brown on, 426, 427, 428, 429; colonized, 33, 117–118, 483 n. 1 (*see also* Back to Africa movement); H.V. Davis on, 825; Du Bois in, 585 n. 4; Du Bois on, 18 n. 1, 33; Europe in, 10–11 n. 1, 18, 22, 51–52, 415, 452, 459, 523, 524, 534, 560–561, 568, 571–572 n. 8, 571–572 n. 9, 595 n. 1, 602, 639 n. 3, 641–642, 643, 644 n. 2, 674, 675, 679, 681 n. 4, 681–682 n. 5, 750, 752 n. 7; exploited, 51, 52, 294; flag of, 480, 569; Garveyism in, 456 n. 4, 569, 572

n. 11; League of Nations mandates on, 10, 18 n. 1, 214, 216–217 n. 1; McGuire on, 620–621, 623, 767; malaria in, 683 n. 3; minerals in, 51, 52, 147, 252, 524; missionaries in, 51–52, 53, 54 n. 1, 443, 674; Muslims in, 23, 26 n. 13; nationalism in, 637, 639 n. 3, 753–754; *Negro World* banned in, 561 n. 3, 681–682 n. 5, 706, 712 n. 4; "new," 311; redemption of, 51, 53, 131, 145, 149, 248, 291, 312, 313, 315, 360, 361, 362, 427, 435, 453, 458–459, 461, 534, 601, 620–621, 649, 739, 753–754, 787, 797, 798, 799, 823; as solution to race problem, 485, 524, 570, 677; slavery in, 214, 216–217 n. 1; United States of, 825; UNIA in, 572 n. 11, 637, 639 n. 3, 706; UNIA on, 7, 10, 18, 435, 443, 560, 823; UNIA Convention on, 594, 595, 674, 675, 739, 741; UNIA Convention to be in, 320–321; whites in, 270, 415, 514, 515, 701, 801 n. 9. *See also* Abyssinia; Egypt; Ethiopia; Liberia; South Africa; Somaliland; Sudan; Uganda; West Africa

African Blood Brotherhood, 192, 228 n. 4, 461, 558–559 n. 1, 843; and Workers party, 842, 845

African Communities League, 125, 622; and *Negro World*, 306, 308 n. 1, 420 n. 2; sued, 420 n. 2, 421, 423 n. 1. *See also* Universal Negro Improvement Association and African Communities League

African Legions. *See* Universal African Legions

African Methodist Episcopal Church, 31, 188 n. 8, 558–559 n. 1, 561, 654, 660 n. 19

African Orthodox Church, 630–631 n. 29, 650 n. 2, 721 n. 1

African Patriotic Committee, 444 n. 1

African Peoples' Organization, 712 n. 4

African Redemption Fund, 173 n. 2, 310

Agent 800. *See* Jones, James Wormley

Agoliagbo, 752 n. 7

Alabama: Birmingham, 416, 484; Garvey in, 484; Ku Klux Klan in, 280, 282–283 n. 3; Prichard, 661, 667 n. 1; race riot in, 220 n. 2; racial legislation in, 832 n. 2; slavery in, 667 n. 1; UNIA in, 219, 661, 667 n. 1

Alabama Polytechnic Institute, 219

Alexander, Judge William D., 55–56, *56 n. 1

Alexander and Baldwin, 681 n. 3

Ali, Dusé Mohamed, 30

Ali, Noble Drew, 681 n. 4

Allah, 23

All Blue Club (of New York), 441–442 n. 3

Allen, Edward, 655, 679, 745, 766, 833, 838

Alleyne, E., 655, *660 n. 14, 686, 833, 838

All-World Negro conference, 559 n. 2

Amalgamated Society of Railway Servants, 549 n. 1

Amalgamation: Du Bois on, 205, 216, 223, 233,

237–239; Garvey on, 138, 205, 216, 223, 233–234, 237, 451, 465, 466, 467

Ambition, 146–147, 249, 250, 468, 469, 491–492, 493, 494, 502–503, 505, 527, 635

American Anti-Slavery Society, 520 n. 2

American Baptist Publication Society, 14 n. 2

American Colonization Society, 586–587, 610, 807

American Federation of Labor, 676 n. 6, 722 n. 3, 755 n. 3, 851

American Jewish Congress, 301 n. 3

American Negro Academy, 688 n. 4

American Negro Labor Congress (ANLC), 846–847, 850

American-West Indian Association on Caribbean Affairs, 4–5 n. 1

Amos, James E., 6, 7, 54–55, 160, 167, 182, 196, 230–231, 243, 275–276, 285, 287, 298, 300, 317, 381, 400, 611, 683; on Eason killing, 181–182 n. 1, 402; on Garvey's bail, 402–403; on Garvey's income tax, 682, 688; on Garvey's trial, 165–166; Garvey on, 404, 405, 406, 408–409; on Cleveland Jacques, 482; threatened, 365 n. 1; on UNIA, 382, 402

Amsterdam News. See New York *Amsterdam News*

Anderson (beef vendor), 284

Anderson, Louis, 159 n. 4

Anderson, Thomas W., 13, 45–46, 172, 178, 192 n. 1, 200 n. 2, 214, 294 n. 1, 297; Bureau of Investigation on, 189–190; on Eason's death, 181; on Garvey, 410; on hardships, 47; on UNIA, 201–202; as UNIA officer, 611, 616

Anderson, Mrs. Thomas, 200 n. 2

S.S. *Antonio Maceo. See* S.S. *Kanawha*

Aptheker, Herbert, 396

Arana, Julio Cesar, 800 n. 8

Archbishop of Canterbury, 594, 673, 729

Arfa-ed-Dowleh, Prince Mirza Riza Khan, 32, *33 n. 1

Arkansas: Blytheville, 652, 657–658 n. 5; Ft. Smith, 656, 660 n. 19; NAACP in, 660 n. 19; UNIA in, 652, 656, 657–658 n. 5, 660 n. 19

Armstrong, S.C., 496 n. 2

Ashanti War, 588, 590 n. 3

Ashwood, Amy (Garvey), 59, 333, 339, 358 nn. 18, 19

Asia, nationalism in, 632, 636. *See also* China; Japan

Askernese, Michael S., 653, 659 n. 10, 678, 686, 744, 786, 833, 838

Assimilation. *See* Amalgamation

Associated Press, 397 n. 1

Astor, John Jacob, 624

Astor Social and Literary Club, 442 n. 4

Aunt Jemima, 569, 572 n. 10

Australia, 602
Azikiwe, Benjamin Nnamdi, 690 n. 4

Bachelor, Richard Hilton, 652, *657 n. 2, 669, 684, 685, 686, 714, 730, 737, 745, 747, 749, 760, 766, 777, 819, 833, 838; on condition of blacks, 678, 679, 742; on missionaries, 748
Back to Africa movement, 31, 219, 229, 231, 428, 429, 507–510, 560, 585 n. 2, 586–587, 591, 592 n. 1, 595–597, 607, 609, 610–611, 708–710, 711, 725–726, 727, 737, 741 n. 2, 758–759, 784, 787–788, 794–795, 796, 797, 798, 800–801 n. 9, 810–811, 812, 815; communists on, 844, 846, 848; Liberian government's response to, xxxvi, lvi, 561 n. 2, 590 n. 1, 591 n. 5, 610–611, 646, 682, 689, 690 n. 4, 773, 774, 775 n. 2, 789–790, 791, 792, 801 n. 10, 807, 810 n. 4. *See also* S.S. *Phyllis Wheatley*
Bagnall, Robert W., 44, 150, 187, 218, 228 n. 12; as anti-Garvey, xxxiii, xxxiv, 47, 217 n. 2; Bureau of Investigation and, 230–231; Garvey on, 219 n. 1, 227 (unnamed), 302, 303, 304, 439, 440, 441; in NAACP, 159 n. 5; as "race traitor," 229
Baker, Lorenzo Dow, 737, *738 n. 1
Baldwin, Roger, 301 n. 3
Baldwin, Stanley, 549 n. 2
Balfour, Lord Arthur, 23, 33 n. 1
Baltimore, Md., 183, 547 n. 1, 653. *See also* Maryland
Baltimore Afro-American, 119 n. 1, 188 nn. 8, 11, 245, 306 n. 1, 547 n. 1, 690 n. 1, 752 n. 6, 797, 801 n. 10
Baltimore Lancet, 187 n. 3
Baltimore Spokesman, 187 n. 3
Bananas, 737, 738 n. 1
Bank of British West Africa, 683 n. 3
Banton, Joab H., 319, *320 n. 2
Barbados, 737, 800 n. 8
Barber, J.D., 687; on Abyssinia, 737–738; on black deity, 666, 671; at UNIA Convention, 674, 675, 679, 684, 686, 729, 828, 833
Barclay, Arthur, 590 n. 2, 591 n. 5, 788, 789, 790, 792, 793, 799 n. 2, 825, 826
Barclay, Edwin, 510 n. 4, 774, 787, 788–789, 797–798, 801 n. 12, 811
Barker, Stephen, 600 n. 2
Barnett, Charles M., 94, 327, 328, *329 n. 13
Barnum, P.T., 9
Barret, Charles L.C.M.P., 7
Battle, Andrew M., 7–8, 27–28, 29–31, 181–186, 190, 197, 229–230, 231, 263–266, 273–275, 293–294, 300 n. 3, 379–380; on black activities, 13–14; on Garcia, 285 n. 1; on Garvey, 174; undercover, 287; on UNIA, 263–264, 383–384, 388 n. 1; on witnesses

threatened, 365 n. 1
Battle, George Gordon, 560 n. 1
Battle, Hannah, 380
Battle, Mrs. J., 380
Baxter, K., 663, 679, 777, 833, 839
Bayne, J.G., 59, 79
Beau, J.B.P., 18 n. 2
Beckett, Joe, 138, 140 n. 1, 141 n. 8
Beet sugar industry, 678, 680 n. 1
Behanzin, King of Dahomey, 750, 752 n. 6, *752 n. 7
Belgium: in Africa, 459, 524, 632; on Garvey, 32, 56–57, 134–135; king of, 800–801 n. 8
Belgrade, Mr. (Garvey's bodyguard), 46–47
Bellegarde, Louis Dantes, 10, 16, 643 n. 2
Benewick, Robert, 262 n. 5
Benin. *See* Dahomey
Bermuda, 561, 654
Bethlehem Steel Corp., 655, 660 n. 15
Bible: blacks in, 629 n. 5, 666; as Ethiopian, 666; quoted, 241, 267, 314, 366, 485, 493, 565, 620, 621–622, 625, 627, 632, 638, 646, 828, 832 n. 1. *See also* Psalms
Birmingham, Ala., 416, 484
Birth of a Nation, 761–762 n. 1
Black(s): American v. West Indian, xxxiv, 45, 180, 185, 217 n. 2, 223, 354, 367–368, 396 n. 1, 442 n. 4; in Bible, 629 n. 5, 666; in British army, 590 n. 3; British policy on, 561 n. 1, 593, 677–680, 684; civilization in Africa, 272, 535, 536; clergy, 686, 728; and communism, 841–854; condition of, 155, 290, 522–523, 529, 531, 536–537, 538, 543, 631, 656, 657–658 n. 5, 661, 662, 677–680, 722 n. 2, 739, 742, 746 n. 4; deity, xxxvii, 603, 604, 605, 625, 647, 649–650, 650 n. 1, 665–667, 669–671, 677, 827–831, 832 n. 3; farmers, 191 n. 1, 657–658 n. 5; films, 761–762 n. 1; franchise, 156, 158 n. 2, 158–159 n. 3, 261 n. 2, 394, 543, 547 n. 5; on Garvey, 9–10, 13; history, 5–6 n. 2; in Italian army, 644 n. 2; leaders, 13, 182–187, 220–227, 377–378, 668 n. 5, 694–695, 700, 740 (*see also* Abbott, Robert S.; Du Bois, W.E.B.; Garvey, Marcus; Johnson, James W.; Moton, R.R.; Owen, Chandler; Pickens, William; Randolph, A. Philip; Washington, Booker T.); and labor unions, 672, 676 n. 6, 852; legal definitions of, 832 n. 2; literature, 747, 748–749; migration, 156, 542; music, 228 n. 5, 801–802 n. 14; in office, 15, 158–159 n. 3, 159 n. 4, 160 n. 7, 543, 545–546, 547 n. 5, 599 n. 1, 637; organizations, 13–14, 396, 557–559 (*see also* African Blood Brotherhood; Friends of Negro Freedom; National Association for the Advancement of Colored People; Universal Negro Improvement Association and African

Communities League); politics (*see* Universal Negro Political Union); self-determination, 848, 850, 854; soldiers, 143, 148, 252, 532, 566, 588, 590 n. 3, 637, 646–647, 797; square deal for, 595, 637, 674, 730, 736; strikebreakers, 676 n. 6, 843; venereal disease among, 720, 722 n. 2. *See also* Press, black

Black Cross Navigation and Trading Co., lv, 714, 778, 816; British on, 591; to buy S.S. *General Goethals*, xxxiv, lvi, 756, 759–760 n. 1; to buy S.S. *Susquehanna*, 600, 606, 607–608; finances of, 607, 608 n. 1; Garvey on, 709, 756, 757, 759; incorporated, 575; for repatriation, 607; USSB on, 600, 606, 607–608

Black Cross Nurses, 480, 569, 572, 616, 777

The Black King, 761–762 n. 1

Blackman, 154 n. 1

The Black Man, 154 n. 1

The Blackshirt, 262 n. 4

Blackshirts, 261 n. 3

"Black Star Line" (song), 801–802 n. 4

Black Star Line (BSL), 10, 58–101, 162, 329 nn. 5, 13, 378, 379; ads by, 307; in Africa, 639 n. 3; assets of, 123; British on, 560; E.E. Brown on, 425, 428; Bureau of Investigation on, 173, 285–286; of Canada, 338; Chirlian on, 76, 114 n. 3; directors of, 59–60; discredited, 391–392; dishonesty in, 37, 38–40; Du Bois on, 33–41, 303; Eason on, 48–49; enemies within, 38, 707; finances of, 35–36, 48–49, 62–69, 70–100, 114 nn. 3, 4, 115–116, 122–126, 150–152, 347, 708–709; Garcia on, 64, 65, 95–96, 125, 347; Garvey on, 37, 38–40, 63, 115–116, 122–123, 150–152, 207, 291, 292, 312–313, 330, 337–338, 339–342, 352–353, 354, 448, 452, 459, 509, 607, 698, 699, 703, 707; Gibson on, 173–174; incorporated, 307; in Jamaica, 63, 475; and Ku Klux Klan, 228 n. 3; mail fraud by, 382–383 n. 4 (*see also* Garvey, Marcus, mail fraud trial of); Merrilees on, 70–100, 114 nn. 3, 4, 122–126; mismanaged, 63, 153, 425, 428, 472, 475, 478; Mulzac on, liv, 472–478; officers of, 58, 59, 60, 61, 62, 63, 69, 73, 77, 78, 80, 81, 391, 425, 472, 475; organization of, 58; press on, 38, 73, 115–116, 150–152, 575; salaries in, 99–100, 330–331, 344, 425; in Seattle, 660 n. 20; ships purchased by, 15, 95–96, 311, 337–338, 351, 352–353, 359 n. 36, 392–393, 432–433, 449, 600 n. 1, 607 (*see also* S.S. *Kanawha*; S.S. *Orion*; S.S. *Shadyside*; S.S. *Phyllis Wheatley*; S.S. *Yarmouth*); stock in, 6, 58, 60–69, 293, 306, 307; stockholders meeting of, 58–59, 65, 73, 81, 114 n. 5; suits/claims against, 33, 34, 35, 80, 81, 116, 125, 150, 151, 152, 153, 298, 347–348; USSB

on, 15–16, 607; UNIA invests in, 58, 59, 69, 97, 112, 122, 123–126, 152, 307; UNIA on, 391–392

Black Star Line Steamship Co. of New Jersey, 98–99, 125, 352

Black Swan Phonograph Co., Inc., 228 n. 5

Blue Vein Society, 227, 438, 440, 441–442 n. 3

Blumstein's Department Store, 444 n. 1

Blyden, Edward Wilmot, 442 n. 6, 683 n. 3

Bolshevism, 193, 250, 555 n. 1

S.S. *Booker T. Washington*, 759–760 n. 1. *See also* S.S. *General Goethals*

Borah, Sen. William E., 482, *483 n. 1

Borno, Louis E.A.F.J., 642, *643 n. 1

Boston Fruit Co., 738 n. 1

Bottomley, Horatio William, 425, *431 n. 3

Bourne, Clifford S., 297, 352, 372, 398, 399, 452, 736, 833, 837; at Garcia's trial, 284; on Garvey, 266, 380 n. 1, 410; as UNIA officer, 207, 611, 616, 818; on V. Williams, 412 n. 2

Boxing, 135, 136–137, 140–141 nn. 1–8

Boyd, Mae E., 671, 672, 686, 721, 736, 760, 764, 767, 777, 779, 806, 833, 837

Boyer, Jean Pierre, 765 n. 2

Boyington, Mrs., 380

Brandeis, Louis, 301 n. 3

Brazil, 294 n. 1

Brennan, Edward J., 276

Brent, A.L., 294–295 n. 1

Brewster, Mr., 664, 833, 836

Briggs, Cyril, 13, 183, 226, 558–559 n. 1, 842, 845, 848

Briggs, James M., 90, 351, 359 n. 36

S.S. *Britannia*, 510 n. 2

British Amalgamated Transport, Ltd., 549 n. 1

British and African Steam Navigation Co., 683 n. 3

British Guiana (Guyana), 712 n. 3, 737

British Honduras (Belize), 709, 712 n. 3, 737

British Union of Fascists, 262 n. 4

British West India Regiment, 590 n. 3, 676 n. 7

Brooklyn, N.Y., 654

Brooklyn Federation of Jewish Charities, 597–598 n. 3

Brooks, George S., 616

Brooks, J.D., 6, 64, 65, 101, 103, 349

Browder, Earl, 849, 850, 852

Brown, Mrs. (of Newark), 748, 767, 833, 836

Brown, Dixon B., 591 n. 5, 790

Brown, E.C., 285 n. 4

Brown, Rev. E. Ethelred: on Africa, 426, 427, 428, 429; on BSL, 425, 428; on Garvey, liv, 368, 423–431; on Garveyism, 424; on Garveyistic devotion, 424, 426–427, 430; on UNIA officials, 430; on West Indian v. American blacks, 367–368

Brown, G., 656, 672, 686, 736, 766, 833, 835

Brown, J.B., 44

Brown, Rev. W.W., 388 n. 1

Browning, Elizabeth Barrett, 324, *328 n. 3

Bruce, Florence, 370, 513, 687, *688 n. 4

Bruce, John E., 370; at *Daily Negro Times*, 11 n. 2; death of, xxxvii, lvi, 687, 688 n. 4; on Du Bois, 513; on Garvey, 396–397; on rival organizations, 396; UNIA prayer by, 657 n. 1

Bruce, Olive, 688 n. 4

Bryan, William Jennings, as candidate for presidency, 261 n. 1; on disfranchisement, 261 n. 2; Garvey on, 258, 259, 260, 261, 269, 277–278, 280, 281, 491, 495; in Panama, 258; racial attitudes of, 258, 259, 260, 261, 277–278, 280, 281; on slavery, 261 n. 2

Bryant, Charles H., 651, 678, 714, 715, 716, 717, 718, 719, 720, 737, 743, 744, 745, 747, 760, 762–763 n. 1, 766, 778, 779, 784, 785, 786, 807, 833, 839; on black deity, 671; on independent black nations, 767; on UNIA, 655

Buchanan, W.L., 294

Bucketing, 308 n. 2, 320 nn. 2, 3

Buffalo, N.Y.: black press in, 294 n. 1; Garvey in, liii, 230, 294; UNIA in, 294 n. 1, 510

Buffalo American, 294 n. 1

Bugge-Wicksell, Anna, 18 n. 2

A.H. Bull Steamship Line, 682, 683 n. 4, 689

Bunche, Ralph, 851

Bundy, Dr. Leroy, 30, 184, 207

Bunner, Alfred E., 364

Bureau of Investigation: agents of, 173, 245 n. 2, 246 n. 1, 285, 294–295 n. 1 (*see also* Amos, James E.; Battle, Andrew M.; Davis, Mortimer J.; Gulley, Harry D.; Jones, James Wormley; Morgan, H.L.; Novario, Rocco C.; Potter, Adrian; Tucker, Joseph G.); on black activities, 13–14, 31; on Black Cross Navigation and Trading Co., 759–760 n. 1; black leaders and, 189, 230–231; on blacks against Garvey, 378 n. 1; on BSL, 173, 285–286; in Buffalo, 294; in Cleveland, 288–289; on *Daily Negro Times*, 31 n. 2; on Eason's assassination, xxxiii, 166–169, 175–180, 181, 195, 196, 197, 198, 199–200, 213–214, 230–231, 232, 242, 243–245, 263, 264–265, 266, 298–300, 380–381, 402; on Garvey, 6, 7–8, 27–28, 29–31, 42–43, 46–47, 54, 160, 164, 165–166, 173, 174–180, 182, 191, 256, 285–286, 287, 294, 316–317, 381–382, 384, 402–403, 463, 548, 556–557, 568–571, 689–690; Garvey on, 404, 405, 406, 408–409; on Cleveland Jacques, 482; in Massachusetts, lii; in New Orleans, 174–180; in Pittsburgh, 41–43; on UNIA, xxxvi, lii, 13–14, 41–43, 47, 164–165, 229–230, 263–264, 276, 293–294, 382, 383–384, 388 n. 1, 397, 402–403,

404, 442–443, 512 n. 1, 568, 597 n. 2; on UNIA Convention, 592–595. *See also* Burns, William; Grimes, W.W.; Hoover, J. Edgar

Burges, Congressman Tristam, 507 n. 1

Burke, Mark, 762–763 n. 1

Burns, John F., 410

Burns, William J., 191, 195, 197, 199, 212, 213 n. 4, 232, 242, 246, 256, 276, 319–320, 384

Burrell, Rev., 176

Burrell, Theo, 13

Burrows, Percival L., 293, *294 n. 1, 432 n. 3, 561 n. 1, 680, 684, 714, 716, 717, 718, 721, 729, 743, 745, 747, 760, 764, 833, 837; as UNIA officer, 609, 611, 616, 818

Burton, P. Eugene, 559 n. 2

Butler, Nicholas Murray, 511, 569

Buxton, Sir Thomas F., 517

Café Savarin, 599 n. 2

California, Garvey in, liv, 482, 484, 490. *See also* Los Angeles

Cambridge Advance, 187 n. 3

Cameroons, 216–217 n. 1

Campbell, D.N,E., 558–559 n. 1

Campbell, Grace, 431 n. 1

Campbell, Gwen, 351

Campbell, M.L., 13

Campbell, Thomas Monroe, 219, *220 n. 2

Canada, liv, 188 n. 8, 338, 435, 602

Cannon, George H., 547 n. 5

Cantor, Eddie, 481 n. 1

Cape Argus, 283 n. 7

Carey, John Jr., 192 n. 1

Cargill, Schuyler, 346, *358 n. 28, 382–383 n. 4

Carmel Baptist Church, 356 n. 1

Carnegie, Andrew, 52, 624

Carnegie Hall: Garvey at, lii, lv, 246, 247–254, 263, 264, 265, 631–638, 723; UNIA at, 229, 230, 631–638

Carpenter, Clarence, 13

Carpentier, Georges, 136, 140 n. 1

Carr, Franklin C., 13

Carranda, D.C., 591 n. 5, 790

Carrington, Annie, 347, *358 n. 32, 403

Carson, Sir Edward Henry, *362 n. 2

Carter, A.M., 197

Carter, G. Emonei, 265, 434, 611, 665, 674, 675, 688 n. 4, 713, 736, 766, 776, 806, 814, 818, 833, 837; on Garvey, 410; report by, 714–715; on UNIA, 383–384

Carter, W.L., 654, 833, 838

Caruso, Enrico, 328, *329 n. 17

Casement, Roger, 253, 309, 362, 800 n. 8

Casimir, J.R. Ralph, 559

Cassatt, Alexander J., 329 n. 8

Castle, Samuel N., 681 n. 3

Castle, William R., *773 n. 1

Castle and Cooke, 681 n. 3

Catholicism, 485, 771, 772, 830

Cauffiel, Joseph, 462 n. 2

Cecil, Lord Robert, 294, *295 n. 2

Century Magazine, 186, 188 n. 14, 217 n. 2, 232

Certain, Jeremiah, 59, 60, 351, 472

Chambers, I., 744, 745, *746 n. 2, 748, 749, 766, 819, 833, 836

Chambers, Jacob, 651, 679, 685, 718, 744, 833, 836

Charles, Linous, 317, 401, 403

Chase, Ella, 762–763 n. 1

Chelsea Exchange Bank, 93, 125, 126, 611

Chesnutt, Charles Waddell, *441–442 n. 3

Chiang Kai-shek, 638 n. 1

Chicago, Ill.: anti-Garveyism in, 183; black organizations in, 557–559; blacks in office in, 156, 159 n. 4, 160 n. 7; Garvey in, lii; housing in, 741 n. 1; Islam in, 681 n. 4; labor strife in, 676 n. 6, 749, 751–752 n. 4; Chandler Owen in, 231, n. 1; proposed meeting in, 389; race riot in, 56, 207, 355, 751 n. 3; UNIA in, 648, 651, 654, 656, 662, 663, 716

Chicago Commission on Race Relations, 751–752 n. 4

Chicago Defender, xxxv, 61, 62, 131, 180 n. 1, 187, 212, 213, 228 n. 6, 243, 245 n. 2

Chicago Tribune, 454, 456 n. 4

Chicago Whip, xxxvi, 55–56, 188 n. 12, 228 n. 7, 585 n. 6

Chilton, Sir Henry Getty, *479 n. 1, 591

China, 539, 638 n. 1, 680 n. 2

Chirlian, H.S., 69, 72, 73, 76, 79, 114 n. 3

Christian, George B. Jr., 396

Christian, Rupert, 590 n. 1

Christianity, 21–22, 514, 515, 635, 673–674

Church and Society World, 765 n. 1

Church Extension Society, 234

Churchill, Winston, 10–11 n. 1, 561

The Churchman, 650 n. 2

Cincinnati, Ohio: black press in, 599 nn. 1, 2; riot in, 55; UNIA in, 55, 184, 506, 655, 661, 715

Cincinnati Union, 599 nn. 2, 4

Cipriani, Arthur A., 676 n. 7

Cipriani, I., 672, *676 n 7, 764, 782, 833, 839

Cipriani, Joseph, 676 n. 7

Cipriani, Lidio, 262 n. 5

Citizens' League for Fair Play, 444 n. 1

Civil rights movement, 853, 854

Clan na Gael, 322–323 n. 2

Clark, H., 654, 833, 838

Clarke, Edward Y., 228 n. 3, 259

Clarkson, Thomas, 517

Clemenceau, Georges, 20, 25 n. 4, 495, 533

Clergy, 654, 660 n. 19, 662, 686, 728, 739

Cleveland, Ohio: black press in, 288; Bureau of Investigation in, 288–289; Garvey in, 294–295 n. 1; Ku Klux Klan in, 289 n. 3;

UNIA in, 183, 288–289, 506, 656, 660 n. 16

Cleveland Call, 288

Cleveland Gazette, liv, 288, 472–478, 599, 599 n. 1

Cleveland Social Circle, 441–442 n. 3

Clinchfield Navigation Corp., 329 n. 13

Club Aristocrat, 442 n. 4

Cockburn, Joshua, 61, 62, 79, 80, 325, 329 n. 5, 351, 358 n. 21, 472–473, 475; competence of, 340; Garvey and, 323, 339–341, 342, 343; removed, 63; salary of, 341; threatened, 196, 317, 403, 408; on *Yarmouth*, 83–84

Cohen, Irvin, 481 n. 1

Cohen, J.E. and Fuchsberg, 382 n. 1

Colban, Erik, *17 n. 1, 18, 28, 29

Coleman, Julia P.H., 186, *189 n. 18, 218, 227 (unnamed), 228 n. 9, 229

Collins, Rev. Frederick H., 168, 175, 176

Collins, Bishop John J., 355 (unnamed), 359 n. 41, 402, 407

Colonial Clubs, 438, 442 n. 4

Colored Citizens Association of Memphis, 188 n. 16

Communist International (Comintern), 549 n. 2, 722 n. 2, 841–854; African Bureau of, 850–851; on American race relations, 841, 842–845, 848, 853–854; as antifascist, 851, 852; on black self-determination, 848, 854; Cyril Briggs and, 842; and CPUSA, 854; Garvey on, 603; on Garveyism, 853; MID on, 841–842; Negro Bureau of, 844–845; Popular Front (People's Front) of, 851, 852, 853, 854; in southern states, 849; Stalin dissolves, 853; State Department on, 843; Second Congress of, 841; Third Congress of, 751 n. 2, 603; Sixth Congress of, 848; Seventh Congress of, 851; first period of, 847; second period of, 847; third period of, 847, 850, 854

Communist International, 846

Communist Party/Communists, 213 n. 3, 841; and African Blood Brotherhood, 842, 845; as antifascist, 852; blacks in, 842, 844, 846, 847, 848, 849, 850, 851, 852; on black state, 848; and CIO, 851–852; and Comintern, 854; Garvey on, 769–771 (*see also* Workers Party); on Garvey, 751 n. 2, 845, 846; Justice Department on, 847; on Ku Klux Klan, 845; on race riot, 842; racism in, 842, 849; on Scottsboro trial, 849, 850; and UNIA, 845–846. *See also* Communist International

Communist Review, 842

Congo Free State (Zaire), 800 n. 8, 812

Congregation Sons of Israel, 597–598 n. 3

Congress of Industrial Organizations (CIO), 851–852

Congress of the International Federation of League of Nations Societies, 643 n. 2

Connecticut, 656
Les Continents, xxxvii, 752 n. 6
Cooke, Amos, 681 n. 3
Coolidge, Calvin, 164 n. 2, *418 n. 1, 433, 434, 434–435 n. 2, 462 n. 2, 513 n. 1, 585 n. 5, 640, 643 n. 2, 649, 690 n. 4, 723, 728 n. 1, 820 n. 3; Garvey on, 491, 495, 797; on Philippines, 592 n. 2; UNIA petition to, 533 n. 1, 573, 812, 824
Coolidge, Calvin Jr., 640 n. 1
Coolidge, John, 820 n. 3
Coombs, A.G., 334
Cooney, William, 345–346
Coryndon, R.T., 10–11 n. 1
Cosmopolitan Tennis Club, 442 n. 4
Coughlan (NYPD inspector), 243, 244
Council of Trent, 666, 669 n. 10
Costa Rica, 655
Craigen, Joseph A., 661–662, *668 n. 4, 762–763 n. 1, 764, 766, 776, 777, 779, 780, 782, 806, 813, 816, 819, 833, 836
Crawford, James, 176
Crichlow, Cyril A., 508
Crim, John W.H., 263, 483
Cripps, Thomas, 761–762 n. 1
Crisis, 153, 158 n. 1, 208, 211, 212, 232, 396 n. 1, 441 n. 1, 800–801 n. 9, 809–810 n. 2; on BSL, 150–152; Garvey on, 302–303, 440, 583, 796; and Ku Klux Klan, 672; *Negro World* on, 598; on UNIA, 584, 585 n. 3. *See also* DuBois, W.E.B.
Crosgrove, R.H., 653, 672, 833, 836
Cross, Robert, 11 n. 2
Cross of African Redemption, 629 n. 1
Crosswaith, Frank, 431 n. 1
Crown Savings Bank of Newport News, 284, 285 n. 4
Crusader, 116, 186, 208, 209, 226, 228 n. 4, 801–802 n. 4
Cuba, 652, 714; condition of blacks in, 694; Haitians in, 658 n. 7; S.S. *Kanawha* in, 150–151; UNIA in, 652–653, 716; S.S. *Yarmouth* in, 473–474, 475
Cunningham, J.B., 166, 191
Curley, C.B., 60, 65, 325
Current History, liii, liv, 436 n. 1, 470, 585 n. 1
Curry, Mrs. I., 661, 665, 785, 833, 838

Dabney, Wendell P., 598–599, 599 n. 1, *599 n. 2
Dabney Publishing Co., 599 n. 1
Dahomey (Benin), xxxvii, 680–681 n. 2, 752 n. 7, 762; *Negro World* banned in, 706, 712 n. 2
Daily Gleaner, 208, 440, 442 n. 6
Daily Negro Times, li, 5–6 n. 2, 10, 28, 30, 31, 134, 154, 363, 421 n. 1; Bureau of Investigation on, 31 n. 2; staff of, 11 n. 2; sus-

pends publication, 56, 115, 149–150
Daily Worker, 558–559 n. 1, 738–741, 741 n. 1, 753–755, 755 n. 4, 768–772, 846, 850, 853. See also *Worker*
Daley, T.R., 745, 833, 837
Dallas News, 141 n. 4
Dancy, Benny, 330, 348–349, *357 n. 7, 381
"Dancy Count," 381, 382–383 n. 4
d'Andrade, Freire, 18 n. 2
Daniel, Rev. Everard W., *117 n. 1, 438, 439
Daniels, D.D., 685, 729, 833, 836
Daniels, M., 654, 679, 745, 747, 764, 766, 833, 836
Darwinism, social, 722 nn. 2, 3
Daugherty, Harry M., 182 n. 1, 192, 245, 246 n. 1, 305, 320 n. 1, 394, 456 n. 6, 479 n. 2; black leaders' letter to, xxxiv, lii, 217–218, 220, 221, 228 n. 14, 305 n. 1, 468, 726, 728 n. 1; Garvey's questionnaire to, 468–470, 483, 488 n. 1; trial of, 301 n. 3
Daugherty, Romeo L., 11 n. 2
Daughters of Ethiopia, 785
Davis, Henrietta V., xxxiii, 30, 43, 163, 274, 333, 388 n. 1, 675, 777, 784, 785, 786, 833, 837; on Africa, 825; on Black Cross Navigation and Trading Co., 709, 778; and BSL, 59, 60, 62, 472; on Dossen, 792, 793–794, 825–826; on Garvey, 826; Garvey on, xxxiv, liii, 350–351, 380, 383, 573, 695, 698, 709, 810; at Garvey's trial, 266, 374; on Liberian anthem, 825–826; on liberty, 792, 793; salary of, 776; on United States of Africa, 825; as UNIA delegate to Liberia, xxxvi, lv, 507, 562, 571–572 n. 8, 573, 591 n. 5, 709, 788, 789, 791–793, 794, 800 n. 7, 810, 825; as UNIA officer, 102, 611, 818; in West Indies, 778
Davis, Jefferson, 746 n. 5
Davis, John W., 659–660 n. 13, 675–676 n. 5
Davis, Lawrence, 192 n. 1, 200 n. 2
Davis, Mortimer J., 160, 164, 166–169, 174, 191, 196, 230–231, 242, 243–245, 246, 285–288, 365 n. 1, 367 n. 2, 380, 381–382; on Eason killing, 298–300; on Garvey, 316–317, 463; on UNIA, 382
R.T. Davis Milling Co., 572 n. 10
Davis, Roy, 289
Davis, Willie, 55
Davitt, Michael, 322–323 n. 2
Dawes Report, 606 n. 4
Death tax/death grant, 109, 110, 112, 113, 188 n. 13, 209, 210, 785–786, 808–809
de Bourg, John Sydney, 30, 101, 181, 197, 287; arrested, 190; Garvey on, 349, 350, 698; at Garvey's trial, 266; threatened, 317, 365, 401, 403; salary of, 103, 698, 712 n. 1
de Cartier de Marchienne, Baron Emile, *134–135 n. 2, 573 n. 1
Delaware, 654

De Lisser, Herbert George, 440
De Mena, Maymie L.T., 785, *786 n. 1, 819, 833, 835
Democratic National Committee, 329 n. 9
Democratic National Convention, 329 n. 8, 611 n. 3, 671–672, 675–676 n. 5
Dempsey, Jack, 136, *140 n. 3
Dennis, W.F., 591 n. 5, 790, 795
de Petrie, Arnold, 11 n. 2, 421 n. 1, 423
De Priest, Oscar, 159 n. 4, 547 nn. 5, 7
de Rivera, Gen. Miguel Primo, 755 n. 2
Detroit, Mich.: black Islam in, 681 n. 4; black leaders in, 668 n. 5; Garvey in, 230, 265; Ramus in, 230, 231 n. 1, 243–244, 246; UNIA in, 231, 245 n. 1, 299, 510 n. 1, 629 n. 1, 662–663
de Valera, Eamon, 568, 706
Devonshire, Duke of (Victor C.W. Cavendish), 560, *561 n. 4
Devount, Prince Imah, 388 n. 1
Dewey, Loring, 765 n. 2
Diagne, Blaise, 136 n. 2
Dickens, Charles, 329 n. 6
Dill, Augustus Granville, 438, *441 n. 1
Dillard, J.B., 230
Dimitroff, Georgi, 851
Diplomacy, 527, 543, 545, 547, 795–796
Direct Leasing Corp., 358 n. 19
Divine, Father, 659 n. 11, 851
Dixon (informant), 244
Dixon, Captain, 475, 478 n. 3
Dixon, Thomas Jr., 583, 761–762 n. 1
Dodds, Gen. Alfred A., 678, *680–681 n. 2, 752 n. 7
Domingo, W.A., 359 n. 33, 431 n. 1, 558–559 n. 1; on death tax, 188 n. 13, 209; Garvey on, 225–226; salary of, 334; on UNIA, 186, 208, 209; on "West Indian," 217 n. 2
Domingue, W.T., 176
Dominican Republic. See Santo Domingo
Donald, W.J., 748, 833, 835
Donohue (NYPD detective), 244
Dorsinville, Luc, 34–35, 153
Dossen, J.J., 591 n. 5, 738 n. 2, 788, 789, 790, 791, 799–800 n. 3, 800 n. 4, 801 n. 13; eulogized, 784, 792, 793–794, 795, 822, 824–827; Garvey on, 784, 796, 797, 799, 822, 824–825
Douglass, Frederick, 24
Dowell, J. Edgar, 801–802 n. 14
Drew, Timothy, 681 n. 4
Drexel family, 327, 329 n. 11
Drummond, Sir Eric, 11, 17, 28, 432, 641
Du Bois, W.E.B., 159 n. 5, 188 n. 16, 207, 301 n. 3, 396, 648, 722 n. 2, 761–762 n. 1, 845; advancement policy of, 437–438; on African mandates, 18 n. 1; on African migration, 33; on amalgamation, 205, 216, 223, 233, 237–239; background/heritage of,

233; banquet for, 599 n. 3; on BSL, 33–41, 303; Bruce on, 513; *Darkwater* of, 236; education of, 236, 239, 240; on Firestone, 805, 809–810 n. 2; v. Garvey, 212, 585 n. 5, 598–599; Garvey compared to, 440, 442 n. 6; on Garvey, lv, 233, 234, 235–236, 238, 239, 303, 583–584, 809–810 n. 2; Garvey on, 204, 205, 215, 216, 223, 225, 226, 232–235, 236–241, 250, 251, 253, 254, 259, 268, 271–272, 282, 302–303, 304, 305, 437–438, 439, 440, 441, 461, 485, 518, 633, 636, 796–797; influence of, 513; in Liberia, 513 n. 1, 585 n. 5, 689, 690 n. 4, 797, 805, 809–810 n. 2; *Negro World* on, 598; on race problem, 237–239; on race war, 583; at Third Pan-African Congress, 513 n. 2, 585 n. 4; threatened, 584; on UNIA, 186, 188 n. 14, 208–209, 210–211, 216, 234, 235, 240; UNIA Convention on, 661, 805–806
Duff, E.H., 327, 328, *329 n. 14
Dujas, Benjamin, 176
Dunbar, Mrs. (of Liberia), 788
Duncan, Luther N., 219, *220 n. 1
Duncan, Samuel, 726
Duncan, William, 762–763 n. 1
Dunn, William E. Jr., *173 n. 3
Dupis (agent), 246 n. 1
Dupont, Abraham, 364, *365 n. 2, 365 n. 3
Dupont, Cornelius, 364–365, 365 n. 2, *365 n. 3
du Pont, T. Coleman, 213 n. 2
Duvall, C.H., 287
Dyer, Constantine (Fred), 166, 172, 175, 176, 177, 178, 179, *180 n. 1, 200, 213, 299; acquitted, lvi; appeal lost by, liii, 381; arrested, lii; as assassin suspect, xxxiii, 185; Bureau of Investigation on, 381, 402; convicted, lii, 300; conviction of reversed, 408; defense fund for, lii, 181–182 n. 1, 185, 192 n. 1, 197 (unnamed), 199, 200 n. 2, 201; indicted, 201; sentenced, liii
Dyer, Mrs. Constantine, 199, 214
Dyer, Leonidas C., *481 n. 1, 486–487, 515, 520 n. 1. (See also Dyer Antilynching Bill)
Dyer Antilynching Bill, 155, 156–157, 158, 486, 515, 516, 517–518, 519, 528
Eason, J.W.H., 6, 64, 183, 188 n. 9; assassinated, xxxiii–xxxiv, lii, liii, lvi, 133 n. 1, 161–162, 166–169, 170, 171, 172, 174, 175–180, 181, 185, 190, 191, 192 n. 2, 195, 196, 197, 198, 199–200, 201, 213–214, 230–231, 232, 242, 243–245, 263, 264–265, 266, 298–300, 374, 380–381, 402, 408, 584; on BSL, 48–49; expelled, xxxiii, 48, 49, 172; membership loan by, 49, 274; in New Orleans, 48, 50, 161–162, 181; salary of, 103; splits from Garvey, 10, 29, 45, 46, 48–50, 162, 166, 167, 168, 175, 179, 181, 185, 190; Universal Negro Alliance of, xxxiii, li, 10, 13, 14, 30, 48, 50, 179; as UNIA officer, 101

East St. Louis, Ill.: blacks in, 679, 682 n. 6; blacks not wanted in, 459; race riot in, 207, 355, 751 n. 3; UNIA in, 651

Eaton, J.B., 664, 665, 670, 671, 720–721, 766, 777, 779, 785, 807, 819, 833, 838; on education, 748; on Negro policy, 679; on Negroes in manufacturing, 742–743; on race problem, 686; on UNIA, 656

Echezabal, Judge Frank T., 411 n. 3

Edison, Thomas Alva, 538, 815, 820 n. 3

Edmunds, Joseph, 585 n. 4

Education: Garvey on, 502, 520–521, 525, 526, 684, 693, 694, 828; McGuire on, 718; new, 520–521, 526; old, 502, 521; as UNIA aim, 520, 521, 525; UNIA Convention on, 592, 593, 717–718, 720–721, 747, 748–749, 760, 763–764

Egypt, 30; Garvey on, 356, 522, 531, 563, 636, 646; nationalism in, 356, 522, 563, 636, 642 n. 1; race relations in, 531; in Sudan, 733 n. 1. See also Psalms

Elder Dempster Line, 682, 683 n. 3

Elevator Men's Union, 227

Elijah Mohammed, 681 n. 4

Ellegor, F. Wilcolm, 64, 65, 102, 103, 616

Ellenberg, A.G., 674, 678, 718, 736, 744, 767, 777, 817, 819, 833, 836; on black deity, 670; on education, 748; on race problem, 686; on steel mills, 653

Ellis (American consul), 825

Emancipation, 649; education for, 684; Garvey on, 47, 143, 145, 156, 157, 223, 308, 313, 314, 315, 360, 361, 449, 517, 542, 604, 633, 684

Emancipation Proclamation (1863), 156, 157, 765 n. 2

Emmet, Robert, 130–131, 309

Endich tradition, 628, 630–631 n. 29

Enoch, Ethiopic First Book of, 669 n. 15

Episcopal Church, 630 n. 20, 650 n. 1

Equality: Garvey on, 118–119, 251, 259, 355, 450, 465, 466, 467, 515, 636, 637; social, 118, 251, 355, 450, 465, 466, 467, 754–755. See also Amalgamation

Eritrea, 644, n. 2

Ethiopia (as Biblical name for Africa): Bible from, 666; Garvey on, 23–24, 440, 502, 646; new, 502. See also Psalms; Abyssinia

Ethiopianism, 692 n. 5

Ethiopian Orthodox Church, 669 n. 15

Eugenics, 720, 722 n. 3

Evans, Mr. (accountant), 63

Evelyn-Graham, Marcus, 358 n. 20

Fabre Line, 510 n. 2

Fangeat, Jean, 752 n. 6

Fard, W.D., 681 n. 4

Farmer-labor convention, 559 n. 2

Farmers Loan and Trust Co., 94

Fascism, 170 n. 1, 261 n. 3, 262 nn. 4, 5; anti-fascism, 851, 852, 853

Federal Bureau of Investigation. See Bureau of Investigation

Federal Council of the Churches of Christ, 674, 676 n. 9

Federated Malay States, 820 n. 4

Fenner, J.J., 767, 833, 838

Ferris, William, 4, 28, 30–31, 43, 135, 163, 275, 287; as BSL director, 60; on Garvey, 27, 181, 190, 263, 265; on Negro World staff, liii, 383, 384 n. 2; at Renaissance Casino, 379; resigns, xxxiv, liii

Finance Corp. of America, 799 n. 1, 809–810 n. 2

Financial World, 386–387

Firestone, Harvey, 799 n. 1, 815, 820 n. 3

Firestone Tire and Rubber Co.: in Liberia, 788, 796, 799 n. 1, 805, 806, 807–808, 809–810 n. 2, 811–812, 815; in Philippines, 800 n. 7

Fisher, Rev. H., 177

Fitzsimmons, John J., 167

Flag, 270, 480, 569

Fletcher, Sir Angus S., 321–322, *323 n. 3

Foley, Ella M., 350, *359 n. 34

Ford, Arnold J., 264 n.2, 388 n.1, 287, 678, 777, 833, 837; on black deity, 670; on education, 748; on Garvey, 28, 264, 288 n. 1; as musical director, 13, 14 n. 1; and UNIA, 380, 616

Ford, Edsel, 668 n. 5

Ford, Henry, 668 n. 5, 815, 820 n. 3

Ford, James W., 849, 850, 851

Ford, Justice John, 420 n. 2

Ford, Patrick, 322–323 n. 2

Ford, Robert, 322–323 n. 2

Ford Motor Co., 662, 668 n. 5

Foreign Policy Association, 295 n. 2

Fortune, T. Thomas, 11 n. 2, 384 n. 2

Fort-Whiteman, Lovett, 559 n. 2, 846, 847

Foster, Mr. (of USSB), 95

Foulkes, A., 736, 833

France: in Africa, 459, 524, 588, 632, 641–642, 674, 675, 679, 680–681 n. 2, 681–682 n. 5, 750, 752 n. 7, 753, 754, 796; bans Negro World, 561 n. 3; boxing in, 140 nn. 1, 2; on Garvey, 378–379; Garvey on, 143, 144, 459, 518–519, 520, 524, 528–529, 588, 601, 602, 632, 641–642, 677, 725, 726, 753, 754, 787, 796, 798; Germany threatened by, 169, 170 n. 1, 270, 518–519, 528–529; on Greco-Turkish War, 26 nn. 8, 10, 12; and Liberia, 796, 800 n. 6; race relations of, 135–136, 137, 138, 140, 155, 594, 677–680, 684; republic in, 143, 144; socialism in, 602, 605 n. 1, 642; on UNIA, 725, 726, 752 n. 6, 796, 797; UNIA ambassador to, liv; UNIA Convention on, 594, 674, 675, 677–

680, 684; and USSR, 605 n. 1

Francis, Lionel, 299, 300, 692, 704

Franco-Prussian War, 528, 533 n. 1

Franklin, Benjamin, 328 n. 1

Franklin, Thomas, 192 n. 1

The Freeman, 288

French Boxing Federation, 140 nn. 1, 2

Freschi, John J., 283, *285 n. 2

Freund, Sanford H.E., 15, 16

Friends of Negro Freedom, 5–6 n. 2, 7, 31, 44, 184, 461, 558–559 n. 1

Fuller, Edward M., 320 n. 3

E.M. Fuller and Co., 320 n. 3, 386–387

Fusion movement, 599 n. 1

Gadsby, G., 380

Gaelic American, 322–323 n. 2

Gaines, E.L., 28, 29–30, 64, 266, 274, 716; discharged, xxxiv, liii, 380, 383; on Garvey, 264–265; Garvey on, 703–704; on guns, 383; in UNIA, 102, 103

Karl Gale and Co., 435

Gambia, 639 n. 3, 560, 561 n. 3

Gandhi, Mohandas (Mahatma), lvi, 119, 253, 645

Garcia, Elie, 81, 94, 97, 102, 343, 344, 351, 353, 801 n. 12; auditor-general's report by, 108–111; on BSL, 64, 65, 95, 96, 114 n. 5, 125, 347; as BSL officer, 60, 77, 308; forgery/theft trial of, lii, 173, 245, 273, 275–276, 283–284; Garvey on, 508; on Garvey, 244–245, 288 n. 1; as mail fraud co-defendant, 173, 302, 308, 323–324, 325–328, 329 n. 15, 357–358 n. 16, 374, 393; salary of, 100, 103, 325, 328; on ship purchases, 95–96, 97, 98, 328 n. 2, 382–383 n. 4; v. UNIA, 274–275, 285 n. 1

Garcia Sugar Corp., 35

Garibaldi, Giuseppe, 261 n. 3

Garrett, John O., 351, 474

Garrett, P., 714, 833, 837

Garrison, William Lloyd, 322–323 n. 2, 517

Garvey, Amy A. *See* Ashwood, Amy (Garvey)

Garvey, Amy J. *See* Jacques, Amy (Garvey)

MARCUS GARVEY

autobiography of, 436 n. 1, 782 n. 2; "Bits of Silver" fund of, 316; bust of, 266; contributions by, lv, 496, 497, 597; deportation efforts against, liv, 188 n. 11, 384, 431 n. 1, 463; v. Du Bois, 212, 585 n. 5, 598–599; editorials/articles by, 51–53, 149–150, 169, 193–195, 217–218, 220–228, 232–241, 312–316, 389, 413–416, 417–418, 437–441, 468, 484–488, 534–536, 724–728, 756–759; flag of, 569; greetings/invitations/condolences by, liii, lv, lvi, 416–417, 433, 442, 496–497, 511, 552–553, 556–557, 640; income tax charge against, 285–286, 682, 683, 688, 689; and

Ku Klux Klan, 10, 44, 154, 183, 228 n. 3, 338, 846; life of in film, 761–762 n. 1; *Philosophy and Opinions* of, xxxv, 406, 411 n. 2, 470, 591 n. 5, 799–800 n. 3; prefers Leavenworth, 385; salary of, 8, 99, 100, 103, 286, 330–331, 345, 370–372; in songs, 801–802 n. 14; speeches by, 19–25, 117–119, 127–132, 135–140, 143–149, 155–158, 214–216, 258–261, 266–273, 277–282, 289–292, 306–309, 308–311, 359–362, 448–455, 456–462, 490–496, 498–505, 513–520, 520–533, 536–547, 549–555, 563–567, 568–570, 572–573, 586–590, 601–605, 646–648, 650–651, 822–823; sued, 54, 347–348, 374, 412 n. 2; suits by, 219 n. 1; travel restrictions on, 191, 560–561; at UNIA Convention (1924), lvi, 640–645, 646–648, 650–651, 661, 663, 665, 669, 671, 677, 684, 690–711, 713, 714, 717, 718, 729, 731, 732, 735, 737, 742, 743, 745, 747, 748, 750, 760, 763, 766, 767, 775, 778, 781, 784, 786, 805, 806, 808, 813, 815, 816, 817, 818, 822–823, 833, 837; violates law, 38, 62; visa difficulties of (1921), 392, 707, 708

ON AFRICA

146; on Africa awakened, 306, 308, 532; on Africa for Africans, 271, 531, 532, 533, 563, 573, 636, 637; on black civilization in, 272, 535, 536; on black government in, 205, 250, 282, 294, 450–451, 452, 467, 468, 469, 470, 485, 486, 506, 507–508, 509, 511, 544, 563, 564, 566, 567, 589–590, 635, 824; on black man's right to, 526; on colonization in, 117–118; on Europe in, 22, 51–52, 415, 452, 459, 523, 524, 534, 560–561, 568, 602, 632, 641–642, 643; on exploitation of, 51, 52, 294; on Egypt, 356, 522, 531, 563, 636, 646; on Ethiopia, 23–24, 440, 502, 646 (*see also* Psalms 68:31); on League of Nations mandates, 214; on minerals in, 51, 52, 147, 252, 254, 524; on missionaries in, 51–52, 54 n. 1; on nationalism in, 637, 639 n. 3, 753–754; on new, 309; on redemption of, 51, 53, 131, 145, 149, 248, 291, 312, 313, 315, 360, 361, 362, 453, 458–459, 461, 534, 601, 753–754, 787, 797, 798, 799; as solution for race problem, 485, 524, 570; on UNIA Convention to be in, 301, 320–321; on West Africa, 454; on whites in, 270, 415, 514, 515, 701, 801 n. 9. *See also* Garvey, Marcus, Topics in Speeches and Writings of, on Liberia

ON BLACK LEADERS AND BLACK ORGANIZATIONS

194, 217–218, 220–227, 228 n. 12, 446, 447, 468, 486, 634, 694–695, 700; on Robert Abbott, 226 (unnamed), 227, 544, 545,

546–547; on African Blood Brotherhood, 192, 461; on Robert Bagnall, 219 n. 1, 227 (unnamed), 302, 303, 304, 439, 440, 441; on black clergy, 686, 728; on black press, 131, 149–150, 219 n. 1, 226, 796–797; on Cyril Briggs, 226, 558–559 n. 1; on *Crisis*, 302–303, 440, 583, 796; on W.E.B. Du Bois, 204, 205, 215, 216, 223, 225, 226, 232–235, 236–241, 250, 251, 253, 254, 259, 268, 271–272, 282, 302–303, 304, 305, 437–438, 439, 440, 441, 461, 485, 518, 633, 636, 796–797; on Friends of Negro Freedom, 192, 461; on "Garvey Must Go" movement, 440; as hindrance to race, 726, 727–728; on J.W. Johnson, 204, 215, 233, 250, 251, 253, 268, 302, 441, 461, 485, 518, 544, 545, 546–547, 633, 636; on Moton, 56, 57; on Nail, 302; on NAACP, 155, 156, 157, 158, 192, 204, 216, 233–234, 235, 237, 238, 248–249, 250–251, 253, 254, 268, 302, 303, 304, 305, 308, 402 n. 1, 437–438, 439, 440, 441, 461, 486, 515, 518, 544, 545, 546–547, 583, 633, 636, 705; on need for new, 251, 490–491, 495, 527, 528, 543, 547; on Negro Sanhedrin, 558–559 n. 1; on old, 757–758, 759; on Chandler Owen, 215, 219 n. 1, 271–272, 461; on Harry Pace, 226 (unnamed), 302; on William Pickens, 215, 219 n. 1, 233, 253–254, 302, 303, 304, 439, 440, 441, 461; on proposed meeting in Chicago of, 389; on A.P. Randolph, 215, 219 n. 1, 271–272, 461; on Booker T. Washington, 24, 490, 491, 493, 494, 496; on Walter White, 439–440

ON BLACKS/NEGROES/RACE

on amalgamation, 138, 205, 216, 223, 233–234, 237, 451, 465, 466, 467; on awakened Negro, 565; on black civilization, 118–119, 205, 241, 458–459; on black deity, 647, 650 n. 1, 665–666, 828, 829, 830, 831; on black franchise, 156, 543; on black migration, 156, 542; on black soldiers, 143, 148, 252, 532, 566, 588, 637, 646–647, 797; on blacks' political power, 155–158, 249–250, 543, 545–546, 637; on black unemployment, 546, 726; on caste aristocracy, 437, 441; on color (light v. dark), 437, 438–439, 509, 570; on condition of blacks, 145–146, 147, 155, 281–282, 290, 459, 522–523, 529, 531, 536–537, 538, 539, 540, 543, 604, 631, 633, 677, 694, 769, 812; on disciplining the Negro, 692, 693; on duty of Negro, 501, 502; on education of race, 131, 206; on future of race, 205, 259, 260, 267, 268, 269–270, 271, 278–279, 281–282, 415, 464, 465, 485, 530, 534, 544, 546–547, 631–632, 636, 701–702, 725, 726, 727; on government of our own, 155, 272–273, 290, 494, 530, 537, 540, 541, 544; on interracial boxing, 135, 136–137; on jimcrowism, 481, 487, 504, 530, 538, 539, 540; on laying Negro low, 360; on Negro as human, 465, 503, 521, 563; on Negro citizenship, 145, 146–147, 148–149; on Negro doesn't understand himself, 498–499; on Negro his own worst enemy, 24, 127, 128, 129–130, 131, 134, 193, 215, 216, 220–223, 227, 314, 315, 436 n. 1, 449–450, 451, 460, 461, 466, 634–635, 727, 757, 797; on Negro in next war, 20–21, 22, 24, 25; on Negro in white man's civilization, 249, 272, 278, 460, 461, 522, 529–530, 531, 540–541, 543, 566, 588, 592; on Negro names, 354; on Negro not fooled, 516; on Negro population, 545, 546, 702; on Negro preparation, 169; on Negro's industrial development, 743; on Negro's opportunity, 270; on Negro's rights, 146–147, 247–248, 249, 479, 481, 503, 522, 533 n. 1, 570, 572; on new Negro, 20, 22–23, 313, 360, 449, 457–458, 460, 468, 516, 522, 526–527, 635, 706, 798; on race attitudes/race relations, liv, 135–140, 155, 205–207, 224, 252, 259, 267, 269, 270–271, 450, 452, 459, 465–466, 468–473, 483, 488, 489, 495, 497, 498, 518, 527, 531, 541, 542, 602, 677, 737, 831; on race competition, 205–206, 267–268, 269, 450–451, 465–466, 467, 566, 567, 635–636; on race consciousness, 493, 495, 530, 567; on race differences, 492, 495, 498–499; on race equality/inequality, 259, 260, 493, 503–504, 564–565; on race idealism, 145, 521, 564–565, 665–666, 831; on race loyalty, 149, 515; on race organization, 24, 632, 634; on race pride, 206, 223–224, 251, 437, 438, 495, 512, 665, 696; on race problem and its solution, 57, 204–205, 206, 238, 260, 270–271, 272, 355, 447, 464, 467, 468–470, 493, 495, 499, 503, 530, 532–533, 542, 543, 566, 684, 686; on race progress, 129, 312, 464, 465, 467–468, 528, 536–537, 543, 632, 636, 742; on race purity, 205, 451, 512, 722 n. 1; on race riots, 207, 355, 749; on race self-interest, 139, 271, 338–339, 361, 493, 514, 515, 516, 517, 519, 521–522, 523, 525, 527, 530, 531, 534, 543, 562, 564, 632–633, 634, 770, 771; on race self-reliance, 449; on race unity, 24, 118, 145, 195, 216, 227, 248, 413, 414, 437–438, 440–441, 508, 512, 521, 562, 636; on race uplift, 118–119, 406, 446, 522; on race war, 21, 479, 481; on respect for Negroes, 534–535, 536–537, 538, 539, 540; on segregation, 538–539, 540; on square deal for Negroes, 637; on stewardship of Negroes, 504, 505; on two types of Negroes, 566–567; on West Indian v. American Negroes, 223

MAIL FRAUD TRIAL OF

xxxiii, li, lii, 38, 116, 160, 162, 174, 316, 846; appeal in, 450, 463, 559; bail for Garvey in, xxxiv, liii, liv, 381–382, 386, 393, 394, 400, 401–403, 404, 406, 407, 409–410, 446–447, 448 nn. 1, 2, 455, 584; black leaders on, 44, 185, 377–378, 428–429, 584, 626, 627; bribery alleged in, 287, 403, 409; British on, 591; bond in, 191, 376; Bureau of Investigation on, 164, 165–166, 173, 191, 256, 287, 317, 381–382, 384, 402–403; character witnesses in, 402, 407; co-defendants in, 173, 302, 308, 374, 376 (*see also* Garcia, Elie; Thompson, O.M.; Tobias, George); Committee on Justice for, liii, 390; compared to Fuller and McGee, 386–387; defense fund for, xxxiv, xxxvi, 47, 164 n. 1, 173, 379, 380 n. 1, 384 n. 3, 401–402, 407, 408, 559; French on, 378–379; Garvey defends himself in, liii, 301–305, 330–356, 357 n. 12, 365, 374–375, 376, 382–383 n. 4, 407, 454, 626, 627, 705–706; Garvey in prison after, liv, 5–6 n. 2, 365–366, 368, 376, 386, 388, 389, 401, 403, 413–416, 417–418, 437–441, 446–447, 450, 452, 453, 457, 462, 634; Garvey on, liii, 132, 301–305, 308–309, 350–353, 366, 368, 386, 402 n. 1, 403, 404–411, 415–416, 439, 446–447, 449–450, 452, 453, 454, 455, 457, 462, 634, 698–699, 705–706, 708; jury addressed in, 306–308, 330–356, 359; jury charged in, 365, 366, 375; jury guarded in, 375; jury threatened in, 364; lawyers in, 336, 381, 386; Mack at, liii, 301–305, 365, 366, 375, 386, 400, 401; Mattuck and, 306–308, 359, 366, 386, 400, 401–402, 404–405, 406, 407–408, 409, 410, 446; press on, 47, 364–365, 373–378, 385–387; reaction to verdict in, 369 n. 1, 377, 385, 397, 401, 410, 479 n. 2, 510, 713; sentencing in, liii, 381, 384, 385, 386, 424, 448; UNIA petition on, liii, 388, 390–394, 396; verdict in, 366, 373, 376, 377–378, 379, 381, 382 n. 4, 384, 404, 448, 449–450, 560, 591; witnesses at, 166, 167, 168, 175, 179, 266, 323–328, 350–353, 374, 600; witnesses threatened in, 169, 196, 317, 364, 365 n. 1, 400, 401, 403, 404–405, 408, 409, 584

METAPHORS USED BY

on being in troubled waters, 526; on being beware of Greeks bearing gifts, 415; on can't serve two masters, 517; on fox and chicken, 487, 517; on handwriting on wall, 266, 273; on having no bananas, 481; on killing a dog, 516, 545, 707; on lion and sheep, 485; on lion and tiger, 632; on living on borrowed goods, 537, 538; on our hand in the lion's mouth, 527–528, 543; on a place in the sun, 468; on princes out of Egypt (*see* Psalms 68:31); on Rome not built in a day, 290; on strangling the bull, 544; on striking the shepherd, 480–481; on survival of fittest, 279, 481, 486, 513, 523; on tiger let loose, 359–360, 362, 402 n. 1

OFFICES AND TITLES OF

378, 480, 560, 639; managing editor of *Negro World*, 182; president of BSL, 58, 59, 60, 61, 62, 63, 69, 73, 77, 78, 80, 81, 83, 84, 85, 86, 88, 89, 93, 97, 98, 99, 311, 391, 425, 472; president-general of UNIA, 101, 125, 126, 192, 207, 247, 391, 392, 589, 609, 611, 616, 724–725, 817; provisional president of Africa, 117, 274

OPINIONS OF OTHERS ON

327, 337, 443, 613, 795; as apostle of new thought, 436; Belgian government on, 32, 56–57, 134–135; as "big black bull," 319; black leaders/black organizations on, xxxiv, lii, liv, lv, 3, 7, 10, 13, 31, 44, 47, 54–55, 182–187, 189, 212, 217 n. 2, 222, 224, 233, 234, 235–236, 238, 239, 263, 303, 306 n. 1, 368, 377–378, 423–431, 497, 578, 579 nn. 1, 2, 583–584, 740, 809–810 n. 2; as (black) Moses, 116, 117, 154, 427, 628, 721 n. 1; black press on, 116, 119 n. 1, 212–213, 254–255, 376–378, 440, 442 n. 6, 498, 585 n. 5, 768 n. 2; blacks against, 9–10, 13, 378 n. 1, 741 n. 1; British on, 479, 560–561, 591; Bureau of Investigation on, 6, 7–8, 27–28, 29–31, 42–43, 46–47, 54, 160, 164, 165–166, 173, 174–180, 189, 191, 256, 285–286, 287, 294, 317, 378 n. 1, 381–382, 384, 402, 463, 548, 556–557, 568–570, 682, 688, 689–690; Communists on, 843, 845, 846, 850; compared to Blyden, 442 n. 6; compared to Du Bois, 440, 442 n. 6; compared to Gandhi, 119; compared to Hitler, 5–6 n. 2; compared to Jesus Christ, 480; compared to John the Baptist, 681 n. 4; compared to Mussolini, 5–6 n. 2; compared to Napoleon, 430; compared to Ponzi, 431 n. 2; compared to Booker T. Washington, 442 n. 6; as dangerous, 570; as demagogue, 182; as exaggerator, 430; French on, 573 n. 1; as great leader, 423, 429–430, 667; Justice Department on, 212; Liberian government on, 610, 773; as martyr, 426; as menace, 378; Panken on, 185; as radical, 463; reaction to meeting with Ku Klux Klan of, 27, 115, 222, 584, 721 n. 1, 751 n. 2, 768–769, 845; threatened, 405; as traitor, lv; UNIA Convention on,

713, 719, 723–724, 739–740; UNIA officers defend, 379, 396–397, 436, 628, 667, 740, 826; white press on, liii, 9–10, 119–120 n. 2

PERSONAL LIFE OF

on Amy Ashwood, 339; on Amy Jacques, 368, 450, 452–453, 700; citizenship of, 401, 406; death of, 5–6 n. 2; described, 480; last will and testament of, 369–370; lived in Harlem, 319, 407, 410; on mother's education, 236; royalty agreement for, 295–297; rumored house in Larchmont of, li, 131, 132; upbringing of, 235–236

TOPICS IN SPEECHES AND
WRITINGS OF

on abolitionism, 517; on ambition, 146–147, 249, 250, 468, 469, 491–492, 493, 494, 502–503, 505, 527, 635; on America as white man's country, 270, 485, 767; on American Indian, 543, 632, 700; appeal to soul of white America, xxxv, liv, 464–468, 470, 567 n. 3, 812; on aristocracy, 251; on arms, 229, 264, 386, 408, 409; on Black Cross Navigation and Trading Co., lvi, 709, 756, 757, 759, 610; on BSL, 37, 38–40, 63, 115–116, 122–123, 150–152, 207, 291, 292, 312–313, 331, 337–338, 339–342, 352–353, 354, 448, 452, 459, 509, 607, 698, 699, 703, 707; on Blue Vein Society, 438, 440; on Bolshevism, 193, 250; on Catholicism, 485, 771, 772, 830; on Christianity, 21–22, 514, 515, 635, 673–674; on Chinese, 539; on classes, 550–551; on Communism, 603, 769–771; on conscience v. belief, 464–465; on *Daily Negro Times*, 10, 149–150; on death, 310–311; on democracy's majority, 143–144, 518, 525, 543, 544, 545, 554; on diplomacy, 527, 543, 545, 547, 795–796; on Dyer Antilynching Bill, 155, 156–157, 158, 486, 515, 516, 517–518, 519, 528; on education, 502, 520–521, 525, 526, 684, 693, 694, 828; on emancipation, 47, 143, 145, 146, 157, 223, 308, 313, 314, 315, 360, 361, 449, 517, 542, 604, 633, 684; on equality, 118, 119, 251, 259, 355, 450, 465, 466, 467, 515, 636, 637; on fairness, 587–588, 646; on fascism, 260; on fear, 362; on fellowship, 514; on France, 140, 144, 270, 459, 518–519, 520, 524, 528–529, 588, 601, 602, 632, 641–642, 677, 725, 726, 753, 754, 787, 796, 797, 798; on Germany, 23, 270, 459, 518–519, 528–529, 602, 641, 798; on Great Britain, xxxv, 22, 43, 146–147, 249, 270, 322, 459, 519, 520, 522, 524, 549 nn. 1, 2, 552, 588, 592, 601, 602, 632, 677, 706–707, 725, 726, 787, 796, 797, 798; on Haiti, 518–519, 529, 642, 750; on his enemies, lii, 38, 43, 47, 131, 203, 217–218, 310–311, 312, 336–339, 341, 365–366,

699, 702–703, 705–706, 708, 710, 711; on human rights, 414, 526, 564; on hypocrisy, 517; on ideals, 315, 521, 604; on industrial development, 756–757; on industry before politics, 527, 545, 546; on initiative, 129; on Islam, 23; on Italy, 459, 519, 524, 539, 643; on Japan, 519, 520, 602; on Jews, 356, 366, 367 n. 3, 485, 522, 539, 563, 573, 771, 772; on justice/injustice, 259, 331, 334, 406, 414, 446–448, 450, 453, 518, 526, 528–529, 563; on Knights of Columbus, 486; on Ku Klux Klan, 222, 258, 260–261, 269, 277, 280–281, 484, 485, 486, 487, 515, 527, 541, 671–672, 749, 771; on League of Nations, 10, 214, 294, 533; on Liberia/emigration to Liberia, 229, 231, 507–510, 586–587, 609–610, 725, 726, 727, 758–759, 787–788, 796, 810–811, 812, 815; on liberty, 253, 332, 563, 564; on Liberty Hall, 234–235; on losing faith, 290–291; on lynching, 120 n. 4, 136, 158, 224, 647, 749, 771; on materialism, 259, 464, 513, 514, 515, 525, 631; on missionaries, 51–52, 53, 54 n. 1, 514, 515; on nationalism/independence movements, 20, 22–23, 43, 127–128, 130–131, 143 144, 270, 291, 356, 362, 457, 158, 522, 539, 550, 551, 553, 563, 573, 588, 601, 602, 603, 632, 636, 641, 706, 737, 750, 753–754; on *Negro World*, 344, 346, 406, 706; on organization, 253, 601–602; on over-population, 701, 702; on perseverance, 456, 457; on Philippines, 592; on Pilgrims, 343, 449, 566, 589, 695; on power, 139, 229, 260, 279, 493–494, 513, 514, 518, 519–520, 528–529; on preparation, 20, 535, 601; on press, 203; quotes Bible, 241, 267, 314, 366, 485, 493, 565, 632, 638, 646, 848; quotes Shakespeare, 220, 356, 620; quotes Walter Scott, 567; on radicalism, 707; on registering to vote, 413, 414–415, 461; on religion, 259–260; on responsibility, 701, 703; on sacrifice, 132, 254, 306–307, 309, 532, 695; on self-preservation, 271; on soldiers, 264; on ships, xxxiv, 36, 37, 93, 97, 98, 99, 332, 342, 343–344, 345, 509, 586, 709–710, 711, 728, 732, 737, 742, 747, 756, 757, 759; on slavery, 128, 354–355, 361–362, 465, 481, 519–520, 565; on socialism, xxxv, 225, 226, 269, 551–552, 602, 603; on South, 494–495, 529, 684, 687 n. 1; on South Africa, 282, 601, 602, 754; on spiritual v. physical, 498–499, 501, 647; on standard of man, 503–504; on Tuskegee, 490–491, 495–496; on unemployment, 546, 694, 726; on United Fruit Co., 737; on United States, 335, 518; on USSB, 291; on victory won from within, 460; on Wall Street, 292; on war clouds gathering, 20–21, 22, 24, 25, 43, 169, 449, 588, 602, 647; on wearing a robe, 604; on West Indies, 238, 602; on white man, xxxv, 138–139, 460, 461, 492, 494–495, 500, 700–702; on white man's civilization, 131, 484, 538, 539, 798; on white philanthropy, 52, 53, 57, 194–195, 235, 236, 237, 239, 486, 487, 495, 517, 523; on work, 250–251; on Workers party, 770, 771–772

TRAVELS OF

591–592, 698; Bermuda trip of prohibited, 561; in Birmingham, Ala., 484; in Buffalo, liii, 230, 294; in California, liv, 184, 482, 484, 490; at Carnegie Hall, lii, lv, 246, 247–254, 263, 264, 265, 631–638, 723; in Chicago, lii; in Cincinnati, 598–599; in Cleveland, 294–295 n. 1; in Detroit, 230, 265; in Kansas, 455, 456 n. 6, 490; at Liberty Hall, 127, 135, 214, 258, 264, 266, 277, 289, 293, 308, 448, 456, 498, 513, 536, 549, 586, 601; at Madison Square Garden, 562–567, 568–570, 572–573; in Newark, lvi, 659 n. 11; in New Orleans, 161, 707–708; in North Carolina, 116, 117–119, 120 n. 4; in Oregon, 490, 496 n. 2; in Panama, 258; in Philadelphia, lv; in Pittsburgh, li, liii, 647; restrictions on, 191, 560–561; in St. Louis, liv, 479, 480–481; at Tuskegee, liv, lv, 484, 490–496, 497; in Virginia, 333; in Washington, D.C., lv, 294–295 n. 1, 520–533, 534, 544; in West Indies (1921), 114 n. 6, 345, 353, 392, 707; world tour (proposed) of, xxxiii, xxxix, lii, 162–163, 191, 229; in Youngstown, Ohio, liv, 464, 470 n. 2

AND UNIA (AND FORMER UNIA) OFFICERS

6, 7, 13–14, 38–39, 389, 405, 421–423, 696–698, 700, 705, 775; and Bourne, 266, 380 n. 1, 410; on Bruce, 688 n. 4; Bruce on, 396–397; and Cockburn, 323, 339–341, 342, 343; on H.V. Davis, xxxiv, liii, 350–351, 379–380, 383, 573, 695, 698, 709, 810; and de Bourg, 349, 350, 698; on Domingo, 225–226; Eason splits from, 10, 29, 45, 46, 48–50, 162, 166, 167, 168, 175, 179, 181, 185, 190, 697; possible involvement in Eason's death of, xxxiii–xxxiv, 167, 172, 174, 181, 190, 192 n. 2, 197, 199, 201, 242, 263, 264, 265, 266, 298, 381, 402, 408, 584; Ferris on, 27, 181, 190, 263, 265; Ford on, 28, 264, 288 n. 1; on Francis, 692, 704; Gaines on, 264–265; on Gaines, 703–704; Garcia on, 244–245, 288 n. 1; on Garcia, 508; has Garcia arrested, lii, 173, 245, 273, 284; on Grey, 333–334, 335; on McGuire, 697, 699; on Marke, xxxiv, liii, 379–380, 383; on Plummer, 818; on Poston, 568, 573, 709, 786; on A. Richardson, 342, 343, 345;

on Silverston, 342–343, 366; on R. Smith, xxxiv, liii, 379–380, 383; on Smith-Green, 340; on Tobitt, 548–549, 698; Tobitt on, 443–444; on Toote, 699, 700; on Van Lowe, 709; on Watkis, 349–350; on V. Williams, 411–412, 419–420; on Yearwood, 276

ON UNIA

379, 456–457, 458, 515, 566, 604, 703, 817; on accomplishments, 634, 637; on aims and objects, 118, 127, 130, 143, 144–145, 146, 202, 203–204, 246, 247–248, 253, 278–279, 289–292, 437–438, 450, 451, 452, 461, 501, 502, 503, 505, 512, 520, 521, 522, 524, 525, 531, 532, 534, 537, 540, 541, 543, 544, 589, 684, 691; on colonization by, 610, 708–710, 711, 725, 726, 787, 797, 798; compares to Christianity, 635; on constitution, 218, 406, 692; on convention of 1920, 696, 697; on convention of 1923, xxxiv, 301, 320–321, 634, 691, 702; on convention of 1924, lv, 301, 320–321, 603; differs from other movements, 143–144, 146–147, 248–249, 250–251, 253, 254, 267, 278, 637; difficulties of, 691–699; duties of members of, 535–536, 781–782, 783; enemies of, 193, 194, 214–216, 252, 312, 313, 314–315, 414, 725–726, 727, 728; flag of, 270; as government, 291; influence of, 603, 797; as international, 753; on League of Nations delegation of, 19, 32, 51, 56–57, 214, 432; on Liberian delegations of, 508, 570–571 n. 1, 573, 586, 587–588, 589, 709, 786–788, 789, 796, 810, 811; on local conventions of, 320–321, 414; on membership, 204, 208, 225, 240, 353, 506, 573; on membership loans, 274; on military branch, 264; misrepresented, 129, 144, 193–194, 203, 204, 218, 247, 508, 509; oath, 695–696; in Philadelphia, 692; as political movement, 144, 525, 601; political role of, 216, 225, 413, 414–415, 637, 663–664; program of, 697; salaries in, 696, 697, 698, 700, 711; secret police of, 408; as spiritual movement, 292, 627; traitors within, 315–316, 692, 695, 696–697, 775; vision of, 268

ON WORLD LEADERS AND HISTORICAL AND RELIGIOUS FIGURES

on Allah, 23; on William J. Bryant, 258, 259, 260, 261, 269, 277–278, 280, 281, 491, 495; on Roger Casement, 253, 309, 362; on Georges Clemenceau, 20, 495, 533; on Calvin Coolidge, 491, 495, 797; on de Valera, 706; on J.J. Dossen, 784, 796, 797, 799, 822, 824–825; on Congressman Dyer, 486–487; on Thomas A. Edison, 538; on Robert Emmet, 130–131, 309; on

Gandhi, 253, 645; on God, 455, 499, 500–501, 502, 504–505, 603, 604–605, 828, 829, 830; on Warren Harding, 294, 416–418, 491, 495, 727; on Jesus Christ, 21, 127, 130, 131, 148, 193, 315, 366, 455, 525, 550, 555, 603, 635, 665, 829, 830, 831; on John the Baptist, 313; on Judas, 316; on Kemal Pasha, 20, 22, 270; on C.D.B. King, 797, 811; on Lenin, 253, 549–550, 551, 552, 553, 554, 555, 556, 557; on Leopold of Belgium, 812; on Abraham Lincoln, 156, 157, 356, 517, 542, 566; on Lloyd George, 20, 495, 533, 554–555; on Martin Luther, 130, 131; on Ramsay MacDonald, xxxv, 552; on Terence MacSwiney, 253, 362; on Mohammed, 21, 22, 127, 130, 132, 315, 665; on Moses, 127, 128, 130, 131, 132; on Mussolini, 495; on Napoleon, 452; on Czar Nicholas, 552; on Orlando, 20, 495; on Poincare, 495; on Theodore Roosevelt, 491; on Simon of Cyrene, 148, 829, 831; on Jan Smuts, 706, 754; on Leo Tolstoy, 143–144; on Leon Trotsky, 23, 253, 550, 551, 552, 553; on Queen Victoria, 517; on George Washington, 143, 144, 250, 253, 341, 356, 362, 450; on white statesmen, 279–280; on Kaiser Wilhelm (William II), 148, 310, 452; on Woodrow Wilson, 20, 148, 491, 495, 533, 647

Marcus Garvey v. *United States*, 302–305. *See also* Garvey, Marcus, Mail Fraud Trial of
Garvey, Marcus Sr., 236, 237
Garvey and Garveyism, 640, 820 nn. 2, 3
Garveyism, 3–4; in Africa, 283 n. 7, 456 n. 4, 569, 572 n. 11; anti-Garveyism, 5–6 n. 2, 183, 212, 235, 442 n. 6; black leaders on, 13; E.E. Brown on, 424, 426–427, 430; in Canada, 188 n. 8; Communists on, 751 n. 2, 843, 845, 846, 850, 851; Episcopal Church on, 630 n. 20; in Harlem, 235, 424, 431 n. 1, 444 n. 1; Perry Howard on, 212–213; Ku Klux Klan compared to, 212, 263 n. 1; McGuire on, 463–464, 621, 626; in North Carolina, 657 n. 4; in West Virginia, 659–660 n. 13
"Garvey Must Go" movement, xxxiii, xxxiv, 9–10, 217 n. 2, 235, 315, 440
Gegan, Lt. James J., 243, 244, 364
S.S. *General Goethals*, xxxiv, lvi, 756, 759–760 n. 1
George, Mrs. A.J., 795
George, John A., 38
King George V, 593
Georgia: Atlanta, 10, 385; Ku Klux Klan in, 671; UNIA in, 654, 663
German Colonial League, 595 n. 1
German East Africa (Burundi, Rwanda, and Tanzania), 19, 214, 216–217 n. 1
German South West Africa (Namibia). *See* South West Africa

Germany, 32 n. 1; in Africa, 10, 18, 214, 595 n. 1, 641; beet sugar industry in, 678, 680 n. 1; fascism in, 170 n. 1; France threatens, 169, 170 n. 1, 270, 518–519, 528–529; Garvey on, 23, 459, 518–519, 528–529, 602, 641, 798; in League of Nations, 595 n. 1; and Liberia, 800 n. 6; mark in, 459; and Mussolini, 643–644 n. 1; nationalists in, 606 n. 4; socialism in, 602, 606, n. 4
George S. Gethen Co., 175
A Giant of His Race, 760–762 n. 1
Gibbons, Floyd, 456 n. 4
Gibson, Dr. Joseph D., 6, 173–174, 178, 189, 781, 783 n. 2
Gibson, Lydia, 741 n. 1
Gill, James R., 670, 675 n. 3, 680, 833, 838
Gillette, William, 262 n. 5
Gimbel Brothers, *207 n. 1, 546
Gitlow, Benjamin, 848–849
Glele, 752 n. 7
God: color of, 603, 604–605, 625, 647–648, 649–650, 650 n. 2, 828, 829, 830; Garvey on, 455, 499–500, 501, 502, 504, 505, 603, 604–605, 638, 647–648, 828, 829, 830; intentions of, 499, 500–501, 502, 504–505; McGuire on, 625, 649–650
Gold Coast (Ghana), 513, 560, 561 n. 3, 639 n. 3, 706
Goltz, Marshal Colmar von der, 26 n. 14
Gompers, Samuel, 676 n. 6, 754, 755 n. 3
Gordon, J.D., 6, 60, 101, 103
Government of Ireland Act of 1920, 362 n. 2
Grace Methodist Episcopal Church (Newark), 283 n. 4
Grant, E.B., 654, *659 n. 12, 665, 679, 833, 838
Grant, Madison, 722 n. 3
Grant, William, 365 n. 1
Great Britain: in Africa, 10–11 n. 1, 22, 459, 524, 572 n. 9, 632, 639 n. 3, 679, 681 n. 4, 681–682 n. 5, 733 n. 1, 796; blacks in army of, 590 n. 3; on Black Cross Navigation and Trading Co., 591; on BSL, 560; communism in, 549 n. 2; educational policy for colonies of, 10–11 n. 1; fascism in, 262 nn. 4, 5; Garvey on, xxxv, 22, 43, 146–147, 249, 270, 322, 459, 519, 520, 522, 524, 549 nn. 1, 2, 552, 588, 592, 601, 602, 632, 677, 706–707, 725, 726, 787, 796, 797, 798; on Garvey, 479, 560–561, 591; on Greco-Turkish War, 22, 23, 26 nn. 10, 12; Islam and, 679; in Jamaica, 679; Labour government in, xxxv, 549 nn. 1, 2, 552; and Liberia, 800 n. 6; McGuire on, 622–623, 677; on *Negro World*, 560, 561 n. 3; passport policy of, 10, 560–561; race relations/race attitudes of, 135–136, 138, 140, 146–147, 155, 249, 522, 561 n. 1, 588, 590 n. 3, 592, 594, 677–680, 684; rubber controlled by, 815, 820 n. 4; socialism in, 552, 602;

Triple Alliance of, 549 n. 1; on Turkish nationalism, 20, 25 nn. 3, 4, 43, 270; UNIA ambassador to, 540, 547 n. 3, 548–549, 560, 561; UNIA in, 561 n. 1; on UNIA, 560–561, 679, 681 n. 4, 706, 725, 726; UNIA Convention on, 594, 677–680, 684

Greater Negro Medical, Inc., 667 n. 2

Greaves, Walter, 42

Greco-Turkish War, 22–23, 25 n. 4, 26 nn. 6, 8, 9, 10, 11, 12, 14, 33 n. 1

Greece, 25 n. 4, 26 n. 6

Green, Miss, 412

Green, Benjamin F., 746 n. 5

Green, Claude, 766, *768 n. 1, 819, 833, 835

Green, William M., 479 n. 2

Green and Wheat, 479 n. 2

Green River Distilling Co., 116, 152, 358 n. 22

Greensboro Daily News, 119 n. 1, 120 n. 4

Grenada, 294 n. 1, 712 n. 3

Grew, Joseph Clark, *27 n. 1

Grey, Edgar M., 58, 59, 61, 333–334, 335, 365 n. 1

Grey, Joseph, 668–669 n. 9

Griffith, D.W., 760–762 n. 1

Griffith, Tiezekiah, 192 n. 1

Grigsley, Roosevelt, 668–669 n. 9

Grimes, W.W., 190–191

Gulley, Harry D., 174–180, *180 n. 4, 197, 198, 200, 214, 380–381

Haile Selassie (Ras Tafari), 5–6 n. 2, 644 n. 1

Haiti, 559 n. 2; colonization of/immigration to, 613 n. 2, 764, 765 n. 2; condition of blacks in, 742; emigration from, 658 n. 7; Garvey on, 518, 519, 529, 642, 750; Spanish in, 765 n. 2; Tribunal de Paix in, 153; United States in, 518, 519, 529, 642, 643 nn. 1, 2; UNIA Convention on independence for, 593, 715, 737, 744, 745, 750, 764, 766, 767–768

Haitian Agricultural Emigration Association, 765 n. 2

Hale, Bryson, 663, *668 n. 7, 686, 833, 838

Hall, Ethel, 559 n. 2

Hall, Otto, 842, 847, 849

Hamid, Sufi Abdul, 444 n. 1

Hamilton, James, 192 n. 1

Hampton, Haywood, 685, 743, 833, 835

Hampton, Milton S., 169 n. 2

Hampton Institute, 52, 54 n. 2, 496 n. 2

Hancock, Louis, 55

Hand, Billings Learned, *164 n. 2

Handy, W.C., 188 n. 16

Harding, Florence Kling, liii, 416, *417 n. 1

Harding, Warren G., 320 n. 1, 329 n. 9, 687 n. 1, 689; in Birmingham, 416; death of, liii, 416–417; Garvey on, 294, 416–418, 491, 495, 727; on ship subsidy bill, 329 n. 10; UNIA petition to, liii, 388 n. 1, 390–394, 396

Harlem: anti-Garveyism in, 9–10, 235; black population of, 411 n. 5, 545, 546, 702; black vote in, 690 n. 1; boycott in, 444 n. 1; businessmen of, 623; communists in, 842, 850; Garveyism in, 235, 424, 431 n. 1, 444 n. 1; Garvey lives in, 319, 407, 410; politicians in, 310; reaction to verdict in, 377; real estate in, 187 n. 2, 188–189 n. 17; rumors in, 287. *See also* New York (city)

Harlem Baptist Church, 241–242 n. 3

Harlem Community Church, 424, 431 n. 1

Harlem Labor Union, 444 n. 1

Harrigan, Ludwig, 745, 762–763 n. 1, 783, 809, 833, 837

Harris, George W., 187, 218, 227 (unnamed), 228 nn. 13, 14, 229, 824; on Garvey, 377–378, 378 n. 2

Harrison, Hubert H., 4–5 n. 1

Harriss, Magill and Co., 84, 85, 86, 87, 336, 337

Harriss, William, 337, 456 n. 1

Harvey, Cecilia, 813, *820 n. 1, 833, 837

Haskell, Lewis W., 27

Hassell, James A., *660 n. 2, 677, 720, 745, 747, 762–763 n. 1, 776, 779, 783, 785, 818, 833, 838; on black deity, 671; on blacks in West Indies, 678; on Ku Klux Klan, 672, 673; on L'Ouverture, 750; on ships, 656–657; on U.S. in Hawaii, 678

Hathaway, Effie, 200 n. 2

Hawaii, 678, 681 n. 3

Hawkins, William Ashbie, 183, *187 n. 3, 224

Hayes, Rutherford B., 242 n. 4

Hayford, Joseph E. Casely, 513

Hayne, Joseph E., 629 n. 5

Haynes, Samuel A., 806, 807, 809, 833, 837

Hayward, William, 122, 400, 409, 456 n. 6

Haywood, Harry, 212, *213 n. 3, 847, 848

Headley, Mrs. E.G., 762–763 n. 1

Healy, Leo, 336–339, 340, 449 (unnamed), 456 n. 1

Heard, Bishop W.H., 717 n. 1

Hebrew Sanhedrin, 558–559 n. 1

Henderson, Rosa, *801–802 n. 4

Henry, Cyril, 59, 60, 62

Henry, Patrick, 793

Herbert, George, 328 n. 1

Herbert, Henry W., 283, *285 n. 3

Hercules, James, 340, 351, 358 n. 21

Herndon, Angelo, 849

Herriot, Édouard, 605 n. 1, 641, *642 n. 1

Hertslet, Godfrey E.P., *479 n. 3

Hertzog, James, 605 n. 1, 755 n. 1

Hessler, F.H., 245 n. 2

Heuisler, Judge, 547 n. 1

Higgins, Frank C., 568–571

Hill, Rev. James, 192 n. 1, 200 n. 2

Hitler, Adolf, 5–6 n. 2, 852, 853

Hodge, Henry, 12
Hoffman, Frederick L., 722 n. 2
Hogues, Ada, 740, 833, 835
Holinseed, Father, 828
Holland, H.C., 652, 833, 837
C.D. Holley Manufacturing Co., 667 n. 2
Holly, Alonzo, 630–631 n. 29
Holly, James T., 765 n. 2
S.S. *Hong Kheng*, 93, 328 n. 2, 353
Hood, ·Solomon Porter, 689, *690 n. 3, 805, 809–810 n. 2
Hoover, J. Edgar, 174, 190, 199 n. 1, 232, 380, 847
Hoover Investigating Committee, 643 n. 1
Hotel Sterling, 598–599, 599 n. 1
Houénou.   *See* Tovalou-Houénou, Prince Kojo Marc
House, Col. Edward M., 295 n. 2
House, Grossman, and Vorhaus, 334
Howard, Mrs., 789
Howard, D.E., 591 n. 5, 788, 790
Howard, Esme, 591–592, *592 n. 3
Howard, Perry W., 212–213, 213 n. 4
Howard University, lv
Hubs, Rev. A., 176, 179–180
Hughes, Charles Evans, 27 n. 2, 352, 633, 773
Huiswoud, Otto, 843, 844, 845, 848, 850
Hunt, Lawrence J., 343–344, 382–383 n. 4
Hunter, W.L., 832, n. 3
Hunton, Addie W., 159 n. 5
Hurley, Reginald, 590 n. 1
Hurley, William L., 3
Husband, Walter W., *384 n. 1
Hutson, Ella Rose, 41
Hyer (U.S. Marshal), 317
Hylan, John F., 689, 690 n. 1
Hymans, Mr., 32

Ifill, J.P., 378, 378 n. 2
Ilgen (of Elder Dempster Line), 682
Illinois: Garvey violates law in, 38, 62; Ku Klux Klan in, 280, 282–283 n. 3. *See also* Chicago; East St. Louis
Immigration Acts: 1917, 384; 1924, 605–606 n. 3, 722 n. 3
Immigration Department, liv, 392
Imperial Fascist League, 262 n. 5
Impis, 569, 571–572 n. 9
India: Garvey on, 356, 602, 603, 636; National Congress of, 639 n. 3; nationalism in, 356; noncooperation movement in, 603, 645 n. 1
Indiana, 653, 654
Indianapolis Ledger, 288
Industrial Workers of the World, 676 n. 6
International Humanity League, 719, 721 n. 1
International Labor Conference, 57 n. 3
International Labor Defense, 849–850
International Longshoreman's Association,

586 n. 1
International Postal Union, 431 n. 2
International Trade Union Committee of Negro Workers, 849
International Uplift League, 558–559 n. 1
Interstate Commerce Commission, 329 n. 8
Intertype Corp., 420 n. 2, 421, 423
Ireland, nationalism in, 130–131, 291, 322–323 n. 2, 356, 362, 362 n. 2, 522, 563, 573, 621, 706
Irish Free State (Ireland), 706
Irish Land League, 322–323 n. 2
Irish Unionist movement, 362 n. 2
Irish Volunteers, 362 n. 2
Irish World, 322
Islam, 25 n. 4, 679, 681 n. 4; in Africa, 23, 26 n. 13
Israelis (Biblical), 531. *See also* Jews
Israel Zion Hospital, 597–598 n. 3
Italy: in Africa, 262 n. 5, 459, 524, 643, 644 n. 2, 852; blacks in army of, 644 n. 2; fascism in, 261 n. 3, 262 n. 5; Garvey on, 459, 519, 524, 539, 643
Izvestia, 844

Jackson, Mr. (of Georgia), 663, 833, 835
Jackson, Charles, 679, 762–763 n. 1, 764, 766, 818, 819, 833, 836
Jackson, Robert R., 159 n. 4
Jacques, Amy (Garvey), liv, 345, 351, 484, 597, 833, 837; edits *Philosophy and Opinions*, 411 n. 2; edits women's page, xxxv, lv, 579, 580 n. 1; *Garvey and Garveyism* of, 640, 820 nn. 2, 3; Garvey on, 368, 450, 452–453, 700; as Garvey's beneficiary, 369; and Garvey's defense fund, 380 n. 1; at Garvey's trial, 374; illness of, 452; influence of, xxxv; Moton on, 497; royalty rights of, 295–297; UNIA to be run by, 398–399, 456 n. 3; UNIA Convention on, 719
Jacques, Cleveland, 482
Jacques, Ida, 762, 833, 837
Jamaica, 180, 737; banana crop in, 738 n. 1; BSL in, 63, 475; British in, 679; *Negro World* banned in, 712 n. 3; race relations in, 237–239; UNIA in, 663; *Yarmouth* in, 474
James, Mrs. E., 383
James, Walter S., 434–435 n. 2
Jamison (accountant), 76
Japan, 519, 520, 539, 568; earthquake in, 442–443 n. 2, 605 n. 2; economic development in, 660–661 n. 21; emigration from, 605–606 n. 3; nationalism in, 638 n. 1; press censorship in, 602, 605 n. 2; ships in, 656, 661 n. 21; shogunates of, 660–661 n. 21
Jaspar, Henri, *32 n. 1, 56, 134
Jeffers (Jeffries), Mr. (of New York), 729, 736, 833

Jefferson, T.L., 245 n. 2

Jeffries, James (or John). *See* Ramus, Esau

Jeffries, James J., 137, 140 n. 3, 141 n. 4

Jekyll and Hyde, 325, 329 n. 6

Jenkins, Janie, 58, 60, 65, 351

Jesus Christ, 649; as black, 603, 665–667, 669–671, 677, 828–831; as creator, 665; embodies all humanity, 21, 665, 831; Garvey compared to, 480; Garvey on, 21, 127, 130, 131, 148, 193, 315, 366, 455, 525, 550, 555, 603, 635, 665, 829, 830, 831

Jethro, 629 n. 5

Jewish Community House of Bensonhurst, 597–598 n. 3

Jews/Judaism, 366, 367 n. 3, 485, 539, 771, 772; excluded from Russia, 772 n. 3; fascism and, 262 n. 5; nationalism of, 356, 522, 563, 573, 596, 610, 621; at Paris Peace Conference, 301 n. 3

Jimcrowism, 481, 487, 504, 530, 538, 539, 540, 559 n. 2, 755

John Bull, 425, 431 n. 3

Johnson, 88

Johnson, Adrian, 54, 190, 781, 783 n. 1

Johnson, Arthur John "Jack," 136, 137, *140 n. 3, 141 nn. 4, 8

Johnson, F., 670, 686, 833, 838

Johnson, Frank, 178

Johnson, Fred E., 651, 665, 675, 679, 687, 713, 716, 729, 730, 737, 743, 745, 762–763 n. 1, 777, 782, 783, 784, 818, 819, 833, 836; on Du Bois, 805–806; on Garvey, 724, 740; on Ku Klux Klan, 672; on Negro Political Union, 815; on square deal for Negroes, 736; on UNIA, 662–663

Johnson, Gabriel, xxxvii, 101, 207, 510 n. 4

Johnson, George, 760–762 n. 1

Johnson, Hattie, 653, 665, 670, 675, 713, 724, 767, 833, 836

Johnson, Henry Lincoln, 46, 357–358 n. 16, 374, 378, 381, 390 n. 2; at Garvey's trial, 323–328, 336

Johnson, James Weldon, 116, 159 n. 5, 188–189 n. 17, 305, 442 n. 5, 488, 489, 558–559 n. 1, 648; on Dyer Antilynching Bill, 158 n. 1; on Garvey, 212, 497, 578, 579 n. 2; Garvey on, 204, 215, 233, 250, 251, 253, 259, 268, 302, 441, 461, 485, 518, 544, 545, 547, 633, 636

Johnson, L., 472

Johnson, L.A., 8–9

Johnson, Noble, 760–762 n. 1

Johnson, P., 715, 834, 836

Johnson, P.E., 656, 714, 834, 837

Johnson-Jeffries fight, 137, 140 n. 3, 141 n. 4

Johnsons, Shipbrokers, 84

John the Baptist, 313, 666, 681 n. 4

St. John the Divine, 464

Jones (of Cleveland), 289

Jones, Alfred L., 683 n. 3

Jones, Ivan, 845

Jones, James Wormley (Agent 800), lii, 195, 197–198, 199–200, 202 n. 2, 213–214, 232, 244, 246

Jones, L., 685, 834, 837

Jones and Laughlin Steel, 41

Jordan, Dr. Lewis A., 717 n. 1

Judas, 316

Judd, Dr. Gerit P., 681 n. 3

Jusserand, Jean-Jules, 378–379, *379 n. 1

Justice/injustice, 259, 331, 334, 406, 414, 446–448, 450, 453, 518, 526, 528–529, 563

Kakaza, Dr. Theodore M., 510, *511 n. 2

Kamenev, 556 n. 3

S.S. *Kanawha*, 80, 115, 307, 325, 326, 353, 354; condition of, 150–151, 476, 477, 478; crew of, 65; in Cuba, 150–151; income from, 92; press on, 35; purchase of, 89–91, 342, 351, 359 n. 36, 476; repairs to, 342, 345, 476–477

Kanet, Roger E., 853

Kansas, 455, 456 n. 6, 490

Kansas City Call, 367 n. 3, 373–376, 385–386, 397

Katayama, Sen, 842, 843, 844, 845

S.S. *Kayo Maro*, 475

Kellum, Isaac, 655, *660 n. 18, 834, 837

Kemal Pasha, Mustapha, 20, 22, 23, *25 n. 2, 26 n. 6, 270

Kemp, Ira, 444 n. 1

Kilroe, Edwin, 333, 334, 335–336, 341, 350, 357–358 n. 16

King, A.L., 851

King, C.D.B., lv, 507, 510 n. 3, 646, 683, 794, 799–800 n. 3, 805, 807, 809–810 n. 2; Garvey on, 797, 811; inauguration of, 513 n. 1, 585 n. 5, 689, 690 n. 4, 810 n. 4; on Liberian colonization, 561 n. 2, 591 n. 5, 789–790, 791, 792, 807, 810 n. 4

King, Mazie, 299

Kirby, Harry W., 383

Kirk, Alexander, 847

Kirnon, Hodge, 3–4, *4–5 n. 1

Knight Commander of the Cross of African Redemption, 629 n. 1

Knight Commander of the Nile, 828

Knights of Columbus, 486, 488 n. 2

Knights of the Black Cross Legion, 480

Knox, George L., 289 n. 2

Knox, Judge John C., 164

Kock, Bernard, 765 n. 2

Kohn, Armin, 381, *382 n. 1, 386

Kohn and Nagler, 382 n. 1, 420 n. 1

Koumintang National Congress, 638 n. 1

Ku Klux Klan, 8 n. 1, 200 n. 2, 229, 488 n. 2, 648–649, 650 n. 1, 687 n. 1, 722 n. 3, 741 n. 2, 751 n. 3; v. black organizations,

559 n. 2, 672; in churches, 280; Congress on, 188 n. 15; and Democratic National Convention, 675–676 n. 5; and Garvey, 10, 27, 44, 115, 154, 183, 222, 228 n. 3, 338, 584, 721 n. 1, 751 n. 2, 768–769, 846; Garveyism compared to, 212, 263 n. 1; Garvey on, 222, 258, 260–261, 269, 277, 280–281, 484–485, 486, 487, 515, 527, 541, 671–672, 749, 771; imitated, 273 n. 2; membership of, 280; in Midwest, 273 n. 2, 280, 282–283 n. 3, 288, 289 n. 3; in North, 280, 282–283 n. 3, 671; in South, 280, 282–283 n. 3, 659–660 n. 13, 671; UNIA compared to, 186, 226; UNIA Convention on, 594, 671–673, 740–741, 749, 755, 768; white politicians on, 280, 675–676 n. 5; white supremacy of, 484, 487, 671; Workers party on, 749, 751 n. 2, 768, 769, 770–771, 772, 845

Kuusinen, Ottomar, 848

Kyle, D.H., 662, 664, *668 n. 6, 671, 674, 675, 678, 720, 729, 747, 749, 762–763 n. 1, 766, 778, 805, 813, 819, 834, 838; on black deity, 670; on Haiti, 750; on *Negro World*, 687

Ladies of the Royal Court of Ethiopia, 688 n. 4, 762, 784–785

La Follette, Robert, 643 n. 2, 648, 650 n. 1

Lagos Record, 397

La Guardia, Fiorello, 329 n. 9, 571 n. 5

Lamar, David, 382 n. 1

Lamos, Enid H., 142, 153–154, 163, 274, 351, 412, 484, 723

La Mothe, Louis, 54

La Rocca, M., *7 n. 1

Lasker, Albert D., 97, 173, 189, 329 n. 9

Lateran Treaty, 645 n. 1

Laundry (of UNIA), lii

Lawrence, Dr. J.F., 795

Lawrence, Isabella, 762–763 n. 1

Lawson, Amy, 656, 834, 835

Lawson, Dorothy, 196, 293, 347, 349, *358 n. 30, 403

Lawton, Charles, 800–801 n. 9

Leadett, Carrie, 334, 351

League of Nations, 295 n. 2, 483 n. 1, 559 n. 2, 643 n. 2, 809–810 n. 2, 823; on Africa, 10, 18, 214, 216–217 n. 1; Ethiopia in, 644 n. 2; Garvey on, 10, 214, 294, 533; Germany in, 595 n. 1; Permanent Mandates Commission of, 17, 18, 18 n. 2; UNIA Convention on, 592, 594; UNIA delegation/petition to, xxxiii, li, liv, 9, 10, 11–12, 16–18, 19, 27, 28–29, 32–33, 51, 56–57, 163, 176, 184, 214, 432, 571 n. 7, 641; 1923 session of, 432

League of Struggle for Negro Rights, 741 n. 1, 850, 851

Leavenworth Prison, 455, 456 n. 6

Ledig, Henry, 177

Lee, Henry, 192 n. 1, 200 n. 2

Lee, S.J., 651, 655, 662, 737, 743, 834, 838

Leese, Arnold, 262 n. 5

Lemam, Mr., 61, 62

Lenin, V.I., 253, 549–550, 551, 552, 553, 554, 555, 556, 557, 751 n. 2, 844, 847

Lennox, Bishop, 289

Lenon, H.J., 548

Leopold of Belgium, 800 n. 8, 812

Le Tellier, Mr., 32

S.S. *Leviathan*, 326, 329 n. 9

Levine, Lawrence, 801–802 n. 14

Levy, Alfred, 846

Lewis, D.D., 102

Lewis, Eunice, 579–580

Lewis, M.N., 255

Lewis, Sir Samuel, 24

Lewis, William, 690 n. 4

Liberator, 226, 228 n. 4, 741 nn. 1, 2

Liberia: anthem of, 825–826; Cape Palmas, 683 n. 5; Cavalla River, 596, 597, 610, 775 n. 2, 784, 790, 811; colonized, 558 n. 1, 586–587, 613 n. 2 (*see also* Back to Africa movement); constitution of, 587, 590 n. 2, 789, 806–807; Du Bois in, 585 n. 5, 689, 690 n. 4, 797, 805, 809–810 n. 2; European influence in, 796, 800 n. 6; Firestone Co. in, 787–788, 796, 799 n. 1, 805, 806, 807–808, 809–810 n. 2, 811–812, 815; Garvey on, 229, 231, 507–510, 586–587, 609, 611, 725, 726, 727, 758–759, 787–788, 796, 810–811, 812, 815; on Garvey, 610, 773; government of, 810–811, 812; government's response to UNIA colonization efforts, xxxvi, lvi, 561 n. 2, 590 n. 1, 591 n. 5, 610–611, 646, 682, 689, 690 n. 4, 773, 774, 775 n. 2, 789–790, 791, 792, 801 n. 10, 807, 810 n. 4; loans to, 108, 188 n. 13, 197, 307, 359 n. 33, 727, 758, 800 n. 6, 809–810 n. 2; motto of, 792; River Cess, 509, 510 n. 4; rubber in, 799 n. 1, 800 n. 7; trade policy of, 590 n. 2; UNIA branch in, 585 n. 4, 795; UNIA Convention on, xxxvi, 593, 715, 737, 744, 745, 767; UNIA delegation (Crichlow's) to, 508; UNIA delegation (Davis, Poston, Van Lowe) to, xxxvi, lv, 507, 510 n. 2, 562, 571 n. 1, 571–572 n. 8, 573, 608–609, 709, 786, 788–793, 794, 796, 799–800 n. 3, 800 n. 7, 805, 810, 811, 825; UNIA ships goods to, 682, 683 n. 5, 797, 801 n. 11; UNIA technical mission to, 586, 587–588, 589, 590 n. 1, 591 n. 5, 610, 774, 775 n. 2, 811

Liberian American Steam Ship Co., 717 n. 1

Liberian Steamship and Sawmill Co., 715, 716, 717 n. 1

Liberty, 252, 332, 563, 564, 792, 793

Liberty Hall, liii, 127, 214, 234–235, 258–264, 277, 285 n. 1, 289, 293, 306, 379, 401, 448, 456, 498, 513, 536, 549, 586, 601, 690 n. 1; mortgaged, 382; new, 266, 443

Ligue Universelle pour la Defense de la Race Noire, 752 n. 6

Lincoln, Abraham, 156, 157, 356, 517, 542, 566, 649

Lincoln Motion Picture Co., 760–762 n. 1

Lineberger, Walter F., 547 n. 6

Liverpool Institute of Tropical Research, 683 n. 3

Liverpool School of Tropical Medicine, 683 n. 3

The Living Church, 630 n. 20

Livingston, Paperne, and Wachtell, 609

Lloyd George, David, 20, 25 nn. 3, 4, 43, 495, 533, 554–555

Logan, G.H., 654, 687, 719, 721, 785, 834, 835

Logau, Friedrich von, 629 n. 12

Longshoremen, 586 n. 1

Lord, F. Levi M., 299, 611, 616, *629 n. 1, 818, 834, 837

Lord, Georgiana W., 629 n. 1

Lord, Samuel Francis, 629 n. 1

Los Angeles, Calif., 164–165, 184, 482

Los Angeles *Daily Express*, 184, 224

Louisiana, 280, 411 n. 3, 663, 668 n. 8. *See also* New Orleans

L'Ouverture, Toussaint, 140, 324, 750

Lovejoy, Elijah Paris, 517, *520 n. 2

Lovestone, Jay, 848

Lowry, H., 656, 664, 674, 834, 835

Luther, Martin, 130, 131, 669 n. 10

Lynching, 120 n. 4, 136, 155, 156, 157, 158, 159–160 n. 6, 224, 559 n. 2, 647, 668–669 n. 9, 749, 751 n. 3, 754, 771. *See also* Dyer Antilynching Bill

Lyon, Ernest, xxxvi, lvi, 611, 680, 773, 774, 775 n. 2, 791

McAdoo, William Gibbs, 675–676 n. 5

McClintic, George W., 682, *683 n. 2, 689

MacDonald, Ramsay, xxxv, lv, lvi, 549 nn. 1, 2, 552, *555–556 n. 2, 591, 641, 733 n. 1

McDougald, Cornelius W., 285, *286 n. 1, 305, 306 n. 1, 357 n. 10, 378

McDowell, R.H., 652, 685, 687, 834, 835

McGee, W. Frank, 320 n. 3, 386–387

MacGregor, Clarence, 510, *511 n. 1

McGuire, Bishop George Alexander, 102, 103, 456 n. 3, 616, 617–629, 665, 674, 675, 719, 721 n. 1, 729, 730, 747, 749, 755, 762, 764, 766, 777, 785, 808, 815, 817, 819, 834, 837; on Africa for Africans, 623, 630; on African redemption, 620–621; on America as white man's country, 767; on black deity, xxxvii, 625, 649–650, 666–667, 671, 677; on British, 622–623, 677; on commercial development, 622, 623, 624; Episcopal church on, 630 n. 20; on Garvey, 626, 627, 628, 667, 713, 724; on Garveyism, 463–464, 621, 626; Garvey on,

697, 699; on Harlem businessmen, 623; as Knight Commander of the Nile, 828; on Ku Klux Klan, 672, 673; on missionaries, 626; on Moses, 617–619, 624, 626, 628, 649; on nationalism, 621; on new Negro, 624; on race education, 718; on race problem, 684–685; on race purity, 685; on race self-determination, 621; on religious freedom, 624, 625, 626, 649; seminary of, 630–631 n. 29; on ships, 622; on UNIA, 619, 620–621, 622, 623, 625, 627, 628, 664; UNIA Convention on, 818

Mack, Judge Julian William, *301 n. 3, 306 n. 1, 316, 317, 345, 358 n. 23, 367 n. 2, 373, 374, 385, 391, 396, 400, 404, 410, 456 n. 6; alleged NAACP membership of, liii, 301 n. 3, 302, 303, 304; charges jury, 357 n. 12, 365, 366, 375; Garvey on, liii, 301–305, 366; on Garvey's self-defense, 365; imposes sentence, 386; threatened, 364, 401, 405

McKay, Claude, 843, 844–845

McKinney, E.B., 657–658 n. 5

McQuillan, Hugh, 285

MacSwiney, Terence, 253, 362

Macy, Rowland, *207 n. 2

Madison Square Garden, lv, 562, 568, 572, 611 n. 3

Mahdi revolt, 681 n. 4

Manghum, Henry E., 432, *433 n. 1, 433 n. 2

Mangin, General Charles, 456 n. 2

Mann, A.J., 659 n. 11

Mann Act, 140 n. 3

Manton, Judge Martin, *400 n. 1, 404, 409, 448 n. 1

Maran, Rene, 752 n. 6

March on Washington movement, 853

Marke, G.O., 28–29, 101, 163, 611, 617, 762, 834, 839; discharged, xxxiv, liii, 380, 383; as UNIA delegate to League of Nations, 11–12, 16, 17, 32–33, 571 n. 7

George O. Marke v. *UNIA*, 609

Marshall, Milton J., 585 n. 3, 793

Martin, Mr., 687

Martin, Rev. Charles, 688 n. 4

Martin, Freeman L., 651, 655, 664, 665, 669, 671, 674, 675, 680, 684, 686, 716, 718, 730, 736, 749, 763, 766, 767–768, 772, 777, 783, 818, 834, 836; on amending constitution, 779, 780–781, 785; on black deity, 670; on death grants, 808; on DuBois, 805; on education, 748; on Garvey, 713, 724; on race policies, 679; on UNIA, 652

Martin, James A., 351, *359 n. 36

Martin, Joseph, 161

Martin, R.A., 652–653, *658 n. 6, 714, 716, 718, 721, 747, 760, 766, 777, 784, 814, 834, 838

Marx, Wilhelm, 606 n. 4

Maryland, segregation in, 538–539, 547 n. 1. *See also* Baltimore

Massachusetts, lii, 359 n. 37, 397, 404, 656
Massachusetts Bonding Co., 91, 150
Massey, Mary, 665, 809, 834
Materialism, 259, 464, 513, 514, 515, 525, 631
Matthews, William C., 60, 64, 94, 96, 102, 103, 378, 381, *382 n. 2
Mattuck, Maxwell, 160, 164, 196, 231, 243, 244, 285, 286, 287, 294–295 n. 1, 298, 299, 317, 330, 336, 345, 362, 367 n. 2, 381–382, 385, 391, 400, 713; addresses jury, 306–308, 359; Garvey on, 366, 402 n. 1, 404–405, 406, 407–408, 409, 410, 446; on Garvey, 386, 401–402; summation by, 394 n. 1; threatened, 405; on UNIA, 376
Maudsley, Dr. Henry, 4, *6 n. 3
Mauk, Capt. Harry G., 41
Meaher, Capt. Tim, 667 n. 1
Mendel, Gregor, 722 n. 3
Mendenhall (accountant), 70
Mensheviks, 555 n. 1
Merchant Fleet Corp., 586 n. 1
Merrilees, Thomas P., 160, 164, 285, 330; on BSL, 70–100, 122–126; on UNIA, 58–114
Merrill, Edward G., 682–683, 689, 690 n. 2
Messenger, xxxiii, 44, 119 n. 1, 121, 182, 183, 187 n. 1, 217 n. 2, 846
Micheaux, Oscar, 760–762 n. 1
Michigan. See Detroit
Military Intelligence Division, 841–842
Miller, George, 55
Miller, Kelly, 558–559 n. 1
Miller, Mildred, 293
Millington, Rev. J.C., 616
Mills, A., 653, 744, 834, 836
Mills Publishing House, 801–802 n. 4
Mines/miners, 572 n. 11, 659–660 n. 13, 668 n. 3, 847
Minor, Robert, *741 n. 1, 741 n. 2, 847; on Garvey, 739–740, 751 n. 2, 768–769, 846; on Ku Klux Klan, 751 n. 2, 768–769; on UNIA, 738–741, 741 n. 2, 751 n. 2, 753–755, 768–772
Minus, Carrie, 671, 685, 715, 721, 729, 736, 764, 834, 837
Miscegenation. See Amalgamation
Missionaries, 514, 515, 626, 678, 681 n. 3, 748; in Africa, 51–52, 53, 54 n. 1, 443, 674
Mississippi: Bolivar County, 746 nn. 4, 5; Ku Klux Klan in, 280, 282–283 n. 3, 671; Mound Bayou, 745, 746 n. 5; Natchez, 653, 658 n. 8; self-governing black cities in, 745, 746 n. 5; UNIA in, 653, 658 n. 8, 663, 668 n. 8, 745, 746 nn. 4, 5
Missouri, 488 n. 3; Caruthersville, 657–658 n. 5, 668–669 n. 9; Charleston, 663, 668–669 n. 9; Ku Klux Klan in, 273 n. 2; New Madrid, 685, 688 n. 3; racial labor trouble in, 267, 269, 270; UNIA in, 663, 668–669 n. 9, 685, 688 n. 3, 716. See also St. Louis

Missouri Herald, 273 n. 2
Mitchell, John Jr., 578
Mohammed, 21, 22, 127, 130, 132, 315, 665
Mollison, W.E., 12
Montague, Marie Louise, 719–720, *721 n. 1
Montgomery, Isaiah, 746 n. 5
Montreal Dawn of Tomorrow, 435
Montserrat Progressive Society, 4–5 n. 1
Moon, 188 n. 16
Moore, Fred, 12, 167, 824
Moore, Richard, 431 n. 1
Moorish Science Temple, 681 n. 4
Moorman-Blackstone, Irene, 444
Morehouse Publishing Co., 630 n. 20
Morgan, H.L., 41–43
Morocco, 459, 462 n. 1, 753–754, 755 n. 2
Morris, Dr. Charles S., 117 n. 1, 183, *187 n. 2
Morris, Russell, 434–435 n. 2
Morse, Mr., 326, 353
Morse Dry Dock Co., 476, 477
Morter, Sir Isaiah, 624
Moses, 127, 128, 130, 131, 132, 464, 649; as black, 666; black wife of, 629 n. 5; Garvey compared to, 116, 117, 154, 427, 628, 721 n. 1; McGuire on, 617–619, 624, 626, 628, 649
Moses, Rev. William H., 13, 14, 569
Mosley, Sir Oswald, 262 nn. 4, 5
Motion pictures, 760–762
Moton, Robert R., 51, 52, 53, 54 n. 1, 120 n. 3, 321, 484, 490, 495, 496; Garvey on, 56, 57; on Garvey, 497
Mound Bayou Oil Mill and Manufacturing Co., 746 n. 5
Mugdal, H.G., 11 n. 2
Muldoon, William, 140 n. 3
Mulzac, Hugh, 317, 342, 401, 403; on BSL, liv, 472–478
Muraskin, William, 444 n. 1
Murphy, Carl, 245, 246 n. 1, *246 n. 2, 256
Muslims. See Islam
Mussolini, Benito, xxxv, lvi, 5–6 n. 2, 261 n. 1, 495, *496 n. 3, 643, 644 n. 2, 645 n. 1

NAACP. See National Association for the Advancement of Colored People
Nagi, George, 358 n. 22
Nagler, Maurice, liv, *420 n. 1, 423 n. 1
Nail, Grace E., 188–189 n. 17
Nail, John E., 186, 187, *188–189 n. 17, 218, 227 (unnamed), 228 n. 8, 229, 302
Nail and Parker, 188–189 n. 17
Napoleon Bonaparte, 430, 452
Napoleon III, 533 n. 1
National Association for the Advancement of Colored People (NAACP), xxxiii, 182, 188–189 n. 17, 230–231, 462 n. 2, 558–559 n. 1, 668 n. 5, 682 n. 6, 689, 752 n. 6, 760–762 n. 1, 824; in Arkansas, 660 n.

19; on blacks' political role, 687 n. 1; and communists, 845, 850, 851; Dyer addresses, 515, 520 n. 1; on Dyer Antilynching Bill, 155–156, 157, 158; founded, 301 n. 3; Garvey on, 155, 156, 157, 158, 192, 204, 216, 233–234, 235, 237, 238, 248–249, 250–251, 253, 254, 259, 268, 302, 303, 304, 305, 310, 402 n. 1, 437–438, 439, 440, 441, 461, 486, 515, 518, 544, 545, 546–547, 583, 633, 636, 705, 706; on Garvey, 212, 306 n. 1, 578, 579 nn. 1, 2; and Ku Klux Klan, 672; on lynching, 155, 156, 157, 158, 159–160 n. 6; Mack rumored in, liii, 301 n. 3, 302, 303, 304; objects of, 157–158; officers of, 54, 159 n. 5; in Philadelphia, 599 n. 4; publishes, 307; political role of, 212; as scheme to destroy race, 439, 440, 441; UNIA compared to, 248–249, 250–251, 253, 254; UNIA Convention on, 814

National Association of Travelers Aid Societies, 442 n. 5

National Baptist Convention, 14 n. 2

National Baptist Publishing Board, 14 n. 2

National City Bank of New York, 800 n. 6

National Colored Republican Conference, 547 n. 5, 643 n. 2

National Congress of British West Africa, 639 n. 3

National Consumer League, 442 n. 5

National Dry Dock and Repair Co., 35, 150, 151

National Emigration Convention, 765 n. 2

National Equal Rights League, 462 n. 2, 558–559 n. 1

Nationalism: Asian, 632, 636, 637, 638 n. 1, 639 n. 3; British on, 20, 25 nn. 3, 4, 43, 270; cost of, 127–128; Egyptian, 356, 522, 563, 636, 642 n. 1; Garvey on, 20, 22–23, 43, 127–128, 130–131, 143–144, 270, 291, 356, 362, 457, 458, 522, 539, 550, 551, 553, 563, 573, 588, 601, 602, 603, 632, 636, 641, 737, 750, 753–754; German, 606 n. 4; Indian, 356, 362, 457; Irish, 130–131, 291, 322–323 n. 2, 356, 362, 522, 563, 573, 621, 706; Islamic, 25 n. 4; Jewish (for Palestine), 356, 522, 563, 573, 596, 621; leaders of, 457, 458; Polish, 356; Turkish, 20, 22–23, 25 nn. 2, 3, 4, 43, 270

National Negro Business League, 54 n. 2, 120 n. 3

National Negro Congress, 851, 853

National Race Congress, 558–559 n. 1

Nauticus, 35

Nazi-Soviet Nonaggression Pact, 852, 853, 854

Negro. *See* Black(s); New Negro; Race

Negro Advancement Associations, 38

Negro Advocate, 167

Negro Bureau, 844–845

The Negro Champion, 847

Negro Churchman, 463–464

Negro Factories Corporation, 622

Negro Industrial and Clinical Alliance, 444 n. 1

Negro Organization Society, 54 n. 2

Negro Political Union. *See* Universal Negro Political Union

Negro Sanhedrin, 557–559, 741 n. 1, 845

Negro Society for Historical Research, 688 n. 4

Negro State Fair, 117

Negro World, 4–5 n. 1, 115, 134, 149–150, 180 n. 1, 222, 294 n. 1, 363, 378, 397, 398, 400, 402 n. 1, 629 n. 1, 752 n. 6, 832 n. 3, 833; ACL owns and publishes, 307, 308 n. 1, 420 n. 2; ads for lighteners and straighteners in, xxxv–xxxvi, 228 n. 7; banned/suppressed, 560, 561 n. 3, 681–682 n. 5, 706, 712 nn. 2, 3, 4; on BSL, 35, 36, 38, 73, 575; BSL ads in, 307, 344–345; British on, 560, 561 n. 3; circulation of, 345–347; in Cleveland, 288; defense fund for Eason murder suspects, 181–182 n. 1, 185; defense fund for Garvey, 47; on Du Bois, 598; on Eason, 172; Ferris and, liii, 383, 384 n. 2; foreign-language editions of, xxxv, lv, 592 n. 2; on Garcia, 283–284; Garvey on, 344, 346, 406, 706; on Garvey, 572–573; good will of, 109, 112, 113; on Islam, 681 n. 4; on Japan, 442–443 n. 2; on Jews, 596; on Moton, 56; on Mussolini, 261 n. 1; on Negro Sanhedrin, 558–559 n. 1; as propaganda, 687; on South Africa, 755 n. 1; staff of, xxxv, lv, 183, 383, 384 n. 2, 579, 580 n. 1, 688 n. 4; on UNIA Convention, 606 n. 7; on UNIA dues, 512; on UNIA Liberian program, 590 n. 1, 591, 592 n. 1, 595–597, 683 n. 5, 811; UNIA notice in, 512; women's page of, xxxv, lv, 579–580

Negro World Publishing Co., 688 n. 4

Negro Year Book, 322 n. 1

Netherlands, 820 n. 4

New Amsterdam Casualty Co., 682

New Deal, 852

New Jersey: Garvey in, lvi, 659 n. 11; Ku Klux Klan in, 280, 282–283 n. 3; Newark, lvi, 653, 659 n. 11; UNIA in, 653, 659 n. 11

New Negro: Garvey on, 20, 22–23, 313, 360, 449, 457–458, 460, 468, 516, 522, 526–527, 635, 706, 798; McGuire on, 624; woman, 579–580

New Orleans: Bureau of Investigation in, 174–180; Eason in, 48, 50, 161–162, 181 (*see also* Eason, J.W.H., assassinated); Garvey in, 161, 707–708; UNIA in, 45–46, 133, 142, 153, 161, 163, 166–167, 175–176, 178–179, 185, 192, 198, 200, 201–202, 298

New Orleans Times-Picayune, 161–162, 369 n. 1

Newport News Star, 255

Newsum, Rev. A., 745, *746 n. 3, 834, 836

New York (city): blacks elected in, 156, 159 n. 4, 160 n. 7; Garvey in, 143–149, 155–158; police department in, 276; U.S. District Court in, 386, n. 1; UNIA (New York local) in, xxxvi, liii, liv, 382, 384 n. 3, 434, 442–443

New York (state): Ku Klux Klan in, 280, 282–283 n. 3; segregation in, 539. *See also* Buffalo; Harlem; New York (city)

New York Age, xxxv, 8, 12 n. 1, 48–50, 134, 141 n. 5, 167, 520 n. 1, 609

New York *Amsterdam News*, 5–6 n. 2, 131, 170, 185, 219 n. 1, 264 n. 1

New York Call, 219 n. 1

New York Central Railroad, 329 nn. 8, 12

New York Evening Bulletin, 639–640, 815, 820 nn. 2, 3

New York Evening Post, 364–365, 397 n. 1

New York *Evening World*, 35

New York Herald, 844

New York Metropolitan Opera, 329 n. 17

New York News, 170–171, 186, 219 n. 1, 378 n. 2

New York Ship Exchange, 15, 64, 93, 94, 95, 96, 97

New York State Athletic Commission, 140 n. 3

New York Sun, 56, 800–801 n. 9

New York Times, 9–10, 119–120 n. 2, 192 n. 2, 219 n. 1, 277, 613 n. 1, 774 n. 1

New York Tribune, 19

New York World, liii, 3, 141 nn. 6, 7, 280, 367, 383 n. 5, 568, 573 n. 1, 603, 605, 605–606 n. 3, 606 nn. 6, 7, 610–611, 774 n. 1, 792

Nicholas, Czar of Russia, 552

Nicholas, Hannah, 669, 671, 672, 674, *675 n. 1, 679, 687, 720, 834, 837

Nicholls, J., 590 n. 1

Nigeria, 456 n. 4, 560, 561 n. 3, 639 n. 3, 706

Nolan, Joseph P., 64, 94, 96, 99, 327, 328, 359 n. 36

Norfolk Journal and Guide, 254–255

Norfolk *National Herald*, 254–255

Norris, J. Austin, xxxiii, 10, 13–14, 30, 183, 230, 231, 243, 265

North Africa, 26 n. 13

North American Steamship Corp., Ltd., 85, 86, 336, 337, 358 n. 17

North Carolina: Garvey in, 116, 117–119, 120 n. 4; Garveyism in, 657 n. 4; Greensboro, 685; Negro State Fair in, 117; segregation in, 652, 657 n. 4; Winston-Salem, 652, 657 n. 4

North Carolina State Interracial Commission, 120

Northeastern Life Insurance Co., 188 n. 16

North State Film Corp., 760–762 n. 1

Nott, Charles C. Jr., *6 n. 1

Novario, Rocco C., 288–289, 294–295 n. 1

O'Brien, Georgianna, 785, 819, 834, 838

O'Brien, John Patrick, 568, 569, *571 n. 5, 573

O'Connor, Thomas V., *586 n. 1

O'Gara, Alice, 351

Ohio: Akron, 289 n. 3, 506; Alliance, 661; Columbus, 506, 655; Dayton, 506, 656; Garvey in, liv, 464, 470 n. 2; Ku Klux Klan in, 288, 289 n. 3; UNIA in, 506, 655, 656, 661, 715; Youngstown, liv, 464. *See also* Cincinnati; Cleveland

O'Keefe, J., 283

O'Kelly, Berry, 119, *120 n. 3

Oliver, Rev. Noel, 178

Omaha, Nebr., 751 n. 3

Omaha New Era, 154

Omdurman, Battle of, 681 n. 4

O'Meally, James, 571 n. 7, 590 n. 1, 608–609, 611, 709, 818, 834

Oregon, Garvey in, 490, 496 n. 1

Oriental Trading Co., 652

S.S. *Orion* (to be known as S.S. *Phyllis Wheatley*): circular on, 382–383 n. 4; deposit on, 36, 37, 189; Garcia on, 95–96; Garvey on, 36, 37, 330, 332; Mulzac on, 477; purchase of, 15, 80, 95–96, 332, 352–353, 432–433, 478, 600, 607; O.M. Thompson on, 80, 478; USSB on, 15–16, 432–433, 478, 600, 607

Orlando, Vittorio E., 20, 495

Ormsby-Gore, W.G., 18 n. 2

Orr, Edward, 33, 34, 347, *359 n. 33

Orts, Pierre, 18 n. 2

O'Shaunnessey, Thomas J., 346, *358 n. 29

Ouny, Fernand, 140 n. 1

Ovington, Mary White, 240, 486

Owen, Chandler, xxxiii, 4, 8, 150, 165 n. 1, 187, 188 n. 11, 217, 218, 227 (unnamed), 228 n. 11, 231 n. 1, 243, 359 n. 33, 548, 716; criticized, 5, 184; Garvey on, 215, 219 n. 1, 271–272, 461; on Garvey, xxxiv, lii, 3, 44, 47, 182, 217 n. 2, 230–231, 263; Sherrill on, 229

Owens, Gordon, 559 n. 2

Owens, Merwin, 42

Oxley, Lionel L., 434–435 n. 2

Pace, Harry Herbert, 186, 187, *188 n. 16, 218, 226 (unnamed), 228 n. 5, 229, 302, 305 n. 2

Pace and Handy Music Co., 188 n. 16

Paderewski, Ignacy, 328, *329 n. 16

Padmore, George, 849, 850–851

Palm Beach, Fla., 434 n. 1

Palmer, Leigh C., 608

Pan-African Congress: Second, 18; Third, 513 n. 2, 585 n. 4, 599 n. 4

Panama, 258, 380, 474, 655

Panama Railroad Co., 759–760 n. 1

Panken, Judge Jacob, 40–41, 185, 225, 359 n. 33

Paragon Credit Union, 629 n. 1

Paris, Nancy, 293–294

Paris Peace Conference, 301 n. 3. *See also* Versailles, Treaty of

Parker, Chauncey G., 600 n. 1

Parker, Henry, 188–189 n. 17

Parker, Gov. John M., 280

Parris, Fritz C. Herbert, 330, *357 n. 6

S.S. *Pasadena*, 472, 478 n. 2

Patespaul, Dr. A.R., 661, *667 n. 2, 686, 745, 747, 834, 837

Pennsylvania: Farrell, 653, 659 n. 10; Johnstown, 459, 462 n. 2; race relations in, 459, 462 n. 2; UNIA in, 41–43, 653, 659 n. 10; Woodlawn, 41–43. *See also* Philadelphia; Pittsburgh

Pennsylvania Central Railroad, 329 n. 8

Pennsylvania Railroad, 326, 329 n. 8

Perry, Rufus Lewis, 629 n. 5

Peru, 800 n. 8, 812

Peruvian Amazon Co., 800 n. 8

Peters, Dr. J.J., 650 n. 2, 651, 664, 665, 675, 680, 687, 714, 716, 718, 720, 744, 745, 749, 764, 766, 767, 770, 776–777, 778, 780, 782, 785, 805, 817, 834, 835; on African redemption, 649; on black deity, 670; on education, 748; on Ku Klux Klan, 650 n. 2, 672; on policy toward Negroes, 677; on UNIA, 648, 663

Peterson, Maurice, 3

Pettiford, Alonzo D., 388 n. 1, 410, *411 n. 7, 412, 420, 422, 629 n. 1

Pettiford Chemical Co., 411 n. 7

Philadelphia: Garvey in, lv; UNIA in, 183, 230, 299, 300, 357 n. 4, 656, 662, 692

Philadelphia Public Ledger, 263

Philbin, J. Harry, 95, 96, 600, 606, 607, 608

St. Philip, 630–631 n. 29

Philippines, 592, 800 n. 7

Phillips, S.V., 559 n. 2

Phillips, William, 45, 133, 141–142, 153, 161, 163, 172, 178, 179, 192 n. 1, 200 n. 2, 201; on Eason, 198–199

The Philosophy and Opinions of Marcus Garvey, xxxv, 228 n. 14, 406, 411 n. 2, 470, 591 n. 5, 799–800 n. 3

S.S. *Phyllis Wheatley*, 37, 293, 307, 354, 425; ads for, 36, 38, 343–345, 382–383 n. 4; fares paid to, 100–101; for public relations, 64–65; purchase of, 65, 93–99, 323–324, 326, 327, 382–383 n. 4, 449; stock sold in, 6. *See also* S.S. *Orion*

Pickens, William, xxxiii, 150, 159 n. 5, 182, 187, 218, 227 (unnamed), 228 n. 10, 243, 648, 649; and La Follette, 650 n. 1; on Garvey, xxxiv, 3, 31, 47, 212, 217 n. 2, 231; Garvey on, 215, 219 n. 1, 233, 253–254, 302, 303, 304, 439, 440, 441, 461; Sherrill on, 229; threatened, 184

Pilgrims, 343, 449, 566, 589, 695

Pilkington, George, 339, 358 n. 18

Pina, Ramon, 18 n. 2

Pinchot, Gifford, 462 n. 2

Pittsburgh, 184; Bureau of Investigation in, 41–43; Garvey in, li, liii, 647; UNIA in, 418, 647

Pittsburgh *American*, 184

Pittsburgh Courier, 288, 376–377, 488, 489, 498, 767, 768 n. 2

Pope Pius XI, lvi, 594 (unnamed), *645 n. 1, 673 (unnamed)

Plummer, Edward, 433 n. 2

Plummer, H. Vinton, 65, 273–274, 297, 299, 305, 370, 388 n. 1, 412, 423, 673, 674, 675, 721, 729, 730, 736, 780, 818, 834, 837

Poincare, Raymond, 170 n. 1, 495

Poland, 329 n. 16, 356

Ponzi, Charles, 425, *431 n. 2

Popular Front. *See* Communist International, Popular Front of

Populist movement, 158–159 n. 3

Porter, Dr. Otey J., 613 n. 2, *613 n. 3

S.S. *Porto Rico*, 95, 96, 97, 98

Portugal, 459, 524, 568, 571–572 n. 8, 674, 675

Poston, Robert L., xxxvii, 43, 118, 119, 181, 192, 201, 207, 274, 297, 388 n. 1, 390, 399, 452, 621, 708, 714; at *Daily Negro Times*, 11 n. 2; eulogized, 568, 573, 786, 792; at Garcia's trial, 284; on Garvey, 174, 379, 410, 436; in New Orleans, 190; on UNIA, 229; as UNIA delegate to Liberia, xxxvi, lv, 507, 562, 571–572 n. 8, 573, 591 n. 5, 709, 789, 800 n. 7; on V. Williams, 398, 412 n. 2

Poston, Ulysses S., 11 n. 2, 30, 181

S.S. *Potomac*, 586

Potter, Adrian L., 397, 404

Powell, Mr. (of Cincinnati), 687, 834, 837

Powell, Rev. Adam Clayton Sr., 117 n. 1, 183, 241–242 n. 3, 853

Powell, Fred, 59, 350

Pravda, 844

S.S. *President Arthur*, 586

S.S. *President Fillmore*, 586

Press, black, 5–6 n. 2, 611 n. 1; in Buffalo, 294 n. 1; in Cincinnati, 599 nn. 1, 2; in Cleveland, 288; on Du Bois, 585 n. 5; on Eason, 184–185; Garvey on, 131, 149–150, 219 n. 1, 226, 796–797; on Garvey, 116, 119 n. 1, 131, 212–213, 254–255, 376–378, 440, 442 n. 6, 498, 585 n. 5, 768 n. 2, 796–797; in Richmond, Va., 585 n. 5. *See also Amsterdam News*; *Baltimore Afro-American*; *Chicago Defender*; *Chicago Whip*; *Crisis*; *Crusader*; *Daily Negro Times*; *Messenger*; *Negro World*; *New York Age*; *New York News*; *Pittsburgh Courier*

Press, non-black: on BSL, 35, 38, 73, 115–116, 150–152, 575; on Eason, 374; on Garvey, liii, 9–10, 47, 119–120 n. 2, 120 n. 5, 364–

365, 373–375, 385–387; Garvey to, 202–207; in Japan, 602, 605 n. 2; on UNIA Convention, 738–741, 753–755, 768–772

Prince, Henry/William Henry. *See* Ramus, Esau

Prince, Mary (Ramus's wife), 141, 230, 231, 242, 243, 245, 246, 298–299

Prince Hall Masonic Society, 688 n. 4

Prinz Oskar. See S.S. *Orion*

Prioleau, Aaron P., 394, *395 n. 2

Profitern, 849

Progressive party, 650 n. 1

Promoter, 4–5 n. 1

Provisional Committee for the Defense of Ethiopia, 851

Psalms 68:31, 23–24, 128, 311, 314, 451, 455, 621, 646, 828, 830

Pulitzer, Ralph, 603 (unnamed), 605, 606 n. 6

Quenum, Georges Tovalou, 752 n. 6

Quenum, Joseph Padonou Tovalou, 752 n. 6

Quezon, Manuel, 592 n. 2

Race: attitudes/relations, liv, 135–140, 146–147, 155, 205–207, 224, 237–239, 249, 252, 259, 267, 269, 270–271, 450, 452, 459, 462 n. 2, 465–466, 468–473, 483, 488, 489, 495, 497, 498, 518, 522, 527, 531, 541, 542, 561 n. 1, 588, 590 n. 3, 592, 594, 602, 668–669 n. 9, 677–680, 684–687, 737, 738–739, 831; William J. Bryan on, 258, 259, 260, 261, 277–278, 280, 281; communists on, 842, 849; competition, 205–206, 267–268, 269, 450–451, 465–466, 467, 566, 567, 635–636; consciousness, 435, 493, 495, 530, 567; Du Bois on, 237–239; extermination, 281–282, 415, 464, 465, 631–632, 636, fascism and, 262 n. 5; future, 205, 259, 260, 267, 268, 269–270, 271, 278–279, 281–282, 415, 464, 465, 485, 530, 534, 544, 546–547, 631–632, 636, 725, 726, 727; idealism, 145, 521, 564–565, 665–666, 831; labor trouble and, 267, 269, 270, 676 n. 6, 749, 751–752 n. 4, 843; legal definitions of, 832 n. 2; loyalty, 149, 515; pride, 206, 223–224, 251, 437, 438, 495, 512, 665, 696; problem and solution, 57, 204–205, 206, 238, 260, 270–271, 272, 355, 447, 464, 467, 468–470, 485, 493, 495, 499, 503, 524, 530, 532–533, 542, 543, 566, 570, 677, 684–685, 686; purity, 205, 451, 512, 685, 717–718, 722 n. 1; radicalism, 4–5 n. 1; riots, 55, 56, 140–141 n. 4, 207, 220 n. 2, 355, 657 n. 4, 749, 751 n. 3, 842; self-determination, 621; self-interest, 139, 271, 338–339, 361, 493, 514, 515, 516, 517, 519, 521–522, 523, 525, 527, 530, 531, 534, 543, 562, 564, 632–633, 634, 770, 771; suicide, 722 n. 3; superiority/inferiority of, 258, 259, 260, 261, 277–278, 280, 281, 493, 503–504,

564–565, 613 n. 1; unity, 24, 118, 145, 195, 216, 227, 248, 364, 413, 414, 437–438, 440–441, 508, 512, 521, 562, 636; uplift, 118–119, 406, 446, 522; war, 21, 479, 481, 583

Ramus, Esau, li, *133 n. 1, 141, 142, 153, 161, 242, 264, 265, 422; aliases of, 230, 243, 244, 298, 381; arrested, lii, 200, 230, 231 n. 2, 243–244, 246; attempt to bribe, 244–245, 265, 266, 298, 299; Bureau of Investigation on, xxxiii, 198, 199 n. 1, 231 n. 2, 232; deportation attempt against, 300 n. 1; and Eason's murder, xxxiii, 191, 197, 199, 200 n. 1, 230, 243, 298; extradited, 298; handwriting analysis of, 243; pleads guilty, 298; in Tombs, 298; on UNIA arms purchase, 299, 300; and UNIA secret police, 191, 198, 213

Ramus, Mrs. *See* Prince, Mary

Randolph, A. Philip, xxxiii, 4, 5, 165 n. 1, 182, 359 n. 33, 851, 853; on Garvey, 3, 7, 10, 47, 217 n. 2; Garvey on, 215, 219 n. 1, 271–272, 461; human hand sent to, 7, 10, 13

Rappard, William, 16, 17, 18 n. 2, 28–29, 33 n. 2

Rawlin, Louis S., 372

Rawlins, Dr. E. Eliot, 720, 721, 722 n. 4, 762–763 n. 1, 834, 837

Razafkeriefo, Andy (Andy Razz), 801–802 n. 4

The Realization of a Negro's Ambition, 761–762 n. 1

Reason, Mamie, 176

Reason, Minnie, 176

Rebel Picketing Committee, 444 n. 1

Redd, Henrietta, 654–655, 685, 686, 687, 762–763 n. 1, 834, 836

Redistricting, 158, 160 n. 7

Redmond, John, 322–323 n. 2

Red Shirts, 261 n. 3, 262 n. 5

Reed, Arthur, 444 n. 1

Reed, Capt. George, 175, 176, 177–178

Reed, John, 841, 842

Reeves, Sir Conrad, 24

Renaissance Casino, 379

Reneau, George C., 762–763 n. 1

Republican party, 231 n. 1, 329 nn. 9, 10, 394, 684, 687 n. 1

Restaurant (of UNIA), li, 154, 275, 334, 335

Reynolds, Ida May, 396

Richards, Rev. R. Van, 616, *738 n. 2, 788, 810, 834, 839; on Dossen, 793–794, 795, 826–827; on Garvey, 795; on UNIA delegation to Liberia, 737, 794–795

Richardson, Adrian, 341, 342, 343, 345, 477

Richardson, J., 686, 834, 838

Richmond Planet, 397, 578, 585 n. 6

Rickard, Ted, 140 n. 3

Ridley, John H., 285 n. 4

Rif people (of Morocco), 462 n. 1, 755 n. 2

Riley, John, 176
Ritter, William C., *597–598 n. 3
Roberson, Wilbur J., 809, 818, 834
Robert, Henry M., 676 n. 8
Robert's Rules of Order, 673, 676 n. 8
Robertson, Mr. (of New York), 672
Robertson, Mrs. A.J., 616
Robertson, Aladia, 180 n. 3, 197–198, 764
Robertson, Eleanora Martines, 180 n. 3
Robertson, James Dewey "Specks," 180 n. 3
Robertson, Sylvester R., 177, 178, 179,*180 n. 3, 197–198, 199, 663, 668 n. 8, 674, 684, 687, 715, 740, 745, 762–763 n. 1, 763, 783, 817, 834, 836; on race problem, 686; on UNIA, 661
Robinson, Dr. J.W., 763
Rockefeller, John D., 259, 327, 624
Rogers, Mr. (of Virginia), 679, 767, 834, 838
Rogers, Henry H., 342
Rogers, Judge Henry Wade, liii, 381–382,*382 n. 3, 400, 410
Rogers, Joel Augustus, 4, *5–6 n. 2, 11 n. 2, 367 n. 3
Rogers, Lelia, 358 n. 20
Rogowski, Henry, 345, 358 n. 27
Roosevelt, Franklin D., 285 n. 2, 852
Roosevelt, Theodore, 141 n. 4, 261 n. 2, 491
Roosevelt, Theodore Jr., 520 n. 1
Rosenwald, Julius, 52, *54 n. 3, 120 n. 3, 367 n. 3
Ross, Donald A., 800 n. 7
Ross, J.W., 656, 834, 835
Royal Poinciana (hotel), 434, 434 n. 1
Royal Union Improvement Co., 599 n. 1
Rubber, 799 n. 1, 800 n. 7, 800–801 n. 8, 812, 815, 820 n. 4
Russia: Garvey on, 144, 550, 551–552, 553, 556, 557; and Greco-Turkish War, 26 n. 11; Jews excluded from, 772 n. 3; recognized by France, 605 n. 1; revolution in, 550, 551, 553; socialism in, 551–552
Russo-Japanese War, 322–323 n. 2, 638 n. 1
Ryan, J.V., 288

Sacrifice, 132, 254, 306–307, 309, 532, 695
St. Joseph Aid Society, 765 n. 1
St. Louis, Mo.: Garvey in, liv, 479, 480–481; segregation in, 652, 657 n. 3; UNIA in, 479, 480–481, 652. *See also* Missouri
St. Louis Observer, 520 n. 2
St. Louis Real Estate Exchange, 657 n. 3
St. Louis Star, 479, 480–481
St. Louis *Times*, 479
St. Luke Herald, 585 n. 6
St. Vincent, 294 n. 1
Salath, Leonard, 177
Salisbury, J.B., 654, 717, 834, 838
Saltus, Harold, 200, 242
Sampson, W.O., 651, 656, 834, 837

Santo Domingo (Dominican Republic), 190, 559 n. 2, 613 n. 2, 643 n. 2, 742
Savannah Tribune, 115–116
Sawmill (of UNIA), 13, 108, 109, 112
Sawyer, Oliver H., 568, *571 n. 4
Saxon, Samuel, 55, 184–185
Sayers, Amelia, 762–763 n. 1, 777, 834, 837
Sayers, Edgar, 330, 357 n. 5
Schenck, Louis A., 330, 348, *356 n. 1
Scherer, Alix, 175
Schomburg, Arthur, 688 n. 4
Schuyler, George S., 558–559 n. 1
Schwartz (Bureau agent), 285
Scott, Emmett J., 12, 761–762 n. 1
Scott, Henry, 175, 176
Scott, John, 762–763 n. 2
Scott, Mrs. John, 762–763 n. 2
Scott, John Smith, 330, *356–357 n. 2
Scott, Maggie, 655, *660 n. 17, 834, 837
Scott, Sir Walter, 567
Scottish Churches Missionary Congress, 54 n. 1
Scottsboro trial, 741 n. 1, 849, 850
Scully, Charles, 463
Segregation, 538–539, 540, 547 n. 1, 652, 657 nn. 3, 4, 659 n. 11, 668–669 n. 9
Seib (Bureau agent), 285
Sélys-Fanson, Florent de, 56–57, *57 n. 1
Senegal, 639 n. 3
Service, A.N., *397 n. 2, 404
S.S. *Shadyside*, 35–36, 80, 88–89, 115, 151, 307, 324, 325, 330, 353, 354, 359 n. 37, 476–478
Shaka (Zulu king), 571–572 n. 9
Shakespeare, William (of England), 220, 355, 359 n. 42, 620
Shakespeare, William (of New Orleans), xxxiii, 166, 175, 178, 179, *180 n. 1, 185, 200, 213, 299; acquitted, lvi; appeal of, liii, 381; arrested, lii; Bureau of Investigation on, 402; convicted, 300; conviction of reversed, 408; defense fund for, lii, 181–182 n. 1, 185, 192 n. 1, 199, 200 n. 2, 201; indicted, 201; sentenced, lii, liii
Shanton, George R., *191 n. 1, 195
Sharecroppers Union, 849
Sharp, Robert S., 568
Shaw, Dr. M.A.N., 558–559 n. 1
Shea (Postal inspector), 160
Sherrill, William Le Van, 28, 29, 163, 188 n. 11, 266, 388 n. 1, 390, 399, 412, 452, 569–570, 573, 611, 665, 675, 720, 740, 743, 763, 782, 785, 805, 818, 834, 837; on Bruce, 688 n. 4; on Garvey, 379, 380 n. 1, 410; on Japanese earthquake, 442–443 n. 2; on Ku Klux Klan, 672; as League of Nations delegate, 18, 19, 27, 184, 571 n. 7; on Negro traveling, 745; on race enemies, 229; scandal involving, 286 n. 1; on UNIA, 664; on V. Williams, 412 n. 2

Shillady, John R., 159 n. 5, 439, *442 n. 5
Ship subsidy bill, 327, 329 n. 9
Shirley, D.D., 59, 79
Sierra Leone, 639 n. 3
Siki, "Battling," 135, 136, 137, 138,*140 n. 1, 140 n. 2, 141 n. 8
Silver, Frank, 481 n. 1
Silverston, Rudolph, 64, 94, 95, 96, 97, 99, 326, 327, 328, 329 nn. 13, 14, 330, 342, 366, 392, 393
Simmons, Mrs. (of Bermuda), 767, 834, 838
Simmons, Archie, 55
Simmons, J.B., 653, 686, 834, 835
Simmons, J.L., 663, 668–669 n. 9, 834, 836
Simmons, William J., 259
Simon of Cyrene, 22 (unnamed), 26 n. 8, 148, 667, 829, 831
Simonoff, Peyser, and Citrin, 68, 69, 72, 81, 82
Sinn Fein, 322–323 n. 2
Slater Foundation, 242 n. 4
Slavery: in Africa, 214, 216–217 n. 1; William J. Bryan on, 261 n. 2; Garvey on, 128, 354–355, 361–362, 465, 481, 519–520, 565; in South, 667 n. 1
Slemp, C. Bascom, 433–434 n. 1
Smith, Mr. (at UNIA Convention), 766, 767
Smith, Al, 394–395 n. 1, 675–676 n. 5, 689, 690 n. 1
Smith, Benjamin, 358 n. 19
Smith, Bessie, 801–802 n. 4
Smith, C.B., 219
Smith, Clifford, 16 n. 1
Smith, Rev. E.J., 654, 686, 834, 836
Smith, J., 654, 834, 837
Smith, Jesse W., 320 n. 1
Smith, Leonard, 743, 744, 745–746, *746 n. 1, 834, 836
Smith, Rudolph, 30, 418, 518, 520 n. 3, 611, 674, 679, 680, 687, 721, 779, 818, 834, 837; discharged, xxxiv, liii, 380, 383; on Garvey, 379, 719; reports to convention, 715–716; on UNIA officers, 783
Smith, Thaddeus S., 330, 349, *357 n. 3
Smith, Wilford H., 60, 64, 94, 95, 97, 102, 103, 325, 352–353
Smith-Green, Edward, 59, 62, 63, 326, 339, 359 nn. 34, 37, 472, 473, 715, 717 n. 1
Smyer, Mr., 161, 201, 231
Smuts, Jan, 295 n. 2, 605 n. 1, 706, 712 n. 4, 753, 755 n. 1
Smyrna, 25 n. 4, 26 n. 6, 33 n. 1
Snowden, Philip, 556–557, *557 n. 1
Social Gospel movement, 676 n. 9
Socialism: European, 552, 602, 606 n. 4, 642; Garvey on, xxxv, 225, 226, 269, 551–552, 602, 603; Russian, 551–552
Social Labor Unionists, 269
Society for Promoting the Emigration of Free Persons of Color to Hayti, 765 n. 2
Sohm, Mr. (of A.H. Bull), 682
Solano, Frances, 365 n. 3
Somaliland, 644 n. 2, 679, 681–682 n. 5
South Africa: British in, 571–572 n. 9; Garvey on, 282, 601, 602, 754; Communist party in, 854; Garveyism in, 283 n. 7, 569, 572 n. 11; independent republican status, 601, 605 n. 1; Negro World banned in, 706, 712 n. 4; political parties in, 605 n. 1, 755 1; and Rand strike, 755 n. 1; UNIA in, 572 n. 11; Zulu rebellions in, 571–572 n. 9, 590 n. 4
South African Chamber of Mines, 755 n. 1
South Carolina, 262 n. 5
Southern Development Co. v. Silva, 331–332
Southern Society of Washington, 261 n. 2, 282 n. 1
Southern Tenant Farmers Union, 273 n. 2, 657–658 n. 5
South West Africa (Namibia), 10, 19
Soviet Union. See Russia
Spain: in Africa, 459, 524, 632; defeated in Morocco, 459, 462 n. 1, 753, 754, 755 n. 2; in Haiti, 765 n. 2
Spear, Allan, 676 n. 6
Spencer, Mrs. Mary, 655, 762–763 n. 1, 834, 837
Spingarn, Joel, 240, 486, 513
Springfield, Charles, 188 n. 9
Stalin, Joseph, 556 n. 3, 849, 853, 854; on American blacks, 847–848
Standard Life Insurance Co. of Atlanta, 188 n. 16
Starr, Frederick, 825, *827 n. 1
Steklov, U., 844
Stephens, Theodore, 750, *752 n. 5, 834, 839
Stephenson, William A., 11 n. 2, 384 n. 2
Stevenson Plan, 820 n. 4
Stevenson, Robert Louis, 329 n. 6
Steward, Joseph H., 434–435 n. 2
Stewart, Rev. G.E., 7, 13, 30, 65, 96, 101, 103, 125, 126
Still, Addie L., 330, 348, *357 n. 4
Stoddard, Theodore L., 722 n. 3
Stokes, H.C., 674, 686, 764, 834, 837
Stokes, Rose Pastor, 769, 772 n. 1, 844, 845
Storey, Moorfield, 240, 304, 486
Strain, E., 200 n. 1
Strange, William W., 590 n. 1
Streseman, Gustav, 595 n. 1
Strikes, 586 n. 1, 676 n. 6, 749, 751–752 n. 4, 843
Sublime Order of the Nile, 547 n. 3
Sudan, uprisings in, 454, 679, 681–682 n. 5, 730, 733 n. 1, 753, 754
Sullivan Law, 243
Sunday, Billy, 118, *119–120 n. 2
Sun Yat-sen, 638 n. 1
S.S. Susquehanna, 600, 606–607, 608

Swift, Leon R., 88, 89, 151, 342, 359 n. 36, 476

Talley, Judge, 298
Tanner, Benjamin Tucker, 629 n. 5
H.D. Taylor Co., 683 n. 5
Temple Beth B'nai Abraham, 14 n. 1
Temple of Islam, 681 n. 4
S.S. *Tennyson*, 324, 328 n. 2, 345
Texas, 280, 282–283 n. 3, 671
Thaele, James, 572 n. 11
Theodoli, Alberto, 18 n. 2
Thomas, Mr. (of New Orleans), 179
Thomas, Allen, 178
Thomas, Rev. J.J., 661, 667 n. 1, 672, 834, 835
Thomas, James Henry, 548, *549 n. 1, 561 n. 1
Thomas, Norton G., 611, 651, 714, 818, 819, 834, 837
Thomas, W.A., 176, 178
Thompson, Frederick I., 16 n. 1, 189 n.1, 433 n. 2
Thompson, Noah, 36, 41, 183–184, 209, 224
Thompson, O.M., 60, 63, 64, 72, 73, 77, 79, 164, 293, 327, 332, 342, 345, 351, 352, 353, 392, 394 n. 1, 475; as co-defendant, 173, 302, 308, 374, 378 n. 2; on purchase of ships, 80, 93–94, 96, 97, 98, 99, 478; and *Phyllis Wheatley* circular, 382–383 n. 4; salary of, 100; threatened, 365 n. 1, 403, 408
Tillman, Pitchfork Ben, 278, 583
Tobago, 294 n. 1
Tobias, David E., 174, 390, 452, 456 n. 7
Tobias, George, 58, 59, 60, 65, 69, 72, 73, 77, 78, 81, 93, 100, 125, 331, 333, 344, 388 n. 1, 472; as co-defendant, 173, 302, 308, 374, 393
Tobitt, R.H., 101, 444, 547, n. 3, 548–549, 560, 561, 698
Togoland, League of Nations mandates in, 19, 214, 216–217 n. 1
Tolstoy, Leo, 143–144
Tombs Prison, liv, 298, 365–366, 376, 386, 388, 389, 401, 413–416, 417–418, 437–441, 634
Tooks, W.H., 265
Toote, Fred A., xxxvii, 30, 43, 60, 94, 102, 103, 190, 274, 348, 714, 729, 730, 767, 807, 834, 838; Garvey on, 699, 700; on Garvey, 266, 713, 724; at Renaissance Casino, 379; on UNIA, 656
Topakyan, H.H., 3
Tovalou-Houénou, Prince Kojo Marc, xxxvii, lvi, 750, 752 n. 6, 762, 823–824, 834, 838
Townsend, Frederic, 35
Treaty of Sevres, 26 n. 12
Treaty of Lausanne, 26 n. 12
Trinidad, 293, 294 n. 1, 561, 676 n. 7, 737
Trinidad Workingman's Association, 676 n. 7
Trotsky, Leon, 23, 26 n. 11, 253, 550, 551, 552, 553, 556 n. 3, 751 n. 2, 844, 845

Trotter, William Monroe, 558–559 n. 1, 845
Tucker, Joseph G., 31, 46–48, 301, 366–367 n. 1, 378 n. 2, 384 n. 3, 443–444, 556–557, 567 n. 3; on UNIA, 43, 512 n. 1, 562, 597 n. 2, 689–690; on UNIA Convention, 592–595
Tulsa, Okla., 459; race riot in, 207, 228 n. 4, 355, 751 n. 3, 842
Turkey, 33 n. 1; nationalism in, 20, 22–23, 25 nn. 2, 3, 4, 43, 270; pan-Islam in, 681 n. 4. *See also* Greco-Turkish War
Turner, Clarence, 55
Tuskegee Institute, liv, lv, 52, 321, 484, 490–496, 497
Tyler, George, 341

Uganda, 10–11 n. 1
Ulster Covenant of Resistance, 362 n. 2
Umberto II, 643–644 n. 1
Underwood, Oscar, 675–676 n. 5
Union, 598, 599 n. 1
Union of Soviet Socialist Republics (USSR). *See* Russia
United Auto Workers, 668 n. 5
United Fruit Co., 322, 658 n. 7, 737, 738 n. 1
United Irish League of America, 322–323 n. 2
United Negro Front Conference, 558–559 n. 1
United States: Constitution of, 158 n. 2, 518, 520 n. 3, 547 n. 1, 765 n. 2; in Haiti, 518–519, 529, 642, 643 nn. 1, 2; in Hawaii, 678; loan to Liberia by, 727, 758, 800 n. 6; racial attitudes in, 135–136, 138, 140, 155, 459, 462 n. 2, 594, 668–669 n. 9, 677–680, 684–687, 738–739
United States Congress, 188 n. 15, 329 n. 10, 824
United States Department of Agriculture, 219
United States Department of Justice, 151, 186, 212, 219 n. 2, 392, 847. *See also* Bureau of Investigation
United States Department of Labor, 300 n. 1
United States Department of State, 3 n. 2, 392, 482 n. 1, 571 n. 4, 773, 843
United States Shipping Board (USSB), xxxiv, lv, 36, 37, 95, 96, 97, 98, 99, 173, 189, 326, 328, 329 n. 9, 382–383 n. 4, 391, 392, 393, 472, 586, 683 n. 5; on Black Cross Navigation and Trading Co., 600, 606, 607, 608; on BSL, 15–16, 607; Emergency Fleet Corp. of, 608; finances of, 291, 292 n. 1; losses of, 354; and S.S. *Orion*, 15–16, 432–433, 478, 600, 607; on ship subsidy bill, 329 n. 10
Universal African Legions, 298, 366, 616, 777; guns for, 299, 300, 380, 383 n. 5, 408, 409
Universal Ethiopian Anthem, 617
Universal Negro Alliance, xxxiii, li, 10, 13, 14, 29, 30, 48, 50, 179

UNIVERSAL NEGRO IMPROVEMENT ASSOCIATION (UNIA) AND AFRICAN COMMUNITIES LEAGUE (ACL)

on Africa, 7, 10, 18, 435, 443, 560, 823; arms and ammunition for, 276, 299, 300, 367 n. 2, 376, 380, 382, 383, 385; Back to Africa movement of, 7, 31, 219, 428, 429, 507 n. 1, 510 n. 3, 560, 591, 592 n. 1, 595–597, 607, 610, 689–690, 725, 726, 737, 773, 775 n. 2, 784, 790, 794–795, 797, 798, 811; BSL controlled by, 58, 59, 69, 97, 112, 122, 123–126, 152, 307; on BSL, 391–392; at Carnegie Hall, 229, 230; and clergy, 654, 660 n. 19, 662; constitution of, 171 n. 1, 182, 184, 186, 188 n. 10, 203–204, 218, 406, 594, 620, 692, 775–777, 778, 779–781, 782, 783, 785, 808, 809; death tax/death fund of, 109, 110, 112, 113, 188 n. 13, 209, 210, 785–786, 808–809; Declaration of Rights of, 620–621, 625; defense fund for Eason murder suspects of, lii; dissension in, xxxiii, xxxiv, xxxvi, 13, 29–30, 165, 184, 379–380, 382, 383–384, 652; dues of, 512; Eason expelled from, 48, 49, 172; enemies/opponents of, xxxiii, 7, 193, 194, 214–216, 252, 312, 313, 314–315, 414, 456–457, 458, 623, 713, 725–726, 727, 728; finances of, 101–114, 134, 208, 209–211, 334, 383–384, 512 n. 1, 584, 585 n. 2, 609, 813, 816; flag of, 270, 568; on Garvey, liii, 379, 388, 390–394, 396, 397, 436, 463, 479 n. 2, 510, 628, 667, 713, 740, 826; greetings/condolences/invitations by, 511, 557, 558–559 n. 1, 573, 646, 687; and Amy Jacques, 295–297, 398–399, 456 n. 3; Liberian Colonization Fund, 610; Liberian construction loan of, 108, 188 n. 13, 197, 310, 359 n. 33; local conventions (1923) of, liv, 320–321, 414, 434 n. 1, 435, 442–443; membership of, 9, 50, 154, 164, 171 n. 1, 178, 186, 188 n. 14, 204, 208–209, 210–211, 216, 225, 240, 353, 391, 506, 511, 572, 573; membership loans to, 49, 274–275; miners in, 659–660 n. 13, 668 n. 3; missionaries of, 443; motto of, 204, 670; petitions Coolidge, 533 n. 1, 573, 812, 824; petitions Harding, liii, 388 n. 1, 390–394, 396; political role of 216, 225, 413, 414–415, 637, 663–664 (see also Universal Negro Political Union); prayer of, 650, 657 n. 1; press release by, 162–163; raided, 198, 200; salaries of, xxxiv, 8, 100, 102, 103, 105, 274, 325, 328, 335, 696, 697, 698, 700, 711, 712 n. 1, 775–777, 778–780; ships goods to Liberia, 682, 683 n. 5, 689, 797, 801 n. 11; sued, xxxiv, 274–275, 285 n. 4, 412, 419–420, 421–423, 609, 698, 712 n. 1; traitors within, 315–316, 692, 695, 696–697; truck, 125, 126; violence and, 357 n. 4; West

Indians in, xxxiv, 45, 216, 223, 263, 293, 388 n. 1

AIMS AND OBJECTS OF

101, 118, 127, 130, 143, 146, 202, 203–204, 246, 247–248, 253, 278–279, 289–292, 293, 450, 451, 452, 501, 502, 503, 505, 512, 531, 532, 534, 616, 620, 670, 684, 691; African redemption as, 312, 435, 461, 823; commercial programs as, 622–623; education as, 520, 521, 525; of human rights, 144–145; nationalism as, 567; Negro nation as, 522, 524, 537, 540, 541, 544, 560; as political movement, 144, 525, 601; race consciousness as, 435; race destiny as, 282; race progress as, 543; race unity as, 145, 437–438, 521; race uplift as, 522; self-development as, 589; as spiritual movement, 292, 627, 628

BRANCHES AND DIVISIONS OF

xxxvi; in Africa, 572 n. 11, 637, 639 n. 3, 706; in Alabama, 219, 661, 667 n. 1; in Arkansas, 652, 656, 657–658 n. 5, 660 n. 19; in Baltimore, 183, 655; in Bermuda, 654; in Brazil, 294 n. 1; in Brooklyn, 654; in Buffalo, 294 n. 1, 510; in California, 164–165, 184; in Canada, liv, 435; in Chicago, 648, 651, 654, 656, 662, 663, 716; in Connecticut, 656; in Costa Rica, 655; in Cuba, 652–653, 716; in Delaware, 654; in Detroit, 231, 245 n. 1, 299, 510 n. 1, 629 n. 1, 662–663; in Georgia, 654, 663; in Great Britain, 561 n. 1; in Grenada, 294 n. 1; in Indiana, 653, 654; in Jamaica, 663; in Liberia, 585 n. 4, 795; in Louisiana, 45–46, 133, 142, 153, 161, 163, 166–167, 175–176, 178–179, 185, 192, 198, 200, 201–202, 298, 661, 663, 668 n. 8; in Massachusetts, 359 n. 37, 397, 404, 656; in Mississippi, 653, 658 n. 8, 663, 668 n. 8, 745, 746 nn. 4, 5; in Missouri, 479, 480–481, 652, 663, 668–669 n. 9, 685, 688 n. 3, 716; in New Jersey, 653, 659 n. 11; in New York City, xxxvi, liii, liv, 307, 382, 384 n. 3, 434, 443–444, 511; in Ohio, 55, 184, 288–289, 506, 655, 656, 660 n. 16, 661, 715; in Panama, 380, 655; in Pennsylvania, 41–43, 183, 230, 299, 300, 357 n. 4, 418, 647, 653, 656, 659 n. 10, 662, 692; in Trinidad, 293, 294 n. 1; in Venezuela, 294 n. 1; in Virginia, 675 n. 2; in Washington (state), 660 n. 20; in Washington, D.C., liv, 434 n. 1, 544; in West Virginia, 654, 656, 659–660 n. 13, 661, 662, 668 nn. 3, 6

CONVENTIONS OF, 1920–1923

1920 convention, 117 n. 1, 659 n. 11, 841; 1921 convention, 183, 209, 294,

n. 1, 392, 626; 1922 convention, xxxiii, xxxvi, 11, 209, 575, 722; 1923 convention (canceled), xxxiv, 301, 320–321, 634, 691, 702. *See also* Universal Negro Improvement Association convention of 1924

OFFICIALS, DELEGATIONS, AND ORGANIZATION OF

xxxiv, 101–102, 430, 723, 782, 783, 813–814, 817, 818; ambassadors of, liv, 540, 547 n. 3, 548–549, 560, 561, 568; auditor-general of, 108; band of, 616, 688 n. 4; chaplain-general of, 776, 780; choir of, 616; counsel-general of, 776, 777; executive council of, 397; international organizer of, 776, 780; juvenile department of, 569, 718, 809; ladies' auxiliary of, 688 n. 5, 762, 784–785; laundry of, lii; League of Nations delegation/petition of, xxxiii, li, liv, 9, 10, 11–12, 16–18, 19, 27, 28–29, 32–33, 51, 56–57, 163, 176, 184, 214, 432, 571 n. 7, 641; Liberian delegations of, xxxvi, lv, 507, 508, 510 nn. 1, 2, 562, 571 n. 1, 571–572 n. 8, 573, 608–609, 709, 737, 786, 788–793, 794–795, 796, 799–800 n. 3, 800 n. 7, 805, 810, 811, 825; Liberian technical mission of, 586, 587–588, 589, 590 n. 1, 591 n. 5, 610, 774, 775 n. 2, 811; military division of, 264, 568–569; minister of education of, 776, 777; motor corp. of, 380, 572; musical director of, 13, 14 n. 1; police and secret service of, 133 n. 1, 142, 153, 166, 175–176, 191, 196, 198, 213, 402–403, 408; press service of, 433–434 n. 1; privy council of, 781; restaurant of, li, 154, 275, 334, 335; surgeon-general of, 776–777, 780

OPINIONS OF OTHERS ON

black leaders on, 182–183, 185, 186, 188 n. 14, 208–209, 210–211, 216, 224, 234, 235, 240; British on, 560–561, 679, 681 n. 4, 706, 725, 726; Bureau of Investigation on, xxxviii, lvi, 13–14, 41–43, 47, 164–165, 229–230, 263–264, 276, 293–294, 382, 383–384, 388 n. 1, 397, 402–403, 404, 442–443, 512 n. 1, 562, 568, 597 n. 2, 689–690; Communists on, lii, 738–741, 751 n. 2, 753–755, 768–772, 843, 845–846; compared to Christianity, 635; compared to Ku Klux Klan, 186, 226; compared to NAACP, 248–249, 250–251, 253, 254; compared to other movements, 143–144, 146–147, 267, 278, 637; *Crisis* on, 584, 585 n. 2; France on, 725, 726, 752 n. 6, 796, 797; Mattuck on, 376; Negro Sanhedrin on, 557–558

Universal Negro Improvement Association Convention of 1924, lvi, 510 n. 1, 616–629, 650–657, 661–667, 669–675, 684–687,

713–721, 729–738, 742–746, 747–751, 763–764, 766–768, 805–809, 813–819, 822–832; on Africa, 594, 595, 739; on amending constitution, 594, 775–777, 778, 779–780, 781, 782, 783, 785, 808, 809; appeals to Archbishop of Canterbury, 595, 673; appeals to Pope, 595, 673, 729; on black deity, 592, 665–667, 669–671, 677, 827–831; on British, 594, 677–680, 684; at Bruce's funeral, 688 n. 4; Bureau of Investigation on, 592–595; at Carnegie Hall, 631–638; on commercial and industrial development, 593–594, 742–743, 744, 745; committee reports to, 729–730; communists and, 845, 846; on condition of Negro, 594, 595, 661, 662, 673, 674, 677–680, 684, 730, 736; court reception of, 762; on death grants, 785–786, 808–809; division reports to, 651–655, 661–663; on Dossen, 822, 824–827; on Du Bois, 661, 805–806; on education, 593, 594, 717–718, 720–721, 747, 748–749, 760, 763–764; on France, 594, 674, 675, 677–680, 684; fund for, 173 n. 2; on Garvey, 713, 719, 723–724, 739–740; Garvey on, lv, 301, 320–321, 603; on Germany, 594; greetings from, 640–645, 714; honors presented by, 762–763 n. 1; on independent Negro nations, xxxvi, 593, 715, 736, 737–738, 744, 745, 750–751, 764, 766, 767–768; on Amy Jacques, 719; on Ku Klux Klan, 594, 671–673, 740–741, 749, 755, 768; on League of Nations, 592, 594; on Liberian colonization, 805, 815–816; Liberian delegates report to, 786, 788–793, 805; location of (proposed), 301, 320–321; on L'Ouverture, 750; on McGuire, 818; motion pictures at, 760, 778; on NAACP, 814; on Negro literature, 594, 747, 748–749; on Negro nation, 674, 675, 741; on Negro political union, xxxvii, 593, 663–665, 730–731, 732, 733–736, 754, 766, 815; Negro Sanhedrin and, 558, 559 n. 3; on officers, 723, 780–783, 817–818; petitions president, 593, 674, 675, 713, 736; press on, 606 n. 7, 738–741, 753–755, 768–772; on purity, 593, 717–718, 720–721, 760, 763–764; on race relations, 594, 595, 674, 675, 677–680, 684–687, 738–739; religious program of, 592, 606 n. 7; on salaries, 775–777, 778–780; secretary-general's report to, 714–715; on ships, 656–657, 743; Rudolph Smith's report to, 715–716; on Sudan, 730; on West Indies, 593; women delegates to, 784–785; on women's division, 763

UNIA v. *Vernal J. Williams*, 412, 419–420, 421–423

Universal Negro Political Union, xxxvii, 592, 663, 665, 730–731, 732, 733–736, 754, 766, 815

Universal Negro Ritual, 616

Universal Printing Shop, 295, 296
Urban League, 851

Vanderbilt family, 327, 329 n. 12
Van Der Zee, James, xxxvii
Van Lowe, J. Milton, *510 n. 1, 762–763 n. 1, 766, 792, 794, 826, 834, 836; on education, 748; on ships, 742; as UNIA delegate to Liberia, xxxvi, lv, 507, 510 n. 1, 562, 571–572 n. 8, 573, 591 n. 5, 709, 786, 788–791, 800 n. 7, 805
Van Rees, D.F.W., 18 n. 2
Vann, Robert L., 488, 489, 497, 498
Vardaman, James K., 278
Vatican City, 645 n. 1
Vaughn, W.S., 778, 814, 819, 834, 837
Venereal disease, 720, 722 nn. 2, 5
Venezuela, 294 n. 1
Verdun, Battle of, 449, 456 n. 2
Versailles, Treaty of (ending World War I), 20, 595 n. 1
Victor Emmanuel III, *643–644 n. 1
Victoria, Queen, 517, 649
Vidimande, R.J., 755, n. 1
Villard, Oswald, 240
Virginia, 588 n. 5, 670, 675 n. 2, 832 n. 2
Vocalion Co., 801–802 n. 14
The Voice of Buffalo, 294 n. 1

Walcott, Charles E., 275, 284
Walcott, James, 590 n. 1
Walker, Mr. (of Delaware), 654, 834, 835
Walker, James J., 571 n. 5
Walker, Rev. Lee, 119
Walker, Dr. Thomas H., 763, *765 n. 1
Wallace, Henry C., *390 n. 1, 483, 571 n. 1
Wallace, William A., 662, 665, 674, 675, 684, 716, 718, 729, 736, 744, 754, 766, 772, 777, 809, 834, 835; on black deity, 671; on death benefits, 785–786; on Ku Klux Klan, 673, 675; on Negro political union, 664; on race relations, 677; on salaries, 778–779; on strikes, 749; on UNIA, 813
Waller, Fats, 801–802 n. 4
Wall Street, 292
Walrond, Eric D., 470 n. 1
Walters, Mr. (of BSL), 65
Wanamaker, John, *208 n. 3, 546
Wanamaker, Lewis Rodman, 207–208 n. 3
Wanamakers' (department store), 206, 207–208 n. 3, 546
War, 22, 43, 169, 602. *See also* World War I; World War II
Ware, William, 55, 56, 352, 353, 661, 665, 675, 715, 819, 834, 837
Warner, Richard E., 58, 59, 317, 333, 334–335, 348, 365 n. 1
Washington (state), 660 n. 20
Washington, Major Allen W., 52, *54 n. 2

Washington, Booker T., 24, 52, 120 n. 3, 321, 322 n. 1, 324, 484, 490, 491, 493, 494, 496, 676 n. 6, 746 n. 5; on black cinema, 761–762 n. 1; dines at White House, 261 n. 2; Garvey compared to, 442 n. 6; *Up from Slavery* of, 761–762 n. 1
Washington, D.C.: Garvey in, lv, 294–295 n. 1, 520–533, 534, 544; race riot in, 207, 355; UNIA in, liii, 434 n. 1, 544
Washington, Dennis, 747, 760, 779, 834, 836
Washington, George, 143, 144, 250, 253, 341, 356, 362, 450
Washington, Josephine, 762–763 n. 1
Washington Star, 213 n. 1
Wasservogel, Judge Isidor, 420 n. 2
Watkis, Harry R., 63–64, 325–326, 349–350
Watson, James, 334
Watterhouse, Florence, 200 n. 2
Wattley, Col. Vincent, 664, 679–680, 686, 762–763 n. 1, 809, 834, 837
Webb, Rev. James, 832 n. 3
Webley, A.N., 177
Welch, M., 783, 834, 836
Wells, "Bombadier," 141 n. 8
Wesley, H.T., 591 n. 5, 790, 793
West Africa, 454. *See also* Dahomey; Gold Coast; Liberia; Nigeria; Senegal; Sierra Leone; Togoland
Western Cape Province African National Congress, 572 n. 11
West Indian (as derogatory term), 217 n. 2
West India Regiments, 590 n. 3; 676 n. 7
West Indies, 593; beet sugar in, 678, 680 n. 1; blacks from in UNIA, xxxiv, 45, 180, 185, 216, 217 n. 2, 223, 263, 293, 367–368, 388 n. 1, 396 n. 1; blacks in office in, 637; BSL in, 62, 63, 475; condition of blacks in, 678, 694; H.V. Davis in, 778; Garvey in (1921), 345, 353, 392, 707; Garvey on, 238, 602; *Negro World* banned in, 706, 712 n. 3; race relations in, 238, 239, 678. *See also* Barbados; Bermuda; Cuba; Grenada; Haiti; Jamaica; St. Vincent; Santo Domingo; Tobago; Trinidad
"West Indies Blues," (song) 801–802 n. 14
Weston, George, 42, 43, 616, 670, 673, 679, 681 n. 4, 686, 687, 717–718, 721, 749, 809, 819, 834, 837
Weston, Mrs. George, 616
West Virginia: Clarksburg, 654, 659–660 n. 13; Garveyism in, 659–660 n. 13; Ku Klux Klan in, 659–660 n. 13; Laura Lee, 662, 668 n. 6; Monongah, 661, 668 n. 3; UNIA in, 654, 656, 659–660 n. 13, 661, 662, 668 nn. 3, 6
Wheat, Samuel R., *479 n. 2, 654, 684, 717, 718, 739–740, 764, 834, 835
Wheatley, Phyllis, 324
White Flag League, 681–682 n. 5

White, George H., 547 n. 5
White, Walter, 54–55, 159 n. 5, 439–440
White Leaguers, 262 n. 5
White Liners of Mississippi, 262 n. 5
Whiteman, Olivia, 559 n. 2, 675, 686, 724, 738–739, 754–755, 834, 835
White Man's Party, 262 n. 5
White supremacy. *See* Race, superiority/inferiority
Whitfield, Louis C., 339, *358 n. 19
Whittingham, Lillian, 334
Whittmore, Ike, 192 n. 1
Wilberforce, William, 517
Wilhelm, Kaiser (William II), 148, 310, 452
William, Crown Prince, 456 n. 2
Williams, Alice A., 176
Williams, Balfour J., 351, *359 n. 37
Williams, Clarence, 801–802 n. 14
Williams, George A., *783 n. 3, 814, 815, 834, 836
Williams, H.B. 656, 744, 834, 836
Williams, Spencer, 801–802 n. 14
Williams, Vernal J., 274, 285, 297, 299, 688; on Garvey, 410; Garvey on, 411–412, 419–420; Poston on, 398, 412 n. 2; on Ramus, 300 n. 1; resigns, xxxiv, liii, 397–398, 411–412, 419–420, 421, 422, 423; salary of, 419, 420, 421, 422, 423; on UNIA, 293; v. UNIA, 412, 419–420, 421–423
Williamson, Alvin, 357 n. 5
Willis, Sen. Frank B., 496–497, *497 n. 1, 506–507
Wills, Harry, 136, *140 n. 3
Wilson, Mr. (of BSL in Jamaica), 63, 475
Wilson, Hugh Robert, *773 n. 2
Wilson, R.R., 13
Wilson, Woodrow, 20, 25 n. 4, 148, 295 n. 2, 491, 495, 533, 647, 823
Winchester Arms and Rifle Co., 403
Winston, E.T., 655, 834, 836
Winston, Robert Watson, 470 n. 1, 585 n. 2, *613 n. 1
Wise, Capt. Jacob, 477
Wise, Stephen S., 301 n. 3
Wizzard, Domengo H., 13
Wolff, J., 99
S.S. *Womachichi*, 15
Wood, William H., 656, 834, 835
Woodley, A.L., 559
Woodville and Woodville, 172
Work, Monroe N., 321 (unnamed), *322 n. 1
Worker, 844. See also *Daily Worker*
Workers Party of America, 558–559 n. 1; and African Blood Brotherhood, 845; American Negro Labor Congress of, 846–847; Central Executive Committee of, 751 n. 2; Garvey on, 770, 771–772; on Garveyism, 751 n. 2; on Ku Klux Klan, 749, 751 n. 2, 768, 769, 770–771, 772, 845; and NAACP, 845; and Negro Sanhedrin, 557–558, 559 n. 2, 845; racism in, 842; and UNIA, lii, 845–846. *See also* Communist International; Communist party/Communists
Workingman's Cooperative Publishing Co., 412 n. 2
World Court, 483 n. 1
World War I, 20, 309, 533 n. 1, 647, 680 n. 2; reparations, 32 n. 1, 170 n. 1
World War II, 852
Wright, Charles, 388 n. 1
Wright, Edward, 159 n. 4

Yanaghita, Kunio, 18 n. 2
S.S. *Yarmouth*, 62–63, 89–90, 151, 308, 330, 340–342, 353, 354, 359 n. 37; claims against, 80; condition of, 35, 473, 475, 476, 477, 478; in Cuba, 473–474, 475; demurrage clause lacking for, 473–474; insurance for, 338; loss on, 33–35, 88, 153; as propaganda, 473, 474; purchase of, 61, 83–87, 325, 329 n. 5, 337–338, 339; sold, 35, 476; voyages of, 86, 340–341, 474–475; whiskey cargo of, 325, 329 n. 7, 337, 341, 472, 473
Yearwood, James B., 65, 101, 103, 190, 197, 266, 276, 287, 380, 388 n. 1, 819, 834, 837; on membership, 208–209; on membership loans, 274, 275
Yokosuka Iron Foundry, 660–661 n. 21
Yorodzu, 605–606 n. 3
Yoshihito, Emperor of Japan, 442
Young, Ambrose, 267
Young, Mary Sharperson, 762–763 n. 1, 785, 834, 837
Young, Judge William, 54
Young Men's Hebrew Association, 597–598 n. 3

Zack, Joseph, 842
Zaghlul Pasha, Saad, 642, 733 n. 1
Zauditu, Empress of Ethiopia, *644 n. 1
Zayas y Alfonso, Alfredo, 714
Zinovyev, Grigori, 549 n. 2, 556 n. 3
Zionist Organization of America, 301 n. 3
Zucker (immigration inspector), 463
Zulu wars, 571–572 n. 9, 588, 590 n. 4

The Type

The text of this book was set in a digitized version of GALLIARD, introduced in 1979 by Mergenthaler and designed by Matthew Carter. It is based on the sixteenth-century type face by Robert Granjon, the French typefounder and printer. The name derives from the combination of elegance and crispness characteristic of the French oldstyles.

The book was composed by Diane L. Hill of the Marcus Garvey and UNIA Papers Project using the TYXSET, version 2.1, computer typesetting system, running under Xenix, version 2.3, and Venix/86, version 7, operating systems.

Printed and bound by

McNaughton and Gunn, Incorporated
Saline, Michigan

Typography and binding design by Linda Robertson